Sir Walter Scott

A Bibliographical History

1796 – 1832

Frontispiece: portrait of Scott by William Smellie Watson

Sir Walter Scott

A Bibliographical History 1796–1832

William B. Todd and Ann Bowden

Oak Knoll Press

First Edition published by:
Oak Knoll Press 308 Delaware Street, New Castle, DE 19720 USA

Authors: William B. Todd and Ann Bowden
Cover design: John von Hoelle and Michael Höhne
Photographer of the author portrait: Don Rogers
Photographer of the Scott portrait: Beth Phillips

ISBN 1-884718-64-7 Oak Knoll Press

Library of Congress Cataloging-in-Publication Data

Todd, William B. (William Burton)
Sir Walter Scott : a bibliographical history, 1796–1832 / by William B. Todd and Ann Bowden. — 1st ed.
p. cm.
Includes indexes.
ISBN 1-884718-64-7
1. Scott, Walter, Sir, 1771–1832—Bibliography. 2. Scotland—In literature—Bibliography.
I. Bowden, Ann, 1924– . II. Title.
Z8802.T63 1998
[PR5332]
016.828'709—dc21 98-26869
CIP

Printed in the United States by Quinn-Woodbine, Inc., Book Manufacturers on 50# Glacier Opaque Natural acid-free archival paper.

CONTENTS
MAJOR WORKS

Chronological lists of all publications in the periods cited below follow the preliminary chapter commentaries. A complete record, ordered alphabetically with entry numbers, is provided in Index 1 (pages 1021-1026), As these entry numbers represent the primary reference, they also appear in the headlines at the outer right margin, with pagination given in the inner margins.

ILLUSTRATIONS

The PORTCULLIS is a device once employed by an ancestor which Scott, in 1809, ordered to be stamped upon the spine of 'a few copies' as a 'decisive mark of appropriation', or sign of his special interest or involvement (*Letters*, ii.168-169). CLAUSUS TUTUS ERO rather loosely represents, as he remarked, an anagram of the name WALTER SCOTT and more precisely translates as 'I shall be safe when closed up'. This gilt symbol exists in several states, one previously reproduced (Daiches, page 96), and another of similar design ca. 1823 observed only once outside the Abbotsford Library (entry 166A). The later stamp is now computer enhanced for illustration here in the original size employed for a narrow book (shown above) or, for more convenient inspection, enlarged to twice that size (page x).

GENERAL INTRODUCTION

There are certain works of Sir Walter Scott, which we have been so much accustomed to admire, that we are disposed to neglect every thing also by the same author. There is, however, no foundation for this prejudice. (*Edinburgh Evening Courant*, 11 August 1834)

This is a comprehensive bibliographical record of Scott's literary career, disclosing further typographical variants among the poems and novels earlier described, extending to a number of editions not previously considered, and citing innumerable issues by other writers or artisans evidently dependent upon his publications. Whatever the genre or significance of Scott's own works, the chronological arrangement of all his *authorized issues* (here designated 'A') corresponds so far as practicable with Scott's original composition, or the final presswork of his printers, and thus facilitates some discussion of their interrelation. Other than the issues accepted as Scott's alone there are also, in this temporal 'A' range, some entries not as yet fixed in the canon, including certain prospectuses of his work, publications formally advertised as imminent but never issued, and books by others which he substantially edited or revised. Since Scott was ever reticent, if not secretive, about the assistance he was constantly providing, as a silent partner in the Ballantyne printing office, a precise account of this editorial activity cannot be presented. For all of his ventures, Scott's complicated fiscal arrangements are also here generally disregarded as irrelevant in a bibliographical report and adequately discussed elsewhere. Like most men of letters it may be stated simply that Scott wrote first for fame, as he more than once conceded, and then, increasingly, for the money required to extend his estate and advance his position.

Immediately precipitated by many of the authorized 'A' entries, and cited in geographical order below them, are the various *reprints* ('R') of little or no authority and other issues which are distinctly *derivative* ('D'), among them all the plays which reached printed form, chapbooks, illustrations, and sheet music.[1] Admittedly these are secondary productions, but an appreciable number were encouraged by Scott himself, a few indeed even preceded his official 'A' issue, and most indirectly served to sustain his work and further enhance his reputation. Though the specific effect of any one production again cannot be measured, it still may be useful to provide, beneath the relevant titles in the separate 'chapter' tables of contents, a total count of all publications identified in these A, R, and D categories, as well as an 'E' count of *extracts* found in numerous anthologies. Certain initial A issues, it will be observed, had an extraordinary impact, the most popular (47A) totaling 435 variants in this English record, along with an uncounted array in other languages.

Chapter divisions, Scott's 'happy points of pause', here allow further commentary on matters that may otherwise pass unnoticed in the welter of bibliographical detail. The first five chapters encompass all of Scott's separate publications, and their consequent issues, through 1832, the year of his death. Later chapters introduce, in VI the collected editions in every genre (A,R,D), 1806-1833 and in VII the final *Magnum Opus* (A), here regarded in its full extent, 1829-1836. The succeeding appendices list: [1] 69 of Scott's legal papers (A), beginning with his 1792 thesis; [2] 164 (E) anthologies reprinting memorable extracts from his work; [3] 38 (S) satires, parodies, and imitations; and [4] 71 (T) tributes and dedications. All of these E,S,T peripheral printings further testify to Scott's dominance in the literary scene, as well as to the high regard and affectionate esteem held for him by his contemporaries. Beyond these indications within Scott's lifetime there are also many others already on record, among them the myriad reviews and discussions cited in J. C. Corson's invaluable 1943 bibliography of secondary works and, by first date entry only, innumerable translations listed in *NCBEL* and the forthcoming *CBEL3*.

Terms and Procedures

In the articulation of entries the initial number-line ordinarily identifies the item bibliographically, not as the publisher's title may read. Though publication dates remain somewhat inexact, given the erratic mode of advertising, two references are regularly used in a special sense: *published*, representing the first announced 'This Day' time of issue, usually in an Edinburgh journal, and *issued*, denoting a later newspaper 'This Day' date, after the books had been shipped to London. (It will become apparent that, while the lapse of time for books in transit—of some two or three weeks usually—was at first of no concern, there is a gradual tendency toward concurrent issue in both cities: an arrangement which then occasionally invited premature disclosures, some few due to Scott himself, others to his indiscreet associates.)

Primary (A) issues are analysed under several descriptive headings, depending upon the extent of Scott's participation. Where he is recognized in his full capacity as author or editor, the title is then given in quasi-facsimile: a procedure which, in a few cases, necessitates breaking a word without hyphen at line end (as in 3rd line, item 5Ab). A hyphen at line end also appears in the original title (as in 7th line, item 13Ac). For these main entries the press figures, as indices of typographical irregularity, are cited throughout, here with the gathering letter given before the page number. Though the figures and other data are essential features of a complete description, the reader usually will turn to the separate chapter commentaries or item *Notes* for matters of more general interest.[2] Unless indicated otherwise, the edition size notation comes from Lockhart's biography. Preceding the first 'A' entry occasionally are one or more epigraphs from Scott himself or, in a few instances, from Lockhart; following the entry are the relevant references and, parenthetically, a further citation of any reprinting in the *Magnum Opus*. As the references often provide illustrations of titles, those few appearing here generally are of a kind deserving further scrutiny.

Under *Copies* the names of certain previous owners (or places) are given in parentheses, if of some importance. The number of copies reported may not be an indication of rarity, but rather of convenience, or of a quest for further particulars (thus the search through twenty-five exemplars of 89Aa in vain pursuit of a true first edition). Copy entry 'E(Abbot)' refers to the distinctive shelfmark assigned by the National Library of Scotland to an item acquired from Abbotsford. Entry 'O(22)', as in *Woodstock*, refers to several copies at the Bodleian Library, and there greatly augmented by the massive Dunston collection of Scott, all uncatalogued at the time of our inspection.

Subsidiary accounts (D,E,R,S,T) are abbreviated, as circumstances may allow, but again the *Notes* will declare anything noteworthy among them. Even in these entries, however, publishers' imprints are given in full as additional witnesses to those advancing the cause of Scott in all of its many aspects. As it was acknowledged in his own day, this author eventually was responsible for a whole literary, musical, and pictorial industry based, near and far, upon his work, and it is therefore appropriate that the present bibliography should mark these further testimonies to his achievement.

11 April 1998 W.B.T. & A.B.

1. Of the countless ephemeral sheets of engraved music, in 1933 still sung 'in many households wherever the English language is spoken' (Van Antwerp[2].12), some of the issues subsequently recorded in unidentified collections now cannot be located; but for every such instance [cited in brackets] two or three other printings are here first listed. The present account still excludes 'derivatives of derivatives,' that is, lyrics in plays by the dramatists themselves or, also under some Scott title, as in the Berlioz *Waverley Overture*, music that is entirely instrumental. Beethoven, Haydn, and other notables, however, are recorded as providing the music for Scott's own lyrics.

Domestic vocal recitals, sadly now defunct since Van Antwerp's day, were increasingly popular during Scott's lifetime. 'Little more than half a century ago, there were but three shops in London for the sale of music and musical instruments . . . and at the present time the number exceeds two hundred.' *Monthly Magazine,* 1 August 1824, page 61.

2. It is to be hoped that the *Notes* on Scott will suffice for most purposes, since in times past there has been a tendency to complicate matters with unnecessary 'points'—for *Waverley* some 388 enforced by Worthington, then another 115 by Poynton. Such proliferations, as Percy Muir recently observed, 'have given bibliophilic interest in Scott a blow from which it has hardly yet recovered' (*Collectible Books: Some New Paths*, ed. Jean Peters, New York & London: Bowker, 1979, page xxii). This bibliography endeavours to ensure a complete recovery, one long delayed and much anticipated.

ACKNOWLEDGEMENTS AND PERMISSIONS

As research on Sir Walter Scott should be conducted, in large measure, at his OWN ROMANTIC TOWN of Edinburgh, our first and many later enquiries were directed to The National Library of Scotland and there to Brian Hillyard, a ready guide in times of uncertainty. Also most helpful at this Library were Iain Gordon Brown, W. A. Kelly, Richard Ovenden, and Ruzena Wood; at the Advocates' Library, Catherine A. Smith; at the Signet Library, G. H. Ballantyne and Joyce Penney; and at the University Library, John Howard and Murray Simpson. Douglas Gifford, honorary librarian of Scott's own collection, and Angus Stewart Q.C., Keeper of the Advocates' Library, formally allowed us access to the Abbotsford library, where we were kindly received by Mrs Patricia Maxwell-Scott and her sister Dame Jean Maxwell-Scott, and there shown certain books not discovered elsewhere. For essential advice on the description of Scott's legal papers, a matter quite beyond our competence, we are further indebted to Donald Davidson, also of the Faculty of Advocates.

Beyond Edinburgh and its environs we have been much encouraged by scholars participating in the ongoing edition of Scott's novels (*EEWN*), especially David Hewitt and J. H. Alexander of the University of Aberdeen. At the University of Glasgow our obligations extend particularly to Larry Schaaf, A. S. Skinner, Nigel Thorpe, David Weston, and at the Mitchell Library, to Karen Cunningham.

In the SISTER KINGDOM, as Scott called it, the varied collections at the Bodleian Library were made more readily accessible by R. J. Roberts, Clive Hurst, Paul W. Nash, and Michael Turner. At the British Library our research was also much facilitated by Lotte Hellinga, Elizabeth James, Robert Parker, and Ian Willison. In London and elsewhere we must acknowledge as well the concern of interested bibliopoles (notably Miles Bartley, James Burmester, Spike Hughes, C. C. and Michèle Kohler, Brian Lake, John V. Price, John Stephens) that we should be aware of Scottiana previously disregarded. At his residence south of London, Bernard C. Lloyd hospitably allowed us on several occasions to examine his unrivalled collection and in our own home twice scrutinized the descriptions we were preparing. At a greater distance, in Melbourne, B. J. McMullin kindly reported on the Poynton collection and gave us the advantage of his own research into Scottish printing. In Germany we are especially indebted to Bernhard Fabian for conducting an extensive campaign to locate in his country English-language editions known to us only in publisher lists.

In the United States our investigations have ranged through the academic or municipal libraries in fifteen cities, and first in Austin at The Harry Ransom Humanities Research Center, where we were assisted considerably by Thomas F. Staley, Richard Oram, and John B. Thomas III. Thereafter, at one time or another, we were helped, in Bethlehem by Philip A. Metzger; in Bloomington by William R. Cagle and Joel Silver; Cambridge: Kenneth E. Carpenter, Roger E. Stoddard, and Leslie Morris; Charlottesville: Terry Belanger and David L. Vander Meulen; Moscow: Terry

Abrahams and Christine Gray; New Haven: Ellen Cordes, Stephen Parks, and Marjorie Gray Wynne; New York (New York University): Chatham Ewing and Marvin J. Taylor, (Pierpont Morgan Library): Anna Lou Ashby, Inge Dupont, H. George Fletcher; Philadelphia (Library Company): James N. Green and John C. Van Horne, (University of Pennsylvania): Daniel Traister; Princeton: William L. Joyce; Providence: Rosemary L. Cullen and Samuel A. Streit; Worcester: Georgia B. Barnhill, Joanne D. Chaison, Ellen S. Dunlap, John B. Hench, and Marcus A. McCorison. Early in our research we were privileged to receive, jointly, Zachariah Poulson fellowships from the Library Company of Philadelphia and Kate B. and Hall J. Peterson fellowships from the American Antiquarian Society in Worcester. To Jimmy Chung, immediately available in Austin, we also extend our thanks for continual assistance in translating our discourse into electronic form.

For permission to reproduce the initial page or title to certain works we are grateful to the Trustees of The British Library (items 38A, 127Aa), The National Library of Scotland (92A, 111A, 248A), and The Pierpont Morgan Library (352A.29). Other illustrations are from our own collection.

As this intriguing enterprise over the last decade now comes to a close, we would lastly express our deep appreciation to Professor Jane Millgate, whose wise counsel has enlightened and sustained us at every stage from start to finish. On many occasions her suggested amendments have greatly enhanced our own endeavours or set aright some misconception. Nonetheless, in a work of this magnitude and complexity, undetected deficiencies will remain, and we would be pleased to know of any that our readers may perceive.

LIBRARIES

Copies at the institutions listed below have been personally examined. Other libraries identified in place have kindly reported variants beyond the range of our inspections.

A	Abbotsford Library
AN	National Library of Wales, Aberystwyth
BCL	Bernard C. Lloyd, East Sussex
C	Cambridge University
CaBVaU	University of British Columbia, Vancouver, Canada
DLC	Library of Congress, Washington, D.C.
DN	National Library of Ireland, Dublin
DT	Trinity College, Dublin
E	National Library of Scotland, Edinburgh
EP	Central Public Library, Edinburgh
ES	Signet Library, Edinburgh
EU	University of Edinburgh
GM	Mitchell Library, Glasgow
GU	University of Glasgow
HS	St Deiniol's Library, Hawarden, Clwyd. The W. E. Gladstone Collection.
IdU	University of Idaho, Moscow. The Earl J. Larrison Collection
InU	Indiana University, Bloomington
L	British Library, London
LU	University of London
LVA	Victoria and Albert Museum Library, London
MB	Boston Public Library, Massachusetts
MH	Harvard University, Widener and Houghton Libraries, Cambridge
MH-M	Harvard University—Music Library
MWA	American Antiquarian Society, Worcester
NjP	Princeton University, New Jersey
NN	New York Public Library
NN-L	New York Public Library—Lincoln Center Music Library
NNC	Columbia University, New York
NNP	Pierpont Morgan Library, New York
NNU-W	New York University—Washington Square. The Fales Collection
O	Oxford University
OCl	Cleveland Public Library, Ohio
P	Bibliothèque Nationale, Paris
PBL	Lehigh University, Bethlehem, Pennsylvania
PHi	Historical Society of Pennsylvania, Philadelphia
PPL	Library Company of Philadelphia
PU	University of Pennsylvania, Philadelphia
RPB	Brown University, Providence, Rhode Island
T/B	Drs. William B. Todd and Ann Bowden, Austin, Texas
TxGR	Rosenberg Library, Galveston, Texas
TxU	University of Texas at Austin
ViU	University of Virginia, Charlottesville

REFERENCES

The following entries were useful in the compilation of this bibliography. Studies concerned with a particular work are cited in the references for that item.

Abbotsford — *Catalogue of the Library at Abbotsford.* John George Cochrane (ed.). [Edinburgh]: M.DCCC.XXXVIII.

Ath — *The Athenaeum or Weekly Review of English and Foreign Literature.* London.

Bell — Alan Bell (ed.). *Scott Bicentenary Essays.* Edinburgh and London: Scottish Academic Press [1973].

Bolton — H. Philip Bolton. *Scott Dramatized.* [London]: Mansell [1992].

Brown, I. — Iain Gordon Brown (ed.). *Scott's Interleaved Waverley Novels . . . An Introduction and Commentary.* [Aberdeen]: Pergamon Books Ltd / Aberdeen University Press / National Library of Scotland [1987].

Brown, P. — Philip A. H. Brown. *London Publishers and Printers 1800-1870.* London: British Library [1982].

Buchan — John Buchan. *Sir Walter Scott.* London: Cassell [1932].

Byron — *Byron's Letters and Journals.* Leslie A. Marchand (ed.). 12 volumes. Cambridge, Mass.: Belknap Press, 1973-1982.

CBEL — *The Cambridge Bibliography of English Literature.* F. W. Bateson (ed.). Volume III: 1800-1900. Cambridge: University Press, 1940.

CM — *The Caledonian Mercury*, Edinburgh.

CPM — *Catalogue of Printed Music in the British Library to 1980.* London: K. G. Saur, 1981.

Church — *A Catalogue of Books . . . forming a Part of the Library of E. D. Church.* George Watson Cole (ed.). Vol. 2. New York: Dodd, Mead, 1909. [Collection now at the Huntington Lbrary.]

Clarkin — William Clarkin. *Mathew Carey: A Bibliography of His Publications, 1785-1824.* New York: Garland, 1984.

Cohn — Albert M. Cohn. *George Cruikshank: A Catalogue Raisonné.* London: The Bookman's Journal, 1924.

Corson(1) — James Clarkson Corson. *A Bibliography of Sir Walter Scott: A Classified and Annotated List . . . 1797-1940.* London: Oliver and Boyd [1943].

Corson(2)	James Clarkson Corson. *Notes and Index to Sir Herbert Grierson's Edition of the Letters of Sir Walter Scott.* Oxford: Clarendon Press, 1979.
Craigie	Sir William Craigie. *The Northern Element in English Literature.* Toronto: University of Toronto Press [1933].
Cruse	Amy Cruse. *The Englishman and His Books in the Early Nineteenth Century.* London: George G. Harrap, 1930.
Curry	Kenneth Curry. *Sir Walter Scott's* Edinburgh Annual Register. Knoxville: University of Tennessee Press [1977].
Daiches	David Daiches. *Sir Walter Scott and His World.* London: Thames and Hudson [1971].
Dibdin	James C. Dibdin. *Annals of the Edinburgh Stage.* Edinburgh: Cameron, 1888.
Duval	K. D. Duval. *Scott & His Scotland: A Catalogue.* Pitlochry: Duval, 1971.
EA	*The Edinburgh Advertiser*
EEC	*The Edinburgh Evening Courant.*
EEWN	*The Edinburgh Edition of the Waverley Novels.* David Hewitt (ed., and others identified in references). Edinburgh: University Press, 1993—.
ELJ	*The Edinburgh Literary Journal.*
1871 Exhibit	*The Scott Exhibition: MDCCCLXXI.* Edinburgh: 1872.
EWJ	*The Edinburgh Weekly Journal*
Faxon	Frederick W. Faxon. *Literary Annuals and Gift Books: A Bibliography 1823-1903.* London: Private Libraries Association, 1973.
Finley	Gerald Finley. *Landscapes of Memory: Turner as Illustrator to Scott.* London: Scolar Press, 1980.
Fiske	Roger Fiske. *Scotland in Music; A European Enthusiasm.* Cambridge: Cambridge University Press [1983].
Ford	Richard Ford. *Dramatisations of Scott's Novels: A Catalogue.* Oxford Bibliographical Society, 1979.
GDS	*Gesamtverzeichnis des deutschsprachigen Schrifttums 1700-1910.* Vol. 132. Munich: K. G. Saur, 1985.
GM	*The Gentleman's Magazine.* London.

G/T	Bryan N. S. Gooch and David S. Thatcher. *Musical Settings of British Romantic Literature.* Two volumes. New York: Garland, 1982.
Garside	Peter Garside. 'Scott as a Political Journalist.' *Review of English Studies,* 37 (1986), 503-517.
Gaskell	Philip Gaskell. *A New Introduction to Bibliography.* Oxford: Clarendon Press, 1972.
Goodhugh	William Goodhugh. *The English Gentleman's Library Manual.* London: Goodhugh, 1827.
Grady	Rose Marie Grady. *The Sources of Scott's Eight Long Poems.* [dissertation]. Urbana: University of Illinois, 1933.
Grove	*The New Grove Dictionary of Music and Musicians,* Stanley Sadie (ed.). 20 volumes. London: Macmillan, 1980.
Grove/ Opera	*The New Grove Dictionary of Opera.* Stanley Sadie (ed.). Four volumes. [London: Macmillan, 1992].
Hart	Francis R. Hart. *Lockhart as Romantic Biographer*. Edinburgh: University Press [1971].
Hewitt	*Scott on Himself: A Selection of the Autobiographical Writings of Sir Walter Scott.* David Hewitt (ed.). Edinburgh: Scottish Academic Press, 1981.
Hopkinson/ Oldman	Cecil Hopkinson and C. B. Oldman. 'Thomson's Collections of National Song with Special Reference to the Contributions of Haydn and Beethoven' *in* the *Edinburgh Bibliographical Society Transactions, V*olume II, Part I (Session 1938-1939), pages *1-2* 3-64. 1940.
H/S	Charles Humphries and William C. Smith. *Music Publishing in the British Isles from the Beginning until the Middle of the Nineteenth Century.* Oxford: Basil Blackwell, 1970.
Hunnisett	Basil Hunnisett. *Steel-Engraved Book Illustration in England.* London: Scolar Press [1980].
Jaboor / McMullin	Nan Jaboor and B. J. McMullin. *James Ballantyne and Press Figures: with a Checklist of Volumes*. Melbourne: Ancora Press, 1994.
Johnson	Edgar Johnson. *Sir Walter Scott: The Great Unknown.* [London] Hamish Hamilton [1970].
Journal	*The Journal of Sir Walter Scott.* W. E. K. Anderson (ed.). Oxford: Clarendon Press, 1972.
Kaser	David Kaser. *The Cost Book of Carey & Lea 1825-1838.* Philadelphia: University of Pennsylvania Press, [1963].

Kohler(1) Michèle Kohler. *Scott Abroad: Catalogue of a Collection.* Dorking: C. C. Kohler, 1989.

Kohler(2) Michèle Kohler. *Scott Abroad Catalogue of a Collection.* Dorking: C. C. Kohler, 1991.

Kohler(3) Michèle Kohler. *British Poetry of the Romantic Period 1789-1839.* Dorking: C. C. Kohler [1995].

Krummel D. W. Krummel. *Bibliographical Handbook of American Music.* Urbana: University of Illinois [1987].

LC *The London Chronicle.*

LG *The Literary Gazette, and Journal of Belles Lettres, Arts, Sciences, &c.* London.

Letters *The Letters of Sir Walter Scott.* H. J. C. Grierson (ed. and others). 12 volumes. London: Constable, 1932-1937.

Lockhart John Gibson Lockhart. *Memoirs of the Life of Sir Walter Scott, Bart.* Second Edition. Ten volumes. Edinburgh: Robert Cadell, 1839.

Loewenberg Alfred Loewenberg. *Annals of Opera: 1597-1940.* Second Edition. Genèva: Societas Bibliographica, 1955.

Lowens Irving Lowens. *A Bibliography of Songsters Printed in America before 1821.* Worcester: American Antiquarian Society, 1976.

Lowndes Walter Thomas Lowndes. *The Bibliographer's Manual of English Literature.* Henry G. Bohn (ed.). Part VIII. London: Bohn, 1863.

MC *The Morning Chronicle.* London.

MH *The Morning Herald.* London.

MLA *The Monthly Literary Advertiser.* London.

MM *The Monthly Magazine, and British Register.* London.

MP *The Morning Post.* London.

MPW *The Miscellaneous Prose Works of Sir Walter Scott.* J. G. Lockhart (ed.). 28 volumes. Edinburgh: Robert Cadell; London: Whittaker and Co. 1834-1836.

McMullin(1) B. J. McMullin. 'Press Figures and Concurrent Perfecting: Walker & Greig.' *The Library*, 6th series, 12 (1990), 236-241.

McMullin(2) B. J. McMullin. 'Volume XI of Scott's *Poetical Works* in Octavo, 1830.' *The Library,* 6th series, 13 (1991), 351-355.

Madison Charles A. Madison. *Book Publishing in America.* New York: McGraw-Hill [1966].

Maggs	Maggs Brothers. Catalogue 1120. 'Charles Dickens and Sir Walter Scott', 1990.
Magnum Opus	[Final collected edition, ranging first to *WN* (1829-1833), then to *PW* and *MPW* (1833-1836)].
Millgate(1)	Jane Millgate. *Walter Scott: The Making of the Novelist.* Edinburgh: Edinburgh University Press [1984].
Millgate(2)	Jane Millgate. 'Scott the Cunning Tailor: Refurbishing the *Poetical Works.*' *The Library*, 6th series, 11 (1989), 336-351.
Millgate(3)	Jane Millgate. 'Making It New: Scott, Constable, Ballantyne, and the Publication of *Ivanhoe.*' *Studies in English Literature,* 34 (1994), 795-811.
Millgate(4)	Jane Millgate. *Scott's Last Edition: A Study of Publishing History.* Edinburgh: Edinburgh University Press [1987].
Millgate(5)	Jane Millgate. 'From Kelso to Edimburgh: The Origins of the Scott-Ballantyne Partnership.' *PBSA*, 92 (1998), 33-51.
Mitchell	Jerome Mitchell. *The Walter Scott Operas, An Analysis of Operas based on the Works of Sir Walter Scott.* University, Alabama: University of Alabama Press [1977].
NCBEL	*The New Cambridge Bibliography of English Literature,* volume 3: 1800-1900. George Watson (ed.). Cambridge: University Press, 1969.
NG	*The National Gazette and Literary Register.* Philadelphia.
NYEP	*The New York Evening Post.*
Neighbour/ Tyson	O. W. Neighbour and Alan Tyson. *English Music Publishers' Plate Numbers in the first half of the Nineteenth Century.* London: Faber and Faber [1965].
PBSA	*The Papers of the Bibliographical Society of America.* New York.
Pearson	Hesketh Pearson. *Walter Scott: His Life and Personality*. London: Hamish Hamilton [1987].
PW	*The Poetical Works of Sir Walter Scott.* J. G. Lockhart (ed.). 12 volumes. Edinburgh: Robert Cadell; London: Whittaker & Co. 1833-1834.
Partington(1)	*The Private Letter-Books of Sir Walter Scott.* Wilfred Partington (ed.). London: Hodder and Stoughton, MCMXXX.
Partington(2)	*Sir Walter's Post-Bag: More Stories and Sidelights*. Wilfred Partington (ed.). London: John Murray [1932].

Randall — David A. Randall. 'Waverley in America.' *The Colophon new series,* 1, no. 1 (Summer 1935), 39-55.

Renwick — W. L. Renwick. *English Literature: 1789-1815.* Oxford: Clarendon Press, 1963.

Rubenstein — Jill Rubenstein. *Sir* Walter *Scott: A Reference Guide*. Boston: G. K. Hall & Co. [1978].

Ruff — William Ruff. 'A Bibliography of the Poetical Works of Sir Walter Scott, 1796-1832.' *Edinburgh Bibliographical Society Transactions., V*ol. I, Part 2 (Session 1936-1937), pages 99-240, 1937; Part 3, pages 279-281, 1938.

SM — *The Scots Magazine.* Edinburgh.

S/S — Ralph R. Shaw and Richard H. Shoemaker (and others). *American Bibliography. A Preliminary Checklist for 1801-1832.* New York and Metuchen, N.J.: Scarecrow, 1958-1977.

Shelley — *The Letters of Percy Bysshe Shelley.* Frederick L. Jones (ed.). Two volumes. Oxford: Clarendon, 1964.

Shine — Hill Shine and Helen Chadwick Shine. *The Quarterly Review: Identification of Contributors 1809-1824.* Chapel Hill: University of North Carolina, 1949.

Southey — *New Letters of Robert Southey.* Kenneth Curry (ed.). Two volumes. New York: Columbia University Press, 1965.

Sterling — *The Sterling Library . . . collected by Sir Louis Sterling . . . and presented by him to the University of London.* Privately Printed, 1954.

Sutherland — John Sutherland. *The Life of Walter Scott: A Critical Biography.* Oxford: Blackwell [1995].

Thomson — John Thomson. *Descriptive Catalogue of the Writings of Sir Walter Scott.* Philadelphia: The Free Library of Philadelphia. Bulletin, Number 1. 1898.

Tinker — *The Tinker Library: A Bibliographical Catalogue of the Books and Manuscripts collected by Chauncey Brewster Tinker.* Robert F. Metzdorf (comp.). New Haven: Yale University Library [1959].

Todd — William B. Todd. *A Directory of Printers and Others in Allied Trades: London and Vicinity 1800-1840.* London: Printing Historical Society [1972].

Van Antwerp(1) — William C. Van Antwerp. *A Collector's Comment on his First Editions of the Works of Sir Walter Scott.* San Francisco: Gelber, Lilienthal, 1932.

Van Antwerp(2)	William C. Van Antwerp. *A Short -Title Catalogue of First Editions of Sir Walter Scott in the Library of William C. Van Antwerp.* [San Francisco]: Privately Printed, 1933.
WN	*Waverley Novels.* 48 volumes. Edinburgh: Cadell & Co.; London: Simpkin & Marshall. 1829-1833.
White	Henry Adelbert White. *Sir Walter Scott's Novels on the Stage.* New Haven: Yale University Press, 1927.
Wolfe	Richard J. Wolfe. *Secular Music in America 1801-1825. A Bibliography.* Three volumes. New York: The New York Public Library, 1964.
Wordsworth	*The Prose Works of William Wordsworth.* W. J. B. Owen and Jane W. Smyser (eds.). Oxford: Clarendon Press, 1974.
Worthington	Greville Worthington. *A Bibliography of the Waverley Novels.* London: Constable & Co.; New York: Richard R. Smith [1931].
Young	Rachel A. Young. *American Songsters to 1860.* [dissertation]. Providence: Brown University [1966].

ONE

1796-1809

On 11 July 1792, a month before his twenty-first birthday, Walter Scott was admitted to the Faculty of Advocates in Edinburgh and, while still engaged in his legal profession, soon thereafter was drawn to several literary pursuits—these leading eventually, in 1802, to his first significant publication, the *Minstrelsy of the Scottish Border*. There, toward the end of his lengthy introduction, Scott avowed his intention of preserving in this collection the history and traditions of his native land, lest this grand inheritance be entirely forgotten. His early commitment, referring especially to the appended 'notes, and occasional dissertations', thus appropriately serves as an epigraph for this literary accomplishment (8Aa) since, as Lockhart later observed, it generally defined Scott's lifetime performance.

Another intimation of this patriotic resolve appears in the dedication of the *Minstrelsy* to the editor's noblest kinsman among the Scott clan, Henry, Duke of Buccleuch, whose 'gallant ancestors' in elder time may have been cheered by these various ballads and tales. In further commemoration of the heroic past, Scott then tendered his first major poem in 1805 (14Ab) to Charles, Earl of Dalkeith, the Duke's older son, and his second in 1808 (28Aa) to Henry, Lord Montagu, the Duke's younger son. Hence in these several acts of fealty, as well as in many other measures, one may readily discern Scott's early literary period as extending from 1796, when he first ventured into print, to 1809, when he temporarily desisted from his poetical chronicles. Within this limited span the present chapter records a total issue of 42 literary publications of all kinds, and in an Appendix (352A) some 68 legal papers in his professional capacity as an Advocate: altogether an extraordinary beginning for an author destined to be the most productive, popular, and influential writer of his time.

Among the several issues of the 1802 *Minstrelsy* there are other indications worth noting: in the first edition (8Aa) early signals of a continuing endeavour to recover from oblivion old works already published but now hardly extant;

in later editions through the fifth (Ah) a steady augmentation of the present text and commentary; and throughout, here and hereafter, the entry into print of a vernacular vocabulary previously existing only in oral or other ephemeral form. Recently a computer analysis of the new *Oxford English Dictionary* divulged the source of all quotations offered over time to establish the varying sense of our national language, with Shakespeare identified as contributing 33,150 and, quite unexpectedly, Scott recognized next as responsible for another 16,548 entries.[1] Even from a linguistic perspective, then, this author's contribution may be regarded as highly significant.

The *Minstrelsy* is also instructive bibliographically, displaying at the outset Scott's constant demand for expensive large-paper issues (8Ab, Ad, Ag) so that his estimable friends and patrons might be properly served. In this respect the author was ever commending James Ballantyne, a 'Scottish Bodoni' (*Letters*, i.282, ii.230), for this printer's fine presswork and, early on, publically criticized a writer for a slovenly produced book on cheap paper (10A). As if to counter this deplorable event, he had Ballantyne prepare in 1803, and issue in 1805, an elaborate edition of Johnson's *Rasselas* (19Aa-Ab), one 'deserving of a high place in the first libraries'. Recovery of the past, then, should not only be done but, for aesthetic and archival reasons, done well.

In subsequent editions of the *Minstrelsy* Ballantyne began to use press figures,[2] these immediately revealing, on some occasions, the presence or absence of cancel leaves (8Ae-Af), on others, the resetting of certain gatherings (Ah)—usually a sign of later issue. Even in an edition as late as the 'Fifteenth', this of *The Lay of the Last Minstrel* (14Au-Aw), the figures may point to as many as three distinct impressions throughout. None of these aberrations, it should be remarked, have been recorded in previous accounts, and numerous others may be expected in the present record.

Some years after the original 1805 issue of *The Lay*, his first major poem (14Aa), Scott alluded to an editorial propensity also of considerable concern throughout this record. In a first edition exemplar now at Windsor Castle, he remarked: 'This copy was prepared for the Second Edition, upon the principle of abbreviating the Notes recommended by the *Edinburgh Review* in their notice of the Poem. But my friend Mr. Constable would not hear of the proposed Abridgment, and so the antiquarian matter was retained . . .' (1871 Exhibit, item 290). Upon the early insistence, then, of his own Edinburgh publisher, Scott is soon observed extending the textual commentary to whatever length the printer's format may require (32Aa), continually augmenting the annotations just provided and adding others (47Aa), and so on at every opportunity to the end of his career. As he more than once confided, he was ever quite capable of providing, for a simple quatrain of verse, a learned commentary filling a handsome quarto (*Letters*, iv.101; *Journal*, pages 451-452).

Scott's *Marmion* (28Aa, 1808), the final poem in these early years, introduces other matters less bibliographical in nature, yet still of some consequence. First is the 1000-guinea proposal received from Scott's enthusiastic publisher:[3] an unprecedented sum which, though satirized by Byron, now established the author as of some considerable value commercially. Next, immediately following the acceptance of these lavish terms, and still a year before issue, is Scott's dispatch of proofs to his confidant, Lady Abercorn: the first recorded instance of a practice which, when conducted by other principals, eventually led to the piracy of printings circulating in advance of official publication.[4] Then also, though *Marmion* upon issue was not so highly praised as the previous performance, Scott's stature as a poet now came into increasing regard, leading several early commentators to assess his epical chronicles as 'Homeric', another recently (in 1932) to cite certain passages as Homeric, and yet another to rank *Marmion* especially above the *Iliad*.[5]

Even in the early years Scott's poetry was quickly disseminated abroad. Matthew Lewis's *Tales of Wonder* 1801 (7Aa), containing five of his poems, within the year was reprinted in Dublin and New York (7Rb, Rd). His own *Lay of the Last Minstrel* 1805 was issued that same year in Philadelphia (14Rm), with identically paged reissues then appearing 1806 by another bookseller in the same city, in New York, and in Charleston, South Carolina (14Rn, Ri, Rf). His less popular *Marmion* 1808 nonetheless was issued that year again in Philadelphia and then, with cancel titles, in Boston (28Rh, Rb).

However received, at home or abroad, *Marmion,* was, for Scott, a debilitating experience, 'a scourging crop' (*Letters*, ii.93), causing him to stop versifying for a while and cultivate more extensively his ongoing editorial projects. The immediate result, to the amazement of all his friends, was the production (discounting large-paper issues and later editions) of thirty substantial volumes, all these before the end of 1809! And yet in this brief interval Scott still found time to engage, additionally, in numerous reviews (or 'articles' as they were then designated), to assist in publishing illustrations for one of his poems (33Aa-Ab), to provide an extensive prospectus for the

Edinburgh Annual Register (35A), and to start an abortive edition of James Thomson (37A).

Among the thirty principal volumes, all hitherto exempt from bibliographical analysis, four editions especially deserve some preliminary notice:
(29A) *The Life of John Dryden*, a much admired biography now first exemplifying Scott's competence in yet another aspect of *belles-lettres*;
(32A) *Queenhoo-Hall*, an edition of Strutt where, as Scott later noted, he anticipated the writing of his own prose romance, that is, *Waverley*;
(34A) *Memoirs of Robert Cary*, an important source-book for Scott, first mentioned in his 1802 *Minstrelsy*, and now formally acclaimed as one of the touchstones of history;
(38A) The 'Somers' Tracts', an immense quarto edition appearing in thirteen volumes, 1-2 in 1809, 3-13 in 1810-1815.
This last edition, though begun in some relief, must rank with the 1827 *Life of Napoleon* as the most exhaustive performance of Scott's entire career, comprising with his 81 additions some 955 tracts in the reigns between Elizabeth and Anne, all here with an enlightened commentary tendered to the historians of that tumultuous period. The historians indeed have gratefully acknowledged this vast encyclopaedia as a primary reference,[6] but literary scholars leave it untouched. Three years after accomplishing this task Scott himself observed that the edition 'made me wonderfully well acquainted with the little traits which mark'd parties & characters in the 17th century' (*Letters*, v.56): an intimate familiarity which would serve him well when, as he said, these traits were 'embodied' in his subsequent literary creations.

1. The computerisation of the *OED* is pleasantly described in *Time* magazine, 27 March 1989, pages 95, 98. From this same numerical analysis the 1990 *Guinness* credits Scott with reclaiming from a 1741 essay the longest word (29 letters) in the *OED*: cf. his *Journal*, pages 107, 536. A further appreciation of Scott's recovery of an archaic language earlier in print was expressed in 1993 when, on behalf of the *EEWN* project, Dr. J. H. Alexander observed (11.419): 'The editorial team has constantly been surprised to find support in the *Oxford English Dictionary* for unusual idioms, often obsolete in Scott's time and employed as part of the period effect by an author steeped in the vernacular of the Elizabethan and Jacobean periods. Restoration of such idioms, especially when they occur in speech, adds considerably to the novel's stylistic vividness.'

2. At Scott's urging, Ballantyne moved his office from Kelso to Edinburgh in 1803, printed several works with figures in 1804, and began using these indices for Scott in *The Lay of the Last Minstrel* (14Ab, published 12 January 1805 in Edinburgh, 24 January in London). Their earliest appearance for Scott, however, occurs in a 1799 London edition (4Aa-Ab),

where again some typographical disturbance has gone unrecognized. For all the Edinburgh issues see the exhaustive checklist in the Jaboor/ McMullin monograph, pages 28-57.

3. It should be observed that the public disclosure of the price for *Marmion* was made in the London *Monthly Magazine*, a journal usually disregarded in literary studies, yet apparently the only source for other revelations concerning Scott, including the price for another of his major poems (64Aa), the issue of some original verse two years before the date generally recognized (63A), commentary on obscure works shortly thereafter edited or translated by Scott (71A, 114A), a previously unknown translation by this author (133A), and apparently his only advance notice of a novel series, this thirteen years before the event (148A). This journal also provides much incidental intelligence, as our record will indicate.

4. A slight lapse, made known to Scott in December 1807, involves William Miller, one of the London publishers of *Marmion*, who imprudently showed parts of the poem to his friends several months before publication (22 February 1808 in Edinburgh, 8 March in London). *Letters*, i.404.

5. Early references to Scott's 'Homeric' discourse were made in 1814 by Thomas Barnes (cf. Corson[1], item 819) and 1832 by Edward Bulwer-Lytton (*The New Monthly Magazine* 35, part 2, pages 300-304); later allusions in 1932 by John Buchan (pages 113-114, 245) and by Thomas Hardy in a conversation with T. E. Lawrence (an encounter represented in Sutherland, page 125). In 1907 Professor George Edward Woodberry placed the author with more recent company in his survey titled *Great Writers: Cervantes, Scott, Milton, Virgil, Montaigne, Shakspere.*

6. Among other citations the two most often given are Conyers Read, *Bibliography of British History: Tudor Period*, 2nd ed. (Oxford 1959) 296, and Godfrey Davies, *Bibliography of British History: Stuart Period*, 2nd ed. (Oxford 1970) 61. A solitary literary article, on Scott's editorial treatment of Stephen Gosson's *The Schoole of Abuse* (in 'Somers' Tracts' iii [1810], 552-574), appears in *PBSA* 59 (1965), 425-429.

THE LAY OF THE LAST MINSTREL, 1809
14Dm. The Westall vignette design,
issued with another engraved suite
illustrated on page 162

CONTENTS OF CHAPTER ONE

THE CHASE, AND WILLIAM AND HELEN

The fate of this, my first publication, was by no means flattering. I distributed so many copies among my friends as, according to the booksellers, materially to interfere with the sale; and the number of translations which appeared in England about the same time, . . . were sufficient to exclude a provincial writer from competition. . . . In a word, my adventure, where so many pushed off to sea, proved a dead loss, and a great part of the edition was condemned to the service of the trunk-maker. Nay, so complete was the failure of the unfortunate ballads, that the very existence of them was soon forgotten. ('Essay on Imitations', April 1830, *PW*, iv.61-62).

1Aa] First Edition, First Issue: 1796

THE | *CHASE,* | AND | *WILLIAM AND HELEN:* | TWO BALLADS, | FROM THE | GERMAN | OF | GOTTFRIED AUGUSTUS BÜRGER. | [*short French rule*] | EDINBURGH: | PRINTED BY *MUNDELL AND SON*, R. BANK CLOSE, | FOR MANNERS AND MILLER, PARLIAMENT SQUARE; | AND SOLD BY T. CADELL, JUN. AND W. DAVIES (SUCCESSORS TO | MR. CADELL) IN THE STRAND, LONDON. | [*dash*] | 1796.

Published 1 November 1796 in Edinburgh (*EEC* 31 October, 'To-morrow'). 3s.6d. Binding: blue or marbled boards with tan/grey spine or (a later issue?) marbled paper with white spine. Paper: Post 4° (268 x 210mm uncut). Watermarks: 1795 / 1795. Collation: π^4(-π4 = *F*1?) A-E^4 *F*1. Pagination: *i* title, *ii blank*, *iii* iv-v note, *vi blank*, *1* 2-41 text, *42 blank*. Figures: none.

Notes: Although the first preliminary advertisement in the *Edinburgh Evening Courant* (15 October) gives the title in its published form, later notices (27, 31 October, 5 November) alter it to read (jokingly?) *Earl Walter's Chase and William and Helen*, a revision reflected in the manuscript 'corrected' copy at the University of Texas. Probably at this time, and certainly by February 1797, the appellation 'Earl Walter' was applied to Scott, then in his new post as quartermaster of the volunteer Edinburgh Light Dragoons. Still later, in 1801 (*see* 7Ab), the first ballad [1], translated from 'Die Wilde Jäger', was more appropriately titled 'The Wild Huntsman' (first words: 'The Wildgrave winds his bugle-horn,').

The later newspaper acoounts further note that the second ballad [2] (first words: 'From heavy dreams fair Helen rose') 'is a new translation of the celebrated Poem *Lenore*, to which the Public attention has of late been attracted in an uncommon degree, by translations of various excellence.' Those mentioned in *PW* are the version of 'Mr [William] Taylor of Norwich, and that of Mr [William Robert] Spencer.' Again, in 1797, 'Earl Walter' chose to name his first charger 'Lenore'. (The supposed advance printing of this second poem—a romantic story first reported by Lockhart, on hearsay from a deathbed, and reiterated thereafter—was early discounted by Robert Cadell who noted in the 1837 Lockhart proof sheets: '[Thomas] Thomson and other comrades doubt the separate printing'. Hart, p.181.)

Presentation copies: E('Miss C[hristian] Rutherford from the Translator'); CtY ('Mrs Fergusson Hermand') NjP('Miss [Sarah] Ponsonby from The Translator'). Other copies: A BCL E(2) ES L O; CtY('Given by Mrs. Christian Ker to Augustus Ross') DLC IdU(J. A. Clerk [of Craighall]) InU MH NNP NNP(Robert Balmanno) NNU-W PPL T/B TxU.

References: Abbotsford, page 271; Ruff 1 (with illustration); Thomson, [1] page 77, [2] page 41; Tinker 1860; Van Antwerp(1) 1. (Magnum Opus Edition 1833: *The Poetical Works*, [1] vi.307-318 as 'The Wild Huntsman', [2] vi.291-306.)

1Ab] First Edition, Second Issue: 1807

THE | **CHASE,** | AND | **WILLIAM AND HELEN**: | TWO BALLADS, | TRANSLATED FROM THE GERMAN | OF | GOTTFRIED AUGUSTUS BÜRGER. | *By WALTER SCOTT, Esq.* | [*diamond dash*] | EDINBURGH: | PRINTED FOR JOHN MURRAY, 32, FLEET-STREET, LONDON. | [*dash*] | 1807.

Binding: Green boards. Notes: Remainder sheets of the original printing reissued eleven years later with a new cancel title leaf, on the verso of which now appears a printer's imprint: [*short rule*] | *Printed by Mundell, Doig, and Stevenson, Edinburgh.* Effective 22 August 1799 the Seditious Societies Act (39 George III, cap.79) required such imprints in all printed work.

Notes: The number of copies extant, both of the first and second issues, would seem to belie Scott's recollection, some thirty years later, (1) that he originally gave away too many copies, and (2) that the larger part of the edition was soon consigned as waste to the trunk-maker.

Copies: BCL E LU O; CtY. Reference: Ruff 2.

THE ERL KING

2A] First Printing: 1798

['THE ERL KING.', (first words: '[O, who rides by night thro' the woodland so wild?]'), *in*:

Kelso Mail or, Roxburgh, Berwickshire, & Northumberland Gazette. March 1, 1798. Printed by James Ballantyne; And sold at the Office in BridgeStreet.]

Published 1 March 1798.

Notes: Five months earlier, in October 1797, Scott had sent a manuscript copy of his rendition of Goethe's 'goblin story' to his aunt, Christian Rutherford, then observing 'there is no small impudence in attempting a version of that ballad, as it has been translated by [Matthew G.] Lewis.' (*Letters,* i.76-77). This 1797 text was considerably revised when printed here in 1798 and again in the 1799 *Apology for Tales of Terror* (5Aa).

Copy: not seen, *Kelso Mail* title and imprint transcribed from a later number.

References: William Ruff, 'Walter Scott and *The Erl-King*,' *Englische Studien* 69 (1934), 106-108 (prints text, but copy not identified). (Magnum Opus Edition: Not reprinted.)

REPRINT

GREAT BRITAIN

2R] EDINBURGH: Constable 1802
'The Erl-King.* From the German.', page 72 (first words: 'O! who rides by night thro' the woodlands so wild?') *in*: The Scots Magazine, for January 1802. Edinburgh: Printed by Alex. Chapman, & Co. Forrester's Wynd, For the Proprietors: And Sold by Archibald Constable, High Street, Edinburgh, And William Coke, Leith. And at the Shops of the Principal Booksellers in the United Kingdom. And, at London, by Messrs Richardson, Royal Exchange; And Murray & Highly, Fleet Street. Published ca. 1 February. Notes: After a laudatory review of *Minstrelsy of the Scottish Border*, here suggested as perhaps by Scott (*see* 8Aa), the reprint of this poem is offered two pages later in the same journal and possibly from the same source. Evidently this new printing was intended to secure a wider audience than that afforded by the limited issues of 1798 and 1799. The long asterisked note reports other translations by Lewis and William Taylor, but concludes: 'For the following version, which was executed before the publication of any of those we have mentioned, we are indebted to a Scotish literary gentleman, whom we do not hesitate to place at the head of those who have cultivated this species of poetry in this country.' Though the reprint bears the subtended initials 'E.F.', we may conjecture that this is an early instance of Scott's self-promotion. Copies: E L; NN TxU.

DERIVATIVE

GREAT BRITAIN

2D] LONDON: Johanning and Whatmore & Whittaker, Treacher 1832
Erlkönig. pages 70-79, *in*: The Cadeau. . . . for 1832. London: Published by Johanning and Whatmore, English and Foreign Music-Sellers, 126, Regent Street; and Whittaker, Treacher & Co. Ave Maria Lane. 1832). Notes: Engraved sheet music preceded by printed text, page 70 (first words: 'O, who rides by night thro' the woodland so wild?'). Music headed: 'Der

Erl-König,(The Erl-King.) The Words by Göthe, translated by Sir Walter Scott. The Music by Fr. Schubert, adapted by F. M. d'Alquen.', has parallel texts in English and German. The text on page 70 is headed 'The Erl=King' and is in English. Copy: L. Reference: G/T 9810.

RULES AND REGULATIONS OF THE ROYAL EDINBURGH LIGHT DRAGOONS

3A] First Edition: 1798[1799]

[*engraved title within an elaborate frame adorned with military and royal symbols*] Rules and Regulations | of the | *ROYAL EDINBURGH* | LIGHT DRAGOONS | *1798*

Privately distributed ca. January 1799 in Edinburgh. Binding: red roan, a.e.g., without label. Paper: Pott 12° in sixes (120 x 71mm cut). Watermarks: none. Collation: π^2 A^6 B^6 C-F^6. Pagination: *i-iv blank*, [*engraved title*], *3* 4-8 Account of the Institution of the Corps, dated from Edinburgh 31 December 1798, *9* fly-title, *10 blank*, *11* 12-26 Rules and Regulations, *27-62* [*blank pages for notes*], *63-66* Words of Command for the Six Divisions of the Sword Exercise, *67-74* [*blank pages for notes*].

Notes: Scott, identified page 7 among the nine members of the Commission as 'Quarter-Master, Pay-Master, and Secretary', held the only 'literary post' and thus may be regarded as particularly responsible for the preliminary Account. This indicates that the first meeting was held 14 February 1797, when an offer of service was transmitted to the Duke of Buccleuch, Lord Lieutenant of the County of Midlothian, and quotes finally a resolution dated 17 March 1798. The several extant copies all appear to have Abbotsford as a common provenance.

Copies: BCL E(presented by Major-General W. J. Maxwell-Scott, C.B., D.S.O., of Abbotsford, 22 May 1932) L; MH('Compiled by Sir Walter Scott as Secretary 1798 given me by Sir Walter Maxwell-Scott Abbotsford 1937. P.P.S. Privately issued').

References: Maggs Catalogue 1120 (1990), no. 168 (now copy L). (Magnum Opus Edition: Not reprinted.)

GOETZ OF BERLICHINGEN

[I]t is necessary not only to be delighted with a work of genius but to be well acquainted with the language in which it was written before we attempt to communicate its beauty to others. I still set a value on my early translation however because it serves to show that I know how to select an object of admiration although from the terrible blunders into which I fell from imperfect acquaintance with the language it was plain I had not adopted the best way of expressing my admiration. (Scott to Goethe, 9 July 1827, *Letters*, x.250.)

4Aa] First Edition, First Issue: 1799

GOETZ of BERLICHINGEN, | *WITH THE IRON HAND:* | A TRAGEDY. | TRANSLATED FROM THE GERMAN OF GOETHÉ, | AUTHOR OF "THE SORROWS OF WERTER," ETC. | [*short French rule*] | BY | WILLIAM SCOTT, Efq. ADVOCATE, Edinburgh. | [*short French rule*] | *LONDON:* | PRINTED FOR J. BELL, NO. 148, OXFORD-STREET, OPPOSITE | NEW BOND-STREET. | [*dash*] | 1799.

Published 14 March 1799 in London (*MC*, also listing the translator as 'William Scott'); issued 4 June in Edinburgh (*EA*). 3s.6d. Binding: grey-green wrappers. Paper: Demy 8° (224 x 140mm uncut). Watermarks: W & Co 97 / 97; 1797 / 1797; 98 / 98. Collation: A-N^8 O^4 P^2. Pagination: *i* half-title, *ii blank*, *iii* title-page, *iv blank*, *v* vi-xiii Preface, dated from Edinburgh, 3 February 1799, *xiv blank*, *xv*-xvi Dramatis Personae, *1* 2-202 text, *203-204 blank*. Typography: The word 'GOETZ' in the title is in a slightly taller and much wider type fount than 'BERLICHINGEN'. Half-title page is signed A. On the title-page the period after ETC. is directly under the first 'E' of 'GOETHÉ'. Long 's' and catchwords are still employed in this London edition.

Figures: A ix-7, B15-2, C27-1 29-3, D38-4, E57-2 59-4, F74-2, G89-1, H108-4 111-2, I 126-3, K144-3, L157-7 159-6, M173-6 175-7, N188-9 191-6, O 194-6, P—.

First Printing of Poetry: An original poem appears in Scene XIX of Act III (page 136), where Scott introduced a ditty sung by a page named George which begins: 'It was a little naughty page, / Ha! ha!'.

Notes: This is the first English translation of Goethe's 1773 play, preceding by two weeks another prepared by Rose Aguilar Lawrence (26 March *MC*, titled *Gortz of Berlingen*, with preface dated 20 March). When some of the manuscript for the play blew out of the compositor's window, M. G. Lewis, then supervising the press work in London, chose to provide his own translation of the missing passages. An allusion to this collaboration appears in the last sentence of the Preface when Scott says: 'Upon the whole, it is hoped the version will be found faithful; of which the translator is less distrustful, owing to the friendship of a gentleman of high literary eminence, who has obligingly taken the trouble of superintending the publication.'

Copies: BCL E L LU; CtY DLC IdU NNP(Van Antwerp) TxU.

References: Ruff 3 (with illustration); Thomson, page 31; Van Antwerp(1) 2. (Magnum Opus Edition 1834: *The Poetical Works*, xii.*443-444* 445-564.)

4Ab] First Edition, Second Issue: 1799

GOETZ of BERLICHINGEN, . . . BY | WALTER SCOTT, Efq. ADVOCATE, Edinburgh. . . . 1799.

Published 27 March 1799 in London (*MC*, now listing the translator as 'Walter Scott' and adding to publisher's imprint 'H. D. Symonds, Paternoster-row; and Messrs. Bell and Bradfute, Edinburgh.')

Notes: A further issue with reset cancel title (period below space between O and E of GOETHÉ) now correcting the translator's name. The resetting and newspaper date would indicate that the alteration was made several weeks after first publication, perhaps when Lewis belatedly advised his London publisher Joseph Bell that the name was erroneously printed.

In this issue gathering N is now in two states: press-figures (1) N188-9 191-6, as in first issue; (2) one figure only N189-5. On opening the inner forme (page 191) to remove figure 6 the bracket after *himself* (line 26) was dislodged. Also apparently at this later time (as noted only in the O copy) figure 1 in the outer forme of G, was moved from page 89 to 96. These disturbances, all occurring after the original impression, would indicate that the type was being held for several printings.

Presentation copy: (state 2) CtY('From the Translator'). Other copies: (state 1) E L; InU.(state 2) BCL E ES L(2) O; CtY DLC MH NjP ViU. Reference: Ruff 4.

REPRINTS

FRANCE

PARIS: Didot and Galignani
[~] Goetz of Berlichingen. 1826. (Collection of Modern English Authors: *see* 292R.1.)

GERMANY

ZWICKAU: Schumann
[~] Goetz of Berlichingen. 1829. (Pocket Library of English Classics. Works of Walter Scott, Esq.: *see* 301R.198.)

UNITED STATES

4R] NEW YORK: Inskeep 1814
Goetz of Berlichingen, with the Iron Hand. . . . By Walter Scott, Esq. New-York, Published by A. H. Inskeep. Van Winkle and Wiley, Printers. 1814. Pages: *1-5* 6-206. Notes: In imprint either a comma or a colon follows New-York. To justify this late issue the publisher quotes

from the *Edinburgh Review*, October 1813: 'Goetz of Berlichingen has been vigorously rendered by a writer whose chivalrous genius, exerted upon somewhat similar scenes of British history, has since rendered him the most popular poet of the age.' Copies: E; CtY MH(H.W. Longfellow) MWA NN NNU-W PPL PU RPB ViU.

AN APOLOGY FOR TALES OF TERROR or TALES OF TERROR

5Aa] First Edition, First Issue: 1799

AN | **APOLOGY** | FOR | *TALES OF TERROR.* | [*double rule*] | [*one-line quotation from* Hamlet] | [*double rule*] | *KELSO:* | PRINTED AT THE MAIL OFFICE. | [*diamond dash*] | 1799.

Privately printed after 26 July 1799. Twelve copies only. Paper: Demy 4° in halfsheets (294 x 221mm uncut). Watermarks: 1794 | J WHATMAN; 1794 I TAYLOR; W ELGAR | 1796. (Obviously remnants of paper stock, with half the sheets unwatermarked, as might be expected in half-sheet imposition.) Collation: $\pi 1$ A^2 B-T^2. Pagination: *i* title-page, *ii blank*, *1* 2-76 text. Typography: Page 55, line 16 the word 'towr' has no apostrophe before the final letter, but in the GM copy there is a slight gap in 'tow r'. The title-page typography, especially evident in the swash Ts, conforms to the text fount, and thus justifies placing this variant as the first issue. In this, the first separate printing by James Ballantyne for Scott, the printer's name does not appear, as the act requiring this identification was not yet in effect.

Notes: Scott's own contributions to his little anthology, all reprints, include 'The Erl-King', pages *1* 2-3 (*see* 2A), 'The Chase' pages *27* 28-40, and 'William and Helen' pages *41* 42-57 (*see* 1Aa). Three others also appear. The 'Apology' of the title in this issue alludes to the long-delayed edition of M. G. Lewis's *Tales of Terror.*

Copies: E+ GM; MH* NNP**.
+With xerox of Abbotsford copy through page 57 (P1r).
*Inscribed 'a Remembrance from his friend John Ballantyne to Mr. Bruce.'
**Book label, No.'437'[MS] of John Ballantyne, Junior, Kelso, and later inscription 'To John Murray Esqr. being the only Copy in their possession With best Compliments from James Ballantyne & Co Edin 26 Feb 1807'.

References: Ruff 6 (with illustration); G. P. Johnston, 'The first book printed by James Ballantyne,' *Edinburgh Bibliographical Society Papers*, 1, sess. 1893-94, no. III and 9, sess. 1904-13, page 90.

5Ab] First Edition, Second Issue: 1799

TALES | OF | *TERROR.* | [*short diamond rule*] | [*short Oxford rule*] | [*one-line quotation from* Hamlet] | [*short reversed Oxford rule*] | KELSO: | *PRINTED BY JAMES BALLANTYNE,* | AT | THE KELSO MAIL PRINT ING OFFICE. | [*diamond dash*] | 1799.

Typography: page 55, line 16, the apostrophe in 'tow'r' is present.

Notes: This single-leaf title apparently was prepared to supplement a short count in the original supply or, possibly, as one more appropriate for presentation. The titletype is now quite dissimilar to the fount represented in the text and includes the name of James Ballantyne as printer: an entry required as of 22 August 1799 according to the Seditious Societies Act. All earlier arguments advancing this issue as the first thus appear to be invalid. (A 'second edition' with this title, dated 1808, is entirely an M. G. Lewis edition, containing only his own poems.)

Copy: CtY(Arms of John Ker, 3d Duke of Roxburghe stamped on covers; armorial book-plate of Sir Robert D'Arcy Hildyard, bart; later Prof. Edward Dowden. Reference: Ruff 5 (with illustration).

THE EVE OF SAINT JOHN

[T]he scene was that of my early childhood. Some idle persons had torn the irongrated door of Smallholm Tower from its hinges, and thrown it down the rock. I was an earnest suitor to my friend and kinsman, Mr Scott of Harden . . . that the dilapidation might be put a stop to, and the mischief repaired. This was readily promised, on condition that I should make a ballad, of which the scene should lie at Smallholm Tower, and among the crags where it is situated. ('Essay on Imitations', April 1830, *PW* iv.68.)

In the beginning of a literary career, which has now been a busy one, I pitched upon Smailhome tower and the crags on which it stands for the scene of a ghost ballad called "The Eve of St. John," and I make a point of making a pilgrimage once a year to the place, in memory of the good people who are gone. (Scott to Eliza Thurburn, ca. 21 June 1830, *Letters*, xi.370.)

6A] First Edition: 1800

THE | EVE OF SAINT JOHN. | *A BORDER BALLAD.* | [*Oxford dash*] | BY | WALTER SCOTT, Esq. Advocate. | [*short double rule*] | KELSO: | *PRINTED BY JAMES BALLANTYNE,* | AT | THE KELSO MAIL PRINTING OFFICE. | 1800.

Privately printed after 22 August 1799. Paper: Post 4° in half-sheets (254 x 198mm cut). Watermarks: laid, but no watermarks. Collation: π^2 ($-\pi 2 = D1$) A^2 B-C^2 $D1$.

Pagination: *i* half-title, *ii blank*, *iii* title-page, *iv blank*, 1-11 text, *12 blank*. Typography: Signature B is signed on B2 verso (page 6). Figures: none.

Notes: (First words: 'The Baron of Smaylho'me rose with day'). Line 7: 'Nor went he 'gainst the English yew'; later: 'He went not 'gainst the English yew'. As for the previous entry, also with Ballantyne's imprint, this issue postdates 22 August, the effective date of the Seditious Societies Act. In 1829 the poem was extracted in the two issues of an anthology titled *The Scottish Ballads* (369E[1-2]).

Copy: L. References: Ruff 7 (with illustration). (Magnum Opus Edition 1833: *The Poetical Works*, iv.183-195.)

TALES OF WONDER

7Aa] First Printings: 1801[1800]

1] 'No. XII. THE FIRE-KING' (first words: 'Bold knights and fair dames, to my harp give an ear,' [37 quatrains]), pages 62-69,

2] 'No. XX. GLENFINLAS, OR LORD RONALD'S CORONACH' (first words: 'O hone a rie! O hone a rie!' [66 quatrains]), pages 122-136,

3] 'No. XXII. FREDERICK AND ALICE' (first words: 'Frederick leaves the land of France,' [22 quatrains]), pages 148-152, *in*:

Tales of Wonder; Written and Collected by M. G. Lewis, Esq. M.P. . . . Vol. I. London: Printed by W. Bulmer and Co. Cleveland-Row, For the Author; and Sold by J. Bell, No. 148, Oxford-Street, Opposite New Bond-Street. 1801.

Published 27 November 1800 in London (*MC*). Two volumes. £1.1.0.

Notes: Because of the ample large paper format (263 x 165mm) and high publication price, this two-volume 8° edition was soon derided as 'Tales of Plunder'. The third poem, 'Frederick and Alice', is a free translation of a song in Goethe's 'Claudina von Villa Bella', but, as Scott observes, 'with such alterations and addi-tions, that it may almost be called original'. Scott's contributions, all confined to the first volume, include the three first printings listed above, as well as reprints of [4] 'No. XXI. The Eve of Saint John', pages 137-147 (*see* 6A), and [5] Scott's translation of Bürger's ballad 'Die Wilde Jäger', now revised but with new title misspelled 'No. XXIII. The Wild Huntsmen'[Huntsman], pages 153-163 (*see* 1A).
Of the three original Scott poems only [3] is extracted in a later anthology (*see* 357E.2).

Presentation copy: NNP('Miss Nicolsen [Jane Nicolson] from Walter Scott'). Other copies: BCL(2) O; CtY(2) DLC IdU(Sir William Augustus Fraser of Ledeclune and Morar, Baronet) InU MH(3) NjP NN PPL T/B TxU(3). References: Ruff 8; Tinker 1496; Van Antwerp(1) 3. (Magnum Opus Edition 1833: *The Poetical Works*, [1] vi.319-326, [2] iv.167-182, [3] vi.327-331.)

7Ab] Second Printings: 1801

Tales of Wonder; . . . The Second Edition. . . . London: Printed by W. Bulmer and Co. Cleveland-Row, St. James's; For J. Bell, No. 148 Oxford-Street, Opposite New Bond-Street. 1801.

Published 28 November 1801 in London (*MC*). One volume issue.

Notes: Though Lewis deleted twenty-eight poems in this selection, all of Scott's are retained, here with different pagination: [1] 'No. XII. The Fire-King' pages 69-77; [2] 'No. XX. Glenfinlas, or Lord Ronald's Coronach', pages 134-152; [3] 'No.XXII. Frederick and Alice', pages 165-169; [4] 'No. XXI. The Eve of Saint John', pages 153-164; and now, in some copies, correctly titled, [5] 'No. XXIII. The Wild Huntsman' pages 170-181.

Copies: BCL O; DLC MH(3) T/B TxU. Reference: Ruff 9.

REPRINTS

AUSTRIA

7Ra] VIENNA: Sammer 1805
Tales of Wonder; . . . Vienna: Printed for R. Sammer, Bookseller. MDCCCV. Three volumes. Pages 1: *i-iv*, 1-248; 2: *i-iv*, 1 2-277; 3: *i-iv*, 1-283 *284*. Copy: MH.

GREAT BRITAIN

7Rb] DUBLIN: Wogan 1801-1805
[1] Tales of Wonder; Written and Collected by M. G. Lewis, Esq. M.P. . . Dublin: Printed by Nicholas Kelly, for P. Wogan, G. Burnet, W. Porter, J. Moore, W. Jones, B. Dugdale, J. Rice, B. Dornin, G. Folingsby, T. Jackson, N. Kelly, J. Stockdale, and J. Parry. 1801. Two volumes. Pages 1: *i-iv*, *1* 2-220; 2: *i-iv*, *1* 2-224. Notes: Second volume title as for 1 except 'Printed by William Porter.' Copies: BCL DN; IdU MH(2) TxU.

[2] Tales of Wonder; . . . Dublin. Printed for P. Wogan, 20 Bridge-Street. 1805. Pages: *i-vi*, *1* 2-376. Copies: InU MH.

7Rc] LONDON: Offor 1817
Tales of Wonder; . . . Two Volumes in One. . . . London: Printed by H. Teape, for G. Offor

and Sons, Tower-Hill. 1817. Pages: *i-vi, 1* 2-376. Notes: A reissue of the Dublin 1805 edition (preceding entry) with cancel title. Copies: OCl PU TxU. References: Ruff 10 (arbitrarily defining this sophisticated piratical remainder as an authorized 'third edition'.)

UNITED STATES

7Rd] NEW YORK: Campbell 1801
Tales of Wonder; . . . New York: Printed by L. Nichols & Co. For Samuel Campbell, Bookseller, No. 124 Pearl-Street. 1801. Two volumes. Pages 1: *i-iv, 1* 2-236; 2: *i-iv*, 1-246. Notes: Volume 1 with woodblock frontispiece, sometimes found as originally printed at the end of volume 2. Copies: CtY MH MWA.

MINSTRELSY OF THE SCOTTISH BORDER

In the notes, and occasional dissertations, it has been my object to throw together, perhaps without sufficient attention to method, a variety of remarks regarding popular superstitions, and legendary history, which, if not now collected, must soon have been totally forgotten. By such efforts, feeble as they are, I may contribute somewhat to the history of my native country; the peculiar features of whose manners and character are daily melting into those of her sister and ally. ('Introduction', pages cix-cx.)

In the text and notes of this early publication, we can now trace the primary incident, or broad outline of almost every romance, whether in verse or in prose, which Sir Walter Scott built in after life on the history or traditions of his country. (Lockhart, 'Advertisement', 12 March 1833, *PW*, i.iv-v.)

8Aa] First Edition, First Impression: 1802

MINSTRELSY | OF THE | **SCOTTISH BORDER:** | CONSISTING OF | HISTORICAL AND ROMANTIC BALLADS, | COLLECTED | IN THE SOUTHERN COUNTIES OF SCOTLAND; WITH A FEW | OF MODERN DATE, FOUNDED UPON | LOCAL TRADITION. | IN TWO VOLUMES. | [*short diamond rule*] | VOL. I [II]. | [*short Oxford rule*] | [*four-line quotation from Warton*] | [*short reversed Oxford rule*] | KELSO: | [*short reversed Oxford rule*] | PRINTED BY JAMES BALLANTYNE, | FOR T. CADELL JUN. AND W. DAVIES, STRAND, LONDON; | AND SOLD BY MANNERS AND MILLER, AND | A. CONSTABLE, EDINBURGH. | 1802.

<SEE ACCOMPANYING ILLUSTRATION>

Published 24 February 1802 in Edinburgh (*EWJ*); issued 9 March in London (*LC*). 18s. On 6 February Ballantyne, writing from Berwick, informed Cadell & Davies that he was then shipping to London on board 'The Neptune' 693 copies. 'One

MINSTRELSY

OF THE

SCOTTISH BORDER:

CONSISTING OF

HISTORICAL AND ROMANTIC BALLADS,

COLLECTED

IN THE SOUTHERN COUNTIES OF SCOTLAND; WITH A FEW
OF MODERN DATE, FOUNDED UPON
LOCAL TRADITION.

IN TWO VOLUMES.

VOL. I.

The songs, to savage virtue dear,
That won of yore the public ear;
Ere Polity, sedate and sage,
Had quench'd the fires of feudal rage.

KELSO:

PRINTED BY JAMES BALLANTYNE,
FOR T. CADELL JUN. AND W. DAVIES, STRAND, LONDON:
AND SOLD BY MANNERS AND MILLER, AND
A. CONSTABLE, EDINBURGH.
1802.

ENTRY 8Aa. THE TODD / BOWDEN COPY

hundred of the remaining copies' (including apparently the 50 large paper) were sent to the Edinburgh publishers and seven retained for himself. (CtY, Osborn MS 43.128.) Binding: grey-green boards with grey-white spine. Paper: Demy 8° (226 x 142mm uncut). Watermarks: (volume 1) 1798 / 1798; 1798 / V F | 1798; 1799 / V F | 1799; 1800 / 1800; B1801 / May 1801; (volume 2) TW 1798.

General Notes: The *Minstrelsy*, at first consisting of 53 ballads, eventually in the 1812 fifth edition ranged through 96 poems, 43 of them printed for the first time, others offered in a 'better text', and all ordered in three categories: Historical, Romantic, and Modern Imitations. Occasionally from one edition to another a poem may be reclassified on the warrant of new advice and the annotation further extended.

A review in the *Scots Magazine* (January 1802, pages 68-70), oddly appearing several weeks before publication, is of a kind which may have originated from Scott himself. This begins with a ringing declaration: 'The Kelso press, which if we regard the execution of an early specimen, promises to vie with the finest exhibitions of typography, in other countries, has just produced a work, which we hesitate not to affirm, will attract the attention of men of literature, not only in Scotland, but in every country which has preserved a taste for poetical antiquities, and popular poetry.' The closing announcement that *Sir Tristrem* would also 'shortly appear' from the Kelso press is the first public intimation of an event still more than two years away and then occurring in Edinburgh.

The reviews immediately following issue, though not fully appreciative of the fine typography, or the old ballads now first appearing, acknowledged 'with particular approbation' the lengthy discourse (ii.167-227) 'On the Fairies of Popular Superstition': a matter of continual interest to Scott (cf. the epigraph above) and one last expressed at much greater length in his 1830 *Letters on Demonology and Witchcraft*.

Copies in two volumes: A* DT L P; CtY DLC MH NjP NNU-W PPL T/B TxU(vol.1). Copies with volume 3 added: (state 1) BCL E ES O; MH InU NNP(Van Antwerp) NNU-W. (2a) A# E L(2) O(Douce); InU. For further information on volume 3 see 8Ac.3.

* A copy with end-papers inscribed 'From His Majesty's Library.'

A copy a presentation, first two volumes the regular issue, third volume large paper: 'Mrs. Scott from her affectionate Son The Editor'.

References: Abbotsford, pages 157, 320; Duval 895 (with illustration); Ruff 11; Thomson, pages 28, 45-46; Van Antwerp(1) 4. (Magnum Opus Edition 1833: *The Poetical Works*, i-iv.)

1] MINSTRELSY | OF THE | **SCOTTISH BORDER:** . . . VOL. I. . . . 1802.

Collation: π^2 $2\pi^2$ a-d^8 e^8(±e8) f-h^8 k^4 i^2(i1+1) A-Q^8 *R*1 *S*1. Pagination: *1* half-title, *2 blank*, *3* title-page, *4 blank*, *5* dedication to Henry, Duke of Buccleuch, dated from Edinburgh 31 December 1801, *6 blank*, *7* fly-title for Introduction, *8 blank*, i-cxxxviii text, *cxxxix* fly-title for Historical Ballads, *cxl blank*, *cxli-cxlii* Contents, 1-258 text, *259* Errata, *260 blank*. Frontispiece: Hermitage Castle, by [Hugh] Williams, engraved by Walker. Typography: Of the four signed leaves in the c gathering, all originally missigned b, b2, b3, b4, the two in the inner forme are later corrected to c2 and c4 (pages xxxv, xxxix), the two in outer forme still retaining the missigned b and b3 (pages xxxiii and xxxvii). A similar 'correction' occurs in the oddly signed k gathering (see collation above), first reading k and i2, then k and k2 (pages cxxix, cxxxi). Figures: none.

Notes: The Contents leaf, printed on the second i leaf, before text, is occasionally withdrawn and inserted after the preliminary dedication. The original readings for cancel e8 (pages lxxix-lxxx) are unknown, even though in several copies (InU, TxU) this leaf is slashed as if it were the original so marked for removal. However, it is still a cancel and typographically identical to other copies.

Among numerous references one frequently cited is Carey's *Memoirs*, here quoted from the 1759 edition, the text Scott edited for issue in 1808. Apart from brief references on pages 122, 123n, there are extensive quotations on pages cxi-cxx, 37-43. A few 'familial' references also occur, to the Haliburton family (lxxiii.n: a manuscript Scott edited in 1820), and to the Scotts of Branxholm and Harden (cxxvi-cxxix).

Of two successive 'historical ballads' in this volume, the first, entitled 'The Laird of Laminton' (pages 216-219), was later withdrawn and the second, 'The Laird of Ochiltrie' (pages 220-225), was subsequently titled 'The Laird o' Logie' with a radically different text.

2] MINSTRELSY | OF THE | **SCOTTISH BORDER:** . . . VOL. II. . . . 1802.

Collation: π1 $2\pi^2$ 3π1 A-$2A^8$ $2B^4$ *2C*1. Pagination: *1* half-title, *2 blank*, *3* title-page, *4 blank*, *5-6* Contents, *7* fly-title for Romantic Ballads, *8 blank*, 1-305 text, *306 blank*, *307* fly-title for 'Imitations', *308 blank*, 309-392 text, *393 Errata*, *394 blank*. Typography: In some copies signatures Y, Y3 (pages 337, 341) are wrongly signed X, X3. For this substantial volume, now for the first time with a collation extending into a second alphabetical sequence, Ballantyne signs this latter sequence oldstyle as 'Aa', 'Bb'. Figures: none.

Scott poem, first printing: 'Thomas the Rhymer, Part Third' (first words: 'When seven years more had come and gone,'), pages 283-294.

Notes: Again as in the preceding volume Scott anticipates a later work, here first in a brief French quotation from 'the voluminous history of Sir Tristrem' (page 128n), then in reference to his own forthcoming 'limited edition' (in 1804, *see* 13A) the several versions known to him, and the first printing of his own modern analogue, titled 'Thomas the Rhymer, Part Third'. The latter 'attempt', he admits, though properly belonging in the ensuing section on modern ballads, is entered here because of 'its immediate connection with the first and second parts of the same story.' (However, in *PW* iv.110-166, all three parts are included.)

The concluding 'modern' section, titled 'Imitations of the Ancient Ballad', here represents only four poems, including reprints of two by Scott ('The Eve of Saint John' pages 309-326 and 'Glenfinlas' pages 373-392). The first of these, now with 'some additional illustratons', appropriately bears a note page 323 on Sir Walter Scott of Buccleuch.

8Ab] First Edition, Second (Large-Paper) Impression: 1802

MINSTRELSY | OF THE | **SCOTTISH BORDER**: . . . IN TWO VOLUMES. . . . VOL. I [-II]. . . . 1802.

Printed in fifty copies. Paper: Royal 8° (210 x 133mm cut). Watermarks: E & P | 1800; 1800 | J WHATMAN; 1801 | J WHATMAN; B1801 / *May* 1801. The May watermark, occurring in six sheets partway through the impression (f-A), also occasionally appears in the title-leaf of the demy paper issue.

Presentation copy: TxU('Mrs Edmonstowne [Barbara Edmonstone] of Newton from The Editor'). Other copy: IdU. Reference: Ruff 12.

1] MINSTRELSY | OF THE | **SCOTTISH BORDER**: . . . IN TWO VOLUMES. . . . VOL. I. . . . 1802.

Notes: Of the two variant preliminary gatherings, the signatures cited for the regular demy issue, little c remains either in the uncorrected or half-corrected state as before, but k is now corrected (k, k2).

2] MINSTRELSY | OF THE | **SCOTTISH BORDER**: . . . IN TWO VOLUMES. . . . VOL. II. . . . 1802.

Notes: In some copies Y and Y3 are again wrongly signed X and X3.

8Ac] Second Edition, First Impression: 1803

MINSTRELSY | OF THE | **SCOTTISH BORDER:** | CONSISTING OF |

HISTORICAL AND ROMANTIC BALLADS, | COLLECTED | IN THE SOUTHERN COUNTIES OF SCOTLAND; WITH A FEW | OF MODERN DATE, FOUNDED UPON | LOCAL TRADITION. | IN THREE VOLUMES. | VOL. I [II-III]. | [*short Oxford rule*] | [*four-line quotation from Warton*] | [*short reversed Oxford rule*] | SECOND EDITION. | EDINBURGH: | PRINTED BY JAMES BALLANTYNE, | FOR LONGMAN AND REES, PATER-NOSTER-ROW, LONDON; | AND SOLD BY MANNERS AND MILLER, AND | A. CONSTABLE, EDINBURGH. | 1803.

Published 25 May 1803 in Edinburgh. £1.11.6. 1000 copies. (500 additional copies of Vol. III were also made available to owners of the first, two-volume edition at 10s.6d.) Binding: grey-green or blue boards with white spine. Paper: Demy 8° (216 x 139mm uncut). Watermarks: none or 1801.

General Notes: On the date of publication in Edinburgh, Scott wrote to Ellis: 'The new edition . . . is published here, but not in London as yet, owing to the embargo on our shipping. An invasion is expected from Flushing, and no measures of any kind taken to prevent or repel it' (*Letters*, i.186). Some thirty years later he observed that, while the original issue was successful, this 'second edition . . . proved, in the language of the trade, rather a heavy concern. The demand in Scotland had been supplied by the first edition, and the curiosity of the English was not much awakened by poems in the rude garb of antiquity, accompanied with notes referring to the obscure feuds of barbarous clans, of whose very names civilized history was ignorant' (*PW*, vi.5-7). Altogether this new edition, published only a year after the initial issue, adds thirty-four ballads: two in the first volume, 21 in the second and—apart from those transferred to the new third volume—another 11 there in the 'Imitations' category.

Among the 'Imitations' in volume III there are four first printings by Scott: [1] 'Cadyow-Castle' (first words: 'When princely Hamilton's abode'), iii.380-401, [2] 'The Gray Brother' (first words: 'The Pope he was saying the high, high mass'), iii.402-414), and [3] 'War-Song of the Royal Edinburgh Light Dragoons' (first words: 'To horse! to horse! the standard flies,'), iii.415-420. Another original printing, [4] 'Christie's Will' (first words: 'Traquair has ridden up Chapelhope,'), iii.105-122, here admittedly 'eked and joined together', yet designated as a legitimate 'historical ballad', was later 'considered as a modern ballad', so transferred to the 'Imitations' group (4th ed., iii. 149-167), and thus occasionally is accepted in modern anthologies as of Scott's composition. (*PW* iv. [1] 200-217, [2] 218-229, [3] 230-234, [4] 91-109.)

Copies: (third volume, state 1) BCL(Francis Jeffrey) E; CtY MH T/B. (2a) E O; NNU-W. (2b) PPL. For additional copies of volume 3, supplementing the first edition, see 8Aa. Reference: Ruff 13.

1] MINSTRELSY | OF THE | **SCOTTISH BORDER:** . . . VOL. I. . . . SECOND EDITION . . . 1803.

Collation: π^4 a-g^8 h^8(±h4) i-k^8 l^4 *m*^{2} A-Q^8 R^8(±R6) S^8 T^2. Pagination: *i-ii blank, iii* half-title, *iv blank, v* title-page, *vi blank, vii* dedication, *viii blank, i* ii-clxviii Introduction and Appendices, *clxix-clxxii* Contents, *clxxi* fly-title, *clxxii blank, 1* 2-291 text, *292 blank.* Typography: In some copies, the direction line page xlix reads incorrectly 'Vol. II'. The direction line page 65 is omitted. Figures: none.

Notes: To the five appendices earlier printed this edition adds, as the first in the series, another titled 'Letter from the Earl of Surrey', pages cxxxv-cxxxix. Compared with the corresponding text in the first edition, cancels h4 (pages cxix-cxx) and R6 (pages 267-268) introduce the following variants: cxix line 2: (p.28)] (p.34); note line 1: says] sayeth; 10: Lindin] Linden; 11: abbacy] abbey; cxx line 8: a . . . told.] "a . . . told."; 19: Brooksby] Brocksby; note line 1: p.167)] p.174.); 267 note line 1: charter book] records. All of these minutiae early testify to Scott's zeal for accuracy, even after publication of the original text.

2] MINSTRELSY | OF THE | **SCOTTISH BORDER:** . . . . VOL. II. . . . SECOND EDITION. . . . 1803.

Collation: π^2 2π^2 A-2C^8 2D1 *2E*^{4}. Pagination: *i* half-title, *ii blank, iii* title-page, *iv blank, v* fly-title, *vi blank, vii-viii* Contents, *1* 2-331 text, *332 blank, 333* fly-title for 'Imitations', *334 blank*, 335-426 text. Typography: In some copies page 355 is misnumbered 553. Again in this and the next volume Ballantyne continues his 'oldstyle' signing practice, Aa, Bb, &c. Figures: none.

3] MINSTRELSY | OF THE | **SCOTTISH BORDER:** . . . . VOL. III. . . SECOND EDITION. . . . 1803.

Collation: π^2 2π^2 A^8 B^8(±B3, ±B8) C-O^8 P^8(±P4) Q-2C^8 2D^2 *2E*1. Pagination: *i* half-title, *ii blank, iii* title-page, *iv blank, v-vi* Contents, *vii* fly-title for Part First, *viii blank, 1* 2-229 text, *230 blank, 231* fly-title for Part Second, *232 blank, 233* 234-293 text, *294 blank, 295* fly-title for Part Third, *296 blank, 297* 298-420 text, 420 printer's imprint, *421* Errata, *422 blank.* Printer's imprint: [*short Oxford rule*] | Printed by James Ballantyne, | At the Border Press, | Holyrood-house. Typography: This is the first Ballantyne volume to include a final printer's imprint. Figures: None.

Notes: Despite the title reading 'SECOND EDITION', this is the original edition of the third volume. Cancels B3 (pages 21-22) and B8 (pages 31-32), original readings remain unknown. Leaf P4 exists in two states, the second in successive settings, page *231* reading:
(1) cancellandum] MINSTRELSY | OF THE | SCOTTISH BORDER. | [*short reversed Oxford rule*] | PART III. | *ROMANTIC BALLADS.*

(2a) cancellans] MINSTRELSY | OF THE | SCOTTISH BORDER. | PART SECOND. | [*reversed Oxford dash*] | *ROMANTIC BALLADS.*
(2b) cancellans] MINSTRELSY | OF THE | SCOTTISH BORDER. | PART SECOND. | [*Oxford dash*] | **Romantic Ballads.**
State 2b, rarely encountered, was probably set later to make up for a short count originally.

Again as in the first edition of the preceding volumes, Scott several times alludes to a work he later edited, now *The Life of Edward Lord Herbert* (*see* 40A). Apart from an extensive quotation pages 123-124n, there is a further reference page 128n. In a long introduction to 'Ellandon Castle' (a ballad contributed by Colin Mackenzie) Scott also provides a summary account of the Lord of the Isles, the subject of his 1815 poem.

After the errata leaf in some copies there is an additional leaf headed 'IN THE PRESS' which announces the forthcoming issue of *The Lay of the Last Minstrel* and *Sir Tristrem*. For this advertisement Scott, as usual, specified the wording (*Letters*, i.183).

8Ad] Second Edition, Second (Large-Paper) Impression: 1803

MINSTRELSY | OF THE | **SCOTTISH BORDER:** . . . IN THREE VOLUMES. | VOL. I [II-III]. . . . SECOND EDITION. . . . 1803

Printed in twelve copies only. Paper: Royal 8° (231 x 146mm uncut). Watermarks: none or J WHATMAN | 1801.

General notes: Writing from London to James Ballantyne, 21 April 1803, Scott mentioned several persons to receive 'ordinary paper' copies and then requests: 'Send one set fine paper to Dalkeith house, addressed to the Duchess [of Buccleuch]; another, by the Inverary carrier, to Lady Charlotte Campbell; the remaining *ten*, fine paper, with any of Vol. III. which may be on fine paper, to be sent to me by sea. I think they will give you some *éclat* here, where printing is so much valued.' However, because of the embargo then in effect on shipping between Leith and London, the ten extra copies apparently remained in Edinburgh and the set noted below thus not dispatched until about 29 June 1803.

Presentation copy: NNP('Mrs [Susan] Murray of Simprim from the Editor').
Reference: *Letters*, i.183.

1] MINSTRELSY | OF THE | **SCOTTISH BORDER**: . . . IN THREE VOLUMES. | VOL. I . . . . SECOND EDITION. . . . 1803

Typography: Page xlix direction line reads incorrectly 'VOL. II'. Page 65 lacks a direction line.

2] MINSTRELSY | OF THE | **SCOTTISH BORDER**: . . . IN THREE VOLUMES. | VOL. II. . . . SECOND EDITION. . . . 1803

Typography: Page 355 is now correctly numbered.

3] MINSTRELSY | OF THE | **SCOTTISH BORDER**: . . . IN THREE VOLUMES. | VOL. III. . . . SECOND EDITION. . . . 1803.

Typography: Leaf B8 (pages 31-32) is of the earlier state. Leaf P4 cancellans (page *231*) is now in a third state: MINSTRELSY | OF THE | SCOTTISH BORDER. | PART SECOND. | [*reversed Oxford dash, 10mm*] | *ROMANTIC BALLADS.*

8Ae] Third Edition: 1806

MINSTRELSY | OF THE | **SCOTTISH BORDER:** | CONSISTING OF | HISTORICAL AND ROMANTIC BALLADS, | COLLECTED | IN THE SOUTHERN COUNTIES OF SCOTLAND; WITH A FEW | OF MODERN DATE, FOUNDED UPON | LOCAL TRADITION. | IN THREE VOLUMES. | VOL. I [II-III]. | [*short Oxford rule*] | [*four-line quotation from Warton*] | [*short reversed Oxford rule*] | THIRD EDITION. | EDINBURGH: | **Printed by James Ballantyne and Co.** | FOR LONGMAN, HURST, REES, AND ORME, PATERNOSTER-ROW, | LONDON; AND A. CONSTABLE AND CO. EDINBURGH. | 1806.

Published November 1806 in Edinburgh (*SM*); issued 19 December in London (*The Times*). £1.11.6. 1250 copies. Paper: Demy 8° (211 x 130mm cut). Water-marks: 1805; 1806.

General Notes: Apart from additions to notes, four ballads are added in this edition: 'The Battle of Pentland Hills' (ii.51-57), 'The Feast of Spurs' (iii.452-456), 'On a Visit paid to the Ruins of Melrose Abbey' (iii.457-459), 'Archie Armstrong's Aith' (iii.460-465). The first of these, a historical ballad, was provided by Mr Livingston of Airds, the remaining three, all imitations, by the Rev. John Marriott, tutor to the Earl of Dalkeith's son. A large-paper impression, not issued separately, it seems, forms part of the *Works of Walter Scott*, 1806, volumes I-III (260Aa).

Copies: (2nd volume, state 1) AN E L O; (2) PU. References: Ruff 14 (noting three additions only).

1] MINSTRELSY | OF THE | **SCOTTISH BORDER:** . . . VOL. I. . . . THIRD EDITION. . . . 1806.

Collation: π^4 a-k^8 l^4 (-l4=*T*1) A-R^8 S^4 *T*1. Pagination: *i* half-title, *ii blank*, *iii* titlepage, *iv blank*, *v* dedication, *vi blank*, *vii-viii* Contents, *i* ii-clxvi Introduction and

Appendices, *1* fly-title for Part First, *2 blank*, *3* 4-282 text, 282 printer's imprint: [*short Oxford rule*] | Edinburgh, | Printed by James Ballantyne & Co. Typography: Page xlix, copied from the second edition, again has a direction line reading incorrectly 'VOL.II.'

Figures: a xiv-1, b xxx-1, c xliii-7, d l-4, e lxx-7, f lxxxix-7, g cv-1, h cxxvii-1, i cxxxix-1, k cxlvii-7 clvi-1, l 7/-, A16-3, B31-1, C47-7, D51-2, E80-3, F87-3, G110-3, H122-4, I 136-3, K152-3, L167-2, M179-3, N208-4, O 221-4, P240-7, Q253-5, R267-5, S—, *T*—.

Notes: The printing of final leaf *T*1 as part of the last preliminary gathering indicates that the introductory matter was being composed concurrently with the text.

2] MINSTRELSY | OF THE | **SCOTTISH BORDER:** . . . VOL. II. . . . THIRD EDITION. . . . 1806.

Collation: π^4 A-Y^8 Z^8(-Z1+*Z*^{2}) 2A-2D^8 *2E*1. Pagination: *i* half-title, *ii blank*, *iii* title-page, *iv blank*, *v-vii* Contents, *viii blank*, *1* fly-title for Part First, continued, *2 blank*, *3* 4-99 text, *100 blank, 101* fly-title for Part Second, *102 blank, 103* 104-434 text, 434 printer's imprint: [*short Oxford rule*] | EDINBURGH, | Printed by James Ballantyne & Co.

Figures: A15-7, B24-5, C46-4 48-7, D—, E74-7, F95-5, G110-5, H128-5, I 132-7, K158-1, L167-5 172-4, M184-5 187-1, N205-2, O 213-4, P231-5, Q246-7, R261-4, S284-7, T296-4 302-2, U320-5, X325-4, Y338-4 349-5, Z354(or 353)-5 361-2, 2A 377-5 378-2, 2B 389-4 391-7, 2C 408-7, 2D 427-3, *2E* 433-1/-.

Notes: Gathering Z exists in two states: (1) single-leaf cancellandum: Z1 signed, pages 353-356 numbered regularly, figure 354-5. (2) doubleton cancellans: introducing further text, Z1 unsigned, pages irregularly numbered 353, 354, [353], [354], figure 353-5.

3] MINSTRELSY | OF THE | **SCOTTISH BORDER:** . . . VOL. III. . . . THIRD EDITION. . . . 1806.

Collation: π^4 A-2F^8 2G^2. Pagination: *i* half-title, *ii blank*, *iii* title-page, *iv blank*, *v-vii* Contents, *viii blank*, *1* fly-title for Part Second, continued, *2 blank*, *3* 4-143 text, *144 blank*, *145* fly-title for Part Third, *146 blank*, *147* 148-471 text, 471 printer's imprint, *472 blank*. Printer's imprint: [*short reversed Oxford rule*] | EDINBURGH: | Printed by James Ballantyne & Co. Typography: Pages 466-467 are misnumbered 470-471.

Figures: A5-4 7-5, B26-3 32-4, C34-7 45-5, D58-4 61-3, E68-7 74-4, F87-2 96-7, G106-5, H116-7 123-3/-, I 141-2 142-4, K160-2, L176-3, M186-5 192-3, N200-7, O 219-2, P227-3 237-5, Q245-3 255-2, R259-4 265-2, S279-4 280-7, T291-7 296-4, U309-5 314-2, X334-2 336-5, Y351-7, Z363-2 364-5, 2A 375-3 384-7, 2B 389-4, 2C 407-2, 2D 421-5 427-7, 2E 437-7, 2F 462-7, 2G '470'[466]-4.

8Af] Fourth Edition, First Impression: 1810

MINSTRELSY | OF THE | **SCOTTISH BORDER:** | CONSISTING OF | HISTORICAL AND ROMANTIC BALLADS, | COLLECTED | IN THE SOUTHERN COUNTIES OF SCOTLAND; WITH A FEW | OF MODERN DATE, FOUNDED UPON | LOCAL TRADITION. | IN THREE VOLUMES. | VOL. I [II-III]. | [*short Oxford rule*] | [*four-line quotation from Warton*] | [*short reversed Oxford rule*] | FOURTH EDITION. | EDINBURGH: | **Printed by James Ballantyne and Co.** | FOR LONGMAN, HURST, REES, AND ORME, PATERNOSTER-ROW, | LONDON; AND A. CONSTABLE AND CO. EDINBURGH. | 1810.

Published 30 May 1810 in Edinburgh (*EWJ*); issued 18 July in London (*MC*). £1.6.0. 1250 copies. Paper: Demy 8° (212 x 132mm cut). Watermarks: 1808; 1809. General Typography: In all three volumes the printer's imprints now read: [*short Oxford rule*] | EDINBURGH: | Printed by James Ballantyne & Co.

General Notes: Apart from additions to notes, five ballads are added to this edition: 'Lord Ewrie' (i.131-135), 'The Death of Featherstonhaugh' (i.233-236; 'originally printed in the notes to Marmion'), 'Raid of Rookhope' (i.252-264), 'Bartham's Dirge' (i.265-269), and 'The Curse of Moy' (iii. 449-464). The 'Raid' piece derives from Joseph Ritson; the 'Curse' was provided by J. B. S. Morritt; the other three 'ballads' are forgeries foisted upon Scott by Robert Surtees.

Copies: E L O(Douce); CtY T/B TxU*. Reference: Ruff 15.
*With undated 8-page Sharpe and Hailes catalogue.

1] MINSTRELSY | OF THE | **SCOTTISH BORDER:** . . . VOL. I. . . . FOURTH EDITION. . . . 1810.

Collation: π^4 a-k^8 l^4(-l4) m^8 *n*1 A-N^8 O^8(±O8) P-T^8 U^4. Pagination: *i* half-title, *ii blank*, *iii* title-page, *iv blank*, *v* dedication, *vi blank*, *vii-viii* Contents, *i* ii-clxxxiii Introduction and Appendices, *clxxxiv blank*, *1* fly-title for Part First, *2 blank*, *3* 4-312 text, 312 printer's imprint.

Figures: a ii-13, b xxv-2, c xxxiv-7 xlviii-6, d 1-6/- lxiv-2, e lxvi-6 lxxx-2, f lxxxii-4 xcvi-8, g xcviii-6 cxii-7, h cxviii-3, i cxxxi-4, k cl-12, l clxiv-8, m clxx-13 clxxxi-3, n—, A*3*-12, B22-12, C46-12, D50-12, E67-12, F82-12, G110-12, H114-11 116-9, I 142-12 144-10, K159-12/-, L163-12, M178-12 180-8/-, N207-10, O213-12 218-7, P239-3 240-6, Q252-15 254-11, R272-14, S274-12 288-3, T290-14, U306-3.

Notes: To the six appendices previously printed in the first two editions, there are now added two others, 'VII. Excommunication of Border Robbers' and 'VIII. Double of the Contract betwixt the King and Several of His Subjects', pages clxvii-clxxxiii. Following leaf l 3 (pages clxv-clxvi) a blank leaf l 4 is ordinarily removed; pagination continues without interruption. Previously, in the third edition, this odd leaf was filled with the last two pages of text. Cancel O 8 (pages 223-224) probably introduces the long paragraph 'Jock o' the Side. . . . Cabala, p. 160.' not in the previous edition.

2] MINSTRELSY | OF THE | **SCOTTISH BORDER:** . . . VOL. II. . . . FOURTH EDITION. . . . 1810.

Collation: π^4 A-2E^8. Pagination: *i* half-title, *ii blank*, *iii* title-page, *iv blank*, *v-vii Contents*, *viii blank*, *1* fly-title for Part First continued, *2 blank*, *3* 4-99 text, *100 blank*, *101* fly-title for Part Second, *102 blank*, *103* 104-446 text, 446 printer's imprint, *447-448 blank*. Typography: Printer's imprint has a comma at end of first line. In some copies page 148 is misnumbered 48.

Figures: A10-12 16-10, B18-4 20-11, C34-6 45-12, D62-7 64-8, E80-12, F83-12, G98-4, H114-12 117-11, I 130-12, K146-12, L162-11, M178-12 189-9, N194-12 204-9, O 217-9 219-11, P240-9, Q247-12 256-8, R258-8, S274-8 276-11, T290-9 304-12, U306-12, X336-9, Y338-9, Z354-12, 2A 370-12 384-11, 2B 394-11 400-3, 2C 407-14 409-5, 2D 425-14 430-5, 2E 434-12 445-13.

3] MINSTRELSY | OF THE | **SCOTTISH BORDER:** . . . VOL. III. . . . FOURTH EDITION. . . . 1810.

Collation: π^4 A-L^8 M^8(±M5) N-2G^8 2H^4. Pagination: *i* half-title, ii *blank*, *iii* title-page, *iv blank*, *v-vii* Contents, *viii blank*, *1* fly-title for Part Second continued, *2 blank*, 3-145 text, *146 blank*, *147* fly-title for Part Third, *148 blank*, 149-486 text, 486 printer's imprint, *487-488 blank*. Typography: In some copies, as noted in the figure record below, the second figure 4 on page 452 has dropped out of the forme.

Figures: A6-14 16-12, B18-8 21-9, C34-12/- 48-11, D50-9 64-12, E68-8 70-12, F82-15 84-13, G98-3 112-12, H114-8 116-14, I 143-6 144-14, K152-6 158-13, L162-13 176-7, M178-12 186-3 192-3, N205-14 206-13, O 210-7 224-14, P237-15 239-12, Q242-10 256-7, R258-11 272-8, S274-3 288-13, T290-15 292-14, U311-15 320-5, X322-11 336-5, Y340-8 342-15, Z354-9 368-7, 2A 370-9 377-7, 2B 386-14 400-3, 2C 402-3 405-7, 2D 431-3 432-8, 2E 436-6 443-1, 2F 450-15 452-14/1, 2G 479-14 480-13, 2H 482-14.

Notes: In gathering M, representing three press-figures, the redundant 3 on inner forme (page 186) appears on cancel leaf M5. As compared with the preceding edition, the only difference in this leaf is at 186 line 2, 'rich' for 'rych'—hardly enough for a substitution. Hence, we may infer, the fault must have originated in this issue.

8Ag] Fourth Edition, Second (Large-Paper) Impression: 1810

MINSTRELSY | OF THE | **SCOTTISH BORDER**: . . . IN THREE VOLUMES. | VOL. I [II-III]. . . .FOURTH EDITION. . . . 1810.

Published concurrently with the previous impression. Binding: Blue-grey boards. Paper: Royal 8° (253 x 152mm uncut). Watermarks: D & A C | 1808; 1809.

General Notes: In all respects identical with the preceding impression except for paper and the variants noted below.

Copies: L; CtY CtY(vols. 2-3: *see* 260Ad[2] note) NN. Reference: Ruff 16.

1] MINSTRELSY | OF THE | **SCOTTISH BORDER**: . . . VOL. I. . . . FOURTH EDITION. . . . 1810.

Typography: Page 220 is misnumbered 20. Figures: E67—, K159-12, M180—.

2] MINSTRELSY | OF THE | **SCOTTISH BORDER**: . . . VOL. II. . . . FOURTH EDITION. . . . 1810.

Typography: Page 445 is misnumbered 436. Figures: S274—.

3] MINSTRELSY | OF THE | **SCOTTISH BORDER**: . . . VOL. III. . . . FOURTH EDITION. . . . 1810.

Figures: A16—, B18—, M186—, 2F 452-14, 2H 482—.

Notes: In this reimpression leaf M5 in its corrected state is integral to the gathering and the redundant figure on page 186 is thus withdrawn.

8Ah] Fifth Edition: 1812

MINSTRELSY | OF THE | **SCOTTISH BORDER:** | CONSISTING OF | HISTORICAL AND ROMANTIC BALLADS, | COLLECTED | IN THE SOUTHERN COUNTIES OF SCOTLAND; WITH A FEW | OF MODERN DATE, FOUNDED UPON | LOCAL TRADITION. | IN THREE VOLUMES. | VOL. I [II-III]. | [*short Oxford rule*] | [*four-line quotation from Warton*] | [*short reversed Oxford rule*] | FIFTH EDITION. | EDINBURGH: | Printed by James Ballantyne and Co. | FOR LONGMAN, HURST, REES, ORME, AND BROWN, PATERNOSTER- | ROW, LONDON; AND A. CONSTABLE AND CO. EDINBURGH. | 1812.

Issued 11 December 1812 in London (*MC*). £1.16.0. 1500 copies. Binding: grey or grey-green boards with printed labels. Paper: Demy 8° (224 x 140mm uncut).

Watermarks: none except for vol.1, sheet M in some copies (J Whatman | 1810) and vol.2 (predominantly none, other sheets: C | 1811 | 3).

General Notes: Apart from additions to the notes, one final ballad has been added to this edition: 'The Daemon-Lover' (ii.427-432), contributed by William Laidlaw, Scott's old confederate in the collecting of ballads..

Copies: (volumes 2-3, issue 1) AN BCL E ES L O P; NjP T/B TxU. (2) BCL IdU PPL. Reference: Ruff 17.

1] MINSTRELSY | OF THE | **SCOTTISH BORDER:** . . . VOL. I. . . . FIFTH EDITION. . . . 1812.

Collation: π^4 a^8 b^8(±b3) c-f^8 g^8(±g8) h-m^8 A-C^8 D^8(-D3-5,+χ^4) E-T^8 U^4 X^2. Pagination: *i* half-title, *ii blank*, *iii* title-page, *iv blank*, *v* dedication, *vi blank*, *vii-viii* Contents, *i* ii-clxxxv Introductions and Appendices, *clxxxvi blank*, *1* fly-title for Part First, *2 blank*, *3* 4-62 *63-*66 65-317 text, 317 printer's imprint, *318 blank*, 319-322 Additional Remarks. Printer's imprint: [*short reversed Oxford rule*] | Edinburgh: | Printed by James Ballantyne and Co.

Figures: a xi-10 xvi-7, b xxiii-3, c xxxiv-5 xl-6, d li-9 lvi-12, e lxxii-1, f lxxxix-7, g cxii-7, h cxxii-5, i cxxx-2, k cxlvi-9, l clxix-3, m clxxviii-5, A21-1, B32-6, C49-2, D56-12 *63-6, E74-5, F97-7, G115-1, H120-1/-, I 136-9, K166-3, L176-8, M190-6, N212-12, O—, P232-1, Q251-6/-, R266-9, S292-3, T299-9, U313-1, X320-1.

Notes: Original readings for the first two cancels are unknown. Cancel g8 bears a press-figure cxii-7. Cancellantia χ^4, replacing three D leaves, at the end of page 59 adds a 15-line passage ('The castle . . . all the vicinity.') and revises as well some later commentary. This insertion also bears a figure *63-6.

2] MINSTRELSY | OF THE | **SCOTTISH BORDER:** . . . VOL II. . . . FIFTH EDITION. . . .1812.

Collation: π^4 A-$2E^8$ $2F^4$. Pagination: *i* half-title, *ii blank*, *iii* title-page, *iv blank*, *v-vii* Contents, *viii blank*, *1* fly-title for Part First, continued, *2 blank*, *3* 4-99 text, *100 blank*, *101* fly-title for Part Second, *102 blank*, *103* 104-456 text, 456 printer's imprint: [*short Oxford rule*] | Edinburgh: | Printed by James Ballantyne and Co.

Figures: A7-12, B20-4, C35-2/- 36-2/-, D52-12, E80-5, F87-9, G98-5, H128-3, I 131-10, K147-6, L172-5, M180-9, N204-2, O 214-1, P240-1, Q244-4, R265-2, S274-8, T293-5, U308-8, X332-9, Y349-2, Z364-10, 2A 384-5, 2B 397-10, 2C 409-8, 2D 418-3, 2E 442-6, 2F 452-8.

Notes: As compared with earlier sheets B and F (1) both figured as noted above, some copies (2) have one or another sheet reset on poor paper watermarked 1806: sheet B, unfigured; sheet F, 95-5. These resettings probably were necessitated by a short count in the original paper layout.

3] MINSTRELSY | OF THE | **SCOTTISH BORDER:** . . . VOL. III. . . . FIFTH EDITION. . . . 1812.

Collation: π^4 A-2G^8 2H^4. Pagination: *i* half-title, *ii blank*, *iii* title-page, *iv blank*, *v-vii* Contents, *viii blank*, *1* fly-title for Part Second, continued, *2 blank*, *3* 4-145 text, *146 blank*, *147* fly-title for Part Third, *148 blank*, 149-488 text, 488 printer's imprint: [*short Oxford rule*] | EDINBURGH: | Printed by James Ballantyne and Co.

Figures: A5-5, B31-8, C40-1, D—, E68-9, F86-7, G110-6, H114-8, I 143-1, K158-7, L176-10, M185-6/-, N204-8, O 213-8, P227-1, Q253-8, R270-6, S282-5, T297-8, U320-6, X332-9, Y338-2, Z355-6, 2A 380-8, 2B 387-2, 2C 404-6, 2D 432-10, 2E 448-6, 2F 460-2, 2G 474-3, 2H 482-5/-.

Notes: Again there are two settings, now of sheet Y, figured either (1) 338-2 or (2) 344-1. Copies with this later setting also have a later setting in the second volume, indicating a later issue of the entire set.

8Ai] Fifth Edition (*Poetical Works*, Variant Issue): 1821

MINSTRELSY | OF THE | **SCOTTISH BORDER:** | CONSISTING OF | HISTORICAL AND ROMANTIC BALLADS, | COLLECTED | IN THE SOUTHERN COUNTIES OF SCOTLAND; WITH A FEW | OF MODERN DATE, FOUNDED UPON | LOCAL TRADITION. | IN THREE VOLUMES. | VOL. I [II-III]. | FIFTH EDITION. | [*short Oxford rule*] | [*four-line quotation from Warton*] | [*short reversed Oxford rule*] | EDINBURGH: | PRINTED FOR LONGMAN, HURST, REES, ORME, AND BROWN, | LONDON; AND A. CONSTABLE AND CO. EDINBURGH. | [*dash*] | 1821.

Published January 1821 at £1.16.0 (advt in Franck, *Northern Memoirs*, 152A). 500 copies. Binding: drab boards or (a later issue?) blue-green cloth with printed labels. Paper: Demy 8° (227 x 145mm uncut). Watermarks: None.

General Typography: The Oxford rule before imprint on title for volumes 2-3 is not reversed. Printer's imprints read invariably:(1) [*short rule*] | *Printed by James Ballantyne and Co. Edinburgh.*; (2) [*short rule*] | EDINBURGH: | Printed by James Ballantyne & Co.

General Notes: A variant issue of the 1821 *Poetical Works*, volumes I-III (263A), with each engraved title replaced by the printed title described above, on the verso of which is entered printer's imprint (1). Ordinarily this 'edition' was issued without half-titles.

Copies: E L O; CtY NN OCl PPL(vols.1,3) PHi T/B. Reference: Ruff 18.

8Aj] Fifth Edition (*Poetical Works*, Second Issue): 1821[1830]

MINSTRELSY | OF THE | **SCOTTISH BORDER:** . . . VOL. I [II-III]. . . . FIFTH EDITION. . . .1821.

Published by 20 April 1830 (advt in *The Doom of Devorgoil*, 239A.) £1.16.0. 300 copies.

General Notes: A remainder issue of the copies originally available in 1821 (cf. preceding entry), now with a new preliminary section inserted after the Contents leaf in volume 1, signed and paged as follows: a*-e*^{8} f*^{2} a†-e†^{8} f†^{2} g*^{8} h†^{4}. Pagination: *i* ii-lxxxiii Introductory Remarks on Popular Poetry, dated from Abbotsford, 1 March 1830, *lxxxiv blank*, *i* fly-title, *ii blank*, *iii* iv-lxxxiii Essay on Imitations of the Ancient Ballad, dated from Abbotsford, April 1830, *lxxxiv blank*, *lxxxv* fly-title, *lxxxvi blank*, *lxxxvii* lxxxviii-cviii Appendix.

Figures: d* lxiv-2, a† vi-15, c† xlviii-5, d† lxii-14, e† lxxx-18, g* lxxxviii-17, h† cvii-14.

Copies: O; CtY. Reference: Ruff 19.

8Ak] Fifth Edition (*Poetical Works*, Third Issue): 1821[1830]

MINSTRELSY | OF THE | **SCOTTISH BORDER:** . . . VOL. I [II-III]. . . . FIFTH EDITION. . . . 1821.

Collation for preliminary section: A-E^{8} F^{2} A†-B†^{8} c†^{8} D†-E†^{8} f†^{2} g†^{8} H†^{4}. Pagination: *1* 2-83 Introductory Remarks, dated from Abbotsford 1 March 1830, *84 blank*, *1* fly-title, *2 blank*, *3* 4-83 Essay on Imitations, dated from Abbotsford April 1830, *84 blank*, *85* fly-title, *86 blank*, *87* 88-108 Appendix.

Figures: D64-2, A†6-15, c†48-5, D†62-14, E†80-18, g†97-17, H†107-14.

General Notes: Evidently copies of the preliminary section prepared in 1830 were insufficient and thus these gatherings were reset.

Copy: O. Reference: Ruff 19, note.

REPRINTS

GREAT BRITAIN

8Ra] EDINBURGH: Constable 1803
'War Song, for The Edinburgh Cavalry Association', pages 725-726 (first words: 'To horse, to horse! The standard flies') *in*: The Scots Magazine, for October 1803. Edinburgh: Printed by Alex. Chapman, & Co. Forrester's Wynd, for the Proprietors. And Sold by Archibald

Constable, High Street, Edinburgh. And to be had of the Principal Booksellers in the United Kingdom. Published ca. 1 November. Notes: A variant reprint of 'War-Song of the Royal Edinburgh Light Dragoons', first issued 25 May in the *Minstrelsy*, volume III (*see* 8Ac). A preliminary notice, possibly deriving from Scott, now observes: 'The reader will peruse with much satisfaction the following admirable effusion of the warlike and animated muse of this ingenious author. It is calculated to produce every effect which a British patriot can desire . . . .' Apart from the title, lines 41 and 47, previously reading 'home' and 'bugle', here read 'Hope' and 'bugles', both amendments perhaps also by Scott. Copies: E; NN.

UNITED STATES

8Rb] PHILADELPHIA: Carey 1813

Minstrelsy of the Scottish Border: . . . By Walter Scott, Esq. Philadelphia, Published by M. Carey, No. 121 Chesnut Street, July 12, 1813. Pages: *i-iii* iv, *5* 6-312. Notes: A selection excerpted from the original. For some reason the Contents pages exclude the last two entries: 'The Douglas Tragedy' (first line: '"Rise up, rise up, now, Lord Douglas," she says,'), pages *301* 302-307, and 'The Original Ballad of the Broom of Cowdenknows' (first line: 'O the broom, and the bonny bonny broom'), pages *308* 309-312. Copies: E; CtY DLC MH MWA NjP NN(Berg-Washington Irving copy) PPL(2). Reference: Clarkin 758.

DERIVATIVES

GREAT BRITAIN

8D] EDINBURGH: Urbani and Liston 1803

Our Word is Law and Liberty. A Favarite[!] New Song Written by W. Scott Esqr. . . . Price 1/ Edinburgh Printed and Sold by Urbani & Liston Music Sellors[!] No. 40 Princes Street. [unwatermarked. 1803]. Pages: i, 1-2. Notes: Engraved sheet music. (first words: 'To horse! to horse! the standard flies, The Bugles sound the call;'). Song composed by P. Urbani for voice and pianoforte. Copy: E.

LONDON: Leigh

~] War-Song, "To Horse! to Horse!—the Standard Flies." 1831. (The Harmonicon: number 6. *see* 336D[4]). Notes: Series initially printed for The Proprietors, published by Leigh. This title was published by Longman, Rees, Orme, Brown, and Green.

EXTRACTS IN ANTHOLOGIES

8E] Of the four Scott poems introduced in the second edition of *The Minstrelsy of the Scottish Border* (8Ac) only two were extracted in the anthologies: [2] 'The Gray Brother' 377E.1 and [3] 'War-Song of the Edinburgh Light Dragoons' 360E.1 379E.5.

LETTER ON HOGG'S JOURNEY

9A] First Printing: 1802

To the Editor of the Scots Magazine, page 812 *in*:

The Scots Magazine, for October 1802. Edinburgh: Printed by Alex. Chapman, & Co. Forrester's Wynd, For the Proprietors: And Sold by Archibald Constable, High Street, Edinburgh. And to be had of the Principal Booksellers in the United Kingdom.

Published ca. 1 November 1802.

Notes: In this letter, dated from Edinburgh 26 September 1802, and inversely initialed 'S.W.', Scott introduces James Hogg's account of his 'Journey through the Highlands of Scotland' (printed pages 813-818 and, in the December number, pages 956-963).

Copies: E L; NN. Reference: (Magnum Opus Edition: Not reprinted, but quoted in *Letters* i.158-159.)

REVIEWS OF SOUTHEY and SIBBALD

10A] First Printings: 1803

1] 'ART. X. *Amadis de Gaul. By Vasco Lobeyra. From the Spanish Version of Garciordonez de Montalvo.* By Robert Southey. . . . *Amadis de Gaul:* A Poem, in Three Books. Freely Translated from the First Part of the French Version of Nicolas de Herberay, . . . With Notes, by William Stewart Rose, Esq.', pages 109-136;

2] 'ART. XVI. *Chronicle of Scotish Poetry, from the* 13*th Century to the Union of the Crowns, with a Glossary*. By J. Sibbald.', pages 198-210, *in*:

The Edinburgh Review, October 1803. No. V. [volume 3 imprint:] Edinburgh: Printed by D. Willison, Craig's Close, For Arch. Constable & Co. Edinburgh, and T. N. Longman & O. Rees, London. 1804.

Published ca. 24 October 1803 (date of an advertisement on verso of Contents leaf).

Notes: The first article—and the first to be accepted unequivocally as Scott's—exemplifies very well the *ER* principle that reviews should be 'a solid work of some magnitude'. The second article, probably uncollected in *MPW* for prudential reasons, contains an interesting commentary on the make-up of Sibbald's book, lamenting the inferior paper, the rough folding, and the poor external appearance. The Sibbald 'Glossary', however, is praised as a 'very important national acquisition'.

Copies: O; PPL TxU. Later issued as 'third edition' 1805 (L) [fourth and fifth editions also reported].

References: Renwick [on Scott and the *ER* generally], pages 197-204; Thomson, [1] page 67. (Magnum Opus Edition 1835: *The Miscellaneous Prose Works*, [1] xviii.*1* 2-43 as 'Amadis of Gaul'; [2] Not reprinted.)

REVIEW OF GODWIN

11A] First Printing: 1804

'ART. XVI.—*Life of Geoffrey Chaucer, the early English Poet:* with Sketches of the Manners, Opinions, Arts, and Literature of England in the 14th Century. By William Godwin.', pages 437-452, *in*:

The Edinburgh Review, January 1804. No. VI. [volume 3 imprint:] Edinburgh: Printed by D. Willison, Craig's Close, For Arch. Constable & Co. Edinburgh, and T. N. Longman & O. Rees, London. 1804.

Published 25 January 1804 (date cited for this issue in previous number).

Notes: On 19 March Scott wrote his friend George Ellis that he here used a 'critical scalping knife' though, 'in general, I think it ungentlemanly to wound any person's feelings through an anonymous publication, unless where conceit or false doctrine strongly calls for reprobation.' Apparently Ellis was not advised that he would shortly be the subject of Scott's next, favourable review (*see* following entry).

Copies: O; PPL TxU. Later issued as 'third edition' 1805 (L) [fourth and fifth editions also reported].

References: *Letters*, i.217. (Magnum Opus Edition 1835: *The Miscellaneous Prose Works*, xvii.55-80 as 'Godwin's Life of Chaucer'.)

REVIEWS OF ELLIS AND GREGORY

12A] First Printings: 1804

1] 'ART. X. *Specimens of the Early English Poets: To which is prefixed, An Historical Sketch of the Rise and Progress of the English Poetry and Language.* By George Ellis Esq. The Third Edition, Corrected.', pages 151-163;

2] 'ART. XVII. *The Works of Thomas Chatterton; containing his Life, by G. Gregory, D.D. and Miscellaneous Poems.'*, pages 214-230, *in*:

The Edinburgh Review April 1804 No. VII [volume 4 imprint:] Edinburgh: Printed by D. Willison, Craig's Close, For Arch. Constable & Co. Edinburgh, and T. N. Longman & O. Rees, London. 1804.

Published 18 April 1804 (date cited for this issue in previous number).

Notes: The headlines for the second review, reading 'Chatterton's Works by Southey and Cottle', are explained by Scott at the beginning of the second paragraph: 'The preface bears the well known and respectable name of Mr Robert Southey; but we are informed that so much of the business has devolved upon Mr Cottle, that it becomes necessary to use the term Editors in the plural.'

Copies: L O; PPL TxU. [fourth edition also reported]

References: (Magnum Opus Edition 1835: *The Miscellaneous Prose Works*, [1] xvii.*1* 2-15 as 'On Ellis's Specimens of the Early English Poets', [2] xvii.215-241 as 'Chatterton'.)

SIR TRISTREM

If the editor has been successful in his statement, two points have been established; 1st, that the minstrels of the south of Scotland . . . became the natural depositaries of the treasures of Celtic tradition, esteemed so precious in the middle ages; 2dly, That from the peculiar circumstances under which the English language was formed in the Lowlands of Scotland, and north of England, it probably was more early fitted for the use of the poet in that country, than in the more southern parts of the sister kingdom, where it was so long confined to the use of the populace. ('Introduction,' pages lxv-lxvi.)

13Aa] First Edition: 1804

SIR TRISTREM; | a | Metrical Romance | of | The Thirteenth Century;| BY | THOMAS OF ERCILDOUNE, | CALLED | *THE RHYMER.* | [*short reversed Oxford rule*] | EDITED FROM THE AUCHINLECK MS. | BY | WALTER SCOTT, ESQ. | ADVOCATE. | [*short Oxford rule*] | [*six-line quotation from Chaucer*] | [*short reversed Oxford rule*] | EDINBURGH: | [*Oxford dash*] | Printed by James Ballantyne, | FOR ARCHIBALD CONSTABLE AND CO. EDINBURGH, | AND LONGMAN AND REES, LONDON. | [*reversed Oxford dash*] | 1804.

Published 14 May 1804 in Edinburgh (*EEC*, which continues to list this limited issue as late as 1 August 1805). £2.2.0. 150 copies. Binding: Marbled paper boards with green paper spine and printed label. Paper: Royal 8° (246 x 154mm cut). Watermarks: J WHATMAN | 1801; single digits of 1 8 0 1 appear on separate leaves of some sheets. Collation: π^2 a^8 b-h^8 A-Z^8 $2A^4$ 2B1 *2C*1. Pagination: *1* half-title, *2 blank*, *3* title-page, *4 blank*, *i* fly-title for Introduction, *ii blank*, *iii* iv-cxxvii text, *cxxviii blank*, *1* 2-200 text of Sir Tristrem, *201* fly-title for Description and Abstract &c., *202 blank*, 203-240 text, *241* fly-title for Notes, *242 blank*, *243* 244-353 text, *354 blank*, *i* fly-title for Glosssary, *ii blank*, *iii* iv-xxiv text, xxiv printer's imprint, *xxv* Errata, *xxvi blank*. Printer's imprint: [*short Oxford rule*] | EDINBURGH: | Printed by J. BALLANTYNE. Figures: none.

Notes: Though intended originally for inclusion in the *Minstrelsy of the Scottish Border*, this work soon became so extensive as to require separate publication. As in the *Minstrelsy*, where Scott added his own modern imitation 'Part Third' to 'Thomas the Rhymer' (8Aa.2), so here, on finding this 'Romance' also to be incomplete, he provided a 15-stanza 'Conclusion', pages 191-200. This considerable addition, though specifically mentioned in the Introduction page xci as 'attempted by the editor', on page 191 is merely described as 'abridged from the French metrical romance, in the stile of Tomas of Erceldoune.'

On 7 May 1804, seven days before publication, Scott advised Francis Douce that the copy sent him was '*one of twelve thrown off without a castration which I adopted in the rest of the edition against my own opinion & in compliance with that of some respectable friends*.' (italics Scott's; letter in the Douce copy.) The reference is to page 124, text line 21, which thus exists in two states:
(1) unexpurgated line, 'Hir queynt abouen hir kne,'
(2) with six asterisks in place of the offensive reading.
The castrated, inscribed E copy also has an explanatory letter of 7 May inserted (H.29.b.55, cf. *Letters*, i.220-21).
Concerning this limited issue George Ellis on 4 July remarked: '. . . in truth I do feel very angry, not indeed with you, but with your bookseller. It is quite scandalous in him to make the book scarce at the moment of publication by printing off no more than 150 copies and selling them at a high price to save himself the trouble of distributing. . . . Your name must have sold 500 copies just as easily as 150, . . .' (*Letters* i.230n). These and other sentiments were also expressed in Ellis's article that same month in the *Edinburgh Review* (July 1804), pages 427-443.

Presentation copies: (state 1) LU('His Excellency The Earl of Moira . . . from the Editor' [not in Scott's hand]) O('Francis Douce Esqr. F.A.S. from the Editor'); NNP('Alexr Hunter Esq. of Blackness from his faithful humble Servant The Editor'). (state 2) E('To the Library of the Honble faculty of Advocates—This copy of a Romance published from a valuable manuscript in that collection is respectfully offerd By the Editor').

Other copies: (state 1) BCL(Charles Kirkpatrick Sharpe) E LU; NjP. (2) BCL (Alexander Ballantyne) ES L(2) O; CtY IdU NNU-W T/B ViU.

References: Duval 897 (with illustration); Ruff 20; Sterling 715; Thomson, pages 73-74. (Magnum Opus Edition 1833: *The Poetical Works*, v.)

13Ab] Second Edition: 1806

SIR TRISTREM; | a | Metrical Romance | of | The Thirteenth Century; | BY | THOMAS OF ERCILDOUNE, | CALLED | *THE RHYMER.* | [*Oxford dash*] | EDITED FROM THE AUCHINLECK MS. | BY | WALTER SCOTT, Esq. | [*short Oxford rule*] | [*six-line quotation from Chaucer*] | [*short reversed Oxford rule*] | THE SECOND EDITION. | EDINBURGH: | [*Oxford dash*] | PRINTED FOR ARCHIBALD CONSTABLE AND CO.; | AND LONGMAN, HURST, REES, AND ORME, | PATERNOSTER-ROW, LONDON. | [*reversed Oxford dash*] | 1806.

Published November 1806 in Edinburgh (*SM*). 12s. 750 copies. Binding: blue-green boards with printed label. Paper: Demy 8° (230 x 144mm uncut). Watermarks: 1803 [1805, 1806]. Collation: π^2 *a*^{8} b-g^8 h^4 *i*1 *k*1 *A*8 B-2A^8 *2B*1. Pagination: *i* half-title, *ii* printer's imprint(1), *iii* title-page, *iv blank*, *i* fly-title, *ii blank*, *iii* iv-cxxiv Introduction, Appendix, and Postcript[!], *1* fly-title, *2 blank*, *3* 4-204 text, *205* fly-title, *206 blank*, *207* 208-358 abstracts of other MSS, and notes, *359* fly-title, *360 blank*, *361* 362-385 Glossary, 385 printer's imprint(2), *386 blank*. Printer's imprints: (1) [*short rule*] | Printed by James Ballantyne and Co. Edinburgh. | [*short rule*]; (2) [*short Oxford rule*] | Edinburgh: | Printed by James Ballantyne & Co. Typography: Additional leaf *k*1, usually on somewhat different paper, has page *cxxiii* heading 'POSTCRIPT' (a Scott misspelling). Page 60 is misnumbered 59.

Figures: *a* x-5 xii-1, b xxx-4, c xxxiv-3, d lxiv-7, e lxxx-7, f lxxxiii-7, g c-3, h cxvii-4, A16-3, B22-7, C34-4, D52-4, E72-3 74-2, F86-4, G111-2, H126-2, I 135-4, K158-4, L174-2, M190-2, N*197*-3, O 222-2, P237-3, Q256-3, R269-5, S282-5/-, T297-5, U312-5, X336-5, Y350-2, Z356-2, 2A 378-4, *2B*—.

Notes: Apart from several minor corrections in the 'Introduction' and notes, as well as the new 'Postcript', the offensive 'queynt' line, deleted in the first edition, has been restored, here as line 23 on page 128. In its first advertisement for this edition the *Edinburgh Weekly Journal* lists as also available (presumably for those now assembling a complete set of Scott), the fifth edition of *Lay of the Last Minstrel*, the second edition of the *Ballads*, and the third edition of the *Minstrelsy of the Scottish Border*. A large-paper impression of this Second Edition of *Sir Tristrem* forms part of the *Works of Walter Scott*, 1806, volume IV (260Aa).

Copies: BCL E(2) L(2) P; CtY DLC IdU NNP OCl* T/B TxU.
*With 16-page Longman catalogue 1 October 1806.

Reference: Ruff 21.

13Ac] Third Edition, First Impression: 1811

SIR TRISTREM; | a | Metrical Romance | of | The Thirteenth Century; | BY | THOMAS OF ERCILDOUNE, | CALLED | *THE RHYMER.* | [*short Oxford rule*] | EDITED FROM THE AUCHINLECK MS. | BY | WALTER SCOTT, Esq. | [*short Oxford rule*] | [*six-line quotation from Chaucer*] | [*short reversed Oxford rule*] | THE THIRD EDITION. | EDINBURGH: | [*Oxford dash*] | PRINTED FOR | ARCHIBALD CONSTABLE AND COMPANY; | AND LONGMAN, HURST, REES, ORME, AND BROWN, | PATERNOSTER-ROW, LONDON. | [*dash*] | 1811.

Issued 15 July 1811 in London (*MC*). 15s. 1000 copies. Binding: drab boards. Paper: Demy 8° (226 x 142mm uncut). Watermarks: W Balston; 1 [4, 5, 6, 7, 8, 9, 10] | W Balston | 1810; 5 [6 7, 8, 10] | W Balston | 1811. Collation: π^2 a-h^8 A-M^8 N^8(-N8=*2C*1) O-2B^8 *2C*1. Pagination: *1* half-title, *2* printer's imprint(1), *3* title-page, *4 blank*, *i* fly-title, *ii blank*, *iii* iv-cxxvi Introduction and Appendix, *cxxvii-cxxviii blank*, *1* fly-title, *2 blank*, *3* 4-204 text, *205* fly-title, *206 blank*, *209*[!] 210-374 abstracts of other MSS and notes, *375* fly-title, *376 blank*, *377* 378-401 Glossary, 401 printer's imprint(2), *402 blank*. Printer's imprints: (1) and (2) [*short Oxford rule*] | EDINBURGH: | Printed by James Ballantyne and Co. Typography: Page xxiii is misnumbered xxviii. Page 319 is misnumbered 219. Pages 207-208 are omitted in the pagination because this leaf (N8, still integral in some copies) was printed for use as *2C*1 (pages 401-*402*).

Figures: a xv-3, b xxv-11, c xxxviii-6, d lxiii-6, e lxxviii-6, f lxxxiv-6, g civ-5, h cxix-9, A6-6, B22-6, C46-6, D57-3, E70-6, F—, G112-3, H127-7, I 139-9, K146-12, L170-1, M189-3, N—, O 222-11, P226-6, Q256-9, R259-9, S279-5, T304-3, U320-9, X322-3, Y338-8, Z356-12, 2A 381-5, 2B 394-12.

Notes: In the 'Introduction' this edition enters as a footnote (pages vii-viii) the information previously conveyed in the 'Postcript', subtends three further notes (pages viii, ix, li), and adds two paragraphs ('Such was the reasoning . . . years and upwards.'; 'But what may be . . . Sir Tristrem.', pages x-xi, xlvii-xlviii). Both of these paragraphs allude to the new section provided by Henry Weber on the German Romances and added to the extracts (pages *249-251* 252-262).

Copies: DN E O P; CtY IdU NNP T/B. Reference: Ruff 22.

13Ad] Third Edition, Second (Large-Paper) Impression: 1811

SIR TRISTREM; . . . THE THIRD EDITION. . . . 1811.

Published concurrently with the previous impression. Paper: Royal 8° (235 x 141mm cut). Watermarks: 1809.

Notes: In all respects identical with the preceding impression, except for paper. Copies: L; CtY(*see* 260Ad[2] note). Reference: Ruff 23.

13Ae] Fourth Edition: 1819

SIR TRISTREM; | a | Metrical Romance | of | The Thirteenth Century; | BY | THOMAS OF ERCILDOUNE, | CALLED | *THE RHYMER.* | [*short Oxford rule*] | EDITED FROM THE AUCHINLECK MS. | BY | WALTER SCOTT, Esq. | [*short Oxford rule*] | [*six-line quotation from Chaucer*] | [*short reversed Oxford rule*] | THE FOURTH EDITION. | EDINBURGH: | PRINTED FOR A. CONSTABLE AND CO. EDINBURGH; | [*short rule*] | LONGMAN, HURST, REES, ORME, AND BROWN, PATERNOSTER-ROW; | AND HURST, ROBINSON, AND CO. 90, CHEAPSIDE, LONDON. | [*dash*] | 1819.

Published at 15s. 500 copies. Binding: drab boards with printed label or (a later issue?) blue/green boards with black pebbled cloth spine and printed label. Paper: Demy 8° (222 x 138mm uncut). Watermarks: [*swash*] J A | 1816; D & A Cowan | 1819. Collation: π^2 a^8 b-g^8 h^8 A-M^8 N^8(-*N*8=*2C*1) O-$2B^8$ *2C*1. Pagination: *1* half-title, *2* printer's imprint(1), *3* title-page, *4 blank*, *i* fly-title, *ii blank*, *iii* iv-xciv Introduction, *xcv* fly-title, *xcvi blank*, *xcvii* xcviii-cxxvi appendices, *cxxvii-cxxviii blank*, *1* fly-title, *2 blank*, *3* 4-204 text, *205* fly-title, *206 blank*, *209* 210-374 abstracts of other mss, and notes, *375* fly-title, *376 blank*, *377* 378-401 Glossary, 401 printer's imprint(2). Printer's imprints: (1) & (2) [*short Oxford rule*] | Edinburgh: | Printed by James Ballantyne and Co. Typography: The first page of gathering *h* (page cxiii) is unsigned, but oddly has in the center signature position a press-figure 6. Page xxxiv is misnumbered xxxxiv. Page numbers 207-208 (=N8) are omitted in pagination.

Figures: *a* xiii-8, b xxxii-8, c xlii-10, d lxiv-6, e lxxvii-8, f lxxxiv-2, g cv-9, *h* cxiii-6, A16-8, B32-8/-, C43-2, D50-9, E80-4, F87-6, G108-9, H128-7, I 142-8, K—, L176-2, M190-2, N201-9, O 218-3, P238-10, Q244-4/-, R*265*-9, S284-10, T304-8, U320-8, X322-6, Y350-10/-, Z365-4, 2A 378-1, 2B 393-9.

Notes: The text is revised, with additions to notes.

Copies: L; CtY InU PU. Reference: Ruff 24.

THE LAY OF THE LAST MINSTREL

The poem . . . was soon finished, proceeding at about the rate of a canto per week . . . and may be regarded as the first work in which the writer, who has been since so voluminous, laid his claim to be considered as an original author. . . . The attempt to return to a more simple and natural style of poetry was likely to be welcomed, at a time when the public had become tired of heroic hexameters, with all the buckram and binding which belong to them of later days. ('Introduction', April 1830, *PW*, vi.29-30.)

14Aa] Pre-publication Issue: 1804

[*fly-title*] THE | **LAY** | OF | THE LAST MINSTREL. | [*short reversed Oxford rule*] | CANTO FIRST.

Privately printed, presumably only in a few copies. Paper: Demy 4° (245 x 205 mm cut). Watermarks: C & S | 1802 / 1802. Collation: *A-B*[4]. Pagination: *1* fly-title, *2 blank*, *3* 4-8 Introduction, *9* fly-title for 'Songs to Ancient British Airs', *10 blank*, *11* 12-16 text, 16 printer's imprint: EDINBURGH: | PRINTED BY JAMES BALLANTYNE, | At the Border Press, | HOLYROOD-HOUSE. | [*Oxford dash*] | 1804. Figures: none.

Notes: The poetic Introduction constitutes a preprint (in the same setting) of the first hundred lines of *The Lay*, followed by first printings of the two 'Airs': [1] 'The Norman Horse Shoe' (first words: 'Red glows the forge in Striguil's bounds'), pages *11* 12-13, and [2] 'The Dying Bard' (first words: 'Dinas Emlinn, lament; for the moment is nigh,' later printed as 'The Last Words of Cadwallon'), pages *14* 15-16: these 'Airs' anticipating texts previously sent to George Thomson, but not yet published. In this hybrid, preliminary form the issue introduces the five stately quarto editions of Scott's narrative poems, each printed by Ballantyne with type specially ordered from the Caslon foundry.

Presentation copy: CtY('The Honble Miss [Anna Maria] Elliot from the Author'). Other copy: GM.

References: Ruff 24A. (Magnum Opus Edition 1833: *The Poetical Works*, [1] vi.363-365, [2] vi.366-372.)

14Ab] First Edition, First Impression: 1805

THE | **LAY** | OF | **THE LAST MINSTREL** | A POEM. | BY | WALTER SCOTT, Esq. | LONDON: | PRINTED FOR LONGMAN, HURST, REES, AND ORME, PATERNOSTER- | ROW, AND A. CONSTABLE AND CO. EDINBURGH, | By James Ballantyne, Edinburgh. | 1805.

Published 12 January 1805 in Edinburgh (*EEC*); issued 24 January in London (*The Times*). £1.5.0. 750 copies. Binding: blue-green or rose boards with printed label or (a later issue?) yellow boards with black cloth spine. Paper: Demy 4° (289 x 224mm uncut). Watermarks: V 1796 / V 1796; C & S | 1802 / 1802; J W 1802 /

1802; 1804 / 1804; M | 1804. Collation: π^4 A^4 B-D^4 E^4 F-Z^4 2A^4(-2A4) 2B^4(-2B1+'2B'^{2}) 2C-2R^4 *2S*1. Pagination: *i* half-title, *ii blank*, *iii* title-page, *iv blank*, *v* dedication to Charles, Earl of Dalkeith, *vi blank*, *vii* preface, *viii blank*, *1* fly-title for Canto first, *2 blank*, *3* 4-194 text, *195* fly-title for Notes, *196 blank*, *197* 198-319 text, *319* printer's imprint, *320 blank*, *321* Errata, *322 blank*. Printer's imprint: [*short Oxford rule*] | EDINBURGH: | Printed by JAMES BALLANTYNE. Typography: In all editions through the 8th, stanza number XXIV is omitted in the 6th canto.

Figures: 2D 216-3, 2E 224-3, 2F 232-3, 2G 238-3. These several figures are the first to appear in a Ballantyne printing of Scott; they occur earlier only in the 1799 London issue of *Goetz of Berlichingen* (4A). On moving to Edinburgh in 1803 Ballantyne reported that his new premises would accommodate only 'two presses, and a proof one' (Lockhart, ii.120), but as noted in Jaboor/McMullin (pages 27-29) his work thereafter progressively exhibits first a figure 3, as here, then later in 1805 a 4 and 5, in 1806 a 6 and 7, and in 1807 an 8: all indicating a rapidly expanding operation.

Notes: On 7 January 1805 Scott advised Richard Heber that his copy was 'now on the road to town' and on the 11th (the day before announced issue) inscribed to Lady Dalkeith, spouse of the dedicatee, a copy of the manuscript specially prepared by his wife Charlotte (*Letters* i.234). Unlike the 1802 or 1804 watermarked text, the cancel 2B doubleton is watermarked V 1796 (a mark which does not otherwise appear before gathering 2 O) and replaces both the last leaf of 2A (pages 191-192) and the first leaf of the original 2B. For this the original readings are unknown.

As in his *Minstrelsy of the Scottish Border*, Scott again quotes at great length (pages 261-264) Robert Carey's *Memoirs*, a work he would edit in 1808. Also entered is a considerable note (pages 211-212) anticipating *The Memoirs of the Duke of Sully*, edited in 1810, and now remarked because the French Bethune [Sully] family were the ancestors of Janet Beaton, Lady Buccleuch, widow of Sir Walter Scott of Branxholm (site of the Minstrel's *Lay*: this Sir Walter was killed 1552 in a feud with the Kerrs). Retrospectively, Scott's own collective *Minstrelsy* is given as a reference on pages 274, 277.

The inexact Errata would suggest the possibility of two states in page 193 ('198' in Errata) line 10: (1) wonder; (2) wander. The list further indicates that the first, incorrect reading appears 'in a very few copies', none of which have been discovered. (Possibly this earlier reading occurs only in the cancellandum 2B1.) The Errata list itself is in a duplicate setting, with the 'w' of 'wander' above either the first or second 'o' of 'good-father'.

Presentation copies: (state 1) not seen. (2) A('Mrs. Scott From her affectionate son The Author') E('Miss [Dorothy] Wordsworth from the Author', [then in Wordsworth's hand] 'Given to my Niece Dora, September 10th, 1835'); CtY[not inscribed, but letter to Richard Heber inserted dated 7 (January) 1805] MH('Miss

Carmichael from Her honourd & obliged humble Servant The Author') TxU ('Miss Domergue [Sophia Dumergue] from her affectionate friend Walter Scott').

Other copies: (state 1) not seen. (2) BCL('Mrs Booker, With most respectful regards from J Ballantyne') E ES L LU O(6); CtY* CtY(2) DLC IdU InU InU (with 12 ink and aquatint illustrations by Thomas Stothard) NNP(2) NNP (Countess of Bandon) NNU-W OCl PPL T/B TxU(Lord Gower) TxU(2). The copy in the library at Windsor Castle has Scott's manuscript annotations.
*Bound with Schetky's 1808 *Illustrations* (*see* 33Aa).

References: Grady, pages 50-113, 394-397; Ruff 25; Thomson, page 40; Tinker 1861; Van Antwerp(1) 5. (Magnum Opus Edition 1833: *The Poetical Works*, vi. *3-5* 6-288.)

14Ac] First Edition, Second (Large-Paper) Impression: 1805

THE | **LAY** | OF | THE LAST MINSTREL | A POEM. . . . 1805.

Privately printed in four copies only. Paper: Royal 4° (305 x 241mm uncut). Watermarks: J WHATMAN | 1801 [1805]. Collation: As for the first impression except that the errata leaf is excluded. Figures: As for first impression.

Notes: Sheet *A* is reset, page *1* Oxford rule is 26mm, page 8 last line LATEST (as compared with Demy impression 22mm and LATEST respectively). Within this new setting three slight corrections, not signalled in the Demy errata list, appear on pages 4, line 6 (Stuart's), page 6, line 15 (But [no comma]), and page 8, line 7 (ecstacy). The copy limitation is noted by A. G. Hunter, of Blackness, partner in the firm of A. Constable, where in his own specimen (NNP) he further remarks 'See W.S's MS Addns. p. 195' (a leaf now affixed to p. 101: note further, 5th edition, 14Ah).

Copy: NNP(Hunter). Reference: Ruff 26.

14Ad] Second Edition, First Impression: 1805

THE | LAY | OF | THE LAST MINSTREL | A POEM. | BY | WALTER SCOTT, ESQ. | [*short Oxford rule*] | [*two-line quotation in Latin*] | [*short reversed Oxford rule*] | THE SECOND EDITION. | LONDON: | PRINTED FOR LONGMAN, HURST, REES, AND ORME, PATERNOS- | TER-ROW, AND A. CONSTABLE AND CO. EDINBURGH, | *By James Ballantyne, Edinburgh.* | 1805.

Published October 1805 (*SM*). 10s.6d. 1500 copies. Paper: Demy 8° (209 x 130 mm cut). Watermarks: In sheets A-L the date 1804 or 1805 appears on each of first four leaves, with the initials W S above the date on one of these leaves; 1805 (sheets M-U as before, but with W S now separately on leaves 5-6 or 7-8). Collation: π^8 A^8 B^8(±B3) C-D^8 E^8(±E7) F-O^8 P^8(±P2,±P6) Q-T^8 U^8(-U4.5=P2,P6). Pagination: *1* half-title, *2 blank*, *3* title-page, *4 blank*, *5* dedication, *6 blank*, *7* preface, *8 blank*, *9* fly-title, *10 blank*, *11* 12-202 text, *203* fly-title, *204 blank*, *205* 206-'334'[332] Notes, '334'[332] printer's imprint: [*short reversed Oxford rule*] | Edinburgh, | Printed by James Ballantyne. Typography: Pages 305-332 are misnumbered 307-334.

Figures: A32-2, B—, C52-2 58-5, D67-4/- 73-2, E94-3/- 95-2 96-3, F111-2 112-3, G124-2 127-3, H130-3 136-4, I 153-3, K—, L178-2, M198-2, N215-2 224-3, O 226-1 232-2, P254-3 256-2, Q271-2 272-3, R286-3, S303-3, T312-4 318-1, U327-2 328-4.

Notes: The original readings of the first two cancels B3 (pages 37-38) and E7 (pages 93-94) are unknown; the corrected texts for both are identical with those in the first edition. The second cancel E7, however, exists in two settings, one with and one without a supernumerary press-figure 3 on page 94. Cancellanda P2 and P6, still retained in several copies, exhibit the following words later corrected: page 244 line 9: order] odour; 251 line 19: reconditus] reconditis; 252 line 26: barell] barrel.

Copies: E+ O; CaBVaU CtY IdU NN NNU-W T/B. Reference: Ruff 27
+Extra-illustrated with 1809 engraved title-page and six plates by Richard Westall (14Dm); additional frontispiece portrait painted by H. Raeburn, engraved by A. Raimbach, and 1 February 1811 imprint of R. H. Cromek and J. Sharpe.

14Ae] Second Edition, Second (Large Paper) Impression: 1805

THE | LAY | OF | THE LAST MINSTREL | A POEM. . . . 1805.

Privately printed (again as for 14Ac perhaps in four copies). Paper: Royal 8° (218 x 129mm cut). Watermarks: J WHATMAN | 1801 [1804]. Collation: π^8 A-T^8 U^6. Pagination and typography as for preceding impression. Figures: As before except D67-4, E94—.

Notes: It would appear that of this impression, unnoticed by Ruff, a few copies were (like 14Ac) privately printed. In this printing the comma is dropped after EDINBURGH in title imprint and all leaves previously cancelled are now in their revised state and integral to their gatherings.

Presentation copy: E('C[hristian] Rutherford from her Affect Nephew Walter Scott'). Another copy: BCL.

14Af] Third Edition: 1806

THE | **LAY** | OF | THE LAST MINSTREL, | A POEM; | BY | WALTER SCOTT, Esq. | [*short Oxford rule*] | [*two-line quotation*] | [*short reversed Oxford rule*] | THE THIRD EDITION. | LONDON: | PRINTED FOR LONGMAN, HURST, REES, AND ORME, | PATERNOSTER-ROW, AND A. CONSTABLE AND CO. EDINBURGH; | *By James Ballantyne, Edinburgh.* | 1806.

Published 22 February 1806 in Edinburgh (*CM*). 10s.6d. 2000 copies. Paper: Demy 8° (225 x 141mm uncut). Watermarks: The two varieties of marks in the second edition first impression recur here, both now dated 1805 and mixed throughout. Collation: *A*[8] B-U[8] X[4] Y[2]. Pagination: *1* half-title, *2 blank*, *3* title-page, *4 blank*, *5* dedication, *6 blank*, *7* preface, *8 blank*, *9* fly-title, *10 blank*, *11* 12-202 text, *203* fly-title, *204 blank*, *205* 206-'334'[332] Notes, '334'[332] printer's imprint: [*short Oxford rule*] | Edinburgh: | Printed by James Ballantyne. Typography: As before, pages 305-332 are misnumbered 307-334. In some copies signature G (page 97) is upside down.

Figures: A15-1, B27-2, C36-2, D50-3, E74-5, F83-1, G107-4, H127-1, I 141-1, K159-6, L175-1, M192-6, N206-6, O 222-1, P239-1, Q256-1, R272-1, S286-1, T303-3, U321-3, X330-1, Y332-1/-.

Notes: The 'trifling improvements' in this edition, as Scott called them, represent two sentences added to the note concluding on page 214, a reference to and quotation from Dante; pages 244-245, and a further citation from *Il Morgante Maggiore*, pages 246-247. Rather than elucidating the text, these several 'trifles' merely exemplify Scott's more arcane reading.

Copies: BCL C E O; CtY T/B. Mixed or sophisticated copy: NN(sheet K from 6th or later edition [with headlines], other sheets with variant figures). References: *Letters*, i.266; Ruff 28.

14Ag] Fourth Edition: 1806

THE | **LAY** | OF | THE LAST MINSTREL, | A POEM; | BY | WALTER SCOTT, Esq. | [*short Oxford rule*] | [*two-line quotation*] | [*short reversed Oxford rule*] | THE FOURTH EDITION. | LONDON: | PRINTED FOR LONGMAN, HURST, REES, AND ORME, | PATERNOSTER-ROW, AND A. CONSTABLE AND CO. EDINBURGH; | *By James Ballantyne & Co. Edinburgh.* | 1806.

Published August 1806 in Edinburgh (*SM*). 10s.6d. 2250 copies. Paper: Demy 8° (212 x 129mm cut). Watermarks: D & A C | 1805 | 1 [2]. Collation: *A*[8] B-U[8] X[4] Y[2].

Pagination: *1* half-title, *2 blank*, *3* title-page, *4 blank*, *5* dedication, *6 blank*, *7* preface, *8 blank*, *9* fly-title, *10 blank*, *11* 12-202 text, *203* fly-title, *204 blank*, *205* 206-332 Notes, 332 printer's imprint: [*short Oxford rule*] | Edinburgh: | Printed by James Ballantyne. Typography: Signature X (page 321) is missigned U.

Figures: *A*16-1, B20-6, C44-6, D62-2 64-7, E80-7, F82-1 84-2, G110-4 112-7, H128-7, I 137-7/- 142-1, K155-2, L172-2 174-3, M192-3, N194-4, O 215-2, P231-2 240-1, Q244-3 246-1, R265-4, S286-7, T303-4, U306-2, U326-7, Y—.

Notes: This edition has numerous additions to text and notes, one of the more significant occurring in Canto 4, stanza VII, where (page 107) a further quatrain has been supplied ('There was . . . gay ladye.'). A large-paper impression, augmented, with different press-figures, forms part of the *Works of Walter Scott*, 1806, volume V (260Aa).

Copies: E O; CaBVaU CtY DLC NN T/B. Reference: Ruff 29.

14Ah] Fifth Edition: 1806

THE | **LAY** | OF | THE LAST MINSTREL, | A POEM; | BY | WALTER SCOTT, Esq. | [*short Oxford rule*] | [*two-line quotation*] | [*short reversed Oxford rule*] | THE FIFTH EDITION. | LONDON: | PRINTED FOR LONGMAN, HURST, REES, AND ORME, | PATERNOSTER-ROW, AND A. CONSTABLE AND CO. EDINBURGH; | *By James Ballantyne & Co. Edinburgh.* | 1806.

Published November 1806 in Edinburgh (*SM*). 10s.6d. 2000 copies. Paper: Demy 8° (220 x 141mm uncut). Watermarks: 1805; 1806. Collation: A^8 B-X^8 Y^2. Pagination: *1* half-title, *2 blank*, *3* title-page, *4 blank*, *5* dedication, *6 blank*, *7* preface, *8 blank*, *9* fly-title, *10 blank*, *11* 12-208 text, *209* fly-title, *210 blank*, *211* 212-340 Notes, 340 printer's imprint: [*short Oxford rule*] | Edinburgh: | Printed by James Ballantyne & Co.

Figures: A13-3, B31-2, C44-7, D58-4, E74-7, F84-1, G110-1, H123-7, I 131-2, K147-4, L163-4, M179-3, N194-3, O 216-4, P239-2, Q256-4, R271-4, S276-3, T299-4, U310-3, X336-7, Y338-4/-.

Notes: Among various additions and corrections, the most notable occurs on pages 109-113, representing three new stanzas X-XII (a total of 82 lines). The manuscript for this addition, with Scott's direction for inserting the text in the fifth edition, may now be found in Hunter's large-paper impression of the first edition (14Ac). Final gathering Y^2 is in a duplicate setting, page 338 with press figure 4, 339 line 14 first word 'telligible' or 338 no figure, 339 line 14 first word 'intelligible'.

Copies: E O(Douce) O*; CtY DLC+ InU T/B. Reference: Ruff 30.
*With undated 4-page Constable and John Murray catalogue of Periodical Works.

+Extra-illustrated with 1809 engraved title-page and six plates by Richard Westall (*see* 14Dm).

14Ai] Sixth Edition: 1807

THE | **LAY** | OF | THE LAST MINSTREL, | A POEM; | BY | WALTER SCOTT, Esq. | [*short Oxford rule*] | [*two-line quotation*] | [*short reversed Oxford rule*] | THE SIXTH EDITION. | LONDON: | PRINTED FOR LONGMAN, HURST, REES, AND ORME, | PATERNOSTER-ROW, AND A. CONSTABLE AND CO. EDINBURGH; | *By James Ballantyne & Co. Edinburgh.* | 1807.

3000 copies. Binding: blue boards with printed label. Paper: Demy 8° (222 x 140mm uncut). Watermarks: 1807. Collation: A^8 B-U^8 X^4 Y^2. Pagination: *1* half-title, *2 blank*, *3* title-page, *4 blank*, *5* dedication, *6 blank*, *7* preface, *8 blank*, *9* fly-title, *10 blank*, *11* 12-208 text, *209* fly-title, *210 blank*, *211* 206-340 Notes, 340 printer's imprint: [*short Oxford rule*] | Edinburgh: | Printed by James Ballantyne & Co.

Figures: A14-1, B18-1, C34-8, D50-5, E66-4, F82-2, G98-5, H114-1, I 130-10 144-3, K146-6, L162-2 176-8, M178-8 192-3, N194-5 208-1, O *211*-2 224-1, P226-5, Q*243*-3, R258-1 272-3/-, S274-1 288-10, T290-8 304-6, U306-10 312-3, X322-7, Y338-7/-.

Notes: The notes, previously 26 lines to a full page, when reset were extended to 27, thus effecting a blank at page *242*, following the notes to Canto I. This is the first edition to employ a running-title across page openings: THE LAY OF | THE LAST MINSTREL.

Copies: BCL E L O; CtY DLC InU NNU-W T/B(2) TxU. Reference: Ruff 31.

EIGHTH (SEVENTH) QUARTO EDITION 1808-1810

Note: As Ruff observed (entry 32) a 'Seventh' edition was advertised in the *Edinburgh Weekly Journal* 24 February 1808 as 'Speedily will be published, in Quarto, printed uniformly with' the first edition of *Marmion.* When this appeared four months later the edition for some reason was labeled the 'Eighth' and then appeared as noted below in several augmented issues through 1810, the date of the first quarto edition of *The Lady of the Lake*. Evidently Scott's publisher at this time was attempting to assemble, as a 4° *Works*, the several poems then published: *see* postscript to 260Ad[4].

14Aj] Eighth Edition, First Impression, First Issue: 1808

THE | **LAY** | OF | THE LAST MINSTREL, | A POEM; | THE EIGHTH EDITION. | WITH | *BALLADS AND LYRICAL PIECES.* | [*short rule*] | BY | WALTER SCOTT, Esq. | [*short rule*] | [*two-line quotation*] | [*short rule*] | LONDON: | [*short Oxford dash*] | PRINTED FOR LONGMAN, HURST, REES, AND ORME, | PATERNOSTER-ROW, AND A. CONSTABLE AND CO. EDINBURGH. | [*dash*] | 1808.

Published June 1808 in Edinburgh (*SM*). £1.11.6. Paper: Demy 4° (272 x 212mm cut). Coarse brown paper *A-B* C-2F (pages *1-11* 12-232) and a-p (pages *i-iii* iv-cxx); fine white paper 2G-2I (pages 233-257 *258*) and q-s (cxxi-cxlii). Watermarks: [coarse paper; indistinct] D & A C | 1807 | *none* [9]; [fine paper] 1807. Collation: *A-B*⁴ C-2I⁴ *2K*1 a-s⁴. Pagination: *1* half-title, *2 blank*, *3* title-page, *4 blank*, *5* dedication, *6 blank*, *7* Advertisement, *8 blank*, *9* fly-title for *The Lay of the Last Minstrel*, *10 blank*, *11* 12-204 text, of *205* fly-title for *Ballads and Lyrical Pieces*, *206 blank*, *207* 208-244 text, *245* fly-title for 'Songs', *246 blank*, *247* 248-257 text, *258 blank*, *i* fly-title, *ii blank*, *iii* iv-cxli Notes to *The Lay of the Last Minstrel*, cxli printer's imprint, *cxlii blank*. Printer's imprint: [*short Oxford rule*] | EDINBURGH: | Printed by James Ballantyne & Co. Typography: Page 171 is misnumbered 170, but page 209 is correctly numbered.

Figures: *A*—, *B*11-10, C18-3, D26-10, E34-11, F46-12, G50-6, H58-3, I 66-2, K74-3, L82-2, M90-6, N104-11, O 106-5, P114-3, Q122-10, R130-10, S138-5, T146-11, U154-3, X162-2, Y170-10, Z178-2, 2A 186-10, 2B 194-1, 2C 202-5, 2D 210-3, 2E 218-3, 2F 226-3, 2G 234-8, 2H 242-3, 2I 250-11, 2K—, a vi-2, b x-6, c xviii-3, d xxvi-3, e xxxiv-2, f xlii-3/-, g l-3, h lviii-11, i lxvi-3, k lxxiv-2, l lxxxii-3, m xc-3, n xcviii-3, o cvi-7, p cxiv-5, q cxxii-3, r cxxx-3, s cxxxviii-8.

Notes: Reset from the sixth edition, with further corrections. Leaf *2K*1 exists with recto page 257 last line reading
(cancellandum): END OF THE BALLADS [without signature]
(cancellans): END OF THE SONGS [with signature 2K].

Copies: BCL; DLC T/B+. Reference : Ruff 33.
+Extra-illustrated with 1809 engraved title-page and six plates by Richard Westall (*see* 14Dm).

14Ak] Eighth Edition, First Impression, Second (Augmented) Issue: 1808

THE | **LAY** | OF | THE LAST MINSTREL, | A POEM; | THE EIGHTH EDITION. | WITH | *BALLADS AND LYRICAL PIECES.* . . . 1808.

Published 20 July 1808 in Edinburgh at £1.11.6 (*EWJ*), issued 7 September in London at £2.2.0 (*MC*). Binding: drab boards with printed label. Paper: Demy 4° (287 x

227mm uncut). Watermarks: [fine paper] 1807; [coarse paper; indistinct] D & A C | 1807 | *none* [9]; [coarse paper; indistinct] D & A C | 1808. Collation: *A-B*^{4} C-2I^4 2K^4(±2K1) 2L-2U^4 a-r4 s^2 t-x^4 y^2. Pagination: *1* half-title, *2 blank*, *3* title-page, *4 blank*, *5* dedication, *6 blank*, [&c. as in previous issue except:] *259* fly-title for 'Ballads from the Minstrelsy of the Scottish Border', *260 blank*, 261-343 text, *344 blank*, *i* fly-title, *ii blank*, *iii* iv-cxli notes to *The Lay of the Last Minstrel*, *cxlii blank*, *cxliii* cxliv-clxviii notes to the 'Ballads', clxviii printer's imprint: [*short Oxford rule*] | EDINBURGH: | Printed by James Ballantyne & Co. Typography: In some copies of this and succeeding issues (1) page 171 is correctly numbered, (2) 209 is misnumbered 092, and (3) the original imprint on page cxli is still retained.

Figures: As in first issue except for the new sheets added to text and notes: 2K 263-5, 2L 266-5, 2M 274-10, 2N 286-10, 2O 290-3, 2P 298-3, 2Q 306-12, 2R 314-2, 2S 322-5, 2T 330(or 331)-11, 2U 338-11, . . . t *cxliii*-13, u cl-11, x clviii-11, y clxviii-1.

Notes: Leaf 2K1 again remains with recto page 257 last line reading
(cancellandum): END OF THE BALLADS. [without signature]
(cancellans): END OF THE SONGS. [with signature 2K].
It will be observed that in this second issue 2K is now extended to a full-gathering, the latter part (page 259+) introducing the supplemental Ballads from the *Minstrelsy* (2K-2U). The four gatherings added at the last (t-y) supply the notes for this supplement and, finally, the displaced printer's imprint.

Copies: E(with 2K1 in both states) L L+ O; CtY TxU. Reference: Ruff 33(?) +Extra-illustrated with 1809 engraved title-page and six plates by Richard Westall (*see* 14Dm).

14Al] Eighth Edition, Second (Large-Paper) Impression, Second (Augmented) Issue: 1808

THE | **LAY** | OF | THE LAST MINSTREL, | A POEM; | THE EIGHTH EDITION. | WITH | *BALLADS AND LYRICAL PIECES*. . . . 1808.

Issued 7 September 1808 in London (*MC*). £3.13.6. Paper: Royal 4° (305 x 241 mm uncut). Watermarks: J WHATMAN | 1805 [1807]. Collation and pagination as in regular augmented issue.

Presentation copy: IdU('The Reverend Mr [Edward] Berwick from his obliged friend The Author'). Other copies: E; NjP. Reference: Ruff 34.

14Am] Eighth Edition, First Impression, Third (Further Augmented) Issue: 1810

THE | **LAY** | OF | THE LAST MINSTREL, | A POEM; | THE EIGHTH EDITION. | WITH | *BALLADS AND LYRICAL PIECES.* | [*short Oxford rule*] | BY | WALTER SCOTT, Esq. | [*short rule*] | [*two-line quotation*] | [*short rule*] | LONDON: | [*short Oxford dash*] | PRINTED FOR LONGMAN, HURST, REES, AND ORME, | PATERNOSTER-ROW, AND A. CONSTABLE AND CO. EDINBURGH; | BY JAMES BALLANTYNE AND CO. EDINBURGH. | [*dash*] | 1810.

Issued 10 March 1810 in London (*MC*). £2.2.0. Paper: Demy 4° (287 x 227mm uncut). Watermarks: 1807; D & A C | 1808; 1809. Collation: *A-B*⁴ C-2U⁴ [&c. as in second issue except:] y-2b⁴. Pagination: *1* title-page, *2-3 blank*, *4* note, *5* dedication, *6 blank*, [&c. as in second issue except:] *clxix* fly-title, *clxx blank*, *clxxi* clxxii-cxcvi appendix of Ballads and Songs, cxcvi printer's imprint: [*short Oxford rule*] | Edinburgh: | Printed by James Ballantyne & Co. Illustration: Frontispiece portrait painted by Saxon, engraved by Heath, with caption 'Walter Scott Esqr' and Ballantyne, Longman imprint, dated 1 March 1810. Typography: In some copies, gathering 2a, properly numbered clxxxi-clxxxviii, is misnumbered clxxix-clxxxvi.

Figures: As in first issue except for three sheets (*B*16-4/-, u—, y clxvii-8) and, in the section further extended, new figures z clxxx-6/-, 2a clxxxiv-10, 2b cxciv-11.

Notes: Page *4* reads: 'To a few copies of this edition [i.e., all of this issue] there is added (*By permission of the author*,) An appendix of poetical pieces, which are to be found in no other edition of Mr Scott's Works. Sold by John Ballantyne and Co. Edinburgh.' Gatherings *A-B* (pages *1-8*) have been reset and, as the figures indicate, 2T, f, u, and y (pages 329-336, xli-xlviii, cxlix-clvi, clxv-clxxii) have been reimpressed, z-2b newly set (pages clxxiii-cxcvi).

Copies: C E+ L; CtY CtY+ MH NNP PU. Reference : Ruff 35.
+Extra-illustrated with 1809 engraved title-page and six plates by Richard Westall (*see* 14Dm).

14An] Eighth Edition, Second (Large-Paper) Impression, Third (Further Augmented) Issue: 1810

THE | **LAY** | OF | THE LAST MINSTREL, | A POEM; | THE EIGHTH EDITION. | WITH | *BALLADS AND LYRICAL PIECES*. . . . 1810.

Issued concurrently with the previous impression. £3.13.6. Paper: Royal 4° (305 x 241mm uncut). Watermarks: 1807; D & A C | 1808; J Whatman | 1805 [1807]. Collation, pagination, and figures as in regular third issue. Notes: This is the last of the 4° 'Eighth Edition' issues, all intended to range with Scott's other poems in the same format.

Copies: L; NNU-W(Auchincruive). Copy without text: NNP+.
+The A. G. Hunter copy, with only the new preliminary and supplementary sections (*see* 14Am above), and his note that this material was given him by Scott; the sections bound with two coloured illustrations and twelve Royal 4° 1810 *Marmion* proof impressions on India paper engraved by Charles Heath (*see* 28Ai).

Reference: Ruff 36.

14Ao] Ninth Edition: 1808

THE | **LAY** | OF | THE LAST MINSTREL, | A POEM; | BY | WALTER SCOTT, Esq. | [*short Oxford rule*] | [*two-line quotation*] | [*short reversed Oxford rule*] | THE NINTH EDITION. | LONDON: | PRINTED FOR LONGMAN, HURST, REES, AND ORME, | PATERNOSTER-ROW; AND A. CONSTABLE AND CO. EDINBURGH: | *By James Ballantyne & Co. Edinburgh.* | 1808.

Published June 1808 (*SM*). 10s.6d. 3550 copies. Paper: Demy 8° (228 x 139mm uncut). Watermarks: occasional sheets have 1807; D & A C | 1808. Collation: A^8 B-Y^8. Pagination: *1* half-title, *2 blank*, *3* title-page, *4 blank*, *5* dedication, *6 blank*, *7* note, *8 blank*, *9* fly-title, *10 blank*, *11* 12-208 text, *209* fly-title, *210 blank*, *211* 212-349 notes, 349 printer's imprint, *350-352 blank*. Printer's imprint: [*short Oxford rule*] | Edinburgh: | Printed by James Ballantyne & Co.

Figures: A15-10 16-3, B18-8 32-5, C34-4 48-13, D50-11 64-1, E66-10 80-11, F82-8 96-4, G98-12 112-7, H114-4 116-5, I 130-4 132-13, K146-11 160-'31'[13], L162-11 176-1, M178-8 192-12, N194-11 200-1, O *211*-8 224-1, P226-4 240-3, Q242-10 *245*-2, R258-11 272-4, S274-12 288-1, T295-10 304-1, U306-5 320-1, X322-10 336-7, Y 338-2/- 341-4/-.

Notes: Text reset with corrections: on page 199, stanza 'XXV' is finally corrected to 'XXIV', the remaining stanzas renumbered and, on page 206, the 'Hymn for the Dead' assigned stanza number XXXI. In this and later octavo formats the press figures have usually been entered on 1v for the inner forme and on 8v for the outer forme: a sign of precisely ordered presswork..

Copies: E L LU O; CtY+ IdU NN PPL TxU. Reference: Ruff 37.
+Extra-illustrated with 1809 engraved title-page and six plates by Richard Westall (*see* 14Dm).

14Ap] Tenth Edition: 1809

THE | **LAY** | OF | THE LAST MINSTREL, | A POEM; | BY | WALTER

SCOTT, Esq. | [*short Oxford rule*] | [*two-line quotation*] | [*short reversed Oxford rule*] | THE TENTH EDITION. | LONDON: | PRINTED FOR LONGMAN, HURST, REES, AND ORME, | PATERNOSTER-ROW, AND A. CONSTABLE AND CO. EDINBURGH: | *By James Ballantyne & Co. Edinburgh.* | 1809.

Issued in 3250 copies. Paper: Demy 8° (213 x 134mm cut). Watermarks: D & A C | 1808 | *none* [1, 2]. Collation, pagination, and printer's imprint as in ninth edition. Typography: In some copies page 163 is misnumbered 631.

Figures: A12-2 15-3, B18-10 32-8, C35-5 48-1, D50-12 64-7, E74-13 80-1, F82-8 96-2, G110-1 112-7, H114-13 117-8, I 130-5 136-12, K146-8 160-6, L162-13 176-12, M178-5 181-13, N194-5 208-12, O 218-12 220-13, P226-3 240-2, Q246-12 248-11, R262-7 272-8, S276-3 278-7, T294-2 296-1, U318-3 320-5, X327-8 333-13, Y339-8 344-12. Generally these figures are again positioned as in the ninth edition.

Copies: BCL DT E L O; CtY T/B*. Reference: Ruff 38.
*Trinity College Dublin prize book.

14Aq] Eleventh Edition, First Impression: 1810

THE | **LAY** | OF | THE LAST MINSTREL, | A POEM; | BY | WALTER SCOTT, Esq. | [*short Oxford rule*] | [*two-line quotation*] | [*short reversed Oxford rule*] | THE ELEVENTH EDITION. | LONDON: | PRINTED FOR LONGMAN, HURST, REES, AND ORME, | PATERNOSTER-ROW, AND A. CONSTABLE AND CO. EDINBURGH; | *By James Ballantyne & Co. Edinburgh.* | 1810.

Paper: Demy 8° (212 x 123mm cut). Watermarks: none. Collation: *A*^{8} B-Y^8. Pagination: *1* fly-title, *2 blank*, *3* title-page, *4 blank*, *5* dedication, *6 blank*, *7* note, *8 blank*, *9* fly-title, *10 blank*, *11* 12-208 text, *209* fly-title, *210 blank*, *211* 212- 351 notes, 351 printer's imprint, *352 blank*. Printer's imprint: [*short Oxford rule*] | Edinburgh: | Printed by James Ballantyne & Co. Typography: Page 32 is correctly numbered.

Figures: A16-8, B26-12 32-13, C*43*-5 48-9, D50-1 64-2, E77-6 78-5, F85-9 95-10, G107-2 112-12, H114-9 116-7, I 133-11 135-3, K147-12 149-1, L170-3 176-6, M182-12 184-2, N203-5, O *211*-2 213-8, P226-2 236-11, Q251-2 253-1, R261-11 270-7, S279-12 280-5, T295-2 300-5, U311-8 317-13, X322-8 324-13, Y340-2 346-12.

Copies: E L; CtY+ NjP+. Reference: Ruff 39.
+Extra-illustrated with 1809 engraved title-page and six plates by Richard Westall (*see* 14Dm).

14Ar] Eleventh Edition, Second (Large-Paper) Impression: 1810

THE | **LAY** | OF | THE LAST MINSTREL, | A POEM; . . . THE ELEVENTH EDITION. . . . 1810.

Published concurrently with the previous impression. Paper: Royal 8° (229 x 137 mm cut). Watermark: 1809.

Notes: In all respects identical with the preceding impression except that page 32 is now misnumbered 23.

Copy: InU. Reference: Ruff 40.

14As] Twelfth Edition: 1811

THE | **LAY** | OF | THE LAST MINSTREL, | A POEM; | BY | WALTER SCOTT, Esq. | [*short Oxford rule*] | [*two-line quotation*] | [*short reversed Oxford rule*] | THE TWELFTH EDITION. | **LONDON:** | PRINTED FOR LONGMAN, HURST, REES, ORME, AND BROWN, | PATERNOSTER-ROW, AND A. CONSTABLE AND CO. EDINBURGH; | *By James Ballantyne & Co. Edinburgh.* | 1811.

Published by 3 July 1811 in Edinburgh (advertisement in *The Vision of Don Roderick*, first edition). 3000 copies. Binding: blue boards with printed label. Paper: Demy 8° (224 x 141mm uncut). Watermarks: 1809 | 4 [6]; 1810 | 1 [4]. Collation: A^8 B-Y^8. Pagination: *1* half-title, *2 blank*, *3* title-page, *4 blank*, *5* dedication, *6 blank*, *7* note, *8 blank*, *9* fly-title, *10 blank*, *11* 12-208 text, *209* fly-title, *210 blank*, *211* 212-349 Notes, 349 printer's imprint, *350-352 blank*. Printer's imprint: [*short Oxford rule*] | Edinburgh: | Printed by James Ballantyne & Co.

Figures: A14-8, B22-1 29-6, C36-3 *43*-1, D61-11 62-6, E77-4 78-12, F85-3 90-4, G106-2 109-9, H121-12, I 130-6 132-12, K147-8 157-2, L162-3 164-4, M178-3 192-1, N203-11 208-9, O217-6 218-1, P226-6 233-2, Q242-4 256-8, R262-1 272-9, S287-12 288-2, T*291*-9 297-1, U*317*-1 318-3, X332-6 335-4, Y338-8 348-11.

Notes: Evidently this issue was set from the ninth or tenth editions, and not from the eleventh, where the notes continue through page 351.

Copies: BCL DT E E* GU L O; T/B TxU. Reference: Ruff 41.
*Trinity College Dublin prize book.

14At] Thirteenth Edition: 1812

THE | **LAY** | OF | THE LAST MINSTREL, | A POEM; | BY | WALTER SCOTT, Esq. | [*short Oxford rule*] | [*two-line quotation*] | [*short reversed

Oxford rule] | THE THIRTEENTH EDITION. | **LONDON:** | PRINTED FOR LONGMAN, HURST, REES, ORME, AND BROWN, | PATERNOSTER-ROW, | AND A. CONSTABLE AND CO. AND JOHN BALLANTYNE | AND CO. EDINBURGH; | *By James Ballantyne & Co. Edinburgh.* | 1812.

Issued in 3000 copies. Paper: Demy 8° (218 x 130mm cut). Watermarks: *none* 1,4,5,6,7,8,9,10] | W BALSTON | 1811. Collation: *A*[8] B-Y[8]. Pagination: *1* half-title, *2 blank*, *3* title-page, *4 blank*, *5* dedication, *6 blank*, *7* note, *8 blank*, *9* fly-title, *10 blank*, *11* 12-208 text, *209* fly-title, *210 blank*, *211* 212-350 Notes, 350 printer's imprint, *351-352 blank*. Printer's imprint: [*short Oxford rule*] | EDINBURGH: | Printed by James Ballantyne & Co.

Figures: A16-10, B23-9, C*43*-2, D54-9, E77-12, F96-5, G103-8, H125-1, I 144-10, K159-9, L169-5, M192-2, N195-1, O 218-5, P239-6, Q—, R268-2, S284-1, T*291*-4, U318-10, X332-5, Y341-3.

Notes: Unlike previous octavo editions, this printing seems to have proceeded at a more leisurely pace, with only one pressman assigned to each sheet. The edition is further revised, including now, page 325, a note for the memorable opening lines of Canto 6 (page 175) 'Breathes there the man, with soul so dead, . . .': this graciously entered upon the importunities of the Rev. Richard Polwhele in what Partridge describes as perhaps 'the world's most impudent letter from a literary man.'

Copies: BCL C E L L+ O; CtY+ DLC+ InU T/B.
+Extra-illustrated with 1809 engraved title-page and six plates by Richard Westall (see 14Dm).

References: Partridge(2), page 73; Ruff 42.

14Au] Fifteenth Edition, First Impression: 1816

THE | **LAY** | OF | THE LAST MINSTREL, | A POEM; | BY | WALTER SCOTT, ESQ. | [*short Oxford rule*] | [*two-line quotation*] | [*short reversed Oxford rule*] | THE FIFTEENTH EDITION. | **LONDON:** | PRINTED FOR LONGMAN, HURST, REES, ORME, AND BROWN, | PATER NOSTER-ROW; AND A. CONSTABLE AND CO. EDINBURGH; | *By James Ballantyne and Co. Edinburgh.* | 1816.

Issued in 3000 copies. Binding: blue boards. Paper: 8° (225 x 142mm uncut). Watermarks: *none* [4,6,8,9] | W BALSTON & Co. | 1815. Collation: *A*[8] B-Y[8]. Pagination: *1* half-title, *2 blank*, *3* title-page, *4 blank*, *5* dedication, *6 blank*, *7* note, *8 blank*, *9* fly-title, *10 blank*, *11* 12-208 text, *209* fly-title, *210 blank*, *211* 212-349 Notes, 349 printer's imprint, *350-352 blank*. Printer's imprint: [*short Oxford rule*] | EDINBURGH: | Printed by James Ballantyne & Co.

Figures: A13-8, B31-5 32-1, C35-4 36-6, D60-11 63-8, E66-10 80-11, F84-2 86-8, G107-2 108-6, H114-1 125-10, I 134-11 141-4, K146-5 149-2, L165-11 175-1, M182-12 184-2, N200-1 203-6, O 217-5 223-2, P228-5 238-8, Q254-10 256-11, R260-5 262-1, S280-11 282-10, T296-2 303-1, U312-11 318-2, X322-11 325-10, Y339-4 345-5.

Notes: Apparently a 14th edition (Ruff 43), so labeled, was never printed. The copytext for this edition is the 12th (1811), reprinting certain stylistic pointing there introduced (e.g. lower case volume references in the notes), but without the Polwhele note introduced in the 13th (1812). As in the 12th edition, past participles in this first impression terminate in 'ed' (e.g. page 113, lines 6, 14, 16: answered, mixed, scattered) and on page 186, line 6, '**Albert Graeme**' is in gothic type. Pages which begin a new section, however, are now numbered (e.g. 141, 175, 325).

Copy: CtY. Reference: Ruff 44 (impressions not differentiated).

14Av] Fifteenth Edition, Second Impression: 1816

THE | **LAY** | OF | THE LAST MINSTREL, | A POEM; . . . THE FIFTEENTH EDITION. . . . 1816.

Watermarks: As above, but with additional vat number 10. Figures: As above, except in some copies E68-2/- 74-8.

Notes: Past participles are now elided (page 113 lines 6, 14, 16: answer'd, mix'd, scatter'd), but page 186 line 6, '**Albert Graeme**' remains in gothic type. Pages 141, 175, 325 now are unnumbered.

Copies: DT L.

14Aw] Fifteenth Edition, Third Impression: 1816

THE | **LAY** | OF | THE LAST MINSTREL, | A POEM; . . . THE FIFTEENTH EDITION. . . . 1816.

Watermarks: as for second impression. Figures: as for second impression, with further variants: B32-1/5/-, M 188-1 190-11.

Notes: As in the second impression, past participles are elided and certain pages unnumbered. On page 186 line 6, however, 'ALBERT GRAEME' is now in small capitals.

Copies: AN C E(2) EP ES L O P; CtY+ T/B+.
+Extra-illustrated with 1809 engraved title-page and six plates by Richard Westall (see 14Dm).

14Ax] Murray's Edition: 1821

THE | LAY | OF | THE LAST MINSTREL. | A POEM. | BY SIR WALTER SCOTT. | [*short double rule*] | [*two-line quotation*] | [*short double rule*] | LONDON: | SOLD BY J. MURRAY, BOOKSELLER, | ALBEMARLE STREET. | [*dash*] | 1821.

Binding: Printed purple wrappers. Paper: Foolscap 12° (182 x 102mm uncut). Watermarks: none. Collation: *A*^{12} B-L^{12} M^{6} N^{4}(-N1). Pagination: *1* half-title, *2 blank*, *3* title-page, *4 blank*, *5* dedication, *6 blank*, *7* note, *8 blank*, *9* 10-145 text, *146 blank*, *147* 148-282 Notes. No printer's imprint. Figures: none.

Notes: As John Murray held a share of the copyright, a separate, reset edition was allowed at this time for his own use and issued somewhat irregularly, it seems, without any notice of the printer then employed.

Copy: NN. Reference: Ruff 45 (Erroneous collation based on the same copy).

14Ay] Sixteenth Edition: 1823

THE | **LAY** | OF | THE LAST MINSTREL, | A POEM; | BY | WALTER SCOTT, BART. | [*short Oxford rule*] | [*two-line quotation*] | [*short reversed Oxford rule*] | THE SIXTEENTH EDITION. | LONDON: | PRINTED FOR LONGMAN, HURST, REES, ORME, AND BROWN, | PATERNOSTER-ROW, AND A. CONSTABLE | AND CO. EDINBURGH. | [*dash*] | 1823.

1000 copies. Paper: Demy 8° (211 x 131mm cut). Watermarks: none, but fine wire lines. Collation: *A*^{8} B-Y^{8}. Pagination: *1* half-title, *2 blank*, *3* title-page, *4* printer's imprint(1), *5* dedication, *6 blank*, *7* note, *8 blank*, *9* fly-title for 'Canto First', *10 blank*, *11* 12-208 text, *209* fly-title for Notes, *210 blank*, *211* 212-352 Notes, 352 printer's imprint(2). Printer's imprint(1) [*short rule*] | PRINTED BY JAMES BALLANTYNE AND CO. EDINBURGH.; (2) [*short rule*] EDINBURGH: | Printed by James Ballantyne and Co. Typography: Signature U (page 305) is missigned T.

Figures: *A*14-3, B32-17, C48-10, D63-13, E80-9, F96-10, G109-11, H128-18, I 144-10, K160-5, L164-16, M192-9, N204-11, O 224-18, P237-2, Q256-2, R272-11, S286-17, T300-10, U316-11, X336-2, Y344-6.

Notes: Text is reset with corrections.

Copies: DLC CtY. Reference: Ruff 46.

14Az] New Edition, First Issue: 1825

[*engraved title*] THE | LAY OF THE LAST MINSTREL, | A POEM; | BY | SIR WALTER SCOTT, BART. | [*short double rule*] | [*two-line quotation*] | [*short double rule*] | A NEW EDITION | [*vignette*] | **LONDON** | PRINTED FOR LONGMAN, HURST, REES, ORME, BROWN, AND GREEN | PATERNOSTER ROW; AND A. CONSTABLE AND CO EDINBURGH. | [*diamond dash*] | 1825.

Published 30 November 1825 in Edinburgh (*EWJ*). 9s. 2000 copies. Paper: Foolscap 8° (162 x 103 mm cut). Watermarks: none, but very fine wire lines. Collation: *A*^{8} B-S^8 2S^8 T-U^8 Y^8. Pagination: *1* half-title, *2 blank*, *3* dedication, *4 blank*, *5* note, *6 blank*, *7* fly-title, *8 blank*, *9* 10-206 text, *207* fly-title, *208 blank*, *209* 210-349 notes, 349 printer's imprint, *350-352 blank*. Printer's imprint: [*short rule*] | EDINBURGH: | Printed by James Ballantyne and Co. Typography: There is no X gathering.

Figures: A16-6, B29-2, C*41*-2, D64-3, E80-2/-, F84-4, G112-5, H128-6, I 144-1, K160-3, L176-1, M192-1, N205-5, O 224-3, P240-6, Q256-2, R270-2, S275-2, 2S 292-2, T320-5, U336-5, Y347-1/-.

Notes: This 'pocket' edition was advertised along with similar issues of *The Lady of the Lake* and *Marmion*, both earlier published 15 June 1825.

Copy: E. Reference: Ruff 47.

14Aaa] New Edition, Second Issue: 1825[1830]

[*engraved title*] THE | LAY OF THE LAST MINSTREL, | A POEM; . . . A NEW EDITION . . . 1825.

Published by 20 April 1830 (advt in *The Doom of Devorgoil*). Collation for additional material: *a-b*^{8}. Pagination: *i* ii-xxx text, *xxxi-xxxii blank*.

Notes: As for the preceding issue except for Scott's new Introduction, dated 'Abbotsford, *April*, 1830'.

Copies: L; CtY(2). Reference: Ruff 48.

REPRINTS

FRANCE

PARIS: Didot and Galignani
[~] The Lay of the Last Minstrel. 1821, 1826. (Collection of Modern English Authors: *see* 290R[1A], [1C].)

PARIS: Galignani
[~] The Lay of the Last Minstrel. 1829. (*see* 293R.7.) Copy: not seen.

14Ra] PARIS: Glashin 1821
The Lay of the Last Minstrel, A Poem; By Sir Walter Scott. . . . Paris: Printed by J. Smith, For D. Glashin, Rue Vivienne, No. 10. 1821. Pages: *1-9* 10-282. Notes: The half-title gives the title, followed by 'In Six Cantos.' Copies: E L(2) P.

Reference: Kohler(1) 87 (with illustration).

GERMANY

ZWICKAU: Schumann
[~] The Lay of the Last Minstrel. 1819. (Pocket Library of English Classics: *see* 302R.7-8.)

UNITED STATES

14Rb] BALTIMORE: Cushing 1811-1812
The Lay of the Last Minstrel: A Poem. By Walter Scott, Esq. . . . Baltimore: Published by Joseph Cushing; and E. Sargeant, New-York. 1811. Pages: *1-7* 8-232. Notes: With an engraved frontispiece. On verso of title is the imprint; 'Printed by D. & G. Bruce, Slote-lane, New-York.' Copies: CtY InU MWA(2) NN PHi PPL RPB.

[~] The Lay of the Last Minstrel. The Twelfth Edition. 1812. (The Poetical Works of Walter Scott: *see* 303R.2.)

14Rc] BOSTON: Bedlington 1828
The Lay of the Last Minstrel, A Poem, by Sir Walter Scott. Boston: Published by Timothy Bedlington. 1828. Pages: *i-iii* iv, *11* 12-304. Notes: The type-set title-page is preceded by a conjugate engraved frontispiece and title-page. Several short poems are added to the main text. The pagination and the reference page 304 'End of Vol. I.' indicates a variant issue. *See also* The Poetical Works of Sir Walter Scott (304R.1). Copies: E; MH.

14Rd] BOSTON: Etheridge and Bliss 1807
The Lay of the Last Minstrel, A Poem; By Walter Scott, Esq. . . . Boston: Published by Etheridge and Bliss, No. 12, Cornhill. Sold also by Said Etheridge, Charlestown. 1807. Pages: *1-9* 10-252. Copies: E; CtY DLC MH MWA NNU-W PU T/B.

14Re] BOSTON: Greenough and Stebbins 1810
The Lay of the Last Minstrel, A Poem; By Walter Scott, Esq. . . . Boston: Published by Greenough and Stebbins, No. 4, Suffolk-Buildings, Congress-Street. 1810. Pages: *1-7* 8-234. Copies: CtY DLC MH MWA(2) NjP.

14Rf] CHARLESTON: Morford 1806
[The Lay of the Last Minstrel, . . . Charleston, S.C., E. Morford, 1806. 252pp.] The only recorded copy, in the Charleston Library Society Library, is now reported as missing; but the page record would indicate that this is probably a variant issue of the 1805 Philadelphia, Maxwell reprint (*see* 14Rm).

FREDERICKSBURG: Withers
[~] Lay of the Last Minstrel. 1824. (The Poetical Works of Sr Walter Scott: *see* 310R.)

14Rg] NEW YORK: Eastburn 1818
The Lay of the Last Minstrel, A Poem. By Walter Scott, Esq. . . . New-York: Published by J. Eastburn & Co. Literary-Rooms, Broadway. 1818. Pages: *1-7* 8-306. Notes: Pages *249-251* 252-306 represent 'The Dance of Death, and Other Poems'. (Also issued in The Poetical Works of Walter Scott, Esq., volume 1. 1819. *see* 312R.1.) Copy: NN.

14Rh] NEW YORK: Elliot and Crissy 1811
The Lay of the Last Minstrel, A Poem. By Walter Scott, Esq. . . . New-York: Printed and Published by Elliot and Crissy, at the Tontine Coffee-House. Sold also by R. Scott, Pearl Street. And A. Devillers, Charleston, 1811. Pages: *i-iv*, *1* 2-'193'[203]. Notes: Some copies have page '193' corrected to 203. Copies: DLC MWA(3) T/B.

14Ri] NEW YORK: Riley and Maxwell 1806
The Lay of the Last Minstrel, A Poem, By Walter Scott, Esq. Published by I. Riley, & Co. New-York, and Hugh Maxwell, Philadelphia. 1806. Pages: *1-9* 10-252. Notes: A variant issue of the 1805 Philadelphia, Maxwell, reprint (*see* 14Rm). Copy: MWA.

14Rj] NEW YORK: Sargeant 1811
The Lay of the Last Minstrel: A Poem. By Walter Scott, Esq. . . . New-York: Published by Ezra Sargeant, No. 86 Broadway; and J. Cushing, Baltimore. 1811. Pages: *1-7* 8-232. Notes: In blue printed boards. With engraved frontispiece copy of a lady and a two-line caption: 'She raised her stately head, And her heart throbbed high with pride.'; with attributions 'drawn by R. Westall./Engraved by F. Kearny.' but engraving only 70 x 50mm. Copy: NjP.

14Rk] PHILADELPHIA: Earle 1810
The Lay of the Last Minstrel, A Poem; By Walter Scott, Esq. . . . The Eleventh Edition. Philadelphia, Published by Edward Earle. Fry and Kammerer Printers. 1810. Pages: *1-7* 8-288. Notes: E copy reads on front endpaper: 'Given me, By Walter Scott Esqr. at Abbotsford. Melrose. August 1813. M. W. H.' (Matthew Weld Hartstonge). This inscription is also present in two other volumes published 1810 by the same publisher: *Marmion* (*see* 28Rg) and *The Lady of the Lake* (*see* 47Ro). Copies: E; MH MWA PPL.

14Rl] PHILADELPHIA: Hopkins 1807
[The Lay of the Last Minstrel, A Poem; by Walter Scott, Esq. Philadelphia: Published by B. & B. Hopkins, No. 170, Market Street. 1807.] Copy located at St. John's College, Annapolis, Maryland.

14Rm] PHILADELPHIA: Maxwell 1805
The Lay of the Last Minstrel, A Poem, by Walter Scott, Esq. Printed and Published by Hugh Maxwell, No. 25, North Second-Street, Philadelphia. 1805. Pages: *1-9* 10-252. Notes: In some copies the comma after 'A Poem,' is missing. The first American edition and, apparently, the prototype for four later issues by other booksellers (*see* 14Rd, Rf, Ri, Rn). Copies: MWA PPL.

14Rn] PHILADELPHIA: Riley 1806
The Lay of the Last Minstrel, A Poem, by Walter Scott, Esq. Philadelphia: Printed for I. Riley & Co. New-York. 1806. Pages: *1-9* 10-252. Notes: A variant issue of the preceding item. Copies: P; MH.

14Ro] SAVANNAH: Seymour and Williams 1811
The Lay of the Last Minstrel, A Poem, By Walter Scott, Esq. . . . Savannah: Printed and Published by Seymour and Williams, and Sold by C. and A. Conrad & Co. and Bradford and Inskeep, Philadelphia; M. and W. Ward, and D. D. Arden, New-York; Charles Williams, and Lincoln and Edmonds, Boston; and E. Morford, Willington & Co. Charleston, S. Carolina. 1811. Pages: *i-v* vi, *7-9* 10-295. Copies: E; CtY MH MWA NN.

DERIVATIVES

GREAT BRITAIN

14Da] DUBLIN: Charles 1811
Border Feuds; or, The Lady of Buccleuch. A Musical Drama, in Three Acts. Founded on Mr. Scott's poem of "The Lay of the Last Minstrel.". . . Dublin: Printed by J. Charles, 57, Mary-Street, (Within three doors of Capel-street.) . . . [1811]. Pages: *1-5* 6-35. Notes: Engraved frontispiece. Drama attributed to Sarah Bartley; the music by John Stevenson (not included). Price: Sixpence British. Copy: L. Reference: Bolton 1.

14Db] DUBLIN: Gilbert and Hodges 1811
Border Feuds; or, The Lady of Buccleuch. A Musical Drama, in Three Acts. Founded on Mr. Scott's poem of "The Lay of the Last Minstrel.". . . Dublin: (Printed by Espy & Cross) for Gilbert and Hodges, No. 27, Dame-Street. 1811. Pages: *1-4, i-v*, 6-41. Notes: Drama attributed to Sarah Bartley (the music by John Stevenson not included). This edition, possibly preceding the previous entry, is not recorded in Bolton. Copy: O.

14Dc] EDINBURGH: Hamilton 1806
Lovely Rosabelle* Written by Walter Scott Esqr. Edinburgh, Printed & Sold by J. Hamilton, Music Seller, No. 24, North Bridge. [unwatermarked. ca.1806]. Pages: *1*-2. Notes: Engraved

sheet music. Asterisk in title refers to footnote: 'From the Lay of the Last Minstrel, by Permission of the Proprietors.' Words from canto 6, stanza 23 (first words: 'O listen, listen, ladies gay,'). Music composed by William Clarke arranged for voice and pianoforte. Price: 1s. Copies: BCL E.

EDINBURGH: Lawrie
[~] The Goblin Groom. 1809. [Parody by R. O. Fenwick. *see* 480S].

14Dd] LONDON: Barker and Son 1806
Songs, Duets, Chorusses, &c. in The White Plume: or, The Border Chieftains; a Musical-Romantick Drama, in Three Acts, . . . London: Printed and published by Barker and Son, Dramatic Repository, Great Russell Street, Covent Garden. 1806. Pages: *1-5* 6-23 *24*. Notes: Drama by Thomas Dibdin. (Music by Mr. Reeve not included.) Price: Ten Pence. Copy: CtY.

14De] LONDON: Birchall 1805-1828
[1] "Breathes there the Man with Soul so dead!". . . . The Poetry from The Lay of the Last Minstrel . . . . London, Printed & Sold by Birchall & Co. 140, New Bond Street. [1828]. Pages: *i-ii*, 1-11. Notes: Engraved sheet music with plate number: '2204'. The caption title reads: 'The Poetry by Sir Walter Scott.' Words from canto 6, stanza 1 (first words as title). Song composed by John Clarke arranged for voice and pianoforte. Price: 3s. Copies: L O. Reference: G/T 10291.

[2] Rosabelle, The Words from the Lay of the last Minstrel, . . . London, Printed & Sold by Rt. Birchall, at his Musical Circulating Library, 133, New Bond Strt. [watermarked 1802. ca.1805]. Pages: 1-7. Notes: Engraved sheet music. Words from canto 6, stanza 23 (first words: 'O listen listen Ladies listen Ladies gay'). Music composed by Dr. Callcott arranged for voice and pianoforte. Price: 2/6. Copy: MH-M.

LONDON: Cadell and Davies
[~] Wallace: or, The Fight of Falkirk. 1809. [Parody by Margaret Hodson. *see* 482S].

LONDON: Cawthorn
[~] The Lay of the Scottish Fiddle. 1814. [Parody by J. K. Paulding. *see* 483S].

14Df] LONDON: Clementi 1807-1825
[1] The Minstrel's Harp, a Cantata, from The Lay of the Last Minstrel; . . . London, Printed by Clementi & Co 26 Cheapside. [watermarked 1807]. Pages: *1* 2-7. Notes: Engraved sheet music. Words from canto 3, stanzas 1-2 (first words: 'And said I that my limbs were old'). Music composed by John Clarke arranged for voice and harp or pianoforte. Price: 1s/6. Copies: E L. Reference: G/T 10289.

[2] The Minstrel's Harp, from The Lay of the Last Minstrel. . . . London, Published by Clementi & Co. 26, Cheapside. [watermarked 1811]. Notes: A reissue of the preceding entry. Price: 2s. Copy: NNP. Again reisssued with 1814 watermark (NN); without watermark (CtY, inscribed 5 January 1816), or with watermark 1819 (L), 1821 (L), 1825 as 'New Edition' (L). Reference: Van Antwerp(2) 42d.

[3] Two Glees "The feast was over in Branksome Tower," . . . The Spirit Scene "Is it the roar of Teviot's Tide", . . . The Poetry from The Lay of the Last Minstrel. . . . London Printed for the Author, by Clementi & Co. & to be had at all the Principal Music Shops. NB. Just Published in Continuation by the same Author, Two Glees for Two Trebles & a Bass, . . [unwatermarked. ca.1809]. Pages: *i-ii, 1* 2-25. Notes: Engraved sheet music with composer's signature in ink to right of imprint. Includes (1) 'The feast was over in Branksome tower,' (first words as title) from canto 1, stanzas 1, 3-4, 11-12; (2) 'The Spirit Scene' (first words: 'Is it the roar of Teviot's tide') from canto 1, stanzas 12, 14-18. Music composed by John Clarke arranged for voice and pianoforte. Price: First Set 6 Shills. Copy: E.

[4] Two Glees, "The Sun had brightened Cheviot Grey", and "Sweet Teviot! on thy Silver Tide," . . London Printed for the Author by Clementi & Co. & to be had at all the Principal Music Shops. . . . [watermarked 1808]. Pages: *i-ii, 1* 2-16. Notes: Engraved sheet music with composer's signature in ink to right of imprint. Words from canto 2, stanzas 25-27 (first words as title) and from canto 4, stanzas 1-2 (first words as title). Songs composed by John Clarke arranged for three voices and pianoforte. Price: Set 2d. 5 Shills. Copies: E L(2). Reissued without watermark (E[2] L). Reference: G/T 10288.

LONDON: Colburn
[~] The Lay of the Last Minstrel. 1811. [Travesty by 'O. Neville'. *see* 484S].

LONDON: Crosby
[~] The Lay of the Poor Fiddler. 1814. [Parody by John Roby. *see* 485S].

14Dg] LONDON: Goulding 1820
Border Feuds, or the Lady of Buccleuch. London: Goulding [1820]. Notes: Music composed by John Stevenson.] Copy: Not seen. Reference: G/T 10311

14Dh] LONDON: Monro and May 1812
The Minstrel's Harp, from The Lay of the Last Minstrel. . . . London, Monro & May, 11 Holborn Bars, near Middle Row. [watermarked 1811. ca.1812]. Pages: *i-ii*, 1-5. Price: 2s/. Copy: L.

14Di] LONDON: Monzani 1807
In Peace Love Tunes the Shepherd's Reed, . . . The Words from the Lay of the Last Minstrel, By Walter Scott, Esqr. . . . London Published by Monzani & Co. Music Sellers to his Royal Highness the Prince of Wales 3 Old Bond Street near Piccadilly. . . . [unwatermarked. ca.1807]. Pages: *i-ii*, 1-9. Notes: Engraved sheet music with plate-number 'No. 108 Vocal English', and composer's initials 'TA' in ink on title-page just before price. Words from canto 3, stanza 2 (first words as title). Glee composed by Thomas Attwood arranged for three voices and pianoforte or harp. Price: 3s. A later issue utilizes page *ii* to list 'Catalogue of Thomas Attwood's music published by Monzani and Co'. Copies: BCL E(3).

14Dj] LONDON: Monzani & Hill 1813-1820
[1] The Harp's Wild Notes. . . . The Words from the Lay of the Last Minstrel, By Walter Scott, Esqr. . . . London. Published by Monzani & Hill Music Sellers to his Royal Highness the Prince Regent No.[ ] Regent Street near Piccadilly. [unwatermarked. ca.1813]. Pages: *i-ii, 1* 2-8. Notes: Engraved sheet music with plate number 'No. 109 Vocal English' and the

composer's initials 'T.A.' in ink on title. Words from canto 5, last stanza (first words: 'The Harp's wild notes though hush'd the song,'). Glee composed by Thomas Attwood arranged for voice and pianoforte. Price 2s/6. Copy: L. Reference: G/T 10279.

[2] In Peace Love Tunes the Shepherds Reed, . . . The Words from the Lay of the Last Minstrel, By Walter Scott, Esqr. . . . London, Published by Monzani & Hill, Music Sellers to his Royal Highness the Prince of Wales 3 Old Bond Street near Piccadilly. [unwatermarked. ca.1813]. Pages: *i-ii*, 1-9. Notes: Engraved sheet music with plate number 'No. 108 Vocal English' and the composer's initials 'T.A.' in ink on title. Words from canto 3, stanza 2 (first words as title). Glee composed by Thomas Attwood arranged for voice, pianoforte and harp. Page *ii* lists 'Catalogue of Thomas Attwood's music published by Monzani & Co'. Copy: BCL. Reimpressed and reissued about 1820 with imprint concluding 'to his Majesty 28 Regent St. Piccadilly.' and without list on page *ii* (BCL L). References: G/T 10280.

14Dk] LONDON: Preston 1813

Two Glees: "The Feast was over in Branksome Tower," . . . and The Spirit Scene, "Is it the roar of Teviot's Tide," . . . London, Preston [unwatermarked. ca.1813]. Pages: *1-3* 4-25. Notes: Engraved sheet music. Words from canto 1, stanzas 1 and 12 (first words as title). Composed by John Clarke arranged for voice and pianoforte. Copy: NN-L.

LONDON: Richardson

[~] The Ass on Parnassus. 1815. [Parody by Jeremiah Quiz. *see* 495S[1-2]].

14Dl] LONDON: Royal Harmonic Institution 1820

[It was an English lady bright. London: Royal Harmonic Institution (1820). Notes: Music by James Fisin.] Copy: not seen. Reference: G/T 10296.

14Dm] LONDON: Sharpe 1809

The Lay of the Last Minstrel. A Poem, by Walter Scott, Esq. . . . London, Published by John Sharpe, Piccadilly. 1809. Engraved vignette title and six plates, issued with the suite prepared for *Marmion* (*see* 28Dt). Illustrations: Title reads 'Illustrated with Engravings from the designs of Richd. Westall'. All plates are labeled 'Drawn by Richd. Westall R A., engraved by Chas. Heath', titled 'Lay of the Last Minstrel' and have an imprint dated 1 June 1809. Advertised in *The Times* 17 November 1809 in [1a] 4° £1.4.0 and in [2] 8° size 12s. An 8 May 1810 *The Lady of the Lake* prospectus (in NNP copy) further notes the availability of [1b] 4° proofs at £1.11.6. and a combined poem-plate issue, [3] in 4° at £3.13.6., [4] in 8° at £1.2.6. The separate [1a] 4° issue bears on outer drab wrapper a printed label indicating as the only publisher, in this state, Gale and Fenner, Paternoster Row; but the [2] 8° issue exhibits in one copy (T/B) around the unlabeled wrapper a portfolio in marbled boards with label designating only Sharpe as the publisher. Separate issue copies: [1a] O; IdU. [1b] not seen. [2] IdU MH T/B. Combined poem-plate issues: [3] 14Aj, Ak, Am. [4] 14Ad, Ah, Ao, At, Aw. Reference: Ruff 49.

Title-page vignette engraved by J. Pye; plates, with page reference below illustration:

(1) [page 28] with a two-line quotation from canto 1, stanza 18 (first line: 'She raised her stately head,');

(2) [page 46] with a two-line quotation (first line: '"And, Dar'st thou, Warrior! seek to see' from canto 2, stanza 5);

(3) [page 90] with a two-line quotation (first line: 'She thought some spirit of the sky' from canto 3, stanza 22);
(4) [page 104] with a three-line quotation (first line: 'Thus to the Ladye did Tinlinn shew' from canto 4, stanza 6);
(5) [page 164] with a two-line quotation (first line: 'Yet not Lord Cranstoun deigned she greet' from canto 5, stanza 25);
(6) [page 206] with a two-line quotation (first line: 'The mitred Abbot stretched his hand,' from canto 6, stanza 30).

14Dn] LONDON: Sutherland 1810
The Dying Bard to his Harp. Written by Walter Scott Esqr. Edinr. Printed & Sold by John Sutherland No. 9 Calton Street. [unwatermarked. ca.1810]. Pages: 1-2. Notes: Engraved sheet music. At the foot of page 2: 'These lines belong to Mr G Thomson's Collection of Welch airs, and are here published by his permission.' (first words: 'Dinas Emlinn lament for the moment is nigh'). Music composed by unidentified composer arranged for voice and pianoforte. Price: 1/. This poem was included in the preprint (14Aa). Copy: E.

14Do] LONDON: Wilkinson 1808
[1] Sweet Teviot! On thy silver tide, . . . the Poetry from The Lay of the Last Minstrel . . . Printed by Wilkinson & Co. Late (Broderip & Wilkinson No.13 Haymarket [unwatermarked. 1808]. Pages: *9-10* 11-16. Notes: Engraved sheet music. Words from canto 4, stanzas 1-2 (first words: 'Sweet Teviot on thy silver tide. . .'). Music composed by John Clarke and arranged for voice and pianoforte. Copy: MH.

[2] Two Glees. "The feast was over in Branksome Tower," . . . and The Spirit Scene "Is it the roar of Teviot's Tide," . . . The Poetry from The Lay of the Last Minstrel. . . . London Printed by Wilkinson & Co. Late Broderip & Wilkinson. No. 43, Haymarket. [watermarked 1808]. Pages: *i-ii*, *1* 2-25. Notes: Engraved sheet music. Words from canto 1, stanzas 1, 3-4, 11-12 (first words as title) and from canto 1, stanzas 12, 14-16, 18 (first words as title). Music composed by John Clarke arranged for chorus and pianoforte. Clark wrote to Scott referring to a performance on 22 May 1808, which Scott belatedly acknowledged 10 January 1809. Price for Set 1st: 6 Shills. Copies: BCL L. References: G/T 10287; *Letters,* ii.147.

UNITED STATES

14Dp] BOSTON: Graupner 1808
The Minstrel's Harp. A Cantata, From the Lay of the Last Minstreal[!]; . . . Boston, Published and Sold by, G. Graupner, at his Music Store, No. 6 Franklin Street. [ca.1808]. Pages: 1-5. Notes: Engraved sheet music with caption title and with plate numbers 269-273. Words from canto 3, stanzas 1-2 (first words: 'And said I that my limbs were old; And said I that my blood was cold,'). Music composed by John Clarke arranged for voice and harp or pianoforte. Copies: E; MWA RPB(3). References: G/T 10289; Wolfe 1843.

14Dq] NEW YORK: Dubois 1818
[The Minstrel's Harp. An Arietta. . . . New York, Publish'd by Wm. Dubois, No. 126 Broadway, [ca.1818]. Notes: A reissue from same plates, with imprint alteration, as entry 14Dr. Copy: not seen. Reference: Wolfe 1844A.

NEW YORK: Inskeep and Bradford
[~] The Lay of the Scottish Fiddle. 1813. [Parody by J. K. Paulding. *see* 501S].

14Dr] NEW YORK: Paff 1812
The Minstrel's Harp. An Arietta from the Lay of the Last Minstrel . . . . New York Sold at J. Paff's Music Store. [1812]. Pages: *1* 2-7. Notes: Engraved sheet music. Words from canto 3, stanza 1-2 (first words: 'And said I that my limbs were old And said I that my blood was cold,'). Music composed by John Clarke arranged for voice and harp or pianoforte. Copies: MH MWA. Reference: Wolfe 1844.

14Ds] PHILADELPHIA: Blake 1812
The Minstrel's Harp, An Arietta, From The Lay of the Last Minstrel; . . . Philadelphia, Published by G. E. Blake. [ca.1812]. Pages: 1-3. Notes: Engraved sheet music with caption title. Words from canto 3, stanzas 1-2 (first words: 'In peace, Love tunes the shepherds reed; In war, he mounts the warriors steed;'). Music composed by John Clarke arranged for voice and harp or pianoforte. Copies: InU MWA PHi RPB(2). Reference: Wolfe 1845.

14Dt] PHILADELPHIA: Willig 1812-1816
[1] The Minstrel's Harp, An Arietta, from the Lay of the Last Minstrel; . . . Philadelphia Publish'd and Sold at G. Willig's Musical Magazine [ca.1812]. Pages: 1-3. Notes: Engraved sheet music. Words from canto 3, stanzas 1-2 (first words: 'In peace, Love tunes the shepherds reed; In war, he mounts the warriors steed;'). Music composed by John Clarke arranged for voice and harp or pianoforte. Copies: MWA(2). Reference: Wolfe 1846.

[2] The Minstrel's Harp An Arietta, from the Lay of the Last Minstrel, . . . Philadelphia. Published and Sold at G. Willig's Music Store. [ca.1816]. Pages: *1* 2-5. Notes: Engraved sheet music. Words from canto 3, stanzas 1-2 (first words: 'And said I that my limbs were old And said I that my blood was cold,'). Music composed by John Clarke arranged for voice and harp or pianoforte. Copy: MWA. Reference: Wolfe 1847.

EXTRACTS IN ANTHOLOGIES

14E] In *The Lay of the Last Minstrel* the two unrelated 'Airs' first printed in the pre-publication issue (14Aa) were later extracted, [1] 'The Norman Horse Shoe in 405E(1).2 413.5; [2] 'The Dying Bard' in 355E.2 389.28 400[2].3 405(1).1 405(3).2. From *The Lay* itself there are 83 extracts in 33 anthologies: 354E.1-2 355.1 356-[2].3-5 358.8-10,13 360.24 361[3].1,3 362.2,5-6 366[2].16 366[3].1 382.1 385.1 386.1,6 388.1,8 389.24,36,38 392.1-4 393 400[2].1 401.1-7 402[1] 406.1-2 408[1].1-3 410[1].1-2 414[1].5 415.7 417.4-6 419.1-3 420.3 423.4,11,13 444.3 450(and 471).1,4-6,9,11-12 463.1-2 464.1-4,7-8.

REVIEWS OF JOHNES AND THORNTON

15A] First Printings: 1805

1] 'ART. VII. *Sir John Froissart's Chronicles of England, France, and the adjoining Countries, from the latter part of the Reign of Edward II. to the Coronation of Henry IV.* Newly Translated from the best French Editions, . . . by Thomas Johnes.', pages 347-362;

2] 'ART. XI. *A Sporting Tour through the Northern Parts of England, and great Part of the Highlands of Scotland, . . . and General Observations on the State of Society and Manners. . . .* By Colonel T. Thornton.', pages 398-405, *in*:

The Edinburgh Review, January 1805. No. X. [volume 5 imprint:] Edinburgh: Printed by D. Willison, Craig's Close, For Arch. Constable & Co. Edinburgh, and Longman, Hurst, Rees, & Orme, London. 1805.

Published 18 January 1805 in Edinburgh (date cited for this issue in previous number).

Copies: L O; PPL TxU. [A fourth edition has also been reported.]

References: (Magnum Opus Edition 1835: *The Miscellaneous Prose Works*, [1] xix.112-138 as 'Johnes's Froissart', [2] xix.*87* 88-99 as 'On Thornton's Sporting *Tour*'.)

REVIEW OF GODWIN

16A] First Printing: 1805

'ART. XV. *Fleetwood: or the New Man of Feeling.* By William Godwin.', pages 182-193, *in*:

The Edinburgh Review, April 1805. No. XI. [volume 6 imprint:] Edinburgh: Printed by D. Willison, Craig's Close, For Archibald Constable & Co. Edinburgh, and Longman Hurst Rees and Orme, London. 1805.

Published 18 April 1805 in Edinburgh (date cited for this issue in previous number).

Copies: O; PPL TxU. [A fourth edition has also been reported.]

Reference: (Magnum Opus Edition 1835: *The Miscellaneous Prose Works*, xviii.118-138 as 'Godwin's Fleetwood'.)

REVIEWS OF HUDSON AND DONAT, HUNTER, MACKENZIE, AND LAING

17A] First Printings: 1805

[1] 'ART. IX. *The New Practice of Cookery, Pastry, Baking and Preserving,* . . . By Mrs Hudson and Mrs Donat, . . . Culina Famulatrix Medicinae; or, *Receipts in Modern Cookery, with a Medical Commentary written by Ignotus, and revised by A. Hunter.* . . . The Second Edition.', pages 350-357;

[2] 'ART. XV. *Report of the Committee of the Highland Society of Scotland, appointed to inquire into the Nature and Authenticity of the Poems of Ossian: . . . by Henry Mackenzie, Esquire, . . . The Poems of Ossian, &c. containing the Poetical Works of James Macpherson . . . with Notes and Illustrations.* By Malcolm Laing', pages 429-462, *in*:

The Edinburgh Review, July 1805. No. XII. [volume 6 imprint:] Edinburgh: Printed by D. Willison, Craig's Close, For Archibald Constable & Co. Edinburgh, and Longman Hurst Rees and Orme, London. 1805.

Published 18 July 1805 in Edinburgh (date cited for this issue in previous number).

Copies: L O; PPL TxU. [A fourth edition has also been reported.]

References: (Magnum Opus Edition 1835: *The Miscellaneous Prose Works*, [1] xix.100-111 as 'On Two Cookery Books', [2] Not reprinted.)

REVIEW OF TODD

18A] First Printing: 1805

'ART. XIV. *The Works of Edmund Spenser, . . . To which are added, Notes, some Account of the life of Spenser,* . . . By the Reverend Henry John Todd', pages *203* 204-217, *in*:

The Edinburgh Review, October 1805. No. XIII. [volume 7 imprint:] Edinburgh: Printed by D. Willison, Craig's Close, For Archibald Constable & Co. Edinburgh, and Longman Hurst Rees and Orme, London. 1806.

Published 17 October 1805 in Edinburgh (date cited for this issue in previous number).

Copies: L O; PPL TxU. [A fourth edition has also been reported.]

Reference: (Magnum Opus Edition 1835: *The Miscellaneous Prose Works*, xvii.80-101 as 'Todd's Edition of Spenser'.)

RASSELAS, BY SAMUEL JOHNSON

19Aa] First Illustrated Edition, First Impression, First State: '1803'[1805]
RASSELAS, | BY | SAMUEL JOHNSON, L. L. D. | [*short Oxford rule*] | WITH | ENGRAVINGS, | FROM | PICTURES BY R. SMIRKE, R. A. | [*short reversed Oxford rule*] | LONDON: | PUBLISHED BY WILLIAM MILLER, OLD BOND-STREET; | AND SOLD BY MANNERS AND MILLER, AND ARCHIBALD CONSTABLE, | EDINBURGH. | The Letter Press by James Ballantyne, Kelso. | 1803.

Notes: A rejected title printed, with the text, two years before publication. On preparing this first title the publishers had not as yet engaged the engraver, A. Raimbach, whose name when employed and the date 1805 appears on the title-page and engravings in the state next described. At that later time the addresses of William Miller and James Ballantyne had also changed.

Copy: GU. For directing us to this early, discarded state we are indebted to the late David Fleeman.

19Ab] First Illustrated Edition, First Impression, Second State: 1805

RASSELAS, | BY | SAMUEL JOHNSON, LL.D. | [*short Oxford rule*] | WITH | ENGRAVINGS, BY A. RAIMBACH, | FROM | PICTURES BY R. SMIRKE, R. A. | [*short reversed Oxford rule*] | LONDON: | PUBLISHED BY WILLIAM MILLER, ALBEMARLE-STREET; | AND SOLD BY MANNERS AND MILLER, AND ARCHIBALD CONSTABLE AND CO. | EDINBURGH. | The Letter Press by James Ballantyne, Edinburgh. | [*dash*] | 1805.

Paper: Demy 4° (274 x 215mm cut). Watermarks: none. Collation: $\pi^4(\pi 4+1)$ A-2A^4 2B^2. Pagination: *1* half-title, *2 blank*, *3* title-page, *4 blank*, *i* ii-iii Advertisement, *iv blank*, *1* 2-197 text, *198 blank*. No printer's imprint. Illustrations: The four engraved plates usually are in the positions given below, but alternately one may be used as a frontispiece; all have the imprint: 'Published by William Miller, London, MDCCCV.' and below the illustration 'R. Smirke R.A. pinxit' and 'A. Raimbach sculp'; the headpiece page *1*, reads 'Drawn by R. Smirke R.A. Published by W. Miller, 1805. Engraved by A. Raimbach.' As this headpiece, above text, required separate presswork the leaf was printed separately. Typography: At this early date Ballantyne still enters double signatures as Aa, Bb. Figures: none.

Notes: This first illustrated edition, sumptuously produced, derives ultimately from the second, 1759 edition. Apart from providing the text, Scott's only editorial service is his anonymous Advertisement where, on page iii, he quotes from one of his favorite pieces to define the moral of this tale as directed to the 'hope, which sickens not the heart, and to the wealth, which has no wings to fly' (anon. 'Castle-Building, an Elegy', variously quoted in the *English Minstrelsy*, i.242, *Redgauntlet*, Letter 12, and *Journal* 18 March 1829). 'In veneration, therefore, for the illustrious Author, and in admiration of the Work itself, the Editor has studied to present it to the public in a form, which may entitle it to a high place in the first libraries.' There are four plates:

(1) [caption title] 'The Attempt of the Mechanist to Use His Wings' usually facing page 22;
(2) 'The Visit of Rasselas to the Hermit', page 82;
(3) 'The Princess Lamenting the loss of Pekuah', page 132;
(4) 'Pekuah Consoling her Attendants', page 142.

Copies: BCL EU L O; T/B.

References: Novels and Novelists (Chapters on Waverley Novels. London: W. H. Allen, 1898) pages 194, 292-293; Gwin J. Kolb, 'Sir Walter Scott, "Editor" of *Rasselas*,' *Modern Philology* 89 (1992), 515-518. (Magnum Opus Edition: Not reprinted.)

19Ac] First Illustrated Edition, Second (Large-Paper) Impression: 1805

RASSELAS, | BY | SAMUEL JOHNSON, LL.D. . . . 1805.

Binding: Brown boards with cloth spine gilt-stamped 'Rasselas'. Paper: Royal 4° (304 x 243mm uncut). Watermarks: none or J WHATMAN | 1801.

Notes: Of this impression there are two issues, with sheet A (1) unwatermarked, (2) reset and watermarked 1814 / 1814. The latter variant apparently was occasioned either by a short count in the original issue, or loss of copy after a nine-year interval.

Copies: (issue 1) BCL; CtY. (2) E O.

19Ad] Second Illustrated Edition: 1819

RASSELAS, | BY | SAMUEL JOHNSON, LL.D. | [*short Oxford rule*] | WITH | ENGRAVINGS, BY A. RAIMBACH, | FROM | PICTURES BY R. SMIRKE, R.A. | [*short reversed Oxford rule*] | **LONDON:** | PUBLISHED BY HECTOR M'LEAN, NO. 8, SOHO SQUARE; | AND SOLD BY MANNERS AND MILLER, AND ARCHIBALD CONSTABLE AND CO. | EDINBURGH. | [*dash*] | 1819

Paper: Demy 4° (261 x 210mm cut). Watermarks: I I SMITH 1818/1818.

Collation and pagination as for first edition except for printer's imprints on verso of title-page and *198*: [*short rule*] | PRINTED BY J. BRETTELL, RUPERT STREET, HAYMARKET, LONDON. Illustrations: The engravings have been reused from the previous edition and hence are still dated by Miller 1805. Typography: No period after title-page date. Brettell's double signatures are entered as AA, BB. Figures: none.

Notes: This paginal resetting of the first illustrated edition may have been issued simply to dispose of the engravings still available after fourteen years.

Copies: BCL O.

REVIEW OF ELLIS AND RITSON

20A] First Printing: 1806

'ART. VI. *Specimens of early English Metrical Romances, . . . To which is prefixed, a Historical Introduction, . . .* By George Ellis, . . . *Ancient Engleish Metrical Romanceës, selected and publish'd by* Joseph Ritson.', pages 387-413, *in*:

The Edinburgh Review, January 1806. No. XIV. [volume 7 imprint:] Edinburgh: Printed by D. Willison, Craig's Close, For Archibald Constable & Co. Edinburgh, and Longman Hurst Rees and Orme, London. 1806.

Published 23 January 1806 in Edinburgh (date cited for this issue in previous number).

Copies: L O; PPL TxU. [A fourth edition has also been reported.]

Reference: Magnum Opus Edition 1835: *The Miscellaneous Prose Works*, xvii.16-54 as 'On Ellis's Specimens of Early English Metrical Romances . . . Ancient English Metrical Romances, Selected by Joseph Ritson'.)

A COLLECTION OF SCOTTISH AIRS

21Aa] First printings in volume 1: 1806

[1] 'HELLVELLYN. BY MR WALTER SCOTT.' (first words: 'I climb'd the dark brow of the mighty Hellvellyn'), pages 16;

[2] 'THE MAID OF TORO. BY WALTER SCOTT, ESQ.' (first words: 'O, low shone the sun on the fair lake of Toro'), pages 37, *in*:

[*engraved title*] A Collection of Scottish Airs, Harmonized for the Voice &

Piano Forte, with introductory & concluding Symphonies; and Accompaniments for a Violin & Violoncello, By Joseph Haydn Mus. Doct. Vol. 1. . . . Edinburgh, Published by the Proprietor, William Whyte, No.1 South St. Andrew's Street, and sold by Clementi & Co. 26, Cheapside, London. The Music engraved by Clementi & Co. London; & the Letter Press, by James Ballantyne, Edinburgh.

[*cover title*] Whyte's Edition of Scottish Songs, Harmonized Exclusively by Haydn; and Containing Two Original Songs, Written Expressly for this Work by Walter Scott, Esq. Edinburgh: Printed by James Ballantyne and Co. For the Proprietor, William Whyte, No. 1. St. Andrew's Street. 1806.

Notes: The Advertisement (page vi) is dated 1 March 1806 and concludes that 'The proprietor is happy to be enabled to add, that the present edition is enriched with two original songs, from the elegant pen of Mr Walter Scott.' An earlier issue of volume 1, with advertisement dated 2 July 1804, has no Scott contributions. Leaves of engraved music are interspersed with leaves of letterpress, with pagination usually duplicated for the facing pages of music and words. The engraved music includes first few lines of poetry. The inspiration for 'Hellvellyn' apparently came from a walking tour in August 1805 when Scott and Wordsworth climbed on the Helvellyn mountain near where Charles Gough had fallen to his death, only to be found three months later still guarded by his faithful dog.

A reissue, undated, retains the 1806 cover, but has the original engraved title imprint removed and another imprint inserted: London, Printed by Goulding, D'Almaine, Potter & Co. 20, Soho Square, & 7, Westmoreland Street, Dublin, and Sold by the Principal Music Sellers in Great Britain.

Copies: L; InU. Reissue: DLC.

References: Ruff 57; *Wordsworth*, ii.387. (Magnum Opus Edition 1833: *The Poetical Works*, [1] vi.370-372, [2] vi.368-369.)

21Ab] First printings in volume 2: 1807

[3] 'THE PALMER. WRITTEN FOR THIS WORK BY WALTER SCOTT, ESQ.' (first words: '"O open the door, some pity to shew," Keen blows the northern wind;'), pages 41. Notes: The composer of the air 'O open the door' is unidentified, but the arranger is Haydn. The closing double quotation mark is lacking in some copies.

[4] 'WANDERING WILLIE. WRITTEN FOR THIS WORK BY WALTER SCOTT, ESQ.' (first words: 'All joy was bereft me the day that you left me,'), pages 45. Notes: The engraved page omits the first word of the poem.

Neither the title of the air, nor the composer is identified, but the arranger is Haydn.

[5] 'THE MAID OF NEIDPATH. WRITTEN FOR THIS WORK BY WALTER SCOTT, ESQ.' (first words: 'O Lovers eyes are sharp to see, And lovers ears in hearing;'), pages 54. Notes: The Scott poem is printed above the Burns' poem 'Anna'; however, the music is engraved with the Burns' words. The composer of the air 'Anna' is not identified, but Haydn was the arranger. Scott is not the author of the song 'Anna' as the 'Contents' imply. These three poems *in*:

[*engraved title*] A Collection of Scottish Airs, Harmonized for the Voice & Piano Forte with introductory & Concluding Symphonies; and Accompaniments for a Violin & Violoncello. By Joseph Haydn Mus. Doct. Vol. 2. . . . Edinburgh, Published by the Proprietor, William Whyte, No.1, South St. Andrew's Street, and Sold by the Principal Music Sellers in Great Britain. The Music engraved by Clementi & Co. London; & the Letter Press, by James Ballantyne, Edinburgh.

Published 8 July 1807 in Edinburgh (*EWJ*). 15s with or 12s without the accompaniments.

Notes: Front cover imprint is dated 1807. The last sentence in the 'Advertisement' reads: 'The Publisher is proud to announce, that he has been so fortunate as to have procured for the present volume three additional songs from the pen of MR WALTER SCOTT.'

Copies: E(2) O.

References: [3] G/T 10576; [4] G/T 10898; [5] G/T 10437]; Ruff 57. (Magnum Opus Edition 1834: *The Poetical Works*, [3] viii.361-362, [4] viii.367-369, [5] viii.365-366.)

DERIVATIVES

GREAT BRITAIN

21Da] LONDON: Chappell 1812

The Maid of Toro, A Song, . . . The Words by Walter Scott Esqr. . . . London, Printed & Sold by Chappell & Co. Music & Musical Instrument Sellers, 124, New Bond Street. [1812]. Pages: 1-6. Notes: Engraved sheet music with plate number 90. (first words: 'O low sunk the Sun on the fair Lake of Toro,'). Music composed by William Horsley arranged for voice and pianoforte. Price: 2s. Copy: L.

21Db] LONDON: Clementi 1811
[The Maid of Toro. London: Clementi (1811). Notes: Music composed by William Horsley.] Copy: not seen. Reference: G/T 10440.

21Dc] LONDON: Clementi, Banger, Collard [and others] 1825
[The Maid of Toro. London: Clementi, Banger, Collard, Davis & Collard (1825). Notes: Music composed by John Charles Clifton.] Copy: not seen. Reference: G/T 10439.

21Dd] LONDON: Goulding and D'Almaine 1828-1829
[1] The Maid of Neidpath, page 71 *in*: The Musical Bijou, An Album of Music, Poetry, and Prose, for MDCCCXXIX. . . . London: Goulding and D'Almaine, 20, Soho Square. [watermarked 1828]. Notes: Edited by F. H. Burney. Letterpress words without music. (first line: 'O lovers' eyes are sharp to see,'). Copy: NN-L.

[2] The Maid of Toro, pages 16-21 *in*: The Musical Bijou, . . . for MDCCCXXX. . . . London: Goulding and D'Almaine, 20 Soho Square. [watermarked 1829]. Notes: Edited by F. H. Burney. Engraved sheet music for voice and pianoforte by John Parry, pages 16-20, letterpress words, page 21. (first line: 'O, low shone the sun on the fair lake of Toro,'). Copies: E; NN-L.

EXTRACTS IN ANTHOLOGIES

21E] Of the five poems by Scott in *A Collection of Scottish Airs* three were extracted in 12 anthologies: [1] 'Hellvellyn' with eight entries: 358E.4 361[3].2 363.4 382.3 385.4 388.7 396 444.1; [2] 'The Maid of Toro' with two entries: 390E 459; [4] 'Wandering Willie' with two entries: 361[2]E.2 423.2.

A HEALTH TO LORD MELVILLE

22A] First Edition: 1806

[*caption title*] A | HEALTH TO LORD MELVILLE; | BEING | AN EXCELLENT NEW SONG. | [*short Oxford rule*] | [*three-line quotation from Shakespeare*] | [*short reversed Oxford rule*]

Privately printed, probably on 27 June 1806 in Edinburgh to serve as text for the singing of this song. Binding: unbound. Paper: Demy 8° in twos. (222 x 141mm uncut). Watermarks: none. Collation: A^2. Pagination: *1* 2-4 text. (first words: 'Since here we are set in array round the table,'). Figures: none.

Notes: Eight ten-line stanzas. The Berg copy is corrected by Scott to read: stanza 2, lines 1-2, 'when boldly] what measures', 'Pitt banished] When Pitt quelled'; stanza 3, line 1, [a footnote:] Blues'*', '* 1st. Regt. Edinburgh Volunteers'. The trimmed E copy, originally enclosed in a letter from W. Imlay to Lockhart 26 February 1834, may represent a large-paper issue, as it now measures 226 x 136mm.

Copies: E; NN(Berg: proof). References: Ruff 50 (with illustration of page *1*). (Magnum Opus Edition: Not reprinted).

REPRINT

GREAT BRITAIN

22R] GLASGOW: Herald Office 1806
A Health to Lord Melville, By Walter Scott, Esquire. Sung at Lord Melville's Dinner, on Friday 28th June, at Edinburgh. . . . Printed in the Herald Office, Glasgow. [1806]. Broadside.
Copy: E.

WRITTEN ON THE OCCASION OF LORD MELVILLE'S ACQUITTAL

23A] First Edition: 1806

[*caption title*] *NEVER BEFORE PRINTED.* | [*short Oxford rule*] | WRITTEN ON THE OCCASION OF | LORD MELVILLE'S ACQUITTAL, | 1806.

Privately printed 28 June 1806 in Edinburgh (date of letter to Robert Dundas, enclosing MS copy now in E). Paper: Broadside (328 x 189mm uncut). Watermarks: none.

[Stanza 1]
Come listen, brave boys, to a story so merry,
'Tis of the Archbishop of fair Canterbury;
How the Mitre did keep the full bottom in awe,
And the Gospel taught manners and justice to Law.
Derry down.

[Stanza 6]
Then here's to the health of that Prelate of fame,
Tho' true Presbyterians, we'll drink to his name;
Long, long may he live, to teach prejudice awe,
And since Melville's got justice, the devil take Law.
Derry down.

Notes: Six numbered quatrains, each with refrain 'Derry down'. A widely variant seven-stanza manuscript with corrections by Scott in the NN Berg Collection is captioned 'The Lawyer and the Archbishop of Canterbury | Being an Excellent New Song | To the Tune of 'King John & The Abbot of Canterbury".' Here the first line reads: 'I'll tell you a story a story so merry'. Perhaps for prudential (or political?)

reasons the penultimate stanza is omitted in the printed version. The manuscript reads:

> The party now find themselves in the wrong box
> Though they praise the Committee and voted with Fox
> They have found out the difference twixt merit & jaw
> And the damnable odds betwixt justice and Law

The manuscript copy sent to Dundas, Lord Melville's son, now at E, also begins 'I'll tell you', but otherwise is only slightly variant.

Copies: E; NN(Berg).

Reference: Ruff 187 (with illustration, page 233). (Magnum Opus Edition: Not reprinted.)

BALLADS AND LYRICAL PIECES

24Aa] First Edition, First Impression: 1806

BALLADS | AND | LYRICAL PIECES. | [*short Oxford rule*] | BY | WALTER SCOTT, Esq. | [*short reversed Oxford rule*] | EDINBURGH: | *Printed by James Ballantyne and Co.* | FOR LONGMAN, HURST, REES, AND ORME, LONDON; | AND ARCHIBALD CONSTABLE AND CO. | EDINBURGH. | [*dash*] | 1806.

Published 20 September 1806 in Edinburgh (*EEC*). 7s.6d. Binding: blue, brown, grey, ochre or pink paper; drab, green, or rose boards with printed label. Paper: Demy 8° (225 x 143mm uncut). Watermarks: 1804/1804.

Collation: π^4 A-L^8 M^2. Pagination: *i* half-title, *ii blank*, *iii* title-page, *iv blank*, *v* Advertisement, *vi blank*, *vii* Contents, *viii blank*, *1* 2-161 text of ballads, *162 blank*, *163* fly-title for 'Songs', *164 blank*, 165-180 text, 180 printer's imprint: [*short Oxford rule*] | Edinburgh: | Printed by James Ballantyne & Co.

Figures: A9-4, B25-1, C35-7, D54-4, E66-7, F83-4, G107-7, H125-4, I 136-4, K157-2, L172-4, M178-2/-.

Notes: In April 1806, five months before issue, the *Scots Magazine* announced that Scott then had 'in the press' not only this collection, but also the fourth edition of *The Lay of the Last Minstrel*, the third of the *Minstrelsy of the Scottish Border*, and the second of *Sir Tristrem*. All of the eight ballads and five songs in this book, as its Advertisement page *v* indicates, were previously published. However, two of the pieces ('The Norman Horse-Shoe' and 'The Dying Bard') were first printed in the 1804 pre-publication issue of *The Lay* (14Aa), and not as here remarked in the musical collections of George Thomson, where they eventually appear in 1809 (405R[1]). The last name in the Advertisement, (state 1) misspelled White in a few copies, was (2) immediately corrected to WHYTE. The final two-leaf gathering M is of a duplicate setting: either page 177 line 4 pointed at the end, '.—' and with figure 2 on page 178; or 177 line 4 '."—' and 178 unfigured.

Presentation copy: (state 1) CtY*(not inscribed, but originally with inserted letter to Richard Heber). Other copies: (state 1) CtY MH. (2) AN BCL E(2) E(Catherine Henrietta Boyle, Countess of Bandon) E(2)* E+ L O; CtY* DLC IdU* NN NNU-W OCl T/B(2) TxU TxU*.
*With 16-page Longman catalogue dated 1 July 1806.
+Extra-illustrated with an 1812 engraved title-page and six plates by Richard Westall. As indicated in the entry for these (341D) the engraved title-page reads 'Glenfinlas [the first ballad in this book] . . . with the Vision of Don Roderick . . . .' The E copy of the latter is 59Af and contains, additionally, the first edition of *The Field of Waterloo* (84Aa).

References: Ruff 51; Tinker 1862. (Magnum Opus Edition: Not reprinted.)

24Ab] First Edition, Second (Large-Paper) Impression: 1806

BALLADS | AND | LYRICAL PIECES. . . . 1806.

Published concurrently with the previous impression. Binding: drab paper boards, printed label. Paper: Royal 8° (245 x 155mm uncut). Watermarks: J WHATMAN | 1804 [1805].

Notes: Typographically in all respects identical with the preceding impression except that the Advertisement is in the second, corrected state, reading 'WHYTE' and figures on page 178 may be 2/-.

Copies: BCL; CtY DLC InU*a MH NNP*b(Van Antwerp).
*With 16-page Longman catalogue dated (a)1 December 1808, (b) 'Corrected to March 1810'.

References: Ruff 52; Van Antwerp(1) 6.

24Ac] Second Edition, First Impression: 1806

BALLADS | AND | LYRICAL PIECES. | [*short Oxford rule*] | BY | WALTER SCOTT, ESQ. | [*short reversed Oxford rule*] | SECOND EDITION. | EDINBURGH: | Printed by James Ballantyne and Co. | FOR LONGMAN, HURST, REES, AND ORME, LONDON; AND | ARCHIBALD CONSTABLE AND CO. EDINBURGH. | [*dash*] | 1806.

Published November 1806 in Edinburgh (*SM*); issued 19 December in London (*The Times*). 7s.6d. Binding: blue-green boards. Paper: Demy 8° (223 x 138mm uncut).

Watermarks: 1804/1804. Collation: π^4 A-L^8 M^4. Pagination: *i* half-title, *ii blank*, *iii* title-page, *iv blank*, *v* Advertisement, *vi blank*, *vii* Contents, *viii blank*, *1* 2-164 text of ballads, *165* fly-title for 'Songs', *166 blank*, 167-182 text, 182 printer's imprint, *183-184 blank*. Printer's imprint: [*short Oxford rule*] | EDINBURGH: | Printed by James Ballantyne & Co.

Figures: A16-3, B19-2, C40-4, D63-3, E75-4, F94-7, G111-5 112-3, H120-5, I 136-5, K154-5, L170-7 173-5, M181-7.

Notes: Text has been reset and 'The Erl-King' added, pages 162-164. The additional piece, first printed in the 1 March 1798 *Kelso Mail* (2A), continues to be printed through the fourth edition of this collection, but then, for the reason noted in the 'fifth' (24Ai), is excluded and thus not collected in *PW*.

Presentation copy: MH('Mrs Gordon confers a high favor by her acceptance of this Volume of [*printed half-title*: Ballads and Lyrical Pieces] 30 March 1811—W.S.'). Other copies: BCL E+ L O; CaBVaU CtY*b InU NNP(Van Antwerp) TxU(2) TxU*a. *With 16-page Longman catalogue dated (a) 1 October 1806, (b) 1 June 1808. +Extra-illustrated with an 1812 engraved title-page and six plates by Richard Westall. As indicated in the entry for these (341D) the engraved title-page reads 'Glenfinlas [the first ballad in this book] . . . with the Vision of Don Roderick . . . .' The E copy of the latter is 59Af.

Reference: Ruff 53.

24Ad] Second Edition, Second (Large-Paper) Impression: 1806

BALLADS | AND | LYRICAL PIECES. . . . SECOND EDITION. . . . 1806.

Published concurrently with the previous impression. Paper: Royal 8° (227 x 143 mm uncut). Watermarks: D & A C | 1805 | 1.

Notes: Apart from the paper the only distinguishing feature of this unrecorded impression is the employment of a dagger, usually to the right of the signature, but twice to the left (for B and I), and twice elsewhere in the forme (F on page 96, M on page 180). This mark usually indicates a reimpression.

Copy: E.

24Ae] Fourth (Third) Edition: 1810

BALLADS | AND | LYRICAL PIECES. | [*short Oxford rule*] | BY | WALTER SCOTT, ESQ. | [*short reversed Oxford rule*] | FOURTH EDITION. | EDINBURGH: | Printed by James Ballantyne and Co. | FOR LONGMAN, HURST, REES, AND ORME, LONDON; AND | ARCHIBALD CONSTABLE AND CO. EDINBURGH. | [*dash*] | 1810.

Issued 18 July 1810 in London (*MC*). 7s.6d. Paper: Demy 8° (212 x 135mm cut). Watermarks: 1808; 1809; 9 | W Balston | 1809; [sheets L-M only] D & A C | 1808 | none [1]; 1809 | 2. Collation and pagination as in Second Edition.

Figures: A4-12 6-13, B26-14 28-2, C40-3 47-13, D50-3 52-13, E67-13 80-3, F83-13 96-12, G107-3 112-13, H126-3 128-9, I 130-9 144-12, K152-5 158-10, L169-10 170-12, M180-13.

Copies: DN DT(2)+ E L+ O+; CtY IdU T/B. Reference: Ruff 54.
+Extra-illustrated with an 1812 engraved title-page and six plates by Richard Westall. As indicated in the entry for these (341D) the engraved title-page reads 'Glenfinlas [the first ballad in this book] . . . with the Vision of Don Roderick . . . .' The latter poem in these copies is 59Ah.

24Af] Fourth Edition, First Impression: 1812

BALLADS | AND | LYRICAL PIECES. | [*short Oxford rule*] | BY | WALTER SCOTT, Esq. | [*short reversed Oxford rule*] | FOURTH EDITION. | EDINBURGH: | *Printed by James Ballantyne and Co.* | FOR LONGMAN, HURST, REES, ORME, AND BROWN, LONDON; | AND ARCHIBALD CONSTABLE AND CO. EDINBURGH. | [*dash*] | 1812.

Paper: Demy 8° (222 x 141mm uncut). Watermarks: 5[8, 10] | W Balston | 1811. Collation and pagination as in Second Edition. Typography: In some copies page 81 or 89 is unnumbered. Figures: A8/9-9, B19-9 28-6, C35-6, D64-5/-, E72-1 75-2, F85-2/- 94-5, G103-3, H118-6, I 144-3, K156-1, L169-6, M178-9.

Copies: O L+; CtY+ MB+ MH*. Reference: Ruff: 55.
*With 16-page undated Longman catalogue.
+Extra-illustrated with an 1812 engraved title-page and six plates by Richard Westall. As indicated in the entry for these (341D) the engraved title-page reads 'Glenfinlas [the first ballad in this book] . . . with the Vision of Don Roderick . . . .' The latter poem in these copies is 59Ah.

24Ag] Fourth Edition, Second (Large-Paper) Impression: 1812

BALLADS | AND | LYRICAL PIECES. . . . FOURTH EDITION. . . . 1812.

Published concurrently with the previous impression. Paper: Royal 8° (225 x 141mm cut). Watermarks: J Whatman | 1810; 6 | J Whatman | 1811. Except for the paper the only difference noted is page 89, now misnumbered 95.

Copy: L+.
+Extra-illustrated with an 1812 engraved title-page and six plates by Richard Westall.

As indicated in the entry for these (341D) the engraved title-page reads 'Glenfinlas [the first ballad in this book] . . . with the Vision of Don Roderick . . . .' The L copy of the latter is 49Ah.

24Ah] Fourth Edition, First Impression, Second Issue: 1812[1815]

BALLADS | AND | LYRICAL PIECES. . . . FOURTH EDITION. . . . 1812.

Paper: Demy 8° (222 x 141mm uncut). Notes: A reissue of the first impression, now without press figures on pages 85 and 169, followed (with pagination continued) by the 'second edition' 1815 of *The Field of Waterloo* (*see* 84Ab).

Copy: E.

24Ai] Fifth Edition, First State: 1819

BALLADS | AND | LYRICAL PIECES. | [*short Oxford rule*] | BY | WALTER SCOTT, Esq. | [*short reversed Oxford rule*] | FIFTH EDITION. | EDINBURGH: | *Printed by James Ballantyne and Co.* | FOR LONGMAN, HURST, REES, ORME, AND BROWN, LONDON; | AND ARCHIBALD CONSTABLE AND CO. | EDINBURGH. | [*dash*] | 1819.

1250 copies. Paper: Demy 8° (219 x 138mm uncut). Watermarks: none. Collation: π^4 A-L^8 M^2. Pagination: *i* half-title, *ii blank*, *iii* title-page, *iv blank*, *v* Advertisement, *vi blank*, *vii* Contents, *viii blank*, *1* 2-161 text of ballads, *162 blank*, *163* fly-title, *164 blank*, 165-180 text of songs, 180 printer's imprint: [*short rule*] | Edinburgh | Printed by James Ballantyne and Co. Typography: The last word of the Advertisement (page *v*), hitherto regularly spelled 'Whyte', is now misprinted 'White' as in a few copies of the first edition.

Figures: A16-11, B19-9, C36-12, D54-10, E69-1, F82-5, G108-2, H126-4, I 144-12, K152-6, L176-7, M—.

Notes: Like the first edition, which may well have served as its copy-text, this has only two leaves in the final gathering and thus also excludes 'The Erl-King'.

Copies: IdU NN T/B+. Reference: Ruff: 36.
+Extra-illustrated with an 1812 engraved title-page and six plates by Richard Westall. As indicated in the entry for these (341D) the engraved title-page reads 'Glenfinlas [*the first ballad in this book*] . . . with the Vision of Don Roderick . . .' The T/B copy of the latter is 59Ai.

24Aj] Fifth Edition, Second State: 1820

BALLADS | AND | LYRICAL PIECES. | [*short Oxford rule*] | BY | WALTER SCOTT, Esq. . . . FIFTH EDITION. . . . 1820.

Notes: This is identical with the preceding state except for the 1820 date and, on page 180, a different reference superseding the imprint: END OF THE BALLADS AND LYRICAL PIECES. This reference would suggest that the issue, as now altered, was to precede another work, probably one of several being adapted to comprise the *Miscellaneous Poems* (261A).

Copy: EU(Corson copy, lacking half-title, bound after *The Vision of Don Roderick*, 1815: *see* 59Ai).

REPRINTS

FRANCE

PARIS: Didot and Galignani
[~] Ballads and Miscellaneous Pieces. 1821, 1826. (Collection of Modern English Authors: *see* 290R[5A], [7C].)

GERMANY

ZWICKAU: Schumann
[~] Ballads and Lyrical Pieces. 1825. (Pocket Library of English Classics: *see* 302R. 117.)

UNITED STATES

24Ra] BALTIMORE: Nicklin [and others] 1811
Ballads and Lyrical Pieces. By Walter Scott, Esq. Baltimore: Published by Philip H. Nicklin: Also by E. Sargeant, New-York; Anthony Finley, Philadelphia; D. Mallory & Co. Boston; J. Milligan, Georgetown; and Joseph Cushing, Baltimore. 1811. Pages: *1-9* 10-215. Notes: Engraved frontispiece published by J. Cushing. The imprint is in two states, with third line reading: (a) 'Also by E. Sargeant'; (b) 'Also by Ezra Sargeant'. Copies: (state a) O; CtY MWA NN(Berg [Washington Irving copy]) NNU-W PHi T/B ViU(2). (b) DLC.

24Rb] BOSTON: Etheridge and Bliss 1807
Ballads and Lyrical Pieces. By Walter Scott, Esq. Boston: Published and sold by Etheridge and Bliss, No. 12, Cornhill. Sold also by said Etheridge, Charlestown. 1807. Pages: *i-viii*, *1* 2-180. Notes: On title verso S. Etheridge of Charlestown is listed as the printer for all three states, the title imprint for each readng, after 'Cornhill.' (a) as above; (b) And by B. and B. Hopkins, Philadelphia. 1807.; (c) And by Thomas and Tappan, Portsmouth, N. H.

1807. Copies: (state a) E O; NjP NN RPB TxU. (b) BCL; InU MH MWA PPL RPB. (c) MWA.

24Rc] NEW YORK: Sargeant and Nicklin 1811
Ballads and Lyrical Pieces. By Walter Scott, Esq. New-York: Published by Ezra Sargeant; and P.H. Nicklin, Baltimore. 1811. Pages: *1-9* 10-215. Notes: Engraved frontispiece published by J. Cushing, Baltimore. A variant issue of 24Ra. Copies: CtY NN NNP.

DERIVATIVE

GREAT BRITAIN

LONDON: Sharpe
[~] Glenfinlas. And Other Ballads Etc. With The Vision of Don Roderick. [1812]. (Westall engravings. *see* 341D).

POPULAR BALLADS AND SONGS

25A] First Scott Edition: 1806

Popular Ballads | AND | Songs, | FROM | TRADITION, MANUSCRIPTS, | AND | SCARCE EDITIONS; | WITH | *TRANSLATIONS OF SIMILAR PIECES* | FROM THE | Ancient Danish Language, | AND | A FEW ORIGINALS BY THE EDITOR. | [*short Oxford rule*] | BY | ROBERT JAMIESON, | A.M. & F.A.S. | [*short reversed Oxford rule*] | VOL. I [II]. | EDINBURGH: | PRINTED FOR ARCHIBALD CONSTABLE AND CO. | EDINBURGH: CADELL AND DAVIES, AND | JOHN MURRAY, LONDON. | 1806.

Published 9 October 1806 in Edinburgh (*EEC*); issued November in London (*MM* 1 December). £1.1.0. Binding: Drab boards with blue-green paper spines and printed labels. Paper: Demy 8° (224 x 141mm. uncut). Watermarks: 1803 [1804, 1805]. Typography: Printer's imprints exist in three variants: (1) [*short Oxford rule*] | *Printed by* | J. BALLANTYNE AND CO. . | *Edinburgh*.; (2) [*short Oxford rule*] | Edinburgh, | Printed by James Ballantyne & Co.; (3) [*short Oxford rule*] | EDINBURGH: | Printed by James Ballantyne & Co.

General Notes: Scott's association with Jamieson extended from 1800, when the two men first compared notes on their ballad collections, and his later participation in this edition is repeatedly acknowledged, first in the 'Advertisement' prefixed to the book (written just before Jamieson departed for a teaching post in Riga), then in headnotes and footnotes (i.20n, 44n, 48-49, &c), and again in the prefatory comment on the five ballads he provided the compiler (i.109, 157, 309; ii.154, 265). Scott himself was early identified as superintending the work in Jamieson's absence (*SM* May 1806, page 365) and in that capacity printed a discursive letter from Riga addressed to him (ii.84-98), inserted various translations from the Danish, apparently composed the dedication to the Duchess of Gordon (*Letters*, i.335), and had the work printed and published by his own associates. By every measure, then, he may be recognized as, in fact, the anonymous co-editor of this companion-piece to his own *Minstrelsy of the Scottish Border*.

Copies: E EU(2); T/B.

References: Duval 503 (with illustration). (Magnum Opus Edition: Not reprinted.)

1] Popular Ballads | AND | Songs, . . . VOL. I. . . . 1806.

Collation: π^4 A^8 $B2^2$ B-I^8 I^8 K-Y^8. Pagination: *1* half-title, *2* printer's imprint(1), *3* title, *4 blank*, *5* dedication to Her Grace the Duchess of Gordon, *6 blank*, *i*-ii Contents, *i* ii-xix Advertisement, dated from London 9 August 1805, *xx blank*, *1* fly-title, *2 blank*, *3* 4-352 text, 352 printer's imprint(2). Typography: As noted in the collation, the third gathering is signed 'B2' and there are two successive gatherings signed I.

Figures: A vii-3 xii-7, B2—, B10-2, C18-4, D42-4, E56-7, F67-4, G96-7, H105-3 106-6, I 121-7, I 141-4, K148-7, L173-1, M179-1, N194-1, O 214-5, P226-5, Q245-5, R259-5, S278-5, T302-5, U307-5, X331-5, Y341-7.

2] Popular Ballads | AND | Songs, . . . VOL. II. . . . 1806.

Collation: π^4 A-$2B^8$ $2C^4$ *2D*^{4}(-*2D*4). Pagination: *1* half-title, *2* printer's imprint(1), *3* title, *4 blank*, *i* ii-iii Contents, *iv blank*, *1* fly-title, *2 blank*, *3* 4-409 text, 409 printer's imprint(3), *410 blank*, *411-414* Works (published by A. Constable & Co.). Typography: Page 124 is misnumbered 24.

Figures: A8-4, B22-4, C38-7, D63-4, E70-2, F82-5, G112-7, H128-2, I 131-2 144-4, K158-2, L169-7, M180-2, N200-7, O 221-7, P231-5, Q256-7, R266-5, S283-3, T291-5 296-2, U320-7, X332-2, Y347-5, Z*367*-1 368-7, 2A 371-4 377-7, 2B 393-5 399-1, 2C 406-3 408-2, *2D*—.

Notes: The Constable list records (as items 3-5) Scott's books and, without acknowledging his editorship, item 13, Slingsby's *Original Memoirs* (27A), issued just after this Jamieson book.

REVIEWS OF BERESFORD AND HERBERT

26A] First Printings: 1807

[1] 'ART. XIII. *The Miseries of Human Life; or, the Groans of Timothy Tesly* [*Testy*], *and Samuel Sensitive*', pages 184-196;

[2] 'ART. XV. *Miscellaneous Poetry*. By the Honourable W. Herbert', pages 211-223, *in*:

The Edinburgh Review, October 1806. No. XVII. [volume 9 imprint:] Edinburgh: Printed by D. Willison, Craig's Close, For Archibald Constable & Co. Edinburgh, and Longman Hurst Rees and Orme, London. 1807.

Published 16 October 1806 in Edinburgh (date cited for this issue in previous number).

Notes: The anonymous first title was later acknowledged to have been written by The Rev. James Beresford.

Copies: L O; PPL. Later issued as a 'fourth edition' (TxU).

References: (Magnum Opus Edition 1835: *The Miscellaneous Prose Works*, [1] xix.139-159 as 'On "The Miseries of Human Life."', [2] xvii.102-118 as 'Herbert's Poems'.)

ORIGINAL MEMOIRS, WRITTEN DURING THE GREAT CIVIL WAR

27Aa] First Edition, First Impression: 1806

ORIGINAL | **MEMOIRS,** | WRITTEN | DURING THE GREAT CIVIL WAR; | BEING | THE LIFE | OF | SIR HENRY SLINGSBY, | AND MEMOIRS OF | CAPT. HODGSON. | WITH | NOTES, &c. | [*short reversed Oxford rule*] | EDINBURGH: | *Printed by James Ballantyne & Co.* | FOR ARCH. CONSTABLE AND CO. EDINBURGH; | AND JOHN MURRAY, 32, FLEET-STREET, LONDON. | [*dash*] | 1806.

Published 30 October 1806 in Edinburgh (*EEC*). 12s. Paper: Demy 8° (220 x 141mm uncut). Watermarks: W S | 1804 (sheets A-D; randomly on first four leaves with date only on other three); R C | 1805 | 1 [or none] (sheet E); W S | 1805 (randomly on first four leaves with date only on other three); 1805 (on first and third and second and fourth of first four leaves); D & A C | 1805 | 1 (sheet M). Collation: π^2 A^8 B-Z^8. Pagination: *1* title-page, *2 blank*, *3-4* Contents, *i* fly-title for Some Account of Sir Henry Slingsby, *ii blank*, *iii* iv-xvii text, *xviii blank*, *19* fly-title for Memoirs of Sir Henry Slingsby, *20 blank*, *21* 22-81 text, *82 blank*, *83* fly-title for Memoirs of Captain John Hodgson, *84 blank*, *85* 86-87 Advertisement (by Joseph Ritson), *88 blank*, *89* 90-198 text, *199* fly-title for Relations of the Campaigns of Oliver Cromwell, *200 blank*, *201* Advertisement, *202 blank*, *203-205* 206-367 texts of ten tracts, each with a type-facsimile of 1650 title, 367 printer's imprint, *368 blank*. Printer's imprint: [*short Oxford rule*] | Edinburgh, | Printed by James

Ballantyne & Co. Illustration: Frontispiece of Sir Henry Slingsby Bart., engraved by Maddocks.

Figures: E83(or 78)-5, F86-3, G112-3, H123-4 128-5, I 132-4 143-5, K152-2, L168-2 170-4, M184-5, N197-3, O 217-3, P234-3, Q247-3, R262-4, S282-4, T293-2, U320-2, X329-2, Y342-2, Z355-7.

Notes: Paper, text, and figures all suggest that this work was begun by a printer other than Ballantyne, but that Ballantyne took over with sheet E—miscalculating as he did so—and thereafter, as elsewhere, figured all of the remaining text. Sheet E exists in two states: (1) Pages misnumbered 81-96 with a disruption of text at the start of this gathering, figure 83-5; (2) pages correctly numbered 65-80, text proceeding regularly, figure 78-5.

Scott refers to his anonymous editorship in a letter to Constable, 7 October 1806. In this book, the first evidence of his antiquarian interest in political affairs, the editor offers no justification, assuming that the subject itself is its own recommendation. The first Memoir apparently derives from an abbreviated transcript (see Scott's note page 87 and DNB s.v. Slingsby); the second Memoir, from an original manuscript previously in Ritson's possession; and the ten printed tracts 'from the originals in possession of Thomas Thomson, Esq. Advocate' (page *201*). These ten published accounts may be identified, in order, as Wing L438, T3023, T2941, S2774, T3040, C7097, L3046, L1782, H1122, A3874).

Copies: (state 1) DLC OCl. (2) E LU* O(2); InU NjP NNU-W(2) TxU.
*With undated 4-page Constable catalogue.

Reference: (Magnum Opus Edition: Not reprinted.)

27Ab] First Edition, First (Large-Paper) Impression: 1806

ORIGINAL | **MEMOIRS,** | WRITTEN | DURING THE GREAT CIVIL WAR; | BEING | THE LIFE | OF | SIR HENRY SLINGSBY, . . . 1806.

Published concurrently with the previous impression. £1.7.6. Paper: Royal 8° (235 x 146mm cut). Watermarks: V 1796 (on each of first four leaves of each gathering).

Notes: Except for paper in all respects identical with the preceding impression, with figure E78-5.

Copy: CtY(Rosebery).

MARMION, A TALE OF FLODDEN FIELD

The Poem was finished in too much haste, to allow me an opportunity of softening down, if not removing, some of its most prominent defects. . . . [but] by good fortune, the novelty of the subject, and, if I may say so, some force and vivacity of description, were allowed to atone for many imperfections. Thus the second experiment on the public patience, generally the most perilous,—for the public are then most apt to judge with rigour, what in the first instance they had received, perhaps, with imprudent generosity,—was in my case decidedly successful. (*PW*, vii.13-14.)

28Aa] First Edition, First Impression: 1808

MARMION; | **A Tale** | **OF FLODDEN FIELD.** | BY | WALTER SCOTT, Esq. | [*short Oxford rule*] | [*four-line quotation from Leyden*] | [*short reversed Oxford rule*] | EDINBURGH: | [*reversed Oxford dash*] | PRINTED BY J. BALLANTYNE AND CO. | FOR ARCHIBALD CONSTABLE AND COMPANY, EDINBURGH; | AND | WILLIAM MILLER, AND JOHN MURRAY, LONDON. | 1808.

Published 22 February 1808 in Edinburgh (*EEC*); issued 8 March in London (*MC* 3 March 'On Tuesday next' [the 8th], earlier announced 20 February for 1 March). £1.11.6. 2000 copies. Binding: drab or grey-blue boards with printed label or (a later issue?) grey-green or yellow boards without label. Paper: Demy 4° (283 x 225mm uncut). Watermarks: 1804 / 1804; 1806; 1807; D & A C | 1805 [1806] | 1; D & A C | 1807 | 1 [2]. Collation: $\pi^4(\pi4+1)$ *A*^{4} B^4(±B1) C-G^4 *H*^{4} I-U^4 X^4(±X3) Y-3A^4 *3B*1 *a*^{4} b^4 c^4(±c1) d-p^4 q^4(-q4). Pagination: *i* half-title, *ii blank*, *iii* title-page, *iv blank*, *v* dedication to Henry, Lord Montagu, *vi blank*, *vii* Advertisement, *viii blank*, *ix* Contents, *x blank*, *1* fly-title, *2 blank*, *3* 4-377 text, *378 blank*, *i* fly-title, *ii blank*, *iii* iv-cxxvi Notes, cxxvi printer's imprint: [*short Oxford rule*] | Edinburgh: | Printed by James Ballantyne & Co.

Figures: A8-3, B10-11, C18-3, D26-3, E34-3, F42-5, G50-8, *H*64-3, I 66-5, K78-10, L82-1, M90-8, N98-10, O 106-8 112-6, P119-8 120-3, Q122-8, R134-1, S138-1 140-2, T146-6 152-10, U154-1 160-10, X162-3 166-12, Y174-3 176-10, Z178-6 181-8, 2A 186-11 192-6, 2B 194-8 200-1, 2C 202-6, 2D 210-1 216-8, 2E 218-6, 2F 227-3 232-10, 2G 234-3 236-1, 2H 242-6 248-11, 2I 250-10 256-3, 2K 258-10, 2L 266-8, 2M 274-3, 2N 282-1, 2O 290-3, 2P 304-2, 2Q 306-12, 2R 320-10, 2S 322-12 328-2, 2T 330-6 336-11, 2U 338-6 344-11, 2X 346-2 352-8, 2Y 354-1 360-11, 2Z 362-7 368-3, 3A 370-2 376-8, *a* vi-10 viii-3, b x-6 xvi-10, c xxiv-3, d xxvi-8 xxix-6, e xl-8, f xlii-7 xlviii-3, g l-10 lvi-1, h lviii-3 lxi-6, i lxvi-1, k lxxiv-1 lxxx-6, l lxxxii-6 lxxxviii-11, m xciii-7 xciv-10, n xcviii-8 civ-2, o cvi-11 cxii-12, p cxiv-10 cxx-1, q cxxiii-7/- cxxiv-2.

Notes: A year before issue, in February 1807, Scott sent the first printed 'sheet' or sheets of the Introduction to Lady Abercorn, confidant of the Princess of Wales, and on 5 February 1808 reported that he had dispatched special copies to London for both of these noble ladies (*Letters*, i.350, ii.11). Meanwhile, five months before publication, readers in Edinburgh were assured that this work would 'appear before Christmas' (*Scots Magazine*, September 1807, page 685) and, at about the same time, other readers in London were surprised to learn that Scott had 'received a thousand guineas for his new Poem, entitled "Marmien[!], or a Tale of Flodden Field."' (*Monthly Magazine*, 1 October 1807, page 275). Probably it was this public fiscal disclosure that prompted Byron in his *English Bards and Scotch Reviewers* (published in March 1809, lines 37-72) to castigate Scott as a paid hireling who had prostituted the Muse.

Apart from the general dedication to Montagu the six cantos have poetic introductions addressed successively to William Stewart Rose, The Rev. John Marriott, M.A., William Erskine, James Skene, George Ellis, and Richard Heber, all close friends who had been helpful in Scott's various literary endeavours. These pieces are addressed from Scott's home at Ashestiel, Ettricke Forest (cantos 1-4), Edinburgh (5), and Mertoun-House, the seat of Hugh Scott of Harden (6). Scott had earlier suggested that these six epistles be printed separately, presumably for the use of his friends, but this proposal was soon aborted (13 Janusry 1807 letter Longman to Scott [E MS 3876,ff.8-8v, also 22 January, ff.14-15] *teste* Jane Millgate).

As on previous occasions, in the 96 discursive notes at first provided for this poem Scott frequently refers to his own *Minstrelsy of the Scottish Border* (pages xxi, xxxviii, lix-lxi, xcv, cxxvi), and now also to later publications: James Hogg's *The Mountain Bard* (1807, a poem dedicated to Scott, pages xl, lvi), *The State Papers and Letters of Sir Ralph Sadler* ('shortly to be published', 1809, pages lxxxiii-lxxxiv, xci), and *The Life of Edward, Lord Herbert of Cherbury* (also edited by Scott in 1809, pages lxxxi-lxxxii).

For the early and middle portions of the book, A-N and 2K-2R, a single press man was employed for both formes of the sheet, regularly figuring (except where a blank page prevents) on 1v of the inner forme. Elsewhere, as the printing became more hurried, a second man was also engaged, figuring usually on 4v of the outer forme.

The three cancels B1, X3, and c1 respectively exhibit in the original and corrected state the following readings:

	CANCELLANDA		CANCELLENTIA
B1]	page 10, line 10:	[+]	For talents mourn, untimely lost,
	[no couplet]		When best employed, and wanted most;
	line 12		
	Mourn genius lost		Mourn genius high,
	line 21		
	And spare the dead's eternal rest		And sacred be the last long rest!
	figure 3		figure 11
X3]	page 166, line 12		
	rein		the rein
	figure *none*		figure 12
c1]	page xvii, line 5		
	First lerges		First derges
	line 7		
	my slid—shillings		my hand slid—shillings
	line 13		
	te t,		text,

From the different paper texture evident in some copies it appears that the cancels were prepared at the end of presswork, together with other single leaves (1 after π^4, *3B*1) and the final gathering q.

When the *Morning Chronicle* of 9 March 1808 complained that the remarkable couplet, page 10, pertaining to Charles James Fox, had not appeared in the earliest copies distributed to the friends of Pitt, the publishers on 7 April explained that the leaf had been cancelled not to suppress but to add this encomium (in the couplet cited above). All three cancellanda were bound in a copy once owned by Charles Scribners Sons, New York.

Copies: A BCL C DT E(2) EP(inscribed by James Ballantyne to Mrs Henry Siddons) L LU+ O(2); DLC CtY CtY* IdU InU(inscribed by C. C. Southey to his wife C. Anne Southey**) InU(with 18 ink and aquatint illustrations by Thomas Stothard) InU(3) MH MH('Presented to Anna Seward by the Publisher', in her hand and with her annotations) NN NNP(2) NNU-W OCl PPL(3) PU+ T/B TxU(3) ViU(2).
*With undated 4-page Miller list of 'Works Now in the Press' (including 'early in April' Scott's edition of Dryden with his extensive prospectus beginning 'It is a circumstance . . .).
**This is in the same elaborately decorated calf binding as three others similarly inscribed (47Aa, 64Aa, 81Aa) and thus was among the four titles of poetry originally presented by Scott to Robert Southey or to his wife Caroline.

+Extra-illustrated with an 1809 engraved title-page and six plates by Richard Westall (*see* 28Dt).

References: Abbotsford, page 271 (noted as presented to Scott's mother, but not inscribed); Grady, pages 114-185, 397-399; Ruff 59 (with illustrations of page 10, both states); Thomson, pages 43-44; Tinker 1863; Van Antwerp(1) 7. (Magnum Opus Edition 1833: *The Poetical Works*, vii.)

28Ab] First Edition, Second (Large-Paper) Impression: 1808

MARMION; | A Tale | OF FLODDEN FIELD. . . . 1808.

Preliminary listing 20 February in London (*MC*) as fifty copies 'on a superior paper' at £3.3.0. Paper: Royal 4° (305 x 243mm uncut). Watermarks: J WHATMAN | 1804 [1805]; [sheet 2C only:] BUTTANSHAW | 1806. Except for paper in all respects identical with the preceding impression; figures now omitted for h lxiii, q cxxiii.

Notes: page 335, last line, in the first impression reading 'stop'd', has been corrected in this impression to 'stopp'd'. As with his large-paper copy of *The Lay of the Last Minstrel* (14Ac) Alexander Gibson Hunter notes in his copy of this work (NNP) that 'only 4 Copies [were] published': an assertion apparently contrary to fact. Copies: E; NNP(A.G. Hunter) NNU-W(Auchincruive) TxU. Reference: Ruff 60.

28Ac] Second Edition, First Impression: 1808

MARMION; | A TALE | OF FLODDEN FIELD. | BY | WALTER SCOTT, ESQ. | THE SECOND EDITION. | [*short Oxford rule*] | [*four-line quotation from Leyden*] | [*short reversed Oxford rule*] | EDINBURGH: | [*short reversed Oxford rule*] | PRINTED BY J. BALLANTYNE AND CO. | FOR ARCHIBALD CONSTABLE AND COMPANY, EDINBURGH; | AND WILLIAM MILLER, ALBEMARLE-STREET, | AND JOHN MURRAY, LONDON. | [*dash*] | 1808.

Published April 1808 in Edinburgh (*SM*); issued 8 July in London (*MC*). 12s. 3000 copies. Paper: Demy 8° (208 x 124mm cut). Watermarks: 1807; D & A C | 1807 | none [1, 2]. Collation: π^4 $2\pi1$ A-Z^8 $2A^4$ 2B1 a-g^8 h^8(-h8=$2\pi1$). Pagination: *i* half-title, *ii blank*, *iii* title-page, *iv blank*, *v* dedication, *vi blank*, *vii* Advertisement, *viii blank*, *ix* Contents, *x blank*, *1* fly-title, *2 blank*, *3* 4-377 text, *378 blank*, *i* fly-title, *ii blank*, *iii* iv-cxxvi notes, cxxvi printer's imprint: [*short reversed Oxford rule*] | EDINBURGH: | Printed by James Ballantyne & Co. Typography: signature c (page *xxxiii*) is wrongly signed b. The original imposition of the Contents leaf $2\pi1$ is confirmed by several copies, where it still remains as the last leaf in the final gathering.

Figures: A15-8/- 16-2, B18-11/- 32-10, C34-11 48-2, D50-8 64-11, E66-8 80-10, F82-10 96-8, G98-8 112-11, H118-10 128-8, I 134-11 144-2, K146-8 160-7, L162-2 176-10, M178-3 192-11, N194-8 208-7, O 210-5, P227-3 232-8, Q242-2 256-10, R258-11 272-4, S274-3 288-8, T294-4/- 304-4, U306-5 320-11, X322-3 336-4, Y338-8 352-10, Z354-5 368-4, 2A 370-11, 2B—, a iii-11 xvi-1, b xviii-11 xxiv-1, c xxxiv-3 xlviii-8/-, d l-8 lxiv-5, e lxvi-5 lxxx-2, f lxxxii-3 xcvi-5, g xcviii-8 cxii-2, h cxix-13 cxxv-7. With few exceptions, the pressmen now figure regularly on 1v (inner forme) and 8v (outer forme).

Notes: Scott observed that this edition was amended with 'some care'. The principal revisions include the correction of a 'point of minute accuracy' mentioned page cxxvi in the first edition, and there referring to page 215 last line, 'By France's king to Scotland given.' Accordingly at the same point the line here reads 'And culverins which France had given.' Among the annotations Scott also revised Canto 5, Note III (page lxxx) upon the advice of his 'noble friend, Lord Napier' and in Canto 6, Note III (page cii) acknowledges 'much elucidation from the learned and extensive labours of Mr Douce.'

Copies: AN BCL E E* O; CtY DLC IdU InU T/B TxU.
*With undated 8-page Constable catalogue.

References: Ruff 61; Tinker 1864 (CtY proof sheets).

28Ad] Second Edition, Second (Large-Paper) Impression: 1808

MARMION; | A TALE | OF FLODDEN FIELD. . . . 1808.
Published concurrently with the previous impression. Paper: Royal 8° (232 x 142mm cut). Watermarks: J WHATMAN | 1805 [1806, 1807]; BUTTANSHAW | 1806.

Notes: Except for paper this unrecoded impression is in all respects identical with the preceding impression; figures present for A15, B18, and c xlviii, but absent for T294. The 8 July 1808 *MC* advertisement notes 'A few Copies' only of this issue, 'making a sixth Volume to the Author's Works' (*see* 260Ab). Another unlocated 'second edition' announced 16 March 1810 in *MC* as two folio volumes (Ruff 62) may well anticipate the reduced format 8° two-volume edition issued later in the year (*see* 28Aj).

Copies: CtY(fore-edge painting of Abbotsford) T/B.

28Ae] Third Edition: 1808

MARMION; | A TALE | OF FLODDEN FIELD. | BY | WALTER SCOTT, ESQ. | THE THIRD EDITION. | [*short Oxford rule*] | [*four-line quotation from Leyden*] | [*short reversed Oxford rule*] | EDINBURGH: | [*Oxford dash*]

| PRINTED BY J. BALLANTYNE AND CO. | FOR ARCHIBALD CONSTABLE AND COMPANY, EDINBURGH; | AND WILLIAM MILLER, ALBEMARLE-STREET, | AND JOHN MURRAY, LONDON. | [*dash*] | 1808.

Published 20 July 1808 in Edinburgh (*EWJ*); issued 3 August in London (*MC*). 12s. 3000 copies. Binding: grey-green boards with printed label. Paper: Demy 8° (225 x 143mm uncut). Watermarks: 1808; D & A C | 1808. Collation: π^4 $2\pi1$ A-Z^8 2A^4 2B1 a-h^8. Pagination: *i* half-title, *ii blank*, *iii* title-page, *iv blank*, *v* dedication, *vi blank*, *vii* Advertisement, *viii blank*, *ix* Contents, *x blank*, *1* fly-title, *2 blank*, *3* 4-377 text, *378 blank*, *i* fly-title, *ii blank*, *iii* iv-cxxviii notes, cxxviii printer's imprint: [*short Oxford rule*] | EDINBURGH: | Printed by James Ballantyne & Co. Typography: In some copies page 88 is misnumbered 84 and page xi is unnumbered.

Figures: A*3*-8 16-13/-, B18-8 32-13, C34-13 48-4, D50-2 64-5, E66-12 80-4, F82-4 96-13, G98-13 112-7, H118-5 128-13, I 137-12 142-13, K146-1 160-10, L162-13 176-7, M178-12 192-11, N194-8 208-1, O 210-10 220-3, P228-12 231-2, Q242-5 256-8, R258-10 272-3, S274-5 288-11, T290-8 304-10, U307-13 320-5, X322-10 336-13, Y338-4 352-12, Z354-1 368-12, 2A 376-7, 2B—, a x-7 xvi-3, b xviii-7 xxxii-12, c xxxiv-13 xlviii-1, d l-11 lxiv-4, e lxvi-5 lxxx-11, f lxxxii-8 xcvi-7, g cii-7 cxii-8, h cxiv-11 cxxviii-2.

Notes: Apart from altered spelling and punctuation in the text, one further annotation is provided (page xxviii [Canto I, Note XV], the only addition in all the early editions through the ninth) and a passing reference to Carey's *Memoirs* (page xiii, 'now reprinting' [and published 19 November 1808]). A few other notes have been expanded (for example, the additional sentence in Canto 5, Note V (page lxxxi) concerning the Battle of Blackheath, 1496).

Copies: BCL C E(2) L O; CtY DLC T/B TxU. Reference: Ruff 63.

28Af] Fourth Edition: 1808

MARMION; | A TALE | OF FLODDEN FIELD. | BY | WALTER SCOTT, ESQ. | THE FOURTH EDITION. | [*short Oxford rule*] | [*four-line quotation from Leyden*] | [*short reversed Oxford rule*] | EDINBURGH: | [*Oxford dash*] | PRINTED BY J. BALLANTYNE AND CO. | FOR ARCHIBALD CONSTABLE AND COMPANY, EDINBURGH; | AND WILLIAM MILLER, ALBEMARLE-STREET, | AND JOHN MURRAY, LONDON. | [*dash*] | 1808.

Published 7 January 1809 in Edinburgh (*EEC*), issued 16 January in London (*MC* as a 'New Edition'). 12s. 3000 copies. Paper: Demy 8° (214 x 132mm cut). Watermarks: none. Collation and pagination as in third edition. Typography: page 368 is misnumbered 386.

Figures: *A*3-8 16-1, B18-13 32-2, C39-7 48-11, D51-4 52-1, E66-10 80-8, F82-1 96-7, G98-8 112-10, H120-13 123-2, I135-4 144-11, K146-10 156-3, L163-2 173-1, M191-3/- 192-11, N194-10 208-11, O 210-4 220-1, P227-8 228-10, Q242-11 256-2, R258-1 272-8, S274-7 288-13, T302-7 304-3, U306-11 320-1, X322-8 328-13, Y343-2 349-11, Z354-7 368-13, 2A 376-2, *2B*—, a *iii*-11 xii-4, b xxv-8 xxvii-10, c xxxiv-2 xlviii-13, d l-8 lvi-4, e lxvi-4 lxix-8, f lxxxii-2 xcvi-4, g xcviii-10 cxii-7, h cxiv-13 cxxv-7.

Notes: In its first advertisement of 7 January, and continuing on to 10 August 1809, the *Edinburgh Evening Courant* listed as also available—presumably for those then desiring a complete Scott collection—the third edition of the *Minstrelsy of the Scottish Border*, the second of *Sir Tristrem*, the ninth of the *Lay of the Last Minstrel*, and the second of the *Ballads and Lyrical Pieces*.

Between the third and the fourth editions of *Marmion* there are a few alterations, for example, page 85 line 19, a change in tense (looked] look); page 254 line 5, an accentuation (pain] pain!); page xiii line 9, an up-date in a reference to the Carey *Memoirs* (of which an edition is now reprinting] published); page cxxv line 12, the correction of a surname (Tunstal] Tunstall). Changes of this order probably may be attributed to the printer.

Copies: AN BCL DT E O+; CtY+ DLC T/B. Reference: Ruff 64.
+Extra-illustrated with an 1809 engraved title-page and six plates by Richard Westall (*see* 28Dt).

28Ag] Fifth Edition, First Impression: 1810

MARMION; | A TALE | OF FLODDEN FIELD. | BY | WALTER SCOTT, Esq. | THE FIFTH EDITION. | [*short Oxford rule*] | [*four-line quotation from Leyden*] | [*short reversed Oxford rule*] | LONDON: | PRINTED BY J. M'CREERY, BLACK-HORSE-COURT, | FOR ARCHIBALD CONSTABLE AND COMPANY, EDINBURGH; | AND WILLIAM MILLER, ALBEMARLE-STREET, | AND JOHN MURRAY, LONDON. | [*dash*] | 1810.

Published 16 May 1810 in London (*MC*), issued 24 May in Edinburgh (*EEC*). 12s. 2000 copies. Paper: Demy 8° (213 x 133mm cut). Watermarks: 7 [8, 9] | W Balston | 1809; 7 [9] | WB | 1809; 1 [4] | W Balston | 1810; 8 | J Whatman | 1810. Collation and pagination as in third edition, except that printer's imprint on page cxxviii reads: [*Oxford dash*] | J. M'Creery, Printer, | Black-Horse-Court, London. Typography: Compared with the next impression, the letters for page-number lxxiv are properly all together. Figures: None used by this printer.

Notes: As on other occasions, this London printing was probably allowed because

of an overload in Ballantyne's Edinburgh printing office.
Copies: E L+ O; CtY+ IdU. Reference: Ruff 65.
+Extra-illustrated with an 1809 engraved title-page and six plates by Richard Westall (*see* 28Dt).

28Ah] Fifth Edition, Second (Large-Paper) Impression: 1810

Published concurrently with the previous impresion. Paper: Royal 8° (241 x 145 mm uncut). Watermarks: 1808; 1809. Except for paper in all respects identical with the preceding impression; the page-number in some copies is now separated as '1 xxiv'.

Copies: L; CtY(*see* 260Ad[2] note). Reference: Ruff 66.

28Ai] Sixth Edition: 1810

MARMION; | A TALE | OF FLODDEN FIELD. | BY | WALTER SCOTT, Esq. | IN TWO VOLUMES. | [*dash*] | SIXTH EDITION. | VOL. I [II]. | [*short Oxford rule*] | [*four-line quotation from Leyden*] | [*short reversed Oxford rule*] | EDINBURGH: | [*Oxford dash*] | PRINTED FOR ARCHIBALD CONSTABLE AND COMPANY, | EDINBURGH: | AND WILLIAM MILLER, ALBEMARLE-STREET, | AND JOHN MURRAY, LONDON. | [*dash*] | 1810.

Published 4 August 1810 in Edinburgh (*EEC*). £1.1.0. 3000 copies. Binding: in boards. Paper: Crown 8° (184 x 122mm cut). Watermarks: W Balston | 1808 [1810]. Illustrations: Twelve engraved plates painted by H. Singleton, engraved by Chas. Heath, dated April 1810, by A. Constable & Co. Edinburgh. Unlike the separate London issues prepared for this and other poems, this integral suite bears no page references or captions, but each plate does identify the canto and stanza then illustrated (cited below in parentheses) and ordinarily is inserted opposite that text page: thus volume 1 (II.6) page 85, (II.30) 110, (III.12) 146, (III.27) 164; volume 2 (IV.8) 26, (V.13) 93, (V.24) 110, (VI.12) 168, (VI.14) 170, (VI.33) 201. Additionally (I.28) and (IV.21) usually serve as frontispieces for the two volumes. (A suite of Royal 4° plate proofs, on India paper, also is bound in A. G. Hunter's large-paper copy of *The Lay of the Last Minstrel*, 8th edition [14An].) Printer's imprints read invariably: (1) [*rule*] | Printed by James Ballantyne and Co. Edinburgh.; (2) [*short Oxford rule*] | Edinburgh: | Printed by James Ballantyne & Co.

General notes: The *Scots Magazine* for July, probably not issued until the first week of August, also lists this attractive edition, the only poetic work to be issued in an illustrated two-volume Crown 8° format. These volumes represent slight changes in punctuation and spelling. The specially designed set was still available in 1815 when, in *The Field of Waterloo*, it was advertised along with the single volume ninth edition of *Marmion*.

Copies: AN BCL DN* DT* E O; CtY NN TxU. Referencce: Ruff 67.
*Trinity College Dublin prize book.

1] **MARMION;** | A TALE | OF FLODDEN FIELD. . . . SIXTH EDITION. VOL. I. . . . 1810.

Collation: $\pi^4(\pi4+1)$ A-P^8 Q^2. Pagination: *i* half-title, *i* printer's imprint(1), *ii blank*, *iii* title-page, *iv blank*, *v* dedication, *vi blank*, *vii* Advertisement, *viii blank*, *ix* Contents, *x blank*, *1* fly-title, *2 blank*, *3* 4-169 text of Cantos 1-3, *170 blank*, *171* fly-title, *172 blank*, *173* 174-244 Notes, 244 printer's imprint(2).

Figures: A*3*-7 16-6, B18-12 20-3, C43-13 48-6, D51-6 64-13, E68-6 70-12, F82-8 96-11, G112-8, H114-6 121-12, I 130-12 140-8, K157-8 158-11, L163-1 176-11, M108-12 192-7, N202-12 204-3, O 218-3 220-1, P238-6 240-15, Q243-1.

2] **MARMION**: | A TALE | OF FLODDEN FIELD. . . . SIXTH EDITION. VOL. II. . . . 1810.

Collation: $\pi^2(\pi2+1)$ A-R^8 S^8(-S8). Pagination: *i* half-title, *i* printer's imprint(1), *ii blank*, *iii* title-page, *iv blank*, *v* Contents, *vi blank*, *1* fly-title, *2 blank*, *3* 4-211 text of Cantos 4-6, *212 blank*, *213* fly-title, *214 blank*, *215* 216-285 Notes, 285 printer's imprint(2), *286 blank.*

Figures: A6-6 12-7, B30-5 32-12, C34-11 48-7, D54-11 64-1, E78-5 80-12, F90-15 96-13, G109-8 111-2, H114-6 128-13, I 138-1 144-7, K153-5 154-7, L171-15, M190-1 192-14, N206-7 208-15, O 222-1 224-13, P227-15 240-3/-, Q242-3 244-12, R270-12 272-1, S278-7 280-2/-

28Aj] Seventh Edition: 1811

MARMION: | A TALE | OF FLODDEN FIELD. | BY | WALTER SCOTT, Esq. | THE SEVENTH EDITION. | [*short Oxford rule*] | [*four-line quotation from Leyden*] | [*short reversed Oxford rule*] | EDINBURGH: | *Printed by George Ramsay and Company*, | FOR ARCHIBALD CONSTABLE AND COMPANY, EDINBURGH; | WILLIAM MILLER, ALBEMARLE-STREET, AND | JOHN MURRAY, FLEET-STREET, LONDON. | [*dash*] | 1811.

Issued 4 March 1811 in London (*MC*). 12s. 4000 copies. Paper: Demy 8° (215 x 130mm cut). Watermarks: *none* [5, 6, 7, 8] | W Balston | 1810. Collation: $\pi1$ $2\pi^4$

A-Z[8] 2A[4] *2B*1 a-h[8]. Pagination: As in third edition, except that printer's imprint on cxxviii reads: [*short rule*] | Printed by George Ramsay and Company, | Edinburgh, 1811. Typography: According to his usual practice Ramsay's double signature is styled as Aa.

Figures: A6-2 16-1, B18-5 32-3, C34-2 48-1, D54-5 64-3, E68-1 70-2, F82-5 96-3, G102-1 108-2, H122-5 128-3, I 134-2 140-1, K148-5 150-3, L172-1 174-2, M178-5 180-3, N202-2 208-1, O 210-2 212-1, P234-1 236-2, Q250-3 252-5, R260-1 270-2, S282-5 288-3, T296-8 302-1, U308-2, X326-3 332-5, Y340-3 342-5, Z364-2 366-5, 2A 370-3 372-1, *2B*—, a x-5 xii-3, b xviii-6 xxviii-8, c xliv-4 xlvi-5, d lii-8 lviii-1, e lxvi-2 lxviii-6, f lxxxiv-1 xciv-8, g xcviii-8 civ-1, h cxx-5 cxxvi-4.

Notes: Again, as with the fifth edition, this edition is printed by someone other than Scott's designated printer, once more, probably, because Ballantyne's commitments exceeded his capacity.

Copies: AN BCL DT E E+ O; CtY+ T/B TxU. Reference: Ruff 68.
+Extra-illustrated with an 1809 engraved title-page and six plates by Richard Westall (*see* 28Dt).

28Ak] Eighth Edition: 1811

MARMION: | A TALE | OF FLODDEN FIELD. | BY | WALTER SCOTT, Esq. | THE EIGHTH EDITION. | [*short Oxford rule*] | [*four-line quotation from Leyden*] | [*short reversed Oxford rule*] | EDINBURGH: | *Printed by George Ramsay and Company,* | FOR ARCHIBALD CONSTABLE AND COMPANY, EDINBURGH; | WILLIAM MILLER, ALBEMARLE-STREET, AND | JOHN MURRAY, FLEET-STREET, LONDON. | [*dash*] | 1811.

Published 5 July 1811 in Edinburgh (*EEC*, edition not stated). 12s. 5000 copies. Binding: blue-grey boards with printed label. Paper: Demy 8° (223 x 140mm uncut). Watermarks: 1809 | 1 [4, 6]; 1810 | 4 [5, 6]; [sheets Z, c, f only:] D & A C | 1808 | 1. Collation: π1 2π^4 A-Z[8] 2A[4] *2B*[2](-*2B*2=π1) a-h[8]. Pagination: As in third edition, except that printer's imprint on cxxviii reads: [*short rule*] | Printed by George Ramsay and Company, | Edinburgh, 1811. Typography: Ramsay's double signature is styled as Aa. In some copies page 253 is misnumbered 256.

Figures: A12-5 14-4/1, B30-5 32-2, C46-2 48-1, D50-4 52-5, E72-5 78-1, F82-5 96-1, G98-5 112-4, H122-2 128-1, I 142-6 144-8, K146-5 160-2, L162-1 172-5, M178-1 192-4, N199-2 208-7, O 216-4 222-2/-, P230-5 236-4, Q254-4, R266-4 272-9, S278-1 284-4, T290-8 300-11, U308-5, X328-1 330-4, Y339-5 340-8, Z362-2 368-1, 2A 370-2 372-1, *2B*—, a viii-2 xiv-1, b xxiv-6 xxvi-3, c xliv-3 xlvi-5, d lvi-1 lxii-5, e lxvi-3 lxviii-2, f lxxxiv-3 xciv-4, g cvi-4 cxii-2, h cxxii-2 cxxiv-4.

Notes: The printing of π1 is exemplified in the TxU copy, where the leaf still follows *2B*1. Gathering R exists in two consecutive settings readily identified by the press-figures: (1) as noted above with 266-4 272-9; (2) 258-10 272-3. In the original setting the black-letter heading '**Lady Heron's Song.**' page 258 is in the large gothic type used elsewhere, with this line measuring 41mm; in the later issue, probably occurring because of a short count in the earlier printing (and thus bearing the final watermark cited above), the heading is in a smaller fount measuring 33mm.

Copies: (issue 1) BCL E L LU O P; CtY DLC*a DLC+(printed title cancelled) NN TxU ViU*b. (2) T/B.
*With fore-edge painting of (a) Bothwell Castle, (b) Norham Castle.
+Extra-illustrated with an 1809 engraved title-page and six plates by Richard Westall (*see* 28Dt).

Reference: Ruff 69.

28Al] Ninth Edition: 1815

MARMION: | A TALE | OF FLODDEN FIELD. | BY | WALTER SCOTT, Esq. | THE NINTH EDITION. | [*short Oxford rule*] | [*four-line quotation from Leyden*] | [*short reversed Oxford rule*] | EDINBURGH: | *Printed by James Ballantyne and Co.* | FOR ARCHIBALD CONSTABLE AND COMPANY, EDINBURGH; | AND LONGMAN, HURST, REES, ORME, AND BROWN, | AND JOHN MURRAY, LONDON. | [*dash*] | 1815.

Published April 1815 in Edinburgh. 3000 copies. Binding: blue boards with printed label. Paper: Demy 8° (224 x 144mm uncut). Watermarks: R T & Co | 1812 [1814]; 1814. Collation: π^4 2π1 A-Z^8 $2A^4$(2A4+1) 2B-$2I^8$. Pagination: *i* half-title, *ii blank*, *iii* title-page, *iv blank*, *v* Advertisement, *vi blank*, *vii* dedication, *viii blank*, *ix* Contents, *x blank*, *1* fly-title, *2 blank*, *3* 4-377 text, *378 blank*, *379* fly-title, *380 blank*, *381* 382-506 Notes, 506 printer's imprint: [*short Oxford rule*] | EDINBURGH: | Printed by James Ballantyne and Co. Typography: Signature 2G (page 459) is missigned 2F.

Figures: A5-9 6-11, B26-10 29-12, C46-9 48-3, D62-4 64-2, E67-12 80-8, F82-4 88-6, G105-1 107-11, H119-2 120-11, I 140-12, K155-9 157-6, L162-11 164-2, M180-5 190-7, N203-4 208-6, O 217-2/- 222-11, P230-6 236-5, Q245-10 255-3, R265-8 270-1, S275-2 276-3, T290-1 304-8, U316-8 318-1, X322-12 332-3, Y347-10 352-5, Z355-2 360-6, 2A 376-7, 2B 390-1 393-8, 2C 400-7 406-5, 2D 421-11 423-6, 2E 429-12 434-9, 2F 448-2 455-7, 2G 465-6 466-11, 2H 483-10, 2I 493-7 498-10.

Notes: This text, at Scott's request, was corrected against the second edition.

Copies: BCL E GU LU O; CtY DLC+ NjP NN+ T/B+. Reference: Ruff 70.
+Extra-illustrated with an 1809 engraved title-page and six plates by Richard Westall (*see* 28Dt).

28Am] Tenth Edition (*Poetical Works*, Reissue): 1821

MARMION; | A TALE | OF FLODDEN FIELD. | BY | SIR WALTER SCOTT, BART. | TENTH EDITION. | [*short Oxford rule*] | [*four-line quotation from Leyden*] | [*short reversed Oxford rule*] | EDINBURGH: | PRINTED FOR ARCHIBALD CONSTABLE AND CO. EDINBURGH; | AND LONGMAN, HURST, REES, ORME, AND BROWN, | AND JOHN MURRAY, LONDON. | [*dash*] | 1821.

Published at 14s. 500 copies. Binding: drab boards with printed label. Paper: Demy 8° (227 x 143mm uncut). Watermarks: none. Printer's imprints: (1) [*rule*] | *Printed by James Ballantyne and Co. Edinburgh.*; (2) [*short rule*] | EDINBURGH: | Printed by James Ballantyne & Co.

Notes: A variant issue of the 1821 *Poetical Works*, volume VI (263A), with the engraved title replaced by the printed title described above, on the verso of which is entered printer's imprint (1).

Copies: AN O; TxU. Reference: Ruff 71.

28An] 'New' (Eleventh) Edition, First Issue: 1825

[*engraved title*] MARMION: | A TALE | OF FLODDEN FIELD. | BY | SIR WALTER SCOTT, BART. | A NEW EDITION. | [*double dash*] | [*vignette*] | EDINBURGH; | PRINTED FOR ARCHIBALD CONSTABLE AND CO. EDINBURGH; | LONGMAN, HURST, REES, ORME, BROWN AND GREEN; | J. MURRAY; AND HURST, ROBINSON, AND Co. LONDON. | [*French dash*] | 1825.

Published 15 June 1825 in Edinburgh (*EWJ*). 9s. 2000 copies. Binding: drab boards with printed label. Paper: Foolscap 8° (174 x 117mm uncut). Watermarks: none. Collation: A-2I^8 *2K*1. Pagination: [*engraved title*], *1* fly-title, *2 blank*, *3* dedication, *4 blank*, *5* Advertisement, *6 blank*, *7* fly-title, *8 blank*, *9* 10-383 text, *384 blank*, *385* fly-title, *386 blank*, 387-513 notes, *514* printer's imprint: [*short rule*] | EDINBURGH: | Printed by James Ballantyne and Co. Illustrations] Title vignette of Linlithgow Castle, engraved by W. Archibald.

Figures: A14-1, B32-6, C48-2, D57-2, E77-3, F96-6, G112-6, H126-6, I—, K160-5, L163-4, M192-6, N208-1, O 222-4, P226-1, Q256-4, R260-5, S285-4, T301-1, U313-1, X335-1, Y349-4, Z368-4, 2A 370-5, 2B 400-4, 2C 413-5, 2D 432-1, 2E 447-6, 2F 464-1, 2G 480-6, 2H 496-6, 2I 510-6, *2K*—.

Notes: With reference to this and *The Lady of the Lake* the periodicals note: 'Travellers and others visiting the Scenes of the above celebrated Poems, will find these editions to form two neat pocket volumes.' There are two states, (1) with title imprint concluding as noted above; (2) with imprint altered to read '. . . ORME, AND BROWN; | AND HURST, ROBINSON, AND CO. LONDON. | [*French dash*] | 1825.

Copies: (State 1) CtY. (2) HS (Inscribed to Gladstone by J. Bruce, afterwards Lord Elgin); RPB (Greenock prize book presented 1839).

Reference: Ruff 72(first state).

28Ao 'New' (Eleventh) Edition, Second Issue: 1830

[*engraved title*] MARMION: | A TALE | OF FLODDEN FIELD. | BY | SIR WALTER SCOTT, BART. | A NEW EDITION. | [*double dash*] | *vignette*] | EDINBURGH; | PRINTED FOR ARCHIBALD CONSTABLE AND CO. EDINBURGH; | LONGMAN, HURST, REES, ORME, AND BROWN; | AND HURST, ROBINSON, AND CO. LONDON. | [*dash*] | 1830.

Published by 20 April 1830 in Edinburgh. 9s. 500 copies. Collation and pagination as in previous issue, except for altered title imprint and Scott's new Introduction, dated from Abbotsford April 1830. Collation for the new material: a^4 b^2. Pagination: *i* ii-xi text, *xii blank*. Figures: As for previous issue except no figure page 112.

Notes: An advertisement dated 20 April 1830 in 'The Doom of Devorgoil' lists this issue together with an 1830 'Twelfth Edition' (28Aq).

Copy: E. Reference: Ruff 73.

28Ap] Twelfth Edition (*Poetical Works*, Reissue): 1825

MARMION; | A TALE | **OF FLODDEN FIELD.** | BY | SIR WALTER SCOTT, BART. | TWELFTH EDITION. | [*short Oxford rule*] | [*four-line quotation from Leyden*] | [*short reversed Oxford rule*] | EDINBURGH: | PRINTED FOR ARCHIBALD CONSTABLE AND CO. EDINBURGH; | AND LONGMAN, HURST, REES, ORME, BROWN, AND GREEN, | AND JOHN MURRAY, LONDON. | [*dash*] | 1825.

Published at 14s. 500 copies. Paper: Demy 8° (223 x 138mm uncut). Watermarks: none. Printer's imprints (1): EDINBURGH: | PRINTED BY JAMES BALLANTYNE AND CO.; (2) [*short rule*] | EDINBURGH: | Printed by James Ballantyne and Co.

Notes: A variant issue of the 1825 *Poetical Works*, volume VI (267Aa), with the engraved title replaced by the printed title described above, on the verso of which is entered printer's imprint (1).

Copies: O; TxU. Reference: Ruff 74.

28Aq] Twelfth Edition, Reissue: 1830

MARMION; | A TALE | **OF FLODDEN FIELD.** . . . 1825.

Published by 20 April 1830 in Edinburgh. 300 copies. Collation and pagination as in previous issue, except for altered title imprint and Scott's new Introduction, dated from Abbotsford April 1830. Collation for the new material: a^4 *b*1. Pagination: *i* ii-x text. Typography: This issue has no imprint on verso of title.

Notes: An advertisement 20 April 1830 in 'The Doom of Devorgoil' lists this issue together with an 1830 'New Edition' (28Ao).

Copies: L; CtY. Reference: Ruff 75.

REPRINTS

FRANCE

PARIS: Didot and Galignani
[~] Marmion. 1821, 1826. (Collection of Modern English Authors: *see* 290R[2A], [2C].)

PARIS: Galignani
[~] Marmion. 1829. (*see* 293R.8.) Copy: not seen.

GERMANY

ZWICKAU: Schumann
[~] Marmion. 1825. (Pocket Library of English Classics: *see* 302R.118-119.)

UNITED STATES

BALTIMORE: Cushing
[~] Marmion. 1812. (The Poetical Works of Walter Scott: *see* 303R.3.)

28Ra] BALTIMORE: Cushing and Sargeant 1811
Marmion: A Tale of Flodden Field. By Walter Scott, Esq. . . . Baltimore: Published by Joseph Cushing; and E. Sargeant, New-York. 1811. Pages: *i-viii 1* 2-319. Notes: Frontispiece drawing by R. Westall; copy re-engraved by J. Boyd, with imprint J. Cushing, Baltimore, 1811. Title verso has imprint: Printed by D. & G. Bruce, Slote-lane, New-York. Copies: MWA NN ViU.

BOSTON: Bedlington
[~] Marmion. 1827. (The Poetical Works of Sir Walter Scott: *see* 304R.2.)

28Rb] BOSTON: Farrand, Mallory 1808
Marmion; A Tale of Flodden Field. By Walter Scott, Esq. . . . Boston, Published by Farrand, Mallory and Co. Suffolk-Buildings. 1808. Two volumes. Pages 1: *1-7* 8 *9-13* 14-219; 2: *1-9* 10-259. Notes: A variant issue of the Hopkins and Earle, Philadelphia edition (*see* 28Rh), with cancel titles of the same setting and date and (for the MWA and RPB copies) identically bound in calf with gilt-lettered labels. Copies: MWA NNU-W RPB.

28Rc] BOSTON: West and Blake 1810
Marmion; A Tale of Flodden Field. By Walter Scott, Esq. . . . Boston: Published by West and Blake, 56, Cornhill. Greenough and Stebbins, Printers. 1810. Pages: *1-7* 8-324. Copies: E; CtY MWA RPB. Reference: Kohler(1) 3 (with illustration).

FREDERICKSBURG: Withers
[~] Marmion. 1824. (The Poetical Works of Sir Walter Scott: *see* 310R.)

28Rd] NEW YORK: Eastburn 1818
[Marmion; A Tale of Flodden Field. By Walter Scott, Esq. . . . New-York: Published by J. Eastburn and Co. Literary-Rooms, Broadway. 1818. Pages: *i-viii, 9-11* 12-359.] Notes: (Also issued in The Poetical Works of Walter Scott, Esq.: volume 3. 1819. *see* 312R.3) Copy: not seen.

28Re] NEW YORK: Elliot and Crissy 1811
Marmion, A Tale of Flodden Field. By Walter Scott, Esq. . . . New-York, Printed and Published by Elliot and Crissy, at the Sign of the Ledger, No. 114, Water-Street; Sold also by T. Powers, No. 116, Broadway, and A. Devillers, Charleston. 1811. Pages: *i-iv, 1* 2-287. Copies: IdU MWA NN.

28Rf] NEW YORK: Sargeant and Cushing 1811
Marmion: A Tale of Flodden Field. By Walter Scott, Esq. . . . New-York: Published by Ezra Sargeant, No. 86 Broadway; and J. Cushing, Baltimore. 1811. Pages: *i-viii 1* 2-319. Notes: A variant issue of the Joseph Cushing, Baltimore edition (*see* 28Ra), with identical frontispiece and printer's imprint. Copies: MWA RPB.

28Rg] PHILADELPHIA: Earle [and others] 1810
[1] Marmion; A Tale of Flodden Field. By Walter Scott, Esq. . . . Philadelphia, Published by Edward Earle; Also by Farrand, Mallory and Co. Boston. Fry and Kammerer, Printers. 1810. Pages: *i-vii* viii *ix-x, 11-13* 14-367. Notes: E copy is inscribed on front endpaper: 'Given me, By Walter Scott Esqr. at Abbotsford. August. 1813. M. W. H.' (Matthew Weld Hartstonge). This inscription is present also in two other volumes issued 1810 by the same publisher: *The Lay of the Last Minstrel* (*see* 14Rk) and *The Lady of the Lake* (*see* 47Ro). Besides (1) the issue described above, with printed title, there is a (2) variant issue with engraved vignette title only, undated imprint: Philadelphia Published by E. Earle & Co. Printed by C. P. Harrison. Copies: (issue 1) E; MWA. (2) CtY.

[2] Marmion: A Tale of Flodden Field. By Walter Scott, Esq. . . . Philadelphia Published by E. Earle & Co. Printed by C. P. Harrison. Notes: A variant issue, with printed title-leaf of the previous issue now replaced by an undated engraved title-page with vignette. Copy: ViU.

28Rh] PHILADELPHIA: Hopkins and Earle 1808-1809

[1] Marmion; A Tale of Flodden Field. By Walter Scott, Esq. . . . Philadelphia: Published by Hopkins and Earle. Fry and Kammerer, Printers. 1808. Two volumes. Pages 1: *1-7* 8 *9-13* 14-219; 2: *1-9* 10-259. Notes: For a variant issue, with cancel titles, *see* Farrand, Boston entry, 28Rb. Copies: E O; CtY IdU InU MWA NjP NNU-W PPL(2).

[2] Marmion; A Tale of Flodden Field. By Walter Scott, Esq. . . . Philadelphia: Published by Hopkins and Earle. Fry and Kammerer, Printers. 1809. Pages: *i-vii* viii *ix-x*, *11-13* 14-367. Copies: E; CtY MWA NN(Berg—Washington Irving's inscribed copy). Reference: Kohler(1) 192 (with illustration).

DERIVATIVES

GREAT BRITAIN

28Da] CORK: Connor 1811

Marmion, A Melo=Drama, Founded upon Walter Scott's Celebrated Poem of Marmion, or, The Battle of Floddenfield[!], . . . Cork: Printed by John Connor, Grand-Parade. 1811. Pages: *i-viii* vii-x, *1* 2-45 *46-48*. Notes: Melodrama by Elizabeth Wright Macauley as performed at The Theatres-Royal, Dublin and Cork. Copy: InU. Reissued as a 'Second Edition' with preliminary pages correctly numbered (DT; NN). Reference: Bolton 9.

28Db] EDINBURGH: Hamilton 1823

[1] Where shall the Lover Rest . . . . Written by Walter Scott Esqr. . . . Price 1/ Edinburgh Printed and Sold at J. Hamiltons[!] Music Library No. 24 North Bridge. [watermarked 1822]. Pages: 1-2. Notes: Engraved sheet music. Words from canto 3, stanzas 10-11 (first words: 'Where shall the lover rest whom the fates sever'). Music composed by William Clarke for voice and pianoforte. Copy: E.

[2] Young Lochinvar ['Lochinvar'] Written by Walter Scott Esqr. . . . Edinburgh, Printed and Sold by J. Hamilton, Music Seller, No. 24 North Bridge. [watermarked 1822]. Pages: 1-2. Notes: Engraved sheet music. Words from canto 5, stanza 12 (first words: 'O, young Lochinvar is come out of the west'). Music composed by William Clarke for voice and pianoforte. Price: 1s. Copy: E.

28Dc] LIVERPOOL: Hime 1818

"Young Lochinvar," ['Lochinvar'] from the Romance of Marmion by Walter Scott Esqr. . . . Liverpool. Printed by Hime & Son, Castle Street & Church Street. [watermarked 1817]. Pages: *1-2* 3. Notes: Engraved sheet music. Words from canto 5, stanza 12 (first words: 'O, young Lochinvar is come out of the West,'). Music composed by Miss Hime arranged for voice and pianoforte. Copy: L. Reference: G/T 10480.

28Dd] LONDON: Birchall 1809

The Spectre Knight, . . . London, Printed & Sold by Rt. Birchall, No. 133, New Bond Street. [watermarked 1808]. Pages: 1-5. Notes: Engraved sheet music. Music composed by William

Hawes arranged for voice and pianoforte. Partly founded on Scott's *Marmion.* Price 1/6. Copy: L.

LONDON: Cadell and Davies
[~] Wallace: or, The Fight of Falkirk. 1809. [Parody by Margaret Holford. *see* 482S].

28De] LONDON: Cahusac 1810
Lochinvar, . . . London Printed for the Author [composer] by W. M. Cahusac 196 Strand. [ca.1810]. Pages: 1-4. Notes: Engraved sheet music with caption title. Words from canto 5, stanza 12 (first words: 'O young Lochinvar is come out of the West, Thro' all the wide Border his Steed was the best,'). Music composed by J. Valentine arranged for voice and pianoforte. Price: 1s./6. Copy: InU.

28Df] LONDON: Cawthorn 1817
Marmion; or, The Fight of Flodden. A Grand Melo-Dramatic Romance, in Three Acts. . . . London: Printed for J. Cawthorn, No. 5, Catherine Street, Strand, Bookseller to Her Royal Highness the Princess of Wales. 1817. Pages: *1-9* 10-47. Notes: Melodrama by D. A. O'Meara (a playwright unrecognized in Bolton). Copy: NN.

28Dg] LONDON: Chappell 1831
New Edition. The Last Words of Marmion, Written by Sir Walter Scott Bart. . . London, Printed & Sold by S. Chappell, Music Seller to His Majesty, 50 New Bond Street and Clementi & Compy. 26, Cheapside. [unwatermarked. ca.1831]. Pages: *i-ii*, 1-9. Notes: Engraved sheet music with plate number: '3818'. Words from canto 6, stanza 32 (first words: 'The war, that for a space did fail'). Music composed by John Clarke arranged for voice and pianoforte. Price: 3s. Copy: E. Reissued with catalogue of vocal music, page *10* (L; NN-L).

28Dh] LONDON: Clementi 1815
Where Shall the Lover rest The Song of Fitseustace[!] in Marmion, . . . London, Printed for the Author [composer], by Clementi & Co. 26 Cheapside. [1815]. Pages: *5* 6-7. Notes: Engraved sheet music with caption title. Words from canto 3, stanza 10 (first words as title). Music composed by David Deane Roche arranged for voice and pianoforte. Copy: L. Reference: G/T 10504.

28Di] LONDON: Dale 1809
Lochinvar Lady Heron's Song from Marmion of Flodden Field . . . Written by Walter Scott, Esqr. . . . Pr.1s/6. Sold by the Author Joseph Dale, at his Music & Instrument Warehouses No. 19 Cornhill; The Corner of Holles Street, & No. 151 New Bond Street. [watermarked 1808]. Pages: 1-4. Notes: Engraved sheet music. Words from canto 5, stanza 12 (first words: 'O Young Lochinvar is come out of the West'). Music composed by Joseph Dale and arranged for voice, pianoforte and harp. Copies: E L; MH.

28Dj] LONDON: D'Almaine 1820
Lochinvar, (Lady Heron's Song.) Marmion, The Poetry Written by Sir Walter Scott, . . .

London, D'Almaine & Co, Soho Square. [unwatermarked. ca.1820]. Pages: 1-3. Notes: Engraved sheet music with plate mark: 'Lochinvar'. Words from canto 5, stanza 12 (first words: 'O Young Lochinvar is come out of the west'). Music composed by Thomas Attwood for voice and pianoforte. Price: 1/6. Copy: O.

28Dk] LONDON: Glendinning 1810
Songs, and Other Vocal Compositions, .. in the Grand Caledonian Aquatic Romance, (Partly founded on the Popular Poem of Marmion,) Called The Spectre Knight. . . . London: Printed by W. Glendinning, 25, Hatton Garden. 1810. Pages: *1-3* 4-32. Notes: The piece by Charles Dibdin, Jun. with the music composed by Mr. Reeve (not included). Copy: L. Reference: Bolton 5.

28Dl] LONDON: Goulding 1808
Where Shall the Lover Rest, A Song . . . The Words from Marmion a Tale of Flodden Field by Walter Scott Esqr. . . . London, Printed by Goulding & Compy. No. 124 New Bond Street & 7, Westmorland Street, Dublin. [watermarked 1807. ca.1808]. Pages: *i-ii*, 1-5. Notes: Engraved sheet music. Additional caption title given on first page of music: 'Fitz Eustace's Song.' Words from canto 3, stanza 10 (first words as title). Music composed by M. Virtue arranged for voice and pianoforte. Copy: PPL. Variant issue has caption title reading: 'Where Shall the Lover Rest' (NN-L).

28Dm] LONDON: Goulding, Phipps, D'Almaine 1808
[1] Where shall the Lover rest A Glee . . . London, Printed by Goulding Phipps, D'Almaine & Co. 124, New Bond Street and No. 7 Westmorland Street, Dublin. [watermarked 1808]. Pages: *1* 2-9. Notes: Engraved sheet music. Words from canto 3, stanzas 10-11 (first words as title). Music composed by Joseph Mazzinghi arranged for voice and pianoforte. Price: 3/ . Copy: L. Reference: G/T 10495.

[2] Young Lochinvar ['Lochinvar']. London, Printed by Goulding, Phipps, D'Almaine & Co. Music Sellers to their R. Hes the Prince & Princess of Wales 124 New Bond Street & 7, Westmorland Street Dublin. [watermarked 1808]. Pages: *1* 2-11. Notes: Engraved sheet music with composer's initial in ink below imprint. Words from canto 5, stanza 12 (first words: 'O, young Lochinvar is come out of the west'). Music composed by Joseph Mazzinghi arranged for chorus and pianoforte. Price: 3/. Copies: E L. Reference: G/T 10496.

28Dn] LONDON: Hawes 1831
Young Lochinvar ['Lochinvar'], Ballad . . . The Poetry by Sir Walter Scott, . . . London, Published by W. Hawes, 355, Strand. [1831]. Pages: *i-ii*, 1-6. Notes: Engraved sheet music with plate number '596'. Words from canto 5, stanza 12 (first words: 'O, young Lochinvar is come out of the west;'). Music composed by C. Challis arranged for voice and pianoforte. Price: 2s. Copy: L. Reference: G/T 10461.

LONDON: Longman, Hurst, Rees, Orme and Brown
[~] Wallace: or The Fight of Falkirk. 1810. [Parody by Margaret Holford. *see* 491S[6]].

28Do] LONDON: Monzani 1808-1810
[1] Christmas Eve, or Full Well our Christian Sires of Old From Marmion of Flodden Field, by Walter Scott Esqr. . . . London Published by Monzani & Co. Music Sellers to H.R.H. the

Prince of Wales, Patentees of the New Improved Ger[man] Flute, No. 3 Old Bond Street. [watermarked 1807]. Pages: *i-ii*, 1-7 *8*. Notes: Engraved sheet music with plate mark 'No. 151 Vocal English'. Words from the Introduction to canto 6 (first words: 'Full well our Christian sires of old lov'd when the year'). Music composed by Thomas Attwood arranged for voice and pianoforte. Price 2s./6. Copies: E L. Reference: G/T 10447.

[2] Lochinvar, Lady Heron's Song, From Marmion of Flodden Field. By Walter Scott Esqr. . . . London Published by Monzani & Co Music Sellers to H.R.H. the Prince of Wales, Patentees & Manufacrs. of the New Improved Ger[man]. Flute. No. 3 Old Bond Street near Piccadilly. [unwatermarked. ca.1808]. Pages: 1-3. Notes: Engraved sheet music with plate mark 'No 149 Vocal English', as well as the composer's initials in ink next to the imprint. Words from canto 5, stanza 12 (first words: 'O, young Lochinvar is come out of the west'). Music composed by Thomas Attwood arranged for voice and pianoforte or harp. There are two issues: (1) unwatermarked and imprint as above; (2) watermarked 1807 and with last words of imprint reading: 'No. 3 Old Bond Street & 100 Cheapside.' Price: 1s./6. Copies: (1) MH-M. (2) E.

[3] Where shall the Lover Rest, . . . From Marmion of Flodden Fields, By Walter Scott, Esqr. . . . London Published by Monzani & Co. Music Sellers to H.R.H. the Prince of Wales Patentees & Manufacs. of the New Improved Ger[man] Flute No. 3 Old Bond Street & 100 Cheapside. [watermarked 1807]. Pages: *1* 2-7. Notes: Engraved sheet music with plate mark 'No. 150 Vocal English' and with the composer's initials in ink below the imprint. Words from canto 3, stanzas 10-11 (first words as title). Music composed by Thomas Attwood arranged for voice and pianoforte or harp. Copy: E.

[4] Where shall the Lover rest. The Song of Fitz-Eustace, From Marmion, . . . Published by the Author [composer] & Sold by Monzani & Co., No. 3 Old Bond Street, London. [unwatermarked. 1810]. Pages: *1* 2-7. Notes: Engraved sheet music. Words from canto 3, stanza 10 (first words as title). Music composed by Barham Livius arranged for voice and pianoforte. Inscribed to Scott (*see* 536T). Copy: L. Reference: G/T 10492.

28Dp] LONDON: Murray 1812

Marmion: or, Floddon[!] Field. A Drama, Founded on the Poem of Walter Scott. London: Published by J. Murray, 32 Fleet-Street, and W. Blackwood, Edinburgh. 1812. Pages: *i-iii* iv-vii *viii*, *1* 2-128. Notes: Drama by James Nelson Barker. Copies: L; NN. Reference: Bolton 6.

28Dq] LONDON: Power 1827

[Day set on Norham's Castle steep. London: Power (1827). Notes: Music composed by John Fane.] Copy: not seen. Reference: G/T 10472.

28Dr] LONDON: Power and Power 1808

Where shall the Lover Rest The Song of Fitz Eustace from Marmion, by Walter Scott Esq . . . London, Published by J. Power, 34, Strand & W. Power, 4, Westmoreland Street, Dublin. [watermarked 1806. ca.1808]. Pages: *i-ii*, 1-5. Notes: Engraved sheet music with title-page as well as caption title. Words from canto 3, stanzas 10-11 (first words: 'Where shall the lover rest, whom the fates sever'). Music composed by John Stevenson arranged for three voices. Price: 2/6. Copies: E(2).

28Ds] LONDON: Preston 1809-1825

[1] The Favorite Song of Fitz-Eustace The Poetry from Marmion, . . . London Printed & Sold by Preston at his Wholesale Warehouses, 97, Strand. [watermarked 1811]. Pages: *i-ii*, 1-16. Notes: Engraved sheet music. Words from canto 3, stanza 10 (first words: 'Where shall the lover rest,'). Music composed by John Clarke arranged for voice and pianoforte. Price: 4s./. Copy: NNP. Reference: Van Antwerp(2) 42f.

[2] The Last Words of Marmion, Expressly written for, . . . London Printed & Sold by Preston, at his Wholesale Warehouses, 97 Strand. [watermarked 1809]. Pages: *i-ii*, 1-10. Notes: Engraved sheet music. Words from canto 6, stanza 32 (first words: 'The war that for a space did fail'). Music composed by John Clarke arranged for voice and pianoforte. Copy: PPL. Reissued with 1811 watermark, 'London,' (E), without watermark, 'London.', '97,' (L).

[3] The Last Words of Marmion, The Poetry by Walter Scott Esqr. . . . London Printed & Sold by Preston, at his Wholesale Warehouses, 97 Strand. [watermarked 1809]. Pages: *i-ii*, 1-10. Notes: Engraved sheet music. Words from canto 6, stanza 32 (first words: 'The war that for a space did fail'). Music composed by John Clarke arranged for voice and pianoforte. Copy: PPL. Reissued with 1811 watermark, 'London,' (E); with 1813 watermark, 'London,', '97.' (L); without watermark, 'London.', '97,' (L, ca.1825).

[4] Lochinvar, Lady Heron's Song, in Marmion, A Tale of Flodden Field, . . . London, Printed & Sold by Preston, at his Wholesale Warehouses, 97, Strand. [unwatermarked. ca. 1810]. Pages: *1* 2-14. Notes: Engraved sheet music. Words from canto 5, stanza 12 (first words: 'O, Young Lochinvar is come out of the west,'). Music by John Clarke arranged for voice and pianoforte and dedicated to Walter Scott (*see also* 28Dw[3]). Price 5s./. Copy: O. Reissued with 1811 watermark (MH-M).

[5] The Song of Fitz Eustace. The Poetry from Marmion, A Tale of Flodden Field, . . . London, Printed and Sold by Preston, at his Wholesale Warehouses, 97, Strand. [1810]. Pages: 1-8. Notes: Engraved sheet music. Words from canto 3, stanza 10-11 (first words: 'Where shall the lover rest,'). Music composed by John Clarke arranged for voice and pianoforte. Price: 2/6. Copies: E L. Reissued with different punctuation in heading and with '&' in imprint. [watermarked 1813 (L; T/B).

[6] Why then a final note prolong, Recitative & Air, From the finale of Marmion, . . . London, Printed & Sold by Preston, at his Wholesale Warehouses, 97, Strand, . . . [watermarked 1810]. Pages: 1-5. Notes: Engraved sheet music. Words from 'L'Envoy To the Reader' (first words as title). Music composed by John Clarke arranged for voice and pianoforte. Price: 2s./. Copy: BCL.

LONDON: Richardson

[~] The Ass on Parnassus. 1815. [Cantos I-IV, including 'Marmion Feats'. A parody. *see* 495S(2)].

28Dt] LONDON: Sharpe 1809

Marmion; A Tale of Flodden Field. By Walter Scott, Esq. . . . London: Published by John Sharpe, Piccadilly. 1809. Engraved vignette title and six plates, issued with the suite prepared for *The Lay of the Last Minstrel* (*see* 14Dm). Title reads 'Illustrated with Engravings, from

the designs of Richd. Westall, Esq. R.A'; all other plates titled 'Marmion', drawn by Richd. Westall R.A., published 1 June 1809. Advertised in *The Times* 17 November as in [1a] quarto at £1.4.0 and in [2] octavo at 12s. An 8 May 1810 *The Lady of the Lake* advertisement (in NNP copy), as well as a Sharpe and Hailes list (8Af), further notes the availability of [1b] quarto proofs at £1.11.6 and indicates a combined poem-plate issue, [3] for quarto £3.3.0, [4] for octavo £1.4.0. Still later [2], separate Colombier quarto proofs were selling for £1.15.0. Separate issue copies: [1a] O. [1b] not seen. [2] O; CtY MH. Combined poem-plate issues: [3] 28Aa. [4] 28Af, Ag, Aj-Al. Reference: Ruff 76.
Title with vignette engraved by John Pye; plates with page reference below illustration:
(1) [page 50] with a three-line quotation (first line: 'For no saluting did he wait,' from canto 1, stanza 28), engraved by F. Engleheart;
(2) [page 100] with a two-line quotation (first line: 'Her look composed, and steady eye,' from canto 2, stanza 21), engraved by Chas. Heath;
(3) [page 138] with a three-line quotation (first line: 'Still fixed on Marmion was his look' from canto 3, stanza 5), engraved by S. Noble;
(4) [page 208] with a two-line quotation (first line: 'High o'er my head, with threatening hand,' from canto 4, stanza 21), engraved by F. Engleheart;
(5) [page 262] with a two-line quotation (first line: 'The monarch o'er the syren hung,' from canto 5, stanza 12), engraved by Jas. Mitan;
(6) [page 366] with a two-line quotation (first line: '"Charge, Chester, Charge! On Stanley, on!' from canto 6, stanza 32), engraved by Jas. Heath.

LONDON: Tegg
[~] Marmion Travestied. 1809. [A parody. *see* 497S(4)].

28Du] LONDON: Walker 1822
Lochinvar, Lady Heron's Song in Marmion, The Words by Walter Scott Esqr. . . . London. Printed for G. Walker at his Music Warehouse 106 Gt. Portland Street. [watermarked 1822]. Pages: 1-5. Notes: Engraved sheet music. Words from canto 5, stanza 12 (first words: 'O young Lochinvar is come out of the west,'). Music composed by John Ross arranged for voice and pianoforte. Price: 1s.6d. Copies: BCL L. Reference: G/T 10506.

28Dv] LONDON: White 1819
Flodden Field: A Dramatick Romance. In Three Acts. . . . London: Published by R. White, 11, Brydges-Street, (opposite the Theatre); By Simpkin and Marshall, Stationers' Court, Ludgate Street; Sherwood, Neely, and Jones, Paternoster Row; C. Chappel, 66, Pall Mall; And T. Earle, Library, Albemarle Street, Piccadilly. 1819. Pages: *i-vi*, *1* 2-42. Notes: Drama by Stephen and Henry Kemble, as first performed at the Theatre Royal, Drury-Lane, 31 December 1818, with music by Thomas Simpson Cooke (music not included). The Preface, signed by the Kembles, reads: 'The compilers of Flodden Field, acknowledge themselves entirely indebted to the Poem of Marmion; from which work it is taken almost verbatim; if the success which attended its representation on the Stage, should induce the elegant author of that Poem to turn his mind towards Dramatic Writings, they shall indeed congratulate themselves in having so materially served the Publick and the Profession.' Price: Two Shillings and Sixpence. Copies: E; InU NjP. Reference: Bolton 18.

28Dw] LONDON: Wilkinson 1808-1810

[1] The Favorite Song of Fitz-Eustace the Poetry from Marmion, . . . Printed by Wilkinson & Co. (Late Broderip & Wilkinson) No. 13 Hay Market, Where may be seen their New Patent Cabinet Piano Fortes. [watermarked 1808]. Pages: *i-ii*, 1-16. Notes: London not cited on title-page. Engraved sheet music. Words from canto 3, stanza 10-11 (first words: 'Where shall the lover rest,'). Music composed by John Clarke arranged for voice and pianoforte. Clarke sent Scott a copy 22 May 1808, which Scott eventually acknowledged 10 January 1809. Price: 4s./. Copy: L.

[2] The Last Words of Marmion, . . . London Printed by Wilkinson & Co. (Late Broderip & Wilkinson) No. 13 Hay Market. Where may be seen their New Patent Cabinet Piano Fortes. [watermarked 1807]. Pages: *i-ii*, 1-10. Notes: Engraved sheet music. Words from canto 6, stanza 32 (first words: 'The war, that for a space did fail'). Music composed by John Clarke arranged for voice and pianoforte, which Clarke undoubtedly included in a package of sheet music sent to Scott on 22 May 1808 and Scott finally acknowledged 10 January 1809. Price: 3s./. Copies: L O; InU MH TxU. Reference: G/T 10463.

[3] Lochinvar, Lady Heron's Song, in Marmion, A Tale of Flodden Field, . . . London, Printed for the Author [composer] by Wilkinson & Compy, (late Broderip & Wilkinson) 13 Haymarket. Where may be had just Published by Dr. Clarke, The Song of Fitz Eustace . . . [watermarked 1807]. Pages: *i-ii*, *1* 2-14. Notes: Engraved sheet music with composer's name, in some copies, signed in ink below imprint. Words from canto 5, stanza 12 (first words: 'O, young Lochinvar is come out of the west'). 'Composed and respectfully dedicated to Walter Scott Esqr.' (*see* 548T). Music composed by John Clarke arranged for voice and pianoforte, two trebles and a bass. Clarke sent Scott a copy 22 May 1808, which Scott acknowledged 10 January 1809. Price: 5s./. Copy: E. References: G/T 10464; *Letters*, ii.147.

[4] The Song of Fitz Eustace, The Poetry from Marmion, a Tale of Flodden Field, . . . London Printed by Wilkinson & Compy, (Late Broderip & Wilkinson) No. 13 Hay Market. [1810]. Just published by the Above Author [composer] Lochinvar . . . Pages: 1-8. Notes: Engraved sheet music. Some copies have composer's signature in ink, just below the name in caption title. Words from canto 3, stanzas 10-11 (first words: 'Where shall the lover rest,'). Music composed by John Clarke arranged for voice, chorus and pianoforte. Price: 2s./6. Copies: E L O; CtY.

[5] Why then a final note prolong, . . . Printed by Wilkinson & Co (Late Broderip & Wilkinson) No. 13. Hay Market. [1810]. Pages: 1-5. Notes: London not cited in imprint. Engraved sheet music. Words from 'L'Envoy' in canto 6 (first words as title). Music composed by John Clarke arranged for voice and pianoforte. Price: 2s. Copy: L. Reference: G/T 10465.

28Dx] LONDON: Williams 1819

Young Lochinvar, Song The Words by Walter Scott Esqr. . . . [watermarked 1818]. Pages: 1-3. Notes: Engraved sheet music. Words from canto 5, stanza 12 (first words: 'O young Lochinvar is come out of the west'). Music composed by Thomas Williams arranged by M. Moss for voice and pianoforte. Price: 1/6. Copy: L. Reference: G/T 10516.

28Dy] LONDON: Wybrow 1820-1825

[1] The Last Words of Marmion. Written by Walter Scott Esqr. . . . London Pubd by W.

Wybrow at his Music Library 24 Rathbone Place Oxford St. [1825]. Pages: *1* 2-3. Notes: Engraved sheet music. Words from canto 6, stanza 32 (first words: 'The War that for a space did fail'). Music composed by Louis Charles Jansen arranged for voice and pianoforte. Price: 1/6. Copy: L. Reference: G/T 10484.

[2] Where shall the Lover Rest? The Song of Fitz Eustace, From Marmion, By Walter Scott Esqr. . . . London Pubd by W. Wybrow at his Public Library 24 Rathbone Place Oxford St. [1820]. Pages: 1-3. Notes: Engraved sheet music. Words from canto 3, stanzas 10-11 (first words as title). Music composed by Louis Charles Jansen arranged for voice and pianoforte. Price: 1/6. Copy: L. Reference: G/T 10483.

28Dz] LONDON: [*publisher unknown*] 1811
[1] The Last Words of Marmion, By Walter Scott, Esqr. [inscribed October 1811. ca.1811]. Pages: *1* 2-3. Notes: Engraved sheet music on green paper, with caption title and no imprint. Words from canto 6, stanza 32 (first words: 'The war that for a space did fail'). Composer not identified, but arranged for voice and pianoforte. The score is dedicated to Dr. John Clarke. This is apparently an instructor's copy; a printing similarly inscribed is listed for *The Lady of the Lake* (*see* 47Dat). Price: 1s. Copy: L. Reference: G/T 10445.

[2] [Marmion, . . . Drama, by James N. Barker. 1826.] Copy reported at DLC but not on shelf and not recorded in Bolton's 'List of Published Versions.' Other editions of Barker's drama are entered as 28Dp and 28Dah.

[~] Sir Albon: A Fragment. 1808. [Parody. *see* 498S].

28Daa] STIRLING: The Booksellers 1829
Young Lochinvar, . . . Stirling: Printed for the Booksellers. [ca. 1829]. Pages: *1-2* 3-8. Notes: In this chapbook only the first of the five titles included was derived from Scott. Copy: L.

UNITED STATES

28Dab] BOSTON: Graupner 1816-1821
[1] The Song of Fitz Eustace From Marmion, A Tale of Flodden Field, . . . Boston, Published and sold by, G. Graupner, at his Music Store, No. 6 Franklin Street. [ca.1816]. Pages: 1-5. Notes: Engraved sheet music with caption title and with plate mark: '515'. Words from canto 3, stanzas 10-11 (first words: 'Where shall the Lover rest, Whom the fates sever, From his true maiden's breast,'). Music composed by John Clarke arranged for voice and pianoforte. Copies: DLC InU MH MWA RPB(4). Reference: Wolfe 1860.

[2] The Song of Fitz Eustace, The Poetry from Marmion A Tale of Flodden Field, . . . Boston, Published by G. Graupner, No. 6 Franklin St. [1821]. Pages: *1* 2-8. Notes: Engraved sheet music. Words from canto 3, stanzas 10-11 (first words: 'Where shall the lover rest, Whom the fates sever From his true maiden's breast,'). Music composed by John Clarke arranged for voice and pianoforte. This is probably the title advertised in the *Euterpeiad* for 8 December 1821. Price: 75 cents. Copy: MWA. Reference: Wolfe 1862. Reissued with additional imprint foot of page *1*: Sold for G. G. by John Ashton. No. 197 Washington St. (DLC MH). Reference: Wolfe 1862A.

28Dac] BOSTON: Hewitt 1812

[Young Lochinvar. . . . Boston, James Hewitt, Musical Library, No 58½ Newberry Street. 1812]. Notes: An edition of this song was advertised by James Hewitt, Musical Library, at the above address in *CC* of 26 September 1812 as 'new music just published.' Copy: not seen. Reference: Wolfe 5746.

28Dad] NEW YORK: Dubois 1818

[1] The Last Words of Marmion . . . . New York Sold by Wm Dubois No 126 Broad-way. [ca.1818]. Pages: *1* 2-8. Notes: Engraved sheet music. Page *1* is the title-page. A reissue from the same plates, with imprint altered, as [Paff] Wolfe 1837 (*see* 28Daj[1]). Words from canto 6, stanza 32 (first words: 'The war, that for a space did fail, Now trebly thund'ring swell'd the gale.'). Music composed by John Clarke arranged for voice and pianoforte. Copies: InU MH MWA(2) RPB(3). Reference: Wolfe 1837A.

[2] The Song of Fitz Eustace The Poetry from Marmion A tale of Flodden Fields . . . New York Published by Wm Dubois. [ca.1818]. Pages: *1* 2-6. Notes: Engraved sheet music with caption title. Words from canto 3, stanzas 10-11 (first words: 'Where shall the lover rest, whom the fates sever'). Music composed by John Clarke arranged for voice and pianoforte. Price: 50 Cents. Copies: CtY InU MH MWA(2) RPB. Reference: Wolfe 1859A. An earlier issue from the same plates was published in New York by John Paff [ca.1812] (*see* 28Daj[2]).

[3] Young Lochinvar from Marmion A Tale of Flodden field . . . . New York Published by W. Dubois. [ca.1818]. Pages: *1* 2-7. Notes: Engraved sheet music. Reissue from same plates [Paff], with imprint altered, as Wolfe 5743 (*see* 28Daj[3]). Words from canto 5, stanza 12 (first words: 'Oh Young Lochinvar is come out of the west Thro' all the wide border his steed was the best'). Music composed by Joseph Mazzinghi arranged for voice and pianoforte. Price: 50 cents. Some copies give price as '50 cts.' Copies: InU MH MWA RPB. Reference: Wolfe 5743A.

28Dae] NEW YORK: Longworth 1812-1816

[1] Marmion; or, Floddon[!] Field. A Drama, Founded on the Poem of Walter Scott. . . New-York: Published by the Longworths, At the Dramatic Repository, Shakspeare-Gallery. May—1812. Pages: *1-3* 4-136. Notes: Drama by James Nelson Barker. The title-page reads: 'from the first London edition, of 1812'. Copies: E(2); CtY DLC InU MWA PU TxU. Reference: Kohler(1) 63 (with illustration).

[2] Marmion; or, The Battle of Flodden Field. A Drama, in Five Acts. . . . New-York: Published by D. Longworth, At the Dramatic Repository, Shakspeare-Gallery. April 1816. Pages: *i-iii* iv-vii *viii, 9* 10-79 *80*. Notes: An 'American' drama by James Nelson Barker, first acted in New York, April 1812. Full credit is given to Scott by name throughout the lengthy Preface, with comments such as 'the play professedly follows the action of the poem'; but regrets are also expressed that since as yet the American 'capitalists in intellectual wealth' have not written for the theatre, 'we must be content to continue the importation of our ideas and sentiments, like our woollen stuffs, from England.' Copies: CtY(2) MWA RPB. Reference: Bolton 10.

[3] [Marmion, or a Tale of Flodden Field. New York: (1816). Notes: Words by James Nelson Barker 'credited for advertising purposes to Thomas Morton'; music may have been composed by John Bray.] Copy: not seen. Reference: G/T 10465.

28Daf] NEW YORK: Mesier 1816
The Last Words of Marmion, Written by Walter Scott, Esq. N- York Published by E. S. Mesier 28 Wall-st. [unwatermarked. ca.1816]. Pages: *1* 2-6. Notes: Engraved sheet music. Words from canto 6, stanza 32 (first words: 'The war, that for a space did fail, Now trebly thund'ring swell'd the gale.'). Copy: MH.

28Dag] NEW YORK: Paff 1812
[1] The Last Words of Marmion . . . . New York Sold at J. Paff's Music Store [ca.1812]. Pages: *1* 2-8. Notes: Engraved sheet music. Page *1* is the title-page. Words from canto 6, stanza 32 (first words: 'The war, that for a space did fail, Now trebly thund'ring swell'd the gale.'). Music composed by John Clarke arranged for voice and pianoforte. Price: [*none*]. Copies: InU RPB(2). Reference: Wolfe 1837.

[2] The Song of Fitz Eustace The Poetry from Marmion, A Tale of Flodden Fields . . . New York Published by John Paff [ca.1812]. Pages: *1* 2-6. Notes: Engraved sheet music. Words from canto 3, stanzas 10-11 (first words: 'Where shall the lover rest, whom the fates sever From his true Maidens Breast,'). Music composed by John Clarke arranged for chorus and pianoforte. Price: 50 cents. Copies: DLC MWA. Reference: Wolfe 1859.

[3] Young Lochinvar ['Lochinvar'] from Marmion A Tale of Flodden field . . . New York Published by J. Paff. [ca.1812]. Pages: *1* 2-7. Notes: Engraved sheet music with caption title. Words from canto 5, stanza 12 (first words: 'Oh Young Lochinvar is come out of the west Thro' all the wide border his steed was the best'). Music composed by Joseph Mazzinghi arranged for voice and pianoforte. Some copies have price added above imprint: 50 Cts. Copies: MWA RPB. Reference: Wolfe 5743(with price).

28Dah] NEW YORK: Riley 1820
[Where shall the Lover rest. . . . New York, Engrav'd, Printed and Sold by E. Riley, 29 Chatham Street. (1820). 9pp. Notes: Music composed by Joseph Mazzinghi arranged by J. Hewitt.] Copy: not seen. Reference: Wolfe 5735.

28Dai] NEW YORK: Willson 1812
[1] The Song of Fitz Eustace The Poetry from Marmion A Tale of Flodden Fields. . . . New York Publish'd at J. Willson's Music Store, No. 58 Maiden Lane. [ca.1812]. Pages: *1* 2-6. Notes: Engraved sheet music. Words from canto 3, stanza 10 (first words: 'Where shall the lover rest'). Music composed by John Clarke arranged for chorus and pianoforte. Price: 50 cts. Copies: DLC NN. Reference: Wolfe 1858. Reissued with imprint address: No. 62 Broadway (DLC InU MH MWA RPB(2)). Reference: Wolfe 1858A.

[2] [Young Lochinvar . . . . New York, Publish'd by J. Willson, No. 62 Broadway. (1812). 17pp. Notes: Music composed by Joseph Mazzinghi.] Copy: not seen. Reference: Wolfe 5745.

28Daj] PHILADELPHIA: Blake 1811-1818
[1] The Last Words of Marmion. Written by Walter Scott. Esqr. . . . Philadelphia, Published by G. E. Blake at his Piano Forte and Music store, no: 13 so: 5th street. [ca.1818]. Pages: 1-6. Notes: Engraved sheet music with caption title and with plate mark: 'Last words of Marmion'. Words from canto 6, stanza 32 (first words: 'The war, that for a space did fail,

Now trebly thund'ring swell'd the gale,'). Music composed by John Clarke arranged for voice and pianoforte. Price: 50 cents. Copies: InU MWA RPB(2). Reference: Wolfe 1838.

[2] Lochinvar. Written by Walter Scott Esqr. . . . Philadelphia. Published by G. E. Blake. [ca.1814]. Pages: 1-5. Notes: Engraved sheet music with caption title. Words from canto 5, stanza 12 (first words: 'Oh Young Lochinvar is come out of the west, Thro' all the wide border, his steed was the best,'). Music composed by Joseph Mazzinghi arranged for voice and pianoforte. Price: 50 cents. Copies: CtY DLC(2) InU(2) MH MWA PHi RPB. Reference: Wolfe 5744.

[3] The Song of Fitz-Eustace, from Marmion, A Tale of Flodden Field, . . . Philadelphia. Published by G. E. Blake. [ca.1811]. Pages: 1-5. Notes: Engraved sheet music with caption title. Words from canto 3, stanzas 10-11 (first words: 'Where shall the Lover rest, Whom the fates sever, From his true maiden's breast,'). Music composed by John Clarke arranged for voice and pianoforte. Copies: DLC InU(2) MH MWA RPB(2). Reference: Wolfe 1856.

PHILADELPHIA: Carey
[~] Marmion Feats. 1815. ['Cantos III-VII.' A Parody. *see* 503S(2)].

28Dak] PHILADELPHIA: Carr and Schetky 1811
Lochinvar . . . . Philadelphia Published by Carr & Schetky. [ca.1811]. Pages: *1* 2-8. Notes: Engraved sheet music with caption title and plate mark 'L' on pages 2-3. Words from canto 5, stanza 12 (first words: 'O Young Lochinvar is come out of the west thro all the wide border his steed was the best'). Music composed by Joseph Mazzinghi arranged for voice and pianoforte. Price: (1) one dollar, (2) 50 cents. Copies: (1) MWA PHi RPB; (2) PU. References: Wolfe 5742 (with price: 50 cents).

PHILADELPHIA: Poole
[~] Marmion; or, The Battle of Flodden Field. 1826. (Lopez and Wemyss' Edition. The Acting American Theatre: number 5. *see* 346D.)

28Dal] PHILADELPLHIA: Willig 1812-1818
[1] The Song of Fitz-Eustace from Marmion, a Tale of Flodden Field, . . . Philadelphia Publish'd and Sold at G. Willig's Musical Magazine. [ca.1812]. Pages: 1-4. Notes: Engraved sheet music with caption title and with plate marks: 'Fitz Eustace' (page 3), 'Fitz Eustace 4' (pages 2, 4). Words from canto 3, stanzas 10-11 (first words: 'Where shall the lover rest, Whom the fates sever from his true maiden's breast'). Music composed by John Clarke arranged for voice and pianoforte. Copies: CtY MWA RPB(3). Reference: Wolfe 1857.

[2] The Song of Fits[!] Eustace, . . . Philadelphia Published and Sold at G. Willig's Musical Magazine [ca.1818]. Pages: *1* 2-4. Notes: Engraved sheet music with caption title and with plate marks: 'Fitz Eustace 4.'(page 2), 'Fitz Eustace.4.'(pages 3-4). Words from canto 3, stanzas 10-11 (first words: 'Where shall the lover rest, Whom the fates sever From his true maidens breast'). Music composed by John Clarke arranged for voice and pianoforte. Copies: InU MWA PHi PU RPB. Reference: Wolfe 1861.

EXTRACTS IN ANTHOLOGIES

28E] From *Marmion* there are 89 extracts in 54 anthologies: 356E[2].2,6-9 357.1 358.12 360.13,16,20 361[1].5 363.8 366[2].15 369[3].7-8 369[4].7-8 372[1].2 373[5] 374 377.2 378.1-2 379.1-2 386.7 388.9 389.5,16 392.5-8 401.8-17 408.4-8 410[1].3 413.11-12 414[2].4-5 415.4-5,11 420.1 423.10 427 430[1] 430[2].1 430[3].1 432 435.2 436.2 440 444.4 448[2] 448[3].1-2 449.3,5 450(and 471).8 452.2 453.2 454.2 457[1].2 462 463.3 467[1].2 467[2].9 468 469.1,12 473 474.1 475.2,4.

THE LIFE OF JOHN DRYDEN

In the mean time, suffice it to say, that I have done with poetry for some time—it is a scourging crop, and ought not to be hastily repeated. Editing, therefore, may be considered as a green crop of turnips or peas, extremely useful for those whose circumstances do not admit of giving their farm a summer fallow. [Then mentioned as underway are editions of Swift, Thomson, Sadler, and Somers.] (Scott to Ellis, 8 October 1808, *Letters*, ii.93.)

29A] First Edition, Separate Impression: 1808

THE | **LIFE** | OF | JOHN DRYDEN. | [*short reversed Oxford rule*] | BY | WALTER SCOTT, ESQ. | [*short reversed Oxford rule*] | LONDON: | PRINTED FOR WILLIAM MILLER, | ALBEMARLE-STREET, | BY JAMES BALLANTYNE AND COMPANY, | EDINBURGH. | [*dash*] | 1808.

Published ca. 8 April 1808 in London. Five days before, on the 3rd, Scott informed Lady Abercorn that he was arranging to send her a copy, and on the 7th Lady Louisa Stuart was advised that she could expect her copy 'in a day or two'. Binding: drab boards with printed label. Paper: Royal 4° (301 x 245mm uncut). Watermarks: J. WHATMAN | 1805 (cream paper, sheets A-3D); unwatermarked (thinner, white paper 3E-3X, preliminaries and cancels). Collation: π^2(π2+1) A-C^4 D^4(±D3) E-I^4 K^4(±K2) L-3U^4 3X^4. Pagination: *1* half-title, *2* certificate, *3* title-page, *4 blank*, *i-ii* Contents, *1* fly-title for 'The Life of John Dryden', *2 blank*, *3* 4-534 text, 534 printer's imprint: [*short Oxford rule*] | EDINBURGH: | Printed by James Ballantyne & Co. Certificate: 'Fifty Copies only of The Life of Dryden are Printed in Quarto. J. Ballantyne & Co.' Frontispiece of Dryden, by James Fittler, dated 1 March 1808 by W. Miller, Albemarle Street.

Figures: These are of a pattern indicating that, as 8° first volume *Works* text-type (30Aa.l) was reimposed for prior issue of this 4° *Life* impression, large blocs were successively assigned to four different pressmen (10, 3, 8, 4), all of whom then regularly entered their identifying figures on 1v of the inner formes. When each man completed his portion of this first extensive job (through sheet 2P), three of them in turn were assigned to type subsequently made ready and another man (5) also enlisted for this later work. Total allocations and work periods:

Pressman	Assignments		Total
	Main	Supplemental	sheets
10	A-Q	2Q-2R 3Q-3X	24
3	R-2A	2Z-3H	17
8	2B-2N	2S-2Y	17
4	2O-2P		2
5		3 I-3P	7
Totals	38	29	67

On 12 November 1807 Scott reported that this separate *Life* was then 'more than half printed', i.e., that it had probably gone through the first, main press assignments recorded above (38 sheets) and was now starting through the supplemental groups (29 sheets).

In paginal order the figures occur: A*3*-10, B10-10, C18-10, D26-10, E34-10, F42-10, G50-10, H58-10, I 66-10, K74-10, L82-10, M90-10, N98-10, O 106-10, P114-10, Q122-10, R130-3, S138-3, T146-3, U154-3, X162-3, Y170-3, Z178-3, 2A 186-3, 2B 194-8, 2C 202-8, 2D 210-8, 2E 218-8, 2F 226-8, 2G 234-8, 2H 242-8, 2I 250-8, 2K 258-8, 2L 266-8, 2M 274-8, 2N 282-8, 2O 296-4, 2P 298-4, 2Q 306-10, 2R 314-10, 2S 322-8, 2T 330-8, 2U 338-8, 2X 346-8, 2Y 354-8, 2Z 362-3, 3A 370-3, 3B 378-3, 3C 386-3, 3D 394-3, 3E 402-3, 3F 410-3, 3G 418-3, 3H 426-3, 3I 434-5, 3K 442-5, 3L 450-5, 3M 458-5, 3N 466-5, 3O 474-5, 3P 482-5, 3Q 490-10, 3R 498-10, 3S 506-10, 3T 514-10, 3U 522-10, 3X 530-10.

Notes: In this 4° *Life* impression the two cancels D3 (pages 29-30) and K2 (pages 75-76) correspond to those also inserted in the previous 8° printing as B7 and E6: see volume 1 (30Aa). Apparently these new white-paper leaves (and so also those in 8°) were belatedly produced some time after work had begun on 3E (page 401), the first sheet of this paper variety. The original readings for these pages are unknown.

Scott's achievement in this account, published only seven years after Malone's life, has recently been acknowledged in a comment by Osborn, reiterated by Sutherland (page 130): 'Almost every page is vitalized by his historical imagination, the power that later found its proper medium in the novel. The biography of Dryden is the first fruit of one of the most productive geniuses in the history of all literature.'

Presentation copy: O('F[rancis] Douce. The valuable gift of the author' [in Douce's handwriting]). Other copies: BCL(2) E L; CtY. Reference: (Magnum Opus Edition 1834: *The Miscellaneous Prose Works*, i.)

REPRINTS

FRANCE

PARIS: Didot and Galignani
[~] Memoirs of John Dryden. MDCCCXXVI. (Collection of Modern English Authors: *see* 292R.4-5.)

GERMANY

ZWICKAU: Schumann
[~] Memoirs of John Dryden. 1829. (Pocket Library of English Classics: *see* 302R.195-197.)

UNITED STATES

BOSTON: Wells and Lilly
[~] Life of John Dryden. 1829. (The Miscellaneous Prose Works. *see* 308R.1)

THE WORKS OF JOHN DRYDEN

30Aa] First Scott Edition, First Impression: 1808

THE | | **WORKS** | OF | JOHN DRYDEN, | NOW FIRST COLLECTED | *IN EIGHTEEN VOLUMES.* | [*short Oxford rule*] | ILLUSTRATED | WITH NOTES, | HISTORICAL, CRITICAL, AND EXPLANATORY, | AND | A LIFE OF THE AUTHOR, | BY | WALTER SCOTT, Esq. | [*short reversed Oxford rule*] | VOL. I [II-XVIII]. | LONDON: | PRINTED FOR WILLIAM MILLER, ALBEMARLE STREET, | BY JAMES BALLANTYNE AND CO. EDINBURGH. | [*dash*] | 1808.

Published 30 April 1808 in Edinburgh (*EEC*); issued 10 June in London (*MC*). The *EEC* does not designate any specific Edinburgh bookseller. £9.0.0. Paper: Demy 8° (212 x 132mm cut). Watermarks: In this first impression three groups of watermarks generally indicate a sequence of printing: (a) 1803; 1804 | none [2, 9]; C & S 1804 / 1804: volumes 2-7; (b) 1805; D & A C | 1805 | 1; H 1806: volumes 8-17 excepting only the sheets cited next; (c) 1807, volumes 11 (sheets M-2G, 12 (a-f), 13 (G), 16 (N-2L), 17 (D-2I), volumes 18 and 1, preliminary leaves for all volumes. A more precise order is observed in the watermarks for the succeeding large-paper impression. Typography: Toward the end of work on the complete edition, as exemplified in the (c) watermark record above, it seems that the title-pages were imposed in duplicate to avoid constant resetting. These double settings, together with their conjugate half-titles, were then impressed concurrently with interruptions as required to change the volume reference. The points for the two title settings are as follows:

B of BY under D of PRINTED. Vols. 4, 6, 7, 9, 12, 13, 15, 17, 1.

B of BY to the right of D. Vols. 2, 3, 5, 8, 10, 11, 14, 16, 18.

General Notes: A forthcoming edition of Dryden was first announced in the *Scots Magazine* for December 1805, where it is stressed that this would be the 'first *complete* collection' (page 935). Earlier, on 20 October, Scott wrote the publisher about some changes in the edition and attached an advertisement for immediate display in the papers (Houghton fMS Eng 890[82], courtesy Jane Millgate). However, the notice seems to have been delayed until time of issue in 1808, when the Edinburgh journals, in their 21-line 'prospectus', present in essence Scott's recommended text, this beginning 'It is a circumstance', deploring the lack of a complete edition, and concluding with the assurance that the present editor has a 'deep sense of the importance of the task.'

Copies: BCL E HS(Gladstone's set, annotated) L O; CtY IdU NN(2) PPL T/B.
Reference: (Magnum Opus Edition: Not reprinted.)

1] THE | **WORKS** | OF | JOHN DRYDEN, . . . VOL. I. . . . 1808.

Collation: π^2 a^8 A^8 B^8(±B7) C-D^8 E^8(±E6) F-$2K^8$ $2L^4$(-2L4). Pagination: *1* halftitle, *2 blank*, *3* title-page, *4 blank*, *i* ii-xi Advertisement, *xii blank*, *xiii* xiv-xv Contents, *xvi blank*, *1* fly-title, *2 blank*, *3* 4-534 The Life of John Dryden, 534 printer's imprint: [*short Oxford rule*] | EDINBURGH: | Printed by James Ballantyne & Co. Illustrations: Frontispiece of Dryden by James Fittler, dated 1 March 1808 by W. Miller, Albemarle Street.

Figures: a ii-11 *xiii*-7, A11-1 16-4, B18-2, C34-11, D50-2, E66-8 76-7 80-3, F82-2/- 96-11, G98-1 109-5, H114-3 124-7, I 130-8 141-11, K146-1 160-7, L162-5 176-7, M178-2 192-5, N194-11/- 204-4, O 210-11, P240-2/-, Q247-5 256-4/-, R258-4 272-1, S277-4/, T290-11 304-5, U306-11, X326-1, Y338-7, Z355-7 364-7, 2A 370-3 384-10, 2B 386-10 400-8, 2C 402-7, 2D 418-4 432-12, 2E 434-12 448-7, 2F 455-6 464-7/-, 2G 466-4 472-6, 2H 482-1 496-2/-, 2I 498-7 500-12, 2K 514-7/- 528-6, 2L 530-7/-. In some copies the figure 1 on page 272 is mashed.

Notes: For separate issue as *The Life of John Dryden see* 29A.. The original state of cancellanda B7 and E6 (pages 29-30, 75-76) is unknown. (In some copies cancel E6 bears the redundant figure 76-7.) Sheet N in this impression (pages 193-208) remains in its first setting, with figures 194-11 204-4, page 193 line 8 first word 'commended'.

2] THE | **WORKS** | OF | JOHN DRYDEN, . . . VOL. II. . . . 1808.

Collation: π^2(π2+1) *A*^{8}(±*A*2,±*A*8) B-F^8 G^8(±G8) H-Q^8 *R*^{8} S-$2F^8$ $2G^4$(-2G3,4+$2G^2$).

Pagination: *i* half-title, *ii blank, iii* title-page, *iv blank, v* Contents, *vi blank, 1* flytitle, *2 blank, 3* Advertisement, *4 blank, 5* 6-12 dedication (to Congreve's 1735 edition), *13* fly-title, *14 blank, 15*-16 note, *17* 18-472 text, 472 printer's imprint: [*short Oxford rule*] | Edinburgh, | Printed by James Ballantyne & Co. Typography: In this impression, page 170 has all page-numbers intact. In some copies signature 2C (page 401) is missigned 2G.

Figures: *A*9-1 11-3, B*19*-5/-, C48-3, D54-1, E—, F92-1, G103-1, H118-4 128-1, I—, K—, L174-4 176-1, M186-5 188-2, N195-1/-, O 211-5/- 224-1, P240-3, Q247-2, R—, S288-4, T304-3, U308-4, X326-5 332-3, Y342-4, Z—, 2A—, 2B *391*-3, 2C 408-1, 2D—, 2E 448-1, 2F—, 2G—.

Notes: Two of the cancels, *A*8 (pages 15-16) and G8 (pages 111-112), both unknown in their prior state, but disclosed here by a direction line 'VOL.II.', apparently represent revisions in the preliminary notes for *The Wild Gallant* and *The Rival Ladies* respectively. The conjugate two-leaf cancel in the final gathering 2G is inferred from the 'Directions' in volume 18.

In view of its superior copy-text, identified as the Congreve 12° 1735 edition further annotated by Malone, the Advertisement *A*2, page *v* line 11, originally discounted any editorial responsibility:

CANCELLANDUM	CANCELLANS
Little was left for the present editors to do in correcting the text.	*Considerable pains have been bestowed by the present editor in correcting the text.*

Doubtless Scott, on reading the notice originally prepared, belatedly decided to assign all credit to himself. (The original Advertisement often is retained since the cancellans, sometimes watermarked 1807, usually is misplaced between the title and contents leaves.)

3] THE | **WORKS** | OF | JOHN DRYDEN, . . . VOL. III. . . . 1808.

Collation: $\pi^2(\pi 2+1)$ A-2C^8 2D^8($\pm$2D7) 2E^2. Pagination: *i* half-title, *ii blank, iii* title-page, *iv blank, v* Contents, *vi blank, 1* fly-title, *2 blank, 3-7* 8-434 *435* text, *435* printer's imprint, *436 blank.* Printer's imprint: [*short Oxford rule*] | Edinburgh, | Printed by James Ballantyne & Co.

Figures: A7-4, B21-5, C45-3, D60-5, E—, F82-4, G111-5, H128-2, I 133-2 134-1, K147-5 156-3, L163-2 169-4, M184-3, N194-5, O 223-1 224-2, P239-3 240-5, Q253-5 254-1, R272-4/-, S276-2 279-5/-, T295-5 301-1, U308-4 318-2, X332-5 334-1, Y351-1 352-4, Z358-5 360-2, 2A 379-2 384-1, 2B 386-5 393-2, 2C 414-1 416-3, 2D 418-5 420-2 430-7, 2E—.

Notes: The original readings of cancellandum 2D7 (pages 429-430) are unknown. The cancellans in this sheet bears the redundant figure 430-7 because it was originally printed (according to the 'Directions' in volume 18) with the last gathering of volume 6, a sheet now lacking a figure..

4] THE | **WORKS** | OF | JOHN DRYDEN, . . . VOL. IV. . . . 1808.

Collation: $\pi^2(\pi 2+1)$ A-2E^8. Pagination: *i* half-title, *ii blank*, *iii* title-page, *iv blank*, *v* Contents, *vi blank*, *1* fly-title, *2 blank*, *3* 4-446 *447* text, *447* printer's imprint, *448 blank*. Printer's imprint: [*short Oxford rule*] | EDINBURGH: | Printed by James Ballantyne. Typography: Page 160 has first page-number missing, in some copies, but page 427 number is intact.

Figures: A11-5, B18-4 24-1, C43-1 45-4, D59-2 64-1, E75-3 80-2, F83-1 85-5, G99-3 101-5, H123-1 124-4, I 137-2 138-4, K148-4 150-2, L162-4 172-5, M183-5 192-2, N200-4, O *211*-5 213-4, P236-4 239-5/-, Q251-1, R260-4, S283-2, T298-5 301-4, U311-5 313-4, X336-4, Y338-5, Z354-5, 2A 383-4, 2B 394-1, 2C 416-3, 2D 424-4, 2E 442-2 444-1.

5] THE | **WORKS** | OF | JOHN DRYDEN, . . . VOL. V. . . . 1808.

Collation: $\pi^2(\pi 2+1)$ A-2B^8 2C^6. Pagination: *i* half-title, *ii blank*, *iii* title-page, *iv blank*, *v* Contents, *vi blank*, *1* fly-title, *2 blank*, *3* 4-410 *411* text, *411* printer's imprint, *412 blank*. Printer's imprint: [*short Oxford rule*] | Edinburgh: | Printed by James Ballantyne & Co. Typography: Page 317 page-numbers are correctly ordered, and page 402 figure 5 is correctly positioned.

Figures: A*13*-5, B21-2 30-6, C48-3, D56-2, E76-6, F82-4, G99-2, H124-5, I 132-2, K160-6, L163-6, M187-4 192-5/-, N208-5, O 224-4, P231-4, Q246-4, R269-5, S*282*-2 288-5, T*296*-5, U308-5, X328-4, Y345-4 347-5, Z361-4 362-5, 2A 377-5/- 383-2, 2B 393-5 394-2, 2C 402-5 408-2.

6] THE | **WORKS** | OF | JOHN DRYDEN, . . . VOL. VI. . . . 1808.

Collation: $\pi^2(\pi 2+1)$ A^8($\pm$A4) B-2G^8 2H^4(-2H1). Pagination: *i* half-title, *ii blank*, *iii* title-page, *iv blank*, *v* Contents, *vi blank*, *1* fly-title, *2 blank*, *3* 4-'450'[486] text, '450' printer's imprint: [*short Oxford rule*] | Edinburgh, | Printed by J. Ballantyne & Co. Illustrations: A large folding engraved plate (324 x 552mm untrimmed), facing page *222*, is titled: 'The Solemn Mock Procession of the POPE Cardinals, Jesuits, Friars, &c. Through the CITY OF LONDON November 17th. 1679.' This exemplifies the extensive note to the final couplet of the Epilogue to *Oedipus*: 'We know not what you can desire or hope, / To please you more, but burning of a Pope.' Typography: Page 486 is misnumbered 450.

Figures: A8-4 10-2, B18-5 20-2, C42-4 48-1/-, D54-4 57-5, E67-4 73-5, F85-5, G107-5, H*117*-5, I 135-4 144-5, K147-7 148-2, L169-1 171-4, M182-4 192-5, N202-5 204-3, O 215-4 224-5, P237-7 239-5, Q250-4 256-5, R*269*-5 271-4, S279-5 281-3, T299-4 301-7, U317-5 318-1/-, X329-1 331-5, Y339-5 348-1, Z362-3 368-5, 2A

373-3 379-7, 2B 388-5 398-4, 2C 408-4 415-7, 2D 431-4 432-1, 2E 438-5 448-2, 2F 453-1 459-4, 2G 471-1 480-2, 2H—.

Notes: Cancel A4 (pages 7-8) carries on verso a press-figure 4. In copy O sheet X is apparently of a different setting, on lighter, unwatermarked paper and without figures. As indicated in the 'Directions', volume 18, the leaf now cancelled in the last 2H gathering was used to print a cancellans 2D7 for volume 3.

7] THE | **WORKS** | OF | JOHN DRYDEN, . . . VOL. VII. . . . 1808.

Collation: $\pi^2(\pi 2+1)$ A-T^8 U^8(±U7) X-$2E^8$. Pagination: *i* half-title, *ii blank*, *iii* title-page, *iv blank*, *v* Contents, *vi blank*, *1* fly-title, *2 blank*, *3* 4-445 text, 445 printer's imprint, *446-448 blank*. Printer's imprint: [*short Oxford rule*] | Edinburgh: | Printed by James Ballantyne & Co.

Figures: A14-2 16-4, B32-5, C35-4, D50-4 64-7, E71-5 73-1, F92-5, G107-5, H119-2, I 143-5, K146-1/- 148-5, L168-1 171-5, M190-5 192-1, N205-5, O 214-4 *216*-2, P*233*-1, Q251-7, R*268*-2, S277-5 279-7, T297-6, U311-2, X324-2, Y339-2, Z362-3, 2A 383-1, 2B 393-2, 2C 416-2, 2D 432-4, 2E 438-2.

Notes: The original readings for cancellandum U7 (pages 317-318) are unknown. The cancellans bears on recto a direction 'VOL. VII.' to guide the binder in its placement.

8] THE | **WORKS** | OF | JOHN DRYDEN, . . . VOL. VIII. . . . 1808.

Collation: $\pi^2(\pi 2+1)$ A-$2F^8$. Pagination: *i* half-title, *ii blank*, *iii* title-page, *iv blank*, *v* Contents, *vi blank*, *1* fly-title, *2 blank*, *3* 4-464 text, 464 printer's imprint: [*short Oxford rule*] | Edinburgh: | Printed by James Ballantyne & Co. Typography: Last page-number in Table of Contents (page *v*), properly 437, is misnumbered 347. Page 335 is misnumbered 353.

Figures: (+1)*i*-7, A9-2 10-3, B21-2 26-4, C39-4, D63-2, E66-7/4/-, F87-1, G99-3, H128-4, I 131-1 141-2, K151-3, L173-2, M186-2, N*196*-3/- 202-4, O 211-4 224-1, P229-2, Q*246*-5/-, R266-1, S279-5, T301-7, U319-2, X323-7, Y350-5, Z362-7 368-5/-, 2A 370-2, 2B 394-2, 2C 402-4, 2D 420-7, 2E *446*-4, 2F 456-7.

9] THE | **WORKS** | OF | JOHN DRYDEN, . . . VOL. IX. . . . 1808.

Collation: $\pi^2(\pi 2+1)$ A-$2E^8$(±2E2) $2F^4$. Pagination: *1* half-title, *2 blank*, *3* title-page, *4 blank*, *i*-ii Contents, *1* fly-title, *2 blank*, *3* 4-455 text, 455 printer's imprint, *456 blank*. Printer's imprint: [*short Oxford rule*] | EDINBURGH: | Printed by James Ballantyne & Co. Illustration: Engraved plate of 'The Medal' facing page *431*.

Figures: A*8*-2/-, B*27*-4, C36-7, D57-2, E*76*-5, F87-7, G107-2, H127-2, I 130-2, K160-4, L168-2, M179-7, N206-4, O 220-2, P228-5 230-3, Q256-2, R267-5 269-4, S279-7, T299-1/- 304-5, U*319*-4 320-5, X326-1 332-7, Y344-5, Z357-7, 2A 375-4,

2B 395-4, 2C 416-2, 2D 429-3, 2E 435-6/7 444-5 447-3, 2F 450-7/-.

Notes: The original readings for cancellandum 2E2 (pages 435-436) are unknown. The cancellans carries a redundant figure for this gathering 435-6 or 7 and, on the same page, a direction line 'VOL. IX.' to guide the binder in its placement.

10] THE | **WORKS** | OF | JOHN DRYDEN, . . . VOL. X. . . . 1808.

Collation: $\pi^2(\pi 2+1)$ A-2E^8 2F^6(-2F6). Pagination: *i* half-title, *ii blank, iii* title-page, *iv blank, v* Contents, *vi blank, 1* fly-title, *2* Argument, *3* 4-457 text with notes interspersed, 457 printer's imprint, *458 blank*. Printer's imprint: [*short Oxford rule*] | Edinburgh, | Printed by James Ballantyne & Co. Typography: Page-number 138 is intact.

Figures: A6-5, B29-5 31-7, C45-4 46-5, D63-3, E76-1, F82-1, G106-4 112-7, H115-5, I 136-4 *139*-2, K154-5, L163-2, M187-5, N201-2, O 217-5 218-4, P238-4, Q250-3, R271-2, S277-7, T300-7, U306-2 316-2/-, X*330*-2, Y*343*-2, Z*368*-5/-, 2A *381*-5 382-2, 2B 387-2, 2C *414*-5, 2D 431-2, 2E 437-5 447-3, 2F 454-5.

Notes: Concerning an inserted leaf occasionally found between gatherings K/L see note to the next volume.

11] THE | **WORKS** | OF | JOHN DRYDEN, . . . VOL. XI. . . . 1808.

Collation: π^2 $2\pi^2$ A-K^8 L^8(L1+1) M-2G^8. Pagination: *1* half-title, *2 blank, 3* title-page, *4 blank, i* ii-iii Contents, *iv blank, 1* fly-title, *2 blank*, 3-480 text, 480 printer's imprint: [*short Oxford rule*] | EDINBURGH: | Printed by James Ballantyne & Co. Typography: Page-number 13 is intact. Gathering 2D (pages 417-432) is misnumbered 433-448.

Figures: A13-5 15-1, B29-7, C44-3, D64-7, E66-10, F88-5, G98-8, H114-3, I 130-3/-, K146-2, L167-10, M178-10, N207-1, O 211-10/- 224-2, P226-7 228-1, Q246-7 256-1, R258—5 260-8, S275-3, T290-7, U306-1 308-2, X322-1 336-8, Y338-1 352-2/-, Z354-1 360-4, 2A 370-10 372-7, 2B 386-8, 2C 406-7/-, 2D 438-1, 2E 434-1 448-2, 2F 450-5, 2G 466-10 477-7.

Notes: The leaf inserted after L1 is paged 161-162 and bears the heading 'Farewell, Fair Armida. A Song.' Since this is set in duplicate (with or without a direction line 'VOL. XI.') a copy without the direction is occasionally misplaced in volume 10. For some reason in this 11th volume only, the pages starting a poem (and so with headings) are, as with the inserted leaf, numbered; hence the absence of italic references in the figure record.

12] THE | **WORKS** | OF | JOHN DRYDEN, . . . VOL. XII. . . . 1808.

Collation: $\pi^2(\pi 2+1)$ a-e^8 f^6 A-2A^8 2B^2. Pagination: *1* half-title, *2 blank, 3* titlepage, *4 blank, i*-ii Contents, *i* fly-title, ii note, *iii* iv-xci text of Chaucer, *xcii blank, 1* fly-title, *2 blank*, *3* 4-388 text of translations, 388 printer's imprint: [*short Oxford rule*] | EDINBURGH: | Printed by James Ballantyne & Co. Typography: Page-number 145 is intact.

Figures: a xv-10, b xviii-10, c xxxiv-1 xlviii-7, d li-7, e lxxx-3, f lxxxii-1 lxxxiv-2, A6-5, B18-4, C36-2, D57-3 *63*-2, E74-7, F91-7, G103-5, H124-7, I 140-3 142-4, K*154*-5 *156*-4, L174-2 176-3, M182-4 192-1, N203-2, O 213-4 223-7, P*231*-4 237-2, Q244-2, R*259*-2 269-3, S288-5, T302-7, U319-2, X*327*-7 328-5, Y*346*-2, Z367-2, 2A 377-5 378-1, 2B—.

Notes: The separate Contents leaf, according to the 'Directions' in volume 18, is a cancel. Evidently, as noted above in the account of watermarks, the long preliminary section a-f, containing Dryden's modernized version of Chaucer, appar-ently as an afterthought was printed off in 1807-1808, some two years later than the main text. A later printing would also explain the use of preliminary lower-case signature letters and roman numerals, since the main text sequence was already finished.

13] THE | **WORKS** | OF | JOHN DRYDEN, . . . VOL. XIII. . . . 1808.

Collation: π^2(π2+1) A-F^8 G^8(±G1) H-S^8 T^8(±T5) U-2C^8 2D^4(-2D4). Pagination: *1* half-title, *2 blank*, *3* title-page, *4 blank*, *i*-ii Contents, *1* fly-title, *2 blank*, *3* 4-421 text, 421 printer's imprint, *422 blank*. Printer's imprint: [*short Oxford rule*] | Edinburgh, | Printed by James Ballantyne & Co.

Figures: (+1)*i*-7/-, A4-7, B23-2/-, C35-4, D56-5/-, E79-5, F95-3, G110-2, H126-2, I *130*-5, K151-2, L175-5, M188-7, N200-2, O 222-5, P231-4 240-2, Q*251*-2 252-1, R264-4 *267*-5, S276-2, T290-7, U307-4, X332-5, Y*345*-4 346-1, Z357-2 362-5, 2A 371(and/or 375)-1 372-2/-, 2B 392-4 395-5, 2C 404-2 414-4, 2D 420-5.

Notes: The original readings for cancellanda G1 (pages 97-98) and T5 (pages 297-298) are unknown. The first cancel, presumably like the original, has the direction notice 'VOL. XIII.'; the second has this reference newly added for the convenience of the binder.

A measure of Scott's exactitude may be observed on page *281* where he correctly insists upon 252 as the total number of 'Second Subscribers' to Dryden's 1697 edition of Virgil, here listed on pages 285-288. (The list of first subscribers is numbered.)

14] THE | **WORKS** | OF | JOHN DRYDEN, . . . VOL. XIV. . . . 1808.

Collation: π^2(π2+1) A-2F^8. Pagination: *1* half-title, *2 blank*, *3* title-page, *4 blank*, *i*-ii Contents, *1* fly-title, *2 blank*, *3* 4-462 text, 462 printer's imprint, *463-464 blank*. Printer's imprint: [*short Oxford rule*] | EDINBURGH, | Printed by James Ballantyne & Co.

Figures: A7-5 16-3, B19-4 32-2, C45-1 47-2, D63-5 64-2/-, E71-2, F87-4 89-1,

G100-1 103-2, H121-1 *127*-4, I 135-1 140-5, K157-4 158-2, L164-2 167-4, M179-5 189-2, N205-1 206-4, O 221-2 222-5, P232-1, Q254-4, R271-2, S287-1, T297-2 298-5, U313-5 314-2, X334-1 336-2, Y349-4/- 350-1, Z364-1 367-4, 2A 379-2, 2B 395-4, 2C 411-2 413-1, 2D 423-1, 2E 436-3 446-5, 2F 456-2.

15] THE | **WORKS** | OF | JOHN DRYDEN, . . . VOL. XV. . . . 1808.

Collation: $\pi^2(\pi2+1)$ A-2C^8 2D1. Pagination: *1* half-title, *2 blank*, *3* title-page, *4 blank*, *i*-ii Contents, *1* 2-417 text, 417 printer's imprint, *418 blank*. Printer's imprint: [*short Oxford rule*] | Edinburgh, | Printed by James Ballantyne & Co. Typography: Page 57 is misnumbered 75 and page 351 is correctly numbered.

Figures: A15-5 16-1, B18-1, C45-5 47-1, D53-1, E74-7, F92-4, G98-7, H119-5, I—, K153-2, L173-7/-, M188-1, N205-1, O 224-7, P230-4, Q248-4 255-8, R*267*-1 268-2, S*283*-8, T290-4, U319-8, X322-7, Y347-5, Z356-3, 2A 372-4 *383*-7, 2B 386-7, 2C 402-7, 2D—.

Notes: Final leaf 2D1 exists in a quadruple impression or setting: between the last line of text page 417 and 'END OF THE FIFTEENTH VOLUME' the interval measures 23, 29, 31, or 37mm.

16] THE | **WORKS** | OF | JOHN DRYDEN, . . . VOL. XVI. . . . 1808.

Collation: $\pi^2(\pi2+1)$ A-2K^8 2L^4. Pagination: *i* half-title, *ii blank*, *iii* title-page, *iv blank*, *v* Contents, *vi blank*, *1* fly-title, *2 blank*, *3* 4-536 text, 536 printer's imprint: [*short Oxford rule*] | EDINBURGH: | Printed by James Ballantyne & Co. Typography: Page 363 is misnumbered 336 and page 519 is correctly numbered.

Figures: A5-7, B18-7, C34-8, D—, E66-8, F82-8, G98-8, H114-7, I 130-8 140-2, K146-2, L162-3, M178-7, N194-2, O 210-5, P226-3, Q242-7, R258-7, S274-2, T290-2, U310-7, X322-5, Y338-7 340-1, Z354-7, 2A 370-8 384-3, 2B 386-7, 2C 402-1, 2D 418-1, 2E 434-7 448-8, 2F 450-1, 2G 466-10, 2H 482-1, 2I 498-1, 2K 514-7, 2L 530-1.

17] THE | **WORKS** | OF | JOHN DRYDEN, . . . VOL. XVII. . . . 1808.

Collation: $\pi^2(\pi2+1)$ A-2H^8 2I^2. Pagination: *1* half-title, *2 blank*, *3* title-page, *4 blank*, *i*-ii Contents, *1* fly-title, *2 blank*, 3-499 text, 499 printer's imprint, *500 blank*. Printer's imprint: [*short Oxford rule*] | EDINBURGH: | Printed by James Ballantyne & Co. Typography: Page 60 is misnumbered 90. In this impression pages 85 and 92 are correctly numbered, but 397 is misnumbered 937.

Figures: (+1)*i*-6, A3-4 13-1, B18-2 32-4, C34-4 48-7, D50-5, E66-2 72-10, F82-4, G98-5, H114-1 116-7, I 130-5 144-1, K146-7 157-11, L162-5 165-7, M178-5 192-1, N194-3 196-5, O 210-1 224-7, P226-4 240-7, Q242-8, R258-5, S274-4 288-5, T290-4, U306-7/-, X322-11 324-4, Y338-8, Z354-11 368-4, 2A 370-2 384-4, 2B

386-5 400-'01'[=10]/-, 2C 402-7 416-8, 2D 419-5 432-4, 2E 434-1 448-2, 2F 450-11 464-8, 2G 466-1 477-7/-, 2H 482-5 496-2, 2I 498-1.

18] THE | **WORKS** | OF | JOHN DRYDEN, . . . VOL. XVIII. . . . 1808.

Collation: $\pi^2(\pi 2+1)$ A-P^8 R^8 a-g^8 h^4. Pagination: *1* half-title, *2 blank*, *3* title-page, *4 blank*, *i* Contents, *ii blank*, *1* fly-title, *2 blank*, 3-182 text, *183* fly-title, *184 blank*, *185* 186-256 Appendix, *i* ii-ciii Index, *civ blank*, *cv* cvi-cxviii General Table of Contents, cxviii printer's imprint, *cxix* Directions to the Binder, *cxx blank*. Printer's imprint: [*short Oxford rule*] | EDINBURGH: | Printed by James Ballantyne & Co. Typography: Pagination is continuous, despite omitted gathering Q. In this impression signature H (page 113) is signed; page 242 has figure 4 correctly entered; pages 244, xxxii, and lxxvi are correctly numbered, but pages 43 and 47 are misnumbered 34 (some copies) and 74 respectively.

Figures: A13-4/-, B30-2, C34-1 48-4, D50-2 64-11, E66-1 80-11, F82-2 96-7, G98-5 112-4, H114-11 128-5, I 130-4, K146-4, L170-5 176-1, M178-3/-, N194-3 208-7, O 210-12, P226-1 240-7, R242-4 244-12, a ii-6, b xviii-4 xxxii-6, c xxxiv-4 xxxvi-12, d l-12 lxi-6, e lxvii-2 lxxvii-7, f lxxxv-6/- lxxxvi-12, g xcviii-5 cxii-11, h cxv-7/-.

Notes: The 'Directions' on page *cxix* advise the binder to correctly place the cancels, one of which is printed on the last sheet of volume 6, the other 13 now 'put up with' volume 2.

30Ab] First Scott Edition, Second (Large-Paper) Impression: 1808

THE | **WORKS** | OF | JOHN DRYDEN, | NOW FIRST COLLECTED | IN EIGHTEEN VOLUMES. | [*short Oxford rule*] | ILLUSTRATED | WITH NOTES, | HISTORICAL, CRITICAL, AND EXPLANATORY, | AND | A LIFE OF THE AUTHOR, | BY | WALTER SCOTT, ESQ. | [*short reversed Oxford rule*] | VOL. I [II-XVIII]. | LONDON: | PRINTED FOR WILLIAM MILLER, ALBEMARLE STREET, | BY JAMES BALLANTYNE AND CO. EDINBURGH. | [*dash*] | 1808.

Published concurrently with the previous impression. £12.12.0. Binding: 'extra boards'. Paper: Royal 8° (236 x 144mm cut). Watermarks: In this later impression four varieties of marks generally establish a certain order of text-printing:
(a) V 1796 [repeated first four leaves of each gathering], volumes 2, 3(-2E2);
(b) BUTTANSHAW | 1803, volumes 3(2E2 only), 4-15 mixed with variant a;
(c) BUTTANSHAW | 1806 mixed with variant b, volumes 16-17, also the same mixture throughout for preliminary gatherings and separate Contents leaves, but apparently unmixed 1806 for twelve of the fourteen cancels or inserts listed in volume 18 'Directions to the Binder';

(d) 1805 | 1805 countermark IIS mixed with variant (c), but unmixed 1805 for the two cancels B7 and E6 in volume 1.
According to this chronology the *Life* volume 1, as the most arduous to prepare, was finally printed (perhaps irregularly) not before the end of work on volume 17, for it comprises sheets K-R of variant (b), A-I and S-X of variant (c), Y-2L and preliminary a of variant (d).

General Notes: In all respects this impression is identical with the previous printing, excepting only the points cited above and below. In seven volumes (3, 6-9, 13-14) no variation has been observed.

Copies: (volume 1, issue 1) E L; TxU. (2) TxU.

1] THE | **WORKS** | OF | JOHN DRYDEN, . . . VOL. I. . . . 1808.

Figures: In this large-paper impression, N194-11/- 204-4/-, P240-2/-, Q247—256-4, 2H 496-2, 2K 514-7. Notes: Sheet N (pages 193-208) now exists in two settings: (1) with figures as in preceding impression (194-11, 204-4), page 193 line 8 first word 'commended'; (2) without figures, first word 'mended'. The first setting is on paper used at this stage of the printing; the second, set apparently to make up for a short initial count, is on paper not used until sheet Y.

2] THE | **WORKS** | OF | JOHN DRYDEN, . . . VOL. II. . . . 1808.

Typography: Page 170 has the first page-number missing.

4] THE | **WORKS** | OF | JOHN DRYDEN, . . . VOL. IV. . . . 1808.

Typography: Page 160 number is intact, but in some copies page 427 first page-number is missing.

5] THE | **WORKS** | OF | JOHN DRYDEN, . . . VOL. V. . . . 1808.

Typography: In some copies page-number 317 is transposed as 173, and on page 402 figure 5 is upside down.

10] THE | **WORKS** | OF | JOHN DRYDEN, . . . VOL. X. . . . 1808.

Typography: Page 138 has first page-number missing. Figures: U316—, Z368-5.

11] THE | **WORKS** | OF | JOHN DRYDEN, . . . VOL. XI. . . . 1808.

Typography: Page 13 has second page-number missing.

12] THE | **WORKS** | OF | JOHN DRYDEN, . . . VOL. XII. . . . 1808.

Typography: In some copies page 145 has first page-number missing.

15] THE | **WORKS** | OF | JOHN DRYDEN, . . . VOL. XV. . . . 1808.

Typography: In some copies page 351 is unnumbered. Unlike the four different intervals previously described for the regular impression, between the last line of text and END OF THE FIFTEENTH VOLUME these intervals measure either 27mm or (somewhat out of register) 40mm.

16] THE | **WORKS** | OF | JOHN DRYDEN, . . . VOL. XVI. . . . 1808.

Typography: Page 519 is misnumbered 195.

17] THE | **WORKS** | OF | JOHN DRYDEN, . . . VOL. XVII. . . . 1808.

Typography: Pages 85 and 92 are misnumbered 58 and 62 respectively, but 397 in some copies is correctly numbered.

18] THE | **WORKS** | OF | JOHN DRYDEN, . . . VOL. XVIII. . . . 1808.

Typography: Pages 43 and 47 are correctly numbered, but signature H (page 113) has dropped. In some copies page 242 has figure 4 upside down; pages 244, xxxii, and lxxvi are misnumbered 214, xxix and xxvi respectively.

30Ac] Second Scott Edition: 1821

THE | **WORKS** | OF | JOHN DRYDEN, | NOW FIRST COLLECTED | *IN EIGHTEEN VOLUMES.* | [*short Oxford rule*] | ILLUSTRATED | WITH NOTES, | HISTORICAL, CRITICAL, AND EXPLANATORY, | AND | A LIFE OF THE AUTHOR, | BY | SIR WALTER SCOTT, BART. | [*short reversed Oxford rule*] | SECOND EDITION. | VOL. I [II-XVIII]. | [*short Oxford rule*] | EDINBURGH: | PRINTED FOR ARCHIBALD CONSTABLE AND CO. EDINBURGH; | AND HURST, ROBINSON, AND CO. LONDON. | [*dash*] | 1821.

Issued 15 August 1821 in London (*MC*). £9.9.0. Paper: Demy 8° (212 x 130mm cut). Watermarks: The marks for this later multi-volumed edition, essentially all available for press work at once, are uniformly 1819 [1820] | none [4], mixed occasionally with unwatermarked paper and, in volume 7, with B | 1816. Volume 8 (by another printer, as noted below) has either (1) no watermarks excepting only sheets S-U, Z, 2B-2D; or (2) B | 1818 marks throughout, excepting only sheet Q: B | 1820 | 2 [none, 6]. Typography: Excepting volumes 8, 13, 15, 17, all printed by others, as noted below, the printer's imprints read uniformly (1) on verso of title: [*short rule*] | *Printed by James Ballantyne and Co. Edinburgh.*; (2) at end of text: [*short rule*] | EDINBURGH: | Printed by James Ballantyne & Co.

General Notes: Scott's Advertisement, volume 1, reprints his earlier essay, but now concludes page xi with a further paragraph: 'Several inaccuracies which had crept into the former edition of this work, are corrected in the present; and the whole has been revised with care.' Transcripts of two Dryden translations, 'Te Deum' and 'Hymn for St John's Eve', both of which reached Scott 'too late to be inserted' in the text, and were therefore cited at length in the 1808 edition of the *Life* (volume 1, pages 343-345), now in 1821 'are inserted in the poet's works' (volume 11, page 343).

Copies: E L P; CtY DLC NN TxU.

1] THE | **WORKS** | OF | JOHN DRYDEN, . . . SECOND EDITION. | VOL. I. . . . 1821.

Collation: π^2 a^8 A-$2K^8$ $2L^4$. Pagination: *1* half-title, *2 blank*, *3* title-page, *4* printer's imprint(1), *i* ii-xi Advertisement, *xii blank*, *xiii* xiv-xv Contents, *xvi blank*, *1* fly-title for *The Life of John Dryden*, *2 blank*, *3* 4-533 text, 533 printer's imprint(2), *534-536 blank*. Illustration: Frontispiece of Dryden, engraved by W. H. Lizars, published by A. Constable, dated 1821.

Figures: a iv-9, A16-7, B32-2, C48-10, D63-2, E80-7, F96-2, G112-2, H128-1, I 144-10, K160-9, L176-6, M192-8, N208-9, O 224-8, P240-10, Q256-8, R272-6, S288-9, T304-9, U320-7, X336-9, Y352-7, Z368-2, 2A 384-15, 2B 400-1, 2C 416-7, 2D 432-9, 2E 448-3, 2F 464-6, 2G 480-8, 2H 496-10, 2I 512-15, 2K 528-7, 2L 532-1. With few exceptions this first volume only is regularly figured in the outer forme last page of the gathering. The volume also exhibits page 512 a figure 15, the highest number recorded thus far.

Notes: Archibald Constable, in his 15 February 1822 letter to Scott, reports that he has 'already printed 1000 copies of Dryden's life' (*Letters*, vii.79n; complete letter E MS 867,ff.168-172), but no separate issue of this volume has been identified.

2] THE | **WORKS** | OF | JOHN DRYDEN, . . . SECOND EDITION. | VOL. II. . . . 1821.

Collation: $\pi^2(\pi 2+1)$ A-$2F^8$ $2G^4$. Pagination: *i* half-title, *ii blank*, *iii* title-page, *iv* printer's imprint(1), *v* Contents, *vi blank*, *1* fly-title, *2 blank*, *3* Advertisement, *4 blank*, *5* 6-12 Congreve dedication, *13* fly-title, *14 blank*, *15* 16-472 text, 472 printer's imprint(2).

Figures: A9-4, B27-6, C46-5, D56-8, E76-3, F93-6, G100-6, H115-3, I 137-3, K148-6, L174-8, M190-5, N*207*-7, O 211-5, P234-9, Q244-7, R266-5, S285-8, T302-1/-, U315-8, X326-9, Y345-12, Z355-6, 2A 384-9, 2B 393-4, 2C 412-10, 2D 430-10, 2E 438-12, 2F 452-5, 2G 468-5.

3] THE | **WORKS** | OF | JOHN DRYDEN, . . . SECOND EDITION. | VOL. III. . . . 1821.

Collation: $\pi^2(\pi 2+1)$ A-2D^8 2E^2. Pagination: *i* half-title, *ii blank*, *iii* title-page, *iv* printer's imprint(1), *v* Contents, *vi blank*, *1* fly-title, *2 blank*, *3* 4-434 *435* text, *435* printer's imprint(2), *436 blank*.

Figures: A13-4/-, B29-2, C35-8, D56-12, E68-3 75-3, F91-6, G109-12, H118-5, I 144-8, K156-9, L173-9, M183-2, N199-6, O 222-12, P239-12, Q247-7, R269-5, S287-6, T290-3, U318-3, X329-3, Y344-12, Z359-14 361-14, 2A 384-3, 2B 398-12, 2C 410-2, 2D 432-6, 2E—.

4] THE | **WORKS** | OF | JOHN DRYDEN, . . . SECOND EDITION. | VOL. IV. . . . 1821.

Collation: $\pi^2(\pi 2+1)$ A-2E^8. Pagination: *i* half-title, *ii blank*, *iii* title-page, *iv* printer's imprint(1), *v* Contents, *vi blank*, *1* fly-title, *2 blank*, *3* 4-446 *447* text, *447* printer's imprint(2), *448 blank*. Typography: In some copies pages 55 and 326 are misnumbered 51 and 226.

Figures: A4-13, B20-5, C46-14, D50-3, E73-8, F94-6, G103-3, H126-14, I 135-10, K154-12, L173-3, M188-8, N207-2, O 220-13, P229-11, Q250-7, R265-3, S278-14, T304-14, U308-3, X332-13, Y*348*-9, Z*359*-7, 2A 378-9, 2B 390-1, 2C 410-5, 2D 432-13, 2E 444-9.

5] THE | **WORKS** | OF | JOHN DRYDEN, . . . SECOND EDITION. | VOL. V. . . . 1821.

Collation: $\pi^2(\pi 2+1)$ A-2B^8 2C^6. Pagination: *i* half-title, *ii blank*, *iii* title-page, *iv* printer's imprint(1), *v* Contents, *vi blank*, *1* fly-title, *2 blank*, *3* 4-410 *411* text, *411* printer's imprint(2), *412 blank*. Typography: Page 49 direction line incorrectly reads 'VOL. IV.'

Figures: A*13*-1, B29-3, C47-3, D56-9, E79-6, F*95*-7, G109-2, H124-11, I 139-5, K157-2, L163-5, M178-8, N207-6, O 223-5, P231-2, Q254-9, R268-5, S276-8, T304-10, U313-5, X335-7, Y349-2, Z368-8, 2A 384-8 2B 392-3, 2C 406-8.

6] THE | **WORKS** | OF | JOHN DRYDEN, . . . SECOND EDITION. | VOL. VI. . . . 1821.

Collation: $\pi^2(\pi 2+1)$ A-2G^8 2H^4(-2H4). Pagination: *i* half-title, *ii blank*, *iii* title-page, *iv* printer's imprint(1), *v* Contents, *vi blank*, *1* fly-title, *2 blank*, *3* 4-486 text, 486 printer's imprint(2), *487-488 blank*.

Figures: A*3*-9, B20-2, C35-7, D61-4, E70-9, F88-2, G107-5, H125-5, I 141-9, K157-6, L169-8, M187-8, N201-6, O 224-9, P233-3, Q256-9, R258-8, S278-5,

T295-8, U318-8, X333-5, Y352-6, Z355-8, 2A 379-8, 2B 400-2, 2C 404-5, 2D—, 2E 448-5, 2F 464-8, 2G 477-6, 2H 485-3.

Notes: In some copies the folding engraved plate, now facing page 223, still carries the first edition imprint of William Miller, dated January 1808. Later plates bear the imprint of A. Constable, 1821.

7] THE | **WORKS** | OF | JOHN DRYDEN, . . . SECOND EDITION. | VOL. VII. . . . 1821.

Collation: $\pi^2(\pi2+1)$ A-2D⁸ 2E⁸. Pagination: *i* half-title, *ii blank*, *iii* title-page, *iv* printer's imprint(1), *v* Contents, *vi blank*, *1* fly-title, *2 blank*, 3-445 text, 445 printer's imprint(2), *446-448 blank*. Typography: Signature 2E (page 433) is wrongly signed 2F. In some copies the figure 12, page 196, is transposed as 21 or is lacking.

Figures: A4-8, B29-3, C48-7, D64-1, E80-5, F84-9, G112-4, H128-3, I 144-3, K156-2, L176-10, M192-7, N196-12/-, O 224-1, P240-6, Q256-5, R267-7, S288-9, T304-5, U320-11, X333-12, Y352-13, Z368-9, 2A 384-2, 2B 400-13, 2C 416-7, 2D 432-3, '2F'[2E] 436-2.

8] THE | **WORKS** | OF | JOHN DRYDEN, . . . SECOND EDITION. | VOL. VIII. . . . 1821.

Collation: $\pi^2(\pi2+1)$ A-2F⁸. Pagination: *1* half-title, *2 blank*, *3* title-page, *4* printer's imprint(1), *i* Contents, *ii blank*, *1* fly-title, *2 blank*, *3* 4-464 text, 464 printer's imprint(2). Printer's imprints: (1) [*short rule*] | *Printed by James Ballantyne and Co. Edinburgh*.; (2) [*short Oxford rule*] | Edinburgh: | Printed by George Ramsay & Co.

Figures: A10-10 16-12, B26-12 32-10, C37-10 42-12, D58-12 60-10, E67-10 76-12, F82-12 92-10, G98-10 100-12, H*125*-10 126-12, I 142-12 144-10, K154-10 156-12, L162-10 172-12, M188-12 *191*-10, N198-12 208-10, O 222-12 224-10, P233-12 238-10, Q255-12 256-10, R262-10 271-10 272-12, S284-12 286-10, T290-12 304-10, U317-10 318-12, X*333*-10 334-12, Y350-12 352-10, Z356-10 366-12, 2A 370-12 384-10, 2B 390-10 392-12, 2C 408-12 410-10, 2D 426-12 428-10, 2E 442-10 444-12, 2F 457-10 *462*-12.

Notes: Unlike Ballantyne's printing elsewhere in this work, all with a full-type page measure of 89mm, and one press-figure per sheet, this single volume assigned to Ramsay measures 88mm and shows that each sheet was regularly worked off by two pressmen 10 and 12. (The redundant 10 in R inner forme, pages 262 or 271, possibly is a mere duplication by a forgetful pressman, since no cancel can be detected here.) Double presswork may also explain, as indicated in general note above, the existence in this volume only of two kinds of paper.

9] THE | **WORKS** | OF | JOHN DRYDEN, . . . SECOND EDITION. | VOL. IX. . . . 1821.

Collation: $\pi^2(\pi 2+1)$ A-H^8(±H1,±H6) I-2E^8 2F^4. Pagination: *1* half-title, *2 blank*, *3* title-page, *4* printer's imprint(1), *i*-ii Contents, *1* fly-title, *2 blank*, *3* 4-455 text, 455 printer's imprint(2), *456 blank*. Illustration: The engraved plate of 'The Medal', inserted in 1808, is not used in this volume.

Figures: A*15*-13, B18-13, C43-8, D57-9, E68-5, F85-6, G99-11, H—, I 132-7, K152-8, L163-3, M183-13, N203-6, O 221-6, P239-12, Q250-13, R268-7, S277-7, T297-5, U309-1, X334-13, Y339-14 349-14, Z365-10, 2A 375-13, 2B 396-9, 2C 404-6, 2D 427-9, 2E 445-12, 2F 453-13.

Notes: One of the H cancellanda (pages 113-114 or 123-124) probably carried the press-figure now missing in this gathering. Between the first, 1808 edition and these 1821 H1, H6 cancellentia (representing stanzas 45-58, 103-114 of *Annus Mirabilis*) no substantive variants appear: a circumstance which would indicate that the textual faults originated in this later printing.

10] THE | **WORKS** | OF | JOHN DRYDEN, . . . SECOND EDITION. | VOL. X. . . . 1821.

Collation: $\pi^2(\pi 2+1)$ A-2E^8 2F^4 2G1. Pagination: *i* half-title, *ii blank*, *iii* title-page, *iv* printer's imprint(1), *v* Contents, *vi blank*, *1* fly-title, *2* Argument, *3* 4-457 text, 457 printer's imprint(2), *458 blank*.

Figures: A*11*-10, B23-1, C34-5, D64-6, E70-11, F91-4, G100-13, H116-1, I 136-9, K151-3, L166-13, M191-10, N204-9, O 217-6, P234-12, Q253-6, R267-2, S281-13, T304-13, U—, X331-3, Y*350*-2, Z364-14/-, 2A 382-5, 2B *393*-10, 2C *409*-13, 2D 421-12, 2E 436-6, 2F 455-10, 2G—.

11] THE | **WORKS** | OF | JOHN DRYDEN, . . . SECOND EDITION. | VOL. XI. . . . 1821.

Collation: π^4 A-K^8 L1 L^8 M^8(-M8+3) N-2G^8. Pagination: *1* half-title, *2 blank*, *3* title-page, *4* printer's imprint(1), *i* ii-iii Contents, *iv blank*, *1* fly-title, *2 blank*, 3-191 192*-195* text, *196* blank*, *193* fly-leaf, *194 blank*, *195* 196-480 text of Fables from Chaucer, 480 printer's imprint(2). Typography: Pages 417-432 are misnumbered 433-448.

Figures: A16-7, B18-8, C45-9, D50-7, E70-9, F88-5, G101-8, H121-9, I 136-9, K160-8, L165-1, M186-6 192*-5, N201-10, O 220-3, P228-8, Q248-6, R272-3, S281-3, T301-8, U318-2, X335-7, Y344-10, Z367-3, 2A 384-3, 2B 392-2, 2C 416-7, 2D 447-6, 2E 439-9, 2F 464-3, 2G 471-2.

Notes: The inserted leaf after gathering K (after page 160), signed L but not included in the pagination, is a fly-leaf reading 'Odes, Songs, and Lyrical Pieces': one now entered separately because of the additional song previously inserted in the 1808 edition (pages 161-162 in both editions). The three leaves replacing M8 (the first recto signed M2, with remaining pages numbered 192*-195*) add 'The Te Deum' (pages 192*-193*) and 'Hymn for St John's Eve' (pages 194*-195*), both of them translations belatedly entered in the *Life* first volume of the 1808 edition and almost overlooked here.

12] THE | **WORKS** | OF | JOHN DRYDEN, . . . SECOND EDITION. | VOL. XII. . . . 1821.

Collation: $\pi^2(\pi 2+1)$ a-e^8 f^6 A-$2A^8$ $2B^2$. Pagination: *1* half-title, *2 blank*, *3* title-page, *4* printer's imprint(1), *i*-ii Contents, *i* fly-title, ii note, *iii* iv-xci translations from Chaucer, *xcii blank*, *1* fly-title, *2 blank*, *3* 4-388 text for other translations, 388 printer's imprint(2). Typography: Page 239 is misnumbered 293.

Figures: a xiv-2, b xxviii-14, c xlviii-7, d li-2, e lxxx-11, f—, A11-9, B*21*-8, C38-3, D64-10, E79-2, F91-2, G107-13, H125-9, I 131-5, K*154*-6, L169-12, M184-1, N*207*-13, O 212-4, P237-8, Q245-1, R272-3, S277-1, T294-6, U320-10, X328-5, Y*346*-8, Z362-8, 2A 377-3, 2B—.

13] THE | **WORKS** | OF | JOHN DRYDEN, . . . SECOND EDITION. | VOL. XIII. . . . 1821.

Collation: $\pi^2(\pi 2+1)$ A-$2C^8$ $2D^4$(-2D4). Pagination: *1* half-title, *2 blank*, *3* title-page, *4* printer's imprint(1), *i*-ii Contents, *1* fly-title, *2 blank*, *3* 4-421 text, 421 printer's imprint(2), *422 blank*. Printer's imprints: (1) [*short rule*] | *Printed by James Ballantyne and Co. Edinburgh*.; (2) [*short rule*] | Printed by Walker & Greig, | Edinburgh.

Figures: A16-47, B31-2, C47-13, D63-47, E79-47, F95-2, G111-47, H127-2, I 144-56, K160-13, L176-13, M192-47, N*207*-47, O 223-13, P240-13, Q255-13, R271-13, S287-56, T303-13, U319-13, X—, Y351-13, Z367-47, 2A 383-47, 2B 399-13, 2C 415-47, 2D 420-47.

Notes: Because of delays in his own presswork Ballantyne originally assigned volume 8 to Ramsay, and later was obliged to submit three others (13, 15, 17) to the firm of Walker & Greig. This firm usually designates double signatures with a double letter (Aa, Bb, Cc) and for some sheets oddly employs double figures (here 13, 47, 56). Figure 2, the one number not combined with any other, appears alone on sheets B, F, and H.

14] THE | **WORKS** | OF | JOHN DRYDEN, . . . SECOND EDITION. | VOL. XIV. . . . 1821.

Collation: $\pi^2(\pi 2+1)$ A-2E^8 2F^8(-2F8). Pagination: *1* half-title, *2 blank*, *3* title-page, *4* printer's imprint(1), *i*-ii Contents, *1* fly-title, *2 blank*, *3* 4-462 text, 462 printer's imprint(2), *463-464 blank*.

Figures: A16-8, B32-5, C38-7, D61-3, E80-13, F96-6, G101-5, H128-8, I 144-10, K160-12, L176-11, M192-3, N208-5, O 224-8, P240-6, Q256-3, R272-9, S288-13, T304-13, U320-8, X336-3, Y352-3, Z368-8, 2A 384-6, 2B 396-11, 2C 413-6, 2D 432-3, 2E 445-6, 2F 461-8.

15] THE | **WORKS** | OF | JOHN DRYDEN, . . . SECOND EDITION. | VOL. XV. . . . 1821.

Collation: $\pi^2(\pi 2+1)$ A-2C^8 2D1. Pagination: *1* half-title, *2 blank*, *3* title-page, *4* printer's imprint(1), *i*-ii Contents, *1* 2-417 text, 417 printer's imprint(2), *418 blank*. Printer's imprints: (1) [*short rule*] | *Printed by James Ballantyne and Co. Edinburgh.*; (2) [*short rule*] | Printed by Walker & Greig, Edinburgh. Typography: In some copies page ii is misnumbered vi.

Figures: A15-13, B28-13, C47-13, D64-13, E79-13, F95-13, G111-13, H127-13, I 143-56, K159-13, L176-13, M191-13, N 207-13, O 224-13, P239-13, Q255-13, R271-13, S287-13, T303-26, U319-13, X335-13, Y351-13, Z367-2 368-13, 2A *383*-13, 2B—, 2C *414*-47.

Notes: In contrast to their earlier performance (volume 13) Walker & Greig now sign regularly, 2A &c., according to Ballantyne's practice. Again the peculiar double figures appear, usually 13, but also once each for 47, 56, and a new combination, T303-26.

16] THE | **WORKS** | OF | JOHN DRYDEN, . . . SECOND EDITION. | VOL. XVI. . . . 1821.

Collation: $\pi^2(\pi 2+1)$ A-2K^8 2L^4. Pagination: *i* half-title, *ii blank*, *iii* title-page, *iv* printer's imprint(1), *v* Contents, *vi blank*, *1* fly-title, *2 blank*, *3* 4-536 text, 536 printer's imprint(2).

Figures: A6-6, B18-3, C46-8, D64-1, E75-5, F93-8, G103-1, H117-2, I 140-3, K153-8, L172-5, M192-1, N204-1, O—, P235-4, Q253-10, R267-3, S280-5, T304-6, U320-11, X331-12, Y347-9, Z365-10, 2A 381-4, 2B 388-7, 2C 404-4, 2D 428-10, 2E 436-13, 2F 452-13, 2G 477-6, 2H 489-7, 2I 498-13, 2K 525-11, 2L—.

17] THE | **WORKS** | OF | JOHN DRYDEN, . . . SECOND EDITION. | VOL. XVII. . . . 1821.

Collation: $\pi^2(\pi 2+1)$ A-2H^8 2I^2. Pagination: *1* half-title, *2 blank*, *3* title-page, *4* printer's imprint(1), *i*-ii Contents, *1* fly-title, *2 blank*, *3* 4-499 text, 499 printer's imprint(2), *500 blank*. Printer's imprints: (1) [*short rule*] | *Printed by James*

Ballantyne and Co. Edinburgh.; (2) [*short rule*] | EDINBURGH: | Printed by James Ballantyne & Co.

Figures: A15-28, B31-13, C47-56, D63-47, E79-56, F95-56, G111-56, H127-28, I 143-56, K159-28, L175-56, M191-28, N208-28, O 223-28, P239-28, Q255-28, R271-47, S287-47, T303-47, U319-47, X335-47, Y—, Z367-47, 2A 383-56, 2B 399-28, 2C 415-56, 2D 431-56, 2E 447-28, 2F 463-56, 2G 479-90, 2H 495-90, 2I—.

Notes: The final unfigured part-gathering 2I (so signed) may in fact have been printed by Ballantyne, as the colophon and a longer text-line would indicate; but all other work in this volume is evidently by Walker & Greig, as again attested first by the double-letter signatures Aa-Hh, secondly, by the double figures. For this third volume of their supplementary work two new figure combinations now appear, 28 and 90.

18] THE | **WORKS** | OF | JOHN DRYDEN, . . . SECOND EDITION. | VOL. XVIII. . . . 1821.

Collation: $\pi^2(\pi 2+1)$ A-P^8 R^8 a-g^8 h^4. Pagination: *i* half-title, *ii blank*, *iii* title-page, *iv* printer's imprint(1), *v* Contents, *vi blank*, *1* fly-title, *2 blank*, 3-182 text, *183* fly-title, *184 blank*, 185-256 Appendix, *i* ii-ciii Index, *civ blank*, *cv* cvi-cxviii General Table of Contents, cxviii printer's imprint(2), *1*-2 list of works published by Constable. Typography: Despite the omitted Q in collation, pagination and text are continuous.

Figures: A14-3, B27-5, C45-4, D64-6, E73-3, F91-10, G112-13, H114-12, I 144-1, K160-5, L176-3, M192-12, N208-11, O 224-11, P230-12, R256-8, a iii-4, b xx-5, c xlviii-5, d lix-5, e lxxiii-10 lxxiv-5, f xcvi-6, g cix-6, h cxvi-3.

MEMOIRS OF CAPT. GEORGE CARLETON

31Aa] First Scott Edition, First Impression: 1808

MEMOIRS | OF | CAPT. GEORGE CARLETON, | AN ENGLISH OFFICER; | INCLUDING | ANECDOTES OF THE WAR IN SPAIN UNDER | THE EARL OF PETERBOROUGH, | AND | MANY INTERESTING PARTICULARS RELATING | TO THE MANNERS OF THE SPANIARDS IN THE BEGIN- | NING OF THE LAST CENTURY. | [*short Oxford rule*] | *WRITTEN BY HIMSELF.* | [*short reversed Oxford rule*] | EDINBURGH: | [*dash*] | PRINTED BY JAMES BALLANTYNE AND CO. | FOR ARCHIBALD CONSTABLE AND CO., EDINBURGH; | AND J. MURRAY, LONDON. | [*dash*] | 1808.

Published April 1808 in Edinburgh (*SM*); issued 8 July in London (*MC*). 12s. Binding: Drab boards with printed label. Paper: Demy 8° (222 x 146mm uncut). Watermarks: D & A C | 1807 | 1 [2]. Collation: π^2 a^8 b^4 A-$2F^8$. Pagination: *1* half-title, *2 blank*, *3* title-page, *4 blank*, *i* ii-xv Preface, *xvi blank*, *xvii* xviii-xix dedication (by Carleton) to Spencer Lord Compton, *xx blank*, *xxi* xxii-xxiii To the Reader, *xxiv blank*, *1* 2-463 text, 463 printer's imprint, *464 blank*. Printer's imprint: [*short Oxford rule*] | EDINBURGH: | Printed by James Ballantyne & Co. Typography: On page 463 the Oxford rule begins either over and to the left of 'E', over the 'E' or over the 'N' in EDINBURGH. Signature Q (page 241) is missigned S.

Figures: a ii-1, b—, A2-7, B18-2 32-10, C34-3, D50-11 52-7/-, E66-7 80-2, F82-7 96-11, G98-2, H114-1 128-10, I 130(or 143)-10 144-3, K146-7, L162-7, M179-7/-, N194-7, O 210-3, P240-3, Q255-11, R258-1, S274-12, T290-11, U306-1, X322-10, Y338-7, Z354-5, 2A 370-2, 2B 386-12, 2C 416-1, 2D 432-6, 2E 434-6 448-4, 2F 450-1.

Notes: Issued on the occasion of Wellington's Peninsular War. Scott in his unsigned Preface begins by remarking that the work was of such a great rarity that it long remained unknown to Dr. Johnson, and concludes by noting that it was 'first printed in 1743'. This, however, was the latest reissue of unsold sheets, first issued with title dated 1728 (three states), then dated 1740. The latest bibliographical scholarship suggests that, while Defoe may have been the first editor of the *Memoirs*, Carleton was a real person.

The Preface is primarily concerned with a biographical sketch of General Peterborough, whose victories in Spain are celebrated in the *Memoirs*, and who is remembered again in 1829 when Scott announced the imminent publication of a full-scale *Life* of this military hero (*see* 231A). To correlate Peterborough's campaign with Wellington's, later advertisements for this 1808 edition (*MC* 14, 23 July, 24 September) display a new heading 'SPANISH PATRIOTS' and additional commentary much in the style of Scott:

> While the eyes of the public are turned with hope and expectance towards the Spanish Kingdom, all information respecting the character of the people and state of the country, particularly in a military point of view, must be highly acceptable. The Memoirs of Carleton were written during that memorable war, in which the Catalonian Insurgents, supported by an auxiliary British Force, drove the French from Madrid, and forced them to recross the Pyrenees; when it was, as now, the common cry in the streets of the Spanish capital, "Paz con la Inglaterra, y con todo el mundo la guerra."
>
> It is the work of an eye-witness, and actor in the scenes he records, and was esteemed by the late Dr. Johnson to contain the best and most authentic account of the campaigns of the gallant Earl of Peterborough.

[This supplememtary remark was somewhat prophetic, for the French were forced to evacuate Madrid 29-31 July, three months after this issue, only to retake the city on 8 December.]

A Constable catalogue in one copy, as noted below, is the first to advertise 'The Works of Walter Scott', 6 volumes, royal 8°, £6.6.0 in boards (260Ab), as well as a regular issue separately of *The Minstrelsy*, 3 volumes, third edition, *Sir Tristrem*, second edition, *Lay of the Last Minstrel*, fifth edition, *Ballads and Lyrical Pieces*, second edition, and *Marmion*, second edition, with a 'few Copies' in royal 8° to make up the 6th volume of the *Works*.

Copies: BCL DN E O; CtY InU* T/B.
*With undated 8-page Constable catalogue.

Reference: (Magnum Opus Edition: Not reprinted.)

31Ab] First Scott Edition, Second (Large-Paper) Impression: 1808

MEMOIRS | OF | CAPT. GEORGE CARLETON, . . . 1808.

Published concurrently with the previous impression. £1.11.6. Reported as 'very few Copies' (*MC*), 17 copies (BCL pencil note), or 25 copies in other references. Paper: Royal 8° (245 x 152mm cut). Watermarks: (a) white paper, unwatermarked or (b) cream paper: BUTTANSHAW | 1806; J WHATMAN | 1805 [1807]. Collation and pagination as for first impression. Typography: On page 463 Oxford rule begins to the right of N in EDINBURGH. Figures: As above, but without figures on pages 7 and 450.

Notes: Apparently there are two printings of this impression of undetermined order with gathering D printed on (a) white paper with figure 7 on page 52; (b) cream paper watermarked as described above and without figure. The variable figure also occurs in the regular paper impression.

Copies: (state a) E; IdU. (b) BCL L.

31Ac] Fourth (Second) Edition: 1809

MEMOIRS | OF | CAPT. GEORGE CARLETON, | AN ENGLISH OFFICER; | INCLUDING | ANECDOTES OF THE WAR IN SPAIN UNDER | THE EARL OF PETERBOROUGH, | AND | MANY INTERESTING PARTICULARS RELATING | TO THE MANNERS OF THE SPANIARDS IN THE BEGINNING OF THE LAST CENTURY. | [*short reversed Oxford rule*] | *WRITTEN BY HIMSELF*. | [*short reversed Oxford rule*] | FOURTH EDITION. | EDINBURGH: | [*short reversed Oxford rule*] PRINTED FOR ARCHIBALD CONSTABLE AND CO.,| EDINBURGH; J. MURRAY, AND | CONSTABLE, HUNTER, PARK & HUNTER, | LONDON. | [*dash*] | 1808.

Published 8 March 1809 in Edinburgh (*EWJ*); issued 20 June in London (*MC*). 12s.

Binding: green boards. Paper: Demy 8° (224 x 143mm uncut). Watermarks: D & A.C. | 1808. Collation: π^2 a^8 b^4 A-2F^8. Pagination: *1* half-title, *2 blank*, *3* title-page, *4 blank*, *i* ii-xv Preface, *xvi blank*, *xvii* xviii-xix dedication, *xx blank*, *xxi* xxii-xxiii To the Reader, *xxiv blank*, *1* 2-463 text, 463 printer's imprint, *464 blank*. Printer's imprint (1) and (2): [*short Oxford rule*] | EDINBURGH: | Printed by James Ballantyne & Co.

Figures: a ii-10 ix-2, b*xxi*-7/-, A7-2 16-8, B22-7 32-1, C34-10 36-12, D59-13 64-7, E79-11 80-2, F82-3, G98-1 112-11, H114-10, I 130-2 132-13, K148-11 154-3, L164-2 167-13, M179-7 181-3, N194-2, O 210-12 224-10, P226-2 229-8, Q243-3 256-7, R272-1, S285-2, T304-1, U306-2, X336-1, Y339-12 352-13, Z368-12, 2A 370-13 384-12, 2B 398-12 400-13, 2C 410-7 416-12, 2D 418-12 432-7, 2E 434-13 448-10, 2F 451-1 456-8.

Notes: A paginal reprint with a few alterations in accidentals. The sudden appearance of a 'fourth edition', without any intervening 'second' or 'third ', represents an early instance of Constable's desire to make a work appear to be more popular than the sales would indicate.

Copies: DN LU; CtY T/B TxU.

QUEENHOO-HALL

[The editing of this work] was a step in my advance towards romantic composition. . . . But I was, on the other hand, so far discouraged by the indifferent reception of Mr Strutt's romance, as to become satisfied that the manners of the middle ages did not possess the interest which I had conceived; and was led to form the opinion that a romance, founded on a Highland story, and more modern events [that is, *Waverley*], would have a better chance of popularity than a tale of chivalry. ('General Preface', 1 January 1829, *WN*, i.xvi-xvii.)

32Aa] First Edition, First Issue: 1808

QUEENHOO-HALL, | A Romance: | AND | ANCIENT TIMES, | A DRAMA. | [*short Oxford rule*] | BY THE LATE | JOSEPH STRUTT, | AUTHOR OF "RURAL SPORTS AND PASTIMES OF THE | PEOPLE OF ENGLAND," &c. | [*short reversed Oxford rule*] | IN FOUR VOLUMES. | VOL. I [II-IV]. | [*short French rule*] | EDINBURGH: | *Printed by James Ballantyne & Co.* | FOR JOHN MURRAY, FLEET-STREET, LONDON; | AND | ARCHIBALD CONSTABLE & CO. EDINBURGH. | [*dash*] | 1808.

Published June 1808 in London (*MM* 1 July). 16s. Binding: drab boards with printed labels or blue boards with cream backs and no labels. Paper: Foolscap 8° (172 x 103mm uncut). Watermarks: Title-leaves occasionally dated 1804, text D & A C | 1806. Typography: The printer's imprint reads invariably: [*short Oxford rule*] | EDINBURGH: | Printed by James Ballantyne & Co.

First Printings of Poetry: In Volume IV Scott included two new poems: (1) [untitled] (first words: 'Waken lords and ladies gay,'), pages 47-48, later titled 'Hunting Song' or 'Sheriff's Fancy'; (2) 'Bridal Song' (first words: 'And did you not hear of a mirth befel'), pages 76-77.

Notes: In an unsigned advertisement in Volume I Scott refers to his own role by stating that 'the tale is brought, by a literary friend, to a hasty conclusion. . . .' This haste is most evident in the last two chapters (Section VIII, Chapters IV and V: pages 43-59 and 60-79 respectively) which Scott supplied because the Strutt manuscript text was 'so indistinct and defaced, that, . . . we can pick out little that is intelligible. . . .' (Volume IV, page 74). Besides the poetry, Scott added two bracketted editorial comments. Consistent with his additions in other work, the editor early inquired of Ballantyne how far this new material extended in print, 'that I may not write more nonsense than enough.'

Copies: BCL E(3) L(2) O; CaBVaU CtY IdU NN(vols 2-4)* NNU-W OCl TxU. *With undated 8-page Constable catalogue.

References: Lockhart, iii.83-84; Ruff 77; Thomson, page 55. (Magnum Opus Edition 1829: chapters IV-V in *Waverley Novels*, i.lxv-xc.)

1] QUEENHOO-HALL, | A Romance: . . . VOL. I. . . . 1808.
Collation: π1 *a*[4] a[4] A-M[8] N[8](±N5) O-P[8] Q[8](-Q7,8+Q7). Pagination: *1* title-page, *2 blank*, *i* ii-vi Advertisement, dated from London, 1 April 1808, *vii* fly-title, *viii blank*, *i* ii-iv Preface, *v* vi-vii Contents, *viii blank*, *1* 2-253 text, 253 printer's imprint, *254 blank*. Typography: The first *a* signature is in italic.

Figures: *a* ii-12, a iv-5, A2-5, B18-1, C34-1, D50-2, E67-2, F82-5, G98-2, H114-2, I 130-2, K146-2, L162-2, M178-1, N194-2 201-7/-, O 210-2, P239-7, Q242-1.

Notes: The first cancellans N5 (pages 201-202) is in a variant state, in some copies carrying on recto the direction VOL. I. and press-figure 7, in others only the first or second of these indices. The later cancellanda (Q7,8), still retained in several copies, begins Chapter III of Section VI (pages 254-256), a passage transferred to volume 2, and replaced with a single leaf containing on recto (page 253) only the last three lines of Chapter II and the printer's imprint.

2] QUEENHOO-HALL, | A Romance: . . . VOL. II. . . . 1808.
Collation: π1 2π1 A-P[8] Q[4]. Pagination: *1* title-page, *2 blank*, *i*-ii Contents, *1* 2-247 text, 247 printer's imprint, *248 blank*.

Figures: A2-5 8-1, B18-1, C48-7, D50-10, E68-12, F82-2, G98-7 112-5, H114-7, I 130-1/- 144-4, K146-2, L162-2, M178-2, N194-5/-, O 210-1 224-4, P226-7, Q243-4.

3] QUEENHOO-HALL, | A Romance: . . . VOL. III. . . . 1808.
Collation: π1 2π1 A-P^8 Q1. Pagination: *1* title-page, *2 blank*, *i*-ii Contents, *1* 2-242 text, 242 printer's imprint.

Figures: A2-2, B18-1, C34-2 48-1, D64-11, E66-4, F82-1 84-4/-, G98-4 112-10, H127-7 128-10, I 130-5 144-7, K146-7 148-4, L162-2, M178-4 180-4/7, N194-4, O 210-4 224-7/-, P226-8, Q—.

4] QUEENHOO-HALL, | A Romance: . . . VOL. IV. . . . 1808.
Collation: π1 2π1 A-E^8 G-N^8 O^2. Pagination: *1* title-page, *2 blank*, *i* Contents, *ii blank*, *1* 2-79 text concluded, *80 blank*, *97* fly-title for 'Ancient Times, A Drama', *98 blank*, 99 Persons Represented, *100 blank*, 101-195 text, *196 blank*, *197* fly-title, *198 blank*, *199* 200-211 Glossary, 211 printer's imprint, *212 blank*.

Figures: A2-5, B18-4 32-11, C48-7, D50-11, E66-12/1/-, G99-5 112-1/-, H114-1 116-5, I 131-5 144-7, K146-5/- 160-11, L162-5 176-2, M178-10 192-2, N194-2 208-7, O—. Page 66 appears to exhibit the progressive elimination (or deterioration) of the figure during presswork.

Notes: Apparently the first text as reconstructed by Scott did not extend as far as expected, thus eliminating the need for sheet F (pages 81-96) in this volume. Meanwhile the printing of 'Ancient Times' had already begun with sheet G (page *97*) in accordance with the earlier estimate.

32Ab] First Edition, Second Issue: 1808

LITERARY RELIQUES | OF | JOSEPH STRUTT: | [*short rule*] | BEING | QUEENHOO-HALL, | A ROMANCE, | AND | ANCIENT TIMES, | A DRAMA. | [*short rule*] | IN FOUR VOLUMES. | [*short rule*] | VOL I [II-IV]. | LONDON: | [*short Oxford rule*] | PRINTED FOR JOHN MURRAY, FLEET-STREET, LONDON; | AND ARCHIBALD CONSTABLE & CO. | EDINBURGH. | [*dash*] | 1808.

Notes: This first lot of remainders, with cancel title-leaves, and a different title, probably was issued five months after original publication, since the variant title for this corresponds to item 46 in the undated Constable catalogue sometimes appended to the Carey *Memoirs* (34Aa), published 19 November 1808. Even with this more informative title, the work did not sell, as indicated in yet another reissue noted below.

Copy: DLC.

32Ac] Second Edition (First Edition, Third Issue): 1812

QUEENHOO-HALL, | A Romance: | AND | ANCIENT TIMES, | A DRAMA. | [*short double rule*] | BY THE LATE | JOSEPH STRUTT, | AUTHOR OF "RURAL SPORTS AND PASTIMES OF | THE PEOPLE OF ENGLAND," &c. | [*short reversed Oxford rule*] | IN FOUR VOLUMES. | VOL. I [II-IV]. | [*French dash*] | Second Edition. | [*rule*] | LONDON: | *Printed by John Dean, 7, Wardour Street, for* | T. MASON, NO. 5, CAMBRIDGE STREET, GOLDEN | SQUARE; MAY BE HAD OF ALL BOOKSELLERS. | [*dash*] | 1812.

Paper: (161 x 98mm cut). Watermarks: Title leaves may have a mark beginning 'J LAF[?]'

Notes: This last group of remainders, again with cancel title leaves, appeared four years after original issue, and now repeats the original title. The John Dean cited as printer was responsible only for the cancels.

Copy: ViU.

DERIVATIVES

GREAT BRITAIN

32Da] LEEDS: Blackburn 1824
['Waken, Lords and Ladies gay'. Leeds: Blackburn (1824). Notes: Music composed by G. F. Broadhead.] Copy: not seen. Reference: G/T 9904.

32Db] LONDON: D'Almaine 1821
The Falconer's Roundelay, Choral Glee The Poetry by Sir Walter Scott, . . . London D'Almaine & Co. Soho Square. Pages: *i-ii*, 1-11. [ca.1821]. Notes: Engraved sheet music with plate mark: 'The Falconer's Roundelay.' Words from 'The Hunting Song' (first words: 'Waken lords and ladies gay, / On the mountain dawns the day;'). Music composed by Henry R. Bishop arranged for voice and pianoforte. Price: [no price given after 'Pr.']. Copy: L.

EXTRACTS IN ANTHOLOGIES

32E] In *Queenhoo Hall* there are apparently no extracts of Scott's second song, but the first, usually titled 'Hunting Song', appears in nine anthologies: 356[2]E.12 369[3-4].12 392.11 397.2 405(3)[1].11 413.7 415.1 423.3.

ILLUSTRATIONS

OF

WALTER SCOTT's

LAY OF THE LAST MINSTREL:

CONSISTING

OF TWELVE VIEWS

ON THE RIVERS

BOTHWICK, ETTRICK, YARROW, TIVIOT, AND TWEED.

ENGRAVED BY JAMES HEATH, R. A. FROM DESIGNS TAKEN ON THE SPOT

BY JOHN C. SCHETKY, OF OXFORD.

WITH

ANECDOTES AND DESCRIPTIONS.

LONDON:

PRINTED FOR LONGMAN, HURST, REES, AND ORME, PATERNOSTER ROW.

1808.

ENTRY 33Aa. THE TODD / BOWDEN COPY
(illustration reduced)

ILLUSTRATIONS OF LAY OF THE LAST MINSTREL

33Aa] First Edition: 1808

ILLUSTRATIONS | OF | WALTER SCOTT's | LAY OF THE LAST MINSTREL: | CONSISTING | OF TWELVE VIEWS | ON THE RIVERS | BOTHWICK, ETTRICK, YARROW, TIVIOT, AND TWEED. | ENGRAVED BY JAMES HEATH, R.A. FROM DESIGNS TAKEN ON THE SPOT | By JOHN C. SCHETKY, of Oxford. | [*short French rule*] | WITH | ANECDOTES AND DESCRIPTIONS. | [*vignette*] | LONDON: | PRINTED FOR LONGMAN, HURST, REES, AND ORME, PATER NOSTER ROW. | [*dash*] | 1808.

<SEE ACCOMPANYING ILLUSTRATION>

Published 7 September 1808 in London (*MC*). £1.11.6. Binding: blue-green or drab boards. Paper: Royal 4° (290 x 225mm uncut). Watermarks: *none* (π, H4); J Whatman | 1805 (2π); D & AC | 1808 | 10 (A-G, H1-3). Collation: π1 2π^2 A-G^4 H^4(±H4). Pagination: *i* title-page, *ii* printer's imprint(1), *iii* dedication (by Schetky) to the Duchess of Buccleuch, *iv blank, v* Advertisement, *vi blank, 1* 2-64 text, 64 engraved tailpiece and printer's imprint(2). Printer's imprints: (1) [*short reversed Oxford rule*] | The Title and Vignette printed by J. M'Creery, | The other Part of the Work by J. Ballantyne and Co. Edinburgh.; (2) [*short reversed Ox-ford rule*] | This leaf printed by J. M'Creery, | Fleet-street, London. Illustrations: Title-vignette, the Scott coat of arms surmounting a recumbent dog; tailpiece, The Last Minstrel; twelve plates, each with caption and facing the descriptive text page [in brackets below], all with Longman, Hurst, Rees, & Orme imprint dated 7 June 1808. It should be noted that the captions below are those given below the plate, not the slightly variant text heading adjacent to the illustration:

(1) [*1*] Newark Tower
(2) [5] Branksome Hall
(3) [11] The Lands of Delorain
(4) [13] The Peel of Goldieland
(5) [15] Hawick
(6) [19] Melrose Abbey
(7) [27] The Eildon Hills from Bowden Moor
(8) [29] Dryhope Tower, St. Mary's Lake
(9) [35] St. Mary's Loch from the Lowes
(10) [39] Wat of Harden's Den
(11) [45] Hermitage Castle
(12) [57] Naworth Castle

Figures: A2-2, B11-13, C24-11, D27-3, E34-3, F42-2, G50-10, H58-13.

Notes: Evidently Scott was early acquainted with young Schetky, also born in Edinburgh and seven years his junior, in 1808 corresponded with him on the subject of these illustrations, arranged with his own printer for the letterpress text and, it may be supposed, secured from his confidant the Duchess her permission for the dedication of the work. Nonetheless, Scott on 9 June, though admitting authorship of the text, advised the Longman firm that the artist should acknowledge only 'further anecdotes traditional and historical' (*Letters*, xii.396); but the newspaper announcements declare that the 'Descriptions and Annotations' are indeed by Scott and, in his own Advertisement, Schetky himself reported that the poet had 'obligingly revised the whole' as well. The Schetky portfolio, based upon the actual landscape, precedes by more than a year the Westall illustrations for *The Lay* and *Marmion* (14Dm, 28Dt), both figments of the artist's imagination and, without Scott's assistance, published concurrently on 17 November 1809.

Scott's collaboration with Schetky is also evident in the ingenious title vignette design, the only one in this bibliography representing his motto and coat of arms, these gracefully poised, it seems, above old Camp, his bull terrier (d. 1809). Both this first decorative leaf and the last, as the printer's imprints declare, were printed in London and on better quality paper. 'Proof Impressions' of the plates only (not located) were also listed at £2.12.6.

Copies: BCL E; CtY(2) IdU* InU NNU-W T/B TxU(2).
*Bound with *The Lay of the Last Minstrel*, eighth edition 1808, Berwick copy (*see* 14Al).

References: Corson(2), page 42. (Magnum Opus Edition: Not reprinted.) For the coat of arms compare the illustrations in 1871 Exhibit, page 200, and Ian Gordon Brown, page 38, both of these in the later state (1820, post baronetcy) with supporters.

33Ab] Second Edition: 1810

ILLUSTRATIONS | OF | WALTER SCOTT's | LAY OF THE LAST MINSTREL: | CONSISTING | OF TWELVE VIEWS | ON THE RIVERS | BOTHWICK, ETTRICK, YARROW, TIVIOT, AND TWEED. | ENGRAVED | BY J. HEATH, R.A. FROM DESIGNS TAKEN ON THE SPOT | BY JOHN C. SCHETKY, OF OXFORD. | [*short French rule*] | WITH | ANECDOTES AND DESCRIPTIONS. | [*vignette*] | LONDON: | PRINTED FOR LONGMAN, HURST, REES, AND ORME, | PATERNOSTER-ROW. | [*dash*] | 1810.

10s.6d. Binding: drab boards. Paper: Royal 8° (230 x 140mm uncut). Watermarks: 1802. Collation: A^2 B-E^8 F^2. Pagination: *i* half-title, *ii blank, iii* title-page, *iv* printer's imprint(1), *1* dedication, *2 blank, 3* Advertisement, *4 blank, 5* 6-68 text, 68 printer's imprint(2). Printer's imprints: (1) [*short Oxford rule*] | J. M'CREERY, Printer, | Black Horse Court, London.; (2) [*short reversed Oxford rule*] | J. M'Creery, Printer, | Black Horse-Court, London. Illustrations: As in first edition, title vignette and tailpiece, with the twelve re-engraved plates now imprinted 1 January 1810 and facing pages *5*, 9, 15, 17, 19, 23, 31, 33, 39, 43, 49, 61. Typography: The second leaf in each gathering is also signed, according to M'Creery's practice. Figures: *none*.

Copies: E*; CtY DLC InU T/B.
*With 16-page Longman catalogue 'Corrected to March 1810'.

MEMOIRS OF ROBERT CARY

Memoirs are the materials, and often the touchstone, of history; and even where they descend to incidents beneath her notice, they aid the studies of the antiquary and the moral philosopher. While, therefore, it is to be regretted, that the reserved temper of our nation has generally deterred our soldiers and statesmen from recording their own story, an attempt to preserve, explain, or render more generally accessible the works which we possess of this nature, seems to have some claim upon public favour. ('Advertisement', page vi.)

34Aa] First Scott Edition, First Impression: 1808

MEMOIRS | OF | **ROBERT CARY,** | EARL OF MONMOUTH. | WRITTEN BY HIMSELF. | [*Oxford dash*] | AND | FRAGMENTA REGALIA; | BEING | *A HISTORY* | OF | QUEEN ELIZABETH'S FAVOURITES. | BY | SIR ROBERT NAUNTON. | WITH EXPLA NATORY ANNOTATIONS. | [*short reversed Oxford rule*] | EDINBURGH: | PRINTED BY JAMES BALLANTYNE AND CO. | FOR ARCHIBALD CONSTABLE AND CO. EDINBURGH, | AND JOHN MURRAY, LONDON. | [*dash*] | 1808.

Published 19 November 1808 in Edinburgh (*EEC*); issued 3 December in London (*MC*). 10s.6d. Paper: Demy 8° (226 x 147mm uncut). Watermarks: D & A C | 1808. Collation: π^4 a-b^8 A-T^8. Pagination: *i* half-title, *ii blank*, *iii* title-page, *iv blank*, *v*-vi Advertisement (by Scott), *vii*-viii Contents, *ix* x-xxxviii Preface (by the first editor, The Earl of Corke), *xxxix* fly-title for the *Memoirs*, *xl blank*, *1* 2-162 text, *163* 164-167 Appendix, *168 blank*, *169* fly-title for the *Fragmenta Regalia*, *170 blank*, *171* 172- 301 text, 301 printer's imprint, *302-304 blank.* Printer's imprint: [*short Oxford rule*] | EDINBURGH: | Printed by James Ballantyne & Co.

Figures: a x-12 xxiv-13, b xxvi-7 xxxvii-8, A3-13, B18-2, C34-8/-, D50-2, E66-2, F82-1, G106-4 112-5, H114-2, I 130-13 144-1, K146-2, L176-5, M178-13 192-5, N194-11 196-8, O 210-7 224-8, P226-7 240-5, Q242-8 256-5, R258-11 272-5, S274-12 288-11, T290-11 296-7.

Notes: As augmented by Scott, this account proved to be very informative, covering the period 1577-1626, and thus including some notice of the 1588 Spanish Armada, affairs on the Scottish border, the death of Elizabeth and the accession of James I.
The spelling of the author's surname varies: Cary on title-page and headlines,

but Carey (correctly) in text, Appendix, &c. Scott's unsigned Advertisement in this work declares that, 'The original edition [published by R. and J. Dodsley, 1759] having now become very scarce, it is presumed that a new impression will be acceptable to the public. Several additions . . . are distinguished by the letter E' [Editor]. Actually for the *Memoirs* there are 207 notes, 55 of them so marked, and for the accompanying *Fragmenta* another 47, all unmarked.

As an historical 'touchstone' Scott had already cited this work at length, first in his 1802 *Minstrelsy of the Scottish Border* (*see* 8Aa.1), then 1805 in *The Lay of the Last Minstrel* (*see* 14Ab)—both works now in these 1808 *Memoirs* noted also as direct references (pages 45-46, 98-99, 108-109). In anticipation of other editions perhaps already contemplated he also twice refers to the *Memoirs* of the Duke of Sully (pages 39, 41: *see* 48A, 1810) and to Osborne's *Secret History of the Court of James the First* (pages 128, 134-135, 158: *see* 56Aa, 1811). Both Osborne and Anthony Weldon are here eventually characterised as 'scandalous authors' (page 294).

Copies: DN E O; CtY* DLC InU NN OCl* PU T/B TxU*.
*With undated 8-page Constable list.

Reference: (Magnum Opus Edition: Not reprinted.)

34Ab] First Scott Edition, Second (Large-Paper) Impression: 1808

MEMOIRS | OF | **ROBERT CARY,** | EARL OF MONMOUTH. . . . 1808.

Published concurrently with the previous impression. £1.5.0. Paper: Royal 8° (235 x 142mm cut). Watermarks: BUTTANSHAW | 1806.

Figures: As above, but without figures on pages 112 and 296.

Copy: IdU(Andrew Fletcher of Saltoun).

PROSPECTUS FOR THE EDINBURGH ANNUAL REGISTER

35A] First Edition: 1808

'PROSPECTUS', pages *v* vi-xii, *in*:

The Edinburgh Annual Register, for 1808. Vol. First—Part First. Edinburgh: Printed by James Ballantyne and Co. For John Ballantyne and Co. Edinburgh; Longman, Hurst, Rees, and Orme; Cadell and Davies; William Miller; John Murray; and Robert Scholey, London. 1810.

Figure: vi-5.

Notes: Issued (1) separately on 9 December 1808 (Corson[2], page 45) and (2) reset(?) as noted above, for inclusion in volume 1 of the *Register*, published after some delay on 6 August 1810 (*see* 51A). The preliminary Advertisement in (2) offers apologies for the delay in issue and indicates various deviations from the original plan as described in the Prospectus, i.e. the omission of essays on morality, literature, and science, as well as articles on biography, the useful arts, and meteorology. The notice serves as a forerunner of an extensive enterprise always somewhat deficient in content, delayed in issue and, eventually, a financial disaster.

On 18 November 1808 Scott promised Ellis a copy of this announcement and, a month later, conceded that the text had perhaps 'too stately a tone'. James Ballantyne, nominally the editor, 'only undertakes for the inferior departments of the work, and for keeping the whole matter in train.' Scott's influence over this publication, now regarded as paramount over the first nine years, still cannot be precisely measured. Beyond doubt, however, the Prospectus may be recognized as primarily, if not entirely his work.

Copies: (issue 1) not seen. (2) E; NN.

References: *Letters*, ii.129, 140, 144; Curry, pages 31-38. (Magnum Opus Edition: Not reprinted, but entire prospectus quoted in Curry, pages *51* 52-60.)

REVIEWS OF BURNS, SOUTHEY, BARRETT, AND CARR

36A] First Printings: 1809

1] 'ART. II. *Reliques of Robert Burns*, . . . Collected and published by R. H. Cromek', pages 19-36;

2] 'ART. XIII. *Chronicle of the Cid* Rodrigo Diaz de Bivar, *the Campeador, from the Spanish,* By Robert Southey', pages 134-153;

3] 'ART. XV. *An Essay on the earlier part of the Life of Swift, by the Rev. John Barrett',* pages 162-177, *and*

4] 'ART. XVI. *Caledonian Sketches, or a Tour through Scotland in* 1807. . . . *By* Sir John Carr', pages 178-193, *in*:

The Quarterly Review. February, 1809. [No.1: volume 1 imprint:] London: Printed by C. Roworth, Bell-yard, Temple-bar; For John Murray, 32, Fleet Street; Hatchard, Piccadilly; Richardson, Cornhill; and John Ballantyne and Co. Edinburgh.

Published 1 March 1809 in London (*MC*; prematurely announced for 23 January in *MLA*); issued 9 March in Edinburgh (*EEC*). 5s.

Notes: As one of the founders of the *Quarterly Review*, Scott here makes a number of significant and highly diverse contributions to the inaugural number. His severe critique of [3], not later reprinted, was undoubtedly influenced by his own research, just now underway, for a complete life and works of Swift (where, nonetheless, in 1814, Scott admits some indebtedness to Barrett [*see* 79Aa, textual notes]). In this 1809 review there are slighting references only (pages 176, 177) to Edmond Malone, whose new 1808 edition Scott was adopting as his primary text, and to John Nichols, Malone's publisher. As noted by Shine, William Gifford, the general editor, supplemented Scott's commentary in article [4].

Copies: BCL L O; PPL(2) TxU. Reissued 1810 as a 'Second Edition' (L).

References: Shine 2, 13, 15, 16. (Magnum Opus Edition 1834-1835: *The Miscellaneous Prose Works*, [1] xvii.242-266 as 'Reliques of Burns', [2] xviii.44-73 as 'Southey's Chronicle of the Cid', [3] Not reprinted, but see *Letters*, ii.157, 161, 200n, [4] xix.160-184 as 'Carr's Caledonian Sketches'.)

THE WORKS OF JAMES THOMSON

37A] Projected Scott Edition: 1809

Notes: James Ballantyne was interested in a Thomson edition as early as 1802 and some further discusson involving Scott is recorded in 1805, but a public notice does not appear until 1808 when, in its section on 'Scottish Literary Intelligence' the *Scots Magazine* for July (page 519) advised its readers that 'Mr Walter Scott will soon present the public with a new edition of the works of Thomson, in three volumes octavo. It will be accompanied by a life of the author, of which little seems hitherto to have been discovered, and which Mr Scott's local connections may be supposed to render him well qualified for illustrating. In particular, it will contain a number of original letters hitherto unknown to the public, which we understand he has been fortunate enough to procure.' Scott's publisher soon realized, however, that Thomson had long been appearing, sometimes twice a year, with editions both of the *Poetical Works* and *The Seasons* in 1808 (the very time of this announcement) and yet another edition of *The Seasons* in 1809, all with an introductory life either by Patrick Murdock or Samuel Johnson. Nonetheless, perhaps at Scott's urging, John Ballantyne had his brother James publish on 16 March 1809 at 5s (*EEC*) yet another pretty little foolscap single-volume edition of *The Seasons*, with vignette title, ten woodcuts in Bewick style, and a preliminary memoir unattributed, but immediately recognized as also from Johnson. The few brief notes in this can hardly be ascribed to Scott, and there is no further mention of the 'original letters' he supposedly 'procured'. Quite possibly this correspondence and other unpublished material was then or later secured by the Earl of Buchan, who is the acknowledged source of the original Thomson printing 1827 in Goodhugh, pages 256-294.

SOMERS' TRACTS

There is, indeed, no repository of fugitive pieces which rivals [the Somers' Tracts] in variety, extent, and importance, excepting the Harleian Miscellany; and it would be difficult to draw a parallel between these celebrated collections. If the Harleian Miscellany exhibits a more curious assortment of ancient pamphlets, and, in general, a greater variety of miscellaneous information, the present work may boast of containing a greater selection of tracts immediately connected with English history, and with English politics. Indeed from the reign of Elizabeth down to that of Queen Anne, the tracts upon all controversies, civil and religious, are so numerous and well selected, that, if the Harleian Miscellany afford most amusement to the antiquary, it may be safely said, that Somers' Tracts promise most information to the historian. . . .

The Editor has only further to hope, that the circumstance of his name having been prefixed to works of a lighter and more popular nature, will not be objected to him as a personal disqualification for his present task. The Muse (to use the established language) found him engaged in the pursuit of historical and traditional antiquities, and the excursions which he has made in her company, have been of a nature which increases his attachment to his original study. ('Advertisement', pages ii, iv.)

38A] First Scott Edition: 1809-1815

A | COLLECTION | OF | SCARCE AND VALUABLE | **TRACTS,** | ON THE MOST | INTERESTING AND ENTERTAINING SUBJECTS: | BUT CHIEFLY SUCH AS RELATE TO THE | *HISTORY AND CONSTITUTION* | OF | THESE KINGDOMS. | SELECTED FROM AN INFINITE NUMBER IN PRINT AND MANUSCRIPT, IN THE ROYAL, | COTTON, SION, AND OTHER PUBLIC, AS WELL AS PRIVATE, LIBRARIES; | PARTICULARLY | THAT OF THE LATE LORD SOMERS. | [*short Oxford rule*] | THE SECOND EDITION, | REVISED, AUGMENTED, AND ARRANGED, | BY | WALTER SCOTT, Esq. | [*short reversed Oxford rule*] | VOLUME FIRST [SECOND-THIRTEENTH]. | [*two quotations in three lines*] | LONDON: | [*Oxford dash*] | PRINTED FOR T. CADELL AND W. DAVIES, STRAND; | W. MILLER, ALBEMARLE-STREET; | R. H. EVANS, PALL-MALL; J. WHITE AND J. MURRAY, FLEET-STREET; | AND J. HARDING, ST JAMES'S-STREET. | 1809 [1810-1815].

<SEE ACCOMPANYING ILLUSTRATION>

Paper: Royal 4° (312 x 248mm. uncut). Watermarks: Volumes 1-8: 1806; 1806 [1807, 1809] | I I S; 1807 / 1807; 1809 / 1809; 1809 [1810, 1811] | I I Smith [I I SMITH]; 1811 / 1811; W & S | 1803 / 1803 (3: 2O-3Q only, in some copies).

A

COLLECTION

OF

SCARCE AND VALUABLE

TRACTS,

ON THE MOST

INTERESTING AND ENTERTAINING SUBJECTS:

BUT CHIEFLY SUCH AS RELATE TO THE

HISTORY AND CONSTITUTION

OF

THESE KINGDOMS.

SELECTED FROM AN INFINITE NUMBER IN PRINT AND MANUSCRIPT, IN THE ROYAL, COTTON, SION, AND OTHER PUBLIC, AS WELL AS PRIVATE, LIBRARIES;

PARTICULARLY

THAT OF THE LATE LORD SOMERS.

THE SECOND EDITION,

REVISED, AUGMENTED, AND ARRANGED,

BY

WALTER SCOTT, Esq.

VOLUME FIRST.

The bent and genius of the age is best known in a free country, by the pamphlets and papers that come daily out, as the sense of parties, and sometimes the voice of the nation. PREFACE TO KENNET'S REGISTER.

Judex qui aliquid statuit, una parte audita tantum et inaudita altera, licet æquum statuerit, haud æquus fuerit. LD. COOK & JUST. INST.

LONDON:

PRINTED FOR T. CADELL AND W. DAVIES, STRAND;
W. MILLER, ALBEMARLE-STREET;
R. H. EVANS, PALL-MALL; J. WHITE AND J. MURRAY, FLEET-STREET;
AND J. HARDING, ST JAMES'S-STREET.

1809.

ENTRY 38A. THE BRITISH LIBRARY (L 750.g.1)
(illustration reduced)

Volumes 9-13: J WHATMAN | 1810; 1811 / 1811; 1812 / 1812; 1814 / 1814; 1814 / I I S; 1808 or 1809 (odd sheets in 9, 11, 12).

General Notes: On 8 April 1808 the publisher William Miller first proposed to Scott a new edition of Somers and intimated that Ballantyne might be pleased to have this extensive printing job. The general plan of the work was then outlined to the present Lord Somers on 4 July and a preliminary announcement made in the *Scots Magazine* for that month, page 519.

Meanwhile on 29 June, when the three London publishing firms first cited in the imprint advertised this Scott work as already 'In the press' (*MC*), a further notice just below, provided by Murray and Harding, cited another issue of Somers in twelve volumes, by an unidentified editor, as also in preparation. If the second notice is not a misprint, then evidently an accomodation was soon made in this editorial jurisdiction, and White, Murray, and Harding went on to announce on 4 August (*MC*) the first of ten volumes, augmented by Thomas Park, of *The Harleian Miscellany*. Thereafter, on 30 October, Scott advised Miller that on the verso of his letter 'you will find all that I think it necessary to say by way of advertisement concerning Somers' Tracts', but a printing of this prospectus, if issued, has not been located.

At 'the expense of some time and labour' Scott in his edition 'revised, augmented, and arranged' systematically the random selections previously issued, four volumes at a time, in 1747-1748, 1750, 1751, 1751-52, and a further selection chronologically ordered and published in 1795. As for Somers' earlier editors, so for Scott, the justification for such a massive undertaking was expressed in the first title-quotation (from the preface to Kennet's *Register*): 'The bent and genius of the age is best known in a free country, by the pamphlets and papers that come daily out, as the sense of parties, and sometimes the voice of the nation.' Judging by the final paragraph in his lengthy Advertisement, cited above in the epigraph, it would appear that Scott in 1809 now regarded historical scholarship as his primary concern and poetry an occasional diversion. Shortly after embarking upon his historical fiction Scott also observed that the Somers project especially made him 'wonderfully well acquainted' with these earlier periods. (*Letters*, v.56.)

To the previous collection of some 882 tracts Scott added another 81 considered to be especially relevant, and extensively annotated the entire edition. All of the 963 pieces now recognized are conveniently listed alphabetically by title in the London Library *Catalogue*, ii.947-959, a reference based upon the Table of Contents. (Another two titles, there overlooked, are cited below in the notes to volumes 10 and 13.) Scott's own additions to the original collection, starred in each Table of Contents and noted below in the volume descriptions, sometimes range well beyond a hundred pages (see note to volume 3 below), but more often are of considerably less extent. After all these had been entered 1809-1812 in the first eight volumes, however, the editor found it unnecessary—or too wearying—to add any more in the five volumes remaining 1813-1815. By the later time, probably, his energies were more inclined to *Waverley* and other immediate interests. Some evidence of this inattention begins to appear in the ninth volume of 1813 and is noticeable thereafter.

Less obvious, and thus cited all together in the following 'Record', are the numerous quotations extracted, often in lengthy head or footnotes, from the various works which Scott himself had just edited or intended to publish. Some of these references are ambiguously identified, others allude only to 'the last editor', and none mention Scott directly; but all discreetly testify to his further involvement in this extraordinary enterprise.

RECORD OF SCOTT EDITIONS CITED IN SOMERS.

The first date is that of Scott's own edition. References in Somers predating this issue are within brackets, with the date of Scott's earlier copytext cited whenever given. It will be noted that while his Herbert and Sadler editions (1809) were published after their citation in his early Somers volumes, certain works such as the *Secret History* (1811, section 1) eventually achieved issue before Scott had issued a later volume.

1808 Dryden, *Works* (30Aa): vi.478; viii.222, 327.
1808 Carleton, *Memoirs* (31Aa): xiii.417.
1808 Carey, *Memoirs* (34Aa): i.445; ii.223.
1809 Herbert of Cherbury, *Life* (40A): [ii.188-190].
1809 Sadler, *State Papers* (41Aa): [i.481].
1811 *Secret History . . . of James the First* (56Aa), 4 sections:
(1) Osborne: [ii.146-147,154,210,223,224(1689), 472; iii.560(1673); iv.146]; vii.83.
(2) Weldon: [ii.275-276, 281, 282, 285, 334, 418-419, 491, 504(1689); v.442].
(3) 'Aulicus Coquinariae': [ii.285, 298-299, 332(1650); v.443].
(4) 'The Court and Kitchin of . . . Joan Cromwel': [vi.421]; vii.53.
1813 Warwick, *Memoirs* (65Aa): [iv.106, 257, 367, 446, 447, 448; v.198 (1701), 211; vi.427; vii.97].
1813 Reresby, *Memoirs* (66A, projected edition): [iii.121; viii.110, 337(1735-1738), 338].
1814 Swift, *Works* (79Aa): xi.513; xiii.86-87, 120-121, 818.

As would appear from this list, Scott's research for the Somers papers may well have persuaded him to edit, as immediately relevant and deserving of separate issue, some of the works here identified.

Copies: AN BCL E(vols 1-7, 9-12) GU L(3) LU O O (Earl of Minto) P+; CtY OCl NN PPL RPB T/B(William Sturges-Bourne).
+With extra leaf following index volume 1 announcing the Thomas Park edition, first two volumes, of the *Harleian Miscellany*.

References: *Letters*, ii.45n.1, 77-79, 112. (Magnum Opus Edition. Not reprinted.)

1] A | COLLECTION | OF | SCARCE AND VALUABLE | **TRACTS,** . . . VOLUME FIRST. . . . 1809.

Announced March 1809 as then published in London (*MLA*), and a copy then sent 1 March to Robert Southey (*Letters*, ii.170). £3.3.0. Collation: π^2 a^4 A-C^4 D^4(±D4) E-G^4 H^4(±H4) I-$4K^4$. Pagination: *1* half-title, *2* printer's imprint(1), *3* title-page, *4 blank, i* ii-iv Advertisement (by Scott), dated from Edinburgh 1 January 1809, *v* vi-viii Table of Contents [King John-Elizabeth], *1* fly-title, *2 blank, 3* 4-621 text, *622 blank, 623* 624-631 Index, 631 printer's imprint (2), *632 blank*. Printer's imprints (1) and (2): [*short double rule*] | EDINBURGH: | Printed by James Ballantyne & Co. Illustrations: Eight folded woodcut engravings by John Derrick labelled to face pages 592, 593, 594, 596, 598, 601, 602, and 612 were prepared later, and thus are occasionally bound at the end of volume 2, or omitted. Scott's first reference to these curious prints occurs in a note to page 584, and a detailed analysis is offered by Corson(2), page 58. Typography: Signature 2Z (page 361) is missigned 2Y.

Figures: a vii-2/- viii-8, A5-7 7-1, B15-7 16-12, C22-11 24-12, D30-2 32-12, E39-7 40-11, F46-11 48-12, G50-12 52-2, H62-13 64-8, I 67-2/- 72-11, K75-8 76-13, L82-11 85-12, M90-7 93-12, N99-8 104-4, O 106-3 112-4, P114-11 117-13, Q122-1/- 128-3, R131-8 136-11, S142-13 144-4, T146-13 152-11, U155-11 157-4, X168-3, Y175-8, Z180-2, 2A 192-3, 2B 198-7 200-10, 2C 202-3 205-12, 2D 211-8 216-11, 2E 218-8 224-11, 2F 226-13 232-12, 2G 234-11, 2H 242-8 248-3, 2 I 251-4 256-7, 2K 258-8 264-13, 2L 266-7 272-11, 2M 274-1 276-8, 2N 287-7 288-2, 2 O 290-12 293-8, 2P 304-8, 2Q 306-11 312-13, 2R 316-11, 2S 325-11 326-3, 2T 330-10 336-3, 2U 339-3 340-12, 2X 346-11 352-8, 2Y 355-7 360-11, 2Z 364-1, 3A 375-11 376-12, 3B 384-8, 3C 386-1, 3D 394-2 400-12, 3E 405-11, 3F 410-2 416-11, 3G 419-7 420-3, 3H 427-12 432-8, 3 I 434-3 440-12, 3K 447-12 448-13, 3L 455-7 456-1, 3M 463-10 464-13, 3N 467-11 472-1, 3 O 478-1 480-11, 3P 482-13 488-2, 3Q 494-2, 3R—, 3S 506-8 508-7, 3T 520-11, 3U 525-13 526-7, 3X 530-11 536-7, 3Y 543-3 544-2/-, 3Z 546-11 549-7, 4A 559-13 560-2, 4B 562-11 568-13, 4C 570-8 576-11, 4D 578-2 580-13, 4E 592-7, 4F 596-11 599-7, 4G 608-2, 4H 611-1 616-8, 4 I 619-8 624-2, 4K 628-8.

Notes: The first section, titled 'Tracts prior to the reign of Queen Elizabeth', extends only to page 57. In this volume Scott provides two commentaries from his own editions (as noted above) and adds six tracts. In the OCl copy, which retains both variants, leaf D4 page 32 has (a) in uncanceled state, press figure 12; (b) in corrected or canceled state, no figure but the additional headline 'HENRY VIII.' Leaf H4 page 63 line 9 reads (a) in uncanceled state 'unmundfull', page 64 no press figure; (b) in canceled state 'unmindfull', page 64 figure 8.

2] A | COLLECTION | OF | SCARCE AND VALUABLE | **TRACTS,** . . . VOLUME SECOND. . . . 1809.

Published October 1809 in London (*MM* 1 November). £3.3.0. Collation: π^2 (π2+1) A-$4H^4$ *4I*1. Pagination: *i* half-title, *ii* printer's imprint(1), *iii* title-page, *iv blank, v*-vi Table of Contents [James I], *1* fly-title, *2 blank, 3* 4-608 text, *609* 610-617 Index,

617 printer's imprint(2), *618 blank*. Printer's imprints: (1) [*short Oxford rule*] | Printed by James Ballantyne & Co. | Edinburgh.; (2) [*short Oxford rule*] | EDINBURGH: | Printed by James Ballantyne & Co. Illustrations: An engraved facsimile plate of a 1651 title faces page 262. Typography: In the title imprint the period before MURRAY is very faint or not present. Signature K (page 73) is missigned H and 4G (page 601) is missigned 4E. Also, in some copies, signature F (page 41) is missigned E.

Figures: A8-10, B16-3, C21-2 23-13, D28-12 31-3, E34-5 40-1, F47-7 48-6, G51-2 52-7, H64-7, I 68-13 70-12, K74-8, L82-2 88-1, M95-11 96-6, N99-6 101-11, O 110-3 112-12, P118-8 120-7, Q122-5 125-3, R134-8, S144-8, T146-8, U158-7 160-8, X167-2 168-7, Y170-5 176-2, Z178-5 184-8, 2A 189-8/- 190-11, 2B 200-11, 2C 205-7, 2D 214-11, 2E 223-1, 2F 226-1, 2G 240-11, 2H 242-10 244-13, 2 I 250-5 256-11, 2K 258-1, 2L 267-2, 2M 278-11, 2N 284-11, 2 O 294-11, 2P 298-7 301-13, 2Q 306-10 312-1, 2R 314-5 317-12, 2S 323-13 328-11, 2T 333-13/- 334-12, 2U 341-5, 2X 348-12, 2Y—, 2Z 362-12 368-13, 3A 370-11, 3B 378-13 384-5, 3C 386-10, 3D 400-10, 3E 408-11, 3F 412-12, 3G 421-10 422-1, 3H 426-1 432-11, 3 I 434-5 440-1, 3K 442-13 448-7, 3L 456-13, 3M 462-13 464-8, 3N 472-5, 3 O 479-2, 3P 488-11, 3Q 490-10 493-12, 3R 499-11 504-13, 3S 511-13 512-10, 3T 514-11 517-1, 3U 522-1 524-11, 3X 535-5 536-13, 3Y 538-10 541-13, 3Z 548-13 551-5, 4A 556-11 558-3, 4B 562-10 565-8, 4C 570-2 576-5, 4D 580-12 582-7, 4E 586-5 589-3, 4F 594-5 600-11, 4G 607-3 608-11, 4H 611-13, *4I* 617-1.

Notes: Since the reign of the Stuarts comes closer to his own interests, Scott provides for this volume no fewer than twenty-four commentaries from his own editions and adds eleven tracts.

3] A | COLLECTION | OF | SCARCE AND VALUABLE | **TRACTS,** . . . VOLUME THIRD. . . . 1810.

Published 9 March 1810 in London (*MC*). £3.3.0. Collation: π^2(π2+1[=4M4]) A-4M^4(-4M4). Pagination: *i* half-title, *ii* printer's imprint(1), *iii* title-page, *iv blank*, *v* Table of Contents [James I, continued], *vi blank*, *1* fly-title, *2 blank*, *3* 4-635 text, *636 blank*, *637* 638-645 Index, 645 printer's imprint(2), *646 blank*. Printer's imprints: (1) [*short Oxford rule*] | Printed by James Ballantyne & Co. | Edinburgh.; (2) [*short Oxford rule*] | EDINBURGH: | Printed by James Ballantyne & Co. Typography: In some copies page 521 is misnumbered 52.

Figures: A8-12, B10-8 16-13, C18-5 20-12, D26-10 32-11, E40-10, F42-10, G50-10 52-12, H59-8 64-6, I 67-10 72-11, K80-5, L82-5, M91-5, N98-5 101-3, O 109-8 111-13, P118-11 120-12, Q125-8 126-12, R131-7 132-5, S144-13, T151-10 152-13/-, U159-5, X166-8, Y170-12 176-5, Z178-8, 2A 188-3 191-13/-, 2B 196-13, 2C 205-7 206-11, 2D 211-4 216-10, 2E 218-4, 2F 226-4, 2G 240-4, 2H 244-2 246-7, 2 I 254-12, 2K 263-2, 2L 271-13, 2M 274-4 276-8, 2N 286-13, 2 O 290-11, 2P 300-11,

2Q 306-7 312-3, 2R 319-13, 2S 327-12, 2T 331-12 336-8, 2U 340-12, 2X 347-12 352-8, 2Y 354-7 360-2, 2Z 362-8 368-4, 3A 370-5 372-9, 3B 383-5, 3C 392-5, 3D 394-4, 3E 403-4, 3F 413-4, 3G 418-4, 3H—, 3 I 439-8, 3K 443-8, 3L 450-8, 3M 464-9, 3N 472-9, 3 O 479-9, 3P 488-11, 3Q 490-13 496-11, 3R 498-11 500-4, 3S 510-4 512-13, 3T 515-9 517-14, 3U 528-11, 3X 534-14, 3Y 538-3, 3Z 546-4, 4A 557-14, 4B 562-9 564-12, 4C 575-9 576-11, 4D 580-9, 4E 589-9 591-4, 4F 595-5 597-14, 4G 607-9 608-11, 4H 610-14 616-12, 4 I 624-14, 4K 629-14, 4L *637*-1 639-14, 4M 642-7 644-15.

Notes: In this further volume relating to James I, Scott provides two commentaries from his own editions and adds seven tracts, including, without sufficient justification (pages 403-551), a late 1599 edition (STC 24385.5 or 24386) of Tusser's *Five Hundred Pointes of good Husbandrie*. Shortly thereafter Sir Egerton Brydges reprinted the first edition (1557, the last year of Mary's reign, STC 24372: this printing in volume 3 of his *British Bibliography* 1812, 200 copies 8°, 120 copies 4°), noting there in his preface of 28 March 1810 the Scott issue and another forthcoming from William Mavor. In the latter, 'variorum' edition of 1812, Mavor abruptly dismisses as irrelevant Scott's 1599 text (page 21n): 'This edition by Short, which is extremely incorrect, is foisted into a late edition of the Somers' Tracts, under the reign of James I' (i.e. 1603-1625). The original position of the Contents leaf, as signified in the collation, is verified in the O(Minto) copy.

4] A | COLLECTION | OF | SCARCE AND VALUABLE | **TRACTS,** . . . VOLUME FOURTH. . . . 1810.

Published ca. October 1810 in London. £3.3.0. Collation: π^4 A-4K^4 *4L*1. Pagination: *i* half-title, *ii* printer's imprint(1), *iii* title-page, *iv blank, v* vi-viii Table of Contents [Charles I], *1* fly-title, *2 blank, 3* 4-626 text, *627* 628-633 Index, 633 printer's imprint(2), *634 blank.* Printer's imprints: (1) [*short Oxford rule*] | Printed by James Ballantyne & Co. | Edinburgh.; (2) [*short Oxford rule*] | EDINBURGH: | Printed by James Ballantyne & Co. Typography: In some copies the second digit in page-number 73 has moved upward or dropped out.

Figures: A6-14 8-15, B15-9 16-1, C18-10 24-13, D26-8 32-3, E36-6 38-13, F47-1 48-6, G54-2 56-12, H58-3 64-8, I 68-'31'[13] 71-14, K79-15 80-5, L86-6 88-14, M90-6 92-7, N103-1 104-7, O 106-5 108-2, P118-3 120-15, Q124-2, R135-13 136-6, S140-14, T148-10, U158-6 160-5, X162-14, Y171-14 172-13, Z182-12 184-1, 2A 188-13, 2B 198-15, 2C 205-12, 2D 215-12 216-3, 2E 224-1, 2F 226-7 232-6, 2G 235-3 236-15, 2H 243-12 248-1, 2 I 252-12, 2K 262-3 264-12, 2L 270-12 272-3, 2M 280-12, 2N 282-1 288-13, 2 O 291-12, 2P 301-3 302-15, 2Q 308-14, 2R 320-3, 2S 326-12, 2T 336-14/-, 2U 338-12 340-14, 2X 346-6 349-5, 2Y 359-13 360-1, 2Z 362-1 368-2, 3A 374-3 376-1, 3B 379-14 381-13, 3C 387-6 392-5, 3D 395-14 397-3, 3E 405-3 406-12, 3F 412-12 415-14, 3G 419-13, 3H 426-13 428-2, 3 I 437-2 439-3, 3K 443-13 445-6, 3L 451-12, 3M 462-12, 3N 471-2 472-12, 3 O 479-12, 3P 483-2

485-13, 3Q 490-1 493-9, 3R 503-2, 3S 507-5 508-10, 3T 514-3, 3U 525-10 527-12, 3X 536-13, 3Y 538-13 544-2, 3Z 546-3, 4A 560-12, 4B 568-8, 4C 570-6 572-13, 4D 584-7, 4E 588-12, 4F 599-3, 4G 603-1 605-7, 4H 612-1, 4 I 623-13, 4K 632-6, *4L*—.

Notes: In this volume Scott provides nine commentaries from his own editions and adds twenty-three tracts (nineteen of them relating to the Earl of Stratford). The heading 'Three Speeches' by the King, page 478, is cited in the Contents as 'Two Speeches'.

5] A | COLLECTION | OF | SCARCE AND VALUABLE | **TRACTS,** . . . VOLUME FIFTH. . . . 1811.

Announced June 1811 in London (*MLA*) but probably not published until 22 July (*MC*). £3.3.0. Collation: π^4 A-4P^4. Pagination: *i* half-title, *ii* printer's imprint(1), *iii* title-page, *iv blank, v* vi-vii Table of Contents [Charles I, continued], *viii blank, 1* fly-title, *2 blank, 3* 4-664 text, *665* 666-672 Index, 672 printer's imprint(2). Printer's imprints: (1) [*short Oxford rule*] | Printed by James Ballantyne & Co. | Edinburgh.; (2) [*short Oxford rule*] | EDINBURGH: | Printed by James Ballantyne & Co. Typography: In the title imprint of some copies the hyphen is omitted after ST JAMES'S.

Figures: A4-6, B15-5 16-7, C18-3, D32-13, E40-13, F47-11, G56-13, H62-3, I 71-5 72-3, K74-12 80-1, L84-7, M90-13, N98-5 100-'31' [13], O 108-12, P—, Q122-13 128-6, R134-3 136-12, S143-4, T152-3, U159-6, X163-6 164-3, Y171-8 176-12, Z180-1 183-9, 2A 186-7, 2B 198-2, 2C 206-2, 2D 212-2, 2E 224-2, 2F 231-2, 2G 237-6, 2H 245-1, 2 I 255-1, 2K 259-1, 2L 270-1, 2M 274-1, 2N 284-1, 2 O 294-1, 2P 304-1, 2Q 312-1, 2R 316-8, 2S 328-3, 2T 332-1, 2U 342-1, 2X 346-3 348-2, 2Y 355-2 356-4, 2Z 367-1, 3A 375-6 376-1, 2B 383-9 384-12, 3C 391-1 392-9, 3D 399-8 400-9, 3E 408-3, 3F 416-2, 3G 421-1, 3H 428-9, 3 I 439-12 440-9, 3K 442-3 444-1, 3L 456-4, 3M 464-4, 3N 467-1, 3 O 479-4, 3P 488-4, 3Q 492-4, 3R 498-4 504-11, 3S 510-4, 3T 515-4, 3U 528-12, 3X 531-4 533-12, 3Y 542-4, 3Z 549-1 551-12, 4A 560-12, 4B 566-9, 4C 572-1, 4D 580-1, 4E 586-1, 4F 595-1, 4G 604-1, 4H 610-12, 4 I 622-6, 4K 628-1, 4L 634-1, 4M 646-1, 4N 651-6, 4 O 661-1, 4P 671-6.

Notes: In this further volume relating to Charles I, Scott provides four commentaries from his own editions and adds eighteen tracts.

6] A | COLLECTION | OF | SCARCE AND VALUABLE | **TRACTS,** . . . VOLUME SIXTH. . . . 1811.

Published September 1811 in London (*MM* 1 October). £3.3.0. Collation: π^4 A-4E^4 4F^2. Pagination: *i* half-title, *ii* printer's imprint(1), *iii* title-page, *iv blank, v* vi-vii Table of Contents [The Commonwealth], *viii blank, 1* fly-title, *2 blank, 3* 4-590 text, *591* 592-596 Index, 596 printer's imprint(2). Printer's imprints: (1) [*short Oxford rule*] | EDINBURGH: | Printed by James Ballantyne & Co.; (2) [*short Oxford rule*] | EDINBURGH: | Printed by James Ballantyne and Co. Typography: In the title imprint of some copies the hyphen is omitted after ST JAMES'S.

Figures: π *v*-3 vii-8, A8-6, B15-4, C22-3, D30-3, E40-1, F44-3, G54-12, H61-3 63-4, I 66-1 68-4, K76-11, L84-12, M91-12, N102-12, O 107-1 108-3, P120-12, Q128-1, R133-1, S140-5, T152-12, U157-9 159-4, X168-1, Y175-1, Z182-4, 2A 189-6, 2B 200-12, 2C 203-1 208-12, 2D 212-1, 2E 223-1, 2F 231-4 232-1, 2G 237-1, 2H 244-4, 2 I 253-1 254-4, 2K 264-9, 2L 266-12 269-3, 2M 274-12, 2N 286-3, 2 O 295-12, 2P 301-3, 2Q 309-3, 2R 316-1, 2S 322-1, 2T 336-3, 2U 338-4, 2X 351-1, 2Y 357-1, 2Z 362-3 364-4, 3A 376-4, 3B 383-12, 3C 389-5, 3D 400-12, 3E 406-3, 3F—, 3G 423-5/-, 3H 429-5, 3 I 440-6, 3K 445-12, 3L 452-12 454-6, 3M 460-1 463-6, 3N 471-12, 3 O 479-9 480-12, 3P 486-12 488-1, 3Q 495-8/- 496-1, 3R 498-3 504-6, 3S 506-8 509-12, 3T 515-6 520-1, 3U 527-3 528-4, 3X 531-8, 3Y 540-12, 3Z 549-4 551-3, 4A 555-3, 4B 563-12 565-4, 4C 574-6 576-1, 4D 582-12 584-1, 4E *591*-8 592-1, 4F 594-4.

Notes: In this volume Scott provides three commentaries from his own editions and adds five tracts. The heading beginning 'Twenty-seven Queries', page 510, is cited in the Contents as 'Thirty-seven Queries'.

7] A | COLLECTION | OF | SCARCE AND VALUABLE | **TRACTS,** . . . VOLUME SEVENTH. . . . 1812.

Published February 1812 in London (*MM* 1 March). (Apparently the entire issue was mistakenly sent to London, leaving Scott still without copies as of 1 April. *Letters*, iii.95.) £3.3.0. Collation: π^4 A-4N^4. Pagination: *i* half-title, *ii* printer's imprint(1), *iii* title-page, *iv blank, v* vi-vii Table of Contents [The Commonwealth, Charles II], *viii blank, 1* fly-title, *2 blank, 3* 4-660 text, *661* 662-666 Index, 666 printer's imprint(2). Printer's imprints: (1) [*short Oxford rule*] | Printed by James Ballantyne & Co. | Edinburgh.; (2) [*short Oxford rule*] | EDINBURGH: | Printed by James Ballantyne & Co. Typography: In title imprint of all copies the hyphen is now omitted after ST JAMES'S. Page 582 is misnumbered 585.

Figures: π vi-1, A6-2, B14-2, C20-8, D32-1, E39-9 40-6, F42-6 44-2, G53-9 54-8, H59-3 61-9, I 71-4 72-8, K76-4 78-3, L88-4, M92-2 94-12, N104-1, O 107-1 108-12, P 116-1 119-3, Q126-12, R136-9, S139-6 144-3, T146-9 152-6, U154-2 157-3, X165-2, Y173-1, Z178-12 181-4, 2A 186-3 192-9, 2B 196-2 198-12, 2C 202-6 204-9, 2D 216-2, 2E 224-6, 2F 229-3 230-1, 2G 237-4 239-2, 2H 242-4 245-1, 2 I 256-12, 2K 261-9, 2L 266-1, 2M 275-9, 2N 286-2, 2 O 290-3 296-6, 2P 300-3 302-9, 2Q 308-12 311-9, 2R 318-12 320-2, 2S 325-1, 2T 330-1, 2U 344-3, 2X 352-6, 2Y 357-12, 2Z 368-6, 3A 375-8 376-12, 3B 380-1, 3C—, 3D—, 3E 403-3 408-12, 3F 411-7 413-1, 3G 423-8 424-9, 3H 431-7 432-3, 3 I 437-7, 3K 456-8

458-7/-, 3L 462-5 465-9, 3M 473-1 474-5, 3N 476-8 478-1, 3 O 488-1 490-3, 3P 498-2, 3Q 506-2, 3R 508-7, 3S 519-2 521-5, 3T 528-7 530-12, 3U 536-2 538-1, 3X 540-12 546-1, 3Y 552-2 554-3, 3Z 559-1 561-9, 4A 569-6 570-2, 4B 573-12 574-2, 4C 580-1 '585'[582]-9, 4D 589-10 594-7, 4E 596-12 602-5, 4F 604-7 610-1, 4G 617-1 618-7, 4H 620-6 626-7, 4 I 628-12 631-6, 4K 636-7 642-2, 4L 644-5 650-8, 4M 652-1 654-5, 4N 662-7.

Notes: In this volume Scott provides three commentaries from his own editions and, to the earlier section on the Commonwealth only, adds eight tracts.

8] A | COLLECTION | OF | SCARCE AND VALUABLE | **TRACTS,** . . . VOLUME EIGHTH. . . . 1812.

Published ca. July 1812 in London (*Letters*, iii.136). £3.3.0. Collation: π[4] A-4 I[4] 4K1. Pagination: *i* half-title, *ii* printer's imprint(1), *iii* title-page, *iv blank, v* vi-vii Table of Contents [Charles II, continued], *viii blank, 1* fly-title, *2 blank, 3* 4-619 text, *620 blank, 621* 622-625 Index, 625 printer's imprint(2), *626 blank.* Printer's imprints: (1) [*Oxford dash*] | Printed by James Ballantyne & Co., | EDINBURGH.; | (2) [*short Oxford rule*] | EDINBURGH: | Printed by James Ballantyne and Co. Typography: In title imprint the hyphen is omitted after ST JAMES'S.

Figures: π vi-8, A8-1, B—, C18-6, D28-1, E39-2, F45-7 47-9, G50-3 56-12, H58-2, I 72-9/-, K79-8, L82-2, M92-7, N104-2, O 106-8, P115-7, Q123-1, R130-1, S141-12, T149-8, U160-9, X165-6, Y172-2, Z183-1, 2A 190-5, 2B 197-1, 2C 202-1, 2D 214-12, 2E 223-12, 2F 229-6, 2G 239-9, 2H 248-5, 2 I 252-12, 2K 264-12, 2L 271-10, 2M 280-10, 2N 286-4, 2 O 294-7, 2P 302-7, 2Q 306-5, 2R 315-2, 2S 328-3, 2T 333-5, 2U 344-8, 2X 347-12, 2Y 355-10, 2Z 363-6, 3A 370-9, 3B 382-9, 3C 392-1, 3D 397-6, 3E 404-6, 3F 413-2, 3G 418-1, 3H 427-9, 3 I 438-2, 3K 447-9, 3L 455-5, 3M 462-12, 3N 469-12, 3 O 475-7, 3P 484-10, 3Q 492-3, 3R 498-7, 3S 509-1, 3T 515-9, 3U 525-6, 3X 534-12, 3Y 544-3, 3Z 552-3, 4A 557-1, 4B 563-6, 4C 573-12, 4D 580-6, 4E 592-6, 4F 600-12, 4G 608-3, 4H 614-5, 4 I 624-2, 4K—.

Notes: In this volume Scott provides six commentaries from his own editions and adds three tracts. On page 89 a heading relating to a bloody massacre 'in Ireland' is cited in the Contents as 'in England'. The final essay 'Of Love', pages 612-619, though still headed 'never published', was in fact printed in the original 1748 Somers collection, ii.401-410.

9] A | COLLECTION | OF | SCARCE AND VALUABLE | **TRACTS,** . . . VOLUME NINTH. . . . STRAND; | J. MURRAY, ALBEMARLE-STREET; | R. H. EVANS, PALL-MALL; J. WHITE, FLEET-STREET; AND J. HARDING, | ST JAMES'S STREET. | 1813.

Published ca. March 1813 in London. £3.3.0. Collation: π[4] A-Q[4] 2R[4](-R1,R2, +R1.2) 2S-4G[4] 4H1. Pagination: *i* half-title, *ii* printer's imprint(1), *iii* title-page, *iv blank, v* vi-vii Table of Contents [James II, William III], *viii blank, 1* fly-title, *2 blank, 3* 4-605 text, *606 blank, 607* 608-610 Index, 610 printer's imprint(2). Printer's imprints: (1) [*Oxford dash*] | Printed by James Ballantyne & Co., | EDINBURGH.; (2) [*Oxford dash*] | EDINBURGH: | Printed by James Ballantyne & Co.

Figures: A8-1, B10-10, C18-6, D29-10, E36-12, F43-2, G54-12, H64-1, I 68-2, K74-2, L86-12, M—, N104-8, O 108-1, P120-6, Q127-12, R136-2, S141-7, T150-10, U157-9, X164-7, Y172-12, Z178-5, 2A 188-7, 2B 196-2, 2C 202-3, 2D 210-12, 2E 224-6, 2F 232-9, 2G *239*-6 240-1, 2H 248-3, 2 I 250-3, 2K 263-5, 2L—, 2M 280-12, 2N 287-6, 2 O 294-7, 2P 301-1, 2Q *309*-1, 2R 316-12, 2S 328-5, 2T 333-6, 2U 340-10, 2X 352-1, 2Y—, 2Z 368-12, 3A 370-10, 3B 381-12, 3C 390-2, 3D 395-7, 3E 408-1, 3F 410-5, 3G 421-10, 3H 428-1, 3 I 437-12, 3K 442-5, 3L 452-1, 3M 460-5, 3N 466-7, 3 O 478-6, 3P 488-2, 3Q 495-3, 3R 504-12, 3S 511-7, 3T 516-7, 3U 528-5, 3X 535-1, 3Y 543-8, 3Z 552-12, 4A 559-2, 4B 568-10, 4C 576-7, 4D 584-7, 4E 591-12, 4F 597-7, 4G—, 4H—.

Notes: No Scott editions are cited here and no tracts added in this and the subsequent volumes, but the editorial commentary continues unabated. Beginning with this issue, as indicated above, there are slight alterations in the publishing arrangements, these necessitated chiefly by the retirement in July 1812 of William Miller, one of the original principals. The 2R cancellation was arranged, at least in part, to admit below the 2R1 fly-title, page *313*, a note: '*ERRATUM.—*Owing to an oversight of the Printer, the head-lines of this Class bear William I. in place of William III.*' [The error, occurring 146 times in the following verso pages, is corrected in the ensuing volumes.]

A further indication of Scott's loss of interest in the details of this publication appears on page 587, where it is admitted that 'This Tract and the following should have preceded page 388, . . .'

10] A | COLLECTION | OF | SCARCE AND VALUABLE | **TRACTS,** . . . VOLUME TENTH. . . . STRAND; | R. H. EVANS, PALL-MALL; WHITE AND COCHRANE, FLEET-STREET; | AND | JOHN MURRAY, ALBEMARLE-STREET. | 1813.

Published ca. July 1813 in London (*Letters*, iii.298). £3.3.0. Collation: $\pi^2(\pi2+1)$ A-4N^4. Pagination: *i* half-title, *ii* printer's imprint(1), *iii* title-page, *iv blank, v*-vi Table of Contents [William III, continued], *1* fly-title, *2 blank, 3* 4-652 text, *653* 654-655 Index, 655 printer's imprint(2), *656 blank.* Printer's imprints: (1) [*short Oxford rule*] | EDINBURGH: | Printed by James Ballantyne & Co.; (2) [*short Oxford rule*] | EDINBURGH: | Printed by James Ballantyne and Co.

Figures: A5-10, B10-13, C18-2, D30-8, E40-5, F48-2, G55-1, H58-10, I 68-8, K80-8, L—, M92-2, N104-5, O 112-5, P120-12, Q128-6, R132-3, S142-1, T150-8, U160-1, X164-5, Y172-6, Z184-6, 2A 186-10, 2B 200-6, 2C 203-12, 2D 212-7, 2E 223-7,

2F 232-5, 2G 238-2, 2H 244-5, 2 I 253-2, 2K 264-10, 2L 270-12, 2M 278-2, 2N—, 2 O 294-2, 2P 301-12, 2Q 311-5, 2R 318-8, 2S 328-6, 2T 336-8, 2U 338-5, 2X 352-6, 2Y 357-1, 2Z 368-2, 3A 370-10, 3B 383-8, 3C 388-1, 3D 398-1, 3E 404-12, 3F 413-5, 3G 423-8, 3H 427-3, 3 I 436-10, 3K 448-3, 3L 452-3, 3M 459-8, 3N 472-6, 3 O 475-10, 3P 484-5, 3Q 495-8, 3R 504-8, 3S 508-1, 3T 519-1, 3U 525-1, 3X—, 3Y 542-8, 3Z 548-1, 4A 557-8, 4B 563-5, 4C 571-2, 4D 582-10, 4E 586-6, 4F 597-1, 4G 602-2, 4H 614-5, 4 I 622-6, 4K 631-10/-, 4L 640-8, 4M 647-10, 4N—.

Notes: The Contents omit 'Animadversion on King James his Letter to the Pope. Published in the Trial of the Lord Preston and Mr Ashton. 1691.', pages 555-559. On page 559 a heading for the next piece, reading 'Great Britain', is cited in the Contents as 'England'.

11] A | COLLECTION | OF | SCARCE AND VALUABLE | **TRACTS,** . . . VOLUME ELEVENTH. . . . 1814.

Published March 1814 in London (*MM* 1 April). £3.3.0. Collation: *a*[2] b1 A-4 I[4] 4K[2] 4L1. Pagination: *i* half-title, *ii* printer's imprint(1), *iii* title-page, *iv blank, v*-vi Table of Contents [William III, continued], *1* fly-title, *2 blank, 3* 4-626 text, *627* 628-630 Index, 630 printer's imprint(2). Printer's imprints: (1) [*Oxford dash*] | EDINBURGH. | Printed by James Ballantyne & Co.; (2) [*short Oxford rule*] | EDINBURGH: | Printed by James Ballantyne and Co.

Figures: b vi-1, A4-5, B16-10, C—, D30-5, E37-2, F48-5, G51-6, H62-8, I 72-2, K76-6, L83-1, M94-3, N101-2, O 111-6, P119-10, Q123-10, R136-8, S138-5, T146-6, U 160-5, X 166-2, Y—, Z184-2, 2A 192-1, 2B 200-10, 2C 204-1, 2D 210-2/-, 2E 218-2, 2F 230-5, 2G 234-5, 2H 244-8, 2 I 252-6, 2K 258-2, 2L 271-1, 2M 280-10, 2N 282-2, 2 O 295-5, 2P 298-5, 2Q 312-10, 2R 315-3, 2S 327-5, 2T 332-8, 2U 340-1, 2X 346-5, 2Y 359-2, 2Z 368-2, 3A 370-6, 3B 384-6, 3C 391-1, 3D 398-5, 3E 404-1, 3F 416-2, 3G 421-5, 3H 429-5, 3 I 437-1, 3K 444-2, 3L 450-6, 3M 460-5, 3N 467-5, 3 O 480-6, 3P 488-5, 3Q 492-7, 3R 501-3, 3S 508-6, 3T 514-8, 3U 526-6, 3X 533-5, 3Y 541-1, 3Z 552-2, 4A 557-6, 4B 564-1, 4C 576-7, 4D 581-6, 4E 591-1, 4F 599-3, 4G 607-5, 4H 616-8, 4 I 620-1, 4K 628-1, 4L—.

Notes: On page 513 Scott finds occasion to cite his edition of Swift. Otherwise, as in volumes 9 and 10, there is some slight evidence of editorial inattention, now at page 485 where the headnote confesses: 'This letter, which should have been taken in among the Civil Tracts, is accidentally misplaced.'

12] A | COLLECTION | OF | SCARCE AND VALUABLE | **TRACTS,** . . . VOLUME TWELFTH. . . . 1814.

Published ca. October 1814 in London. £3.3.0. Collation: π^4 A-4X[4]. Pagination: *i* half-title, *ii* printer's imprint(1), *iii* title-page, *iv blank, v* vi-vii Table of Contents [William III, Anne], *viii blank, 1* fly-title, *2 blank, 3* 4-725 text, *726 blank, 727*

728-730 Index, 730 printer's imprint(2). Folding table placed to face page '382' [372]. Printer's imprints (1) and (2): [*short Oxford dash*] | EDINBURGH: | Printed by James Ballantyne & Co. Typography: Pages 372-720 are misnumbered 382-730. Signature 3H (page 435) is missigned 2H.

Figures: π *v*-3, A3-1, B11-7, C24-7, D30-2, E34-10, F43-5, G52-5, H61-7, I—, K76-3, L82-7, M91-1, N—, O 110-8, P114-3, Q122-2, R131-2, S140-8, T150-7, U156-2, X168-2, Y176-7, Z180-2, 2A 189-9, 2B 199-5, 2C 207-2, 2D 214-7, 2E 219-1, 2F 228-3, 2G 240-2, 2H 248-2, 2 I 251-2, 2K 260-2, 2L 267-2, 2M 275-5, 2N 284-3, 2 O 292-1, 2P—, 2Q 309-3, 2R 317-5, 2S—, 2T 335-5, 2U 341-6, 2X 349-9, 2Y—, 2Z 363-2, 3A 386-6, 3B 393-8, 3C 402-6, 3D—, 3E 417-1/-, 3F 420-3, 3G 431-5, 3H 437-3, 3 I 447-1, 3K 454-7, 3L 460-7, 3M 468-5, 3N 480-5, 3O 484-5, 3P 494-3, 3Q—, 3R 514-8, 3S 519-5, 3T 530-1, 3U 532-2, 3X 540-7, 3Y 552-2, 3Z 560-2, 4A 566-8, 4B 574-7, 4C 580-1, 4D 590-5, 4E 598-5, 4F 606-3, 4G 616-1, 4H 622-2, 4 I 634-3, 4K 639-8, 4L 646-10, 4M 657-8, 4N 666-3, 4 O 670-2, 4P 678-7, 4Q 687-2, 4R 697-8, 4S 705-7, 4T 710-8, 4U 720-7, 4X 729-5.

Notes: The final total in the folding table facing page '382' [372], appears to be incorrectly calculated.

13] A | COLLECTION | OF | SCARCE AND VALUABLE | **TRACTS,** . . . VOLUME THIRTEENTH. . . . 1815.

Published ca. March 1815 in London. £3.3.0. Collation: π[4] A-5T[4]. Pagination: *i* half-title, *ii* printer's imprint(1), *iii* title-page, *iv blank, v* vi-vii Table of Contents [Anne, George I], *viii blank, 1* fly-title, *2 blank, 3* 4-892 text, *893* 894-895 Index, 895 printer's imprint(2), *896 blank.* Printer's imprints (1) and (2): [*short double rule*] | EDINBURGH: | Printed by James Ballantyne & Co. Typography: Pages 213, 241, 575, 785 are misnumbered 215, 243, 755, 795 respectively. Certain page sequences are also misnumbered, 369-391 as 367-389, and 585-887 as 593-895. Signature 3M (page 457) lacks the first digit.

Figures: π vii-11, A5-2, B11-9, C20-9, D30-9, E40-7, F42-11, G56-2, H58-1, I 71-5, K77-2, L82-7, M92-11, N100-4, O 112-4, P116-4, Q124-5, R130-12, S144-6, T147-4, U155-3, X168-2, Y172-12, Z182-14, 2A 190-5, 2B 200-12, 2C 205-6, 2D 210-12, 2E 219-1, 2F 227-6, 2G 240-14, 2H 243-14, 2 I 251-3, 2K 258-4 264-4, 2L 271-9, 2M 278-14, 2N 285-6, 2 O 292-3, 2P 299-7, 2Q 311-2, 2R 319-14, 2S 328-9, 2T 333-2, 2U 339-3, 2X 349-6, 2Y 354-4, 2Z 362-3, 3A 368-7 3B 376-10, 3C—, 3D 398-3, 3E 405-7, 3F 415-4, 3G—. 3H 432-8, 3 I 435-7, 3K 445-4, 3L 456-5, 3M 461-2, 3N 471-7, 3 O 475-2, 3P 482-2, 3Q 496-4, 3R 500-5, 3S 510-4, 3T 516-7, 3U 523-5, 3X 536-9, 3Y 544-5, 3Z 548-5, 4A 559-3, 4B 566-4, 4C 573-5, 4D 579-4, 4E 597-9, 4F 606-9, 4G 612-5, 4H 619-6, 4 I 631-1, 4K 636-6, 4L 645-7, 4M 652-6 654-6, 4N 660-11, 4 O 666-11, 4P 674-7, 4Q 687-8, 4R 694-3, 4S 699-5, 4T 706-1, 4U 720-6, 4X 724-8, 4Y 731-3, 4Z 739-10, 5A 746-9, 5B 756-1, 5C 763-5,

5D 773-8, 5E 782-2, 5F 791-6, 5G 796-2, 5H 808-1, 5 I 815-2, 5K 824-5, 5L 829-10, 5M 840-2, 5N 847-2, 5 O 853-10, 5P 861-9, 5Q 871-9, 5R 876-10, 5S 885-5, 5T 894-10. Two pressmen accidentally figure both formes of a gathering, 4 in 2K and 6 in 4M.

Notes: On this last occasion Scott for the first time (page 417) offers a long quotation from his 1808 edition of Carleton, and in three other places (pages 86-87, 120-121, 818) again quotes extensively from the 'late edition' of Swift. The Contents omit 'A Further Search into the Conduct of the Allies. . . . 1712.', pages 182-205.

REVIEWS OF CAMPBELL AND CUMBERLAND

39A] First Printings: 1809

1] 'ART. I. *Gertrude of Wyoming, a Pensylvanian[!] Tale, and other Poems, by Thomas Campbell'*, pages *241* 242-258,

2] 'ART. VII. *John de Lancaster: a Novel.* By Richard Cumberland, Esq.', pages 337-348, *in*:

The Quarterly Review. May, 1809. [No.2: volume 1 imprint:] London: Printed by C. Roworth, Bell-yard, Temple-bar; For John Murray, 32, Fleet Street; Hatchard, Piccadilly; Richardson, Cornhill; and John Ballantyne and Co. Edinburgh.

Published 30 May 1809 in London (*MC)*; issued 10 July in Edinburgh (*EEC*).

Copies: BCL O; PPL(2) TxU. Later issue labelled 'Second Edition. . . 1810' (L).

References: Shine 19, 25. (Magnum Opus Edition 1835: *The Miscellaneous Prose Works*, [1] xvii.267-291 as 'Campbell's Gertrude of Wyoming, &c.', [2] xviii.138-157 as 'Cumberland's John de Lancaster'.)

THE LIFE OF EDWARD LORD HERBERT, OF CHERBURY

40A] First Scott Edition: 1809

THE | **LIFE** | OF | Edward Lord Herbert, | OF | CHERBURY. | [*short rule*] | WRITTEN BY HIMSELF. | [*short rule*] | WITH | A PREFATORY MEMOIR. | [*short Oxford rule*] | EDINBURGH: | Printed by James Ballantyne and Co. | FOR JOHN BALLANTYNE AND CO. EDINBURGH, | AND JOHN MURRAY, LONDON. | [*dash*] | 1809.

Published ca. June 1809 in Edinburgh. Paper: Demy 8° (218 x 134mm cut). Watermarks: D & A C | 1808 | *none* [1, 2]. Collation: π^2 a^8 b^8 c^2 a^8 A-R^8 S^4 *T*1.

Pagination: *1* half-title, *2 blank, 3* title-page, *4 blank, i* ii-xxxvi Prefatory Memoir (by Scott), *i* ii-iii Original Dedication (by Horace Walpole), *iv blank, v* vi-xvi Advertisement to the First Edition (1764), *1* 2-281 text, 281 printer's imprint, *282 blank*. Printer's imprint: [*short Oxford rule*] | EDINBURGH: | Printed by James Ballantyne & Co. Illustration: copperplate frontispiece portrait drawn by Oliver, engraved by C. Pye, with caption 'Edward Lord Herbert of Chirbury[!].' Typography: The second signature a, in italic type, constitutes Walpole's dedication and advertisement: a full gathering which is sometimes bound first.

Figures: *a* vii-8, b xviii-12, c xxxiv-4, *a* xi-3, A2(or 15)-12, B21-7, C48-1, D64-13, E80-11, F82-8 85-13, G98-12, H114-2, I138-7, K160-11, L162-3, M178-11, N201-5, O 210-8, P240-11, Q242-11, R272-11, S276-1, *T*—.

Notes: The date below Herbert's portrait is in two states: (1) 'June 31st' [an impossibility!]; (2) 'June 13th'. At the beginning of his lengthly memoir Scott notes that 'this spirited and valuable piece of biography' was first printed 1764 at Strawberry Hill, but that Walpole added his dedication in the 1770 London edition. Scott's intention now is to 'unite' with Walpole's account the observations 'scattered in some other authors, and to give a catalogue and some notices' of Herbert's writings.

Copies: (state 1) AN BCL LU; CtY. (2) O; CaBVaU DLC T/B.

Reference: (Magnum Opus Edition: Not reprinted.)

REPRINT

GREAT BRITAIN

40R] LONDON: Warwick 1824

The Life of Edward Lord Herbert of Cherbury. Written by Himself. With a Prefatory Memoir. London, J. Warwick, Brooke Street, Holborn. 1824. Pages: *i-v* vi-lii, *1* 2-243 *244*. Scott's 'Prefatory Memoir', printed anonymously, is on pages *xx* xxi-lii. Later editions were published under the title: The Autobiography of Edward, Lord Herbert of Cherbury. Copies: L; TxU.

BIOGRAPHICAL MEMOIR OF SIR RALPH SADLER

41Aa] First Printing: 1809

BIOGRAPHICAL MEMOIR OF SIR RALPH SADLER. Volume 1, pages *i* ii-xxxix, *in*:

The State Papers and Letters of Sir Ralph Sadler, Knight-Banneret. Edited by Arthur Clifford, Esq. In two volumes. To which is added, A Memoir of

The Life of Sir Ralph Sadler, with Historical Notes, by Walter Scott, Esq. Vol. I [II]. Edinburgh: Printed for Archibald Constable and Co. Edinburgh; and for T. Cadell and W. Davies, William Miller, and John Murray, London. 1809.

Published 4 November 1809 in Edinburgh (*EEC*); issued 22 November in London (*MC*). £5.5.0.

Notes: Ralph Sadler was the English Ambassador to the Scottish Court 1539-40, 1543, involved in the 1560 treaty between the two countries, and appointed guardian of Mary Queen of Scots 1580-81. A preliminary Advertisement, by Clifford, is dated from 3 North Castle Street, Edinburgh, 1 May 1809. Scott, dwelling next door at number 2 (redesignated 39 Castle in 1811), doubtless was interested in his neighbour's edition because of the references therein to other 16th-century names and places already mentioned or yet to appear in his own works, e.g. 'Branksome Castle', Sir Walter Scott of Buccleuch (killed 1552 in a feud with the Kerrs), Baron Somerville, Sir Francis Slingsby, Henry Slingsby, Cardinal David Bethune, and James Bethune, Archbishop of Glasgow. Among the several hundred textual notes, however, Scott's intervention is not readily perceived; generally these entries are styled as coming from the editor, a Sadler descendent and evident enthusiast.

Copies: BCL DN GU O P; DLC InU NNU-W T/B.

References: Thomson, page 57. (Magnum Opus Edition 1834: *The Miscellaneous Prose Works*, iv.71-136.)

41Ab] Second (Large-Paper) Printing: 1809

BIOGRAPHICAL MEMOIR OF SIR RALPH SADLER. Volume 1, pages *i* ii-xxxix, *in*:

The State Papers and Letters . . . In Three Volumes . . . Vol. I [II-III]. . . . 1809.

Published concurrently with the earlier printing and then described as 'forming one of the most splendid large paper books that has ever been published'. £8.8.0.

Notes: Due to the extraordinary extent of the two volumes in the regular issue (text 732, 623 pages) it was necessary to redistribute the pages into three volumes in this Royal 4° impression (312 x 244mm uncut, text '463'[465], 513, 385 pages) and alter the page numbers and cross references accordingly. In Scott's 'Memoir' leaves d2, d4, and e1 (pages xxvii-xxviii, xxxi-xxxii, xxxiii-xxxiv) now are cancels, perhaps because the footnote references had not been changed. For these leaves the press figures occur earlier, in the uncancelled state, as xxviii-13, xxxi-2, xxxiv-none, here in the cancels as xxviii-7, xxxi-none, xxxiv-1.

Copies: BCL E GU O; IdU MH T/B.

REVIEW OF CROKER

42A] First Printing: 1809

'ART. XVII. *The Battles of Talavera. A Poem.*', pages 426-433, *in*:

The Quarterly Review. November, 1809. [No.4: volume 2 imprint:] London: Printed by C. Roworth, Bell-yard, Temple-bar; For John Murray, 32, Fleet Street; Hatchard, Piccadilly; Richardson, Cornhill; John Ballantyne and Co. Edinburgh; and M. N. Mahon, Dublin.

Published 23 December 1809 in London (*MC*); announced 30 December as shipped from London to Edinburgh on the 24th and expected within 'a few days' (*EEC*).

Notes: The poem was later acknowledged to be written by John Wilson Croker. The irregular Pindaric measure, 'first applied to serious composition by Mr. Walter Scott' (page 428) is here graciously conceded to be of better effect.

Copies: BCL L O; PPL(2) TxU. References: Shine 63. (Magnum Opus Edition 1835: *The Miscellaneous Prose Works*, xvii.291-300.)

MARMION; A TALE OF FLODDEN FIELD, 1809
28Dt. The Westall vignette design, issued with
another engraved suite illustrated on page 5

TWO

1810-1813

With the publication in 1810 of *The Lady of the Lake* (47Aa) Scott reached the first summit of his literary career, but only after careful preparation. As on previous occasions (28A, 43A) Lady Abercorn was taken into his confidence prior to issue, now with the further purpose of securing through her the approbation of her husband the Marquess, to whom the poem was to be dedicated.

Other parties were also in great expectation. Where before a single London publisher, John Sharpe, had belatedly engaged an artist to illustrate the earlier poems (14Dm, 28Dt), now two publishers, Sharpe and the Longman firm, each hired an illustrator, much to Scott's amusement, six weeks before publication (47Dab[3], 47Dam). This extra embellishment, merely tolerated by Scott, was continued for later verse by one or the other firm and regularly involved three artists as well as scores of engravers (64Dp, 81Dj, 341D). Hence all of Scott's major poems, published 1805-1815 in Edinburgh, may be intermittently adorned by a series of plates issued, for each, somewhat later in London. As noted for all, these plates were also available separately in various formats or states and thus could be admired, apart from the poems, simply as works of art.

Other signs in 1810 of an increasing impetus, and wider impact, began to appear a few months after issue with the appearance of the first dramatized adaptations of a Scott poem (again by two rivals)[1] and a rapid increase in metrical renditions of the lyrics intercalated within the text. The total outcome of these and various other aftereffects is best represented, perhaps somewhat imprecisely, in the accompanying statistical Table: one exhibiting the marked ascendency of this poem, in Scott's time, over those before and after. As a recent biographer has observed, the critics were now unanimous in their praise,[2] the verse had transformed the unexplored Trossachs into classic tourist country,[3] and certain of the lyrics even inspired Wellington's troops far afield. Today one can still immediately recall, in another vein, the 'Ave Maria' as arranged by Schubert (47Da[5]) and 'Hail to the Chief' which, to the Sanderson strains (47Dau[2]), formally announces the President of the United States.

Recognizing the 1810 poem as a happy augury, the publishers in 1813 issued 3000 copies of *Rokeby* (64Aa), 1000 more than before, and again raised their payment to the author, only to discover that the earlier momentum was now lost. Coincidentally in this year of issue Byron drew his famous pyramid with Scott still at the apex,[4] but our Table illustrates in all measurable particulars the beginning of a decline. Even so, eight months after issue of the poem, recognition from the highest authority was publically announced:

We understand, that the Laurel has, by express desire of his Royal Highness the Prince Regent, been tendered, in the most handsome and flattering manner, to Mr Walter Scott, and declined by that distinguished poet, from motives, not less creditable to his literary character, than to the gracious partiality with which he has been honoured by his Royal Highness. (*Edinburgh Weekly Journal*, 15 Septemner 1813; see also *Letters*, iii.342-348).

Scott declined the honour himself but was eager in his recommendation that Robert Southey be appointed Laureate.

However regarded, *Rokeby* marks one new bibliographical circumstance. Hitherto, as observed in the ongoing record, shipments to London from Leith, the Edinburgh port, if not interrupted by embargoes against a threatened French invasion, storms at sea, or wayward tides in the Thames, would on average take several weeks—perhaps even longer for work in little demand—but for the poems, especially, adjustments in the shipping schedule soon brought the Edinburgh and London issue dates closer together: two weeks apart at first, as the Table shows, then one, and then for this poem four days only. Though the shorter interval, as Scott said, was intended this once to give the London publisher a 'fair start', it eventually led, for many issues, to concurrent publication. As before, the production of sequels also continues to accelerate, with Scott providing John Clarke several lyrics four months before issue and, ten days afterward, the actual publication of five songs by an eager music-sheet seller (64Dd). Thus, it appears, Scott remained in *Rokeby* a valuable commodity of himself, and an ever increasing source of profits to those awaiting his performance.

Besides the two major poems in this period there are two works from the French now deserving further notice. For these two and several others of later time it is well to recall the enduring Scottish remembrance of the 'ancient alliance', Scott's own marriage to a French woman, and further, as he was aware, the Gallic ancestry of his noble friends. This antiquarian's repeated allusions 1805-1828 to the Bethunes or Beatons among the Buccleuch forbears, as recited in the entry for *The Memoirs of the Duke of Sully* (48A), may not only have inclined him to edit that work, but could very well have prompted him, later on, to devise the name 'Martha Bethune Baliol' (where another evocative allusion is added), the fictional lady of 'quality and fortune' 1827 in 'The Highland Widow'. Similarly, after dedicating *The Lady of the Lake* to the First Marquess of Abercorn, Scott doubtless was reminded of that noble lord's collateral ancestor, Count Anthony Hamilton, a son of the First Earl of Abercorn and author of *Memoirs of Count Grammont* (53Aa). Should it be argued that these remote relations offer little pretext for literary treatment, it might be urged that the more romantic Scots, and Walter Scott first among them, acknowledged no limit to the bonds of consanguinity. This much conceded, the editions of Sully and Grammont may therefore be regarded as further compliments to the nobility whom Scott had already celebrated in a more direct way. From this elevated plane it was only a short rise to royal affairs: to a secret history of James I in 1811 (56Aa) and a memoir of Charles I in 1813 (65Aa), both frequently cited also in the 'Somers' Tracts' (38A).

THE FIVE MAJOR POEMS 1805-1815: A SUMMARY TABLE

The record disregards Scott's authorized collected works, where the count is constant, but includes all separate issues in English, domestic and foreign (A and R entries), printed derivatives of every kind (D), extracts in anthologies (E), and the record of productions given in Bolton. First publication date: Edinburgh, second: London.]

No.	Title / Date	1st Issue Copies	All eds.	Derivatives	Extracts	Play productions
14A	The Lay of the Last Minstrel 1805 January 12/24	750	47	31	83	1
28A	Marmion 1808 February 22/March 8[5]	2000	36	74	89	21
47A	The Lady of the Lake 1810 May 8/16	2000	52	281	102	132
64A	Rokeby 1813 January 11/15	3000	28	166	52	3
81A	The Lord of the Isles 1815 January 5/13	1750	18	63	20	9

1. Printed issues are recorded by publisher in the derivative 'D' section. Earliest performances as noted by Bolton (reference number, place and dramatist in parentheses): *The Lady of the Lake*: 24 September 1810 (49/ London, Dibdin), 15 January 1811 (50/ Edinburgh, Eyre). *Marmion*: 25 October 1810 (3/ London, [unknown]). *The Lay of the Last Minstrel*: late 1811 (1/ Dublin, [unknown]}. *Rokeby*: 19 April 1813 (338/ London, Dibdin). *The Lord of the Isles*: 27 February 1815 (344/ London, Faulkner?). Altogether, as the Table indicates, Scott's poems were unsuitable for dramatic treatment, one reaching the astonishing total of 132 productions in his lifetime, but the other four not exceeding twenty-one.

2. This assessment, by John Buchan (pages 85-86), is not quite right, for among the sixteen reviews cited in Corson(1) two are described as hostile (entries 924, 956).

3. To assist the sudden onrush of tourists Scott's publishers hastened to provide a map (64Aa), and present-day visitors may continue to voyage on Loch Katrine in the s.s. *Sir Walter Scott.*

4. Byron's pyramid, a triangular 'Gradus ad Parnassum' drawn in his journal 24 November 1813 and first printed in 1830 (237A), is reproduced below.

5. As noted in the entry for 28A the London publisher originally advertised first issue for 1 March, but then for some reason was obliged to delay publication for a week.

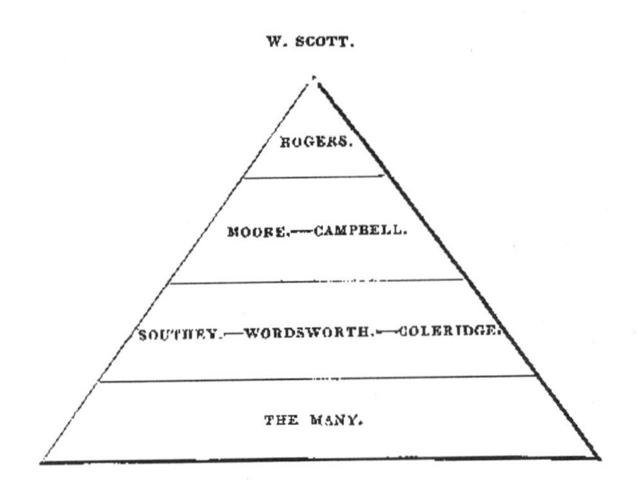

BYRON'S PYRAMID
1813

CONTENTS OF CHAPTER TWO

ENGLISH MINSTRELSY

43A] First Edition: 1810

ENGLISH MINSTRELSY. | BEING | A Selection of Fugitive Poetry. | FROM THE | BEST ENGLISH AUTHORS; | WITH SOME | ORIGINAL PIECES | HITHERTO UNPUBLISHED. | [*short Oxford rule*] | IN TWO VOLUMES. | [*short reversed Oxford rule*] | Vol. I [II]. | [*rule*] | [*two-line quotation from Gray*] | [*rule*] | EDINBURGH: | PRINTED FOR JOHN BALLANTYNE AND CO. | MANNERS AND MILLER, AND BROWN AND CROMBIE, | EDINBURGH; AND JOHN MURRAY, | LONDON. | [*dash*] | 1810.

Published 1 February 1810 in Edinburgh (*EEC*); issued 15 February in London (*MC*). 14s. Binding: grey-blue boards. Paper: Foolscap 8° (177 x 105mm uncut). Watermarks: O M | 1807 [1808]. Typography: Printer's imprints read invariably: (1) [*short rule*] | Printed by James Ballantyne and Co. Edinburgh. | [*short rule*]; (2) [*short reversed Oxford rule*] | EDINBURGH: | Printed by James Ballantyne & Co.

General Notes: A week before issue, on 21 January, Scott wrote to Lady Abercorn, 'I want to send your Ladyship two little trumpery volumes of Miscellanies containing some scraps of my own, with others better worthy of your perusal which I begged and borrowed from some friends to help off a selection of pieces made by some booksellers here whom I wish to encourage.' In the Advertisement, volume 1, pages vi-vii, the publishers implicitly acknowledge Scott's work: 'To one eminent individual, whose name they do not venture to particularize, they are indebted for most valuable assistance in selection, arrangement, and contribution; . . .'. All five of the Scott poems identified below were reprinted in the *Edinburgh Annual Register for 1808*, published 6 August 1810.

Copies: BCL E(2) L O(2); CaBVaU CtY DLC IdU(James Hogg) InU NjP NNU-W PPL(2) PU TxU(3) ViU. References: *Letters*, ii.286; Ruff 84.

1] ENGLISH MINSTRELSY. . . . Vol . I. . . . 1810.

Collation: π^4 $2\pi^2$ A^8(±A4) B-N^8 O^4 P-S^8. Pagination: *i* half-title, *ii* printer's imprint(1), *iii* title-page, *iv blank*, *v* vi-vii Advertisement, dated from Edinburgh 1 January 1810, *viii blank*, *ix* x-xii Contents, *1* fly-title, *2 blank*, *3* 4-280 text, 280 printer's imprint(2). Typography: In the title of some copies the period is dropped at the end of the third line.

Figures: 2π x-5, A*3*-10 8-8, B31-10, C34-10, D50-10, E66-10, F82-10, G—, H114-10, I—, K147-3/-, L162-10, M178-10, N194-10, O 216-10, P—, Q234-10, R250-10, S270-10. In this consecutive press-work, with one press figure to a sheet, the superfluous figure 8 on page 8 identifies the cancellans A4, original readings unknown.

Notes: First Printing of a Scott poem [1] 'LVIII. THE RESOLVE.—ANONYMOUS.' (first words: 'My wayward fate I needs must plain,'), pages 212-214. This volume also includes a reprinting of 'Hunting Song', pages 26-266, which first appears untitled in *Queenhoo-Hall*, 1808.

2] ENGLISH MINSTRELSY. . . . Vol. II. . . . 1810.

Collation: π^4 A-I^8 K^4(-K1,2,+K1.2) χ^4 L-M^8 N^8(±N2) O-Q^8 R^4. Pagination: *i* half-title, *ii* printer's imprint(1), *iii* title-page, *iv blank*, *v* vi-viii Contents, *1* fly-title, *2 blank*, *3* 4-264 text, 264 printer's imprint(2).

Figures: π vi-10, A15-10/-, B18-10, C34-10, D50-10, E66-10, F82-10, G98-10, H114-10, I 142-10, K148-10 153-2, L162-10, M183-10, N200-2, O 223-2, P228-3 230-1, Q243-2, R259-2. The additional figure 10 on page 148 identifies the second leaf of the conjugate cancellentia K1.2, original readings unknown. In several copies leaves K1.2 and N2 are uncancelled, with invariant text.

Notes: First Printings of Scott's poems, all now in the Contents attributed to him and marked * as original: [2] 'XLIII. WITH FLOWERS FROM A ROMAN WALL.—WALTER SCOTT.', (first words: 'Take these flowers which, purple waving,'), page 191; [3] 'XLIV. *THE BARD'S INCANTATION.—WALTER SCOTT.' (first words: 'The Forest of Glenmore is drear,'), pages 192-196; [4] 'XLV. THE VIOLET.—WALTER SCOTT.' (first words: 'The violet, in her green-wood bower,'), pages 197-198.

References: (Magnum Opus Edition 1834: *The Poetical Works*, [1] viii.374-376, [2] viii.373 as 'To a Lady, with Flowers from a Roman Wall.', [3] viii.*357* 358-360, [4] viii.372.)

EXTRACTS IN ANTHOLOGIES

43E] The four original poems by Scott were extracted in fourteen anthologies:
[1] 'The Resolve' with four entries: E360.21 389.18 405(2)[3] note [one line only] 405(3)[1].8
[2] 'With Flowers from a Roman Wall' with three entries: E356[2].14 392.13 423.5
[3] 'The Bard's Incantation' wth three entries: E356[2].15 378.14 392.14
[4] 'The Violet' with four entries: E356[2].13 392.12 399 423.6

THE ANCIENT BRITISH DRAMA

44A] First Edition: 1810

THE | **Ancient** | **BRITISH DRAMA**. | IN THREE VOLUMES. | [*short Oxford rule*] | VOLUME FIRST [SECOND-THIRD]. | [*vignette*] | LONDON: |

PRINTED FOR WILLIAM MILLER, ALBEMARLE STREET, | BY JAMES BALLANTYNE AND CO. EDINBURGH. | 1810.

Published 28 February 1810 in London (*MC*). £3.8.0. Paper: Royal 8° in fours (224 x 156mm cut). Watermarks: [none]; 1801; 1807; J WHATMAN | 1808. About half of the gatherings are unwatermarked, as would be expected in half-sheet imposition. Conjugate half-title and title in each volume are printed on heavy plate paper.

General Notes: The Preface indicates that this edition is intended to form, with *The British Drama* (1804, a text superseded in 1811 by the *Modern British Drama*: see 54A) and *Shakspeare's Dramatic Works* (1778), a uniform edition of the best English plays. Here only 'the Publisher' assumes responsibility, without reference to Scott, expressed or implied, but the correspondence with Miller indicates his continual involvement. In an unpublished letter (NNP, postmarked 17 February 1809) the editor suggests that the third volume be postponed since it is 'impossible for me to look out & arrange the copy as I am very busy just now . . .'
Three of the editorial initials below the text were employed by John Nichols in his 1780 printing of Dodsley's *Select Collection of Old Plays*, the 'ground-work of the present Collection': 'S.' (George Steevens, apparently); 'S.P.' (identity still unknown); and 'N.' (Nichols himself). Two other initials occasionally appear in this 1810 edition: 'T.' (Thomas Tyrwhitt) and 'E.' (probably signifying the present editor, an initial previously used by Scott in his 1808 edition of the *Memoirs of Robert Cary*). Short bio/bibliographical notes before each play as well as numerous other footnotes appear without initials and may thus also be attributed to Scott.
Again, as for the *English Minstrelsy*, Ballantyne in the first two volumes uses only one press figure for each sheet, indicating leisurely consecutive presswork.

Copies: BCL E EU; CtY DLC IdU NN(2) TxU. Sophisticated copy: CaBVaU (inserted in vol. 3 is the essay 'Remarks on English Opera and Farce', taken from vol. 5 of the 1811 *Modern British Drama*). Reference: Magnum Opus Edition: Not reprinted.)

1] THE | Ancient | **BRITISH DRAMA**. . . . VOLUME FIRST. . . 1810.

Collation: a^2 b^4 A-E^4 $4F^2$. Pagination: *i* half-title, *ii blank*, *iii* title-page, *iv blank*, *v* vi-vii Preface, *viii blank*, *ix* x-xi Contents, *xii blank*, *1* 2-595 text, 595 printer's imprint, *596 blank*. Printer's imprint: [*short Oxford rule*] | EDINBURGH: | Printed by James Ballantyne & Co. Illustration: Title vignette, of a clown and child, is unsigned. Typography: In some copies page-number 497 is transposed as 479.

Figures: A2-8, B16-10, C18-3, D26-2, E34-2, F42-1, G50-3, H58-10, I 66-1, K74-3, L82-4, M90-8, N104-8, O 112-12, P114-2, Q122-8, R136-7/-, S138-10/-, T148-1, U154-12, X162-2, Y176-8, Z180-2, 2A 190-2, 2B 194-10, 2C 203-8, 2D 210-10, 2E—, 2F 226-13, 2G 234-7, 2H 242-12, 2 I *250*-5, 2K 258-10, 2L 266-12, 2M

274-5, 2N 288-4, 2 O 291-2, 2P 304-1, 2Q 312-6, 2R 320-5, 2S 328-6, 2T 330-5, 2U 344-4, 2X 346-5, 2Y 354-2, 2Z 362-5, 3A 374-4, 3B 378-1, 3C 392-8, 3D 400-13, 3E 408-7, 3F 416-1, 3G 424-12, 3H 432-12, 3 I 440-7, 3K 442-8, 3L 456-11, 3M 462-8, 3N 472-13, 3 O 474-7/-, 3P 482-2, 3Q 492-13, 3R 498-7, 3S 506-4, 3T 514-8, 3U—, 3X 530-8, 3Y 538-7, 3Z 546-7, 4A 554-4, 4B 562-1, 4C 570-2, 4D 578-13, 4E 586-2, 4F 594-11.

2] THE | Ancient | **BRITISH DRAMA**. . . . VOLUME SECOND. . . . 1810.

Collation: π^2 A-4H[4]. Pagination: *i* half-title, *ii blank*, *iii* title-page, *iv blank*, *1* 2-614 text, 614 printer's imprint, *615-616 blank*. Printer's imprint: [*short Oxford rule*] | EDINBURGH: | Printed by James Ballantyne & Co. Illustration: Title vignette, of a mourning figure, is unsigned. Typography: On page 591 the page-number 1 has dropped out.

Figures: A2-1, B10-7, C24-4, D26-3, E34-4, F43-8, G56-10, H58-4, I *66*-4, K74-2, L88-2, M96-1, N98-4, O 108-2, P—, Q128-2, R136-1, S138-8, T150-4, U*160*-8, X162-13, Y170-10, Z178-7, 2A 186-8, 2B 200-2, 2C 208-1, 2D 215-2, 2E 223-2, 2F 232-4, 2G 234-2, 2H 244-10, 2 I 256-7, 2K 262-3, 2L 269-2, 2M 280-7, 2N 288-13, 2 O 296-2, 2P 304-10/-, 2Q 312-11, 2R 319-7, 2S 328-7, 2T 330-11, 2U 338-7, 2X 346-3, 2Y 360-7, 2Z 368-10, 3A 376-7, 3B—, 3C 392-8, 3D 400-7, 3E 408-2, 3F 416-1, 3G 421-2, 3H 432-11, 3 I 437-2, 3K 442-8, 3L 450-5, 3M 459-7, 3N 469-7, 3 O 480-8, 3P 488-7, 3Q 496-13, 3R 500-5, 3S 512-5, 3T 517-13, 3U 528-7/-, 3X 536-12, 3Y 543-12, 3Z 552-12, 4A 557-13, 4B 562-7, 4C 576-10, 4D 584-11, 4E 592-11, 4F 600-5, 4G 607-12, 4H 612-12.

3] THE | Ancient | **BRITISH DRAMA**. . . . VOLUME THIRD. . . ALBEMARLE STREET, | BY JAMES MOYES, GREVILLE STREET, HATTON GARDEN. | 1810.

Collation: π^2 A-4F[4]. Pagination: *i* half-title, *ii blank*, *iii* title-page, *iv blank*, *1* 2-598 text, 598 printer's imprint, *599-600* list of books published by William Miller. Printer's imprint: [*short rule*] | J. MOYES, PRINTER, | Greville Street, Hatton Garden, London. Illustration: Title vignette, of a nymph and two cupids, is engraved by F. Engleheart. Figures: None for this volume printed by James Moyes.

Notes: Some indication of haste appears towards the end of this project, pages 508-598, where Webster's controversial *Dutchesse of Malfy* and the two succeeding plays are printed essentially without any annotation other than the few slight notes earlier provided by Dodsley and Nichols.

BIOGRAPHICAL MEMOIR OF DANIEL DE FOE

45A] First Printing: 1810

'BIOGRAPHICAL MEMOIR OF DANIEL DE FOE', volume 1, pages *i* ii-xxxii, *in*:

The Novels of Daniel De Foe. Volume First; [Second-Twelve] . . . Containing Life of De Foe, and Robinson Crusoe. Edinburgh: Printed by James Ballantyne and Co. For John Ballantyne and Co. and Brown and Crombie, Edinburgh; and Longman, Hurst, Rees, and Orme, [and John Murray,] London. 1810.

Publication dates are indeterminate. The first three volumes were announced as 'now ready' 16 March 1809, but only volumes 4-5 are so dated, with Murray there cited as an additional publisher. All twelve volumes were available on 28 April 1810 at £3.12.0 (*EEC*).

Notes: As the publication details would suggest, this is a bibliographical puzzle since the Biographical Memoir originally was credited to John Ballantyne, with Scott's intervention, if any, not readily ascertained. In 1840-1841 and certain later editions of the *Novels* the titles declare, rather ambiguously, the presence of 'a biographical memoir, literary prefaces to the various pieces, illustrative notes, etc., including all contained in the edition attributed to the late Sir Walter Scott. . . .' Nonetheless, the memoir itself, as originally composed for this edition, does not yet contain the many revisions and additions later provided by Scott in 1827 (*see* 287A.4) and thus, in 1810, may still be attributed, in some measure, to John Ballantyne.

Copies: BCL E. Reference: (Magnum Opus Edition 1834: *The Miscellaneous Prose Works*, iv.228-296 as 'Daniel De Foe'.)

PROLOGUE FOR THE FAMILY LEGEND

46Aa] First Printing: 1810

'PROLOGUE. WRITTEN BY WALTER SCOTT, ESQ.' (first words: ''Tis sweet to hear expiring Summer's sigh,'), pages *iii*-iv, *in*:

The Family Legend: A Tragedy. By Joanna Baillie. Edinburgh: Printed by James Ballantyne and Co. For John Ballantyne and Co. Hanover-Street; and Longman, Hurst, Rees, and Orme, Paternoster-Row, London. 1810.

Published 28 April 1810 in Edinburgh (*EEC*).

Notes: The play is dedicated to Scott (*see* 505T), who is the first, in 'To the Reader', to receive (page xiii) the author's 'warmest acknowledgements' in facilitating the stage production, first performed 22 January in the Edinburgh Theatre-Royal. The reviewer in the *Scots Magazine* (February 1810, page 107) 'could not relish' Daniel Terry's recitation, though the prologue itself 'appeared to be worthy' of Scott. The play, issued the same day as the *Novels of Daniel Defoe*, is entered after that work since it is not listed there among the titles 'lately published'.

The text is described as being from the original copy given to the Theatre, rather than from the play as presented. At this performance Scott first met Terry, soon to become one of his closest friends and confidants. The 'Prologue' was later extracted, 1814, in an anthology (408[2]E.2).

Copies: O; CtY InU TxU. References: Duval 32 (with illustration). (Magnum Opus Edition 1834: *The Poetical Works*, viii.387-389.)

46Ab] Second Printing: 1810

PROLOGUE. WRITTEN BY WALTER SCOTT, ESQ. SPOKEN BY MR TERRY.', pages *iii*-iv, *in*:

The Family Legend: A Tragedy. . . The Second Edition. Edinburgh: Printed by James Ballantyne and Co. For John Ballantyne and Co., Hanover-Street; and Longman, Hurst, Rees, Orme, and Brown, Paternoster-Row, London. 1810.

Published 15 September 1810 in Edinburgh (*EEC*).

Notes: A different setting, with 'Spoken by Mr Terry' added to the heading and, in line 21, 'groupe' altered to 'group'.

Copies: DT E O; InU NjP NN(2) OCl TxU(2).

REPRINT

UNITED STATES

46R] NEW YORK: Longworth 1810

'Prologue. Written by Walter Scott, Esq.', page *vii*, *in*: The Family Legend: A Tragedy, in Five Acts. . . . New-York: Published by D. Longworth, At the Dramatic Repository, Shakspeare-Gallery. Nov.--1810. Notes: Drama by Joanna Baillie, which as in the authorized editions is dedicated to Scott (*see* 557T). Title-page reads '(First american[!] from the first Edinburgh edition of 1810).' Copies: E; MH MWA NjP NN-L(prompt copy) PPL PU.

THE LADY OF THE LAKE

This poem, the action of which lay among scenes so beautiful, and so deeply imprinted on my recollections, was a labour of love, and it was no less so to recall the manners and incidents introduced. The frequent custom of James IV., and particularly of James V., to walk through their kingdom in disguise, afforded me the hint of an incident, which never fails to be interesting if managed with the slightest address or dexterity. . . . [The success of the poem] was certainly so extraordinary as to induce me for the moment to conclude that I had at last fixed a nail in the proverbially inconstant wheel of Fortune . . . . ('Introduction', April 1830, *PW,* viii.4-5, 10.)

47Aa] First Edition, First Impression: 1810

THE | **LADY OF THE LAKE;** | A POEM. | BY | WALTER SCOTT, Esq. | [*short Oxford rule*] | EDINBURGH: | [*short Oxford rule*] | PRINTED FOR | JOHN BALLANTYNE AND CO. EDINBURGH; | AND | LONGMAN, HURST, REES, AND ORME, AND WILLIAM MILLER, | LONDON; | *By James Ballantyne and Co. Edinburgh.* | [*Oxford dash*] | 1810.

Published 8 May 1810 in Edinburgh (*EEC* 28 April, 10 May); issued 16 May in London (*MC*). £2.2.0. 2000 copies. Binding: drab, blue, or dark blue boards with printed label; grey boards without label, or (a later issue?) cream boards with green cloth spine. Paper: Demy 4° (277 x 220mm uncut). Watermarks: 1807; 1809; 4 | W Balston | 1810. Collation: π^4 2π1 A-2N^4 2 O 1 a-q^4 *r*1. Pagination: *i* half-title, *ii blank*, *iii* title, *iv blank*, *v* dedication to John James, Marquis of Abercorn, *vi blank*, *vii* Argument, *viii blank*, *ix* Contents, *x blank*, *1* fly-title, *2 blank*, *3* 4-290 text, *i* fly-title, *ii blank*, *iii* iv-cxxix Notes, cxxix Errata, author's apology, printer's imprint, *cxxx blank*. Printer's imprint: [*short Oxford rule*] | Edinburgh: | Printed by James Ballantyne & Co. Illustrations: Engraved frontispiece portrait of Scott and his dog Camp, painted by Saxon, engraved by Heath, with caption: 'Walter Scott Esqr.'; published by Ballantyne & Co. and Longman, Hurst, Rees & Orme, & W. Miller', dated 1 March 1810.

Figures: A7-11 8-8, B10-11, C22-8, D26-8 32-11, E34-5 36-6, F42-8 48-1, G50-8 56-11, H58-11 64-8, I 70-8, K74-11, L82-8, M90-11, N98-8, O 106-6 112-5, P114-11 120-5, Q128-8, R130-11, S138-8 144-6, T146-11, U154-8 160-9, X162-9 168-8, Y170-11 176-9, Z178-9 184-8, 2A 186-8 192-9, 2B 194-9 200-8, 2C 202-8 208-9, 2D 216-9, 2E 218-8 224-11, 2F 226-8 232-9, 2G 234-11, 2H 244-9 247-8, 2 I 250-8 256-9, 2K 258-11 264-5, 2L 266-9 272-8, 2M 274-5/- 277-8, 2N 282-9 284-11, 2 O—, a iv-13 vii-14, b x-11, c xxii-5 xxiv-11/-, d xxviii-11 xxxi-5, e xxxv-14 xl-6, f *xliii*-11 xlviii-8, g l-7 lvi-1, h lxi-5 lxii-8, i lxvii-1 lxxii-6, k lxxv-6 lxxx-7, l lxxxiii-6 lxxxviii-7, m xc-6 xcvi-7, n *ciii*-8 civ-9, o cvii-13 cxii-6, p cxviii-6 cxx-11, q cxxv-13 cxxvii-6, *r*—.

Notes: Some six weeks before publication, on 14 March, Scott sent to Lady Abercorn printed copy of the first two cantos for Lord Abercorn's approval as the dedicatee. Shortly thereafter, on the 30th, he reported, in some amusement, that two rival sets of illustrations were then being prepared, one again by Richard Westall, who had previously embellished his earlier poems, and the other by Richard Cook, an artist now employed by Longman. (As noted below [47Ae] the Cook plates were still being prepared on 1 August.) When finally issued, one or another of these suites were occasionally applied to the first and later edition copies. On 7 May, the day before official issue, an advance copy was sent to Lady Dalkeith, another to Anne Arden, baroness Alvanley, and a royal-paper copy to Richard Heber. Robert Southey received his copy at Durham 10 May.

Page 86, line 11 of text, reads: 'but e'er'. Two states occur in the original printing, page 288 below text (a) 'END OF CANTO SIXTH.' (b) line withdrawn in view of the same reference below text on page 290. It would appear that the printer had assumed the poem was at an end before receiving Scott's memorable peroration beginning 'Harp of the North, farewell!', this requiring an extra leaf of text (2 0: pages 289-290) and rendering the earlier END statement superfluous.

The textual notes exhibit, more clearly than before, Scott's increasing tendency to augment the commentary previously supplied: this brought on perhaps by his unrestrained annotation in the Somers Tracts 1809-1815. To the 1808 *Marmion* he later added, in the third edition, only one further note. To this poem, in 1810, he immediately provided, in the second edition, eleven more as well as extending various others.

Presentation copies: [state a] LU('The Honble Lady [Mary Elizabeth] Hood From her faithful & much honoured freind The Author'); InU('These four volumes were presentation copies from Sir Walter Scott to my mother'*) NN('Lady Charlotte Campbell From her Ladyships Most obedient & very faithful humble Servant The Author'). [state b] TxU('Miss Joanna Baillie from her sincere freind & the arden[!] admirer of her sublime genius Walter Scott').
*The statement is signed by the son, C. C. Southey, who presented the volumes to his wife Anne in August 1844. For other Southey copies *see* 28Aa.

Other copies: [state a] A E(2); IdU NN(2) PU+w. [b] AN(2) BCL E ES(2) LVA+w (Forster) O(2) O+w O+w,c; CtY(2) InU(2) InU# MH NjP* NjP(2) NN(3) NNP(Van Antwerp) NNP(with Scott's ms corrections) NNP## OCl PPL T/B TxU ViU.
*Hester Lynch Piozzi 'May 1810' with her annotations.
+Extra-illustrated with an 1811 engraved title-page and six plates by (w) Richard Westall (47Dam) or (c) Richard Cook (47Dab[3]).
#With 11 ink and aquatint illustrations by Thomas Stothard.
##Original boards, but notes bound in first; with prospectus inserted for Westall plates.

References: Abbotsford, page 271(noted as presented to Scott's mother, but not inscribed); *Letters*, ii.311,321, 330-331; xii.318; Grady, pages 186-234, 399-401; Ruff 86 (illustration of Scott's ms corrections, page 243, NNP copy); Sterling 716; Thomson, pages 39-40; Tinker 1865; Van Antwerp(1) 8(Lady Alvanley). (Magnum Opus Edition 1834: *The Poetical Works*, viii.*1-3* 4-353.)

47Ab] First Edition, Second (Large-Paper) Impression: 1810

THE | **LADY OF THE LAKE;** | A POEM. . . . 1810.

Published concurrently with the previous impression. £4.4.0. A 'very few' (20) copies on 'plate paper'. Binding: (for the Princess of Wales copy) yellow glazed boards without label. Paper: Royal 4° (318 x 252mm uncut, bulking 54mm). Watermarks: 1803; 1805. Typography: Though the three errata cited page cxxix in the preceding impression remain unaltered, page 86, line 12, is corrected to read: 'but ere' and page 288 is in its corrected state, without line below text.

Figures: Perhaps because of its large size (some 13mm taller than other special impressions), a condition rendering it somewhat unmanageable at press, this reimposed issue exhibits a repeated disturbance in the figure register. In eight of the sheets previously double-figured one of the numbers has now dropped out or been withdrawn (pages D32, F48, P120, S144, U160, 2K 264, 2M 274[as in some of the earlier copies], h lxi). In eleven others the number has been withdrawn in one forme and a new number substituted in the other (pages E4— 36-8, O 106-11 112—, a iv-11 vii—, e xxxv-8 xl—, g l-11 lvi—, i lxvii-8 lxxii—, k lxxv-8 lxxx—, m xc-8 xcvi—, o cvii— cxii-10, p cxviii— cxx-10, q cxxv— cxxvii-8). In yet another sheet (R, page 130) the only number has been changed from 11 to 10.

Notes: After its main entry in the 10 May *Edinburgh Evening Courant* John Ballantyne and Co. further report that they have, 'at considerable expence, made up six sets of the above works [*The Lay of the Last Minstrel, Marmion,* and this poem], in royal and demy quarto, embellished with TWENTY SEVEN quarto plates, almost all proofs, illustrative of the subjects and scenery of the poems. . . .' For this special grangerized issue no price is given, but a partial accounting may be found, for *The Lay of the Last Minstrel* and *The Lady of the Lake* in a description of Ballantyne's own copies (Abbotsford, page 338), for *Marmion* in a copy once owned by A. G. Hunter (see 28Ab).

Presentation copies: CtY('Richard Heber Esquire from his affectionate friend The Author' [with letter from Scott to Heber dated 8 May 1810]) InU('To Her Royal Highness The Princess of Wales From Her Royal Highness's most dutiful much honoured & most obliged humble servant The author'). Other copies: BCL L+c; MH NNP NNU-W(Auchincruive) ViU.
+Extra-illustrated with an 1811 engraved title-page and six plates by (c) Richard Cook (47Dab[3]).

Reference: Ruff 87.

47Ac] Second Edition, First Impression: 1810

THE | **LADY OF THE LAKE.** | A POEM. | BY | WALTER SCOTT, Esq. | THE SECOND EDITION. | [*short Oxford rule*] | EDINBURGH: | [*short Oxford rule*] | PRINTED FOR | JOHN BALLANTYNE AND CO. EDINBURGH; | AND | LONGMAN, HURST, REES, AND ORME, AND W. MILLER, | LONDON; | *By James Ballantyne and Co. Edinburgh.* | [*dash*] | 1810.

Published 5 July 1810 in Edinburgh (*EEC*). 12s. 3000 copies. Binding: blue-green boards with printed label. Paper: Demy 8° (226 x 144mm uncut). Watermarks: 7 | WB | 1809; 7 [9] | W Balston | 1809; *none* [4] | W Balston | 1810; *none* [2, 4] | J Whatman | 1810. Typography: The semicolon at the end of the third line of the imprint has dropped. Collation: π^4 $2\pi 1$ A-S^8 T1(=$2\pi 2$) U-2E^8. Pagination: *i* half-title, *ii blank*, *iii* title-page, *iv blank*, *v* dedication, *vi blank*, *vii* Argument, *viii blank*, *ix* Contents, *x blank*, *1* fly-title, *2 blank*, *3* 4-290 text, *291* fly-title, *292 blank*, *293* 294-433 Notes, 433 author's apology and printer's imprint, *434 blank.* Printer's imprint: [*short Oxford rule*] | Edinburgh: | Printed by James Ballantyne & Co.

Figures: A*3*-8 16-11, B18-1 29-9, C34-11 36-8, D55-9 64-8, E66-5 68-10, F86-8 88-9, G100-8 110-10, H116-6 118-11, I 134-8 144-11, K151-9 153-7, L162-8 176-11, M183-6 192-7, N195-1 208-9, O 215-8 224-6, P229-1 230-5, Q246-7 256-6, R263-6 265-5, S279-10 285-7, T290-10/-, U296-9 298-7, X310-6 313-5, Y326-1, Z341-2 354-13, 2A *359*-1/- 361-10, 2B 378-11 384-5, 2C 388-12 402-7, 2D 404-6 411-3, 2E 423-13 432-2.

Notes: Two months after initial issue, this second edition displays Scott's inclination to multiply his notes, here in cantos 3 (from 11 to 16), 4 (12 to 14) and 5 (9 to 13), and even when the notes remain essentially the same, as in canto 5 note 12 (note 9 in the first edition), to augment these, here from nine to 58 lines. Also of interest is his repeated reference to Burt's *Letters from a Gentleman in the North of Scotland* (canto 2 notes 1, 10, 16, 17 in the first edition and, newly added here in canto 3, notes 13, 16): an allusion that eventually implicated him as the author of *Waverley* (*see* 77Aa, Ac). Both in the first edition (page xli) and in this setting (page 331) canto 2 note XVII is misnumbered VIII: see further the fifth and sixth editions described below. A note on page 346 refers to an erroneous explanation in the first edition. As revealed in several copies the two single leaves $2\pi 1$ and T1 were imposed together and, to fill the forme, set in duplicate, page *ix* with short Oxford rule measuring either 15 or 19mm, page 289 with signature T below 'id' of 'idle' and 290 figure 10, or T below 'l' of 'idle' and 290 unfigured. (As may be surmised from the intermittent 290 figure this same arrangement appears to hold for later editions and thus will not be noted further.)

Copies: BCL E(3) ES L LVA(Dyce) O(Douce); NN NNP T/B TxU+w.
+Extra-illustrated with an 1811 engraved title-page and six plates by (w) Richard

Westall (47Dam).

Reference: Ruff 88.

47Ad] Second Edition, Second (Large-Paper) Impression: 1810

THE | **LADY OF THE LAKE.** . . . THE SECOND EDITION. . . . 1810.

Published concurrently with the previous impression. £1.1.0. Paper: Royal 8° (232 x 144mm cut). Watermarks: J WHATMAN | 1807. Collation and pagination as for the preceding impression. Figures: as for first impression except B18-11 and K150-8 151—. Also four figures at pages D55, E66, F88, and S285 dropped out upon the reimposition for this issue.

Copies: BCL L LU+c; CtY T/B+w#. Reference: Ruff 89.
+Extra-illustrated with an 1811 engraved title-page and six plates by (w) Richard Westall (47Dam) or (c) Richard Cook (47Dab[3]).
#With the Raeburn frontispiece imprinted 1 February 1811.

47Ae] Third Edition: 1810

THE | **LADY OF THE LAKE.** | A POEM. | BY | WALTER SCOTT, ESQ. | THE THIRD EDITION. | [*short Oxford rule*] | EDINBURGH: | [*short Oxford rule*] | PRINTED FOR | JOHN BALLANTYNE AND CO. EDINBURGH; | AND LONGMAN, HURST, REES, AND ORME, AND W. MILLER, | LONDON; | *By James Ballantyne and Co. Edinburgh.* | [*dash*] | 1810.

Published 2 August 1810 in Edinburgh (*EEC*). 12s. 3250 copies. Binding: blue-green boards with printed label. Paper: Demy 8° (226 x 144mm cut). Water-marks: 3 | 1809; 7 [9] | W BALSTON | 1809; 7 [9] | J WHATMAN | 1809; 2 [4,5,6,7,8] | W BALSTON | 1810; 2 | J WHATMAN | 1810. Collation and pagination for this and all succeeding 1810 issues as for Second Edition.

Figures: A4-12 6-13, B22-10 28-3, C36-9 42-13, D52-3 58-9, E67-2 80-6, F82-7 88-8, G98-9 109-13, H126-1 128-5, I 130-10 132-1, K150-2/- 160-3, L162-8 176-11, M183-6 192-7, N195-1 208-9, O 215-8 224-6, P229-1 230-5, Q245-7 250-9, R263-6, S279-10 285-7, T290-10/-, U296-9 298-7, X321-7 322-9, Y326-3, Z341-2 354-13, 2A *359*-1 361-10, 2B 378-11 384-5, 2C 388-12 402-7, 2D 404-6 411-3, 2E 423-13 432-2.

Notes: The decision to go into a third edition was apparently made after some ten or twelve sheets had been printed for the second, and the issue increased accordingly. As the figures would suggest, sheets A-K and Q of this new edition were reset, R, X-Y reimpressed from the previous setting, and L-P, S-U, Z-2E continued now in a larger impression used for both editions. As before T1 is in a duplicate setting, page 290 with or without the press figure. On reimpressed page 331 (in gathering Y) the note is now correctly numbered XVII.

Copies: E O; CtY T/B TxU* ViU. Reference: Ruff 90.
*With 1 August 1810 slip announcing preparation of the Cook plates.

47Af] Fourth Edition, First Issue: 1810

THE | **LADY OF THE LAKE.** | A POEM. | BY | WALTER SCOTT, Esq. | THE FOURTH EDITION. | [*short Oxford rule*] | EDINBURGH: | [*short Oxford rule*] | PRINTED FOR | JOHN BALLANTYNE AND CO. EDINBURGH; | AND | LONGMAN, HURST, REES, AND ORME, AND W. MILLER, | LONDON; | *By James Ballantyne and Co. Edinburgh.* | [*dash*] | 1810.

Published 22 September 1810 in Edinburgh (*EEC*). 12s. 6000 copies. Binding: grey-green boards with printed label. Paper: Demy 8° (223 x 143mm uncut). Watermarks: 9 | W Balston | 1809; 2 [4, 5, 6, 7, 8] | W Balston | 1810. Collation and pagination as for the Second Edition.

Figures: A13-6 15-9, B20-8 27-2, C35-3 48-9, D50-6 64-9, E70-7 80-9, F88-8 91-7, G98-1 109-13, H128-12, I 130-10 132-1, K150-2/- 160-3, L163-9 176-6, M182-9 192-7, N206-13 208-7, O 210-1 224-6, P227-5 237-6, Q245-7 250-9, R258-7 260-13, S274-12 288-6, T290-1/-, U296-8 303-9, X321-2 322-5, Y324-8 326-13, Z340-8 343-5, 2A 360-12 363-7, 2B 373-9 374-1, 2C 388-7 395-6, 2D 405-6 414-13, 2E 423-9 428-4.

Notes: Again the demand for this poem soon required a further issue: this edition being thus reset through sheet E in the text, X only in the Notes, partially reimpressed in most other gatherings, and of the same impression in gatherings I-K and M. On reset page 331 the note is still correctly numbered XVII.

Copies: E+w L; CtY+w* CtY+c T/B. Reference: Ruff 91.
+Extra-illustrated with an 1811 engraved title-page and six plates by (w) Richard Westall (47Dam) or (c) Richard Cook (47Dab[3]).
*With an undated 16-page Sharpe and Hailes catalogue advertising the Westall plate issue of this and earlier Scott poems as available 'in a Variety of Morocco and other elegant Bindings.'

47Ag] Fourth Edition, Second Issue: 1810

THE | **LADY OF THE LAKE.** | A POEM. . . THE FOURTH EDITION. . . . LONGMAN, HURST, REES, ORME, AND BROWN, AND | W. MILLER, LONDON; | *By James Ballantyne and Co. Edinburgh.* | [*dash*] | 1810.

Note: As for first issue except that conjugate leaves π2-3 have been cancelled to allow for the title-page imprint reading as above. This now includes a new partner, Thomas Brown, who joined the firm between 27 July and 9 August 1810, but whose name for some reason was excluded in the previous issue.

Copies: AN O; CtY ViU. Reference: Ruff 91 note.

47Ah] Fifth Edition, First Issue: 1810

THE | **LADY OF THE LAKE.** | A POEM. | BY | WALTER SCOTT, Esq. | THE FIFTH EDITION. | [*short Oxford rule*] | EDINBURGH: | [*short Oxford rule*] | PRINTED FOR | JOHN BALLANTYNE AND CO. EDINBURGH; | AND LONGMAN, HURST, REES, ORME, AND BROWN, AND | W. MILLER, LONDON; | *By James Ballantyne and Co. Edinburgh.* | [*dash*] | 1810.

Published 25 October 1810 in Edinburgh (*EEC*). 12s. 6000 copies. Binding: Paper: Demy 8° (223 x 140mm uncut). Watermarks: *none* [1, 2, 4, 5, 6, 7, 8, 9] | W Balston | 1810; 4 | W Balston | 810; 4 [8] | W Balston | 18 0; (sheet S only, now usually discoloured) D & A C | 1808 | 1; 1809 | 1 [2]. Collation and pagination as for the Second Edition. Typography: page 214 is misnumbered 124.

Figures: A5-11 6-8, B18-7 28-12, C36-1 43-6, D56-8 63-13, E70-4 73-2, F82-7/-[or]85-11, G107-5 112-6, H114-9 116-8, I 138-5 144-6, K147-8 160-2/—, L167-7 176-11, M180-5 183-8, N199-4 208-6, O '124'[214]-11 224-7, P229-8 230-13, Q246-3 256-1, R258-13 272-9, S283-7 284-8, T290-11/-, U301-12 306-, X317-318-2, Y336-9 338-1, Z340-8 343-5, 2A 360-12 363-7, 2B 373-9 374-1, 2C *399*-12 400-13, 2D 405-6 414-13, 2E 423-9 428-4.

Notes: The whole of sheet S (pages 273-288), now discoloured and with variant watermarks, may represent a cancel. As the figures illustrate, final sheets Z-2B, 2D-2E are of the same impression as those in the fourth edition, indicating a deliberate over-printing in anticipation of this later issue. In reset Y page 331 for this (and the next three 1810 'editions') now again has note XVII incorrectly numbered VIII, indicating the second edition as copytext for at least some of these printings. This fifth edition, however, on pages 316-317 correctly orders as Notes VI, VII two entries previously misnumbered as VII, VIII.

As might be supposed from the irregular numbering of subsequent issues through the 'eighth edition' detailed below, the '6000' issue reported by Lockhart probably comprehends not only this but all the remaining 1810 variants.

Copies: E L O; CtY T/B TxU. Reference: Ruff 92.

47Ai] Sixth Edition (Fifth Edition, Second Issue): 1810

THE | **LADY OF THE LAKE.** | A POEM. . . . THE SIXTH EDITION. . . . 1810.

Issued 29 November 1810 in London (*MC*). 12s. Collation, pagination, and figures as for the preceding issue, but sheets R and S in some copies are now of fine unwatermarked paper. Typography: As before page 214 is misnumbered 124. Additionally, in some copies, the 1 in page-number 194 has dropped out.

Notes: Except for the preliminary gathering the figures indicate that this 'edition' is of the same impression as the 'fifth edition', but now newly labelled to dispose of remainder copies before issue of the legitimate 'sixth edition' next described.

Copies: E O; CtY T/B. Reference: Ruff 93.

47Aj] Sixth Edition, First Issue: 1810

THE | **LADY OF THE LAKE.** | A POEM. | BY | WALTER SCOTT, Esq. | THE SIXTH EDITION. | [*short Oxford rule*] | EDINBURGH: | [*short Oxford rule*] | PRINTED FOR | JOHN BALLANTYNE AND CO. EDINBURGH; | AND | LONGMAN, HURST, REES, ORME, AND BROWN, AND | W. MILLER, LONDON; | *By James Ballantyne and Co. Edinburgh.* | [*dash*] | 1810.

Issued 29 November 1810 in London (*MC*). 12s. Paper: Demy 8° (205 x 127mm cut). Watermarks: 1809 | 1 [2]. Collation and pagination as for the Second Edition. Typography: In a few copies of this reset sixth through the eighth 'edition', signature C (page 33) is missigned D, the 1 in page number 316 is lacking, and (as copied from the 'fifth edition') pages 194 and 214 are misnumbered 94 and 124, respectively: all confirming other evidence of an identical type-setting. Printer's imprint: [*short Oxford rule*] | Edinburgh: | Printed by Jas. Ballantyne & Co.

Figures: A6-8 16-9, B19-13 24-4, C40-2 42-1, D54-7 64-6, E74-13 80-12, F89-6 90-9, G99-2 109-1, H117-4, I 139-2 144-6, K150-3 156-4, L165-12 166-6, M186-4 192-6, N196-3 207-1, O 210-4 217-2, P227-11 229-6, Q246-9 256-4, R258-13 272-9, S283-7 284-2, T290-11, U301-12 306-4, X315-2 320-7, Y*333*-4 338-13, Z340-12 347-13, 2A 369-9 370-12, 2B 372-2 386-11, 2C 392-9 *399*-11, 2D 408-6 415-11, 2E 427-2 429-4.

Notes: Excepting only sheets R-U which, as the figures indicate, are generally of the same impression as the preceding 'sixth edition', this issue is of an entirely new setting.

Copy: L.

47Ak] Seventh Edition (Sixth Edition, Second Issue): 1810

THE | **LADY OF THE LAKE.** | A POEM. . . . THE SEVENTH EDITION. . . . 1810.

Binding: drab boards with printed 'Sixth Edition' label in one of the E copies. Paper: Demy 8° (223 x 141mm cut). Collation, pagination, and figures as for the preceding issue, but paper occasionally bearing a 1810 | 5 watermark.

Notes: This is a further issue of the preceding 'edition' and thus exhibits all the points previously described.

Copies: BCL E* E+w GU O; CtY InU T/B# TxU. Reference: 94.
*With 16-page Longman catalogue March 1810.
#Volume 8 of a Trinity College Dublin prize.
+Extra-illustrated with an 1811 engraved title-page and six plates by (w) Richard Westall (47Dam).

47Al] Eighth Edition (Sixth Edition, Third Issue) 1810

THE | **LADY OF THE LAKE.** | A POEM. . . . THE EIGHTH EDITION. . . . 1810.

Paper: Demy 8° (223 x 141mm uncut). Watermarks: 1809 | 1 [2, 6]. Collation, pagination, and figures as in the preceding issues.

Notes: This is a further reissue of the 'Sixth Edition', again with a new 'edition' title-page.

Copies: E L+w O*; CtY T/B TxU. Reference: Ruff 95.
+Extra-illustrated with an 1811 engraved title-page and six plates by (w) Richard Westall (47Dam).
*With an undated 16-page Sharpe and Hailes catalogue advertising the Westall issue of this and earlier Scott poems as available 'in a Variety of Morocco and other elegant Bindings.'

47Am] Ninth Edition: 1811

THE | **LADY OF THE LAKE.** | A POEM. | BY | WALTER SCOTT, Esq. | THE NINTH EDITION. | [*short Oxford rule*] | EDINBURGH: | [*short Oxford* *rule*] | PRINTED FOR | JOHN BALLANTYNE AND CO. EDINBURGH; | AND LONGMAN, HURST, REES, ORME, AND BROWN, AND | W. MILLER, LONDON; | *By James Ballantyne and Co. Edinburgh.* | [*dash*] | 1811.

3000 copies. Paper: Demy 8° (215 x 132mm cut). Watermarks: 6 [7] | W BALSTON | 1810; 8 | W BALSTON | 1811; 1809 | 6 (sheets O and Q only, both of the same impression as the three issues of the sixth edition). Collation: π^4 $2\pi1$ A-S^8 T1(=$2\pi2$) U-$2E^8$. Pagination: *i* half-title, *ii blank*, *iii* title-page, *iv blank*, *v* dedication, *vi blank*, *vii* Argument, *viii blank*, *ix* Contents, *x blank*, *1* fly-title, *2 blank*, *3* 4-290 text, *291* fly-title, *292 blank*, *293* 294-433 Notes, 433 author's apology, printer's imprint, *434 blank*. Printer's imprint: [*short Oxford rule*] | EDINBURGH: | Printed by Jas. Ballantyne & Co.

Figures: A12-9, B18-6, C38-11, D50-3, E70-4 73-2, F88-11, G99-3, H120-9, I 139-2 144-6, K153-8, L165-12 166-6, M186-4 192-6, N203-11, O 210-4 217-2, P230-11, Q246-9 256-4, R265-11, S278-8 288-11, T—, U297-11 298-6, X317-4 318-2, Y326-8 336-3, Z341-2 354-13, 2A 365-11, 2B 372-2 386-11, 2C *399*-9, 2D 404-9, 2E 428-6.

Notes: As revealed partly by the paper and figures, this edition consists of several amalgams, the first combination noted above (1) consisting of remainder sheets from the second edition (Z), the fifth edition (E, X), the 'sixth-eighth edition' (I, L-M, O, Q, 2B); a new impression of type still composed (2C-2E); and a new setting for type already distributed (A-D, F-H, K, N, P, R-U, Y, 2A). In a later issue (2), nine of these sheets having run out, a new setting was prepared, thus with different figures: E70-8, I 144-9, L162-6, M180-9, O 217-6, Q253-6, X322-9, Z354-9, 2B 385-11/-. Unlike all previous settings the various sheets reset in this edition, it will be observed, generally were printed in a leisurely manner, each by a single pressman. In this and later editions the note page 331 is again numbered, correctly, XVII.

Copies: (issue 1) L. (2) AN BCL E O; NNU-W('To Isabella M[ary] M[ontague] Scott from Charlotte Scott Oct.r 24. 1815.') T/B. Reference: Ruff 96.

47An] Tenth Edition, First Impression: 1814

THE | **LADY OF THE LAKE.** | A POEM. | BY | WALTER SCOTT, ESQ. | THE TENTH EDITION. | [*short Oxford rule*] | EDINBURGH: | [*short Oxford rule*] | *Printed by James Ballantyne and Co.* | FOR | LONGMAN, HURST, REES, ORME, AND BROWN, | LONDON; AND ARCHIBALD CONSTABLE AND CO., AND | JOHN BALLANTYNE AND CO. EDINBURGH. | [*dash*] | 1814.

Published 25 June 1814 in Edinburgh (*EEC*). 14s. 2000 copies. Paper: Demy 8°

(213 x 130mm cut). Watermarks: 7 | W Balston | 1812; none [5, 6, 8, 9] | W Balston | 1813. Typography: In some copies the colon has dropped from the printer's imprint. Collation: π^4 $2\pi^2$(-2π2=T1) A-S^8 T1(=2π2) U-2E^8. Pagination: *i* half-title, *ii blank*, *iii* title-page, *iv blank*, *v* dedication, *vi blank*, *vii* Argument, *viii blank*, *ix* Contents, *x blank, 1* fly-title, *2 blank, 3* 4-290 text, *291* fly-title, *292 blank, 293* 294-433 Notes, 433 author's apology, printer's imprint, *434 blank*. Printer's imprint: [*short Oxford rule*] | Edinburgh: | Printed by James Ballantyne & Co.

Figures: A6-1, B32-1, C42-2, D50-1, E80-6, F87-1, G104-1, H118-2, I 132-1, K154-3, L176-8, M181-2, N199-7 204-5, O 210-2 220-1, P233-5 234-9, Q244-6 250-1, R259-8 260-5, S283-8 284-6, T290-9, U294-5, X321-2, Y335-2, Z352-1, 2A 362-6, 2B 374-6, 2C 395-5, 2D 405-2, 2E 429-3.

Notes: In this reset edition the work again is done in a leisurely fashion, in large part by pressmen 1, 2, 6. As a result of copyright rearrangements the publishers are now differently ordered in the imprint, with John Ballantyne appearing last.

Copies: BCL L O+w O+w,c; NN+c T/B. Reference: Ruff 97.
+Extra-illustrated with an 1811 engraved title-page and six plates by (w) Richard Westall (47Dam) or (c) Richard Cook (47Dab[3])

47Ao] Tenth Edition, Second (Large-Paper) Impression: 1814

THE | **LADY OF THE LAKE.** | A POEM. . . . THE TENTH EDITION. . . 1814.

Paper: Royal 8° (232 x 143mm cut). Watermarks: none [9] | W Balston & Co | 1813. Typography: Final printer's imprint has no colon.

Figures: A—, B32-6, C37-6, D50-6, E80-6, F82-6, G104-10, H114-10, I 130-10, K154-3, L178-8, M181-10, N199-6, O 220-6, P233-6, Q244-6, R259-8 260-5, S284-6, T—, U295-6 300-6, X321-6, Y324-10, Z350-6, 2A 362-6, 2B 374-6, 2C 395-3, 2D 415-5, 2E 429-10.

Notes: With few exceptions (in K, Q, R-S, 2A-2B) none of the sheets for this impression carry the figures for the previous issue: an unusual circumstance..

Copy: CtY(*see* 260Ad[2]). Reference: Ruff 98.

47Ap] Eleventh Edition, First Issue: 1816

THE | **LADY OF THE LAKE,** | A POEM. | BY | WALTER SCOTT, Esq. | THE ELEVENTH EDITION. | [*short Oxford rule*] | EDINBURGH: | [*short Oxford rule*] | *Printed by James Ballantyne and Co.* | FOR | LONGMAN, HURST, REES, ORME, AND BROWN, | LONDON; AND ARCHIBALD

CONSTABLE AND CO., AND | JOHN BALLANTYNE AND CO. EDINBURGH. | [*dash*] | 1816.

Issued 3 October 1816 in London (*MC*). 14s. 2000 copies. Paper: Demy 8° (210 x 130mm cut). Watermarks: 7 | W BALSTON & Co | 1814; *none* [6, 7, 8, 9] | W BALSTON & Co | 1815. Typography: Page 433 is misnumbered 423. Leaf 2A (page 369) is missigned A2.

Collation: π^4 2π1 A-K^8 L^8(±L2) M-2D^8 *2E*1. Pagination: *i* half-title, *ii blank*, *iii* title-page, *iv blank*, *v* dedication, *vi blank*, *vii* Argument, *viii blank*, *ix* Contents, *x blank*, *1* fly-title, *2 blank*, *3* 4-290 text, *291* fly-title, *292 blank*, *293* 294-'423' [433] Notes, '423'[433] author's apology, printer's imprint, 4*34 blank*. Printer's imprint: [*short Oxford rule*] | EDINBURGH: | Printed by Jas. Ballantyne & Co.

Figures: A7-11 16-6, B25-5, C35-1/- 48-8, D50-9 60-6, E74-6 76-1, F83-11 88-10, G100-8 111-9, H114-10 128-11/-, I 135-11 137-6, K154-6 156-8, L171-6 176-11, M178-5/- 185-2, N205-10 206-8, O 215-8 217-11, P234-5 237-8, Q249-4 250-2, R268-4 270-1, S274-1 280-2, T295-1 296-10, U315-10 320-8, X322-6 336-9, Y339-11 345-10, Z363-8 364-10, 2A 374-6, 2B 387-1 400-8, 2C 402-1 408-8, 2D 420-9 427-3, *2E*—.

Notes: The original readings for cancel L2 (pages 163-164) are unknown; present text is identical with that of the tenth edition.

Copies: E L O; NjP T/B+c. Reference: Ruff 99.
+Extra-illustrated with an 1811 engraved title-page and six plates by (c) Richard Cook (47Dab[3]).

47Aq] Eleventh Edition, Second Issue: 1816

THE | **LADY OF THE LAKE,** | A POEM. . . . THE ELEVENTH EDITION. . . . 1816.

Collation: The previous eleventh edition issue is now interspersed with remainder sheets, in part or whole, from the fifth (H), sixth (X), or tenth edition (F,L,T-U,Y-2A,2C-2E), collation, with these substitute gatherings cited here in parentheses: π 2π1 A-E^8 (F^8) G^8 (H^8) I-K^8 (L^8) M-S^8 (T1 U-Z^8 2A^8[-2A8]) 2A-2B^8 (2C8 2D-2E^8). So constituted, the issue still represents a continuous text.

Figures: Substitute sheets/leaves are again represented in the following record by parentheses: A7-11 16-6, B25-5, C48-8, D50-9 60-6, E74-6 76-1, (F87-1), G100-8 111-9, (H114-9 116-8), I 135-11 137-6, K154-6 156-8, (L176-8), M178-5/- 185-2, N205-10 206-8, O 215-8 217-11, P234-5 237-8, Q249-4 250-2, R268-4 270-1, S274-1 280-2, (T—, U294-5, X315-2 320-7, Y335-2, Z352-1, 2A 362-6) 2A 374-6, 2B 387-1 400-8, (2D 405-2, 2E 429-3).

Notes: The figures demonstrate that, *pace* Ruff, some sheets derive from editions other than the tenth, but it may well be, as he suggests, that this is a later, remainder issue rather than (as in 47Ai above), an earlier clearance of stock.

Copy: CtY. Reference: Ruff 100.

47Ar] Twelfth Edition: 1819

THE | **LADY OF THE LAKE,** | A POEM. | BY | WALTER SCOTT, Esq. | THE TWELFTH EDITION. | [*short Oxford rule*] | EDINBURGH: | PRINTED FOR ARCHIBALD CONSTABLE AND CO. EDINBURGH; | AND LONGMAN, HURST, REES, ORME, AND BROWN, LONDON. | [*dash*] | 1819.

Published in 2000 copies. Binding: crushed brown buckram. Paper: Demy 8° (211 x 139mm cut). Watermarks: none. Collation: π^4 2π1 A-2B^8 2C^8(±2C5) 2D^8 *2E*1. Pagination: *i* half-title, *ii* printer's imprint(1), *iii* title-page, *iv blank*, *v* dedication, *vi blank*, *vii* Argument, *viii blank*, *ix* Contents, *x blank*, *1* fly-title, *2 blank*, *3* 4-290 text, *291* fly-title, *292 blank*, *293* 294-433 Notes, 433 author's apology, printer's imprint(2), *434 blank*. Printer's imprint(1): [*short rule*] | *Printed by James Ballantyne and Co. Edinburgh*.; (2): [*short rule*] | Edinburgh: | Printed by James Ballantyne and Co. Typography: Signature 2A (page 369) is missigned A2 and in some copies 2C5 is a cancel.

Figures: A7-9, B20-4, C36-5, D55-13, E68-7, F82-12, G112-12, H126-9, I 144-1, K160-9, L176-8, M179-5 185-9, N201-1, O 224-8, P226-6, Q255-4/-, R265-5, S288-4, T294-8, U319-7, X336-12, Y352-8, Z366-12, 2A 372-8, 2B 389-14, 2C 415-6, 2D 420-9, 2E—.

Notes: John Ballantyne, appearing last in the imprint of the two preceding editions, now is no longer entered as a publisher, since his erratic performance in that capacity finally ceased in October 1817.

Copies: AN E; CtY T/B. Reference: Ruff 101.

47As] New (Thirteenth) Edition: 1825

[*engraved title*] THE | LADY OF THE LAKE, | A POEM. | BY | Sir WALTER SCOTT, Bart. | A NEW EDITION. | [*short reversed Oxford rule*] | [*vignette of Stirling Castle*] | EDINBURGH; | PRINTED FOR ARCHIBALD CONSTABLE AND CO. EDINBURGH; | LONGMAN, HURST, REES, ORME, AND BROWN; | AND HURST ROBINSON AND CO LONDON. | [*short French rule*] | 1825.

Published 15 June 1825 in Edinburgh (*EWJ*). 9s. 2500 copies, a count perhaps including the fourteenth edition. Paper: Foolscap 8° (164 x 103mm cut). Watermarks: none. Collation: A-2E⁸. Pagination: *1* half-title, *2 blank*, [*engraved title*], *3* dedication, *4 blank*, *5* Argument, *6 blank*, *7* fly-title, *8 blank*, *9* 10-296 text, *297* fly-title, *298 blank*, *299* 300-445 Notes, 445 author's apology, printer's imprint, *446-448 blank*. Printer's imprint: [*short rule*] | EDINBURGH: | Printed by James Ballantyne & Co. Typography: Leaf A5 (page 9) is signed A2.

Figures: A13-5, B—, C48-47, D61-6, E80-2, F96-7, G112-1, H128-6, I 144-6, K160-1, L176-3, M192-2, N208-4, O 223-6, P240-1, Q—, R272-3, S285-6, T304-4, U317-2, X336-6, Y352-6, Z368-4, 2A 384-2, 2B 400-6, 2C 416-2, 2D—, 2E 444-5.

Notes: With reference to this and *Marmion* the periodicals note that 'Travellers and others visiting the Scenes of the above celebrated Poems, will find these editions to form two neat pocket volumes.' This edition exists in two issues: third line of title imprint ends (1) 'ORME, AND BROWN;' (2) 'ORME, BROWN, AND GREEN;'.

Copies: (issue 1) L; T/B. (2) C. Reference: Ruff 102.

47At] Fourteenth Edition (*Poetical Works*, Reissue): 1825

THE | **LADY OF THE LAKE,** | A POEM. | BY | SIR WALTER SCOTT, BART. | FOURTEENTH EDITION. | [*short Oxford rule*] | EDINBURGH: | PRINTED FOR ARCHIBALD CONSTABLE AND CO. EDINBURGH; | AND LONGMAN, HURST, REES, ORME, BROWN, AND GREEN, | LONDON. | [*dash*] | 1825.

Typography: Printer's imprints (1): EDINBURGH: | PRINTED BY JAMES BALLANTYNE AND CO.; (2) [*short rule*] | EDINBURGH: | Printed by James Ballantyne and Co.

Notes: A variant issue of the 1825 *Poetical Works*, volume VII (267Aa) with new preliminaries, imprint(1) added to verso of the half-title, but (as with earlier separate editions) imprint(2) entered on page 439, excluding the 'Miscellaneous Poems' added in the *Works* volume.

Copies: O; T/B. Reference: Ruff 103.

47Au] Fourteenth Edition (*Poetical Works*, Reissue): 1830

[THE | **LADY OF THE LAKE,** | A POEM. . . . FOURTEENTH EDITION. . . . 1830.]

Published: by 20 April 1830 at 14s (advertisement in *Doom of Devorgoil*). 2500 copies (a count including thirteenth edition?). Paper: Demy 8°. Collation and pagination as in the preceding 1825 issue, but title now of later date and including

Scott's introduction dated Abbotsford, April 1830.

Copy: not seen. Reference: Ruff 104.

47Av] New (Fifteenth) Edition, First Issue: 1830

[*engraved title*] THE | LADY OF THE LAKE, | A POEM. | BY | SIR WALTER SCOTT, BART. | A NEW EDITION. | [*short reversed Oxford rule*] | [*vignette*] | EDINBURGH; | PRINTED FOR ROBERT CADELL EDINBURGH; | AND SIMPKIN AND MARSHALL LONDON. | [*short French rule*] | 1830.

Published 26 June 1830 in Edinburgh (*EEC*). 9s. Paper: Foolscap 8° (162 x 102mm cut). Watermarks: none. Collation: a[8] A-2E[8]. Pagination: *i* half-title, *ii blank*, [*engraved title*], *iii* iv-xv Introduction, dated Abbotsford, April 1830, *xvi blank*, *1* fly-title, *2 blank*, *3* dedication, *4 blank*, *5* Argument, *6 blank*, *7* fly-title, *8 blank*, *9* 10-296 text, *297* fly-title, *298 blank*, *299* 300-445 Notes, 445 author's apology, printer's imprint, *446-448 blank*. Printer's imprint: EDINBURGH: | PRINTED BY ANDREW SHORTREED, | THISTLE LANE. Figures: none.

Notes: This edition is essentially a paginal resetting of the 1825 'New Edition' (47As), now with Scott's new 1830 introduction, without press figures, and with variant title and printer's imprint.

Copy: L. Reference: Ruff 105.

47Aw] New (Fifteenth) Edition, Second Issue: 1832

[[*engraved title*] THE | LADY OF THE LAKE, | A POEM. . . . A NEW EDITION. . . . PRINTED FOR ROBERT CADELL EDINBURGH; | AND WHITTAKER & CO. LONDON. | [*dash*] | 1832.]

Paper: Foolscap 8° (162 x 102mm cut).

Notes: A reissue of the 1830 'New Edition' (47Av) with title of later date and indicating a different London publisher.

Copy: not seen. Reference: Ruff 106.

REPRINTS

FRANCE

47Ra] PARIS: Baudry 1822
The Lady of the Lake, A Poem. By Sir Walter Scott, Bart. Paris, Printed for Baudry, English, Italian, Spanish, Portuguese, and German Library, Rue du Coq-St.-Honoré. 1822. Pages: *1-9* 10-355. Notes: Vignette title-page. Copy: T/B.

PARIS: Didot and Galignani
[~] Lady of the Lake. 1821, 1826. (Collection of Modern English Authors: *see* 290R[3A], [3C].)

PARIS: Galignani
[~] The Lady of the Lake. 1829. (*See* 293R.9) Copy: not seen.

GERMANY

ZWICKAU: Schumann
[~] The Lady of the Lake. 1819, 1825. (Pocket Library of English Classics: *see* 302R. 12-13.)

UNITED STATES

47Rb] ALBANY: Shaw 1823
The Lady of the Lake: A Poem. By Walter Scott, Esq. Albany: Published by S. Shaw, 47 State-Street. Packard & Van Benthuysen, Printers. 1823. Pages: *1-9* 10-177. Notes: Engraved frontispiece and title-page precede typeset title-page. Copies: DLC NN.

BALTIMORE: Cushing
[~] The Lady of the Lake. 1812. (The Poetical Works of Walter Scott: *see* 303R.4.)

47Rc] BALTIMORE: Cushing and Sargeant 1811
The Lady of the Lake: A Poem. By Walter Scott, Esq. Baltimore: Published by Joseph Cushing; and E. Sargeant, New-York. 1811. Pages: *1-9* 10-288. Notes: With frontispiece of The Lady, imprinted Nicklin, Baltimore. Copies: E; IdU MWA NN ViU. Variant state with imprint reading 'Baltimore, Joseph Cushing; and E. Sergeant, New-York. 1811.' and frontispiece portrait of Scott (NN).

BALTIMORE: Sargeant
[~] The Lady of the Lake: A Poem. 1811. (*See* preceding entry).

47Rd] BOSTON: Allen 1823
The Lady of the Lake; A Poem, in Six Cantos, By Walter Scott, Esq. Boston: Printed and Published by Ebenezer K. Allen, No. 1, Congress Street. 1823. Pages: *1-5* 6-164. Copies: E; CtY DLC. Reference: Kohler(1) 4 (with illustration).

BOSTON: Bedlington
[~] The Lady of the Lake. 1827. (The Poetical Works of Sir Walter Scott: *see* 304R.3)

47Re] BOSTON: Wells and Wait 1810
The Lady of the Lake; A Poem. By Walter Scott, Esq. Boston, Published by W. Wells and T. B. Wait and Co. T. B. Wait and Co. Printers. 1810. Pages: *1-9* 10-224, *iii* iv-cxxv. Notes: With The Lady (Nicklin, Baltimore) frontispiece in some copies. Pages *i-ii* apparently represented a fly-title, now cancelled. The following Notes section oddly bears direction

lines 'Vol. II.' and omits page numbers lxxv-lxxviii between gatherings D and E. In some copies page cxxv is misnumbered cxxi. Copies: MH MWA RPB ViU.

FREDERICKSBURG: Withers
[~] The Lady of the Lake. 1824. (The Poetical Works of Sir Walter Scott: *see* 310R)

47Rf] MONTPELIER: Bowles 1813
The Lady of the Lake. A Poem, In Six Cantos. By Walter Scott, Esq. Montpelier, Vt. Published by Lucius Q. C. Bowles. 1813. Pages: *1-9* 10-320. Copies: BCL E; CtY MWA NNU-W OCl PPL. Reference: Kohler (1) 47 (with illustration).

47Rg] NEW YORK: Eastburn 1818
The Lady of the Lake: A Poem. By Walter Scott, Esq. New-York: Published by J. Eastburn and Co. Literary-Rooms, Broadway. 1818. Pages: *i-viii*, *9-11* 12-348. Notes: The final pages, *315-321* 322-348, are a printing of *The Field of Waterloo*. Frontispiece of the Lady drawn by Westall, engraved by P. Maverick & Durand. (Also issued in The Poetical Works of Walter Scott, Esq.: volume 4. 1818, 1819. *see* 312R.4.) Copies: E; CtY.

47Rh] NEW YORK: Elliot and Crissy 1810
The Lady of the Lake, A Poem. By Walter Scott, Esq. New-York, Printed and Published by Elliot and Crissy, At the Sign of the Ledger, No. 114, Water-Street; Sold also by T. Powers, No. 116, Broadway. 1810. Pages: *i-iv*, *1* 2-260. Copy: T/B.

47Ri] NEW YORK: Huntington 1813
The Lady of the Lake: A Poem. By Walter Scott, Esq. New-York: Published by D. Huntington, C. S. Van Winkle, Printer. 1813. Pages: *1-9* 10-264. Notes: With a crude copy of The Lady frontispiece, imprinted D. Huntington. In some copies the colon in title is dropped. Copies: E; CtY MWA NjP PU. Reference: Kohler (1) 64 (with illustration.)

47Rj] NEW YORK: King 1827-1831
[1] The Lady of the Lake; A Poem. By Walter Scott, Esq. New York, Published by S. King, 150, William Street. 1827. Pages: *1-6*, *i*-ii, *7-9* 10-'275'[265]. Notes: Engraved frontispiece of The Lady and title-page, with publisher's name given as Solamon King, precede printed title-page. Copies: MWA PPL.

[2] The Lady of the Lake. A Poem: By Walter Scott, Esq. New-York: Published by S. King, 18 Fulton Street. D. Mitchell, Printer. 1831. Pages: *1-9* 10-234. Notes: With engraved title and frontispiece of The Lady. Copy: DLC.

47Rk] NEW YORK: Lomax 1831
The Lady of the Lake; A Poem. By Walter Scott, Esq. New-York: John Lomax, Publisher. 1831. Pages: *1-9* 10-232. Notes: With additional engraved title-page. Copy: DLC.

47Rl] NEW YORK: Sargeant 1810-1811
[1] The Lady of the Lake; A Poem. By Walter Scott, Esq. New-York: Published by Ezra Sargeant, Opposite Trinity Church. 1810. Pages: *i-viii*, *1* 2-279. Copies: MWA NN RPB ViU.

[2] The Lady of the Lake: A Poem. By Walter Scott, Esq. New-York: Published by Ezra Sargeant, No. 86 Broadway; and J. Cushing, Baltimore. 1811. Pages: *1-9* 10-288. Notes: Issued with the Nicklin, Baltimore frontispiece. (*see also*: Baltimore: Cushing and Sargeant, 47Rc). Copies: MWA ViU(2).

47Rm] NEW YORK: Scott 1813
The Lady of the Lake: A Poem. By Walter Scott, Esq. New-York, Published by Richard Scott, 276 Pearl-Street. 1813. Pages: *1-9* 10-176. In some copies the comma after New-York is replaced with a colon. Copies: MWA PPL RPB TxU.

47Rn] NEW YORK: Sickels 1829
The Lady of the Lake; A Poem. By Walter Scott, Esq. New=York, Published by George G. Sickels, 68 William-Street. 1829. Pages: *1-9* 10-155. Notes: Engraved frontispiece and title-page precede typeset title-page. Issued without notes. Copies: CtY PHi. Variant issue with notes extending to page 232 (NN PPL RPB[2] TxU.)

47Ro] PHILADELPHIA: Earle [and others] 1810
The Lady of the Lake; A Poem. By Walter Scott, Esq. Published by Edward Earle, Philadelphia. Also by M. Carey, Philadelphia; D. Mallory & Co., Boston; Lyman, Hall & Co., Portland; Swift & Chipman, Middlebury; P. H. Nicklin & Co., Baltimore; and John W. Campbell, Petersburgh. Fry and Kammerer, Printers. 1810. Pages: *1-13* 14-307. Notes: Engraved frontispiece portrait of Scott, engraved by D. Edwin. E copy is inscribed 'Given me, By, Walter Scott Esqr. at Abbotsford. Melrose. August 1813. M. W. H.' (Matthew Weld Hartstonge). This inscription is present also in two other volumes published 1810 by the same publisher: *The Lay of the Last Minstrel* (*see* 14Rk) and *Marmion* (*see* 28Rg). Copies: E; CtY IdU InU MWA PPL ViU. Reference: Van Antwerp(1) 9 (with illustration of Scott's inscription 2 August 1818 in Edward Everett's copy.)

47Rp] PHILADELPHIA: Towar 1824-1828
The Lady of the Lake; A Poem. By Walter Scott, Esq. Philadelphia: Published by A. Towar, 255, Market-St. J. H. Cunningham, printer. 1824. Pages: *1-9* 10-282. Notes: Engraved frontispiece and title-page precede typeset title-page. Copies: NN PHi ViU(2). Reissued 1826(NN) 1828(CtY).

47Rq] PHILADELPHIA: Wright 1823
The Lady of the Lake: A Poem. By Walter Scott, Esq. Philadelphia: Printed and Published by Robert Wright, Back of 110 Walnut-Street. 1823. Pages: *1-9* 10-172. Notes: Scott's notes are not included. Copy: MH.

DERIVATIVES

AUSTRIA

47Da] VIENNA: Artaria 1826
Sieben Gesänge aus Walter Scott's Fräulein vom See in Musik gesetzt. . . . Wien, bey Math. Artaria, Kohlmarkt No. 258. [1826] [watermarked U F F]. Two parts. Pages I: *i-ii*, *1* 2-23; II: *1-2* 3-19. Notes: Engraved sheet music with plate numbers M.A. 813 and M.A. 814. Words in English and/or German by Frau Sophie Gräfin v. Weissenwolf. Music by Franz Schubert arranged for voice and pianoforte. The songs listed below are ordered as in the Harvard copy; in other copies the gatherings are differently arranged. Copies: L(Hirsh); MH NNP. References: G/T 10243; Schubert no. 530; Van Antwerp (2) 43.
Part 1: [1] Bootgesang (first words: 'Hail to the Chief who in triumph advances!') from canto 2, stanza 19;
[2] Coronach (first words: 'Angus, the heir of Duncan's line'); from canto 3, stanza 18;
[3] Ellens Gesang I (first words: 'Soldier, rest! thy warfare o'er') from canto 1, stanza 31;
[4] Ellens Gesang II (first words: 'Huntsman, rest! thy chase is done') from canto 1, stanza 32; Part 2:
[5] Ellens Gesang III (first words: 'Ave Maria! maiden mild!') from canto 3, stanza 29;
[6] Lied des gefangenen Jägers (first words: 'My hawk is tired of perch and hood') from canto 6, stanza 24;
[7] Normans Gesang (first words: 'The heath this night must be my bed') from canto 3, stanza 23.

GREAT BRITAIN

47Db] DUBLIN: Charles 1811
[1] The Lady of the Lake. A Drama, In Three Acts; Founded on the Popular Poem written by W. Scott, Esq. . . . Dublin: Printed by J. Charles, 49, Mary-Street. [1811]. Pages: *1-3* 4-46. Notes: 'Arranged as it is now performed, at the Theatre-Royal, Dublin.' A manuscript note in the L copy attributes this play to Miss Smith, later Mrs [Sarah] Bartley. However, the text appears to have been taken from the Dublin, Figgis printing (*see* 47Dc). Copy: L. Reference: Bolton 59.

[2] [The Lady of the Lake and Knight of Snowdoun: A Drama, in Three Acts. . . . The Eighth Edition. . . . Dublin: J. Charles [ca.1811]. 53pp. 24° bound as 16°. Notes: Words by Thomas John Dibdin ; music composed by James Sanderson. 'Enlarged and arranged as it is now performed at the Theatre-Royal, Crow-Street.'] Copy: not seen.

[3] The Lady of the Lake, and Knight of Snowdown: A Drama in Three Acts. . . . The Eleventh Edition, . . . Dublin: Printed by J. Charles, 57, Mary-Street [ca. 1811]. Pages: *1-3* 4-44. Notes: 'Enlarged and Arranged as it is now Performed at the Theatre-Royal, Hawkins'-Street.' Copy: AN

47Dc] DUBLIN: Figgis 1811
The Lady of the Lake: A Grand Dramatic Romance, in Three Acts; Founded on the Popular Poem Written by W. Scott, Esq. . . . Dublin: Published by W. Figgis, Nassau-Street. 1811.

Pages: *i-iv*, *1* 2-32. Notes: Words by Thomas John Dibdin. Music composed by James Sanderson. 'Arranged and performed at the Theatre-Royal, Dublin', but first performed 24 September 1810 at the London Surrey Theatre. Copy: L. Reference: Bolton 49.

47Dd] DUBLIN: O'Flanagan 1825

The Lady of the Lake, and Knight of Snowdoun: A Drama, in Three Acts. . . . The Twelfth Edition. Dublin: Printed by T. O'Flanagan, 26, Bachelor's-Walk. 1825. Pages: *1-3* 4-44 (mispaged throughout). Notes: Words by Thomas John Dibdin (music by James Sanderson not included). 'Enlarged and Arranged as it is now Performed at the Theatre Royal, Hawkins'-Street.' Copy: DT.

47De] EDINBURGH: Corri 1810

[1] Ave Maria Hymn to the Virgin From the Popular Poem of the Lady of the Lake Written by Walter Scott Esqr, . . . Edinburgh Printed and Sold by N. Corri at his Music and Musical Instrument Warehouse front of the Theatre Royal head of Leith Walk, and at Birchall's 133 New Bond Street London. [1810]. Pages: 1-5. Notes: Engraved sheet music. Words from canto 3, stanza 29 (first words: 'Ave Maria! maiden mild'). Song composed by Natale Corri arranged for voice and pianoforte. Copy: L. Reference: G/T 10151.

[2] Blanche of Devan's Song "They bid me Sleep, They bid me Pray" From the Celebrated Poem of The Lady of the Lake Written by Walter Scott Esqr. . . Edinburgh Printed and Sold by N. Corri at his Music and Musical Instrument Warehouse Front of the Theatre Royal head of Leith Walk and at Birchall's 133. New Bond Street London Where all the other songs from the same poem may be had and every other article in the Musical line. [unwatermarked. ca.1810]. Pages: 1-5. Notes: Engraved sheet music. Words from canto 4, stanza 22 (first words as the title, but in quotation marks). Song composed by N. Corri for voice and pianoforte. Copies: E(2).

[3] Boat Song From the admired Poem of The Lady of the Lake. . . Dedicated to Walter Scott Esqr. Edinburgh Printed and Sold by N. Corri at his Music and Musical Instrument Warehouse front of the Theatre Royal head of Leith Walk. [unwatermarked. ca.1810]. Pages: *i-ii*, 1-2. Notes: Engraved sheet music with a caption title. Words from canto 2, stanza 19 (first words: Hail to the Chief who in triumph advances). Music composed 'By an Amateur' adapted from an 'Ancient Perthshire Huting[!] Song.' and arranged for voice and pianoforte. Price: 1/. Copy: MH.

[4] Mary From the Celebrated Poem of The Lady of the Lake. Wrote by Walter Scott Esqr. . . . Edinburgh Printed and Sold by N. Corri at his Music and Musical Instrument Warehouse front of the Theatre Royal head of Leith Walk. [1810]. Pages: 1-2. Notes: Engraved sheet music with paging beginning on verso of first leaf. Words from 'Song' canto 3, stanza 23 (first words: 'The heath this night must be my bed, The bracken curtain for my head,'). Music composed as a Canzonett by N. Corri arranged for voice and pianoforte. Price: 1/. Copies: E(2) L.

47Df] EDINBURGH: Gow & Shepherd 1810

The Lonely Isle, A Song from the Lady of the Lake; Written by Walter Scott Esqr. . . Edinburgh; Printed & Sold by Gow & Shepherd, 16 Princes Street. [unwatermarked. ca.1810]. Pages: *1* 2-5. Notes: Engraved sheet music. Words from canto 2, stanzas 2-3 (first words:

'Not faster yonder rowers might flings from their oars the spray'). Music composed by J. G. C. Schetky arranged for voice and pianoforte. Price: 2/. Copy: E.

47Dg] EDINBURGH: Hamilton 1810
[1] Ave Maria Maiden Mild from the Third Canto of the Lady of the Lake . . . and Dedicated to Walter Scott Esq, . . . Edinburgh Printed and Sold by J. Hamilton Music Seller 24 North Bridge. [unwatermarked. ca.1810]. Pages: 1-3. Notes: Engraved sheet music. Words from canto 3, stanza 29 (first words: 'Ave Maria maiden mild Listen to a maiden's prayer'). Music composed by G. F. Graham arranged for voice, pianoforte or harp. Copies: E(2).

[2] The Heath this Night must be My Bed Written by Walter Scott Esqr. . . . Edinburgh. Printed & Sold by J. Hamilton, Music Seller 24. North Bridge. [watermarked 1809. ca.1810]. Pages: 1-2. Notes: Engraved sheet music. Words from canto 3, stanza 23 (first words as title). Music composed by William Clarke arranged for voice and pianoforte. Price 1/. Copy: MH.

47Dh] EDINBURGH: Mather 1812
'Hail to the Chief' . . . The Poetry from the Lady of the Lake. . . Edinburgh, Published at J. Mather's Musical Repository, No 9 Greenside Place. [watermarked 1811. 1812]. Pages: *1* 2-8. Notes: Engraved sheet music. Words from canto 2, stanzas 19-20 (first words: 'Hail, hail, hail! Hail to the chief who in triumph advances,'). Music composed by J. Mather arranged for voice and pianoforte. Price: 3/6. Copy: E.

47Di] EDINBURGH: Schetky 1815
Normans Song and the Coronach from the Lady of the Lake Written by Walter Scott Esqr. . . Edinburgh: Published by G: Schetky Junr. 58 Hanover Street, and to be had at all the Music Shops. [Title-page continues, as an afterthought, in lower third with dedication in script 'To Walter Scott Esqr.' signed 'J. G. C. Schetky.' *see* 514T.] [1815]. In two parts. Pages II: *1-2* 3-6. Notes: Engraved sheet music with plate number: '106'. 'The Coronach' starts on page *2* with a caption title reading 'Coronach or Funeral Song from the Lady of the Lake Written by Walter Scott Esqr. . . .' Presumably 'Normans Song' was published as part I of this issue. Price: [both parts] 3/ or 1/6 each. Copy: InU.

47Dj] EDINBURGH: Wood 1810
The Heath this Night must be my Bed. From the Lady of the Lake. To Music. . . Edinburgh Printed & Sold by Muir Wood & Co Leith Str. [unwatermarked. ca.1810]. Pages: 1-4. Notes: Engraved sheet music. Words from canto 3, stanza 23 (first words as title). The caption title reads 'Mary or The Heath this Night must be my Bed Written by Walter Scott Esqr.' Music composed by John Ross arranged for voice and pianoforte or harp. Price: 1/ 6. Copy: E.

47Dk] EDINBURGH: [unknown] 1813
['Pocket Map of the Scenery of the Lady of the Lake, taken from an actual Survey, and beautifully coloured.' (ca. 1813).] Copy: not seen. Reference: Listed in *Rokeby* (64Aa) advertisement page 3.

47Dl] GLASGOW: Neil 1829
The Lady of the Lake, a Melo=Drama, in Three Acts, by Sir Walter Scott. Glasgow; Printed

by Carmichael, Neil & Co. 43, Trongate, and sold by James Neil, 17, Bazar. 1829. Pages: *1-3* 4-36. Notes: Drama, as written by Thomas Dibdin with simple frontispiece portrait. Copy: InU.

47Dm] LONDON: Birchall 1810-1815

[1] [Ave Maria, Hymn to the Virgin. London: Birchall (1810). Notes: Issued simultaneously in Edinburgh by the composer. Music composed by Natale Corri.] Copy: not seen. Reference: G/T 10151.

[2] The Coronach or Funeral Song from the Lady of the Lake, Walter Scott Esqr. . . . London, Printed & Sold by Rt. Birchall, No. 133, New Bond Street. [watermarked 1810]. Pages: 1-4. Notes: Engraved sheet music, with caption title. Words from canto 3, stanza 16 (first words: 'He is gone on the mountain,'). Music composed by John Ross arranged for voice and pianoforte. Price: 1/6. Copies: E L(2). Reference: G/T 10231.

[3] Hymn to the Virgin, from the Lady of the Lake, by Walter Scott Esqr. . . . London, Printed & Sold by Rt. Birchall, No. 133 New Bond Street. [watermarked 1814]. Pages: 1-4. Notes: Engraved sheet music with caption title. Words from canto 3, stanza 29 (first words: 'Ave Maria! maiden mild!'). Music composed by John Ross arranged for voice and pianoforte. Price: 1/6. Copies: E L. Reference: G/T 10232.

[4] The Rose is fairest when 'tis budding, . . . The Poetry from the Lady of the Lake . . . London, Printed & Sold by Rt. Birchall No. 133, New Bond Street. [1811]. Pages: 1-5. Notes: Engraved sheet music. Words from canto 4, stanza 1 (first words as title). Music composed by Robert Cooke arranged for voice. Price: 2s. Copies: L O. Reference: G/T 10148.

[5] Some feelings are to mortals given, . . . The Poetry from the Lady of the Lake, . . . London, Printed for the Author [composer], by Rt. Birchall, 133, New Bond Street. [1812]. Pages: *i-ii*, 1-7. Notes: Engraved sheet music with page 1 on verso of first leaf. Words from canto 2, stanza 22 (first words as title). Music composed by Robert Cooke arranged for chorus and pianoforte. Price: 2/6. Copies: L O. Reference: G/T 10149.

47Dn] LONDON: Bland & Weller 1810

[Soldier rest! thy warfare o'er. London: Bland & Weller's Music Warehouse (1810). Music composed by James Hook.] Copy: not seen. Reference: G/T 10170.

47Do] LONDON: Bown 1810

Our Vicar still preaches that Peter & Poule (Sung with the most unbounded Applause) in the Lady of the Lake. By Walter Scott, Esqr. Printed by G. Bown, Music Seller, No. 11 St. Martins Church Yard. [ca. 1810]. Pages: *1-2* [?]. Notes: Engraved sheet music with caption title, cropped copy. Words from canto 6, stanza 5 (first words as in title). The composer is unidentified, the music apparently for voice with bass accompaniment. Price: 1s.6. Copy: MH.

47Dp] LONDON: Brettell 1828-1829

[1] La Donna Del Lago. The Lady of the Lake, A Melo-dramatic Opera, in Two Acts. . . . London: Printed by T Brettell, Rupert Street; Published and sold at the King's Theatre; Also by Andrews, Bond Street; Sams, Pall Mall; M'Clary, St. James's Street; Hookham, Old

Bond Street; Ebers, Old Bond Street; Marsh, Oxford Street; and Seguin, Regent Street. [Price Two Shillings.] 1829. Pages: *1-5* 6-68. Notes: This edition has no half-title and only one title-page, in English, but the libretto by Leone Tottola has text on facing pages in Italian and English, except for page 68 which has both Italian and English (music by Gioachino Rossini not included). The text is as performed at the King's Theatre, Haymarket, January 1829. Copy: L.

[2] The Lady of the Lake, A Melo-dramatic Opera, in Two Acts. . . . London: Printed by T. Brettell, Rupert Street; Published and sold at the King's Theatre; Also by Andrews, Bond Street; Sams, Pall Mall; M'Clary, St. James's Street; Hookham, Old Bond Street; Ebers, Old Bond Street; Marsh, Oxford Street; and Seguin, Regent Street. [Price Two Shillings.] 1828. Pages: *1-7* 8-69 *70*. Notes: Half-title reads: 'La Donna del Lago.' as does the title-page in Italian. Libretto by Leone Tottola with text and title on facing pages in Italian and English (music by Gioachino Rossini not included). The text is as performed at the King's Theatre, Haymarket, May 1828. For an earlier date and translator *see* 47Dt. Copies: E; InU PU.

47Dq] LONDON: Button and Whitaker 1824-1827

The Imprisoned Huntsman, A Favorite Song, The Poetry from the Celebrated Poem The Lady of the Lake, Written by Walter Scott, Esqr. . . . London Printed by Button & Whitaker 75 St. Paul's Church Yard. [*start of music*] Printed and sold by W & S Wybrow, 24 Rathbone Place. [watermarked 1824]. Pages: 1-3. Notes: Engraved sheet music in frame with plate mark reading 'The Imprison'd Huntsman'. Words from canto 6, stanza 24 (first words: 'My hawk is tir'd of perch and hood,'). Song composed by John Whitaker arranged for voice and pianoforte. Price: 1s.6. Copy: E. Reissued on paper watermarked 1827(L).

LONDON: Clarke

[~] For publications with imprint reading 'London; Published for the Author [composer] by Messrs. Phipps & Co. *see* LONDON: Phipps.

47Dr] LONDON: Clementi 1810

Hymn to the Virgin Selected from the Popular Poem called The Lady of the Lake, Written by Walter Scott Esqr. . . . London: Printed for the author [composer], by Clementi & Co. 26 Cheapside. may be had also at the Great Room Spring Gardens. [watermarked 1807. ca.1810]. Pages: *i-ii*, *1* 2-5. Notes: Engraved sheet music. Words from canto 3, stanza 29 (first words: 'Ave Maria! maiden mild! Listen to a maiden's prayer;'). Music composed by Henry R. Bishop arranged for voice and harp or pianoforte. Copy: BCL. Reference: G/T 10124. Variant issue watermarked 1810(L).

LONDON: Cooke

[~] For sheet music with the imprint 'London, Printed for the Author by Rt. Birchall, 133 New Bond Street' *see* title under Birchall.

LONDON: Cumberland

[~] The Lady of the Lake: A Melo-dramatic Romance. [1829] (Cumberland's Minor Theatre: number 22: *see* 330D.22)

47Ds] LONDON: D'Almaine 1815

[1] Ave Maria, From the Lady of the Lake, Written by Walter Scott Esqr, . . . London

D'Almaine & Co. Soho Square. [ca.1815]. Pages: *i-ii*, *1* 2-7 *8*. Notes: Engraved sheet music. Words from canto 3, stanza 29 (first words: 'Ave Maria! Maiden mild!'). Music composed by Joseph Mazzinghi arranged for voice and harp. Price: 2s./6. Copy: L.

[2] Huntsman rest! thy chace is done, Recitative & Air, In continuation of the Song. "Soldier rest, thy warfare o'er," from the Lady of the Lake, Written by Walter Scott Esqr. . . . D'Almaine & Co. Soho Square, London. [1815]. Pages: 1-4. Notes: Engraved sheet music with plate number '4002'. Words from Canto 1, stanza 32 (first words for recitative: 'She paused then blushing, led the lay, To grace the stranger of the day;' and from canto 1, stanza 32 for song: 'Huntsman rest! thy chase is done, While our slumbrous spells assail ye,'). Music composed by Joseph Mazzinghi arranged for voice and pianoforte. Price: 1/6. Copy: BCL.

47Dt] LONDON: Ebers 1823

La Donna Del Lago. The Lady of the Lake; A Melo-Dramatic Opera, in Two Acts. . . . London: Printed for John Ebers, Bookseller to His Majesty, Old Bond-Street. And Sold also at the King's Theatre. Price 2s. 6d. [1823]. Pages: *i-iv*, *1-3* 4-67 *68*. Notes: Opera in Italian and English with libretto by Tottola (music by Rossini not included) as presented at the King's Theatre [Haymarket], 18 February 1823. The text throughout has parallel texts in Italian on left, facing the English on right. The English translation is by W. J. Walter. Price: 2s.6d. Copy: O. Reference: Bolton 106.

47Du] LONDON: Goulding 1810-1812

[1] [The Boat Song . . . . London. Printed by Goulding & Co. 20 Soho Square, 124 New Bond Strt. & 7 Westmoreland Stt(!). Dublin. (1810). Notes: Music composed by John Stevenson.] Copy: not seen. Reference: Advertised in 'Lay of the Imprisoned Huntsman', item 6 below.

[2] [The Favorite Airs from The Lady of the Lake. London: Goulding (1810). Notes: Music composed by Tom Cooke.] Copy: not seen. Reference: G/T 10150.

[3] He is Gone on the Mountain The Coronach or Funeral Song from the Lady of the Lake by Walter Scott Esqr. . . . London. Printed by Goulding & Co. 20 Soho Square 124 New Bond St. & 7 Westmoreland St. Dublin. [watermarked 1810]. Pages: *i-ii*, 1-7. Notes: Engraved sheet music. Words from canto 3, stanza 16 (first words: 'He is gone on the mountain, He is lost to the forest,'). Music composed by John Stevenson for three voices and pianoforte. Price: 3s/. Copy: E.

[4] [Hunter rest thy Chace is done . . . . London. Printed by Goulding & Co. 20 Soho Square, 124 New Bond Strt. & 7 Westmoreland Stt(!). Dublin. (1810). Music composed by Joseph Mazzinghi.] Copy: not seen. Reference: Advertised in 'Lay of the Imprisoned Huntsman', item 6 below.

[5] [The Hymn to the Virgin . . . . London. Printed by Goulding & Co. 20 Soho Square, 124 New Bond Strt. & 7 Westmoreland Stt(!). Dublin. (1810). Notes: Music composed by T.Cooke. Price: 2/.] Copy: not seen. Reference: Advertised in 'Lay of the Imprisoned Huntsman', item 6 below.

[6] Lay of the Imprisoned Huntsman, A Song from the Lady of the Lake, by Walter Scott Esqr. . . . London. Printed by Goulding & Co. 20 Soho Square, 124 New Bond Strt. & 7

Westmoreland Stt[!]. Dublin. [unwatermarked. ca.1810]. Pages: *i-ii*, 1-5. Notes: Engraved sheet music, with advertisements on title leaf. Words from canto 6, stanza 24 (first words: 'My hawk is tired of perch and hood'). Music composed by John Stevenson arranged for voice and pianoforte. Copy: PPL.

[7] Loch Katrine. From the Lady of the Lake by Walter Scott Esqr. . . . London. Printed by Goulding & Co. 20 Soho Square 124 New Bond Stt[!]. & 7 Westmoreland St. Dublin. Pages: *i-ii*, 1-5. Notes: Engraved sheet music with 'The Words by Walter Scott Esqr.' below the caption title. Words from canto 3, stanza 2 (first words: 'The Summer dawns reflected hue, To purple chang'd Loch Katrine blue,'). Music by T. Cooke arranged for voice and pianoforte. Price: 2/. Copy: PPL.

[8] [The Lonely Isle . . . . London. Printed by Goulding & Co. 20 Soho Square, 124 New Bond Strt. & 7 Westmoreland Stt(!). Dublin. (1810). Notes: Music composed by Joseph Mazzinghi. Price: 1/6.] Copy: not seen. Reference: Advertised in 'Lay of the Imprisoned Huntsman', item 6 above.

[9] The Maniac Song, from the Lady of the Lake by Walter Scott Esqr. . . . London. Printed by Goulding & Co. 20 Soho Square, 124 New Bond Strt. & 7 Westmoreland Stt[!]. Dublin. [1810]. Pages: *1* 2-4. Notes: Engraved sheet music. Words from canto 4, stanza 22 (first words: 'They bid me sleep, they bid me pray,'). Music composed by John Stevenson arranged for voice and pianoforte. Price: 1s.6d. Copy: E. Reissued with imprint corrected to 'Street' (L).

[~] The Minstrel's Tale *see* W. W. Phipps 47Daf[13].

[10] [The Soldier Bridegrooms Song . . . . London. Printed by Goulding & Co. 20 Soho Square, 124 New Bond Strt. & 7 Westmoreland Stt(!). Dublin. (1810). Notes: Music composed by John Stevenson. Price: 2s.] Copy: not seen. References: G/T 10256; Advertised in 'Lay of the Imprisoned Huntsman', item 6 above.

[11] [Soldier rest thy warfare oe'r . . . . London. Printed by Goulding & Co. 20 Soho Square, 124 New Bond Strt. & 7 Westmoreland Stt(!). Dublin. (1810). Notes: Music composed by Joseph Mazzinghi. Price: 1/6.] Copy: not seen. Reference: Advertised in 'Lay of the Imprisoned Huntsman', item 6 above.

[12] Whoop Barnaby! The Soldiers Song from the Lady of the Lake by Walter Scott Esqr. . . . London. Printed by Goulding & Co. 20 Soho Squar.[!] 124 New Bond St. & 7 Westmoreland St. Dublin. [ca.1810]. Pages: *i-ii*, 1-6. Notes: Engraved sheet music. Words from canto 6, stanza 5 (first words: 'Our Vicar still preaches that Peter and Poule'). Music composed by T. Cooke arranged for voice and pianoforte. Price: 2s. Copy: E.

47Dv] LONDON: Goulding and D'Almaine 1830
[For publications for W. W. Phipps by Goulding and D'Almaine *see* Phipps (47Daf).]

Lay of the Imprisoned Huntsman, from the Lady of the Lake, Written by Walter Scott Esqr. . . . London, Published by Goulding & D'Almaine, 20, Soho Square. [1830]. Pages: 1-4. Notes: Engraved sheet music: a late reissue from plates first used in 47Dw[14]. Words from canto 6, stanza 24 (first words: 'My hawk is tired of perch and hood,'). Music composed by Joseph Mazzinghi arranged for voice and pianoforte. Price: 1/6. Copies: L; MH.

47Dw] LONDON: Goulding, D'Almaine, Potter 1810-1825

[1] Alice Brand, from the Lady of the Lake, . . Dedicated to Walter Scott Esqr. (Author of the Words) . . . London, Printed by Goulding, D'Almaine, Potter & Co. 20, Soho Square, & 7, Westmoreland Street, Dublin. [watermarked 1820]. Pages: *1* 2-12. Notes: Engraved sheet music. Words from canto 4, stanza 12 (first words: 'Merry it is in the good greenwood when the Mavis and Merle are singing,'). Music composed by John Stevenson arranged for voice and pianoforte. Price: 3s. Copies: E; NN-L.

[2] Ave Maria, From the Lady of the Lake, Written by Walter Scott Esqr. . . . London Printed by Goulding, D'Almaine, Potter & Co. Musical Instrument Makers & Music Sellers to their Royal Highnesses the Prince & Princess of Wales 20 Soho Square, 124 New Bond Street & 7 Westmorland St. Dublin. [watermarked 1808]. Pages: *1* 2-7. Notes: Engraved sheet music with composer's initial 'M' in ink on title. Words from canto 3, stanza 29 (first words: 'Ave Maria! maiden mild'). Music composed by Joseph Mazzinghi arranged for voice and harp. Price: 2s./6. Copies: E; MH-M. Reference: G/T 10195. Reissued without watermark [1815?] (L O).

[3] The Boat Song, from the Lady of the Lake, By Walter Scott Esqr. . . . London, Printed by Goulding, D'Almaine, Potter, & Co. Music Sellers, 20, Soho Square, & No. 7, Westmoreland St. Dublin. [ca.1815]. Pages: *i-ii*, 1-26. Notes: Engraved sheet music. Words from canto 2, stanzas 18-19 (first words: 'The war pipes ceas'd;'). The familiar song (stanza 19) does not begin until page 16. Music composed and arranged by John Stevenson for voice and pianoforte. Price: 5.Shs. Copy: L. Reissued with watermark 1820 and imprint 'Square, & to be had at No. 7' (NNP). References: G/T 10254; Van Antwerp(2) 42p.

[4] The Crazed Bride, from the Lady of the Lake, Written by Walter Scott Esqr. . . . London, Printed by Goulding, D'Almaine, Potter & Co. 20, Soho Square, 124, New Bond Street, & 7, Westmoreland Strt. Dublin. [watermarked 1810]. Pages: 1-4. Notes: Engraved sheet music with composer's characteristic 'M' in ink next to imprint. Words from canto 4, stanza 22 (first words: 'They bid me sleep, they bid me pray,'). Music composed by Joseph Mazzinghi for voice and pianoforte. Price: 1/6. Copy: E.

[5] The Elfin King, from the Lady of the Lake, Written by Walter Scott Esqr. . . . London, Printed by Goulding, D'Almaine, Potter & Co. 20, Soho Square, 124, New Bond Street, & 7, Westmoreland Street Dublin. [watermarked 1809]. Pages: 1-4. Notes: Engraved sheet music with composer's initial 'M' in ink to right of imprint. Words from canto 4, stanza 13 (first words: '"Tis merry, 'tis merry, in good greenwood,"'). Music composed by Joseph Mazzinghi arranged for voice and pianoforte. Price: 1/6. Copies: E L; NN-L. Reference: G/T 10196.

[6] He is Gone on the Mountain, from the Lady of the Lake, Written by Walter Scott Esqr. . . . London, Printed by Goulding, D'Almaine, Potter, & Co. 20, Soho Square, 124 New Bond Street & 7, Westmoreland Strt. Dublin. [unwatermarked. ca.1810]. Pages: *1* 2-7. Notes: Engraved sheet music. Words from canto 3, stanza 16 (first words as title). Music composed by Joseph Mazzinghi as duet. Price: 2/6. Copy: L. Reissued with 1820 watermark (E). Reference: G/T 10197.

[7] The Heath this Night must be my Bed from the Lady of the Lake, written by W. Scott Esqr. . . . London, Printed by Goulding, D'Almaine, Potter, & Co. 20, Soho Square, 124, New Bond Street, & to be had at 7, Westmoreland Strt. Dublin. [unwatermarked. ca.1810].

Pages: *1* 2-4. Notes: Engraved sheet music. Words from canto 3, stanza 23 (first words as title). Music composed by Joseph Mazzinghi for voice and pianoforte. Price: 1/6. Copy: E.

[8] Huntsman rest! thy chace is done, Recitative & Air, . . . In Continuation of the Song, "Soldier rest, thy warfare o'er," from the Lady of the Lake, written by Walter Scott Esqr. . . . London, Printed by Goulding, D'Almaine, Potter, & Co. 20, Soho Square. 124, New Bond Street & 7, Westmoreland Street, Dublin. [watermarked 1809]. Pages: *1* 2-4. Notes: Engraved sheet music with composer's initial 'M' in ink on the title. Words from canto 1, stanza 32 (first words of recitative: 'She paused then blushing, led the lay, To grace the stranger of the day;') and from *ibid.* for song (first words: 'Huntsman rest! thy chase is done, / While our slumbrous spells assail ye,'). Music composed by Joseph Mazzinghi arranged for voice, flute, harp, and pianoforte. Price: 1/6. Copies: BCL L; NNP. References: G/T 10198; Van Antwerp(2) 42a. Reissued ca. 1822-1824 with arrangement for voice and pianoforte only, page 1 numbered, paper unwatermarked, with imprint as above (E O[2]), and with phrase inserted '& to be had at 7' (L; MH).

[9] Hush thee poor Maiden, from the Lady of the Lake, Written by Walter Scott Esqr. . . . London. Printed by Goulding, D'Almaine, Potter, & Co. Music Sellers to their Royal Highnesses the Prince, & Princess of Wales, 20, Soho Square, & to be had at No. 7, Westmoreland St. Dublin. [ca. 1810]. Pages: *i-ii*, *1* 2-7. Notes: Engraved sheet music. Words from canto 4, stanzas 23-24 (first words: 'See the grey pennons I prepare, To seek my true-love'). Music composed by Joseph Mazzinghi for voice and pianoforte. Price: 2.6. Copy: E.

[10] John of Brent, The Soldier's Song from The Lady of the Lake, Written by Walter Scott, Esqr. . . . London, Printed by Goulding, D'Almaine, Potter, & Co. 20, Soho Square, 124, New Bond Street, & 7, Westmoreland Strt. Dublin. [watermarked 1808. ca.1810]. Pages: *1* 2-7. Notes: Engraved sheet music with composer's characteristic 'M' in ink next to imprint. Words from canto 6, stanza 5 (first words: 'Our vicar still preaches that Peter and Poule Laid a swinging long curse'). Music composed by Joseph Mazzinghi for three voices and pianoforte. Price: 2/6. Copy: BCL. Reissued without watermark (E).

[11] Lament, from The Lady of the Lake, Written by Walter Scott Esqr. . . London, Printed by Goulding, D'Almaine, Potter & Co. 20, Soho Square, 12, New Bond Street, & 7, Westmoreland Street, Dublin. [watermarked 1811]. Pages: 1-4. Notes: Engraved sheet music with the composer's characteristic 'M' in ink on the title-page. Words from canto 6, stanza 22 (first words: 'And art thou cold, and lowly laid, Thy foeman's dread,'). Music composed by Joseph Mazzinghi arranged for voice and pianoforte. Price 1/6. Copies: BCL E. Reference: G/T 10204.

[12] Lay of the Imprisoned Huntsman, a Song, the Words from the Lady of the Lake, Written by Walter Scott Esqr. . . London, Printed by Goulding, D'Almaine, Potter, & Co. Music Sellers to their Royal Highnesses the Prince & Princess of Wales, 20, Soho Sqe. & 7, Westmorland St. Dublin. [watermarked 1810]. Pages: *i-ii*, 1-5. Notes: Engraved sheet music with plate mark: 'Imprisoned Huntsman'. Words from canto 6, stanza 24 (first words: 'My hawk is tired of perch and hood'). Music composed by John Stevenson for voice and pianoforte. Price: 2s. Copies: E(2); NN-L.

[13] Lay of the Imprisoned Huntsman, from the Lady of the Lake, Written by Walter Scott Esqr. . . . London, Printed by Goulding, D'Almaine, Potter & Co. 20, Soho Square, 124,

New Bond Street, & to be had at 7, Westmoreland Street, Dublin. [watermarked 1809. ca.1810]. Pages: 1-4. Notes: Engraved sheet music. Words from canto 6, stanza 24 (first words: 'My hawk is tired of perch and hood'). Music composed by Joseph Mazzinghi for voice and pianoforte. Price: 1/6. Copy: MH. Reissued with watermark 1821 and imprint phrase added 'and to be had at' 7 (E), also watermark 1823 (NNP), and with variant imprint in 1830 (*see* 47Dv). Reference: Van Antwerp(2) 42q.

[14] The Lonely Isle, from the Lady of the Lake, Written by W. Scott Esqr. . . . London, Printed by Goulding, D'Almaine, Potter, & Co. 20, Soho Square, and to be had at No. 7, Westmoreland Street, Dublin. [watermarked 1821]. Pages: 1-4. Notes: Engraved sheet music. Words from canto 2, stanzas 2-3 (first words: 'Not faster yonder rowers' might'). Music composed by Joseph Mazzinghi arranged for voice and pianoforte. Price: 1/6. Copy: E. Reference: G/T 10202.

[15] The Maniac Song, from the Lady of the Lake, by Walter Scott Esqr. . . London, Printed by Goulding, D'Almaine, Potter & Co. 20, Soho Square, 124, New Bond Street & 7, Westmoreland Strt. Dublin. [watermarked 1809]. Pages: 1-4. Notes: Engraved sheet music. Words from canto 4 , stanza 22 (first words: 'They bid me sleep, they bid me pray'). Music composed by John Stevenson for voice and pianoforte. Price: 1/6. Copy: E. Reference: G/ T 10255.

[16] Merry it is in Good Greenwood, from the Lady of the Lake, Written by Walter Scott Esqr. . . . London, Printed by Goulding, D'Almaine, Potter & Co. 20, Soho Square, 124, New Bond Street & 7, Westmoreland Strt. Dublin. [watermarked 1810]. Pages: 1-4. Notes: Engraved sheet music with composer's characteristic 'M' in ink next to imprint. Words from canto 4, stanza 12 (first words as title). Music composed by Joseph Mazzinghi arranged for voice and pianoforte. Price: 1/6. Copy: E.

[17] Roderigh vich Alpine, From the Lady of the Lake, Written by Walter Scott, Esqr. . . . London, Printed by Goulding D'Almaine Potter & Co. . . . 117 New Bond Street & Westmorland Street Dublin. [watermarked 1810]. Pages: *1* 2-8. Notes: Engraved sheet music. Words from canto 2, stanza 19 (first words: 'Hail to the Chief who in triumph advances,'). Music composed by Joseph Mazzinghi arranged for voice and pianoforte. Price 3s. Copy: L. Reference: G/T 10199.

[18] . . . Roderigh vich Alpine, . . . Written by Walter Scott, Esqr. [unwatermarked]. Notes: Variant issue of next entry with heading above title: 'Sung at the Bath Concerts, by Mrs. Ashe, Mr. Magrath, & Mr. Bellamy,'. Copy: NN-L.

[19] Roderigh vich Alpine, . . . The Poetry by Sir Walter Scott Bart. . . . London, Published by Goulding, D'Almaine, Potter & Co. 20, Soho Sq. & to be had of all Music Sellers in the United Kingdom. [ca.1825]. Pages: *1* 2-8. Notes: Engraved sheet music with plate mark reading 'Roderigh Vich Alpine. Mazz:'. Words from canto 2, stanzas 19-20 (first words: 'Hail to the Chief who in triumph advances!'). Music composed by Joseph Mazzinghi, arranged for three voices and pianoforte. Price: 3s/. Copy: E.

[20] The Soldier Bridegroom's Song, a Ballad . . . the Words from The Lady of the Lake by Walter Scott Esqr. . . . London, Printed by Goulding, D'Almaine, Potter & Co. Music Sellers, 20, Soho Square & to be had at 7. Westmorland Street, Dublin. [watermarked 1809]. Pages: *i-ii*, 1-5. Notes: Engraved sheet music. Words from canto 3, stanza 23 (first words: 'The heath this night must be my bed'). Music composed by John Stevenson for voice and pianoforte. Price: 2s/. Copy: E. Reference: G/T 10256.

[21] The Soldier Bridegoom's Song, a Ballad . . . the Words from The Lady of the Lake By Walter Scott Esqr. . . London, Printed by Goulding, D'Almaine, Potter & Co. Music Sellers. 20 Soho Square, 124, New Bond Strr. & 7. Westmoreland Street, Dublin. [1811] (CtY ms date: 9 November 1811). Pages: *i-ii*, 1-5. Notes: Engraved sheet music. Words from canto 3, stanza 23 (first words: 'The heath this night must be my bed'). Music composed by John Stevenson for voice and pianoforte. Price: [indistinct]. Copies: L; CtY.

[22] Soldier rest thy warfare o'er from The Lady of the Lake, written by W. Scott Esqr. . . . London, Printed by Goulding, D'Almaine, Potter, & Co. 20 Soho Square, 124, New Bond Street, & 7, Westmoreland Street, Dublin. [watermarked 1809. ca.1810]. Pages: 1-4. Notes: Engraved sheet music with composer's characteristic initial 'M' in ink on the title-page. Words from canto 1, stanza 31 (first words: 'Soldier rest thy warfare o'er, Sleep the sleep that knows not breaking,'). Music by Joseph Mazzinghi arranged for voice and pianoforte. Price: 1/6. Copy: BCL.

[23] 'Tis Merry 'Tis Merry in Fairyland, from the Lady of the Lake, by Walter Scott Esqr. . . . London, Printed by Goulding, D'Almaine, Potter & Co. 20, Soho Square, & 7, Westmoreland Strt. Dublin. [watermarked 1810]. Pages: 1-4. Notes: Engraved sheet music with composer's characteristic 'M' in ink beside his name on title. Words from canto 4, stanza 15 (first words: ''Tis merry, 'tis merry, in Fairy-land, When fairy birds'). Music composed by Joseph Mazzinghi arranged for voice and pianoforte. Price: 1/6. Copy: E. Reissued without watermark, but inscribed '1811' (L). Reference: G/T 10200.

[24] 'Tis Merry 'Tis Merry in Good Greenwood, from the Lady of the Lake, Written by Walter Scott Esqr. . . . London, Printed by Goulding, D'Almaine, Potter & Co. 20, Soho Square, 124 New Bond Street, & 7, Westmoreland Strt., Dublin. [watermarked 1808. ca.1810]. Pages: 1-4. Notes: Engraved sheet music with composer's initial in ink next to imprint. Words from canto 4, stanza 14 (first words: ''Tis merry, 'tis merry, in good green wood, Though the birds'). Music composed by Joseph Mazzinghi arranged for voice and pianoforte. Price: 1/6. Copy: NN-L. Reissued ca. 1815 with no watermark (L). Reissued with 1823 watermark and imprint 'Square, and to be had at 7,' (E).

47Dx] LONDON: Goulding, D'Almaine, Potter and Wood 1814
Soldier rest thy warfare o'er, from The Lady of the Lake, written by W. Scott Esqr. . . . London, Printed by Goulding, D'Almaine, Potter, & Wood. 20 Soho Square & to be had at 7, Westmorland Street, Dublin. [watermarked 1813. ca.1814]. Pages: 1-4. Notes: Engraved sheet music with plate-mark 'Soldier, rest!'. Words from canto 1, stanza 31 (first words as title). Music composed by Joseph Mazzinghi arranged for voice and pianoforte. Copies: E(2); MH.

47Dy] LONDON: Holloway 1810-1820
[1] Ellens[!] Song Ave Maria Hymn to the Virgin The Poetry from the Popular Poem of the Lady of the Lake Written by Walter Scott. Esqr. . . . London, Publish'd by Holloway & Co. Wholesale Music Sellers & Musical Inst. Makers. No. 40 Hart Street. Bloomsbury Square. Where may be had by the same Author, . . [watermarked 1817]. Pages: *1* 2-10. Notes: Engraved sheet music. Words from canto 3, stanza 29 (first words: 'Ave Maria! maiden mild'). Music composed by John Clarke for four voices and organ. Price: 3s/. Copy: E.

[2] The heath this night must be my bed, Norman's Song The Poetry from the popular Poem of the Lady of the Lake Written by Walter Scott, Esqr. . . . London, Pubd. by Holloway & Co. Wholesale Music Sellers, & Musical Inst. Makers No. 40 Hart Street. Bloomsbury Square. [watermarked 1819]. Pages *i-ii,* 1-5. Notes: Engraved sheet music. Words from canto 3, stanza 23 (first words as title). Music by John Clarke for voice and piano forte. Price: 2s/. Copy: O.

[3] Huntsman rest, thy chace is done, . . . From the Lady of the Lake, Written by Walter Scott Esqr., . . . London, Pubd. by Holloway & Co. Wholesale Music Sellers, & Musical Inst. Makers, 40 Hart Street, Bloomsbury Sqre. [1814]. Pages: *1* 2-4. Notes: Engraved sheet music. Words from canto 1, stanza 32 (first words: 'She paused—then, blushing, led the lay,'). Music composed by John Clarke arranged for voice and pianoforte. Copy: L. Reference: G/T 10141.

[4] Lay of the Imprisoned Huntsman, from the Lady of the Lake . . . Written by Walter Scott, Esqr . . . . London. Pubd. by Holloway & Co. Wholesale Music Sellers & Musical Inst. Makers. 40 Hart Stt. Bloomsbury Sqa[!] Where may be had as Perform'd at the London & Bath Concerts, Ave Maria. . . [unwatermarked. ca.1810]. Pages: *i-ii,* 1-4. Notes: Engraved sheet music. Words from canto 6, stanza 24 (first words: 'My hawk is tired of perch and hood'). Music composed by John Clarke arranged for voice and pianoforte. Price: 2/. Copy: E.

[5] 'Roderigh Vich Alpine Dhu, Ho! Ieroc,' The Boat Song, in The Lady of the Lake, Written by Walter Scott Esqr. . . . London Pubd. by Holloway & Co. Wholesale Music Sellers & Musical Ins Makers 10, Hart St. Bloomsbury Square. [watermarked 1817]. Pages: *1* 2-7. Notes: Engraved sheet music. Words from canto 2, stanzas 19-20 (first words: 'Hail to the Chief who in triumph advances!'). Music composed by John Clarke arranged for voice and pianoforte. For an earlier impression see 47Daf[16] under Phipps. Copy: E.

47Dz] LONDON: Hubert 1815

[1] Allen bane the Harper. The Words from The Lady of the Lake, . . . London Printed for the Author [composer] and sold by H. Hubert. 402, Strand, opposite Salisbury Street. [watermerked 1815]. Pages: 1-3. Notes: Engraved sheet music. Words from canto 2, stanzas 6-10 (first words: 'Wake Allen bane aloud she cried,'). Music composed by Anton Radiger arranged for voice and pianoforte. Copy: L.

[2] Four Songs Being the Leading subject in Canto the first Section the 15th to 24th from the Lady of the Lake, . . . [London] Sold by H. Hubert, 402, Strand Opposite Salisbury Street. Where may be had all the Works of the Above Author. [1815]. Pages: *i-ii, 1* 2-9. Notes: Engraved sheet music, with composer's signature in ink to right of imprint. Music composed by Anton Radiger arranged for voice and pianoforte. Copy: L. Reference: G/T 10225. The songs include:

'The Bewilder'd Knight' from canto 1, stanzas 15-17 (first words: 'From the steep promontory gazed');

'The Nymph of Loch Katrine' from canto 1, stanzas 18-19 (first words: 'And ne'er did Grecian chizzel[!] trace,');

'The Royal Huntsman' from canto 1, stanzas 20-21 (first words: 'Impatient of the silent horn,');

'The Mountain Maid' from canto 1, stanzas 22-24 (first words: 'A while the maid the stranger eyed,').
A variant issue of 'Four Songs' was published by George Shade (*see* 47Dal[2]).

47Daa] LONDON: Lavenu 1810-1812
[1] Hymn to the Virgin Selected from the Popular Poem called The Lady of the Lake, Written by Walter Scott Esqr. . . . London, Printed & Sold by L. Lavenu, 26, New Bond Strt. Where may be had all the above Author's Works. [unwatermarked. ca.1810]. Pages: *i-ii, 1* 2-5. Notes: Engraved sheet music. Words from canto 3, stanza 29 (first words: 'Ave Maria! maiden mild'). Music composed by Henry R. Bishop arranged for voice with harp or pianoforte. Price: 2s.6d. Copy: L. Reference: G/T 10124. Reissued with watermark 1812 (E).

[2] Mary or Normans[!] Song from the Lady of the Lake, by Walter Scott Esqr. . . . London, Printed & Sold by L. Lavenu, Music Seller to his Royal Highness the Prince of Wales at his Musical Circulating Library, 26, New Bond Strt. [watermarked 1806. 1810]. Pages: *i-ii, 1* 2-5. Notes: Engraved sheet music. Words from canto 3, stanza 23 (first words: 'The heath this night must be my bed'). Music composed by Thomas Ludford Bellamy arranged for voice and pianoforte. Price: 2/-. Copy: E.

47Dab] LONDON: Longman, Hurst, Rees, Orme, and Brown 1811-1812
[1] Dr. Kemp's Musical Illustrations of The Lady of the Lake. . . . The Poetry Written by Walter Scott Esqr. London, Printed for Longman, Hurst, Rees, Orme, & Brown, Paternoster Row. And for the Author, 20 Kenton Street, Russell Square. [1811]. Notes: Engraved sheet music, with each title [except for 1] in a separate gathering, separately paged, probably for separate sale. Music composed by Joseph Kemp arranged for voice, harp and pianoforte. The music is followed by a leaf, which may be the last recto of the wrapper which lists 'Various other parts of The Lady of the Lake, that constitute pieces, which may be sung to the foregoing Lays.' Copy: L. The twelve titles include:
(1) 'The Surprise' from canto 1, stanza 16 (first words: 'I am alone, my bugle strain), plate mark: 'Lay 1', pages 1-4.
(2) 'Fitz-James. The Parting' from canto 2, stanza 6 (first words: 'While yet he loitered on the spot,'), plate mark: 'Lay 2', pages 1-4.
(3) 'Brian & Roderick Dhu. The Incantation' from canto 3, stanza 9 (first words: 'Woe to the Clansman who shall view'), plate mark: 'Lay 3', pages 1-4.
(4) 'The Anathema' from canto 3, stanza 9 (first words: 'Woe to the wretch, who fails to rear At this dread sign'), plate mark: 'Lay 9', page 4. Notes: Printed on last page of the gathering for the preceding song.
(5) 'Ellen & Fitz-James. The Return' from canto 4, stanza 16 (first words: '"O Stranger! in such hour of fear,'), plate mark: 'Lay ', pages 1-4.
(6) 'The Maniac' from canto 4, stanza 21 (first words: 'Now wound the path its dizzy ledge'), plate mark: 'Lay.', pages 1-*2*.
(7) 'Clan-Alpine's Warriors. The Defiance' from canto 5, stanza 8 (first words: 'Twice have I sought Clan Alpine's glen'), plate mark: 'Lay 5', pages 1-4.
(8) 'The Court. The Discovery' from canto 6, stanza 27 (first words: 'As wreath of snow on mountain breast,'), plate mark: 'Lay 6', pages 1-4.
(9) 'The Interview' from canto 1, stanza 20 (first words: 'Impatient of the silent horn, Now

on the gale her voice was borne:'), plate mark: 'Lay 7', pages 1-2.
(10) 'The Hare-Bell' from canto 2, stanza 9 (first words: '"For me, whose memory scarce conveys'), plate mark: 'Lay 8', pages 1-2.
(11) 'The Procession' from canto 5, stanza 20 (first words: '[But] Hark! what blithe and jolly peal'), plate mark: 'Lay 11', pages 1-2.
(12) 'Lay of the Imprisoned Huntsman' from canto 6, stanza 24 (first words: 'My hawk is tired of perch and hood,'), plate mark: 'Lay 12', pages 1-2.

[2] Dr. Kemp's Musical Illustrations of The Lady of the Lake. . . . Expressly composed to the Subjects of the Pictures, now engraving, to illustrate The Lady of the Lake; By Walter Scott, Esq. . . . Second Edition with Additions. London: Printed by A. J. Valpy, Took's-Court, Chancery-Lane; Published for Longman, Hurst, Rees, Orme, and Brown, Paternoster-Row; and the Author, No.20, Kenton-Street, Russell-Square. [1811]. Notes: Title from printed wrapper, with reference to the pictures by Richard Cook (*see* 47Dab[3]); also engraved title identifying composer as Joseph Kemp, music for voice and pianoforte or harp. Engraved music in 2 to 4 pages, each identified by a 'Lay' number and title. Despite the reference to 'additions' the contents are as for the first edition, previous entry. Printed wrapper at foot cites two sizes 'to bind up with each Edition of the Poem, if required': (a) 4°, 12s; (b) 8°, 9s. Copy: (a) not seen, (b) P.

[3] The Lady of the Lake, A Poem by Walter Scott, Esqr. . . . London: Published by Longman, Hurst, Rees, Orme & Brown, & W. Miller; & J. Ballantyne & Co. Edinburgh. 1811. Notes: Engraved vignette title-page and six plates. Title-page reads 'Illustrated with engravings from paintings by Richard Cook.'; all other plates titled 'Lady of the Lake', painted by Richard Cook, published by Longman & Co. Paternoster Row, 20 March 1811. Two preliminary advertisement slips have been noted, the first dated 1 August 1810 (TxU copy, 47Ae) indicating that with the illustrations, then in preparation, 'will be given a Portrait of the Author, engraved by Fittler, from a Painting by Saxon'; the second dated 21 January 1811 (47Ak) again announcing the portrait and now reporting issue in 'the ensuing month'. Advertised in the *Scots Magazine* for June 1811 (page 53) in [a] quarto proofs £1.10s. and in [b] octavo proof size 15s. (Lowndes notes modern impressions at 6s.) Separate copies: [issue a] not seen. [b] CtY MH. Combined poem-plate issues: see 47Aa, Ab, Ad, An, Ap. Reference: Ruff 107.
Title-page with vignette of Scottish hunting symbols engraved by F. Engleheart. Plates:
(1) [page 25] with a two-line quotation from canto 1, stanza 20 (first line: 'Then safe though fluttering and amazed,'), engraved by Chas. Heath
(2) [page 57] with a two-line quotation from canto 2, stanza 9 (first line: 'This little flower that loves the lea,'), engraved by Chas. Heath
(3) [page 110] with a two-line quotation from canto 3, stanza 10 (first line: 'Woe to the wretch, who fails to rear'), engraved by Chas. Warren Coincidentally, this is the same quotation earlier used for Richard Westall's illustration (*see* 47Dam).
(4) [page 173] with a two-line quotation from canto 4, stanza 21 (first line: 'The Tartan plaid she first descried'), engraved by A. Smith
(5) [page 222] with a two-line quotation from canto 5, stanza 21 (first line: 'As slowly down the steep descent,'), engraved by F. Engleheart
(6) [page 288] with a two-line quotation from canto 6, stanza 29 (first line: 'Then gently drew the glittering band,'), engraved by C. Armstrong

[~] Poetical Vagaries. 1812, 1814 [Parody by George Colman: *see* 491S(3-4)]

[~] The Prince of the Lake. 1815. [Imitation by M. J. Sullivan: *see* 491S(5)

[~] Wallace: or The Fight of Falkirk. 1810. [Parody by Margaret Holford: *see* 491S(6)]

LONDON: Leigh
[~] "Ave Maria!". 1832. (The Harmonicon: number 9: *see* 337D.7). Notes: Series initially printed for The Proprietors, published by Leigh. This title was published by Longman, Rees, Orme, Brown, Green, and Longman.

47Dac] LONDON: Macleish 1811
Airs, Duets, Choruses, &c. &c. in the New Musical Drama . . . . called The Knight of Snowdoun. . . . London: Printed by E. Macleish, 2, Bow-Street. [1811]. Pages: *1-7* 8-23 *24*. Notes: Page *6* notes that this drama is 'founded on the Poem of the Lady of the Lake.' Words by Thomas Morton; music composed by Sir Henry Bishop (not included). Copy: L.

47Dad] LONDON: Mallett 1823
[A Selection from the Sacred Oratorio, The Redemption . . . . London, Printed by J. Mallett (1823). 23pp. Notes: Libretto by Leone Tottola; music composed by Gioachino Rossini. The opera was first performed in London 18 February 1823.] Copy: not seen. Reference: Loewenberg, col. 665.

47Dae] LONDON: Monzani & Hill 1810
[1] Ellen's Song, Ave Maria, From the Lady of the Lake, By Walter Scott, Esqr. . . . London, Published by Monzani & Hill, Music Sellers to HRH the Prince of Wales. 3, Old Bond Street. [1810]. Pages: *i-ii*, 1-7. Notes: Engraved sheet music with plate number 'No. 175 Vocal English' and with composer's initials 'T.A.' in ink on title. Words from canto 3, stanza 29 (first words: 'Ave Maria! maiden mild'). Music composed by Thomas Attwood arranged for voice and pianoforte. Price: 2/6. Copies: BCL E. Reference: G/T 10118.

[2] He is gone on the Mountain, The Coronach or Funeral Song, From The Lady of the Lake, by Walter Scott Esqr. London Published by Monzani & Hill Music Sellers to H.R.H. the Prince of Wales No. 3, Old Bond St. [1810]. Pages: 1-4. Notes: Engraved sheet music with plate number 'No. 174 Vocal English' and with composer's initials 'T.A.' in ink on title. Words from canto 3, stanza 16 (first words as title). Music composed by Thomas Attwood arranged for voice and pianoforte. Price 1/6. Copy: L. Reference: G/T 10119.

[3] The heath this night must be my bed, Norman's Song From the Lady of the Lake, by Walter Scott, Esqr. . . . London Published by Monzani & Hill, Music Sellers to HRH the Prince of Wales, 3, Old Bond Street. [unwatermarked. ca.1810]. Pages: *i-ii* 1-8. Plate mark 'No. 173 Vocal English'. Notes: Engraved sheet music. Words from canto 3, stanza 23 (first words as title). Music composed by Thomas Attwood arranged for voice and pianoforte. Price 2/6. Copies: L O. Reference: G/T 10120.

LONDON: Phillips
[~] The Knight of the Cross. [1814]. [Parodic sheet music: *see* 494S(1)]

[~] Liberty. [1814]. [Parodic sheet music: see 494S(2)]

47Daf] LONDON: Phipps 1810-1820

[1] Allan-bane's Song, from the Lady of the Lake, . . . Written by Walter Scott, Esqr. . . London Printed for the Author [composer] by Messrs. Phipps & Co. 25 Duke St. Grosvenor Sqr. [watermarked 1810]. Two parts. Pages 1: *1* 2-5 *6*; 2: *5* 6-9 *10*. Notes: Engraved sheet music with composer's initials 'JC' handstamped on both titles. Words from canto 2, stanza 2 (first words: 'Not faster yonder rower's might flings from their oars the spray, ' and Part 2 from canto 2, stanza 3 (first words: 'But if beneath yon southern sky A plaided stranger roam,'). Music composed by John Clarke arranged for voice and pianoforte. Price: 1/6. Copy: BCL; MH(part 2).

[2] Allan-Bane's Song, from the Lady of the Lake, . . . Written by Walter Scott, Esqr. . . London Printed for the Author [composer] by Messrs. Phipps & Co. 25 Duke St. Grosvenor Sqr. [watermarked 1810]. Pages: *i-ii*, *1* 2-9. Notes: Engraved sheet music, with title-page modified in ink from the title-page used above: the Part number is left blank, and the price is changed to read 2/6. Words from canto 2, stanzas 2-3 (first words: "'Not faster yonder rowers' might flings from their oars the spray,'"). Music composed by John Clarke arranged for voice and pianoforte. Copy: E.

[3] Blanche of Devan's Song "They bid me sleep, they bid me Pray" The Poetry from the Popular Poem of The Lady of the Lake; Written by Walter Scott, Esqr. London; Published for the Author [composer] by Messrs. Phipps & Co. at their Music Warerooms, No. 25 Duke Street, Grosvenor Squae[!]. [watermarked 1810]. Pages: *i-ii*, *1* 2-5. Notes: Engraved sheet music with composer's initials 'JC' handstamped on title. Words from canto 4, stanza 22 (first words: 'They bid me sleep, they bid me pray'). Music composed by John Clarke arranged for voice and pianoforte. Copy: MH. Reference: G/T 10138. Reissued with watermark 1811 (E); 1813 (MH); 1815 (BCL E).

[4] The Coronach or Funeral Song, ("He's gone on the Mountain",) The Poetry from The Lady of the Lake, written by Walter Scott, Esqr. . . . London, Published for the Author [composer], by Messrs. Phipps & Co. at their Music Warerooms, No.25, Duke Street, Grosvenor Square. [watermarked: S | 1810]. Pages: *1* 2-7. Notes: Engraved sheet music with plate mark 'The Coronach.' and with composer's monogram ink-stamped on the title page. Imprint in some copies has semi-colon after London. Words from canto 3, stanza 16 (first words: 'He's gone on the mountain,'). Music composed by John Clarke arranged for voice and pianoforte. Price 2/. Copies: O; MH MH-M NN-L.

[5] The Coronach, (Third Edition) The Poetry from The Lady of the Lake, written by Walter Scott, Esqr.... London. Ent. at Sta. Hall. [watermarked 1816]. Pages: *1* 2-7. Notes: Apparently a private impression, without imprint, of the preceding issue. Engraved sheet music with plate mark 'The Coronach'. Words from canto 3, stanza 16 (first words: 'He's gone on the mountain'). Music composed by John Clarke arranged for voice and pianoforte. Price 2s/-. Copies: L O.

[6] The Coronach. (Third Edition) The Poetry from The Lady of the Lake, written by Walter Scott, Esqr. . . . London. Published for the Proprietor W. W. Phipps, by Goulding, D'Almaine & Co. 20, Soho Square. & to be had of all Music & Booksellers in the United Kingdom. [watermarked 1824]. Pages: *1* 2-7. Notes: Apparently a later impression of the preceding issue, with imprint. Engraved sheet music with plate mark 'The Coronach'. Words from canto 3, stanza 16 (first words: 'He's gone on the mountain'). Music composed by John Clarke arranged for voice and pianoforte. Price: 2s/. Copy: E. Reference: G/T 10139.

[7] The Coronach "He's gone on the Mountain," The Poetry from The Lady of the Lake, Written by Walter Scott, Esqr. . . . London, Published for the Author [composer] by Messrs. Phipps & Co. at their Music Warerooms, No. 25 Duke Street, Grosvenor Square. [1810]. Pages: *i-ii*, 1-9. Notes: Engraved sheet music with composer's initials 'JC' handstamped on title. Words from canto 3, stanza 16 (first words: 'He's gone on the mountain'). Music composed by John Clarke arranged for four voices and pianoforte. Copies: BCL E.

[8] Ellen's Song, "Ave Maria"; (Hymn to the Virgin,) The Poetry from the Popular Poem of The Lady of the Lake Written by Walter Scott, Esqr. . . . London, Published for the Author [composer] by Messrs. Phipps & Co. at their Music Warerooms, No. 25, Duke Street, Grosvenor Square. [watermarked 1809. 1810]. Pages: *i-ii*, *1* 2-10. Notes: Engraved sheet music with composer's initials 'JC' handstamped on the title. Words from canto 3, stanza 29 (first words: 'Ave Maria! maiden mild!'). Music by John Clarke arranged for voice and organ. Price: 3/. Copy: L. Reissued with watermark 1810 (BCL; MH) and without watermarks (L O). Reference: G/T 10142.

[9] The Heath this Night must be my Bed, Norman's Song. The Poetry from the Popular Poem of the Lady of the Lake Written by Walter Scott Esqr. . . . London, Published for the Proprietor W. W. Phipps by Goulding, D'Almaine & Co. 20 Soho Square. & to be had of all Music & Booksellers in the United Kingdom. [watermarked 1824]. Pages: *i-ii*, 1-5. Notes: Engraved sheet music. Words from canto 3, stanza 23 (first words as title). Music composed by John Clarke arranged for voice and pianoforte. Price: 2s/. Copies: BCL E.

[10] Huntsman rest thy chace is done, Recitative & Air, In Continuation of the Song Soldier Rest, Thy Warfare O'er, From the Lady of the Lake, Written by Walter Scott, Esqr. . . . London Published by Messrs. Phipps & Co. 25, Duke St. Grosvenor Square Where may be had the whole of the Songs from the above Poem compd. by Dr. Clarke. [watermarked: S | 1810]. Pages: *1-4*. Engraved sheet music. Words from canto 1, stanza 32, recitative (first words: 'She paused—then blushing') and song (first words as title). Music by John Clarke for voice and pianoforte. Price: 1/6. Copy: O.

[11] The Lady of the Lake's Song. . . . The Poetry by Walter Scott Esqr. . . . London Publish'd for the Author [composer] by Messrs. Phipps & Co. at their Music Rooms, 25 Duke Street, Grosvenor Square. [unwatermarked. ca.1810]. Pages: *1* 2-9. Notes: Engraved sheet music with composer's initials 'JC' handstamped on the title. Words from canto 1, stanzas 31-32 (first words: 'Soldier, rest! thy warfare o'er'). Music composed by John Clarke arranged for voice and pianoforte. Copy: E.

[11a] Lay of the Imprisoned Huntsman, From the Lady of the Lake, . . . Written by Walter Scott, Esqr, . . . London Printed for the Author by Messrs. Phipps & Co. at their Music Rooms. 25 Duke St. Grosvenor Square. [unwatermarked. ca.1810]. Pages: *1-2* 1-4. Notes: Engraved sheet music. Words from canto 6, stanza 24 (first words: 'My hawk is tir'd of perch and hood,'). Music composed by John Clarke arranged for voice and pianoforte. Copy: AN.

[12] The Minstrel's Tale, or Alice Brand, in Four Parts Glee and Solo, The Poetry from The Lady of the Lake, Written by Walter Scott Esqr. . . . London, Published by Messrs. Phipps & Co. 25, Duke Strt. Grosvenor Square. [watermarked 1808. ca.1810]. Four parts. Pages 1: *i-ii*, *1* 2-11; 2: *i-ii*, *1* 2-7; 3: *i-ii*, 1-9; 4: *i-ii*, *1* 2-13. Notes: Engraved sheet music with handstamped 'P&Co' on title-page and with plate marks 'Minstrel[!] Tale. Part 1 [2-4]'.

Each part has a separate title-page with the words 'Part' and 'Price' engraved and the part number and amount of the price added in ink after each word just above the imprint. Music composed by John Clarke 'respectfully dedicated to Mrs. Walter Scott' and arranged for three voices and pianoforte. Prices: (1) 5/; (2) 3/; (3) 4/; (4) 5/. Copies: BCL; MH. Reissued with watermark 1809 [1810](L), and 1813 (E, parts 2-4). The four parts represent: (1) Words from canto 4, stanza 12 (first words: 'Merry it is in the good green wood'); (2) Words from canto 4, stanza 13 (first words: 'Tis merry, 'tis merry, in good green wood, So blithe Lady Alice is singing'); (3) Words from canto 4, stanza 14 (first words: 'Tis merry, 'tis merry, in good green wood, Though the birds have still'd their singing'); (4) Words from canto 4, stanza 15 (first words: 'Tis merry, 'tis merry, in fairy land, When fairy birds are singing,').

[13] The Minstrel's Tale, or Alice Brand, Glee and Solo, The Poetry from The Lady of the Lake, written by Sir Walter Scott Bart. . . . [no part or price information] London, Published for the Proprietor W. W. Phipps, by Goulding & Co. 20, Soho Square. [ca.1820]. Pages: *1* 2-11. Notes: Engraved sheet music with plate mark 'Minstrel[!] Tale. (Part 1.)'. Words from canto 4, stanza 12 (first line: 'Merry it is in the good greenwood'). Music composed by John Clarke 'respectfully dedicated to Lady Walter Scott' and arranged for three voices and pianoforte. Except for the title-page this is a reimpression of part 1 of the preceding issue, with due regard now for the baronetcy. Copy: E.

[14] Norman's Song, The Poetry from the Popular Poem, of The Lady of the Lake, written by Walter Scott, Esqr. . . . London; Published for the Author [composer] by Messrs. Phipps & Co. at their Music Warerooms, No. 25 Duke St. Grosvenor Sq. [watermarked 1808]. Pages: *i-ii,* 1-5. Notes: Engraved sheet music with composer's initials 'JC' handstamped left below title-page frame and 'pr.2/' in ink on right below title-page frame. Words from canto 3, stanza 23 (first words: 'The heath this night must be my bed'). Music composed by John Clarke arranged for voice and pianoforte. Copies: BCL E O. Reissued with watermarks dated 1809 (O), 1810 (O; MH[2] NNP), 1815 (L), and unwatermarked (MH-M). References: G/T 10140; Van Antwerp(2) 42c.

[15] The Overture, And whole of the Music in The Knight of Snowdoun, . . . London Published by Messrs. Phipps & Co. At their Music Warehouse, No. 25 Duke Street Grosvenor Sqr. [watermarked 1809. 1810]. Pages: *i-ii, 1* 2-114. Notes: Engraved sheet music with plate mark 'The Knight of Snowdoun'. Words for musical drama by Thomas Morton. Music composed by Henry R. Bishop arranged for voice, chorus and pianoforte, opus 16. Price 12s. Copy: L. Reference: G/T 10125.

[16] "Roderigh Vich Alpine dhu, ho! ieroe," The Boat Song, in The Lady of the Lake, Written by Walter Scott, Esqr. . . . London Published for the Author [composer] by Messrs. Phipps & Co. 25 Duke Street Grosvenor Square. [watermarked 1810]. Pages: *1* 2-7. Notes: Engraved sheet music with composer's initials 'JC' handstamped on title. Words from canto 2, stanza 19 (first words: 'Hail to the Chief who in triumph advances!'). Music 'composed expressly for Mr. Braham' by John Clarke arranged for voice and pianoforte. Price: 2/. Copy: NNP. Reference: Van Antwerp(2) 42b. Reissued without watermark (BCL).

47Dag] LONDON: Power 1819

[1] Roderigh vich Alpine dhu, Boat Song from the Lady of the Lake, Written by Walter Scott Esqr. . . . No. 4. . . . London, Published by J. Power, 34, Strand. [watermarked 1819]. Pages: 1-3. Notes: Engraved sheet music with plate number '143'. Words from canto 2,

stanzas 19-20 (first words: 'Hail to the Chief who in triumph advances'). Music composed by C. E. Horn arranged for voice and pianoforte. Price: 1/6. Copy: E.

[2] Soldier, Rest! Ellen's Song from the Lady of the Lake, by Walter Scott Esqr. . . . London, Published by J. Power, 34, Strand. [watermarked 1819]. Pages: *1* 2-7. Notes: Engraved sheet music with plate number '108'. Words from canto 1, stanza 31 (first words: 'Soldier, rest! Thy warfare o'er,'). Music composed by Joseph Kemp arranged for voice and pianoforte. Price: 2/6. Copy: MH.

47Dah] LONDON: Power and Power 1810-1815

[1] Blanche of Devans song from The Lady of the Lake by Walter Scott Esqr. . . . London [Published by J. Power, 34, Stra]nd & W Powers[!] (4) Westmorland Street Dublin. [ca. 1815]. Pages *i-ii, 1* 2-5. Words in brackets defaced from copy. Notes: Engraved sheet music. Words from canto 4, stanza 25 (first words: 'The toils are pitch'd & the stakes are set,'). Music composed by T. Cooke arranged for voice and pianoforte. Price: 2/. Copy: L.

[2] The Emblem The Words from Walter Scott's admired poem of the Lady of the Lake, . . . London, Published by J. Power 34, Strand, and W. Power, 4, Westmoreland Street, Dublin. [ca. 1815]. Pages *1-2* 3-7. Notes: Engraved sheet music, plate mark '144'. Words from canto 4, stanza 1 (first words: 'The Rose is fairest when tis budding new'). Music composed by C. E. Horn for voice, pianoforte, flute, and violin.. Price: 2/. Copy: MH.

[3] The Heath this Night Must be my Bed, Norman's Song, from the Lady of the Lake, Written by Walter Scott Esqr. . . . No. 1. London, Published by J. Power, 34, Strand, & W. Power, 4, Westmoreland Street, Dublin. [unwatermarked. ca.1810]. Pages: 1-4. Notes: Engraved sheet music with plate mark '106'. Words from canto 3, stanza 23 (first words: 'The heath this night must be my bed,'). Music composed by Joseph Kemp for voice and pianoforte. Price: 1/6. Copy: E.

[4] The Lonely Isle, Minstrels Song, from the Lady of the Lake, Written by Walter Scott Esqr. . . . No. 5. London, Published by J. Power, 34, Strand, and W. Power, 4, Westmoreland Street, Dublin. [unwatermarked. ca.1810]. Pages: *1-2* 3-10. Notes: Engraved sheet music with plate mark '119'. Words from canto 2, stanza 2 (first words: 'Not faster yonder rowers' might'). Music composed by C. E. Horn arranged for voice and pianoforte. Price: 3/. Copy: E.

[5] Roderigh Vich Alpine Dhu, Ho! Ieroe, the Celebrated Boat Glee, from the Lady of the Lake, written by Walter Scott Esqr. . . . No. 4. London, Published by J. Power, 34, Strand, and W. Power, 4, Westmoreland Street, Dublin. [1810]. Pages: *i-ii, 1-2* 3-7. Notes: Engraved sheet music with plate number 112. Words from 'Boat Song', canto 2, stanza 19 (first words: 'Hail to the chief who in triumph advances Honour'd and bless'd be the evergreen pine!'). Music composed by E. E. Horn arranged for voice and piano-forte. Price: 3/-. Copy: L.

[6] Soldier, Rest! Ellen's Song from the Lady of the Lake, by Walter Scott Esqr. . . . London, Published by J. Power, 34, Strand, & W. Power, 4, Westmoreland Strt. Dublin. [unwatermarked. ca.1810]. Pages: 1-3. Notes: Engraved sheet music with plate number '108'. Words from canto 1, stanza 31 (first words: 'Soldier rest! thy warfare o'er'). Music composed by Joseph Kemp arranged for voice and pianoforte. Price: 1/6. Copy: E. Reissued with watermark 1811(L).

[7] Soldier, Rest! Ellen's Song from the Lady of the Lake, Written by Walter Scott Esqr. . . . London, Published by J. Power, 34, Strand, & W. Power, 4, Westmoreland Strt. Dublin. [watermarked 1809. 1810]. Pages: 1-3. Notes: Engraved sheet music with plate mark '142'. Words from canto 1, stanza 31 (first words: 'Soldier rest! thy warfare o'er'). Music composed by Joseph Kemp arranged for voice and pianoforte. Price: 1/6. Copy: E. Reissued with watermark 1811(L). Reference:G/T 10177 (watermark 1812).

[8] They Bid me Sleep, Blanche of Devan's Song from The Lady of the Lake, Written by Walter Scott Esqr. . . . No.2. London, Published by J. Power, 34, Strand & W. Power, 4, Westmoreland Strt. Dublin. [1815]. Pages: 1-3. Notes: Engraved sheet music with plate number '107'. Words from canto 4, stanza 22 (first words: 'They bid me sleep, they bid me pray,'). Music composed by Joseph Kemp and arranged for voice and pianoforte. Price: 1/6. Copies: E L. Reference: G/T 10178.

47Dai] LONDON: Radiger 1812
Allen[!] Bane the Harper, The Words from The Lady of The Lake, . . . London Printed for the Author and sold by H. Hubert. 402, Strand, opposite Salisbury Street. [1812]. Pages: 1-3. Notes: Engraved sheet music with caption title. Words from canto 2, stanza 6 (first words: 'Wake Allenbane[!] aloud she cried,'). Music composed by Anton Radiger arranged for voice and pianoforte or harp. Copy: L. Reference: G/T 10224.

LONDON: Richardson
[~] The Ass on Parnassus. Cantos I-II. [1815]. [Parody: *see* 495S(1)]

[~] The Ass on Parnassus. Cantos I-IV. [1815]. [Parody: *see* 495S(2)]

47Daj] LONDON: Royal Harmonic Institution 1820
"It was an English Lady bright," . . . From the Lady of the Lake, London, Printed by the Royal Harmonic Institution. (Lower Saloon, Argyll Rooms.). [1820]. Pages: 1-8. Notes: Engraved sheet music with caption title and plate number '572'. Words from canto 6, stanza 11 (first words: 'It was an English Lady[!] bright, The sun shines fair on Carlisle wall,'). Music composed by James Fisin arranged for voice and pianoforte. Price: 2s/-. Copy: L.

47Dak] LONDON: Schetky 1810-1815
[1] [Blanche of Devan's Song. London: Schetky (1815). Notes: Music composed by J. G. C. Schetky.] Copy: not seen. Reference: G/T 10239.

[2] [Coronach. London: Schetky (1815). Notes: Music composed by J. G. C. Schetky.] Copy: not seen. Reference: G/T 10240.

[3] The Lonely Isle, A Song from the Lady of the Lake; Written by Walter Scott Esqr. . . . London, Published by G. Schetky Junr. No. 6. Gt. Pulteney Street Golden Square, And to be had at Mr. Birchall's & Mr. Chappel's Music Shops New Bond Street. [unwatermarked. ca.1810]. Pages: *1* 2-5. Notes: Engraved sheet music. Words from canto 2, stanzas 2-3 (first words: 'Not faster yonder rowers might'). Music composed by J. G. C. Schetky. Price 2/6. Copy: L. Reference: G/T 10238.

[4] Norman's Song, and the Coronach. From the Lady of the Lake Written by Walter Scott Esqr. . . . London, Published by G. Schetky Junr. No. 6. Gt. Pulteney Street, Golden Square,

And to be had at Mr. Birchall's & Mr. Chappel's Music Shops New Bond Street. [unwatermarked. ca. 1810]. Pages: *i-ii*, 1-6. Notes: Engraved sheet music with plate number 106. Dedicated to Scott (*see* 542T). Words from canto 3, stanza 23 (first words: 'The heath this night must be my bed') and from canto 3, stanza 16 ('He is gone on the mountain'). Music composed by J. G. C. Schetky arranged for voice and pianoforte. Price: 3s/. Copy: L.

47Dal] LONDON: Shade 1822-1830

[1] The Bewilder'd Knight. London Printed for G. Shade East Side of Soho Sqr. [1822]. Pages: *1* 2-3. Engraved sheet music with caption title. Words from Canto 1, stanzas 15-17 (first words: 'From the steep promontory gazed'). Music composed by Anton Radiger. Copy: L.

[2] Four Songs being the Leading subject in Canto the first Section the 15th. to 24th. from the Lady of the Lake, . . . London Printed by Geo: Shade, Soho Square. . . . [1830]. Pages: *1* 2-9. Notes: Engraved sheet music. Titles and plot-lines for the four songs are listed on the title-page, each of which was also reimposed and made available separately. Music composed by Anton Radiger arranged for voice and pianoforte. Price: 4s; separate nos. 1/6. Copies: L L(no.8). The songs include:
(1) 'The Bewilder'd Knight' from canto 1, stanzas 15-17 (first words: 'From the steep promontory gazed'), pages 2-3;
(2) 'The Nymph of Loch Katrine' from canto 1, stanzas 18-19 (first words: 'And ne'er did Grecian chizzel[!] trace,'), pages 4-5;
(3) 'The Royal Huntsman' from canto 1, stanzas 20-21 (first words: 'Impatient of the silent horn,'), pages 6-7;
(4) 'The Mountain Maid' from canto 1, stanzas 22-24 (first words: 'A while the maid the Stranger eyed, And, reassured'), pages 8-9.
A variant issue of 'Four Songs' was published by H. Hubert (*see* 47Dz[2]).

[3] The Lay, of the Imprisoned Huntsman From the Lady of the Lake. By Walter Scott Esqr. . . . Printed for G. Shade East Side of Soho Square. [unwatermarked. ca.1830]. Pages: *1-2* 3. Notes: Engraved sheet music. Words from canto 6, stanza 24 (first words: 'My hawk is tired of perch and hood,'). Music composed by W. S. Stevens, arranged for voice and pianoforte. Price: 1/. Copy: MH.

[4] Soldier Rest, Ellen's Song from the Lady of the Lake, By Walter Scott Esqr. London. Published by Geo. Shade, Soho Square. [unwatermarked. ca.1830]. Pages: 1-3. Notes: Engraved sheet music. Words from canto 1, stanza 31 (first words: 'Soldier rest! thy warfare o'er'). No composer cited. Music arranged for voice and pianoforte. Price: 1s./. Copy: E.

47Dam] LONDON: Sharpe 1810

The Lady of the Lake, A Poem by Walter Scott, Esq. . . . London, Published by John Sharpe, Piccadilly, 1811. Notes: A suite usually with frontispiece of Scott dated 1 February 1811, this after H. Raeburn, engraved by A Raimbach. Engraved vignette title-page and six plates dated 1 December 1810, all after Richard Westall by the engravers first cited below and advertised in a Prospectus dated 8 May 1810 (issue date of the poem itself, copy NNP). The 1810 plates were available in [a] 4° proofs £1.15.0. and in [b] 8° size 12s. As noted in Ruff, certain of these plates were later dated 1 June 1811 and produced by other engravers (here identified in parentheses). Separate suites: [issue a] not seen. [b] EP. Combined poem-

plate issues: *see* 47Aa, Ac, Ad, Ak, An. References: Ruff 108-109.
Title-page with vignette of tree, harp, and lake, engraved by John Pye. Plates:
(1) [page 22] with a two-line quotation from canto 1, stanza 17 (first line: 'In listening mood, she seemed to stand,') engraved by Chas. Heath
(2) [page 52] with a two-line quotation from canto 2, stanza 6 (first line: 'But when he turned him to the glade,') engraved by F. Engleheart (Anker Smith)
(3) [page 110] with a two-line quotation from canto 3, stanza 10 (first line: '"Woe to the wretch, who fails to rear') engraved by Abr. Raimbach (John Romney). Coincidentally, this is the same quotation later used for Richard Cook's illustration (*see* 47Dab[3].)
(4) [page 166] with a two-line quotation from canto 4, stanza 16 (first line: '—Ellen beheld as in a dream,') engraved by Anker Smith (F. Engleheart)
(5) [page 204] with a two-line quotation from canto 5, stanza 9 (first line: '"These are Clan-Alpine's warriors true;') engraved by Saml. Noble (Richard Golding)
(6) [page 284] with a two-line quotation from canto 6, stanza 27 (first line: 'No word her choaking voice commands,—') engraved by Richd Golding (James Fittler).

47Dan] LONDON: Sharpe and Hailes 1811
The Knight of Snowdoun; A Musical Drama, in Three Acts, . . . London: Printed by Whittingham and Rowland, Goswell Street; For Sharpe and Hailes, Opposite Albany, Piccadilly. 1811. Pages: *1-7* 8-79. Notes: Words by Thomas Morton (music by Henry Bishop not included), as it was performed at the Theatre Royal, Covent Garden, 5 February 1811. The 'Advertisement' reads: 'This musical Drama is founded on the Poem of the Lady of the Lake, but as the writer's humble judgment has directed him to select, rather than to copy, he trusts the admirers of the Poem will concede to him the indulgence of making such alterations in the original story, as stage necessity has induced him to adopt.' A chorus in this drama is revived in Pocock's *Rob Roy Macgregor* (see 112Dk). Price: 2s. 6d. Copies: BCL C DT E O; CtY DLC InU NjP. Reference: Bolton 51.

47Dao] LONDON: Tegg 1810
The Lady of the Lake: A Romance, In Two Volumes. Founded on the Poem so called by Walter Scott, Esq. . . . London: Printed for Thomas Tegg, No. 111, Cheapside. And sold by Wm. Allason, No. 31, New Bond Street. 1810. Two volumes. Pages 1: *i-iv*, *1* 2-186; 2: *i-iv*, *1* 2-178 *179-180*. Notes: A prose version. One year later this derivative story was advertised in Edinburgh, for 10s., at Sutherland's Circulating Library (*EEC* 20 September 1811). Copies: E; MH.

47Dap] LONDON: Walker 1810-1822
[1] Allan-Bane, The Minstrel's Song, The Words from The Lady of the Lake, by W. Scott Esqr. . . . London Published by G. Walker at his Music Warehouse 106 Gt. Portland Street, . . . [watermarked 1809. 1810]. Pages: *1* 2-7. Notes: Engraved sheet music. Words from canto 2, stanza 2 (first words: 'Not faster yonder rowers might Flings from their oars the spray'). Music composed by James Lacy arranged for voice and harp or pianoforte. Price: 2s. Copy: BCL.

[2] Blanche of Devan's Song from the Admired Poem of the Lady of the Lake, Written by Walter Scott Esq, . . London: Printed & Sold by G. Walker, for the Author [Composer], at his Wholesale Music Warehouse 106 Grt. Portland Street. [unwatermarked. ca.1810]. Pages: *i-ii*, *1* 2-5 *6*. Notes: Engraved sheet music. Words from canto 4, stanza 22 (first words:

'They bid me sleep, they bid me pray, They say my brain is warp'd and wrung'). Music composed by Augustus Meves arranged for voice and harp or pianoforte. Price: 2s/. Copy: E.

[3] Ellen's Song, The Words from The Lady of the Lake, . . . London, Published by G. Walker at his Music Warehouse 106 Gt. Portland Str. [watermarked 1806. 1810]. Pages: *1* 2-8. Notes: Engraved sheet music. Words from canto 1, stanzas 30-32 (first words: 'Weird women we! by dale and down,'). Music composed by James Lacy arranged for voice with harp or pianoforte. Price: 2s. Copies: L; NN-L. Reference: G/T 10183.

[4] Norman's Song, The words from the Lady of the Lake, Written by Walter Scott, Esqr. . . . London Printed for the Author [composer] & Sold by G. Walker 106 Gt. Portland Street. . . . [unwatermarked. ca. 1815]. Pages: *i-ii*, 1-5. Notes: Engraved sheet music. Words from canto 3, stanza 23 (first words: 'The heath this night must be my bed'). Music composed by James Lacy arranged for voice and harp or pianoforte. Price: 2s. Copy: L. Reference: G/T 10184.

[5] Rodorich[!] Vich Alpine, or the Boat Song, . . The words from the Lady of the Lake, . . . London Printed by G. Walker 106 Gt. Portland Street. [watermarked 1818]. Pages: *i-ii*, 1-6. Notes: Engraved sheet music. Words from canto 2, stanza 19 (first words: 'Hail to the Chief, who in Triumph advances!'). Music by Augustus Meves arranged for voice and pianoforte. Copy: E.

47Daq] LONDON: Wheatstone 1810
Ave Maria, from the Lady of the Lake, Written by W. Scott Esqr. . . . London Printed for C. Wheatstone & Co. 436 Strand. [watermarked 1809. ca.1810]. Pages *1-3*. Notes: Engraved sheet music. Words from 'Hymn to the Virgin', canto 4, stanza 29 (first words: 'Ave Maria maiden mild listen to a maiden's prayer,'). Music composed by Louis Jansen arranged for voice and harp or pianoforte. Price: 1s. Copy: L.

47Dar] LONDON: Wyatt 1811
The Lady of the Lake: A Melo-Dramatic Romance, in Three Acts; Taken from the Popular Poem of that Title, . . . London: Printed for W. H. Wyatt, Picket Street, Temple-Bar; by B. McMillan, Bow Street, Covent Garden. 1811. Pages: *i-vi*, *1* 2-49 *50*. Notes: Drama by Edmund John Eyre, as 'Now Performing with Undiminished Applause, at the Theatre Royal, Edinburgh.' A preliminary note reports that the playwright was 'very sensible, that Mr. Scott's Poem of "*The Lady of the Lake*," afforded materials for a much superior Drama than the one here presented', but that at the urgent request of the Theatre Manager, Mr. Siddons, 'the whole piece was arranged, written, and copied, in the short space of ten days.' The first full-scale dramatic version of Scott's works, by Thomas J. Dibdin, was first produced in London at the Surrey Theatre 24 September 1810, and first published in Dublin by Figgis (*see* 47Dc). On 18 December Scott wrote at length to the young actress Sarah Smith (later Mrs Bartley), commenting on what he had heard about the Dibdin performance and the preparations then underway for this Eyre version, produced in Edinburgh 15 January 1811. Copies: BCL E; CtY(2) DLC InU NjP NN ViU. References: *Letters*, ii.410-413; Bolton 49-50.

47Das] LONDON: Wybrow 1826
[1] The Lay of the Imprisoned Huntsman, from The Lady of the Lake Words by Walter Scott Esqr. . . London Pub by W Wybrow at his Public Library 24 Rathbone Place Oxford

St. [unwatermarked. ca.1826]. Pages: *1* 2-3. Notes: Engraved sheet music. Words from canto 6, stanza 24 (first words: 'My hawk is tir'd of perch and hood,'). Music by Louis Jansen arranged for voice and pianoforte. Price: 1s. Copies: E(2).

[2] Soldier Rest! Ellen's Song From the Lady of the Lake, By Walter Scott Esqr. . . . London Pubd by W Wybrow at his Public Library 24 Rathbone Place Oxford Street. [unwatermarked. ca.1826]. Pages: 1-3. Notes: Engraved sheet music. Words from canto 1, stanza 31 (first words: 'Soldier rest thy warfare o'er'). Composer not identified: arranged for voice and pianoforte. Price: 1s/. Copy: L.

[3] The Vicar still preaches, Soldiers[!] Song from the Lady of the Lake. Words by Walter Scott Esqr. . . . London. Pubd. by W. Wybrow at his Public Library 24 Rathbone Place Oxford Street. [unwatermarked. ca.1826]. Pages: *1* 2-3. Notes: Engraved sheet music. Words from canto 6, stanza 5 (first words: 'Our vicor[!] still preaches that Peter and Poule, Laid a swinging long Curse'). Music composed by Louis Jansen arranged for voice and pianoforte. Price: 1s. Copy: E.

47Dat] LONDON: [no publisher] 1811

Roderick Vich Alpine, (Boat Song) in the Lady of the Lake, By Walter Scott, Esqr. [inscribed October 1811]. Pages: *1* 2-*3*. Notes: Engraved sheet music on green paper, without imprint and with caption title. Words from canto 2, stanzas 19-20 (first words: 'Hail to the chief who in triumph advances'). Composer not identified, but arranged for voice and pianoforte. Apparently an instructor's copy; a printing similarly inscribed is listed for *Marmion* (*see* 28Daa). Price: 1s. Copy: L.

UNITED STATES

47Dau] BALTIMORE: Carr 1814

[1] The Invisible Chorus in the Melo-dramatic Romance, The Lady of the Lake. . . . Baltimore, Printed and Sold at Carrs Music Store 36 Baltimore Street. [ca.1814]. Pages: *1-2*. Notes: Engraved sheet music. Lyrics by Thomas John Dibdin from canto 1, stanza 31 (first words: 'Soldier rest thy warfare o'er,'). Music by James Sanderson, arranged for voice and pianoforte by T. Carr. Copy: PPL. Reference: Wolfe 7812.

[2] The much admired March & Chorus "Hail to the Chief" in the celebrated Melo-Dramatic Romance, The Lady of the Lake. . . . Baltimore, Printed and Sold at Carr's Music Store, 36 Baltimore Street. [ca.1814]. Pages: *1-3*. Notes: Engraved sheet music with caption title. Page *1* is blank. Words by Thomas John Dibdin adapted from canto 2, stanza 19 (first words: 'Hail, to the Chief who in triumph advances!'). Music composed by James Sanderson arranged for voice and pianoforte by T. Carr. Some copies have a period after the first Baltimore and there is no apostrophe, nor space, in the same line. Beginning in 1815 the words for 'Hail to the Chief' were adapted for use with the title 'Wreaths for the Chieftain'. The occasion then was to celebrate both the end of the 1812-1814 war with Britain and George Washington's birthday. The Sanderson arrangement, frequently reprinted as noted below, is now used to herald the arrival of the President of the United States. Copies: MH MWA PPL RPB. Reference: Wolfe 7770.

47Dav] BALTIMORE: Le Pelletier 1810

[1] Blanche of Devan's Song From the Lady of the Lake . . . *In* Journal of Musick [part 2, number 24]. Published by Madame Le Pelletier, [Baltimore]. 1810. Pages: 166-169. Notes: Engraved sheet music with caption title for music. Words from canto 4, stanza 22 (first words: 'They bid me sleep, they bid me pray'). Music composed by John Clarke arranged for voice and pianoforte. Page 169 of this last number notes that the engraving was done by G. Willig 'at his Musical Magazine Philadelphia.' Copies: DLC MWA RPB. References: G/T 10138; Wolfe 1823, 4696.

[2] The Coronach A Funeral Song From the Lady of the Lake . . . *In* Journal of Musick [part 2, number 23]. Published by Madame Le Pelletier, [Baltimore]. 1810. Pages: 158-162. Notes: Engraved sheet music. Words from canto 3, stanza 16 (first words: 'He's gone on the mountain, He's lost to the forest,'). Music composed by John Clarke arranged for voice and pianoforte. Copies: DLC MH MWA RPB. References: G/T 10139; Wolfe 1827, 4696.

[3] The Soldier Bridegroom's Song From the Lady of the Lake . . . *In* Journal of Musick [part 2, number 24]. Published by Madame Le Pelletier, [Baltimore]. 1810. Pages: 163-165. Notes: Engraved sheet music. Words from canto 3, stanza 23 (first words: 'The heath this night must be my bed, The bracken curtain for my head,'). Music composed by John A. Stevenson arranged for voice and pianoforte. Copies: DLC MWA RPB. References: Wolfe 8956, 4696.

47Daw] BALTIMORE: Robinson 1826

The Lady of the Lake; A Melo-Dramatic Romance, in Three Acts. . . . Baltimore: Printed and Published by J. Robinson, Circulating Library and Dramatic Repository. 1826. Pages: *1-3* 4-36. Notes: Play by Edmund John Eyre. Copy: MH.

47Dax] BOSTON: Bradlee 1827

Roderigh vich Alpine. Poetry by Sir Walter Scott, . . . Boston: Published by C. Bradlee Washington Street. [ca.1827]. Pages: *1* 2-8. Notes: Engraved sheet music. Words from canto 2, stanzas 19-20 (first words: 'Hail to the Chief who in triumph advances,'). Music composed by Joseph Mazzinghi arranged for voice and pianoforte. In two issues: (a) with 'O. L. No. 2.' at upper right of page *1*; (b) without designation. Copies: (a) MWA; (b) MH(3) MWA.

47Day] BOSTON: Graupner 1811

Soldiers[!] Rest A Song from the Lady of the Lake, . . . Boston, Published and Sold, by G. Graupner, at his Music Store, No. 6 Franklin Street. [ca.1811]. Pages *1* 2-3. Notes: Engraved sheet music with plate numbers 457-458. Words from canto 1, stanza 31 (first words: 'Soldier rest thy warfare's o'er Sleep the sleep that knows no breaking dream',). Music composed by James Hook arranged for voice and pianoforte. Copies: DLC MWA. Reference: Wolfe 4209.

47Daz] BOSTON: Hewitt 1812

[The Imprisoned Huntsman. A Favorite Song. Notes: In *CC* 26 September 1812 this 'new music just published' was advertised by James Hewitt, Musical Library, 58 Newbury Street, Boston. Music composed by John Whitaker.] Copy: not seen. Reference: Wolfe 9823.

47Dba] CHARLESTON: Gilfert 1813-1817

[1] [Alice Brand. *In* Chas. Gilfert & Cos. Monthly Publication, number 3. Charleston (ca.1817). 38-39pp. Notes: Music composed by James Hook.] Copy: not seen. Reference: Wolfe 3948.

[2] [The Coronach, or Funeral Song. . . . Charleston, Publish'd by G. Gilfert & Co., No. 40 Broad Street. (ca.1813). 6pp. Notes: Music composed by John Clarke.] Copy: not seen. Reference: Wolfe 1830.

[3] [Huntsman Rest Thy Chace is Done. *In* Chas. Gilfert & Cos. Monthly Publication, number 6. Charleston (ca.1817). 84-86pp. Notes: Music composed by Joseph Mazzinghi.] Copy: not seen. Reference: Wolfe 5693.

47Dbb] CHARLESTON: Siegling 1821

[March & Chorus in the Dromatic[!] Romance of The Lady of the Lake. Charleston, Published by J. Siegling at His Musical Warehouse, 69 Broad Street. (ca.1821). Pages: 1-4. Notes: With publication number 15. Lyrics by Thomas John Dibdin. Music composed by James Sanderson.] Copy: not seen. Reference: Wolfe 7782.

47Dbc] NEW YORK: Bourne 1827

Huntsman rest thy chace is done A favourite Huntingsong[!] in the Lady of the Lake written by Walter Scott. . . . [*rubber stamp*] Depository of Arts Bourne's 359 Broadway [1827]. Pages: *1* 2-4. Notes: Engraved sheet music. Words from canto 1, stanza 32 (first words: 'She paused then blushing led the lay, To grace the stranger of the day;'). Music composed by Joseph Mazzinghi arranged for voice and pianoforte. Copy: MWA.

47Dbd] NEW YORK: Bradish 1810-1811

[1] [Alice Brand. A Favorite Ballad. . . . New York, Publish'd by Mrs. Bradish, No. 124 Broadway. (ca.1811). Pages: 1-2. Notes: Music composed by James Hook.] Copy: not seen. References: G/T 10171; Wolfe 3947.

[2] Blanche of Devan's Song From The Lady of the Lake Written by W Scott. . . . New York Published by Mrs Bradish No. 124 Broad Way. [ca.1811]. Pages: *1* 2-4. Notes: Engraved sheet music with caption title. Words from canto 4, stanza 22 (first words: 'They bid me sleep, they bid me pray,'). Music composed by John Clarke arranged for voice and pianoforte. Copies: MWA RPB. Reference: Wolfe 1824.

[3] [Boat Song. . . . New York, Publish'd by Mrs. Bradish, No. 124 Broad Way. (ca.1811). Pages: 1-2.] Notes: Composer unknown. Copy: not seen. Reference: Wolfe 907.

[4] The Coronach, or Funeral Song from The Lady of the Lake Written by W. Scott. . . New York Published by Mrs Bradish, No. 124 Broad Way. [ca.1810]. Pages: *1-2* 3-7. Notes: Engraved sheet music with caption title and with plate mark on pages 3-7: 'The Coronach'. Page *1* is blank. Words from canto 3, stanza 16 (first words: 'He's gone on the mountain, He's lost to the forest'). Music composed by John Clarke arranged for voice and pianoforte. Some copies have variant pointing in imprint. Copies: MH MWA RPB. Reference: Wolfe 1828.

[5] Ellen's Song, "Ave Maria;" (Hymn to the Virgin,) The Poetry from the Popular Poem of the Lady of the Lake written by Walter Scott, Esqr. . . . New York, Publish'd by Mrs. Bradish

No. 124 Broadway. [ca.1811]. Pages: 1-9. Notes: Engraved sheet music with caption title. Words from canto 3, stanza 29 (first words: 'Ave Maria! maiden mild!'). Music composed by John Clarke arranged for voice and pianoforte. Copies: PPL RPB. Reference: Wolfe 2674.

[6] Huntsman Rest! Thy Chace is Done, Recitative & Air, in Continuation of the Song, Soldier rest thy warfare o'er from the Lady of the Lake Written by Walter Scott Esqr. . . New York Publish'd by Mrs. Bradish No. 124 Broadway. [1811]. Pages: 1-4. Notes: Engraved sheet music. Words from canto 1, stanza 32 (first words: 'She paused then blushing led, the lay,'). Music composed by Joseph Mazzinghi arranged for voice and pianoforte. In some copies page number 1 is excised. Advertised by Mrs. Bradish in *NYEP* 12 January 1811. Copies: DLC MH MWA. Reference: Wolfe 5690.

[7] Norman's Song, The Poetry from the Popular Poem, of The Lady of the Lake, Written by Walter Scott Esqr . . . . New York, Publish'd by Mrs. Bradish, 124 Broadway. [1810]. Pages: *i-ii*, 1-5. Notes: Engraved sheet music. Words from canto 3, stanza 23 (first words: 'The heath this night must be my bed, The bracken curtain for my head,'). Music composed by John Clarke arranged for voice and pianoforte. Copy: MWA. Reference: *see note* Wolfe 1851.

47Dbe] NEW YORK: Clayton 1811

The Lady of the Lake; A Melo-Dramatic Romance, in Three Acts. . . . Printed from the Acting Copy, with Stage Directions. New-York:— E. B. Clayton, 9 Thames-street. Philadelphia:—C. Neal, 16 South Seventh-street. [1811]. Pages: *1-3* 4-39. Notes: Play by Edmund John Eyre. At head of title: Clayton's Edition. Copies: MH(prompt copy) NN-L(2:prompt copies).

47Dbf] NEW YORK: Dubois 1817-1818

[1] Chorus Hail to the Chief Lady of the Lake, . . . New York Published by Wm. Dubois [ca.1817]. Pages: *1* 2-3. Notes: Engraved sheet music with caption title. Reissue from same plates as Wolfe 7769 [Paff] with altered imprint. Words adapted by Thomas John Dibdin from canto 2, stanzas 19-20 (first words: 'Hail! Hail! Hail to the Chief who in Triumph advances'). Music composed by James Sanderson arranged for voice and pianoforte. Copies: DLC InU(2) MH MWA RPB. Reference: Wolfe 7769A. Reissued with slight plate revisions and pagination removed, as Wolfe 7769B (RPB).

[2] Huntsman Rest! Thy Chace Is Done Recitative and Air, from Lady of the Lake . . . New York Published by Wm. Dubois. [ca.1818]. Pages: *1* 2-4. Notes: Engraved sheet music with caption title. Words from canto 1, stanza 32 (first words: 'She paus'd then blushing led, the lay, To grace the Stranger'). Music composed by Joseph Mazzinghi arranged for voice and pianoforte. Reissue from the same plates as Wolfe 5691 (47Dbk[2]) with altered imprint. Copies: MWA RPB. Reference: Wolfe 5691A.

47Dbg] NEW YORK: Firth and Hall 1823

Hail to the Chief Lady of the Lake Written by Sr. Walter Scott . . . New York, Published by Firth & Hall, 358, Pearl Street. [unwatermarked. ca.1823]. Pages: *1* 2-3. Notes: Engraved sheet music. At head of title: 'Chorus'. Words from canto 2, stanza 19 (first words: 'Hail! Hail! Hail to the Chief who in triumph advances,'). Music composed by James Sanderson arranged for voice and pianoforte. Copy: NN-L. Variant issue with address reading '7, Franklin Sqr.' (MH).

47Dbh] NEW YORK: Hall and Son 1825

Hail to the Chief Lady of the Lake Written by Sr. Walter Scott . . . New York. Published by William Hall & Son. 239 Broadway. [ca.1825]. Pages *1* 2-3. Notes: Another impression of the preceding entry with a different publisher and a plate mark now entered as '505'. Copy: MH.

47Dbi] NEW YORK: Inskeep and Bradford 1811

The Lady of the Lake, A Melo-Dramatic Romance, in Three Acts: Taken from the Popular Poem of that Title, . . . New-York: Printed for Inskeep and Bradford, No. 128, Broadway, By Southwick and Pelsue, No. 3, New-street. 1811. Pages: *1-7* 8-63. Notes: Drama by Edmund John Eyre. Scott is not cited on title-page, but is given due credit in the author's preface. Copies: MWA NN.

47Dbj] NEW YORK: Longworth 1811-1815

[1] The Knight of Snowdoun: A Musical Drama, In Three Acts. . . . New-York: Published by D. Longworth, at the Dramatic Repository, Shakspeare-Gallery, April-1811. Pages: *1-3* 4-58. Notes: Drama by Thomas Morton (music by Henry Bishop not included) as performed at the Theatre Royal, Covent Garden, London. Although only partially derived from *The Lady of the Lake*, the preliminary 'Remarks' quote a London publication: 'The title of this musical drama indicates Walter Scott's celebrated poem, the Lady of the Lake, as its origin. Perhaps there is no story in poetical romance more formed to win and rivet the attention, or more suitable to the wildness and irregularity of the modern drama.' Copies: MWA NN.

[2] The Lady of the Lake: A Melo-dramatic Romance, in Three Acts. . . . New-York: Published by D. Longworth, at the Dramatic Repository, Shakspeare-Gallery. May-1811. Pages: *1-3* 4-36. Notes: Drama by Edmund John Eyre. In some copies the last page number is lacking. Copies: CtY MH NN.

[3] [The Lady of the Lake; A Melo Dramatic Romance, in Three Acts. . . . Second Edition. New-York, D. Longworth, 1815. 43pp. Notes: Drama by Edmund John Eyre.] Copy: not seen.

47Dbk] NEW YORK: Paff 1810-1815

[1] Chorus Hail to the Chief. Lady of the Lake, . . . New York Published by John Paff. [ca.1815]. Pages: *1* 2-3. Notes: Engraved sheet music with caption title. Words from canto 2, stanzas 19-20 (first words: 'Hail! Hail! Hail to the Chief who in Triumph advances'). Music composed by James Sanderson arranged for three-part chorus and pianoforte. Copy: DLC. References: G/T 10235; Wolfe 7769.

[2] Huntsman rest! Thy Chace Is done Recitative and Air. from Lady of the Lake . . . New York Published by John Paff [ca.1811]. Pages: *1* 2-4. Notes: Engraved sheet music with caption title. Words from canto 1, stanza 32 (first words: 'She paus'd then blushing led, the lay,'). Music composed by Joseph Mazzinghi arranged for voice and pianoforte. Copies: MH RPB. Reference: Wolfe 5691.

[3] [The Imprisoned Huntsman.... John Paff, Music Store, 7 Park Street (1812). Notes: An edition of this was advertised by Paff in the *NYEP* 28 March 1812 as 'just published.'] Copy: not seen. Reference: Wolfe 9822.

47Dbl] NEW YORK: Paff and Hewitt 1825

The Heath this Night must be My Bed. From the celebrated Poem . . . The Lady of the Lake . . . New York Publish'd by the Author, Sold by J. & M. Paff, Broadway, & J. Hewitt, Maiden Lane [ca.1825]. Pages *1-2* 3. Engraved sheet music with caption title, engraver identified foot of page *1* as E. Riley. Words from canto 3, stanza 23 (first words as title). Music composed by J. Willson arranged for voice and pianoforte. Copy: MH.

47Dbm] NEW YORK: Riley 1827

Hail to the Chief The Chorus in the Lady of the Lake Written by Sir Walter Scott.... New York, Engraved, Printed & Sold by, E. Riley, 29, Chatham Street. [ca.1827]. Pages: *1* 2-3. Notes: Engraved sheet music with plate mark '(Hail to the Chief. 3.)' at foot of each page. Words from canto 2, stanzas 19-20 (first words: 'Hail! Hail! Hail! to the Chief who in triumph advances'). Music composed by James Sanderson arranged for voice and pianoforte. Copies: DLC MWA.

47Dbn] NEW YORK: Singleton 1820

[The Heath This Night. *In* The Melodist, volume 1. New York, Published by George Singleton at the Office of The Ladies' Literary Cabinet, 194 Greenwich Street. 1820. Pages: 218-219. Notes: Music composed by Joseph Willson, arranged by G. S. Thornton. Advertised in *NYEP* 2 February 1820.] Copy: not seen. Reference: Wolfe 3578.

47Dbo] NEW YORK: Smith 1824

Ave, Maria. From "The Lady of the Lake."—By Walter Scott. *In* The Melodist, Comprising A Selection of the most Favourite English, Scotch, and Irish Songs, . . . New-York, Sold by W. & P. C. Smith, Printers and Booksellers, 59 Fulton-Street. 1824. Pages: 105-106. Notes: Engraved sheet music. Words from canto 3, stanza 29 (first line: 'Ave Maria! maiden mild'). Music by John Clarke arranged for voice and flute or violin. Copy: PPL. Reference: Wolfe 358.

47Dbp] NEW YORK: Willson (occasionally spelled *Wilson*) 1810-1817

Note: For references below to Mrs Bradish *see* 47Dbd.

[1] [Alice Brand. A Favorite Ballad. New York: Joseph Willson (1812). Notes: Music composed by James Hook. An edition of this song was advertised by Willson, music store, in *NYEP* 16 May 1812, probably reissued from Mrs Bradish's plates.] Copy: not seen. References: Wolfe 3947 and 3947A.

[2] Blanche of Devan's Song From The Lady of the Lake Written by W Scott.... New York, Published by J. Wilson, No. 62. Broad Way. [1812]. Pages: *1* 2-4. Notes: Engraved sheet music with caption title. Words from canto 4, stanza 22 (first words: 'They bid me sleep, they bid me pray'). Music composed by John Clarke arranged for voice and pianoforte. Reissue from Mrs Bradish's plates, with imprint altered as above. Copy: RPB. Reference: Wolfe 1824A .

[3] [The Coronach, or Funeral Song. . . . Joseph Willson, Music Store (1812). Notes: Music composed by John Clarke. An edition of this song was advertised by Willson in *NYEP* 16 May 1812, probably a reissue from Mrs Bradish's plates.] Copy: not seen. References: Wolfe 1828 and 1828A.

[4] [Ellen's Song, "Ave Maria" (Hymn to the Virgin). . . . Joseph Willson, Music Store (1812). Notes: Music composed by John Clarke. An edition of this song was advertised by Willson in *NYEP* 16 May 1812, probably a reissue from Mrs. Bradish's plates.] Copy: not seen. References: Wolfe 2674 and 2674A.

[5] The Heath This Night Must Be My Bed. From the celebrated Poem—The Lady of the Lake written by Walter Scott. . . . New York—Publish'd by the Author [composer], Sold by J. & M. Paff, Broadway. & J. Hewitt, Maiden Lane. [1810]. Pages: *1-2* 3. Notes: Engraved sheet music with caption title. Words from canto 3, stanza 23 (first words: 'The heath this night must be my bed The braken curtain for my head,'). Music composed by Joseph Willson arranged for voice and pianoforte. Advertised by Willson in *NYEP* 22 September 1810, 3 November 1811, and 16 May 1812. Copies: InU MWA PHi RPB. References: G/T 10274; Wolfe 9984. *See also* Wolfe 9984A.

[6] Huntsman Rest! Thy Chace Is Done, Recitative & Air, In Continuation of the Song, Soldier rest thy warfare o'er from the Lady of the Lake written by Walter Scott Esqr. . . New York—Publish'd by J. Wilson—No. 62 Broadway. [1812]. Pages: 1-4. Notes: Engraved sheet music with caption title and plate mark 'Huntsman rest'. Words from canto 1, stanza 32 (first words: 'She paused then blushing led, the lay,'). Music composed by Joseph Mazzinghi arranged for voice and pianoforte. Reissue from Mrs Bradish's plates with altered imprint and, in some copies, with page number 1 excised. Advertised by Willson in *NYEP* 16 May 1812. Copies: DLC MH MWA RPB(2). Reference: Wolfe 5690A.

[7] The Imprisoned Huntsman, A Favorite Song, The Poetry from the celebrated Poem The Lady of the Lake, written by Walter Scott, Esqr. . . . Published by Joseph Willson [New York] 62 Broadway. [1812]. Pages: 1-3. Notes: Engraved sheet music. Words from canto 6, stanza 24 (first words: 'My Hawk is tir'd of perch and hood,'). Music composed by John Whitaker arranged for voice and pianoforte. Advertised by Willson in *NYEP* 26 October 1812 as 'just published'. Copies: DLC MH PHi. References: G/T 10271; Wolfe 9824.

[8] Norman's Song, The Poetry from the Popular Poem, The Lady of the Lake, Written by Walter Scott Esqr . . . . New York, Publish'd by J. Willson. 62 Broadway [1812]. Pages: *i-ii*, 1-5. Notes: Engraved sheet music with four leaves and title on page *i* and page *ii* blank. Words from canto 3, stanza 23 (first words: 'The heath this night must be my bed'). Music composed by John Clarke arranged for voice and pianoforte. Reissued obviously from the plates of an earlier publisher, probably Mrs. Bradish, whose edition would date ca. 1810. Copy: RPB. References: G/T 10140; Wolfe 1851. Variant issue with three leaves and same plates. Pagination: *i*, 1-5. Copy: RPB.

47Dbq] NEW YORK: [no publisher] 1817
The Lady of the Lake; A Melo Dramatic Romance, in Three Acts. . . . New-York: Printed and Published, in the year 1817. Pages: *1-5* 6-8. Notes: Play by Edmund John Eyre. Copy: MH.

47Dbr] PHILADELPHIA: Bacon 1816-1817

[1] March & Chorus in the Dramatic Romance of The Lady of the Lake. . . . Philadelphia, Published by A. Bacon & Co No 11 So 4th Street. [ca.1816]. Pages: 1-4. Notes: Engraved sheet music in two states: (1) without price and plate number; (2) with price (37__12 cts) and plate number '16' added. Words adapted by Thomas John Dibdin from canto 2, stanzas 19-20 (first words: 'Hail! Hail! Hail! to the Chief who in triumph advances,'). Music by James Sanderson, arranged for voice and pianoforte. Copies: (1) not seen; (2) MWA PPL. References: Wolfe 7781 and 7781A.

[2] Soldier Rest! from the Celebrated Poem of the Lady of the Lake. . . . Philadelphia, Published by A. Bacon & Co. [ca.1817]. Pages: *1* 2-4. Notes: Engraved sheet music with plate number '24'. Page *1* is blank. Words from canto 1, stanza 31 (first words: 'Soldier rest thy war fare's[!] o'er Sleep the sleep that knows not breaking;'). Music composed by James Hook arranged for voice and pianoforte. Price: 25 cents. In some copies 'cts.' Copies: MWA RPB. References: G/T 10170; Wolfe 4210.

47Dbs] PHILADELPHIA: Blake 1812

[1] Blanche of Devan's Song. From the Lady of the Lake Written by Walter Scott Esqr. . . . Philadelphia. Published by E. Blake. [ca.1812]. Pages: 14-16. Notes: Engraved sheet music in two issues: (1) with pagination as above; (2) repaginated 1-3. Words from canto 4, stanza 22 (first words: 'They bid me sleep, They bid me pray'). Music composed by John Clarke arranged for voice and pianoforte. Issue (1) is also included in an untitled collection: *Six Favorite Songs* (item [6] below). Copies: (1) DLC; (2) MWA. References: Wolfe 1825 and 1825A.

[2] The Coronach. A Funeral Song, From the Lady of the Lake, Written by W. Scott Esqr. . . . Philadelphia. Published by G. E. Blake. [ca.1812]. Pages: *11* 12-13. Notes: Engraved sheet music with caption title. Page *11* is blank. Words from canto 3, stanza 16 (first words: 'He's gone on the mountain, He is lost to the forest,'). Music composed by John Clarke arranged for voice and pianoforte. Also included in an untitled collection: *Six Favorite Songs* (item [6] below). Copies: DLC InU MWA RPB(2). Reference: Wolfe 1829.

[3] The Heath this Night, from the Lady of the Lake, the Poetry by Walter Scott Esqr. . . Philadelphia, Published by G. E. Blake. [1812]. Pages: 9-11. Notes: Engraved sheet music with caption title. Words from Canto 3, stanza 23 (first words: 'The heath this night must be my bed,'). Music by John Bray arranged for voice and pianoforte. Also included in an untitled collection: *Six Favorite Songs* (item [6] below). Copies: DLC PPL RPB. References: G/T 10128; Wolfe 1297.

[4] The Imprisoned Huntsman, . . . The Poetry from The Lady of the Lake, written by Walter Scott Esqr. . . . Philadelphia: Published by G. E. Blake. [ca.1812]. Pages: 1-3. Notes: Engraved sheet music. Words from canto 6, stanza 24 (first words: 'My Hawk is tir'd of perch and hood'). Music composed by John Whitaker arranged for voice and pianoforte. Copy: DLC. Reference: Wolfe 9825.

[5] March & Chorus, in the Dramatic Romance, of the Lady of the Lake, . . . Philadelphia, Published by G. E. Blake. [ca.1812]. Pages: 5-8. Notes: Engraved sheet music with caption title. Words adapted by Thomas John Dibdin from canto 2, stanzas 19-20 (first words: 'Hail! Hail! Hail to the Chief who in triumph advances,'). Music composed by James

Sanderson arranged for voice and pianoforte. Also included in an untitled collection: *Six Favorite Songs* (item [6] below). Copies: DLC MH MWA(2) RPB(2). Reference: Wolfe 7779.

[6] [Six Favorite Songs from The Lady of the Lake. Philadelphia, George E. Blake (1812). Pages: 1-16. Notes: A collected issue, paged continuously. Wolfe derives the title from J. R. Parker's (Boston) catalogue of 1820. Each piece bears an individual imprint, but lacks a series note. Music arranged for voice and pianoforte.] Copy: not seen. Reference: Wolfe 8448. The songs include:
(1) ['Soldier Rest!'. Notes: Music composed by James Sanderson.] References: G/T 10236; Wolfe 7811;
(2-3) ['March & Chorus in the Dramatic Romance'. Notes: Music by James Sanderson.] Reference: Wolfe 7779;
(4) ['The Heath This Night'. Notes: Music by John Bray.] References: G/T 10128; Wolfe 1297;
(5) ['The Coronach'. Notes: Composer unknown.] Reference: Wolfe 1829;
(6) ['Blanche of Devan's Song'. Notes: Composer unknown.] Reference: Wolfe 1825.

[7] Soldier Rest! Duett and Chorus in The Lady of the Lake, written by Walter Scott Esqr. . . . Philadelphia, Published by G. E. Blake. [ca.1812]. Pages: 1-4. Notes: Engraved sheet music. Words adapted by Thomas John Dibdin from canto 1, stanza 31 (first words: 'Soldier rest! thy warfare o'er, Sleep the sleep that knows not breaking;'). Music composed by James Sanderson arranged for voice and pianoforte. Also included in an untitled collection: *Six Favorite Songs* (item [6] above). Copies: MB MWA PPL. Reference: Wolfe 7811.

PHILADELPHIA: Carey
[~] The Ass on Parnassus. 1815. [Parody: *see* 503S(1)]

47Dbt] PHILADELPHIA: Carr and Schetky 1810
[1] Alice Brand. Pages: *i-iii, 1* 2-12. Notes: Engraved sheet music. Words from canto 4, stanza 12 (first words: 'Merry it is in the good greenwood'). Music composed by Benjamin Carr arranged for three voices. This title is number 5 in a collection titled 'Six Ballads from the Poem of The Lady of the Lake' (item[6] below).

[2] Blanche of Devan. Pages: *i-iii, 1* 2-3. Notes: Engraved sheet music. Words from canto 4, stanza 22 (first words: 'They bid me sleep they bid me pray'). Music composed by Benjamin Carr arranged for voice and pianoforte. This title is number 4 in a collection titled 'Six Ballads from the Poem of The Lady of the Lake' (item [6] below).

[3] Coronach. Pages: *i-iii, 1-2 3*. Notes: Engraved sheet music. Words from canto 3, stanza 16 (first words: 'He is gone on the mountain'). Music composed by Benjamin Carr arranged for voice and pianoforte. This title is number 6 in a collection titled 'Six Ballads from the Poem of The Lady of the Lake' (item [6] below).

[4] Hymn to the Virgin Ave Maria. Pages: *i-ii, 1* 2-9. Notes: Engraved sheet music. Words from canto 3, stanza 29 (first words: 'Ave Maria maiden mild'). Music composed by Benjamin Carr arranged for voice and harp. This title is number 3 in a collection titled 'Six Ballads from the Poem of The Lady of the Lake' (item [6] below).

[5] Mary. Pages: *i-iii, 1* 2-3. Notes: Engraved sheet music. Words from canto 3, stanza 23

(first words: 'The heath this night must be my bed'). Music composed by Benjamin Carr arranged for voice and pianoforte. This title is number 1 in a collection titled 'Six Ballads from the Poem of The Lady of the Lake' (item [6] below). Reimpressed with '2d. edition' on series title, unpaged, and this part priced at 38 cents (InU).

[6] Six Ballads from the Poem of The Lady of the Lake. . . . Carr & Schetky, Philadelphia [1810]. Pages: 1-50. Notes: Engraved sheet music in three issues: (1) no pagination; (2) paged continuously through page 35; (3) paged separately as noted elsewhere in this record. Collective title for numbers 1-6. Music composed by Benjamin Carr. The title-leaf reads on recto: 'Published in 6 Periodical Numbers by Carr & Schetky, Philadelphia.' and has a copyright statement on the verso. Copies: (1) E; (2) DLC ViU; (3) NN-L. References: G/T 10135; Wolfe 1579 and 1579A. The six ballads (with one-word plus plate-numbers) include:
(1) 'Mary' from canto 3, stanza 23 (first words: 'The heath this night must be my bed'). References: Wolfe 1617, 1617A;
(2) 'Soldier Rest' from canto 1, stanza 31 (first words: 'Soldier rest thy warfare o'er'). References: Wolfe 1655, 1655A;
(3) 'Hymn to the Virgin' from canto 3, stanza 29 (first words: 'Ave Maria maiden mild!'). Reference: Wolfe 1606;
(4) 'Blanche of Devan' from canto 4, stanza 22 (first words: 'They bid me sleep they bid me pray'). Reference: Wolfe 1580;
(5) 'Alice Brand' from canto 4, stanza 12 (first words: 'Merry it is in the good greenwood'). Reference: Wolfe 1573;
(6) 'Coronach' from canto 3, stanza 16 (first words; 'He is gone on the mountain'). Reference: Wolfe 1591.

[7] Soldier Rest. Pages: *i-iii*, *1* 2-3. Notes: Engraved sheet music. Words from canto 1, stanza 31 (first words: 'Soldier rest thy warfare o'er'). Music composed by Benjamin Carr arranged for voice and pianoforte. This title is number 2 in a collection titled 'Six Ballads from the Poem of The Lady of the Lake' (item [6] above).

47Dbu] PHILADELPHIA: Field 1828
The Scottish Exiles, Rendered into Prose, from Sir Walter Scott's Lady of the Lake. . . . Philadelphia: Published by J. Field. 1828. Pages: *1-3* 4-180. Notes: The reference on title, 'By a Lady of Philadelphia', sometimes identified as Sarah Ewing Hall, is more commonly understood to be Ernestine Chapman. The dedication to Henley Chapman, Esq., of Mount Prospect, Giles County, Virginia, is signed 'Ernestine' and dated from Philadelphia 1 February 1827. Copies: CtY(2) MWA PPL RPB ViU.

47Dbv] PHILADELPHIA: Klemm 1823-1825
[1] [March and Chorus in the Dramatic Romance of The Lady of the Lake . . . . Philadelphia, Published by J. G. Klemm. No. 3 South Third street. (ca.1824). Pages: 1-4. Notes: Words by Thomas John Dibdin. Music composed by James Sanderson.] Copy: not seen. References: Wolfe 7781A and 7781B.

[2] March and Chorus in the Dramatic Romance of The Lady of the Lake. . . . Philadelphia, Published by John G. Klemm. [1825?] Pages: 1-4. Notes: Engraved sheet music with plate number '16'. First page has four stanzas of 'March'; page 2 has caption title reading 'Chorus. Hail to the Chief. Written by Walter Scott Esqr.' from canto 2, stanza 19 (first words: 'Hail!

Hail! Hail! to the Chief who in triumph advances,'). Music composed by James Sanderson arranged for voice and pianoforte. Price: 37 1/2 cts. Copy: CtY. Reference: Printed from plates that differ from Wolfe 7781B (item [1] above].

[3] Soldier Rest! from the Celebrated Poem of the Lady of the Lake . . . . Philadelphia, Published by John G. Klemm. [ca.1823]. Pages: *1* 2-4. Notes: Engraved sheet music with plate number '24'. Words from canto 1, stanza 31 (first words: 'Soldier rest thy war fare's o'er Sleep the sleep that knows not breaking;'). Music composed by James Hook arranged for voice and pianoforte. Price: 25 cents. Reissue of same title published by Bacon (47Dbr[2]). Copy: MWA. References: G/T 10170; Wolfe 4210A.

47Dbw] PHILADELPHIA: Palmer 1824

The Lady of the Lake; A Melo-Dramatic Romance. In Three Acts. . . . Philadelphia: Published by Thomas H. Palmer, 1824. Pages: *1-3* 4-40. Notes: Romance by Edmund John Eyre. Copy: MH.

47Dbx] PHILADELPHIA: Willig 1810-1827

[1] Blanche of Devan's Song from the Lady of the Lake . . . . Published by G: Willig at His Musical Magazine Philadelphia. [1810]. Pages: 1-4. Notes: Engraved sheet music with imprint at foot of page and with plate mark reading 'B: of D: S:' on pages 2-4. Words from canto 4, stanza 22 (first words: 'They bid me sleep, they bid me pray,'). Music composed by John Clarke arranged for voice and pianoforte. Reissue from same plates as a Baltimore printing (47Dav[1]), repaged with engraver's note on page 169 altered to read as imprint above. Copy: MWA. References: G/T 10138; Wolfe 1823A. Variant issue with imprint at foot of page 4: (MH.)

[2] The Coronach A Funeral Song From the Lady of the Lake . . . . Philada[!] Published & sold by Geo: Willig 171 Chesnut str: [ca.1819]. Pages: *1-2* 3-4. Notes: Engraved sheet music with caption title and with plate mark on pages 3-4: 'The Coronach'. Page *1* is blank. Words from canto 3, stanza 16 (first words: 'He's gone on the mountain, He's lost to the forest,'). Music composed by John Clarke arranged for voice and pianoforte. Copy: RPB.

[3] The Coronach A Funeral Song From the Lady of the Lake . . . . Notes: Caption title and imprint as for [2], but music paged *1-3*, plate mark on pages *2-3*. Copy: MH.

[4] The Coronach A Funeral Song from the Lady of the Lake . . . . Philadephia[!] Printed for G Willig. [ca.1810]. Pages: *1-2* 3-6. Notes: Engraved sheet music with imprint at foot of page *2*. Words from canto 3, stanza 16 (first words: 'He's gone on the mountain, He's lost to the forest,'). Music composed by John Clarke arranged for voice and pianoforte. Reissue from same plates as a Baltimore printing (47Dav[2]), with imprint added to title-page, and with repagination. Copy: MWA. Reference: Wolfe 1827A.

[5] The Coronach A Funeral Song From the Lady of the Lake . . . Philadelphia Printed for G. Willig [ca. 1810]. Pages: 12-16 (but first digit of each number partly defaced). Notes: Engraved sheet-music. Words from canto 3, stanza 16 (first words: 'He's gone on the mountain, He's lost to the forest,). Music composed by John Clarke arranged for voice and pianoforte. Copies: CtY DLC. Reference: Wolfe 1827A.

[6] The Coronach A Funeral Song from the Lady of the Lake . . . Philadelphia Published & Sold by Geo: Willig 171 Chesnut str:. [ca.1826]. Pages: *1-2* 3-4. Notes: Engraved sheet

music. Words from canto 3, stanza 16 (first words: 'He's gone on the mountain, He's lost to the forest,'). Music composed by John Clarke arranged for voice and pianoforte. Copies: InU MWA.

[7] Hail to the Chief March in the Lady of the Lake . . . Philadelphia, George Willig 171 Chesnut St. For sale by E. Johns & Co. New Orleans. [1827]. Pages: *1* 2-4. Notes: Engraved sheet music. Page 2 has caption heading 'Hail to the Chief written by Sir Walter Scott'. Words from canto 2, stanzas 19-20 (first words: 'Hail! Hail! Hail to the Chief who in triumph advances,'). Music composed by James Sanderson arranged for voice and pianoforte. Copy: MWA.

[8] Huntsman Rest Thy Chace Is Done. . . . from the Lady of the Lake Written by Walter Scott Esqr. Philadelphia, Published and Sold at G. Willig's Musical Magazine. [ca.1811]. Pages: *1* 2-4. Notes: Engraved sheet music with plate mark: 'Huntsman rest'. Words for recitative from canto 1, stanza 32 (first words: 'She paused then blushing led the lay,') and words for the Air from *loc. cit.* (first words: 'Huntsman rest thy chase is done while our slumb'rous spells assail ye'). Music composed by Joseph Mazzinghi arranged for voice and pianoforte. Copies: InU(2) MH PPL. Reference: Wolfe 5692.

[9] [I hate to learn the ebb of time. Philadelphia: Willig (1812). Notes: Music composed by Victor Pelissier. (Pelissier's Columbian Melodies: number 3.)] Copy: not seen. Reference: G/T 10216.

[10] March and Chorus In the Dramatic Romance of The Lady of the Lake, . . . Philadelphia Published and Sold by G: Willig. [ca.1815]. Pages: *1* 2-4. Notes: Engraved sheet music with plate mark: 'Hail to.4.' Caption title on page 2 reads 'Chorus Hail to the Chief written by Walter Scott Esqr.' Words adapted by Thomas John Dibdin from canto 2, stanzas 19-20 (first words: 'Hail! Hail! Hail to the Chief who in triumph advances,'). Music by James Sanderson arranged for voice and pianoforte. Copies: DLC InU MWA RPB. Reference: Wolfe 7780.

[11] The Soldier Bridegroom's Song From the Lady of the Lake . . . . Engravd by G: Willig at his Musical Magazin[!] Philadelphia [ca.1812]. Pages: 163-169. Notes: Engraved sheet music with caption title on first page and imprint on last. Words from canto 3, stanza 13 (first words: 'The heath this night must be my bed,'). Music by Sir John Stevenson arranged for voice and pianoforte. Copy: MH.

[12] [Soldier Rest. Philadelphia: Willig (1813). Notes: Music composed by Joseph Mazzinghi.] Copy: not seen. Reference: G/T 10201.

[13] [What groans shall yonder vallies[!] fill. Philadelphia: Willig (1812). Notes: Music composed by Victor Pelissier. (Pelissier's Columbian Melodies: number 4.)] Copy: not seen. Reference: G/T 10217.

EXTRACTS IN ANTHOLOGIES

47E] From *The Lady of the Lake* there are 102 extracts in 64 anthologies: 354E.4 355.4 356[2].10 358.2,6,15,18 359.2 360.3,14 363.7 365 366[1].8,10 367[1].2 368 372[1].3

372[2].3 373[1].2 373[4] 377.1 378.3-5 379.3-4 386.2,4-5 388.2-3 389.3-4,11,21,29-30,40 391.1-4 392.9 398.1-4 401.18-22 404.4 405(2)[2].2 405(2)[3].11 405(3)[2].1 408[1].9-14 413.9 414[1].6-7 415.10 417.2 420.2 423.8 430[2].2-3 430[3].2-3 435.1 436.1 443.1 445[1] 445[2].2 446[1].2 447 448[1].1 449.1 450(and 471).10 454.1 455 456[1].2 456[2] 457[2].1 460 461.2 463.4 464.5-6 467[1-2].1 469.5,7 474.2 475.1 477.3 478.

THE MEMOIRS OF THE DUKE OF SULLY

The Bethunes were of French origin, and derived their name from a small town in Artois. There were several distinguished families of the Bethunes in the neighbouring province of Picardie; they numbered among their descendants the celebrated Duc de Sully; and the name was accounted among the most noble in France, while aught noble remained in that country.[1] The family of Bethune, or Beatoun, in Fife, produced three learned and dignified prelates; namely, Cardinal Beaton, and two successive archbishops of Glasgow, all of whom flourished about the date of the romance. Of this family was descended Dame Janet Beaton, Lady Buccleuch, widow of Sir Walter Scott of Branksome.

1. This expression and sentiment were dictated by the situation of France, in the year 1803, when [*The Lay of the Last Minstrel*] was originally written. 1821. ('Note E', *PW*, vi.235.)

48A] First Scott Edition: 1810

THE | MEMOIRS | OF | THE DUKE OF SULLY, | PRIME-MINISTER TO | HENRY THE GREAT. | [*short rule*] | TRANSLATED FROM THE FRENCH BY | CHARLOTTE LENNOX. | [*short rule*] | A NEW EDITION, | REVISED AND CORRECTED; WITH ADDITIONAL NOTES, SOME | LETTERS OF HENRY THE GREAT, | AND | A BRIEF HISTORICAL INTRODUCTION. | [*short rule*] | EMBELLISHED WITH PORTRAITS. | [*short rule*] | IN FIVE VOLUMES. | VOL. I [II-V]. | LONDON: | [*short reversed Oxford rule*] | PRINTED FOR WILLIAM MILLER, ALBEMARLE STREET; | BY W. BULMER, AND CO. CLEVELAND-ROW, ST. JAMES'S. | 1810.

Published 16 May 1810 in London (*MC*). £3.13.6. Paper: Royal 8° (242 x 148 mm uncut). Watermarks: none, except for several sheets dated 1803 in volume 4, printed by J. Moyes.

General Notes: The original occasion for Scott's eventual edition of this work in 1810, not directly avowed in the text, may be traced to a comment in *The Lay of the Last Minstrel* (1805), where the note cited above as an epigraph first appears on page 211. Obviously Scott, as another, remote descendant, would have a certain affinity for these *Memoirs* of his illustrious ancestor. Sully's work is also noted in

Scott's edition of Carey's *Memoirs* (1808), pages 39, 41, the ecclesiastical Beatons in *The State Papers of Sir Ralph Sadler* (1809), and 'Dame Janet Betoun' as late as 1828 in Scott's letter to the 5th Duke of Buccleuch (*Letters*, xi.64).

In the first volume, Scott's anonymous Advertisement reports that the Lennox translation has been 'carefully collated with the French', further adjusted by reference to an early commentary, additional notes then added 'to correct or explain any passage in the text' and, in the last volume, the provision of relevant letters of Henri IV to one of his mistresses are supplied. The editor's own 'brief' introduction extends to 48 pages and itself is extensively annotated. Though the Lennox translation differs widely from the five-volume 1805 edition issued in Edinburgh by Bell and Bradfute, most of the notes when applicable for Scott's purpose in 1810 are directly transferred from this earlier 1805 issue. Occasionally, however, as at the end of Book VII (volume 2, pages 81-83), Scott intervenes at considerable length, here with a 1000-word commentary. Such extended comments are usually signalled by the reference 'Edit.'

As in the Scott edition of Count Grammont 18ll (*see* 53Aa) the portraits are all engraved by E. Scriven, and all now with imprint 'Published 1810, by W. Miller, London.' Bulmer's handsome presswork, done without press figures, varies also in signing double-letter sheets as Aa, Bb, &c. The printer's imprint for his work (volumes 1-3, 5) is: [*short rule*] | London: Printed by W. Bulmer and Co. | Cleveland-Row, St. James's. Typography: Title imprints in volumes 3-4 have a very bold hyphen between 'ALBEMARLE-STREET' while other volumes have very indistinct hyphens, if at all. The printer's imprints in volumes 2-3 have first letter of 'printed' and 'row' in lower case, and the fifth volume has 'row' in lower case.

Copies: L; DCL(vols.1-2) NjP.

1] THE | MEMOIRS | OF | THE DUKE OF SULLY, . . . VOL. I. . . . 1810.

Collation: a^4 b-e^8 f^4 B-2G^8 2H^2. Pagination: *1* half-title, *2 blank*, *3* title-page, *4 blank*, *5-6* Advertisement, dated 20 March 1810, *7-8* dedication by Charlotte Lennox, dated 5 September 1755, *i ii*-xxiii The Preface to the French Edition, *xxiv blank*, *xxv* xxvi-lxxii A Brief Historical Introduction, *1* 2-468 text, 468 printer's imprint. Illustration: Frontispiece portrait of the Duke of Sully. Typography: Pages 209-222, 224 are misnumbered 207-220, 222. Figures: none.

2] THE | MEMOIRS | OF | THE DUKE OF SULLY, . . . VOL. II. . . . 1810.

Collation: A^2 B-2L^8 2M^4. Pagination: *i* half-title, *ii blank*, *iii* title-page, *iv blank*, *1* 2-536 text, 536 printer's imprint. Illustration: Frontispiece portrait of Henri IV. Typography: In some copies pages 465-480 are misnumbered 463-478. Figures: none.

3] THE | MEMOIRS | OF | THE DUKE OF SULLY, . . . VOL. III. . . . 1810.

Collation: A² B-2G⁸ 2H1. Pagination: *i* half-title, *ii blank*, *iii* title-page, *iv blank*, *1* 2-465 text, 465 printer's imprint, *466 blank*. Illustration: Frontispiece portrait of Mary de Medicis. Figures: none.

4] THE | MEMOIRS | OF | THE DUKE OF SULLY, . . . VOL. IV. . . . PRINTED FOR WILLIAM MILLER, ALBEMARLE-STREET; | BY J. MOYES, GREVILLE-STREET, HATTON-GARDEN. | 1810.

Collation: A² B-2I⁸ 2K⁴ 2L². Pagination: *i* half-title, *ii blank, iii* title-page, *iv blank*, *1* 2-507 text, 507 printer's imprint, *508 blank.* Printer's imprint: [*short rule*] | J. MOYES, PRINTER, | Greville Street, Hatton Garden, London. Illustration: Frontispiece portrait of Gabrielle d'Estrées. Typography: Like Bulmer, Moyes uses double letter signatures, but in the style AA, BB, &c.

Figures: H103-2, I—, K—, L157-1, M169-1 175-2, N186-2 189-1, O 199-1 204-2, P216-2 218-1, Q—, R250-1 252-2, S268-2 270-3, T—, U296-1 298-1, X—, Y332-1, Z—, 2A—, 2B 382-2, 2C—, 2D 410-2. It is unusual for Moyes to employ figures, and here only in the middle of the one volume assigned to him. Possibly sheets H-2D were worked by another printer.

5] THE | MEMOIRS | OF | THE DUKE OF SULLY, . . . VOL. V. . . . PRINTED FOR WILLIAM MILLER, ALBEMARLE STREET; | BY W. BULMER, AND CO. CLEVELAND-ROW, ST. JAMES'S. | 1810.

Collation: A² B-T⁸ U-2S⁴ 2T1. Pagination: *i* half-title, *ii blank, iii* title-page, *iv blank*, *1* 2-157 text of the Memoirs concluded, *158 blank*, *159* 160-195 Observations on the Assassination of Henry IV, *196 blank*, 197-237 The Trial of Francis Ravaillac, for the Murder of King Henry IV. 1610, *238 blank*, 239-274 Appendix, *275* fly-title, *276 blank*, *277* 278-466 General Index, 466 printer's imprint. Illustration: Frontispiece portrait of the Marchioness de Verneuil. Figures: none.

Notes: The Appendix prints 41 letters 1570-[1608?] from Henri IV to his mistress Corisande d'Andoin, afterwards the Countess of Guiche. After this gathering, beginning with signature U, the format was reduced to half-sheet imposition so that the limited quantity of smaller type could be reused more expeditiously for the very lengthy index.

REPRINT

UNITED STATES

48R] PHILADELPHIA: Earle 1817

The Memoirs of the Duke of Sully, . . . Philadelphia: Published by Edward Earle. J. Maxwell,

Printer. Five volumes. Pages 1: *i-vii* viii-lxxvii *lxxviii, 1* 2-467; 2: *i-ii, 1* 2-535; 3: *i-ii, 1* 2-465; 4: *i-ii, 1* 2-506; 5: *i-ii, 1* 2-424. Copy: CtY.

REVIEWS OF MATURIN, EVANS and AITKIN

49A] First Printings: 1810

1] 'ART. III. *Fatal Revenge; or, the Family of Montorio: a Romance.* By Dennis Jasper Murphy.', pages 339-347;

2] 'ART. XVI. *Old Ballads, Historical, &c.* By Thomas Evans.'; '*Essays on Song Writing, &c.* By John Aikin. A new Edition, with Additions and Corrections, . . . By R. H. Evans.'; '*Vocal Poetry, or a select Collection of English Songs*. . . . By John Aikin, M.D.', pages 481-492, *in*:

The Quarterly Review. May, 1810. [No.6: volume 3 imprint:] London: Printed by C. Roworth, Bell-yard, Temple-bar; For John Murray, 32, Fleet Street. Hatchard, Piccadilly; Richardson, Cornhill; Parker, Oxford; Deighton, Cambridge; John Ballantyne and Co. Edinburgh; and M. N. Mahon, Dublin.

Notes: The issue, delayed because of 'unforeseen accidents' (page 517), was eventually published 23 July 1810 in London (*MC*). The first title reviewed is pseudonymously attributed to Dennis Jasper Murphy, although it was later acknowledged to have been written by C. R. Maturin. Immediately following the second entry is a long review (by George Ellis) of *The Lady of the Lake*, pages 492-517.

Article XIV, on James Grahame's *British Georgics*, sometimes attributed to Scott on the warrant of *Letters*, ii.397 and note, on better evidence is assigned to Robert Southey in Shine 98. Other early contributions doubtfully ascribed, at least in part, to Scott (Shine 71, 74, 90), have not been accepted in this bibliography.

Copies: BCL L O; TxU. References: Shine 87, 100. (Magnum Opus Edition 1835: *The Miscellaneous Prose Works*, [1] xviii.157-172 as 'Maturin's Fatal Revenge', [2] xvii.119-136 as 'Evans's Old Ballads'.)

THE POETICAL WORKS OF ANNA SEWARD

50A] First Edition: 1810

THE | POETICAL WORKS | OF | ANNA SEWARD; | WITH | EXTRACTS FROM HER LITERARY CORRESPONDENCE. | EDITED BY | WALTER SCOTT, E$^{SQ.}$ | [*short rule*] | IN THREE VOLUMES. | [*short rule*] | VOL. I

[II-III]. | EDINBURGH: | Printed by James Ballantyne and Co. | FOR JOHN BALLANTYNE AND CO. EDINBURGH; | AND LONGMAN, HURST, REES, AND ORME, PATER- | NOSTER-ROW, LONDON. | 1810.

Published 26 July 1810 in Edinburgh (*EEC*), issued 8 August in London (*MC*). £1.11.6. Binding: drab boards with printed labels. Paper: Post 8° (191 x 120mm uncut). Watermarks: BUTTANSHAW | 1807 [1808]. Printer's imprints read: [*short Oxford rule*] | EDINBURGH: | Printed by James Ballantyne & Co. ['and Co.' vol.3].

General Notes: Scott's Biographical Preface quotes an undated letter from Anna Seward (pages xxxiii-xxxvii) notifying him that he has been appointed literary executor, to produce, as he may decide, 'a miscellaneous edition' of her works. Most of her verse he had earlier complained to Joanna Baillie was 'absolutely execrable' and the publication was a commercial disaster.

Copies: AN BCL; DLC IdU NjP(2) NN NNU-W OCl.
References: *Letters*, ii.314-315; Thomson, page 62. (Magnum Opus Edition 1834: *The Miscellaneous Prose Works*, iv.199-227 as 'Miss Anna Seward'.)

1] THE | POETICAL WORKS | OF | ANNA SEWARD; . . . VOL. I. . . . 1810.

Collation: π^4(-π4) a-b^8 c^4 d-n^8 o^4 A-L^8 M^4 N^2. Pagination: *i* half-title, *ii blank*, *iii* title-page, *iv blank*, *v*-vi Contents, *i* fly-title, *ii blank*, *iii* iv-xxxix Biographical Preface, *xl blank*, *xli* fly-title, *xlii blank*, *xliii* xliv-ccvi Literary Correspondence, *ccvii* fly-title, *ccviii blank*, *1* 2-187 text, *188* printer's imprint. Typography: In some copies page 133 is misnumbered 33.

Figures: a vi-5/-, b xxx-5, c xxxix-11, d xlviii-6 liv-8, e lviii-10, f lxxiv-1 lxxxiv-10, g civ-5, h cxiv-1, i cxxxii-1, k cxxxviii-1 cxlix-6, l clviii-5 clxviii-6, m clxxii-6, n cxcv-5, o ccv-10, A4-6 6-5, B19-5 28-10, C36-10 46-5, D50-5 60-10, E70-5 80-1, F82-1 96-10, G98-5, H115-1 127-5 128-1, I 138-10, K152-9 158-1, L162-7 169-5, M179-6/-, N—. In some copies the redundant 1 (page 115) in gathering H either was added by mistake, after some intermission, or withdrawn.

2] THE | POETICAL WORKS | OF | ANNA SEWARD; . . . VOL. II. . . . 1810.

Collation: π^4 A-Z^8 $2A^4$ $2B^2$. Pagination: *i* half-title, *ii blank*, *iii* title-page, *iv blank*, *v* vi-viii Contents, *1* 2-380 text, 380 printer's imprint.

Figures: A2-2, B27-2, C47-2, D55-1, E76-2, F86-2, G98-2, H126-2, I 143-2, K159-2, L172-2, M192-2, N207-2, O 211-2, P238-2, Q251-2, R271-2, S287-2, T298-2, U315-2, X335-2, Y348-10, Z361-10, 2A 370-10, 2B—.

3] THE | POETICAL WORKS | OF | ANNA SEWARD; . . . VOL. III. . . 1810.

Collation: a^4 *b*1 A-2B^8 2C1. Pagination: *i* half-title, *ii blank*, *iii* title-page, *iv blank*, *v* vi-ix Contents, *x blank*, *1* 2-402 Poems, 402 printer's imprint. Typography: Page 236 is misnumbered 326.

Figures: *a* vii-1, *b*—, A11-10, B22-10, C46-10, D51-9, E79-10, F96-10, G105-10, H—, I 131-9, K160-9, L162-9, M178-9, N208-9, O 224-9, P240-9, Q246-10 256-6, R261-5 266-11, S288-9, T302-5 304-6, U311-5 320-11/6, X325-11, Y343-10 352-5, Z356-9 362-5, 2A 382-5 384-6, 2B 386-5 389-6, 2C—.

VIEW OF JUSTICE IN SCOTLAND and GENERAL VIEW OF LITERATURE

51A] First Printings: 1810

1] 'VIEW OF THE CHANGES PROPOSED AND ADOPTED IN THE ADMINISTRATION OF JUSTICE IN SCOTLAND.', pages 342-372;
2] 'GENERAL VIEW OF LITERATURE. OF THE LIVING POETS OF GREAT BRITAIN.', pages 417-443, *in*:

The Edinburgh Annual Register, for 1808. Vol. First—Part Second. Edinburgh: Printed by James Ballantyne and Co. For John Ballantyne and Co. Edinburgh; Longman, Hurst, Rees, and Orme; Cadell and Davies; William Miller; John Murray; and Robert Scholey, London. 1810.

Published 6 August 1810 in Edinburgh (*EEC*).

Notes: The Prospectus for the *Register* was issued 9 December 1808 (*see* 35A), but the publication of this first volume then delayed for want of contributions. Both of these substantial articles are attributed to Scott on sufficient evidence. To fill up another department, five of his poems from *English Minstrelsy* (43A) are reprinted: 'The Bard's Incantation', pages xxi-xxiii; 'To a Lady, With Flowers from a Roman Wall', page xxiii; 'The Violet', page xxiii; 'Hunting Song', page xxviii; 'The Resolve', pages xxxvi-xxxvii. (The first printing of 'Hunting Song' was in *Queenhoo-Hall* [32Aa], published in 1808.)

Copies: O; PPL TxU. References: (Magnum Opus Edition: Not reprinted, but quoted with commentary in Curry, pages [1] 170-211, [2] 60-99.)

LETTER ON WELLINGTON'S VICTORIES

52A] First Printing: 1810

'TO THE SPY.' page 72, *in*:

The Spy. 1810. Numb. IX. Saturday, October 27. [General title-page supplied at completion of the 52nd issue:] Edinburgh: Printed for the Proprietors and Sold by Archibald Constable & Co. Edinburgh, and by all the principal booksellers. 1811].

Published 27 October 1810 in Edinburgh (*EEC*).

Notes: This brief letter begins 'Sir, The late distinguished achievements of Lord Wellington, against the rest of all Buonaparte's Generals, have in some degree obliterated the memory of his Indian victories', then mentions the enclosed poem by John Leyden on the latter subject and concludes as the paper's 'Well-wisher, and Constant Reader.' Though another letter, on card-playing, ends with the same 'signature' (no. 20, 12 January 1811, pages *153* 154-157), the editor James Hogg formally attributed only the shorter piece to Scott, yet informally in jest ascribed several others also to this same author. Several marked-up sets of the periodical are extant: the Sinton copy noted by Batho, the Gibson Craig entries further annotated by Andrew Linton [E copy, L.C. 1241], and the D. Bridges copy [University of Guelph]).

Copies: E(3). Edith C. Batho, *The Library*, 4th ser, (1935), 321. (Magnum Opus Edition: Not reprinted.)

MEMOIRS OF COUNT GRAMMONT

53Aa] First Scott Edition, First Impression: 1811

MEMOIRS | OF | **COUNT GRAMMONT,** | BY | ANTHONY HAMILTON. | [*short rule*] | A NEW EDITION. | TO WHICH ARE PREFIXED, A BIOGRAPHICAL SKETCH | OF COUNT HAMILTON, AND A TRANSLATION OF THE EPISTLE | TO COUNT GRAMMONT. | [*short rule*] | Illustrated with Sixty-four Portraits, | ENGRAVED BY EDWARD SCRIVEN, &c. | [*short reversed Oxford rule*] | IN TWO VOLUMES. | VOL. I [II]. | LONDON: | PRINTED | FOR WILLIAM MILLER, ALBEMARLE STREET, | AND | JAMES CARPENTER, OLD BOND STREET. | 1811.

Published 16 March in London (*MC*), issued 30 March in Edinburgh (*EEC*). £3.13.6. On the same first date Miller and Carpenter also issued an edition in French (*see* 53Ac). Paper: Royal 8° (225 x 146mm uncut). Watermarks: 1802; 1804; John Dickinson & Co | 1810.

General Notes: Of the numerous editions preceding Scott's 1811 version of these scandalous 'Memoirs' of the Court of Charles II, apparently the one serving as his copy-text is the quarto English issue of 1793, an edition based essentially upon the original 1714 translation of Abel Boyer, as supplemented by the 'Notes and Illustrations' first appearing in Horace Walpole's 1772 French edition. Scott's 1811 issue, volume 2, page 239, incorrectly reprints from the 1793 printing a heading 'CHAPTER XI' (properly 'CHAPTER III' in this second volume): a reference altered to XII in the octavo redaction of 1809.

Scott's interest in this account possibly was quickened by his close friendship with the Earl of Abercorn, a collateral descendant of Count Anthony Hamilton and the dedicatee, in the previous year, of *The Lady of the Lake.* His own contribution here was to prefix a biographical sketch of Hamilton and Hamilton's Epistle to Grammont (his brother-in-law), to alter the text wherever it was deficient stylistically and, of greater importance, to revise throughout the extensive notes following each volume: e.g. in volume I, page 215, where, in a long annotation on Viscount Turenne's death (some 570 words in the 1793 text) he intervenes after the 255th word to say, 'In former editions, the quotation from Voltaire was yet longer. It is more germain to the present matter to observe [then 96 words based on an earlier reference]'. Instead of proclaiming the 'intrinsic value' of the work, or the editor's own efforts therein, the preliminary Advertisement is content to report: 'The principal claim of the present Edition to public favour consists in the extreme beauty of its Typographical Execution, and in the delicacy and truth of the Portraits; . . . [all] finished in a manner which cannot fail to afford general satisfaction.' As compared with the editions of 1793 (with 78 portraits) or 1809 (which reprints 39 of these) the 64 now offered, on imported Auvergne plate-paper, would seem to justify this claim. Some 31 of these bear the publishers' names ordered Miller and Carpenter; the 33 others have the names reversed as Carpenter and Miller.

Less justified in the Advertisement is the final assertion: 'That the lovers of Fine Books may in every respect be gratified, a small Edition is taken off upon Large Paper, of a quarto size, with proof impressions of the plates.' The later quarto impression is printed on the same paper and has *Proof* etched in the lower right corner of the plate, it would seem, only after completion of the ordinary lettered run. One or two of these 'Proofs' may appear in the octavo, and eight or ten of the ordinary issue still may reappear in the quarto.

Of this issue there are two variant states of indeterminate order, with each publisher accorded precedence in the title imprint: (1) LONDON: | PRINTED | FOR WILLIAM MILLER, ALBEMARLE STREET, | AND | JAMES CARPENTER, OLD BOND STREET. | 1811.; (2) LONDON: | PRINTED FOR JAMES CARPENTER, OLD BOND STREET, | AND | WILLIAM MILLER, ALBEMARLE STREET. | 1811.

Copies: (state 1) BCL; CtY(vol.1) MH T/B. (2) EU; CtY(vol.2) MH(2) MWA.

Reference: (Magnum Opus Edition: Not reprinted.)

1] MEMOIRS | OF | **COUNT GRAMMONT,** | BY | ANTHONY HAMILTON. . . . | VOL. I. . . . 1811.

Collation: $\pi^4(-\pi 4)$ $2\pi^2$ a-b^8 c^4(-c4) A-Q^8 R^4. Pagination: *i* half-title, *ii* printer's imprint(1), *iii* title-page, *iv blank*, *v*-vi Advertisement, *vii* viii-ix Directions for placing the Portraits, *x blank*, *i* fly-title, *ii blank*, *iii* iv-xx Biographical Sketch of Anthony Hamilton, *xxi* xxii-xxxvii Epistle to Grammont, *xxxviii blank*, *1* 2-210 text, *211* fly-title, *212 blank*, *213* 214-262 Notes and Illustrations, 262 printer's imprint(2), *262-263 blank*. Printer's imprints: (1) [*short Oxford rule*] | EDINBURGH: | Printed by James Ballantyne & Co.; (2) [*short Oxford rule*] | EDINBURGH: | Printed by J. Ballantyne & Co.

Figures: a v-8, b xxiii-8, c xxxv-6, A2-1, B18-10, C48-1, D50-10, E66-1, F96-1, G98-10, H114-1, I 130-1, K146-10, L163-2, M181-1, N203-2, O 219-10 220-6, P238-5 240-6, Q243-6 244-5, R260-5.

Notes: Evidently presswork at first proceeded at a leisurely pace, with one press only used for both formes of a sheet, but starting with sheet O two presses were employed, and R[4] finished off by half-sheet imposition.

2] MEMOIRS | OF | **COUNT GRAMMONT,** | BY | ANTHONY HAMILTON. . . . VOL. II. . . . 1811.

Collation: π[2] A-Y[8] Z[2]. Pagination: *i* half-title, *ii* printer's imprint(1), *iii* title-page, *iv blank*, *1* 2-303 text, *304 blank*, *305* fly-title, *306 blank*, *307* 308-351 Notes and Illustrations, *352 blank*, *353* 354-356 Index of Names, 356 printer's imprint(2). Printer's imprints: (1) [*short Oxford rule*] | EDINBURGH: | Printed by Jas. Ballantyne & Co.; (2) [*short Oxford rule*] | EDINBURGH: | Printed by James Ballantyne & Co.

Figures: A2-1, B18-10/-, C48-1, D53-1, E66-1, F94-1, G98-1, H114-10, I 130-10, K146-1 160-10, L162-10 172-1, M187-1, N194-1, O 210-10, P233-11, Q243-5, R258-5, S282-5, T294-5, U314-11, X329-11, Y346-11, Z—.

53Ab] First Scott Edition, Second (Large-Paper) Impression: 1811

MEMOIRS | OF | **COUNT GRAMMONT,** | BY | ANTHONY HAMILTON. | [*short rule*] | A NEW EDITION. . . . 1811.

Published concurrently with the preceding impression. £6.6.0. Paper: Royal 4° (282 x 226mm cut). Watermarks: 1802; 1804; JOHN DICKINSON & CO | 1810.

General Notes: The octavo type-page, averaging 150 x 80mm, when reimposed in quarto format now appears suspended in an excessively wide expanse of paper. Since two quarto gatherings are thus required to accommodate one in octavo format, generally twice as many press-figures appear in this impression. As before the title imprint order may read either (1) Miller and Carpenter, or (2) Carpenter and Miller.

Copies: (state 1) IdU NN NNP NNP(extra-illustrated). (2) T/B.

1] MEMOIRS | OF | **COUNT GRAMMONT,** | BY | ANTHONY HAMILTON. . . . VOL. I. . . . 1811.

Collation: π1 2π^4 a-d^4 e^4(-e4) A-2K^4. Pagination: as in first impression. Typography: Signature e (page xxxiii) still retains the little c reference of the earlier octavo impression. Signature 2K (page 257), earlier in octavo signed R, is now missigned 2 I. The second printer's imprint has no period at the end.

Figures: a v-8, b x-8/-, c xxiii-8, d xxvi-8, 'c'[e] xxxv-8/-, A2-1, B10-1, C18-10, D26-10, E35-1, F48-1, G50-10, H58-10, I66-1, K74-1, L82-1, M96-1, N98-10, O 106-10, P114-1, Q126-1, R130-1, S143-1, T146-10, U154-10, X163-2, Y174-2, Z181-1, 2A 187-1, 2B—, 2C 203-2, 2D 216-10, 2E 219-10, 2F 226-11, 2G 235-11, 2H 244-10, 2 I 250-10, '2 I'[2K] 260-11.

2] MEMOIRS | OF | **COUNT GRAMMONT,** | BY | ANTHONY HAMILTON. . . . VOL. II. . . . 1811.

Collation: π^2 A-2X^4 2Z^2. Pagination: as in first impression. Typography: Signature 2Z (page *353*) is missigned Z.

Figures: A2-1, B10-1, C18-10, D27-10/-, E38-1, F48-1, G51-1, H59-1, I 66-1, K75-1, L86-1, M94-1, N98-1, O 106-1, P114-10, Q122-10, R130-10, S138-10, T146-1, U154-1, X164-2, Y172-2, Z—, 2A 187-1, 2B 194-8, 2C 202-8, 2D 210-10, 2E 218-10, 2F 226-11, 2G 234-11, 2H 244-10, 2 I 252-10, 2K 258-10, 2L 266-10, 2M 275-10, 2N 282-10, 2 O 290-10, 2P 298-10, 2Q 308-11, 2R 314-11, 2S 324-11, 2T 336-11, 2U 341-11, 2X 346-11, 'Z' [2Z] 355-11/-.

53Ac] First Scott Edition in French: 1811

MEMOIRES | DU | COMTE DE GRAMMONT | PAR | ANTOINE HAMILTON. | [*short rule*] | NOUVELLE EDITION | EN DEUX VOLUMES | PRÉCÉDÉ | D'UNE NOTICE BIOGRAPHIQUE SUR LE | COMTE HAMILTON, | ET | ENRICHIE DE SOIXANTE-QUATRE PORTRAITS | GRAVÉS PAR EDOUARD SCRIVEN, &c. | [*short rule*] | TOME I [II]. | A LONDRES: | CHEZ JACQUES CARPENTER, OLD-BOND-STREET, ET | WILLIAM MILLER, ALBEMARLE-STREET: | *Imprimé par W. Bulmer et Co. Cleveland-row, St. James's.* | 1811.

Published concurrently with the English edition. £3.13.6. Paper: Demy 8° (212 x 136mm cut). Watermarks: 1804; [JOHN DICKINSON & Co | 1810 only for 'Table des Chapitres'].

General Notes: This edition reprints the entire work in French, including Scott's preliminaries and the 64 Scriven plates. Each of the plates bears an English imprint: London, Published 1810 by W. Miller & J. Carpenter (or, as before, with the two names reversed). The title-pages would indicate that the typesetters did not have a wide-ranging French type base, since there is a dearth of capitals with the proper diacriticals.

Copy: L. Reference: Ruth Clark, *Anthony Hamilton*. London: John Lane, 1921, page 318 (citing fourteen other French editions in the period 1812-1831, none however with any Scott material).

1] MEMOIRES | DU | COMTE DE GRAMMONT . . . . TOME I. . . . 1811.

Collation: $\pi^2[\pi 2+1]$ a-c^8 d^4 e^2 B-K^8 L-P^4. Pagination: *1* title-page, *2 blank*, *3* Avertissement, *4 blank*, *5* Avis au Relieur pour Placer les Portraits, *6 blank*, *i* fly-title, *ii blank*, *iii* iv-xxxii Note Biographique sur Antoine Hamilton, *xxxiii* fly-title, *xxxiv blank*, *xxxv* xxxvi-lvi Epitre a Monsieur le Comte de Grammont, *lvii* Table des Chapitres, *lviii blank*, *lix* fly-title, *lx blank*, *1* 2-145 text, *146 blank*, *147* fly-title, *148 blank*, *149* 150-184 Notes et Eclaircissemens, 184 printer's imprint: [*short rule*] | Londres: imprimé par W. Bulmer et Co. | Cleveland-Row, St. James's. Figures: none.

2] MEMOIRES | DU | COMTE DE GRAMMONT . . . . TOME II. . . . 1811.

Collation: *A*^{2}[*A*2+1] B-X^8 Y-Dd^4 Ee^2. Pagination: *i* title-page, *ii blank*, *iii*-iv 'Avis au Relieur pour Placer les Portraits, *v* Table des Chapitres, *vi blank*, *1* 2-316 text, *317* fly-title, *318 blank*, *319* 320-367 Notes et Eclaircissemens, *368 blank*, *369-371* Table, *371* Printer's imprint: [*short rule*] | Londres: imprimé par W. Bulmer et Co. | Cleveland-Row, St. James's. Typography: Page 299 is misnumbered 292. Figures: none.

THE MODERN BRITISH DRAMA

54A] First Scott Edition: 1811

THE | Modern | BRITISH DRAMA. | IN FIVE VOLUMES. | [*short Oxford rule*] | VOLUME FIRST [SECOND-FIFTH]. | [*short rule*] | TRAGEDIES [COMEDIES, OPERAS AND FARCES]. | [*short rule*] | [*vignette*] | LONDON: | PRINTED FOR WILLIAM MILLER, ALBEMARLE STREET, | BY JAMES BALLANTYNE AND CO. EDINBURGH. | 1811.

Published 16 March 1811 in London (*MC*); issued 30 March in Edinburgh (*EEC*). £5.10.0. Paper: Royal 8° (234 x 152mm cut). Conjugate half-title and title-page in each volume printed on heavy plate paper. Watermarks: J Whatman | 1808.

General Notes: Unlike the companion 1810 edition of *The Ancient British Drama* (*see* 44A), which benefits from John Nichols' antiquarian interests, this collection contains no reference to earlier texts and, as noted below, relatively few explanatory notes. However, the prefatory 'Remarks' to volumes 1, 3, and 5 may be attributed to Scott, as well as the selection of plays, tragic, comic, and farcical. Many of these plays appear in the Miller/Ballanyne 1804 compilation simply titled

The British Drama, a work of comparable size and bearing the vignettes recurring here in volumes 1, 3, 5; but this earlier selection is probably not by Scott, as occasionally alleged, for the works then presented, as he realized, generally exclude all preliminary or final matter. As early as 7 December 1808 he was suggesting to Miller expedient procedures for 'replacing the prologues & epilogues'. Thus the present edition, both in its range and in its fidelity to text, exhibits the work of a more judicious editor.

Copies: (Volume 1, state 1) CaBVaU CtY(2). (2) EU; NN(2) TxU(vols 2,3). Reference: *Letters*, xii.398. (Magnum Opus Edition: Not reprinted.)

1] THE | Modern | BRITISH DRAMA. . . . VOLUME FIRST | [*short Oxford rule*] | *TRAGEDIES*. . . . 1811.

Collation: $\pi^2(\pi2+1)$ $a^4(-a4)$ A-2U^8. Pagination: *1* half-title, *2 blank*, *3* title-page, *4 blank*, *5* Contents, *6 blank*, *i* ii-vi Remarks on English Tragedy, *1* 2-688 text, 688 printer's imprint: [*short reversed Oxford rule*] | EDINBURGH: | Printed by James Ballantyne & Co. Illustration: Title vignette, of the Tragic Muse and three putti, was drawn by H. Howard, engraved by Noble & Raimbach.

Figures: a ii-5, A3-12 16-10, B31-12 32-10, C34-10 48-12, D53-12 54-10, E66-10 72-12, F82-3 88-10, G98-3 112-10, H114-1 125-10/-, I 130-10 133-1, K154-1/- 160-10, L162-4 172-10, M178-10, N194-10 204-1, O 210-10/- 224-1, P226-1 240-10/-, Q242-10 256-4, R259-10 272-3, S274-4 280-3, T290-4 304-3, U318-8 320-4, X322-8 328-4, Y338-8 352-4, Z358-2 368-13, 2A 383-7 384-13, 2B 398-7 400-13, 2C 403-7 416-13, 2D 418-7 429-13, 2E 443-7 448-13, 2F 450-13 456-7, 2G 475-7 480-13, 2H 490-4 496-7, 2 I 500-10 506-7, 2K 526-10, 2L 541-4 543-7, 2M 546-4, 2N 562-4 576-10, 2O 579-10 580-4, 2P 598-4 608-7, 2Q 612-4 618-10, 2R 635-7 640-4, 2S 642-4 656-7, 2T 664-4, 2U 679-4 684-7.

Notes: There are only two notes in this volume, pages 258 and 462, the first on a play not in the 1804 edition, the second following an 'Epilogue' again not there represented. First text gathering A was apparently short-counted (or accidentally pied) in the printing, the first setting (1) as noted above exhibiting press figures 3-12 16-10. The later, supplemental setting (2) has no figures, unlike normal procedure.

2] THE | Modern | BRITISH DRAMA. . . . [*short reversed Oxford rule*] | VOLUME SECOND | [*short rule*] | *TRAGEDIES*. . . . 1811.

Collation: $\pi^2(\pi2+1)$ A-2O^8 2P^4 2Q1. Pagination: *1* half-title, *2 blank*, *i* title-page, *ii blank*, *iii*-iv Contents, *1* 2-602 text, 602 printer's imprint: [*short Oxford rule*] | EDINBURGH: | Printed by James Ballantyne & Co. Illustration: Title vignette, of the Tragic Muse veiled and two suppliants, was drawn by M. W. Sharp, engraved by J. Romney.

Figures: A2-8 16-4, B18-8 32-4, C35-4 40-13, D50-13 64-4, E66-13 80-2, F82-7 96-13, G103-13 109-7, H126-7, I 139-7 144-13, K148-13 154-7, L175-7 176-13, M178-10 192-7, N199-7 208-10, O 222-7 224-4, P226-10 233-7, Q251-10 252-7, R263-10 272-4, S274-7 288-4, T298-7 301-4, U312-4 314-7, X334-7 336-4, Y350-13 352-6, Z357-7 359-4, 2A 384-4, 2B 391-4 400-3/-, 2C 407-3 413-7, 2D 418-4 432-13, 2E 442-7 448-4, 2F 462-13 464-7, 2G 479-13 480-3, 2H 482-6 489-13, 2 I 498-13 504-10, 2K 514-13 528-10, 2L 537-7 539-6, 2M 546-6 553-13, 2N 563-6 564-1, 2O 579-7 592-5, 2P 600-3/5, 2Q—.

Notes: Annotations occur seven times only, two for obscure plays early in the volume (pages 124, 287), five in reference to Walpole's *Mysterious Mother* (pages 553[2], 559, 563, 566) and one for Milton's *Comus* (page 571). Among these four plays only the first is in the 1804 edition, there without a note. The misplaced Milton entry, here dated 1637, reappears properly in volume 5.

3] THE | Modern | BRITISH DRAMA. . . . [*short reversed Oxford rule*] | VOLUME THIRD. | [*short rule*] | *COMEDIES*. . . . 1811.

Collation: $\pi^2(\pi2+1)$ a^4 A-$2S^8$ $2T^4$ $2U^2$. Pagination: *1* half-title, *2 blank*, *3* title-page, *4 blank*, *5* Contents, *6 blank*, *i* ii-vii Remarks on English Comedy, *viii blank*, *1* 2-668 text, 668 printer's imprint: [*short Oxford rule*] | Edinburgh: | Printed by James Ballantyne & Co. Illustration: Title vignette, of the Comic Muse and three putti, was drawn by H. Howard, engraved by Noble. Typography: Page 153 is unnumbered. Page 265 is misnumbered 266. In some copies a malformed 5 occurs in page-numbers 519 and 579.

Figures: a ii-6/5, A2-7 16-4, B19-3 32-13, C47-7 48-4, D51-13 64-10, E75-10 80-7, F95-13 96-10, G110-10 112-13, H123-13 128-1, I 139-13 141-5, K148-6 158-5, L162-6 176-7, M191-5 192-6, N207-1 208-7, O 210-7 221-5, P228-6 238-5, Q249-12 250-5, R260-2 270-5, S275-6 285-2, T298-5 304-6, U307-6 320-1, X327-8 332-6, Y338-7 349-1, Z358-5 368-6, 2A 370-13 380-11, 2B 387-12 400-6, 2C 403-5, 2D 423-5, 2E 434-5, 2F 451-5, 2G 466-5, 2H 483-5, 2 I 499-5, 2K 514-7, 2L 532-7, 2M 557-7, 2N—, 2O 592-7, 2P 608-5, 2Q—, 2R 640-1/-, 2S 643-5, 2T 664-7, 2U 667-7.

Notes: A single note appears on page 579, this to a 'Prologue' not included in the 1804 edition.

4] THE | Modern | BRITISH DRAMA. . . . VOLUME FOURTH. | [*short rule*] | *COMEDIES*. . . . 1811.

Collation: $\pi^2(\pi2+1)$ A-$2R^8$ $2S^4$. Pagination: *i* half-title, *ii blank*, *iii* title-page, *iv blank*, *v* Contents, *vi blank*, *1* 2-648 text, 648 printer's imprint: [*short Oxford rule*] | Edinburgh: | Printed by James Ballantyne & Co. Illustration: Title vignette, of the Comic Muse being crowned, was drawn by M. W. Sharp, engraved by J. Noble.

Figures: A14-5 16-13, B20-5 22-13, C34-7 48-6, D62-6 64-7, E74-6 80-5, F94-13 96-6, G112-1, H116-7 127-10, I 143-5 144-1, K146-1 148-5, L162-13 176-2, M180-12 183-2, N197-12 207-3, O 212-6 223-2, P230-5 240-7, Q242-2 256-7, R264-6, S274-10 276-2, T290-6, U306-11 316-12, X331-12 336-6, Y339-7 352-2, Z356-7 362-6, 2A 275-7 384-2, 2B 386-11 400-8, 2C 415-7 416-1, 2D 422-5 432-7, 2E 441-1 447-6, 2F 451-7 457-2, 2G 466-7 472-, 2H 482-7 496-1, 2 I 504-5 507-1, 2K 514-6 517-11, 2L 536-2, 2M 546-5 560-6, 2N 568-6, 2O 578-7 584-6, 2P 606-2 608-3, 2Q 610-6 612-7, 2R 635-6 640-4, 2S 642-5.

Notes: A single note appears on page 287, this to an 'Epilogue' not included in the 1804 edition.

5] THE | Modern | BRITISH DRAMA. . . . VOLUME FIFTH. | [*short rule*] | *OPERAS AND FARCES* . . . STREET, | BY WILLIAM SAVAGE, BEDFORD BURY. | 1811.

Collation: π^2 $2\pi^4$($-\pi 1$) A-2S^8 2T^6. Pagination: *1* half-title, *2 blank*, *3* title-page, *4 blank*, *iii* iv-vi Remarks on English Opera and Farce, *vii*-viii Contents, *1* 2-668 text. No printer's imprint. Illustration: Title vignette, of a Giant Jester, was drawn by R. Smirke, engraved by J. Fittler. Typography: This volume, indicated on title as by a different printer, has no volume direction lines. Page 359 is misnumbered 459.

Figures: A*8*-3 10-1, B18-1 29-4, C41-4 *46*-1, D60-4, E72-1 74-4, F82-1 92-2, G102-1 104-1, H116-4, I 132-1 134-4, K146-1 156-2, L164-1 174-2, M183-4 184-1, N198-2 200-1, O 211-4 212-1, P226-1, Q244-1 254-2, R258-1 268-2, S*274*-1 276-1, T290-1 292-1, U306-1 316-2, X324-1 326-2, Y342-1 348-2, Z354-1 364-2, 2A 370-1 372-2, 2B 388-1, 2C 404-1 406-2, 2D 418-1 420-2, 2E 436-1 442-2, 2F 462-2, 2G 466-1 468-2, 2H 482-1 496-2, 2 I 498-1 504-2, 2K 514-1, 2L 530-1 532-2, 2M 546-1 548-1, 2N 562-1 564-1, 2O 578-1 580-1, 2P 594-1 596-1, 2Q 610-1 *612*-1, 2R 626-1 628-1, 2S *642*-1 644-1, 2T 658-1.
Unlike James Ballantyne's printers, who in the preceding four volumes regularly avoid figuring an unnumbered page, those employed by Savage here randomly, on five occasions, figure these pages.

Notes: This volume has no annotation, but the selection here is widely different from that in 1804, beginning with Milton's *Comus* (now dated 1634) and concluding with Sheridan's *The Critic* (1779) and Frances Brooke's *Rosina* (1783). The Milton, 'altered for the stage by Colman', is of a different text from that wrongly entered in volume 2.

REVIEW OF SOUTHEY

55A] First Printing: 1811

'ART. II. *The Curse of Kehama*. By Robert Southey', pages 40-61, *in*:

The Quarterly Review. February, 1811. [No.9: volume 5 imprint:] London: Printed by C. Roworth, Bell-yard, Temple-bar; For John Murray, 32, Fleet Street; Hatchard, Piccadilly; Richardson, Cornhill; Parker, Oxford; Deighton, Cambridge; William Blackwood, Edinburgh; and M. N. Mahon, Dublin.

Published 8 April 1811 in London (*MC* 5 April; earlier announcements 2, 3 April were premature); 'just arrived' in Edinburgh 17 April (*EWJ*), issued 18 April (*EEC*).

Notes: For this performance Scott offered measured praise in a letter to the author, but earlier commented to George Ellis that in the forthcoming review he had tried 'to throw as much weight as possible upon the beautiful passages, of which there are many, and to slur over the absurdities, of which there are not a few.'

In the final paragraph there is extravagent praise of the manner in which the printing of the poem is executed: 'We hope that every "wire wove, hot pressed" poem, composed upon this model, will be printed with the same attention to picturesque beauty, . . .' Quite possibly this and other concluding sentiments were supplied by William Gifford, editor of *The Quarterly Review*.

Article XV in the previous number 8, possibly with some slight assistance by Scott, is here disregarded (Shine 129).

Copies: BCL L O; PPL TxU. References: *Letters*, ii.36, 15-16; Shine 131. (Magnum Opus Edition 1835: *The Miscellaneous Prose Works*, xvii.301-337 as 'Southey's Curse of Kehama'.)

SECRET HISTORY OF THE COURT OF JAMES THE FIRST

56Aa] First Scott Edition, First Impression: 1811

SECRET HISTORY | OF | THE COURT | OF | James the First: | CONTAINING, | I. OSBORNE'S TRADITIONAL MEMOIRS. | II. SIR ANTHONY WELDON'S COURT AND CHARACTER | OF KING JAMES. | III. AULICUS COQUINARIAE. | IV. SIR EDWARD PEYTON'S DIVINE CATASTROPHE OF | THE HOUSE OF STUARTS. | WITH | NOTES AND INTRODUCTORY REMARKS. | [*short rule*] | IN TWO VOLUMES. | VOL. I [II]. | [*short Oxford rule*] | EDINBURGH: | *Printed by James Ballantyne and Co.* | FOR JOHN BALLANTYNE AND CO., EDINBURGH; AND | LONGMAN, HURST, REES, ORME, AND BROWN, | LONDON. | [*dash*] | 1811.

Published 30 May 1811 in Edinburgh (*EEC*); issued 24 July in London (*MC*). £1.4.0. Paper: Demy 8° (222 x 142mm uncut, bulking 27, 30mm). Watermarks: none.

General Notes: The text Advertisement, observing that these are 'scarce Works . . . here republished in a uniform shape', defines the function of the edition as adding notes 'for the purpose of explaining or correcting, or corroborating, the statements in the text' and prefixing a 'short introduction' to each of the tracts. The Introduction to the Appendix in volume 2 further remarks that while the four tracts listed on title were at press the publishers were 'favoured with the perusal of a very rare pamphlet' (The Court and Kitchin of Elizabeth, Commonly Called Joan Cromwel, . . . 1664), the first part of which is then reprinted. The author, title, and date of all five pieces may be more precisely identified in Wing: numbers O515, W1274, S645, P1952, C7036.

The author of the first group of 'Memoirs' is Francis Osborne. Sir Anthony Weldon's name is spelled correctly on both title-pages, but usually given as 'Welldon' in the introductions and text. Scott had earlier described both authors as 'scandalous' (34Aa), but was making good use of them nonetheless in the Somers' Tracts (38A).

Copies: BCL O; CtY IdU NNU-W OCl PPL T/B. Reference: (Magnum Opus Edition: Not reprinted.)

1] SECRET HISTORY | OF | THE COURT | OF | James the First: . . . VOL. I. . . . 1811.

Collation: π^4 A-2G^8 2H1. Pagination: *i* title-page, *ii blank*, *iii*-iv Advertisement, *v*-vi Contents, *vii* fly-title for [Osborne's] 'Historical Memoirs on the Reigns of Elizabeth and King James', *viii blank*, *i* ii-iii Introduction, *iv blank*, *v* vi-ix 'Osborne's Traditional Memoirs. The Epistle', *x blank*, *xi* xii-xvi To the Reader, *17* 18-297 text, *298 blank*, *299* fly-title for [Weldon's] 'The Court and Character of King James', *300 blank*, *301* 302-303 Introduction, *304 blank*, *305* 306-482 text, 482 printer's imprint: [*short Oxford rule*] | Edinburgh: | Printed by James Ballantyne & Co. Illustration: Engraved frontispiece portrait engraved by Kirkwood, with caption reading 'Mars, Puer, Alecto, Virgo, Vulpes, Leo, Nullus. James the First', published by John Ballantyne & Co. Edinburgh and Longman & Co. London. Typography: In some copies pages *91* and *343* are unnumbered.

Fgures: A vii-9, B18-8, C38-8, D55-2, E80-2, F90-9, G103-6, H128-12, I 130-12 144-1, K151-12 160-3, L165-2 167-9, M178-12 180-4, N199-1 208-3, O 223-8, P238-3/- 240-12, Q242-8 253-3, R258-8 268-9, S280-8, T294-6 296-4, U*313*-8 319-11, X327-3 328-11, Y*343*-1 349-12, Z365-4, 2A 379-1, 2B 399-9, 2C 416-3, 2D 432-3, 2E 439-8, 2F 458-12, 2G 470-12 480-4, 2H—.

2] SECRET HISTORY | OF | THE COURT | OF | James the First: . . . VOL. II. . . . 1811.

Collation: π^2 A-I^8 K^8(±K7) L-$2H^8$ 2 I^4 2K1. Pagination: *i* title-page, *ii blank*, *iii*-iv Contents, *1* 2-89 Weldon text concluded, *90 blank*, *91* 92-97 Introduction to 'Aulicus Coquinariae', *98 blank*, *99* fly-title, *100 blank*, *101* 102-300 text, *301* fly-title for 'The Divine Catastrophe . . . of the House of Stuarts', *302 blank*, *303* 304-466 text, *467* fly-title for 'Appendix', *468 blank*, *469* 470-472 Introduction, *473* fly-title for 'The Court and Kitchin of Elizabeth', *474 blank*, *475* 476-506 text, 506 printer's imprint: [*short Oxford rule*] | Edinburgh: | Printed by James Ballantyne & Co. Illustration: Woodcut frontispiece with caption: 'James 1. About to Take Assay of the Deer. See [volume 1] Page 196.'

Figures: A7-4, B30-4, C35-12, D51-4, E70-8, F96-4, G106-12, H118-12, I 137-3 143-6, K152-1, L171-12, M192-3, N208-12, O 222-4, P226-4 240-1, Q254-6, R262-6, S282-6, T296-9, U316-1, X335-9 336-8, Y352-3, Z367-12, 2A 371-12, 2B 386-3 389-12/-, 2C 415-6, 2D 419-6 428-12/-, 2E 441-12 447-1, 2F 451-12, 2G 477-4, 2H 90-4 496-9, 2 I 498-'2 I'[12], 2K—.

Notes: Both in its integral and cancel form K7 (pages 157-158) is short one line on each page and in some copies is inserted out of register.

56Ab] First Edition, Second (Large-Paper) Impression: 1811

SECRET HISTORY | OF | THE COURT | OF | James the First: . . . 1811.

Published concurrently with the preceding impression. £2.2.0. A 'few copies'. Paper: Royal 8° apparently in two printings: (a) 222 x 140mm cut, bulking 45mm, 47mm; (b) 227 x 140mm cut, bulking 34mm, 38mm. Watermarks: none.

Notes: In all respects identical with the regular paper impression except as noted above and below.
1] Typography: Pages 91 and 343 are correctly numbered. Figures: none on pages vii, 319, 416.
2] Figures: 389-12 and 428-12.

Copies: (a) E; CtY(William Beckford, annotated) CtY(W. S. Lewis, extra-illustrated). (b) GU.

INTRODUCTION to THE CASTLE OF OTRANTO

57A] First Printing: 1811

'INTRODUCTION', pages *iii* iv-xliii, *in*:

The Castle of Otranto; A Gothic Story. [*vignette of giant helmet and sword*] Edinburgh: Printed by James Ballantyne and Co. For John Ballantyne and Company, Edinburgh; and Longman, Hurst, Rees, Orme, and Brown, London. 1811.

Published 30 May 1811 in Edinburgh (*EEC*); issued 24 July in London (*MC*). £1.6.0. Typography: The authorship of the novel, not given on the title, is provided on the half-title: 'By the Honourable Horace Walpole.'

Notes: Scott's inscription in the E copy reads: 'The introduction to this book was written by W. Scott and the frontispiece [*title-page vignette*] was drawn by Daniel Terry of Covent Garden Theatre W. Scott 29th December 1813.' The opening sentence of his long commentary evinces Scott's especial concern: 'The Castle of Otranto is remarkable not only for the wild interest of the story, but as the first modern attempt to found a tale of amusing fiction upon the basis of the ancient romances of chivalry.' Quite appropriately, therefore, this is an edition 'which the publishers have endeavoured to execute in a style of elegance corresponding to the estimation in which they hold the work, and the genius of the author' (page xvi). (Another compelling reason, perhaps, was the appearance in London, the year before, of a miserable chapbook version published by T. Hughes, 35, Ludgate-Street.) Scott concludes his essay by reprinting Walpole's 'The Entail. A Fable' (pages xxxvii-xxxix) and, as he says elsewhere (xi), by offering for the first time 'an elegant French version of that lively apologue' (xl-xliii).
Copies: BCL E(H. Macdonald Buchanan [Principal Clerk of Session]); CtY InU MH* NjP RPB T/B.
*Lacking preliminaries and pages xxxvii-xliii, but with extensive MS revisions by Scott in the 'Introduction', none of which were incorporated in this or, apparently, in any subsequent edition.

Reference: (Magnum Opus Edition: Not reprinted.)

REPRINT

GERMANY

57R] DRESDEN: Arnold 1826
[The Castle of Otranto. New Edition. Dresden: Arnold, 1826.] Copy: not seen.
Reference: GDS 132, page 337.

LETTERS OF ANNA SEWARD

58A] First Printing: 1811

Letters of Anna Seward: Written between the Years 1784 and 1807. In Six Volumes. Volume I [II-VI]. Edinburgh: Printed by George Ramsay &

Company, For Archibald Constable and Company, Edinburgh; and Longman, Hurst, Rees, Orme, and Brown, William Miller, and John Murray, London. 1811.

Published May 1811 in Edinburgh (*SM*); issued 9 August in London (*MC*). £3.3.0.

Notes: Scott had been a confidant of Miss Seward since 1802, and at her expressed desire edited her poetry in 1810 (50A) as well as inscribing an epitaph for her father (60A). The preliminary Advertisement cites a letter from Seward to Constable 17 July 1807 inviting this publisher to edit her correspondence (this apparently after Scott had declined the honour); but an appreciable number of the footnotes are signed 'S' (for 'Seward' or 'Scott'?) and Scott's own letters to Constable indicate his active participation in selecting, and sometimes modifying, the author's correspondence. Ten of her letters to Scott are printed in the sixth volume. The entire edition, Corson reports, was finally edited, anonymously, by Robert Morehead.

An informative review, both of Scott's 1810 edition of Seward's *Poetical Works* and of this publication, appears in the *Scots Magazine*, July 1811, pages 520-535.

Copies: BCL E. References: *Letters*, ii.273, 315; Corson(2), page 56; Thomson, page 62. (Magnum Opus Edition: Not reprinted.)

THE VISION OF DON RODERICK

59Aa] First Issue (Author's copy): 1811

THE | **VISION** | OF | DON RODERICK; | A POEM. | [*Oxford dash*] | BY | WALTER SCOTT, ESQ. | [*reversed Oxford dash*] | [*two-line quotation from Claudian*] | [*Oxford dash*] | (*Author's Copy.*) | EDINBURGH: | [*Oxford dash*] | *Printed by James Ballantyne and Company,* | AT | *The Border Press.* | [*Oxford dash*] | 1811.

Privately printed by 1 July 1811 in Edinburgh. 50 copies. Binding: drab printed wrappers. Paper: Crown 4° (229 x 185mm uncut). Watermarks: BUTTANSHAW | 1809. Collation: π^4 A-G^4. Pagination: *i* half-title, *ii blank, iii* title, *iv blank*, *v* dedication to John Whitmore, Esq. and to the Committee of Subscribers for Relief of the Portugueze Sufferers, *vi blank, vii*-viii preface dated from Edinburgh 24 June 1811, *1* fly-title, *2* 'Of these private Copies, 50 only are printed.', *3* 4-7 Introduction, *8 blank*, *9* 10-37 text, *38 blank*, *39* fly-title for Notes, *40 blank, 41* 42-56 notes, 56 printer's imprint: [*Oxford dash*] | EDINBURGH: | Printed by James Ballantyne and Co.

Figures: π *vii*-8, A*3*-8, B10-8, C18-8, D32-7, E35-7, F44-7, G*52*-7.

Notes: *The Vision of Don Roderick* is not divided into cantos, as in earlier long poems, but rather, in this preliminary extract, into eighteen nine-line stanzas.

Although printed as a Crown quarto this issue is sometimes described as an octavo. Page *3* line 2 begins 'May rise', as in the corrected state of the succeeding Demy quarto impression. Thus, while issued earlier for presentation, this would appear to be of a later printing.

Presentation copies: E('These 2 Poems [with *The Field of Waterloo*] were given by her Friend the Author, to A[nne] D[orothea] Alvanley') LU('The Honble Lady [Mary Elizabeth] Hood from the Author'); CtY('Henry Weber Esq from Walter Scott') IdU('From the Author') MH('Amelia M. Ramsay, from the Author' [not in Scott's hand]) NN('William Erskine Esq from his affectionate freind Walter Scott') NNP('From the Author 1823'[W(illiam) Laidlaw signature above Scott's inscription])

Other copies: BCL O; CtY MH NjP NNP TxU. References: Grady, pages 235-259, 401; Ruff 110(illustration of title-page: page 171); Thomson, page 7; Tinker 1866(recipient wrongly identified as Henry Wilson, rather than Henry Weber); Sterling 717. (Magnum Opus Edition 1834: *The Poetical Works*, ix.*355-357* 358-440.)

59Ab] First, Quarto Edition, First Impression: 1811

THE | **VISION** | OF | **DON RODERICK;** | A POEM. | [*short Oxford rule*] | BY | WALTER SCOTT, Esq. | [*short reversed Oxford rule*] | [*two line quotation from Claudian*] | [*short Oxford rule*] | EDINBURGH: | Printed by James Ballantyne and Co. | FOR JOHN BALLANTYNE AND CO. HANOVER STREET, EDINBURGH; | AND LONGMAN, HURST, REES, ORME, AND BROWN, | LONDON. | [*dash*] | 1811.

Published 2 July 1811 in Edinburgh (*EEC* 29 June); announced 14 June as 'a few days' in London (*MC*, no further listing). 15s. Binding: drab boards with or without printed label, or (a later issue?) blue boards and tan cloth back. Paper: Demy 4° (286 x 227mm uncut). To 'strengthen' a rather slim performance, typographically, one or more of the earlier gatherings were usually printed on heavier paper. Watermarks: primarily J L | 1808 [1809], but occasional sheets of 1794 | J Whatman; J Whatman | 1801 1807, 1809, 1810]; R C | 1807 [1808]; 1809; John Dickinson & Co | 1810.

Collation: π^4 $2\pi^2$ A-H^4 $(H)^2$[(H2)+1] I-P^4 Q^2. Pagination: *i* half-title, *ii blank*, *iii* title-page, *iv blank*, *v* dedication, *vi blank*, *vii* viii-ix preface, dated from Edinburgh 24 June 1811, *x blank*, *xi* Contents, *xii blank*, *1* fly-title, *2 blank*, *3* 4-69 text, *70 blank*, *65* fly-title, *66 blank*, *67* '68-122'[*71-73* 74-128] Notes, *129-130* advertisement, *130* printer's imprint: [*short rule*] | Edinburgh: Printed by J. Ballantyne & Co. | [*short rule*]. Typography: Because of the belated insertion of a second, half-sheet (H) there is a repetition of numbered pages 68-69, resulting in the misnumbering of all subsequent pages. The leaf inserted after the half-sheet to provide the last five lines of text is of a duplicate setting, with initial C of the headline CONCLUSION (page 69) directly above either 'a' or 'n' of 'and'.

Figures: π *vii*-8 viii-1, 2π ix-6, A8-6, B15-9, C18-8 20-3, D28-6 31-8, E35-8 40-6, F43-7 45-8, G53-7 55-3, H59-1 64-5, (H)66-7, I 70-1 72-7, K77-6 78-3, L86-12 88-3, M94-7 96-5, N99-3 101-8, O 109-12 110-6, P114-1 116-12, Q*129*-3.

Notes: This edition exists in two states, page *3* line 2 beginning: (1) 'May swell', (2) 'May rise'. The entire poem (in second state) with notes was reprinted 'for a valuable consideration' in the 1811 *Edinburgh Annual Register for 1809* (volume 2, part 2, pages 601-635): an odd circumstance for an author sharing profits in this Ballantyne enterprise.

Copies: (state 1) E(2) E(with two 1812 Westall plates); CtY InU(2) InU* NNP(2) PU TxU(2). (2) AN+ E(2) ES O+; IdU InU MH NN NN(Berg) NNP+ NNU-W OCl T/B+ TxU(2).
*'To Henry MacKenzie Esqr with respectful Compliments from The Publishers'.
+With 16-page Longman catalogue 'Corrected to February, 1811.'

Reference: Ruff 111.

59Ac] First, Quarto Edition, First Impression, Variant Issue: 1811

THE | **VISION** | OF | **DON RODERICK;** ... EDINBURGH; | LONGMAN AND CO. LONDON; AND JOHN CUMMING, | DUBLIN. | [*dash*] | 1811.

Notes: Except for title—now with Longman imprint abbreviated to accomodate the Cumming entry on line—this variant is in all respects identical with the main London issue, page *3* in second state, line 2 beginning 'May rise'.

Copies: E; NN(Berg).

59Ad] First, Quarto Edition, Second (Large-Paper) Impression): 1811

THE | **VISION** | OF | **DON RODERICK;** ... LONDON. | [*dash*] | 1811.

Published concurrently with the preceding impression. £1.10.0. 60 copies. Binding: drab boards with printed label on front board identifying the impression as 'Royal Copy'. Paper: Royal 4° (302 x 240mm uncut). Watermarks: *none*; 1803; J WHATMAN | 1810.

Notes: Title imprint corresponds with the main London issue (excluding the Dublin variant). Page *3* is in the corrected state, line 2 beginning 'May rise'.

Copies: E O+; CtY CtY* InU+.

*Bound as a remainder in original blue-gray boards with the 1815 large-paper impression of *The Lord of the Isles* (*see* 81Ab).
+With 16-page Longman catalogue 'Corrected to February, 1811.'

References: Ruff 112; Tinker 1867.

59Ae] First, Quarto Edition, Third Impression: 1811

THE | **VISION** | OF | **DON RODERICK;** . . . LONDON. | [*dash*] | 1811.

Binding: Grey-green boards with printed label. Paper: Demy 4° (282 x 221mm uncut). Watermarks: C | 1811. Collation: π^4 $2\pi^2$ A-H^4 I^4(-I ^{4}) K-Q^4 R^2. Pagination: *i* half-title, *ii blank*, *iii* title-page, *iv blank*, *v* dedication, *vi blank*, *vii* viii-ix preface, *x blank*, *xi* Contents, *xii blank*, *1* fly-title, *2 blank*, *3* 4-69 text, *70 blank*, *71* fly-title, *72 blank*, *73* 74-128 Notes, *129-130* advertisement, *130* printer's imprint: [*short rule*] | EDINBURGH: PRINTED BY J. BALLANTYNE & CO. | [*short rule*]. Typography: The irregularities in collation and pagination, noted in the first impression, have now been corrected.

Figures: π *vii*-8, 2π—, A4-6, B14-3, C24-9, D27-4, E39-6, F43-1, G50-4, H60-6/-, I 66-8, K76-3, L85-4, M94-1, N99-12, O 105-1 107-9, P115-9, Q120-6 122-12, R*129*-1.

Notes: The term 'impression' is retained for this issue, in deference to long established usage, though sheets A-G are now reset. Evidently, upon the original printing of H, it was decided to increase the issue, thus requiring a recomposition of the A-G type then already distributed.

Copies: BCL; InU NNP(Van Antwerp) T/B TxU. References: Ruff 113; Van Antwerp(1) 10.

59Af] Second Edition, First Impression: 1811

THE | **VISION** | OF | **DON RODERICK,** | AND | OTHER POEMS. | [*short Oxford rule*] | BY | WALTER SCOTT, ESQ. | [*short reversed Oxford rule*] | THE SECOND EDITION. | [*short rule*] | EDINBURGH: | PRINTED FOR AND SOLD BY JOHN BALLANTYNE AND CO., | EDINBURGH: | ALSO BY LONGMAN AND CO., WILLIAM MILLER, | WHITE AND CO., AND GALE AND CO., | LONDON. | [*dash*] | 1811.

Published 1 January 1812 in Edinburgh (*EWJ*). 9s. Binding: drab, blue-green or grey-brown boards with printed label. Paper: Demy 8° (228 x 12mm uncut). Again to give greater solidity to the book, some copies of sheets K-L and all copies of sheet *A* are on thick paper. Watermarks: 1809 | 5 [6]; R C | 1807 [1808, 1809, 1810].

Collation: *A*[8] B-K[8] L[4]. Pagination: *1* half-title, *2* printer's imprint (1), *3* title-page, *4 blank*, *5* Advertisement, *6 blank*, *7* Contents, *8 blank*, *9* dedication, *10 blank*, *11* 12-13 preface, *14 blank*, *15* fly-title for *The Vision of Don Roderick*, *16 blank*, *17* 18-83 text, *84 blank*, *85* fly-title for Notes, *86 blank*, *87* 88-131 text, *132 blank*, *133* fly-title for 'Miscellaneous Poems', *134 blank*, *135* 136-164 text, *165-167* 'Books Lately Published' by Scott, *167* printer's imprint(2), *168 blank*. Printer's imprints: (1) [*short Oxford rule*] | EDINBURGH: | Printed by James Ballantyne & Co.; (2) [*rule*] | EDINBURGH: PRINTED BY JAMES BALLANTYNE AND CO. | [*rule*].

Figures: *A*12-9, B20-9 23-5, C37-12 47-1/-, D51-2 61-9, E74-3 77-5, F82-8 88-3/-, G110-6 112-7, H126-5 128-8, I 139-12 141-1, K146-3 160-12, L*166*-5.

Notes: The Advertisement states that there are now added 'several . . . smaller poems' not previously collected. In fact, nine have been added.

Copies: AN BCL E* E+ O P; CtY(3) IdU NN(2) NNP PPL TxU(2).
*Bound with first edition of *Ballads and Lyrical Pieces* (24Aa).
+Extra-illustrated with an 1812 engraved title-page and six plates by Richard Westall (four for the first and two for the second work: *see* 341D). As indicated in this entry, the later engraved title reads 'Glenfinlas [first ballad in the first work] . . . with The Vision of Don Roderick . . . .'

*References: Ruff 114; Tinker 1868.

59Ag] Second Edition, Second (Large-Paper) Impression: 1811

THE | **VISION** | OF | **DON RODERICK,** | AND | OTHER POEMS. . . . THE SECOND EDITION. . . . 1811.

Published concurrently with the previous impression. Binding: drab boards with pink backstrip and printed label. Paper: Royal 8° (243 x 150mm uncut). Watermarks: J WHATMAN | 1810.

Copies: L+; CtY InU. Reference: Ruff 115.
+Extra-illustrated with an 1812 engraved title-page and six plates by Richard Westall (four for the first and two for the second work: *see* 341D). As indicated in this entry, the later engraved title reads 'Glenfinlas [first ballad in the first work] . . . with The Vision of Don Roderick . . . .'

59Ah] Second Edition, Third Impression: 1811

THE | **VISION** | OF | **DON RODERICK,** | AND | OTHER POEMS. . . . THE SECOND EDITION. . . . 1811.

Binding: drab or grey-brown boards with printed label. Paper: Demy 8° (224 x 138mm uncut). Watermarks: 1809 | *none* [5]; C | 1811. Figures: *A*12-9/-, B24-3

27-1, C37-2 39-12, D50-9 53-6, E67-4 72-1, F82-4 88-12, G105-1 110-2, H115-12 121-2, I 139-6 141-1, K146-1 152(or 153)-3, L*166*-5/7.

Notes: With this regular impression the pattern established in the three quarto issues is repeated, all exhibiting a total publication which as Scott remarked on 4 August 'has greatly exceeded my calculation as to popularity.'

Copies: L L+ LU LVA(Forster); CtY* InU.
+Extra-illustrated with an 1812 engraved title-page and six plates by Richard Westall (four for the first and two for the second work: *see* 341D). As indicated in this entry, the later engraved title reads 'Glenfinlas [first ballad in the first work] . . . with The Vision of Don Roderick . . . .'
*Bound with second edition of *The Field of Waterloo* (84Ab)..

59Ai] Third Edition: 1815

THE | VISION | OF | Don Roderick, | THE | FIELD OF WATERLOO, | AND | OTHER POEMS. | [*short Oxford rule*] | BY | WALTER SCOTT, Esq. | [*short reversed Oxford rule*] | EDINBURGH: | *Printed by James Ballantyne and Co.* | FOR LONGMAN, HURST, REES, ORME, AND BROWN, AND | JOHN MURRAY, LONDON; | AND ARCHIBALD CONSTABLE AND COMPANY, | EDINBURGH. | [*dash*] | 1815.

Issued 22 March 1816 in London (*MC*). 10s.6d. Paper: Demy 8° (218 x 137mm cut). Watermarks: 7 | W Balston & Co | 1814; 6 [9] | W Balston & Co | 1815.
Collation: a^8(a4+1) B-Q^8 R^4. Pagination: *1-2 blank*, *3* half-title, *4 blank*, *5* title-page, *6 blank*, *7* dedication, *8 blank*, *9*-10 Contents, *11* 12-13 Preface, *14 blank*, *15* fly-title for *The Vision of Don Roderick*, *16 blank*, *17* 18-131 text and notes, *132 blank*, *133* fly-title for 'Miscellaneous Poems', *134 blank*, *135* 136-188 text, *189* fly-title for *The Field of Waterloo*, *190 blank*, *191* dedication, *192 blank*, *193* 194-238 text and notes, *239* fly-title for 'Miscellanies', *240 blank*, *241* 242-264 text, 264 printer's imprint: [*short rule*] | Edinburgh: | Printed by James Ballantyne & Co.
Typography: Recto first leaf bears only the signature 'a'. Page 159 is misnumbered 156.

Figures: a 12-10, B23-7, C37-2, D50-5, E77-7, F95-3, G98-2, H124-10, I 144-8, K154-5, L171-3, M188-1, N197-8, O 218-1, P228-10, Q243-2, R258-2.

Notes: The Contents leaf is inserted in the initial gathering. Only the concluding miscellaneous poem, 'Saint Cloud' (pages 186-188), is dated, from Paris 5 September 1815. As suggested by the press figures, there are two issues: (1) sheet O figured 218-1 as usual, page 224 line 3 'Wellington.'; sheet R figured 258-2, page 263 line 12 'herd's'. Later, because of a short count in these sheets, they were reset: (2) sheet O unfigured, page 224 line 3 'Wellington!'; sheet R figured 260-2, page 263 line 12 'Herd's'.

Copies: (issue 1) AN E+ EU*(Corson) GU L O; InU NN(2) T/B T/B+. (2) InU.
+Extra-illustrated with two Westall engravings dated 4 June and 4 May 1812 respectively, these representing the latter part of a suite with *Glenfinlas* engraved title and *Ballads and Lyrical Pieces* printed title (*see* 341D).
*Followed, in the original binding, by a unique issue of *Ballads and Lyrical Pieces*, fifth edition, 1820 (*see* 24Aj).

Reference: Ruff 116.

59Aj] Fourth Edition: 1821

THE | VISION | OF | Don Roderick, | THE | FIELD OF WATERLOO, | AND | OTHER POEMS. | [*short rule*] | BY | SIR WALTER SCOTT, BART. | [*short rule*] | FOURTH EDITION. | [*short reversed Oxford rule*] | EDINBURGH: | PRINTED FOR ARCHIBALD CONSTABLE AND CO. | [*dash*] | 1821.

Paper: Demy 8° (209 x 125mm cut). Watermarks: none. Collation: *A*^{8} B-Q^{8} R^{4}. Pagination: *1-2 blank*, *3* half-title, *4* printer's imprint(1), *5* title-page, *6 blank*, *7* dedication, *8 blank*, *9*-10 Contents, *11* 12-13 Preface, *14 blank*, *15* fly-title, *16 blank*, *17* 18-131 text and notes for *The Vision of Don Roderick*, *132 blank*, *133* fly-title, *134 blank*, *135* 136-188 text of 'Miscellaneous Poems', *189* fly-title, *190 blank*, *191* dedication, *192 blank*, *193* 194-238 text and notes for *The Field of Waterloo*, *239* fly-title, *240 blank*, 241-264 text of 'Miscellanies', 264 printer's imprint(2). Printer's imprints: (1) [*short rule*] | EDINBURGH: | Printed by James Ballantyne and Co.; (2) [*short rule*] | EDINBURGH: | Printed by James Ballantyne & Co.

Figures: *A*12-10, B32-6, C35-7, D52-6, E80-10, F82-9, G112-8, H*119*-10, I 130-5, K146-7, L169-1, M180-3, N208-3, O 214-3, P228-9, Q242-3, R260-8.

Copies: L; NN(2). Reference: Ruff 117.

REPRINTS

FRANCE

PARIS: Didot and Galignani
[~] The Vision of Don Roderick. 1821, 1826. (Collection of Modern English Authors: *see* 290R[7A], [7C])

GERMANY

ZWICKAU: Schumann
[~] The Vision of Don Roderick. . . . The Field of Waterloo. 1821. (Pocket Library of English Classics: *see* 302R.23)

INDIA

CALCUTTA: [*no publisher known*]
59Ra] The Vision of Don Roderick; A Poem. By Walter Scott, Esq. Calcutta, Re-Printed, 1812. One Volume. Pages: *i-vii* viii-ix *x-xii, 1-3* 4-92, 97-101. Notes: Despite the irregular pagination there is no break in the text. Copy: E(information kindly provided by Dr. Brian Hillyard).

UNITED STATES

BALTIMORE: Cushing
[~] The Vision of Don Roderick. Ballads and Lyrical Pieces. 1813. (The Poetical Works of Walter Scott: *see* 303R.1)

59Rb] BOSTON: Greenleaf 1811
The Vision of Don Roderick; A Poem. By Walter Scott, Esq. . . . Boston, Published by J. Greenleaf. 1811. Pages: *i-vi* viii-ix *x, 11* 12-131. Notes: Original printed boards list on back *Marmion, The Lady of the Lake, The Lay of the Last Minstrel, Ballads and Lyrical Pieces*. Copies: MH MWA(2) NjP NN RPB.

59Rc] BOSTON: Wait 1811-1812
The Vision of Don Roderick. A Poem. By Walter Scott, Esquire. . . . Boston: Published by T. B. Wait & Company. 1811. Pages: *i-v* vi, *7* 8-74. Notes: Often issued bound with *The Lay of the Last Minstrel*, Boston, Greenough and Stebbins, 1811. (*see* 14Re). Copies: DLC MWA. Reissued 1812 (DLC).

59Rd] NEW YORK: Eastburn 1818
The Vision of Don Roderick. Ballads and Lyrical Pieces. By Walter Scott, Esq. New York: Published by J. Eastburn and Co., Literary-Rooms, Broadway. 1818. Pages: *i-vii* viii-ix *x, 11-15* 16-286. Notes: With engraved frontispiece. Pages *83-89* 90-286 represent *Ballads and Lyrical Pieces*. (Also issued in The Poetical Works of Walter Scott, Esq.: volume 2. 1818. *see* 312R.) Copies: E; MWA.

59Re] NEW YORK: Sargeant 1811
The Vision of Don Roderick: A Poem. By Walter Scott, Esq. . . . New-York: Published by Ezra Sargeant, No. 86 Broadway. 1811. Pages: *i-v* vi-vii *viii, 13-15* 16-123. Copies: CtY IdU MH MWA NN(4) NNU-W PHi.

59Rf] PHILADELPHIA: Finley and Hopkins 1811

[1] The Vision of Don Roderick; A Poem. By Walter Scott, Esq. . . . Philadelphia, Published by Anthony Finley, and B. B. Hopkins & Co. Sold also by P. H. Nicklin, and J. Cushing, Baltimore; J. West & Co., and D. Mallory, Boston; Whiting & Watson, and J. Thompson, New-York; Patterson & Hopkins, Pittsburg; A. Montgomery, Frankford (Ky.); Seymour & Williams, Savannah; and M. R. Lockerman, Wilmington (Del.) T. & G. Palmer, printers. 1811. Pages: *i-vii* viii-x *xi-xii, 13-15* 16-136. Notes: With engraved vignette title-page. Bound in printed boards with the back board advertising *The Poetical Works of Walter Scott* in 'an elegant miniature edition, with five beautiful engravings' (an edition as yet unidentified). Copies: E O; CtY DLC MWA NN(2) PPL(2) T/B.

[2] . . . The Vision of Don Roderick; A Poem. . . . By Walter Scott, Esq. . . . Philadelphia, Published by Anthony Finley, and B. B. Hopkins & Co. Sold also by P. H. Nicklin, and J. Cushing, Baltimore; J. West & Co., and D. Mallory, Boston; Whiting & Watson, and J. Thompson, New-York; Patterson & Hopkins, Pittsburg; A. Montgomery, Frankford (Ky.); Seymour & Williams, Savannah; and M. R. Lockerman. Wilmington (Del.) T. & G. Palmer, printers. 1811. Pages: *i-v* vi-vii *viii, 9* 10-'92'[84]. Notes: At head of title: Finley's Second Edition. With engraved title-page. Some copies, bound with *Ballads and Lyrical Pieces*, Baltimore: Philip H. Nicklin. 1811. (*see* 24Ra.) Copies: O; MH NN(Berg—Washington Irving copy).

DERIVATIVES

GREAT BRITAIN

EDINBURGH: Ballantyne
[~] The Magic Mirror. 1810, 1812. [Imitation by John Wilson: *see* 479S(1-2)]

LONDON: Sharpe
[~] Glenfinlas. And Other Ballads Etc. With The Vision of Don Roderick. (Westall engravings: *see* 341D).

EXTRACTS IN ANTHOLOGIES

59E] From *The Vision of Don Roderick* there are six extracts in the anthologies: 363E.3 366[1].7 370 385.2 388.5 471.7

ESSAYS AND POEMS

60A] First Printings: 1811

1] 'CURSORY REMARKS UPON THE FRENCH ORDER OF BATTLE, PARTICULARLY IN THE CAMPAIGNS OF BUONAPARTE.', pages 526-540 *541*;

2] 'ON THE PRESENT STATE OF PERIODICAL CRITICISM.', pages 556- 581;

3] 'THE INFERNO OF ALTISIDORA.', pages 582-599;

4] 'EPITAPH', pages 643-644, *in*:

The Edinburgh Annual Register, for 1809. Vol. Second—Part Second. Edinburgh: Printed by James Ballantyne and Co. For John Ballantyne and Co. Edinburgh; Longman, Hurst, Rees, Orme, and Brown, and John Murray, London. 1811.

Published 1 August 1811 in Edinburgh (*EEC*).

First Printings of Poetry: The letter [3] on the 'Inferno', signed 'Caleb Quotem, Argyle's Square, April 1', is in reality a humourous critique of the state of periodical criticism (that is, essay [2]), concluding with poetic imitations, in three 'fragments', of Crabbe, Moore, and Scott: [3a] 'The Poacher' (first words: 'Welcome, grave Stranger, to our green retreats'), [3b] Song (first words: 'Oh say not, my love with that mortified air'), and [3c] 'The Vision of Triermain'. The last, Scott's own imitation of himself, was later slightly revised to form the first 133 lines of Canto First of *The Bridal of Triermain* (*see* 68Aa). Of these verses only 3b was extracted, twice, in the anthologies: 360E.2, 419E.6

The 'Epitaph' [4] (first words: 'Amid these aisles, where once his precepts show'd'), the only entry bearing Scott's name, is headed: 'Designed for a Monument to be erected in Lichfield Cathedral, agreeably to the Bequest of the late Miss Anna Seward, to designate the Burial Place of her Father, The Rev. Thomas Seward, a Canon of that Cathedral, in which she is herself interred.' On reprinting Scott's inscription the *Monthly Magazine* (1 October 1811, page 291) observed that this 'costly monument, designed and executed by Bacon, will soon be placed in a recess of the northern transcept' and that the symbols upon it are reflected in the verse. Also included in this volume 'for a valuable consideration' is a reprint of *The Vision of Don Roderick*, pages *601-605* 606-635. As editor of the journal, as well as a silent partner with both printer and publisher, it is difficult to explain how Scott could arrange some further payment.

Copies: O; PPL TxU. References: (Magnum Opus Edition 1833: [1] and [2] not reprinted, but quoted with commentary in Curry (pages [1] 99-118, [2] 132-170, [3] 119-132); *The Poetical Works*, [3a] vi.375-381, [3b] vi.382, [4] viii.377-378.)

LETTER COMMENDING ALEXANDER MURRAY

61A] First Printing: 1812

No. X. *Letter from Walter Scott, Esq. Advocate, and one of the Principal*

Clerks of Session, to Principal Baird.', page 519 *in:*

The Scots Magazine, and Edinburgh Literary Miscellany, for July 1812. imprint for vol. 7:] Edinburgh: Printed for Archibald Constable and Company, By J. Ruthven and Sons. 1812.

Published ca. 1 August 1812 in Edinburgh.

Notes: This letter, dated from Edinburgh 25 June 1812, is one of thirty-four documents printed in support of the candidacy of the Reverend Alexander Murray as Professor of Hebrew and Oriental Languages in the University of Edinburgh. Copies: EP L. References: *Scott Newsletter* 16 (Summer 1990), 6-9. (Magnum Opus Edition: Not reprinted.)

ACCOUNT OF THE POEMS OF PATRICK CAREY

62A] First Printing: 1812

'ACCOUNT OF THE POEMS OF PATRICK CAREY, A POET OF THE 17TH CENTURY.', pages lxvii-lxxvi, *in*:

The Edinburgh Annual Register, for 1810. Vol. Third—Part Second. Edinburgh: Printed by James Ballantyne and Co. for John Ballantyne and Co. Edinburgh; Longman, Hurst, Rees, Orme, and Brown; and John Murray, London. 1812.

Published 6 August 1812 in Edinburgh (*EEC*).

Notes: This review includes a first printing of six poems by Patrick Carey, all later reprinted in Scott's edition of Carey's poems published in 1819 (*see* 131A).

Copies: L O; PPL TxU. Reference: (Magnum Opus Edition: Not reprinted.)

LINES ADDRESSED TO RANALD MACDONALD

63A] First Printing: 1812

[Lines addressed to Ranald Macdonald], pages 309-310 *in*:

The Monthly Magazine. No. 233. November 1, 1812. 4 of Vol. 34. [Volume title imprint:] London: Printed for Richard Phillips, . . . J. Adlard, Printer, 23, Bartholomew-Close, and 39, Duke-Street, Smithfield.

Published ca. 1 November 1812 in London.

Notes: These fifteen lines, beginning 'Staffa! sprung from high Mac-Donald', were written by Scott in an album at Ulva 18 July 1810 and there discovered by one J. T. Mayne of Trowbridge who, in his letter of 20 August 1812, transmitted them to the *Monthly Magazine* as perhaps constituting the 'idea' or 'foundation' for a forthcoming poem. Line 13 in this first state reads 'All thou lov'st, and all that love thee,'. This printing precedes by two years the variant text previously regarded as the first (Ruff 137: *see next entry*) and later adopted with this line omitted and other variants introduced.

Copies: E; T/B. References: *Letters*, ii.358-360. (Magnum Opus Edition 1834: *The Poetical Works*, x.356.)

REPRINT

GREAT BRITAIN

63R] LONDON: Rivington 1814
The Poetical Register, and Repository of Fugitive Poetry, for 1810-1811. London: Printed for F. C. and J. Rivington, No 62, St. Paul's Church Yard. 1814. Notes: Includes, page 231, 'Lines Addressed to Ronald[!] Macdonald Esq. . . . As an anthology this work is also entered as 408[2]E. Copies: L(2) NN. Reference: Ruff 137(listed as a first printing).

ROKEBY

If subject and scenery could have influenced the fate of a poem, that of "Rokeby" should have been eminently distinguished; for the grounds belonged to a dear friend, with whom I had lived in habits of intimacy for many years, . . . But the Cavaliers and Roundheads, whom I attempted to summon up to tenant this beautiful region, had for the public neither the novelty nor the peculiar interest of the primitive Highlanders. ('Introduction', April 1830, *PW*, ix.12.)

64Aa] First Edition, First Impression: 1813

ROKEBY; | A POEM. | BY | WALTER SCOTT, Esq. | [*short Oxford rule*] | EDINBURGH: | [*short Oxford rule*] | PRINTED FOR | JOHN BALLANTYNE AND CO. EDINBURGH; | AND | LONGMAN, HURST, REES, ORME, AND BROWN, LONDON; | *By James Ballantyne and Co. Edinburgh.* | [*Oxford dash*] | 1813.

Published 11 January 1813 in Edinburgh (*EEC*); issued 15 January in London (*MC*). £2.2.0. About 3000 copies. Binding: drab or grey-green boards with printed label. Paper: Demy 4° (285 x 225mm uncut). Watermarks: (first appear in sheet H) J Whatman | 1810 [1812]. Collation: a^2 b^2 c1 A^4 B-$2S^4$ 2T1 a-p^4. Pagination: *i* half-title, *ii blank*, *iii* title-page, *iv blank*, *v* dedication to John B. S. Morritt, Esq., *vi blank*, *vii* Advertisement, *viii blank*, *ix* Contents, *x blank*, *1* fly-title, *2 blank*, *3* 4-330 text, *i* fly-title, *ii blank*, *iii* iv-cxvi Notes, cxvi printer's imprint, *1* 2-3 'New Editions of . . . Walter Scott', *4 blank*. Printer's imprint: [*short Oxford rule*] | EDINBURGH: | Printed by James Ballantyne and Co. Typography: Page 81, with signature L, also oddly bears press figure 7. In some copies page number 39 is lacking and signature 2T (page 329) is missigned T.

Figures: b *vii*-1, *A4*-9 6-2/-, B10-6 12-12, C19-12 21-8, D26-10 28-2, E35-1/- 36-5, F44-7 46-12, G50-8 56-2, H58-12 61-7, I 69-6 71-12, K76-10 78-8, L81-7 82-1, M90-12, N*101*-5 103-2, O 108-12 110-6, P114-2 120-1, Q125-8 127-5, R130-12 132-7, S141-10 142-2, T147-10 148-1, U159-8 160-10, X163-5 164-7/-, Y171-7 176-8, Z178-10 181-2, 2A 189-7/- 191-10, 2B 197-2 198-5, 2C 207-6 208-1, 2D 215-8 216-7/-, 2E 218-6 220-8, 2F 226-7 228-1, 2G 234-7 237-12, 2H 245-6 247-12, 2 I 254-8 256-10, 2K 261-6 262-2, 2L 266-10 272-5, 2M 274-10 280-5, 2N 285-2 287-7/-, 2 O 293-5 294-10, 2P 300-7 303-2, 2Q 307-1 308-5, 2R 314-7 316-2, 2S 323-1 328-10, 2T—, a vi-5 viii-7, b xi-5 xiii-8, c xxi-2 xxiii-7, d xxx-6 xxxii-12, e xxxvi-6 xxxviii-5, f xliii-2 xlv-6/-, g li-8 liii-1, h lx-6 lxiii-5, i lxvii-2 lxix-10, k lxxv-5 *lxxvii*-12, l lxxxiii-8 lxxxv-2/-, m xci-5 xcii-6, n cii-1 civ-8, o cvii-12 cix-1, p *1*-12 2-5/- or 3-8/-.

Notes: Scott completed the first version of Canto I in July 1812 and a revision of this the following month. Though he was sending proof to Morritt, at Rokeby, as early as September, and about then forwarding the songs to John Clarke, in Cambridge, for musical renditions, he was greatly annoyed to discover that Longman in October was showing the first printed sheet to several literary friends in London, including Joanna Baillie. The Edinburgh publication was delayed until 11 January 1813, as Scott wrote Morritt the following day, in order 'to give the London publishers a fair start' (*Letters*, iii.224): the first intimation that publishers in both cities are now attempting to coordinate their issue.

In his commentary Scott once again refers to his other work, quoting at length first, pages vii-ix, the Hodgson account in the 1806 *Original Memoirs* (27A), then, pages xiv-xviii, the Somerville history he is now editing (93A). As on an earlier occasion for *Marmion* (*see* 28Aa), so again for this poem, the *Monthly Magazine* 1 October 1812 (page 243) soon disclosed the financial arrangement: 'The public opinion of the muse of Mr. Scott may be inferred from that of his publishers, who have agreed to give him three thousand guineas for this new production.' A month later (pages 309-310) this same journal cites 15 lines advanced by a correspondent as Scott's supposed 'foundation' for the poem (*see* 63A), and on 1 May 1813 (page 348) reports that, by then, 3000 copies had been purchased.

Along with the formal Longman notice on 15 January 1813, only four days after the Edinburgh issue, and now listing as well the receipt of illustrations by Stothard, the *Morning Chronicle* carried a further notice: 'A few copies of ROKEBY have been received by Mail, and may be had by applying to J. Murray, 50, Albemarle-street.' This special despatch by three-day mail-coach to an unlisted publisher could only benefit certain privileged clients, among them Lord Byron (*see* 81Aa). Meanwhile on the 25th (*MC*, 21 January, 'On Monday next'), ten days after the London issue, a music publisher announced the issue of five songs based upon *Rokeby* (64Dd), these not by Clarke, Scott's designated composer, but by one John Whitaker.

In their booklist of 'New Editions' Ballantyne and Longman now cite, for all previous poems, the separately produced illustrations by Westall or Cook, as well as the earlier Schetky issue, the two different portraits of Scott by Saxon and Raeburn, and a half-sheet map of the scenery of *The Lady of the Lake*.

Presentation copies: InU('Robert Southey from the Author. Jany.11. 1813' [in the recipient's hand]) NN('To Miss [Maria] Edgeworth from the Author') TxU('Miss [Sophia] Dumergue from her affectionate friend The Author')
Other copies: A AN* BCL(2) E(2) E(with Raeburn frontispiece portrait) ES LU O; CaBVaU CtY CtY* IdU InU(4) InU* MH NN(5) NNP* NNP*(Van Antwerp) NNU-W* OCl PU+ T/B* TxU(2) TxU*.
*With additional, undated 8-page 'New Books . . . by John Ballantyne.'
+Extra-illustrated with engraved title-page and one plate by R. Smirke dated 1823 (*see* 64Do).

References: Abbotsford, page 271(noted as presented to Scott's mother, but not inscribed); Grady, pages 260-302, 401-403; Ruff 119; Thomson, page 58; Tinker 1869; Van Antwerp(1) 11. (Magnum Opus Edition 1834: *The Poetical Works*, ix.5-7 8-353.)

64Ab] First Edition, Second (Large-Paper) Impression: 1813

ROKEBY; | A POEM. | BY | WALTER SCOTT, ESQ. . . . 1813.

Published concurrently with the previous impression. A 'very few copies'. Binding: blue-grey boards with maroon roan spine and printed label noting 'Twenty-five Printed.' Paper: Royal 4° (301 x 245mm uncut). Watermarks: J WHATMAN | 1810. Typography: Signature 2T (page 329) is now correctly entered but again, in some copies, page number 39 is lacking.

Presentation copy: CtY(Richard Heber [not inscribed, but with accompanying letter dated 4 January 1813, a week before issue]).

Other copies: L+; CtY NNU-W(Auchincruive). Reference: Ruff 120.
+Extra-illustrated with engraved title-page and six plates by Thomas Stothard, first issued 10 April 1813 (*see* 64Dp).

64Ac] Second Edition, First Impression, First Issue: 1813

ROKEBY; | A POEM. | BY | WALTER SCOTT, Esq. | [*short Oxford rule*] | THE SECOND EDITION. | EDINBURGH: | [*short Oxford rule*] | PRINTED FOR | JOHN BALLANTYNE AND CO. EDINBURGH; | AND | LONGMAN, HURST, REES, ORME, AND BROWN, LONDON; | *By James Ballantyne and Co. Edinburgh.* | [*short Oxford dash*] | 1813.

Published 8 April 1813 in Edinburgh (*EEC*); issued 15 April in London (*MC*). 14s. 6000 copies. Binding: blue-grey or drab boards and printed label. Paper: Demy 8° (224 x 145mm uncut). Watermarks: 1809 [1810] | 4; 1810 | 8; 1812 | 12; J Whatman | 1812. Collation: a^4 b1 A-2C^8. Pagination: *i* half-title, *ii blank*, *iii* title-page, *iv blank*, *v* dedication, *vi blank*, *vii* Advertisement, *viii blank*, *ix* Contents, *x blank*, *1* fly-title, *2 blank*, *3* 4-413 text, 413 printer's imprint, *414-416 blank*. Printer's imprint: [*short Oxford rule*] | Edinburgh: | Printed by James Ballantyne and Co. Typography: The Contents page is of a duplicate setting: short Oxford rule either 13mm or 18mm. In either setting the signature b may be lacking.

Figures: A8-1 10-12, B18-7 20-2, C36-5 43-10, D53-12 59-8, E75-7 80-1, F87-3 93-2, G107-10 109-1, H121-12 127-8, I 140-3 143-5/-, K153-8 155-12, L175-2 176-1, M179-5 192-6, N204-10 207-7, O 214-5 224-2, P226-3 240-1, Q246-10 256-6, R258-12 269-7, S283-1 288-5, T290-8 292-6, U313-5 314-12, X334-3 336-1, Y*339*-6 349-2, Z358-8 368-7, 2A 371-8, 2B 399-6 400-1, 2C 402-12 412-5.

Presentation copy: E('Miss [Christian] Rutherford from her Affectionate Nephew The Author'). Other copies: BCL E LU O; CtY InU OCl T/B. Sophisticated copy: IdU(sheets A, 2B-2C supplied from later editions). Reference: Ruff 121.

64Ad] Second Edition, Second (Large-Paper) Impression: 1813

ROKEBY; . . . THE SECOND EDITION. . . . 1813.

Published concurently with the previous impression. £1.8.0. Binding: drab boards without label. Paper: Royal 8° (253 x 158mm uncut). Watermarks: J Whatman | 1810; 1810; 1812. Figures: As for the previous printing except: A16-7, B29-10, I 143—.

Notes: When it was decided to issue, again for this poem, a large-paper impression, the type for sheets A-B had already been distributed and thus required a resetting. Apart from the distinctive press-figures, this new setting introduces a misprint in the stanza number page 6: previously IV, but now VI.

Copies: E+; CtY(*see* 260Ad[2]). Reference: Ruff 122.
+Extra-illustrated with 1813 engraved title-page and six plates by Thomas Stothard (*see* 64Dp).

64Ae] Third Edition (Second Edition, First Impression, Second Issue): 1813

ROKEBY; . . . THE THIRD EDITION. . . . 1813.

Notes: Sheets of Second Edition, First Impression, with the title-page altered to read 'THE THIRD EDITION'. The alteration must have been effected before the resetting for the large-paper 'SECOND EDITION' as the earlier press-figures for sheets A-B still appear (A8-1 10-12, B18-7 20-2) and the stanza number page 6 still reads 'IV.' One of the E copies is inscribed 'April 1813', the same month as the second edition.

Copies: AN BCL(2) E(2) O; CtY CtY*a InU PPL T/B*b TxU(3).
*With fore-edge painting of (a) Barnard Castle, (b) Greta Bridge near Rokeby (in Edwards of Halifax binding).

Reference: Ruff 123.

64Af] Fourth Edition: 1813

ROKEBY; | A POEM. | BY | WALTER SCOTT, Esq. | [*short Oxford rule*] | THE FOURTH EDITION. | EDINBURGH: | [*short Oxford rule*] | PRINTED FOR | JOHN BALLANTYNE AND CO. EDINBURGH; | AND | LONGMAN, HURST, REES, ORME, AND BROWN, LONDON; | *By James Ballantyne and Co. Edinburgh.* | [*short Oxford rule*] | 1813.

Binding: blue-green boards with printed label. Paper: Demy 8° (228 x 144mm uncut). Watermarks: 1812; J Whatman | 1812; W Balston | 1812. Collation: a^4 b1 A-2C^8. Pagination: *i* half-title, *ii blank*, *iii* title-page, *iv blank*, *v* dedication, *vi blank*, *vii* Advertisement, *viii blank*, *ix* Contents, *x blank*, *1* fly-title, *2 blank*, *3* 4-413 text, 413 printer's imprint, *414-416 blank*. Printer's imprint: [*short Oxford rule*] | Edinburgh: | Printed by James Ballantyne & Co. Typography: In some copies the page number '9' on page 349 is inverted.

Figures: A11-6 13-12, B18-5 20-2, C37-1 42-12, D56-12 59-2, E78-8 80-10, F94-5 96-1, G98-5 109-1, H126-5, I 141-6 142-12, K147-2 149-1, L168-2 175-1, M187-6 192-8, N203-2, O 210-6 212-12, P234-1 240-8, Q255-2 256-5, R261-6 270-12, S279-1 288-5, T290-2 296-6, U308-5 318-2, X334-5 336-1, Y341-8 351-3, Z366-1 368-5, 2A 377-6, 2B 399-2 400-12, 2C 404-10.

Copies: E O; CtY CtY* InU T/B TxU(2). Reference: Ruff 124.
*With fore-edge painting of Barnard Castle.

64Ag] Fifth Edition, First Issue: 1813

ROKEBY; | A POEM. | BY | WALTER SCOTT, Esq. | [*short Oxford rule*] | THE FIFTH EDITION. | EDINBURGH: | [*short Oxford rule*] | PRINTED FOR | JOHN BALLANTYNE AND CO. EDINBURGH; | AND LONGMAN, HURST, REES, ORME, AND BROWN, LONDON; | *By James Ballantyne and Co. Edinburgh.* | [*short Oxford rule*] | 1813.

Published 19 August 1813 in Edinburgh (*EEC*). 14s. Paper: Demy 8° (214 x 131mm cut). Watermarks: 1812 | 11 [12]. Collation: a^4 b1 A-2C^8. Pagination: *i* half-title, *ii blank*, *iii* title-page, *iv blank*, *v* dedication, *vi blank*, *vii* Advertisement, *viii blank*, *ix* Contents, *x blank*, *1* fly-title, *2 blank*, *3* 4-413 text, 413 printer's imprint, *414-416 blank*. Printer's imprint: [*short Oxford rule*] | Edinburgh: | Printed by James Ballantyne & Co. Typography: In some copies the page numbers '6' on page 86 and '9' on page 349 are inverted.

Figures: A5-1 7-5, B26-12 28-6, C36-6 38-5, D54-2 64-12, E72-5 78-3, F82-1 96-5, G98-12 105-6, H121-7 122-10, I 139-2 144-5, K148-8 150-6, L175-7 176-2, M191-3 192-1, N207-5 208-1, O 218-8 224-12, P235-8 237-1, Q255-3 256-5, R261-6, S279-1 288-5, T290-2 296-6, U310-3 320-6, X334-6 336-8, Y341-12 351-3, Z366-1 368-5, 2A *375*-5 384-2, 2B 387-1 396-12, 2C 402-3 *409*-1.

Notes: In their advertisements for this edition the *Edinburgh Evening Courant* and *Edinburgh Weekly Journal* both again (and for the last time) advise their readers of the editions of Scott now available, in order: the thirteenth edition of *The Lay of the Last Minstrel*, the fourth of *Minstrelsy of the Scottish Border*, the third of *Sir Tristrem*, the eighth of *Marmion*, the third of *Ballads and Lyrical Pieces*, the eighth of *The Lady of the Lake*, and the second of *The Vision of Don Roderick*. Scott's imitation of himself in *The Bridal of Triermain* is of course excluded from this listing.

As partly divulged by the figures, as well as the inverted page-number 349, sheets R-T, Z (pages 257-30, 353-368) are of the same impression as those in the fourth edition; sheets U-Y, 2A-2C (pages 305-352, 369-413) are reimpressed. The figure 12 on page 270 was dropped when the final pointing in the last line was altered from a comma to a semicolon.

Copy: T/B.

64Ah] Fifth Edition, Second Issue: 1813

ROKEBY; . . . THE FIFTH EDITION. . . . PRINTED FOR | A. CONSTABLE AND CO. AND | JOHN BALLANTYNE . . . . 1813.

Notes: Apart from the addition of Constable's name in the title imprint the only other variation appears to be, in some copies, an omitted press-figure on page 121. As Constable had belatedly secured a copyright share in this poem before the original issue of the fifth edition (*Letters*, iii.289) the altered imprint may simply represent a correction at press. However, in his *Scots Magazine,* Constable does not list this edition until the October number, some six weeks after the initial issue. Under his entry 126 Ruff notes in the *Morning Chronicle* for 11 December 1813 an advertisement for a large-paper 'Fifth Edition', but this appears not to have been issued.

Copies: E L O; CtY+ DLC+(2). Reference: Ruff 125.
+Extra-illustrated with 1813 engraved title-page and six plates by Thomas Stothard (*see* 64Dp).

64Ai] Sixth Edition, First Issue: 1815

ROKEBY; | A POEM. | BY | WALTER SCOTT, Esq. | [*short Oxford rule*] | THE SIXTH EDITION. | EDINBURGH: | [*short Oxford rule*] | *Printed by James Ballantyne and Co.*, | FOR | LONGMAN, HURST, REES, ORME, AND BROWN, LONDON; | AND | ARCHIBALD CONSTABLE AND CO., EDINBURGH. | [*short Oxford rule*] | 1815.

Issued 21 July 1815 in London (*MC*). 14s. Paper: Demy 8° (217 x 134mm cut). Watermarks: W Balston & Co | 1814; *none* [7, 8] | W Balston & Co | 1815. Collation: $\pi^4(\pi4+1)$ A-2C^8. Pagination: *i* half-title, *ii blank*, *iii* title-page, *iv blank*, *v* dedication, *vi blank*, *vii* Advertisement, *viii blank*, *ix* Contents, *x blank*, *1* fly-title, *2 blank*, *3* 4-413 text, 413 printer's imprint, *414-416 blank*. Printer's imprint: [*short Oxford rule*] | Edinburgh: | Printed by James Ballantyne & Co.

Figures: A5-9 7-1/-, B19-8 24-7, C41-1 42-13, D57-4 58-8, E66-4 80-3, F85-11 87-3, G105-1 110-4, H115-8 121-2, I 143-4 144-9, K150-3 160-8, L166-9 173-2, M186-3 189-7, N194-8 208-10, O 211-3 224-9, P232-9 234-1, Q251-11 256-7, R262-11 272-7, S274-11 288-6, T296-9, U310-4 316-3, X326-4 329-3, Y347-8 349-4, Z*355*-9 364-5, 2A 371-3 384-7, 2B 389-8 395-7, 2C 406-9 *409*-7.

Copies: BCL E+ GU O; CtY* InU PPL T/B+. Reference: Ruff 127.
*With fore-edge painting of Barnard Castle.
+Extra-illustrated with 1813 engraved title-page and six plates by Thomas Stothard (*see* 64Dp).

64Aj] Sixth Edition, Variant Issue: 1815

ROKEBY; . . . THE SIXTH EDITION. . . . 1815.

Collation: As determined by the press figures, the regular issue is here interspersed with remainder sheets Q, Z from the second edition, N, X from the fourth, and B-M, O-P, R-S, U from the fifth, all of these substitutes now designated in parentheses:

π^4[π4+1] A^8 (B-S^8) T^8 (U-X^8) Y^8 (Z^8) 2A-2C^8. So constituted, this mixed issue still represents a continuous text, with pagination as before.
Figures: Substitute sheets from other editions are again represented here by a parenthesis. A5-9 7-1, (B26-12 28-6, C36-6 38-5, D54-2 64-12, E72-5 78-3, F82-1 96-5, G98-12 105-6, H121-7 122-10, I 139-2 144-5, K148-8 150-6, L175-7 176-2, M191-3 192-1, N203-2, O 218-8 224-12, P235-8 237-1, Q246-10 256-6, R261-6, S279-1 288-5), T296-9, (U310-3 320-6, X334-5 336-1), Y347-8 349-4, (Z358-8 368-7), 2A 371-3 384-7, 2B 389-8 395-7, 2C 406-9 *409*-7.

Notes: Ruff, in describing this copy, wrongly indicates that it is made up of sheets from the fifth and sixth editions only: a matter clarified here by reference to the press figures.

Copy: CtY. Reference: Ruff 128.

64Ak] Seventh Edition (Reissue of *Poetical Works*): 1821

ROKEBY; | A POEM. | BY | SIR WALTER SCOTT, BART. | [*short reversed Oxford rule*] | SEVENTH EDITION. | EDINBURGH: | PRINTED FOR ARCHIBALD CONSTABLE AND CO. EDINBURGH; | AND LONGMAN, HURST, REES, ORME, AND BROWN, LONDON. | [*dash*] | 1821.

Printer's imprints: (1) [*short rule*] | *Printed by James Ballantyne and Co. Edinburgh*.; (2) [*short rule*] | EDINBURGH: | Printed by James Ballantyne & Co. Typography: Some copies have imprint (1) repeated on page *iv*.

Notes: A variant issue of the first item in the 1821 *Poetical Works*, volume 8 (263A), with a new printed title-leaf, printer's imprint (1) on verso, and a resetting of pages 417-419.

Copies: E; CtY. Reference: Ruff 129.

REPRINTS

FRANCE

PARIS: Didot and Galignani
[~] Rokeby. 1821, 1826. (Collection of Modern English Authors: *see* 290R.[4A], [4C])

PARIS: Galignani
[~] Rokeby. 1829. (*See* 293R.10) Copy: not seen.

GERMANY

ZWICKAU: Schumann
[~] Rokeby. 1821. (Pocket Library of English Classics: *see* 302R.17-18)

UNITED STATES

BALTIMORE: Cushing
[~] Rokeby. 1813. (The Poetical Works of Walter Scott: *see* 303R.5)

BOSTON: Bedlington
[~] Rokeby. 1828. (The Poetical Works of Sir Walter Scott: *see* 304R.4)

64Ra] BOSTON: Bradford & Read 1813
[1] Rokeby; A Poem, By Walter Scott, Esq. Boston: Published by Bradford & Read. J. Maxwell, Printer. 1813. Pages: *i-viii, 1* 2-172, *1-3* 4-95. Notes: A variant issue of the first 1813 Philadelphia, Bradford and Inskeep edition (*see* 64Re[1]). Copies: MH MWA.

[2] Rokeby; A Poem, In Six Cantos. By Walter Scott, Esq. Boston: Published by Bradford and Read. William Fry, Printer. 1813. Pages: *i-viii, 1* 2-267. Notes: A variant issue of the second 1813 Philadelphia, Bradford and Inskeep edition (*see* 64Re[2]). Copies: MWA NjP.

64Rb] BOSTON: Waldo 1813
Rokeby; A Poem. By Walter Scott, Esq. Boston: Published by Henry S. Waldo. S. Etheridge, Printer. 1813. Pages: *1-9* 10-180, *1-3* 4-83. Notes: A variant issue of the Charlestown, Etheridge edition (*see* next enry).
Copy: RPB.

64Rc] CHARLESTOWN: Etheridge 1813
Rokeby; A Poem, By Walter Scott, Esq. Charlestown, Published by S. Etheridge, Jun. Sold by C. Williams, H. S. Waldo, Cummings & Hilliard, West & Richardson, and William Wells, Boston. 1813. Pages: *1-9* 10-180, *1-3* 4-83. Copies: E; CtY MB MWA T/B ViU. Reference: Kohler (1) 13 (with illustration).

FREDERICKSBURG: Withers
[~] Rokeby. 1824. (The Poetical Works of Sir Walter Scott: *see* 310R)

64Rd] NEW YORK: Eastburn 1818
Rokeby: A Poem. By Walter Scott, Esq. New-York: Published by J. Eastburn and Co. Literary-Rooms, Broadway. 1818. Pages: *i-viii, 9-11* 12-300. Notes: With engraved frontispiece. (Also issued in The Poetical Works of Walter Scott, Esq.: volume 5. 1819. *see* 311R.5). Copy: NN.

64Re] PHILADELPHIA: Bradford and Inskeep 1813
[1] Rokeby; A Poem, By Walter Scott, Esq. Philadelphia: Published by Bradford and Inskeep, and Inskeep and Bradford, NewYork[!]. J. Maxwell, Printer. 1813. Pages: *i-viii, 1*

2-172, *1-3* 4-95. Copies: CtY InU MH MWA NN(Berg—Washington Irving copy) PPL.

[2] Rokeby; A Poem, In Six Cantos. By Walter Scott, Esq. Philadelphia: Published by Bradford and Inskeep, and Inskeep and Bradford, New-York. William Fry, Printer. 1813. Pages: *i-viii*, *1* 2-267. Copies: E(cover lists J. Maxwell as printer); CtY MH ViU(cover lists William Fry as printer).

DERIVATIVES

GREAT BRITAIN

64Da] ABERDEEN: Davie 1813
To the Moon An Admired Song in the Celebrated Poem of Rokeby, by Walter Scott Esqr. . . Aberdeen, Published by James Davie at his Musical Repository Union St. [ca.1813]. Pages: 1-4. Notes: Engraved sheet music. Words from canto 1, stanza 33 (first words: 'Hail to thy cold clouded beam, Pale pilgrim of the troubled sky!'). Music by John Ross arranged for voice and pianoforte. Price: 1/6. Copy: E.

64Db] DUBLIN: Tyrrell 1814
Rokeby; or, The Buccaneer's Revenge; A Drama; in Three Acts; Founded on Mr. Walter Scott's Last Popular Poem. . . . Dublin: Printed by W. H. Tyrrell, 17, College-Green. 1814. Pages: *1-5* 6-47. Notes: Drama by C. Pelham Thompson, with dramatic variations and additions. Apparently this is the only dramatic version to be printed in the 19th century. Copies: DT E; NN. Reference: Bolton 339.

64Dc] LONDON: Birchall 1813-1817
[1] Allen a Dale, . . . The Poetry from Rokeby, Written by Walter Scott Esqre. . . . No. 6. London, Printed & Sold by Rt. Birchall, No. 133 New Bond Street. [watermarked 1811. ca.1813.] Pages: *1* 2-9. Notes: Engraved sheet music with plate mark: 'Rokeby 6'. Words from canto 3, stanza 30 (first words: 'Allen-a-dale has no fagot for burning'). Glee composed by John Clarke arranged for voice and pianoforte. Price: 2/6. Copies: L O; MH. Reference: G/T 10745.

[2] "And whither would you lead me then?" quoth the Friar of the Orders Gray;—. . . . from Rokeby, Written by Walter Scott Esqr. . . . No. 5. London, Printed for Rt. Birchall, 133, New Bond Street. [watermarked 1811. ca.1813]. Pages: *1* 2-5. Notes: Engraved sheet music with plate mark: 'Rokeby 5.'. Words from Canto 5, stanza 27 (first words as title). Glee composed by John Clarke arranged for voice and pianoforte. Price: 1/6. Copies: E L O. Reissued on unwatermarked paper (MH-M). Reference: G/T 10746.

[3] Ballad A weary lot is thine fair Maid, The Poetry from Rokeby, Written by Walter Scott Esqre. . . . No. 1. London, Printed & Sold by Rt. Birchall No. 133, New Bond Street. [watermarked 1811. ca.1813]. Pages: *1* 2-5. Notes: Engraved sheet music with plate mark: 'Rokeby 1.' Words from canto 3, stanza 28 (first words: 'A weary lot is thine, fair maid,'). Ballad composed by John Clarke arranged for voice and pianoforte. Price: 1/6. Copies: L O. Reference: G/T 10754.

[4] Brignal Banks, Song & Chorus, The Poetry from Rokeby, Written by Walter Scott Esqre. . . . No. 7. London, Printed & Sold by Rt. Birchall, No. 133, New Bond Street. [unwatermarked. 1817 ms date]. Pages: *i-ii*, 1-11. Notes: Engraved sheet music with plate mark: 'Rokeby 7.'. Words from canto 3, stanzas 15-16 (first words: 'With desperate merriment he sung, The cavern to the chorus rung;'). Music composed by John Clarke arranged for voice with pianoforte. Another issue spells 'Brignal' as 'Brignall'. Price: 3/-. Copies: E L O; CtY. Reference: G/T 10747[dated 1814].

[5] The Cavalier, The Poetry from Rokeby, Written by Walter Scott Esqr. . . . No. 10. London, Printed for Rt. Birchall, 133, New Bond Street. [watermarked 1811. ca.1813]. Pages: *1* 2-7. Notes: Engraved sheet music with plate mark: 'Rokeby 10.' Words from canto 5, stanza 20 (first words: 'While the dawn on the mountain was misty and grey'). Music composed by John Clarke arranged for voice and pianoforte. Price: 2/6. Copies: L O. Reference: G/T 10748.

[6] The Cypress Wreath, The Poetry from Rokeby, Written by Walter Scott Esqr. . . . No. 2. London, Printed for Rt. Birchall, 133, New Bond Street. [watermarked 1811. ca.1813]. Pages: *1* 2-9. Notes: Engraved sheet music with plate mark: 'Rokeby 2'. Words from canto 5, stanza 13 (first words: 'O, Lady, twine no wreath for me, Or twine it,'). Music composed by John Clarke arranged for voice and pianoforte. The title-page notes that the piece is 'Respectfully Inscribed to Mrs. Walter Scott.' Price: 2/6. Copies: L O. Reissued on watermarked paper 1817 (E). Reference: G/T 10749.

[7] Edmund's Song, or The Harp. The Poetry from Rokeby Written by Walter Scott Esqr. . . No. 8. London, Printed for Rt. Birchall, 133, New Bond Street. [watermarked 1811]. Pages: *1* 2-9. Notes: Engraved sheet music with plate mark reading: 'Rokeby 8.'. Words from canto 5, stanza 18 (first words: 'I was a wild and wayward boy'). Music composed by John Clarke arranged for voice and harp or pianoforte. Price: 2/6. Copies: E L O. Reference: G/T 10750.

[8] The Harper A Glee for Three Voices with an Accompaniment for the Piano Forte as Sung at the Nobility's Concerts The Words by Walter Scott Esqr. . . . London, Printed for the Author [composer] & Sold by Rt. Birchall, 133 New Bond St. [watermarked 1811. ca.1813]. Pages: *1* 2-10. Notes: Engraved sheet music with plate mark reading: 'The Harper. (Glee)'. Words from canto 5, stanza 7 (first words: 'Summer eve is gone and past,'). Glee composed by T.R. Hobbes arranged for voice and pianoforte. Copy: L. Reference: G/T 10789.

[9] Matilda's Song, or The Farewell, from Rokeby, Written by Walter Scott Esqre. . . . No. 9. London, Printed & Sold by Rt. Birchall, No. 133, New Bond Street. [watermarked 1811. ca.1813]. Pages: *1* 2-6. Notes: Engraved sheet music with plate mark: 'Rokeby 9.'. Words from canto 5, stanza 23 (first words: The sound of Rokeby's woods I hear'). Music composed by John Clarke arranged for voice and harp or pianoforte. Price: 1/6. Copies: L O. Reference: G/T 10751.

[10] My harp Alone, A Song, Written by Walter Scott Esqre. . . . London, Printed & Sold for the Author [composer], by Rt. Birchall, 133, New Bond Street . . . . [watermarked 1813]. Pages: *1* 2-7. Notes: Engraved sheet-music with plate mark: 'My harp alone.' Words from canto 5, stanza 18 (first words: 'I was a wild and wayward boy,'). Music composed by T. R. Hobbes arranged for voice and pianoforte. Copy: L. Reference: G/T 10790.

[11] Song To the Moon, The Poetry from Rokeby, Written by Walter Scott Esqre. . . . No. 4. London, Printed & Sold by Rt. Birchall, No. 133, New Bond Street. [watermarked 1811. ca.1813]. Pages: *1* 2-7. Notes: Engraved sheet music with plate mark: 'Rokeby 4.'. Words from canto 1, stanza 33 (first words: 'Hail to thy cold and clouded beam'). Music composed by John Clarke arranged for voice and pianoforte. Price: 2/6. Copies: L O. Reference: G/T 10752.

[12] Summer eve is gone and past, The Harper's Song in Rokeby, Written by Walter Scott Esqr. . . . No. 3. London, Printed for Rt. Birchall 133 New Bond Street. [watermarked 1811. ca.1813]. Pages: *1* 2-5. Notes: Engraved sheet music with plate mark: 'Rokeby 3.'. Words from canto 5, stanza 7 (first words: 'Summer eve is gone and past, / Summer dew is falling fast;'). Music composed by John Clarke arranged for voice and harp or pianoforte. Price: 1/6. Copies: E(2) L O. Reissued on unwatermarked paper (L). Reference: G/T 10753.

64Dd] LONDON: Button and Whitaker 1813

Note: Five of the songs (each here starred in the Notes entry) were published 25 January 1813 (*MC* 21, 28 January), with an indication that 'the rest of the Songs' would be issued 'in a few days'.

[1] Allen-a-Dale, The Poetry from The Celebrated Poem, Rokeby, Written by Walter Scott, Esqr. . . . London Published by Button & Whitaker, 75. St. Paul's Church-Yard. [watermarked 1809. 1813]. Pages: *1* 2-4. Notes: *Engraved sheet music with plate mark 'Allen-a-Dale'. Words from canto 3, stanza 30 (first words: 'Allen-a-Dale has no faggot for burning,'). Music composed by John Whitaker arranged for voice and harp or pianoforte. Price: 1/6. Copy: L. Reference: G/T 10840.

[2] The Cavalier, The Poetry from The Celebrated Poem, Rokeby, Written by Walter Scott Esqr. . . London Published by Button & Whitaker, 75, St. Paul's Church Yard. [unwatermarked. 1813]. Pages: *1* 2-7. Notes: *Engraved sheet music with plate mark 'The Cavalier' within a frame. Words from canto 5, stanza 20 (first words: 'While the dawn on the mountain was misty and grey'). Music composed by John Whitaker arranged for voice and harp or pianoforte. Copy: NN-L. Reference: G/T 10841.

[3] A Collection of Popular Songs . . . London, Printed by Button & Whitaker, 75 St. Paul's Church Yard. [watermarked 1813]. Pages: *1* 2-25. Notes: Engraved sheet music within frames. Contains twelve songs of which the three by Scott have words from *Rokeby*, not so identified: [9] The Wandering Harper, pages 18-19; [10] The Cypress Wreath, pages 20-21; [11] My Harp Alone, pages 22-23. Numbers [9] and [11] were published separately (see under titles). Music for each composed by John Whitaker and arranged for voice and lute by M. Levien. Price: 6s. Copy: NN-L.

[4] Edmund's Song, "O Brignal Banks are wild & fair," The Poetry from The Celebrated Poem Rokeby, Written by Walter Scott, Esqr. . . . London Button & Whitaker, No. 75, St. Paul's Church Yard. [1813]. Pages: *1* 2-7. Notes: *Engraved sheet music. Words from canto 3, stanza 16 (first words: 'O Brignal banks are wild and fair,'). Music composed by John Whitaker arranged for voice and harp or pianoforte. Price: 2/6. Price: 2/6. Copy: L. Reissued on watermarked paper 1814 (L). Reference: G/T 10844.

[5] My Harp Alone! The Poetry from the Celebrated Poem, Rokeby, Written by Walter Scott, Esqr. . . . London Published by Button & Whitaker, 75, St. Paul's Church Yard.

[1813]. Pages: *1* 2-[incomplete]. Notes: *Engraved sheet music within a frame. Words from canto 5, stanza 18 (first words: 'I was a wild and wayward boy'.). Music composed by John Whitaker arranged for voice and harp or pianoforte. Also issued without separate title-page in *A Collection of Popular Songs* (*see* item [3] above). Copy: NN-L. Reference: G/T 10842.

[6] The Wandering Harper, the Poetry from the Celebrated Poem, Rokeby, Written by Walter Scott, Esqr. . . . London Published by Button & Whitaker, 75, St. Paul's Church Yard. [watermarked 1811. 1813]. Pages: *1* 2-3. Notes: *Engraved sheet music with plate mark: 'The Wandering Harper'. Words from canto 5, stanzas 7, 9 (first words: 'Summer eve is gone and past, / Summer dew is falling fast,'). Also issued without separate title-page in *A Collection of Popular Songs* (*see* item [3] above). Price: 1/6. Copy: L.

[7] A Weary Lot is Thine Fair Maid, The Poetry from The Celebrated Poem Rokeby, Written by Walter Scott, Esqr. . . . London Published by Button & Whitaker, 75 St. Paul's Church Yard. [watermarked 1809. ca.1813]. Pages: *1* 2-3. Notes: Engraved sheet music with plate mark: 'A weary lot is thine fair maid.' within frame. Words from canto 3, stanza 28 (first words as title'). Music composed by John Whitaker arranged for voice and harp or pianoforte. Copy: NN-L. Reference: G/T 10843.

[8] Wilfrid's Song, The Cypress Wreath, The Poetry from The Celebrated Poem, Rokeby, Written by Walter Scott, Esqr. . . . London Published by Button & Whitaker, 75, St. Paul's Church Yard. [unwatermarked. ca.1813]. Pages: *1* 2-3. Notes: Engraved sheet music with plate mark 'The Cypress wreath.' Words from canto 5, stanza 13 (first words: 'O Lady twine no wreath for me,'). Price: 1/6. Copy: L.

64De] LONDON: Clementi 1815
The Cavalier, The Poetry from Rokeby, Written by Walter Scott, Esqr. . . . London, Printed for the Author [composer], by Clementi & Compy. 26, Cheapside. [1815]. Pages: *1* 2-6. Notes: Engraved sheet music. Words from canto 5, stanza 20 (first words: 'While the dawn on the mountain was misty and gray'). Music composed by James Hunter arranged for voice and harp or pianoforte. Price: 1s.6d. Copy: L. Reference: G/T 10793.

64Df] LONDON: Clementi, Banger, Collard, Davis and Collard 1813-1815
[1] The brave Cavalier, that fights for the Crown. Song from Rokeby, A New Poem, Written by Walter Scott, Esqr. . . . London, Printed by Clementi, Banger, Collard, Davis, & Collard, 26, Cheapside. [watermarked 1811]. Pages: *1* 2-7. Notes: Engraved sheet music. Words from canto 5, stanza 20 (first words: 'While the dawn on the mountain was misty and grey'). Music composed by Samuel Webbe, Jr. arranged for voice and pianoforte. Price: 2s. Copies: L; NN NN-L. Reference: G/T 10838.

[2] My Harp alone, Song from the New Poem of Rokeby, by Walter Scott, Esqr. . . . London, Printed by Clementi, Banger, Collard, Davis, & Collard, 26, Cheapside. [watermarked 1814 or 1815]. Pages: *i-ii*, 1-7. Notes: Engraved sheet music. Words from canto 5, stanza 18 (first words: 'I was a wild and wayward boy my childhood scorned each childish toy'). Music composed by Samuel Webbe, Jr. arranged for voice and harp or pianoforte. Price: 2s. Copies: E L; MH NN-L. Reference: G/T 10839.

64Dg] LONDON: Dale 1813

[1] Allen-a-Dale, From the Celebrated Poem Rokeby Written by Walter Scott Esqr. . . . London, Printed for & Sold by W. Dale 8, Poultry. [unwatermarked. ca.1813]. Pages: *1* 2-3. Notes: Engraved sheet music. Words from canto 3, stanza 30 (first words: 'Allen-a-dale has no fagot for burning,'). Music composed by John Addison arranged for voice and pianoforte. Price: 1/6. Copy: L. Reference: G/T 10733.

[2] The Sound of Rokeby's wood I hear The Poetry from Rokeby, Written by Walter Scott Esqre. . . . London, Printed for & Sold by W. Dale 8, Poultry. [unwatermarked. ca.1813]. Pages: 1-3. Notes: Engraved sheet music. Words from canto 5, stanza 23 (first words as title). Music composed by John Addison arranged for voice and pianoforte. Price: 1/6. Copy: L. Reference: G/T 10734.

[3] Summer Eve is Gone and Past, The Harper's Song in Rokeby, Written by Walter Scott Esqre. . . . London Printed for & Sold by W. Dale 8, Poultry. [watermarked 1809. ca.1813]. Pages *1* 2-3. Notes: Engraved sheet music. Words from canto 5, stanzas 7 and 9 (first words as title). Music composed by John Addison arranged for voice and pianoforte. Price: 1/6. Copy: L.

[4] A Weary Lot is Thine Fair Maid, The Poetry from Rokeby, Written by Walter Scott Esqre. . . . London, Printed for & Sold by W. Dale 8, Poultry. [watermarked 1809. ca.1813]. Pages: 1-3. Notes: Engraved sheet music. Words from canto 3, stanza 28 (first words as title). Music composed by John Addison arranged for voice and pianoforte. Price: 1/6. Copy: L. Reference: G/T 10735.

64Dh] LONDON: Falkner and Christmas 1813-1815

[1] [Allen A Dale. Notes: Music composed by William Edward Heather.] Copy: not seen. Reference: G/T 10787.

[2] "Brignall[!] banks are Wild and Fair," Song and Chorus, from Rokeby, Written by Walter Scott Esqr. . . . London, Published by Falkner & Christmas, at the Opera Saloon, 9, Pall Mall. Of whom may be had Allen a dale, The Harp, . . . [watermarked 1812 or 1813]. Pages: *i-ii*, 1-10. Notes: Engraved sheet music with plate mark 'Brignal Banks'. Words from Canto 3, stanzas 16-17 (first words: 'O Brignal banks are wild and fair,'). Music composed by William Edward Heather arranged for voice and harp or pianoforte. Price: 3s. Copies: L; NN-L. Reference: G/T 10783.

[3] [The Cavalier. Notes: Music composed by William Edward Heather.] Copy: not seen. Reference: G/T 10787.

[4] The Cypress Wreath, Wilfred Wycliffe's Song From the admired Poem of Rokeby Written by Walter Scott Esqr. . . . London Published by Falkner & Christmas (late M. Kelly) 9 Pall Mall. Of whom may be had Allen a Dale, The Harp, . . . [watermarked 1812.] Pages: *1* 2-9. Notes: Engraved sheet music with plate mark: 'Cypress Wreath. Rokeby'. Words from canto 5, stanza 13 (first words: 'O, Lady, twine no wreath for me'). Music composed by William Edward Heather arranged for voice and harp or pianoforte. Price: 3s. Copies: E L. Reference: G/T 10784.

[5] [The Harp Song. Notes: Music composed by William Edward Heather.] Copy: not seen. Reference: G/T 10787.

[6] The Harp, Third Song, From Canto Five of Walter Scott's Popular Poem of Rokeby, . . .

London, Printed by Falkner & Christmas (Late M. Kelly) 9, Pall Mall. Where may be had all the Songs from the above poem by the same Author. [watermarked 1812]. Pages: *i-ii*, 1-7. Notes: Engraved sheet music. Words from canto 5, stanza 18 (first words: 'I was a wild and wayward boy, My childhood scorn'd each childish toy;'). Music composed by William Edward Heather arranged for voice and 'with an accompanyment[!] expressly for Harp or Piano Forte, and respectfully inscribed to Walter Scott Esqr.' (*see* 529T). Price: 3s./. Copies: E; NN-L.

[7] [Matilda's Song. Notes: Music composed by William Edward Heather.] Copy: not seen. Reference: G/T 10787.

[8] Song to the Moon, From the admired Poem of Rokeby, Written by Walter Scott Esqr. . . London Published by Falkner & Christmas, (Late M. Kelly) 9, Pall Mall. Where may be had Allen a Dale, The Harp, . . . [watermarked 1812]. Pages: 1-4. Notes: Engraved sheet music with plate mark 'Moon Song Rokeby'. Words from canto 1, stanza 33 (first words: 'Hail! to thy cold and clouded beam'). Music composed by William Edward Heather arranged for voice and harp or pianoforte. Price: 1s./6. Copies: E L. Reference: G/T 10785.

[9] "The tear down Childhood's cheek that flows." A Beautiful Simile, From Walter Scott's Poem of Rokeby, . . . London Published by Falkner & Christmas (Late M. Kelly) 9 Pall Mall. watermarked 1812]. Pages: 1-3. Notes: Engraved sheet music. Words from canto 4, stanza 11 (first words as title). Music composed by John Parry arranged for vocal duet, pianoforte, and flute. Price 1s./6. Copy: L. Reference: G/T 10818.

[10] A Weary Lot is Thine Fair Maid, From Walter Scott's Poem of Rokeby, . . . London Published by Falkner & Christmas at the Opera Saloon Pall Mall. Where may be had Allen a Dale . . . [watermarked 1812]. Pages: *i-ii*, 1-4. Notes: Engraved sheet music with plate mark 'A weary lot'. Words from canto 3, stanza 28 (first words as title). Music composed by William Edward Heather arranged for voice and harp or pianoforte. Price: 2s./. Copies: E L; NN-L. Some copies appear to be an unwatermarked reissue, ca.1820. Reference: G/T 10786.

64Di] LONDON: Goulding 1814-1818

The Harp, From the celebrated Poem, Rokeby, Written by Walter Scott Esqr. . . . London, Printed by Goulding & Co. 20, Soho Square, & to be had at 7, Westmorland St. Dublin. [watermarked 1811. ca.1814]. Pages: *1* 2-3. Notes: Engraved sheet music with caption title, plate mark 'The Harp.', lower right corner page *1* initialed 'M' by the composer. Words from canto 5, stanza 18 (first words: 'I was a wild and wayward boy'). Music composed by Joseph Mazzinghi arranged for voice and harp. Copy: MH. Reissued with watermark 1818 (O).

64Dj] LONDON: Goulding and D'Almaine 1825

And Whither would you lead me? London: Goulding, D'Almaine & Co. (ca.1825). Notes: Glee composed by Joseph Mazzinghi.] Copy: not seen. Reference: G/T 10813.

64Dk] LONDON: Goulding, D'Almaine, Potter 1813-1820

[1] Allen A Dale, from the Celebrated Poem Rokeby Written by Walter Scott Esqr. . . London. Printed by Goulding D'Almaine, Potter & Co. 20, Soho Square and 7. Westmorland Street, Dublin. [watermarked 1810. ca.1813]. Pages: *i-ii*, 1-5. Notes: Engraved sheet

music with plate number: '108'. Words from canto 3, stanza 30 (first words: 'Allen-a-Dale has no fagot for burning,'). Music composed by J. A. Stevenson arranged for three voices. Copy: E.

[2] And wither would you lead me then. From the Celebrated Poem Rokeby Written by Walter Scott Esqr. . . London, Printed by Goulding, D'Almaine, Potter & Co, 20, Soho Square & 7, Westmorland Street, Dublin. [watermarked 1811. ca.1813]. Pages: *1* 2-7. Notes: Engraved sheet music with plate mark: 'And whither &c.' as well as the composer's usual initial in ink below imprint. Words from canto 5, stanza 27 (first words as title). Music by Joseph Mazzinghi arranged for voice and pianoforte. Price: 2/6. Copies: E; MH.

[3] The Cypress Wreath, A Canzonet, The Words from Rokeby, By W. Scott Esqr. . . . London, Printed by Messrs. Goulding, D'Almaine, Potter & Co., 20, Soho Square, and 7, Westmorland Strt, Dublin. [watermarked 1811. ca.1813]. Pages: *1-2* 3-7. Notes: Engraved sheet music with plate mark 'Cypress wreath, S.J.S.', L copy with inscribed date 1814. Words from canto 5, stanza 13 (first words: 'O Lady twine no wreath for me'). Music composed by John Stevenson arranged for voice and pianoforte. Copy: L.

[4] The Cypress Wreath. From the Celebrated Poem Rokeby Written by Walter Scott Esqr. . . . London, Printed by Messrs. Goulding, D'Almaine, Potter & Co., No. 20, Soho Square, and 7, Westmorland Street, Dublin. [watermarked 1811. ca.1813]. Pages: *1* 2-9. Notes: Engraved sheet music with plate mark 'The Cypress wreath'. Words from canto 5, stanza 13 (first words: 'O Lady, twine no wreath for me'). Music composed by Joseph Mazzinghi arranged for voice and pianoforte. Price: 3/. Copies: MH NN-L NNP. Reissued on unwatermarked paper (L). References: G/T 10808; Van Antwerp(2) 42e.

[5] The Cypress Wreath from the Celebrated Poem Rokeby Written by Walter Scott Esqr. . . London, Printed by Messrs. Goulding, D'Almaine, Potter & Co. No. 20, Soho Square and to be had at 7. Westmorland Street, Dublin. [watermarked 1820]. Pages: *1* 2-9. Notes: Engraved sheet music with imprint altered by engraving 'to be had at' on last line in space between 'Entd. at Stat. Hall.' and '7, Westmorland Street, Dublin'. Words from canto 5, stanza 13 (first words: 'O, Lady, twine no wreath for me'). Music composed by John Stevenson arranged for voice and pianoforte. Copy: E. Reference: G/T 10833.

[6] [The Harper's First Song. London: Goulding, D'Almaine, Potter & Co. Notes: Music composed by Joseph Mazzinghi.] Copy: not seen. Reference: G/T 10810.

[7] The Harper's Second Song. From the Celebrated Poem Rokeby Written by Walter Scott Esqr. . . . London, Printed by Messrs. Goulding, D'Almaine, Potter & Co 20, Soho Square and 7, Westmorland Strt. Dublin. [watermarked 1811. ca.1815]. Pages: *i-ii,* 1-5. Notes: Engraved sheet music, 'No.2.' at head of title, with plate mark 'The Harper's (Second) Song' and the composer's initial 'M' in ink on title-page lower outer corner. Words from canto 5, stanza 9 (first words: 'I have a song of war for Knight,'). Music composed by Joseph Mazzinghi arranged for voice and harp. Price: 2/6. Copy: MH.

[8] O Brignal banks are wild and fair. From the Celebrated Poem Rokeby Written by Walter Scott Esqr. . . . London. Printed by Messrs. Goulding, D'Almaine, Potter & Co. 20, Soho Square and No. 7, Westmorland Strt. Dublin. [watermarked 1811. ca.1815]. Pages: *1* 2-11. Notes: Engraved sheet music with plate mark 'O Brignal Banks' and the composer's initial 'M' in ink on title-page lower outer corner. Words from canto 3, stanzas 16-18 (first words

as title). Music composed by Joseph Mazzinghi arranged for three voices and pianoforte. Price: 3/-. Copies: E; MH. Reference: G/T 10811.

64Dl] LONDON: Goulding, D'Almaine, Potter and Wood 1813-1815

[1] [The Harp. London: Goulding, D'Almaine, Potter and Wood (1815). Notes: Music composed by Joseph Mazzinghi.] Copy: not seen. Reference: G/T 10809.

[2] Let our Halls & Towers Decay, From the Celebrated Poem, Rokeby, Written by Walter Scott Esqr. . . . London, Printed by Goulding, D'Almaine, Potter and Wood, 20, Soho Square & 7, Westmorland Street, Dublin. [watermarked 1811. ca.1813]. Pages: 1-3 *4*. Notes: Engraved sheet music with plate mark 'Let our halls'. Words from canto 5, stanza 24 (first words as title). Music composed by Joseph Mazzinghi arranged for voice and pianoforte. Price: 1/6. Copies: L(2). Reference: G/T 10807.

[3] The Sound of Rokeby's Woods I Hear, From the Celebrated Poem, Rokeby, Written by Walter Scott Esqr. . . . London Printed by Goulding, D'Almaine, Potter and Wood, 20, Soho Square & 7, Westmorland Street, Dublin. [watermarked 1811. ca.1813]. Pages: 1-4. Notes: Engraved sheet music with plate mark 'The sound of Rokeby's'. Words from canto 5, stanza 23 (first words as title). Music composed by Joseph Mazzinghi arranged for voice and pianoforte. Price 1/6. Copies: L; NN-L. Reference: G/T 10812.

LONDON: Hawes

[~] For sheet music printed for William Hawes *see* LONDON: The Royal Harmonic Institution (64Dt).

64Dn] LONDON: Hodsoll 1813

[1] Allen A Dale from the Celebrated Poem, Rokeby Written by Walter Scott Esqr. London: Printed & Sold by W. Hodsoll, 45, High Holborn. . . . [1813]. Pages: *1* 2-3. Notes: Engraved sheet music. Words from canto 3, stanza 30 (first words: 'Allen-a-Dale has no faggot for burning'). Music composed by William Russell arranged for voice and pianoforte. Price: 1s/6d. Copy: L. Reference: G/T 10823.

[2] The Cypress Wreath. from the Celebrated Poem Rokeby Written by Walter Scott Esqr. . . . London, Printed & Sold by W. Hodsoll, 45 High Holborn. . . . [1813]. Pages: *i-ii*, 1-4. Notes: Engraved sheet music. Words from canto 5, stanza 13 (first words: 'O Lady twine no wreath for me,'). Music composed by William Russell arranged for voice and harp or pianoforte. Price: 2s. Copy: L. Reference: G/T 10824.

[3] The Harp from the Celebrated Poem Rokeby, Written by Walter Scott Esqr. . . . London Printed & Sold by W. Hodsoll, 45, High Holborn. . . . [1813]. Pages: 1-2. Notes: Engraved sheet music, with caption title. Words from canto 5, stanza 18 (first words: 'I was a wild and wayward boy'). Music composed by William Russell arranged for voice and harp or pianoforte. Price: 1/6. Copy: L. Reference: G/T 10825.

[4] The Harpers[!] First Song from the Celebrated Poem Rokeby Written by Walter Scott Esqr. . . . London Printed & Sold by W. Hodsoll, 45, High Holborn. . . . [1813]. Pages: *1* 2-6. Notes: Engraved sheet music. Words from canto 5, stanza 7 (first words: 'While thus in peaceful guise they sate'). Music composed by William Russell arranged for voice and harp or pianoforte. Price: 2s. Copy: L. Reference: G/T 10826.

[5] The Harpers[!] Second Song from the Celebrated Poem Rokeby Written by Walter Scott Esqr. . . . London Printed & Sold by W. Hodsoll, 45, High Holborn. . . . [1813]. Pages: 1-'3'[5]. Notes: Engraved sheet music, with caption title. Words from canto 5, stanza 9 (first words: 'I have song of war for knight'). Music composed by William Russell arranged for voice and harp or pianoforte. Price: 1/6. Copy: L. Reference: G/T 10827.

[6] A Weary Lot is Thine, Fair Maid from the Celebrated Poem Rokeby Written by Walter Scott Esqr. . . . London. Printed & sold by W. Hodsoll, 45, High Holborn. . . . [1813]. Pages: 1-3. Notes: Engraved sheet music, with caption title. Words from canto 3, stanza 28 (first words as title). Music composed by William Russell arranged for voice and harp or pianoforte. Price: 1/6. Copy: L. Reference: G/T 10828.

64Do] LONDON: Hurst, Robinson 1823
[Rokeby. . . . London: Hurst, Robinson. 1823. Engraved vignette title-page and six plates dated 1823. Notes: Illustrated with engravings from R. Smirke.] Copy: PU [only one plate seen, in octavo format, inserted in a PU quarto (64Aa), marked for Canto 5, stanza 35].

64Dp] LONDON: Longman, Hurst, Rees, Orme, and Brown 1813
Rokeby A Poem in Six Cantos by Walter Scott, Esq. . . . London Published by Longman, Hurst, Rees, Orme, and Brown. 1813. Notes: Engraved vignette title-page and six plates. Title-page reads 'Illustrated with Engravings from Thomas Stothard Esq. R.A.'; all other plates titled 'Rokeby', painted by Thos. Stothard, published 10 April 1813. Listed 28 July (*MC*) in [1] folio, 25 proofs on India paper, £2.2.0; [2] 4° proofs on French paper, £1.16.0; [3] 8° prints, 18s; [4] 8° bound with the poem, £1.12.0. Separate issue copies: [1] not seen; [2] EP; [3] MH. Combined poem-plate issues: see 64Ab, Ad, Ah, Ai. Reference: Ruff 130.
Title-page with vignette engraved by John Pye. Plates:
[1] [page 23] with a two-line quotation from Canto 1, stanza 15 (first words: 'What carest thou for beleaguered York,'), engraved by Chas. Heath;
[2] [page 85] with a two-line quotation from Canto 2, stanza 21 (first words: 'With Monarch's voice forbade the fight,'), engraved by F. Engleheart;
[3] [page 129] with a three-line quotation from Canto 3, stanza 18 (first words: 'But, far apart, in dark Divan,'), engraved by Chas. Heath;
[4] [page 192] with a two-line quotation from Canto 4, stanza 25 (first words: 'Bertram, forbear!—We are undone'), engraved by W. Finden;
[5] [page 252] with a three-line quotation from Canto 5, stanza 28 (first words: 'She saw too true. Stride after stride,'), engraved by W. Lewis and C. Heath;
[6] [page 325] with a two-line quotation from Canto 6, stanza 33 (first words:'Full levelled at the Baron's head,'), engraved by Chas. Heath.

64Dq] LONDON: Mitchell 1815
[1] The Cypress Wreath, from the Poem of Rokeby, Written by Walter Scott Esqr. . . . London, Published at Mitchell's Musical Library & Instrument Warehouse, 159 New Bond Street, Opposite Clifford Street. [watermarked 1811. ca.1815]. Pages: 1-7. Notes: Caption title, No. 3. Engraved sheet music with plate number 405. Words from canto 5, stanza 13 (first words: 'O, Lady, weave no wreath for me'). Music composed by George Kiallmark arranged for voice and harp or pianoforte. Price: 2/6. Copy: L. Reference: G/T 10796.

[2] I was a wild & wayward Boy, from Rokeby, Written by Walter Scott Esqr. . . . London,

Published at Mitchell's Musical Library, 159 New Bond Street, opposite Clifford Street. [unwatermarked. ca.1815]. Pages: 1-3. Notes: Caption title, No.2. Engraved sheet music with plate number 406. Words from Canto 5, stanza 18 (first words as title). Music composed by George Kiallmark arranged for voice and harp or pianoforte. Price 1/6. Copy: L. Reference: G/T 10797.

64Dr] LONDON: Phipps 1813-1815

[1] [Adieu for Evermore. London: Phipps & Co. (1815). Notes: Music composed by William Hawes.] Copy: not seen. Reference: G/T 10780.

[2] The Cypress Wreath, A Favorite Song, . . . The Poetry from the Popular Poem, Rokeby, Written by Walter Scott Esqr. . . . London: Phipps [1815]. Pages: *1* 2-8. Notes: Engraved sheet music. Words of recitative are from canto 5, stanza 12-13 (first words of Recitative: 'The mournfull[!] youth, a space aside'). Price: 2/0. Music composed by William Hawes arranged for voice and pianoforte. Copy: L. Reference: G/T 10778.

[3] The Harpers (1st) Song, . . . The Poetry from the Popular Poem Rokeby, Written by Walter Scott Esqr, . . . London, Pubd by Phipps & Co., 25, Duke Street, Grosvenor Square. [1815]. Pages: *1* 2-4. Notes: Engraved sheet music, letters in parentheses in ink. Words from canto 5, stanza 7 (first words: 'While thus in peaceful guise they sate'). Music composed by Thomas Attwood arranged for voice and harp or pianoforte. Copy: L. Reference: G/T 10737.

[4] [My Harp Alone. London: Phipps & Co. (1815). Notes: Music composed by William Hawes.] Copy: not seen. Reference: G/T 10780.

[5] [O Brignal Banks. London: Phipps & Co. (1815). Notes: Music composed by William Hawes.] Copy: not seen. Reference: G/T 10780.

[6] To the Moon! A Favorite Song, . . . The Poetry from the Popular Poem, Rokeby, Written by Walter Scott Esqr. . . . London, Pubd. by Phipps & Co. 25, Duke St. Grosvenor Square. [watermarked 1811. ca.1813]. Pages: *i-ii*, 1-5. Notes: Engraved sheet music. Words from the 'Song To the Moon' in canto 1, stanza 33 (first words: 'Hail to thy cold and clouded beam,'). Music composed by William Hawes arranged for voice and harp or pianoforte. Price: [*space blank*]. Copy: L. Reference: G/T 10779.

64Ds] LONDON: Preston 1815

[1] Allen a Dale, a Song from Rokeby Written by Walter Scott Esqr. . . . London. Printed & Sold by Preston at his Wholesale Warehouses, 97, Strand. [1815]. Pages: *1* 2-7. Notes: Engraved sheet music with title signed 'W Gresham 195'. Words from canto 3, stanza 30 (first words: 'Allen-a-Dale has no faggot for burning,'). Music composed by William Gresham arranged for voice and pianoforte. Price 2s. Copy: L. Reference: G/T 10773.

[2] The Cypress Wreath, a Song from Rokeby written by Walter Scott Esqr. . . . London, Printed & Sold by Preston, at his Music Warehouses, 97, Strand. for the Author [composer]. [ca.1815]. Pages: *i-ii, 1* 2-9. Notes: Engraved sheet music with title signed 'W Gresham 20'. Words from canto 5, stanza 13 (first words: 'O, Lady, twine no wreath for me'). Music composed by William Gresham arranged for voice and pianoforte. Price: 3s. Copy: L. Reference: G/T 10774.

[3] [The Cypress Wreath. London: Preston, 1814. Notes: Music composed by Harriet Hague.] Copy: not seen. Reference: G/T 10777.

[4] The Harper's Song from Rokeby Written by Walter Scott Esqr. . . . London Printed & Sold by Preston, at his Wholesale Warehouses, 97, Strand. [1815]. Pages: *i-ii, 1* 2-5. Notes: Engraved sheet music with title signed 'W. Gresham 189'. Words from canto 5, stanzas 7 and 9 (first words: 'Summer eve is gone and past,'). Music composed by William Gresham arranged for voice and pianoforte. Price: 2s. Copy: L. Reference: G/T 10775.

[5] A Weary lot is thine fair Maid, A Ballad, The Words from Rokeby, Written by Walter Scott, Esqr. . . . London, Printed & Sold for the Author [composer], by Preston, at his Wholesale Warehouses, 97, Strand [1815]. Pages *1* 2-3. Notes: Engraved sheet music. Words from canto 3, stanza 28 (first words as title). Music composed by Charles Stedman Cobham arranged for voice and pianoforte. Price: 1s. Copies: L(2). Reference: G/T 10755.

64Dt] LONDON: Royal Harmonic Institution 1822

[1] "Allen A Dale," A Favorite Glee, . . . The Words from Rokeby, A Poem, by Sir Walter Scott. . . . London, Printed for the Author by the Royal Harmonic Institution Lower Saloon, Argyll Rooms, Regent St. [1822]. Pages: *i-ii, 1* 2-9. Notes: Engraved sheet music with composer's signature on title-page lower right, and with plate number 112. Words from canto 3, stanza 30 (first words: 'Allen a Dale has no faggot for burning'). Music composed by William Hawes arranged for voice and pianoforte. Price: 3/-. Copy: L. Reference: G/T 10781.

[2] Song, "To the Moon" from Rokeby, a Poem written by Sir Walter Scott, . . . London, Printed for the Author, by the Royal Harmonic Institution, Lower Saloon, Argyll Rooms, Regent Stt. . . . [1822]. Pages: *i-ii,* 1-5 *6*. Notes: Engraved sheet music with plate number 1138 and with composer's signature in ink at lower right of title-page. Words from canto 2, stanza 33 (first words: 'Hail to thy cold and clouded beam,'). Music composed by William Hawes arranged for voice and harp or pianoforte. Price: 2/0. Copies: L O.

64Du] LONDON: Shade 1824

O Lady, twine no wreath for me, . . . The Words by Walter Scott Esqr. London, Printed, by G. Shade, East Side of Soho Square. [ca.1824]. Pages: *1* 2-3. Notes: Engraved sheet music with plate mark 'O Lady twine.' Words from canto 5, stanza 13 (first words as title). Music composed by 'A Lady of Devonshire' arranged for voice and pianoforte. Copy: L. Variant issues with page *1* blank, but still retaining plate mark (L), with page 1 numbered and without plate mark (L) and, further, with imprint reading 'Printed for G: Shade' (CtY). Reference: G/T 10799.

LONDON: Tegg

[~] Jokeby, A Burlesque on Rokeby. 1813. [Parody by John Roby: *see* 497S(1-3)]

64Dv] LONDON: Walker 1816

[1] O Brignal Banks are Wild & Fair, A Song from the Poem of Rokeby, Written by Walter Scott Esqr. . . London Published by G. Walker Publisher of Books & Music 105 & 106 Gt. Portland Street. [watermarked 1815]. Pages: *i-ii,* 1-5 *6*. Notes: Engraved sheet music. Words from canto 3, stanzas 16-18 (first words as title). Music composed by John Ross arranged for voice and pianoforte. Copy: E.

[2] A Weary Lot is Thine, Fair Maid, . . The Words from the Poem of Rokeby, By W. Scott Esqr. . . London, Published by G. Walker, Publisher of Books & Music, No. 106 Gt. Portland Street. [watermarked 1815]. Pages: *i-ii*, 1-5 *6*. Notes: Engraved sheet music. Words from canto 3, stanza 28 (first words as title). Music composed by Louis Charles Jansen arranged for voice and pianoforte or harp. Copy: E. Reference: G/T 10794.

64Dw] LONDON: Wheatstone 1815
The Harper's Song, from Rokeby . . . London Published for the Author [composer] by Wheatstone & Co. 436, Strand. [1815]. Pages: 1-3. Notes: Engraved sheet music. Words from canto 5, stanza 7 (first words: 'Summer eve is gone and past,'). Music composed by Dr. Spiker arranged for voice and pianoforte. Price: 1/6. Copy: L. Reference: G/T 10831.

64Dx] LONDON: Willis 1825
Brignal Banks . . . London, Published by I. Willis & Co. Royal Musical Repository, 55, St. James's Street and 7, Westmorland St. Dublin. [1825]. Pages: *i-ii*, 1-11. Notes: Engraved sheet music with plate number 161. Words from canto 3, stanzas 16-17 (first words: 'Oh! Brignal banks are wild and fair,'). Music by Mrs. J. M. Miles for voice and pianoforte. Price 3s/. Copy: L. Reference: G/T 10815.

64Dy] LONDON: Wybrow 1820
The Cypress Wreath, Written by Sir Walter Scott, ... London Printed by W. & S. Wybrow, 24 Rathbone Place, . . . [1820]. Pages: *1* 2-3. Notes: Engraved sheet music. Words from canto 5, stanza 13 (first words: 'O, Lady twine no wreath for me'). Music composed by Maria Foote arranged for voice and pianoforte or harp. Copy: L. Reference: G/T 10759.

UNITED STATES

64Dz] BALTIMORE: Carr 1813-1820
[1] Allen a Dale from Rokeby Poetry by Walter Scott Esq Printed for J: Carr, Baltimore. [ca.1814]. Pages: 6-8. Notes: Engraved sheet music with caption title. Words from canto 3, stanza 30 (first words: 'Allen-a-Dale Allen-a-Dale Allen-a-Dale has no fagot for burning'). Music by Benjamin Carr arranged for voice and pianoforte. Price: 38 Cents. (Carrs Musical Miscellany in Occasional Numbers: 11). Copies: DLC MH. References: G/T 10743; Wolfe 1574 (cf. Wolfe 1687 and 1687A).

[2] [Brignall(!) Banks. . . . Printed for J. Carr, Baltimore. [ca. 1813]. Pages: 9-12. Notes: Music composed by Benjamin Carr. (Carrs Musical Miscellany in Occasional Numbers: 12)]. Copy: not seen. References: G/T 10743; Wolfe 1583 (cf. Wolfe 1687 and 1687A).

[3] [Brignall(!) Banks. . . . Baltimore (ca.1814). Notes: Music composed by Benjamin Carr. ('Four Ballads from the Celebrated New Poem of Rokeby:' 12). Reissue from the same plates as Wolfe 1583.] Copy: not seen. References: G/T 10743 [without 'new' in collective title]; Wolfe 1583A (cf. Wolfe 1687 and 1687A).

[4] Duett—the words from—Rokeby. "The Tear Down Childhoods Cheek that Flows". . . Printed for J. Carr Baltimore [ca.1814]. Pages: *1-3*. Notes: Engraved sheet music with caption title. Page *1* is blank. Words from canto 4, stanza 11 (first words: 'The tear down childhoods cheek that flows'). Music composed by Benjamin Carr arranged for voice and

pianoforte. (Carrs Musical Miscellany in Occasional Numbers. number 22). Price: 25 cents. Copies: PPL PHi RPB. Reference: Wolfe 1662.

[5] . . . Four Ballads from the celebrated Poem of Rokeby Written by Walter Scott Esq . . . . Printed for J. Carr, Baltimore. Sold also in Philadelphia at the Music Stores of C. Taws, South Third St. and G. Willig, South Fourth St. [ca.1814]. Pages: *1* 2-12. Notes: Engraved sheet music. A collected issue with the following statement at head of each title: 'No. — of Carr's Musical Miscellany in Occasional Numbers'. Comprises a second state of four Scott numbers (cited as 9 through 12). Music composed by Benjamin Carr. Copy: RPB. References: G/T 10743; Wolfe 1578. The Ballads:
(1) 'The Wandering Harper'. Pages: 2-3. References: Wolfe 1671, 1671A;
(2) 'A Weary Lot is Thine Sweet[!] Maid'. Pages: 4-5. References: Wolfe 1672, 1672A;
(3) 'Allen a Dale'. Pages: 6-8. References: Wolfe 1574, 1574A;
(4) 'Brignal Banks'. Pages: 9-12. References: Wolfe 1583, 1583A.

[6] [The Tear Down Childhood's Cheek That Flows. Baltimore: Carr (1820). Notes: Music composed by Benjamin Carr.] Copy: not seen. Reference: G/T 10744.

[7] The Wandering Harper From Rokeby Poetry by Walter Scott Esq . . . . Printed for J Carr Baltimore [ca.1813]. Pages: *1* 2-3. Notes: Engraved sheet music. Words from canto 5, stanza 7 (first words: 'Summer eve is gone and past Summer dew is falling fast',). Music by Benjamin Carr arranged for voice and pianoforte. (Carrs Musical Miscellany in Occasional Numbers: 9). Price: 25 cents. Imprint at foot of page 3. Copies: DLC MWA. References: Wolfe 1671 (cf. Wolfe 1687 and 1687A).

[8] [The Wandering Harper. Baltimore: Carr (ca.1814). Notes: Music composed by Benjamin Carr. (also in 'Four Ballads from the Celebrated Poem of Rokeby': 9). Reissue from same plates as item [5](1) above.] Copy: not seen. References: G/T 10743; Wolfe 1671A (cf. 1687 and 1687A).

[9] A Weary Lot is Thine Sweet[!] Maid from Rokeby Poetry by Walter Scott Esq . . . . Printed for J Carr Baltimore [1813]. Pages: *3* 4-5. Notes: Engraved sheet music. Words from canto 3, stanza 28 (first words: 'A weary lot is thine sweet maid A weary lot is thine to pluck the thorn'). Music composed by Benjamin Carr arranged for voice and pianoforte. (also in 'Four Ballads from the Celebrated Poem of Rokeby': 10). Imprint at foot of page 3. Price: 25 cents. Copy: MWA. References: G/T 10743; Wolfe 1672; (cf Wolfe 1687 and 1687A).

64Daa] BOSTON: Bradlee 1827
Brignal Banks, Song & Chorus, Poetry by Walter Scott Esqr. . . . Boston: Published by C. Bradlee, No. 164 Washington St. [ca.1827]. Pages: *1* 2-8. Notes: Engraved sheet music. Words from canto 3, stanzas 15-18 (first words: 'With desperate merriment he sung, The cavern to the chorus rung;'). Music composed by John Clarke for voice and pianoforte. Copies: E; CtY(3) InU MB MH(2) MWA PHi PPL.

64Dab] BOSTON: Graupner 1821
The Harper's Song. Words from Rokeby . . . . Boston: Published by G. Graupner, No. 6 Franklin Street. [1821]. Pages: *1*-2. Notes: Engraved sheet music and caption title. Verso of page *1* is blank with engraved music page facing. Words from canto 5, stanza 7 (first words:

'Summer eve is gone and past, Summer dew is falling fast;'). Scott is not cited. Music composed by Thomas Van Dyke Wiesenthal arranged for voice and harp or pianoforte. (At head of title: Cottage Melodies no. 1). Copies: DLC MH(2) MWA PPL RPB. Reissue from same plates as Wolfe 9896, with 'Sold by John Ashton, No. 197 Washington St.' added above imprint (MWA). References: G/T 10847; Wolfe 9896, 9896A.

64Dac] BOSTON: Hewitt 1829
Brignal Banks, Poetry by Walter Scott Esqr. . . . Boston, Published by James L. Hewitt & Co. at their Music Store No. 36 Market St. [ca. 1829]. Pages: *1* 2-4. Notes: Engraved sheet music. Words from canto 3, stanza 16 (first words: 'O Brignal banks are wild and fair, And Greta woods are green,'). Music composed by John Clarke arranged for voice and pianoforte. (*See also* New York: Hewitt, 64Dao). Copy: MWA.

BOSTON: Wells and Wait
[~] Jokeby, A Burlesque on Rokeby. 1813. [Parody by John Roby: *see* 500S]

64Dad] CHARLESTON: Siegling 1819-1828
[1] [Allen a Dale. From Rokeby. . . . Charleston, Published by J. Siegling, 69 Broad Street. (ca.1819). Pages: 1-2. Notes: Music in two issues: see next entry. Music composed by Charles Gilfert.] Copy: not seen. Reference: Wolfe 3030.

[2] [Allen a Dale. From Rokeby. . . . Charleston, Published by J. Siegling, 109 Meetings Street. (1828). Notes: The same as preceding entry except for address change in imprint.] Copy: not seen. Reference: Wolfe 3030A.

[3] [The Harper's Song. Words by Rokeby. . . . Charleston, Published by J. Siegling, No. 69 Broad Street. (ca.1821). Pages: 1-2. Notes: No publication number. Music composed by Thomas Wiesenthal.] Copy: not seen. Reissued with plate number '42' (not seen). References: Wolfe 9898 and 9898A.

64Dae] NEW YORK: Appel 1813
[1] Allen a Dale. From Rokeby. . . . New York__Publish'd by J. Appel, No. 208 Broadway. [1813]. Pages: *1* 2-3. Notes: Engraved sheet music with caption title. Page *1* is blank. Words from canto 3, stanza 30 (first words: 'Allen-a-Dale has no faggot for burning'). Music composed by Charles Gilfert arranged for voice and pianoforte with optional flute accompaniment. Advertised in *NYEP* of 1 October 1813 as 'just published.' Copy: RPB. References: G/T 10763; Wolfe 3028.

[2] The Cypress Wreath. From Rokeby . . . . New York __ Publish'd by J. Appel, 208 Broadway. [1813]. Pages: *1-3*. Notes: Engraved sheet music with caption title. Page *1* is blank. Lower margin of page *2* reads: 'E. Riley, engraver, 23 Chatham Street, N.Y.' Words from canto 5, stanza 13 (first words: 'Oh lady twine no wreath for me'). Music composed by Charles Gilfert arranged for voice and pianoforte. Advertised in *NYEP* of 1 October 1813 as 'just published, new music'. Copy: RPB. References: G/T 10764; Wolfe 3032.

[3] Farewell From Rokeby . . . . New York Publish'd by J. Appel, No 208 Broadway. [ca.1813]. Pages: *1-3*. Notes: Engraved sheet music with caption title. Page *1* is blank. Lower margin of page *2* reads: 'E Riley, Engraver, 23 Chatham St. N.Y.' Words from canto 5, stanza 23 (first words: 'The sounds of Rokeby's woods I hear, They mingle with the

song,'). Music by Charles Gilfert arranged for voice and pianoforte. Advertised in *NYEP* of 1 October 1813 as 'just published'. Copies: MWA RPB. References: G/T 10765; Wolfe 3037.

[4] [The Harp From Rokeby . . . . New York Publish'd by J. Appel, No 208 Broadway (1813). Pages: 1-4. Notes: Engraved sheet music. Words from canto 5, stanza 18 (first words: 'I was a wild and wayward boy,'). Music composed by Charles Gilfert. Advertised in *NYEP* of 1 October 1813 as 'published and for sale'.] Copy: not seen. References: G/T 10766; Wolfe 3040.

[5] The Harp From Rokeby . . . . New York Publish'd by J. Appel, No 208 Broadway [1813]. Pages: 2-4. Notes: The same as preceding entry except that the plates are imposed so that there is no page 1. Copies: MH RPB. Reference: Wolfe 3040A.

[6] To the Moon From Rokeby . . . . New York __ Publish'd by J Appel 208 Broadway [1813]. Pages: *1-3*. Notes: Engraved sheet music with caption title. Page *1* is blank. Words from canto 1, stanza 33 (first words: 'Hail to thy cold and clouded beam'). Music composed by Charles Gilfert arranged for voice and pianoforte. Advertised in *NYEP* of 1 October 1813 as 'just published'. Copy: RPB. References: G/T 10767; Wolfe 3070.

[7] A Weary Lot is Thine Fair Maid From Rokeby . . . . New York __ Publish'd by J. Appel, No. 208 Broadway [ca.1813]. Pages: 1-3. Notes: Engraved sheet music with caption title. Words from canto 3, stanza 28 (first words as title). Music composed by Charles Gilfert arranged for voice and pianoforte. Advertised in *NYEP* of 1 October 1813 as 'just published, new music'. Copy: RPB. References: G/T 10767; Wolfe 3084.

64Daf] NEW YORK: Bourne 1827

The Harper's Song Words from Rockeby[!] . . . . Published & Sold by Bourne, 359 Broabway[!] N York [1827]. Pages: *1*-2. Notes: Engraved sheet music. Words from canto 5, stanza 7 (first words: 'Summer eve is gone & past Summer dew is falling fast,'). Music composed by Thomas Van Dyke Wiesenthal arranged for voice and pianoforte or harp. Copy: MWA.

64Dag] NEW YORK: Dubois 1818

[The Harp. From Rokeby. . . . New York (Dubois, 1818). Pages: 1-2. Notes: Music composed by Theodore Marschausen. Probably reissued from the same plates used in Wolfe 5589.] Copy: not seen. Reference: Wolfe 5589A(not seen).

64Dah] NEW YORK: Dubois & Stodart 1829

O Brignal Banks are wild and fair. A Scotch Song Written by Sir Walter Scott . . . . New York Published by Dubois & Stodart No. 167 Broadway. [copyright 25 February 1829]. Pages: *1* 2-3. Notes: Engraved sheet music. Words from canto 3, stanza 16 (first words: 'O Brignal banks are wild and fair, and Greta woods are green,'). Music arranged by J. F. Hance for voice and pianoforte. Copies: MH MWA.

64Dai] NEW YORK: Firth and Hall 1815

Brignal Banks Poetry by Walter Scott, Esqr. . . . New York Firth & Hall 1 Franklin Square. [unwatermarked. ca.1815]. Pages: *1-3*. Notes: Engraved sheet music with caption title and plate mark '146' at center foot of each page. Words from canto 3, stanza 16 (first words: 'O Brignal banks are wild and fair, and Greta woods are green,'). Music by John Clarke arranged for voice and pianoforte. Copy: MH.

64Daj] NEW YORK: A. Geib 1815
[1] The Cypress Wreath. From Rokeby. . . . New York Publish'd by A. Geib, 9 Maiden Lane. (1815). Pages 3-4. Notes: Engraved sheet music with caption title, E. Riley identified as engraver at foot of page 3. Words from canto 5, stanza 13 (first words: 'Oh lady twine no wreath for me'). Music by Charles Gilfert. Copy: MH. Reference: Wolfe 3032A.

[2] [The Harp. From Rokeby. . . . New York, Published by A. Geib, No. 9 Maiden Lane. (1815). Notes: Music by Charles Gilfert. Reissue from same plates as Wolfe 3040 (64Dae[4]) with original pagination, and imprint altered as above.] Copy: not seen. Reference: Wolfe 3040B.

64Dak] NEW YORK: A. and W. Geib 1822
[The Cypress Wreath. . . . New York, Published by A. & W. Geib, 23 Maiden Lane. [ca.1822]. Notes: The same as 64Daj[1] except that this issue has a variant imprint. Copy: not seen. Reference: Wolfe 3032B.

64Dal] NEW YORK: J., A. and W. Geib 1818-1820
[1] Allen a Dale. From Rokeby. . . . New York: Published by J. A. & W. Geib, 23 Maiden Lane. [ca.1818]. Pages: *1* 2-3. Notes: Engraved sheet music. Words from canto 3, stanza 30 (first words: 'Allen-a-Dale has no faggot for burning'). Music composed by Charles Gilfert arranged for voice and pianoforte. Includes optional flute accompaniment. First reissue from same plates as Wolfe 3028 (64Dan), with imprint altered to read as above. Copies: RPB(2). Reference: Wolfe 3028A.

[2] [My Harp Alone. . . . New York. Pr. 63 cts. Published by J. A. & W. Geib, 23 Maiden Lane. (ca.1820). Notes: The same as following entry with variant imprint.] Copy: not seen. Reference: Wolfe 3874.

64Dam] NEW YORK: Geib and Co. 1816
My Harp Alone A Much admired song written by Walter Scott Esqr. . . . New York: Published by Geib & Co. No. 23 Maiden Lane. [ca.1816]. Pages: *1* 2-7. Notes: Engraved sheet music with plate mark 83. In two issues: see also preceding entry. Music composed by T. R. Hobbes arranged for voice, pianoforte or harp. Copy: MH. Reference: Wolfe 3878.

64Dan] NEW YORK: Geib and Walker 1829
Allen a Dale. From Rokeby . . . . New York: Published by Geib and Walker. 23 Maiden Lane. [ca.1829]. Pages: *1* 2-3. Notes: Engraved sheet music with caption title. This title exists in two reissues of Wolfe 3028 (*see also* 64Dal[1]). Words from canto 3, stanza 30 (first words: 'Allen-a-Dale has no faggot for burning'). Music composed by Charles Gilfert arranged for voice and pianoforte and with optional accompaniment for flute. Copy: not seen. Reference: Wolfe 3028B. Reissued in a variant state with price '25 cts' above imprint. Copies: RPB(2). Reference: Wolfe 3028C.

64Dao] NEW YORK: Hewitt 1829

Brignal Banks, Poetry by Walter Scott Esqr. . . . New York Published by James L. Hewitt & Co. at their Music Store No. 137 Broadway [unwatermarked. ca.1829]. Pages: *1* 2-4. Notes: Engraved sheet music. Page *1* is blank. Words from canto 3, stanza 16 (first words: 'O Brignal banks are wild and fair, And Greta woods are green,'). Music composed by John Clarke arranged for voice and pianoforte. (*See also* Boston: Hewitt, 64Dac). Copies: InU MH(2) MWA NN-L.

64Dap] NEW YORK: Mesier 1813

The Harper's Song. Words from Rockeby [!] . . . N. York Lithd. Published by E. S. Mesier 28 Wall st. [unwatermarked. ca. 1813]. Pages: *1-2*. Notes: Lithographed sheet music, noted at end as 'Corrected by D. McCarthy. Professor of Music.' Words from canto 5, stanza 7 (first words: 'Summer Eve is gone and past,'). Music composed by T. V. Wiesenthal arranged for voice and harp or pianoforte. Copies: MH(2).

64Daq] NEW YORK: Paff 1813

The Harp. From Rokeby written by Walter Scott. . . New York Published by John Paff. [ca.1813]. Pages: *1-3*. Notes: Engraved sheet music with caption title. Page *1* is blank. Words from canto 5, stanza 18 (first words: 'I was a wild and wayward boy'). Music composed by Theodore Marschausen arranged for voice and pianoforte. Copy: RPB. References: G/T 10805; Wolfe 5589.

64Dar] NEW YORK: Riley 1819-1828

[1] Brignal Banks The Poetry by Sir Walter Scott . . . . New York, Engraved Printed & Sold by, E. Riley, 29, Chatham Street [ca.1828]. Pages: 1-2 *3*. Notes: Engraved sheet music with plate mark centered at foot of each page.' Words from canto 3, stanzas 16-18 (first words: 'O Brignal banks are wild and fair And Greta woods are green,'). Music composed by John Clarke arranged for voice and pianoforte. Copies: MH MWA.

[2] The Harpers Song from Rokeby . . . New-York, Published by E. Riley, 29, Chatham Street [ca.1819]. Pages: *1-2*. Notes: Engraved sheet music with caption title. Words from canto 5, stanzas 7, 9 (first words: 'Summer eve is gone and past, Summer dew is falling fast'). Music composed by T. V. Wiesenthall[!] arranged for voice and pianoforte or harp. Copies: InU MH.

[3] Summer's Eve is gone and past The Harpers Song in Rokeby. New York, Engraved Printed & Sold by E. Riley, 29, Chatham Street. [ca.1820]. Pages: *1-2*. Notes: Engraved sheet music with caption title. Words from canto 5, stanzas 7, 9 (first words: 'Summer eve is gone and past Summer dew is falling fast'). Music composed by John Clarke arranged for voice and pianoforte. Copy: DLC.

64Das] NEW YORK: Willson 1812

The Cypress Wreath. From Rokeby. . . . New York_Publish'd by the Author No 62 Broadway [1812]. Pages: *1-3*. Notes: Engraved sheet music with caption title. Page *1* is blank. Words from canto 5, stanza 13 (first words: 'Oh lady twine no wreath for me'). Music composed by Joseph Willson arranged for voice and pianoforte. Price: 25 cts. Copies: MH RPB. References: G/T 10848; Wolfe 9980.

64Dat] PHILADELPHIA: Bacon 1818
Oh! Lady Twine no Wreath for Me. From Rokeby. . . . Philadelphia; Published by Bacon & Co., 11. South Fourth Street. [ca.1818]. Pages: *1* 2-3. Notes: Engraved sheet music with caption title. Page *1* is blank. Words from canto 5, stanza 13 (first words: 'Oh! Lady twine no wreath for me, Or twine it of the Cypress tree,'). Music composed by Thomas Van Dyke Wiesenthal arranged for voice and pianoforte. (At head of title: 'American, Musical Miscellany No. 6.' Some copies have the final 'l' in 'Musical' lacking and closed up.) Advertised in *NYEP* on 23 December 1818 as 'just published'. Price: 25 cents (or '25' only). Copies: InU MWA RPB(2). References: G/T 10846; Wolfe 9912.

64Dau] PHILADELPHIA: Blake 1813-1826
[1] Allen-a-Dale. From Rokeby, . . . Philadelphia: Published by G. E. Blake. [ca.1813]. Pages: *1-3*. Notes: Engraved sheet music with caption title. Page *1* is blank. Words from canto 3, stanza 30 (first words: 'Allen-a-Dale has no faggot for burning'). Music composed by Charles Gilfert arranged for voice and pianoforte. Copies: MH PPL RPB(3). Reference: Wolfe 3029.

[2] Brignal Banks A Song The Words by Sir Walter Scott, . . . Philadelphia, Published by G. E. Blake No: 13 south Fifth street. [unwatermarked. ca.1821.] Pages: *1* 2-3. Notes: Engraved sheet music with caption title. Words from canto 3, stanza 16 (first words: 'O Brignal banks are wild and fair, And Greta woods are green,'). Music composed by John Clarke arranged for voice and pianoforte. Copies: MH.

[3] The Cypress Wreath. From Rokeby. Written by Walter Scott Esqr. . . . Philadelphia, Published by G. E. Blake. [ca.1813]. Pages: *1-3*. Notes: Engraved sheet music with caption title. Page *1* is blank. Words from canto 5, stanza 13 (first words: 'Oh Lady, twine no wreath for me, Or twine it of the Cypress tree!'). Music composed by John Bray arranged for voice and pianoforte. Copies: DLC RPB. References: G/T 10739; Wolfe 1285.

[4] The Harper's Song . . . . Philadelphia: Published by G. E. Blake. . . . 1826. Pages: [single leaf numbered '41']. Notes: Engraved sheet music. Leaf has 'No: 4' at foot. Words from canto 5, stanza 7 (first words: 'Summer eve is gone and past, Summer dew is failing fast'). Music arranged by B F Peale for voice and spanish guitar. Copy: MWA.

[5] The Harper's Song. Words from Rockeby[!] . . . . Philadelphia, Published by G. E. Blake, No. 13 South 5th. street. [ca.1821]. Pages: *1-2*. Notes: Engraved sheet music with caption title and plate mark: 'Harper's song'. Verso of first page blank with pages facing. Words from canto 5, stanzas 7, 9 (first words: 'Summer eve is gone and past, Summer dew is falling fast;'). Music composed by Thomas Van Dyke Wiesenthal arranged for voice and pianoforte or harp. Copies: MWA RPB(2). Reference: Wolfe 9897.

[6] [My Harp Alone. From Rokeby. . . Philadelphia, Published by G. E. Blake, No. 13 South 5th Street. (ca.1818). Notes: Music composed by George Kiallmark.] Copy: not seen. Reference: Wolfe 4957.

[7] A weary lot is thine fair Maid! From Rokeby, written by Walter Scott Esqr. . . . Philadelphia: Published by G. E. Blake. [ca.1813]. Pages: *1-3*. Notes: Engraved sheet music with caption title. Page *1* is blank. Words from canto 3, stanza 28 (first words as title). Music composed by Charles Gilfert arranged for voice and pianoforte. Copies: InU MH PPL RPB. Reference: Wolfe 3085.

64Dav] PHILADELPHIA: Klemm 1823-1824

[1] The Harper's Song. Words from Rockeby[!]. . . . Philadelphia Published by John G. Klemm. [1824]. Pages: *1-2*. Notes: Engraved sheet music with plate mark: '277'. Words from canto 5, stanzas 7, 9 (first words: 'Summer eve is gone and past, Summer dew is falling fast;'). Music composed by Thomas Van Dyke Wiesenthal arranged for voice and Spanish guitar. Copies: InU MWA. Reference: G/T 10847.

[2] Oh! Lady twine no wreath for me. From Rokeby. . . . Philadelphia; Published by J. G. Klemm, No3 South Third Street. [ca.1823]. Pages: *1* 2-3. Notes: Engraved sheet music with plate number: '111'. Words from canto 5, stanza 13 (first line as title). Music composed by Thomas V. Wiesenthal arranged for voice and pianoforte. Price: 25. Reissue from the same plates as Wolfe 9912 (64Dat), but with the imprint altered as above. Copy: InU. Reference: Wolfe 9912A.

64Daw] PHILADELPHIA: Willig 1816-1823

[1] Allen A Dale from Rokeby . . . Philad. Pub. & sold by Geo. Willig 171 Chesnut St. [ca.1823]. Pages: *1* 2-3. Notes: Engraved sheet music. Words from canto 3, stanza 30 (first words: 'Allen-a-Dale has no faggot for burning'). Music composed by C. Gilfert arranged for voice and pianoforte. Copy: InU.

[2] The Harper's Song. Words from Rockeby[!] . . . . Philadelphia Published & sold by Geo. Willig 171 Chesnut Street. [ca.1823]. Pages: *1-3*. Notes: Engraved sheet music on either pink or white paper with caption title. Page *1* is blank. Words from canto 5, stanzas 7, 9 (first words: 'Summer eve is gone and past, Summer dew is falling fast;). Music composed and arranged by Thomas Van Dyke Wiesenthal for voice and harp or pianoforte. Some copies have imprint ending with 'St.' Copies: CtY InU MWA RPB(2). Reference: Wolfe 9899.

[3] [I was a Wild & Wayward Boy. From Rokeby. . . Philadelphia, Published and sold at G. Willig's Musical Magazine. (ca.1816). Pages: 1-2. Notes: Music composed by George Kiallmark.] Copy: not seen. Reference: Wolfe 4956.

[4] The Tear down Childhoods Cheek that Flows Duett The words from Rokeby . . . Philadelphia G. Willig 171 Chesnut St. [ca.1815]. Pages: *1-2*. Notes: Engraved sheet music. Words from canto 4, stanza 11 (first words: as title). Music composed by Benjamin Carr arranged for voice and pianoforte. Copy: MH.

EXTRACTS IN ANTHOLOGIES

64E] From *Rokeby* there are 52 extracts in 29 anthologies: 354E.3 355.3 356[2].11 357.3-4 358.11 360.4,6-7,12 361[1].3,7 367[1].3 369[3].1,6 369[4].1,6 373[1].1 376.2-3 378.6-9 382.2 388.4 389.2,7,10,25,27 392.10 405(3)[1].17 413.6,10,13-14 414.3-4 423.1 452.1 453.3 457[1].1 467[1-2].3 467[2].5,7 469.2,6 474.3 477.4.

MEMOIRS OF THE REIGN OF KING CHARLES THE FIRST

65Aa] First Scott Edition, First Impression: 1813

MEMOIRS | OF | THE REIGN | OF | King Charles the First. | [*short Oxford rule*] | BY | SIR PHILIP WARWICK, KNIGHT. | [*short reversed Oxford rule*] | EDINBURGH: | Printed by James Ballantyne and Co. | FOR JOHN BALLANTYNE AND CO., EDINBURGH; AND | LONGMAN, HURST, REES, ORME, AND BROWN, | LONDON. | [*dash*] | 1813.

Issued 9 February 1813 in London (*MC*). 12s. Binding: drab boards with printed label. Paper: Demy 8° (225 x 142mm uncut). Watermarks (indistinct): 1811 | 11; C | 1811 [1812, 1813]; C | 1812 | 5.

Collation: a^6 A-2F^8 2G^6. Pagination: *i* title-page, *ii blank*, *iii* facsimile of 1702 title-page, *iv blank*, *v* Contents, *vi blank*, *vii* viii-x Introduction, *xi*-xii Original Preface, *1* 2-387 text of *Memoirs of the Reign of King Charles I*, *388 blank*, *389* fly-title, *390 blank*, *391* 392-473 text of 'Memoirs, or Reflections on The State of Affairs after the King's Murder', *474* printer's imprint, *475* advertisement for two other works published by John Ballantyne, *476 blank*. Printer's imprint: [*short Oxford rule*] | EDINBURGH: | Printed by James Ballantyne and Co. Illustrations: Two engraved plates, a frontispiece portrait of King Charles the First and a portrait of Sir Philip Warwick facing facsimile title-page. Typography: Preliminary signature a is in italic.

Figures: *a vii*-2, A11-3, B19-3, C36-1, D64-3, E80-9, F85-8, G98-3, H115-2, I 144-5, K147-3, L173-7, M178-6, N206-7, O 223-2, P237-1, Q254-12, R270-2, S—, T298-5, U318-7, X323-9, Y350-10, Z359-12, 2A 383-2, 2B—, 2C 414-2, 2D 427-7, 2E 448-5, 2F 464-6, 2G 472-10 *475*-6.

Notes: Concerning his new edition Scott concludes (page x) that 'this authentic and curious book' preserves 'more personal anecdotes of interesting characters during the civil wars, than in any other work of the period.' An array of royalist figures are sharply portrayed, as well as Cromwell and Hampden. For such an evocative work about eighty footnotes are supplied, some of considerable length, and the book itself in its earlier edition was much used in the Somers' Tracts (38A).

The original sale of this edition may have been greatly enhanced by a report, two months after its issue, that the body of Charles I had been discovered (in Henry VIII's vault) at Windsor Castle on 1 April (*MM* 1 May 1813, pages 344-345). Shortly thereafter Scott received a lock of the King's hair and had a ring made for it.

Copies: BCL E(2); MB CaBVaU NN. References: *Letters*, iii.264 *passim*, 391. (Magnum Opus Edition: Not reprinted.)

65Ab] First Scott Edition, Second (Large-Paper) Impression: 1813

MEMOIRS | OF | THE REIGN | OF | King Charles the First. . . .1813.
Published concurrently with the previous impression. £1.1.0. Paper: Crown 4° (235 x 188mm cut). Watermarks: BUTTANSHAW | 1809. Collation: π^2 $2\pi^4$ A-3N[4] *3O* 1. Pagination as for the previous 8° impression, except that concluding advertisement is omitted. Figures: On same pages as before except for omitted figures on *vii*, 36, 98, 144.

Notes: Because of the larger size all pages were reimposed in a different format, differently signed, for 4° imposition, yet essentially retaining their previously assigned figures.

Copy: L.

MEMOIRS OF SIR JOHN RERESBY

66A] Projected Scott Edition: 1813

Notes: The advertisement, page *475*, *Memoirs of. . . King Charles the First* (65Aa) lists as 'lately published' the *Secret History of. . . James the First* (56Aa) and now also, to accompany these two issues: 'In the Press, and speedily will be Published . . . Memoirs of Sir John Reresby'. This further work, also presumably by Scott and based on the original 1734 edition already consulted by him for the Somers' Tracts (38A), was to be issued 'uniformly with the preceding volumes with Engravings, price 12s. in boards. . . . A few Copies of these works are taken off on Royal Octavo paper of the first quality, and carefully hot-pressed, price 21s. per volume.' Unfortunately this third book, though apparently far advanced in the press, was preëmpted in 1813, the same year as the advertisement, by a more extensive London edition titled *The Memoirs and Travels of Sir John Reresby*, containing some 40 portraits and views.

ON THE DEATH OF SIMON DE MONTFORT

67A] First Printing: 1813

'Ballad XXVIII. ON THE DEATH OF SIMON DE MONTFORT, EARL OF LEICESTER, AT THE BATTLE OF EVESHAM, 1266. (Literally versified from the Norman-French) BY WALTER SCOTT, ESQ.*' (first words: 'In woeful wise my song shall rise, My heart impells[!] the strain;'), pages 380-384 *in*:

A Select Collection of English Songs, with their Original Airs: and a Historical Essay on the Origin and Progress of National Song, by the late Joseph Ritson, Esq.

In three Volumes. The Second Edition, with Additional Songs and Occasional Notes. By Thomas Park, F. S. A. Vol. II. London: Printed for F. C. and J. Rivington; Longman, Hurst, Rees, Orme, and Brown; Lackington, Allen, and Co.; Cadell and Davies; C. Law; S. Bagster; J. Booker; Black, Parry, and Co.; J. M. Richardson; J. Booth; R. Priestley; R. Scholey; Cradock and Joy; R. Baldwin; and J. Major. 1813.

Published 20 February 1813 in London (*MC*); issued 8 March in Edinburgh (*EEC*).

Notes: In the preliminary 'Advertisement' in volume 1, Thomas Park, the editor of the second edition, reports (pages *6-7*) that 'more than a hundred songs have been added to the present edition', of which Scott's verse is the last in volume 2. The footnote in the title above refers to the late Joseph Ritson's 'desire' that this version be issued.

Copies: BCL E; CaBVaU CtY NN-L.

References: Ruff 188. (Magnum Opus Edition: Not reprinted.)

THE BRIDAL OF TRIERMAIN

68Aa] First Edition: 1813

THE | Bridal of Triermain, | OR | THE VALE OF ST JOHN. | IN THREE CANTOS. | [*short Oxford rule*] | [*six-line quotation from* Rime of Sir Thopas] | [*short reversed Oxford rule*] | EDINBURGH: | [*Oxford dash*] | *Printed by James Ballantyne and Co.* | FOR JOHN BALLANTYNE AND CO. HANOVER-STREET; | AND FOR LONGMAN, HURST, REES, ORME, AND BROWN; | AND GALE, CURTIS, AND FENNER; | LONDON. | [*dash*] | 1813.

Published 9 March 1813 in Edinburgh (*EEC* 8 March). 7s.6d. Binding: drab or blue-grey boards with printed label. Paper: Foolscap 8° (172 x 106mm uncut). Watermarks: none. Collation: $\pi^8(\pi8+1)$ A-F^8 G^8(±G5) H-O^8 P^4 *Q*1 *R*1. Pagination: *i* half-title, *ii blank*, *iii* title-page, *iv blank*, *v* Contents, *vi blank*, *vii* viii-xvii Preface, *xviii blank*, *1* 2-203 text, *204 blank*, *205* fly-title, *206 blank*, *207* 208-216 Notes, *217* fly-title for 'Fragments', *218 blank*, *219* 220-233 text, 233 printer's imprint, *234 blank*, *235* Errata, *236 blank*. Printer's imprint: [*short reversed Oxford rule*] | EDINBURGH: | Printed by James Ballantyne & Co. Typography: Page xiii is misnumbered xv.

Figures: π xiv-10, A5-10, B29-10, C38-10, D—, E74-10, F82-5, G—, H118-10, I 139-10, K155-10, L169-10, M189-10, N—, O 213-5, P230-1/8, *Q*—, *R*—.

Notes: In his Preface the anonymous author alludes to the three 'fragments' he had first printed in the *Edinburgh Annual Register* for 1809 (*see* 60A) and his present effort to complete one in the manner of 'the master whom he has here adopted as his model', i.e. Scott himself. The earlier printing of this fragment in the *Register*, citing the first 133 lines of Canto First, concludes:

'But ere his errand he could tell, / The sage his answer gave.'

In this 1813 text, the poem continues after these lines (page 26, lines 3-4) have been altered to read, transitionally:

'And then his master's tale did tell, / And then for counsel crave.'

So that this spoof Arthurian romance might still appear to be, at first, by another hand, Scott had his friend William Erskine 'write over' the preface in order to further mystify its readers.

There are two states of this edition, the first (1), observed only in a single copy, without the errata leaf later supplied and containing, with a press figure for the G gathering [106-10], the uncancelled leaf for that sheet. This exhibits the readings 105.4 Defies/Exceeds, 105.13 noisy/boisterous, 106.5 Fancy's/ Fashion's. State (2) without the figure, and with the errata, has the revised reading in each instance.

Copies: (State 1) T/B(R[obert] Lundie). (2)BCL E EU O P; CtY(2) IdU NNP RPB*.
*With Scott's signature on the title-page: an unusual practice not seen elsewhere.

References: Grady, pages 303-325, 403; Lockhart iv.13, 59; Ruff 131, Thomson, page 17; Van Antwerp(1) 12. (Magnum Opus Edition 1834: *The Poetical Works*, xi.*1-3* 4-11).

68Ab] Second Edition: 1813

THE | Bridal of Triermain, . . . SECOND EDITION. | [*short Oxford rule*] | EDINBURGH: . . . FOR JOHN BALLANTYNE AND CO. HANOVER-STREET; . . . 1813.

Paper: Foolscap 8° (173 x 105mm uncut). Drab boards with printed label. Watermarks: C Wilmott | 1811. Collation: $\pi^8(\pi8+1)$ A-O^8 P^4 *Q*1. Pagination: *i* half-title, *ii blank*, *iii* title-page, *iv blank*, *v* Contents, *vi blank*, *vii* viii-xvii Preface, *xviii blank*, *1* 2-203 text, *204 blank*, *205* fly-title, *206 blank*, *207* 208-216 Notes, *217* fly-title, *218 blank*, *219* 220-233 Fragments, 233 printer's imprint, *234 blank*. Printer's imprint: [*short reversed Oxford rule*] | Edinburgh: | Printed by James Ballantyne & Co.

Figures: π xii-10, A11-5, B28-10, C44-10, D64-8, E69-8, F92-8, G112-8, H128-10, I 140-10/-, K146-8, L176-8, M190-8, N194-10, O 224-5, P230-8, *Q*—.

Copies: BCL O P; CtY InU T/B TxU. Reference: Ruff 132.

68Ac] Third Edition: 1813

THE | Bridal of Triermain, . . . THIRD EDITION. | [*short Oxford rule*] |

EDINBURGH: . . . FOR JOHN BALLANTYNE AND CO. HIGH-STREET; . . . 1813.

Binding: drab boards with printed label. Paper: Foolscap 8° (171 x 107mm uncut). Watermarks: W[P] | [*crossed pens*] | 1811. Collation: $\pi^8(\pi2+1)$ A-O^8 $P^4(\pm P2)$ *Q*1. Pagination: *i* half-title, *ii blank*, *iii* title-page, *iv blank*, *v* Contents, *vi blank*, *vii* viii-xvii Preface, *xviii blank*, *1* 2-203 text, *204 blank*, *205* fly-title, *206 blank*, *207* 208-216 Notes, *217* fly-title, *218 blank*, *219* 220-233 Fragments, 233 printer's imprint, *234 blank*. Printer's imprint: [*short reversed Oxford rule*] | EDINBURGH: | Printed by James Ballantyne and Co.

Figures: π xiv-8, A12-8, B30-8, C34-10, D64-6, E69-1, F90-8, G102-2, H*127*-6, I 133-10, K159-1, L166-1, M181-6, N200-10, O 223-6, P226-5, *Q*—.

Notes: It may be observed that since the issue of the preceding edition shortly before, John Ballantyne has in effect now given up as publisher, for financial reasons, and moved across to another address in old town. Original readings for cancel P2 (pages 227-228) are unknown; text remains as for the second edition.

Copies: AN L O; CtY NNU-W RPB. Reference: Ruff 133.

68Ad] Fourth Edition: 1814[1813]

THE | Bridal of Triermain, . . . FOURTH EDITION. | [*short Oxford rule*] | LONDON: | PRINTED FOR LONGMAN, HURST, REES, ORME, AND | BROWN, PATERNOSTER-ROW. | [*dash*] | 1814.

Issued 23 December 1813 in Edinburgh (*EEC*). 7s.6d. Paper: Foolscap 12° (161 x 98mm cut). Watermarks: W BALSTON | 1813; W BALSTON [with countermark heart design and 1813]. Collation: a^6 b^4(-b4) A-K^{12}. Pagination: *i* half-title, *ii* printer's imprint(1), *iii* title-page, *iv blank*, *v* Contents, *vi blank*, *vii* viii-xvii Preface, *xviii blank*, *1* 2-203 text, *204 blank*, *205* fly-title, *206 blank*, *207* 208-220 Notes, *221* fly-title, *222 blank*, *223* 224-237 Fragments, 237 printer's imprint(2), *238-240 blank*. Printer's imprints (1) and (2): [*short Oxford rule*] | EDINBURGH: | Printed by James Ballantyne and Co. Typography: In gathering C only the fifth leaf (page 57) is signed. In some copies page-number 55 is missing a digit. Page-number 169 is transposed as 196, and 195 is turned to 165.

Figures: *a vii*-10/-, b xiv-1, A24-8, B47-8, C72-8, D94-8, E99-8, F136-8, G162-8, H178-8, I 213-10, K226-8.

Notes: Neither James Ballantyne nor John Ballantyne now appears in the title imprint. Another 'Fourth' edition was issued in 1819 combined with *Harold the Dauntless*: *see* 68Af.

Copies: AN L O; CaBVaU PPL. Reference: Ruff 134.

68Ae] Fifth Edition: 1817

THE | Bridal of Triermain, . . . FIFTH EDITION. | [*short rule*] | [*short Oxford rule*] | EDINBURGH: | *Printed by James Ballantyne and Co.* | FOR LONGMAN, HURST, REES, ORME, AND BROWN, LONDON; | AND ARCHIBALD CONSTABLE AND CO. EDINBURGH. | [*dash*] | 1817.

Published 5 February 1817 in Edinburgh (*EWJ*); issued 12 February in London (*MC*). 7s. Paper: Foolscap 8° (158 x 97mm cut). Watermarks: J WHATMAN | 1812. Collation: $\pi^2(\pi2+1)$ $2\pi^6$ A-K[8] L[8](±L7) M[8] N[8](±N8) O-P[8]. Pagination: *i* half-title, *ii blank*, *iii* title-page, *iv blank*, *v* Contents, *vi blank*, *vii* viii-xvii Preface, *xviii blank*, *1* 2-203 text, *204 blank*, *205* fly-title, *206 blank*, *207* 208-220 Notes, *221* fly-title, *222 blank*, *223* 224-237 Fragments, *237* printer's imprint, *238-240 blank*. Printer's imprint: [*short Oxford rule*] | EDINBURGH: | Printed by James Ballantyne & Co. Typography: Pages 63 and 217 read 68 and 117 respectively. In some copies the 'I' in the direction line page 65 is lacking.

Figures: 2π xiii-3, A10-10, B21-10, C44-10, D57-10, E70-10, F96-10, G103-6, H*117*-10, I 143-6, K152-10, L166-6, M186-6/-, N208-6/-, O 210-1, P236-10.

Notes: Leaf L7 (pages 173-174) is uncancelled in some copies, but text remains invariant with the cancel. Cancel N8 in some copies has a press-figure on page 208; original readings are unknown. Because this edition was sold both (1) separately and (2) with *Harold the Dauntless* (for a combined price of 15s) the direction lines throughout read VOL. I. and below the text now on page 237 a line reads: END OF VOLUME FIRST.

Copies: (issue 1) TxU. (2) BCL E O; CtY. Reference: Ruff 135.

68Af] Fourth (Combined) Edition: 1819

THE | **BRIDAL OF TRIERMAIN,** | AND | **HAROLD THE DAUNTLESS.** | TWO POEMS. | [*short rule*] | BY | WALTER SCOTT, ESQ. | [*short rule*] | FOURTH EDITION. | [*short reversed Oxford rule*] | EDINBURGH: | PRINTED FOR ARCHIBALD CONSTABLE AND CO. EDINBURGH; | [*short rule*] | LONGMAN, HURST, REES, ORME, AND BROWN, PATERNOSTER-ROW; | AND HURST, ROBINSON, AND CO. 90, CHEAPSIDE, LONDON. | [*short rule*] | 1819.

Issued 12 February 1819 as a 'fifth edition' in London (*MC*). Paper: Demy 8° (227 x 147mm uncut). Watermarks: none. Collation: π^2 *A*[8] B-U[8] X[4] Y[2]. Pagination: *1* half-title, *2* printer's imprint(1), *3* title-page, *4 blank*, *i* fly-leaf for *The Bridal of Triermain*, *ii blank*, *iii* iv-xii Preface, *1* 2-158 text and notes, *159* fly-title for Fragments, *160 blank*, *161* 162-171 text, *172 blank*, *173* fly-title for *Harold the Dauntless*, *174 blank*, *175* 176-318 *319* text, *319* printer's imprint(2), *320 blank*.

Printer's imprints: (1) [*short Oxford rule*] | EDINBURGH: | Printed by James Ballantyne and Co.; (2) [*short rule*] | EDINBURGH: | Printed by James Ballantyne & Co.

Figures: *A* ix-10, B12-6, C—, D41-7, E58-5, F75-5, G93-10, H116-5, I 132-10, K144-10, L*161*-5, M168-8, N193-9, O 212-10, P219-12, Q235-5, R254-5/-, S266-13, T280-5, U302-12, X314-6, Y—.

Notes: *Harold the Dauntless* was first issued separately on 30 January 1817. The first impression noted by Ruff actually is (1) an early state of gatherings of C, L, and X, all mispaged as 213-226 *227-228* (2d state properly 21-34 *35-36*), *342* 342-356 (*149* 150-164), 501-508 (309-316). In the earlier state X is also missigned 2K and has no figure; both states of C are unfigured and both of L are figured, the earlier mispaginated as *353*-5 (*161*-5).

Copies: (state 1) CtY. (2) E; T/B. Reference: Ruff 155.

REPRINTS

FRANCE

PARIS: Didot and Galignani
[~] The Bridal of Triermain. 1821, 1826. (Collection of Modern English Authors: *see* 290R.[7A], [7C])

GERMANY

ZWICKAU: Schumann
[~] The Bridal of Triermain. 1827. (Pocket Library of English Classics: *see* 302R.136)

UNITED STATES

BOSTON: Bedlington
[~] The Bridal of Triermain. 1828. (The Poetical Works of Sir Walter Scott: *see* 304R.6)

FREDERICKSBURG: Withers
[~] Bridal of Triermain. 1824. (The Poetical Works of Sir Walter Scott: *see* 310R)

68Ra] PHILADELPHIA: Bradford and Inskeep 1813
The Bridal of Triermain, . . . Philadelphia: Published by Bradford and Inskeep, and Inskeep and Bradford, New-York. William Fry, Printer. 1813. Pages: *1-5* 6-187 *188-192*. Notes: Since pages *189-192* list books published by Moses Thomas, it may be presumed that the Thomas issue (*see* next entry) is primary and this imprint a variant. Copies: CtY MWA NN.

68Rb] PHILADELPHIA: Thomas 1813

The Bridal of Triermain, or The Vale of St. John. Philadelphia: Published by Moses Thomas. William Fry, Printer. 1813. Pages: *1-5* 6-187 *188-192*. Copies: MH MWA NN(2) PPL ViU.

DERIVATIVES

GREAT BRITAIN

LONDON: Hookham
[~] The Bridal of Caölchairn. 1822. [Parody by John Hay Allan: *see* 488S(1)]

LONDON: Hurst, Robinson
[~] The Bridal of Caölchairn. 1822. [Parody by John Hay Allan: *see* 489S]

MINSTRELSY OF ERIN

69A] First Edition: 1812[1813]

Minstrelsy of Erin, | OR | POEMS | LYRICAL, PASTORAL, AND DESCRIPTIVE. | BY | MATTHEW WELD HARTSTONGE, Esq. | [*short Oxford rule*] | [*two-line quotation from Ovid*] | [*short reversed Oxford rule*] | EDINBURGH: | *Printed by James Ballantyne and Co.* | FOR JOHN BALLANTYNE AND CO. EDINBURGH; | LONGMAN AND CO. LONDON; | AND J. CUMMING, AND M. N. MAHON, DUBLIN. | 1812.

Issued apparently April 1813 in London (*MLA*) but not advertised there until 25 June (*MC*). 7s.6d. Binding: drab boards with printed label. Paper: Foolscap 8° in half-sheets (172 x 105mm uncut). Watermarks: none. Collation: π^4 A-M^8 N^4(-N4). Pagination: *i* title, *ii blank*, *iii* dedication to Walter Scott, Esq., *iv* blank, *v* vi-vii Contents, *viii blank*, *1* fly-title, *2 blank*, *3* 4-158 text, *159* fly-title for Notes, *160 blank*, *161* 162-198 text, 198 printer's imprint: [*short Oxford rule*] | Edinburgh: | Printed by James Ballantyne and Co.

Figures: A14-10, B23-'01'[10], C48-5, D57-10, E67-10, F94-5, G108-5, H118-10, I 136-10, K148-5, L176-5, M187-5, N*197*-5.

Notes: One of these poems, 'Trumpet and Church Bell', pages 47-52, Scott had earlier revised and included in the *Edinburgh Annual Register, for 1810*, page xciii, eventually published 6 August 1812. Though there is no evidence of further editorial intervention to rescue the poetaster in his complete text, Scott's complicity is admitted in a letter to Hartstonge, 22 December 1811: 'I have made some alterations and in one or two cases some omissions in the poems now under Ballantyne's charge. I am sensible how delicate a matter it is to correct the works of another author, but I am confident in your good nature and that you will give me credit in every case for having acted to the best of my judgement.' Scott's editorship is implicitly recognized in the Irish poetaster's versified dedication (*see* 505T).

The author earlier had requested, presumably for private distribution 1812 in Ireland, only a 'small and limited impression' of his verses and, as Scott later conceded 23 April 1813, their sale in Great Britain was disappointing: a circumstance evident in the early lack of publicity by the inept John Ballantyne and present scarcity of copies. Another of Hartstonge's productions, again dedicated to Scott (548T), and known only by one copy, also appears to have a curious Irish history.

Copies: L O. References: *Letters*, iii.12, 105, 261; Corson(2), page 83. (Magnum Opus Edition: Not reprinted.)

BIOGRAPHICAL MEMOIR OF JOHN LEYDEN, M.D.

70A] First Printing: 1813

'BIOGRAPHICAL MEMOIR OF JOHN LEYDEN, M.D.', pages *xli* xlii-lxviii, *in*:

The Edinburgh Annual Register, for 1811. Vol. Fourth.—Part Second. Edinburgh: Printed by James Ballantyne and Co. For John Ballantyne and Co. Edinburgh; Longman, Hurst, Rees, Orme, and Brown, London; and the Other Proprietors. 1813.

Published 23 December 1813 in Edinburgh (*EEC*).

Notes: Leyden, a long-time personal friend of Scott's, died in Java 28 August 1811 while accompanying Lord Minto on the British occupation.
Copies: L O; PPL. Reference: (Magnum Opus Edition 1834: *The Miscellaneous Prose Works*, iv.137-198.)

THE SCOTT-BUCCLEUCH EMBLEMATIC FRONTISPIECE:1825
(Entry 543T. Todd / Bowden copy)

THREE

1814-1817

In 1814, just before his forty-third birthday, the acclaimed author most recently of *Rokeby* silently brought forth a work representing an entirely different genre in literature. Yet within a month of its appearance, on 7 July, several reviewers of *Waverley*, though admitting that this anonymous fiction was quite unlike anything done before, casually attributed it to Walter Scott, one going so far as to question 'Why a poet of established fame, should dwindle into a scribbler of novels' (77Aa). As if in response to such demurrals, Scott shortly thereafter, in his own review of Jane Austen's *Emma* (90A), for the first time advanced a few generalities about novel writing, observing that these frivolous compositions still had a certain 'universal charm of narrative.' A reader even of the worst novel, he continued, might prefer 'to yawn over it, rather than to open the page of the historian, moralist, or poet.'[1] As an admired practitioner of one or another of these more serious disciplines, in times past, it is not surprising that Scott, on attempting a new literary mode, should prefer to be known, in this more demeaning activity, simply as 'The Author of Waverley.'

One unintended sign of authorship, also immediately recognized, was the continual use of Edmund Burt's *Letters from a Gentleman in the North of Scotland*, first 1810 in *The Lady of the Lake* and now 1814 implicitly in several episodes in this novel: a source admitted three months later by the author himself in the 'Preface' to the third edition (77Ac). As another of his historical 'touchstones', Scott also repeatedly cited this same work in his 1816 review of the *Culloden Papers* (95A), as well as in the Magnum Opus introduction to *Rob Roy* (112A[1817], 348A.7[1829]), and assisted in a further edition of Burt in 1818 (127A). It is no wonder, then, as Scott indicated in the opening sentence of his 1816 review: 'Every thing belonging to the Highlands of Scotland has of late become peculiarly interesting', for he himself was a primary cause of it all. Early or late the eventual consequence, now everywhere declared, was that his highland *Waverley* 'marked the emergence of the modern novel in the western world'.[2]

With his new Scottish novels as with his earlier epical poetry one may again trace a rapid ascent in Scott's popularity and a further increase in the number of derivatives, especially among his 'theatrical grandchildren'. The initial printing of his widely acclaimed verse romances, as already remarked in the previous chapter, ranged in 1805-1813 only from 750 to 3000 copies, but his prose fiction 1814-1817, having as he said a more 'universal charm', now surged from a tentative issue of *Waverley* in 1000 to *Rob Roy* in 10,000 copies—a record hardly equalled by any subsequent publication. Again, however, with the novels, as before with the poetry, the eager publisher overshot the mark with the larger order for *Rob Roy*, and was here obliged to shuffle off some of the first edition printing as 'Second' or 'Third Editions'; yet the upward tendency is clear and established the supposedly unknown author appreciably beyond his contemporaries.

The sudden and rapidly extending production of theatrical versions begins not with the first, but with Scott's second novel. On 12 March 1816 Daniel Terry's *Guy Mannering; or, The Gipsey's Prophecy* (82Dj) opened at the Theatre Royal, Covent Garden, and, within Scott's lifetime, attained a record of 348 productions (Bolton 409-756), far surpassing the 132 count previously reported for *The Lady of the Lake* (49-180) and exceeded only by the 360 later recorded for *Rob Roy* (1448-1807), a subject already celebrated in song and story. It was only after these hugh successes that Scott's other fiction began to appear, much less frequently, in dramatic form, 'The Black Dwarf' first in 1817 with only 19 productions all told (1428-1446), then during 1820, in quick succession, 39 for *The Antiquary* (1275-1313, beginning 25 January), 21 for 'Old Mortality' (1316-1336, 22 May), and 31 for *Waverley* (367-397, 11 September). Evidently, as these figures seem to indicate, some of Scott's early prose fiction was not readily amenable to dramatic treatment, and all of it, as noted in the record of derivatives, inspired much less sheet music, relatively, than the poems earlier issued. No illustrations for these works appear before 1820 and thus are best considered in the next chapter when *Ivanhoe*, Scott's next great success, inaugurates a series of pictorial suites.

Apart from issuing six Scottish novels and tales in this brief period, the indefatigable author is responsible for at least twenty-eight other publications, among them in 1814 an extensive 19-volume edition of Swift (79Aa, this with an ingenious imposition of the preliminaries and misleading imprints in volumes 6, 9, and 10), then in the same year a 'Coasting Voyage' around the Northern and Western Isles of Scotland (first printed partially in a journal 80A, then immediately used again in Scott's last 4° poem, 81Aa), and within

the next several years four substantial works relevant to Napoleon's climactic defeat in 1815, each of these exhibiting certain bibliographical peculiarities:
(84Aa) *The Field of Waterloo*: a poem now in modern 8° format, as Lockhart observed, and the only work in Scott wherein another printer (here of Ac) counterfeits both the imprint and press figures of a previous impression;
(89Aa) *Paul's Letters to His Kinsfolk*: a report anticipated two weeks before by the issue of two poems in a journal (88Aa) and in its total issue exhibiting both for the first edition (all copies) and second edition (Scott's own copy) press figures for later impressions;
(97A) 'History of Europe, 1814': an 1816 journal printing of 367 pages, with a preliminary notice possibly by Scott;
(108A) 'History of Europe, 1815': an 1817 journal printing of 373 pages, again with an accolade which might be attributed to Scott.

The four journal printings noted above (80A, 88Aa, 97A, 108A) all occur in the *Edinburgh Annual Register*, first announced by Scott in his 1808 'Prospectus' (35A) for a volume issued initially in 1810 (51A), then edited by him through the volume for 1816, published in 1820. Throughout in *EAR* his influence is all-pervasive, but the total extent of his silent contributions is beyond calculation. Besides the seventeen evident entries recorded in this bibliograhy there are five other possibilities mentioned in Curry's admirable study,[3] and uncounted pieces belatedly inserted to fill up the volumes. Excepting his own original work, Scott's general intent in *EAR* was to 'rescue from oblivion' various ephemerae—the same intention that impelled him to issue his *Minstrelsy of the Scottish Border* in 1802, numerous separate editions beginning in 1808, the 81 pieces entered in the first eight volumes of the Somers Tracts, 1809-1812, the 'Antiquarian Repertory' established 1817 in yet another journal (104A), and in 1823 the inception of the Bannatyne Club, founded and presided over by Scott for this same purpose. Though this constant endeavour to place 'beyond the reach of accident' all of the perishable past is commendable, the burden for the publisher, especially when confronted with such ponderous and eventually unsalable productions as the annual *EAR*, occasionally threatened all the participants with some fiscal insolvency. To find a way out of this predicament Constable eventually resorted to a stratagem appropriately considered in the next chapter commentary.

1. Scott had earlier reviewed three other contemporary novelists (Godwin 16A, Cumberland 39A, Maturin 49A), but then refrained from any opinion of the novel as a genre. Now, as a newly committed participant, he is evidently less restrained in his account of Jane Austen's latest work (90A). Since that review, unlike the others, was not originally collected, the relevant passage (page 188) is quoted in full:

'There are some vices in civilized society so common that they are hardly acknowledged as stains upon the moral character, the propensity to which is nevertheless carefully concealed, even by those who most frequently give way to them; since no man of pleasure would willingly assume the gross epithet of debauchee or a drunkard. One would almost think that novel-reading fell under this class of frailties, since among the crowds who read little else, it is not common to find an individual of hardihood sufficient to avow his taste for these frivolous studies. A novel, therefore, is frequently 'bread eaten in secret;' and it is not upon Lydia Languish's toilet alone that Tom Jones and Peregrine Pickle are to be found ambushed behind works of a more grave and instructive character. And hence it has happened, that in no branch of composition, not even in poetry itself, have so many writers, and of such varied talents, exerted their powers. It may perhaps be added, that although the composition of these works admits of being exalted and decorated by the higher exertions of genius; yet such is the universal charm of narrative, that the worst novel ever written will find some gentle reader content to yawn over it, rather than to open the page of the historian, moralist, or poet.'

2. The quotation is from the opening statement in David Daiches' 'Foreword' to the *EEWN* volumes (1993 to date), where Balzac, Stendhal, Manzoni, Gogol, and Tolstoy are mentioned as literary descendants. A similar declaration appears in *Printing and the Mind of Man* (1967, entry 273), where ten descendant novels of national fame are cited, including, most recently, Margaret Mitchell's *Gone with the Wind* (1936).

3. Curry suggests (pages 32-35) that Scott secured the letters of Shenstone, Hume, and Spence, reprinted William Davidson's *Bloody Journal*, and inserted from a 'curious manuscript' the Book of Clanranald, but admits the possibility of various other inclusions.

CONTENTS OF CHAPTER THREE

THE LETTING OF HUMOURS BLOOD IN THE HEAD VAINE

71Aa] Facsimile Edition, First Issue: 1814

The | Letting of Humours Blood | In | The Head Vaine, &c. | BY | S. ROWLANDS. | [*short Oxford rule*] | EDINBURGH: | *Reprinted by James Ballantyne and Co.* | FOR | WILLIAM BLACKWOOD, SOUTH-BRIDGE STREET. | [*dash*] | 1814.

Published ca. April 1814 in Edinburgh. [Hyphen in transcript present in titlepage.] 100 copies (BCL copy, ms note). Binding: drab boards. Foolscap 8° (166 x 135mm uncut). Watermarks: *none.* Collation: π^4 'A-C^8 D^6'*E*^{4}. Pagination: *1* title-page, *2 blank*, *i* ii-vi Advertisement, dated from Abbotsford 1 April 1814, *1* facsimile of 1611 title, *2 blank*, *3-60* facsimile text, *i* ii-viii Notes. Figure (in Notes): iv-6.

Notes: Some incentive for this reprint, of a kind quite unlike others by Scott, may have come from a special feature in the *Monthly Magazine* called 'Scarce Tracts', among which the very first (1 February 1810) is an account of *Letting of Humours Blood.* 'This is one of those curious little tracts', it observes (pages 49-50), 'which the commentators on Shakespeare have occasionally called in to their assistance.'

As if in response to this notice Scott's Advertisement declares that 'the curious antiquary' will be gratified by this 'very limited impression'. The first edition of 1600, he adds, was ordered burned, and three subsequent editions to 1611 are also very rare. Excepting 'this preliminary advertisement, and a few trifling notes, the present edition is an exact fac-simile of that of 1611.' The predominately vertical chainlines would indicate that despite the 1611 collation faithfully reproduced, this replica was imposed in 4° full or half-sheets. The 1814 issue exists in two states, with title-page imprint concluding:
(1) WILLIAM BLACKWOOD, SOUTH-BRIDGE STREET. | [*dash*] | 1814.
(2) WILLIAM LAING, AND WILLIAM BLACKWOOD. | [*dash*] | 1814.
[As a matter of fact, the 'burned' 1600 edition is accorded three entries in STC: 21392.7; 21393; 21393.5.]

Presentation copies: (state 1) NN('Alexander Boswell Esq. of Auchinlech from his sincere & obliged friend Walter Scott') NN('Charles Kirkpatrick Sharpe Esq from his feal freind The Editor' with letter beginning: 'Will you accept the inclosed trifling publication or rather private reprint—for they are very scarce for sale + not worth buying— . . .'). Other copies: (state 1) BCL. (2) BCL E(David Laing).

Reference: (Magnum Opus Edition: Not reprinted.)

71Ab] Facsimile Edition, Second Issue: 1815

The | Letting of Humours Blood | In | The Head Vaine, &c. | BY | S. ROWLANDS. | [*short Oxford rule*] | EDINBURGH: . . . 1815.

Notes: After the 1814 issue the date was altered to 1815 in both states:
(1) WILLIAM BLACKWOOD, SOUTH-BRIDGE STREET. | [*dash*] | 1815.
(2) WILLIAM LAING, AND WILLIAM BLACKWOOD. | [*dash*] | 1815.

Copies: (state 1) O; TxU. (2) E; CtY IdU NN.

A SELECT COLLECTION OF ORIGINAL IRISH AIRS

72A] First Printings: 1814

1] 'The Return to Ulster. WRITTEN FOR THIS WORK *By WALTER SCOTT, Esq.*' (first words: 'Once again, but how chang'd, since my wand'rings began—'), pages 1[l p (letterpress)], 2-3[e m (engraved music)];
2] 'On the massacre of Glencoe.—O tell me, Harper. WRITTEN FOR THIS WORK *By WALTER SCOTT, Esq.*' (first words: 'O tell me, Harper, wherefore flow'), pages 11[l p], 12-13[e m];

3] 'The British Light Dragoons; OR, THE PLAIN OF BADAJOS. WRITTEN FOR THIS WORK *By WALTER SCOTT, Esq.*' (first words: ''Twas a Marechal of France, and he fain would honour gain,'), pages 65[e m], 66[l p]; *in*:

[*engraved title*] A Select Collection of Original Irish Airs for the Voice United to Characteristic English Poetry Written for this Work. With Symphonies & Accompaniments for the Piano Forte, Violin, & Violoncello, Composed by Beethoven. Vol: [1] Price One Guinea... London. Printed & Sold by Preston 97 Strand. And by G. Thomson the Editor & Proprietor Edinburgh.

Published ca. April 1814 in Edinburgh (preface dated March 1814).

Notes: The engraved title is in two states: (a) price and address as given above—'One Guinea'; (b) 'Price 15 Shillings . . . Preston 71 Dean St. Soho & G. Thomson . . .', [colophon dated '1816']. Preston moved to this second address in 1822. The first Scott poem is combined with music of the air, 'Young Terence Macdonough' by Carolan, which is arranged by Beethoven and to be found under Beethoven's works as 'Heimkehr nach Ulster', translated by G. Pertz. For the second, the heading on the first engraved page uses only the first line of poem as given above. The composer of the air is unknown, but the arrangement is by Beethoven.

The third Scott poem was written for a cavalry dinner in April 1812. The first engraved page uses the more common title: "Twas a Marechal of France'. The composer of the air 'The Bold Dragoon' is unknown, but the arrangement is by Beethoven.

Several issues exist of this work. The earliest two (1, 2) in the two title states noted above, are to be distinguished by a single footnote on the first page of the Preface and by the date 'March 1814' at the end of the Preface. A further issue (3), probably postdating 1822, has two footnotes on the first page of the Preface and the date 'Anno 1814' at the end of the Preface. A lithographed issue (4), perhaps of later date than this bibliography, may be determined, among other points, by a lithograph statement at the lower left corner of the title-page frame, by a change in price from 'One Guinea' to 15/—, and by the date 'Anno 1814' at the end of the Preface.

Copies: (issue 1) BCL E(2); DLC. (2) CtY. (3) E O*; CtY. (4) E.
*Volume 1 title-page inscribed 'For Stationers hall'.

References: [1] G/T 10725; [2] G/T 10523; Ruff 79. (Magnum Opus Edition 1834: *The Poetical Works*, [1] viii.379-381, [2] viii.382-386, [3] x.357-359 as 'The Bold Dragoon'.)

EXTRACTS IN ANTHOLOGIES

72E] Scott's three poems were extracted in four anthologies: [1] 405(3)[1]E.10; [2] 362E.1 378.12; [3] 405(3)[2]E.2.

THE BORDER ANTIQUITIES OF ENGLAND AND SCOTLAND

73Aa] First Volume Printing: 1814

The Border Antiquities of England and Scotland; Comprising Specimens of Architecture and Sculpture, . . . Together with Illustrations of Remarkable Incidents in Border History and Tradition, and Original Poetry. By Walter Scott, Esq. Vol. I [II]. London: Printed for Longman, Hurst, Rees, Orme, and Brown, Paternoster-Row; J. Murray, Albemarle-Street; John Greig, Upper-Street, Islington; And Constable and Co. Edinburgh. 1814 [1817].

Published 1 June 1812-September 1817 at London in 17 parts; May 1814 part 7 (the first to involve Scott); 8 December 1814, volume 1 (parts 1-9) issued in Edinburgh (*EEC*). Typography: The three 4° volume issues of the first edition listed below are the only ones to represent part numbers in the volume direction lines and to carry the 1817 date on the engraved title-page of the second volume. Though the index gives only six references to 'Walter Scott', his poetic work is frequently mentioned or quoted, sometimes at considerable length, and his name cited on ten occasions. In three of these the name is unchanged in all settings (87.10, 102.note,

105.8), but in the third and later settings (*post* 1820) further reference may be changed to 'Sir W. Scott' (97.15) and six others altered to 'Sir Walter Scott' (*51*.note, 145.note, 147.13-14, *149*.2-3, 152.1, 156.10).

General Notes: Though the text in large measure seems to have been provided by William Mudford, some indeterminate assistance by Scott was acclaimed by the publishers in their advertisement to the 7th part (May 1814) and reiterated thereafter: this in view of his letter of 28 March and early provision of some of the illustrations. Nonetheless, in his later correspondence, Scott admits that it was a 'foolishly conducted publication' (3 June 1814) and that, as far as he was concerned, it 'must be given up' (19 January 1815). Even so, in August 1817, he had separately printed his extensive 'Introduction' and appendices to this work (*see* 109A), which were then reimpressed as volume 1, pages *iii* iv-cxxvii for the two-volume 1814-1817 issue of the *Border Antiquities.*

As finally issued with Scott's 'Introduction', the two-volume work included two engraved vignette titles and ninety-four plates, with the first edition published at differing prices in three impressions:
(1) Super-royal (380 x 273mm uncut). Watermarks: J WHATMAN | 1808 [1811, 1813, 1815]. £27.0.0. With proof illustrations on India paper.
(2) Royal (343 x 260mm uncut). Watermarks: 1806 [1808]. £13.13.0. With illustrations printed directly on cartridge paper.
(3) Medium (294 x 230mm uncut). Watermarks: 1809 [1815]. £9.0.0. With illustrations printed directly on cartridge paper.

Copies: (impression 1) MH T/B. (2) L LU; CaBVaU CtY(Sir James Mackintosh) InU NN(Berg) PPL RPB(3) TxU(2). (3) BCL C E(2) E(vol.1) ES O; TxU(2).

References: *Letters*, i.517, iii.423-424, 449, iv.16; J. C. Corson, *The Bibliotheck* 1 (1956), 23-26, 3 (1960) 15-23; Thomson, page 16; W. B. Todd, *Studies in Bibliography* 9 (1957), 244-251. (Magnum Opus Edition 1834: *The Miscellaneous Prose Works*, vii.*1-3* 4-153 as 'Essay on Border Antiquities'.)

73Ab] Second Printing: 1823

The Border Antiquities of England and Scotland; . . . 1814.

Published: ca. 1823, though both volumes dated 1814. Paper: 4°. Watermarks: 1821 [1822]; J WHATMAN | 1821 [1822]; J WHATMAN | TURKEY MILL | 1822. With illustrations printed directly on cartridge paper.

Notes: In this setting Scott is still not accorded his title. A variant issue watermarked 1815 and with plates on India paper is listed in Maggs Catalogue 1120 (190), item 180.

Copies: CtY NN(Draper).

73Ac] Third Printing: 1823-1826

The Border Antiquities of England and Scotland; . . . 1814.

Published ca.1823-1826, though both volumes dated 1814. Paper: 4° in twos. Watermarks: *none*. With illustrations printed on India paper.

Notes: In this and subsequent settings the contributor is now generally styled 'Sir Walter Scott'.

Copies: E; InU MH TxU.

73Ad] Fourth Printing: 1823-1826

The Border Antiquities of England and Scotland; . . . 1814.

Published ca. 1823-1826, though both volumes dated 1814. Paper: 4°. Watermarks: *none*. With illustrations printed directly on cartridge paper.

Copies: O; IdU NN(Williams) PHi PPL.

73Ae] Fifth Printing: 1832

The Border Antiquities of England and Scotland; . . . 1814.

Published ca. 1832, though both volumes dated 1814. Paper: 4°. Watermarks: 1831 or *none*. With illustrations re-engraved and printed on India paper.

Copies: GU LU; CaBVaU.

FOR THE ANNIVERSARY MEETING OF THE PITT CLUB

74A] First Printing: 1814

For the Anniversary Meeting of the PITT CLUB | *of Scotland*, 1814. | [*short diamond rule*] | [*five eight-line stanzas*] (first words: 'O Dread was the time, and more dreadful the omen,').

Privately printed ca. 3 June 1814 in Edinburgh. Paper: Broadside. (322 x 197 mm cut). Watermarks: C WILMOTT | 1810.

Notes: In all probability this broadside was printed for use at the dinner. Lockhart seems to have been lately advised of this earlier broadside poem, since he entered it in *The Poetical Works* separately from the other piece cited in the next entry. This poem was extracted in two anthologies: 360E.18, 378E.10.

Copy: EU. References: *Letters*, iii.449-450; Corson(2), page 104; (Magnum Opus Edition 1834: *The Poetical Works*, xi.309-311.)

SONGS SUNG AT THE ANNIVERSARY DINNER OF THE PITT CLUB

75A] First Printing: 1814

'FOR A' THAT AN' A' THAT. *Being a new Song to an old Tune.*'. (first words: 'Though right be aft put down by strength,) pages 13-14 *in*:
Songs sung at the Anniversary Dinner of the Pitt Club of Scotland, May 28, 1814. Edinburgh: Printed by James Ballantyne and Co.

Printed for private issue ca. 3 June 1814 in Edinburgh.

Notes: In a postscript to his letter of 3 June, Scott notes that all five songs were printed together but, as Corson indicates, his first song was also issued separately as a broadside, probably, as noted in the preceding entry, before this combined printing. Scott's first poem is a reprint of this song '*For the Anniversary Meeting of the* Pitt Club of *Scotland*, 1814.', pages 5-6, (first words: 'O, dread was the time, and more dreadful the omen'). Scott's second contribution, an original printing, is not to be confused with a quite different poem by Robert Burns which has the same refrain, but a first line reading 'Is there for honest poverty'.

Copy: E(Abbot). References: *Letters*, iii.449-450; Corson(2), page 104; Ruff 136 (with illustration). (Magnum Opus Edition 1834: *The Poetical Works*, x.360-362 [erroneously noted as published first in *Scots Magazine*, July 1814])

ILLUSTRATIONS OF NORTHERN ANTIQUITIES

The purpose of the present Publication is to introduce the reader to the Metrical Poems and Romances of the ancient Gothic Dialects, a subject intimately connected with the earlier history of European literature, but to which English antiquaries have as yet but partially turned their eyes. ('Advertisement', page *v*.)

76A] First Edition 1814

ILLUSTRATIONS | OF | **Northern Antiquities,** | FROM THE EARLIER | TEUTONIC AND SCANDINAVIAN | ROMANCES; | BEING AN | **Absract of the Book of Heroes, and Nibelungen Lay;** | WITH TRANSLATIONS OF | METRICAL TALES, | FROM THE | **Old German, Danish, Swedish, and Icelandic Languages;** | WITH | NOTES AND DISSERTATIONS. | [*short Oxford rule*] | EDINBURGH: | [*Oxford dash*] | *Printed by James Ballantyne and Co.* | FOR LONGMAN, HURST, REES, ORME, AND BROWN, LONDON; | AND JOHN BALLANTYNE AND CO., EDINBURGH. | [*dash*] | 1814.

Published June 1814 in Edinburgh (*SM* May, 'in a few days'); issued 4 August in London (*MC*). Binding: drab boards with printed label. £3.3.0. Paper: Royal 4° (310 x 245mm uncut). Watermarks: 1807; 1809 / 1809 (*countermark*: I I S); I I SMITH | 1810; 1810 / I I SMITH; 1812 / 1812; 9 | W BALSTON | 1813. Collation: $\pi^4(\pi4+1)$ A-3T^4 3U1. Pagination: *i* half-title, *ii blank*, *iii* title-page, *iv blank*, *v*-vi Advertisement, *vii* viii-ix Contents, *x blank*, *1* fly-title, *2 blank*, *3* 4-513 text, *514 blank*, *515* 516-522 Glossary, 522 printer's imprint: [*short Oxford rule*] | EDINBURGH: | Printed by James Ballantyne & Co. Typography: Signature 2R (page 313) is signed R. Because of the wide outer margins, of some 70 millimeters, copies are sometimes wrongly described as of a variant 'large-paper' impression, but all exhibit the same watermarks.

Figures: π *v*-10, A8-11, B16-11, C23-11, D31-11, E40-11, F47-6, G54-11, H58-11, I 66-8, K78-6, L83-6, M93-8 94-3, N99-6, O 106-1 109-3, P119-1 120-3, Q126-3 128-6, R130-8 132-9, S139-3, T152-6, U160-6, X163-3 164-4, Y170-3 172-1, Z179-11, 2A 187-6 189-1, 2B 199-6 200-3, 2C 202-11, 2D 212-11, 2E 222-11, 2F 226-8 229-3, 2G 238-8, 2H 247-4 248-3, 2 I 253-9, 2K 263-8, 2L 267-8 268-11, 2M 275-8, 2N 288-3, 2 O 293-3, 2P 298-9, 2Q 312-3, 2R 314-9, 2S 326-9, 2T 335-3, 2U 343-8, 2X 350-11, 2Y 357-12, 2Z 368-6, 3A 375-8, 3B 379-6, 3C 390-11, 3D 394-3, 3E 407-8, 3F 411-8, 3G 420-7, 3H 427-7, 3 I 435-6, 3K 444-8, 3L 454-6, 3M 460-3, 3N 470-1, 3 O 474-1, 3P 488-2, 3Q 496-3, 3R 502-2, 3S 507-1, 3T *515*-7, 3U—.

Notes: Among the three editors of this collection, Henry Weber was chiefly responsible for the Old German section (pages *3* 4-230), Robert Jamieson for the northern languages and concluding glossary (pages *233* 234-474, *515* 516-522), and Scott for the 'Abstract of the Eyrbiggia-Saga' (pages 477-513), this last contribution on page 513 initialed 'W.S.' and dated from Abbotsford, October 1813. However, much of the Old German section, according to Lockhart, may be attributed to Scott. Quite possibly Scott was also responsible for the preliminary Advertisement, which immediately sets forth the occasion, as stated in the epigraph above, and promises various sequels should the present volume be favourably received. Even so (page vi), 'the Editors cannot augur brilliant or extensive success for a work which relishes too much of pure antiquity to be generally popular, . . .' Essentially this same language appears in the earliest preliminary advertisements, three years before eventual issue (*EEC* 31 January 1811, *EWJ* 26 June 1811).

Presentation copy: GU ('To Sir John McGregor Murray of Lanrick, Bart—with Mr Jamieson's Compliments. Edinburgh, April 15th 1816.'). Other copies: BCL E(3) GU L(2) P(2); IdU NN(2) NNP OCl PPL.

References: Lockhart iv.154. (Magnum Opus Edition 1834: *The Miscellaneous Prose Works*, v.*355-357* 358-413 as 'Abstract of the Eyrbiggia-Saga'.)

WAVERLEY

My original motive for publishing the work anonymously, was the consciousness that it was an experiment on the public taste which might very probably fail, and therefore there was no occasion to take on myself the personal risk of discomfiture. ('General Preface', 1 January 1829, *WN*, i.xx.)

77Aa] First Edition: 1814

WAVERLEY; | OR, | *'TIS SIXTY YEARS SINCE.* | IN THREE VOLUMES. | [*rule*] | [*one-line quotation from* Henry IV. Part II.] | [*rule*] | VOL. I [II-III]. | [*short Oxford rule*] | EDINBURGH: | *Printed by James Ballantyne and Co.* | FOR ARCHIBALD CONSTABLE AND CO. EDINBURGH; AND | LONGMAN, HURST, REES, ORME, AND BROWN, | LONDON. | [*dash*] | 1814.

Published 7 July 1814 in Edinburgh (*EEC*); issued 30 July in London (*MC*); dedication copy dispatched 2 July (see below). £1.1.0. 1000 copies. Binding: drab, blue, or blue-grey boards with or without printed labels. Paper: Royal 12° (190 x 115mm uncut). Watermarks: B | 1812 [1813]. Typography: Printer's imprints read invariably: [*short Oxford rule*] | EDINBURGH: | Printed by James Ballantyne & Co.

General Notes: Scott early confided to J.B.S. Morritt that, after delivery of the first volume to the printer, 'the other two were begun and finishd between the 4th June & the 1st July during all of which I attended my duty in court': a swift dispatch at the last marked in the printing by the appearance of two press figures, generally, for all gatherings beginning with sheet O of the second volume. The doubling of figures signals a shift from consecutive to simultaneous printing of the two formes in the sheet.

To preserve his anonymity at the time of issue, Scott then directed Constable to forward a set to the dedicatee, Henry Mackenzie. The publisher's informative letter is dated 2 July (a day after work was done) and reads:

> It is with great pleasure, and in obedience to the unknown Authors Wishes I send you the first Copy from Press of "Waverly[!] or 'tis Sixty years since" It is the only Novel I have yet ventured on publishing a proof of the Sentiments which I entertain of the merit & which I would fain flatter myself will be confirmed by the high sanction of your own favorable opinion—
>
> I have additional pleasure in transmitting these Volumes from the happy & appropriate conclusion with which the Author has closed his Work . . . . (E MS.789, p.85)

Under such direction Mackenzie's set, signed by him, may be considered as indirectly presented by the author: one of the very few presentations known in the anonymous series of novels now underway. His 'first Copy', however, though the first perhaps to be collated by the binder, does not necessarily exhibit the earliest printing of the sheets: note the presence of press figures in volume 2, but their absence in volume 3.

Even before the reference to Burt's *Letters*, in the Preface to the third edition, a commentator on the first edition, in the *Monthly Review* for November 1814, quickly remarked that this novel is commonly attributed to Scott (page 275) and later notes that Burt was a primary source for *The Lady of the Lake*, a circumstance serving 'to strengthen the very prevalent opinion as to the identity of the poet and the historian' (page 280). Another writer, commenting on the second edition, in the *Critical Review* for March 1815, immediately observed: 'This romance, lavishly extolled by the Scotch reviewers, is attributed to the pen of Walter Scott. Why a poet of established fame, should dwindle into a scribbler of novels, we cannot tell' (page 288). Despite these and other early surmises, however, the general public acceded to Scott's subterfuge, no publisher thereafter venturing to enter his name upon the title of any Waverley novel before a Zwickau issue in 1822 (*see* 302R.24-25).

Presentation copy: (volume 3, state 1) NNP('Henry Mackenzie'). Other copies: (volume 3, state 1) BCL(2) C E(4) L LU O(4) P; CtY ICN InU MH NjP(Parrish) NN(Berg) NNP NNU-W TxU ViU. (2) T/B(Joseph Marryat). Mixed or sophisticated copies: ES(vol.3 with title-leaf supplied from 7th edition 1817); CtY(6th edition, lacking 'Preface', with imitation lst edition title-pages); NN(Berg, vol.3 is 2nd edition).

References: *Letters*, iii.479; Church 530(with illustration); Duval 933(J.B.S. Morritt copy); P. D. Garside, *The Bibliotheck* 13 (1986), 61-81; Claire Lamont (ed.), *Waverley*, Oxford: Clarendon Press, 1981; Orde Poynton, *The Private Library* 2d ser. 4 (1971), 85-92; Sterling 722; Thomson, pp.75-76; Van Antwerp (1) 1; Van Antwerp(1) 2(with illustration of Mackenzie copy); Worthington 1. (Magnum Opus Edition 1829: *Waverley Novels*, i-ii.)

1] **WAVERLEY;** . . . VOL. I. . . . 1814.

Collation: π^2 A^{12}(±A4) B-P^{12}. Pagination: *i* half-title, *ii blank*, *iii* title-page, *iv blank*, *1* fly-title, *2 blank*, *3* 4-358 text, *359* printer's imprint, *360 blank*.

Figures: *A*10-8, B35-5, C72-1, D93-2, E99-3, F142-3, G147-10, H192-7, I 216-5, K240-1, L264-6, M288-1, N309-2, O 336-2, P338-6.

Notes: Contrary to Poynton's conclusion (page 88) that in one of his copies A4 is a cancellandum (with page 8 line 3 beginning 'purple') it is more reasonable to suppose that the revision was effected very late in the presswork, and that this leaf accordingly represents the only one known still in original setting but with the text then in corrected state. The earlier readings in that setting thus remain unknown.

2] **WAVERLEY;** . . . VOL.II . . . 1814.

Collation: π^2 A^{12}(±A2) B-P^{12} Q^6. Pagination: *i* half-title, *ii blank*, *iii* titlepage, *iv blank*, *1* fly-title, *2 blank*, *3* 4-370 text, *371* printer's imprint, *372 blank*. Typography: On page 136, line 1, the y in 'your' has dropped, leaving an en space vacant in the text of all copies examined. (A contrary supposition occasionally advanced, that 'our' represents an early uncorrected state, cannot be sustained.)

Figures: A12-6, B26-7/-, C72-6, D82-2, E—, F124-2, G168-3, H192-1, I 216-8, K219-1/-, L264-8, M268-3, N312-8, O 324-7/- 335-1, P339-7 357-1, Q366-3. The Mackenzie volume, still representing figures for the variable sheets B, K, and O, would thus indeed appear, in this instance, to be 'first Copy' as described by Constable; but note volume 3.

Notes: For the unlocated A2 cancellandum, a printer's mock-up copy (E: RB.s. 207) indicates page *3* was originally headed 'Chapter XXIV', a reference erroneously carrying on from the numbering in volume 1, and possibly representing an earlier plan to number chapters continuously from volume to volume.

3] **WAVERLEY;** . . . VOL. III. . . . 1814.

Collation: π^2 A-E^{12} F^{12}(±F12) G-P^{12} Q^6. Pagination: *i* half-title, *ii blank*, *iii* title-page, *iv blank*, *1* fly-title, *2 blank*, *3* 4-371 text, 371 dedication to Henry Mackenzie, 371 printer's imprint, *372 blank*. Typography: In some copies signature G2 (page 153) is signed 2G and page 323 is misnumbered 32. Chapter headings, irregularly numbered in the first three editions from page 213 onward, are only partly corrected in certain later editions.

Figures: A10-8 12-6/-, B45-10 47-1, C60-7, D91-10, E107-9/6/-, F136-3 142-5, G—, H181-6, I 213-10 214-8/-, K229-6 230-7, L255-5 264-8, M272-5 282-8, N300-7/- 311-6, O 324-8 334-5/-, P351-6/- 360-1/-, Q362-7/-. The Mackenzie copy, now with figures dropped in all the variable later sheets (I, N, O, P, P, Q), apparently does not represent the earliest press work done on this volume.

Notes: Cancellandum F12 according to the mock-up copy originally read 'maudite' page 143, line 20, corrected to 'maudit' in the cancellans. The original leaf, torn for cancellation, also occurs in the MH(Lowell) copy. Gathering C exists in two previously unrecognized settings, now readily identified by the variant press figures: (1) as noted above with C60-7; (2) without C60-7, but with C53-3 71-1. The later setting, observed only in the T/B copy, apparently was necessitated by a short count in the earlier printing. Since its variant lineation (for example, page 56, line 1, beginning 'self') was soon copied in the second edition setting, the shortage must have been quickly discovered and remedied.

77Ab] Second Edition, First Issue: 1814

WAVERLEY; | OR, | '*TIS SIXTY YEARS SINCE.* | IN THREE VOLUMES. | [*rule*] | [*one-line quotation from* Henry IV. Part II.] | [*rule*] | SECOND EDITION. | VOL. I [II-III]. | [*short Oxford rule*] | EDIN BURGH: | *Printed by James Ballantyne and Co.* | FOR ARCHIBALD CONSTABLE AND CO. EDINBURGH; AND | LONGMAN, HURST, REES, ORME, AND BROWN, | LONDON. | [*dash*] | 1814.

Published 13 August 1814 in Edinburgh (*EEC*); issued 2 September in London (*MC*). £1.1.0. 2000 copies. Binding: Blue or blue-grey boards with or without printed labels. Paper: Royal 12° (190 x 115mm uncut). Watermarks: B | 1813. Typography: Printer's imprints read invariably: [*short Oxford rule*] | EDINBURGH: | Printed by James Ballantyne & Co.

General Notes: Through volume 3 page 216 (sheet I), this edition has been reset, and thereafter is generally of a reimpression, but throughout slightly revised. The most extensive revision occurs in volume 2 page 294, which introduces a new paragraph: "'It is the ancient . . . *commilitones*.'" In all of this issue, as in the latter half of the first edition, press work has proceeded full-speed, generally with two men to a sheet.

Copies: BCL C L(2) O(2) O*; CtY(vols.2-3) IdU InU NNU-W(C. Sneyd Edgeworth) T/B TxU(2). Mixed or sophisticated copy: LU(vol. 1 text of first edition).
*With 4-page Longman catalogue April 1814.

1] **WAVERLEY;** . . . SECOND EDITION. | VOL. I. . . . 1814.

Collation: π² A-P¹². Pagination: *i* half-title, *ii blank*, *iii* title-page, *iv blank*, *1* fly-title, *2 blank*, *3* 4-358 text, *359* printer's imprint, *360 blank*.

Figures: A12-6/- 22-1, B45-9 46-2, C61-5 63-8, D87-5/-, E99-7, F141-1, G166-3, H192-9/-, I 214-6 216-5, K238-1 240-7, L263-5 264-3, M267-5 268-9, N290-2, O 324-6 334-7/-, P340-5 346-8/-.

2] **WAVERLEY;** . . . SECOND EDITION. | VOL. II. . . . 1814.

Collation: π² A-P¹² Q⁶. Pagination: *i* half-title, *ii blank*, *iii* title-page, *iv blank*, *1* fly-title, *2 blank*, *3* 4-370 text, *371* printer's imprint, *372 blank*. Typography: In some copies page 214 is misnumbered 142 and page 295 misnumbered 592.

Figures: A10-1 21-9, B39-3 48-5, C50-1 72-3, D82-2 85-5, E99-7 120-3, F133-8 135-6/-, G155-5 168-8, H171-3 192-9, I 202-3 205-5, K238-2/-, L253-1 262-8, M278-10 280-6, N298-5 312-3, O 333-5 335-7, P339-3 340-7, Q366-1.

3] **WAVERLEY;** . . . SECOND EDITION. | VOL. III. . . . 1814.

Collation: π^2 A-P^{12} Q^6. Pagination: *i* half-title, *ii blank*, *iii* title-page, *iv blank*, *1* fly-title, *2 blank*, *3* 4-371 text, 371 dedication, 371 printer's imprint, *372 blank*. Typography: In some copies page 56 is misnumbered 6.

Figures: A10-1 12-6, B39-5 45-1, C63-1 72-3, D84-6 94-9, E108-3 118-5, F122-1 133-9, G157-10 159-8, H171-2, I 202-5 213-3, K240-3, L262-7, M288-3, N300-7, O 334-1, P349-8, Q362-7/- 369-5/-.

77Ac] Third Edition (Second Edition, Second Issue): 1814

WAVERLEY; | OR, | '*TIS SIXTY YEARS SINCE.* | IN THREE VOLUMES. | [*rule*] | [*one-line quotation from* Henry IV. Part II.] | [*rule*] | THIRD EDITION. | VOL. I [II-III]. | [*short Oxford rule*] | EDINBURGH: | *Printed by James Ballantyne and Co.* | FOR ARCHIBALD CONSTABLE AND CO. EDINBURGH; AND | LONGMAN, HURST, REES, ORME, AND BROWN, | LONDON. | [*dash*] | 1814.

Published 22 October 1814 in Edinburgh (*EEC*); issued 1 November in London (*MC*). £1.1.0. 1000 copies (a count presumably including two subsequent issues and the genuine 'third edition').

General Notes: Apart from an additional preliminary gathering for the new 'Preface' and the various mixed impressions noted below for volume 1 only, this 'third edition' in its first two issues consists of an overrun of the second edition sheets, and thus exhibits for volumes 2 and 3 the same typographical irregularities and press figures. A reference to Burt's *Letters* in the preface, as noted earlier, links the unknown author of this novel to the known author of *The Lady of the Lake* (*see* 47Ac).

Copies: E LU; CtY.

1] **WAVERLEY;** . . . THIRD EDITION. | VOL. I. . . . 1814.

Collation: π^2 $2\pi^4$ A-P^{12}. Pagination: *i* half-title, *ii blank*, *iii* title-page, *iv blank*, *v* vi-x Preface to the Third Edition, *xi-xii blank*, *1* fly-title, *2 blank*, *3* 4-358 text, *359* printer's imprint, *360 blank*. Printer's imprint: [*short Oxford rule*] | EDINBURGH: | Printed by James Ballantyne & Co. Typography: page 351 is misnumbered 35.

Figures: π ix-7, A22-1, B45-9 46-2, C61-5 63-8, D87-5, E99-7, F141-1, G166-3 168-8/-, H192-9/-, I 214-6 216-5, K240-7, L263-5 264-3, M267-5 268-9, N290-2, O 324-6 334-7, P340-5.

Notes: Except for the new 'Preface' this volume, as the figures signify, is essentially of the same impression as the second edition. Gatherings G and K are partially reimpressed.

2] **WAVERLEY;** . . . THIRD EDITION. | VOL. II. . . . 1814.

Notes: Except for title-page, this is an overrun of second edition sheets.

3] **WAVERLEY;** . . . THIRD EDITION. | VOL. III. . . . 1814.

Notes: Except for title-page, this is an overrun of second edition sheets.

77Ad] Third Edition (Second Edition, Third Issue): 1814

WAVERLEY; | OR, | *'TIS SIXTY YEARS SINCE*. . . . THIRD EDITION. | VOL. I [II-III]. . . . 1814.

Notes: Again in the first volume a shortage of sheets required several other reimpressions or resettings as the press figures further signify: C72-1, H192-7, P348-7 355-2. Reset gathering P now introduces (page 338, line 14, upon the advice of J. B. S. Morritt) the name of 'Poussin' as a better choice than 'Claude'.

Mixed copies: NN(Vol.1: with vols. 2-3 of succeeding third edition) T/B(Vol.1: with vols. 2-3 of second edition).

77Ae] Third Edition, First Issue: 1814

WAVERLEY; | OR, | '*TIS SIXTY YEARS SINCE*. | IN THREE VOLUMES. | [*rule*] | [*one-line quotation from* Henry IV. Part II.] | [*rule*] | THIRD EDITION. | VOL. I [II-III]. | [*short Oxford rule*] | EDINBURGH: | *Printed by James Ballantyne and Co.* | FOR ARCHIBALD CONSTABLE AND CO. EDINBURGH; AND | LONGMAN, HURST, REES, ORME, AND BROWN, | LONDON. | [*dash*] | 1814.

Paper: Royal 12° (190 x 115mm uncut). Watermarks: B | 1813; B | 1814 | 1 [2]. Collation and Pagination as for the first 'third' edition, with the new 'Preface', except that in volume 2 the printer's imprint has been moved to the preceding text page 370 and final blank leaf Q6 cancelled.

Notes: In this issue the final gathering P of volume 1 (pages 337-358) was reimpressed in its inner forme, as well as the greater part of volume 3 (B-G, H1-4, I: pages 25-176, 193-216). As indicated by variant press figures, all other pages appear to be reset.

Copies: BCL O; InU MH.

1] **WAVERLEY;** . . . THIRD EDITION. | VOL. I. . . . 1814.

Typography: Page 351 is misnumbered 35. Figures: π ix-7, A13-7 15-2, B46-4 48-8, C63-5 64-2, D82-6 84-3, E106-5 108-4, F136-3 142-8, G154-2 168-10, H181-5

183-8, I 207-1 216-2, K232-5 238-10, L252-2 262-4, M282-5 285-1, N291-4 301-7, O 323-2 336-6, P348-7 358-3.

2] **WAVERLEY;** . . . THIRD EDITION. | VOL. II. . . . 1814.

Figures: A13-3 15-2, B27-7 48-6, C67-1 72-8, D86-1 89-8, E116-6 119-3, F133-10 135-4, G163-3 168-6, H178-2 189-5, I 196-7 198-8, K220-1 239-3, L243-7/- 245-8, M276-5 279-2, N303-3 312-5, O 315-2 336-6, P351-7 352-1, Q362-8.

3] **WAVERLEY;** . . . THIRD EDITION. | VOL. III. . . . 1814.

Typography: Page 333 is unnumbered. Figures: A13-8, B42-5 48-1, C51-3, D86-8, E106-5, F124-2 142-7/-, G147-7, H179-2 181-6/-, I 195-3, K226-7 240-1, L264-1, M279-6, N292-3 303-2, O 324-4 334-1, P346-5 348-7, Q369-8/-.

77Af] Fourth Edition (Third Edition, Second Issue): 1814[1815]

WAVERLEY; | OR, | '*TIS SIXTY YEARS SINCE.* | IN THREE VOLUMES. | [*rule*] | [*one-line quotation from* Henry IV. Part II.] | [*rule*] | FOURTH EDITION. | VOL. I [II-III]. | [*short Oxford rule*] | EDINBURGH: | *Printed by James Ballantyne and Co.* | FOR ARCHIBALD CONSTABLE AND CO. EDINBURGH; AND | LONGMAN, HURST, REES, ORME, AND BROWN, | LONDON. | [*dash*] | 1814.

Published 19 January 1815 in Edinburgh (*EEC*). £1.1.0. 1000 copies (a count presumably including, as well, the subsequent issue). Lockhart's date for this 'fourth' edition (November 1814), as well as the fifth, appears to be confused.

General Notes: Collation and pagination correspond to the third edition, with the third issue sheets again used, now with some slight variation as recorded below.

Copies: BCL E L O; CtY TxU. Reference: Lockhart iv.395.

1] **WAVERLEY;** . . . FOURTH EDITION. | VOL. I. . . . 1814.

Figures: as for 77Ae.1 except, in some copies, pages 238 and 285 are unfigured.

2] **WAVERLEY;** . . . FOURTH EDITION. | VOL. II. . . . 1814.

Notes: No variation observed.

3] **WAVERLEY;** . . . FOURTH EDITION. | VOL. III. . . . 1814.

Figures: as for 77Ae.3 except, in some copies, one or the other of the two figures in sheet B is lacking or both replaced with B43-1.

77Ag] Fourth Edition (Third Edition, Third Issue): 1814

WAVERLEY; | OR, | *'TIS SIXTY YEARS SINCE*. . . . FOURTH EDITION. | VOL. I [II-III]. . . . 1814.

General Notes: Generally this is a further mixture of earlier printings, the first volume from second edition, second issue sheets, the other volumes again from the third edition.

Copy: E.

1] **WAVERLEY;** . . . FOURTH EDITION. | VOL. I. . . . 1814.

Figures: as for 77Ae.1 except 2π vii-8, D—, H192-7.

2] **WAVERLEY;** . . . FOURTH EDITION. | VOL. II. . . . 1814.

Figures: as for 77Ae.2 except sheet I only one figure: I 213-7.

3] **WAVERLEY;** . . . FOURTH EDITION. | VOL. III. . . . 1814.

Typography: Printer's imprint, page 371, previously beginning with a short Oxford rule, now has a short double rule.

77Ah] Fifth Edition: 1815

WAVERLEY; | OR, | '*TIS SIXTY YEARS SINCE*. | IN THREE VOLUMES. | [*rule*] | [*one-line quotation from* Henry IV. Part II.] | [*rule*] | FIFTH EDITION. | VOL. I [II-III]. | [*short Oxford rule*] | EDINBURGH: | *Printed by James Ballantyne and Co.* | FOR ARCHIBALD CONSTABLE AND CO. EDINBURGH; AND | LONGMAN, HURST, REES, ORME, AND BROWN, | LONDON. | [*dash*] | 1815.

Published 19 October 1815 in Edinburgh (*EEC*), probably a late notice. 1000 copies. Binding: blue boards with printed label. Paper: Royal 12° (188 x 114mm uncut). Watermarks: M 1814 | 2 [3, 8]; MELWARD[? | 1815. Typography: Printer's imprints read invariably: [*short rule*] | EDINBURGH: | Printed by James Ballantyne & Co.

General Notes: A legitimate edition, entirely reset, and slightly revised throughout. Volume 1, page 82, line 21, hitherto 'L.297:13:6', now reads 'L 294:13:6'. Lockhart cites publication as January 1815, actually the date of the 'fourth' edition.

Copies: E L O; CtY.

1] **WAVERLEY;** . . . FIFTH EDITION. | VOL. I. . . . 1815.

Collation: π^2 $2\pi^4$ A-P^{12}. Pagination: *i* half-title, *ii blank*, *iii* title-page, *iv blank*, *v*

vii-x Preface to the Third Edition, *xi-xii blank*, *1* fly-title, *2 blank*, *3* 4-358 text, *359* printer's imprint, *360 blank*.

Figures: π ix-1, A21-7 22-3, B—, C69-2 71-1, D95-1, E109-2 119-6, F123-9 136-10, G146-2 165-9, H172-3 191-5, I 207-4, K227-4, L262-3, M286-7, N310-5 312-1/-, O 314-3 325-6/-, P340-5 350-9.

2] **WAVERLEY;** . . . FIFTH EDITION. | VOL. II. . . . 1815.

Collation: π^2 A-P^{12} Q^6. Pagination: *i* half-title, *ii blank*, *iii* title-page, *iv blank*, *1* fly-title, *2 blank*, *3* 4-370 text, 370 printer's imprint, *371-372 blank*.

Figures: A13-4 23-9, B26-5 48-3, C62-9 64-2, D83-3 84-5, E117-7 119-3, F123-2 144-3, G148-11 166-7, H170-2 192-3, I 202-9 209-8, K226-3 237-1, L242-9 256-11, M267-8 268-9, N290-11 296-2, O 327-9 336-7, P347-3 353-10, Q362-11.

3] **WAVERLEY;** . . . FIFTH EDITION. | VOL. III. . . . 1815.

Collation: π^2 A-P^{12} Q^6. Pagination: *i* half-title, *ii blank*, *iii* title-page, *iv blank*, *1* fly-title, *2 blank*, *3* 4-371 text, 371 dedication, 371 printer's imprint, *372 blank*.

Figures: A*3*-8 24-9, B40-7 47-5, C52-3 71-1, D84-7 87-1, E106-3 117-7, F133-1 134-6, G154-10 165-7, H174-11 184-3, I 214-11 216-7, K229-2 230-3, L250-3 264-5, M279-3 285-9, N291-9 312-11, O 327-3 336-8, P338-9 348-8, Q362- 11/6.

77Ai] Sixth Edition: 1816

WAVERLEY; | OR, | '*TIS SIXTY YEARS SINCE.* | IN THREE VOLUMES. | [*rule*] | [*one-line quotation from* Henry IV. Part II.] | [*rule*] | SIXTH EDITION. | VOL. I [II-III]. | [*short Oxford rule*] | EDINBURGH: | *Printed by James Ballantyne and Co.* | FOR ARCHIBALD CONSTABLE AND CO. EDINBURGH; AND | LONGMAN, HURST, REES, ORME, AND BROWN, | LONDON. | [*dash*] | 1816.

Published June 1816 in Edinburgh (Lockhart). 1500 copies. Binding: drab or blue green boards with printed label. Paper: Royal 12° (188 x 114mm uncut). Watermarks: 1815; 4 [5, *none*] | LM | 1815.

General Notes: Collation and pagination correspond to the fifth edition, but reset throughout. Again there are numerous alterations, here somewhat more consequential, including a revision of Flora MacIvor's song in volume 1 page 342, previously beginning: 'Mist darkens the mountain, night darkens the vale,' now reading 'There is mist on the mountain, and night on the vale,'.

Copies: BCL E L LU O; NNU-W* T/B.
*With 4-page Longman catalogue February 1817.

1] **WAVERLEY;** . . . SIXTH EDITION. | VOL. I. . . . 1816.

Figures: A10-9/- 24-8, B37-2 46-9, C64-2 70-10/-, D88-7 94-8, E100-11 118-3, F123-10 136-8, G154-8 165-11, H172-11 182-5, I 195-11 216-5, K219-8 237-11, L244-6 262-11, M276-4 279-7, N290-3 292-10, O 314-7 333-8, P339-4 352-6.

2] **WAVERLEY;** . . . SIXTH EDITION. | VOL. II. . . . 1816.

Figures: A4-7 10-4, B27-8 40-5, C50-2 64-3, D94-10 96-4, E111-10 120-11, F126-4 144-3, G163-10 168-3, H178-10 198-7, I 209-11 214-3, K218-10 240-3, L262-7, M274-8 288-10, N303-5 304-3, O 316-6 322-11, P339-10 360-6, Q362-7 366-11.

3] **WAVERLEY;** . . . SIXTH EDITION. | VOL. III. . . . 1816.

Figures: A21-4 22-6, B45-7 47-8, C50-10 52-4, D89-4 94-5, E106-11 117-5, F123-3 141-11, G154-3 156-6, H170-7 181-11, I 205-3 207-7, K219-3 229-7, L251-5 264-8, M266-8 285-6, N300-3 311-6, O 316-5 327-11, P348-11 358-4, Q—.

77Aj] Seventh Edition: 1817

WAVERLEY; | OR, | '*TIS SIXTY YEARS SINCE.* | IN THREE VOLUMES. | [*rule*] | [*one-line quotation from* Henry IV. Part II.] | [*rule*] | SEVENTH EDITION. | VOL. I [II-III]. | [*short Oxford rule*] | EDINBURGH: | *Printed by James Ballantyne and Co.* | FOR ARCHIBALD CONSTABLE AND CO. EDINBURGH; AND | LONGMAN, HURST, REES, ORME, AND BROWN, | LONDON. | [*dash*] | 1817.

Published October 1817 in Edinburgh (Lockhart). 2000 copies. Paper: Royal 12° (194 x 109mm uncut). Watermarks: 1816 | 3 [4, 5].

General Notes: Collation and pagination correspond to the fifth edition. After a three-year interval this edition still represents a few alterations, e.g. volume 2, page 202 line 23 the correction of the Archbishop's name from Sharpe to Sharp.

Copies: BCL E(3) L*a O*b; T/B. Mixed copy: CtY(vol. 3 text of 6th edition).
*Extra-illustrated with (a) 1820 Allan plates, (b) 1832 Chapman & Hall plates.

1] **WAVERLEY;** . . . SEVENTH EDITION. | VOL. I. . . . 1817.

Figures: π vi-8/-, A10-9 21-3, B28-4 39-8, C50-9 52-3, D74-10 96-1, E106-8 108-3/-, F141-9 143-1, G147-6 168-11, H172-11 182-6, I 202-8 205-9, K218-5 228-9, L262-9, M266-11 288-6, N301-11 310-5, O 314-5 328-11, P338-8 352-5.

2] **WAVERLEY;** . . . SEVENTH EDITION. | VOL. II. . . . 1817.

Figures: A20-5 23-11, B27-6 45-4, C60-10 63-3, D76-9 94-8, E112-11 119-5, F135-8

144-6, G147-4 168-9, H170-8 184-1, I 203-9 213-10, K221-9 227-5, L261-3 263-11, M268-4 279-11, N310-1 312-8, O 333-8 335-11, P346-4 357-8, Q—.

3] **WAVERLEY;** . . . SEVENTH EDITION. | VOL. III. . . . 1817.

Figures: A17-3/- 22-1, B27-9 40-8, C69-5, D94-9 96-6, E111-3 120-1, F142-8 144-3, G146-11 157-3, H172-3 178-11, I 205-8 214-5/-, K230-9 240-1, L254-5 264-8, M266-11 288-3, N290-4 292-9, O 333-3 335-1, P349-4 358-11, Q366-5 368-3.

77Ak] Eighth Edition, First Impression: 1821

WAVERLEY; | OR, | '*TIS SIXTY YEARS SINCE.* | IN THREE VOLUMES. | [*rule*] | [*one-line quotation from* Henry IV. Part II.] | [*rule*] | EIGHTH EDITION. | VOL. I [II-III]. | [*short Oxford rule*] | EDINBURGH: | PRINTED FOR ARCHIBALD CONSTABLE AND CO. EDINBURGH; | AND HURST, ROBINSON, AND CO. LONDON. | [*dash*] | 1821.

Published April 1821 in Edinburgh (Lockhart). 2000 copies. Binding: blue boards with printed labels. Paper: Royal 12° (188 x 114mm uncut). Watermarks: *None* except for the beginning of volume 2: 1819 | 2.

General Notes: Another four years elapse before the appearance of this edition, one now published without any printers' imprints, thus probably printed by someone other than Ballantyne. Where in the previous edition Ballantyne used a number of press figures ranging through 10 and 11, this anonymous printing exhibits only two, 1 and 4. For a typographically-related issue, also dated 1821, but here without figures, see further the note to *The Antiquary* (94Ae).

Copies: L*a; CtY T/B*b.
*With printed spine labels reading (a) '5TH EDITION' [a sophistication?], (b) 'EIGHTH EDITION'.

1] **WAVERLEY;** . . . EIGHTH EDITION. | VOL. I. . . . 1821.

Collation: π^6 A-P^{12}. Pagination: *i* half-title, *ii blank*, *iii* title-page, *iv blank*, *v* vi-x Preface to the Third Edition, *xi-xii blank*, *1* fly-title, *2 blank*, *3* 4-358 text, *359-360 blank*.

Figures: A16-1, B45-4/-, C51-1 52-4, D75-1/- 88-4, E110-4 117-1/-, F133-4 142-1/-, G165-1 166-4, H172-4 179-1, I 196-4 215-1/-, K239-4, L244-1 262-4, M266-1 277-4, N300-1 310-4, O 328-1 334-4, P340-1 350-4.

2] **WAVERLEY;** . . . EIGHTH EDITION. | VOL. II. . . . 1821.

Collation: π^2 A-P^{12} Q^6. Pagination: *i* half-title, *ii blank*, *iii* title-page, *iv blank*, *1* fly-title, *2 blank*, *3* 4-370 text, *371-372 blank*. Typography: A dagger mark, indicatng a reimprssion, occasionally appears to the right of the signature on page 73.

Figures: A4-1 15-4, B27-1 48-4, C51-1 52-4, D83-4 96-1, E107-4 120-1, F122-4 141-1, G168-4, H190-1 192-4, I 205-4 214-1, K219-4 240-1/-, L243-1 253-4, M266-4 288-1, N309-1, O 326-4 333-1, P357-1 359-4, Q362-4.

3] **WAVERLEY;** . . . EIGHTH EDITION. | VOL. III. . . . 1821.

Collation: π^2 A-P^{12} Q^6. Pagination: *i* half-title, *ii blank*, *iii* title-page, *iv blank*, *1* fly-title, *2 blank*, *3* 4-371 text, 371 dedication, *372 blank*. Typography: A dagger mark, indicatng a reimprssion, occasionally appears to the right of the signature on page 361.

Figures: A10-4 16-1, B40-1 47-4, C52-4 70-1, D88-1, E98-4 109-1, F131-1/- 133-4, G146-1 168-4, H191-4 192-1, I 194-4 216-1, K220-1/- 239-4, L263-4 264-1, M267-1 285-4, N292-4 298-1, O 323-4 333-1, P346-1 360-1, Q362-1.

77Al] Eighth Edition, Second Impression: 1821

WAVERLEY; | OR, | *'TIS SIXTY YEARS SINCE*. . . . EIGHTH EDITION. | VOL. I [II-III]. . . . 1821.

Binding: Blue boards with printed labels. Paper: Royal 12° (188 x 114mm uncut). Watermarks: *none*.

General Notes: Except for volume 1 pages *1* and 193 (in some copies), and volume 3 page 49, dagger marks now appear to the right of all signatures, indicating a reimpression throughout.

Copies: C E*.
*With 4-page Longman catalogue February 1827.

REPRINTS

FRANCE

PARIS: Baudry, Barrois [*and others*]
[~] Waverley. 1831. (Collection of Ancient and Modern British Novels and Romances: *see* 288R.1)

PARIS: Didot and Galignani
[~] Waverley. 1821, 1825, 1830 (Collection of Modern English Authors: *see* 291R.1-3)

PARIS: Galignani
[~] Waverley. 1827. One volume. (*See* 294R[3].1)

PARIS: Ledoux
[~] Waverley. 1830. (The Works of Sir Walter Scott: *see* 296R.1)

GERMANY

LEIPZIG: Wigand
[~] Waverley. 1831. (Complete Edition of the Waverley Novels: *see* 300R.1-3)

ZWICKAU: Schumann
[~] Waverley. 1822. (Pocket Library of English Classics: *see* 302R.24-25) Apparently the first edition to display Scott's name on the title-page.

UNITED STATES

77Ra] BOSTON: Parker 1820-1832
Waverley; or, 'Tis Sixty Years Since.... Boston: Samuel H. Parker, No. 12, Cornhill. 1820. Pages: *i-iii* iv, *5* 6-384. Notes: Title-page reads 'Complete in One Volume'. Page 327 is misnumbered 237. (Also reissued in The Novels Tales and Romances. 1822: *see* 305R.1) Copies: MH MWA TxU.

[~] Waverley. 1826, 1829. (Waverley Novels: *see* 306R.1-2)

[~] Waverley. 1829, 1830, 1832. (Waverley Novels, Parker's Edition Revised: *see* 307R.1-2)

77Rb] BOSTON: Wells and Lilly, and Bradford and Read 1815
Waverley; or, 'Tis Sixty Years Since.... Boston: Published by Wells and Lilly, and Bradford and Read. 1815. Two volumes. Pages 1: *1-3* 4-300; 2: *1-3* 4-314. Copies: E; InU. Reference: Kohler(1) 5 (with illustration).

77Rc] EXETER: Williams 1824
Waverley; or, 'Tis Sixty Years Since.... Exeter: Published by J. & B. Williams. 1824. Two volumes. Pages 1: *1-5* 6-203; 2: *1-3* 4-205. Notes: On back paper boards 'The Publishers would give notice that GUY MANNERING is now in press, and they intend if possible, to pursue the printing of all the Novels in their order. All the other uniform editions of these works in this country, have been of an expensive kind, and the number and cost of the whole series have rendered them inaccessible to the mass of readers. It is hoped, that the execution of this will not be considered much, if at all inferior, to that of any heretofore published, while its cheapness will make it easy of acquisition to all....' Copies: E; MWA NNU-W.

[~] Waverley; ... 1831. (Waverley Novels: *see* 309R.1)

77Rd] HARTFORD: Goodrich, and Huntington and Hopkins 1821
Waverley; or, 'Tis Sixty Years Since.... Hartford: Samuel G. Goodrich, and Huntington and Hopkins, 1821. Pages: *1-5* 6-282. Copy: CtY.

77Re] NEW YORK: Burgess 1828
Waverley; or, 'Tis Sixty Years Since.... New=York: Published by William Burgess, Jun.

No. 97 Fulton-Street. 1828. Two volumes. Pages 1: *1-3* 4-266; 2: *1-3* 4-254. Copies: O(2); MWA.

77Rf] NEW YORK: Duyckinck 1821-1822
[1] [Waverley; or 'Tis Sixty Years Since. . . . New-York: Printed for Evert Duyckinck, 1821.] Copy: not seen; once reported at Boston University but not now located. Possibly this is a variant issue of the next entry.

[2] Waverley; or 'Tis Sixty Years Since. By the Author of Guy Mannering, Antiquary, Ivanhoe, Rob Roy, Monastery, &c. &c. . . . New=York: Published by Evert Duyckinck, No. 68 Water-Street. 1822. Two volumes. Pages 1: *1-3* 4-244; 2: *i-ii*, *1* 2-188. Copies: CtY(vol.1) MB MWA NN T/B(vol.1).

77Rg] NEW YORK: Eastburn 1819
Waverley; or, 'Tis Sixty Years Since. . . . New-York: Published by James Eastburn and Co. At the Literary Rooms, Broadway. G. Long, Printer. 1819. Two volumes. Pages 1: *1-3* 4-276; 2: *1-3* 4-220. Notes: Title-page reads: 'Three Volumes in Two', referring to the Edinburgh edition. Copy: NN.

NEW YORK: Harper
[~] Waverley. 1829. (Novels and Tales by Sir Walter Scott: *see* 312R.1)

77Rh] NEW YORK: Riley 1815
Waverley; Or, 'Tis Sixty Years Since. . . . New-York: Published by I. Riley. 1815. Two volumes. Pages 1: *1-3* 4-292; 2: *1-3* 4-248. Notes: The title-pages read 'Three volumes in Two', referring to the Edinburgh edition. This reprint is a piracy of the Van Winkle and Wiley reprint (*see* 77Ri), typeset almost entirely as a line-for-line facsimile, with even the press figures, although different, placed on the same pages. Copies: InU MWA NjP NNU-W PPL T/B.

77Ri] NEW YORK: Van Winkle and Wiley 1815
Waverley; or, 'Tis Sixty Years Since. . . . New-York: Printed and Published by Van Winkle and Wiley, Corner of Wall and New-streets. 1815. Two volumes. Pages 1: *1-3* 4-292; 2: *1-3* 4-248. Notes: Apparently the first Amercan edition, preceding the 1815 Boston issue (77Rb). The title-pages read 'Three volumes in Two', referring to the Edinburgh edition. This reprint is the copy-text for the piracy issued by Riley (77Rh). Copies: BCL E; CtY InU MWA NNU-W NNU-W(vol.1) PPL.

77Rj] NEW YORK: White [and others] 1829
Waverley, . . . New York; Published for White, Gallaher & White, George Long, Collins & Hannay, E. Bliss, G. & C. & H. Carvill, James E. Betts, W. Burgess, Jr. New-York.—T. DeSilver, Jr., J. Grigg, Stoddard & Atherton, H. K. Cowperthwaite, Bennet & Walton, E. Littell, Philadelphia—And Sold by Booksellers Generally. G. G. Sickels, Publisher, Broadway and Liberty-street. 1829. Two volumes. Pages 1: not seen; 2: *1-3* 4-254, *1* 2-12. Notes: At head of title: 'Sickels' Corrected Stereotype Edition of Waver-ley, By Sir W. Scott.' No author reference in main title. Copy: NN(vol.2).

77Rk] PHILADELPHIA: Crissy 1825
Waverley; or 'Tis Sixty Years Since. . . . Philadelphia: J. Crissy, 177 Chesnut Street. 1825. Two volumes. Pages 1: not seen; 2: *1-3* 4-244. Copy: T/B(vol.2).

77Rl] PHILADELPHIA: Scott 1821
Waverley; or, 'Tis Sixty Years Since. . . . Philadelphia: Published by Edwin T. Scott, 61, North Eighth Street. 1821. Two volumes. Pages 1: *1-3* 4-292; 2: *1-3* 4-248. Notes: The titlepage reads 'Three volumes in Two', referring to the Edinburgh edition. This is in general a line-for-line type-facsimile of the Riley issue (*see* 77Rh above), which itself as noted is a piracy of another edition. The title-page, volume 2, lacks the comma after '61' in the imprint. Copies: E; CtY MWA PPL T/B(vol.2) ViU.

DERIVATIVES

GREAT BRITAIN

77Da] BIRMINGHAM: Beilby and Knotts [and others] 1822
Waverley; A Tale. Founded on the Rebellion in the Year 1745. London. Printed for Beilby & Knotts, Birmingham; J. & C. Evans, London; Henry Mozley, Derby; and Oliver & Boyd, Edinburgh. 1822. Pages: *1-5* 6-36. Notes: A chapbook with handcoloured woodcut frontispiece included in the pagination, as well as a title-page vignette. Copies: E L.

77Db] EDINBURGH: Anderson 1824
[Waverley. Edinburgh: Published by John Anderson, Jun. 55, North Bridge Street. 1824.] Copy: not seen. (Also issued in: Edinburgh Select British Theatre, 1824: number 12 [*see* 319D] and in: The Waverley Dramas, 1824: volume 2, play 7[*see* 321D]. No copy of either variant has been seen.)

77Dc] LONDON: Birchall 1819
"They came upon us in the Night," Davie Gellatly's Song in Waverley, . . . London, Printed & Sold by Messrs. Birchall & Co. 133, New Bond Street. [1819]. Pages: 1-4. Notes: Engraved sheet music with caption title. Words from chapter 63 (first words as title). Song composed by John Clarke arranged for voice and pianoforte. Price: 1/6. Copies: L(2) O. Reference: G/T 10910.

77Dd] LONDON: Company of Booksellers 1822
Waverley; and Rose of Bradwardine: A Scottish Tale, of the Last Century. From the pen of the Celebrated Author of "The Pirate," &c. &c. London: Printed and Sold by The Company of Booksellers. Price Sixpence. [1822]. Pages: *1-2*, *7* 8-40. Notes: A chapbook with coloured frontispiece showing two scenes. Copy: E.

LONDON: Cumberland
[~] Waverley; . . A Scottish Drama. [1831]. (Cumberland's Minor Theatre: number 44: *see* 330D)

77De] LONDON: Dean and Munday 1821
Waverley; or, The Castle of Mac Iver: A Highland Tale, of Sixty Years Since. From the Pen of the Celebrated Author of "Kenilworth," &c. . . . London: Printed and Sold by Dean and Munday, Threadneedle-Street. Price: Sixpence. [1821]. Pages: *1-2*, *5* 6-34. Notes: A chapbook with coloured woodcut fold-out frontispiece dated 1 May 1821; epitomized by Sarah Scudgell Wilkinson. Copy: E.

LONDON: Evans
[~] Waverley; A Tale. 1822. [Copies occasionally classified by this publisher are entered under Birmingham: *see* 77Da]

77Dg] LONDON: Leigh 1815
Sir Wilibert de Waverley; or, The Bridal Eve. A Poem. . . . London: Printed for Samuel Leigh, 18, Strand, By W. Clowes, Northumberland-court, Strand. 1815. Pages: *i-v* vi *vii-viii, 1* 2-87. Notes: On page *viii* the author Eliza A. Francis remarks: 'The following Tale is an amplification, in verse, of a little romantic sketch, in one of the first Chapters of the Novel, . . .' Copy: E.

77Dh] LONDON: Lowndes 1823
Waverly[!]; or, Sixty Years Since: A Dramatic Romance, in Three Acts, Founded on the Popular Novel of the Same Name. . . . London: Printed by and for John Lowndes, 36, Bow Street, Covent Garden. [watermarked 1823]. Pages: *1-5* 6-44. Notes: Drama by Edward Ball [Fitzball] (music by George Herbert Rodwell not included), as first performed 8 March 1824 at the Adelphi Theatre, Strand. 'Waverley' is misspelled 'Waverly' throughout. In his 'Preface' the dramatist states: 'I can only entertain a degree of surprise, that the *very best* of the Scotch Novels, amid the existing multitude of Dramatic Authors, should have been left for my pen to dramatise;'. Lithographed frontispiece portrait of Mrs. Waylett as Davie Gelletley. Price: Two Shillings and Sixpence. Copies: E O; CtY MH NN. References: Bolton 372; Ford X2.

77Di] LONDON: Mitchell 1815-1817
Hie away! A Favorite Air, Written by the Author of Waverley, . . . London, Published at Mitchells[!] Musical Library & Instrument Warehouse, 159 New Bond Street, Opposite Clifford Strt. [1815 (ms date)]. Pages: 1-4. Notes: Engraved sheet music with plate number: (548). Words from chapter 12 (first words: 'Hie away! Hie away! Over bank and over brae,'). Music composed by George Kiallmark arranged for voice and pianoforte. Price 1/6. Copy: CtY. Reissued on paper watermarked 1817 and with imprint address: 28, New Bond Street, near Conduit Street. (NNP). References: G/T 10922[1820]; Van Antwerp(2) 42 (1).

77Dj] LONDON: Novello 1830
[Hie Away, Hie Away. London: J. Alfred Novello (1830). Notes: Glee composed by Thomas Henry Severn.] Copy: not seen. Reference: G/T 10934.

77Dk] LONDON: Walker 1814
Hie Away, The Song to the two Deer Greyhounds. Selected from Waverly [!] . . . London. Printed for G. Walker, Publisher of Books and Music 105 & 106 Gt. Portland Stt. [watermarked 1814]. Notes: Engraved sheet music. Words from chapter 12 (first words: 'Hie away, hie away, over bank over brae,'). Music composed as a Glee by Wm. Leeves arranged for voice and pianoforte. Price: 1/6. Copy: E.

EXTRACTS IN ANTHOLOGIES

77E] From *Waverley* there are nine extracts in eight anthologies: 360E.19 361[1].4 366[1].1 375[1].1 375[2].1,4 389.12 394 418.

PROSPECTUS FOR THE WORKS OF JONATHAN SWIFT

78A] '[EDITOR'S ADVERTISEMENT.]', pages *ii-iv, in:* 1814

[*i announcement:*] Swift's Works, by Walter Scott, Esq. This Day were Published, handsomely printed in 19 Volumes Octavo, Price L.9, 19s. 6d. boards, with a Portrait, and other Plates, The Works of Jonathan Swift, D.D. Dean of St Patrick's Dublin; Containing Additional Letters, Tracts, and Poems, not hitherto Published; with Notes, and A Life of the Author, by Walter Scott, Esq. Edinburgh: Printed for Archibald Constable and Co. Edinburgh; Gale, Curtis, and Fenner, London; and John Cumming, Dublin. Published ca. July 1814 in Edinburgh. Notes: Scott's text is the same as that constituting the last two paragraphs of the 'Advertisement' prefixed to volume 1 of the *Works*. The first thirteen words ('The present edition . . . Public') are also identical with the notice forwarded to Constable 22 January 1809, where it was bravely announced that the work would 'appear in the course of 1810.'

This 1814 prospectus exists in three settings: (1) title with no comma after 'Patrick's', page iii first word 'and'; (2) title with comma after 'Patrick's', page 3 first word 'Mr'; (3) title with comma after 'Patrick's', imprint adds 'White, Cochrane, and Co. and' before Gale, page iii first word 'dant', with printer's imprint on page iv. Issues (1) and (2) are of eight pages, (3) of four pages only (two conjugate leaves). A reimpression of setting (3) appears 1815 in *Lord of the Isles*, 2nd edition, here repaged as *444* 445-447 *448* (*see* 81Ac).

Copies: (setting 1) O(2:J.Johnson). (2) O(J.Johnson). (3) O(J.Johnson).

References: *Letters* ii.80-81, 154n. (Magnum Opus Edition: Not reprinted.)

THE WORKS OF JONATHAN SWIFT

79Aa] First Scott Edition, First Impression: 1814

THE | **WORKS** | OF | JONATHAN SWIFT, D.D. | DEAN OF ST PATRICK'S, DUBLIN; | CONTAINING | ADDITIONAL LETTERS, TRACTS, AND POEMS, | NOT HITHERTO PUBLISHED; | WITH | NOTES, | AND | A LIFE OF THE AUTHOR, | BY | WALTER SCOTT, ESQ. | [*short Oxford rule*] | VOLUME I [II-XIX]. | [*short reversed Oxford rule*] | EDINBURGH: | PRINTED FOR ARCHIBALD CONSTABLE AND CO. EDINBURGH; | WHITE, COCHRANE, AND CO. AND GALE, CURTIS, AND FENNER, | LONDON; AND JOHN CUMMING, DUBLIN. | [*short rule or dash*: *see notes below*] | 1814.

Published 6 August 1814 in Edinburgh (*EEC*); issued 31 August in London (*MC*). (Lockhart's date of 1 July, preceding the issuance of *Waverley*, is erroneous; see note to volume 1.) £9.19.6. 1250 copies. Binding: blue boards with printed labels. Paper: Demy 8° (222 x 140mm uncut).

Watermarks: Again in this multi-volume work the marks indicate a certain progression, here apparently through several phases:
(*a*) D & A C | 1808 | 1 [2, 10, 11]; 1808 | 2; D & A C | 1809 | 2 [10]; 1809 | 1 [2]: volumes 2-6, 8, 9(A-2K), 10(A-2D), 11-13, all but the last of these printed by James Ballantyne;
(*b1*) 1809 | 1 [2]; 1810 | 9 [10]; 1811 | 9 [10]; 1812 | 11 [12]: volumes 7, 9(final sheets *2L-*2N), 10(final sheets 2 O-2P), all printed by George Ramsay;
(*b2*) 1809 | 6; D & A C | 1810 | 10; 1810 | 4 [5, 10]; 1811 | 10 [11, 12]: volumes 14-18 printed by Ramsay [15-18 with his final imprint dated '1811'];
(*b3*) 1810 | 9; 1811 | 9 [10, 11, 12]; 1812 | 1 [12]; 1814 | 9 [10]; 1815 | *none* [11]: volumes 1, 19 by Ramsay [both with his final imprint dated '1814'] and preliminary gatherings for all 19 volumes.

General Notes: The printing done by James Ballantyne (*a* in the above watermark record) is recognized by press figures ranging to 18 and double letter signatures given as 2A &c. According to these criteria volume 6, although lacking a final imprint, may be assigned to him. The other work undertaken by George Ramsay (*b*), first to complete what was left undone by Ballantyne (volumes 7, 9-10), then continuing on with undated or dated terminal imprints (volumes 11-19, 1), is revealed by a lower range of press figures, usually not extending beyond 10 and by double letter signatures entered as Aa &c.

For the 19-volume π preliminaries, the last to be printed, Ramsay prepared four titles to be imposed together in a single forme, and then reimpresed as required with new volume numbers. These four are readily differentiated by the length of the short rule (or dash) above date: 10mm (volumes 2, 9, 14, 17); 11mm (volumes 5, 7, 10, 15); 14mm (volumes 4, 6, 8, 13, 18, 19); 17mm (volumes 3, 11, 12, 16, 1). While arranging these π preliminaries Ramsay, after wasting a preliminary blank leaf π1 in three volumes (2, 4, 5), perceived that in five others (3, 6, 8, 11, 12) he could reimpose this 'spare' as π4, print thereon an additional half-title / printer's imprint leaf, then excise and prefix this to the five later volumes (14-18) where a lengthy contents listing already occupied the full π^4 gatherings. To accommodate the newly supplied preliminary leaf (*i-ii*) before title (*iii-iv*) the first contents leaf was accordingly numbered *v*-vi.

Despite these elaborate arrangements, however, only two of the copies examined (O, MWA) exhibit the desired 'ideal state', with half-titles in the later volumes. An exemplar of the large-paper impression (TxGR) still retains the spare half-titles as originally imposed. All other copies have the duplicate half-titles removed from 3, 6, 8, 11, 12, but none of them transferred to 14-18.

Textual Notes: Though Scott based his text (without sufficient acknowledgement) primarily upon the John Nichols edition of 1808, his own discursive annotations are extensive and the material newly printed ranges, according to the Potter listing (pages 130-150) to 122 items. Among the new entries are 83 letters, 22 poems, and 17 prose pieces, many of them forwarded, as Scott duly acknowledged, through his Irish correspondent Matthew Weld Hartstonge. Also frequently mentioned, in the extensive Appendix to volume 1, is an indebtedness to Dr John Barrett, librarian of Trinity College Dublin, whose *Essay* on Swift had been severely reviewed by Scott in 1809 (*see* 36A). As noted in the entry for the ninth volume, several anthologies reprint a new attribution.

Copies: (volume 1 issue 1) AN BCL O; CtY MWA T/B TxU ViU. (2) TxU (Evelyn Waugh).

References: Lee H. Potter, *Walter Scott's Edition of Jonathan Swift's Works* (dissertation, Chapel Hill, N.C. 1954); also his further analysis in *Studies in Bibliography* 22 (1969), 140-255. (Magnum Opus Edition 1834: *The Miscellaneous Prose Works*, ii.)

1] THE | **WORKS** | OF | JONATHAN SWIFT, D.D. . . . VOLUME I. . . . 1814.

Collation: π^8 A-O^8 P^8(±P1) Q-2H^8 2I^4(-2I4) *a-i*^{8}. Pagination: *i* half-title, *ii* printer's imprint(1), *iii* title-page, *iv blank*, *v* vi-x Advertisement, dated from Abbotsford 1 July 1814, *xi* xii-xv Contents, *xvi blank*, *1* fly-title, *2 blank*, *3* 4-502 Memoirs of Jonathan Swift, *i* fly-title, *ii blank*, *iii-iv* v-cxliv Appendix, cxliv printer's imprint(2). Printer's imprints: (1) [*short rule*] | Printed by George Ramsay & Co.; (2) [*short rule*] | Printed by G. Ramsay & Co. | Edinburgh, 1814. Illustrations: Frontispiece portrait of Swift after Bindon, painted by J. Burgess. In some copies an engraving of a copper medal, by E. Mitchell, faces page *3*. The cancel P1, signed *P, bears on verso, page 226, a copperplate engraving by T. Badge of Wood's Halfpenny, this perhaps belatedly received by the editor and bearing the inscription 'To Walter Scott Esqr. from Doctor Hill Reg. Prof. Phy, T.C.D.' Typography: Gatherings 2A-2I are signed Aa-Ii, according to Ramsay's practice. Direction line 'VOL. I.' (page 417) is represented as 'VO. IL.' Signature letters for the Appendix are in italic.

Figures: π xiv-1, A14-10/6/-, B20-5 22-1, C46-6/- 48-3, D54-6 60-3, E76-5 78-1, F86-1/- 88-5, G98-3, H114-6 120-3, I 132-1, K146-6 152-5, L174-5, M188-6, N206-3 208-1, O 210-4 224-5, P228-3, Q242-1 248-3, R260-1 270-5, S286-3 288-1, T296-3 298-1, U308-3 310-1, X324-2 326-1, Y338-1 340-3, Z354-3, 2A 370-5 384-3, 2B 386-5 392-3, 2C 406-1 408-3, 2D 424-3 426-5, 2E 446-4 448-5/-, 2F 450-3 464-1, 2G 472-5, 2H 484-1 494-3, 2 I 498-4, *a* vi-1, *b* xviii-5 xxiv-3/-, *c* xxxvi-3/- xlii-1, *d* lii-4 lxii-5/-, *e* lxvi-3 lxviii-5, *f* xciv-5, *g* cxii-1, *h*—, *i*—.

Notes: Sheet A exists in two settings: (1) page *3* last line first word 'nied', page 14 figure 10 or 6; (2) page *3* 'denied', no figure. Setting (2) may have been considerably delayed, probably to make up for a short count, since type-setting (1) was still available for the later large-paper impression.

Some copies of this volume of Memoirs, 'very near printed' by 10 February 1814, were separately distributed to Byron and other close associates, but the complete *Works* destined for the Prince Regent and Scott's Irish confederates apparently were still awaiting shipment on 10 July. (*Letters*, iii.410, 461.)

2] THE | **WORKS** | OF | JONATHAN SWIFT, D.D. . . . VOLUME II. . . . 1814.

Collation: π^4 A-2E^8. Pagination: *i-ii blank*, *iii* half-title, *iv* printer's imprint(1), *v* title-page, *vi blank*, *vii*-viii Contents, *1* fly-title, *2 blank*, 3-446 text, 446 printer's imprint(2), *447-448 blank*. Printer's imprints: (1) [*short rule*] | Printed by George Ramsay & Co.; (2) [*short Oxford rule*] | Edinburgh: | Printed by James Ballantyne & Co.

Figures: A14-2 16-7, B19-11 32-10, C38-4 48-12, D50-11 64-2, E66-4 76-1, F82-11 96-3, G98-8 112-1, H114-7 128-1, I 130-8 144-10, K146-7 160-4, L163-10 176-2, M178-13 192-7, N194-3 208-4, O 210-2 224-10, P226-1 232-8, Q243-1 253-3, R258-1 272-7, S274-13 288-4, T294-4 304-2, U307-11 320-4, X326-10 336-8, Y338-4 352-11, Z354-11, 2A 378-13 384-3/-, 2B 398-3, 2C 415-3 416-13, 2D 418-10 432-2, 2E 440-7.

Notes: The first blank leaf in this and volumes 4, 5 is usually excised. However, as the Contents verso indicates, this leaf was counted in the preliminary pagination.

3] THE | **WORKS** | OF | JONATHAN SWIFT, D.D. . . . VOLUME III. . . . 1814.

Collation: π^4(-π4) A-P^8 Q^8(±Q8) R-2D^8 2E^4 2F^2. Pagination: *i* half-title, *ii* printer's imprint(1), *iii* title-page, *iv blank*, *v*-vi Contents, *1* 2-444 text, 444 printer's imprint(2). Printer's imprints: (1) [*short rule*] | Printed by George Ramsay & Co.; (2) [*short Oxford rule*] | Edinburgh; | Printed by James Ballantyne & Co.

Figures: A2-11, B19-3 32-7, C34-11 48-4, D50-10 52-2, E66-11 76-1, F83-4, G98-11 112-10, H114-11 128-3, I 143-2 144-10, K146-11, L176-3, M178-8 180-7, N194-11 205-1, O 210-1 224-11, P226-3 233-7, Q246-7 256-1, R270-2 272-4, S286-2 288-1, T290-12 304-13, U306-2 320-11, X322-8 336-11, Y338-11 352-2, Z354-11 368-7, 2A 370-13 384-12, 2B 386-8/- 400-12, 2C 402-12 412-8, 2D 418-13 432-1, 2E 440-10, 2F 442-12.

Notes: Concerning the extra, cancelled half-title π4 see introductory General Notes above. Cancel Q8 has figure 1 on its verso, page 256.

4] THE | **WORKS** | OF | JONATHAN SWIFT, D.D. . . . VOLUME IV. . . . 1814.

Collation: π4 A-2G8. Pagination: *i-ii blank*, *iii* half-title, *iv* printer's imprint(1), *v* title-page, *vi blank*, *vii*-viii Contents, *1* fly-title, *2 blank*, 3-478 text, 478 printer's imprint(2), *479-480 blank*. Printer's imprints: (1) [*short rule*] | Printed by George Ramsay & Co.; (2) [*short Oxford rule*] | EDINBURGH: | Printed by James Ballantyne & Co. Typography: Page 357 is missing right bracket; page 441 is misnumbered 443.

Figures: A11-8 16-10, B18-13 25-11, C34-13 37-2, D51-13 53-11, E67-12, F90-8, G98-1 112-12, H118-13 128-3, I 130-1 144-7, K151-12 157-11, L168-7 175-2, M180-3 182-7, N196-2/- 207-13, O 223-1 224-8, P226-10 240-12, Q242-10 256-18, R258-10 272-5, S287-8 288-1, T290-7 304-13, U314-7 320-11, X325-2 330-11, Y346-13 352-8, Z366-5 368-1, 2A 370-5 381-11, 2B 386-11 400-2, 2C 402-3/- 416-11, 2D 430-7, 2E 434-8 445-6, 2F 461-1 463-8, 2G 470-13 476-7.

Notes: Concerning the preliminary blank leaf, see Notes to volume 2.

5] THE | **WORKS** | OF | JONATHAN SWIFT, D.D. . . . VOLUME V. . . . 1814.

Collation: π4 A-2C8 2D2. Pagination: *i-ii blank*, *iii* half-title, *iv* printer's imprint(1), *v* title-page, *vi blank*, *vii* Contents, *viii blank*, *1* fly-title, *2 blank*, 3-'418'[420] text, '418' printer's imprint(2). Printer's imprints: (1) [*short rule*] | Printed by George Ramsay & Co.; (2) [*short Oxford rule*] | EDINBURGH: | Printed by J. Ballantyne & Co. Typography: Page 46 is misnumbered 36; page 420 is misnumbered 418.

Figures: A14-13 16-11, B23-13 28-8, C34-11 48-5, D50-2, E74-11 80-3, F91-3 96-11, G99-2 112-11, H114-1 125-5, I 133-13 142-3, K155-2, L162-13 168-5, M179-11 184-2, N208-12, O 223-5 224-12, P240-13, Q242-13 256-8, R258-5 269-7, S286-1, T290-12 304-8, U315-1 320-11, X322-10 336-11, Y342-12 352-'01'[10], Z354-5 368-11, 2A 370-12 380-5, 2B 399-5 400-10, 2C 402-4 413-8, 2D 418-6/-.

Notes: Concerning the preliminary blank leaf, see Notes to volume 2.

6] THE | **WORKS** | OF | JONATHAN SWIFT, D.D. . . . VOLUME VI. . . . 1814.

Collation: π4(-π4) A-2E8 2F4 2G1. Pagination: *i* half-title, *ii* printer's imprint, *iii* title-page, *iv blank*, *v*-vi Contents, *1* fly-title, *2 blank*, *3* 4-458 text. Printer's imprint: [*short rule*] | Printed by George Ramsay & Co.

Figures: A4-1 10-11, B22-5 32-8, C34-8 48-11, D54-8 57-5, E75-3 80-10, F82-6/-, G98-3 101-2, H118-5, I 134-12, K146-11 148-12, L163-12/- 169-13, M178-6 192-12, N194-12, O 210-8 220-5, P240-4, Q251-12 256-5, R258-6 272-10, S276-9 282-11, T290-8 304-4, U310-5, X336-10, Y338-13, Z360-13/-, 2A 384-13, 2B 386-14 396-11, 2C 403-9 416-14, 2D 418-14 420-5, 2E 439-3 441-5, 2F 456-6, 2G—.

Notes: Concerning the extra, canceled half-title π4 see introductory General Notes above. Though there is no imprint on the final page, it appears both from the figures (ranging through 14) and from the '2A' mode of signing that the text of this volume was printed by James Ballantyne.

7] THE | **WORKS** | OF | JONATHAN SWIFT, D.D. . . . VOLUME VII. . . . 1814.

Collation: π^4 A-2 O^8. Pagination: *i* half-title, *ii* printer's imprint, *iii* title-page, *iv blank*, *v* vi-vii Contents, *viii blank*, *1* fly-title, *2* note, *3* 4-592 text. Printer's imprint: [*short rule*] | Printed by George Ramsay & Co.

Figures: A8-10 10-4, B20-1 22-3, C38-10, D54-4/- 64-3, E66-3 72-4, F86-1 88-3, G98-3 104-1, H118-10 128-4/-, I 130-10 132-10/-, K146-4 148-10, L176-1, M182-4/- 188-10, N198-5 200-1, O 210-1 212-5, P234-10 236-5, Q244-5, R270-10 272-3, S278-10 288-1, T304-5, U314-10 320-5, X326-4/- 328-10, Y338-10 344-5/-, Z360-10, 2A 374-4 384-5, 2B 398-10 400-4, 2C 402-10 408-5, 2D 418-3 424-10, 2E 434-4 436-10, 2F 450-5 456-1, 2G 468-10 470-3, 2H 488-3 494-5/-, 2 I 510-4 512-3, 2K 514-1 516-5, 2L 530-1 544-10, 2M 550-5 556-3, 2N 568-3, 2 O 578-1 588-10.

Notes: Though there is no imprint on the final page, it is evident from the figures (ranging only through 10) and from the 'Aa' mode of signing that the complete text, as well as the preliminary gathering, was printed by George Ramsay.

8] THE | **WORKS** | OF | JONATHAN SWIFT, D.D. . . VOLUME VIII. . . . 1814.

Collation: $\pi^4(-\pi4)$ A-T^8 $U^8(\pm U4)$ X-2E^8. Pagination: *i* half-title, *ii* printer's imprint(1), *iii* title-page, *iv blank*, *v*-vi Contents, *1* fly-title, *2 blank*, 3-446 text, 446 printer's imprint(2), *447-448 blank*. Printer's imprints: (1) [*short rule*] | Printed by George Ramsay & Co.; (2) [*short Oxford rule*] | EDINBURGH: | Printed by James Ballantyne & Co. Typography: Page 328 in some copies has first number missing.

Figures: A3-8/- 16-9, B20-4, C35-5 37-13, D50-11 60-12, E66-9 80-11, F83-9 84-4, G98-11, H114-14, I 131-11 137-6, K146-9 160-11, L162-12 164-11, M191-12, N204-5 206-11, O 210-14, P237-12 238-13/-, Q246-12/-, R259-14 272-5, S281-14, T304-14, U320-5, X322-8 328-9, Y338-9 340-11, Z358-4 365-9, 2A 370-5 384-9, 2B 387-5 389-12, 2C 402-8 404-4, 2D 418-14 432-4, 2E 434-6 436-5.

Notes: Concerning the extra, canceled half-title π4 see introductory General Notes above. The original text for cancel U4 (pages 311-312) is unknown.

9] THE | **WORKS** | OF | JONATHAN SWIFT, D.D. . . . VOLUME IX. . . . 1814.

Collation: π[4] A-2I[8] 2K[4](-2K4) *2L[8] *2M[4] *2N1. Pagination: *i* half-title, *ii* printer's imprint(1), *iii* title-page, *iv blank*, *v* vi-vii Contents, *viii blank*, *1* fly-title, *2 blank*, *3-4* 5-544 text, 544 printer's imprint(2). Printer's imprints: (1) and (2) [*short rule*] | Printed by George Ramsay & Co. Typography: The second parenthesis is missing in some copies after page-number 279 and in all copies after page-number 475.

Figures: A5-13 6-9, B18-8/- 24-7, C38-12 40-2, D56-15 58-3, E66-12 69-3, F87-14 96-1, G101-14/- 107-11, H114-14 124-15, I 131-6 144-3, K153-11 154-13, L162-7 169-5, M180-14 183-6, N196-3 206-14, O 210-14 216-3, P226-13 237-10, Q243-2 244-6, R264-15 266-12, S286-9 288-15, T290-12 292-14, U310-12 312-14, X334-2 336-7, Y348-14 351-10, Z361-6 367-5, 2A 379-12 384-7, 2B 398-14 400-3, 2C 404-12 406-8, 2D 422-3 425-5, 2E 447-12 448-14, 2F 459-12 464-5/-, 2G 468-15, 2H 482-12, 2I 510-12, 2K 514-13, *2L 522-1 529-5, *2M—, *2N—.

Notes: Despite the final printer's imprint, it is evident from Ballantyne's original imprint on cancellandum 2K4v (page 520 in a TxU copy), as well as from the figures and paper, that he worked off the greater portion of this volume and George Ramsay printed (besides the preliminaries, as usual) only the later starred sheets *2L-*2N. These supplementary gatherings now add (pages 521-544) as 'indisputedly written by Swift' the satire entitled 'A Serious and Useful Scheme to make an Hospital for Incurables'. The first leaf of this later insert (pages 519- 520) necessarily reprints the same concluding paragraphs earlier provided in the cancellandum for 'The History of the Second Solomon'. Five years later this newly identified satire was extracted in three anthologies (384E.1, 412, 466.1), all apparently copied one from another

10] THE | **WORKS** | OF | JONATHAN SWIFT, D.D. . . . VOLUME X. . . . 1814.

Collation: π[4] A-2M[8] 2N[8](±2N3) 2 O[8] 2P[2]. Pagination: *i* half-title, *ii* printer's imprint(1), *iii* title-page, *iv blank*, *v* vi-viii Contents, *1* fly-title, *2 blank*, *3-4* 5-595 text, 595 printer's imprint(2), *596 blank*. Printer's imprints: (1) [*short rule*] | Printed by George Ramsay & Co.; (2) [*short rule*] | Printed by G. Ramsay & Co. | Edinburgh, 1814. Typography: Page 416 is misnumbered 414; page 524 is misnumbered 526; page 561 in some copies is misnumbered 156; double signatures 2A-2N are recorded thus, but OO-Pp thus.

Figures: A14-11 16-3, B31-5/- 32-7, C43-13 45-3, D53-12 59-3, E74-6 80-14, F96-6, G105-13 106-12, H117-13 122-6, I 132-14, K158-15 160-3, L162-14 176-7, M184-15 190-1, N198-15 208-14, O 210-11 221-6, P228-14 235-3, Q251-5/- 252-12, R258-14 260-2, S280-6 287-12/-, T291-12 296-14, U306-14 317-7, X322-1 325-3, Y351-13 352-5, Z354-12 357-14/- 2A 371-14 373-1/-, 2B 386-14 388-12, 2C '414'[416]-3, 2D 418-9 432-2, 2E 442-5 448-6, 2F 452-3 462-5, 2G 468-5/- 470-1, 2H 486-5, 2 I 508-5, 2K 514-5 516-1, 2L 530-6 540-1, 2M 556-5, 2N 562-5/- 568-4, 2 O 584-3/- 586-1, 2P—.

Notes: Cancel 2N3 (pages 565-566) has direction line reading 'VOL. X.' and at center *. Despite the final printer's imprint, it is evident from the figures, the paper, and the styling of double-letter signatures that James Ballantyne worked off the greater portion of this volume and George Ramsay printed only the last two sheets (signed OO, Pp), as well as the preliminaries.

11] THE | **WORKS** | OF | JONATHAN SWIFT, D.D. . . . VOLUME XI. . . . 1814.

Collation: π^4(-π4) A-2D^8. Pagination: *i* half-title, *ii* printer's imprint(1), *iii* title-page, *iv blank*, *v* Contents, *vi blank*, 1-429 text, 429 printer's imprint(2), *430-432 blank*. Printer's imprints: (1) [*short rule*] | Printed by George Ramsay & Co.; (2) [*short Oxford rule*] | EDINBURGH: | Printed by James Ballantyne & Co.

Figures: A14-5 16-3, B20-3 23-12, C34-2 36-13, D63-1 64-11, E79-3 80-1, F82-3 89-2, G99-3 112-2, H116-13 118-2, I 132-10 143-2, K148-13 150-12, L162-3 168-12, M192-3 200-12, N200-12/-, O 224-12, P230-3, Q245-3, R263-3, S285-3, T304-12, U306-3, X329-13 335-2, Y342-1, Z354-6 356-13, 2A 371-3 384-5, 2B 386-1 397-10, 2C 409-3 415-12, 2D 422-8.

Notes: Concerning the extra, canceled half-title π4 see introductory General Notes above.

12] THE | **WORKS** | OF | JONATHAN SWIFT, D.D. . . VOLUME XII. . . . 1814.

Collation: π^4(-π4) A-2F^8 2G^2. Pagination: *i* half-title, *ii* printer's imprint(1), *iii* title-page, *iv blank*, *v* Contents, *vi blank*, *1* fly-title, *2 blank*, *3* 4-467 text, 467 printer's imprint(2), *468 blank*. Printer's imprints: (1) [*short rule*] | Printed by George Ramsay & Co.; (2) [*short Oxford rule*] | EDINBURGH: | Printed by Jas. Ballantyne & Co.

Figures: A9-1, B26-5 32-7, C36-3, D51-13 64-6, E79-6, F94-3, G112-12, H120-12, I 135-9 136-3, K146-12, L172-7, M187-12, N194-13, O 210-13 212-9, P238-3, Q242-7 256-13, R260-12 267-3, S279-3 285-12, T290-3, U308-12 319-13, X326-11 333-5, Y342-8 348-13, Z358-8 365-11, 2A 372-2 379-3, 2B 390-4, 2C 403-4 409-3, 2D 422-3 432-4, 2E 434-2, 2F 450-9 464-2, 2G—.

Notes: Concerning the extra, canceled half-title π4 see introductory General Notes above.

13] THE | **WORKS** | OF | JONATHAN SWIFT, D.D. . . VOLUME XIII. . . . 1814.

Collation: π^4 A-2H^8. Pagination: *i* half-title, *ii* printer's imprint(1), *iii* title-page, *iv blank*, *v* vi-vii Contents, *viii blank*, *1* fly-title, *2 blank*, *3-4* 5-493 text, 493 printer's imprint(2), *494-496 blank*. Printer's imprints: (1) [*short rule*] | Printed by George

Ramsay & Co.; (2) [*short Oxford rule*] | EDINBURGH: | Printed by George Ramsay & Co. Typography: Gatherings 2A-2H are signed Aa-Hh, according to Ramsay's practice.

Figures: A10-1, B22-1, C—, D62-12, E67-1, F93-1, G106-1, H126-13, I 134-8, K150-7 152-9/-, L176-8, M184-11/-, N202-9, O 220-13, P240-13, Q246-13, R264-13, S278-13, T294-8, U316-13, X—, Y348-13, Z368-7, 2A 373-13/-, 2B—, 2C 412-9/-, 2D—, 2E—, 2F 453-1 462-5, 2G 472-2 474-3, 2H 482-9 488-13.

Notes: Sheet M exists in two settings (1) watermarked as with other paper for this volume 1809 | 1, figure 184-11; (2) watermarked 1813 and unfigured.

14] THE | **WORKS** | OF | JONATHAN SWIFT, D.D. . . VOLUME XIV. . . . 1814.

Collation: π1 2π[4] A-2H[8] 2I[4] 2K[2]. Pagination: *i* half-title, *ii* printer's imprint(1), *iii* title-page, *iv blank*, *v* vi-ix Contents, *x blank*, *1-3* 4-507 text, 507 printer's imprint(2), *508 blank*. Printer's imprints: (1) [*short rule*] | Printed by George Ramsay & Co.; (2) [*short Oxford rule*] | EDINBURGH: | Printed by George Ramsay & Co. Typography: Page ix has page-number at inner position rather than outer. Gatherings 2A-2K are signed Aa-Kk, according to Ramsay's practice.

Figures: A16-12, B24-13, C48-12, D64-13, E78-13 80-12, F96-12, G108-13, H128-12, I 141-12, K160-10, L174-4, M192-6, N198-10, O 220-3 222-10, P234-6, Q246-10, R270-1, S286-10, T300-10, U314-10, X334-10, Y346-3, Z354-1, 2A 374-6, 2B 394-3 400-6, 2C 406-6/- 412-3, 2D 418-6 424-3, 2E 434-7 448-6, 2F 450-7 464-6, 2G 474-6 480-7, 2H 488-6, 2I 498-6, 2K 506-1.

15] THE | **WORKS** | OF | JONATHAN SWIFT, D.D. . . VOLUME XV. . . . 1814.

Collation: π1 2π[4] A-2F[8] 2G[4] *1. Pagination: *i* half-title, *ii* printer's imprint(1), *iii* title-page, *iv blank*, *v* vi-ix Contents, *x blank*, *1* fly-title, *2 blank*, *3* 4-471 text, 471 printer's imprint(2), *472 blank*, 473 note, *474 blank*. Printer's imprints: (1) [*short rule*] | Printed by George Ramsay & Co.; (2) [*short rule*] | EDINBURGH | Printed by George Ramsay & Co. | 1811. Typography: Gatherings 2A-2G are signed Aa-Gg, according to Ramsay's practice. The right bracket is missing after page-number 473.

Figures: A16-6, B18-1, C42-6 48-8, D60-8 62-6, E66-11 68-8, F94-8 96-11, G112-1, H114-1 128-1, I 136-4 138-1, K152-1 154-4, L174-1 176-4, M184-1/-, N198-1 200-2, O 213-3/- 222-1, P230-1 232-4, Q246-1 256-9, R258-1, S284-4, T292-4 302-11, U318-4, X326-4, Y342-4, Z366-4, 2A 376-4, 2B 388-6 390-4/-, 2C 410-4, 2D 428-4 430-6, 2E 446-4, 2F 464-4, 2G 466-6.

Notes: Sheet O, with press figure 3 not appearing elsewhere in the volume, seems to be a 16-page cancellans, sometimes bearing (in both regular and large-paper impression) an 1812 watermark: one year later than the date in the final printer's imprint. Leaf 2B5, torn for cancellation in some copies, mistakenly refers page 394 line 7 to the '13th book of Tacitus', a reference corrected to the '15th' in the second edition. Apparently, however, the cancel if prepared was never inserted. The additional leaf after text (pages 473-*474*), signed * on recto, carries further lines to follow verses printed on pages 187 and 188.

16] THE | **WORKS** | OF | JONATHAN SWIFT, D.D. . . VOLUME XVI. . . . 1814.

Collation: $\pi 1$ $2\pi^4$ A-$2G^8$ $2H^2$. Pagination: *i* half-title, *ii* printer's imprint(1), *iii* title-page, *iv blank*, *v* vi-x Contents, *1* fly-title, *2 blank*, *3* 4-483 text, 483 printer's imprint(2), *484 blank*. Printer's imprints: (1) [*short rule*] | Printed by George Ramsay & Co.; (2) [*short rule*] | EDINBURGH: | Printed by Geo. Ramsay & Co. | 1811. Typography: Gatherings 2A-2H are signed Aa-Hh, according to Ramsay's practice.

Figures: A10-8 12-9, B27-8, C36-3 46-4, D62-4 64-7, E80-7, F82-4 84-9, G102-4, H126-4 128-8, I 142-4 144-8, K146-6 156-1, L174-3, M184-2 186-1, N200-8 206-1, O 218-2 224-6, P236-1 238-7, Q244-7 250-1, R258-1 272-4, S286-3 288-1, T290-4 304-1, U306-4 320-10, X328-1 334-8, Y350-1 352-8, Z358-1 360-8, 2A 380-2, 2B 390-7 400-5, 2C 410-5 412-1, 2D 420-1 430-5, 2E 446-1 448-2, 2F 452-8 462-7, 2G 476-1, 2H 482-8.

17] THE | **WORKS** | OF | JONATHAN SWIFT, D.D. . . . VOLUME XVII. . . . 1814.

Collation: $\pi 1$ $2\pi^4$ A-U^8 X^8(±X3) Y-$2E^8$ $2F^4$ $2G^2$. Pagination: *i* half-title, *ii* printer's imprint(1), *iii* title-page, *iv blank*, *v* vi-x Contents, *1* fly-title, *2 blank*, *3* 4-460 text, 460 printer's imprint(2). Printer's imprints: (1) [*short rule*] | Printed by George Ramsay & Co.; (2) [*short rule*] | EDINBURGH: | Printed by Geo. Ramsay & Co. | 1811. Typography: Gatherings 2A-2G are signed Aa-Hh, according to Ramsay's practice. In some copies page 417 is misnumbered 471.

Figures: A4-2 10-1, B26-1, C36-1, D58-7 60-8, E77-5, F92-5, G112-9, H126-5, I 132-5, K148-5 159-5/-, L167-6 176-5, M184-5, N203-6/- 208-2, O 218-5, P237-6 238-9, Q242-10 256-4, R268-4 271-5, S282-5 284-4, T291-10 297-4, U306-4 312-5, X328-5 334-6/4, Y338-4 352-5, Z354-10 356-6, 2A 370-4 372-5, 2B 394-5, 2C 406-10 416-5, 2D 426-10 428-5, 2E 446-7 448-5, 2F 456-5, 2G 458-7.

Notes: Cancel X3 (pages 325-326) has a direction reference line and an * at center.

18] THE | **WORKS** | OF | JONATHAN SWIFT, D.D. . . . VOLUME XVIII. . . . 1814.

Collation: π1 2π[4] A-2F[8] 2G[4] *2H1. Pagination: *i* half-title, *ii* printer's imprint(1), *iii* title-page, *iv blank*, *v* vi-ix Contents, *x blank*, *1-3* 4-471 text, 471 printer's imprint(2), *472 blank*, 473 Corrigenda et Addenda, *474 blank*. Printer's imprints: (1) [*short rule*] | Printed by George Ramsay & Co.; (2) [*short rule*] | EDINBURGH: | Printed by Geo. Ramsay & Co. | 1811. Typography: Gatherings 2A-2G and *2H are signed Aa-Gg and *Hh, according to Ramsay's practice.

Figures: A4-7 6-5, B30-5 32-7, C34-7 36-5, D62-1 64-4, E74-5 76-10, F90-4 96-6, G104-5 110-4, H124-2 126-6/-, I 130-4 132-5, K158-5 160-10, L166-10 176-5, M186-5 192-10, N194-5, O 218-10 221-4, P236-10 238-6, Q250-5 252-4, R272-4, S281-10 283-7, T300-6 302-4, U316-4, X327-6/- 336-10, Y342-6 344-4, Z362-6, 2A 380-6 382-4, 2B 394-4 396-6, 2C 416-4/-, 2D 426-6 428-4/-, 2E 442-8 444-1, 2F 464-6, 2G 467-11, *2H—.

19] THE | **WORKS** | OF | JONATHAN SWIFT, D.D. . . . VOLUME XIX. . . . 1814.

Collation: *a*[2] *b*[4] A-2M[8] 2N[2]. Pagination: *i* half-title, *ii blank*, *iii* title-page, *iv blank*, *v* vi-xi Contents, *xii blank*, *1* fly-title, *2 blank*, *3* 4-457 text, 457 Errata, *458 blank*, *i* ii-cvi Index, cvi printer's imprint: [*short rule*] | Printed by George Ramsay & Co. | Edinburgh, 1814. Typography: Signature *b* is italicized. Gatherings 2A-2N are signed Aa-Nn, according to Ramsay's practice.

Figures: *b* viii-1, A14-10, B18-6, C48-10/-, D52-6/-, E80-6, F84-11, G102-6, H—, I 140-6/-, K150-6 152-6, L162-3/- 164-4, M180-1, N194-8 200-6, O 214-8, P240-8, Q245-8, R260-5 266-4, S282-5 288-4, T298-8 304-4, U306-6 320-10, X328-5 330-10/-, Y346-6 352-5/-, Z354-6/-, 2A 380-5, 2B 400-1, 2C 406-5/- 416-3, 2D 429-3 430-4, 2E 448-1, 2F 452-5, 2G x-4 xxi-5, 2H—, 2I xlii-3 lii-1, 2K lvi-2 or 3 lxvi-1, 2L lxxii-5 lxxviii-1, 2M lxxxviii-3 cii-5, 2N—.

Notes: 'A Cantata' on two engraved leaves follows X8 (page 336).

79Ab] First Scott Edition, Second (Large-Paper) Impression: 1814

THE | **WORKS** | OF | JONATHAN SWIFT, D.D. | DEAN OF ST PATRICK'S, DUBLIN; . . . VOLUME I [II-XIX]. . . . 1814.

Published concurrently with the previous impression. £15.4.0. A 'few copies'. Paper: Royal 8° (245 x 153mm uncut). Watermarks: These again indicate, as in the preceding impression, several progressions:

(*a*) D & AC | 1808, occasionally mixed with date only of 1806 or 1808, volumes 2-6, 8, 9(A-2K), and mixed further with 1809: volumes 10(A-2D), 11-12, all these printed by James Ballantyne;

(*b1*) 1809, 1810, 1812 mixed: volumes 7, 9(final sheets *2L-*2N), 10(final sheets 2O-2P), 13-15, 18, and mixed further with WS 1803, volumes 16-17, all printed by

George Ramsay [15-18 with his final imprint dated '1811'];
(*b2*) 1810, 1812, 1814 mixed: volumes 1, 19 [both with George Ramsay's imprint dated '1814'];
(*b3*) undated preliminary gatherings volumes 2-6, 1812 volumes 7-13, 1814 volumes 14-19, 1.

General Notes: Apart from the paper described immediately above, all volumes are identical with the previous regular paper impression, except as noted below. The rule above title-page date varies according to the pattern described for the earlier printing.

Copy: TxGR*.
*With π4 representing duplicate half-title in volumes 3, 6, 8, 11, 12, all printed, apparently, according to the procedure described in 79Aa, General Notes..

1] THE | **WORKS** | OF | JONATHAN SWIFT, D.D. . . VOLUME I. . . . 1814.

Figures: A10-6, C46—, F86—, 2E 448—, *b* xxiv—, *d* lx——.

2] THE | **WORKS** | OF | JONATHAN SWIFT, D.D. . . VOLUME II. . . . 1814.

Figures: 2A 384—.

3] THE | **WORKS** | OF | JONATHAN SWIFT, D.D. . . VOLUME III. . . . 1814.

Typography: In this impression page 192 is missing page number 1; page 224 is missing first page number 2; page 235 has page number 5 upside down. Figures: 2B 386—. Notes: Q8, now integral in its corrected state, has figure 10 on its verso, page 256.

4] THE | **WORKS** | OF | JONATHAN SWIFT, D.D. . . VOLUME IV. . . . 1814.

Typography: In this impression 432 is missing the first two page-numbers. Figures: M180—, N196-2, 2A 370—, 2C 402-3.

5] THE | **WORKS** | OF | JONATHAN SWIFT, D.D. . . VOLUME V. . . . 1814.

Typography: In this impression page 396 is unnumbered and signature U (page 305) has no volume number in the direction line. Figures: Y352-10, 2D 418-6.

6] THE | **WORKS** | OF | JONATHAN SWIFT, D.D. . . VOLUME VI. . . . 1814.

Figures: F82—, L163—, Z360—.

7] THE | **WORKS** | OF | JONATHAN SWIFT, D.D. . . VOLUME VII. . . . 1814.

Figures: D54—, H128—, I 132—, M182—, X326—, Y344-5, 2H 494—.

8] THE | **WORKS** | OF | JONATHAN SWIFT, D.D. . . VOLUME VIII. . . . 1814.

Typography: In this impression U4 (pages 311-312) is now integral to the gathering. Figures: A3—, P238-13, Q246-12, 2B 389-'21'[12].

9] THE | **WORKS** | OF | JONATHAN SWIFT, D.D. . . . VOLUME IX. . . . 1814.

Typography: In this impression page 166 the first word now is above the line; page 176 the first parenthesis is missing; page 279 the first parenthesis is broken; page 363 has no page number; page 412 has the '4' in the page number missing. Figures: B18—, G101-14 107—, 2F 464—.

10] THE | **WORKS** | OF | JONATHAN SWIFT, D.D. . . . VOLUME X. . . . 1814.

Figures: B31—, Q251—, S287—, Z354-'21'[12] 357—, 2A 373—, 2G 468—, 2N 562—, 2 O 584-3.

11] THE | **WORKS** | OF | JONATHAN SWIFT, D.D. . . .VOLUME XI. . . . 1814.

Typography: In this impression page 97 has the page number transposed as '79'. Figures: Present, but invariable.

12] THE | **WORKS** | OF | JONATHAN SWIFT, D.D. . . .VOLUME XII. . . . 1814.

Typography: In this impression pages 4 and 140 are unnumbered. Figures: A9—.

13] THE | **WORKS** | OF | JONATHAN SWIFT, D.D. . . VOLUME XIII. . . . 1814.

Typography: In this impression page 466 has the first page number missing. Figures: K152—, 2A 373—, 2C 412—.

14] THE | **WORKS** | OF | JONATHAN SWIFT, D.D. . . VOLUME XIV. . . . 1814.

Figures: 2C 406—.

15] THE | **WORKS** | OF | JONATHAN SWIFT, D.D. . . VOLUME XV. . . . 1814.

Figures: M184-1. Notes: For the reasons given in the note to the regular issue, sheet O appears to be of a later, cancel setting in both impressions.

16] THE | **WORKS** | OF | JONATHAN SWIFT, D.D. . . VOLUME XVI. . . . 1814.

Notes: In all respects except paper this volume appears to be invariable.

17] THE | **WORKS** | OF | JONATHAN SWIFT, D.D. . . . VOLUME XVII. . . . 1814.

Typography: In this impression page 417 is misnumbered 471. Figures: K159-5, N203—, X334-4.

18] THE | **WORKS** | OF | JONATHAN SWIFT, D.D. . . . VOLUME XVIII. . . . 1814.

Typography: In this impression page number vi is transposed as 'iv'. Figures: H126—, 2C 416—, 2D 428—.

19] THE | **WORKS** | OF | JONATHAN SWIFT, D.D. . . . VOLUME XIX. . . . 1814.

Typography: In this impression page 179 has the last page number upside down as '6'. Figures: C48—, D52—, I 140—, L162-3, X330-10, Y352—, Z354—, 2C 406—, 2K lvi-3.

79Ac] Second Scott Edition: 1824

THE | **WORKS** | OF | JONATHAN SWIFT, D.D. | DEAN OF ST PATRICK'S, DUBLIN; | CONTAINING | ADDITIONAL LETTERS, TRACTS, AND POEMS, | NOT HITHERTO PUBLISHED; | WITH | **NOTES,** | AND | A LIFE OF THE AUTHOR, | BY | SIR WALTER SCOTT, BART. | SECOND EDITION. | [*short Oxford rule*] | VOLUME I [II-XIX]. |

[*short reversed Oxford rule*] | EDINBURGH: | PRINTED FOR ARCHIBALD CONSTABLE AND CO. EDINBURGH; | AND HURST, ROBINSON, AND CO. LONDON. | [*short rule*] | 1824.

Announced July 1824 in London (*MM* 1 August), issued 16 August (*MC*). £8.11.0. 1250 copies. Binding: drab or blue boards with printed labels. Paper: Demy 8° (225 x 142mm uncut). Watermarks: *none*. Typography: Printer's imprints read: (1) [*short rule*] | EDINBURGH: | PRINTED BY JAMES BALLANTYNE AND CO.; (2a) [*short rule*] | EDINBURGH: | Printed by James Ballantyne and Co. For volumes 2-5, all the work of another printer, the final imprint is changed to (2b) [*short rule*] | Printed by George Ramsay & Co.

General Notes: To the original 1814 Advertisement, reprinted in volume 1 of this 1824 edition, Scott adds two further paragraphs, the first mentioning some improvements in the arrangement of the contents, the second alluding to the discovery of previously unpublished letters. Altogether, as indicated in the Potter listing (pages 130-150), only two new letters are added in this edition, as well as supplementary verses to three poems previously printed, and four prose pieces; but as usual Scott's commentary, as suggested below in volume 6, continues to be enlarged.

Copies: BCL E O P; CtY IdU InU*a NNU-W*b(vols.6-10, 12-18) TxU.
*(a) copy marked for some later edition; (b) James Ballantyne's marked copy.

1] THE | **WORKS** | OF | JONATHAN SWIFT, D.D. . . . SECOND EDITION. | [*short Oxford rule*] | VOLUME I. . . . 1824.

Collation: $\pi^2(\pi 2+1)$ a^4 A-2K^8 2L^2. Pagination: *1* half-title, *2 blank*, *3* title-page, *4* printer's imprint(1), *i*-ii Contents, *iii* iv-ix Advertisement, dated from Abbotsford 1 June 1824, *x blank*, *1* fly-title, *2 blank*, *3* 4-495 Memoirs, *496 blank*, *497* fly-title, *498 blank*, *499-500* 501-532 Appendix, 532 printer's imprint(2a). Illustrations: Frontispiece portrait painted by J. Burgess after Bindon, engraved by W. H. Lizars, and published by A. Constable with 1824 imprint date (*see* des-cription page 458n); facing second page *1*, or in some copies page *4*, three medal designs engraved by W. H. Lizars. Typography: Preliminary signature *a* is in italic.

Figures: *a* ix-1, A16-9, B32-12, C48-11, D64-17, E80-17, F96-12, G112-10, H128-5, I 144-9, K160-12, L176-10, M192-11, N208-10, O 224-3, P240-2, Q256-2, R272-9, S288-5, T304-3, U320-7, X336-6, Y352-4, Z368-11, 2A 384-9, 2B 400-6, 2C 416-7, 2D 432-8, 2E 448-4, 2F 464-6, 2G 480-5, 2H 492-15, 2 I 512-12, 2K 528-8, 2L—. Excepting 2H, where 8v (page *496*) is a blank (and the figure 15 therefore entered elsewhere in the outer forme), each figure is centered below text in the last page of the gathering: a reflection of the niceties now observed in the Ballantyne printing office.

2] THE | **WORKS** | OF | JONATHAN SWIFT, D.D. . . . SECOND EDITION. | [*short Oxford rule*] | VOLUME II. . . . 1824.

Collation: $\pi^2(\pi 2+1)$ A-2I^8 2K^2. Pagination: *1* half-title, *2 blank*, *3* title-page, *4* printer's imprint(1), *i*-ii Contents, *1* fly-title, *2 blank*, *3* 4-516 text, 516 printer's imprint(2b). Typography: Gatherings 2A-2K are signed Aa-Kk, according to printer Ramsay's practice. In some copies page 4 is unnumbered.

Figures: A12-1, B22-4, C38-1, D60-4, E66-6, F92-6, G102-6, H118-6, I 138-4, K156-6, L174-1, M186-1, N206-4, O 222-4, P226-4, Q242-1, R260-10, S277-4, T299-10, U314-1, X330-4, Y352-6, Z354-4 364-4/-, 2A 372-6, 2B 400-4, 2C 412-4, 2D 418-1, 2E 442-6, 2F 464-4, 2G 476-4, 2H—, 2I—, 2K 514-1. In contrast to the regular procedure in the first Ballantyne volume, the figuring in Ramsay's printing office was done randomly, if at all.

3] THE | **WORKS** | OF | JONATHAN SWIFT, D.D. . . . SECOND EDITION. | [*short Oxford rule*] | VOLUME III. . . . 1824.

Collation: π^2 $2\pi^2$ A-2I^8 2K^4 2L^2. Pagination: *1* half-title, *2 blank*, *3* title-page, *4* printer's imprint(1), *i* ii-iii Contents, *iv blank*, *1* fly-title, *2 blank*, *3* 4-523 text, 523 printer's imprint(2b), *524 blank*. Typography: Gatherings 2A-2L are signed Aa-Ll, according to printer Ramsay's practice.

Figures: A4-1 10-11, B24-1 26-11, C41-11, D60-1, E66-10 80-4, F92-11 94-1, G106-4 112-10, H118-1 124-11, I 137-4 142-10, K146-11 160-1, L172-10 174-4, M178-11 180-1, N194-10 208-4, O 218-10 220-4, P234-10 240-4, Q256-10, R270-4, S284-10 286-11, T292-11 302-1, U315-1, X334-11, Y350-1, Z366-11, 2A 384-4, 2B 394-10, 2C 416-4, 2D 424-10, 2E 442-1, 2F 458-11, 2G 480-1, 2H 489-11, 2 I 512-4, 2K 518-10, 2L 522-10.

4] THE | **WORKS** | OF | JONATHAN SWIFT, D.D. . . . SECOND EDITION. | [*short Oxford rule*] | VOLUME IV. . . . 1824.

Collation: $\pi^2(\pi 2+1)$ A-2D^8. Pagination: *1* half-title, *2 blank*, *3* title-page, *4* printer's imprint(1), *i*-ii Contents, *1* fly-title, *2 blank*, *3* 4-432 text, 432 printer's imprint(2b). Typography: Gatherings 2A-2D are signed Aa-Dd, according to printer Ramsay's practice.

Figures: A8-10, B22-6, C34-6, D54-6, E72-10, F90-1, G102-10, H120-10, I 142-10, K154-1, L176-6, M184-1, N204-10, O 221-10, P236-10, Q254-6, R268-2 271-1, S286-10, T298-4, U310-4, X330-2, Y352-4, Z365-11, 2A 374-2, 2B 400-4, 2C 410-2, 2D 420-4.

5] THE | **WORKS** | OF | JONATHAN SWIFT, D.D. . . . SECOND EDITION. | [*short Oxford rule*] | VOLUME V. . . . 1824.

Collation: $\pi^2(\pi 2+1)$ A-$2F^8$ 2G1. Pagination: *1* half-title, *2 blank*, *3* title-page, *4* printer's imprint(1), *i*-ii Contents, *1* fly-title, *2 blank*, *3* 4-466 text, 466 printer's imprint(2b). Typography: Gatherings 2A-2G are signed Aa-Gg, according to printer Ramsay's practice.

Figures: A4-1, B24-6, C48-10, D62-6, E74-4, F82-6 84-10, G110-4, H128-2, I 130-4, K153-1, L170-4 176-1, M188-4 190-1, N202-1, O 218-1, P230-1, Q248-1/-, R262-1, S288-1, T298-1, U310-1, X322-1, Y348-1, Z368-1, 2A 374-1, 2B 400-1, 2C 412-1, 2D 428-1, 2E 446-1, 2F 458-1, 2G—.

6] THE | **WORKS** | OF | JONATHAN SWIFT, D.D. . . . SECOND EDITION. | [*short Oxford rule*] | VOLUME VI. . . . 1824.

Collation: π^2 $2\pi^4(-2\pi 4)$ A-X^8 $Y^8(\pm Y6)$ Z-$2I^8$. Pagination: *1* half-title, *2 blank*, *3* title-page, *4* printer's imprint(1), *i* ii-v Contents, *vi blank*, *1* fly-title, *2 blank*, *3* 4-512 text, 512 printer's imprint(2a). Typography: In some copies page 297 is misnumbered 29.

Figures: 2π ii-15, A16-5, B32-2, C41-7, D64-11, E80-3, F96-11, G112-12, H128-10, I 131-2, K160-13, L*176*-12, M181-7, N208-9, O 224-15, P240-19, Q256-18, R272-3, S288-10, T*303*-19, U317-19, X336-18/-, Y352-10, Z368-15, 2A 384-19, 2B *400*-1, 2C 416-5, 2D 432-15, 2E 448-16, 2F 464-19, 2G 480-1, 2H 496-3, 2 I 509-8. As for the first volume, also printed throughout by Ballantyne, so for this and the remaining volumes, the figures with few exceptions are carefully centered below text on the last page of the gathering.

Notes: In his introduction to *The History of John Bull* (page 4) Scott refers to a manuscript satiric parable by Adam Ferguson (died 1816, two years after Scott's first edition of Swift), given him by the author's family, and possibly used by Scott himself in a 24 January 1821 communication to the *Edinburgh Weekly Journal* (*see* 151A). The engraving of Wood's Halfpenny, appearing belatedly on cancel P1 volume 1 of the first edition (a volume printed last), now appropriately occurs here as a headpiece on Y6 (page 347): again a cancel to permit this separate press work, with printed text on verso.

7] THE | **WORKS** | OF | JONATHAN SWIFT, D.D. . . . SECOND EDITION. | [*short Oxford rule*] | VOLUME VII. . . . 1824.

Collation: π^2 $2\pi^2$ A-$2I^8$ $2K^2$. Pagination: *1* half-title, *2 blank*, *3* title-page, *4* printer's imprint(1), *i* ii-iii Contents, *iv blank*, *1* fly-title, *2 blank*, *3-4* 5-515 text, 515 printer's imprint(2a), *516 blank*. Typography: Page 139 is misnumbered 339.

Figures: A16-15/5, B32-10, C48-16, D64-1, E80-6, F93-15, G112-19, H128-17, I 144-6, K160-4, L174-4, M192-9, N208-13, O 212-19, P240-10, Q256-3, R272-18, S288-15, T304-2, U320-3, X324-18, Y352-6, Z368-4, 2A 384-5, 2B 400-16, 2C 416-15, 2D 432-7, 2E 448-5, 2F 464-8, 2G 480-16, 2H 496-13, 2 I 512-10, 2K—.

8] THE | **WORKS** | OF | JONATHAN SWIFT, D.D. . . . SECOND EDITION. | [*short Oxford rule*] | VOLUME VIII. . . . 1824.

Collation: $\pi^2(\pi 2+1)$ A-2H[8] 2I[4]. Pagination: *i* half-title, *ii blank*, *iii* title-page, *iv* printer's imprint(1), *v*-vi Contents, *1* fly-title, *2 blank*, *3* 4-502 text, 502 printer's imprint(2a), *503-504 blank*.

Figures: A14-19, B32-12, C—, D61-7, E80-16, F96-2, G112-8, H128-9, I 142-8, K160-10, L176-'21'[12], M192-15, N208-13, O 224-15, P240-18, Q256-13, R272-14, S288-10, T304-18, U320-2, X336-8, Y352-10, Z368-13, 2A 384-18, 2B 400-14, 2C 416-13, 2D 428-10, 2E 448-8, 2F 464-14, 2G 480-7, 2H 496-7, 2 I 498-15. Probably figure '21' (page 176) is transposed, for the highest number otherwise recorded in this work is 19.

9] THE | **WORKS** | OF | JONATHAN SWIFT, D.D. . . . SECOND EDITION. | [*short Oxford rule*] | VOLUME IX. . . . 1824.

Collation: π^2 $2\pi^2$ A-2G[8] 2H1. Pagination: *1* half-title, *2 blank*, *3* title-page, *4* printer's imprint(1), *i* ii-iii Contents, *iv blank*, *1* fly-title, *2* note, 3-482 text, 482 printer's imprint(2a). Typography: Page number 459 is transposed as 495.

Figures: A16-5, B32-15, C48-2, D64-7, E80-5, F96-15, G109-10, H128-15, I 144-18, K160-19, L176-16, M192-2, N205-10, O 224-19, P240-2, Q—, R269-7, S288-11, T304-3, U320-13, X336-12, Y349-20, Z368-12, 2A 384-6, 2B 400-12, 2C 414-16, 2D 432-11, 2E 448-6, 2F 464-18, 2G 480-8, 2H—.

10] THE | **WORKS** | OF | JONATHAN SWIFT, D.D. . . . SECOND EDITION. | [*short Oxford rule*] | VOLUME X. . . . 1824.

Collation: π^2 $2\pi^2$ A-2D[8] 2E[4]. Pagination: *1* half-title, *2 blank*, *3* title-page, *4* printer's imprint(1), *i* ii-iii Contents, *iv blank*, *1* fly-title, *2 blank*, *3* 4-440 text, 440 printer's imprint(2a).

Figures: A16-15, B32-12, C48-15, D64-1, E80-17, F96-8, G112-2, H128-11, I 144-3, K160-7, L176-12, M192-9, N208-8, O 224-4, P240-12, Q256-17, R272-17, S288-7, T304-6, U320-5, X336-9, Y352-10, Z368-7, 2A 384-15, 2B 397-10, 2C 416-10, 2D 432-17, 2E 439-11.

Notes: Fly-title verso, page *2*, originally blank, in later copies was provided with three classical quotations.

11] THE | **WORKS** | OF | JONATHAN SWIFT, D.D. . . . SECOND EDITION. | [*short Oxford rule*] | VOLUME XI. . . . 1824.

Collation: π^2 $2\pi^2(2\pi 2+1)$ A-2E[8] 2F[4] 2G[2]. Pagination: *i* half-title, *ii blank*, *iii* title-page, *iv* printer's imprint(1), *v* vi-ix Contents, *x blank*, *1* fly-title, *2 blank*, *3* 4-460 text, 460 printer's imprint(2a). Typography: In a few copies the name in final imprint was pied and then reinserted (by the pressman?) as 'Jamesla Balntyne'. In some copies page 436 is misnumbered 33.

Figures: 2π ix-1/-, A13-7, B32-1, C48-7, D64-4, E80-7, F96-7, G98-14 112-13, H128-16, I 144-20, K160-19, L176-16, M192-14, N208-12, O 224-17, P240-19, Q256-17, R272-19, S288-13, T304-2, U320-12, X336-19, Y352-17, Z368-12, 2A 384-6, 2B 400-11, 2C 416-12, 2D 432-11, 2E 448-15/-, 2F 456-5, 2G—.

12] THE | **WORKS** | OF | JONATHAN SWIFT, D.D. . . . SECOND EDITION. | [*short Oxford rule*] | VOLUME XII. . . . 1824.

Collation: π^2 $2\pi^2$ A-2H^8 2I^4(-2I4). Pagination: *1* half-title, *2 blank*, *3* title-page, *4* printer's imprint(1), *i* ii-iii Contents, *iv blank*, *1* fly-title, *2 blank*, *3-4* 5-501 text, 501 printer's imprint(2a), *502 blank.*

Figures: 2π iii-17, A13-15, B32-9, C48-15, D64-7, E80-16, F96-7, G112-12, H—, I 144-16/20, K160-11, L176-5, M192-7, N208-17, O 224-14, P240-5, Q256-6, R272-12, S288-18, T302-19, U320-6, X336-4, Y352-9, Z368-2, 2A 376-10, 2B 400-10, 2C 413-15, 2D—, 2E 448-14, 2F 464-10, 2G 477-4, 2H 496-10, 2 I—.

13] THE | **WORKS** | OF | JONATHAN SWIFT, D.D. . . . SECOND EDITION. | [*short Oxford rule*] | VOLUME XIII. . . . 1824.

Collation: π^2 $2\pi^2(2\pi2+1)$ A-2G^8 2H^4 *2 I*1. Pagination: *1* half-title, *2 blank*, *3* title-page, *4* printer's imprint(1), *i* ii-v Contents, *vi blank*, *1* fly-title, *2* Preface, *3* 4-489 text, 489 printer's imprint(2a), *490 blank*. Typography: Page number 368 is transposed as 386.

Figures: A16-7, B32-1, C48-10, D64-14, E80-17, F96-11, G109-10, H125-15, I 140-5, K160-15, L176-11, M192-5, N208-11, O 224-6, P240-14, Q256-5, R272-4, S285-11, T300-9, U320-8, X—, Y352-8, Z '386'[368]-6, 2A—, 2B 397-12, 2C 416-2, 2D 432-17, 2E 448-15, 2F 464-6, 2G 480-14, 2H 488-8, *2 I*—.

14] THE | **WORKS** | OF | JONATHAN SWIFT, D.D. . . . SECOND EDITION. | [*short Oxford rule*] | VOLUME XIV. . . . 1824.

Collation: π^2 $2\pi^2(2\pi2+1)$ A-2L^8. Pagination: *1* half-title, *2 blank*, *3* title-page, *4* printer's imprint(1), *i* ii-vi Contents, *1* fly-title, *2 blank*, *3* 4-544 text, 544 printer's imprint(2a). Typography: Pages 145-176 (sheets K-L) are misnumbered 137-168. Page 347 is misnumbered 247.

Figures: A16-13, B32-15, C48-3, D61-6, E80-13, F96-9, G112-9, H125-15, I 144-14, K152-1/19, L168-2, M192-16, N208-12, O 224-16, P240-3, Q252-6, R272-17, S288-4, T304-5, U320-6, X336-4, Y352-1, Z368-9, 2A 384-17, 2B 400-14, 2C 416-2, 2D 432-5, 2E 448-9, 2F 464-10, 2G 480-12, 2H 496-17, 2 I 512-7, 2K 528-10, 2L 544-7.

15] THE | **WORKS** | OF | JONATHAN SWIFT, D.D. . . . SECOND EDITION. | [*short Oxford rule*] | VOLUME XV. . . . 1824.

Collation: π^2 $2\pi^4$ A-2K^8 *2L*1. Pagination: *1* half-title, *2 blank*, *3* title-page, *4* printer's imprint(1), *i* ii-vii Contents, *viii blank*, *1* fly-title, *2 blank*, *3* 4-529 text, 529 printer's imprint(2a), *530 blank*.

Figures: 2π v-5, A16-9/11, B32-15, C48-1, D64-7, E80-17, F96-2, G112-16, H128-4, I 144-1, K160-15, L176-8, M192-7, N208-12, O 224-6, P240-2, Q256-11, R272-15, S288-5, T304-9, U320-10, X336-6, Y352-4, Z361-15, 2A 384-17, 2B 400-11, 2C 413-8, 2D 432-7, 2E 444-6, 2F 464-2, 2G 480-5, 2H 496-7, 2 I 512-4, 2K 528-9, *2L*—.

16] THE | **WORKS** | OF | JONATHAN SWIFT, D.D. . . . SECOND EDITION. | [*short Oxford rule*] | VOLUME XVI. . . . 1824.

Collation: π^2 $2\pi^4$ A-2G^8 2H^4 2I1 *2K*1. Pagination: *1* half-title, *2 blank*, *3* titlepage, *4* printer's imprint(1), *i* ii-vii Contents, *viii blank*, *1* fly-title, *2 blank*, *3* 4-491 text, 491 printer's imprint(2a), *492 blank*.

Figures: 2π iv-15, A16-10, B32-7, C45-16, D64-5, E80-7, F96-3, G112-14, H128-4, I 144-15, K160-2, L176-15, M192-5, N208-10, O 224-12, P240-4, Q256-8, R272-12, S288-6, T304-12, U320-17, X336-15, Y352-11, Z 368-10, 2A 384-2, 2B 400-3, 2C 403-8, 2D 432-17, 2E 445-14, 2F 456-17, 2G 480-16, 2H 488-6, 2 I—, *2K*—.

17] THE | **WORKS** | OF | JONATHAN SWIFT, D.D. . . . SECOND EDITION. | [*short Oxford rule*] | VOLUME XVII. . . . 1824.

Collation: π^2 $2\pi^2(2\pi2+1)$ A-2H^8 2I^4 2K1. Pagination: *1* half-title, *2 blank*, *3* title-page, *4* printer's imprint(1), *i* ii-vi Contents, *1* fly-title, *2 blank*, *3* 4-506 text, 506 printer's imprint(2a).

Figures: 2π *i*-5, A16-6, B32-5, C48-15, D64-11, E80-14, F96-7, G112-15, H128-7, I 144-12, K160-2/-, L176-5, M192-12, N208-10, O 224-11, P236-12, Q256-17, R272-8, S288-11, T304-7, U320-1, X336-2, Y352-9, Z368-17, 2A 384-9, 2B 400-12, 2C 416-7, 2D 432-3, 2E 448-17, 2F 464-8, 2G 480-15, 2H 496-17, 2 I 504-3/-, 2K—.

18] THE | **WORKS** | OF | JONATHAN SWIFT, D.D. . . . SECOND EDITION. | [*short Oxford rule*] | VOLUME XVIII. . . . 1824.

Collation: π^2 $2\pi^2(2\pi2+1)$ A-2K^8 2L^4. Pagination: *1* half-title, *2 blank*, *3* titlepage, *4* printer's imprint(1), *i* ii-vi Contents, *1* fly-title, *2 blank*, 3 4-535 text, *536* printer's imprint(2a).

Figures: A16-2, B32-5, C48-14, D64-6, E80-12, F96-1, G112-11, H128-15, I 144-5, K160-6, L176-17, M192-11, N208-12, O 224-3, P240-11, Q256-3, R272-15,

S288-17, T304-1, U320-17, X336-15, Y352-17, Z367-1/-, 2A 384-7, 2B 400-11, 2C 416-11, 2D 432-15, 2E 448-15, 2F 464-8, 2G 480-15, 2H 496-12, 2 I 509-4, 2K 527-11, 2L 533-1.

19] THE | **WORKS** | OF | JONATHAN SWIFT, D.D. . . . SECOND EDITION. | [*short Oxford rule*] | VOLUME XIX. . . . 1824.

Collation: π^2 $2\pi^2(2\pi2+1)$ A-2G^8 2G^4 2H^2. Pagination: *1* half-title, *2 blank*, *3* title-page, *4* printer's imprint(1), *i* ii-vi Contents, *1* fly-title, *2 blank*, *3* 4-382 text, *383* fly-title, *384 blank*, *385* 386-491 Index, 491 printer's imprint(2a), *492 blank*. Illustrations: 'A Cantata' on two leaves, engraved by Lizars, follows X8 (page 336).

Figures: A16-1, B32-7, C48-10, D64-6, E77-10, F96-11, G112-6, H128-8, I 144-17, K160-3, L176-1, M189-7, N208-17, O 224-8, P240-12, Q256-1, R272-1, S284-15, T297-15, U320-17, X336-1, Y352-15, Z 365-1, 2A 381-9, 2B 399-13, 2C 416-1, 2D 432-12, 2E 448-15, 2F 464-10, 2G 480-11, 2G 488-12, 2H—.

REPRINTS

FRANCE

PARIS: Didot and Galignani
[~] Memoirs of Jonathan Swift, D. D. MDCCCXXVI. (Collection of Modern English Authors: *see* 292R.2-3)

GERMANY

ZWICKAU: Schumann
[~] Memoirs of Jonathan Swift, D.D. 1829. (Pocket Library of English Classics: *see* 302R.192-194)

UNITED STATES

BOSTON: Wells and Lilly
[~] Life of Jonathan Swift. 1829. (The Miscellaneous Prose Works: *see* 308R.2)

79R] PHILADELPHIA: Mitchell, Ames, and White 1819
Select Poems of Jonathan Swift. With a Life of the Author, from Johnson, and Scott. (*in* The Works of the British Poets . . . Vol. XVIII. . . Philadelphia: Published by Mitchell, Ames, and White. William Brown, Printer. 1819.) Pages: *1* 2-36. Notes: A single paraphrase by Robert Walsh, Jr., with quotations from the two biographical essays. Copies: DLC MH.

EXTRACTS FROM A JOURNAL KEPT DURING A COASTING VOYAGE

80A] First Printing: 1814

'EXTRACTS FROM A JOURNAL KEPT DURING A COASTING VOYAGE THROUGH THE SCOTTISH ISLANDS.', pages *431* 432-446, *in*:

The Edinburgh Annual Register, for 1812. Vol. Fifth.—Part Second. Edinburgh: Printed by James Ballantyne and Co. for John Ballantyne and Co. Edinburgh; Longman, Hurst, Rees, Orme, and Brown, London; and the Other Proprietors. 1814.

Published 26 December 1814 in Edinburgh (*EEC*). £1.4.0.

Notes: Four of Scott's diary entries for August 1814, all unsigned, are entered here, rather curiously, as a space-filler in an annual for 1812. A fuller and more accurate version, 'contained in five little paper-books' and dating from 29 July to 8 September, is printed in Lockhart.

Copies: E L O; PPL TxU.

References: Curry, pages 36-37. (Magnum Opus Edition: Not reprinted, but quoted in Lockhart, iv.182-370.)

THE LORD OF THE ISLES

As for the *Lord of the Isles* I think it is my last poetical adventure at least upon a large scale—I swear not because I do not make any positive resolution. But I think I have written enough and it is unlikely that I shall change my opinion. (Scott to Lady Abercorn, 10 January 1815, *Letters*, iv.6-7.)

81Aa] First Edition, First Impression: 1815

THE | **LORD OF THE ISLES,** | A POEM. | BY | WALTER SCOTT, Esq. | [*short Oxford rule*] | EDINBURGH: | [*short Oxford rule*] | PRINTED FOR | ARCHIBALD CONSTABLE AND CO. EDINBURGH; | AND | LONGMAN, HURST, REES, ORME, AND BROWN, LONDON; | *By James Ballantyne and Co. Edinburgh.* | [*Oxford dash*] | 1815.

Recorded 2 January 1815 in Edinburgh (E MS.789, p.173); published 5 January (*EEC*); issued 13 January in London (*MC*). On 10 January Byron noted that he had received a 'mail-coach copy . . . by special licence of Murray' (*Byron*, iv.252). £2.2.0. 1750 copies (E MS.321, f.295). Binding: drab or slate boards with printed label. Paper: Demy 4° (287 x 223mm. uncut). Watermarks: 3 [5, 7, 9, 10] | W BALSTON | 1814. Collation: π^4 A-D^4 E^4(±E1) F-K^4 L^4(±L4) M-X^4 Y^4(±Y1) Z-2L^4 2M^2 a-b^4 c^4(±c3) d-u^4 x^2 *y*1. Pagination: *i* half-title, *ii blank*, *iii* title-page, *iv blank*, *v* Advertisement dated from Abbotsford, 10 December 1814, *vi blank*, *vii* Contents, *viii blank*, *1* fly-title, *2 blank*, *3* 4-275 text, *276 blank*, *i* fly-title, *ii blank*, *iii* iv-clxv Notes, clxv printer's imprint, *clxvi blank*. Printer's imprint: [*short Oxford rule*] | EDINBURGH: | Printed by James Ballantyne & Co. Typography: page li is misnumbered il. In some copies, page 37, line 8, the initial quotation mark is depressed.

Figures: A*3*-8, B11-10, C18-10, D30-7, E36-5, F46-10, G56-5, H58-10 61-3, I 66-2 69-8, K77-5 78-1, L87-10, M93-1, N100-10, O 107-1, P116-7/-, Q122-3, R136-2, S139-10, T148-2, U155-9, X162-5, Y175-3, Z180-10, 2A 188-5, 2B 195-2, 2C 208-2, 2D 211-5, 2E 223-1, 2F 231-3, 2G 237-8, 2H 244-7, 2 I 250-9, 2K 261-4, 2L 269-11 270-1, 2M 274-7, a vii-5, b xvi-3, c xviii-1 xxi-3, d xxviii-7, e xxxvi-1, f xlviii-7, g liv-3, h lxi-6, i lxxi-10, k lxxviii-9, l lxxxv-6, m xcvi-2, n civ-1, o cx-6, p cxvi-7/-, q cxxiii-10, r cxxxvi-7, s cxli-3, t cxlviii-11, u cliv-9 clvii-1/-, x clxiv-7, *y*—.

Notes: By the date of this poem general delivery to the London publisher had been expedited, issue there now occurring only a week later, usually, with special mail-coach copies arriving even earlier. The production of a dramatic version was also accelerated, with a premiere at the London Olympic Theatre on 27 February, two months after the Edinburgh publication. (Bolton 344)

The original readings of the first two cancelled leaves E1, L4 (pages 33-34, 87-88) are unknown. According to Van Antwerp the cancellandum Y1 (pages 169-170) omitted twelve lines 'It shall be so. . . he slowly went'—a shorter state which would originally leave 170 blank. Leaf c3 recto (page xxi) lines 4 and 7-8 read: (cancellandum) 'more likely. . . disown or divorce his original lady'; (cancellans) 'much more probable. . . disinherit to a certain extent his eldest son Ronald, . . .' Two of the cancels, L4 and c3, carry press figures on pages 87 and xxi respectively. Cancellandum c3 has been discovered only in E copy of the large-paper impression.

A variant collation, with preliminary π in two 2-leaf gatherings, may be detected in certain copies still uncut or in original bindings. More evident are, first, a correction at press:

[1a] page 56, line 8 'hunters' spears', [1b] 'hunters, spears,' and secondly, some disorder as a forme was repeatedly returned to press:

[2a] page 175 with figure 3, [2b] without figure 3, [2c] page misnumbered 157 and without the figure. At the end, beginning with page lxxvii, notes 3 and 5 in Canto 3, as well as note 5 in Canto 4, quote the 'Journal' published just the week before (80A).

Presentation copies: [states 1a, 2a] InU('Presentation Copy from the Author to my Mother' [Caroline Southey, inscription by C. C. Southey]) PBL('Miss [Maria] Edgeworth From the Author'). Other copies: [states 1a, 2a] AN BCL E(2) O; IdU

MH(2) NN(5) NNU-W(2) TxU(2). [1b, 2a] A BCL E ES O; CtY NNU-W PU T/B. [1b, 2c] TxU.

References: Abbotsford, page 271(noted as presented to Scott's mother, but not inscribed); Grady, pages 326-356, 403-404; Ruff 138(reproduces both states of c3); Tinker 1870; Van Antwerp(1) 14.

81Ab] First Edition, Second (Large-Paper) Impression: 1815

THE | **LORD OF THE ISLES,** | A POEM. . . . 1815.

Published 5 January 1815 concurrently with the previous impression. 50 copies (E MS 321. f.295). Paper: Royal 4° (305 x 245mm uncut). Watermarks: *none* or 1794 | J WHATMAN; J WHATMAN | 1810 [1811, 1813].

Notes: In all respects typographically identical with the preceding impression, points in later state 1b, 2b, a combination not observed in the regular issue. The NNU-W copy appears to be of a separate printing on unwatermarked paper.

Copies: E; CtY NNU-W(Auchincruive). Reference: Ruff 139.

81Ac] Second Edition, First Impression: 1815

THE | **LORD OF THE ISLES;** | A POEM. | BY | WALTER SCOTT, ESQ. | [*short Oxford rule*] | THE SECOND EDITION. | EDINBURGH: | [*short reversed Oxford rule*] | *Printed by James Ballantyne and Co.* | FOR ARCHIBALD CONSTABLE AND COMPANY, EDINBURGH; | AND LONGMAN, HURST, REES, ORME, AND | BROWN, LONDON. | [*Oxford dash*] | 1815.

Published 1 March 1815 (*EEC* 2 March) in Edinburgh; issued 29 March in London (*MC*). 14s. 6000 copies. (E MS.789, pp. 236-237). Binding: blue-green boards and printed label. Paper: Demy 8° (226 x 142mm uncut). Watermarks: *none* or 6 [7, 8, 9, 10] | W BALSTON & Co | 1814. Collation: π^4 A-R^8 S^2 a-k^8 1^4(±1 4) m^2. Pagination: *i* half-title, *ii blank*, *iii* title-page, *iv blank*, *v* Advertisement, *vi blank*, *vii* Contents, *viii blank*, *1* fly-title, *2 blank*, *3* 4-275 text, *276 blank*, *277* fly-title, *278 blank*, *279* 280-443 Notes, 443 printer's imprint, *444* 445-447 *448* advertisement for Scott's works, *449-450 blank*. Printer's imprint: [*short rule*] | EDINBURGH: | Printed by James Ballantyne & Co. Typography: In some copies page 378 footnote number has dropped.

Figures: A14(or 7)-2 12-5, B21-6 22-8, C34-10 44-3, D58-9 61-1, E78-6, F85-2, G106-3, H121-7, I 134-9, K148-6, L166-2 *173*-4, M187-10 189-2, N197-5 207-11, O 212-2 215-10, P227-4 232-12, Q252-1 255-3, R259-6 272-12, S274-2/-, a 287-1, b 297-2 306-8, c 321-10, d 337-3 339-5, e 355-1 356-11, f *365*-7 371-1, g 386-6 388-3, h 391-11 396-4, i 406-7 420-9, k 424-12 431-9, l 438-6, *m*—. The next impression and 'third edition', both of the same setting, exhibit figure 7 in its second position page 7.

Notes: The final gathering of text S^2 is in a duplicate setting, page 274 figure 2 and 275 line 1 'fair;—' or 274 unfigured and 275 line 1 'fair:'. Bruce is identified, incorrectly, as the author of the verse last text line page 425. Both in this and in the 'third edition' (a) final leaf l 4 is integral, without advertisement on page *444*, page 443 line 19 reading 'Scottish'; (b) the leaf is a cancel, with an advertisement for Swift on *444*, page 443 line 19 reading 'Scotish'. Depending upon the binder, the continuing advertisements (in gathering m^2) may or may not be included. If present they are of the first setting, page 446 first word 'dant' (the last variant of the earlier Swift prospectus, *see* 78A).

Presentation copy: (state a) E('J[ane] B[oston] Russell from the Author'). Other copies: (state b) AN BCL E(3) GU O; InU NjP PPL T/B TxU.

Reference: Ruff 140.

81Ad] Second Edition, Second (Large-Paper) Impression: 1815

THE | **LORD OF THE ISLES;** | A POEM. . . . THE SECOND EDITION. . . . 1815.

Published concurrently with the preceding impression. 250 copies. (E MS.789, p. 165). Paper: Royal 8° (232 x 141mm cut). Watermarks: 9 | W Balston | 1813; W Balston | 1814.

Notes: Except for paper, in all respects identical with the preceding impression; page 443 line 19 reads 'Scotish', remaining pages lacking.

Copy: CtY (*see* 260Ad[2]). Reference: Ruff 141.

81Ae] Third Edition (Second Edition, First Impression, Second Issue): 1815

THE | **LORD OF THE ISLES;** | A POEM. | BY | WALTER SCOTT, Esq. | [*short Oxford rule*] | THE THIRD EDITION. | EDINBURGH: | [*short reversed Oxford rule*] | *Printed by James Ballantyne and Co.* | FOR ARCHIBALD CONSTABLE AND COMPANY, EDINBURGH; | AND LONGMAN, HURST, REES, ORME, AND | BROWN, LONDON. | [*Oxford dash*] | 1815.

Published 23 March 1815 (*EEC*). 14s. Paper: 8° (211 x 130mm cut). Watermarks, collation, and pagination as for first impression. Figures: As for first impression, first gathering A7-2 12-5.

Notes: As this is an overrun of first mpression sheets; leaf I 4 remains in two states, (a) without or (b) with an advertisement on page 444.

Copies: (state a) E; NjP OCl. (b) E O; CtY T/B. Reference: Ruff 142.

81Af] Fourth Edition (Third Edition, First Issue): 1815

THE | **LORD OF THE ISLES;** | A POEM. | BY | WALTER SCOTT, Esq. | [*short Oxford rule*] | THE FOURTH EDITION. | EDINBURGH: | [*short Oxford rule*] | *Printed by James Ballantyne and Co.* | FOR ARCHIBALD CONSTABLE AND COMPANY, EDINBURGH; | AND LONGMAN, HURST, REES, ORME, AND | BROWN, LONDON. | [*Oxford dash*] | 1815.

Published 6 April 1815 (*EEC*). 14s. 6000 copies. (E MS.789, pp.257-258). Paper: Demy 8° (212 x 133mm cut). Watermarks: R T & Co | 1812 [1814]; 6 [9] | W Balston & Co | 1814. Collation: π^4 A-R^8 S^2 T-2E^8 2F^4 2G^2. Pagination: *i* half-title, *ii blank*, *iii* title-page, *iv blank*, *v* Advertisement, *vi blank*, *vii* Contents, *viii blank*, *1* fly-title, *2 blank*, *3* 4-275 text, *276 blank*, *277* fly-title, *278 blank*, *279* 280-443 Notes, 443 printer's imprint, *444* 445-447 *448* advertisements for Scott's works. Printer's imprint: [*short rule*] | Edinburgh: | Printed by James Ballantyne & Co.

Figures: A11-8 13-5, B18-5/- 32-3, C38-8 45-6, D55-7 64-2, E73-11 74-1, F93-6 95-9, G107-14 112-7, H114-14 117-10, I 134-9 141-3, K148-1 159-8, L165-7 167-5, M180-11 190-4, N200-3 202-1, O 214-9 217-2, P227-4 229-8, Q246-4 252-8, R259-2/- 268-5, S274-6/-, T280-7 286-13, U298-12 304-5, X319-7 320-2, Y326-11 337-12, Z346-3 356-13, 2A 367-5 369-2, 2B 375-6 377-10, 2C 398-14 401-11, 2D 415-3 416-11, 2E 425-5 427-10, 2F 441-13 (or 437-13). In one copy (E), possibly of the earliest state, the 2F figure 13 is improperly placed on signature page 437.

Notes: Text represents a few corrections, e.g. Burns as the author of the verse last line page 425. Again, depending upon the binder, the final advertisements may consist of one or five pages, but these, though unaltered, have now been reset: page 446 first word 'jor'.

Copies: BCL E GU O; CtY*+ InU T/B+ TxU(2). Reference: Ruff 143.
*With fore-edge painting of Stirling Castle.
+Extra-illustrated with 1815 engraved title-page and six plates by Richard Westall (*see* 81Dj).

81Ag] Fifth Edition, (Third Edition, Second Issue): 1815

THE | **LORD OF THE ISLES;** . . . THE FIFTH EDITION. . . . 1815.

Paper: Demy 8° (212 x 133mm cut). Watermarks: R T & Co | 1811 [1812, 1814]; 6 | W BALSTON & Co | 1814. Figures: As previous issue with the first MH copy still reflecting the misplacement of figure 13 on page 437.

Notes: Sheets of the previous issue with an altered title-page.

Copies: E O; CtY MH MH* NN. Reference: Ruff 144.
*With fore-edge painting of Berwick on Tweed.

81Ah] Fifth Edition, (Third Edition, Third Issue): 1830

[THE | **LORD OF THE ISLES;** . . . THE FIFTH EDITION. . . . 1815.]
Published 20 April 1830. 14s. 140 copies. (E MS.794, p.373). Not seen; described as a reissue with Scott's new introduction dated from Abbotsford, April, 1830, between the contents [p.viii] and p.[1]. The introduction is gathered π^2 $2\pi1$, and the pagination is *i* ii-vi. Advertised in *The Doom of Devorgoil* (page *1* of advertisement dated 20 April 1830). Reference: Ruff 145.

REPRINTS

FRANCE

PARIS: Didot and Galignani
[~] The Lord of the Isles. 1821, 1826. (Collection of Modern English Authors: *see* 290R.[6A], [5C])

PARIS: Galignani
[~] The Lord of the Isles. 1829. (*See* 293R.11). Copy: not seen.

ZWICKAU: Schumann
[~] The Lord of the Isles. 1821-1822. (Pocket Library of English Classics: *see* 302R. 24-25.)

UNITED STATES

BOSTON: Bedlington
[~] The Lord of the Isles. 1828. (The Poetical Works of Sir Walter Scott: *see* 304R.5)

81Ra] BOSTON: Wells & Lilly 1815
The Lord of the Isles, A Poem. By Walter Scott, Esq. Boston: Published by Wells & Lilly. 1815. Pages: *1-4*, *9-10* 11-222, *i-iii* iv-clxv. Copies: L; CtY MWA(2) PPL.

FREDERICKSBURG: Withers
[~] The Lord of the Isles. 1824. (The Poetical Works of Sir Walter Scott: *see* 310R.5)

81Rb] NEW YORK: Eastburn 1818
The Lord of the Isles. A Poem. By Walter Scott, Esq. New-York: Published by J. Eastburn and Co. Literary-Rooms, Broadway. 1818. Pages: *i-vi, 7-9* 10-324. Notes: (Also issued in The Poetical Works of Walter Scott: volume 6. 1819. *see* 312R.6.) Copies: BCL E; MWA.

81Rc] NEW YORK: Scott 1815
The Lord of the Isles, A Poem. By Walter Scott, Esq. New-York: Published by Richard Scott, 276 Pearl-street. 1815. Pages: *i-viii, 1-3* 4-175 *176* [*177-184*], *177-179* 180-302. Notes: Page numbers in brackets represent, after text, the last four leaves in gathering H, now blank but left uncancelled. Copies: MWA RPB.

81Rd] PHILADELPHIA: Thomas 1815
The Lord of the Isles, A Poem. By Walter Scott, Esq. Philadelphia: Published by Moses Thomas, No. 52, Chesnut-Street, 1815. Pages: *i-viii, 1-3* 4-307 *308-312*. Notes: Titlepage varies slightly in capitalization and punctuation. Copies: CtY IdU InU(2) MWA NN(2) NNU-W PHi PPL(2) RPB.

DERIVATIVES

GREAT BRITAIN

81Da] DUBLIN: Tyrrell 1818
Robert Bruce; or, The Lord of the Isles: A Poetical Play, in Three Acts: founded on Walter Scott's popular poem of "The Lord of the Isles". First performed at the Theatre-Royal, Crow-Street, on Saturday, June 13th, 1818. Dublin, Printed by William H. Tyrrell, No. 17, College-Green. 1818. Pages: *i-iii* iv-v *vi 7-9* 10-72. Notes: The anonymous adapter's dedication to his friends is dated from Dublin 6 June 1818. This appears to be the only printed version of a drama based upon the poem. Copy: CtY. Reference: Bolton 349 (attributing the play to Faulkner).

81Db] DUBLIN: Willis 1815-1822
[1] The Bark before the Gale . . . From Scott's Celebrated Poem The Lord of the Isles . . . Dublin Printed by I. Willis, Music & Musical Instrument Seller, 7, Westmorland St. [unwatermarked. ca.1815]. Pages: *1-2* 3-10. Notes: Engraved sheet music without plate number seen in later issues. Title-page with engraving of sailing ship. Words from canto 4, stanza 11 (first words: 'Merrily merrily goes the bark before the gale she bounds,'). Music composed by I. Willis arranged as a glee for three voices and piano-forte. Price: 3/-. Copy: E.

[2] The Bark before the Gale. . . . From Scott's Celebrated Poem The Lord of the Isles. . . . Dublin Printed by I. Willis, Music & Musical Instrument Seller, 7, Westmorland St. & 55 St. James St. London. Entd. in Sta. Hall. [ca.1820]. Pages: *1-2* 3-10. Notes: Engraved sheet music with vignette title-page, plate number '28', and the publisher/ composer's ink

stamp at foot of the title-page. The additional caption title reads: 'Merrily Merrily goes the Bark. The Words by Walter Scott Esq.' Words from canto 4, stanza 11 (first words: 'Merrily merrily goes the bark before the gale she bounds,'). Music composed by I. Willis arranged for three voices and pianoforte. Price: 3s. Copy: E.

[3] (Second Edition) The Bark before the Gale.... From Scott's Celebrated Poem The Lord of the Isles .... Dublin Printed by I. Willis, Music & Musical Instrument Seller, 7, Westmorland St. & 55 St. James St. London. Entd. in Sta. Hall. [watermarked 1822]. Pages: *1-2* 3-10. Notes: Engraved sheet music with vignette title-page, plate number '28', and the publisher/composer's ink stamp at foot of title-page. The additional caption title reads: 'Merrily Merrily goes the Bark. The Words by Walter Scott Esq.' Words from canto 4, stanza 11 (first words: 'Merrily merrily goes the bark before the gale she bounds,'). Music composed by I. Willis arranged for three voices and pianoforte. Price: 3s. Copies: E; MH

81Dc] LONDON: Bland and Weller 1815
Merrily, Merrily Bounds the Bark The Words from the Lord of the Isles, A New Poem by Walter Scott, Esqr.... London, Printed & Sold at Bland & Weller's Music Warehouse, 23, Oxford Strt. [watermarked 1815]. Page: *1* 2-4. Notes: Engraved sheet music with caption title. Words from canto 4, stanza 7 (first words: 'Merrily, merrily bounds the bark, / She bounds before the gale,'). Music composed by John Parry arranged for voice and pianoforte. Price: 1/6. Copy: L. Reference: G/T 10368.

81Dd] LONDON: Clementi 1815
[1] Edith of Lorn,.. The Poetry from The Lord of the Isles, Written by Walter Scott, Esqr. ... London, Printed by Clementi & Co. 26. Cheapside. [unwatermarked. ca.1815.] Pages: *1* 2-11. Notes: Engraved sheet music with a plate mark: 'Edith of Lorn'. Music composed by John Clarke and arranged as a glee for three voices and pianoforte. Words from canto 1, stanzas 1-3 (first words: '"Wake maid of Lorn!" the Minstrels sung'). Price: 2/6. Copies: E; MH-M.

[2] Go Forth My Song, Conclusion to The Lord of the Isles... London, Printed by Clementi & Co. No. 26, Cheapside. [unwatermarked. ca.1815]. Pages: *1* 2-6. Notes: Engraved sheet music. Words from Conclusion in full (first words: 'Go Forth My Song, upon thy venturous way;'). A cantata composed by John Clarke for voice and pianoforte. The cantata is 'respectfully inscribed to Mrs. Walter Scott'. Price: 2s. Copies: E L. Reference: G/T 10345.

[3] "It was a Night of Lovely June," glee for three voices.... London, Printed by Clementi & Co. 26, Cheapside. [watermarked 1814.] Pages: *1* 2-7. Notes: Engraved sheet music with a plate mark: 'It was a night'. Words from canto 6, stanza 19 (first words: 'It was a night of lovely, lovely June,'). Glee composed by John Clarke arranged for voice and pianoforte. Price: 2s. Copy: MH-M. Reference: G/T 10347.

[4] Merrily, merrily, bounds the bark,... The Poetry from The Lord of the Isles, Written by Walter Scott, Esqr.... London, Printed by Clementi & Co. 26, Cheapside. [1815.] Pages: *1* 2-12. Notes: Engraved sheet music with plate mark: 'Merrily bounds the bark.' Words from canto 4, stanzas 7, 9-12 (first words: 'Merrily, merrily, bounds the bark / She bounds before the gale'). Glee composed by John Clarke arranged for voice and pianoforte. Price: 2/6. Copy: L. Reference: G/T 10346.

[5] Wake Maid of Lorn, Song from the Poem of The Lord of the Isles Written by Walter Scott, Esqr. . . . London, Printed by Clementi, and Co. No. 26, Cheapside [watermarked 1814]. Pages: *1* 2-6. Notes: Engraved sheet music. Words from canto 1, stanza 4 (first words: '"Wake, Maid of Lorn!" the moments fly,'). Music composed by John Clarke arranged for voice and pianoforte. Price: 2s. Copies: BCL L. Reference: G/T 10344.

81De] LONDON: Falkner 1815

[1] O Wake while dawn, From the celebrated Poem, The Lord of the Isles, Written by Walter Scott, Esqr. . . . London, Published for the Composer at Falkner's Opera Music Warehouse, 3, Old Bond St. [unwatermarked. ca.1815]. Pages: *1* 2-3. Notes: Engraved sheet music with caption title. Words from canto 1, stanza 3 (first words: 'O wake while dawn with dewy shine / Wakes nature's charms'). Music composed by John Addison arranged for voice and pianoforte. Price: 1s/6. Copy: L.

[2] Wake, Maid of Lorn! The Invocation from the Celebrated Poem the Lord of the Isles, Written by Walter Scott, Esqr. . . . London. Published for the Composer at Falkner's Opera Music Warehouse. 3 Old Bond Street. [watermarked 1815]. Pages: *i-ii*, *1* 2-5. Notes: Engraved sheet-music with composer's signature in ink below imprint. Words from canto 1, stanza 4 (first words: 'Wake, Maid of Lorn! The moments fly Which yet that name,'). Music composed by John Addison arranged for voice and harp or pianoforte. Price: 2/s. Copy: L. Reference: G/T 10343.

81Df] LONDON: Gerock 1820

Wake Edith Wake, from the Celebrated Poem The Lord of the Isles, Written by Walter Scott Esqr. . . . [London] Publish'd by C. Gerock, Musical Instrument Manufacturer and Music Seller, 1, Gracechurch Street, and 76, Bishopsgate Street (within.) [unwatermarked. ca. 1820]. Pages: 1-3. Notes: Engraved sheet music with caption title and plate mark: 'Wake Edith Wake.' Words from canto 1, stanza 4 (first words: 'Wake, Maid of Lorn the moments fly, / which yet that maiden that maiden name allow;'). Music composed by Charles Jones arranged for voice and pianoforte. Copy: L. Reference: G/T 10358.

81Dg] LONDON: Goulding, D'Almaine 1820

(Second Edition.) Merrily merrily goes the Bark, from the Celebrated Poem The Lord of the Isles, Written by Sir Walter Scott, Bart. . . . London, Printed by Goulding, D'Almaine & Co. 20, Soho Square & to be had at, 7, Westmorland St. Dublin. [ca.1820.] Pages: 1-4. Notes: Engraved sheet music with caption title and plate mark reading: 'Merrily, merrily, &c.'. Words from canto 4, stanza 11 (first words: 'Merrily, merrily goes the bark, / Before the gale she bounds;'). Music composed by Joseph Mazzinghi arranged for voice and pianoforte. Price: 1/6. Later date assigned in view of Scott's baronetcy. Apparently a variant issue of the 1815 plates listed in next entry below. Copy: L. Reference: G/T 10363.

81Dh] LONDON: Goulding, D'Almaine, Potter 1815

[1] Merrily, Merrily, goes the Bark, from the Celebrated Poem The Lord of the Isles, Written by Walter Scott Esqr. . . . London, Printed by Goulding, D'Almaine, Potter & Co., 20, Soho Sq & to be had at 7, Westmorland Strt. Dublin. [ca.1815]. Pages: 1-4. Notes: Engraved sheet music with caption title and plate mark: 'Merrily, merrily, &c.'. Words from canto 4, stanza 11 (first words: 'Merrily, merrily, goes the bark, / Before the gale she bounds;'). Music composed by Joseph Mazzinghi arranged for voice and pianoforte. Price: 1/6. Copy: L.

[2] The Minstrel's Summons from the Celebrated Poem The Lord of the Isles, Written by Walter Scott, Esqr. . . . London Printed by Goulding, D'Almaine, Potter & Co. 20, Soho Sque. & 7, Westmorland Strt. Dublin. [watermarked 1814]. Pages: *1* 2-8. Notes: Engraved sheet music with plate mark reading: 'The Minstrel's Summons'. Words from canto 1, stanza 3 (first words: '"Wake, Maid of Lorn!" 'twas thus 'twas thus they sung,'). Glee composed by Joseph Mazzinghi arranged for three voices. Copies: L; NNP. Reference: Van Antwerp(2) 42t.

[3] O wake while Dawn with dewy Shine from the Celebrated Poem The Lord of the Isles, Written by Walter Scott Esqr. . . . London, Printed by Goulding, D'Almaine, Potter & Co. 20, Soho Square & 7, Westmorland Street, Dublin. [watermarked 1814]. Pages: 1-3. Notes: Engraved sheet music with caption title and composer's initial 'M' beside the imprint. Words from canto 1, stanza 3 (first words as title). Music composed by Joseph Mazzinghi arranged for voice and pianoforte. Price: 1/6. Copy: L. Reference: G/T 10360.

[4] Wake, Edith, Wake! London; Printed by Goulding, D'Almaine, Potter & Co. 20, Soho Square & 7, Westmorland Strt. Dublin. [watermarked 1815.] Pages: 1-4. Notes: Engraved sheet music with caption title and plate mark: 'Wake, Edith, Wake!'. The composer's initial is in ink just above the price. Words from canto 1, stanza 4 (first words: 'Wake, Edith, wake! the moments fly'). Music composed by Joseph Mazzinghi arranged for voice and pianoforte. Price: 1/6. Copy: L.

[5] Wake Maid of Lorn, from the Celebrated Poem The Lord of the Isles. Written by Walter Scott Esqr. . . . London, Printed by Goulding, D'Almaine Potter & Co. 20, Soho Sqr. & 7, Westmorland St. Dublin. [1815.] Pages: *1* 2-4. Notes: Engraved sheet music with composer's initial in ink to the right of the caption title. Also with plate mark: 'Wake Maid of Lorn!'. Words from canto 1, stanza 1 (first words: '"Wake, Maid of Lorn!" the Minstrels sung.—'). Music composed by Joseph Mazzinghi arranged for chorus and pianoforte. Price: 1/6. Copy: L. Reference: G/T 10362.

81Di] LONDON: Hodsoll 1815
[1] The Maid of Lorn. . . . from the celebrated Poem The Lord of the Isles Written by Walter Scott Esq. London Printed & Sold by W. Hodsoll 45 High Holborn Where may be had . . . . [watermarked 1814.] Pages: *i-ii*, 1-5. Notes: Engraved sheet music. Words from canto 1, stanza 4 (first words: 'Wake Maid of Lorn the moments fly / Which yet that maiden name allow'). Music composed by William Thomas Parke arranged for voice and pianoforte or harp. Price: 2/s. Copy: L. Reference: G/T 10366.

[2] Merrily, Merrily Goes the Bark from the Celebrated Poem "The Lord of the Isles." Written by Walter Scott Esqr. . . . London Printed & Sold by W. Hodsoll 45, High Holborn, where may be had by the same composer from the above Poem Maid of Lorn . . . [1815]. Pages: 1-3. Notes: Engraved sheet music with caption title. Words from canto 4, stanza 11 (first words: 'Merrily, merrily goes the Bark / Before the gale she bounds'). Music composed by William Thomas Parke arranged for voice and pianoforte or harp. Price: 1/6. Copies: E L. Reference: G/T 10367.

81Dj] LONDON: Longman [and others] 1815
Lord of the Isles A Poem in Six Cantos by Walter Scott, Esq. . . . London. Published by

Longman, Hurst, Rees, Orme, and Brown. 1815. Pages: Engraved vignette title-page and six plates. Notes: The one copy seen in original condition (L) is in drab wrappers within drab boards with printed label. Engraved title-page reads 'Illustrated with Engravings from the designs of Richard Westall Esqr. R.A.'; all other plates titled 'Lord of the Isles', drawn [or 'painted'] by Richard Westall'. The publication date is April 1815 unless noted differently below. Since order may vary, the plates are listed below in the order planned for insertion. Advertised on the printed label and in a March 1816 Longman catalogue as [1] 4° proofs 'on French paper' £1.16.0 and in [2] 8° size 18s. and indicating an 8° combined poem-plate issue, for £1.12.0. A further note indicates [3] a 'few Copies of Proof Impressions on India Paper', no price cited. Separate issue copies: [1] not seen. [2] L; CtY. [3] not seen. Combined poem-plate issue: see 81Af. Reference: Ruff 146.

Title-page with vignette engraved by John Pye; plates:
(1) [page 35] two-line quotation (first line: 'The younger Knight that maiden bare' from canto 1, stanza 28), engraved by Charles Heath;
(2) [no page given] three-line quotation (first line: 'I Bless thee, and thou shalt be bless'd—''' from canto 2, stanza 31), engraved by F. Engleheart; published 1 June 1815;
(3) [page 118] four-line quotation (first line: '__Hark! hears he not the sea-nymph speak' from canto 3, stanza 28), engraved by Charles Heath;
(4) [page 166] four-line quotation (first line: 'With sudden impulse forward sprung' from canto 4, stanza 28), engraved by James Heath;
(5) [page 212] two-line quotation (first line: 'He raised the page, where on the plain' from canto 5, stanza 30), engraved by Charles Heath;
(6) [page 269] two-line quotation (first line: 'Then foremost was the generous Bruce' from canto 6, stanza 33), engraved by Charles Heath.

81Dk] LONDON: Phipps 1815

[1] [The Breach of Lorn. London: Phipps (ca.1815). Notes: Music composed by James Hook.] Copy: not seen. Reference: G/T 10356.

[2] [Hush Daughter Hush. London: Phipps (ca.1815). Notes: Music composed by James Hook.] Copy: not seen. Reference: G/T 10356.

[3] [Merrily Merrily Goes the Bark. London: Phipps (ca.1815). Notes: Music composed by James Hook.] Copy: not seen. Reference: G/T 10356.

[4] Morag's Song, Hush daughter hush, from the Lord of the Isles, Written by Walter Scott Esqre. . . . London. Pubd. by Phipps & Co. 25, Duke St. Grosvenor Sqe. where may be had by the same Author from the same Poem, Wake Maid . . . . [watermarked 1815]. Pages: *1* 2-5. Notes: Engraved sheet music. Words from canto 1, stanza 12 (first words: 'Hush, Daughter, hush! Thy doubts Remove, / More Nobly think of Ron-alds[!] love,). Music composed by James Hook arranged for voice and harp or piano-forte. Price: [in ink] 1/6. Copy: L.

[5] [O Wake while Dawn with Dewy Shine. London: Phipps (ca.1815). Notes: Music composed by James Hook.] Copy: not seen. Reference: G/T 10356.

[6] 'Tis Morning & the Convent Bell, Lady Isabell, from the Lord of the Isles, Written by Walter Scott Esqre. . . . London. Pubd. by Phipps & Co. 25, Duke St. Grosvenor Sqe. where may be had by the same Author from the same Poem, Wake, Maid . . . . [watermarked 1813]. Pages: *i-ii*, 1-5. Notes: Engraved sheet music. Words from canto 4, stanza 21 (first words:

''Tis Morning, and the Convent Bell, / long time had ceas'd its Matin Knell,'). Music composed by James Hook arranged for voice and pianoforte or harp. Price: 1/6. Copy: L. Reference: G/T 10355.

[7] [Wake, Maid of Lorn. London: Phipps (ca.1815.) Notes: Music composed by James Hook.] Copy: not seen. Reference: G/T 10356.

81Dl] LONDON: Power 1815
Wake Maid of Lorn, A Ballad from The Lord of the Isles, Written by Walter Scott Esqr. . . . London, Published by J. Power, 34, Strand. [1815.] Pages: *i-ii*, 1-5. Notes: Engraved sheet music with plate number '260'. Words from canto 1, stanza 4 (first words: '"Wake Maid of Lorn" the moments fly'.) Music composed by John Stevenson arranged for voice and pianoforte. Copies: L O. Reference: G/T 10372.

81Dm] LONDON: Preston 1815
Wake Maid of Lorn, a Song from The Lord of the Isles Written by Walter Scott Esqr. . . London. Printed & Sold for the Author by Preston, at his Music Warehouses, 97, Strand. Where also may be had . . . . [watermarked 1814 ca.1815.] Pages: *i-ii*, *1* 2-5. Notes: Engraved sheet music signed by the composer in ink under the imprint. Words from canto 1, stanza 1 (first line: 'Wake Maid of Lorn!" the moments fly, / Which yet that maiden name allow,'). Music composed by Wiliam Gresham arranged for voice and pianoforte. Price: 2s/. Copy: L. Reference: G/T 10351.

81Dn] LONDON: Walker 1815-1817
[1] Merrily, Merrily Goes the Bark, The Words Selected from Walter Scott's Celebrated Poem, The Lord of the Isles, . . . London, Printed by G. Walker, Publisher of Books and Music, 105 & 106, Gt. Portland Street. . . [watermarked 1817.] Pages: *i-ii*, 1-6. Notes: Engraved sheet music. Words from canto 4, stanza 11 (first words: 'Merrily merrily goes the Bark / Before the gale she bounds'). Music composed by Louis Charles Jansen arranged as a glee for voice and pianoforte. Price: 2s. Copies: L(2). Reference: G/T 10357. Variant issue without watermark (MH).

[2] Wake, Maid of Lorn! The Minstrel's Song, Written by W. Scott, Esqr. In the poem of the Lord of the Isles, . . London. Printed for G. Walker, Publisher of Books and Music 105 & 106 Gt. Portland Stt. [watermarked 1815.] Pages: 1-3. Notes: Engraved sheet music. Words from canto 1, stanza 4 (first words: 'Wake, wake, wake Maid of Lorn,'). Music composed by Louis Jansen arranged for voice and pianoforte. Price: 1s. Copies: E(2).

81Do] LONDON: Willis 1825
(Third Edition) The Bark before the Gale. . . From Scott's celebrated Poem The Lord of the Isles . . . London, Published by I. Willis & Co. 55, St. James's Street, opposite Jermyn Strt. No. 7. Westmorland Street, Dublin, & 4, bis Rue de la Paix, Paris. [ca.1825]. Pages: *1-2* 3-10. Notes: Engraved sheet music with two plate numbers: (1) '(28)' and (2) '716'. Apparently a reissue of the 'Second Edition' Dublin, Willis plates (81Db[3]). The sheets now are worn, with a re-engraved title-page and illustration of a sailing ship. Words from canto 4, stanza 11 (first words: 'Merrilly merrily goes the bark before the gale she bounds,'). Music composed by I. Willis arranged as a glee for three voices and pianoforte. Price: 3/-. Copy: E.

UNITED STATES

81Dp] BALTIMORE: Carr 1815-1817

[1] The Convent of Saint Bride. From the Celebrated Poem, The Lord of the Isles. Written by Walter Scott Esqr. . . . Price 25 cents. Printed and Sold at Carrs Music Store Baltimore. [1815.] Pages: 1-2. Notes: Engraved sheet music. Words from canto 4, stanza 21 (first words: 'Tis morning, and the Convent Bell'). Music composed by William Thomas Parke arranged for voice and pianoforte. Copy: PPL. References: G/T 10365; Wolfe 6790.

[2] Merrily, Merrily, Goes the Bark, From the Celebrated Poem, The Lord of the Isles. Written by Walter Scott Esqr. . . . . Printed and sold at Carrs Music Store, Baltimore. [1815]. Pages: 1-3. Notes: Engraved sheet music. Words from canto 4, stanza 10 (first words: 'Merrily, merrily goes the bark / On a breeze from the northward free,'). Music composed by Joseph Mazzinghi arranged for voice and pianoforte. Price: 38 cents. Copy: PPL. Reference: Wolfe 5699.

[3] Wake, Maid of Lorn! From the Celebrated Poem The Lord of the Isles written by Walter Scott Esqr. . . . Printed and Sold at Carrs Music Store Baltimore. [ca.1817.] Pages: 1-4. Notes: Engraved sheet music. Words from canto 1, stanza 4 (first words: '"Wake, Maid of Lorn!" the moments fly, Which yet that maiden name that maiden name allow;'). Music composed by Joseph Mazzinghi arranged for voice and pianoforte. Two issues (1) Price: 50 cents; (2) no price. Copy: (1) not seen; (2) MWA. Reference: Wolfe 1872.

81Dq] BOSTON: Bradlee 1815

[1] The Bark before the Gale . . . Words by Walter Scott, . . . Boston: Published by C. Bradlee, No. 164 Washington Street. [unwatermarked. ca.1815.] Pages: *1* 2-8. Notes: Engraved sheet music with caption title. Words from canto 4, stanza 11 (first words: 'Merrily merrily goes the bark before the gale she bounds,'). Music by I. Willis arranged for voice and pianoforte. Composer's name in italic type. Copy: MH.

[2] The Bark before the Gale . . . Words by Walter Scott, . . . Boston: Published by C. Bradlee, No. 107 Washington Street. [unwatermarked. ca.1815.] Pages: *1* 2-8. Notes: Engraved sheet music with caption title. A variant setting with composer's name in hollow Roman capitals. (*See* preceding entry and also same title published by Wade, entry 81Dt.) Music by I. Willis arranged for voice and pianoforte. Copy: MH.

81Dr] BOSTON: Hewitt 1815

[Wake, Edith, Wake! . . . Boston, Published & Sold by J. Hewitt. (1815.) Pages: 1-4. Notes: Music composed by Joseph Mazzinghi.] Copy: not seen. Reference: Wolfe 5730.

81Ds] BOSTON: Parker 1816

[1] Edith of Lorn. . . . *in:* The Orphean Lyre, . . . Boston Published by S. H. Parker at the Union Circulating Library. No. 4. Cornhill. [1816.] Pages: 28-33. Notes: Engraved sheet music with caption title for music. Words from canto 1, stanzas 1-3 (first words: '"Wake Maid of Lorn!" The minstrels sung.'). Music composed by John Clarke arranged for voice and pianoforte. Copy: RPB. Reference: Wolfe 1870.

[2] It was a Night of Lovely June. . . . *In* The Orphean Lyre, . . . Boston Published by S. H. Parker at the Union Circulating Library. No. 4. Cornhill. [1816.] Pages: 6-9. Notes: Engraved Sheet music with caption title for music. Words from canto 6, stanza 19 (first words 'It was

a night of lovely, lovely June'.) Music composed by John Clarke arranged for voice and pianoforte. Copy: RPB. Reference: Wolfe 1833.

[3] Merrily, Merrily, bounds the Bark. . . . *in:* The Orphean Lyre, . . . Boston Published by S. H. Parker at the Union Circulating Library. No. 4. Cornhill. [1816.] Pages: 14-20. Notes: Engraved sheet music with caption title for music. Words from canto 4, stanza 7, 9-12 (first words as title). Music composed by John Clarke arranged for voice and pianoforte. Copy: RPB. Reference: Wolfe 1841.

81Dt] BOSTON: Wade 1815
The Bark before the Gale . . . Words by Walter Scott, . . Boston: Published by E. H. Wade 197 Washington Street. [unwatermarked. ca.1815.] Pages: *1* 2-8. Notes: Engraved sheet music with caption title. Printed from same plates as those used by C. Bradlee for his variant printing (*see* 81Dq[2]). Words from canto 4, stanza 11 (first words: 'Merrily merrily goes the bark before the gale she bounds,'). Music by I. Willis arranged for voice and pianoforte. Copy: MH.

81Du] NEW YORK: Riley 1816-1818
[1] Wake, Maid of Lorn Written by W. Scott Esqr. . . . New York__ Engrav'd, Printed and Sold, by E Riley, 23 Chatham Street. [1816.] Pages: *1* 2-3. Notes: Engraved sheet music with caption title. Words from canto 1, stanza 4 (first words: 'Wake Maid of Lorn! the moments fly, Which yet that maiden name allow'). Music composed by John Clarke arranged for voice and pianoforte. Advertised by Riley in *NYEP* of 1 April 1816 as 'new music'. Copies: PPL RPB. Reference: Wolfe 1869.

[2] Wake Maid of Lorn from the Poem of The Lord of the Isles Written by Walter Scott Esqr. . . . New York__ Engrav'd, Printed and Sold, by E. Riley, 23 Chatham Street [ca.1818.] Pages: *1-2* 3. Notes: Engraved sheet music with caption title. Words from canto 1, stanza 4 (first words: 'Wake Maid of Lorn the moments fly / Which yet that maiden name allow'). Music composed by John Clarke arranged for voice and pianoforte. Price: cents 25. Copy: RPB. Reference: A resetting of only the first plate, otherwise as Wolfe 1869 for pages *2* and 3.

81Dv] NEW YORK: Willson 1815
Wake Maid of Lorn; A Song from the Poem of The Lord of the Isles: Written by Walter Scott, Esq. . . . New York: Publish'd by Joseph Willson, No. 16 Maiden Lane. [1815.] Pages: *1* 2-6. Notes: Engraved sheet music with title on page *1* and plate marks: '12' (page *1*), '(Maid of Lorn.)' (pages 2-6.) Words from canto 1, stanza 4 (first words: 'Wake Maid of Lorn! the moments fly'). Music composed by John Clarke arranged for voice and pianoforte. Copy: RPB. Reference: Wolfe 1868.

81Dw] PHILADELPHIA: Bacon 1815-1817
[1] Merrily Goes the Bark. From the Celebrated Poem, The Lord of the Isles. Written by Walter Scott. . . . Philadelphia, Published by A. Bacon & Co No 11 S 4th Street. . . . [ca.1816.] Pages: 1-3. Notes: Engraved sheet music with plate number: '20'. Words from canto 4, stanza 11 (first words: 'Merrily, merrily, goes the bark, / Before the gale she bounds;'). Music composed by Joseph Mazzinghi arranged for voice and pianoforte. Price: 25 cents. Copies: InU MWA. Reference: Wolfe 5700.

[2] Merrily Goes the Bark. From the Celebrated Poem, The Lord of the Isles. Written by Walter Scott. . . Philadelphia, Published by A. Bacon & Co No 11 S 4th Street. [ca. 1815]. Pages: 1-3. Notes: Engraved sheet music with caption title and plate mark: '8'. Words from canto 4, stanza 11 (first words: 'Merrily, merrily, goes the bark, Before the gale she bounds;'). Music composed by Joseph Mazzinghi arranged for voice and pianoforte. Copy: RPB. Reference: Wolfe 5698.

[3] [Wake Maid of Lorn. . . . Philadelphia, Published by A. Bacon & Co., No. 11 S. 4th Street. (1817.) 3pp. Notes: Music composed by John Clarke.] Copy: not seen. References: Wolfe 1873 and 1873A.

81Dx] PHILADELPHIA: Blake 1816-1817

[1] Go Forth My Song. Conclusion to The Lord of the Isles, . . . Published by G. E. Blake, No. 13. South 5h. Street, Philadelphia [1817.] Pages: *1* 2-4. Notes: Engraved sheet music. Words from the Conclusion: (first words: 'Go forth my Song, upon thy venturous way; / Go boldly forth nor yet thy master blame,'). Music composed by John Clarke arranged for voice and pianoforte. Price: 38 cents. Song dedicated to Mrs. Walter Scott . Copy: MWA. Reference: Wolfe 1832.

[2] It was a Night of Lovely June . . . . The Poetry from The Lord of the Isles Written by Walter Scott, Esqr. . . . Philadelphia, Published by G. E. Blake, No. 13 South 5th Street. [ca.1816.] Pages: *1* 2-4. Notes: Engraved sheet music. Words from canto 6, stanza 19 (first words: 'It was a night of lovely, lovely June, / High rode in cloudless blue the moon;'). Music composed by John Clarke arranged for voice and pianoforte. Price: 38 cents. Copies: InU MWA. References: G/T 10347; Wolfe 1834.

[3] Merrily, Merrily, Bounds the Bark. . . . The Poetry from The Lord of the Isles, Written by Walter Scott, Esqr. . . . Published by G. E. Blake, No. 13. South 5h Street. Philadelplhia. [1816.] Pages: *1-2* 3-7. Notes: Engraved sheet music. Words from canto 4, stanza 7 (first words: 'Merrily, merrily, bounds the bark, / She bounds before the gale;'). Glee composed by John Clarke arranged for voice and pianoforte. Price: 50 cents. Copy: MWA. Reference: Wolfe 1842.

[4] Wake Maid of Lorn Song from the Poem of The Lord of The Isles Written by Walter Scott, Esqr. . . . Published by G. E. Blake, No. 13 South 5h Street, Philadelphia [ca.1817.] Pages: *1* 2-4. Notes: Engraved sheet music with plate mark: 'Wake Maid of Lorn'. Words from canto 1, stanza 4 (first words: 'Wake, Maid of Lorn! the moments fly, Which yet that maiden name allow;'). Music composed by John Clarke arranged for voice and pianoforte. Price: 38 c. Copy: InU. Reference: Wolfe 1871.

81Dy] PHILADELPHIA: Klemm 1823-1824

[1] Merrily goes the Bark. From the Celebrated Poem, The Lord of the Isles. Written by Walter Scott. . . . Philadelphia, Published by J. G. Klemm. No 3 S. 3d. Street. [ca.1824.] Pages: 1-3. Notes: Engraved sheet music with caption title and plate number: '20'. Words from canto 4, stanza 11 (first words: 'Merrily, merrily, goes the bark, Before the gale she bounds;'). Music composed by Joseph Mazzinghi arranged for voice and pianoforte. Price: 25 cents. Some copies read '25 cts.' Reissue from same plates as 81Dw[1] (Wolfe 5700) published by A. Bacon. Copies: MWA PPL RPB. Reference: Wolfe 5700A.

[2] Wake, Maid of Lorn. . . . Philadelphia, Published by J. G. Klemm. No 3 S. 3d Street.

[ca.1823.] Pages: 1-3. Notes: Engraved sheet music with caption title and with plate number: '47'. Words from canto 1, stanza 4 (first words: 'Wake Maid of Lorn! the moments fly, / Which yet that maiden name allow;'). Music composed by John Clarke arranged for voice and pianoforte. Price: 25 cts. Copies: PPL RPB. Reference: Wolfe 1873B.

EXTRACTS IN ANTHOLOGIES

81E] From *The Lord of the Isles* there are 20 extracts in 12 anthologies: 358E.16-17, 19 360.23 389.13,15 415.3,8-9 416 417.1 439.1-3 451 467[2].8 469.8 476.1-2 477.2.

GUY MANNERING

The Novel or Romance of WAVERLEY made its way to the public slowly, of course, at first, but afterwards with such accumulating popularity as to encourage the author to a second attempt. . . . The tale was originally told me by an old servant of my father's, an excellent old Highlander, without a fault, unless a preference to mountain-dew over less potent liquors be accounted one. ('Introduction', January 1829, *WN*, iii.i-ii.)

82Aa] First Edition: 1815

GUY MANNERING; | OR, | *THE ASTROLOGER.* | BY THE AUTHOR OF "WAVERLEY." | [*short Oxford rule*] | [*four-line quotation from* Lay of the Last Minstrel.] | [*short reversed Oxford rule*] | IN THREE VOLUMES. | VOL. I [II-III]. | EDINBURGH: | *Printed by James Ballantyne and Co.* | FOR LONGMAN, HURST, REES, ORME, AND BROWN, | LONDON; AND ARCHIBALD CONSTABLE AND CO. | EDINBURGH. | [*dash*] | 1815.

Published 24 February 1815 in Edinburgh (Lockhart v.21); issued 24 March in London (*MC,* previously announced 3, 8 December 1814 as 'In the course of the Month'). £1.1.0. 2000 copies. Binding: blue, green or blue-green paper boards with printed labels. Paper: Royal 12° (191 x 112mm uncut). Watermarks: 1813; M 1813; 1814 | 9 [10, 11, 12]. Typography: Printer's imprint reads invariably: [*short rule*] | EDINBURGH: | Printed by James Ballantyne & Co.

Copies: (volume 3, state 1a) BCL E* O LU; IdU(2) MH NN(Berg-2) T/B ViU. (1b) LU O; CtY InU MH NNU-W. (state 2a) BCL* E L O P; InU. (state 2b) MH(2). Mixed or sophisticated copy: CtY(counterfeit type-facsimile 1st edition titles, 2d edition text).
*With 4-page Longman catalogue dated January 1815.

References: Church 531; Sterling 723; Thomson, pages 32-33; Van Antwerp(1) 3; Worthington 2. (Magnum Opus Edition 1829: *Waverley Novels*, iii-iv.)

1] **GUY MANNERING;** . . . VOL. I. . . . 1815.

Collation: π^2 A-H^{12} $I^{12}(\pm I1,9)$ K-O^{12} $P^2(P2+1)$. Pagination: *i* half-title, *ii blank*, *iii* title-page, *iv blank*, *1* fly-title, *2 blank*, *3* 4-341 text, 341 printer's imprint, *342 blank*. Typography: In some copies the first digit in page-number 16 is missing and the first digit in page number 163 is in the wrong fount.

Figures: A15-3 17-2, B26-7 28-10, C52-10 63-3, D90-7 96-5, E100-7 119-3, F122-9 137-7, G159-1 168-5, H183-9 189-3, I 210-7 214-7 216-5, K231-9 232-3, L244-8 263-7, M274-11 276-6, N291-11 309-9/-, O 329-9 331-6, P—.

Notes: The separate final P leaf, representing only seven lines of type, is in a duplicate setting, the colon of the imprint on page 341 being either above the 'nt' or above the 'y' of 'Ballantyne'. Leaf I1 (pages 193-194) in some copies is a cancel, with invariant text. Cancel leaf I9 is immediately signaled by the redundant figure 7 on page 210. The original readings for both I leaves are unknown.

2] **GUY MANNERING;** . . . VOL. II. . . . 1815.

Collation: π^2 A-G^{12} H^{12}(-H3,4 +H3.4) I-O^{12} P^6. Pagination: *i* half-title, *ii blank*, *iii* title-page, *iv blank*, *1* fly-title, *2 blank*, *3* 4-346 text, *347* printer's imprint, *348 blank*. Typography: Signature G2 (page 153) is transposed as 2G.

Figures: A10-9 24-4, B35-5 48-10, C71-4 72-6/-, D84-2 86-8, E99-1/- 104-5, F122-12, G146-3 165-1, H179-11, 180-9/-, I 194-5 204-9, K218-9 220-4, L252-9 263-5, M275-5 280-9, N302-6 312-7, O 314-3 333-11, P340-9.

Notes: In his close analysis of the manuscript Van Antwerp discovered 101 variants from the readings in the cancels, practically all of them merely differences in spelling or punctuation, but one clearly a substantive revision: 175.14 youngster/ fellow whom I enquire after.

3] **GUY MANNERING;** . . . VOL. III. . . . 1815.

Collation: π^2 A-P^{12}. Pagination: *i* half-title, *ii blank*, *iii* title-page, *iv blank*, *1* fly-title, *2 blank*, *3* 4-358 text, *359* Errata and printer's imprint, *360 blank*.

Figures: A13-7 22-12, B39-5 45-9/-, C52-2 55-5, D80-4 82-8, E117-1 119-4, F122-11/- 141-3, G147-5 164-11, H172-4 191-1/-, I 204-5 214-3, K219-7 224-11, L244-1 250-10, M275-1 277-10, N298-11 304-7, O 322-6 324-4/-, P340-12 343-9.

Notes: Worthington reports in 'some copies' a figure 10 on page 60 ($C6^v$): a superfluous mark in the outer forme which, if it occurs, would probably signal a cancel (as in the first volume described above). As the errata leaf notes, there are two states of the text in this volume, page 309 line 13 reading (1) 'minute' or (2) 'minutely'. The errata list itself is also in two states, reading

(a) 'Vol. III. p.309. For *minute*, read *minutely.*'

(b) 'Vol. III. p.309. (In some copies) For *minute*, read *minutely.*'

82Ab] Second Edition, First Issue: 1815

GUY MANNERING; | OR, | *THE ASTROLOGER.* | BY THE AUTHOR OF "WAVERLEY." | [*short Oxford rule*] | [*four-line quotation from* Lay of the Last Minstrel.] | [*short reversed Oxford rule*] | IN THREE VOLUMES. | VOL. I [II-III]. | SECOND EDITION. | EDINBURGH: | *Printed by James Ballantyne and Co.* | FOR LONGMAN, HURST, REES, ORME, AND BROWN, | LONDON; AND ARCHIBALD CONSTABLE AND CO. | EDINBURGH. | [*dash*] | 1815.

Published: 20 March 1815 in Edinburgh (*EEC*). £1.1.0 5000 copies (a count including the third edition). Binding: blue boards with printed labels. Paper: Royal 12° (188 x 112mm uncut). Watermarks: 1814 | 9 [10, 11]. Typography: Printer's imprint reads invariably: [*short rule*] | EDINBURGH: | Printed by James Ballantyne & Co.

Copies: BCL E*b EU(Edward Fitzgerald) L*a O(3); CtY T/B.
*With 4-page Longman catalogue dated (a) January 1815; (b) February 1816.

1] **GUY MANNERING**; . . . VOL. I. | SECOND EDITION. . . . 1815.

Collation: π^2 A-O^{12} P^2(P2+1). Pagination: *i* half-title, *ii blank*, *iii* title-page, *iv blank*, *1* fly-title, *2 blank*, *3* 4-341 text, 341 printer's imprint, *342 blank*. Typography: Page number 163 is now in the correct fount.

Figures: A15-3 24-7, B36-2 39-6, C60-9 67-8, D82-5 93-4, E107-7 120-1, F143-7 144-5, G155-1 160-3, H174-9 184-2 192-2, I 202-8 205-1, K238-4 240-5, L261-7 263-1, M280-9 286-10, N290-8 312-3, O 316-5 327-12, P339-1/-.

Notes: Possibly the entire four-leaf inserted section H4-7, with supernumerary figure 184-2, represents a cancel. The entire gathering P is now in a duplicate setting, with or without figure 1 on page 339. The errata in an 1815 Boston edition (*see* 82Rc) indicate that, while that text apparently was set from the original issue, a later proofing there against this revised second edition exhibited three corrections, located in this setting as: 207 line 2: Mr Mervyn] Mrs Mervyn; 258 line 23: Miss Bertram's] Miss Mannering's; 272 line 14: first] latter.

2] **GUY MANNERING**; . . . VOL. II. | SECOND EDITION. . . . 1815.

Collation: π^2 A-O^{12} P^6. Pagination: *i* half-title, *ii blank*, *iii* title-page, *iv blank*, *1* fly-title, *2 blank*, *3* 4-346 text, *347* printer's imprint, *348 blank*. Typography: Signature G2 (page 153) in some copies remains transposed as 2G.

Figures: A15-5 24-1, B39-9 41-8, C62-12 72-2, D83-11 96-7, E111-11 120-8, F135-9, G146-10 168-7, H184-4, I 206-3 216-8, K233-9 239-6, L247-12 264-3, M272-9 286-8, N291-7 312-4/6/-, O 322-9/- 336-1, P343-5.

3] **GUY MANNERING**; . . . VOL. III. | SECOND EDITION. . . . 1815.

Collation: π^2 A-O^{12} P^{12}. Pagination: *i* half-title, *ii blank*, *iii* title-page, *iv blank*, *1* fly-title, *2 blank*, *3* 4-358 text, *359* printer's imprint, *360 blank*. Typography: Signatures C2 and G2 (pages 57, 153) are missigned 2C and 2G respectively.

Figures: A12-6 22-9, B27-3 36-9, C63-2 69-4, D94-7 96-10, E118-3 120-10, F124-2 135-6, G148-1 154-3, H181-12 190-4, I 215-3 216-5, K229-4 231-6, L244-7 250-6, M275-12 277-8, N303-2 309-3, O 322-4 324-3, P343-5 357-8.

82Ac] Second Edition, Second Issue: 1815

GUY MANNERING; | OR, | *THE ASTROLOGER*. . . . VOL. I [II-III]. | SECOND EDITION. . . . 1815.

Notes: All collations and paginations as in the previous issue, but there is now some further reimpression and resetting as noted below.

Copy: L.

1] **GUY MANNERING**; . . . VOL. I. | SECOND EDITION. . . . 1815.

Figures: A15-8 21-4, B26-14 37-4, C58-5 60-10, D78-8 88-6, E99-6 112-5, F122-9 144-14, G148-4 159-3, H170-6 192-9, I 195-7 216-3, K221-3 238-4, L253-9 263-7/-, M280-9 286-10, N303-12 309-2, O 327-12, P339—. It will be observed that, essentially, this new setting is again used for the third edition.

2] **GUY MANNERING**; . . . VOL. II. | SECOND EDITION. . . . 1815.

Figures: A15-5 24-1, B39-9 41-8, C62-12 72-2, D83-11 96-7, E111-11 120-8, F135-9, G146-10 168-7, H184-4, I 206-3 216-8, K233-9 239-6, L247-12 264-3, M272-9 286-8, N291-7 312-6/4, O 322-9/- 336-1, P343-5. Sheets A-G and M are reset, the others are of the same impression both of the previous issue and the third edition.

3] **GUY MANNERING**; . . . VOL. III. | SECOND EDITION. . . . 1815.

Notes: Of the same impression throughout, and so with the same figures, as the previous issue. The issue thus retains the missigned signatures on C2 and G2.

82Ad] Third Edition: 1815

GUY MANNERING; | OR, | *THE ASTROLOGER*. | BY THE AUTHOR OF "WAVERLEY." | [*short Oxford rule*] | [*four-line quotation from* Lay of the Last Minstrel.] | [*short reversed Oxford rule*] | IN THREE VOLUMES. | VOL. I [II-III]. | THIRD EDITION. | EDINBURGH: | *Printed by James*

Ballantyne and Co. | FOR LONGMAN, HURST, REES, ORME, AND BROWN, | LONDON; AND ARCHIBALD CONSTABLE AND CO. | EDINBURGH. | [*dash*] | 1815.

Published 19 October 1815 in Edinburgh (*EEC*). £1.1.0. Binding: blue-green boards with printed labels. Paper: Royal 12° (190 x 114mm uncut). Watermarks: none.

Copies: BCL E(3) L O(2); CtY(2) DLC InU MH NN T/B TxU.

1] **GUY MANNERING;** . . . VOL. I. | THIRD EDITION. . . . 1815.

Collation: π^2 A-O^{12} P^2(P2+1). Pagination: *i* half-title, *ii blank*, *iii* title-page, *iv blank*, *1* fly-title, *2 blank*, *3* 4-341 text, 341 printer's imprint, *342 blank*. Printer's imprint: [*short rule*] | EDINBURGH: | Printed by James Ballantyne & Co. Figures: Of the same impression as the previous issue except for L263-7/-, M267-7 277-6, P339-1/-.

2] **GUY MANNERING;** . . . VOL. II. | THIRD EDITION. . . . 1815.

Collation: π^2 A-O^{12} P^6. Pagination: *i* half-title, *ii blank*, *iii* title-page, *iv blank*, *1* fly-title, *2 blank*, *3* 4-346 text, *347* printer's imprint, *348 blank except for* printer's imprint: [*short rule*] | EDINBURGH: | Printed by James Ballantyne & Co. Figures: A14-6 16-11, B34-3 40-6, C59-11 72-12, D84-2 86-9, E107-12 109-7, F130-1 133-9, G166-4 168-14, H184-4, I 206-3 216-8, K233-9 239-6, L247-12 264-3, M280-9 286-14, N291-7 312-6/4, O 322-9/- 336-1, P343-5. See note for previous issue.

3] **GUY MANNERING;** . . . VOL. III. | THIRD EDITION. . . . 1815.

Collation: π^2 A-P^{12}. Pagination: *i* half-title, *ii blank*, *iii* title-page, *iv blank*, *1* fly-title, *2 blank*, *3* 4-358 text, *359* printer's imprint, *360 blank*. Printer's imprint: [*short rule*] | EDINBURGH: | Printed by James Ballantyne and Co. Typography: Section signature H2 (page 177) is omitted. Figures: A12-9 22-4, B27-8 36-13, C50-11 60-10, D75-13 93-1, E109-9 110-4, F134-4 144-9, G155-4 160-3, H179-11 189-4, I 207-3 216-4, K220-9 231-7, L242-9 244-4, M279-2 288-14, N304-11 311-14, O 324-3 334-2, P343-13 352-4.

82Ae] Fourth Edition: 1817

GUY MANNERING; | OR, | *THE ASTROLOGER.* | BY THE AUTHOR OF "WAVERLEY." | [*short Oxford rule*] | [*four-line quotation from* Lay of the Last Minstrel.] | [*short reversed Oxford rule*] | IN THREE VOLUMES. | VOL. I [II-III]. | FOURTH EDITION. | EDINBURGH: | *Printed by James Ballantyne and Co.* | FOR LONGMAN, HURST, REES, ORME, AND

BROWN, | LONDON; AND ARCHIBALD CONSTABLE AND CO. | EDINBURGH. | [*dash*] | 1817.

Binding: blue boards with printed labels. Paper: Royal 12° (190 x 110mm uncut). Watermarks: *none* or 1816 | 3. Printer's imprint reads invariably: [*short rule*] | EDINBURGH: | Printed by James Ballantyne & Co.

Copies: BCL E(3) L O; CtY T/B TxU.

1] **GUY MANNERING;** . . . VOL. I. | FOURTH EDITION. . . . 1817.

Collation: π^2 A-O^{12} P^4. Pagination: *i* half-title, *ii blank*, *iii* title-page, *iv blank*, *1* fly-title, *2 blank*, *3* 4-341 text, 341 printer's imprint, *342-344 blank*. Figures: A21-10 23-6, B26-9 40-1, C69-11, D87-4 96-3, E99-6 120-10, F138-9 140-4, G165-8 167-9, H189-3 190-9, I 204-4 206-5, K220-11 226-9, L252-4 262-1, M280-10 286-11, N302-9 304-10, O 327-4, P339-11.

2] **GUY MANNERING;** . . . VOL. II. | FOURTH EDITION. . . . 1817.

Collation: π^2 A-O^{12} P^6. Pagination: *i* half-title, *ii blank*, *iii* title-page, *iv blank*, *1* fly-title, *2 blank*, *3* 4-346 text, *347* printer's imprint, *348 blank*. Figures: A14-11 24-1, B40-6 42-8, C58-4 65-11, D74-4 93-11, E115-8 117-11, F132-4 135-11, G154-9 168-8, H170-9 184-5, I 196-11 202-4/-, K231-5/- 237-9, L243-9 257-4, M272-8 282-11, N291-3 292-6, O 322-9 336-4, P343-5.

3] **GUY MANNERING;** . . . VOL. III. | FOURTH EDITION. . . . 1817.

Collation: π^2 A-P^{12}. Pagination: *i* half-title, *ii blank*, *iii* title-page, *iv blank*, *1* fly-title, *2 blank*, *3* 4-358 text, *359* printer's imprint, *360 blank*. Typography: In some copies section signature H2 (page 177) is unsigned and the press figure on page 268 is transposed as '01'. Figures: A4-10 23-4, B47-10 48-11, C61-6 70-8, D88-10 91-9, E119-10 120-11, F133-11 135-1, G148-8 150-11, H171-5 172-3, I 213-11 215-4, K219-11 224-4, L243-5 256-10, M268-10 275-8, N310-10 312-4, O 324-11 326-5, P339-9 353-5.

82Af] Sixth Edition (Fifth Edition, First Impression): 1820

GUY MANNERING; | OR, | *THE ASTROLOGER.* | BY THE AUTHOR OF "WAVERLEY." | [*short Oxford rule*] | [*four-line quotation from* Lay of the Last Minstrel.] | [*short reversed Oxford rule*] | IN THREE VOLUMES. | VOL. I [II-III]. | SIXTH EDITION. | EDINBURGH: | *Printed by James Ballantyne and Co.* | FOR ARCHIBALD CONSTABLE AND CO. EDINBURGH. | [*dash*] | 1820.

Paper: Royal 12° (174 x 99mm cut). Watermarks: *none* or E | 1819. Printer's imprint reads invariably: [*short rule*] | EDINBURGH: | Printed by James Ballantyne & Co.

General Notes: As there is no record of a 'fifth' edition, this impression, here mislabeled a 'sixth', may have been regarded as the earlier edition. It is most easily distinguished from the 'sixth' next described by the absence of any dagger on the signature pages. As noted below, volume 1 consists in part of two issues.

Copies: (Issue 1) EP; (2) BCL; CtY T/B.

1] **GUY MANNERING;** . . . VOL. I. | SIXTH EDITION. . . . 1820.

Collation: π^2 A-O^{12} P^4(-P4). Pagination: *i* half-title, *ii blank*, *iii* title-page, *iv blank*, *1* fly-title, *2 blank*, *3* 4-341 text, 341 printer's imprint, *342 blank*. Figures: A24-6, B26-9/- 40-1, C72-2, D87-4 96-3, E120-2, F143-7 144-5, G155-1 160-3, H190-7, I 204-4 206-5, K220-11 226-9, L252-4 262-1, M280-10 286-11, N302-9 304-10, O 316-5 327-12, P340-15.

Notes: This volume only consists of two issues, (1) a printing in which, generally, sheets with two press figures, as noted above, constitute an overrun from the preceding 'fourth edition'; (2) a later printing of ten of these sheets, each now with a single figure: B46-2/7, D78-15, F133-9, G146-15, I 194-9, K229-15, L262-1, M279-4, N311-9, O 316-10. Of this later impression all but sheets B and D were, in turn, overrun for the next 'sixth edition'. It will be observed that, in this first 'sixth edition', a single press was used also for each sheet in volumes 2 and 3: a circumstance which would suggest that the new 'sixth edition' was being impressed at the same time as the later volumes of the original 'sixth edition'.

2] **GUY MANNERING;** . . . VOL. II. | SIXTH EDITION. . . . 1820.

Collation: π^2 A-O^{12} P^6(-P6). Pagination: *i* half-title, *ii blank*, *iii* title-page, *iv blank*, *1* fly-title, *2 blank*, *3* 4-346 text, *347* printer's imprint, *348 blank*. Figures: A15-10, B27-9, C72-15, D82-9, E117-6, F124-10, G147-10, H183-6, I 213-9, K226-1, L250-10, M285-15, N312-1, O 336-2, P343-12.

3] **GUY MANNERING;** . . . VOL. III. | SIXTH EDITION. . . . 1820.

Collation: π^2 A-P^{12}(-P12). Pagination: *i* half-title, *ii blank*, *iii* title-page, *iv blank*, *1* fly-title, *2 blank*, *3* 4-358 text, *359* printer's imprint, *360 blank*. Figures: A22-10, B27-4, C72-15, D93-2, E109-6, F144-9, G147-5, H171-10, I 205-15, K220-9, L264-5, M274-12, N298-15, O 327-10, P339-11.

82Ag] Sixth Edition (Fifth Edition, Second Impression): 1820

GUY MANNERING; . . . VOL. I [II-III]. | SIXTH EDITION. . . 1820.

Binding: blue boards with printed labels. Paper: Royal 12° (195 x 117mm uncut). Watermarks: *none*.

General Notes: In general this reimpression may be distinguished by the insertion of a dagger † to the right of each signature letter. Except as noted below all other points are identical with the preceding impression.

Copy: E*.
*With 4-page Longman catalogue February 1827

1] **GUY MANNERING;** . . . VOL. I. | SIXTH EDITION. . . . 1820.

Figures: A22-2, B46-2, C72-2, D78-15, E120-2, F133-9, G146-15, H190-7, I 194-9, K229-15, L262-1, M279-4, N311-9, O 316-10, P340-15. Generally this single figure sequence conforms to that of the second printing differentiated in the preceding impression.

2] **GUY MANNERING;** . . . VOL. II. | SIXTH EDITION. . . . 1820.

Typography: No dagger appears after signature letter I (page 193). Figures: As in the preceding impression except for an additional figure I 214-9 and a substitute figure N310-1.

3] **GUY MANNERING;** . . . VOL. III. | SIXTH EDITION. . . . 1820.

Typography: No dagger appears after signature letter P (page 337). Figures: As in the preceding impression except for a substitute figure P351-8.

REPRINTS

FRANCE

PARIS: Baudry
[~] Guy Mannering. 1831. (Collection of Ancient and Modern British Novels and Romances: *see* 288R.2)

PARIS: Didot and Galignani
[~] Guy Mannering. 1821, 1826, 1830. (Collection of Modern English Authors: *see* 291R.4-6)

PARIS: Ledoux
[~] Guy Mannering. 1830. (The Works of Sir Walter Scott: *see* 296R.2)

GERMANY

82Ra] BERLIN: Schlesinger 1823
[Guy Mannering, . . . Berlin, Printed for Adolph Martin Schlesinger. 1823.] Copy: not seen. Reference: GDS 132, page 343.

LEIPSIC: Wigand
[~] Guy Mannering. 1831. (A Complete Edition of the Waverley Novels: *see* 300R.4-6)

ZWICKAU: Schumann
[~] Guy Mannering. 1822. (Pocket Library of English Classics: *see* 302R.32-35)

HUNGARY

[~] PEST, LEIPSIC and LONDON: Wigand. *see* GERMANY. LEIPSIC: Wigand.

UNITED STATES

82Rb] BOSTON: Parker 1821-1831
[Guy Mannering; or, The Astrologer. By the Author of "Waverley." . . . Boston: Samuel H. Parker, No. 12, Cornhill. 1821. Pages: *1-3* 4-360.] Copy: not seen. Notes: (Also reissued in The Novels, Tales and Romances. 1822: *see* 305R.2.)

[~] Guy Mannering. 1826, 1829. (Waverley Novels: *see* 306R.3-4)

[~] Guy Mannering. 1830, 1831. (Waverley Novels, Parker's Edition Revised: *see* 307R.3-4)

82Rb] BOSTON: Vinall 1829
[Guy Mannering; or, The Astrologer. By the Author of Waverly[!] and the Antiquary. . . . Boston: Published by Gordon M. Vinall. William Bellamy—printer. 1829. Two volumes.] Copy located at University of Minnesota.

82Rc] BOSTON: West and Richardson 1815
Guy Mannering; or The Astrologer. By the Author of "Waverly."[!] . . . Boston: Published by West and Richardson, No. 75, Cornhill. And Eastburn, Kirk, and Co. New-York. T. W. White, Printer. 1815. Two volumes. Pages 1: *1-3* 4-308; 2: *1-3* 4-295 *296*. Notes: Cited as 'Three volumes in Two' referring to the first edition, and also cited as 'First American Edition'. Judging by the errata given at the end of the second volume for the first, this text was copied from the original Edinburgh edition, but proofed against a later setting: *see* 82Ac. In some copies the spelling of 'Waverley' is corrected. Copies: CtY InU MH NNU-W(2) RPB.

82Rd] EXETER: Williams 1824
Guy Mannering; or, The Astrologer. By the Author of "Waverley." . . . Exeter: Published by J. & B. Williams. 1824. Two volumes. Pages 1: *1-3* 4-190; 2: *1-3* 4-188. Copy: MWA.

82Re] HARTFORD: Goodrich, and Huntington and Hopkins 1821

Guy Mannering; or, The Astrologer. By the Author of "Waverley." . . . Hartford: Samuel G. Goodrich, and Huntington and Hopkins, 1821. Pages: *1-3* 4-268. Copy: CtY. (Certain references suggest a possible reissue in 1822.)

82Rf] NEW YORK: Duyckinck [and others] 1820

Guy Mannering; or, The Astrologer. By The Author of "Waverley," &c. &c. . . . New=York: Published by E. Duyckinck, W. B. Gilley, L. & F. Lockwood, and E. Bliss. James & John Harper, Printers. 1820. Two volumes. Pages 1: *1-3* 4-237; 2: *1-3* 4-244. Notes: Title-pages read: 'Three Volumes in Two.' referring to the original Edinburgh edition. This is a paginal reprint of the 1818 Eastburn edition next cited. Copies: E; MWA PPL. Reference: Kohler(1) 65 (with illustration).

82Rg] NEW YORK: Eastburn 1818

Guy Mannering; or, The Astrologer. By the Author of Waverly[!] and The Antiquary. . . New-York: Published by James Eastburn and Co. Literary Rooms, Broadway. 1818. Two volumes. Pages 1: *1-3* 4-237; 2: *1-3* 4-244. Notes: Covers and title-pages read 'Three Volumes in Two.' referring to the Edinburgh edition. Copies: MH RPB(vol.1) ViU.

82Rh] PHILADELPHIA: Conrad 1822

Guy Mannering; or, The Astrologer. By the Author of Waverly[!] and The Antiquary. . . . Philadelphia: Published by John Conrad. J. Harding, Printer. 1822. Two volumes. Pages 1: *1-3* 4-292; 2: *1-3* 4-288. Copy: E.

82Ri] PHILADELPHIA: Crissy 1826

Guy Mannering; or, The Astrologer. By the Author of Waverley and The Antiquary. . . . Philadelphia: James Crissy, No. 14, South Seventh Street. 1826. Two volumes. Pages 1: *1-3* 4-260; 2: *1-3* 4-256. Copies: CtY IdU NN T/B(vol.2).

82Rj] PHILADELPHIA: Maxwell 1820-1823

[1] Guy Mannering; or, The Astrologer. By the Author of Waverly[!] and The Antiquary. . . . Philadelphia: Printed and published by J. Maxwell. 1820. Two volumes. Pages 1: *1-3* 4-295; 2: *1-3* 4-293. Copies: L; MWA NN PPL T/B..

[2] Guy Mannering, or, The Astrologer. By the Author of Waverley, &c. . . . Philadelphia: J. Maxwell, S. E. Corner of Fourth and Walnut Streets. R. Wright, Printer, 1823. Two volumes. Pages 1: *1-3* 4-243; 2: *1-3* 4-235. Copies: NN PPL.

DERIVATIVES

GREAT BRITAIN

82Da] EDINBURGH: Huie 1823

Guy Mannering; or, The Gypsey's Prophecy. A Musical Drama, Founded on the Celebrated Novel of the Same Name, by The Author of "Waverley," &c. &c. . . . [no imprint: Edinburgh, James L. Huie, 1823]. [Page *3* reads 'Stevenson & Co. Printers, 32 Thistle Street'.] Pages: *1-5* 6-60. Notes: Drama by Daniel Terry (music composed by Henry R. Bishop not included), first performed at the Theatre-Royal, Covent Garden, London, in 1816 (*see* 82Dj) was apparently revived in this version 25 February 1817 in Edinburgh (note in Ford H1). Engraved frontispiece portrait 'Mr. Denham late of the Theatre Royal Edinburgh as Dandie Dinmont. Edinburgh Printed for James L. Huie. Reprinted for Stirling Kenney & Co.' Signatures: A-C. Notes: After 1817 there are references to other Edinburgh productions 6 February 1818; 12 May 1819; 14 February, 25 May, 22 October 1822 (Bolton 440, 458, 498, 505, 514, with Denham identified as Dandie Dinmont only in the last two entries). See further the next entry. Copy: NN. (A variant issued in: Dramas from the Novels, Tales, and Romances, 1823: volume 2, number 8: *see* 323D)

82Db] LEITH: Burnet 1827
Guy Mannering; or, The Gypsey's Prophecy. A Musical Play, . . . Leith: Printed by James Burnet, and Sold by the Booksellers. 1827. Pages: *i-iv*, *1* 2-80. Notes: Drama with libretto by Daniel Terry (music composed by Henry R. Bishop not included) as performed at the Theatre-Royal, Edinburgh. In addition to the earlier productions in Edinburgh, as cited in the previous entry, Bolton notes later performances there beginning 3 June 1824; 1 February, 27 October 1825, 15 October 1826, 15 October 1827 (529, 541, 548, 577, 608, with Denham again noted in the last three entries). Copies: E(2) (no plates).

82Dc] LONDON: Chappell 1815
Twist ye, twine ye! The Song of Meg Merrilies the Gipsey, from Guy Mannering, . . London, Printed & Sold by Chappell & Co. Music & Musical Instrument Sellers, 124, New Bond Street. [unwatermarked. ca.1815]. Pages: 1-5. Notes: Engraved sheet music with plate number: '416', and the composer's initials in ink at the foot of page 1. Words by Scott from chapter 4 (first words as title). Music composed by George Kiallmark for voice and pianoforte. Price: 2/. Copy: E.

LONDON: Clementi
[~] The Favorite Scotch Song, The Blue Bonnets are over the Borders. *See* 144Dc[2].
LONDON: Cumberland
[~] Guy Mannering; or, The Gipsy's Prophecy. [1831]. (Cumberland's British Theatre: *see* 329D)

82Dd] LONDON: Duncombe 1821
The Gipsey of Derncleugh, A Melo-Drama, in Three Acts, Adapted to Stage Representation from the novel of "Guy Mannering;" . . . London: Published by Duncombe, 19, Little Queen Street; And Sold by all Booksellers. [1821]. Pages: *1-3* 4-36. Notes: Drama adapted by Douglas William Jerrold, and published as it was performed at Sadler's Wells Theatre, 26 August 1821, with coloured woodcut frontispiece portrait of Mrs Egerton as Meg Merrilies. At head of title: Duncombe's Edition. Text ends on page 35: page 36 has graphic sketch of 'Disposition of the Characters when the Curtain falls.' As Bolton observes, an opening date of 26 August is an impossibility, as that was a Sunday. Copies: E; CtY. References: Bolton 487('27 Aug'); Ford H3.

82De] LONDON: Goulding, D'Almaine, Potter 1816
[1] The Overture, Songs, Duett, Glees & Choruses, in the Musical Play of Guy Mannering, or, the Gipsey's Prophecy; . . . London, Printed by Goulding, D'Almaine, Potter & Co.

[ca.1816.] Pages: *i-ii*, 1-66. Notes: Engraved sheet music with plate mark: 'Guy Mannering.' Libretto by Daniel Terry. Music composed by Henry R. Bishop and arranged for the pianoforte by Thomas Attwood and Henry R. Bishop, as performed at the Theatre Royal Covent Garden. Price: 12s. Copy: O.

[2] The Overture. Songs, Duett, Glees & Chorusses, In the Musical Play of Guy Mannering, or the Gipsey's Prophecy; . . . London, Printed by Goulding, D'Almaine, Potter & Co. 20, Soho Square & to be had at 7 Westmorland Str.t Dublin. [1816]. Pages: *i-ii*, 1-82. Notes: Libretto by Daniel Terry. Music composed by Henry R. Bishop and arranged for the pianoforte by Thomas Attwood and Henry R. Bishop. Pagination is continuous and the collective price is 15s/-, but each of the fourteen songs is priced separately as well. Copy: L.

LONDON: Hodgson
[~] Guy Mannering; or, The Gipsey's Prophecy. [1822]. (Hodgson's Juvenile Drama: *see* 333D.1)

82Df] LONDON: Hone 1816
Guy Mannering, The Astrologer, or The Prophecy of Meg Merrilies, The Gipsey. . . . London, Printed for W. Hone, 55 Fleet Street. 1816. Price Sixpence. Pages: *1-5* 6-28. Notes: There is no type-set title-page. At head of woodcut title: 'Hone's Popular Cabinet Edition'. Woodcut hand-coloured frontispiece and title-page with vignette both by George Cruikshank, and both counted in the pagination. The frontispiece shows Mrs. Egerton as 'Meg Merrilies' and the title vignette portrays Mr. Liston as 'Dominic Sampson'. A 'Postscript' (pages 27-28), possibly prepared later, contains lyrics from the play. Judging by the illustrations, this would appear to be a reprint of the 1816 London: Miller issue (*see* 82Dj[1]). In some copies page number '6' is lacking. Copies: InU without Postscript) MH NjP TxU. Reference: Cohn 374.

82Dg] LONDON: Hurst, Robinson 1821
[*printed wrapper*] Illustrations of Guy Mannering; or, The Astrologer: A Novel. By "The Author of Waverley," &c. . . . London: Printed for Hurst, Robinson, and Co. (Late Boydell), 90, Cheapside. 1821. Moyes, London. Published 20 April 1821 in London (*MC*), as the fourth in the Hurst, Robinson series. Notes: Following printed title, engraved vignette title-page and six plates, all drawn by R. Westall and engraved by Chas. Heath. Since the one copy examined is before letters, the captions are taken from a separate listing. The printed title lists five states of this issue: (1) 12° prints, 9s.6d.; (2) Medium 8° prints, 12s.6d.; (3) Imperial 4° proofs, £1.4.0; (4) Imperial 4° proofs on India paper, £1.10.0; (5) Columbier 4° proofs on India paper, before the letters, £1.16.0. Copy: (5) T/B.
Title vignette: 'Meg Merrilies predicting the fall of Ellangowan'; plates:
(1) 'The dead body of Kennedy discovered on the Beach';
(2) 'Meg Merrilies attending upon the dying Smuggler';
(3) 'The Meeting of Meg Merrilies, Brown, and Dinmont';
(4) 'Julia Mannering serenaded from the Lake';
(5) 'The sudden appearance of Meg Merrilies on Gibbie's-Knowe';
(6) 'The Death of Meg Merrilies'.

82Dh] LONDON: Lowndes 1821
Songs, Duets, Glees, and Chorusses, in a New Musical Drama, . . . Called the Witch of

Derncleugh, being a New Dramatick Version of Guy Mannering. . . . London: Printed by C. Lowndes, Marquis Court, Drury Lane; And Sold in the Theatre. [1821]. Pages: *1-5* 6-15. Notes: Drama by J. R. Planché (music by Henry R. Bishop not included) as performed at the Theatre Royal, English Opera House, Strand, 30 July 1821. Price: Ten pence. Copy: C. References: Bolton 486; Ford H2.

82Di] LONDON: Mason 1819

The History of Guy Mannering, The Astrologer; Founded on the Romantic Drama performed This Season . . . . To which is added, The Libertine, or History of Don Juan; . . . . London: Printed and Published by W. Mason, 21, Clerkenwell Green. [ca. 1819.] Pages: *i-ii, 1-3* 4-25 Guy Mannering, 25-32 The Libertine. Notes: A chapbook version of the two plays. Price: Sixpence. Copy: BCL.

82Dj] LONDON: Miller 1816-1818

[1] Guy Mannering; or, The Gipsey's Prophecy: A Musical Play, in Three Acts, . . . London: Printed for John Miller, 25, Bow Street, Covent Garden; By W. Smith and Co. King Street, Seven Dials. 1816. Pages: *i-ii, 1* 2-71 *72-74.* Notes: Libretto by Daniel Terry (music by Henry R. Bishop not included) as first performed at The Theatre Royal, Covent Garden, 12 March 1816. This play includes a poem composed by Scott for his friend Daniel Terry: 'Lullaby of an Infant Chief' (first words: 'O, hush thee, my babie, thy sire was a knight,') and hence is also listed as an authorized printing (*see* 91A). Price: Two Shillings and Sixpence.

This is the first dramatic adaptation of a Scott novel, the only one (as indicated below) to go through a number of editions by the original publisher, and the first of Terry's several 'Waverley' plays, all staged with Scott"s encouragement. Copies: BCL E O; InU (inscribed) NjP NNP(Van Antwerp) TxU TxU(prompt copy). References: Bolton 409; Ford H1; Van Antwerp(2) 18a. (Apart from several Scottish issues [82Da-Db], and others issued in the U.S. [82D0-Dp, Dr], further London editions 1820-1824 were printed in the 'Oxberry' series: *see* 340D[2a-2b]).

[2] Guy Mannering; or, The Gipsey's Prophecy: A Musical Play, in Three Acts. . . Second Edition. London, Printed for J. Miller, 25, Bow-Street, Covent-Garden; By B. M'Millan, Bow-Street, Covent-Garden. 1816. Pages: *i-ii, 1* 2-70. Notes: Libretto by Daniel Terry (music by Henry R. Bishop not included) as first performed at The Theatre Royal, Covent Garden, 12 March 1816. Price: Two Shillings and Sixpence. Copies: L(2) O; NN. Reference: Ford H1.

[3] Guy Mannering; or, The Gipsey's Prophecy: . . . Third Edition. London: Printed for John Miller, 25, Bow-Street, Covent-Garden; By B. M'Millan, Bow-Street, Covent-Garden. 1817. Pages: *1-3* 4-60. Notes: Libretto by Daniel Terry (music by Henry R. Bishop not included). Price: Two Shillings and Sixpence. Copies: L; CtY(2) TxU. Reference: Ford H1.

[4] Guy Mannering; or, The Gipsey's Prophecy: . . . Fourth Edition. London: Printed for John Miller, 25, Bow-Street, Covent-Garden; Printed by B. M'Millan, Bow-Street, Covent-Garden. 1818. Pages: *1-3* 4-60. Notes: Libretto by Daniel Terry (music by Henry R. Bishop not included). Price: Two Shillings and Sixpence. Copies: L; TxU.

82Dk] LONDON: Phipps 1815

Twist Ye Twine Ye, The Favorite Gipsy Song in Guy Mannering . . . London Pub/d by

Phipps & Co. 25 Duke St. Grosvenor Sq. [watermarked 1815]. Pages: *1* 2-4. Notes: Engraved sheet music. Words from chapter 4 (first words: 'Twist ye, twine ye, even so, Mingle shades of joy and woe.'). Music composed by Francis Joseph Klose arranged for voice and pianoforte. Copy: L. Reference: G/T 9833.

LONDON: The Proprietors
[~] Guy Mannering; or, The Gipsey's Prophecy! 1820, 1821, 1824. (The New English Drama: *see* 340D.2)

82Dl] LONDON: Schetky 1815
[1] [Meg Merrilies' Prophecy. London: Schetky (1815.) Notes: Music composed by G. C. Schetky.] Copy: not seen. Reference: G/T 9837.

[2] Meg Merrilies' Song, from Guy Mannering, . . . London, Published by G. Schetky Junr. No. 6, Gt. Pulteney Strt. Golden Square, & to be had at Mr. Birchall's & Mr. Chappell's Music Shops New Bond Strt. [1815]. Pages: 1-4. Notes: Engraved sheet music with composer's first three initials in ink next to imprint. Words from chapter 4 (first words: 'Twist ye Twist ye twine ye twine ye even even so'). Music composed by J. G. C. Schetky arranged for voice and pianoforte. Price: 1/6. Copy: InU. Reference: G/T 9838.

UNITED STATES

82Dm] BALTIMORE: Cole 1831
[La Dame Blanche, or The White Lady; A Comic Opera, . . . Baltimore. Cole, 1831. Pages: 70pp. Notes: Libretto by Eugene Scribe, translated into English by W. P. W. (music by François Adrien Boieldieu not included)]. Copy: not seen.

82Dn] BOSTON: Bangs 1818
Rosalvo Delmonmort, A Tale: by Guy Mannering. . . . Boston: Published by Thomas G. Bangs, No. 7, State-Street. 1818. Pages: *1-5* 6-196. Copy: CtY.

BOSTON: Bradlee
[~] The Favorite Scotch Song. The Blue Bonnets are over the Border, . . . in the Opera of Guy Mannering. [ca.1827.] *See* The Monastery 144Di).

82Do] BOSTON: Wells and Lilly 1823
Guy Mannering; or, The Gipsey's Prophecy! A Musical Play, . . . Boston: Published by Wells and Lilly—Court-Street: A. T. Goodrich & Co.—New-York. 1823. Pages: *1-3* 4-88. Notes: Libretto by Daniel Terry (music composed by Henry R. Bishop not included.) Prefatory remarks say that 'Guy Mannering, like all his brethren, is a very near kinsman of the melo-drama; pathos, comedy, music, incident, are skillfully blended; . . .' At head of title: 'Oxberry's Edition.' This edition is described as being 'selected and arranged from the novel with the hand of a master' and 'the only edition existing which is faithfully marked with the stage business, and stage directions, as it is performed at the Theatres Royal. By W. Oxberry, comedian.' Copies: CtY DLC MWA NN NN-L(prompt copy.)

82Dp] NEW YORK: Longworth 1816
Guy Mannering; or, The Gipsey's Prophecy: A Musical Play, in Three Acts. . . New-York: Published by David Longworth, At the Dramatic Repository, Shakspeare-Gallery. 1816. Pages: *1-5* 6-64. Notes: An abridged libretto by Daniel Terry (music composed by Henry R. Bishop and others not included.) From the first London edition of 1816. Copies: MWA(2).

82Dq] NEW YORK: Spear & Nesbitt 1832
Songs, Duetts, Choruses &c. in The White Lady, or, Spirit of Avenel, a Romantic Opera in Three Acts, . . . New York, Spear & Nesbitt, 1832. Pages: 1-42. Notes: Libretto by Eugene Scribe translated into English by J. H. Payne; music composed by François Adrien Boieldieu, with additions from Weber, Rossini, Auber and Guglielmi, as produced at The Theatre, New York, 21 May 1832, from the Covent Garden version. Copy: NN.

82Dr] PHILADELPHIA: Palmer 1823
Guy Mannering; or, The Gipsey's Prophecy. A Musical Play in Three Acts. . . . Philadelphia: Published by Thomas H. Palmer. 1823. Pages: *1-3* 4-60. Notes: Libretto by Daniel Terry (music by François Adrien Boieldieu not included.) Page 25 misnumbered 2. Copy: NN.

EXTRACTS IN ANTHOLOGIES

82E] From the novel *Guy Mannering* there are only three extracts in the anthologies: 384E.5 389.9 466.5. For Scott's poem in Terry's play of the same title (82Dj) there are eleven extracts recorded in entry 91E below.

AN ESSAY OF THE NATURE AND ACTIONS OF INVISIBLE PEOPLE

83A] First Scott Edition: 1815

AN ESSAY | OF | The Nature and Actions of the Subterranean (and, for the | moſt Part,) Inviſible People, heretofoir going under the | Name of ELVES, FAUNES, and FAIRIES, or the lyke, among | the Low-Country Scots, as they are deſcribed by thoſe who | have the SECOND SIGHT; and now, to occaſion further | Inquiry, collected and compared, by a Circumſpect Inquirer | reſiding among the Scottiſh-Iriſh in Scotland; with an Ap- | pendix, conſiſting of Extracts from a Treaſise on SECOND | SIGHT, by Theophilus Inſulanus. | [*double rule*] | *EDINBURGH: Reprinted by JAMES BALLANTYNE & Co. for LONGMAN, | HURST, REES, ORME, & BROWN, Paternoſter- Row, LONDON. | 1815.*

Privately distributed in March 1815. 100 copies. Binding: drab boards with diamond-shaped printed label on front. Paper: laid Demy 4° (246 x 195mm uncut). Watermarks: Crown shield with posthorn and BANK MILL | 1813.

Collation: π4(-π4) A-M4 *N*1(=π4). Pagination: *i* title-page, *ii 'One Hundred Copies only reprinted. J. Ballantyne & Co.'*, *iii* type-facsimile of manuscript title 'Secret Commonwealth, or, A Treatife difplayeing the Chiefe Curiofities . . . By Mr Robert Kirk, Minifter at Aberfoill. 1691.', *iv blank*, *v*-vi preface, *1* 2-45 text, *46 blank*, *47* fly-title for Appendix, *48 blank*, *49* 50-97 Extracts from A Treatise on the Second Sight, dated Edinburgh 1763, 97 printer's imprint, *98 blank*. Printer's imprint: [*short rule*] | EDINBURGH: | Reprinted by James Ballantyne & Co. .

Figures: A8-10, B16-10, C24-10, D32-10, E40-10, F44-6, G56-10, H64-10, I 72-6/10, K80-6/10, L88-10, M96-10, *N*—.

Notes: On 3 March 1815 Scott advised Lady Macleod that this 'very curious treatise' would be issued 'in a few weeks', but the inscribed copy cited below might indicate an earlier printing, if the editor's dating is to be trusted. The preface notes that the first 'curious Tract' is 'printed literally from a Manuscript copy preserved in the Advocates' Library.' To 'complete the Examples of Second Sight' the Extracts from the second, printed Treatise, 'a very scarce Work', are then provided. In some copies, when the first title is misplaced after the facsimile, the work is then erroneously described as titled 'Secret Commonwealth . . . .' Scott himself used the first, imprint title, as transcribed above, when he next referred to the *Essay* in a review of the Culloden Papers (95A, page 290). The edition itself is occasionally, and wrongly, attributed to Robert Jamieson.

Presentation copy: IdU('Alexander Boswell Esq of Auchinleck from his sincere & obliged friend Walter Scott Edin. 20 february'). Other copies: BCL EU(stamped: 'Edinburgh College from Stationers Hall') L(3) O(2); NjP T/B(Frances Mary Richardson Currer).

Reference: (Magnum Opus Edition: Not reprinted.)

THE FIELD OF WATERLOO

The poem was the first upon a subject likely to be sufficiently hackneyed; and, having the advantage of coming out in a small cheap form—(prudently imitated from Murray's innovation with the tales of Byron, which was the deathblow to the system of verse in quarto)—it attained rapidly a measure of circulation above what had been reached either by Rokeby or the Lord of the Isles. (Lockhart, v.106-107.)

84Aa] First Edition, First Impression: 1815

THE | FIELD | OF | **WATERLOO;** | A POEM. | BY | WALTER SCOTT, ESQ. | [*short Oxford rule*] | [*six-line quotation from Akenside*] | [*short reversed Oxford rule*] | EDINBURGH: | *Printed by James Ballantyne & Co.* | FOR ARCHIBALD CONSTABLE AND CO. EDINBURGH; AND | LONGMAN,

HURST, REES, ORME, AND BROWN, | AND JOHN MURRAY, LONDON. | [*dash*] | 1815.

Published 23 October 1815 in Edinburgh (*EEC*); issued 2 November in London (*MC*). 5s. 6000 copies (E MS.789, p.377). Binding: drab paper wrappers. Paper: Demy 8° (228 x 143mm uncut). Watermarks: 5 [7, 9, 10] | W Balston & Co | 1814; R T & Co | 1815. Collation: A^8 B-C^8 D^4 E^2 *F*1. Pagination: *1* half-title, *2 blank*, *3* title-page, *4 blank*, *5* dedication to the Duchess of Wellington, *6 blank*, *7* Advertisement, *8 blank*, *9* 10-45 text, *46 blank*, *47* fly-title, *48 blank*, *49* 50-54 Notes, *55*-56 advertisement for Scott's works, *56* printer's imprint, *1*-2 advertisement for Scott's edition of Swift's *Works* and *3*-4 (dated September 1815) a supplement to the *Encyclopaedia Britannica*, *5* Proposal for Publishing two prints by Richard Sasse, *6 blank*. Printer's imprint: [*short rule*] | Edinburgh: | Printed by James Ballantyne & Co.

Figures: *A*13-10 14-11, B18-8 29-6, C36-11 43-1, D53-2.

Notes: Lockhart v.100-104 transcribes certain of the proofs to illustrate the banter between printer and poet as this work was being perfected for issue, all indicating, as he remarks, Scott's 'habitual good-nature.' The Proposal for the Sasse prints relating to Waterloo, printed separately on a single leaf, was included at Scott's request.

Presentation copies: E('A[nne] D[orothea] Alvanley given by the Author 1815') E('Miss [Christian] Rutherford with the Authors Compts'); IdU('Harriet Scott From the Author') NN('To J[ames?]. Paterson with the best respect of the Author') TxU('The Reverend Mr [Edward] Berwick from his sincere friend The Author'). Other copies: BCL E(John Stuart, 12th Earl of Moray) E(3) ES O; CtY(3) IdU InU MH(2) NN(2) PPL T/B(2) TxU(4) ViU.

References: Ruff 147; Thomson, page 28; Tinker 1871; Van Antwerp(1) 15. (Magnum Opus Edition 1834: *The Poetical Works*, xi.*255-259* 260-291.)

84Ab] Second Edition (First Edition, Second Impression): 1815

THE | FIELD | OF | **WATERLOO;** | A POEM. | BY | WALTER SCOTT, Esq. | [*short Oxford rule*] | [*six-line quotation from Akenside*] | [*short reversed Oxford rule*] | SECOND EDITION. | [*short rule*] | EDINBURGH: | *Printed by James Ballantyne & Co.* | FOR ARCHIBALD CONSTABLE AND CO. EDINBURGH; AND | LONGMAN, HURST, REES, ORME, AND BROWN, | AND JOHN MURRAY, LONDON. | [*dash*] | 1815.

Published 9 November 1815 in Edinburgh (*EEC*). 5s. 1000 copies (E MS.789, p.438). Binding (for issue 1): drab paper wrappers. Paper: Demy 8° (228 x 143 mm uncut). Watermarks: 7 | W Balston & Co | 1814. Collation: $\pi^4(\pm\pi 2)$ N-P^8.

Pagination: *1* half-title, *2 blank*, *3* title-page, *4 blank*, *5* dedication, *6 blank*, *7* Advertisement, *8 blank*, *193* 194-229 text, *230 blank*, *231* fly-title, *232 blank*, *233* 234-238 Notes, *239*-240 advertisements, 240 printer's imprint: [*short rule*] | EDINBURGH: | Printed by James Ballantyne & Co. Typography: A semicolon, following the last word in the original impression (page 15), has dropped in this reimposed reimpression (page 199).

Figures: N208-5, O 214-10/-, P234-11.

Notes: When the first edition was nearly sold out, Constable had the original setting reimposed, inserted a cancel title-page reading 'Second Edition', and issued the piece (1) separately or, as the page numbers now indicate, (2) bound after the fourth edition of *Ballads and Lyrical Pieces*. With his type so rearranged it was impractical for the publisher to continue issuing a 'first edition'; hence the extraordinary expedient described in the next issue.

Copies: (1) O P; CtY*. (2) E. Reference: Ruff 148(refers to copy bound with and following *Vision of Don Roderick*).
*Bound with second edition of *The Vision of Don Roderick* (59Ah).

84Ac] Third (Second) Edition: 1815

THE | FIELD | OF | **WATERLOO;** | A POEM. | BY | WALTER SCOTT, ESQ. | [*short Oxford rule*] | [*six-line quotation from Akenside*] | [*short reversed Oxford rule*] | THIRD EDITION. | EDINBURGH: | *Printed by James Ballantyne & Co.* | FOR ARCHIBALD CONSTABLE AND CO. EDINBURGH; AND | LONGMAN, HURST, REES, ORME, AND BROWN, | AND JOHN MURRAY, LONDON. | [*dash*] | 1815.

Published 11 November 1815 in London (*MC*). 5s. 3000 copies. (E MS.789, p.452). Paper: Demy 8° (211 x 132mm cut). Watermarks: *none*. Collation: A^8 B-C^8 D^4. Pagination: As for first edition, first impression, except for an additional printer's imprint verso of title (page *4*): [*short rule*] | T. DAVISON, Lombard-street, | Whitefriars, London.

Figures: As for first edition, first impression, except no figure on page 43.

Notes: This is a reset type-facsimile of the first edition, even including the Edinburgh press figures and, in its (1) first issue, page 56, Ballantyne printer's imprint, but printed in London with Scott's permission to meet a continuing demand for copies. Davison, the printer, occasionally prepared 'private issues' for the Longman firm.

In a (2) later issue the fourteen entries for Scott's works listed pages *55*-56 are closed up to admit a listing of four sets of illustrations, and the final Ballantyne imprint is displaced by one for the Longman publishing firm: *Published by Longman, Hurst, Rees, Orme, and Brown, Paternoster-row,* | *London*.

Copies: (issue 1) BCL E; NN T/B T/B(inscribed 27 November 1815) TxU(2). (2) O; CtY InU.

Reference: Ruff 149.

84Ad] Fourth Edition: 1821

THE | VISION | OF | Don Roderick, | THE | FIELD OF WATERLOO, | AND | OTHER POEMS. | | [*short rule*] | BY | SIR WALTER SCOTT, BART. | [*short rule*] | FOURTH EDITION. | [*short reversed Oxford rule*] | EDINBURGH: | PRINTED FOR ARCHIBALD CONSTABLE AND CO. | [*dash*] | 1821.

Notes: This 'Fourth Edition' is conjoined in a single setting, with a 'Fourth Edition' of *The Vision of Don Roderick,* an issue fully described in entry 59Aj.

REPRINTS

FRANCE

PARIS: Didot and Galignani
[~] The Field of Waterloo. 1821. (Collection of Modern English Authors: *see* 290R. [7A])

84Ra] PARIS: Galignani 1816
The Field of Waterloo; A Poem By Walter Scott, Esq. Third Edition. Paris: Printed for, and sold at Galignani's French, English, Italian, German, and Spanish Library, No. 18, Rue Vivienne. 1816. Pages: *i-viii*, *9* 10-54. Notes: This issue, some four years before any of the Galignani series, appears to follow the Edinburgh second edition. Copy: P.

UNITED STATES

84Rb] BOSTON: Wait 1815
The Field of Waterloo; A Poem. By Walter Scott, Esq.... Boston: Printed and Published by T. B. Wait & Sons, 1815. Pages: *1-9* 10-56. Copies: E; CtY DLC IdU InU MH(2) MWA. Reference: Kohler(1) 6 (with illustration).

84Rc] BURLINGTON: Mills 1816
The Field of Waterloo. A Poem By Walter Scott, Esq. Burlington: Printed and Published by Samuel Mills. 1816. Pages: *i-ii*, *1-3* 4-47. Copies: MWA TxU.

84Rd] HUDSON: Norman 1816
The Field of Waterloo; A Poem. By Walter Scott, Esq.... Hudson: Published by William E. Norman, No. 63, Warren-Street. 1816. Pages: *1-9* 10-48. Notes: The same pagination, but not a paginal resetting from the 1815 New York/Philadelphia issues (*see* 84Rf-Rg). Copies: E; InU MWA.

84Re] LEXINGTON: Bradford 1816
The Field of Waterloo; A Poem. By Walter Scott, Esq. Lexington, (Ky.) Printed by F. Bradford, Jr. 1816. Pages: *1-3* 4-23. Copy: DLC.

84Rf] NEW YORK: Van Winkle & Wiley 1815
The Field of Waterloo; A Poem. By Walter Scott, Esq. . . . New-York: Printed and Published by Van Winkle & Wiley, No. 3 Wall-Street. 1815. Pages *1-9* 10-48. Notes: Apparently the first American issue, preceding the 1815 Philadelphia reprint issued by Thomas. The original boards, when present, are in several states: the first in tan boards listing on back as in press 'An Exposition of the Political Conduct of Carnot' and 'Says She to Her Neighbour'; the second in green or grey boards and citing these works as already published. This title is often seen bound with *The Lay of the Last Minstrel*, Boston, Greenough and Stebbins, 1810 (*see* 14Re) or with *The Poetical Works* (*The Vision of Don Roderick*), Baltimore, Joseph Cushing, 1813 (*see* 303R.1). Copies: E; CtY DLC InU(2) MWA NN(3) RPB TxU(3). Reference: Kohler(1) 66 (with illustration).

84Rg] PHILADELPHIA: Thomas 1815
The Field of Waterloo; . . . Philadelphia: Published by M. Thomas, No. 52 Chesnut Street. Van Winkle & Wiley, Printers. 1815. Pages: *1-9* 10-48. Notes: Printed from the same type as that used for the 1815 New York issue by Van Winkle & Wiley. Copies: DLC MWA PPL(2).

DERIVATIVE

GREAT BRITAIN

84D] LONDON: Birchall 1818
Waterloo, . . . The Poetry by Walter Scott Esq. . . . London, Printed & Sold for the Author, by Rt. Birchall, 133, New Bond Street. [unwatermarked. ca.1818.] Pages: 1-5. Notes: Engraved sheet music. Words from stanza 23 (first words: Farewell sad field, whose blighted face, wears desolations'). Music composed by John Wall Callcott arranged for voice and pianoforte. Price: 2s. Copies: E L. Reissued with price as '2/-' and a catalogue on page *6* (MH-M). Reference: G/T 9815.

EXTRACTS IN ANTHOLOGIES

84E] From *The Field of Waterloo* there are four extracts in the anthologies: 363E.1 385.3 388.6 423.12.

ANECDOTES OF MUNGO PARK

85A] First Printing: 1815

[Anecdotes of Mungo Park], pages 100-105 *in*:

The Journal of a Mission to the Interior of Africa, in the Year 1805. By Mungo Park. . . . The Second Edition, Revised and Corrected, with Additions. London: Printed for John Murray, Albemarle-Street, by W. Bulmer and Co. Cleveland-Row, St. James's. 1815.

Notes: In his 'Advertisement' to this edition, dated 1 August 1815, John Whishaw recognizes several further anecdotes relating to Park 'obtained from different sources, but principally through the kind and liberal communications of WALTER SCOTT, Esq., to whom the acknowledgements of the editor are particularly due' (page *v*). Nonetheless only the six pages noted above seem to derive directly from Scott, and these sentiments are conveyed chiefly in the third person.

Before (2) the book printing described above the section including Scott's anecotes appeared as (1) a separate pamphlet entitled: 'Addenda to the Life of Mr. Park, prefixed to a Journal . . .', this consisting of 27 pages (*Monthly Review*, October 1815, pages 196-200). It was then remarked (*ibid.*, page 197): 'The information obtained from Mr. Walter Scott does not assist materially in the delineation of the traveller's character.'

Twenty-one years after Park's death, in 1827, an anthology published in Cornish, Maine (444E.2, pages 128-129), attributed to 'W. Scott' a poetic 'Dirge' consisting of four quatrains (first words: 'Hope no more! in peace he sleepeth,').

Copies: (issue 1) not seen. (2) BCL GM. References: *Letters*, iv.52-55; Duval 807(for 1815 first edition) and page 135.

THE LIFTING OF THE BANNER

86A] First Printing: 1815

'THE LIFTING OF THE BANNER' (first words: 'From the brown crest of Newark its summons extending,') pages *3* 4-5, *in*:

[*vignette of banner, shield, sword, ribbon, all in front of a stunted tree*] The Ettricke Garland; Being Two Excellent New Songs on The Lifting of the Banner of the House of Buccleuch, at the Great Foot-Ball Match on Carterhaugh, Dec. 4, 1815. Edinburgh: Printed by James Ballantyne and Co. 1815.

Printed for distribution 'among the spectators' on the date of the match 4 December 1815 (final paragraph of *EWJ* entry, *see* 87A).

Notes: Both the first song, by the 'Sheriff of the Forest' (Scott) and the second, 'To the Ancient Banner of the House of Buccleuch' by the 'Ettricke Shepherd' (James Hogg) are dated 'Dec. 1, 1815.', three days before the event. See further the next entry.

Copies: E L; NNP(Baron Montague[Montagu]).

References: Ruff 150 (with illustration); Van Antwerp(1) 13. (Magnum Opus Edition 1834: *The Poetical Works*, xi.312-314.)

EXTRACTS IN ANTHOLOGIES

86E] Scott's poem 'The Lifting of the Banner' was extracted in six anthologies: 360E.17 369[4].3 389.26 405(2)[3].2 405(3)[1].3 423.7.

FOOT-BALL MATCH

87A] First Printing: 1815

'*FOOT-BALL MATCH.*' page 414 *in*:

The Edinburgh Weekly Journal. Vol. XVIII. No. 939. Wednesday, December 13, 1815. [Price 7d. Edinburgh—Printed by Michael Anderson, Lady Stair's Close, Lawnmarket, For himself, The Heirs of William Brown, and other Proprietors.

Published 13 December 1815.

Notes: This long account, concluding with a reprint of the two poems written for the occasion (*see* 86A), may be attributed to Scott on Lockhart's assurance that it was 'written, I can have no doubt, by the Sheriff of the Forest', who would certainly be proud to see 'his boy ride about Carterhaugh with the pennon of Bellenden' (Lockhart, v.112, 120, with the *EWJ* article itself reprinted 116-120).

The 'football' (rugby) match and its splendid pagentry, all largely organized by Scott, is fully represented as the last event, again reprinted but without attribution, in Fisher's book on 1815, this date identified on the dust-jacket as 'the most dramatic, exciting, and pivotal year in history'.

Copy: E. Reference: John Fisher, *1815: An End and a Beginning,* New York: Harper [1963], pages 278-282.

THE DANCE OF DEATH and ROMANCE OF DUNOIS

88A] First Printings: 1815[1816]

1] 'THE DANCE OF DEATH.' (first words: 'Night and morning were at meeting', pages *cccxxxv* cccxxxvi-cccxxxix, includes 'SONG.' (first words: 'Wheel the wild dance') sections 4-7 of 8;

2] 'ROMANCE OF DUNOIS.' (first words: 'It was Dunois, the young and brave, was bound for Palestine,') page cccxxxix *in*:

The Edinburgh Annual Register, for 1813. Vol. Sixth.—Parts I. and II. Edinburgh: Printed by James Ballantyne and Co. For John Ballantyne and Co. Edinburgh; Longman, Hurst, Rees, Orme, and Brown, London; and the Other Proprietors. 1815.

Published 11 January 1816 in Edinburgh (*EEC* 8 January); issued 10 February in London. £1.1.0.

Notes: The first poem is dated from Abbotsford 1 October 1815. The second poem 'Romance of Dunois' is one of three which Scott offered as a 'strictly literal' translation from a manuscript in French 'given me by a lady, whose father had found it upon the field of battle' at Waterloo (*Paul's Letters*, page 209). The original author appears not to have been Hortencia (former Queen of Holland), as Scott was first informed, but rather the Duchesse de St Leu (*see* 89Ac). The other two translations were first printed in *Paul's Letters* (89Aa), issued two weeks after this journal. Apart from the two first printings listed above there are two reprints not related to Waterloo: [3] 'Song, for the Anniversary Meeting of the Pitt Club of Scotland', page cccxl, and [4] 'The Lifting of the Banner', pages cccxli-cccxlii (*see* 74A and 86A.)

Copies: E L O; PPL T/B.

References: Thomson, page 64. (Magnum Opus Edition 1834: *The Poetical Works*, [1] xi. 297-303; [2] xi.304-305.)

REPRINT

UNITED STATES

PHILADELPHIA: Carey and Wells and Lilly 1816
[~] The Dance of Death, and Other Poems. 1816. (*see* 315R).

DERIVATIVES

GREAT BRITAIN

88Da] DUBLIN: Willis 1820
It was Dunois the Young and Brave.... The translation of the words by Sir Walter Scott, Bt. Published by Willis & Co. 7 Westmorland Street Dublin & 55 St. James's Street, London. [watermarked 1811. ca.1820]. Pages: *1-2* 3-10. Notes: Engraved sheet music with plate number '591'. (first words as title). Music composed by T. Philipps arranged for voice and pianoforte. Price: 3/0. Copy: MH-M.

88Db] LONDON: Birchall 1816
[Twelve Vocal Pieces (Second Set.) London: Birchall (1816.) Notes: Music composed by John Clarke.] Copy: not seen. Reference: G/T 10852.

88Dc] LONDON: Goulding, D'Almaine, Potter 1816-1817
[1] The bravest Knight and the fairest fair, . . . London Published by Goulding D'Almaine Potter & Co. 20, Soho Square, & to be had at 7, Westmorland Street Dublin. [ca.1817]. *in* The Overture Marches & Vocal Music, In the Opera of Montrose. Pages: 14-17. Notes: Engraved sheet music with plate mark: 'Montroce[!]'. (first words: 'It was Dunois the young and brave, was bound for Palestine'). Music arranged by Henry R. Bishop for voice and pianoforte. Price: 1/6. Copy: MH-M.

[2] Dunois the Brave, A Popular French Ballad, also with English Poetry from Pauls Letters to his Kinsfolk, . . . London Publish'd by Goulding, D'Almaine, Potter & Co. 20, Soho Sq. & to be had at 7, Westmorland St. Dublin. [ca.1816.] Pages: 1-3. Notes: Engraved sheet music with plate mark: 'Dunois the brave'. (first words in English: 'It was Dunois the young and brave, was bound for Palestine'; in French: 'Partant pour la Syrie le jeune et beau Dunois,'). Music by an anonymous composer arranged for voice and pianoforte. Price: 1/6. Copy: L.

88Dd] LONDON: Phillips and Mayhew 1816
Dunois the Young and Brave, A Popular French Romance, . . . In the Opera of Henri Quatre, . . . London, Printed by Phillips & Mayhew, Music Sellers to H.R.H. The Duchess of Kent, 17, Old Bond Street. and to be had at Ellard's Music Warehouse, 27, Sackville Street, Dublin. [watermarked 1816.] Pages: 1-3. Notes: Engraved sheet music with plate mark: 'Dunois the Young & Brave'. Music arranged by J. D. Loder for voice and pianoforte. Price: 1s/6. Copy: L.

88De] LONDON: Williams 1816
Partant pour la Syrie, (Dunois the Brave) The English Words by Sir Walter Scott . . . London, Published by B. Williams, 11, Paternoster Row & 170, Gt. Dover Road. [ca.1820]. Pages: 77-80. Notes: Engraved sheet music with caption title headed 'No. 20. Gentlemen's Series____Cyclopedia of Music.' In English and French (first words: 'It was Dunois the young and brave'). Arranged with characteristic symphonies and accompaniments by unidentified musicians. Price: Threepence. Copy: MH.

UNITED STATES

Note: The original French manuscript of The 'Romance of Dunois', at first attributed by Scott to Hortencia Beauharnais, former Queen of Holland, and so represented in much of the sheet music listed below, was finally ascribed by him to the Duchesse de St Leu in the third edition of *Paul's Letters* (*see* 89Ac.) The attributions below have all been modified to reflect the St Leu ascription.

88Df] BALTIMORE: Carr 1820
[The Knight Errant. . . . Baltimore, Printed and sold at T. Carr's music store, 78 1/2 Baltimore Street. (ca.1820). Pages: 1-2. Notes: Original French by Duchesse de St Leu. (*see note above)*]. Copy: not seen. Reference: Wolfe 4348.

88Dg] BALTIMORE: Cole 1825
[The Knight Errant. . . . Published by John Cole, Baltimore. (ca. 1825.) Pages: 1-2. Notes: Original French by Duchesse de St Leu.] Copy: not seen. Reference: Wolfe 4356.

88Dh] BALTIMORE: Willig 1823
[The Knight Errant. . . . Baltimore, Published and sold by Geo. Willig. (1823.) Broadside. Notes: Original French by Duchesse de St Leu. Copyright secured 4 August 1823.] Copy: not seen. References: Wolfe 4352, 4352A.

BOSTON: Graupner
[~] The Knight Errant. (*See* 88Di)

88Di] CHARLESTON: Muck 1820
The Knight Errant, . . . Translated from the French by Walter Scott. . . . Published for Mr. P. Muck, Charleston, S.C., by G. Graupner & Co. Boston. [1820.] Pages: *1-2* 3. Notes: Engraved sheet music with caption title. Page *1* is blank. (first words: 'It was Dunvis[!] the young and brave, was bound for Palestine,'). Original French by Duchesse de St Leu and arranged for voice and pianoforte. Copies: DLC MWA. Reference: Wolfe 4346. Reissued with plate number '104' added (RPB); with plate number now reading '(104)' (InU MH RPB[8]); [1824] with phrase 'Sold by John. Ashton. No. 197 Washington St.' added as last line page *2*, below plate number '(104)' (MH MWA RPB). [References: Wolfe 4346A,B,C].

88Dj] CHARLESTOWN: 1822
The Knight Errant. Charlestown, 1822. Pages: 13-15. Notes: In *The Musical Cabinet,* vol.1, no.1. Orginal French by Duchesse de St Leu. *See* 442E. Reference: Wolfe 4351.

88Dk] NEW YORK: Dubois 1819
The Knight Errant. . . . Translated from the French by Walter Scott. New York Published by W. Dubois at his Piano Forte and Music Store No. 126 Broadway. [1819.] Pages: *1-3*. Notes: Engraved sheet music with caption title. Page *1* is blank. (first words: 'It was Dunvis[!] the young and brave, was bound for Palestine,'). Original French by Duchesse de St Leu and arranged for voice and pianoforte. Listed in the *NYEP* 24 April 1819 as 'just published'. Copies: DLC(2) InU MWA PPL RPB(4). Reference: Wolfe 4342.

88Dl] NEW YORK: Geib 1820
The Knight Errant. . . . Translated from the French by Walter Scott New York: Published by J. A. & W. Geib 23 Maiden Lane. [ca.1820]. Pages: *1-3*. Notes: Engraved sheet music with caption title. Page *1* is blank. (first words: 'It was Dunvis[!] the young & brave was bound for Palestine'). Original French by Duchesse de St Leu and arranged for voice and pianoforte. Price: 25 cts. Copies: InU MH MWA RPB(2). Reference: Wolfe 4341.

88Dm] NEW YORK: Riley 1820
The Knight Errant, . . . New York, Engrav'd, Printed & Sold by E. Riley, 29 Chatham Street. [ca.1820]. Pages: *1-3*. Notes: Engraved sheet music with caption title. Page *1* is blank. (first words: 'It was Dunvis[!] the young & brave was bound for Palestine,'). Original French by Duchesse de St Leu and arranged for voice and pianoforte. Copy: MWA. Reissued with plate mark 'Knight Errant.2.' added to page *2* and the price added above imprint: 25 cents. (RPB). References: Wolfe 4345, 4345A.

88Dn] PHILADELPHIA: Blake 1826
The Knight Errant, . . . Translated from the French by Walter Scott. Philadelphia, Published by G. E. Blake, No: 13 south 5th Street. [1826]. Pages: *1* 2-3. Notes: Engraved sheet music with caption title and plate mark reading: 'The Knight Errant.' Page *1* blank. (first words: 'It was Dunvis[!], the young and brave, was bound for Palestine,'). Original French by Duchesse de St Leu and arranged for voice and pianoforte. Copies: DLC MWA RPB(5). References: G/T 10851; Wolfe 4340.

88Do] PHILADELPHIA: Carr 1821-1822
[1] [The Knight Errant. . . . Published by B. Carr, Philadelphia. (ca.1821.) Pages: 1-7. Notes: In Carr's Musical Miscellany in Occasional Numbers: number 69. Original French by Duchesse de St Leu with variations for the pianoforte by Joseph C. Taws.] Copy: not seen. References: G/T 10851; Wolfe 4347.

[2] [The Knight Errant. . . . Printed for B. Carr, Philadelphia. (ca. 1822.) Broadside. Notes: Music composed by Duchesse de St Leu and arranged for pianoforte by B. Carr.] Copy: not seen. Reference: Wolfe 4353.

[3] [The Knight Errant. (ca.1822), Book 2. Broadside paged 5. Notes: *Musical Bagatelles*; reissue from same plate as Wolfe 4353. Music composed by Duchesse de St Leu and arranged for pianoforte by B. Carr.] Copy: not seen. Reference: Wolfe 4353A.

88Dp] PHILADELPHIA: Willig 1819
The Knight Errant. . . . Translated from the French by Walter Scott. Philadelphia. Published by G: Willig No. 171 Chesnut Street. [ca.1819]. Pages: *1-2*. Notes: Engraved sheet music with caption title. Page *1* is blank. (first words: 'It was Dunvis[!] the young and brave, was bound for Palestine,'). Original French by Duchesse de St Leu and arranged for voice and pianoforte. Copies: DLC InU MWA PPL RPB(2). Reference: Wolfe 4343.

88Dq] PHILADELPHIA: 1824
[Romance of Dunois. . . . Philadelphia (ca.1824). 6-8pp. Notes: In Guilbert's *Twelve English Songs*. Original French by Duchesse de St Leu and arranged for voice and guitar or lyre.] Copy: not seen. Reference: Wolfe 4354.

EXTRACTS IN ANTHOLOGIES

88E] Compared to poem [1] 'The Dance of Death', which was extracted only once (372E.6), the second poem [2] 'Romance of Dunois', has 25 entries: 360E.15 373[3] 389.1 403.1 405(3)[1].15 414[1].2 431.2 433 434.2 438 441 442 443.2 445[2].1 446[1].1 448[1].3 449.2 456[1].1 457[2].3 461.1 467[1-2].4 475.3. Among the 18 U.S. anthologies (431.2-475.3) only one retains the original title (441), all the others having a variant heading 'The Knight Errant'—obviously a sign of some interrelationship.

PAUL'S LETTERS TO HIS KINSFOLK

[I]f the reader has not perused Paul's Letters . . . he will refresh his memory . . . by bestowing an hour on that genuine fragment of the author's autobiography. . . . The kindest of husbands and fathers never portrayed himself with more unaffected truth . . . mixed up with an equally growing enthusiasm, at which many may smile, for the tiniest relics of feudal antiquity—and last, not least, a pulse of physical rapture for the "circumstances of war," . . . (Lockhart, v.62-63.)

89Aa] First Edition: 1816

PAUL'S LETTERS | TO | HIS KINSFOLK. | [*short Oxford rule*] | EDINBURGH: | *Printed by James Ballantyne and Co.* | FOR ARCHIBALD CONSTABLE AND COMPANY, | EDINBURGH; | AND LONGMAN, HURST, REES, ORME, AND BROWN, | AND JOHN MURRAY, LONDON. | [*dash*] | 1816.

Published 25 January 1816 in Edinburgh (*EEC*); issued 10 February in London (*MC*). 12s. 6000 copies. Binding: drab, blue, or blue-green boards with printed label. Paper: Demy 8° (223 x 141mm uncut). Watermarks: *none*; 1815 | 3 [5]; E D D S | 1815; J E D D S | 1815. (Sheets O, Y-2G are generally browned.) Collation: π^2 A-C^8 D^8(±D2) E^8 F^8(±F4) G-2F^8 2G^2. Pagination: *i* half-title, *ii blank*, *iii* title-page, *iv blank*, *1* 2-468 text, 468 printer's imprint: [*short rule*] | EDINBURGH: | Printed by James Ballantyne & Co.

Figures: A7-5/- 13-1, B25-1 27-9, C34-9 48-8, D—, E75-8 80-11, F93-2, G112-8, H120-11/- 123-8, I 139-10 140-3, K153-10 155-3, L171-4 172-2, M189-3 190-9, N194-6 204-2, O 220-6 223-1, P232-6 239-3, Q250-11 253-10, R260-2 263-9, S283-10 285-11, T300-3 302-6, U317-8 319-4, X330-9 336-11, Y351-3 352-10, Z366-5 368-1, 2A 374-8 380-2, 2B 394-10 400-11, 2C 402-2 408-10, 2D 428-6 430-5/8, 2E 434-11 437-4, 2F 450-2 464-10/-, 2G 466-5.

First printings: In addition to 'Romance of Dunois', reprinted here (page 210), and issued unrevised two weeks earlier (*see* 88A), two other poems in first printings, translated by Scott, were included in *Paul's Letters*: [1] 'The Troubadour' (first words: 'Glowing with love, on fire for fame') pages 211-212, and [2] 'It chanced that Cupid on a season' (first words as title), pages 212-213.

Notes: This is the last of Scott's several accounts relating to the Battle of Waterloo, and one no less popular than his early poem on the subject (84Aa-Ad). Cancel D2 (pages 51-52), of a single setting in the states described below, represents revisions now unknown, for the leaf is missing in Scott's corrected 'rough copy' (L: C.28.g.4). This copy, however, does retain the original F4, and there shows page 87 a press-figure 4, as well as the earlier misprint line 12 'elocution' for 'eloquence'. Of some interest in this copy is the publisher's imprint, here in title proof transposed to read: FOR LONGMAN, HURST, REES, ORME, AND BROWN, | AND JOHN MURRAY, LONDON; | AND ARCHIBALD CONSTABLE AND COMPANY, | EDINBURGH.

Of greater consequence in Scott's copy are the non-figured proof-sheets O and Y-2G (pages 209-222, 337-467) with revisions generally incorporated in the first edition. (These same sheets, as noted above, were later printed on paper that is now discoloured.) Many of these alterations affect (in Letter 9) Scott's translations of the verse there printed.

Possibly as the result of an early decision 3 November 1815 (*Letters*, iv.115) to increase the issue from 3000 to 6000 copies, there are two states of this edition, exemplified even in Scott's presentation and corrected copies, as well as the one retained in his Abbotsford library, the first (1) representing sheets A-H of an earlier impression, as defined by the figures cited above, the second (2) exhibiting one or more of these eight sheets in a later impression indicated by the figures A3-8, B26-5 29-6, C41-11 47-5, D64-11, E73-9 75-2, F89-8 94-6, G106-9 109-8, H123-5 125-6. An unmixed first impression, it will be noted, has yet to be located among the 25 copies examined. All eight sheets of the later printing intermixed with the first were overrun and thus reappear in the second edition.

Presentation copy: (state 2) NNU-W('James Wedderburn Esq from his faithful friend Paul'; with later impression sheets A,C-D,G). Other copies: state (1) not seen; (2:later sheets noted in parentheses) A(A,C,G) BCL(A-B,E,G) E[John Stuart, 12th Earl of Moray](C) E(F,H) E(A,C-D,G) ES(E) L[Scott's corrected copy](C,E,F) L(A,B,E,G) LU(D,F,H) O(C) O(A-B,D-E,G) O(A-H); CtY[William Beckford, annotated](D,F,H) CtY(A-B,E,G)* IdU(A-B,G) MH(H) NN[Berg](C) NNU-W(C,F) PPL(C-D,F-G) RPB(A-B,E,G) T/B(B) TxU(2:D,F,H) ViU(A,C-D,G).
*With 4-page undated Henry Colburn catalogue.

References: Abbotsford, page 319; Ruff 152; Thomson, page 52; Van Antwerp(1) 16(Maria Edgeworth), 17(manuscript). (Magnum Opus Edition 1834: *The Miscellaneous Prose Works*, v.*1* 2-354.)

89Ab] Second Edition: 1816

PAUL'S LETTERS | TO | HIS KINSFOLK. | [*short reversed Oxford rule*] | SECOND EDITION. | [*short reversed Oxford rule*] | EDINBURGH: | *Printed* *by James Ballantyne and Co.* | FOR ARCHIBALD CONSTABLE AND COMPANY, | EDINBURGH; | AND LONGMAN, HURST, REES, ORME, AND BROWN, | AND JOHN MURRAY, LONDON. | [*dash*] | 1816.

Issued 18 April 1816 in London (*MC*). 12s. 1500 copies. Binding: drab or blue-grey boards with printed label. Paper: Demy 8° (223 x 141mm uncut). Watermarks, collation, and pagination as in first edition.

Figures: A3-8, B26-5 29-6, C41-11 47-5, D64-11/-, E73-9 75-2, F89-8 94-6, G106-9 109-8, H123-5 125-6, I 139-10 140-3, K153-10 155-3, L171-4 172-2, M189-3 190-9, N194-6 204-2, O 220-6 223-3, P232-6 239-3, Q250-11 253-10, R260-2 263-9, S283-10 285-11, T300-3 302-6, U317-8 319-4, X330-9 336-11, Y351-3 352-10, Z361-8(or 368-1) 366-5, 2A 374-2 381-5, 2B 394-3 400-10, 2C 402-2 408-10, 2D 430-8/5 432-8/-, 2E 434-11 437-4, 2F 450-2 464-10, 2G 466-5/-.

Notes: As the figures partly signify, this edition consists essentially of the previous issue in its second state, including the two cancels D2 and F4, but now exhibits a further reimpression of five sheets toward the end of the book (O, Z, 2A, 2B, 2D). A few copies have been noted with one or more stray sheets of the first state (A, D-F, G-H or 2B), each exhibiting the figures for that printing.

Copies: BCL E(2) O P; CtY InU T/B TxU. Mixed copy: A (three text sheets (E,G,X) of the third edition, as determined by the press figures, the remaining 27 of the fourth). Reference: Abbotsford, page 319, 'Second Edition' (without comment).

89Ac] Third Edition: 1816

PAUL'S LETTERS | TO | HIS KINSFOLK. | [*short Oxford rule*] | THIRD EDITION. | EDINBURGH: | *Printed by James Ballantyne and Co.* | FOR ARCHIBALD CONSTABLE AND COMPANY, | EDINBURGH; | AND LONGMAN, HURST, REES, ORME, AND BROWN, | AND JOHN MURRAY, LONDON. | [*dash*] | 1816.

Published 13 June 1816 in Edinburgh (*EEC*). 12s. 1500 copies. Binding: Grey-blue or green boards. Paper: Demy 8° (223 x 141mm uncut). Watermarks: 1815 | 1 [2, 4]. Collation: π^2 A-2I^8 2K^4. Pagination: *i* half-title, *ii blank*, *iii* title-page, *iv blank*, *1* 2-481 text, *482 blank*, *483* fly-title, *484 blank*, *485* 486-519 appendices, 519 printer's imprint, *520 blank*. Printer's imprint: [*short rule*] | EDINBURGH: | Printed by James Ballantyne & Co.

Figures: A7-7 13-9, B23-3 32-2, C45-9 46-3, D51-5 57-7, E68-10/'01' 75-2, F82-7 85-5, G110-4 112-3, H114-9 128-7, I 133-10 142-4, K147-10 149-6, L165-8 175-11, M187-11 189-5, N200-6 207-7, O 214-8 224-2, P229-8 231-6, Q245-11 255-2, R270-5 272-3, S279-2 284-5, T302-7 304-8, U310-11 320-6, X334-5 336-2, Y342-6 348-8, Z362-2 364-10, 2A 371-11 377-7, 2B 391-5 396-2, 2C 406-6 413-4, 2D

427-7 429-8, 2E 436-6 442-3, 2F 451-3 452-11, 2G 469-6 475-4, 2H 489-8 490-2, 2 I 503-2 508-4, 2K 515-11.

Notes: This edition is extensively revised and extended. One significant alteration occurs in a note page 222, where Scott, in reference to the 'Romance of Dunois' and 'The Troubadour', admits that these poems, previously attributed to Hortencia Beauharnais, former Queen of Holland, were actually 'written by no less a personage than the Duchesse de St Leu.'

Copies: AN O; NjP T/B.

89Ad] Fourth Edition: 1817

PAUL'S LETTERS | TO | HIS KINSFOLK. | [*short Oxford rule*] | FOURTH EDITION. | EDINBURGH: | *Printed by James Ballantyne and Co.* | FOR ARCHIBALD CONSTABLE AND COMPANY, | EDINBURGH; | AND LONGMAN, HURST, REES, ORME, AND BROWN, | AND JOHN MURRAY, LONDON. | [*dash*] | 1817.

Paper: Demy 8° (206 x 127mm cut). Watermarks: C | 1816. Collation and pagination as in third edition. Typography: Page 135 is misnumbered 134.

Figures: A4-10, B20-1 23-3, C39-3 45-5, D57-6 58-8, E67-7 76-10, F85-1 90-6, G98-3 109-1, H115-8 116-1, I 144-3, K148-10 150-1, L171-5, M192-11, N197-11, O 218-4 224-5, P27-4 240-11, Q255-6 256-11, R261-1 266-7, S277-4 278-3, T290-4 301-11, U319-6, X322-8 328-4, Y338-10 344-3, Z355-8 356-4, 2A 373-4 383-1, 2B 397-8 399-10, 2C 410-4 412-1, 2D 431-6, 2E 444-4, 2F 450-4, 2G 474-4, 2H 496-6, 2 I 500-4, 2K 517-1.

Copies: E HS(Gladstone); CtY TxU.

REPRINTS

GERMANY

ZWICKAU: Schumann
[~] Paul's Letters. 1826. (Pocket Library of English Classics: *see* 302R.128-129)

UNITED STATES

89R] PHILADELPHIA: Thomas 1816
Paul's Letters to His Kinsfolk. Philadelphia: Re-published by Moses Thomas, from the Edinburgh Edition. 1816. Pages: *i-ii*, *1* 2-275. Notes: The back cover lists the Thomas address as 52, Chesnut-Street. Copies: E; InU MH MWA NjP PPL(2) ViU. Reference: Kohler(1) 193 (with illustration).

DERIVATIVES

GREAT BRITAIN

89Da] LONDON: Power 1816
The Gallant Troubadour. London, Published by J. Power, 34, Strand. [1816]. Pages: *1-2* 3-7. Notes: Engraved sheet music. Words from Letter 9, 'The Troubadour', stanza 1 (first words: 'Glowing with love, on fire for fame,'). Music composed by John Stevenson arranged for voice and pianoforte. Price: 2/-. Copy: L. Reference: G/T 10889.

89Db] LONDON: Walker 1815
The Gallant Troubadour, the Poetry from Paul's Letters to his Kinsfolk, . . . London. Printed for G. Walker, Publisher of Books & Music 105 & 106 Great Portland Street. [watermarked 1815.] Pages: 1-3. Notes: Engraved sheet music. Words from Letter 9 (first words: 'Glowing with love on fire for fame, A Troubadour that hated sorrow'). Music composed by unidentified individual, arranged for voice and harp or pianoforte. Price: 1s. Copy: InU.

UNITED STATES

89Dc] PHILADELPLHIA: Willig 1820
The Troubadour. Translated from the French by Walter Scott. . . . Philadelphia. Published and sold by Geo. Willig. [ca.1820.] Pages: *1-2* 3. Notes: Engraved sheet music. Words from Letter 9 (first words: 'Glowing with love on fire for fame'). Original French by the Duchess St Leu with this music composed by S. Cristiani arranged for voice and pianoforte or harp. Copies: MWA PHi. References: G/T 10877; Wolfe 2217.

EXTRACTS IN ANTHOLOGIES

89E] From *Paul's Letters to His Kinsfolk* there are 13 extracts in 12 anthologies: 360E. 8,11 371.3 387[2] 389.14 405(2)[2].1 405(2)[3].8 405(3)[1].12 414[1].1 448[1].2 449.4 457[2].2 469.3.

REVIEW OF JANE AUSTEN

90A] First Printing: 1816

'ART. IX. *Emma; a Novel.*', pages 188-201, *in*:

The Quarterly Review. October, 1815. [No. 27. volume 14 imprint:] London: Printed for John Murray, Albemarle Street. 1816.

Published 9 March 1816 (*MC*); listed as 'just arrived' in Edinburgh 16 March (*EEC*, earlier noted 7 March as to be published in London 'on Saturday next' [the 9th], 14 March 'shipped on Thursday last' [the 7th]).

Notes: No explanation is offered for the long delay in issuing this number. The author of *Emma*, later identified as Jane Austen, at this time was recognized only as 'the Author of Sense and Sensibility, Pride and Prejudice, &c.' Lockhart, aware that Scott had once reviewed Austen, mistakenly reprinted in *MPW* (xviii.209-249 as 'Miss Austen's Novels') a piece actually written by Richard Whateley. Though the authorship was set aright finally in 1929 (*see* Corson[1] 2058) Buchan in 1932 (page 341) also quotes at length from the Whateley review, still believing it to be Scott's.

Several other articles issued in 1812-1815, and doubtfully attributed to Scott (Shine 184, 218, 348), are here disregarded.

Copies: BCL O; PPL TxU. References: Shine 361. (Magnum Opus Edition: Not reprinted.)

LULLABY OF AN INFANT CHIEF

91A] First Printing: 1816

['Lullaby of an Infant Chief'] (first words: 'Oh! slumber, my darling, / Thy Sire is a knight') page 28 *in*:

Guy Mannering; or, The Gipsey's Prophecy: A Musical Play, in Three Acts. . . . London: Printed for John Miller, 25, Bow Street, Covent Garden; By W. Smith and Co. King Street, Seven Dials. 1816. (Price Two Shillings and Sixpence). Pages: *i-ii*, *1* 2-71 *72-74*.

Notes: The first of the Waverley novels to be adapted as a play. This song in Act 2, Scene 1, was written anonymously by Scott for his friend Daniel Terry, the dramatist. The play does not give the two eight-line stanzas a title, other than to call it an 'Air—([sung by] Miss Bertram.)' The words of the play and many other songs were written by Terry (music by Henry R. Bishop not included) and are as first performed at The Theatre Royal, Covent Garden, Tuesday 12 March 1816. A variant text of Scott's poem was printed four months later in *Albyn's Anthology* where the commonly used title is first given (92A, 96A.1). For other editions of the play in Terry's version see under *Guy Mannering* Derivatives: the four original Miller issues (82Dj) and six other printings (82Da- Db, Df, Do-Dp, Dr).

Copies: BCL E; InU(inscribed) NjP NNP TxU TxU(prompt copy).

References: Bolton 409; Ford H1; Van Antwerp(2) 18a. (Magnum Opus Edition 1834: *The Poetical Works*, xi.317-318.)

DERIVATIVES

GREAT BRITAIN

91Da] LONDON: Button and Whitaker 1816
Oh! Rest Thee Babe. Rest Thee Babe. The Celebrated Ballad . . . in Guy Mannering To which is added the Stanza sung in the Scene of the Gypsies Haunt, in the same Play, . . . London, Printed by Button, Whitaker, & Compy. 75, St. Paul's Church Yard. [water-marked 1815. ca.1816]. Pages: 1-4. Notes: Engraved sheet music within a single-rule frame with type ornament at each corner and with a plate mark reading 'Oh! Slumber my Darling.' Some copies have an elaborate paste-on at foot of page 1 reading: 'Sold at White's Music and Musical Instrument Warehouses, No. 1, Milsom Street and No. 3, George Street, Bath.' Words by Walter Scott (first words: 'Oh! slumber my darling, Thy Sire is a Knight,'). Music composed by John Whitaker arranged for voice and pianoforte as performed at Covent Garden. Price: 2/-. Copies: E L; NNP. References: G/T 9822; Van Antwerp(2) 42g. Reissued as a 'Second Edition' (E[2] L; NNP). Reference: Van Antwerp(2) 42h.

91Db] LONDON: Mayhew 1825
Oh! Rest Thee Babe, The Celebrated Ballad, . . . in Guy Mannering, To which is added the Stanza, sung . . . . in the Scene of the Gypsies Haunt, . . . London, Mayhew & Co. Music Sellers to the Royal Family 17, Old Bond St. [watermarked 1824]. Pages: 1-4. Notes: At head of title: 'Fifth Edition.' Engraved sheet-music with caption title. Words by Walter Scott. (first words: 'Oh! slumber my darling, Thy Sire is a Knight,'). Music composed by John Whitaker arranged for voice and pianoforte. Presumably a reissue of the London, Whitaker 'Fifth Edition' (91Dc). Price: 2/-. Copy: L. Reissued again as a 'Sixth Edition' (L), with some copies watermarked 1827 (MH).

91Dc] LONDON: Whitaker 1820-1821
Fourth Edition. Oh! Rest Thee Babe, The Celebrated Ballad, . . . in Guy Mannering, . . . London, Printed by Whitaker & Co. 75, St. Paul's Church Yard. [ca.1820]. Pages: 1-4. Notes: Engraved sheet music with caption title and plate mark: 'Oh! Rest thee Babe.' Each plate/page is in a single rule frame. Music composed by John Whitaker arranged for voice and pianoforte. Presumably a reissue of the London, Button and Whitaker 'Second' (or 'Third'?) edition (*see* 91Da). Price: 2/. Copy: L. Reissued again as a 'Fifth Edition' [watermarked 1821]. (E).

UNITED STATES

91Dd] NEW YORK: Dubois and Stodart 1823
[Oh Rest thee Babe. Dubois & Stodart, 126 Broadway. (ca.1823). Pages: 2pp. Notes: Music composed by John Whitaker.] Copy: not seen. References: Wolfe 9842.

91De] NEW YORK: Riley 1820
Oh! Rest Thee Babe The Celebrated Ballad . . . in Guy Mannering. . . . New York Engraved Printed & Sold by E. Riley, 29 Chatham Street [ca.1820]. Pages: *1-2* 3. Notes: Engraved sheet music. Words by Walter Scott (first words: 'Oh! slumber my darling, Thy Sire is a

Knight, Thy Mother, a Lady') from the play Guy Mannering first performed at Covent Garden, London, on 12 March 1816. Music composed by John Whitaker arranged for voice and pianoforte. In two states: without numeral '(3)' in lower right margin of page 1 (RPB); with numeral '(3)' (MWA). References: Wolfe 9841, 9841A.

91Df] PHILADELPHIA: Balls 1817
Oh! Rest Thee Babe, The Celebrated Ballad, . . . in Guy Mannering . . . . Philadelphia, Printed & Sold by G. Balls, 151, Chesnut Street. [ca.1817]. Pages: *1* 2-3. Notes: Engraved sheet music. Words by Walter Scott adapted by Eugene Scribe (first words: 'Oh! slumber my darling, Thy Sire is a Knight, Thy Mother a Lady'). Music composed by John Whitaker arranged for voice and pianoforte. Price: 25 cents. Copy: MWA. Reference: Wolfe 9840.

91Dg] PHILADELPHIA: Blake 1816
Oh! Rest Thee Babe, Rest Thee Babe. The Celebrated Ballad. . . . in Guy Mannering, To which is added, the Stanza sung . . . in the Scene of the Gypsies' Haunt in the same Play . . . . Philadelphia, Published by G. E. Blake, No. 13 S. 5h. Street. [ca.1816]. Pages: *1-2*. Notes: Engraved sheet music. Words by Walter Scott adapted by Eugene Scribe (first words: 'Oh! slumber my darling, Thy Sire is a Knight, Thy Mother a lady'). Music composed by John Whitaker arranged for voice and pianoforte. At head of title: No. 9 of Blake's Musical Miscellany. Copies: DLC MWA. Reference: Wolfe 9839.

91Dh] PHILADELPHIA: Klemm 1823
Oh! Rest Thee Babe. The Celebrated Ballad . . . in Guy Mannering. . . . Philadelphia Published by John G. Klemm. [ca.1823]. Pages: *1-2*. Notes: Engraved sheet music. Words by Walter Scott adapted by Eugene Scribe (first words: 'Oh! slumber my darling, Thy Sire is a Knight, Thy Mother a lady'). Music composed by John Whitaker arranged for voice and pianoforte. Copy: MWA.

EXTRACTS IN ANTHOLOGIES

91E] In whole or part Scott's ballad is extracted in eleven anthologies: 360E.5 361[1].2 369[3].5 369[4].5 400[1].1 403[2] 405(2)[1].1 405(2)[3].3 405(3)[1].5 405(3)[3].2 415.6.

PROSPECTUS FOR ALBYN'S ANTHOLOGY

92A] First Edition: 1816

Albyn's Anthology; | OR, | A SELECT COLLECTION | OF THE | Melodies, Songs, Dancing Measures, and | Military Music, | PECULIAR TO THE | DIFFERENT DISTRICTS OF SCOTLAND AND THE ISLES, | *HITHERTO UNPUBLISHED;* | COLLECTED AND ARRANGED | By ALEXANDER CAMPBELL, | . . . | INSCRIBED, BY GRACIOUS PERMISSION, | To His Royal Highness the PRINCE REGENT.

<SEE ACCOMPANYING ILLUSTRATION>

Written by Mr W. Scott

Albyn's Anthology;

OR,

A SELECT COLLECTION

OF THE

Melodies, Songs, Dancing Measures, and Military Music,

PECULIAR TO THE

DIFFERENT DISTRICTS OF SCOTLAND AND THE ISLES,

HITHERTO UNPUBLISHED;

COLLECTED AND ARRANGED

BY ALEXANDER CAMPBELL,

Author of "The History of Poetry in Scotland, a Journey through different parts of Scotland," &c. &c.

INSCRIBED, BY GRACIOUS PERMISSION,

To His Royal Highness the PRINCE REGENT.

IT is well known that there exists no general Collection of the Music peculiar to the Highlands of Scotland; and it is also certain, that notwithstanding the numerous Publications relating to the Lowland Scottish Music, there are to be found in the remote, and especially in the pastoral, Districts, many beautiful Tunes which have hitherto escaped the research of every former Collector.

THE Highland Society of Scotland have been pleased to honour with their approbation the present attempt to collect and preserve Relics so very interesting in themselves, and so intimately connected with the History and Literature of the Country. Under their

ENTRY 92A. THE NATIONAL LIBRARY OF SCOTLAND (MS 677, f.139)
(illustration reduced)

Published in Edinburgh March 1816. Demy 4° (255 x 198mm cut). Pages *1* caption title and text, 2-3 text continued, *4 blank.*

Notes: This elaborate proposal, marked by Constable in the E copy as written by Scott, credits him with five lyrics, including 'Lullaby of an Infant Chief'. Since that accidental disclosure would immediately identify Scott as the author of *Guy Mannering* (*see* previous entries), Scott arranged to have the editor delete this reference when the anthology was published 18 July 1816 (96A.1).

Copy: E. Reference: *Letters,* iv.217-219.

MEMORIE OF THE SOMERVILLES

[This is] one of the most curious pieces of family history ever produced to the world, on which he [Scott] laboured with more than usual zeal and diligence, from his warm affection for the noble representative of its author. (Lockhart, v.14.)

93A] First Edition: 1815[1816]

MEMORIE | OF | The Somervilles; | BEING | A HISTORY | OF THE | BARONIAL HOUSE OF SOMERVILLE. | BY | JAMES, | ELEVENTH LORD SOMERVILLE. | [*short Oxford rule*] | IN TWO VOLUMES. | [*short reversed Oxford rule*] | VOL. I [II]. | EDINBURGH: | *Printed by James Ballantyne and Co.* | FOR ARCHIBALD CONSTABLE AND COMPANY, EDINBURGH; | AND LONGMAN, HURST, REES, ORME, AND BROWN, | LONDON. | [*dash*] | 1815.

Published March 1816 in Edinburgh (*SM*); issued 21 June in London (*MC*). £2.2.0. Binding: drab boards with printed labels. Paper: Demy 8° (227 x 145mm uncut). Watermarks: J. WHATMAN | 1812. Typography: The spelling throughout in the headlines is 'Somervills'.

General Notes: Though Scott on 9 October 1814 reported that 'Somerville is finishd & I presume deliverd', he later, on the 22nd, reminded the publisher that, even if unfinished, thirty copies should be given the present Baron 'in lieu of the plates', all of which (as noted below) were eventually imprinted 1 May 1815. Even then, it seems, this restricted printing was not made available to the public until the following March, 1816.

As stated in the Preface to this 'limited edition', Scott as the editor of the original manuscript was chiefly intent upon 'correcting the more obvious errors, by comparing the Memoirs with other sources of evidence' and commenting on the more 'severe remarks upon the conduct of others' (Vol. I, pages *vii* viii-ix). In his concluding remarks (Vol. II, pages 486-487) the editor then welcomed the present Baron (1765-1819) as a neighbor along the banks of the Tweed. Scott later described the Baron's new home as: '*Alwyn*, the seat of the Lord Somerville, now, alas! untenanted, by the lamented death of that kind and hospitable nobleman, the author's nearest neighbour and intimate friend' (*Miscellaneous Poems*, 1820, page 155n). In the map provided by Sutherland (page *359*) this Alwyn manor is identified as 'The Pavilion'.

Copies: (volume 2, state a) BCL; NN NNU-W PPL(3). (b) O(plates on India paper) P; CtY InU. References: *Letters*, iii.505, 511. (Magnum Opus Edition: Not reprinted.)

1] MEMORIE | OF | The Somervilles; . . . Vol. I. . . . 1815.

Collation: π1 a1 *b*⁴ A-K⁸ *L*⁸ M-2H⁸ *2I*1. Pagination: *i* title-page, *ii blank*, *iii*-iv Directions for Placing Engravings, *v* dedication to John, [15th] Lord Somerville, *vi blank*, *vii* viii-xii Preface, *1* 2-497 text, 497 printer's imprint, *498 blank*. Printer's imprint: [*short Oxford rule*] | EDINBURGH: | Printed by James Ballantyne & Co. Illustrations: Frontispiece of John Lord Somerville and six engravings facing pages 45, 47, 63, 176, 361, 409, all published by Longman, Hurst and Rees, and dated 1 May 1815. Typography: In some copies page number 105 is transposed as 501.

Figures: *b* ix-7, A13-8, B32-12, C44-2, D58-2, E79-1, F90-10, G105-6, H125-5, I 144-6, K148-8, *L*161-2, M181-3, N200-10, O 215-7/-, P232-6, Q253-8, R272-7, S288-6, T297-10, U—, X327-5, Y340-7, Z368-1, 2A 379-2, 2B—, 2C 407-1, 2D 428-7, 2E 435-5, 2F 454-9, 2G 478-7, 2H 495-2, *2I*—. Figure 2, oddly displacing signature L on page 161, was eventually withdrawn and L entered on this page in later copies.

2] MEMORIE | OF | The Somervilles; . . . Vol. II . . . 1815.

Collation: π1 2π1 a1 A-2F⁸ 2G⁴ 2H⁸. Pagination: *i* title-page, *ii blank*, *iii* Errata, *iv blank*, *v* Directions for Placing Engravings, *vi blank*, *1* 2-476 text, *477* 478-487 Conclusion, *488 blank*. No final printer's imprint. Illustrations: Frontispiece of William Somerville (Author of 'The Chase'), three engravings facing pages 385, 482, 486, all published by Longman, Hurst & Rees, dated 1 May 1815, and, at the end, a folding genealogical chart of maternal descent from King William the Conqueror. Typography: In some copies, the first digit in page-number 359 has dropped.

Figures: 2π *iii*-3, A5-1, B25-6, C47-1, D54-2, E80-3, F90-1, G104-5/-, H125-9, I 133-3, K149-6, L167-9, M183-6, N198-6, O 210-5, P233-7/-, Q255-3, R269-3/-, S288-7, T304-1, U—, X330-1, Y352-7/-, Z354-7, 2A 370-2, 2B 389-5, 2C 413-1, 2D 427-5, 2E 434-2, 2F 456-1, 2G 469-3, 2H 486-3.

Notes: The corrections in the Errata, (a) listed for page 486, are all entered in the copies examined. In a later state (b) two other errata are listed for pages 51 and 422, both uncorrected.

93Ab] First Edition, Second (Large-Paper) Impression: 1815[1816]

[MEMORIE | OF | The Somervilles; . . . IN TWO VOLUMES. | [*short reversed Oxford rule*] | VOL. I [II] . . . 1815.]

Published concurrently with the previous impression. £3.3.0. Royal 4°

Notees: The royal paper impression was advertised as issued 'in a few copies', most of which, presumably, were delivered to Baron Somerville and his friends.

Copy: not seen..

THE ANTIQUARY

The present Work completes a series of fictitious narratives, intended to illustrate the manners of Scotland at three different periods. WAVERLEY embraced the age of our fathers, GUY MANNERING that of our own youth, and the ANTIQUARY refers to the last ten years of the eighteenth century. ('Advertisement', page *3*.)

94Aa] First Edition: 1816

THE | **ANTIQUARY.** | BY THE | AUTHOR OF "WAVERLEY" AND "GUY MANNERING." | [*short Oxford rule*] | [*eight lines of verse*] | [*short reversed Oxford rule*] | IN THREE VOLUMES. | VOL. I [II-III]. | EDINBURGH: | *Printed by James Ballantyne and Co.* | FOR ARCHIBALD CONSTABLE AND CO. EDINBURGH; AND | LONGMAN, HURST, REES, ORME, AND BROWN, | LONDON. | [*dash*] | 1816.

Published 4 May 1816 in Edinburgh (*EEC*); issued 8 May in London (*EEWN3*. 370). £1.4.0 (a three shilling advance over the price quoted for *Waverley* and *Guy Mannering*). 5000 copies, of which 1500 in sheets were shipped to London on 30 April, together with two complete copies by post, followed on the next day by a 'Coach parcel' containing the last sheet and the two cancels (*EEWN3*.360). Binding: blue or blue-grey boards with printed labels. Paper: Royal 12° (192 x 116mm uncut). Watermarks: *none* or 3 [5, 6, 7, 8, 9] | S M | 1814; *none* or 4 [5, 6, 7, 8, 9, 10] | S M | 1815. Typography: Printer's imprints read invariably: [*short rule*] | EDINBURGH: | Printed by James Ballantyne and Co.

General Notes: The contract for this novel was signed in January 1815 with publication date then specified as 4 June; subsequent delays are reviewed in *EEWN3*. 358-361. The verse on title-page is probably by Scott (first line: 'I knew Anselmo. He was shrewd and prudent'). In correcting the proof-sheets for this novel Scott now also began to fabricate chapter mottoes whenever his recollection did not provide an appropriate quotation.

Copies: A AN BCL(2) E E*a E*b EU L O(6) O*b P; CtY IdU InU NN(2) MH MH*a NNU-W T/B TxU(Wolff) TxU ViU. Mixed or sophisticated copies: O(with

5th edition title-pages: see note to 94Ac) P(with volume 2 title-page created from a volume 1).
*With 4-page (a) Longman catalogue February 1816, (b) Constable catalogue March 1816.

References: Church 532; David Hewitt (ed.), *EEWN3*; Sterling 724; Thomson, pages 11-12; Van Antwerp(1) 4; Worthington 3. (Magnum Opus Edition 1829: *Waverley Novels*, v-vi.)

1] THE | **ANTIQUARY.** . . . VOL. I. . . . 1816.

Collation: π^2 a^2 A^{12} B^{12}(-B2,3,+B2.3) C-O^{12}. Pagination: *i* half-title, *ii blank*, *iii* title-page, *iv blank*, *v* vi-viii Advertisement, *1* fly-title, *2 blank*, *3* 4-336 text, 336 printer's imprint.

Figures: a vii-10/-, A10-10 12-1, B29-7/- 39-2 40-5, C63-4 69-11, D75-1 85-5, E118-10 120-3, F135-4 144-5, G154-3 168-8, H178-1/- 184-3, I 205-6 207-4, K237-2 239-3, L250-6 253-10, M274-5 285-8, N304-10 310-3, O 315-4 333-2.

Notes: Preliminary gathering 'a' is of a duplicate setting, with or without press figure 10 on page vii. In his extensive account Van Antwerp cites twenty manuscript readings which were altered in the doubleton cancel, among them 28.15 younger/juvenile, 29.11 brother/proprietor, 29.16 Josiah/Jonathan.

2] THE | **ANTIQUARY.** . . . VOL. II. . . . 1816.

Collation: π^2 A-O^{12} P^6. Pagination: *i* half-title, *ii blank*, *iii* title-page, *iv blank*, *1* fly-title, *2 blank*, *3* 4-348 text, 348 printer's imprint.

Figures: A8-8 22-6, B45-4 47-11, C61-5 63-1, D87-10 96-2, E100-4 119-11, F123-5 144-8, G167-3 168-2, H170-2 184-8, I 208-11 215-3, K228-10 231-8, L255-4 264-1, M277-11 279-5, N311-11 312-3, O 322-8 333-10, P342-1.

3] THE | **ANTIQUARY.** . . . VOL. III. . . . 1816.

Collation: π^2 A-O^{12} P^6 Q^{12}. Pagination: *i* half-title, *ii blank*, *iii* title-page, *iv blank*, *1* fly-title, *2 blank*, *3* 4-355 text, *356 blank*, *357* 358-372 Glossary. Typography: No printer's imprint appears since the Glossary completely fills the last page in a full gathering. Page 138 is misnumbered 318.

Figures: A4-6 15-5, B34-4 48-3, C52-1 70-10, D94-8 96-5, E117-4 119-6, F143-1 144-10, G147-11 168-3, H176-4 178-2, I 204-2 207-5, K238-6 240-11, L261-4 262-3, M267-7 285-10, N301-8 311-4/-, O 335-5 336-2, P343-8, Q351-6 369-4.

Notes: Like the opening sentence of Scott's Advertisement, given above as an epigraph, the final Glossary encompasses all three of the novels now published, further indicating that this work concludes a 'cycle'.

94Ab] Second Edition: 1816

THE | **ANTIQUARY.** | BY THE | AUTHOR OF "WAVERLEY" AND "GUY MANNERING." | [*short Oxford rule*] | [*eight lines of verse*] | [*short reversed Oxford rule*] | IN THREE VOLUMES. | VOL. I [II-III]. | SECOND EDITION. | EDINBURGH: | *Printed by James Ballantyne and Co.* | FOR ARCHIBALD CONSTABLE AND CO. EDINBURGH; AND | LONGMAN, HURST, REES, ORME, AND BROWN, | LONDON. | [*dash*] | 1816.

Published 27 July 1816 in Edinburgh (*EEC*); issued 3 August as a 'new Edition' in London (*MC*). £1.4.0. Paper: Royal 12° (192 x 116mm uncut). Watermarks: 1814 | 2; 3 [5] | S M | 1814; 1815 | 1; *none* or 3 [4, 5, 6, 7, 8, 9, 10] | S M | 1815.

General Notes: Of some 830 variants discovered in this edition, 111 were incorporated in the *EEWN3* text (cf. pages 371, 395 et seq). Here in the final Glossary, applicable to all three of the Waverley novels published thus far, sixteen additional terms have also been supplied, together with appropriate definitions (Brawly, Chancy, Clarty, Cosie, Dwam, Fain, Haud, Howlit, Jalouse, Knave-bairn, Mousted, Single-soldier, Tale-pyet, Ivy Tod [after 'Tod'], Tramping, and Whiles). Further, the definition of six other terms has been revised (Scaur 1, Scaur 2, Snecked, Sneck, Tirling, Wear the jacket) and the spelling of two words has been altered (Jeeding/Jeedging, Shriegh/Skriegh).

Copies: E; T/B TxU.

1] THE | **ANTIQUARY.** . . . VOL. I. | SECOND EDITION. . . . 1816.

Collation: π^2 a^2 A-H^{12} I^{12}(±I 11) K-O^{12}. Pagination: *i* half-title, *ii blank*, *iii* title-page, *iv blank*, *v* vi-viii Advertisement, *1* fly-title, *2 blank*, *3* 4-336 text, 336 printer's imprint: [*short rule*] | EDINBURGH: | Printed by James Ballantyne and Co. Typography: Page numbers 50 and 52 are transposed as 05 and 25.

Figures: A3-11 12-4, B27-5 48-8, C63-4 69-7, D95-5 96-11 E99-3 117-6, F142-10 144-5, G147-7 165-8, H170-7 172-10, I215-3, K237-7 238-3, L253-7 263-5, M286-1 288-5, N290-4 309-6, O 323-3 324-6.

Notes: Presumably in gathering I, now exhibiting only an inner forme figure, the one in outer forme appeared on the cancellandum, page 213. Though the original readings are unknown, the cancellans alters the first edition quotation page 214 line 20 from 'sonné' to 'sonne'.

2] THE | **ANTIQUARY.** . . . VOL. II. | SECOND EDITION. . . . 1816.

Collation: π^2 A-O^{12} P^6. Pagination: *i* half-title, *ii blank*, *iii* title-page, *iv blank*, *1* fly-title, *2 blank*, *3* 4-348 text, 348 printer's imprint: [*short rule*] | EDINBURGH: | Printed by James Ballantyne & Co.

Figures: A15-5 21-10, B46-3 48-10, C63-8 72-6, D83-5 (or 86-5) 93-3, E98-5, F122-4 144-6, G148-11 163-3, H179-4 181-8, I 205-5 207-6 216-5, K220-7 227-5, L262-11 264-10, M280-4 286-5, N310-6 312-4, O 323-7 325-3, P338-10.

Notes: Coincidentally, in the I gathering there is again a peculiarity with figure 5 twice entered in the outer forme, but now no evidence of a cancel.

3] THE | **ANTIQUARY.** . . . VOL. III. | SECOND EDITION. . . . 1816.

Collation: π^2 A-O^{12} P^6 Q^{12}. Pagination: *i* half-title, *ii blank*, *iii* title-page, *iv blank*, *1* fly-title, *2 blank*, *3* 4-355 text, *356 blank*, *357* 358-372 Glossary, 372 printer's imprint: [*short rule*] | EDINBURGH: | Printed by James Ballantyne & Co.

Figures: A4-4 15-11, B36-3 46-10, C59-6 69-10, D78-8 88-4, E106-8 117-6, F124-8, G156-7 157-3/- 167-8, H190-3 192-7, I 194-7 208-5, K229-5 239-8, L255-4 264-6, M286-11 288-7, N 309-3 310-4, O 315-4 325-7, P338-5, Q360-8 371-10. The superfluous 3 in the G gathering, immediately adjacent to 7 in the outer forme, apparently was withdrawn in the course of printing.

Notes: Despite the many additions noted above, the Glossary has been compressed typographically in this edition to allow space for the printer's imprint on the last page.

94Ac] Fifth Edition (Second Edition, Second Issue) 1818

THE | **ANTIQUARY.** . . . IN THREE VOLUMES. | VOL. I [II-III]. | FIFTH EDITION. | EDINBURGH: | *Printed by James Ballantyne and Co.* | FOR ARCHIBALD CONSTABLE AND CO. EDINBURGH; AND | LONGMAN, HURST, REES, ORME, AND BROWN, | LONDON. | [*dash*] | 1818.

General Notes: A remainder issue of the second edition, with all points identical excepting only those noted below. The reset preliminaries π^2 occasionally exhibit an 1818 watermark. By passing these unsold sheets off as a 'fifth edition' Scott's publishers evidently wished to convey the notion that this third novel in the series was as successful as the previous two. Very probably, as in the O copy noted above, a few first edition strays were also shuffled off as a ''fifth'.

Copy: T/B.

1] THE | **ANTIQUARY.** . . . VOL. I. | FIFTH EDITION. . . . 1818.

Typography: Page number 50, transposed in the previous issue, is correctly registered, but page number 52 remains uncorrected. Figures: As before except for gathering I: 213-8 215-3.

2] THE | **ANTIQUARY.** . . . VOL. II. | FIFTH EDITION. . . . 1818.

Figures: As before except for gathering E: 98-5 117-10.

3] THE | **ANTIQUARY.** . . . VOL. III. | FIFTH EDITION. . . . 1818.
Notes: No variation observed.

94Ad] Fifth (Third) Edition: 1818

THE | **ANTIQUARY**. | BY THE | AUTHOR OF "WAVERLEY" AND "GUY MANNERING." | [*short Oxford rule*] | [*eight lines of verse*] | [*short reversed Oxford rule*] | IN THREE VOLUMES. | VOL. I [II-III]. | FIFTH EDITION | EDINBURGH: | *Printed by James Ballantyne and Co.* | FOR ARCHIBALD CONSTABLE AND CO. EDINBURGH; AND | LONGMAN, HURST, REES, ORME, AND BROWN, | LONDON. | [*dash*] | 1818.

Paper: Royal 12° (175 x 104mm cut). Watermarks: 1818 | 1 but usually *none*.

General Notes: Once the 1816 remainder sheets had been cleared away in the previous 1818 'fifth edition' issue, the book was finally reset and thus displays, as cited below, an entirely new range of press figures. Excepting only second volume sheet A (accidentally figured twice with the same number) and sheet L (without figure) all sheets now bear only one figure each, indicating more leisurely press-work.

The slow sale of *The Antiquary* apparently substantiates Scott's concluding remark (*WN*, v.xix) that this novel 'was not so well received on its first appearance as either of its predecessors, though in course of time it rose to equal, and with some readers, superior popularity.' One of those readers was Scott himself.

Copies: E; CtY(vols.1-2).

1] THE | **ANTIQUARY**. . . . VOL. I. | FIFTH EDITION. . . . 1818.

Collation: π^2 a^2 A-O^{12}. Pagination: *i* half-title, *ii blank*, *iii* title-page, *iv blank*, *v* vi-viii Advertisement, *1* fly-title, *2 blank*, *3* 4-336 text, 336 printer's imprint: [*short rule*] | Edinburgh: | Printed by James Ballantyne and Co. Typography: The title-page imprint lacks a colon after the first 'EDINBURGH'.

Figures: a vi-5, A16-1, B48-4, C56-4, D96-9, E109-6, F144-4, G159-1, H178-1, I 207-9, K229-6, L250-1, M288-4, N300-4, O 324-9.

2] THE | **ANTIQUARY**. . . . VOL. II. | FIFTH EDITION. . . . 1818.

Collation: π^2 A-O^{12} P^6. Pagination: *i* half-title, *ii blank*, *iii* title-page, *iv blank*, *1* fly-title, *2 blank*, *3* 4-348 text, 348 printer's imprint: [*short rule*] | Edinburgh: | Printed by James Ballantyne and Co.

Figures: A11-8 12-8, B37-9, C64-9, D96-9, E111-3, F144-8, G167-1, H191-1, I 205-3, K—, L264-3, M288-6, N310-5, O 326-8, P340-3.

3] THE | **ANTIQUARY**. . . . VOL. III. | FIFTH EDITION. . . . 1818.

Collation: π² A-O¹² P⁶ Q¹². Pagination: *i* half-title, *ii blank*, *iii* title-page, *iv blank*, *1* fly-title, *2 blank*, *3* 4-355 text, *356 blank*, *357* 358-372 Glossary, 372 printer's imprint: [*short rule*] | EDINBURGH: | Printed by James Ballantyne & Co.

Figures: A8-3, B39-9, C63-4, D84-3, E106-5, F130-9, G160-3, H181-3, I 214-5, K238-4, L244-3, M285-8, N309-3, O 334-3, P344-5.

94Ae] Sixth (Fourth) Edition: 1821

THE | **ANTIQUARY.** | BY THE | AUTHOR OF "WAVERLEY" AND "GUY MANNERING." | [*short Oxford rule*] | [*eight lines of verse*] | [*short reversed Oxford rule*] | IN THREE VOLUMES. | SIXTH EDITION. | VOL. I [II-III]. | EDINBURGH: | PRINTED FOR ARCHIBALD CONSTABLE AND CO. EDINBURGH; | AND HURST, ROBINSON, AND CO. LONDON. | [*dash*] | 1821.

Paper: Royal 12° (187 x 110mm uncut). Watermarks: 1819 | 2 [3] but primarily *none*.

General Notes: Collation and pagination as for the preceding 1818 edition except that volume 3 concludes P¹² Q⁶. More significant is the omission of any reference to the printer, either on title-pages or at the end of the volumes, and the absence throughout of any press figures: a constant feature of Ballantyne's work. As a Ballantyne imprint is also lacking in an 1821 eighth edition of *Waverley* (77Ak-Al), one may surmise that both of these editions were arranged perhaps in London under the aegis of the publisher newly identified on the title-page. (The last separate, 1820 edition of *Guy Mannering* [82Af] is perfectly regular in all respects.)

Copies: BCL; CtY(2).

REPRINTS

FRANCE

PARIS: Baudry, Barrois [and others]
[~] The Antiquary. 1831. (Collection of Ancient and Modern British Novels and Romances: *see* 288R.3)

94Ra] PARIS: French, English and American Library 1831
The Antiquary A Romance By Sir Walter Scott, Bart. . . . Paris French, English and American

Library, No. 55, Rue Neuve Saint Augustin, One Door from No. 11, Rue de la Paix. 1831. Two volumes. Pages 1: *1-2*, *i-iii* iv, *5* 6-238; 2: *i-ii*, *1-3* 4-242. Notes: Apparently a remainder of a book printed in Boston. French title-pages and preliminaries (imprinted 'Printed by Paul Renouard, No. 5, Rue Garencière.) have been applied to a Boston: Parker issue with Parker engraved frontispieces first issued in 1827 (Waverley Novels: *see* 306R.5-6). Copy: E.

PARIS: Didot and Galignani
[~] The Antiquary. M DCC XXI. (Collection of Modern English Authors: *see* 291R.7-9)

PARIS: Ledoux
[~] The Antiquary. 1830. (The Works of Sir Walter Scott: *see* 296R.3)

GERMANY

94Rb] BERLIN: Schlesinger 1822
The Antiquary. By the Author of "Waverley" and "Guy Mannering." . . . Fifth Edition. Berlin, Printed for Adolph Martin Schlesinger. 1822. Three volumes. Pages 1: *1-5* 6-170; 2: *1-3* 4-178; 3: *1-3* 4-197 *198*. Copy: L. Reference: GDS 132, page 336.

LEIPSIC: Wigand
[~] The Antiquary. 1831. (A Complete Edition of the Waverley Novels: *see* 300R.7-9)

ZWICKAU: Schumann
[~] The Antiquary. 1822. (Pocket Library of English Classics: *see* 302R.36-39)

HUNGARY

PEST, LEIPSIC and LONDON: Wigand
[~] The Antiquary. 1831. (A Complete Edition of the Waverley Novels: *see* 300R.7-9)

UNITED STATES

94Rc] BOSTON: Parker 1821
The Antiquary. A Romance. . . . Boston, Samuel H. Parker, No. 12, Cornhill. 1821. Pages: *1-3* 4-360.] Copy: not seen. Notes: (Also reissued in The Novels Tales and Romances '1820' [1822]: *see* 305R.3.)

[~] The Antiquary. 1827, 1829. (Waverley Novels: *see* 306R.5-6)

[~] The Antiquary. 1830, 1832. (Waverley Novels, Parker's Edition Revised: *see* 307R.5-6)

94Rd] EXETER: Williams 1824
The Antiquary. By the Author of "Waverley." . . . Exeter: Published by J. & B. Williams, 1824. Two volumes. Pages 1: *1-3* 4-190; 2: *1-3* 4-192. Copy: MWA.

94Re] HARTFORD: Goodrich, Huntington and Hopkins 1821
The Antiquary. By the Author of "Waverley" and "Guy Mannering." . . . Hartford: Samuel G. Goodrich, and Huntington and Hopkins, 1821. Pages: *1-5* 6-271. Copy: PU.

94Rf] NEW YORK: Duyckinck, Gilley, Wiley, Lockwood 1820
The Antiquary. By the Author of "Waverley" and "Guy Mannering." . . . New-York: Published by E. Duyckinck, W. B. Gilley, C. Wiley & Co. and L. & F. Lockwood. James & John Harper, Printers. 1820. Two volumes. Pages 1: *i-'v'*[*iv*], *5* 6-238; 2: *1-3* 4-244. Notes: Title-page reads 'Three volumes in Two', referring to the Edinburgh edition. This is a paginal resetting of the 1818 Eastburn edition next cited. Copies: CtY IdU MWA.

94Rg] NEW YORK: Eastburn 1818
The Antiquary. By the Author of "Waverley" and "Guy Mannering." . . . New-York: Published by James Eastburn and Co. Literary Rooms, Broadway. 1818. Two volumes. Pages 1: *i-iii* iv *5* 6-238; 2: *1-3* 4-244. Notes: The title-page reads 'Three volumes in Two', referring to the Edinburgh edition. Copies: InU MWA(vol.2.)

94Rh] NEW YORK: Van Winkle and Wiley 1816
The Antiquary. By the Author of "Waverley" and "Guy Mannering." . . . New-York: Published by Van Winkle and Wiley, No. 3 Wall-Street. 1816. Two volumes. Pages 1: *i-iii* iv, *5* 6-248; 2: *1-3* 4-260. Notes: First American edition. The title-page reads 'Three volumes in Two', referring to the Edinburgh edition. Imprint on original boards adds: Sold by Wells and Lilly, Boston. Copies: E; MWA NN NNU-W(2) PPL(vol.1) RPB.

94Ri] PHILADELPHIA: Crissy 1821-1826
[1] The Antiquary. By the Author of "Waverley" and "Guy Mannering." . . . Philadelphia: Published by James Crissy, No. 177, Chesnut Street. G. Goodman, Printer, 1821. Two volumes. Pages 1: *i-iii* iv, *5* 6-244; 2: *1-3* 4-254. Notes: The spelling of 'Waverley' and the punctuation varies. Volume 2 has no printer's statement on the title-page, but on the last page of text reads: Griggs & Dickinson, Printers. Copies: E(vol.2); MWA PPL T/B.

[2] The Antiquary. By the Author of "Waverley," and "Guy Mannering." . . . Philadelphia: James Crissy, No. 14, South Seventh Street. 1826. Two volumes. Pages 1: *i—i* iv, *5* 6-263; 2: *1-3* 4-272. Copies: IdU MWA T/B(vol.1).

DERIVATIVES

GREAT BRITAIN

94Da] EDINBURGH: Huie 1823
The Antiquary; A National Drama, Founded on the Celebrated Novel of the Same Name, by the Author of "Waverley," &c. &c. . . . [no imprint. Edinburgh: Printed for James L. Huie, 14 Infirmary Street. 1822.] Pages: *i-ii*, *1-5* 6-64. Notes: Drama by Daniel Terry (music not included) as performed at the Theatre-Royal, Edinburgh, with Edinburgh casts of 1820 and 1822. Engraved frontispiece portrait 'Mrs. Nicol of the Theatre Royal Edinburgh as Miss Grizelda Oldbuck Drawn and Engraved for the National Dramas by W. H. Lizars and Published by James L. Huie 14, Infirmary Street 1823.' Copies: E(3) DN L; NjP. (A

variant issued in: Dramas from the Novels, Tales, and Romances, 1822: *see* 323D4) Collation is *T*[6] U-2A[6]. Reference: Ford B3.

LONDON: Cumberland
[~] The Antiquary; A Musical Play. [1832]. (Cumberland's British Theatre: *see* 329D. 231)

94Db] LONDON: Goulding, D'Almaine, Potter 1820
The Music in The Antiquary, A Musical Drama in Three Acts, . . . London, Published by Goulding, D'Almaine, Potter, and Co. 20, Soho Square, & to be had at 7, Westmoreland St, Dublin. [unwatermarked. ca.1820.] Pages: *1* 2-65. Notes: Engraved sheet music with the composer's rubber-stamped monogram above the price and with plate marks: 'Ov: H.of Mid Lothian The Antiquary' (for the Overture) and 'The Antiquary' (for the remaining plates). There is double pagination throughout, first the continuous paging, second a separate pagination and price for each of the eleven songs. The poetry written by Daniel Terry with music composed and arranged by Henry R. Bishop for voice and pianoforte. Price 15/. Copies: L O.

94Dc] LONDON: Stockdale 1820
The Antiquary; A Musical Play, in Three Acts; Taken from the Celebrated Novel of that Name, . . London: Printed for William Stockdale, No 181, Piccadilly. 1820. Pages: *i-vii* viii, *1* 2-64. Notes: Libretto by Daniel Terry, compiled from Isaac Pocock's operatic drama. (Music by Henry R. Bishop not included, but notice is given that it is available from Messrs. Goulding and Co. *see* preceding entry). First produced at the Theatre Royal, Covent Garden, on 25 January 1820. Price: Three Shillings. First edition of the play to be produced and, unlike Terry's immediate performance of *Guy Mannering*, delayed for some five years after publication of the novel. Copies: BCL DT E(prompt copy) L O; CtY InU(2) NNU-W ViU(inscribed.) References: Bolton 1275; Ford B2.

EXTRACTS IN ANTHOLOGIES

94E] From *The Antiquary* there are eight extracts in four anthologies: 358E.7 366[3].3 384.3-4,7 466.3-4,7.

REVIEWS OF CULLODEN PAPERS and of POLWHELE

95A] First Printings: 1816

1] 'ART. I. *Culloden Papers*', pages *283* 284-333,

2] 'ART. IV. *The Fair Isabel of Cotchele. A Cornish Romance*, pages 402-405, *in*:

The Quarterly Review. January, 1816. [No.28; volume 14 imprint:] London: Printed for John Murray, Albemarle Street. 1816.

Published 25 May 1816 in London (*MC*; in view of the announcement 20 May the entry 21 May is erroneous).

Notes: Article I contains on pages 294, 311, and 325 references to Burt's *Letters from a Gentleman in the North of Scotland*. Scott had the original 1754 edition (Abbotsford, page 19), refers to this book repeatedly at this time, and assisted in a later edition of 1818 (127A).

Article IV, not previously in the canon, is accepted on the evidence given in Shine. The opening paragraph reads: 'The valuable manuscript of the poem before us was inclosed, it seems, in a bureau of Mr. Walter Scott, which was "for some time inaccessible." (p.371). The key, however, was at length luckily found, or a blacksmith procured; and the *Cornish Romance* emerged from the obscurity of its seclusion.' Attributing the poem to 'Mr. Polwhele' Scott continues: 'In the drawer of this mystic cabinet were some papers belonging to Mr. Scott himself; and the reader will not fail to remark a fortunate result of this contiguity, in the spirit communicated to these pages from the lays of the Northern Minstrel. Thus the Lady of the Lake has stanzaic introductions, so has Fair Isabel; the Lady of the Lake is in short lyric measure, so is Fair Isabel; The Lady of the Lake is interspersed with songs, so, beyond all possibility of cavil, is Fair Isabel; for the songs alone would form a very respectable "Complete Songster," adapted to the vocal paradise of Vauxhall. We must, however, admit a wonderful improvement on the plan of Mr. Scott, inasmuch as these songs are not always incidental, but are made to supply the place of dialogue.' (pages 402-403).

Copies: BCL L O; PPL. References: Shine 366, 369. (Magnum Opus Edition 1835: *The Miscellaneous Prose Works*, [1] xx.*1* 2-93, [2] not reprinted.)

POEMS IN ALBYN'S ANTHOLOGY

96A] First Printings in volume 1: 1816

1] 'JOCK OF HAZELDEAN. WRITTEN BY WALTER SCOTT, Esq.', (first words: '"Why weep ye by the tide, ladie?"'), pages 18[l p (letterpress)]-19[e m (engraved music)];

2] 'NORA'S VOW. WRITTEN BY WALTER SCOTT, Esq.', (first words: 'Hear what Highland Nora said,') pages 20[e m]-21[l p]. Arranged to the air 'Cha teid mis a chaoidh' and also with Gaelic song and translation on page 21;

3] 'PIBROCH OF DONUIL DHU. WRITTEN BY WALTER SCOTT, Esq.', (first words as title), pages 82-88[e m] and 89[l p]. In some copies the engraved title varies: 'Pibroch of Donuil Dubh' or 'Pibroch of Donald Dubh.';

4] 'MACGREGORS' GATHERING. WRITTEN BY WALTER SCOTT, ESQ.' (first words: 'The moon's on the lake, and the mist's on the brae,'), pages 90[1 p] and 91-97[e m], *in*:

[*engraved title*] Albyn's Anthology or A Select Collection of the Melodies & Vocal Poetry Peculiar to Scotland & The Isles Hitherto Unpublished Collected and Arranged by Alexander Campbell . . . . The Modern Scotish & English Verses Adapted to the Highland, Hebridean & Lowland Melodies Written by Walter Scott Esq. and other living Poets of the first Eminence Vol: I. Edinburgh Published by Oliver & Boyd, And Sold by Clementi & Co. & Law & Whittaker London; & the Principal Music & Booksellers in the United Kingdom. 1816.

Volume 1 published 16 July 1816 in Edinburgh (*SM*.lxxviii.533); issued 7 September in London (*MC*). £1.1.0.

General Notes: Scott's prospectus for this work was issued in March 1816 (*see* 92A). Several months later, on 30 May, he advised Lady Compton that he had provided the engraved title, featuring his deerhound Maida 'with other emblems of highland sport and song', and on 8 July forwarded the first copy to the Prince Regent.

The two volumes, with the exception of preliminaries, consist of interspersed leaves of engraved sheet music (e m) and leaves of letterpress (l p). The collection was edited by Alexander Campbell with the close association of Scott. In fact, the first volume preface, dated 20 June 1816, reads, page ix: 'In the course of the Editor's labours in arranging materials for publication, Mr Walter Scott, whom the Editor may emphatically call *Friend*, generously offered his assistance in the progress and execution of the present extensive plan, . . . Through Mr Scott's means, the Prince Regent was applied to, for permission to inscribe this collection to his Royal Highness, who was graciously pleased to signify his sanction to a gentleman high in office, . . .'

Scott's first poem (1) is founded upon a well-known ballad usually titled 'Jock of Hazelgreen'—a ballad to which Scott added stanzas two, three and four. Another poem by Scott, reprinted here, 'Lullaby of an Infant Chief' (pages 22-23), was first printed in March 1816 as a part of the musical drama 'Guy Mannering' (*see* 91A).

Copies: AN BCL E(3) L O(2); CtY(2) DLC(2) MH.

References: *Letters*, iv.246, 259-260; [1] G/T 10043; [2] G/T 10565; [3] G/T 10583; [4] G/T 10427; Ruff 151. (Magnum Opus Edition 1834: *The Poetical Works*, [1] xi.315-316, [2] xi.322-324, [3] xi.319-321, [4] xi.325-327.)

First Printings in volume 2: 1818

5] 'MACKRIMMON'S LAMENT. WRITTEN FOR THIS WORK BY WALTER SCOTT, ESQ.' (first words: 'Macleod's wizzard flag from the grey castle sallies,'), pages 54-56[e m] and 57[l p]. Engraved page uses title 'Lament';

6] '"DONALD CAIRD'S COME AGAIN!" WRITTEN FOR THIS WORK BY WALTER SCOTT, ESQ.' (first words of song: 'Donald Caird can lilt and sing,'; first words of chorus as title), pages 80-82[e m] and 83[l p], *in*:

Albyn's Anthology . . . . Vol: 2. Edinburgh; Printed for the Editor & Proprietor; & Sold by Oliver & Boyd, And also by Clementi & Co; & Law & Whittaker London; and the Principal Booksellers. 1818. To be had at Purdies Music Warehouse, 70, Princes Street, Edinr. where orders for this work are received.

Volume 2 published 14 February 1818 in Edinburgh (*EEC*). £1.1.0.

Notes: The preface, dated 2 February 1818, promises a third volume 'early in the year 1819' which did not materialize.

Copies: AN BCL E(3) L O; CtY(2) DLC MH.

References: [5] G/T 10431; [6] G/T 9776; Ruff 151. (Magnum Opus Edition 1834: *The Poetical Works*, [5] xi.332-333, [6] xi.328-331.)

DERIVATIVES

GREAT BRITAIN

96Da] EDINBURGH: Robertson 1820

[1] Jock of Hazeldean, A Popular Border Ballad Written by Sir Walter Scott Bart. and Published by his express permission . . . Edinburgh Published by Alexr. Robertson at his Music Saloon 47 Princes St. [ca.1820]. Pages: *1* 2-3. Notes: Engraved sheet music with caption title (first words: 'Why weep ye by the tide ladye'). With symphonies and accompaniment composed by Alexander Robertson for pianoforte and arranged for voice. Price: 1/6. Copies: BCL L; NNP. Reference: Van Antwerp(2) 42s.

[2] Pibroch of Donuil Dhu. The Pipe Summons of Black Donald, Written by Sir Walter Scott Bart. & Published by his express permission. . . . Edinburgh Published by Alexr Robertson at the Music Saloon 47 Princes St. [ca.1820]. Pages: *1* 2-3. Notes: Engraved sheet music with caption title. (first words as title). With symphonies and accompaniment composed by R. A. Smith for pianoforte and arranged for voice. Price: 1/6. Copy: MH.

96Db] LONDON: Chappell 1825
Jock o' Hazledean[!], A Scotch Ballad. written by Sir Walter Scott, . . . London, Printed & Sold by Chappell & Co. Music Sellers to His Majesty, 50, New Bond Street. NB. This Song is Copyright. [1825]. Pages: *i-ii*, *1* 2-5. Notes: Engraved sheet music with plate number 2603. Music composed by Mary Ann Paton arranged for voice and pianoforte. Price 2/-. Copy: L. Reference: G/T 10072.

96Dc] LONDON: Cramer, Addison and Beale 1825
Jock o' Hazledean(!), A Scotch Ballad, Written by Sir Walter Scott Bart. . . London, Published by J. B. Cramer, Addison & Beale, 201 Regent Street, Corner of Conduit Street. [watermarked 1825]. Pages: 1-5. Notes: Engraved sheet music with plate marks: 'Jock o' Hazeldean' and '256'. Music composed by T. P. Chipp arranged for pianoforte or harp. Price: 1/6. Copy: L.

96Dd] LONDON: Cumberland 1825
['Jock of Hazledean(!)' London: Cumberland [1825]. Music composed by Mary Ann Paton.] Copy: not seen. Reference: G/T 10072.

96De] LONDON: Gow 1821
Jock of Hazeldean The admired Scotish Ballad . . . The Words Written by Sir Walter Scott and Published by permission. London, Published by John Gow & Son Music Sellers to His Majesty 162, Regent St. [ca.1821] Pages: 1-3. Notes: Engraved sheet music with plate number '105'. The symphonies and accompaniments composed by John Whitaker arranged for voice and pianoforte. Price: 1/6. Copy: NNP.

96Df] LONDON: Latour 1827
Jock o' Hazledean[!], A Scotch Ballad. Written by Sir Walter Scott, . . . London. Printed & Sold by F. T. Latour Music Seller to his Majesty. 50, New Bond Street. NB. This song is Copyright. [1827]. Pages: *i-ii*, *1* 2-5. Notes: Engraved sheet music with plate number 'L 2603'. The song arranged by Mary Ann Paton for voice and pianoforte. Price: 2/-. Copy: L.

LONDON: Leigh
[~] Scottish Air, "Jock O' Hazeldean." 1828. (The Harmonicon: number 1. *see* 337D.)

96Dg] LONDON: Mayhew 1824
The Moon's on the Lake, The Celebrated Scotch Song of the Macgregor's Gathering, dedicated to Sir Walter Scott, (Author of the Poetry.) . . . London, Mayhew & Co. Music Sellers to the Royal Family, 17, Old Bond Strt. [watermarked 1824]. Pages: *i-ii*, 1-4. Notes: Engraved sheet music. (first words: 'The moon's on the lake, and the mist's on the brae, And the clan has a name that is nameless by day,'). Music composed by Alexander Lee arranged for voice and pianoforte. Price: 2/-. Copies: L; InU. Refer-ence: G/T 10429.

96Dh] LONDON: Preston 1825
[Jock O'Hazeldean Ballad sung by Miss Paton . . written by Sir Walter Scott, Bart., . . . London: Published by Preston, No. 71, Soho. 1825. Notes: 'now published by the express permission of Messrs. Archibald Constable and Co., the sole Proprietors, and no where else

by authority, except in Albyn's Anthology and Thomson's Collection of Scotish Songs. Advertised in *MC* 7 July 1825. Price: 1s. 6d.] Copy: not seen.

LONDON: The Proprietors
[~] Scottish Air, "Jock O' Hazeldean." 1828. (The Harmonicon, number 1. *see* 337D.)

96Di] MONTROSE: Smith 1820
[~] Bauldy Baird. [1820]. [*Slip-ballad parody: see* 499S.]

Donald Caird's Come Again, . . . Printed for, and Sold by John Smith, Bookseller, &c. Montrose. [ca. 1820]. Notes: Slip-ballad. [Popular Songs—No. 4.] Copy: NN.

UNITED STATES

96Dj] BALTIMORE: Cole 1826
Jock O' Hazeldean, A favorile[!] Scottish Ballad . . . The words by Sir Walter Scott Bart. Published by John Cole, Baltimore [1826]. Pages: *1-3*. Notes: Engraved sheet music with caption title and plate number: '364'. (first words: 'Why weep ye by the tide Lady? Why weep ye by the tide,'). Music composed by [Alex.] Campbell and arranged for voice and pianoforte. Copies: InU MH(2) MWA.

96Dk] BALTIMORE: Willig 1826
Jock O' Hazeldean, A favorile[!] Scottish Ballad . . . The words by Sir Walter Scott Bart. Published by G. Willig, Baltimore [1826]. Notes: A variant issue of the preceding entry. Copy: InU.

96Dl] BOSTON: Bradlee 1827
Jock O' Hazeldean. A Scotch Ballad, Written by Sir Walter Scott . . . . Boston, Published by C. Bradlee No. 164 Washington St. [1827]. Pages: *1-2*. Notes: Engraved sheet music with caption title. Song composed by Alexander Campbell, arranged by T. T. Craven for voice and pianoforte or harp. Copies: MH MWA.

96Dm] BOSTON: Hewitt 1826-1828
The Moon's on the Lake The celebrated Scotch Song, of the Macgregors Gathering . . . the Poetry by Sir Walter Scott . . . . Boston, Published by James L. Hewitt & Co. at their Music Saloon No. 36 Market Street. [ca.1826]. Pages: *1* 2-5. Notes: Engraved sheet music. (first words: 'The moon's on the lake, and the mist's o the brae, And the clan has a name'). Song composed by Alexander Lee arranged for voice and pianoforte. Copies: CtY MWA. Reissue [ca.1828] with additional address: 'and No. 129 Broadway, New York.' (InU MH[2] MWA).

96Dn] CINCINNATI: Church 1828
The Moon's on the lake or The Macgregor's Gathering, A Favorite Scotch Song . . . Written by Walter Scott, Cincinnati, J. Church, Jr. Pages: *1* 2-5. Notes: Engraved sheet music with plate mark '370' which ties this issue to the Philadelphia: Klemm edition [1828] (*see* 96Dt). Copy: MH.

96Do] NEW YORK: Dubois and Stodart 1828
The Moon's on the Lake or the Macgregor's Gathering, A Favorite Scotch Song . . . Written by Walter Scott, . . . New York Published by Dubois & Stodart No. 167 Broadway. [ca.1828]. Pages: *1* 2 *3-5*. Notes: Engraved sheet music. Song composed by Alexander Lee arranged for voice and pianoforte with oboe. (first words: 'The moon's on the lake, and the mist's on the brae,'). A reissue of the preceding entry. The earliest issue (1) no plate number; (2) plate number '5' on page *1*. Price: (1) 50 cents; (2) Pr. 50. Copies: (1) PPL. (2) MH[2] MWA.

96Dp] NEW YORK: Hall 1821
The Moon's on the Lake The celebrated Scotch Song, of the Macgregors Gathering . . . the Poetry by Sir Walter Scott . . . New York, Published by William Hall & Son 545 Broadway. [ca.1821]. Pages: *1-2* 3 *4* 5. Notes: Engraved sheet music with plate number: '950'. (first words: 'The moon's on the lake, and the mist's on the brae, And the clan has a name that is nameless by day,'). Music composed by Alexander Lee arranged for voice and pianoforte. Copy: InU.

96Dq] New York: Mesier 1830
The Moon's on the Lake or The Macgregor's Gathering, A favorite Scotch Song . . . Written by Walter Scott, . . . N.Y. Published by E.S. Mesier 28 Wall-st & Bourne 359 Broadway. [1830]. Pages: *1* 2-5. Notes: Engraved sheet music with caption title (first words: 'The moon's on the lake, and the mist's on the brae,'). Music composed by Alexr. Lee arranged for voice, pianoforte, and oboe. Copy: MH.

96Dr] NEW YORK: Riley 1826
Jock of Hazeldean . . . Written by Sir Walter Scott . . . New-York, Publish'd by E. Riley, 29, Chatham Street. [ca.1826]. Pages: *1* 2-3. Notes: Engraved sheet music with caption title. (first words: 'Why weep ye by the tide ladye, why weep ye by the tide;'). Music composed by Alex. Campbell, arranged by Alexander Robertson for voice and pianoforte. Copies: E; InU MH MWA PHi. Reference: G/T 10074.

96Ds] PHILADELPHIA: Blake 1830
The Moon's on the lake. or The Macgregor's Gathering, A Favorite Scotch Song . . . Written by Walter Scott. Philadelphia Published and sold by G. E. Blake No: 13 south Fifth Street. [1830]. Pages: *1* 2-3. Notes: Engraved sheet music with plate mark on pages 2-3 reading : 'The Moon is on the Lake'. (first words: The moon's on the lake, and the mist's on the brae, . . .'). Music composed by Alexr. Lee and arranged for voice, pianoforte and oboe. Price: Pr. 25 cents. Copy: MH.

96Dt] PHILADELPHIA: Klemm 1828
The Moon's on the Lake or the Macgregors Gathering, A favorite Scotch Song . . . Written by Walter Scott, . . . Philadelphia Published by John G. Klemm. [ca.1828]. Pages: *1* 2-5. Notes: Engraved sheet music with plate number: '370'. (first words: 'The moon's on the lake, and the mist's on the brae, And the clan has a name that is nameless by day,'). Music composed by Alexander Lee arranged for voice and pianoforte. A variant of rhe Cincinnati and New York issues (*see* 96Dn-Do). Copies: InU(2) MH MWA.

96Du] PHILADELPHIA: Willig 1819
The Moon's on the Lake or the Macgregors Gathering a favorite Scotch Song. . . Written by Walter Scott . . . Philadelphia, George Willig 171 Chesnut St. [ca.1819]. Pages: *1* 2-5. Notes: Engraved sheet music with plate mark: 'The moon's on the lake.' on all but page *1*. (first words: 'The moon's on the lake, and the mist's on the brae, And the clan has a name that's nameless by day,'). Music composed by Alexander Lee arranged for voice and pianoforte. Price: 50 Cts. Copies: InU MH(2).

EXTRACTS IN ANTHOLOGIES

96E] Though only one of Scott's six poems in *Albyn's Anthology* was reprinted in the United States ([4],item 458), these lyrics were often extracted in Great Britain:
[1] 'Jock of Hazeldean' with 17 entries: 357E.5 361[1].8 369[1-2] 369[3].10 369[4].10 371.1 387[1].2 389.31 405(2)[3].17 405(3)[1].7 413.3 414[2].2 419.4 422.2 428 429[2].
[2] 'Nora's Vow' with 9 entries: 360E.25 369[3].4 369[4].4 375 389.17 405(2)[1].2 405(2)[3].4 405(3)[1].1 413.2.
[3] 'Pibroch of Donuil Dhu' with 12 entries: 360E.22,26 366[2].14 369[3].11 369[4]. 11 371.2 375[1].2 376.1 405(2)[3].18 405(3)[1].6 413.1 415.2.
[4] 'MacGregor's Gathering' with 7 entries: 359E.1 369[3-4].14 375[1].3 421 425 458.
[5] 'Mackrimmon's Lament' with one entry in 358E.14.
[6] 'Donald Caird's Come Again!' with 10 entries: 357E.6 359.3 361[1].10 362.3 369[3].2 369[4].2 405(2)[2].6 405(2)[3].15 405(3)[1].9 413.15.

HISTORY OF EUROPE, 1814

97A] First Printing: 1816

'HISTORY OF EUROPE, 1814' pages *3* 4-367, *in*:

The Edinburgh Annual Register, for 1814. Vol. Seventh.—Parts I. and II. Edinburgh: Printed by James Ballantyne and Co. for Archibald Constable and Co. Edinburgh; Longman, Hurst, Rees, Orme, and Brown, London; and the other Proprietors. 1816.

Published 10 October 1816 in Edinburgh (*EEC*); issued 26 October 1816 in London (*MC*). £1.1.0.

Notes: The *Monthly Literary Advertiser*, September 1816, in its notice that this volume is now 'In the Press', grandly remarks that 'it can hardly be necessary to mention, that the period which it embraces is one of the most fertile in important events that has ever occurred in the history of the world. . . . The Publishers have the satisfaction of being enabled to state, that the historical part of the volume now about to be presented to the Public, is written by a gentleman of the *highest literary eminence*, who adds to the other qualifications requisite for such an undertaking, a minute and accurate knowledge of the *locale* of most of the great battles recently fought, founded on personal inspection, and assisted by military and scientific co-operation; and who has possessed unwonted opportunities of intercourse with the most illustrious among those who directed the movements of the grand political machine.' Quite possibly this accolade was prepared with Scott's assistance, for the 'History', in an annual under his direction, was of some considerable extent.

Copies: E L; PPL. Reference: (Magnum Opus Edition: Not reprinted.)

TALES OF MY LANDLORD
[First Series]
'THE BLACK DWARF' and 'OLD MORTALITY'

[T]here are two tales—the last of which I really prefer to any fictitious narrative I have yet been able to produce—the first is wishy-washy enough. . . . To give the go-by to the public, I have doubled and leaped into my form, like a hare in snow; that is, I have changed my publisher, and come forth like a maiden knight's white shield (there is a conceit!) without any adhesion to fame in former adventures (another!) or, in other words, with a virgin title-page (another!) . . . . (Scott to Daniel Terry, 12 November 1816, *Letters*, iv.288.)

98Aa] First Edition: 1816

TALES OF MY LANDLORD, | COLLECTED AND ARRANGED | BY | JEDEDIAH CLEISHBOTHAM, | SCHOOLMASTER AND PARISH-CLERK OF GANDERCLEUGH. | [*short rule*] | [*six-line quotation from Burns*] | [*short rule*] | IN FOUR VOLUMES. | VOL. I [II-IV]. | [*short Oxford rule*] | EDINBURGH: | PRINTED FOR WILLIAM BLACKWOOD, PRINCE'S STREET: | AND JOHN MURRAY, ALBEMARLE STREET, LONDON. | [*dash*] | 1816.

Published 2 December 1816 in Edinburgh (*EEC*, the date also earlier announced 21 and 28 November); issued 5 December in London (*MP*). £1.8.0. 2000 copies. Binding: drab or blue boards with printed labels. Paper: Royal 12° (192 x 114mm uncut). Watermarks: *none* or 6 [7, 8, 9, 0] | S M | 1814; *none* or 5 [7, 8, 9, 10] | S M | 1815; 9 | W Balston & Co | 1815. Typography: Printer's imprints read: (1) [*short rule*] | *Edinburgh, Printed by James Ballantyne and Co.*; (2) [*short rule*] | Edinburgh: | Printed by James Ballantyne & Co.

General Notes: Though Scott readily confided in Terry, as evident in the epigraph quoted above, he still dissembled when sending an advance copy to Lady Abercorn on 29 November. Yet on 21 December he implicitly admitted his authorship to Joseph Train (who had provided him with the plot of 'Old Mortality') and dated the copy sent to Train 'by Portpatrick mail' 25 December. By 30 January, as he then informed Morritt, another confidant, 6000 copies (of the first three editions) had been sold and 3000 more 'are pressing forward'. Still another recipient, who from now on regularly received the novels upon issue, was Lady Louisa Stuart.

It seems that the first fly-title (A1) was cancelled throughout because of the unnecessary repetition of the five-line quotation which already appeared on the verso of the half-title. Confusion resulted in the issue of this and later editions when binders casually cancelled either the half-title (with no volume or signature 'A') or the fly-title (with the volume and signature 'A') and then substituted one for the other.

Presentation copies: (Volume 1, state 1) E('given me by the author while secret 1816' [Lady Louisa Stuart]). Other copies: (volume 1, state 1) BCL E O(2) P; ICN InU MH NN(Berg[2]) NNP(3). (state 2) BCL E L(3) O(3); CtY IdU NNU-W T/B. Mixed or sophisticated copies: CtY([vols.1-3] and [vols.1,4] imitation first edition title-pages dated 1817 with second edition texts).

References: Church 533; P. D. Garside (ed.), *EEWN4a*; Douglas Mack (ed.), *EEWN4b*; Sterling 725; Thomson, [1] page 16, [2] page 51; Van Antwerp(1) 5; Van Antwerp(2) 49-50(Joseph Train); Worthington 4. (Magnum Opus Edition 1830: *Waverley Novels*, ix.*i-iii* iv-xiv, [1] ix.*xv-xvii* xviii-xxix *xxx*, *1* 2-217—[2] ix.*219-221* 222-374—x-xi.*1-3* 4-138.)

1] **TALES OF MY LANDLORD,** . . . VOL. I. . . . 1816.

Collation: $\pi^2(\pi 2+1)$ $A^{12}(-A1)$ $B\text{-}P^{12}$ Q^2. Pagination: *i* half-title, *ii* five-line quotation in Spanish from *Don Quixote* with Jarvis's six-line translation into English, *iii* title-page, *iv* printer's imprint(1), *1* dedication 'To His Loving Countrymen,' *2 blank*, *3* 4-21 Introduction, *22 blank*, *23* fly-title for Tale I. 'The Black Dwarf', *24 blank*, *25* 26-363 text, 363 printer's imprint(2), *364 blank*. Typography: Printer's imprint(2) is below a short Oxford rule. In some copies page number 46 is upside down or represented only by the 6 and page number 328 is transposed as 238.

Figures: A*3*-6 13-7, B38-10, C61-11 71-9, D87-8 88-10, E109-5 110-10, F123-7 141-8, G159-10 168-8, H183-4 184-9, I 196-'01'[10] 202-6, K219-4 229-9, L244-7 262-5, M267-6 288-9, N298-5 309-7, O 316-7 327-8, P357-5 359-6, Q362-10. Early sheets of M and N, bearing no press figures, have been reported in the University of Keele copy.

Notes: The inserted dedication leaf was originally printed in volume 3, as Q2 and occasionally remains in that position. The last leaf of sheet B (pages 47-48) was corrected at press, a circumstance which results in two textually identical variants: (a) an uncancelled state for copies then corrected; (b) a cancel B12 to replace the faulty reading in copies previously printed. In another instance further along, involving a grammatical fault on page 234, lines 20-21, the leaf was left uncancelled, reading incorrectly (state 1) 'were heard. . . was perceived'; correctly (state 2) 'was heard. . . were perceived'.

2] **TALES OF MY LANDLORD,** . . . VOL. II. . . . 1816.

Collation: π^2 A^{12}(-A1) B^{12}(±B9) C-O^{12} P^2. Pagination: *i* half-title, *ii* quotation, *1* title-page, *2* printer's imprint(1), *3* 4-340 text of Tale II, 'Old Mortality', chapters 1-13, 340 printer's imprint(2). Typography: In some copies the title has no comma at the end of the first line.

Figures: A11-4 12-11, B28-5 46-8, C51-10 60-11, D83-6 85-4, E111-10/- 120-5, F132-8 142-11, G147-4 168-7, H170-8/9, I 196-6 214-8/-, K226-11 237-8, L243-4 252-10, M276-5 286-9, N298-7 300-6, O 327-7 336-10, P—.

Notes: Leaf B9 reads page 42 line 3: (a) 'Tower' in cancellandum; (b) 'tower' in cancellans. Again, for this two-page text, Van Antwerp discovers a number of manuscript variants, here nine. As in the preceding volume there is also some further correction at press in B12, C5 and E9, pages 47-48, 57-58, and 113-114, with: (a) an uncancelled state for copies then corrected; (b) cancels in other copies to replace the faulty leaves. In either state the text is identical.

3] **TALES OF MY LANDLORD,** . . . VOL. III. . . . 1816.

Collation: π^2 A^{12}(-A1) B-O^{12} P^6 Q^2(-Q2=vol.1,+1 after π2). Pagination: *i* half-title, *ii* quotation, *1* title-page, *2* printer's imprint(1), *3* 4-349 text of Tale II. 'Old Mortality', continued, 349 printer's imprint(2), *350 blank.*

Figures: A22-7 24-5, B34-9 36-5, C55-9 69-4, D94-6, E109-10 118-7, F135-7 136-10, G157-8 166-11, H170-11 180-4, I 206-7 213-8, K232-8 238-5, L255-7 256-10, M276-7 287-4, N299-8 304-10, O 323-7 332-5, P343-5.

4] **TALES OF MY LANDLORD,** . . . VOL. IV. . . . 1816.

Collation: π^2 A^{12}(-A1) B-O^{12} P^6. Pagination: *i* half-title, *ii* quotation, *1* titlepage, *2* printer's imprint(1), *3* 4-345 text of Tale II, 'Old Mortality', concluded, 346-347 Peroration, dated 'Gandercleugh' 15 November 1816, 347 printer's imprint(2), *348 blank.*

Figures: A22-4 24-6, B38-5 45-11, C62-11 69-7, D86-5 96-10, E107-11 116-7, F124-10 143-4, G148-5 159-6, H170-10 180-7, I 196-4 214-8, K237-8 239-11, L243-6 253-4, M286-10 288-5, N303-8 309-6, O 316-4 327-5, P338-10.

98Ab] Second Edition: 1817

TALES OF MY LANDLORD, | COLLECTED AND ARRANGED | BY | JEDEDIAH CLEISHBOTHAM, | SCHOOLMASTER AND PARISH-CLERK OF GANDERCLEUGH. | [*short rule*] | [*six-line quotation from*

Burns] | [*short rule*] | IN FOUR VOLUMES. | VOL. I [II-IV]. | SECOND EDITION. | [*short Oxford rule*] | EDINBURGH: | PRINTED FOR WILLIAM BLACKWOOD, PRINCE'S STREET: | AND JOHN MURRAY, ALBEMARLE STREET, LONDON. | [*dash*] | 1817.

Published 2 January 1817 in Edinburgh (*EEC*). £1.8.0. Binding: blue boards with printed labels. Paper: Royal 12° (192 x 114mm uncut). Watermarks: 7 [8, 9, O] | S M | 1814; 7 | S M | 1815; M 1816 | 1 [2, 3, 4, 5, 6]; W BALSTON & Co | 1816(only in volume 4, gathering H, pages 169-192). General Typography: Printer's imprints read invariably: (1) [*short rule*] | *Edinburgh, Printed by James Ballantyne and Co.*; (2) [*short rule*] | EDINBURGH: | Printed by James Ballantyne & Co.

General Notes: For an explanation of the A1 cancel in each volume see First Edition (98Aa), General Notes.

Copies: (volume 2, issue 1) TxU. (2) BCL E(vols.2-4) L(2) O; CtY(vols.1-3) IdU InU T/B. Mixed copy: L(vol.2, 4th edition).

1] **TALES OF MY LANDLORD,** . . . VOL. I. | SECOND EDITION. . . 1817.

Collation: $\pi^2(\pi2+1)$ $A^{12}(-A1)$ B-P^{12} Q^2. Pagination: *i* half-title, *ii* quotation, *iii* title-page, *iv* printer's imprint(1), *v* dedication, *vi blank*, *3* 4-21 Introduction, *22 blank*, *23* fly-title, *24 blank*, *25* 26-363 text of Tale I: 'The Black Dwarf', 363 printer's imprint(2), *364 blank*. Typography: In some copies page number 35 is omitted.

Figures: A4-10 14-11, B35-4 45-7, C58-6 60-4, D87-4 96-5, E120-8/-, F123-5, G166-7 168-4, H175-4, I 215-10 216-8, K227-5 240-8, L262-4 264-7/-, M277-10 286-5, N293-5 302-7, O 328-5 334-7, P357-10, Q—.

2] **TALES OF MY LANDLORD,** . . . VOL. II. | SECOND EDITION. . . . 1817.

Collation: π^2 $A^{12}(-A1)$ B-O^{12} P^2. Pagination: *i* half-title, *ii* quotation, *iii* title-page, *iv* printer's imprint(1), *3* 4-340 text of Tale II: 'Old Mortality', chapters 1-13, 340 printer's imprint(2). Typography: In some copies page number 13 is omitted.

Figures: A11-4 12-11, B27-10 48-6, C59-7 72-6, D82-11 96-8, E111-10/- 117-5, F132-8 142-11, G147-4 168-7, H181-10 190-5, I 208-7 214-11, K224-8, L243-4 252-10, M276-5 286-9, N303-2 304-10, O 322-7 336-8, P—.

Notes: As the figures indicate (1) the first issue consists in part of five over-run sheets (A, F-G, L-M) from the first edition, (2) the second issue has three to five of these sheets newly reset and figured A21-10 23-6, F126-7 141-5, G147-2 157-6, L254-7 264-5, M287-5 288-1/-. Additionally, in the second issue some copies have sheet O partly reimpressed, here figured 327-11 336-8.

3] **TALES OF MY LANDLORD,** . . . VOL. III. | SECOND EDITION. . . . 1817.

Collation: π^2 A^{12}(-A1) B-O^{12} P^6 Q^2(-*Q*2=vol.1,+1 after π2). Pagination: *i* half-title, *ii* quotation, *iii* title-page, *iv* printer's imprint(1), *3* 4-349 text of Tale II: 'Old Mortality', continued, 349 printer's imprint(2), *350 blank.*

Figures: A24-8, B26-5 28-6, C61-11 71-8, D88-8 94-7, E120-7, F133-10 135-8, G148-5 166-8, H179-8 189-5, I 208-10 215-4, K231-10 240-7, L253-5 262-11, M278-1 280-8/-, N300-8 303-11, O 323-2 324-6/-, P342-6, *Q*—.

4] **TALES OF MY LANDLORD,** . . . VOL. IV. | SECOND EDITION. . . . 1817.

Collation: π^2 A^{12}(-A1) B-O^{12} P^6. Pagination: *i* half-title, *ii* quotation, *iii* titlepage, *iv* printer's imprint(1), *3* 4-345 text of Tale II: 'Old Mortality', concluded, 346-347 Peroration, 347 printer's imprint(2), 348 *blank.*

Figures: A24-6, B27-5, C51-5 52-6, D85-5 95-7, E107-11 116-7, F124-10 143-4, G148-5 159-6, H170-10 180-7, I 196-4 214-8, K237-8 239-11, L243-6 253-4, M286-10 288-5, N303-8 309-6, O 316-4 327-5, P338-10.

Notes: As the figures testify, sheets E-P (pages 97-347) are an over-run of the first edition impression.

98Ac] Third Edition: 1817

TALES OF MY LANDLORD, | COLLECTED AND ARRANGED | BY | JEDEDIAH CLEISHBOTHAM, | SCHOOLMASTER AND PARISH-CLERK OF GANDERCLEUGH. | [*short rule*] | [*six-line quotation from Burns*] | [*short rule*] | IN FOUR VOLUMES. | VOL. I [II-IV]. | THIRD EDITION. | [*short Oxford rule*] | EDINBURGH: | PRINTED FOR WILLIAM BLACKWOOD, PRINCE'S STREET: | AND JOHN MURRAY, ALBEMARLE STREET, LONDON. | [*dash*] | 1817.

Published 20 February 1817 in Edinburgh (*EEC*). £1.8.0. Binding: Drab boards with printed labels. Paper: Royal 12° (190 x 111mm uncut). Watermarks: M 1816 | 1 [2, 3, 5]. Typography: Printer's imprints read invariably: (1) [*short rule*] | *Edinburgh, Printed by James Ballantyne and Co.*; (2) [*short rule*] | EDINBURGH: | Printed by James Ballantyne & Co.

General Notes: For an explanation of the A1 cancel in each volume see First Edition (98Aa), General Notes.

Copies: AN E E(vols.2-4) L; CtY MH T/B T/B(vols.1,4).

1] **TALES OF MY LANDLORD,** . . . VOL. I. | THIRD EDITION. . . . 1817.

Collation: $\pi^2(\pi2+1)$ A^{12}(-A1) B-P^{12} Q^2. Pagination: *i* half-title, *ii* quotation, *iii* title-page, *iv* printer's imprint(1), *v* dedication, *vi blank*, *3* 4-21 Introduction, *22 blank*, *23* fly-title for Tale I: 'Black Dwarf', *24 blank*, *25* 26-363 text, *364 blank*. Typography: Page 60 is misnumbered 66. In some copies page 94 has mashed type appearing to be 84.

Figures: A6-6 13-11, B27-5 45-6, C50-1 72-5, D94-8 96-7, E102-3 108-10, F143-1 144-5, G157-4 167-10, H171-8 173-4, I 205-5 214-10, K238-10 240-4, L250-7 264-4, M268-7 287-11, N290-10 304-1, O 325-4 334-3, P357-1 358-8, Q—.

Notes: Unlike the second edition, this printing carries no legend 'END OF VOLUME FIRST.' or printer's imprint(2) below last page of text, though ample space was available for these entries.

2] **TALES OF MY LANDLORD,** . . . VOL. II. | THIRD EDITION. . . . 1817.

Collation: π^2 A^{12}(-A1) B-O^{12} P^2. Pagination: *i* half-title, *ii* quotation, *iii* title-page, *iv* printer's imprint(1), *3* 4-340 text of Tale II: 'Old Mortality', chapters 1-13, 340 printer's imprint(2). Typography: Pages 287 and 299 are misnumbered 207 and 331.

Figures: A8-8 23-7, B26-7 40-5, C52-5 59-1, D82-11 96-8, E107-8 117-5, F126-7 141-5, G147-2 157-6, H189-3 190-6, I 195-4 200-8, K235-7, L259-7 261-6, M'207'[287]-7 288-2, N304-10, O 322-7 336-8, P—.

Notes: Final gathering P is of a duplicate setting, page 340 line 4 reading either 'guard' or 'guards'.

3] **TALES OF MY LANDLORD,** . . . VOL. III. | THIRD EDITION. . . 1817

Collation: π^2 A^{12}(-A1) B-O^{12} P^6 *Q*^{2}(-*Q*2=vol.1,+1 after π2). Pagination: *i* half-title, *ii* quotation, *iii* title-page, *iv* printer's imprint(1), *3* 4-349 text of Tale II: 'Old Mortality', continued, 349 printer's imprint(2), *350 blank*. Typography: Section signature I2 (page 201) is unsigned.

Figures: A17-7 22-5/-, B28-5 34-4, C50-4 72-8, D74-1 85-7, E107-10 117-7, F123-10 141-6, G146-7 148-8, H180-4 182-5, I 194-11 208-6, K230-6 237-4, L253-4 255-5, M267-8 268-7, N291-3 301-11, O 334-6 336-4, P344-1, *Q*—.

4] **TALES OF MY LANDLORD,** . . . VOL. IV. | THIRD EDITION. . . 1817

Collation: π^2 A^{12}(-A1) B-O^{12} P^6. Pagination: *i* half-title, *ii* quotation, *iii* titlepage, *iv* printer's imprint(1), *3* 4-345 text of Tale II: 'Old Mortality', concluded, 346-347 Peroration, 347 printer's imprint(2), *348 blank*.

Figures: A13-1 14-7, B37-5 47-8, C62-10 69-7, D85-5 87-6, E108-4 111-6, F136-5 142-8, G155-4 156-7, H184-6 190-3, I 194-7 205-4, K233-4 235-6, L253-3 258-1, M287-7 288-11, N303-11, O 322-8 325-3, P*346*-10.

98Ad] Fourth Edition: 1817[1818]

TALES OF MY LANDLORD, | COLLECTED AND ARRANGED | BY | JEDEDIAH CLEISHBOTHAM, | SCHOOLMASTER AND PARISH-CLERK OF GANDERCLEUGH. | [*short rule*] | [*six-line quotation from Burns*] | [*short rule*] | IN FOUR VOLUMES. | VOL. I [II-IV]. | FOURTH EDITION. | [*short Oxford rule*] | EDINBURGH: | PRINTED FOR WILLIAM BLACKWOOD, PRINCE'S STREET; | AND JOHN MURRAY, ALBEMARLE STREET, LONDON. | [*dash*] | 1817.

Published 1 January 1818 in Edinburgh (*EEC*). £1.8.0. Paper: Royal 12° (173 x 104mm cut). Watermarks: MAVOR & Co | 1816.

General Notes: Collation and pagination as in the third edition. This resetting, however, varies in other particulars, as noted below. For a detailed explanation of the A1 cancel in each volume see First Edition (98Aa), General Notes.

Copies: E(with three 1820 Allan plates); CtY(vol.2) TxU(2).

1] **TALES OF MY LANDLORD,** . . . VOL. I. | FOURTH EDITION. . . . 1817.

Typography: Page 199 is misnumbered 991. Page 363 now carries printer's imprint(2).

Figures: A15-6 17-5, B36-7 38-5, C51-10 72-5, D82-7 96-11, E106-5 120-8, F130-1 141-6, G156-1 159-3, H182-5 184-8, I 202-6 208-8, K234-4 240-1, L252-1 262-11, M275-11 288-4, N304-4 310-9, O 327-9 328-5, P350-8 360-10, Q—.

2] **TALES OF MY LANDLORD,** . . . VOL. II. | FOURTH EDITION. . . . 1817.

Figures: A23-10 24-4, B39-8 40-4, C70-4, D93-5 94-8, E107-3 112-5, F135-5 136-8, G156-1 159-11, H170-10 180-11, I 194-4 209-3, K218-1 240-10, L250-8 264-4, M286-9 288-5, N299-11 304-1, O 315-8 333-1, P339-9/-.

3] **TALES OF MY LANDLORD,** . . . VOL. III. | FOURTH EDITION. . . . 1817.

Figures: A16-11 22-1, B26-10 28-8, C50-4 60-6, D83-11 96-8, E117-7, F131-4 132-1, G148-7 167-1, H190-5 192-4, I 208-6, K230-6 237-4, L253-4, M287-10, N291-3 301-11, O 327-8 336-5, P344-1, *Q*—.

Notes: As the figures indicate, three sheets are in part (C, E, I) and two others entirely (N, P) of the same impression as the third edition.

4] **TALES OF MY LANDLORD,** . . . VOL. IV. | FOURTH EDITION. . . . 1817.

Typography: Section signature I2 (page 201) is missigned 2I.

Figures: A*3*-6 4-9, B45-11 47-1, C51-8 69-4, D84-9, E99-10 109-6, F124-3 130-5, G146-8 165-6, H173-1 179-10, I 208-9 215-4, K227-9 237-3, L262-5 264-11, M267-10 288-4, N300-11 310-8, O 314-8 325-6, P342-9.

98Ae] Fourth Edition (Fifth Edition, First Issue): 1818

TALES OF MY LANDLORD, | **First Series,** | COLLECTED AND ARRANGED | BY | JEDEDIAH CLEISHBOTHAM, | SCHOOLMASTER AND PARISH-CLERK OF GANDERCLEUGH. | [*short rule*] | [*six-line quotation from Burns*] | [*short rule*] | IN FOUR VOLUMES. | VOL. I [II-IV]. | FOURTH EDITION. | [*short Oxford rule*] | EDINBURGH: | PRINTED FOR WILLIAM BLACKWOOD, PRINCE'S STREET; | AND JOHN MURRAY, ALBEMARLE STREET, LONDON. | [*dash*] | 1818.

Possibly the 'Fourth Edition' listed 30 May 1818 in London (*MC*).

General Notes: Paper, collation and pagination as in the third edition, except that, in this resetting, the dedication leaf was imposed as A1. Apparently this issue is intermediate between the one before and the one after.

Copy: O(vol.1 only, later volumes constitute 6th, 5th, 5th editions respectively)

1] **TALES OF MY LANDLORD,** | **First Series,** . . . VOL. I. | FOURTH EDITION. . . . 1818.

Collation: π^2 A^{12} B-P^{12} Q^2. Pagination: *i* half-title, *ii* quotation, *iii* title-page, *iv* printer's imprint(1), *1* dedication To His Loving Countrymen, *2 blank*, *3* 4-21 Introduction, *22 blank*, *23* fly-title for Tale I: 'The Black Dwarf', *24 blank*, *25* 26-363 text, 363 printer's imprint(2), *364 blank*. Typography: Page 140 is numbered 14. Page 363 now carries printer's imprint(2).

Figures: A6-4 17-9, B30-8 37-9, C51-1 72-8, D76-3 94-4, E106-8 109-9, F130-9 141-7, G155-8 168-9, H171-1 181-4, I 195-8 205-1, K230-6 232-7, L254-3 264-9, M266-9 285-6, N290-3 300-7, O 334-3 336-8, P338-8 340-7, Q—.

98Af] Fifth Edition, Second Issue: 1819

TALES OF MY LANDLORD, | First Series, | COLLECTED AND ARRANGED | BY | JEDEDIAH CLEISHBOTHAM, | SCHOOLMASTER AND PARISH-CLERK OF GANDERCLEUGH. | [*short rule*] | [*six-line quotation from Burns*] | [*short rule*] | IN FOUR VOLUMES. | VOL. I [II-IV]. | FIFTH EDITION. | [*short Oxford rule*] | EDINBURGH: | PRINTED FOR ARCHIBALD CONSTABLE AND COMPANY. | [*dash*] | 1819.

Published 6 May 1819 in Edinburgh (*EEC*, listed as 'New Edition'). £1.8.0. Binding: pink boards with printed labels. Paper: Royal 12° (188 x 111mm uncut). Watermarks: C | 1818. Typography: Printer's imprints read (1) [*short rule*] | *Edinburgh, Printed by James Ballantyne and Co.*; (2) [*short rule*] | EDINBURGH: | Printed by James Ballantyne & Co.

Copies: BCL E(2) L O(vols.3-4); CtY.

1] **TALES OF MY LANDLORD,** | First Series, . . . VOL. I. | FIFTH EDITION. . . . 1819.

Collation: π^2 A^{12} B-P^{12} Q^2. Pagination: *i* half-title, *ii* quotation, *iii* title-page, *iv* printer's imprint(1), *1* dedication To His Loving Countrymen, *2 blank*, *3* 4-21 Introduction, *22 blank*, *23* fly-title for Tale I: 'The Black Dwarf', *24 blank*, *25* 26-363 text, 363 printer's imprint(2), *364 blank*. Figures:As for 'Fourth Edition' (Fifth Edition, First Issue, 98Ae).

2] **TALES OF MY LANDLORD,** | First Series, . . . VOL. II. | FIFTH EDITION. . . . 1819.

Collation: π^2 A-O^{12} P^2. Pagination: *i* half-title, *ii* quotation, *iii* title-page, *iv* printer's imprint(1), *1* fly-title for Tale II: 'Old Mortality', *2 blank*, *3* 4-340 text, chapters 1-13, 340 printer's imprint(2). Typography: Leaf A1 (page *1*) is unsigned. Page 253 last line the 'y' in 'your' is missing. Printer's imprint(2) ends 'and Co.'

Figures: A11-7 12-1, B34-9 40-4, C50-8 68-1, D74-6 85-3, E108-7 110-9, F141-9 142-8, G165-4 166-8, H189-7 190-3, I 208-9 215-3, K226-4 240-7, L250-4 264-6, M288-9, N301-3 310-8, O 315-1 328-9, P338-1.

3] **TALES OF MY LANDLORD,** | First Series, . . . VOL. III. | FIFTH

EDITION. . . . 1819.

Collation: π^2 A-O^{12} P^6 *Q*^{2}. Pagination: *i* half-title, *ii* quotation, *iii* title-page, *iv* printer's imprint(1), *1* fly-title for Tale II: 'Old Mortality', *2 blank*, *3* 4-349 text continued, 349 printer's imprint(2), *350-352 blank*. Typography: Leaf A1 (page *1*) is signed.

Figures: A16-3 22-7, B34-7 36-9, C64-8 70-6, D94-8 96-3, E102-9 120-6, F142-3 144-7, G158-6 168-8, H192-9, I 202-1 216-5, K239-6 240-5, L256-8 263-9, M268-3 287-5, N309-6 311-9, O 334-8 336-7, P340-7, *Q*—.

4] **TALES OF MY LANDLORD,** | First Series, . . . VOL. IV. | FIFTH EDITION. . . . 1819.

Collation: π^2 A-O^{12} P^6. Pagination: *i* half-title, *ii* quotation, *iii* title-page, *iv* printer's imprint(1), *1* fly-title for Tale II: 'Old Mortality', *2 blank*, *3* 4-345 text concluded, 346-347 Peroration, 347 printer's imprint(2), *348 blank*. Typography: Leaf *A*1 (page *1*) is unsigned. Section signatures I 2 and P2 (pages 201 and 341) are missigned 2 I and O 2. Page 271 is misnumbered 217.

Figures: A12-5 22-3, B40-7, C64-7 70-8, D82-5 93-8, E99-7 109-3, F130-4 136-5, G146-9 160-5, H181-5 191-6, I 203-7 208-8, K218-6 232-7, L262-10 264-2, M274-11 280-9, N296-6, O *336*-11, P338-6.

98Ag] 'Sixth Edition': 1819

TALES OF MY LANDLORD, | First Series, | COLLECTED AND ARRANGED | BY | JEDEDIAH CLEISHBOTHAM, | SCHOOLMASTER AND PARISH-CLERK OF GANDERCLEUGH. | [*short rule*] | [*six-line quotation from Burns*] | [*short rule*] | IN FOUR VOLUMES. | VOL. I [II-IV]. | SIXTH EDITION. | [*short Oxford rule*] | EDINBURGH: | PRINTED FOR ARCHIBALD CONSTABLE AND COMPANY. | [*dash*] | 1819.

Paper: Royal 12° (182 x 108mm uncut). Watermarks: C | 1818 but usually *none*.

General Notes: This edition is apparently made up from remainders of earlier editions, volume 1 from sheets of the 'Fourth Edition' (Fifth Edition, First Issue), volumes 2-4 from sheets of the Fifth Edition, Second Issue.
Copy: BCL; CtY(vols.1-2,4).

REPRINTS

FRANCE

PARIS: Baudry, Barrois [and others]
[~} Tales of My Landlord. . . . First Series. 1831. (Collection of Ancient and Modern British Novels and Romances: *see* 288R.12)

PARIS: Didot and Galignani
[~] Tales of My Landlord, First Series, . . . M DCCC XXI. (Collection of Modern English Authors: *see* 291R.10-13)

PARIS: Galignani
[~] Tales of My Landlord [*with two other titles*] 1827. One volume. (*See* 294R[3].2)

PARIS: Glashin, Robertson [*and others*]
[~] Tales of My Landlord, First Series. 1827. (The Complete Works of Sir Walter Scott, Bart.: *see* 295R.4-7)

GERMANY

98Ra] BERLIN: Schlesinger 1823
[Black Dwarf. . . . Berlin, Printed for Adolph Martin Schlesinger. 1823.] Copy reported at Staatsbibliothek zu Berlin (Haus 1). Reference: GDS 132, page 344.

[Old Mortality. . . . Berlin, Printed for Adolph Martin Schlesinger. 1822.] Copy reported by James Burmester.

LEIPZIG: Wigand
[~] The Black Dwarf.1831. (A Complete Edition of the Waverley Novels: *see* 300R.13)

[~] Old Mortality. 1831. (A Complete Edition of the Waverley Novels: *see* 300R.14-16)

ZWICKAU: Schumann
[~] Tales of My Landlord. The Black Dwarf. 1822. (Pocket Library of English Classics.*see* 302R.46-47.)

[~] Tales of My Landlord. Old Mortality. 1822. (Pocket Library of English Classics: *see* 302R.48-51)

HUNGARY

PEST, LEIPSIC and LONDON: Wigand
[~] The Black Dwarf. 1831. (A Complete Edition of the Waverley Novels. *see* 300R.13)

[~] Old Mortality. 1831. (A Complete Edition of the Waverley Novels. *see* 300R.14-16)

UNITED STATES

98Rb] BOSTON: Parker 1821-1832
[Tales of My Landlord. First Series. Black Dwarf and Old Mortality. Boston: Samuel H. Parker, No. 12, Cornhill. 1821. Pages: *i-iii* iv-vii *viii*, *9* 10-483.] Copy: not seen. (Also reissued 1821 in Novels Tales and Romances: *see* 305R.5)

[~] Tales of My Landlord. First Series. 1827, 1829. (Waverley Novels: *see* 306R.9-10.)

[~] Tales of My Landlord. First Series. 1830, 1832. (Waverley Novels, Parker's Edition Revised: *see* 307R.9-10)

98Rc] EXETER: Williams 1829
Tales of My Landlord, Collected and Reported by Jedediah Cleishbotham, Schoolmaster and Parish-Clerk of Gandercleugh. First Series. . . . Exeter: J. & B. Williams. 1829. Two volumes. Pages 1: *i-v* vi-x, *11* 12-294; 2: *1-3* 4-291 *292-293*. Notes: Volume 1 contains *The Black Dwarf* and the beginning of *Old Mortality*; 2 *Old Mortality* concluded. Copy: E. Reference: Kohler(1) 16 (with illustration).

98Rd] HARTFORD: Goodrich, and Huntington and Hopkins 1821
Tales of My Landlord, Collected and Arranged by Jedediah Cleishbotham. . . . Hartford: Samuel G. Goodrich, and Huntington and Hopkins. 1821. Pages: *1-5* 6-357 *358-359*. Copies: PU T/B.

98Re] NEW YORK: Duyckinck (*and others*) 1820
Tales of My Landlord, Collected and Arranged by Jedediah Cleishbotham, . . . NewYork: Published by Evert Duyckinck, W. B. Gilley, L. and F. Lockwood, and E. Bliss. J. & J. Harper, printers, 189 Pearl-st. 1820. Four volumes. Pages 1: *1-5* 6-182; 2: *1-3* 4-173; 3: *1-3* 4-178; 4: *1-3* 4-178. Copies: MH(vols.3-4) MWA(vols.1-2) NNU-W.

98Rf] NEW YORK: Eastburn 1817-1818
[1] Tales of My Landlord, Collected and Arranged by Jedediah Cleishbotham, . . . Second American Edition. New-York: Published by James Eastburn & Co. At the Literary Rooms, Broadway. E. & E. Hosford's Print, Albany. 1817. Four volumes. Pages: 1: *1-7* 8-152; 2: *1-5* 6-140; 3: *1-5* 6-144; 4: *1-5* 6-143. Copies: MWA NN (vols.3-4) NNU-W PHi.

[2] Tales of My Landlord, Collected and Arranged by Jedediah Cleishbotham, . . . NewYork: Published by James Eastburn & Co. At the Literary Rooms, Broadway. 1818. Four volumes in two. Pages 1: *i-vii* viii-xiv, *15-17* 18-170; 2: *1-3* 4-157; 3: *1-5* 6-162; 4: *1-5* 6-158. Copies: MH(vol.2) MWA PPL ViU.

98Rg] PHILADELPHIA: Crissy 1826
Tales of My Landlord, Collected and Arranged by Jedediah Cleishbotham, . . . Philadelphia: James Crissy, No. 14, South Seventh Street. 1826. Three volumes. Pages 1: *i-v* vi-xii, *13-15* 16-253; 2: *1-3* 4-235; 3: *1-3* 4-256 *257*. Copies: IdU NN T/B.

98Rh] PHILADELPHIA: Maxwell 1820

Tales of My Landlord, Collected and Arranged by Jedediah Cleishbotham, . . . Philadelphia: Printed and Published by James Maxwell. 1820. Three volumes. Pages 1: *i-vii* viii-xv *xvi, 17-19* 20-284; 2: *1-7* 8-259; 3: *1-7* 8-279 *280*. Notes: Volume 1 has an engraved vignette title-page preceding the type-set title-page. Copies: MWA NN PPL T/B.

98Ri] PHILADELPHIA: Thomas 1817
Tales of My Landlord, Collected and Arranged by Jedediah Cleishbotham, . . . Philadelphia: Published by M. Thomas, No. 52 Chesnut Street. J. Maxwell, Printer. 1817. Four volumes in two. Pages 1: *1-7* 8-189; 2: *1-5* 6-179; 3: *1-5* 6-183; 4: *1-3* 4-180 *181-184*. Notes: Apparently the first American edition. Imprint varies: volumes 2-3: Philadelphia: Published by M. Thomas, no. 52, Chesnut street. W. Fry, Printer.; volume 4: Philadelphia: Published by M. Thomas, 52, Chesnut-street. Copies: MH MWA PPL ViU.

98Rj] PHILADELPHIA: Wright 1823
Tales of My Landlord, Collected and Arranged by Jedediah Cleishbotham, . . . Philadelphia. Robert Wright—63, South Fifth Street. 1823. Three volumes. Pages 1: *i-vii* viii-xiii *xiv-xvi, 17* 18-238; 2: *1-7* 8-223; 3: *1-7* 8-235 *236*. Copies: MB NjP PPL(with additional engraved title first used in the Phladelphia 1820 Maxwell edition) RPB.

DERIVATIVES

GREAT BRITAIN

98Da] DUBLIN: M'Mullen 1822
The Black Dwarf; or, The Recluse of Mucklestaine Moor. A Dramatic Piece in Five Acts. . . . Dublin: Printed by M'Mullen, 21, Duke-Street. 1822. Pages: *1-3* 4-56. Notes: Drama by William Fawcett. Copy: DN. References: Bolton 1435; Ford D5.

98Db] EDINBURGH: Anderson 1823
[The Battle of Bothwell Bridge. Edinburgh: Published by John Anderson, Jun. 55, North Bridge Street. 1823.] Copy: not seen. (Also issued in: Edinburgh Select British Theatre, 1823: *see* 319D.3 and in: The Waverley Dramas, 1823: *see* 321D.3). Reference: Bolton 1320(?).

98Dc] EDINBURGH: Chambers [*and others*] 1820
The Life and Anecdotes of the Black Dwarf, or David Ritchie, . . . The Celebrated Original of the Character of Elshender, in the Tales of My Landlord; . . . To Which is Added, An Abridgement of the Tale of "The Black Dwarf." Edinburgh: Printed and Sold by W. Chambers, Leith Walk, Also Sold by J. Dick, Edinburgh; William Reid, Leith; R. Griffin & Co. Glasgow; Alex. Elder, Peebles; and All Other Booksellers. 1820. Pages: *i-iii* iv, *7* 8-149. Notes: A coloured woodcut frontispiece is captioned 'The Black Dwarf'. Pages 37-149 contain the abridgement, which the preliminary advertisement states 'cannot in the least injure the sale of the Tales of my Landlord, . . . but at the same time, he [the compiler] is proud to acknowledge, that the proprietors of that work, with their known liberality, have kindly permitted him the use which he has made of it.' Copy: IdU.

98Dd] HAMILTON: Borthwick 1821
A History of The Rencounter at Drumclog, and Battle at Bothwell Bridge, in the Month of June, 1679, with an Account of What is Correct, and What is Fictitious in the "Tales of my Landlord," . . . Hamilton: Printed by W. M. Borthwick and Co. 1821. Pages: *1-5* 6-131 *132*. Notes: Text by William Aiton includes 'Reflections on Political Subjects'. A folding woodcut frontispiece is included in the pagination. Copy: TxU.

98De] LONDON: Goulding, D'Almaine, Potter 1820
The Battle of Bothwell Brigg, A Scottish Musical Romance, in Two Acts, . . . London Published by Goulding D'Almaine Potter & Co. 20, Soho Square, & to be had at 7, Westmoreland Street Dublin. [1820]. Pages: *i-ii* 1-45. Notes: Engraved sheet-music with plate mark: 'Bothwell Brigg'. Music derived from 'Old Mortality', transcribed from 'Scotch tunes' by Henry R. Bishop, arranged for voice and pianoforte. Pagination is given continuously for the entire work and also given separately with separate price for each of the seven vocal numbers, the overture and the marches. Price 10/6. Copies: L O. Reference: G/T 10570.

LONDON: Iley
[~] Tales of My Landlady. 1818. [Parody: *see* 490S]

98Df] LONDON: Lowndes 1820
The Battle of Bothwell Brigg, A Scottish Romance, in Two Acts, Founded on the Story of Old Mortality, in the Popular "Tales of My Landlord," . . . London: Printed by G. Auld, Greville Street, for John Lowndes, 25, Bow Street, Covent Garden. 1820. Pages: *i-iv*, *1* 2-35 *36-40*. Notes: Play by Charles Farley (music by Henry R. Bishop not included) as performed at the Theatre Royal Covent Garden 22 May 1820. Price: Two Shillings. First edition of this adaptation. Copies: DT E; CtY NN PU ViU. References: Bolton 1316; Ford O 1.

EXTRACTS IN ANTHOLOGIES

98E] The story 'Old Mortality' was extracted in three anthologies: 360E.28 366[1].3 372[2].2

VERSES, COMPOSED FOR THE OCCASION

99A] First Edition: 1816

VERSES, | Composed for the Occasion, and adapted to Haydn's | celebrated air, | "*God Save the Emperour Francis,*" | And sung by a Professional Band, after the Dinner given | BY THE | LORD PROVOST | TO THE | GRAND DUKE OF RUSSIA, | AND HIS SUITE, | *At Charlotte Square,* 19*th December* 1816.

Printed at Edinburgh, presumably, in time for the performance 19 December 1816.

Paper: Post 8° (201 x 124mm cut). Watermarks: none. Collation: A^2. Pagination: *1* text, *2-4 blank*. Figures: none.

Notes: The three eight-line stanzas begin as follows: (1) 'God protect brave ALEXANDER!'; (2) 'Bless him! mid his land's disaster'; (3) 'Hail! then, hail! ILLUSTRIOUS STRANGER!'. These were later arranged as two twelve-line stanzas with the second stanza beginning 'O'er his just resentment victor'.

Copy: E(Abbot). References: Ruff 153(with illustration page 193); Thomson, page 51. (Magnum Opus Edition 1834: *The Poetical Works*, x.365-366 in two twelve-line stanzas.)

HAROLD THE DAUNTLESS

This [letter] accompanies *Harold the Dauntless*. I thought once I should have made it something clever, but it turned vapid upon my imagination; and I finished it at last with hurry and impatience. Nobody knows, that has not tried the feverish trade of poetry, how much it depends upon mood and whim . . . . (Scott to Lady Louisa Stuart, 31 January 1817, *Letters*, iv.380.)

100A] First Edition: 1817

Harold the Dauntless; | A POEM, | IN SIX CANTOS. | BY | THE AUTHOR OF "THE BRIDAL OF TRIERMAIN." | [*short Oxford rule*] | EDINBURGH: | *Printed by James Ballantyne and Co.* | FOR LONGMAN, HURST, REES, ORME, AND BROWN, LONDON; | AND ARCHIBALD CONSTABLE AND CO. EDINBURGH. | [*dash*] | 1817.

Published 30 January 1817 in Edinburgh (*EEC*). First advertised at 7s, but corrected on 1 February to 7s.6d (*EEC*). Binding: blue-green boards with printed label citing price at 7s.6d. Paper: Pott 8° (170 x 107mm uncut). Watermarks: J. WHATMAN | 1812. Collation: π1 A-B[8] C[8](±C8) D-M[8] N[4]. Pagination: *i* title-page, *ii blank*, *1* 2-199 *200* text, *200* printer's imprint, *201-202 blank*. Printer's imprint: [*short Oxford rule*] | EDINBURGH: | Printed by James Ballantyne & Co. Typography: Direction line throughout reads 'VOL. II'. In some copies page 65 reads only 'VOL.'. Page numbers 129-130 are omitted, but text is continuous.

Figures: A16-8, B26-11, C37-11, D61-11, E79-6 80-3, F93-6, G110-11, H127- 11, I *137*-6, K161-11, L177-11, M190-6, N196-11.

Notes: As indicated above Scott sent Lady Louisa Stuart a complete copy the day after publication, but this relatively brief poem must have been long 'at press', for fifteen months earlier, on 2 November 1815, he was ready to send her, presumably in printed form, 'the first canto under the seal of secrecy' (*Letters*, iv.114). On that earlier occasion he was more excited about the prospects for this verse, describing it as 'A strange piece of work . . . a sort of tale of errantry and magic which, *entre nous*, I am very fond of, though ashamed to avow my frailty.'

In its direction line this anonymous edition is styled 'VOL II' so that it might sell separately as well as with the counterpart fifth edition (1817) of *The Bridal of Triermain* (*see* 68Ae). The cancel C8 is in a duplicate setting, (1a) page 47 with page number, and with line 6 reading 'maid'; (1b) page 47 without page number, line 6 reading 'maid,'. Apparently even when duplicated the cancel issue was short, requiring later a further setting of conjugate leaves C1.8 (2), page 47 with page number, and with line 6 reading 'maid,'.

Copies: (state 1a) ES; MH NNU-W. (1b) BCL; NNP. (2) E O; CtY(Hartstonge) DLC IdU InU(2) T/B TxU.

References: Grady, pages 357-380, 404-405; Ruff 154; Thomson, page 33; Tinker 1872; Van Antwerp(1) 18. (Magnum Opus Edition 1834: *The Poetical Works*, xi.*143-144* 145-254.)

REPRINTS

GERMANY

ZWICKAU: Schumann
[~] Harold the Dauntless. 1827. (Pocket Library of English Classics: *see* 302R.137)

UNITED STATES

BOSTON: Bedlington
[~] Harold the Dauntless. 1828. (The Poetical Works of Sir Walter Scott: *see* 304R.7)

FREDERICKSBURG: Withers
[~] Harold the Dauntless. 1824. (The Poetical Works of Sir Walter Scott: *see* 310R.7)

100R] NEW YORK: Eastburn 1817
Harold the Dauntless; A Poem, in Six Cantos. By the Author of "The Bridal of Triermain." New-York: Published by James Eastburn & Co. Van Winkle, Wiley, & Co., Printers. 1817. Pages: *1-3* 4-143 *144*. Notes: In some copies the comma after 'A Poem,' on the title-page is missing. Copies: DLC MH MWA NN PPL ViU.

EXTRACTS IN ANTHOLOGIES

100E] From *Harold the Dauntless* there are four extracts in three anthologies: 360E.9-10 417.7 419.5.

THE SEARCH AFTER HAPPINESS

101A] First Printing: 1817

'THE SEARCH AFTER HAPPINESS; OR, THE QUEST OF SULTAUN SOLIMAUN' (first words: 'O, for a glance of that gay Muse's eye,') pages *33* 34-39, *in*:

The Sale-Room, No. V. Saturday, 1 February 1817. Edinburgh, 1817. [Printer's imprint:] Edinburgh, printed by James Ballantyne & Co. For John Ballantyne, Hanover-Street.

Number V published 1 February 1817 in Edinburgh. The first number was issued 4 January (*EEC* 2 January). 6d. each number.

Notes: The entire fifth number of this weekly periodical is devoted to this twenty-two stanza poem. There is no mention of Scott, and in fact the prefatory statement makes a point that the piece was left at the Sale-Room office by an unknown person. In his account of this journal, projected and published through 28 numbers by Scott and the Ballantynes, W. Forbes Gray also attributes to Scott part or the whole of numbers 2-3, 9-11, 13, 17 (*Quarterly Review*, 255 [1930], 116-132). On the other hand the extensively annotated BCL exemplar ascribes to Scott (besides the unquestioned number 5), numbers 1-3, 6, 18-19. In the Gilbert J. French copy (CtY) number 1 is also attributed entirely to Scott—not an unreasonable assumption, given Scott's proclivity for starting periodicals.

Copies: BCL E(2); CtY(2) IdU TxU. Reference: (Magnum Opus Edition 1834: *The Poetical Works*, xi.352-366.)

REPRINT

UNITED STATES

PHILADELPHIA: Carey
[~] The Search after Happiness. 1820. (*See* 313R)

REVIEW OF LORD BYRON

102A] First Printing: 1816[1817]

'ART. IX.—1. *Childe Harold's Pilgrimage, Canto III. . . .* 2. *The Prisoner of Chillon, a Dream; and other Poems.* By Lord Byron.', pages 172-208, *in*:

The Quarterly Review. October, 1816. [No.31. volume 16 imprint:] London: Printed for John Murray, Albemarle Street. 1817.

Published 11 February 1817 in London (*Byron,* v.183n); issued 15 February in Edinburgh (*EEC*).

Notes: In a letter to Murray 9 March 1817, Lord Byron, then unaware of the reviewer's identity, gratefully remarked, 'he must be a gallant as well as a good man—who has ventured in that place—and at this time—to write such an article even anonymously. . . . It is not the mere praise, but there is a *tact* & a *delicacy* throughout not only with regard to me—but to *others*—which as it had not been observed *elsewhere*—I had till now doubted—whether it could be preserved *any where.*' Murray later told Byron that the author was Scott. The review was extracted in one anthology, 366[2]E.13

Copies: BCL L O; PPL.

References: *Byron,* v.178; Shine 407. (Magnum Opus Edition 1834: *The Miscellaneous Prose Works*: iv.351-399 as 'Lord Byron'.)

THE FAREWELL ADDRESS

103A] First Printing: 1817

'THE FAREWELL ADDRESS. WRITTEN BY WALTER SCOTT, ESQ.' (first words: 'As the worn war-horse, at the trumpet's sound,') pages 111-112, *in*:

The Sale-Room, No. XIV. Saturday 5 April 1817. Edinburgh, 1817. [Printer's imprint:] Edinburgh, printed by James Ballantyne & Co. For John Ballantyne, Hanover-Street.

Number XIV published 5 April 1817 in Edinburgh.

Notes: This entire number is a tribute to John Philip Kemble and Scott's thirty-six line address is that which Kemble delivered on Saturday 29 March 1817 after the conclusion of his last performance in *Macbeth.* A fifty-six line version subsequently appeared in the April number of the *Scots Magazine*, page 296, issued about 1 May. In 1822 the thirty-six line version was printed in one anthology: 366[1].9.

Copies: BCL E(2); CtY(2) IdU.

Reference: (Magnum Opus Edition 1834: *The Miscellaneous Prose Works*, xi. 348-

351 as 'Mr Kemble's Farewell Address' in the fifty-six line version.)

REPRINTS

GREAT BRITAIN

103Ra] EDINBURGH: Constable 1821
'Farewell Address', pages 348-349 *in*: The Edinburgh Annual Register, for 1817. Vol. Tenth.—Parts I. and II. Edinburgh: Printed by James Ballantyne and Co. For Archibald Constable and Co., Edinburgh; Longman, Hurst, Rees, Orme, and Brown; and Hurst, Robinson, and Co., London. 1821. Notes: The fifty-six line version. Copies: L; PPL.

103Rb] LONDON: Miller 1817
'(E). Poetical Address, written by Walter Scott, Esq.' pages 76-77, *in:* An Authentic Narrative of Mr Kemble's Retirement from the Stage; including Farewell Address, Criticisms, Poems, &c. Selected from various Periodical Publications; with an Account of the Dinner Given at the Freemasons' Tavern, June 27, 1817; . . . London: Printed for John Miller, 25, Bow-Street, Covent-Garden. 1817. Copy: L. Reference: Ruff 157.

NOTICES CONCERNING THE SCOTTISH GYPSIES

104A] First Printing: 1817

'NOTICES CONCERNING THE SCOTTISH GYPSIES.', pages 43-58; 154-161, 167-168; 615-620, *in*:

The Edinburgh Monthly Magazine. April [May, September] 1817. No I [II, VI] [vol. I imprint:] Edinburgh: Printed for William Blackwood, No 17, Prince's Street, Edinburgh; and Baldwin, Cradock, and Joy, Paternoster Row, London.

First part published about 20 April in Edinburgh; issued 1 May in London. [schedule as noted in No. II].

Notes: The periodical title 'Blackwood's Edinburgh Magazine' was not adopted until the October 1817 number. Early numbers with this later title consequently are reprints. On the verso of the original volume 1 title a notable feature of this new periodical, the 'Antiquarian Repertory', is mentioned as enabling the proprietors, 'not only to lay before their readers articles calculated to gratify curiosity, but also to rescue from oblivion such materials as may throw some light on the disputed points in British history, and on such minute features in the state of society in former ages, as might necessarily be excluded from the pages of the historian.' This language is very reminiscent of Scott, the 'Repertory' is used to document the second part of his essay on Gypsies (pages 167-168), and other documents in subsequent volumes may well have been entered upon his recommendation.

Scott dictated the substance of his original article on the Kirk Yetholm gypsies to Thomas Pringle. Later he quoted from the first part in his review of *Tales of My Landlord* (106A) and subsequently used the same accounts in his 1829 introduction to *Guy Mannering* (348A.3). Sequels to his article, relating to the gypsies in Fife, and initialed 'W.S.', are by Walter Simson, later a frequent correspondent with Scott on the subject.

Copies: L O; NjP.

References: *Letters*, v.282n. (Magnum Opus Edition 1835: *The Miscellaneous Prose Works*, [*short excerpt in*] xix.18-20, otherwise not reprinted.)

THE FORAY

105A] First Printing in Volume 1: 1817

'No I. THE FORAY. WRITTEN EXPRESSLY FOR THIS WORK, BY WALTER SCOTT, ESQ.', (first words: 'The last of the steers on our board has been spread,'), pages 3[letterpress], 18-24[engraved music], *in*:

Twelve Vocal Pieces, Most of them with Original Poetry, Written Expressly for this work by Mrs Joanna Baillie, Walter Scott Esqr. William Smyth Esqr. Jas. Hogg, the Scots Shepherd, John Stewart, Esqr. Lord Byron. Composed . . . by John Clarke, Mus:Doc:Cam: Vol. 1. London, Printed for the Author [composer]. Orders for this Work will be received at Mr. Birchall's, 133. New Bond Street. Entd. at Stats. Hall. [watermarked 1811]. Reissued without watermarks (L).

Published May 1817 in London (Corson[2] page 94).

Notes: In contrast to this first printing, *PW* transposes the words 'the' and 'our', thus reading: 'The last of our steers on the board . . . '. The subscription list includes Scott and his daughter Sophia, both of whom were much interested in Clarke's musical renditions. Publication of this title was long delayed, as evidenced by the 1811 watermark in the paper of both volumes. In addition to the first song, volume 2 page 14 contains a reprint of 'The Romance of Dunois'. John Clarke later in life changed his surname to read 'Whitfeld', not 'Whitefield' as Lockhart reports.

Copies: E L(2) O; CtY(2).

References: G/T 9817; Ruff 156. (Magnum Opus Edition 1834: *The Poetical Works*, xi.340-341.)

DERIVATIVES

GREAT BRITAIN

EDINBURGH: Preston
[~] 'The Foray' *in*: The Melodies of Scotland, with symphonies and accomps. for the pianoforte, violin, &c. by Pleyel, Haydn, Beethoven . . . (*see* 405R(2)[3].9)

UNITED STATES

105D] BOSTON: Graupner 1820
The Foray The words by Walter Scott Esqr. . . Boston: Published by G. Graupner. and Sold for him by John. Ashton. No. 197 Wahington[!] Street. [ca.1820]. Pages: *1* 2-6. Notes: Engraved sheet music. First words: 'The last of the steers on our board has been spread,'. Music composed by John Clarke arranged for voice and pianoforte. Copy: DLC(lacking inner leaf, pages 4-5).

EXTRACTS IN ANTHOLOGIES

105E] The poem titled 'The Foray' is extracted in six anthologies: 367E.1 369[3-4].13 389.34 405(2)[3].9 413.8.

REVIEW OF TALES OF MY LANDLORD

106A] First Printing: 1817

'ART. VIII. *Tales of My Landlord*. . . . Third Edition', pages 430-480, *in*:

The Quarterly Review. January, 1817. [No.32, volume 16 imprint:] London: Printed for John Murray, Albemarle Street. 1817.

Published ca. May 1817 in London.

Notes: Although William Erskine (Lord Kinedder) may have drafted part of this review, the original manuscript is entirely in Scott's handwriting. In this account he immediately discovers that the piece is of the same authorship as *Waverley* and *Guy Mannering*, all exhibiting 'insipid' heroes, and provides further particulars concerning 'Old Mortality'. The review concludes with a discussion of other possible authors.

Copies: BCL L O; PPL.

References: Shine 417; Thomson, page 71. (Magnum Opus Edition 1835: *The Miscellaneous Prose Works*, xix.*1* 2-86.)

THE MONKS OF BANGOR'S MARCH

107A] First printing in Volume 3: 1817

1] 'No. 62. *Ymdaith Mwnge.* THE MONKS OF BANGOR'S MARCH. WRITTEN FOR THIS WORK *By WALTER SCOTT, Esq.*' (First words" 'When the heathen trumpets clang / Round beleaguered Chester rang,'), pages 64-65[engraved music], 66[letterpress], *in*:

[*engraved title*] A Select Collection of Original Welsh Airs Adapted for the Voice United to Characteristic English Poetry never before Published With Introductory & Concluding Symphonies and Accompaniments for the Piano Forte Violin & Violoncello Composed Partly by Haydn but chiefly by Beethoven . . . Vol 3 Entd. at Stationers Hall. London. Printed & Sold by Preston 97 Strand. And by G. Thomson the Editor & Proprietor Edinburgh. [1817].

Published ca. June 1817 in Edinburgh. £1.1.0.

Notes: The engraved title represents two issues, the concluding lines reading (1) as above, with the price given at £1.1.0; (2) 'Composed Chiefly by Haydn and Beethoven . . . Preston 71. Dean St. Soho . . .' and priced at 15s. This issue is signed G. Thomson. Some copies have a frontispiece drawn by D. Thomson, engraved by R. Scott, with caption 'Conway Castle' and date May 1817. The air for the Scott song, by an unknown composer, has the introductory and concluding music arranged by Beethoven, as credited in the 'Index to the Airs'. The volume also includes a reprint of 'The Sheriff's Fancy', pages 91-92, first printed in Scott's addition to Strutt's *Queenhoo Hall* (32Aa.1). Scott's new printing here was extracted in one anthology, 405(3)[1]E.13.

Copies: (issue 1) E L; CtY(2) PU. (2) CtY DLC.

References: Ruff 78. (Magnum Opus Edition 1834: *The Poetical Works*, xi.342-344.)

HISTORY OF EUROPE, 1815

108A] First Printing: 1817

'HISTORY OF EUROPE, 1815', pages *3* 4-373, *in*:

The Edinburgh Annual Register, for 1815. Vol. Eighth.—Parts I. and II. Edinburgh: Printed by James Ballantyne and Co. for Archibald Constable and Co. Edinburgh; Longman, Hurst, Rees, Orme, and Brown, London; and the Other Proprietors. 1817.

Published 21 August 1817 in Edinburgh (*EEC*). £1.1.0.

Notes:. Again as for the previous contribution (*see* 97A) the *Monthly Literary Advertiser* for September takes special notice of the historical review: 'This volume will be found to include that memorable series of military and political events, which terminated with the battle of Waterloo, and the final downfall of Bonaparte's dominion. The narrative is written by the highly eminent individual who contributed the same department of this work for the year 1814, and who has possessed peculiar opportunities of intercourse with the most illustrious among those who directed the movement of the grand political machine.' As before this accolade would appear to come, at least indirectly, from Scott and, toward the end, repeats the language almost verbatim.

The volume also includes, reprinted from *The Sale Room*, 'The Search after Happiness', pages cclviii-cclxvi (*see* 101A).

Copies: E L O; PPL. Reference: (Magnum Opus Edition: Not reprinted.)

INTRODUCTION TO BORDER ANTIQUITIES

109A] First Separate Impression: 1817

INTRODUCTION | TO | BORDER ANTIQUITIES. | [*short Oxford rule*] | BY WALTER SCOTT, Esq. of Abbotsford. | [*short rule*] | [*four-line quotation from* The Aeneid] | [*short rule*] | EDINBURGH: | **Printed at the Border Press,** | BY | **James Ballantyne and Company.** | [*dash*] | 1817.

Printed in August 1817 (*Letters*, iv.499). Paper: Royal 4° (326 x 251mm cut). Watermarks: 1806 (infrequently).

Collation: π^2 a^4 b-q^4, *a*-n^4. Pagination: *1-2 blank, 3* title, *4 blank, i* fly-title, *ii blank, iii* iv-cxxvii Introduction, *cxxviii blank, i* fly-title, *ii blank, iii* iv-ci appendices, ci printer's imprint, *cii-civ blank.* Printer's imprint: [*short rule*] | Edinburgh: | Printed by James Ballantyne and Co. Typography: Second signature sequence is in italic, excepting c (page xvii). In the same sequence page number xcv, misprinted xvc in this separate large-paper impression, is correctly printed in the complete book printings.

Figures: d xxxii-11, e xxxix-3, f xlvi-6, g lvi-3, h lx-3, i lxx-3, k lxxv-6, l lxxxv-3, m xcii-3, n ci-8, o cix-3, p cxvii-1, q cxxvi-8; *a* vii-3, *b* x-11, c xviii-6, *d*—, *e*—, *f* xlvii-3, *g* lvi-6, *h* lxiv-8, *i*—, *k*—, *l* lxxxiv-1, *m* xciii-6, *n*—.

Notes: Upon the removal of the preliminary fold, the final blank leaf, and the alteration of several press figures in the appendices (*f* xlvii-6, *k* lxxiv-6, *n* c-8) this 1817 piece was overprinted for inclusion in the book edition of *The Border Antiquities* (73Aa), the introductory section before text in the '1814' first volume, the appendices before the General Index in the 1817 second volume.

Presentation copy: E('For William Scott Esq younger of Raeburn from his affectionate Cousin The Author Abbotsford Septr 1817').

References: (Magnum Opus Edition 1834: *The Miscellaneous Prose Works*, vii.*1-3* 4-153 as 'Essay on Border Antiquities'.)

ALARMING INCREASE OF DEPRAVITY AMONG ANIMALS

110A] First Printing: 1817

'ALARMING INCREASE OF DEPRAVITY AMONG ANIMALS', pages 82-86, *in*:

Blackwood's Edinburgh Magazine. October 1817. Edinburgh: Printed for William Blackwood, No 17, Prince's Street, Edinburgh; and Baldwin, Cradock, and Joy, Paternoster Row, London.

Published 20 October 1817 in Edinburgh; 1 November 1817 in London (according to the schedule listed in number V).

Notes: Imprints now appear on title-page of the monthly issue. This anonymous jeu d'esprit, dated from Tweedside, 30 September, largely concerns dogs, with the author quoting from the 'Last Dying Words of Bonny Heck', a poem Scott later reprinted in full (*see* 220A).

Copies: E L O; NjP PPL. References: (Magnum Opus Edition: Not reprinted.)

PROSPECTUS FOR PROVINCIAL ANTIQUITIES AND PICTURESQUE SCENERY OF SCOTLAND

111A] First Edition: 1817

ADDRESS [for Provincial Antiquities and Picturesque Scenery of Scotland].

Published 1 November 1817 (*BEM* October 1817, page 106, noting that this prospectus is included with the first number). Two-page broadside with single-word headline, pagination: *1*-2.

Notes: Scott's interest is implicit in the opening sentence as illustrated below. After outlining the general plan, the Address, page 2, identifies the artists, engravers, and

Scott as the principal conductor of the 'Historical Descriptions'. It is then indicated that the first portion, 'Antiquities and Scenery of the Lothians', would consist of twelve numbers, each with five engravings: a large undertaking somewhat restricted by the time issue had begun on 1 May 1819 (*see* 132A).

Copy: E (L175.a <see first page illustration below>).

ADDRESS.

THE encouragement which has been of late so liberally offered to Works upon Topographical Antiquities, in which Art is brought into alliance with History, has encouraged the undertakers of the present Work to submit their plan and names to public consideration.

Without depreciating the labours of others, it may be safely assumed, that the Antiquities of Scotland have hitherto been rendered interesting, rather by the Pen than by the Pencil. Yet they are in many respects highly susceptible of the latter mode of illustration; since, though generally inferior in architectural beauty and importance to the remains of Antiquities in England, they have frequent advantages over them from the grander and more picturesque characters of the adjacent scenery. It is needless to remark how much they have been of late years the object of attention, or how desirable it would be that the Traveller should possess accurate, and at the same time graceful representations, of the scenes which he has viewed with interest, and that those who cannot visit them in person may have an opportunity of becoming acquainted with their beauties through the medium of the Pencil. To the natives of Scotland, a publication must be interesting, which can, as it were, arrest the course of time, and preserve an accurate remembrance of the present state of those objects of Historical Antiquity which are themselves gradually decaying under the influence of time, or suffering from more active causes. How far the present Publication may be qualified to attain objects so desirable, can only be estimated by reference to the well-known and generally respected names of the Artists engaged.

Some written description will, of course, be necessary, for the explanation of the Engravings. It is the wish of the Publishers that this part of the Work should supply, as nearly as possible, the place of an agreeable and intelligent Cicerone, who, without loading his conversation with dry and uninteresting details, can communicate in an authentic, and, at the same time, a popular form, the history of the building, and of the events, real or traditional, with which it is connected. Every stranger, while he views a venerable ruin, must desire to have the advantage of such a companion; or, if he has enjoyed his conversation, would willingly have it placed upon record, in order to refresh his own recollection, and satisfy the curiosity of others. The proposed descriptions will, at the same time, contain such remarks on the general plan, situation, and architecture of the building, as may be judged necessary to explain the Engravings.

ROB ROY

No introduction can be more appropriate to the work than some account of the singular character whose name is given on the title-page, and who, through good report and bad report, has maintained a wonderful degree of importance in popular recollection. . . . He owed his fame in a great measure to his residing on the very verge of the Highlands, and playing such pranks in the beginning of the 18th century, as are usually ascribed to Robin Hood . . . . ('Introduction', undated, but published 1 December 1829, *WN*, vii.*vii*-viii.)

112Aa] First Edition, First Issue: 1818[1817]

ROB ROY. | BY THE | AUTHOR OF "WAVERLEY," "GUY MANNERING," AND | "THE ANTIQUARY." | [*short Oxford rule*] | [*four-line quotation from* Rob Roy's Grave *by Wordsworth*] | [*short reversed Oxford rule*] | IN THREE VOLUMES. | VOL. I [II-III]. | EDINBURGH: | *Printed by James Ballantyne and Co.* | FOR ARCHIBALD CONSTABLE AND CO. EDINBURGH; AND | LONGMAN, HURST, REES, ORME, AND BROWN, | LONDON. | [*dash*] | 1818.

Published 30 December 1817 in Edinburgh (*EWJ* 24 December, 'on Tuesday the 30th'); issued 13 January 1818 in London (*MC*). £1.4.0. 10,000 copies (a count presumably including the 'second' and 'third editions'). The *MC* 13 January notice is by William Sams (an enterprising bookseller at 62, Pall-Mall), the official Longman advertisement not appearing until 24 January. Binding: blue-grey boards with printed labels. Paper: Royal 12° (190 x 111mm uncut). Watermarks: 1814 | 3; 1816 | 2 [3, 4, 5]; 1817 | *none* or 1; M 1817 | 5. Typography: Printer's imprints: [*short rule*] | EDINBURGH: | Printed by James Ballantyne & Co.

Presentation copies: E('given me by the author while secret' [Lady Louisa Stuart]). Other copies: BCL(3) E(3) E('To Dr [Daniel] Rutherford from his Affct sister Ann Scott' [Sir Walter Scott's mother]) L(2) O(8); CtY(2) IdU InU(2) MH* MH NN PPL T/B ViU. Mixed or sophisticated copies: LU(Sterling: text for volumes 1,3 corresponding to the 'Third Edition').
*With 'Popular Novels' catalogue from Longman, Hurst, Rees, Orme, and Brown, dated December 1817.

References: Church 534; Sterling 726; Thomson, page 58; Van Antwerp(1) 6; Worthington 5. (Magnum Opus Edition 1829-1830: *Waverley Novels*, vii-viii.)

1] **ROB ROY.** . . . VOL. I. . . . 1818.

Collation: π^2 $2\pi^2$ A-N^{12} O^6. Pagination: *i* half-title, *ii blank*, *iii* title-page, *iv blank*, *v* vi-viii Advertisement, *1* fly-title, *2 blank*, *3* 4-321 text, 321 printer's imprint, *322-324 blank*. Typography: Signature H2 (page 177) is missigned 2H. In some copies page numbers 25 and/or 248 are misnumbered 52 and 842, and at foot of page 321 the colon may be lacking after EDINBURGH in the printer's imprint.

Figures: A16-9 22-1, B37-6 46-1, C59-9 60-8, D79-10 96-3, E119-8 120-10, F135-11 136-6, G159-1 160-9, H184-6 190-11, I 203-8 208-10, K219-4 220-5, L242-3 261-1, M276-11 286-6, N291-4 312-8, O 318-10. Both in this and in the second and third 'editions' page 60 figure 8 may be under either the 'e' of 'accidental', or the second 'e' of 'every': a clear sign of successive printings mixed in a common setting.

Notes: The Advertisement is in a duplicate setting, page *v* with reversed Oxford rule (22mm) or in regular order (12mm). Both of these textually invariant settings also reappear in the later 'editions'. Shortly after her introduction, Diana Vernon, the heroine, is wrongly identified as 'Miss Osbaldistone' (page 99, line 6), an error also persisting in the later 'editions'.

2] **ROB ROY.** . . . VOL. II. . . . 1818.

Collation: π^2 A-N^{12} O^6. Pagination: *i* half-title, *ii blank*, *iii* title-page, *iv blank*, *1* fly-title, *2 blank*, *3* 4-324 text, 324 printer's imprint. Typography: Page 193, last line of text begins either with quotation marks correctly placed, or with these inverted—both states recurring in later 'editions'. In a few copies the colon is lacking after EDINBURGH in the printer's imprint.

Figures: A10-6 24-10, B36-9 46-3, C67-5 72-10/-, D84-10 87-3, E103-1 112-6, F130-9 133-8, G157-1 167-8, H170-6 184-4, I 194-11 213-10, K227-5 237-9, L248-3 250-4, M285-8 287-1, N302-9 304-10, O 320-11.

3] **ROB ROY.** . . . VOL. III. . . . 1818.

Collation: π^2 A-O^{12} P^6. Pagination: *i* half-title, *ii blank*, *iii* title-page, *iv blank*, *1* fly-title, *2 blank*, *3* 4-348 text, 348 printer's imprint. Typography: In some copies section signatures F2 and P2 (pages 129 and 341) are transposed as 2F and 2P and page 343 lacks the page number. The same variations occur in the 'Second Edition'.

Figures: A4-9 11-4, B26-5 37-3, C59-10 72-5, D82-4 93-11, E114-8 117-1, F142-9 144-5, G159-3 165-10, H180-4/- 182-11, I 213-9 215-6, K230-5 237-8, L244-1 263-4, M266-11 277-10, N303-3 304-4/-, O 333-9 335-5, P338-6.

Notes: A CtY copy of this volume occasionally marked 'Proof sheet' (title-page and at the beginnning of gatherings L-P), and lacking the last six press figures, contains a number of earlier readings, for example, 95.25 preserver] prisoner, 266.22 upsetting man] upsetting, serving-man, 272.9 apprehension] arrest.

112Ab] Second Edition (First Edition, Second Issue): 1818

ROB ROY. . . . VOL. I [II-III]. | SECOND EDITION. . . . 1818.

Published 7 January 1818 in Edinburgh (*EWJ*). £1.4.0. Binding: Blue-green cloth with printed labels.

General Notes: Essentially, as noted below, this 'second edition' constitutes an overrun of first edition sheets.

Copies: (volumes 1 and 3 state 1) E; CtY. (volumes 1 and 3 state 2) E L; T/B. Mixed copy: BCL(vol 1 state 2; in all three vols, Mary Curteis ms date 29 January 1818, but volume 3 is 'third edition').

1] **ROB ROY.** . . . VOL. I. | SECOND EDITION. . . . 1818.

Figures: (1) A16-9 22-1 &c. as in first edition; (2) A4-11 22-1.

Notes: This is another printer's deception, reading 'Second Edition' on title, and existing in two states: (1) remainder of first edition sheets, page 10 line 3 first word: 'the'; (2) still a remainder except for first sheet A now reset, page 10 line 3 first word: 'gales'.

2] **ROB ROY.** . . . VOL. II. | SECOND EDITION. . . . 1818.

Figures: Throughout as in first edition. Notes: This volume is entirely of the same impression as before and thus still exhibits either variant of quotation marks on page 193.

3] **ROB ROY.** . . . VOL. III. | SECOND EDITION. . . . 1818.

Figures: As in first edition except (1) D82— 93-5 . . . F142— 144-9 . . . L244-11 263-4/-. In the second state (2) three more sheets are variant: C61-10 62-5, K230-1 237-9, O 333-8 335-5.

Notes: Except for the sheets with variant figures, indicating resettings or reimpressions, this volume also is of the same impression as the first edition.

112Ac] Third Edition (First Edition, Third issue): 1818

ROB ROY. . . . VOL. I [II-III] | THIRD EDITION. . . . 1818.

Published 10 January 1818 in Edinburgh (*EEC*), three days after the 'second edition'; issued 26 June in London (*MC*). £1.4.0.

General Notes: Except as noted below this 'third edition' represents a further overrun of previous printings.

Copies: (volume 3, state 1) InU T/B. (2) BCL E(2) L O(2); CtY InU.

1] **ROB ROY.** . . . VOL. I. | THIRD EDITION. . . . 1818.

Notes: The first A sheet is of the same impression as the 'second edition' state 2, with press figures 4-11 22-1.

2] **ROB ROY.** . . . VOL. II. | THIRD EDITION. . . . 1818.

Figures: As in the first edition except B46-3/-.

3] **ROB ROY.** . . . VOL. III. | THIRD EDITION. . . . 1818.

Figures: A4-9 11-4, B26-5 37-3/11, C59-10 72-5, D93-5, E114-1/8 117-1, F144-9, G159-3 165-10, H180-4/- 182-11, I 213-9 215-6, K230-1 237-9, L244-11, M266-11 277-10, N303-3 304-4, O 333-8/9 335-5, P338-6.

Notes: Essentially in its first issue (1) four sheets (A-C, E) are further overruns of the first edition, four others (D, K-L, O) overrun from the 'second edition', the remainder finally of a new setting. Eventually, however, (2) another overrun sheet from the second edition is used (C61-10 62-5) and, in some copies, a further sheet reset (E100-1). In this further E resetting a variant reading occurs at page 97 line 23, previously 'imminent', now 'eminent'.

112Ad] Fourth Edition: 1818

ROB ROY. | BY THE | AUTHOR OF "WAVERLEY," "GUY MANNERING," AND | "THE ANTIQUARY." | [*short Oxford rule*] | [*four-line quotation from Wordsworth*] | [*short reversed Oxford rule*] | IN THREE VOLUMES. | VOL. I [II-III]. | FOURTH EDITION. | EDINBURGH: | *Printed by James Ballantyne and Co.* | FOR ARCHIBALD CONSTABLE AND CO. EDINBURGH; AND | LONGMAN, HURST, REES, ORME, AND BROWN, | LONDON. | [*dash*] | 1818.

Published 31 January 1818 in Edinburgh (*EEC*), three weeks after the 'third edition'; issued 24 November in London (*MC*). 3000 copies ('within a fortnight a 'second impression' (Lockhart, v.269). £1.4.0. Binding: blue boards with printed labels. Paper: Royal 12° (190 x 111mm uncut). Watermarks: 1818 | 1 but usually *none*. Typography: Printer's imprints read invariably: [*short rule*] | EDINBURGH: | Printed by James Ballantyne & Co.

General Notes: This is the first 'edition' to be reset throughout, now with slight alterations. For example in volume 1, page *v* line 15 changes from 'in the' to 'in', page 317 line 14 from 'confess' to 'to confess'.

Copies: BCL E; CtY TxU.

1] **ROB ROY.** . . . VOL. I. | FOURTH EDITION. . . . 1818.

Collation: π² 2π² A-N¹² O⁶(-O6). Pagination: *i* half-title, *ii blank*, *iii* title-page, *iv blank*, *v* vi-viii Advertisement, *1* fly-title, *2 blank*, *3* 4-321 text, 321 printer's imprint, *322 blank*. Typography: Page number 25 is transposed as 52.

Figures: A12-4 14-6, B34-10 37-8, C69-9 71-2, D84-10 95-6, E107-10 108-2, F133-8 143-9, G159-8 160-6, H178-6 189-4, I 206-9 213-8, K228-2 231-8, L251-9 253-5, M274-6 288-9, N290-10 309-8, O 316-6.

2] **ROB BOY.** . . . VOL. II. | FOURTH EDITION. . . . 1818.

Collation: π² A-N¹² O⁶. Pagination: *i* half-title, *ii blank*, *iii* title-page, *iv blank*, *1* fly-title, *2 blank*, *3* 4-324 text, 324 printer's imprint.

Figures: A4-5 23-2, B34-8 40-10, C58(or 66)-8 60-9, D82-6 96-5, E110-5 117-9, F132-2 143-10, G157-2 159-8, H189-9 191-10, I 196-4 214-1, K231-9 240-2, L255-10 256-9, M274-5 276-6, N302-4 312-1, O 320-5.

3] **ROB ROY.** . . . VOL. III. | FOURTH EDITION. . . . 1818.

Collation: π² A-O¹² P⁶. Pagination: *i* half-title, *ii blank*, *iii* title-page, *iv blank*, *1* fly-title, *2 blank*, *3* 4-348 text, 348 printer's imprint.

Figures: A15-9 24-2, B37-8 38-5, C51-2 72-6, D87-8 88-10, E109-10 118-9, F122-1 133-8, G167-2 168-8, H171-5 192-10, I 207-10, K226-5 232-2, L262-2, M267-9 277-10, N301-1 311-8, O 334-8 336-10, P338-5.

REPRINTS

FRANCE

PARIS: Baudry, Barrois [and others]
[~] Rob Roy. 1831. (Collection of Ancient and Modern British Novels and Romances: *see* 288R.10)

PARIS: Didot and Galignani
[~] Rob Roy. M DCCC XXI. (Collection of Modern English Authors: *see* 291R18-20)

GERMANY

112Ra] BERLIN: Schlesinger 1822
[Rob Roy . . . Berlin: Schlesinger, 1822.] Copy: not seen. Reference: GDS 132, page 346.

LEIPZIG: Wigand

[~] Rob Roy. 1831. (A Complete Edition of the Waverley Novels: *see* 300R.10-12)

ZWICKAU: Schumann
[~] Rob Roy. 1822. (Pocket Library of English Classics: *see* 302R.40-43)

HUNGARY

PEST, LEIPSIC and LONDON: Wigand
[~] Rob Roy. 1831. (A Complete Edition of the Waverley Novels: *see* 300R.10-12)

UNITED STATES

112Rb] BOSTON: Parker 1821-1832
[Rob Roy. A Romance, By the Author of "Waverley," etc. . . . Boston: Samuel H. Parker, No. 12, Cornhill. 1821. Pages: *i-iii* iv, *5* 6-352.] Copy: not seen. (Also reissued 1822 in Novels Tales and Romances: *see* 305R.4.)

[~] Rob Roy. 1827, 1828. (Waverley Novels: *see* 306R.7-8.)

[~] Rob Roy. 1830, 1832. (Waverley Novels, Parker's Edition Revised: *see* 307R.7-8.)

112Rc] HARTFORD: Goodrich, Huntington and Hopkins 1821
Rob Roy. By the Author of Waverley, Guy Mannering, and The Antiquary. . . . Hartford: Samuel G. Goodrich, and Huntington and Hopkins, 1821. Pages: *1-5* 6-260. Copy: PU.

112Rd] NEW YORK: Duyckinck [and others] 1821
[Rob Roy. New York, pub. by E. Duyckinck, William B. Gilley, L. and F. Lockwood, and E. Bliss, J. & J. Harper, printers, 1821.] Copy: not seen.

112Re] NEW YORK: Eastburn 1818
[1] Rob Roy. By the Author of Waverley, Guy Mannering, and The Antiquary. . . . New-York: Published by James Eastburn and Co. Literary Rooms, Broadway. 1818. Two volumes. Pages 1: *i-v* vi-vii *viii*, *9-11* 12-255; 2: *1-5* 6-252. Notes: Volume 1 page 255 due to careless pagination throughout in some copies is numbered 245. Imprint second state reads '& Co.' in both volumes. A later variant of this state, volume 2 only, continues: At the Literary Rooms, Broadway, Corner of Pine-Street. Clayton & Kingsland, Printers. 1818. Copies: E L; MH MWA NjP NNU-W.

[2] Rob Roy. By the Author of Waverley, Guy Mannering and The Antiquary. . . . New-York: Published by James Eastburn & Co. Literary Rooms, Broadway. G. Long, Printer. 1818. Two volumes. Pages 1: *i-v* vi-vii *viii*, *9-11* 12-252; 2: *1-5* 6-252. Notes: The second volume apparently is a variant issue of the previous entry. Copy: CtY.

112Rf] NEW YORK: Kirk and Mercein 1818
Rob Roy. By the Author of Waverly[!], Guy Mannering, and The Antiquary. . . New-York: Published by Kirk and Mercein. 22, Wall-street. E. & E. Hosford, Printers, Albany. 1818.

Two volumes. Pages 1: *i-v* vi, *7-9* 10-252; 2: *i-v*, 6-252. Notes: In some copies punctuation varies in imprint. Copies: CtY MH.

112Rg] PHILADELPHIA: Crissy 1824
Rob Roy. By the Author of "Waverley," "Guy Mannering," &c. . . . Philadelphia: J. Crissy, No. 177, Chestnut Street. 1824. Two volumes. Pages 1: *i-iii* iv, *5* 6-246; 2: *1-3* 4-246. Copies: E(2); IdU NN PPL T/B(vol.2).

112Rh] PHILADELPHIA: Hickman & Hazzard 1821
Rob Roy. By the Author of "Waverley," "Guy Mannering," and "The Antiquary." . . . Philadelphia: Published by Hickman & Hazzard, No. 121, Chesnut Street. William Brown, Printer. 1821. Two volumes. Pages 1: *1-3* 4-250; 2: *1-3* 4-244. Copies: PPL T/B(vol.1).

112Ri] PHILADELPHIA: Thomas 1818
[1] Rob Roy. By the Author of "Waverley," "Guy Mannering," and "The Antiquary." . . . Philadelphia: Published by M. Thomas, No. 52, Chesnut Street; J. Maxwell, Printer. 1818. Two volumes. Pages 1: *i-iii* iv-v *vi, 1-3* 4-297; 2: *i-ii, 1-3* 4-294. Copies: E; DLC(vol.1) MWA.

[2] Rob Roy. By the Author of "Waverley," "Guy Mannering," and "The Antiquary." . . . Second Philadelphia Edition. Philadelphia: Published by M. Thomas, No. 52, Chesnut Street. 1818. Two volumes. Pages 1: *i-iii* iv, *5* 6-324; 2: not seen. Copy: CtY(vol.1).

112Rj] PHILADELPHIA: Thomas and Kirk and Mercein 1818
Rob Roy. By the Author of "Waverley," "Guy Mannering," and "The Antiquary." . . . Philadelphia: Published by M. Thomas, No. 52, Chesnut Street; and by Kirk and Mercein, New-York. 1818. Two volumes. Pages 1: *i-iii* iv-v *vi, 1-3* 4-297 *298, 1*-2; 2: *i-ii, 1-3* 4-294. Notes: A variant issue of 112Ri[1] with an extended imprint and, in volume 1, a two-page advertisement for *The Analectic Magazine*. In some copies, in one or both volumes, a leaf is inserted which reads: 'The publishers of this edition have printed one on an inferior paper, but same type, at 175 cents.' Copies: InU MWA PPL.

DERIVATIVES

GREAT BRITAIN

112Da] ALNWICK: Davison 1820
Rob Roy, A Tale. From the Author of "Waverley."... Alnwick: Published by W. Davison. Price Twopence. [1820]. Pages: *1-5* 6-31. Notes: Chapbook with woodcut frontispiece and title-page vignette, as well as woodcuts throughout text. Copy: L.

112Db] BIRMINGHAM: Beilby & Knotts [and others] 1822
Rob Roy, The Celebrated Highland Freebooter; or, Memoirs of The Osbaldistone Family. London: Printed for Beilby & Knotts, Birmingham; J. & C. Evans, London; Henry Mozley, Derby; and Oliver & Boyd, Edinburgh. [1822]. Pages: *1-5* 6-36. Notes: Chapbook with hand-coloured woodcut frontispiece and title-page vignette, both included in pagination. Copy: E.

112Dc] EDINBURGH: [no publisher identified] 1822
Rob Roy; A National Drama, Founded on the Celebrated Novel of the Same Name, by The Author of "Waverley,". . . . [1822]. Pages: *1-5* 6-68. Notes: Drama by Isaac Pocock. Frontispiece of 'Mr. Mackay of the Theatre Royal Edinburgh, as Bailie Nicol Jarvie.' Page *4* lists 'Dramatis Personae. As Performed before His Majesty, Tuesday, August 27, 1822.' This is one of the copies printed without imprint for use in the theatre. The grand occasion, unremarked by Scott, is fully represented by his biographer. Copy: MH. References: Bolton 1475; Lockhart, vii.65-67.

EDINBURGH: Hay
[~] The Trials of James, Duncan, and Robert M'Gregor . . . 1818. (*See* 112Dg)

112Dd] EDINBURGH: Huie 1822
Rob Roy; A National Drama, Founded on the Celebrated Novel of the Same Name, by The Author of "Waverley," &c. &c. . . [no imprint. Edinburgh: Printed for James L. Huie, 14 Infirmary Street. 1822]. Pages: [*i-ii*], *1-5* 6-68. Notes: Drama by Isaac Pocock (music by John Davy not included) as performed at the Theatre-Royal, Edinburgh, in 1819 and before His Majesty, 27 August 1822. This text is the version which saved the Theatre Royal from bankruptcy. With engraved portrait frontispiece 'Mr. Mackay, of the Theatre Royal Edinburgh, as Bailie Nicol Jarvie.' Copies: E: CtY(2) InU NN. (A variant issued in: Dramas from Novels, Tales, and Romances, 1822: *see* 323D.1.) References: Bolton 1475; Lockhart, vii.65-67.

112De] GLASGOW: Hutchison 1823
Rob Roy Macgregor, . . . Glasgow: Published and Sold, Wholesale and Retail, by R. Hutchison, Bookseller, 19. Salt-market. 1823. Pages: *1-2* 3-8. Notes: A ballad in three octaves followed by four other songs. Copies: L(2).

112Df] LEITH: Burnet 1828
Rob Roy; A National Drama, . . . Leith: Printed by James Burnet, and Sold by the Booksellers. 1828. Pages: *i-iv*, *1* 2-90[?]. Notes: Drama by Daniel Terry with Dramatis Personae as performed before His Majesty at the Theatre-Royal, Edinburgh, 27 August 1822. Crude woodcut frontispiece titled 'Mr. Mackay'. Copy: RPB[incomplete].

112Dg] LONDON: Baldwin, Cradock, and Joy 1818
The Trials of James, Duncan, and Robert M'Gregor, Three Sons of the Celebrated Rob Roy, . . . To which is prefixed a Memoir relating to the Highlands with Anecdotes of Rob Roy. Edinburgh: Printed by J. Hay and Co. And sold by Baldwin Cradock, and Joy, Paternoster-Row London; and J. Taylor Smith and Co. Hunter Square, Edinburgh. 1818. Pages: *1-2*, *i* ii-cxxix *cxxx*, *1* 2-244. Copy: InU.

112Dh] LONDON: The Company of Booksellers 1822
The Life and Atchievements of Rob Roy Macgregor, The Celebrated Scotch Free-booter! . . . London: Printed for The Company of Booksellers. [1822]. Pages: *1-2*, *7* 8-40. Notes: Chapbook with coloured woodcut frontispiece. At head of title: Fifth Edition. Headlines throughout read 'Memoirs of Rob Roy'. Copy: E.

LONDON: Cumberland
[~] Rob Roy; A Romantic Drama. [1831]. (Cumberland's British Theatre: *see* 329D. 285.)

LONDON: Hodgson
[~] Rob Roy MacGregor; or, Auld Lang Syne. [1822]. (Hodgson's Juvenile Drama: *see* 333D.5)

112Di] LONDON: Hodsoll 1818
Rob Roy Macgregor Musical Drama, . . . London Printed & sold by W. Hodsoll at his Music Warehouse 45 High Holborn. [watermarked 1815. ca.1818]. Pages: *i-ii*, 1-57. Notes: Engraved sheet music with plate-mark: 'Rob Roy'. Words by Isaac Pocock. Music composed by John Davy and compiled from old Scottish Airs, with twelve separate songs, each with its own title-page or caption title, price, and imprint, as for separate sale, but with single pagination. Price: 10s/6d. Copy: E. Reference: G/T 10729.

112Dj] LONDON: McLean 1826
Mr. Liston in the Character of Baillie Nicol Jarvie in Rob Roy. "My Conscience." London. Published by Thos. McLean, 26, Haymarket. 1826. Illustration: Engraving on cartonnage (plate measure 302 x 201mm). Copy: E.

112Dk] LONDON: Miller 1818
Rob Roy Macgregor; or, Auld Lang Syne! A Musical Drama, in Three Acts. Founded on the Popular Novel of Rob Roy. . . . London: Printed for John Miller, 25, Bow-Street, Covent-Garden; Sold also by W. Sams, 62, Pall-Mall. Printed by B. M'Millan, Bow-Street, Covent-Garden. 1818. [Price Three Shillings.] Pages: *i-vi*, *1* 2-80. Notes: Words by Isaac Pocock (music by John Davy not included) as first performed at the Theatre-Royal, Covent-Garden, 12 March 1818. A revised version of Pocock's drama, later performed at the Edinburgh Theatre Royal 15 February 1819, has been described as 'the most meritorious and successful of all the dramas', appearing in Edinburgh for forty-one consecutive nights, especially performed there at the request of George IV on 27 August 1822, and eventually played 285 times by 14 March 1837. (Lockhart, vi.28-30; Ford T4). (Possibly there was another play first performed at Edinburgh on 17 January 1818: *see* Bolton 1448.) Copies: BCL C L; InU(2) NjP PU. References: Bolton 1450; Ford T3. Reissued as 'Second Edition' (L).

112Dl] LONDON: The Proprietors 1820-1826
[1] Rob Roy Macgregor; or, Auld Lang Syne! A Musical Drama, in Three Acts. . . . Third Edition. London. Published for the Proprietors, by W. Simpkin, and R. Marshall, Stationers' Court, Ludgate-Street; and C. Chapple, 66, Pall-Mall. 1820. Pages: *i-iv*, *1* 2-69. Notes: Drama by Isaac Pocock, first performed at the Theatre-Royal, Covent-Garden, Thursday, 12 March 1818. Title-page reads, 'Founded on the Popular Novel of Rob Roy.' Copy: DT.

[2] Rob Roy Macgregor; or, Auld Lang Syne. An Opera: . . . London. Published for the Proprietors, by W. Simpkin, and R. Marshall, Stationers' Court, Ludgate Street; and C. Chapple, 59, Pall-Mall. 1820. Pages: *1-2*, *i* ii-iii *iv-vi*, *1* 2-69. Notes: Adapted by Isaac Pocock (music by John Davy not included) with engraved frontispiece portrait. At head of title: Oxberry's Edition. With concluding graphic of the position of characters when the curtain falls. (Also issued with collective title: The New English Drama, 1820, 1821, 1822,

1826. *see* 340D.1A,B,C.) Copies: E E(no illustration; prompt copy); CtY(frontispiece) PBL(no illustration). Reissued 1821(MB[frontispiece]).

112Dm] LONDON: White 1818

Rob Roy, the Gregarach. A Romantick Drama, in Three Acts: . . . London: Published by Richard White. (At the Office for the Sale of the Acting Drama.) 11, Brydges-Street, opposite the Theatre; Sherwood, Neely and Jones, Paternoster Row, and T. Earle, Library, Albemarle Street, Piccadilly. 1818. Pages: *i-vi* vii-xii, *1* 2-84. Notes: Drama which borrows in part from *Rob Roy* with libretto by George Soane (music not included), as performed at the Theatre Royal, Drury Lane, 25 March 1818. Copies: E; CtY(2) MH(prompt copy). Reference: Ford appendix 16.

112Dn] STIRLING: Macnie 1818

The Life and Exploits of Rob Roy M'Gregor, The Highland Freebooter. . . . Stirling: Printed by William Macnie, And Sold Wholesale and Retail [1818]. Pages: *1-3* 4-24. Notes: Chapbook. No mention of Scott or the play. Copy: L.

UNITED STATES

112Do] BOSTON: Wells & Lilly 1823

Rob Roy Macgregor; or, Auld Lang Syne. An Opera: . . . Boston: Published by Wells & Lilly—Court-Street: A. T. Goodrich & Co.—New-York. 1823. Pages: *1-3* 4-96. Notes: Words by Isaac Pocock (music by John Davy not included). With prefatory remarks and other directions by W. Oxberry. At head of title: Oxberry's Edition. Price: Three Shillings. Copies: CtY NN.

112Dp] NEW YORK: Longworth 1818

Rob Roy MacGregor; or, Auld Lang Syne! A Musical Drama, in Three Acts. Founded on the Popular Novel of Rob Roy. . . . New-York: Published by D. Longworth, At the Dramatic Repository, Shakspeare-Gallery. June.—1818. Pages: *1-3* 4-66 *67-68*. Notes: Libretto by Isaac Pocock (music composed by John Davy not included). As performed at the Covent Garden and New-York theatres. This edition is from the London edition of 1818 (112Dk). Dramatis personae are lsted for both Covent Garden and New York. Copies: L; MWA NN.

112Dq] PHILADELPHIA: Carey 1818

Memoir relating to the Highlands; With Anecdotes of Rob Roy, and His Family. Philadelphia: Published by M. Carey and Son. John Bioren, Printer. 1818. Pages: *1-3* 4-152. Notes: This compilation, though avoiding any direct reference to Scott's novel, obviously was prepared as a result. Copy: IdU.

112Dr] PHILADELPHIA: Dobson 1818

[Rob Roy Macgregor; . . . Philadelphia, Dobson, 1818. Pages: 1-76. Notes: Words by Isaac Pocock.] Copy reported at MH but not located.

EXTRACTS IN ANTHOLOGIES

112E] From *Rob Roy* there are only three extracts in the anthologies: 360E.27 366[1]. 4,5

LETTERS ON THE HISTORY OF SCOTLAND

113A] Projected Scott Edition: 1817

Notes: Though Lockhart doubted that Scott 'ever wrote any part' of a history, at least this early and under this title, it appears that he had first proposed such a work in 1814 and two years later was ready to have it advertised as 'Letters on the History of Scotland addressed to a family of young persons'. Shortly after Scott's last written comment on the subject, the *Monthly Magazine* 1 December 1816 had a further report:

Mr. Walter Scott, whose literary productions in verse fill eleven large volumes (over and above his ill-omened Waterloo), and whose original or annotated prose works exceed fifty volumes, surprises his friends by announcing a new History of Scotland, from the earliest records to the year 1745, in three volumes octavo. While Mr. Scott writes so well as he has often written, and while he does not lend his powerful talents to flatter *the mischievous prejudices of weak princes*, we think his works cannot be too extensive or various. (page 441)

The italicized remark, alluding to Scott's increasing familiarity with the Prince Regent, comes not unexpectedly in a Whiggish periodical; but the specific occasion for it is obscure. On 1 September 1817 this same journal reported that the History was 'rapidly advancing at press' (page 166), but nothing further is related.

References: *Letters*, iii.504, iv.69, 277-278; Lockhart, v.164.

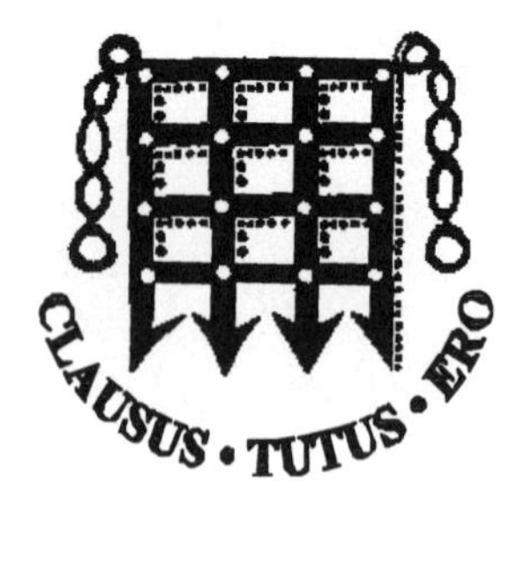
CLAUSUS · TUTUS · ERO

FOUR

1818-1825

The year 1818 marks the inception of a more expeditious scheme for issuing Scott in America, where this author, all unprotected by any copyright, was in ever-increasing demand. For some time Archibald Constable, his Edinburgh publisher, had been unloading out-of-date or otherwise unsalable books through the firm of Robinson & Co., wholesalers in Leeds with useful American connections, and as a further inducement to these intermediaries now offered to provide as well early proofs or sheets of works at press, chief among them the popular novels of the Author of Waverley. Though it has recently been determined that the first of these to be dispatched was *Rob Roy*, on 19 December 1817,[1] the full extent of this clandestine activity still eludes discovery. In general it appears that, from the beginning, the advance book-sheets, usually in uncorrected state, for security reasons were sealed for shipment, then forwarded successively in at least two packets, the first so that the American publisher could get a 'head start' over his competitors, the second as this later text was printed. For some years the Robinson agent in Philadelphia was one Thomas Wardle, who supplied the first two Scott novels to persons still unidentified,[2] then a third work to Moses Thomas, a bookseller whose advertisement frankly admits a partial issue based only upon the earlier shipment (135Ri).

Starting in 1819 with *Ivanhoe*, the fourth novel, Wardle entered into a more enduring agreement with Mathew Carey & Son, and later declared that all copy for that firm, through *Peveril of the Peak* (1822), was still derived from his original supplier, then designated as Hurst, Robinson & Co. of London. When after some enquiry Constable, in Edinburgh, was apprised of this roundabout scheme, he appears to have concluded his own direct arrangement with Carey, thus eliminating two intermediaries.[3] Meanwhile in Philadelphia, as indicated in one or another communication, the Carey firm began to post around the country its own first volume of each novel in order to forestall any competition, and then print off the subsequent volume(s) as the later text became available: a practice which, to his great annoyance, caused him initially to omit Scott's afterthoughts as conveyed, still later, for at least four works.[4]

After publishing several of Scott's novels, it then occurred to Carey that he might get advance publicity by issuing extracts from proofs just off his own press, and for this purpose allowed the Philadelphia *National Gazette and Literary Register* to print two sections of *Kenilworth* in its issues for 3 and 9 March 1821 (149Aa, Rg). Thus begins an uninterrupted sequence of quotations, with some 10,400 words cited for this book and, as detailed in the relevant entries, about 103,500 quoted altogether for the thirteen novels issued in the period 1821-1831.[5] The extracts for three of these appeared one or two weeks before publication of the novel in Edinburgh (157Aa, 167Aa, 227A), yet another a month before (171Aa), and still another five months before (253A), with this last extract in turn twice reprinted in London before the Edinburgh issue! The whole performance, it will be agreed, is unparalleled in bibliographical history, of immeasurable consequence in any textual evaluation, and certainly quite beyond previous assessments of the early Philadelphia printings.[6]

In this same period it is also apparent that the issue of Scott's works elsewhere abroad was quickening apace, all exempt from the jurisdiction of the author, his publishers, or copyright law. Hitherto these publications were sporadic, as local demand might require. Now in 1819 the Brothers Schumann in Zwickau incorporated the author in their 'Pocket Library of the English Classics', beginning with *The Lay of the Last Minstrel* (302R.7-8) and continuing for a total of 156 Scott volumes: a record number in any language. A year later Didot and Galignani in Paris started their series of 73 volumes with *The Abbot* (291R.31-33), an appropriate story for French readers. And again in 1820 Samuel Parker of Boston started with a few novels separately, but within two years began his series of 23 volumes (305R): all typographically superior to any previous American printing and, as occasionally with the others, several times completely reprinted. Though not fully cognizant of such rapid proliferations, Scott was somewhat aware of these foreign issues and, whenever a few appeared in Abbotsford, usually bestowed them upon his Irish and American visitors.

Along with multiplication of issue there are also, in increasing measure, an undetermined number of prints from reprints, these no longer directly related, textually, to the original publication. Some of the Carey and Schumann issues, as noted, appear to derive from Galignani, and anthologies as well as sheet-music often seem to be interdependent. Among American prints especially the perpetuation of a misprint obviously links certain of these related issues (*see* prefatory remarks in Appendix 2).

Beginning in 1819 there are also several significant developments in the illustration of Scott's work. First, in its August number, *The Lady's Magazine* (324D) began to embellish practically every issue with one or more rather crude plates relating to its extensive extracts, totaling some 41 special inserts over the next ten years. Then on 19 December the first collected British issue of Scott's fiction was published: a handsome royal octavo in twelve volumes titled *Novels and Tales* (269Aa) and now bearing, in addition to Constable and Longman, the imprint of Hurst, Robinson, all with lettering on engraved titles superseding the printed pages previously employed for separate publications. Both for this and for the corresponding ten-volume '1821' issue of *The Poetical Works* (263A, issued 2 December 1820) the title vignettes, probably arranged by Constable, were drawn by Alexander Nasmyth and engraved by W. H. Lizars. This same publisher also commissioned William Allan to draw a separate series of thirteen plates for the novels (*Letters*, v.350), all engraved by Lizars and others and eventually published on 11 December 1820 (322D).

Though the Nasmyth titles seem to have been printed in Edinburgh, the separate 1820 Allan suite apparently was impressed at the direction of Constable's agent in London, for the preliminary letterpress title bears the surname of James Moyes, the same printer who (together with Thomas Davison) was accountable for a number of issues with Hurst, Robinson only identified as publisher. Presumably with Constable's acquiescence, this firm had already published under its own imprint another set of illustrations, these for *Ivanhoe* on 19 February 1820 (140Dk), just two months after that novel had been issued, and then in rapid succession issued three other suites (*The Monastery* on 26 December [144De], *Kenilworth* on 8 January 1821 [149Dj] and *Guy Mannering* on 20 April 1821 [82Dg][7]) with *The Monastery* sequence displaying the first plate (here illustrated) to be 'Engraved on Steel': a technical advance of some consequence.[8] All of these four issues have after the solitary Hurst, Robinson imprint address the phrase '(late Boydell)', indicating that the London firm was, with these pictorial suites, also carrying on the business of the previous publisher, one that specialized in artistic prints. So designed, all of these suites, as separate entities, rarely appear with the relevant text, printed in Edinburgh, and thus may be regarded as somewhat removed from the Scott canon in the more restricted sense.

Even further removed, yet exemplifying even more effectively Scott's widening influence, are the splendid operas which, in this brief period, now make their appearance, notably first at Naples:

(1) 'La Donna del Lago' by Rossini in 1819 (Bolton 86), first performed in

THE MONASTERY, 1820: FIRST ENGRAVING ON STEEL
(Entry 144De.1. Todd / Bowden copy: plate enlarged to show detail)

London 1823 (106), and often printed there in 1823-1829 (47Dp[1,2], 47Dt);
(2) 'Il Castello di Kenilworth' by Donizetti in 1829 (3860); and then at Paris;
(3) 'La Dame Blanche' [from *Guy Mannering*] by Boieldieu in 1825 (552), first performed in London 1826 (575), the most successful opera in Scott's lifetime; and
(4) 'Ivanhoe' by Rossini in 1826 (3372), first performed in London 1829 (3384). Scott attended the original production of this operatic pastiche at the Odeon on 31 October 1826, but then as on other occasions large and small,[9] near or remote from his own work, was disinclined to admit any responsibility. Even so, by now his name was assigned to many printings on the continent, direct and indirect, and his elevation to a baronetcy in 1820 only enhanced his reputation and increased his sales.

In the few years remaining before Scott and his publishers were forced into bankruptcy the busy author continued to prosper, further expanding his estate at Abbotsford, selling at a good price eight novel copyrights to Constable, and thereafter through 1825 issuing nine more novels and tales. Bibliographically three of these works are unusual, *Ivanhoe* for the hurried impressions and increased issues of this first non-Scottish and highly successful novel (140Aa-Ac); *The Pirate* for the only occurrence of two 'first editions', necessitated here by another unexpected success (156Aa-Ab); and *Quentin Durward*, the first 'European' novel, here especially distinguished by two Parisian editions for different publishers, both issued the same year, in separate settings, from the same printing office (167Aa; 291R.43-45; 295R.1-3).

1. Much valuable information on the Constable-Robinson connection is provided by Jane Millgate, 'Archibald Constable and the Problem of London,' *The Library*, 6th series, 18 (1996), 110-123. Other accounts particularly relating to Wardle and Carey are given in David Kaser, 'Waverley in America,' *PBSA* 51 (1957), 163-167, and to the unrevised proofs used for the Carey editions in Randall's 1935 article. See also the Green reference in the Carey *Ivanhoe* entry (140Rg).

2. For the first two novels, *Rob Roy* and *Tales of My Landlord (Second Series)*, the Philadelphia booksellers might well have been Moses Thomas and Mathew Carey respectively (112Ri, 122Rf), both later involved in this enterprise.

3. It remains inexplicable why Constable in 1822 should enter a formal protest with the Edinburgh authorities about sheets being 'abstracted' from his printing office for transmittal to Philadelphia (Kaser, pages 163-164; Randall, page 41) when in 1819 he in effect demanded £50 for further shipments (Millgate, page 121, note 45). In any event, the new agreement is made clear in the Philadelphia *National Gazette and Literary Register*, 28 June 1823, where

Carey complains that he had 'paid Messrs. Constable & Co. a large sum' for *Quentin Durward* (cf. next note), only to discover that the copy was incomplete. In the confusion over piracies it should be recalled that, to deny the publishers any advance clue, this was the first novel to be printed without title headlines.

Since the *National Gazette*, a scarce tri-weekly journal, has not been consulted in previous investigations, we should note that we examined the relatively complete set at CtY for the period 1820-1832, then supplemented this with the earlier numbers 1820-1822 at PPL.

4. Apart from *Ivanhoe* where, because the shipping route was frozen up, Carey had to secure some copy from a New York bookseller (140Rg), the missing texts provided too late for this publisher include: an additional chapter in *The Pirate* (156Ri), the 'Introductory Epistle' in *The Fortunes of Nigel* (157Rg), the 'Conclusion' to *Quentin Durward* (167Rd) and, somewhat later, the 'Introduction' for *Chronicles of the Canongate* (206Re). With so much admitted, rather reluctantly, in communications to the *National Gazette*, it may be suspected that other deficiencies occur throughout.

5. In 1827 Carey also provided for his own journal 22 extracts from his edition of Scott's *Life of Napoleon Buonaparte* (200Aa) and on this occasion, following Constable's bankruptcy, agreed to pay the author directly. This publisher also received advance sheets for all except the last series of the *Tales of a Grandfather* (208Aa, 219Aa, 234A), but apparently none of this juvenalia was abstracted in the Philadelphia papers.

6. Of the sixteen novels now documented as printed in Philadelphia from advance proofs or sheets (three early by others, thirteen later by Carey) David Randall's 1935 analysis encompassed only nine, and then only of the text represented by cancels in the earlier Edinburgh edition. Nonetheless, as Corson has remarked ([1],entry 23), this is an important article on a matter hitherto unexplored.

7. Six additional Hurst, Robinson series dated 1823-1825 are described as entries 146Dd, 156Dk, and 334D.1-4.

8. The 1820 steel engraving, by Charles Heath, anticipates by more than a year the one illustrated in Hunnisett and dated September 1822. Heath in 1823 also provided all the steel-engraved title vignettes for the 18° edition of *The Poetical Works* (266Aa). Basil Hunnisett, *Steel-engraved book illustration in England*, London: Scolar Press [1980], pages 30-31.

9. Two other famous operas, both first performed after Scott's death in 1835, are Bellini's 'I Puritani di Scozia' in Paris (distantly related to 'Old Mortality') and, most successful among all Scott derivatives, Donizetti's 'Lucia di Lammermoor' in Naples.

CONTENTS OF CHAPTER FOUR

THE BATTLE OF SEMPACH

114A] First Printing: 1818

'THE BATTLE OF SEMPACH' (first words: ''Twas when among our linden trees') pages 530-532, *in*:

Blackwood's Edinburgh Magazine. February 1818. No. XI. Vol. II [imprint:] Edinburgh: Printed for William Blackwood, No 17, Prince's Street, Edinburgh; and Baldwin, Cradock, and Joy, Paternoster Row, London. 1818.

Published 20 February 1818 in Edinburgh; issued 28 February in London. (notice in no. X).

Notes: This anonymous contribution of forty-one quatrains has a prefixed notice that it is a 'literal translation of an ancient Swiss ballad upon the Battle of Sempach, fought 9th July, 1386, being the victory by which the Swiss cantons established their independence; . . .' The author was recognized to be Albert Tchudi, a Swiss minstrel. Quite possibly, as on an earlier occasion (71Aa), Scott may have been first directed to this unusual subject (for him) by a long prose account of the battle in the *Monthly Magazine* (1 July 1802, pages 563-564), then later reminded of it in 1810 on reading some 'old Swiss ditties' (*Letters*, ii.399; Corson[2], page 65). Coincidentally, in the same issue of the *Monthly Magazine* (page 559), there is some remarkably spirited verse on the temporary cessation of hostilities with France (this upon ratification of the Treaty of Amiens) which was anonymously contributed from Edinburgh in April 1802. Scott might well have known the author of this martial poem, or perhaps have been himself responsible.

Copies: E L. Reference: (Magnum Opus Edition 1833: *The Poetical Works*, vi.332-342.)

CHIVALRY

115A] First Printing: 1818

['CHIVALRY.' Vol. III, Part 1, pages 115-140 141*-*144, *in*:

Supplement to the Fourth, Fifth, and Sixth Editions of the Encyclopaedia Britannica. With Preliminary Dissertations on the History of the Sciences. Illustrated by Engravings. Volume Third. Part I. Edinburgh: Printed for Archibald Constable and Company, Edinburgh; and Hurst, Robinson, and Company, London. 1818.]

Published 23 February 1818 in Edinburgh (*EEC*). £1.5.0.

Notes: The starred pagination occurs on a two-leaf insert; the following essay, printed earlier, begins on a page regularly numbered 145. This and two other essays by Scott in the *Encyclopaedia* (129A, 173A) are initialled at end '(N.N.)'.

Copies: (Original part issue) not seen; (reissue with 1824 volume title) E GM. Reference: (Magnum Opus Edition 1834: *The Miscellaneous Prose Works*, vi.*1-3* 4-126 as 'An Essay on Chivalry'.)

REPRINT

FRANCE

PARIS: Didot and Galignani
[~] Essays by Sir Walter Scott. 1828. (*see* 292R.8-9.) Also included are the two other *Encyclopaedia* essays titled 'Romance' and 'The Drama'.

EPILOGUE

116A] First Printing: 1818

'Epilogue, By a Friend of the Author' (first words: 'A cat of yore (or else old Aesop lied)') pages *53*-54, *in*:

The Appeal: A Tragedy, in Three Acts: . . . Edinburgh: Printed for Archibald Constable and Company; and Longman, Hurst, Rees, Orme, and Brown, London. 1818.

Published ca. February 1818 in Edinburgh.

Notes: Play by John Galt, first performed at the Theatre-Royal, Edinburgh, on 16 February 1818. Scott's contribution, performed by Mrs Henry Siddons, has thirty lines, with two footnotes. The nostalgic epilogue, 'addressed only to the Edinburgh audience', alludes regretfully to the construction of a new jail nearby on Calton Hill and the high towers now rising on North Bridge.

Copies: E O; InU. References: Thomson, page 65. (Magnum Opus Edition 1834: *The Poetical Works*, xi.367-368.)

REVIEW OF MARY SHELLEY

117A] First Printing: 1818

'REMARKS ON FRANKENSTEIN, OR THE MODERN PROMETHEUS; A NOVEL.', pages *613* 614-620, *in*:

Blackwood's Edinburgh Magazine. March 1818. No. XII. Vol. II [imprint:] Edinburgh: Printed for William Blackwood, No 17, Prince's Street, Edinburgh; and Baldwin, Cradock, and Joy, Paternoster Row, London. 1818.

Published 20 March 1818 in Edinburgh; issued 1 April in London. (notice in no. XI).

Notes: As a 'slight tribute of high admiration' for Scott, Percy B. Shelley had forwarded his wife's novel 2 January 1818 and, on receiving a copy of the review, Mary on 14 June wrote also to affirm that she was the author. According to James Ballantyne, Scott 'greatly preferred' this book even to his own romances.

Copies: E L O; NjP PPL.

References: *Letters*, v.109. (Magnum Opus Edition 1835: *The Miscellaneous Prose Works*, xviii.250-269.)

PHANTASMAGORIA

118A] First Printing: 1818

'*To the Veiled Conductor of Blackwood's Edinburgh Magazine.*', pages 211-215, *in*:

Blackwood's Edinburgh Magazine. May 1818. No XIV. VOL. III [imprint:] Edinburgh: William Blackwood, No 17, Prince's Street, Edinburgh; and Baldwin, Cradock, and Joy, Paternoster Row, London 1818.

Published ca. 20 May 1818 in Edinburgh; issued ca. 1 June in London (schedule according to previous notices).

Notes: The author, signing himself 'Simon Shadow', introduces as No. 1 of a series called 'Phantasmagoria', the tale of an apparition appearing to a woman in Argyleshire. Though the series was not continued, this journal several months later (August 1818, pages 589-596) carried a perceptive review, headed 'Phantasmagoriana', of several works on the same subject. In 1826 Scott's tale was extracted in an anthology (395E.2).

Copy: E. Reference: (Magnum Opus Edition: Not reprinted.)

POEMS in A SELECT COLLECTION

119A] First Printings: 1818

1] 'THE MAID OF ISLA, *(Imitated from the Gaelic.)* WRITTEN FOR THIS WORK *By WALTER SCOTT, Esq.*', (first words: 'O Maid of Isla, from yon cliff, / That looks on troubled wave and sky,'), pages 209[e m (engraved music)],

209[l p (letterpress)]. Notes: The air titled 'The Maid of Isla', by an unknown composer, has symphonies and accompaniments by Beethoven, as credited to him in 'Index to Airs'.

2] 'THE SUN UPON THE WEIRDLAW HILL. WRITTEN FOR THIS WORK *By WALTER SCOTT, Esq.'* (first words: 'The sun upon the Weirdlaw hill, / In Ettrick's vale, is sinking sweet;'), pages 215[l p], 215[e m]. Notes: The engraved page has the heading: 'Sun Set'. The air titled 'Sunset[!]', by an unknown composer, has symphonies and accompaniments by Beethoven, as credited to him in 'Index to Airs'.

3] 'FAREWELL TO THE MUSE. WRITTEN FOR THIS WORK *By WALTER SCOTT, Esq.*', (first words: 'Enchantress, farewell, who so oft has decoy'd me,'), page 217. Notes: Engraved page has heading 'Enchantress Farewell'. An 1822 publication of this poem is titled 'Kinloch', after the composer of the air, George Kinloch, Esq. of Kinloch. According to the 'Index to Airs', the symphonies and accompaniments were composed by Beethoven.

4] 'ON ETTRICK FOREST'S MOUNTAINS DUN. WRITTEN FOR THIS WORK *By WALTER SCOTT, Esq.'* (first words as title), page 227[l p]. Notes: This Scott poem is printed below the Burn's poem, 'Now Bank and Brae are clothed in Green', which the engraved page uses with the air titled 'I Canna come Ilka day to woo'. Notice is given that Scott's poem can be performed to the same air with symphonies and accompaniments by Haydn. All four first printings *in*:

[*engraved title*] A Select Collection of Original Scottish Airs with Introductory & Concluding Symphonies & Accompaniments for the Piano Forte, Violin & Violoncello by Haydn & Beethoven. With Select Verses adapted to the Airs, including upwards of one hundred new Songs by Burns, Together with his celebrated Poem of The Jolly Beggars Set to music by Henry R. Bishop. . . . Vol.5. Entd. at Stationers hall. London, Printed & Sold by Preston, 97, Strand. And by G. Thomson the Editor and Proprietor Edinburgh. [1818].

Published according to the 'Preface [To the Public]' which states that 'On the 1st June 1818, was published . . . the fifth volume'.

Notes: Sometimes bound with 'The Jolly Beggars', with music by Henry R. Bishop; pages *1-3* 4-30; imprint: George Thomson, Edinburgh, 1818. Scott lyrics in the subsequent Thomson publications recorded in Ruff as 81, 82, 83, are identified as reprints and thus entered here, respectively, as 405E(3), 405E(2)[1], and 371R.

Copies: BCL E(3) L L(Hirsch) O(2).

References: G/T 9809; [1] G/T 10435; [2] G/T 10867; Ruff 80. (Magnum Opus Edition 1834: *The Poetical Works*, [1] xi.338-339, [2] xi.336-337, [3] xi.345-346, [4] 334-335.)

EXTRACTS IN ANTHOLOGIES

119E] With one exception (423E.9) these four poems were extracted only in George Thomson's later 'Selections': [1] 405(2)[2]E.3 405(2)[3].12 405(3)[1].14; [2] 405(2)[2]E.4 405(2)[3].13; [3] 405(2)[2]E.5 405(2)[3].14 405(3)[1].18 423.9; [4] 405(2)[2]E.7 405-(2)[3].16 405(3)[1].16. Nonetheless, though the least even among these Thomson reprints, [2] 'The Sun upon the Weirdlaw Hill', was regarded by one of Scott's recent biographers as 'his best short poem' (Pearson, page 134).

REVIEWS OF DOUGLAS and KIRKTON

120A] First Printing: 1818

1] 'ART. VII. *An Essay on the Principles and Construction of Military Bridges, and the Passage of Rivers in Military Operations.* By Colonel Sir Howard Douglas, Bt. FRS.', pages 423-431;
2] 'ART. XIII. *The Secret and True History of the Church of Scotland,* . . . By The Rev. Mr. James Kirkton, &c. *With an Account of the Murder of Archbishop Sharp.* By James Russell. . . Edited from the MS. by Charles Kirkpatrick Sharpe.', pages 502- 541, *in*:

The Quarterly Review. January, 1818. [No. 36; volume 18 imprint:] London: John Murray, Albemarle Street. 1818.

Published 9 June 1818 in London (*EEC* 4 June, preliminary notice); 'just arrived' 11 June in Edinburgh (*EEC*).

Copies: BCL O; PPL.

References: Shine 460, 466. (Magnum Opus Edition 1835: *The Miscellaneous Prose Works*, [1] Not reprinted, but cited in *Letters*, v.109, [2] xix.213-282 as 'Kirkton's Church History'.)

BIOGRAPHICAL AND LITERARY MEMOIR OF WEBER

121A] First Printing: 1818

'BIOGRAPHICAL AND LITERARY MEMOIR OF HENRY WILLIAM WEBER, Esq. THE LITERARY PART By WALTER SCOTT, Esq.', *in*:

The Literary Journal and General Miscellany of Science, Arts, History, Politics. [London, July 1818].

Notes: After preliminary comment by 'M.D.F.', contributor of the 'biographical part' on Weber, dated 2 July 1818, Scott's extensive 'literary' tribute, dating from 'Edinburgh, 12th June, 1818' continues for fifteen paragraphs. The original manuscript of Scott's contribution only, at NNP, without place or date, is transcribed at length with commentary by Grierson (*Letters*, xii.290-292n), who was unaware of any subsequent publication.

As the only recorded copy of the journal (L) 'was destroyed by bombing in the war', the present description is taken primarily from a clipping in James Maidment's commonplace book, also at NNP, where title-pages and pagination have been cut away.

Copy: NNP(Maidment). Reference: (Magnum Opus Edition: Not reprinted.)

TALES OF MY LANDLORD
[Second Series]
THE HEART OF MID-LOTHIAN

The reader is now able to judge how far the author has improved upon, or fallen short of, the pleasing and interesting sketch of high principle and steady affection displayed by Helen Walker, the prototype of the fictitious Jeanie Deans. ('Introduction', 1 April 1830, *WN*, xi.147.)

122Aa] First Edition, First Issue: 1818

TALES OF MY LANDLORD, | Second Series, | COLLECTED AND ARRANGED | BY | JEDEDIAH CLEISHBOTHAM, | SCHOOLMASTER AND PARISH-CLERK OF GANDERCLEUGH. | [*short rule*] | [*six-line quotation from Burns*] | [*short rule*] | IN FOUR VOLUMES. | VOL. I [II-IV]. | [*short Oxford rule*] | EDINBURGH: | PRINTED FOR ARCHIBALD CONSTABLE AND COMPANY. | [*dash*] | 1818.

Published 25 July 1818 in Edinburgh (*EEC*); 'now ready for delivery' 28 July in London (*MC*). £1.12.0. 10,000 copies, total printing apparently of all three issues (E MS. 790, page 119). The first London publication notice was provided both by the 'Ebers Library' and again (as for *Rob Roy*) the bookseller William Sams, the official Longman listing appearing three days later. Binding: drab or blue boards with printed labels. Paper: Royal 12° (190 x 112mm uncut). Watermarks: 1817 1 [4,5]; M 1817 | 4 [5]; 1818; 1818 | 4 [6]; M 1818 | *none* [3, 5]. Typography: Printer's imprints read: (1) [*short rule*] | *Printed by James Ballantyne and Co*.; (2) [*short rule*] | EDINBURGH: | Printed by James Ballantyne & Co.

General Notes: To give Daniel Terry some advantage over his competitors, Scott on 18 May 1818 promised him the text of this Tale, 'The Heart of Mid-Lothian', as soon as it was in proof. The novel, originally intended for issue on the King's birthday 4 June, was finally shipped from Leith on the 'Caledonia' 17 July, the date of one of the inscribed copies. This work was extracted only in one anthology, 372[1]E.4

Presentation copy: (volume 1, state 1): E('The gift of Mr Walter Scott while secret 1818 [Lady] Louisa Stuart'). Other copies: (volume 1, state 1): BCL*b BCL E(2) E*b L O(4) O*a; CtY+*b InU*b InU*c MH NN NN*b# NNU-W NNU-W(vols.1-3) T/B*b. (state 2): BCL*b E E*b L O(4) O(with Finden plates) O*b##; CtY MH NN.
+Inserted after vol.1 page 314, 8 leaves of Scott's corrected proof with numerous alterations.
*With (a) 4-page Longman catalogue April 1818, (b) 12-page Constable catalogue June 1818, (c) both catalogues.
'With the Publishers[!], best Compliments Edinb 17 July 1818'.
'R. Gordon A present from the Publishers'.

References: *Letters*, v.149-150; Church 535; Sterling 727; Thomson, page 34; Tinker 1873; Van Antwerp(1) 7; Worthington 6. (Magnum Opus Edition 1830: *Waverley Novels*, xi.*139-141* 142-419; xii-xiii.*1-3* 4-234.)

1] **TALES OF MY LANDLORD,** | Second Series, . . . VOL. I. . . . 1818.

Collation: π^2 *A*^{12} B-O^{12}. Pagination: *i* half-title, *ii* advertisement and printer's imprint(1), *iii* title-page, *iv* quotation and (in some copies) printer's imprint(1), *1* 2-10 introduction signed 'J.C.', Gandercleuch, 1 April 1818, *11* fly-title, *12 blank*, *13* 14-333 text, 333 printer's imprint(2), *334-336 blank*. Typography: The 4-page preliminary gathering, with its intricate layout, was nonetheless set in duplicate, with half-title verso first rule starting under 'F' of 'OF' and title verso with printer's imprint, or with rule starting under 'M' of 'MID-' and title verso with or without imprint. Section signature A2 (page 9) is omitted.

Figures: A2-5 21-1, B34-10 48-2, C59-1 61-4, D93-8 95-4, E111-2 120-10, F131-4 144-8, G158-5 168-2, H171-10 172-9, I 204-6 215-4, K227-5 240-8, L242-10 261-6, M276-2 286-9, N304-4 310-5, O 323-8 328-4.

Notes: Page *1* is (1) without direction-line, (2) with added directions 'VOL. I.' and signature 'A'. The latter state is retained for the 'second' and 'third' editions. The advertisement is for *Criminal Trials, Illustrative of* . . . "The Heart of Mid-Lothian", a work once ascribed in part to Scott and here (*see* 123A), in the absence of any contrary evidence, again tentatively admitted to the canon.

2] **TALES OF MY LANDLORD,** | Second Series, . . . VOL. II. . . . 1818.

Collation: π^2 A-N^{12} O^6. Pagination: *i* half-title, *ii* quotation and printer's imprint(1), *iii* title-page, *iv blank*, *1* fly-title, *2 blank*, *3* 4-322 text, 322 printer's imprint(2), *323-*

324 blank. Typography: Page 52 first word of text reads 'WICHTCRAFT', a misprint persisting in the later 'editions'.

Figures: A21-2 23-5, B39-10 48-9, C63-6 69-9, D76-10 86-8, E119-5 120-2, F122-10 124-4, G148-8 158-2, H170-6 176-1, I 202-8 216-9, K237-2 238-5, L243-10 264-2, M281-4 286-1, N310-5 312-8, O319-6.

3] **TALES OF MY LANDLORD,** | Second Series, . . . VOL. III. . . . 1818.

Collation: π^2 A-N^{12} O^6 P^2. Pagination: *i* half-title, *ii* quotation and printer's imprint(1), *iii* title-page, *iv blank*, *1* fly-title, *2 blank*, *3* 4-328 text, 328 printer's imprint(2). Typography: Again the preliminary gathering is set in duplicate, with first rule on title starting over the 'nd' of 'Land' or over the following "o"'.

Figures: A21-3 22-9, B37-8 46-2, C60-5 70-10, D84-6 87-4, E110-3 117-2, F132-1/- 142-9, G166-4 168-9, H190-10 192-5, I 198-1 216-8, K236-5 239-6, L252-10 262-8, M280-2 287-3, N299-3 312-2, O 323-7, P327-8.

4] **TALES OF MY LANDLORD,** | Second Series, . . . VOL. IV. . . . 1818.

Collation: π^2 A-P^{12} Q^6 R^2. Pagination: *i* half-title, *ii* quotation and printer's imprint(1), *iii* title-page, *iv blank*, *1* fly-title, *2 blank*, *3* 4-375 text, 375 printer's imprint(2), *376 blank*. Typography: In some copies page 348 is misnumbered 438, a fault recurring in the next 'edition'. Gathering R is in a duplicate setting, with printer's imprint(2), page 375, ending either '& Co.' or 'and Co.'

Figures: A22-9 24-6, B37-4 47-10, C63-5 69-8, D74-3 84-7, E111-2 113-1, F130-5 141-9, G159-7 161-2, H189-10 190-8, I 195-6/- 216-8, K228-11 239-9, L253-5 255-4, M266-3 277-7, N310-3 312-9, O 322-10 324-2, P339-2 340-11, Q366-6, R—.

122Ab] Second Edition (First Edition, Second Issue): 1818

TALES OF MY LANDLORD, | Second Series, . . . VOL. I [II-IV]. | SECOND EDITION. . . . 1818.

General Notes: An overrun of first edition sheets with altered title-pages and printed labels, thus in all respects identical with that issue except that volume 4 page 195 has no press figure.

Copies: O; CtY.

122Ac] Third Edition (First Edition, Third Issue): 1818

TALES OF MY LANDLORD, | Second Series, . . . VOL. I [II-IV]. | THIRD EDITION. . . . 1818.

General Notes: A further overrun of first edition sheets with altered title-pages and printed labels, thus essentially identical with that issue. In some copies, volume 3, page 132, as well as volume 4, page 195, lack press-figures, and volume 4, page 348, is correctly numbered.

Copies: E O; CtY T/B.

REPRINTS

FRANCE

PARIS: Baudry, Barrois [and others]
[~] Tales of My Landlord. . . . Second Series. The Heart of Mid-Lothian. 1831. (Collection of Ancient and Modern British Novels and Romances: *see* 288R.13.)

PARIS: Didot and Galignani
[~] Tales of My Landlord. . . . Second Series. 1821. (Collection of Modern English Authors: *see* 291R.14-17.)

GERMANY

122Ra] BERLIN: Schlesinger 1822
[The Heart of Mid-Lothian, . . . Second Edition. Berlin, Printed for Adolph Martin Schlesinger. 1822.] Copy: not seen. Reference: GDS 132, page 339.

LEIPZIG: Wigand
[~] The Heart of Midlothian. 1831. (A Complete Edition of the Waverley Novels: *see* 300R. 17-20.)

ZWICKAU: Schumann
[~] The Heart of Mid-Lothian. 1822. (Pocket Library of English Classics: *see* 302R.52-56.)

UNITED STATES

122Rb] BOSTON: Parker 1821-1832
[Tales of my Landlord. Second Series. . . . The Heart of Mid-lothian. . . . Boston: Samuel H. Parker, No. 12, Cornhill. 1821. Pages: *i-iii* iv-vi, *7* 8-480.] Copy: not seen. Notes: (Also reissued in Novels Tales and Romances. 1821. *see* 305R.6).

[~] Tales of My Landlord. . . . Second Series. 1827, 1829. (Waverley Novels. *see* 306R.11-12].

[~] Tales of My Landlord. Second Series. 1830, 1832. (Waverley Novels: [Parker's Edition Revised] *see* 307R.11-12).

122Rc] HARTFORD: Goodrich, and Huntington and Hopkins 1821
Tales of My Landlord; Second Series: Collected and Arranged by Jedediah Cleishbotham. . . Hartford: Samuel G. Goodrich, and Huntington and Hopkins. 1821. Pages: *1-3* 4-353. Copies: CtY PU T/B.

122Rd] NEW YORK: Duyckinck, Gilley, Lockwood, and Bliss 1820
Tales of My Landlord. Second Series: Collected and Arranged by Jedediah Cleishbotham. . . . New-York: Published by Evert Duyckinck, W. B. Gilley, L. & F. Lockwood, and Elam Bliss. James & John Harper, Printers. 1820. Two volumes. Pages 1: *1-3* 4-340; 2: *1-3* 4-364. Copy: E.

122Re] NEW YORK: Van Winkle 1818
Tales of My Landlord, Second Series, Collected and Arranged by Jedediah Cleishbotham, . . . New-York: Printed and Published by C. S. Van Winkle, No. 101 Greenwich-street. 1818. Four volumes. Pages 1: *1-3* 4-157; 2: *1-3* 4-151; 3: *i-iv, 1* 2-156; 4: *1* 2-180. Volume 2 has imprint: Published by M. Carey and Son, 126 Chesnut-street. C. S. Van Winkle, Printer, New-York. 1818.: the imprint also on front board for combined volumes. These boards read: The Second Philadelphia Edition. Volumes 3-4 have latter part of a single title reading: The Second Philadephia Edition. In Four Volumes. Vols. III. and IV. Philadelphia: Published by M. Carey & Son, No. 126, Chesnut street. 1818. Copies: MWA NN PPL PPL(vols.1-2) T/B(vols.1-2).

122Rf] PHILADELPHIA: Carey and Son 1818
Tales of My Landlord: Second Series: Collected and Arranged by Jedediah Cleishbotham, . . . Philadelphia: Published by M. Carey & Son, No. 126, Chesnut-Street. 1818. Four volumes separately paged but bound in two: the 4th without separate title. Pages 1: *i-iv*, *1* 2-161; 2: *i-ii*, *1* 2-154; 3: *i-iv*, *1* 2-156; 4: *3* 4-182. Notes: For another setting of volumes 3-4 *see* New York, Van Winkle edition (122Re). As remarked in note 2 of this chapter, this edition may well derive from advance copy; it certainly marks Carey's first appearance as a publisher of Scott novels and (in view of the statement preceding entry) can be regarded as the first American edition. Copies: E; CtY MH MWA NN TxU ViU(vols.1-2). Reference: Clarkin 1080-1083.

122Rg] PHILADELPHIA: Crissy 1826
Tales of My Landlord: Second Series: Collected and Arranged by Jedediah Cleishbotham, . . . Philadelphia: James Crissy, No. 14, South Seventh Street. 1826. Three volumes. Pages 1: *1-3* 4-249; 2: *1-3* 4-250; 3: *1-3* 4-240. Copies: IdU NN NN(vol.3) T/B.

122Rh] PHILADELPHIA: Dickinson 1821
Tales of My Landlord: Second Series: Collected and Arranged by Jedediah Cleishbotham, . . . Third Philadelphia Edition. Philadelphia: Published and Sold at No. 18 South Front street. Printed by D. Dickinson, Corner of Market and Decatur Streets. 1821. Four volumes bound in two. Pages 1: *i-v* vi-x, *11* 12-155; 2: *1-5* 6-150; 3: *i-iv*, *1* 2-147; 4: *1-5* 6-169. Copies: E; NjP NN PPL RPB.

DERIVATIVES

GREAT BRITAIN

122Da] DUBLIN: The Booksellers 1819
The Heart of Mid-Lothian; or, The Lily of St. Leonard's, a Melo-dramatic Romance in Three Acts. Founded on the second series of the popular Tales of my Landlord. Dublin: Printed for and Sold by All the Booksellers. 1819. Pages: *1-5* 6-55. Notes: Drama by Thomas John Dibdin, first performed at the Theatre-Royal, Crow-Street, on Tuesday, 13 April 1819. Copies: DN DT; MH. References: Bolton 2425 (conjectural); Ford I 1.

122Db] EDINBURGH: Caw and Elder 1818
The Heart of Mid-Lothian: or The Lily of St. Leonard's.... Edinburgh: Published by Caw & Elder, High Street, and Alex. Peat, 35, South Bridge. [ca.1818]. Price Twopence. Two parts. Pages 1: (not seen); 2: *1-2* 3-24. Notes: Chapbook. The text of the second part begins with the heading: 'Conclusion of the Story of Jeanie and Effie Deans.' The imprint above is taken from the wrapper since the title-page with wood-cut vignette has no imprint. Copy: E(part 2).

122Dc] EDINBURGH: Huie 1822
The Heart of Mid-Lothian; A Romantic National Drama, Founded on the Popular Tale of the Same Name, In the Second Series of the "Tales of My Landlord:" [no imprint. 1822]. Pages: *1-7* 8-66. Notes: Drama by Thomas J. Dibdin, as performed at the Theatre-Royal, Edinburgh, in 1820. With engraved frontispiece portrait 'Mr. Jones of the Theatre Royal Edinburgh, as the Duke of Argyle.', this facing left or right, but with the same imprint. Drawn and Engraved for the National Dramas by E. Mitchell and Published by James L. Huie 14 Infirmary Street Edinburgh 1822. Signatures: *A* B-F. Copies: E(2); InU NjP NN. (A variant issued in: Dramas from the Novels, Tales, and Romances, 1822: volume 1, number 2. *see* 323D.) Reference: Bolton 2448 (erroneous entry).

122Dd] LONDON: Bailey 1823
Heart of Mid Lothian; or, The Lily of St. Leonard. A Caledonian Tale of Great Interest, On which is Founded the Piece of that Name, Performed at the London Theatres... London: Published by J. Bailey, Printer, 116, Chancery Lane. [ca.1823]. Pages: *1-3* 4-24. Notes: Chapbook with coloured woodcut frontispiece. Price: Sixpence. Copies: A BCL E. Reference: Abbotsford, page 320.

122De] LONDON: The Company of Booksellers 1822
Heart of Mid Lothian; or The Lily of St. Leonard, A Caledonian Tale of Great Interest, On which is founded the Piece of that Name, Performed with unbounded Applause, at the Different Theatres.... London: Printed for The Company of Booksellers. [1822]. Pages: *1-2*, 7 8-34. Notes: Chapbook with coloured woodcut frontispiece. Price: Sixpence. Copy: E.

LONDON: Cumberland
[~] The Heart of Mid-Lothian: A Melo-Dramatic Romance. [1830]. (Cumberland's Minor Theatre: number 2. *see* 330D).

122Df] LONDON: Duncombe 1820
The Heart of Midlothian, or The Lily of St. Leonard's: A ... Romance. From the "Tales of My

Landlord," London, Duncombe [ca.1820] Pages: *1-3* 4-24. Notes: A chapbook consisting of four extracts labelled chapters I-IV from Scott's novel by Joseph Claude Mauris, with coloured engraving. Copy: L.

122Dg] LONDON: Goulding, D'Almaine, Potter 1819
The Overture and Whole of the Music in The Heart of Mid-Lothian; A musical drama in three acts... The poetry by D. Terry Esqr. London Published by Goulding, Dalmaine, Potter & Co. 20, Soho Square & to be had at 7 Westmorland Strt. Dublin. [1819]. Pages: *1* 2-48. Notes: Engraved sheet music with plate marks: 'Ov.H.of Mid Lothian' and 'The Heart of Mid-Lothian'. Drama by Daniel Terry. Music composed by Henry R. Bishop arranged for voice and pianoforte. Price: 10s. Copy: E. Reference: G/T 9850.

LONDON: Hodgson
[~] The Heart of Mid Lothian; or, The Lily of St. Leonard's. [1822]. (Hodgson's Juvenile Drama: number 2. *see* 333D.)

122Dh] LONDON: Macleish 1819
Airs, Choruses, &c. &c. in the New Drama, (in Three Acts,) Called the Heart of Mid=Lothian. ... London: Printed by E. Macleish, 2, Bow-street, Covent-Garden. 1819. Pages: *1-7* 8-14. Notes: Words only for the airs, choruses in the drama by Daniel Terry (music arranged by Henry R. Bishop not included) as performed at the Theatre Royal, Covent-Garden, 17 April 1819. In some copies page 14 is blank. Copies: E O; CtY InU.

122Di] LONDON: Macpherson 1819
Filial Duty; or, The Maid of Oban. A Dramatic Piece, with Songs... London: Printed and Sold for the Author, By A. Macpherson, Russell Court, Covent Garden. 1819. Pages: *1-3* 4-24. Notes: Drama by A. Maclaren. Copy: MH.

122Dj] LONDON: Stockdale 1819
The Heart of Mid-Lothian, A Musical Drama, in Three Acts; ... London: Printed for William Stockdale, No. 181, Piccadilly. 1819. Pages: *i-iv*, *1* 2-66 *67-68*. Notes: Words by Daniel Terry (music composed by Henry R. Bishop not included) but with note stating that the music of this 'Opera' may be had of Messrs. Goulding and Co. This publication is as first performed at The Theatre Royal, Covent Garden, 17 April 1819. Price: Two Shillings and Sixpence [with 'and Sixpence' carefully inked out in one CtY copy]. Though Scott sent proofs of the novel so that Terry could anticipate other dramatizations (*see* 122Aa above), it is evident that, beginning 13 January, Dibdin and others were first on the stage (*see* next entry and Bolton 2421-2425). Copies: BCL E L O; CtY(3) IdU InU ViU(inscribed). References: Bolton 2426; Ford I 3; Maggs Catalogue 1120 (1990), item 238.

122Dk] LONDON: Stodart 1819
The Heart of Mid-Lothian; or, The Lily of St. Leonard's: A Melo-Dramatic Romance, in Three Acts. From "Tales of My Landlord." ... London: Printed for Robert Stodart, 81, Strand. 1819. Pages: *i-v* vi *vii-viii*, *1* 2-66 *67-68*. Notes: Melodrama by Thomas John Dibdin. First performed at the Surrey Theatre on 13 January 1819. In his preliminary Advertisement Dibdin mentions a critic's remark that this 'required little more than an amanuensis to construct' and indicates that the composition required only a week before the first reading on 6 January 1819,

just one week before the first performance. Pages *67-68* (integral with pages 65-66) list books published and sold by Robert Stodart, with page *68* also publishing terms of subscription to the Library and Reading Room at No. 81 Strand. Price: Two Shillings and Sixpence. Copies: C; InU(inscribed by Dibdin) InU NN-L(prompt copy) PU(inscribed by Dibdin). References: Bolton 2421; Ford I 1. Reissued as 'Second Edition' (BCL L; CtY InU NN NNU-W), 'Third Edition' (E; InU NN T/B).

122Dl] NEWCASTLE UPON TYNE: Mackenzie and Dent 1819
The Heart of Mid-Lothian, or The Affecting History of Jeanie and Effie Deans. Abridged from the Original by D. Stewart. . . . Newcastle upon Tyne: Printed by Mackenzie and Dent, St. Nicolas' Church-Yard. [watermarked 1819]. Pages: *1-3* 4-52. Notes: Chapbook. Price: One Shilling. Copy: E(no plate).

UNITED STATES

122Dm] BALTIMORE: Robinson 1828
The Heart of Mid-Lothian: A Melo-Dramatic Romance, In Three Acts. . . Baltimore: Published by Jos. Robinson. [1828]. Pages: *1-7* 8-47. Notes: Drama by Thomas John Dibdin, as performed at the London Royal Surrey in 1819 and in American theatres in 1828. (At head of title: Robinson's Edition). Imprint on wrapper: New-York: Edward Dunigan's Shakspeare Dramatic Repository, 137 Fulton Street. Copies: CtY DLC(2) NN TxU.

CRIMINAL TRIALS

123A] First Printing: 1818

'PREFACE, INCLUDING SOME PARTICULARS OF THE LIFE OF CAPTAIN JOHN PORTEOUS.' pages *i* ii-xxxvi, *in*:

Criminal Trials, Illustrative of the Tale Entitled, "The Heart of Mid=Lothian," Published from the Original Record: With a Prefatory Notice, Including Some Particulars of the Life of Captain John Porteous. . . . Edinburgh: Printed for Archibald Constable and Company. 1818.

Published 1 August 1818 in Edinburgh (*EEC*); issued 22 August in London (*MC*). 8s.

Notes: The engraved frontispiece, drawn and engraved by W. and D. Lizars, is captioned 'The Tolbooth of Edinburgh, taken down 1817.' The illustrative *Criminal Trials* is advertised in the first edition, volume 1, on the verso of the half-title of the *Tales of My Landlord*, Second Series, representing *The Heart of Mid-Lothian*. Like that edition, it was issued by Constable and, as occasionally with some of Scott's other work, was printed by George Ramsay. Moreover, the anonymous Preface may be attributed to Scott as a person conversant in legal matters, with access to papers from the High Court of Justiciary, and immediately involved in the preparation of this novel, page xxxiv of the Preface referring the reader to volume 2, page 155, where there is some comment on a Parliamentary Act respecting the murder of Porteous. Possibly the text itself, as occasonally alleged, was 'edited' by Scott's friend C. K. Sharpe (cf. note below), but this consists only of legal documents, all without annotation.

Copies: BCL E(2) O; CtY IdU NN* NNU-W T/B.
*With ms note 'This work was edited anonymously by Charles Kirkpatrick Sharpe. G.F. B[lack].'

References: CBEL (ascribes the Preface to Scott), NCBEL (attribution withdrawn). (Magnum Opus Edition: Not reprinted.)

REVIEW OF MATURIN

124A] First Printing: 1818

'ART. IX. *Women; or Pour et Contre: A Tale.* By the Author of Bertram, &c.', pages 234-257, *in*:

The Edinburgh Review, June, 1818. No. LIX. [volume 30 imprint:] Edinburgh: Printed by David Willison, for Archibald Constable and Company, Edinburgh; and Longman, Hurst, Rees, Orme and Brown, London. 1818.

Published 10 August 1818 in Edinburgh (*EEC*); issued 14 August in London (*MC*).

Notes: The author, well known to Scott, was Charles Robert Maturin, whom Scott mentions by name throughout the review. This is the first appearance of Scott in *The Edinburgh Review* since October 1806 (*see* 26A), when he withdrew for political reasons.

Copies: L O; PPL.

Reference: (Magnum Opus Edition 1835: *The Miscellaneous Prose Works*, xviii.172-208.)

MY MITHER IS OF STURDY AIRN

125Aa] First Edition: 1818

[*headnote*] The following Lines, are written by Walter Scott | Esq.—The first Verse is a literal translation of a | GERMAN MOTTO, . . . | [*poem's first line:*] My Mither is of sturdy airn, | A copper Dwarf am I, her Bairn; . . . PRINTED at GRAY HOUSE Sept.1st.1818

Privately printed, as noted, 1 September 1818. Paper: Broadside (222 x 140mm uncut). Watermarks: none.

Notes: The eight-line informational headline is followed by two quatrains and a couplet. Ruff suggests that this was 'presumably printed at the home of Francis, 14th Lord Gray.'

Copy: EU. References: Ruff 158 (with illustration). (Magnum Opus Edition: Not reprinted.)

125Ab] Second Edition: 1823

[*in a border of ornamental type*] [*headnote*] The following Lines, are written by Sir | Walter Scott Bart.—The first Verse is a lit- | eral translation of a GERMAN MOTTO, . . . [*poem*] My Mither is of sturdy airn, | A copper Dwarf am I, her Bairn; | . . . . Printed at KINFAUNS CASTLE, Novr. 19th. 1823.

Privately printed, as noted, 19 November 1823. Paper: Broadside (230 x 192mm uncut). Watermarks: none.

Notes: This second printing divides the information at head into two paragraphs, the second reading: 'The two other Verses are in compliment to LORD GRAY'S Family.' The couplet alluded to reads: 'Long have they flourish'd, long may they, | Still flourish in the House of GRAY.'

Copy: E. Reference: Ruff 159 (with illustration).

REVIEWS OF WALPOLE and BYRON

126A] First Printing: 1818

1] 'ART. IV. *Letters from the Hon. Horace Walpole to George Montague Esq.*', pages 118-131;

2] 'ART. IX.—*Childe Harold's Pilgrimage. Canto IV.* By Lord Byron.', pages 215-232, *in*:

The Quarterly Review. April, 1818. [No. 37; volume 19 imprint:] London: John Murray, Albemarle Street. 1818.

Published 26 September in London (*MC*).

Copies: BCL O; PPL. References: Shine 470, 475. (Magnum Opus Edition 1835: *The Miscellaneous Prose Works*, [1] Not reprinted, [2] xvii.337-366.)

LETTERS FROM A GENTLEMAN IN THE NORTH OF SCOTLAND

127Aa] First Scott Printing, First Issue: 1818

1] 'THE HISTORY OF DONALD THE HAMMERER.', vol. 1, pages *lxiv* lxv-lxxvi, and

2] 'No. IV. EXTRACTS FROM "*An Inquiry into the Causes which facilitate the Rise and Progress of Rebellions and Insurrections in the Highlands of Scotland, &c." written in* 1747., vol. 2, pages *338* 339-370, *in*:

Letters from a Gentleman in the North of Scotland to His Friend in London; Containing the description of a Capital Town in that Northern Country, with an Account of some uncommon customs of the Inhabitants. . . . The Fifth Edition, with a Large Appendix. . . . With an Introduction and Notes, by the Editor, R. Jamieson, . . . and The History of Donald the Hammerer, From an Authentic Account of the Family of Invernahyle; a MS. communicated by Walter Scott, Esq. Vol. I [II]. London: Printed for Rest Fenner, Paternoster-Row. 1818.

<SEE ACCOMPANYING ILLUSTRATION>

Published 31 October 1818 in London (*MC*). £1.1.0.

Notes: The first, 1754 edition of Edmund Burt's *Letters* (written ca. 1726) evidently was a primary source for Scott and remains in his Abbotsford library beside this 1818 publication. In 1815 the edition issued just before the present text prompted the *Monthly Magazine* to remark, indiscreetly, that this was the work 'so often quoted in the Lady of the Lake, and in Waverly[!]' (1 February 1815, page 56), a comment immediately repeated in the *Scots Magazine* (February, page 132) and shortly thereafter in the *Critical Review* (May, page 436). Since the reiterated assertion could be verified (for the poem, in Canto 2, notes 1, 10, 16, 17, Canto 3, notes 13, 16 and, for the novel, in the new Preface to the third edition) the known author thus was directly linked to the 'Great Unknown', here six years before J. L. Adolphus drew this and similar parallels. If Scott was rather vexed by this early disclosure of his continual reliance upon Burt, all further confirmed in some reviews of *Waverley* (*see* 77Aa), the further link on the titles of Jamieson's 1818 edition must have been all the more exasperating. It also must have been a considerable embarrassment for the new editor constantly to allude to him now in text or notes, on eight occasions as the editor of various works, twice as the known author of *Marmion* (i.53) and *The Lady of the Lake* (i.202-203), and three times indirectly as the 'wonderful author' of *The Antiquary* (i.108), *Waverley* (ii.124) and *Tales of My Landlord* first series (ii.127).

There are two 1818 states, with sentence before 'Vol. I.' in title (1) identifying Scott, as noted above; (2) title a cancel, Scott's name removed, and the sentence

LETTERS

FROM A

GENTLEMAN IN THE NORTH OF SCOTLAND

TO

HIS FRIEND IN LONDON;

CONTAINING THE DESCRIPTION OF A CAPITAL TOWN IN THAT NORTHERN COUNTRY, WITH AN ACCOUNT OF SOME UNCOMMON CUSTOMS OF THE INHABITANTS;

LIKEWISE

An Account of the Highlands,

WITH

THE CUSTOMS AND MANNERS OF THE HIGHLANDERS.

TO WHICH IS ADDED,

A LETTER RELATING TO THE MILITARY WAYS AMONG THE MOUNTAINS, BEGUN IN THE YEAR 1726.

THE FIFTH EDITION,

WITH

A LARGE APPENDIX,

CONTAINING VARIOUS IMPORTANT HISTORICAL DOCUMENTS, HITHERTO UNPUBLISHED; WITH AN

INTRODUCTION AND NOTES,

BY THE EDITOR,

R. JAMIESON, F. A. S. LOND. & EDIN.

Corresponding Member of the Scandinavian Literary Society of Copenhagen, &c.

AND

THE HISTORY OF DONALD THE HAMMERER,

From an Authentic Account of the Family of Invernahyle; a MS. communicated by WALTER SCOTT, Esq.

VOL. I.

LONDON:

PRINTED FOR REST FENNER, PATERNOSTER-ROW.

1818.

ENTRY 127Aa. THE BRITISH LIBRARY (287.f.21)
(illustration reduced)

ending 'Invernahyle.' In view of Scott's sensitivity about this work, as just remarked, and his reaction to a further issue of the edition (*see* 127Ab, next entry), the cancellation would seem to have been executed immediately upon his demand and the original issue at once suppressed. Yet within this new 1818 edition, a headnote to the first contribution still reads, page *lxiv*: 'From an authentic Account of the Family of Invernahyle. [MS. communicated by Walter Scott, Esq.]'. In this Scott interpolated a nine-line comment in italics and supplied three notes.

Not mentioned on the title, and thus disregarded hitherto, is Scott's provision also of the last Appendix IV in the second volume—a considerable addition with a headnote reading, page *338*: '[From a MS. in the possession of the Gartmore Family, communicated by Walter Scott, Esq.]'. To this Scott subtended sixteen notes, some of considerable length, the last concluding in its final line with a misprint (page 367): 'Satistical'.

Copies: (State 1) L(King's Library: title here reproduced) P. (2) E L(Grenville) O.

References: Abbotsford, page 19; Craigie, pages 30, 59-60, 70-71, 80, 98-99, 101-103. (Magnum Opus Edition: Not reprinted.)

127Ab] First Scott Printing, Second Issue: 1822

'THE HISTORY OF DONALD THE HAMMERER.', [&c. as in first issue] *in*:

Letters from a Gentleman in the North of Scotland. . . The Fifth Edition, with Engravings, and A large Appendix, . . . Invernahyle; a MS. communicated by Sir Walter Scott, Bart. . . . London: Printed for Ogle, Duncan, and Co. 37, Paternoster Row, and 295, Holborn; Oliver and Boyd, Edinburgh; M. Ogle, Glasgow; and M. Keene, Dublin. 1822.

Published 11 March 1822 in London (*MC*). Illustration: The newly added frontispiece for volume 1, dated 1 January 1822 (and directly relating to Scott's first piece), is painted by E. F. Burney, engraved by R. Baker, with caption 'The Secreting of Donald the Hammerer'.

Notes: Identical except for cancel title-pages now again (as in the 1818 first issue, first state) identifying the contributor. After four years Scott once more was greatly disturbed that his name should appear, if only incidentally, and demanded, now to no avail, that this leaf (already in cancelled state) should be cancelled again. As compared with the initial, suppressed issue, this unauthorized reissue, continuing in defiance of Scott, apparently had a much wider circulation.

Copies: BCL E GU O P; InU T/B TxU. Reference: *Letters* v.274-275.

REMARKS ON GENERAL GOURGAUD'S ACCOUNT

128A] First Printing: 1818

'REMARKS ON GENERAL GOURGAUD'S ACCOUNT OF THE CAMPAIGN OF 1815.', pages 220-228, *in*:

Blackwood's Edinburgh Magazine. November 1818. No. XX. Vol. IV. [imprint:] William Blackwood, No 17, Prince's Street, Edinburgh; and John Murray, Albemarle Street, London.

Published ca. 20 November 1818 in Edinburgh; issued ca. 1 December in London. (schedule according to previous notices).

Notes: Although the article is noted '(To be continued.)' and a further account was promised in Scott's letter to Morritt on 21 November, no further continuation appears.

Copies: E L O; NjP PPL.

Reference: *Letters*, v.226. (Magnum Opus Edition: Not reprinted.)

DRAMA

129A] First Printing: 1819

['DRAMA.' Vol. III, Part 2, pages 629-671, *in*:

Supplement to the Fourth, Fifth, and Sixth Editions of the Encyclopaedia Britannica. With Preliminary Dissertations on the History of the Sciences. Illustrated by Engravings. Volume Third. Part II. Edinburgh: Printed for Archibald Constable and Company, Edinburgh; and Hurst, Robinson, and Company, London. 1819.]

Published 28 January 1819 in Edinburgh (*EEC*); issued 12 February in London (*MC*). £1.6.0.

Notes: This and the two other essays by Scott in the *Encyclopaedia* (115A, 173A) are initialled at the end '(N.N.)'.

Copies: (Original part issue) not seen; (reissue, with 1824 volume title) E GM.

References: Thomson, page 26. (Magnum Opus Edition 1834: *The Miscellaneous Prose Works*, vi.*217-219* 220-395 as 'Essay on the Drama'.)

REPRINT

FRANCE

PARIS: Didot and Galignani
[~] Essays by Sir Walter Scott. 1828. (*see* 292R.8-9.) Also included are the two other *Encyclopaedia* essays titled 'Romance' and 'Chivalry'.

THE LATE DUKE OF BUCCLEUCH AND QUEENSBERRY

130Aa] First Edition: 1819

[wrapper title, within a black border] The Late | DUKE OF BUCCLEUCH | AND | QUEENSBERRY.

Privately printed in Edinburgh after 20 April 1819. Binding: side-sewed wrappers of text paper. Paper: 8° (206 x 134mm uncut). Watermarks: none. Collation: *A*⁸. Pagination: *1* wrapper title, *2 blank*, *3* 4-16 text. Figures: none.

Notes: This undated obituary with black-bordered title has no imprint, but was undoubtedly printed by Ballantyne immediately after the 4th Duke's death on 20 April 1819. Though no author is cited, Scott's affection for the family and his style immediately identify the text as his. The same text was reprinted in the *Edinburgh Weekly Journal* of 12 May 1819, cited in the following entry

Copy: E(Abbot).

References: Thomson, page 18. (Magnum Opus Edition 1834: *The Miscellaneous Prose Works*, iv.297-308 as 'Character of the late Charles Duke of Buccleuch and Queensberry'.)

130Ab] First Journal Printing: 1819

'THE LATE DUKE OF BUCCLEUCH AND QUEENSBERRY', page 150 *in*:

The Edinburgh Weekly Journal. Vol. XXII. No. 1117.] Wednesday, May 12, 1819. Price 7d. Edinburgh—Printed by James Ballantyne, For himself and the other Proprietors.

Published 12 May 1819 in Edinburgh.

Copy: E.

TRIVIAL POEMS, AND TRIOLETS

131Aa] First Scott Edition, First Issue: 1819

TRIVIAL POEMS, | AND | **TRIOLETS.** | WRITTEN | IN OBEDIENCE TO MRS TOMKIN'S COMMANDS, | BY PATRICK CAREY. | 20TH AUG. 1651. | [*coat of arms*] | LONDON: | JOHN MURRAY, ALBEMARLE-STREET. | [*short rule*] | 1819.

Published in a limited issue ca. April 1819 in London. 18s. Binding: Drab boards. Paper: Demy 4° (262 x 210mm cut). Watermarks: [twice in each sheet, Prince of Wales feathers] | J & M | 1817 [1818]. Collation: π^2 A^4 B-H^4 I^2. Pagination: *i* title-page, *ii blank*, *iii*-iv Introduction, dated from Abbotsford 1 April 1819, *1* An Octaue[!] [*poetic dedication by Carey to Mrs. Tomkin*], *2 blank*, *3* 4-40 text of 'Ballades', *41* fly-title reading: 'I will sing unto the Lord. Psalm XIII. Vers. VI.', *42 blank*, *43* 44-63 text of 'Triolets', *64 blank*, *65* 66-67 Notes, *68* printer's imprint: [*short rule*] | EDINBURGH: | Printed by James Ballantyne and Co. Typography: In some copies the printer's imprint is lacking. Page 34 is misnumbered 44. Figures: *none*.

Notes: After referring to his earlier printing of six of Carey's poems (in 'Account of the Poems of Patrick Carey', *Edinburgh Annual Register for 1810*, 1812, *see* 62A) Scott says that he 'has been induced to place them beyond the chance of total oblivion, by the present very limited edition', this based on a manuscript given him by John Murray. The headlines divide the text into 'Ballades' and 'Triolets' although the pagination is continuous. This first issue has an uncancelled title dated 1819.

Presentation copies: BCL('Richard [! Robert] Surtees Esq of Mainsforth from the editor') E*('Margaret E[lizabeth] Hughes from her friend, the editor Sir Walter Scott') InU('A Gift from Sir Walter Scott J.R.'). Another copy: O.
*Now excised apparently in this cropped copy, inscription copied from bookseller's note. At the end Mrs Hughes refers to a letter from Scott 12 October 1824 noting that he then had 'two copies left'.

Reference: (Magnum Opus. Not reprinted.)

131Ab] First Edition, Second Issue: 1820

TRIVIAL POEMS, | AND | **TRIOLETS.** . . . 1820.

Published 20 April 1820 in London (*MC*); issued 15 May in Edinburgh (*EEC*). 18s.

Notes: As for first issue, except for a paste-on cancel carefully applied to title with the later date. The 1820 *EEC* advertisement, noting the printing only of a 'very few copies', lists Oliver and Boyd as the Edinburgh booksellers.

Copies: O(2); CtY(2) MH NjP NN(Robert Southey, 18 January 1836) NNU-W TxU.

THE PROVINCIAL ANTIQUITIES AND PICTURESQUE SCENERY OF SCOTLAND

132Aa] First Edition, Part Issue: 1819-1826

[*On brown wrappers headed* 'No. I [II-VIII] *Proofs*, 30*s*. [£1,10*s*. in III-VIII]', *then below within a ribbon frame:*] The | Provincial Antiquities | And | Picturesque Scenery of Scotland. | [*short Oxford rule*] | WITH | DESCRIPTIVE ILLUSTRATIONS, | BY | WALTER SCOTT, Esq. [*Nos. X-XX:* Sir WALTER SCOTT, Bart.] | [*vignette: regalia of Scotland*] | LONDON: | PRINTED FOR RODWELL AND MARTIN; | AND SOLD BY J. AND A. ARCH, CORNHILL, LONDON; AND | WILLIAM BLACKWOOD, EDINBURGH.

Number 1 issued 1 May 1819 in Edinburgh (*EWJ* 28 April). 16s for the ordinary part issue; thereafter the nine remaining parts at irregular intervals to 14 December 1826 (*EEC*). Illustrations: The earlier numbers of this work are somewhat less extensive than those outlined 1 November 1817 in Scott's prospectus (*see* 111A). In the original impression the first 51 plates, as noted below, were published by Rodwell & Martin with imprints dated 2 April 1819—1 June 1826, and the final plate by John and Arthur Arch 1 September 1826, most of these with a McQueen printer's imprint. (A later impression with undated plates, published by J. Menzies, 61 Princes Street, Edinburgh, postdates 1832.) Since Scott refused payment for *The Provincial Antiquities*, once the success of the title was assured, the publishers presented him with some of the original drawings. Twelve of these were prepared by J. M. W. Turner, here marking his first appearance in a Scott enterprise. Seven other artists were also engaged for this grand project, as well as fourteen engravers, all identified in the record given below. No imprint is provided for Scott's accompanying letterpress descriptions of the scenes, but in all printings, part or volume, of the early impressions there are press figures, as noted below, and part number II is cited on the first leaf recto of gatherings E-H.

Either in part or volume issue it is impractical to differentiate the various proofs, since all bear the same Whatman watermark and are usually cut. Lowndes, describing the proof issues as, in his time, 'all much reduced in price', quotes the original charges for the volumes as: Large paper proofs, imperial 4° at £15. Proofs on India paper, imperial 4°, 2 vols. at £21. Large paper, India Proofs and Etchings, imperial 4°, at £26.5.0. To complicate matters further, some of these plate 'proofs' are with and some without lettering.

Binding: Brown printed wrappers as described above for numbers 1-8, plain drab wrappers only for 9-10. Paper: Imperial 4° (384 x 278mm uncut). Letterpress watermarks for part issues and (1) large-paper impressions: J WHATMAN | 1818 [1819, 1821 to 1825]; (2) ordinary impression: as before but usually unwatermarked. Collation, pagination, and figures: see below.

Copies: E; NN(text to page 146 only).

References: Maggs Catalogue 1120 (1990), item 219 (with illustrations of Turner etchings); Thomson, pages 54-55. (Magnum Opus Edition 1834: *The Miscellaneous Prose Works*, vii.*155-157* 158-457 as 'Provincial Antiquities of Scotland'.)

132Ab] First Edition, Volume Issue: 1826

Published December 1826 in Edinburgh upon issue of the 10th part. £7. Paper: as for part issue.

Copies: (1) first, large-paper impression: E(2) GU LU; InU. With 'proof' plates: BCL* E(37 plates) ES. (2) second, ordinary impression: O; CtY(2) NN TxU. Later issue: First volume Arch/Blackwood title retained, but thereafter an undated Menzies reimpression: P; T/B.
*With pencil note indicating 25 copies.

1] [*engraved title*] PROVINCIAL ANTIQUITIES | and | PICTURESQUE SCENERY | *of* | SCOTLAND, | *with descriptive illustrations* | by | SIR WALTER SCOTT. BART. | [*beneath 14 stars and a thistle, vignette of Edinburgh Castle*] | VOLUME 1. | *LONDON*, | PUBLISHED BY JOHN AND ARTHUR ARCH, CORNHILL, | *and by William Blackwood, Edinburgh*, | 1826.

Collation: *a*1 b-g^4 h1 A-H^4 I^2(I 2+1) K-M^4 N2. Pagination: [*engraved title*], *i*-ii Regalia of Scotland (description of the plate), *iii* iv-xli Regalia of Scotland (essay), xlii-lii appendixes, *1* 2-95 *96* text, *97* Directions for Placing the Plates, *98 blank*. Illustrations: See list below. Typography: In some copies page 62 is misnumbered 26. Figures: A3-1, B16-1/-, C19-12/1, H61-6, K77-1, L81-1 92-1/-.

Notes: Leaf *a*1 is in a duplicate setting, page ii first word reading either *the* or *in*. Though the first sentence page *i* states that the Regalia illustrated on part cover and title-page were *drawn accurately, from the originals by Mr Lizars*, it appears that this first volume printed title was cancelled, for it is admitted at the foot of page *97* that 'The representation of the Crown, Sceptre, and Sword, referred to in page 1, having been found to be incorrect, a new drawing of them has been made by Mr. Geddes, from which a beautiful engraving by Mr. Goodall, has been substituted for that mentioned in the text.' Here reference is to the plate facing page *iii*, as listed below.

The accompanying essay on the Regalia, now occupying all of the subsequent preliminary gatherings, was first issued with parts 3 and 4 (cf. references on pages *65*, *83*), 1820-1821, shortly after Scott's brief account in pamphlet form (*see* 134Aa).

Depending upon the somewhat erratic plate order, Scott's commentary on the illustrations is highly variable—ranging from a single paragraph on a monument (cf. page *31*) to a series of disjointed essays on eleven aspects of Edinburgh (cf. pages *65* 66-88, *96-97* 98-126)—and is accordingly not analyzed in the list of plates which follows. A more systematic order is imposed in *MPW*, but even this oddly interposes the Regalia essay after the Edinburgh sequence and before eleven other entries. Sheet C provides clear evidence, in this book, of the priority of the large-paper (Whatman) impressions, these with figure 12 page 19 and footnote paragraphs 1, 3, pages 19-20, each ending with a single word: 'bank.' and 'Castle.' In the other, generally unwatermarked printing, with figure 1 on page 19, each of these single word 'widows' is driven up into the preceding full line.

2] [*engraved title*] Provincial Antiquities and Picturesque Scenery | *of* | SCOTLAND, | *with descriptive illustrations* | BY SIR WALTER SCOTT. BART. | [*beneath a star and a flying horse, vignette of a naval battle*] | VOLUME II. | *LONDON.* | PUBLISHED BY JOHN AND ARTHUR ARCH, CORNHILL, | *and by William Blackwood, Edinburgh,* | 1826.

Collation: O-Q^4 R^2(R2+1) S-T^4 U^2 X-Y^4 Z^2 2A1 2B-2E^4 Aa^4 Bb^2. Pagination: *97* 98-208 *209* text, *210-211* Directions for Placing the Plates, *212 blank*. Illustrations: See list below. Typography: In some copies page 128 is misnumbered 12 and in some copies the 'Directions for Placing the Plates' precedes the text in volume 1. Figures: O 104-1, P111-1, Y162-5, Aa 168-5/-.

Illustrations: The following record cites in order: Plate (facing descriptive text page); Artist/Engraver and Caption; Date (in publisher's imprint). For the late-dated plate facing page *iii* see Note above.

VOLUME I: Title vignette; J.M.W. Turner 1825/George Cooke [provided for volume issue]; plates:

(1)	*iii*	A. Geddes/E. Goodall; Regalia of Scotland	1 December 1824
(2)	*1*	J.M.W. Turner/George Cooke; Crichton Castle	1 August 1819
(3)	23	E. Blore/W. Lizars; Crichton Castle. Interior Court	2 April 1819
(4)	28	E. Blore/J. LeKeux; Crichton Church	2 April 1819
(5)	*29*	I.M.W.[!] Turner/H. LeKeux; Borthwick Castle	2 April 1819
(6)	31	E. Blore/G. Cooke; Monument in Borthwick Church	2 April 1819
(7)	*33*	H.W. Williams/W. Finden; Borthwick Castle	1 August 1819
(8)	*34*	E. Blore/R. Sands; Hall of Borthwick Castle	1 August 1819
(9)	*51*	Revd. J. Thomson/G. Cooke; Crichton Castle	23 April 1819
(10)	67	Revd. J. Thomson/H. LeKeux; Dalkeith	1 August 1819
(11)	63	E. Blore/G. Hollis; Dalkeith Church	1 August 1819

Plate	Artist/Engraver; Subject	Date
(12) *65*	A.W. Callcott/George Cooke; Edinburgh. From St. Anthony's Chapel	20 December 1819
(13) 66	Edwd. Blore[drawn/engraved]; Interior of Holyrood Chapel	1 July 1821
(14) *67*	Revd. I.[!] Thomson/W. Woolnoth; Edinburgh. From Corstorphin[!] Hill	20 December 1819
(15) *68*	I.M.W.[!] Turner/H. LeKeux[1]; High Street, Edinburgh	20 December 1819
(16) *83*	J.M.W. Turner/George Cooke; Edinburgh. From the Calton Hill	1 November 1820
(17) *86*	A.W. Calcott/H. LeKeux[1]; The Castle. From the Grass Market	1 November 1820
(18) *89*	Revd. I.[!] Thomson/W. Woolnoth; Craig Millar Castle	4 August 1820
(19) 90	Revd. J. Thomson/J.C. Allen; Craig-Millar Castle	1 September 1826
(20) *91*	Revd. J. Thomson/J. Stewart; Merchiston Tower	1 November 1820
(21) *96*	E. Blore[drawn/engraved]; Holyrood Chapel. West Entrance	20 December 1819

VOLUME II: Title vignette; J.M.W. Turner/R. Wallis; [provided for volume issue]; plates:

Plate	Artist/Engraver; Subject	Date
(22) 97	J.M.W. Turner/H. Le Keux[1]; Heriot's Hospital, Edinburgh	1 November 1822
(23)*106*	A.W. Callcott/G. Cooke; Edinburgh. From Braid Hill	1 July 1821
(24)114	A. Nasmyth/G. Hollis; Edinburgh. From the Glasgow Road	1 July 1821
(25)*117*	E. Blore/G. Hollis; Holyrood House	1 January 1820
(26)*127*	J.M.W. Turner/W.R. Smith; Roslin Castle	1 November 1822
(27)129	Revd. S. Thomson/W. Cooke Junr; Roslin Castle	1 June 1822
(28)131	J. Schetky/J.C. Allen; Hawthornden	1 November 1822
(29)1*39*	E. Blore/G. Hollis; Seton Church	1 July 1821
(30)*145*	Revd. J. Thomson/W. Miller; Inverwick[!] Castle	1 October 1822
(31)*147*	I.M.W.[!] Turner/I.C. Allen; Dunbar	1 May 1824
(32)148	I. Schetky[!]/E. Goodall; Dunbar Castle	1 August 1823
(33)*160*	P.M.W. Turner[!]/E. Goodall; Tantallon Castle	1 June 1822
(34)162	Revd. I.[!] Thomson/Robt. Wallis; Tantallon Castle	1 November 1823
(35)*169*	I.M.W.[!] Turner/R. Wallis; Linlithgow Palace	1 July 1822
(36)171	E. Blore[drawn/engraved]; Linlithgow Church and Entrance to the Palace	1 September 1823
(37)175	E. Blore/H. LeKeux; Interior of the Hall of Linlithgow Palace	November 1823
(38)177	E. Blore[drawn/engraved]; Court of Linlithgow Palace	1 June 1822
(39)178	A.W. Callcott/W.R. Smith; Linlithgow	1 November 1823
(40)*181*	J.M.W. Turner/Willm. Miller; Bass Rock	1 May 1826
(41)*188*	Revd. I.[!] Thomson/Willm. Miller; Fast Castle	1 May 1826
(42)*197*	Revd. I.[!] Thomson/W. Miller; Dirlton[!] Castle	1 May 1824
(43)*199*	E. Blore/G. Hollis; Dalmeny Church	1 June 1822

(44)200	E. Blore[drawn/engraved]; South Porch of Dalmeny Church	1 July 1821
(45)200	Edw. Blore[drawn/engraved] Interior of Dalmeny Church	1 December 1824
(46)*201*	E. Blore[drawn/engraved]; South Entrance to Kirkliston Church	1 November 1822
(47)*202*	A.W. Callcott/George Cooke; Entrance to Leith Harbour	1 May 1826
(48)*205*	Edwd. Blore/G. Cook[!]; Roslyn Chapel[2]	1 May 1824
(49)206	E. Blore/H. LeKeux; Roslyn Chapel. Interior of the East End	1 August 1821
(50)207	E. Blore/H. LeKeux; Interior of Roslyn Chapel	1 June 1826

1. With additional note, 'The figures engraved [*or* etched] by G. Cooke.', evidently because LeKeux was admittedly incompetent to inscribe these lines. 2. This caption on a slip-cancel pasted over the erroneous reference 'Linlithgow Palace.'

LINES ON THE CALEDONIAN CANAL

133A] First Printing: 1819

'Lines on the Caledonian Canal . . . Imitation of the above, by the Modern Bard of Caledonia.', pages 98-99 *in*:

Two Excursions to the Ports of England, Scotland, and Ireland, in 1816, 1817, and 1818; . . . Translated from the French of Charles Dupin, . . . London: Printed for Sir Richard Phillips and Co. Bride-Court, Bridge-Street. 1819.

Published 17 May 1819 in London (*MC*). 3s sewed, 3s.6d in boards.

Notes: The essay containing Scott's verse, separately paged, later constituted the third section volume 1 of *New Voyages and Travels*, this with a title more accurately defining the third piece as 'Dupin's Excursions among the Public Establishments of Great Britain.' The essay itself, presumably, was translated by Phillips, the publisher, who offered his thanks (page viii) for the 'elegant version of M. Dupin's lines . . . with which we have been favoured by the Modern Bard of Caledonia.' The identity of the Bard is made clear in Phillips' own *Monthly Magazine* 1 June 1819 (pages 442-443) where it is remarked that 'Mr. Walter Scott has obligingly anglicized' Dupin's verse. The translation, in fourteen couplets, begins, 'Far in the desert Scottish bounds I saw'.

Copies: CtY TxU. Reference: (Magnum Opus Edition: Not reprinted.)

DESCRIPTION OF THE REGALIA OF SCOTLAND

I have never been more pleased since the battle of Waterloo than with this discovery. Who may get the merit of it I know not but I think I should have had my full share of blame had the research been unsuccessful. (Scott to William Dundas, 14 February 1818, *Letters*, v.82.)

134Aa] First Edition, First Impression: 1819

DESCRIPTION | OF THE | **REGALIA OF SCOTLAND.** | [*short Oxford rule*] | [*four-line quotation from* Albania, a Poem] | [*short reversed Oxford rule*] | EDINBURGH: | PRINTED BY JAMES BALLANTYNE AND COMPANY. | [*dash*] | 1819.

Published ca. May 1819 in Edinburgh. Binding: blue-green wrappers. Paper: Demy 12° (167 x 107mm uncut). Watermarks: R C | 1818. Collation: A^{12} B^{6}. Pagination: *1* title-page, *2 blank*, *3* 4-34 text, *35-36 blank*. No printer's imprint. Typography: Page 10, line 6, incorrectly gives the date of the coronation of David II as 1331. Figures: A22-11 24-8, B32-10.

Notes: On pages 28-29 Scott identifies himself as one of the ten persons commissioned to enter the Crown-Room at the Castle, where in a chest the Regalia of Scotland were discovered on 4 February 1818, after being sequestered from public view since 1707. The Room, 'handsomely fitted up for the exhibition of the Regalia', was opened for public inspection 26 May 1819 (page 30).

Scott's summary account, prepared it would seem for the exhibit, was later greatly expanded for insertion in parts 3-4 (1820-1821) of his *Provincial Antiquities* (*see* 132Ab). A copy of this earlier pamphlet was sent to James Skene before 26 June 1819.

Copies: E O; CtY MH NN NN(Berg) TxU.

References: *Letters*, v.400,n.2 (as amended by Corson[2], page 163). (Magnum Opus Edition: Not reprinted.)

134Ab] First Edition, Second (Large-Paper) Impression: 1819

DESCRIPTION | OF THE | **REGALIA OF SCOTLAND.** . . . 1819.

Published concurrently with the previous impression. Binding: blue-green wrappers. Paper: Demy 8° (175 x 117mm cut). Watermarks: J WHATMAN | 1816. Collation: A-B^{8} C1. Pagination: *1* title-page, *2 blank*, *3* 4-34. Figures: A—, B22-12, C—.

Notes: For this larger paper issue the type was reimposed in octavo format.

Copy: E.

134Ac] Second Edition: 1824

DESCRIPTION | OF THE | **REGALIA OF SCOTLAND.** | [*short rule*] | [*four-line quotation from* Albania, A Poem] | [*short rule*] | EDINBURGH: | **Printed by James Ballantyne and Company.** | [*dash*] | 1824.

Binding: Drab wrappers. Paper: Demy 12° (169 x 109mm cut). Watermarks: RC | 1820. Collation: A^{12} B^{6}. Pagination: *1* title-page, *2 blank*, *3* 4-34 text, 34 printer's imprint, *35-36 blank*. Printer's imprint: [*short rule*] | EDINBURGH: | Printed by James Ballantyne & Co. Figures: A—, B30-15.

Notes: This page-for-page resetting changes the incorrect date for the coronation of David II (page 10, line 6) from 1331 in the first edition to 1329.

Copies: GU O; IdU MH NNP.

References: Van Antwerp(2) 27(incorrectly described as first edition).

134Ad] Third Edition: 1830

DESCRIPTION | OF THE | **REGALIA OF SCOTLAND.** | [*short rule*] | [*four-line quotation from* Albania, A Poem] | [*short rule*] | EDINBURGH: | **Printed by James Ballantyne and Company.** | [*dash*] | 1830.

Paper: Demy 12° (174 x 107mm cut). Watermarks: *none*. Collation: A^{6} B^{12} (-B12). Pagination: *1* title-page, *2 blank*, *3* 4-34 text, 34 printer's imprint: [*short rule*] | EDINBURGH: | Printed by James Ballantyne & Co. Figures: *none*.

Copy: BCL; NN.

REPRINTS

GREAT BRITAIN

134Ra] EDINBURGH: Shaw 1827
Description of the Regalia of Scotland. . . . Edinburgh, Printed by J. Shaw and Co. Riddel's Court, Lawnmarket. 1827. Pages: *1-3* 4-34. Copies: E(2); MH.

134Rb] EDINBURGH: University 1830
Description of the Regalia of Scotland. . . Edinburgh: Printed at the University Press. 1830. Pages: *1-3* 4-34. Notes: On the verso of a leaf before title it is noted that four additional jewels were deposited in the crown-room by order of King William IV, 18 December 1830. Copies: BCL; MH.

DERIVATIVE

GREAT BRITAIN

134D] EDINBURGH: Walker and Anderson 1819
The Regalia of Scotland A Medley . . . . Walker & Anderson Edinr. [unwatermarked. ca.1819]. Pages: *1* 2-3. Notes: Engraved sheet music with caption title. Medley composed of five favorite tunes by F. W. Grant. Price 2/. Footnote on page *1* to The Regalia of Scotland reads: 'Discovered 4th. Feby. 1818'. Copy: E.

TALES OF MY LANDLORD
[Third Series]
THE BRIDE OF LAMMERMOOR and A LEGEND OF MONTROSE

Reader! The Tales of my Landlord are now finally closed, . . . I have the vanity to suppose, that the popularity of these Novels has shewn my countrymen, and their peculiarities, in lights which were new to the Southern reader; and that many, hitherto indifferent upon the subject, have been induced to read Scottish history, from the allusions in these works of fiction.

I retire from the field, conscious there remains behind not only a large harvest, but labourers capable of gathering it in. (iv.319-320.)

135Aa] First Edition, First Issue: 1819

TALES OF MY LANDLORD, | Third Series, | COLLECTED AND ARRANGED | BY | JEDEDIAH CLEISHBOTHAM, | SCHOOLMASTER AND PARISH-CLERK OF GANDERCLEUGH. | [*short rule*] | [*six-line quotation from Burns*] | [*short rule*] | IN FOUR VOLUMES. | VOL. I [II-IV]. | [*short Oxford rule*] | EDINBURGH: | PRINTED FOR ARCHIBALD CONSTABLE AND CO. EDINBURGH; | [*short rule*] | LONGMAN, HURST, REES, ORME, AND BROWN, PATERNOSTER-ROW; | AND HURST, ROBINSON, AND CO. 90, CHEAPSIDE, LONDON. | [*dash*] | 1819.

Published 21 June 1819 in Edinburgh (*EEC*); issued 26 June in London (*MC*). (First London advertisement again is by William Sams; Longman announced on 14 June for 'Monday next' [21st] but no further listing appears). £1.12.0. Probably 10,000 copies for the three issues (*EEWN7a*.274). All of the seven 'Waverley' novels issued thus far are occasionally cited in the advertisements as a set of 24 volumes, price £9.2.0. Binding: drab or blue boards with printed labels. Paper: Royal 12° (190 x 112mm uncut). Watermarks: 1818 | 9; C | 1818 [1819]. General Typography: Printer's imprints: (1) [*short rule*] | *Printed by James Ballantyne and Co.*; (2) [*short rule*] | EDINBURGH: | Printed by James Ballantyne and Co. ['& Co.' vols.2-3]

General Notes: Volumes 1-3 represent 'The Bride of Lammermoor'; volumes 3-4 'A Legend of Montrose.' Of these Constable on 22 May posted to Hurst, Robinson an advance copy of the first three volumes only 'for your foreign Correspondent' (Thomas Wardle), but then neglected to send the fourth: a circumstance leading eventually to a partial issue in Philadelphia (*see* 135Ri). Meanwhile, on 11 June, a complete shipment of 5000 copies was shipped to London on the 'Wellington' (*EEWN7a.*273-274).

Presentation copies: E('given to me by Mr Walter Scott while a secret 1819' [Lady Louisa Stuart]). Other copies: AN BCL(3) E L(2) O(9) O*; CtY IdU InU(3) MH NN(3) NNU-W.
*With 4-page Longman catalogue February 1819.

References: J. H. Alexander (ed.), *EEWN7a-7b*; Church 536; Sterling 728; Thomson, pages 17, 40-41; Van Antwerp(1) 8; Worthington 7. (Magnum Opus Edition 1830: *Waverley Novels*, [1] xiii.*235-237* 238-392—xiv. [2] xv.)

1] **TALES OF MY LANDLORD,** | Third Series, . . . VOL. I. . . . 1819.

Collation: π^2 A-O^{12}. Pagination: *i* half-title, *ii* quotation and printer's imprint(1), *iii* title-page, *iv blank*, *1* fly-title for 'The Bride of Lammermoor', *2 blank*, *3* 4-333 text, chapters 1-12, 333 printer's imprint(2), *334-336 blank*. Typography: Section signature N2 (page 297) is transposed as 2N.

Figures: A14-9 24-6, B37-5 43-8, C63-9 69-6, D88-9 94-6/-, E117-8 118-1, F131-3 141-5, G166-9 168-4, H178-1 181-4, I 202-8 205-7, K222-3 236-6, L252-9 258-3, M277-4 286-5, N303-7 312-8, O 315-2 325-5/10.

2] **TALES OF MY LANDLORD,** | Third Series, . . . VOL. II. . . . 1819.

Collation: π^2 A-N^{12} O^6. Pagination: *i* half-title, *ii* quotation and printer's imprint(1), *iii* title-page, *iv blank*, *1* fly-title for 'The Bride of Lammermoor', *2 blank*, *3* 4-324 text continued, 324 printer's imprint(2). Typography: In some copies page 117 is misnumbered 11. Section signature N2 (page 297) is missigned N3.

Figures: A15-3 24-7, B35-5 48-9/-, C53-6 59-11, D74-10 85-2, G106-7 113-3, F122-11 133-7, G154-2 160-5, H171-3 192-8, I 195-5 205-4, K229-7 239-2, L250-5 256-10, M285-3 286-11, N310-10 312-6/-, O 321-8/-.

3] **TALES OF MY LANDLORD,** | Third Series, . . . VOL. III. . . . 1819.

Collation: π^2 A-O^{12}. Pagination: *i* half-title, *ii* quotation and printer's imprint(1), *iii* title-page, *iv blank*, *1* fly-title for 'The Bride of Lammermoor', *2 blank*, *3* 4-131 text concluded, *132 blank*, *133* fly-title for 'A Legend of Montrose', *134 blank*, *135* 136-147 Introduction, *148 blank*, *149* 150-333 text, chapters 1-8, 333 printer's imprint(2), *334-336 blank.* Typography: In some copies the colon in printer's imprint(2) is dropped.

Figures: A4-8 14-3, B34-7/- 37-10, C62-6 72-5, D83-4 96-8, E109-10 110-11, F124-10 130-5, G154-12 168-6, H171-8 184-7, I 195-11 196-13, K232-8 238-7, L254-5, M267-11 268-2, N298-12 312-3, O 324-7 327-8.

Notes: In some copies of this and of the later 'editions' the quotation page *ii* is replaced by an advertisement citing the forthcoming issue in November of *Illustrations of the Novels and Tales* in 12 prints after designs by William Allan (see 322D).

4] **TALES OF MY LANDLORD,** | Third Series, . . . VOL. IV. . . . 1819.

Collation: π^2 A-O^{12}. Pagination: *i* half-title, *ii* quotation and printer's imprint(1), *iii* title-page, *iv blank*, *1* fly-title for 'A Legend of Montrose', *2 blank*, *3* 4-330 text concluded, 330 printer's imprint(2), *1* 2-4 Archibald Constable catalogue, dated June 1819, *5-6 blank*. Typography: Title imprint has a comma after the last 'CO'.

Figures: A4-10 15-5/-, B46-11 48-8, C58-9 61-13, D74-7 76-12, E98-10 112-5, F122-11 132-3, G154-8 157-13, H171-7 180-5, I 202-10 216-12, K220-3 226-8, L256-11 263-6, M266-10 288-4, N302-2 312-7, O 314-13 328-1.

Notes: As in volume 3 in some copies of this and of the later 'editions' the quotation page *ii* is replaced by an advertisement, now citing as published 'This day' the *Memoirs of the Most Renowned James Graham* (135Dc).

135Ab] Second Edition (First Edition, Second Issue): 1819

TALES OF MY LANDLORD, | Third Series, . . . VOL. I [II-IV]. | SECOND EDITION. . . . 1819.

Issued 19 August 1819 in London (*MC*). £1.12.0. Notes: A further issue with 'Second Edition' titles, the book representing the later state of imprints and advertisements noted above. On 13 August Constable mentioned that, of 'the last thousand' (i.e., it seems, the final printing of the 10,000 total issue), 'there were 800 with Second Edition [titles] and 200 with *third*' (*EEWN7a*.303, n.33).

Copies: C E(2) O.

135Ac] Third Edition (First Edition, Third Issue): 1819

TALES OF MY LANDLORD, | Third Series, . . . VOL. I [II-IV]. | THIRD EDITION. . . . 1819.

Notes: A further issue of 200 copies with all points again in later state. See preceding note.

Copies: E L; CtY.

REPRINTS

FRANCE

PARIS: Baudry, Barrois [and others]
[~] Tales of My Landlord. . . . Third Series. 1831. (Collection of Ancient and Modern British Novels and Romances: *see* 288R.14.)

PARIS: Didot
[~] A Legend of Montrose. 1826. (Select British Novels, Tales, and Historical Romances: *see* 289R.1-2.)

PARIS: Didot and Galignani
[~] Tales of My Landlord, Third Series. M DCCC XXI. (Collection of Modern English Authors: *see* 291R.21-24.)

135Ra] PARIS: Doyen 1826
Legend of Montrose. By Sir Walter Scott. . . . Paris: Printed by G. Doyen, Rue St. Jacques, N. 38. 1826. Two volumes. Pages 1: *i-v* vi-xvi, *1* 2-200; 2: *i-iv*, *1* 2-227. Copy: E.

PARIS: Galignani
[~] A Legend of Montrose. 1829. Two volumes. (*see* 293R.12-13.) Copy: not seen.

GERMANY

135Rb] BERLIN: Schlesinger 1823
[1] [The Bride of Lammermoor. . . . Berlin, Printed for Adolph Martin Schlesinger. 1823.] Copy reported at Stadtbibliothek Worms. Reference: GDS 132, page 337.

[2] [A Legend of Montrose. . . . Berlin, Printed for Adolph Martin Schlesinger. 1823.] Copy reported at Stadtbibliothek Worms. Reference: GDS 132, page 342.

LEIPZIG: Wigand
[~] The Bride of Lammermoor. 1832. (A Complete Edition of the Waverley Novels: *see* 300R.21- 22.)

[~] A Legend of Montrose. 1832. (A Complete Edition of the Waverley Novels. *see* 300R. 23-24.)

ZWICKAU: Schumann
[~] The[!] Legend of Montrose. 1823. (Pocket Library of English Classics: *see* 302R.60-61.)

[~] Tales of My Landlord. . . . The Bride of Lammermoor. 1823. (Pocket Library of English Classics: *see* 302R.57-59.)

UNITED STATES

135Rc] BOSTON: Parker 1821-1832
[Tales of My Landlord. Third Series. 1821. Pages: *1-3* 4-460, *1* 2-14.] Copy: not seen. (Also reissued 1822 in Novels Tales and Romances: *see* 305R.7).

[~] Tales of My Landlord. Third Series. 1827, 1829. (Waverley Novels: *see* 306R.13-14).

[~] Tales of My Landlord. Third Series. 1830, 1832. (Waverley Novels: [Parker's Edition Revised] *see* 307R.13-14).

135Rd] HARTFORD: Goodrich, and Huntington and Hopkins 1821
Tales of My Landlord; Third Series: Collected and Arranged by Jedediah Cleishbotham, . . . Hartford: Samuel G. Goodrich, and Huntington and Hopkins. 1821. Pages: *1-3* 4-340. Copies: E; PU.

135Re] NEW YORK: Duyckinck, Gilley, Lockwood, Bliss 1821
Tales of My Landlord. Third Series. Collected and Arranged by Jedediah Cleishbotham, . . . New-York; Published by Evert Duyckinck, W. B. Gilley, L. & F. Lockwood, and Elam Bliss. James & John Harper, Printers, 1821. Two volumes. Pages 1: *1-3* 4-342; 2: *1-3* 4-340. Notes: Volume 1 'The Bride of Lammermoor'; 2 'The Bride of Lammermoor', 'A Legend of Montrose'. Copy: MWA.

135Rf] NEW YORK: Wiley 1819
Tales of My Landlord: Third Series. Collected and Arranged by Jedediah Cleishbotham, . . . New-York: Published by Charles Wiley & Co., W. B. Gilley, and A. T. Goodrich & Co. Clayton and Kingsland, Printers. 1819. Four volumes bound in two. Pages 1: *1-3* 4-151 *152*; 2: *153* 154-297; 3: *1-3* 4-152; 4: *1-3* 4-153 *154-156*, *1* 2-7. Notes: This book has only two title-pages, one for volumes 1-2, and a second for 3-4. 'A Legend of Montrose' has the only half-title. The pagination for volumes 1-2 runs continually, but not the chapter numbers or signatures. Volume 2, chapter heading VIII, is correct on page 204, but repeated on page 215, a mistake which disorders all later headings in volume 2. In volume 2, there are two 'N' signatures. Contents: Volumes 1-3 'The Bride of Lammermoor'; 4 'A Legend of Montrose'. Copies: E; CtY NN(2) PPL ViU.

135Rg] PHILADELPHIA: Crissy 1826
Tales of My Landlord: Third Series: Collected and Arranged by Jedediah Cleishbotham, . . . Philadelphia: James Crissy, No. 14, South Seventh Street. 1826. Three volumes. Pages 1: *1-3* 4-240; 2: *1-3* 4-236; 3: *1-3* 4-235. Notes: volumes 1-2 'The Bride of Lammermoor'; 2-3: 'A Legend of Montrose'. Copies: IdU NN T/B.

135Rh] PHILADELPHIA: Maxwell 1822
Tales of My Landlord: Third Series. Collected and Arranged by Jedediah Cleishbotham, . . . Philadelphia: Published by James Maxwell. 1822. Three volumes. Pages 1: *1-3* 4-'542'[254]; 2: *1-3* 4-226; 3: *1-3* 4-236. Notes: In some copies the final page number volume 1 correctly reads '254'; volume 3 imprint 'Printed and Published'. Volumes 1 and 2: 'The Bride of Lammermoor'; 2 and 3: 'A Legend of Montrose'. Chapter numbers for 'A Legend of Montrose' run continuously for volumes 2 and 3. Copies: CtY MWA NN NjP PPL RPB T/B.

135Ri] PHILADELPHIA: Thomas [and others] 1819
Tales of My Landlord: Third Series. Collected and Arranged by Jedediah Cleishbotham, . . . Philadelphia: Published by M. Thomas, No. 108, Chesnut-Street and J. Haly & C. Thomas, No. 55 Maiden Lane, New York. 1819. Four volumes in two. Pages 1: *1-5* 6-162; 2: *1-3* 4-156; 3: *i-ii*, *1-3* 4-160; 4: *1-3* 4-159 *160*, *1-3* 4-8. Notes: Title-pages vary in punctuation. Two title-pages serve for volumes 1-2 and for 3-4, the text for 2 and 4 identified only by a half-title. An extraordinary preliminary notice, volume 1, page *4*, is quoted in full:

ADVERTISEMENT

The copy from which the present edition is printed, was sent from Edinburgh previous to the publication of the work there. Three volumes only (of the four) were ready at the time—the fourth was to have been sent as soon as printed. Being uncertain, however, when it may arrive, it has been thought advisable to publish the first Tale separately.

The American edition will be printed volume for volume with the Edinburgh, but the four volumes *will be bound in two*. "The Bride of Lammermoor," being longer than the "Legend of Montrose," extends 63 pages into the third volume, which pages, in order to complete the Tale, are put at the end of this volume instead of the beginning of the next. Of the copies thus done up, the first volume will be much the larger, but the binder can put these pages in their proper place when the work is bound, and the volumes will then be of the same size.

[*pointing hand*] Those who take the first volume will be required to pay for the set, and receive a due bill which will entitle them to the second volume.

Philadelphia, August, 1819.

Though the book in this provisional arrangement has not been seen, the occasion for it arises from the fact that, while the first lot of advance sheets (through the third Edinburgh volume: see 135Aa) was shipped as early as 22 May, no further copy was supplied. Thus, presumably, Thomas some time after August had to secure his remaining text in another way—perhaps from a New York edition (135Rf). Copies: MH NNU-W PPL ViU.

DERIVATIVES

GREAT BRITAIN

135Da] BATH: White 1822
Wert thou like me in life's low vale, The Song of Annot Lyle, from A Legend of Montrose in the Tales of my Landlord; . . . Bath, Published at White's Music Warehouses, No. 1, Milsom Street & 3, George Street. [1822]. Pages: *1-2* 3-7 *8*. Notes: Engraved sheet music with composer's signature in ink at foot of first page and plate number: '(64)'. Words from 'A Legend of Montrose', chapter 21 (first words as title). Music composed by John Charles White arranged for voice and pianoforte. Copies: L O. Reference: G/T 10341.

135Db] EDINBURGH: Anderson 1823
[1] The Bride of Lammermoor. A Drama; In Five Acts. . . Taken from the Celebrated Story of the Same Name in the Third Series of the "Tales of My Landlord." . . . Edinburgh: Printed for John Anderson, Jun. 55, North Bridge Street, Edinburgh; and Simpkin and Marshall, Stationers'

Hall Court, Ludgate Street, London. 1823. Pages: *i-v* vi-viii *ix-x*, *1* 2-62. Notes: Drama by John William Calcraft [Cole]. The Preface begins 'In the following Drama, the language and incidents of the beautiful and affecting Tale from which it is taken, have been carefully preserved.' The Preface, signed with the dramatist's initials, is dated 15 January 1823. Copies: L O; CtY DLC. References: Bolton 2776; Ford E4.

[2] [Montrose or the Children of the Mist. Second Edition. Edinburgh: Published by John Anderson Junr. 55. North Bridge Street. 1823.] Notes: Dramatized anonymously by Isaac Pocock, but apparently not published in a 'first edition'. Copy: not seen. (Also issued in: Edinburgh Select British Theatre, 1823: volume 8 [*see* 319D] and in: The Waverley Dramas, 1823: volume 2, play 6 [*see* 321D].) Reference: Bolton 3289.

135Dc] EDINBURGH: Constable 1819

Memoirs of the most renowned James Graham, Marquis of Montrose. . . . Edinburgh: Printed for Archibald Constable & Co. Edinburgh; Longman, Hurst, Rees, Orme, & Brown, Paternoster-Row; and Hurst, Robinson, & Co., 90, Cheapside, London. 1819. Pages: *i-v*, vi-xvi, *1* 2-530. Notes: Translated from the Latin of The Rev. Dr George Wishart. The relevance of this substantial work is made apparent in the opening paragraph of the 'Preface', page *v*: 'As the last series of the Tales of My Landlord will probably call the attention of the public towards the biography of the Marquis of Montrose, it has been deemed expedient to republish this translation of Bishop Wishart's Memoirs, adding a few Notes to those already subjoined, and increasing the original Appendix with various interesting documents, some of which are now for the first time printed.' Copy: E.

135Dd] GLASGOW: Johnston [and others] 1820

Montrose; A National Melo-Drama. In Three Acts. Glasgow: Printed for C. Johnston & Co, J. Brash & Co. Reid & Henderson, William Turnbull and Thomas Ogilvie; A. Constable & Co. William Blackwood and Fairburn & Anderson, Edinburgh; Longman & Co and C. Chapple, 66, Pall Mall, London. 1820. Pages: *1-7* 8-49. Notes: The anonymous writer dedicates the play to Scott, as 'The Unknown, but Immortal Author of Waverley' and confesses in the Advertisement 'that the Author of WAVERLEY is the literary "god of his idolatry."' Copies: BCL; CtY. Reference: Bolton 3288.

135De] LONDON: Birchall 1822

Wert thou like me in Life's low Vale, Song, taken from the Third Series of Tales of my Landlord, ... London, Printed & Sold by Birchall & Co. 133, New Bond Street. [1822]. Pages: 1-3. Notes: Engraved sheet music with caption title and plate number: '1220'. Words from 'A Legend of Montrose', chapter 21 (first words as title). Music composed by Thomas Miles arranged for voice and pianoforte. Price 1/6. Copies: L(2). Reference: G/T 10332.

135Df] LONDON: Chappell and Goulding 1819

Him I Love, A Song from the Tales of My Landlord, . . . London, Printed & Sold by Chappell & Co. 50, New Bond Street, & Goulding & Co. 20. Soho Square. [1819]. Pages: 1-4. Notes: Engraved sheet music with caption title and plate number: '1020'. Words from 'A Legend of Montrose', chapter 21 (first words: 'Wer't thou like me, in life's low vale,'). Song composed by George Kiallmark arranged for voice and pianoforte. Price: 1/6. Copies: E L.

135Dg] LONDON: Clementi 1819
[Him I Love. London: Clementi. (1819). Notes: Music composed by George Kiallmark.] Copy: not seen. Reference: G/T 10330.

135Dh] LONDON: Goulding, D'Almaine, Potter 1819-1822
[1] 'The Forester's Roundelay' from the Bride of Lammermoor! In the Tales of my Landlord. (Third Series) . . . London, Published by Goulding, D'Almaine, Potter & Co. 20, Soho Sq. & to be had at 7, Westmorland St. Dublin. [watermarked 1816. 1819]. Pages: *i-ii*, 1-9. Notes: Engraved sheet music. Words from chapter 2 or 3 (first words: 'The monk must arise when the matins ring, The abbot may sleep to their chime;'). Music composed by Henry R. Bishop arranged for voice and pianoforte. In two impressions (1a) watermarked 1816 with the title word 'Forester's' misspelled 'Forrester's', (1b) same watermark with title word corrected. Copies: (1a) L. (1b) BCL L; InU NNP. References: G/T 9760(1a); Van Antwerp(2) 42n.

[2] Him I Love, Canzonet, from "A Legend of Montrose" in the Tales of my Landlord, (Third Series) . . . . London, Published by Goulding, D'Almaine, Potter & Co. 20, Soho Square, & to be had at 7, Westmoreland Street, Dublin. [watermarked 1816. 1819]. Pages: *i-ii*, *1* 2-5. Notes: Engraved sheet music. Words from chapter 21 (first words: 'Wert thou, like me, in life's low vale,'). Canzonet composed by Henry R. Bishop for voice and pianoforte. Price 2/. Copy: L.

[3] Look not thou on Beauty's Charming. Canzonet from "The Bride of Lammermoor," . . . London Published by Goulding, D'Almaine, Potter & Co. 20, Soho Sq. & to be had at 7, Westmorland St. Dublin. [watermarked 1816. 1819]. Pages: *i-ii*, *1* 2-4. Notes: Engraved sheet-music with plate mark: 'Look not thou &c.'. Words from chapter 3 (first words as title). Music composed by Henry R. Bishop arranged for voice and pianoforte. Price: 2s. Copy: NNP. Later reissued on unwatermarked paper. References: G/T 9759[1815?]; Van Antwerp(2) 42j.

[4] The Overture Marches & Vocal Music, In the Opera of Montrose or The Children of the Mist. . . London. Published by Goulding, D'Almaine, Potter and Co. 20, Soho Square, & to be had at 7, Westmorland Street, Dublin. [unwatermarked. ca.1822]. Pages: *i-ii*, *1* 2-58. Notes: Engraved sheet music with the composer's rubber-stamped monogram below imprint and with plate marks: 'Ov: Montrose' and 'Montrose'. The words adapted by Isaac Pocock with music composed and arranged by Henry R. Bishop for voice and pianoforte. Price: 10/6. Copy: E.

LONDON: Hodgson
[~] Montrose; or, The Children of the Mist. [1822]. (Hodgson's Juvenile Drama: number 3. *see* 333D).

LONDON: Leigh
[~] Annot Lyle's Song. 1831. (The Harmonicon: number 5. *see* 337D.3). Notes: Series initially printed for The Proprietors, published by Leigh. This title published by Longman, Rees, Orme, Brown, and Green.

135Di] LONDON: Power 1819
The Song of Annot Lyle, From "A Legend of Montrose" in the Tales of My Landlord, . . London, Published by J. Power, 34, Strand. [1819]. Pages: *1-2* 3-7. Notes: Engraved sheet music (1) without plate number; (2) with plate number: '462'. Words from chapter 21 (first

words: 'Wert thou, like me, in life's low vale, With thee, how blest, that lot I'd share;'). Music composed by Wesley Doyle arranged for voice and pianoforte. Price: 2/-. Copies: (1) L. (2) E. Reference: G/T 10325.

135Dj] LONDON: Preston 1830
To Weep and pray for him, I Love from Tales of my Landlord. . . . London. Printed & Sold by Preston, at his Wholesale Warehouses, 97 Strand. [1830]. Pages: *1* 2-[3-4?]-5. Notes: Engraved sheet music with plate mark: 'Wer't thou like me.' Words from 'A Legend of Montrose', chapter 21 (first words: 'Wer't thou like me, in life's low vale,'). Price: 1/6. Copy: L.

135Dk] LONDON: Regent's Harmonic Institution 1819
"Wert thou like Me?" Annot Lyle's Song, from the Tales of my Landlord, . . . London, Printed by the Regent's Harmonic Institution, (Lower Saloon, Argyll Rooms.). [1819]. Pages: 1-5. Notes: Engraved sheet music with caption title and with plate number: '360'. Words from 'A Legend of Montrose' chapter 21 (first words: 'Wert thou like me in life's low vale, with thee how blest, that lot I'd share;'). Music composed by John Goss arranged for voice and pianoforte. Price: 2s/-. Copy: L. Reference: G/T 10328.

135Dl] LONDON: Royal Harmonic Institution 1820
"Wert thou, like me, in Life's Low Vale," Annot Lyles Song, from "A Legend of Montrose," one of the Tales of my Landlord, . . . London, Printed for the Author [composer] by The Royal Harmonic Institution, Lower Saloon, Argyll Rooms. [1820]. Pages: *i-ii*, 1-3 *4*. Notes: Upon the ascendency of George IV the name of the sponsoring Institution was restyled (*see* preceding entry). Engraved sheet music with plate number: '587'. Words from chapter 21 (first words: 'Wert thou, like me, in life's low vale'). Music composed by William Hawes arranged for voice and pianoforte. Price: 1/6. Copies: L O. Reference: G/T 10329.

135Dm] LONDON: Simpkin and Marshall 1822
Montrose; or the Children of the Mist. A Musical Drama, in Three Acts, Founded on The[!] Legend of Montrose. . . . London: Printed for W. Simpkin & R. Marshall Stationers'-Hall-Court, Ludgate Street; By W. Molineux, Bream's Buildings, Chancery Lane. 1822. Pages: *i-iv*, *1* 2-70 *71-72*. Notes: Drama with words by Isaac Pocock (the overture by Henry Bishop and other music not included) as first performed at The Theatre-Royal, Covent-Garden, 14 February 1822. Price: Three Shillings. Copies: BCL E GM L; CtY(2) NjP NNU-W ViU. References: Bolton 3289; Ford M4.

UNITED STATES

135Dn] BALTIMORE: Robinson 1822-1829
Montrose; or, The Children of the Mist. A Musical Drama, in Three Acts. Founded on The[!] Legend of Montrose. . . . Baltimore: Printed and Published by J. Robinson, Circulating Library and Dramatic Repository, 94, Market-street. 1822. Pages: *1-3* 4-60. Notes: Libretto by Isaac Pocock (music composed by Henry R. Bishop not included) as first performed at the Theatre=Royal, Covent=Garden, 14 February 1822. Copies: CtY MWA NN. Reissued 1829 (not seen).

135Do] NEW YORK: Riley 1819
Annot Lyle's Song from Musical Illustrations of the Waverly[!] Novels . . . New-York, Publish'd by E. Riley, 29, Chatham Street. [ca.1819]. Pages: *1-3*. Notes: Engraved sheet music with caption title. Words from 'A Legend of Montrose' chapter 21 (first words: 'Wert thou, like me in life's low vale, With thee how blest that lot I'd share,'). Copy: InU.

135Dp] PHILADELPHIA: Carey and Lea 1822
Valdemar; or, The Castle of the Cliff. A Tragedy. . . . Philadelphia: H. C. Carey and I. Lea, Chesnut Street. J. Maxwell, Printer. 1822. Pages: iv, *5* 6-50. Notes: Play by James Wright Simmons. Page iv: 'Those who read his tragedy will perceive, what we always meant to acknowledge, that it is founded upon the beautiful romance of the Bride of Lammermoor.' Copy: MH. Reference: Clarkin 1326.

EXTRACTS IN ANTHOLOGIES

135E] From these two tales there are 11 extracts in nine anthologies: (1) 'The Bride of Lammermoor': 366[2]E.12; (2) 'A legend of Montrose': 375[2]E.2,3 380 386.8 389.33 405-(2)[3].10,19 417.3 469.9 472.2.

THE POETICAL REMAINS OF JOHN LEYDEN

136A] First Printing: 1819

'NOTES BY THE EDITOR OF THE MINSTRELSY OF THE SCOTTISH BORDERS, pages 71-72, *in*:

The Poetical Remains of the Late Dr. John Leyden, with Memoirs of his Life, by The Rev. James Morton. London: Printed by Strahan and Spottiswoode, Printers-Street, For Longman, Hurst, Rees, Orme, and Brown; And A. Constable and Co. Edinburgh. 1819.

Published 20 August 1819 in London (*MC*). 12s.

Notes: Scott's notes refer to a lengthy poem titled 'Lord Soulis' which had first appeared in his *The Minstrelsy of the Scottish Border*. While only the pages noted above are specifically attributable to Scott, there are intimations throughout that he was involved in the publication of this volume. The Memoirs end (page xcii) with a note pointing out that Scott alludes to the death of Leyden in *The Lord of the Isles* (stanza 11):

His bright and brief career is o'er,
  And mute his tuneful strains; . . .
A distant and a deadly shore
  Has LEYDEN'S cold remains!

Copy: CtY. Reference: (Magnum Opus Edition: Not reprinted.)

LETTER VINDICATING THE MAGISTRATES AT MANCHESTER

137A] First Printing: 1819

'TO THE EDITOR OF THE EDINBURGH WEEKLY JOURNAL.' pages 305-306, *in*:

The Edinburgh Weekly Journal. Vol. XXII. No. 1134.] Wednesday, September 8, 1819. [Price 7d. Edinburgh—Printed by James Ballantyne, For himself and the other Proprietors.

Published 8 September 1819 in Edinburgh. Notes: In rejoinder to an editorial commentary (by James Ballantyne) this extensive report notes that the magistrates, as GUARDIANS OF THE PUBLIC PEACE, are obliged to put down riotous gatherings of the kind assembled by 'Mr Hunt and his friends.' The signature initials 'L.T.' probably signify Laurence Templeton, the pseudonym Scott used in *Ivanhoe* (*see* 140Aa), published a few months later.

Copy: E. References: Garside, pages 504-505. (Magnum Opus Edition: Not reprinted.)

THE LATE LORD SOMERVILLE

138A] First Printing: 1819

'THE LATE LORD SOMERVILLE.', page 362, *in*:

The Edinburgh Weekly Journal. Vol. XXII. No. 1141.] Wednesday, October 27, 1819. [Price 7d. Edinburgh—Printed by James Ballantyne, For himself and the other Proprietors.

Published 27 October 1819 in Edinburgh. Notes: Somerville, deceased at Vevey on 5 October, was Scott's closest neighbor, with his family seat at The Pavilion, one mile east of Abbotsford across the Tweed.

Copy: E. Reference: (Magnum Opus Edition 1834: *The Miscellaneous Prose Works*, iv.309-321 as 'Character of the Late John Lord Somerville'.)

THE VISIONARY

139Aa] First Printing: 1819

'THE VISIONARY, No. I [II, III]. TO THE EDITOR OF THE EDINBURGH WEEKLY JOURNAL.', pages 402, 410, 418, *in*:

The Edinburgh Weekly Journal. Vol. XXII. No. 1146 [1147, 1148].] Wednesday, December 1 [8, 15], 1819. [Price 7d. Edinburgh—Printed by James Ballantyne, For himself and the other Proprietors.
Published 1, 8, 15 December 1819 in Edinburgh.

Notes: The three letters are signed SOMNAMBULUS. See further the next entry.

Copy: E. References: Garside, pages 507-509. (Magnum Opus Edition: Not reprinted.)

139Ab] First Book Edition: 1819[1820]

THE | VISIONARY. | Nos. I. II. III. | [*rule*] | [*one-line quotation from* Romeo and Juliet] | [*rule*] | EDINBURGH: | PRINTED FOR WILLIAM BLACKWOOD, EDINBURGH; AND | T. CADELL AND W. DAVIES, STRAND, LONDON. | [*dash*] | 1819.

Published 1 January 1820 in Edinburgh (*EEC*); issued 27 January in London. 6d. Binding: sewed with π1 leaf wrapped around the text gatherings. Paper: Royal 12° (194 x 120mm uncut). Watermarks: *none*. Collation: π^2(-π1=*D*1) A-B^{12} C^4 *D*1. Pagination: *i* half-title, *ii blank*, *1* title-page, *2* printer's imprint(1), *3* 4-16 Preface (unsigned), *17* 18-55 text of the three letters, each signed 'Somnambulus', 55 printer's imprint(2), *56 blank*, *57* advertisement, *58 blank*. Printer's imprints: (1) [*short rule*] | *Printed by James Ballantyne and Co.*; (2) [*short rule*] | EDINBURGH: | Printed by James Ballantyne & Co. Typography: Section signature B2 (page 33) is omitted. Figures: A12-6 23-13, B47-5 48-15, C51-11.

Notes: The new Preface, noting the earlier issue of these essays in a newspaper, indicates that the present printing might still 'do some good at this very peculiar crisis' relating to the insane idea of Radical Reform and Universal Suffrage (page *3*), admits the necessity of 'two parties in this and in every free state' (page 5), but still feels 'obliged to separate the leaders and more respectable part of the followers of the Whig party in Scotland, from the more unworthy part of their own body, as well as from the mob of Radicality, . . .' (page 7).

Copies: BCL E E(Abbot) ES GU O; InU MH NN(Berg) NNU-W TxU.

Reference: Duval 946 (with illustration).

REPRINT

GREAT BRITAIN

139R] SUNDERLAND: Reed 1819
Reform and Ruin! A Dream. [Printer's imprint: Sunderland; printed by Reed & Son.] [1819]. Pages: *1* 2-4. Notes: A tract signed Somnambulus, reprinted from Number 2 of 'The Visionary'. Copy: L.

IVANHOE

Ivanhoe was highly successful upon its appearance, and may be said to have procured for its author the freedom of the Rules, since he has ever since been permitted to exercise his powers of fictitious composition in England, as well as Scotland. ('Introduction', 1 September 1830, *WN*, xvi.xx.)

140Aa] First Edition, First Issue: 1820[1819]

IVANHOE; | A ROMANCE. | BY "THE AUTHOR OF WAVERLEY," &c. | [*short rule*] | [*two-line quotation from Prior*] | [*short rule*] | IN THREE VOLUMES. | VOL. I [II-III]. | [*short Oxford rule*] | EDINBURGH: | PRINTED FOR ARCHIBALD CONSTABLE AND CO. EDINBURGH; | AND HURST, ROBINSON, AND CO. 90, CHEAPSIDE, LONDON. | [*dash*] | 1820.

Published 20 December 1819 in Edinburgh (*EEC*); issued 29 December in London (*MC*). £1.10.0. (In an undated note Scott reports that 'by an unhappy accident a vessel containing 6000 [*recte* 5750] copies was forced to put into Shields and there is not even yet advice of her having reached London' [*Letters,* v.404]; total printing for all issues through 140Ac apparently reached 10,000 copies [E MS. 742,f.191r]. Binding: drab, rose, or blue-green boards with printed labels. Paper: Post 8° (198 x 122mm uncut). Watermarks: irregular, but occasionally BATH | 1817; 1818; 1819.

Typography: In all three volumes the first doubleton, consisting of half-title and title, is set in duplicate, with the same two settings used for all three volumes in an indiscriminate way. The exclamation point after 'depart!' (in the title quotation) is either over the second 'R' in 'PRIOR' and the dash above date measures 13mm; or the exclamation point is over the space between 'O' and 'R' and the dash above date measures 10mm. Printer's imprints read: (1) [*short rule*] | *Printed by James Ballantyne and Co. Edinburgh*.; (2) [*short rule*] | EDINBURGH: | Printed by James Ballantyne and Co. ['& Co.' vol.1.]

General Notes: That author, printer, and publisher were intent upon differentiating this more 'expansive' novel from all that had gone before is readily evident in many particulars: the imprint alteration (with Hurst, Robinson now listed as the sole London agent), a shift in format (from 12° to 8°), paper generally of a better quality, type of a smaller design, and the appearance of a new narrator, 'Laurence Templeton'. With so much carefully arranged, Scott on 4 July 1819, six months before issue, advised his associates that this forthcoming work should 'be communicated to no person whatsoever out of the office' (*Letters*, v.402, vi.4 as amended in Corson[2], page 168). Nonetheless, advance sheets were promptly shipped when printed to the Carey publishing firm in Philadelphia (140Rg), as previously arranged, and on 10 November the author agreed to forward to his trusted dramatist friend Daniel Terry, in London, the manuscript portion of whatever was then finished in print (*Letters*, vi.10-12), this to give him an advantage over the competition. As before, then, repeated injunctions from the author seem to bear little relation to prevailing practice.

The initial arrangements for and early publication history of *Ivanhoe*, as detailed by Jane Millgate and Graham Tulloch, again represent a frantic endeavour to keep a suddenly popular novel constantly in print, here by proceeding through two 'first' and two 'second' editions, all sharing some type in common. Though the original printing was of 6,000 copies only, even before first issue the press-runs were twice extended and soon reached a total of 10,000, as noted above. A year later a new typesetting for a third edition was required, and in 1822 this novel appropriately became the first in a new collected series entitled *Historical Romances* (274A).

Copies: BCL(2) E** L LU O(10); CtY InU MH NN(3) NNU-W(Countess of Jersey) RPB T/B TxU* TxU ViU(2). Mixed or sophisticated copies: LU(text throughout of third edition: Sterling 729); MH(with volume 1 mixed first edition, second issue and second edition; volumes 2-3 entirely second edition); NN(text of second edition, extra-illustrated with engraved Westall titles and plates).
*With 12-page Sherwood, Neely, and Jones catalogue January 1820.
**With 4-page Longman catalogue February 1820.

References: Church 538; Lockhart vi.175(with facsimile of MS page); Millgate(3); Thomson, pages 36-37; Graham Tulloch (ed.), *EEWN8*; Van Antwerp(1) 9; Worthington 8. (Magnum Opus Edition 1830: *Waverley Novels*, xvi-xvii.)

1] **IVANHOE;** | A ROMANCE. . . . VOL. I. . . . 1820.

Collation: $\pi^2(\pi2+1)$ A-X^8 Y^2. Pagination: *1* half-title, *2 blank*, *3* title-page, *4* printer's imprint(1), *5* Advertisement, *6 blank*, *i* fly-title, *ii blank*, *iii* iv-xxxiii Dedicatory Epistle signed 'Laurence Templeton, Toppingwold, near Egremont, Cumberland, Nov. 17, 1817.', *xxxiv blank*, *1* 2-'298'[306] text, '298'[306] printer's imprint(2). Typography: Pages 159-306 (sheets N-Y) are misnumbered 151-298. The single Advertisement leaf appears to be set in quadruplicate, with Oxford rule measuring 13, 14, 15, or 16mm. Final gathering Y is of a duplicate setting, either with single quotation mark after 'journey' [pagination as printed] page 296 line 11 and in some copies figure 3 page 297, or with double mark and no figure.

Figures: The following list gives the pagination as it is printed and disregards the many misnumbered pages: A *iii*-9 v-6, B xxviii-9 xxx-12, C7-4 9-2, D17-6 30-12/-, E43-9 44-10/2, F55-4 57-9, G77-1 78-13, H88-4 91-6, I 101-2 107-1, K124-13 126-9, L128-10 131-7, M147-3 148-14 (or 152-4), N165-13 166-11, O 168-8 178-3, P191-10 192-6, Q211-2 213-13, R226-7 229-11, S241-3 246-2, T250-1 260-8, U265-10 266-9, X287-7 292-4, Y297-3/-.

2] **IVANHOE;** | A ROMANCE. . . . VOL. II. . . . 1820.

Collation: π^2 A-U^8 X^4. Pagination: *i* half-title, *ii blank*, *iii* title-page, *iv* printer's imprint(1), *1* fly-title, *2 blank*, *3* 4-327 text, 327 printer's imprint(2), *328 blank*.

Figures: A10-6 16-13, B30-10 32-12, C41-2 43-8, D63-11 64-7, E71-13/5 72-2, F83-7 89-4, G111-14 112-3, H119-12 125-5, I 136-3 139-14, K156-13 159-11, L169-7 170-10, M184-3 191-4, N195-2 201-1, O 210-12 224-6, P239-11 240-8, Q243-10 244-3/-, R259-7 268-5, S287-9 288-14, T299-2 304-12, U 310-10 320-11, X323-14.

3] **IVANHOE;** | A ROMANCE. . . . VOL. III. . . . 1820.

Collation: π^2 A-Z^8 2A^4. Pagination: *i* half-title, *ii blank*, *iii* title-page, *iv* printer's imprint(1), *1* fly-title, *2 blank*, *3* 4-371 text, 371 printer's imprint(2), *372 blank*, *1* 2-3 advertisement for works published by Constable, *4 blank*.

Figures: A10-7 13-3, B18-9 25-2/-, C35-10 48-5, D52-13 62-8, E76-7 78-4, F84-6 94-2, G105-7 107-9, H116-1 126-3, I 131-11 140-13, K153-9 154-7, L173-14 174-10, M185-5 190-6, N198-4 201-2, O 223-3 224-12, P231-13 237-11, Q243-9 256-8, R262-7 272-14, S283-1/- 284-2, T291-4 304-10, U313-13 314-5, X329-11 334-3, Y340-6 350-8, Z361-7 363-14, 2A 370-12.

Notes: As noted by Graham Tulloch (*EEWN8*.433, 461.n.134) Scott's term at page 187 line 17 originally was 'pregnant' in an archaic sense, then mistakenly corrected to 'frequent' in this setting, and finally amended to 'flagrant' in a cancel leaf M6 located in a single copy at the Baillieu Library, Melbourne University.

140Ab] First Edition, Second Issue: 1820[1819]

IVANHOE; | A ROMANCE. . . . VOL. I [II-III]. . . . 1820.

Watermarks: As for the first issue except for the reset portion, which is unwatermarked. Notes: As indicated below, sheets A-G of the first volume, with variant figures, are in a second setting, but all later sheets and volumes 2-3 are of the same impression as the earlier issue. By 29 November 1819 it was decided, in view of advance orders, that the original issue should be increased to 8,000: a decision then necessitating a new press run of 2,000 copies for the first seven sheets of an issue extending only to 6,000.

Since this increase would serve his own purposes, Constable thereupon shipped most of the earlier printing, some 5750 copies, to London. Judging by an inscription in one copy, the further work appears to have been accomplished within a few days of original publication, yet in time to admit of a number of corrections and one important revision in the Dedicatory Epistle (xv.3 from 'toilsome' to 'trivial').

Copies: BCL E(2) O(2); CtY(covers inscribed 'Decr 1819') NN* ViU.
*With engraved title and six plates by Westall (140Dk).

1] **IVANHOE;** | A ROMANCE. . . . VOL. I. . . . 1820.

Figures: A *iii*-2/- xvi-10, B xix-7 xxiv-3, C12-6, D26-3, E45-5, F56-15/1 62-4/-, G73-5 78-8, H88-4 &c. as in first issue. Figures for sheet M are in final order: 147-3 152-4.

140Ac] Second Edition (First Edition, Third Issue) 1820

IVANHOE; | A ROMANCE. . . . VOL. I [II-III]. | SECOND EDITION. . . . 1820

Published 15 January 1820 in Edinburgh (*EEC*); issued 16 February in London (*MC*). £1.10.0. Notes: Probably because of the delayed arrival of copies, Hurst, Robinson still had a good supply of the original printing at the time a second edition was in preparation. Accordingly on 15 January, the very date of his own announcement in the Edinburgh papers, Constable forwarded to London '*by this coach parcel* 500 titles with *Second Edition*, and we think on receipt of this you ought to use a little Clap trap, and announce a *new Edition* as just arrived!' (*EEWN8*.429). Evidently, as the copy states would suggest, Constable also prepared some extra cancel titles for his own use—or sent further sheets on to London—as there is occasionally a mixture from the legitimate second edition (140Ad) then underway.

Copies: (Vols 1-3, state 1) O. (Vol. 1, state 2, 2-3 state 1) L. Vols. 1-3, state 2) L.

1] **IVANHOE;** | A ROMANCE. . . . VOL. I. | SECOND EDITION. . . . 1820.

Figures: (state 1) As for the first issue. (2) sheets A-C, F-G of the second issue, D-E of the first.

2] **IVANHOE;** | A ROMANCE. . . . VOL. II. | SECOND EDITION. . . . 1820.

Figures: (state 1) As for the first issue. (2) A later state which, as the figures reveal, is mixed with eight other sheets again used for the true second edition noted below. These sheets are A-B, D, I, M, R-S, and U.

3] **IVANHOE;** | A ROMANCE. . . . VOL. III. | SECOND EDITION. . . . 1820.

Figures: (state 1) As for the first issue. (2) Again a later state of two sheets, L and M, both again used for the true second edition next described.

140Ad] Second Edition: 1820

IVANHOE; | A ROMANCE. | BY "THE AUTHOR OF WAVERLEY," &c. | [*short rule*] | [*two-line quotation from Prior*] | [*short rule*] | IN THREE VOLUMES. | VOL. I [II-III]. | SECOND EDITION. | [*short Oxford rule*] | EDINBURGH: | PRINTED FOR ARCHIBALD CONSTABLE AND CO. EDINBURGH; | AND HURST, ROBINSON, AND CO. 90, CHEAPSIDE, LONDON. | [*dash*] | 1820.

Paper: Post 8° (195 x 118mm cut). Watermarks: 1818; 1819; A NASMYTH; CUARI \ 1[*illegible*] 1819. Typography: Printer's imprints read: (1) [*short rule*] | *Printed by James Ballantyne and Co. Edinburgh.*; (2) [*short rule*] | EDINBURGH: | Printed by James Ballantyne and Co. ['& Co.' vols. 2-3].

General Notes: This issue, essentially reset, apparently results from a decision reached by 17 December 1819, immediately after the printing of cancel 'Second Edition' titles (previous entry), now to increase the press-run by yet another 2000 copies, for a total of 10,000 thus far. There are further corrections, but none whch can be attributed to the author.

Copies: BCL E O; InU MH T/B. Sophisticated copy: AN(vol. 3, text of the 1st edition, first issue).

1] **IVANHOE;** | A ROMANCE. . . . VOL. I. | SECOND EDITION. . . . 1820.

Collation: π^2 $2\pi^2$($-2\pi 2$) A-X^8 Y^2. Pagination: *1* half-title, *2 blank*, *3* title-page, *4* printer's imprint(1), *5* Advertisement, *6 blank*, *i* fly-title, *ii blank*, *iii* iv-xxxiii Dedicatory Epistle, *xxxiv blank*, *1* 2-306 text, 306 printer's imprint(2). Typography: This second setting is now correctly paged.

Figures: A *iii*-2 xvi-10, B xix-7 xxiv-3, C12-6, D28-3 30-3/7, E34-13 44-11, F56-1 62-4, G73-5/- 78-8, H84-2 94-3, I 101-12 110-1, K115-9 120-10, L128-7 142-10, M146-2 149-9, N171-10 173-2, O 185-5 190-4, P194-9 201-5, Q212-5 222-4, R237-9 238-12, S243-10 244-7, T267-14 268-3, U279-6 285-14, X291-2 296-10, Y304-8/-.

Notes: In the earlier part of this volume sheets A-C and G are of the same impression as in the first edition, second issue, E-F are reimpressed, and D is reset.

2] **IVANHOE;** | A ROMANCE. . . . VOL. II. | SECOND EDITION. . . . 1820.

Collation: π^2 A-U^8 X^4. Pagination: *i* half-title, *ii blank*, *iii* title-page, *iv* printer's imprint(1), *1* fly-title, *2 blank*, *3* 4-327 text, 327 printer's imprint(2), *328 blank*. Typography: Page 89 is misnumbered 98.

Figures: A15-11 16-9, B29-10 31-6, C39-3 48-11, D59-9 64-5, E70-1 76-6, F82-15 93-11, G101-12 107-3, H118-1 128-8, I 132-4 142-6, K152-15 159-5, L171-7 176-11, M191-10 192-12, N197-8 206-1, O 220-14 223-3, P232-7 235-11, Q243-3 245-15, R263-4 272-6, S283-5 288-2, T293-3 299-14, U312-8 319-5, X326-4.

3] **IVANHOE;** | A ROMANCE. . . . VOL. III. | SECOND EDITION . . . 1820.

Collation: π^2 A-Z^8 $2A^4$. Pagination: *i* half-title, *ii blank*, *iii* title-page, *iv* printer's imprint(1), *1* fly-title, *2 blank*, *3* 4-371 text, 371 printer's imprint(2), *372 blank*, *1* 2-3 advertisement for works published by Constable, *4 blank*. Typography: In some copies the advertisement extends to page *4*.

Figures: A12-5 14-3, B20-2 23-9, C47-10 48-11, D59-10 64-14, E66-5 77-3, F83-2 93-14/-, G110-11 112-9, H119-8 128-14, I 132-14 135-4, K146-10 153-7, L165-13 175-3, M187-5 192-15, N202-6 208-9, O 223-4 224-8, P240-14, Q255-11 256-5, R266-15 269-9, S283-13 284-14, T294-3 304-5, U313-14, X334-14 336-3, Y348-9, Z355-12 357-9, 2A 370-4. The first press figure numeral on page 132 is in the wrong fount and upside down.

Notes: The last five sheets U-2A are reimpressed from the first edition setting.

140Ae] Third Edition: 1821

IVANHOE; | A ROMANCE. | BY "THE AUTHOR OF WAVERLEY," &c. | [*short rule*] | [*two-line quotation from Prior*] | [*short rule*] | IN THREE VOLUMES. | VOL. I [II-III]. | THIRD EDITION. | [*short Oxford rule*] | EDINBURGH: | PRINTED FOR ARCHIBALD CONSTABLE AND CO.; | AND JOHN BALLANTYNE, EDINBURGH; | AND HURST, ROBINSON, AND CO., | LONDON. | [*dash*] | 1821.

Issued in London 18 July 1821 (*MC*, called 'new Edition'). Binding: drab or blue-green boards with printed labels. Paper: Post 8° (194 x 121mm uncut). Watermarks: *none* or BATH | 1820. Typography: Printer's imprints read invariably: (1) [*short rule*] | *Printed by James Ballantyne and Co. Edinburgh.*; (2) [*short rule*] | EDINBURGH: | Printed by James Ballantyne & Co.

General Notes: This reset edition, issued a year later, is printed in a more leisurely fashion, with only one figure to a sheet (excepting volume 2, sheet N). It derives from the first issue of the first edition and thus, in general, does not incorporate the intervening corrections.

Copies: E(2) L; CtY InU. Mixed or sophisticated copy: T/B(vol.1 sheets A-B from first edition, second issue).

1] **IVANHOE;** | A ROMANCE. . . . VOL. I. | THIRD EDITION. . . . 1821.

Collation: $\pi^2(\pi2+1)$ A-X^8 Y^2. Pagination: *1* half-title, *2 blank*, *3* title-page, *4* printer's imprint(1), *5* Advertisement, *6 blank*, *i* fly-title, *ii blank*, *iii* iv-xxxiii Dedicatory Epistle, *xxxiv blank*, *1* 2-'298'[306] text, '298'[306] printer's imprint(2). Typography: Page 234 the last word omits the 'w', thus reading 'Je ?"'

Figures: A vi-7, B xx-7, C14-14, D21-9, E33-13, F58-5, G75-8, H93-7, I 108-9, K115-6, L141-4, M151-8, N172-3, O 189-3, P201-12, Q212-13, R230-10, S249-6, T265-9, U285-13, X302-14, Y'296'[304]-3.

Notes: A revision at press is noted in some copies, page 147 line 1, where the description of Rebecca's neck, first given as 'snow-white', is changed to 'lovely'. Pages 303-306 (Y^2) are misnumbered 295-298: an obvious sign that this gathering, at least, was set from the misnumbered first edition. Even here, however, there is some deviation, page '296' line 15 first word reading in the first 'shrink', in this 'from'.

2] **IVANHOE;** | A ROMANCE. . . . VOL. II. | THIRD EDITION. . . . 1821.

Collation: π^2 A-U^8 X^4. Pagination: *i* half-title, *ii blank*, *iii* title-page, *iv* printer's imprint(1), *1* fly-title, *2 blank*, *3* 4-327 text, 327 printer's imprint(2), *328 blank*. Typography: In some copies the 9 of page-number 59 has started to move off the line.

Figures: A16-3, B18-10, C45-7, D57-6, E80-5, F95-2, G106-13, H125-12, I 131-7, K159-4, L169-6, M185-9, N198-13 201-11(or 208-2), O 222-10, P233-8, Q242-7, R268-5, S284-9, T301-6, U309-12, X324-8.

3] **IVANHOE;** | A ROMANCE. . . . VOL. III. | THIRD EDITION. . . . 1821.

Collation: π^2 A-Z^8 2A^4. Pagination: *i* half-title, *ii blank*, *iii* title-page, *iv* printer's imprint(1), *1* fly-title, *2 blank*, *3* 4-371 text, 371 printer's imprint(2), *372 blank*, *1* 2-3 *4* advertisement for works published by Constable.

Figures: A6-14, B25-10, C48-6, D63-9, E69-10, F84-9, G106-2, H128-6, I 131-4, K151-10, L176-8, M180-6, N197-5, O 224-7, P240-6, Q256-2, R263-10, S284-4, T291-7, U317-6, X330-5, Y339-10, Z368-7, 2A 370-10.

Notes: The concluding advertisement now lists, on the final unnumbered page, as 'Just Published' in Royal 8°, price 28s, the first volume of *Ballantyne's Novelist's Library* (148A), noting that this was intended several years before and announced in the *Quarterly Review*. 'Circumstances, wholly uninteresting to the Public, have retarded the publication till now.'

REPRINTS

FRANCE

PARIS: Baudry, Barrois [and others]
[~] Ivanhoe. 1831. (Collection of Ancient and Modern British Novels and Romances: *see* 288R.6.)

PARIS: Didot and Galignani
[~] Ivanhoe. M DCCC XXI, MDCCCXXV. (Collection of Modern English Authors: *see* 291R.25-27.)

PARIS: Lequien
[~] Ivanhoe. 1832. (Collection of the Best British Authors: *see* 297R.1-4.)

140Ra] PARIS: Richard 1821
Ivanhoe, A Romance. By the Author of Waverley. Third edition. Paris, Sold by Madame Richard, Rue Neuve de Seine, No 54. 1821. Two volumes. Page 1: *i-vii* viii-xxv *xxvi*, *1* 2-309; 2: *i-iv*, *1* 2-356. Notes: A contemporary hand has inked-out the last part of the printer's imprint in both volumes which begins: 'Printed by Cellot . . .' Copy: P.

GERMANY

140Rb] BERLIN: Schlesinger 1822
Ivanhoe, A Romance. By "The Author of Waverley," &c. . . . Second edition. Berlin, Printed for Adolph Martin Schlesinger. 1822. Three volumes. Pages 1: *I-V* VI-XXIV, *1* 2-207 *208*; 2: *1-3* 4-223 *224*; 3: *1-3* 4-251 *252*. Notes: One of the E copies is a presentation copy from Frau Ahlefeldt, translator of an edition in German [Goedeke 48]. Copies: E(2) P(vol.1).

ZWICKAU: Schumann
[~] Ivanhoe. 1823. (Pocket Library of English Classics: *see* 302R.62-65.)

UNITED STATES

140Rc] BOSTON: Allen 1823
[Ivanhoe, . . . Boston, pr. and pub. by Ebenezer K. Allen, 1823. Pages: 164pp.] Copy: not seen, probably an abridgement. Reference: S/S 14064.

140Rd] BOSTON: Parker 1820-1832
[Ivanhoe, A Romance. By the Author of "Waverley," etc. . . . Boston: Samuel H. Parker, No. 12, Cornhill. 1820. Pages: *i-v* vi-xiv, *15* 16-412.] Copy: not seen. Notes: (Also reissued 1822 in Novels Tales and Romances: *see* 305R.8).

[~] Ivanhoe. 1827, 1829. (Waverley Novels: *see* 306R.15-16).

[~] Ivanhoe. 1831, 1832. (Waverley Novels [Parker's Edition Revised] *see* 307R.15-16).

140Re] HARTFORD: Goodrich, and Huntington and Hopkins 1821
Ivanhoe: A Romance. By the Author of "Waverley," etc. . . . Hartford: Samuel G. Goodrich, and Huntington and Hopkins. 1821. Pages: *1-3* 4-305. Copies: PU T/B TxU.

140Rf] NEW YORK: Van Norden 1823
Ivanhoe; A Romance. By the Author of Waverly[!], &c. . . . New York: Printed by William Van Norden. 1823. Two volumes. Pages 1: *i-iii* iv-xiii *xiv*, *15* 16-252; 2: *1-3* 4-235. Copies: CtY MH RPB.

140Rg] PHILADELPHIA: Carey 1820
[1] Ivanhoe; A Romance. By the Author of "Waverley," &c. . . . Philadelphia: Published by M. Carey and Son, No. 126, Chesnut Street. 1820. Two volumes. Pages 1: *i-v* vi-xx, *21* 22-288; 2: *1-3* 4-309. Notes: This edition consists of two successive printings, the first (through volume 2 gathering B [page 24]) from advance sheets received 10 January 1820; the second (volume 2 gatherings C-CC [pages 25-309]), hurriedly worked by three pressmen from a copy provided by Charles Wiley in New York (a publisher of the preceding novel [135Rf], but not apparently of this). The Wiley copy was sent to Philadelphia on 7 February at Carey's entreaty since further advance sheets could not be shipped up the frozen Delaware River. All copies were printed and bound by 17 February 1820. Copies: InU MH MWA(vol.1) PPL. References: Clarkin, 1168; James Green, 'Ivanhoe in America', *The Annual Report of the Library Company of Philadelphia for the Year 1994* (1995), pages 8-14.

[2] Ivanhoe; A Romance. By the Author of "Waverley," &c. . . . Second American Edition. Philadelphia: Published by M. Carey and Son, No. 126, Chesnut Street. 1820. Two volumes. Pages 1: *i-v* vi-xx, *21* 22-288; 2: *1-3* 4-309. Notes: In anticipation of this issue, necessitated by an unexpected demand, Carey overprinted the latter section described for the first edition (*see* previous entry) and then, using several printers, reset the first section, the type for which had already been distributed. All copies were ready for issue on 28 February, eleven days after the first edition. Copies: CtY MWA[vol.2] NNU-W PPL. References: Clarkin 1169; Green (as for [1]).

140Rh] PHILADELPHIA: Crissy 1823-1828
[1] Ivanhoe; A Romance. By the Author of "Waverley," &c. &c. . . . Fourth American Edition. Philadelphia: James Crissy, No. 177, Chestnut Street. 1823. Two volumes. Pages 1: *i-v* vi-xx, *21* 22-288; 2: *1-3* 4-309. Notes: A paginal reprint of the Philadelphia, Carey editions. At this later date there appears to be a renewed interest among Philadelphia readers (see subsequent entries and 140Dt-Du), due probably to a rumor that the character Rebecca was modeled upon Rebecca Gratz, a young lady resident in that city. Copies: MH(vol.2) NN PPL.

[2] Ivanhoe; A Romance. By the Author of "Waverley," &c. &c. . . . Philadelphia: James Crissy, No. 14, S. Seventh Street. 1827. Two volumes. Pages 1: *i-iii* iv-xiii *xiv*, *15* 16-252; 2: *1-3* 4-309. Copies: IdU NN.

[3] Ivanhoe; A Romance. By the Author of "Waverley," &c. &c. . . . Philadelphia: James Crissy, No. 14, S. Seventh Street. 1828. Two volumes. Pages 1: *i-iii* iv-xv *xvi*, *17* 18-272; 2:

1-3 4-270. Notes: Again as with the Carey editions (140Rg) this Philadelphia firm, in view of the continuing demand for copies, was obliged to issue several editions. Copy: ViU.

140Ri] PHILADELPHIA: DeSilver 1823
Ivanhoe; A Romance. By the Author of "Waverley," &c. &c.... Fourth American Edition. Philadelphia: Thomas Desilver, No. 253, Market Street. 1823. Notes: Another issue, with variant imprint, of the 1823 Philadelphia, Crissy edition (140Rh[1]). Copy: NN.

140Rj] PHILADELPHIA: Scott 1820
Ivanhoe; A Romance. By the Author of "Waverley," &c. &c. . . . Third American Edition. Philadelphia: Published by Edwin T. Scott, No. 61, N. Eighth Street. 1820. Two volumes. Pages 1: *i-v* vi-xx, *21* 22-288; 2: *1-3* 4-309. Notes: A paginal reprint of the Philadelphia, Carey 'second' edition (140Rg[2]). Copies: CtY(vol.1) MWA T/B(vol.2).

140Rk] PHILADELPHIA: Wright 1823
[Ivanhoe; . . . Philadelphia, R. Wright, 1823. Pages: 1-172.] Copy: not seen; probably an abridgement. Reference: S/S 14065.

DERIVATIVES

GREAT BRITAIN

140Da] BIRMINGHAM: Beilby and Knotts [and others] 1820-1821
[1] Ivanhoe; or, The Jew of York. A New Grand Chivalric Play, in Three Acts.... Birmingham, Sold by Beilby and Knotts; Also by Gold and Northouse, 19, Great Russell Street, Covent Garden; Lowndes, 25, Bow Street; Miller, Lisle Street, Leicester Square, London; and all Booksellers. 1820. Pages: *1-2*, *i-iv*, *3* 4-76. Notes: Play compiled 'from the celebrated novel of that name, and from the cotemporary[!] plays on the subject' by Alfred Bunn (music composed by Henry Bishop [and others] not included) as performing at the New Theatre Royal, Birmingham, 1 September 1820. Copies: E(prompt copy); NN(2). References: Bolton 3347; Ford K6 (variant title).

[2] Rebecca, The Jewess. A Tale. Founded on the Romance of Ivanhoe. London: Printed for Beilby & Knotts, Birmingham; J. & C. Evans, London; Henry Mozley, Derby; and Oliver & Boyd, Edinburgh. [watermarked 1821]. Pages: *1-3* 4-33. Notes: Chapbook with hand-coloured woodcut frontispiece and title-page vignette. The text is preceded by a paragraph beginning: 'The following Tale is a condensed view of some of the principal scenes and leading characters in the popular romance of Ivanhoe, . . .' Copies: E L.

140Db] EDINBURGH: Anderson 1823
Ivanhoe or The Jewess, A Drama Founded on the Celebrated Romance of Ivanhoe, By the Author of Waverley. Published by John Anderson Junr. 55. North Bridge Street Edinburgh. 1823. Pages: *i-iv*, *1* 2-79. Notes: Drama by John William Calcraft [John William Cole]. Engraved frontispiece and vignette title-page. There is no type-set title-page. Copy: MH (prompt book). Reference: Bolton 3362. (Also issued in: Edinburgh Select British Theatre, 1823: number 2 [*see* 319D] and in: The Waverley Dramas, 1823: volume 1, play 2 [*see* 321D].) No copy of the second variant has been seen.)

140Dc] EDINBURGH: Huie 1823
Ivanhoe; A Historical Drama, Founded on the Celebrated Romance of the Same Name, By the Author of "Waverley", &c. &c. . . . Edinburgh: Printed for James L. Huie, and sold by Oliver & Boyd, and Stirling & Slade, Edinburgh; G. & W. B. Whittaker, and Black, Young and Young, London. 1823. Pages: *1-7* 8-76. Notes: Drama adapted by William Henry Wood Murray from Samuel Beazley's 'Ivanhoe' and John William Calcraft's [John William Cole] 'Ivanhoe' (music by Henry R. Bishop, arranged by Dewar, not included). Copies: E; InU. (Also issued in Dramas from the Novels, Tales, and Romances: volume 2, number 7: *see* 323D, no copy seen).

140Dd] LONDON: Bailey 1821
Ivanhoe; or, The Knight Templar, and the Jew's Daughter. An Ancient Tale of English Chivalry: From the Celebrated Romance of "Ivanhoe," by the Author of "Tales of My Landlord," &c. &c. London: Printed and Published by J. Bailey, 116, Chancery Lane. [ca. 1821]. Pages: *1-3* 4-24. Notes: Chapbook with coloured woodcut frontispiece of Blois Guilbert. Price Sixpence. Copies: A BCL O; InU NjP. Reference: Abbotsford, page 320.

140De] LONDON: Birchall 1820
[1] Anna Marie, love, Song of the Knight & Wamba, in the Romance of Ivanhoe, (written by the Author of Waverley &c.) . . . London, Printed & Sold by Messrs. Birchall & Co. 133, New Bond Street. [1820]. Pages: *1* 2-5. Notes: Engraved sheet-music with caption title. Words from chapter 41 (first words: 'Anna-Marie, love, up is the sun'). Music composed by John Clarke arranged for voice with pianoforte. Price: 2s. Copies: L O; MH. Reference: G/T 9990.

[2] There came three merry men, A Comic Ditty, Sung by the Knight & Wamba, in the Romance of Ivanhoe. . . . London, Printed & Sold by Messrs. Birchall & Co. 133, New Bond Street. [1820]. Pages: 1-6. Notes: Engraved sheet-music. Words from chapter 41 (first words: 'There came three merry men from south, west, and north,'). Music composed by John Clarke arranged for voice and pianoforte. Price: 2s. Copies: L(2) O. Reference: G/T 9991.

140Df] LONDON: Chappell and Goulding 1820
The Black Knight, a Duet from Ivanhoe, . . . London, Printed & Sold by Chappell & Co. 50, New Bond Street, & Goulding & Co. 20, Soho Square. [unwatermarked. 1820]. Pages: 1-7. Notes: Engraved sheet music with caption title and plate number: '1425'. Words from chapter 41 (first words: 'Anne-Marie, love, up is the Sun,'). Song composed by George Kiallmark arranged for voice and harp or pianoforte. Price: 2/6. Copies: E(2) L.

140Dg] LONDON: The Company of Booksellers 1822
Ivanhoe; or, the Knight Templar, and the Jew's Daughter. An Ancient Tale of English Chivalry. From the Celebrated Romance of "Ivanhoe," by the Author of "Tales of My Landlord," &c. &c. London: Printed for the Company of Booksellers. Price Sixpence. [1822]. Pages: *1-2*, 7 8-33. Notes: Chapbook with coloured frontispiece. Copy: E.

140Dh] LONDON: Cumberland 1819-1831
['The Black Knight'. London: Cumberland (1819). Notes: Music composed by George Kiallmark.] Copy: not seen. Reference: G/T 10002.

[~] The Maid of Judah; or, The Knights Templars. [1829]. (Cumberland's British Theatre: number 177. *see* 329D).

[~] Ivanhoe; or, the Jew's Daughter: . . . [1820 and 1831] (Cumberland's Minor Theatre: number 17. *see* 330D).

LONDON: Evans
[~] Rebecca, The Jewess. 1830. [Copies cccasionally classified by this publisher are entered under Birmingham:: *see* 140Da.]

140Dj] LONDON: Goulding, D'Almaine, Potter 1820
[1] Barefooted Friar, . . In the Musical Drama of Ivanhoe. at the Theatre Royal, Covent Garden, (The Words from the Romance of Ivanhoe.) . . . London, Published by Goulding, D'Almaine, Potter & Co. 20, Soho Square, & to be had at 7, Westmoreland St. Dublin. [watermarked 1816. ca.1820.] Pages: 1-3. Also paged in center top margin: 37-39. Notes: Engraved sheet music with caption title. Issued with 'The Grand March of the Knights Templars' on page 4 (40). Music composed by William Kitchiner[!] arranged for voice and pianoforte. Price: 1:6. Copy: MH.

[2] Ivanhoe or the Knight Templar, A Musical Drama . . . London, Printed by Goulding, D'Almaine, Potter & Co., 20 Soho Square, & to be had at 7, Westmorland Street, Dublin. . . . [1820]. Pages: *i-ii*, *1* 2-4, 1-52, *1* 2-4. Notes: Engraved sheet music with plate mark: 'Ivanhoe'. Operatic libretto by Samuel Beazley. Music composed and selected chiefly from the works of Stephen Storace by William Kitchener with orchestral accompaniment by John Parry, as performed at the Theatre Royal, Covent Garden. This and *The Hebrew* (*see* 140Dl[1]) both opened in London on the same night, 2 March 1820. Each of the thirteen musical pieces is also paged individuallly to allow for impression as separate issues. Price for whole: 12/-, (1) and (2) 2s., remaining 1/6. Copies: L; NN-L(numbers 1-13). References: Bolton 3338; Ford K4; G/T 10020.

LONDON: Hodgson
[~] Ivanhoe; or, The Jew of York. [1822]. (Hodgson's Juvenile Drama: number 4: *see* 333D).

140Dk] LONDON: Hurst, Robinson 1820
[*printed wrapper*] Illustrations of Ivanhoe; A Romance. By "The Author of Waverley," &c... London: Printed for Hurst, Robinson, and Co., (Late Boydell,) 90, Cheapside. 1820. Davison, Whitefriars. Published 19 February 1820 in London (*MC*), two months after issue of the novel, as the first of a series of illustrative plate sequences primarily under the direction of Hurst, Robinson. Notes: Following printed title cover, engraved vignette title-page and six plates, all drawn by R. Westall, engraved by Chas. Heath, and bearing the Hurst, Robinson 1820 imprint. The printed title lists four states of this issue: (1) Medium 8° prints, 16s.; (2) Imperial 4° proofs, £1.5.0; (3) Imperial 4° proofs, on India paper, £1.10.0; (4) Colombier 4° proofs on India paper before letters, £1.15.0. Apparently the first printed title, citing prices, was intended only as a temporary cover, the second, engraved, for use when bound in the book or, for the larger sizes, in collections of artwork. Copies: (1) NN(bound in 140Ab, first edition, second issue); (2) T/B; (4) T/B.

The vignette inscription is "Do you dispute with me slave!" [vol.1] page 34, elsewhere described as 'Gurth disputing with Sir Brian de Bois-Guilbert.' Plate captions:

(1) 'The Palmer's introduction to Rowena.' vol.1, page 103;
(2) 'The Tournament.' vol.1, page 235;
(3) 'Fortitude of Rebecca.' vol.2, page 173;
(4) 'Wamba before Front-de-Boeuf.' vol.2, page 236;
(5) 'Rowena rescued from the Flames.' vol.3, page 21;
(6) 'Rebecca at the Stake.' vol.3, page 337.

140Dl] LONDON: Lowndes 1820-1822

[1] The Hebrew, A Drama, in Five Acts, . . . London: Printed for John Lowndes, 25, Bow-Street, Covent-Garden. 1820. Pages: *1-9* 10-64. Notes: As performed at the Theatre Royal, Drury Lane, 2 March, the same night as the musical drama *Ivanhoe* [*see* 140Dj(2)]. Tragi-comedy by George Soane, without reference to Scott although adopting the *Ivanhoe* plot and the names of his characters, and using a prologue alluding apologetically to an unnamed novelist. In some copies, a period follows the second word of the title. Price: 2s. 6d. Copies: L; CtY(3). References: Bolton 3337; Ford K5.

[2] Ivanhoe! or, The Jewess. A Chivalric Play, in Three Acts; Founded on the Popular Romance of "Ivanhoe," . . . London: Printed for John Lowndes, 25, Bow Street, Covent Garden, By F. Marshall, Kenton St. Brunswick Sq. 1820. Pages: *i-iv, 1* 2-80. Notes: Play by W. T. Moncrieff, who requests 'that the Author of the Romance of "Ivanhoe," in consideration of the tenderness I have shewn in mangling his Work, will do me the favour in future to let me have the proof sheets of his productions the moment he receives them from the Printer.' Price: 2s. 6d. Copies: L; CtY InU NjP. Reference: Ford K2.

[3] Maid Marian; or, The Huntress of Arlingford. A Legendary Opera, in Three Acts. . . . London: Printed for John Lowndes, 36, Bow Street, Covent Garden. [1822]. Pages: *i-iv, 1* 2-52. Notes: First performed at the Theatre Royal, Covent Garden, 3 December 1822. Play by J. R. Planché, who observes that his opera is founded 'principally' upon Thomas Love Peacock's novel of that title, but also 'of some undramatized situations in the Romance of "Ivanhoe". . . .' (The music by Henry R. Bishop not included). Price: Two Shillings and Sixpence. Copies: L; CtY. Reference: Ford appendix 12.

140Dm] LONDON: Mason 1820

Ivanhoe; or the Jew and his Daughter, An Interesting Old English Tale. . . . London: Printed and Published by W. Mason, 21, Clerkenwell Green. 1820. Pages: *1-3* 4-36. Notes: Chapbook 'Founded on Facts', with coloured woodcut frontispiece. The wrapper identifies 'Mason's Pamphlet Warehouse' at the same address. Price: Sixpence. Copy: L.

140Dn] LONDON: Regent's Harmonic Institution 1820

[1] "Anne Marie Love", The Words from Ivanhoe, . . . London, Printed by the Regent's Harmonic Institution. (Lower Saloon, Argyll Rooms.) [1820]. Pages: 1-4. Notes: Engraved sheet-music with caption title and with plate number: '404'. Words from chapter 41 (first words: 'Anne Marie love up is the sun'). Music composed by James Hunter arranged for voice and pianoforte. Price: 1s/6. Copy: L. Reference: G/T 9998.

[2] The Crusader's Return, A Romance, from Ivanhoe, . . . London Printed by the Regent's Harmonic Institution, (Lower Saloon, Argyll Rooms) [1820]. Pages: 1-4. Notes: Engraved sheet-music with caption title and with plate number: '405'. Words from chapter 18 (first

words: 'Joy to the fair thy knight behold return'd from yonder land of gold'). Music composed by John Beale arranged for voice and pianoforte. Price: 1/6. Copy: L. Reference: G/T 9982.

LONDON: Richardson
[~] The Young Jewess. 1826. (Old English Tales of Love and Chivalry: *see* 407E).

140Do] LONDON: Roach 1820
Ivanhoe; or, The Jew's Daughter; A Melo Dramatic Romance, in Three Acts. . . . London: Printed and Published by Roach and Co: Public Library, Russell Court, Drury Lane. 1820. Pages: *i-vii* viii, *9* 10-71 *72*. Notes: Drama by Thomas J. Dibdin, announced 30 December 1819 as 'in preparation' (ten days after publication of the novel) and first performed at the Surrey Theatre on 20 January 1820. Dedicated to Jedediah Cleishbotham and Lawrence Templeton[!]. In some copies, page *72* is blank, but in others it lists books published by Roach and Co. Price 2s.6d. Copies: DT E GU O; CtY InU MH. References: Bolton 3333; Ford K1.

140Dp] LONDON: Robins 1828
Rebecca. *in* The Gentleman's Pocket Magazine; and Album of Literature and Fine Arts. . . . 1828. Joseph Robins, Bride-Court, Bridge-Street, London. Pages: Frontispiece engraving, drawn by C. R. Leslie, of Rebecca. Notes: An explanation, headed 'Rebecca in Prison', appears on pages 50-51. For another commentary in 1826 see Philadelphia, Carey issue (140Dt). Copy: NNP.

140Dq] LONDON: Simpkin and Marshall [and others] 1820
Ivanhoe; or, The Knight Templar: Adapted from the Novel of That Name. . . . London: Printed by W. Smith, King Street, Long Acre; Sold by Simpkin and Marshall, Stationers' Court, Ludgate Street; Sherwood, Neely, and Jones, Paternoster Row; And C. Chappel[!], 66, Pall Mall. 1820. Pages: *1-5* 6-72. Notes: Drama by Samuel Beazley (music selected by William Kitchener not included) as first performed 2 March 1820 at the Theatre Royal, Covent Garden. Dedicated 'To the unknown Author of Ivanhoe,' (*see* 544T). Price: Two Shillings and Sixpence. Copies: AN BCL C E L; CtY DLC InU TxU ViU. References: Bolton 3338; Ford K4.

140Dr] LONDON: Wheatstone 1820
Rebecca's Song, from the Romance of Ivanhoe adapted to an Hebrew Melody, . . London Published by C Wheatstone 436 Strand. [unwatermarked. ca.1820]. Pages: 1-4. Notes: Words from chapter 40 (first words: 'When Israel of the Lord belov'd, Out from the land of bondage came,'). Music composed by John Davy arranged for voice and pianoforte. Price: 1/6. Copy: E.

UNITED STATES

140Ds] NEW YORK: Circulating Library 1823
Maid Marian; or The Huntress of Arlingford. An Opera, in Three Acts, Some of the Incidents taken from the Romance of "Ivanhoe." . . . New-York: Published at the Circulating Library and Dramatic Repository, No. 4 Chamber-Street. E. M. Murden, print.[!] 1823. Pages: *1-3* 4-63 *64*. Notes: Drama by J. R. Planché (music by Henry R. Bishop not included) as performed at the Theatre Royal, Covent Garden. Copy: CtY.

140Dt] PHILADELPHIA: Carey and Lea 1825
Rebecca in the Prison at Templestowe, pages *264* 265-268, *in* The Atlantic Souvenir; A Christmas and New Year's Offering. 1826. Philadelphia: H. C. Carey & I. Lea. Notes: This anonymous article focuses on a drawing of 'Rebecca' by the American artist, Charles R. Leslie. It was early presumed that Rebecca was modeled upon a lady in a Philadelphia family: see further 140Rh. Copy: MWA.

140Du] PHILADELPHIA: Scott 1822
[Ivanhoe; Or, The Knight Templar: And The Jew's Daughter. Philadelphia: Published and Sold by E. T. Scott, No. 61, North Eighth-street. 1822. Pages: 24pp.] Copy: not seen. Reference: Heartwood Books, Charlottesville, Virginia, catalogue 40 [1996], item 8, presumably the copy now [1998] reported at PPL.

EXTRACTS IN ANTHOLOGIES

140E] From *Ivanhoe* there are nine extracts in seven anthologies: 366[1]E.2 366[2].11 366[3].2 372[1].1,7 375[2].5,6 405(2)[3].5 472.1.

MEMORIAL FOR KING GEORGE III

141A] First Printing: 1820

'TUESDAY, FEBRUARY 8.', pages 44-46, *in*:

The Edinburgh Weekly Journal. Vol. XXIII. No. 1156.] Wednesday, February 9, 1820. [Price 7d. Edinburgh—Printed by James Ballantyne, For himself and the other Proprietors.

Published 9 February 1820 in Edinburgh.

Notes: Following a two-paragraph factual report, Scott's commentary begins, 'George the Third was the first of his family who could be termed a British Monarch; . . .'

Copy: EP. References: Thomson, page 30. (Magnum Opus Edition 1834: *The Miscellaneous Prose Works*, iv.322-342.)

TO THOSE INHABITANTS OF THE REGALITY OF MELROSE

142A] First Printing: 1820

[*caption title*] *To those Inhabitants of the Regality of Melrose, who offered, or proposed to offer, | their services to form a Corps of Marksmen under Mr Walter Scott of Abbots- | ford.*
[*no imprint*].

Privately circulated February 1820 in Melrose and vicinity. Paper: Post 4° (252 x 202mm cut). Watermarks: D & A Cowan | 1819. Typography: Text on first page only of a doubleton leaf. Page *1*: 32 lines of text, three paragraphs, dated at foot Abbotsford 8 February 1820 and signed WALTER SCOTT, *2-4 blank*.

Notes: The 'unfortunate circumstances' two months before, as Scott advised Lady Abercorn on 15 January, involved uprisings across the border chiefly in Cumberland and Northumberland, against which Scott and his loyal band of yeomanry were prepared to take action. 'The Scotch,' he further remarked, 'certainly seem to have a natural turn for war for they learn military discipline in an incredibly short time and are very fond of the exercise'. Even so, as his proclamation now concedes, the occasion for alarm has, 'through the wise measures of Parliament, in a great measure disappeared.'

Copies: E(3); NNP(Maidment).

References: *Letters*, vi.114-115. (Magnum Opus Edition: Not reprinted.)

THE NOBLE MORINGER

143A] First Printing: 1820

'THE NOBLE MORINGER, AN ANCIENT BALLAD, TRANSLATED FROM THE GERMAN.' (first words: 'O, will you hear a nightly tale of old Bohemian day,'), pages ccccxcv-ccccci, *in*:

The Edinburgh Annual Register, for 1816. Vol. Ninth.—Parts I. and II. Edinburgh: Printed by James Ballantyne and Co. For Archibald Constable and Co. Edinburgh; Longman, Hurst, Rees, Orme, and Brown; and Hurst, Robinson, and Co. London. 1820.

Published 16 March 1820 in London (*MC*); issued 25 March in Edinburgh (*EEC*). £1.1.0. The early appearance of this Edinburgh volume in London is not readily explained. After a prefatory note, this poem consists of 43 numbered quatrains.

Copies: EP O; PPL.

References: Ruff 163A. (Magnum Opus Edition 1833: *The Poetical Works*, vi.343-359.)

THE MONASTERY

It would be difficult to assign any good reason why the author of Ivanhoe, after using, in that work, all the art he possessed to remove the personages, action, and manners of the tale, to a distance from his own country, should choose for the scene of his next attempt, the celebrated ruins of Melrose, in the immediate neighbourhood of his own residence. But the reason, or caprice, which dictated his change of system, has entirely escaped his recollection . . . . ('Introduction', 1 November 1830, *WN*, xviii.*iii.*)

144Aa] First Edition, First Issue: 1820

THE | **MONASTERY.** | A ROMANCE. | BY THE AUTHOR OF "WAVERLEY." | [*short Oxford rule*] | IN THREE VOLUMES. | VOL. I [II-III]. | [*short reversed Oxford rule*] | EDINBURGH: | PRINTED FOR LONGMAN, HURST, REES, ORME, AND BROWN, | LONDON; | AND FOR ARCHIBALD CONSTABLE AND CO., | AND JOHN BALLANTYNE, BOOKSELLER TO THE KING, | EDINBURGH. | [*dash*] | 1820.

Published 23 March 1820 in Edinburgh (*EEC*); issued 30 March in London (*MC*). £1.4.0. Binding: drab, blue, or grey-green boards with printed labels. Paper: Royal 12° (192 x 115mm uncut). Watermarks: M 1817; 1818 [1819, 1820] | 1; M 1819 [1820] | 5. Typography: Printer's imprints read: (1) [*short rule*] | *Printed by James Ballantyne & Co. Edinburgh.*; (2) [*short rule*] | EDINBURGH: | Printed by James Ballan tyne & Co. ['and Co.' vols 2-3.]

General Notes: All of the typographical and other innovations exhibited in the previous novel (140Aa) are abandoned in this and succeeding works, which revert to the earlier models. Two modifications in the publishers' imprint, however, are of some significance: first the entry of John Ballantyne, now claiming a dignity not apparent elsewhere; secondly the removal of Hurst, Robinson both from this and the succeeding publication (146Aa). As this London firm was the intermediary for shipping advance sheets to Philadelphia, its absence from any effective participation in the issue may well have deprived it, temporarily, of the privilage earlier allowed (*see* 144Rh, 146Re).

Copies: AN BCL(3) E(3) ES L(2); CtY(2) IdU InU(2) MH NN(2) NNC NNU-W(3) T/B TxU ViU.

References: Church 539; Sterling 730; Thomson, page 48; Van Antwerp(1) 10; Worthington 9. (Magnum Opus Edition 1830: *Waverley Novels*, xviii-xix.)

1] THE | **MONASTERY.** . . . VOL. I. | [*short reversed Oxford rule*] . . . . 1820.

Collation: π^2 A-N^{12} O^6 P^4. Pagination: *i* half-title, *ii* printer's imprint(1), *iii* title-page, *iv blank*, *1* 2-58 Introductory Epistle signed by 'Cuthbert Clutterbuck', dated Village of Kennaquhair, '— *of April* 18—', *59* 60-76 Answer by 'The Author of Waverley,' *77* fly-title, *78 blank*, *79* 80-331 text, 331 printer's imprint(2), *332 blank*. Typography: In some copies page 263 is misnumbered 268.

Figures: A22-13 24-11, B27-7 45-10, C70-3 72-8, D87-12 96-14, E118-7 120-11, F130-8 144-12/-, G147-13 168-15, H191-14 192-13, I 212-11 214-7, K218-4 240-3, L253-5 262-6, M276-9 287-12, N302-5 312-11, O 318-13, P326-3.

Notes: The correction of 'attentoin' to 'attention' (page 226, last line) may no longer be cited as two states of the first edition only, for either reading appears in the identically set 'Second Edition.'

2] THE | **MONASTERY.** . . . VOL. II. | [*short Oxford rule*] . . . . 1820.

Collation: π^2 A-O^{12}. Pagination: *i* half-title, *ii* printer's imprint(1), *iii* title-page, *iv blank*, *1* fly-title, *2 blank*, *3* 4-333 text, 333 printer's imprint(2), *334-336 blank*. Typography: On title-page the second Oxford rule is regular. Chapter numbers on pages 26 and 63 both read 'II.' and those for 89 and 123 read 'III.'; thus all later numbers are short by two (for example, page 309 'XI.' is actually 'XIII.').

Figures: A4-14 23-8, B39-14 45-3, C59-13 72-7, D95-12 96-8, E100-1 119-6, F141-14 143-5, G167-13 168-11, H170-10 189-3, I 194-12 212-2, K219-11 232-5, L261-14 263-7, M266-13 285-3, N306-8 312-12, O 327-3 328-13.

3] THE | **MONASTERY.** . . . VOL. III. | [*short Oxford rule*] . . . 1820.

Collation: π^2 A-O^{12} P^6 Q^2. Pagination: *i* half-title, *ii* printer's imprint(1), *iii* title-page, *iv blank*, *1* fly-title, *2 blank*, *3* 4-351 text, 351 printer's imprint(2), 352 blank. Typography: On title-page the second Oxford rule is regular.

Figures: A13-14 19-11, B37-7 39-5, C58-8 65-11, D84-12 91-13, E108-14 110-2, F136-3 143-4, G147-7 168-8, H187-11 189-13, I 198-9 213-2, K237-14 239-3, L263-12 264-5, M276-7 286-6, N311-13 312-11, O 328-8 334-15, P344-4, Q—.

144Ab] Second Edition (First Edition, Second Issue): 1820

THE | **MONASTERY.** | A ROMANCE. . . . VOL. I [II-III]. | SECOND EDITION. . . . 1820.

General Notes: Except for 'Second Edition' on title-page, in all respects identical to the preceding issue, with volume 1 page 226 last line spelled either 'attentoin' or 'attention'. The failure of this novel to be continually printed into a 'Third Edition' is an indication that it was not a complete success. (A 'third edition' reported at MB is in error.)

Copies: E L O(2); CtY.

REPRINTS

FRANCE

PARIS: Baudry, Barrois [and others]
[~] The Monastery. 1832. (Collection of Ancient and Modern British Novels and Romances: *see* 288R.19.)

PARIS: Didot and Galignani
[~] The Monastery. M DCCC XXI. (Collection of Modern English Authors: *see* 291R.28-30)

144Ra] PARIS: Glashin 1821
The Monastery. A Romance. By the Author of "Waverley." . . . Paris: Printed by J. Smith, For D. Glashin, Rue Vivienne, No. 10. 1821. Three volumes. Pages 1: *1-5* 6-244; 2: *1-5* 6-242; 3: *1-5* 6-263. Copies: E P(vols.1,3); TxU(vols.1,3). Reference: Kohler(1) 124 (with illustration).

GERMANY

144Rb] BERLIN: Schlesinger 1822
The Monastery. A Romance. By the Author of "Waverley." Second Edition. Berlin: Printed for Adolph Martin Schlesinger. 1822. Three volumes. Pages 1: not seen; 2: *1-3* 4-207 *208*; 3: *1-3* 4-215 *216*. Copy: P(vols.2-3). Reference: GDS 132, page 344.

ZWICKAU: Schumann
[~] The Monastery. 1824. (Pocket Library of English Classics: *see* 302R.66-69.)

UNITED STATES

144Rc} BOSTON: Parker 1820
The Monastery. A Romance. By the Author of "Waverley," etc. . . . Boston: Samuel H. Parker, No. 12, Cornhill. 1820. Pages: *i-iii* iv-xxxix *xl*, *41* 42-384. Copy: MWA. Notes: (Also reissued 1822 in Novels Tales and Romances: *see* 305R.9).

[~] The Monastery. 1827, 1829. (Waverley Novels: *see* 306R.17-18).

[~} The Monastery. 1831, 1832. (Waverley Novels [Parker's Edition Revised]: *see* 307R.17-18).

144Rd] HARTFORD: Goodrich, and Huntington and Hopkins 1821
The Monastery. A Romance. By the Author of "Waverley," etc. Hartford: Samuel G. Goodrich, and Huntington and Hopkins. 1821. Pages: *1-3* 4-273. Copies: PU T/B TxU.

144Re] NEW YORK: Clayton & Kingsland 1820
The Monastery; A Romance. By the Author of Waverley, &c. . . . New-York: Printed by

Clayton & Kingsland, 84 Maiden-lane, and 64 Pine-street. 1820. Two volumes. Pages 1: *1-3* 4-271; 2: *1-3* 4-272. Copies: MWA NN.

144Rf] NEW YORK: Duyckinck, Collins & Hannay, and Gilley 1822
[The Monastery; A Romance. . . . New-York: E. Duyckinck, Collins & Hannay, and William B. Gilley, pr. by J. & J. Harper, 1822.] Copy: not seen. Reference: S/S 10202.

NEW YORK: Harper
[~] The Monastery; A Romance. 1820, 1822. (*see* 144Rf and 144Rg).

144Rg] NEW YORK: Seymour 1820
The Monastery; A Romance. By the Author of "Waverley," &c. . . . New=York: Printed by J. Seymour, 49 John-Street. 1820. Two volumes. Pages 1: *1-3* 4-275; 2: *1-3* 4-272. Notes: Vol. 2 has imprint: New=York: Printed by James and John Harper, No. 189 Pearl-Street. 1820. Bound in pink printed boards. Copies: NjP RPB.

144Rh] PHILADELPHIA: Carey 1820
The Monastery; A Romance. By the Author of Waverley, etc. . . . Philadelphia: Published by M. Carey & Son. 1820. Two volumes. Pages 1: *i-ii*, *1* 2-275; 2: *1-3* 4-272. Notes: Volume 2 has page 65 misnumbered 56 and the last page, 272, reading below text: 'End of Volume Third.': a reference taken from the original Edinburgh issue of 23 March 1820. By a previous agreement for *Ivanhoe* Carey was apparently entitled to advance sheets for this novel, but for reasons given above (*see* 144Aa) these seem not to have been delivered.. Accordingly his edition was not listed in the Philadelphia *National Gazette* until 5 August; but a bookseller named James Maxwell was advertising an edition as early as 6 May, this perhaps representing one of the New York publications. The book itself was reviewed in the same journal on 13 May. Copies: E; CtY MH MWA NN NNU-W PPL RPB TxU ViU. References: Clarkin 1170; Kohler(1) 194 (with illustration).

144Ri] PHILADELPHIA: Crissy 1821-1827
[1] The Monastery; A Romance. By the Author of Waverley, etc. . . . Philadelphia: Published by James Crissy, No. 177, Chesnut Street. 1821. Two volumes. Pages 1: *1-3* 4-276; 2: *1-3* 4-272. Copies: E; MH MWA PPL T/B ViU.

[2] The Monastery; A Romance. By the Author of "Waverley, Antiquary," &c. . . . Philadelphia: James Crissy, No. 14, South Seventh Street. 1827. Two volumes. Pages 1: *1-3* 4-252; 2: *1-3* 4-259. Copies: IdU NN T/B.

144Rj] PHILADELPHIA: M'Carty & Davis, De Silver, Clarke 1825
The Monastery; A Romance. By the Author of Waverley, etc. . . . Philadelphia: Published by M'Carty & Davis, No. 171, and Thos. De Silver, No. 253, Market Street, and L. B. Clarke, No. 4, South Front St. 1825. Two volumes. Pages 1: *1-3* 4-228; 2: *1-3* 4-230. Copies: NjP NN PU.

DERIVATIVES

GREAT BRITAIN

144Da] LONDON: Birchall 1820-1827

[1] March, March, Ettrick and Teviotdale. London, Printed & Sold by Birchall & Co. 140, New Bond Street. [1827]. Pages: 1-4. Notes: Engraved sheet music with caption title and plate mark: '1986'. Words from chapter 25 (first words: 'March, march, Ettrick and Teviotdale, / Why my lads dinna ye march forward in order;'). Music composed by Thomas Miles for voice and pianoforte. Price: 1/6. Copy: L. Reference: G/T 10551.

[2] "Merrily swim we, the moon shines bright,["] The White Lady's Song to the Sacristan, in the Romance of The Monastery, Written by the Author of Waverley, . . . London, Printed & Sold by Messrs. Birchall & Co. 133, New Bond Street. [1820]. Pages: 1-9. Notes: Engraved sheet music with caption title and plate number: '1068'. Words from chapter 5 (first words as title). Music composed by John Clarke arranged for voice and pianoforte. Price: 2s/6d. Copies: L(2) O. Reference: G/T 10529.

[3] "Thrice to the Holly Brake," Invocation to the White Lady, and "Youth of the Dark Eye, Wherefore didst thou call me?["] The White Lady's Answer, in the Romance of The Monastery, . . . London, Printed & Sold by Messrs. Birchall & Co. 133, New Bond Street. [1820]. Pages: 1-7. Notes: Engraved sheet-music with caption title and plate number: '1056'. First poem from chapter 11 (first words: '"Thrice to the holly brake / Thrice to the well I bid'); second poem from chapter 12 (first words as title'). Music composed by John Clarke arranged for voice and pianoforte. Price: 2s. Copies: L(2) O. Reference: G/T 10530.

144Db] LONDON: Chappell and Goulding 1820

"Merrily swim we, the Moon shines bright!" Song, of the White Lady, from the Monastery, . . . London, Printed & Sold by Chappell & Co. No. 50. New Bond Street. & Goulding & Co. 20, Soho Square. [1820]. Pages: 1-5. Notes: Engraved sheet music with caption title and plate number: '1650'. Words from chapter 5 (first words as title). Music composed by a Lady and arranged by George Kiallmark for voice and pianoforte. Price: 2s/-. Copy: L.

144Dc] LONDON: Clementi 1820-1825

[1] Blue Bonnets, A Scotch Song, . . . The Poetry from the Popular new Novel, The Monastery, by the Author of Waverly[!]. . . London, Printed by Clementi & Co. No. 26, Cheapside. [unwatermarked. 1820]. Pages: 1-4. Notes: Engraved sheet music with caption title and the plate mark: '(Blue Bonnets)'. Words from chapter 25 (first words: 'March, Eltrick[!] and Teviotdale, why the deil dinna ye march forward in order?'). Music composed by William Thomas Parke for voice and pianoforte or harp. Price: 1/6. Copies: L; NN-L. Reference: G/ T 10553.

[2] The favorite Scotch Song, The Blue Bonnets are over the Borders, . . . in the Opera of Guy Mannering, . . . London, Published by Clementi & Co. 26, Cheapside. [watermarked 1825]. Pages: *1* 2-3. Notes: Engraved sheet music with caption title and plate mark: 'Blue Bonnets.' Words from chapter 25 (first words: 'March, March, Ettrick and Teviotdale! Why, my lads, dinna ye march forward in order?'). No composer cited. Music arranged for voice and pianoforte. Price: 1/6. Copy: NNP.

144Dd] LONDON: Falkner 1825
Blue Bonnets over the Border, . . . London, Published by H. Falkner, 3, Old Bond Street. [watermarked 1824]. Pages: 1-4. Notes: Engraved sheet music. Words from chapter 25 (first words: 'March march Ettrick and Teviotdale!'). Music composed by John Charles Clifton arranged for voice and pianoforte. Price: 1/6. Copy: L. Reference: G/T 10531.

144De] LONDON: Hurst, Robinson 1821[1820]
[*printed wrapper*] Illustrations of The Monastery; A Romance. By "The Author of Waverley," &c. . . . London: Printed for Hurst, Robinson, and Co. (Late Boydell), 90, Cheapside. 1821. Moyes, London. Published 26 December 1820 (*MC*) as the third in the Hurst, Robinson series. Notes: Portfolio containing engraved vignette title-page and six plates, all drawn by R. Westall and engraved by Chas. Heath. As remarked in the Chapter Four commentary, note 8, the first plate apparently is the first in any production to be engraved on steel, a new process that eventually (as in Scott's 1829-1833 'Magnum Opus') allowed thousands of copies to be run off on duplicate plates.

The printed wrapper lists five states of this issue: (1) 12° prints, 9s.6d.; (2) Medium 8° prints, 12s.6d.; (3) Imperial 4° proofs, £1.4.0; (4) Imperial 4° proofs on India paper, £1.10.0; Columbier 4° proofs on India paper. Copies: (1) NN; (2) T/B.

The vignette, without caption, is advertised as depicting 'The Disastrous Adventure of Peter the Sacristan with the Maid of Avenel.' The plates are captioned:

(1) 'The Lady of Avenel and Her Daughter in the Dwelling of Dame Elspeth.';
(2) 'Halbert Glendinning's First Invocation of the White Maid of Avenel.';
(3) 'The Spirit of Avenel appearing to Halbert the Night Previous to His Duel with Sir Piercie Shafton.';
(4) 'Warden reproving Julian Avenel for His Injustice to Catherine.';
(5) 'Mysie Happer's visit to Sir Piercie Shafton.';
(6) 'Catherine discovered by Halbert lamenting over the body of Julian Avenel.'

144Df] LONDON: Lavenu 1820
March, March, Etrick[!] and Teviot Dale[!], (all the Blue Bonnets are over the Border) A National Scotch Ballad, . . London, Published by Lavenu & Co. 24, Edward Street, (corner of Duke Street) Manchester Square, & W. Card, 98, Quadrant Regent Street. [unwatermarked. ca. 1820]. Pages: *i-ii*, 1-4. Notes: Engraved sheet music with publisher's rubber stamp below imprint. Words from chapter 25 (first words: 'March, March, Etrick[!] and Teviot dale[!], Why my lads dinna ye March forward in order,'). Composer not identified, but arrangement for voice and pianoforte. Price: 2/-. Copy: E.

144Dg] LONDON: Willis 1826-1830
[1] Blue Bonnets over the Border, or March, March, Ettrick & Teviot-Dale, . . . London, Published by I[saac] Willis & Co. Royal Musical Repository, 55, St. James's Street, and 7, Westmorland Street, Dublin. [watermarked 1825]. Pages: *1-2* 3-7 *8*. Notes: Engraved sheet music with plate mark: '242'. The title-page has an inked stamp of John Braham's (the soloist's) signature on lower outer corner. Words from chapter 25 (first words: 'March! March! Ettrick and Teviot dale!'). Music 'partly' composed by Alexander Lee as sung by Mr Braham, at the Theatres Royal London, Edinburgh & Dublin. On 13 June 1826 Scott indicated that he would accept £50 for the use of this song. (*Letters*, x.57). Price: 2/. Copy: E. Variant issue on unwatermarked paper (L).

[2] Third Edition. Blue Bonnets Over The Border, or March, March Ettrick & Teviot-Dale. . . . The Words by Sir W. Scott, Bart. . . . London, Printed by J. Willis & Co. Royal Musical Repository, 55, St. James's Street, (opposite Jermyn St.) & 7. Westmorland Street, (corner of Fleet Street.) Dublin. . . . [1830]. Pages: *i-ii*, 1-5 *6*. Notes: Engraved sheet music with plate number: '242'. Words from chapter 25 (first words: 'March! March! Ettrick and Teviotdale! Why my lads dinna ye march forward in order!). Music 'partly' composed and arranged by Alexander Lee for voice and pianoforte. Price: 2/:. Copy: L. Reference: G/T 10546.

144Dh] MONTROSE: Smith 1820

Blue Bonnets over the Border. [Printed for, and Sold by John Smith, Bookseller, &c. Montrose. ca. 1820]. Notes: Slip-ballad with Scott poem preceded by 'Hey the Bonny, ho the Bonny.' Words from chapter 25 (first words: 'March, march, Ettrick and Teviotdale, / Why, my lads, dinna ye march forward in order?) [Popular Songs—No. 2]. Copy: NN.

UNITED STATES

144Di] BOSTON: Bradlee 1827

The Favorite Scotch Song. The Blue Bonnets are over the Border, . . . in the Opera of Guy Mannering. Boston: Published by C. Bradlee, No. 164 Washington St. [ca.1827]. Pages: *1* 2-3. Notes: Engraved sheet music. Words from *The Monastery*, chapter 25 (first words: 'March, March, Ettrick and Teviotdale! Why, my lads, dinna ye march forward in order?'). Composer unknown. Copy: MWA.

144Dj] NEW YORK: Riley 1820

The White Maid of Avenel, A Serenade. The Words from the Romance of the Monastery. . . . New York Published by E. Riley. 29 Chatham St. [ca.1820]. Pages: *1* 2-3. Notes: Engraved sheet music. Words from chapter 11 (first words: 'Thrice to the Holly brake thrice to the well, I bid thee awake'). Music composed by Mrs Colonel Stewart arranged for voice and pianoforte. The song is also dedicated to Scott (*see* 559T). Price: 25 cents. Copies: MH MWA.

EXTRACTS IN ANTHOLOGIES

144E] From *The Monastery* there are 20 extracts in 19 anthologies, all but five representing the lyric generally titled 'Blue Bonnets over the Border': 367[1]E.4 369[3-4].9 373[2] 375[1].4 384.2,6 387.1 389.3 414[2].1 422.1 424 429[1] 431.1 434.1 437 443.3 466.2,6 467[2].6 469.4. The exceptions are 358.3 384E.2,6, and 466.2,6.

MEMORIALS OF THE HALIBURTONS

145Aa] First Edition: 1820

MEMORIALS | OF | **THE HALIBURTONS.** | [*short reversed Oxford rule*] | EDINBURGH: | PRINTED BY JAMES BALLANTYNE AND COMP ANY, | **At the Border Press.** | [*short rule*] | 1820.

Privately printed March 1820; 'Thirty copies have been thrown off of these Genealogical Memorials, intended only to gratify the wish of some respectable friends of the present possessor of the Manuscript, whose families are mentioned' (page *iii*).

Binding: pink silk or drab boards with printed label on front. Paper: Demy 4° (265 x 208mm uncut). Watermarks: [Prince of Wales feathers] | [script] J & M | 1818. [repeated twice on each sheet]. Collation: π^2 A-H^4. Pagination: *i* title-page, *ii blank*, *iii*-iv Preliminary Notice dated from Abbotsford, March 1820, *1* 2-63 text, *64 blank*. No printer's imprint. Illustration: Frontispiece engraving 'from the pencil of James Skene of Rubislaw' (page *iii*) of the Haliburton burial aisle in Dryburgh Abbey. Figures: *none*.

Notes: In his 'Preliminary Notice' (page iv) Scott identifies himself as the representative of the 'extinguished families' in this record and, further, as the declared heir 'to his grand uncle, Robert Haliburton of Newmains, by a respectable jury at Selkirk, the 14th day of February, 1820.' As the newly declared legal heir Scott thus was entitled in 1820 to bear on his escutcheon the Supporters of the Haliburtons (this in anticipation of his baronetcy), in 1826 to inter his wife in this family aisle at Dryburgh Abbey, and in 1832 to be buried there himself.

Presentation copies: BCL([inscribed by E.W.A. Drummond-Hay] 'This copy of Memorials of the Haliburtons given me by Sir Walter Scott 9 November 1828'); L(with MS note dated 6 May and stressing the rarity of this issue to an unidentified recipient [Baron Grenville? shelfmark G.1146] signed 'Your faithful humble Servant'); CtY([no inscription, but attached autograph letter reading] 'I beg your acceptance of the Haliburton Tract and think Mrs. [Archibald] Constable will do me the favor to accept a brace of Tarmigan[!] Yours truly W Scott Tuesday Castle Street') InU('Walter Scott Esq of Harden from his affectionate friend & most faithful humble Servant Walter Scott Abbotsford 13 October 1820') NN('For Mr David Laing / Bookseller As a mark of sincere sense of his successful researches into Scottish Antiquities from his obliged Servant Walter Scott'). Other copy: E(James Scott [Sir Walter Scott's cousin]).

References: Maggs Catalogue 1120 (1990), no. 199; Van Antwerp(2) 21. (Magnum Opus Edition: Not reprinted.)

145Ab] Second Edition: 1824

MEMORIALS | OF | **THE HALIBURTONS.** | [*short reversed Oxford rule*] | EDINBURGH: | PRINTED BY JAMES BALLANTYNE AND COMP ANY, | **At the Border Press.** | [*short rule*] | 1824.

Binding: rose cloth with printed label on front. Paper: Demy 4° (280 x 220mm uncut). Watermarks: C Wilmott | 1819. Collation: π^2 A-H^4 I^2. Pagination: *i* title-page, *ii blank*, *iii*-iv Preliminary Notice now dated from Abbotsford, November 1824, *1* 2-68 text. No printer's imprint. Illustration: As for 1820 edition. Figures: *none.*

Notes: This second limited edition apparently exists in two issues: (1) with the memorials extended in gathering I, as noted above, to four additional pages; (2) with this text further supplemented, by an additional gathering a², to a four-page [*i* ii-iv] 'Declaration . . . anent Muirhouselaw's Death.'

Presentation copy (Issue 1): NNP('The Right Honble Lord Chief Commissioner [William] Adam from his affectionate & grateful friend Walter Scott'). Other copies: (Issue 1) E O. (2) BCL; NNU-W. Reference: Van Antwerp(1) 23.

THE ABBOT

[W]hen I considered myself as having been unsuccessful in the Monastery, I was tempted to try whether I could not restore, even at the risk of totally losing, my so called reputation, by a new hazard—I looked round my library and could not but observe, that, from the time of Chaucer to that of Byron, the most popular authors had been the most prolific. Even the aristarch Johnson allowed that the quality of readiness and profusion had a merit in itself, independent of the intrinsic value of the composition. ('Introduction', 1 January 1831, *WN*, xx.v.)

146Aa] First Edition, First Issue: 1820

THE | **ABBOT.** | BY THE AUTHOR OF "WAVERLEY." | [*short Oxford rule*] | IN THREE VOLUMES. | VOL. I [II-III]. | [*short reversed Oxford rule*] | EDINBURGH: | PRINTED FOR LONGMAN, HURST, REES, ORME, AND BROWN, | LONDON; | AND FOR ARCHIBALD CONSTABLE AND COMPANY, | AND JOHN BALLANTYNE, EDINBURGH. | [*dash*] | 1820.

Published concurrently 2 September 1820 in Edinburgh (*EEC*) and 4 September in London (*MC*). £1.4.0. Both Longman and Sams advertise this issue on 4 September. Binding: drab, blue, or green boards with printed labels. Paper: Royal 12° (192 x 115mm uncut). Watermarks: *none*; 1818 | 2; 1819 | 1; M 1819 | 5; D & A COWAN | 1819 | *none* or 7; 1820 | 1 [2, 4]; M 1820 | *none* or 1 [3, 4, 6]; D & A COWAN | 1820 | 5 [9]. Typography: Printer's imprints: (1) [*short rule*] | *Printed by James Ballantyne & Co. Edinburgh.*; (2) [*short rule*] | EDINBURGH: | Printed by James Ballantyne & Co. ['and Co.' vols. 2-3. In some copies there is no period after 'Co'].

General Notes: As the Hurst, Robnson firm was excluded from the publishers imprint, both in this and the preceding novel (144Aa), this London intermediary for shipping advance sheets to Philadelphia may have been temporarily denied the privilege earlier allowed (*see* 146Re).

Copies: AN BCL(2) E(4) L(2) O(9); CtY IdU InU InU* MH*(2) NN(3) NN(Berg—

Lord Rancliffe) NNC NNU-W T/B TxU(2) ViU.
*With 4-page Longman catalogue September 1820.

References: Church 537; Sterling 731; Thomson, page 10; Van Antwerp(1) 11; Worthington 10 (with illustration). (Magnum Opus Edition 1831: *Waverley Novels*, xx-xxi.)

1] THE | **ABBOT.** . . . VOL. I. . . . 1820.

Collation: π^2 a^2 A-O^{12} P^6. Pagination: *1* half-title, *2* printer's imprint(1), *3* title-page, *4 blank*, *i* ii-iv Introductory Epistle to Captain Clutterbuck, signed 'The Author of Waverley', *1* fly-title, *2 blank*, *3* 4-348 text, 348 printer's imprint(2). Typography: In some copies signature E (page 97) is missigned F.

Figures: a iii-2/-, A13-13 14-12, B26-10 37-3, C62-10 72-5, D86-3 96-8, E110-3 120-1, F123-11 144-8, G146-8 168-5, H183-11 184-3, I 207-11 216-3, K219-8 228-5, L250-1 261-7, M278-2 288-5, N304-3 310-11, O 316-10 335-9, P339-12.
Notes: The Introductory Epistle (a^2) is in a duplicate setting, page ii, line 10 reading 'travellers' and page iii, figure 2, or page ii, line 10 reading 'traveller' and page iii no press figure. Some copies, including several in original boards, lack the Epistle, suggesting that this letter to 'Captain Clutterbuck' may have been printed after the earliest copies had been distributed.

2] THE | **ABBOT.** . . . VOL. II. . . . 1820.

Collation: π^2 A-O^{12} P^6 Q^2. Pagination: *i* half-title, *ii* printer's imprint(1), *iii* title-page, *iv blank*, *1* fly-title, *2 blank*, *3* 4-351 text, 351 printer's imprint(2), *352 blank*.

Figures: A10-6 24-4, B46-10 48-3, C52-5 62-8, D91-2 96-9, E110-3 113-6, F131-12 136-11, G156-5 167-8, H170-4 189-3, I 195-9 216-10, K218-5 220-13, L263-12 264-8, M277-1 279-7, N311-3 312-13, O 335-11 336-6, P348-5, Q350-6/-.

Notes: Again duplicate settings, now of the final fold (Q^2), may be differentiated most readily by the figure 6, present or absent on page 350.

3] THE | **ABBOT.** . . . VOL. III. . . . 1820.

Collation: π^2 A-P^{12} Q^6. Pagination: *i* half-title, *ii* printer's imprint(1), *iii* title-page, *iv blank*, *1* fly-title, *2 blank*, *3* 4-367 text, *368* printer's imprint(2), *369* advertisement, *370-372 blank*. Typography: Section signature P2 (page 345) is missigned 2P.

Figures: A15-2 21-13, B45-3 47-11, C58-13 69-2, D93-8 95-12, E98-11 109-5, F123-7 144-8, G155-10 168-1, H171-12 189-13, I 204-3 215-5, K226-4 229-11, L242(or 250)-8 261-13, M274-12 276-1, N300-3 310-5, O 320-4 322-8(or 334-9), P349-12 351-13, Q366-11.

Notes: Chapter VI heading (page 143) is misnumbered V, a miscalculation that disorders all subsequent chapter numbers. The advertisement, apart from listing 'new editions' of all the novels to date, announces as *Nearly ready* 'Illustrations of the Novels and Tales . . . original designs by William Allan' (*see* 322D).

146Ab] First Edition, Second Issue: 1820

[THE | **ABBOT.** | BY THE AUTHOR OF "WAVERLEY." | [*short Oxford rule*] | IN THREE VOLUMES. | VOL. I [II-III]. | [*short reversed Oxford rule*] | EDINBURGH: | PRINTED FOR ARCHIBALD CONSTABLE AND CO. EDINBURGH; | AND HURST, ROBINSON, AND CO. LONDON. | [*dash*] | 1820.]

Notes: Worthington describes this unlocated variant as a 'remainder' title, printed possibly for some sheets which were found some time after the book was published.' The failure of this novel to be continually printed into a 'Second' or 'Third Edition' is an indication that it was not a complete success. However, as it featured Mary Queen of Scots, the novel was the first to be printed in the series started by Galignani in Paris (*see* 291R.31-33).

Copy: not seen. Reference: Worthington, page 105 (with illustration).

REPRINTS

FRANCE

PARIS: Baudry, Barrois [and others]
[~] The Abbot. 1832. (Collection of Ancient and Modern British Novels and Romances: *see* 288R.20.)

PARIS: Didot and Galignani
[~] The Abbot. M DCCC XX, M DCCC XXI. (Collection of Modern English Authors: *see* 291R.31-33.)

PARIS: Galignani
[~] The Abbot [with four other titles]. 1827. One volume. (*see* 294R.3.)

GERMANY

146Ra] BERLIN: Schlesinger 1822
The Abbot. By the Author of "Waverley." . . . Berlin, Printed for Adolph Martin Schlesinger. 1822. Three volumes. Pages 1: *I-III* IV-VI, *7* 8-220; 2: *1-3* 4-222; 3: *1-3* 4-230. Copy: E. Reference: GDS 132, page 336.

ZWICKAU: Schumann
[~] The Abbot. 1824. (Pocket Library of English Classics: *see* 302R.70-73.)

UNITED STATES

146Rb] BOSTON: Parker 1820
The Abbot; being the sequel of The Monastery. . . . Boston: Samuel H. Parker, No. 12, Cornhill. 1820. Pages: *1-2*, *i*-ii, *3* 4-382. Copy: MH. Notes: (Also reissued 1822 in Novels Tales and Romances: *see* 305R.10).

[~] The Abbot. 1827, 1829. (Waverley Novels: *see* 306R.19-20).

[~] The Abbot. 1831, 1832. (Waverley Novels [Parker's Edition Revised]: *see* 307R.19-20).

146Rc] HARTFORD: Goodrich, and Huntington and Hopkins 1821
The Abbot; being the sequel of The Monastery. by the Author of "Waverley," etc. Hartford: Samuel G. Goodrich, and Huntington and Hopkins. 1821. Pages: *1-3* 4-285. Copies: NN PU.

146Rd] NEW YORK: Harper 1820
The Abbot; Being the Sequel of The Monastery. By the Author of "Waverley," "Ivanhoe," &c. &c. . . . New-York: Printed by James & John Harper, No. 189 Pearl-Street. 1820. Two volumes. Pages 1: [*i-ii*] *iii-iv*, *1* 2-278; 2: [*1-2*] *3-5* 6-290. Notes: Volume 2, page 289 is misnumbered 288. Copy: CtY.

146Re] PHILADELPHIA: Carey 1820
The Abbot; being the sequel of The Monastery. By the Author of "Waverley," "Ivanhoe," &c. &c. . . . Philadelphia: Published by M. Carey & Son, Corner of Chesnut and Fourth Streets. 1820. Two volumes. Pages 1: *i-iv*, *1* 2-278 *279-280*; 2: *1-5* 6-290 *291-292*. Notes: By a previous agreement for *Ivanhoe* Carey was apparently entitled to advance sheets for this novel, but for reasons given above (*see* 146Aa) these seem not to have been delivered. Though the original Edinburgh edition was published 2 September 1820, the Carey issue was not advertised until 14 October (*NG*), three days after the novel, from some other publisher (146Rd?), had been listed by the Philadelphia booksellers J. Maxwell and M. Thomas. Copies: E; CtY MH(vol.2) NN NNU-W MWA PPL. References: Clarkin 1167; Kohler(1) 195 (with illustration).

146Rf] PHILADELPHIA: Crissy 1825
The Abbot; being the sequel of The Monastery. By the Author of "Waverley," "Ivanhoe," &c. &c. . . Philadelphia: Published by James Crissy. 1825. Two volumes. Pages 1: *1-3* 4-257; 2:

1-3 4-266. Notes: In some copies of the first volume, the title-page has one '&c.' at the end of the sixth line. Copies: CtY IdU NN(2) RPB T/B.

146Rg] PHILADELPHIA: Hickman & Hazzard 1821
The Abbot; being the sequel of The Monastery. By the Author of "Waverley," "Ivanhoe," &c. &c.... Philadelphia: Published by Hickman & Hazzard, No. 121, Chesnut Street. D. Dickinson, Printer. 1821. Two volumes. Pages 1: *i-iv*, *1* 2-248; 2: *1-5* 6-253. Copies: E(2); MWA NN PPL(vol.1) T/B.

146Rh] PHILADELPHIA: Warner 1821
The Abbot; being the sequel of The Monastery. By the Author of "Waverley," "Ivanhoe," &c. &c.... Philadelphia: Published by B. Warner—sold also at his store, in Richmond, (Vir.) and by William P. Bason, Charleston, (S. C.) 1821. Two volumes. Pages 1: *i-iv*, *1* 2-278; 2: *1-5* 6-290. Copies: O; PPL.

DERIVATIVES

GREAT BRITAIN

146Da] EDINBURGH: Anderson 1825
[Mary Queen of Scots or Loch-Leven Castle. Edinburgh: Published by John Anderson Junr. 55. North Bridge Street Edinburgh. 1825.] Copy: not seen. (Also issued in: Edinburgh Select British Theatre, 1825: number 14 [*see* 319D] and in: The Waverley Dramas, 1825: volume 2, play 9 *see* 321D].)

146Db] LONDON: Company of Booksellers 1822
The Abbot; or, The Heir of Avenel. By the Author of Waverley. Epitomized by a Favourite Author. London: Printed for the Company of Booksellers. Price Sixpence. [1822]. Pages: *1-2*, *7* 8-40. Notes: Chapbook with a coloured woodcut frontispiece with two scenes. Copy: E.

146Dc] LONDON: Dean & Munday 1820
The Abbot; or, The Heir of Avenel. By the Author of Waverly[!].... London: Printed and Sold by Dean & Munday, Threadneedle-Street. [ca.1820]. Pages: *1-7* 8-40. Notes: Chapbook with a folding coloured woodcut frontispiece with two scenes. The woodcut is apparently counted as four pages in the pagination. Epitomized by William Francis Sullivan, A. M. Price: Sixpence. Copies: A BCL; CtY. Reference: Abbotsford, page 320.

146Dd] LONDON: Hurst, Robinson 1824
[*printed wrapper*] Illustrations of The Abbot; A Romance, by "The Author of Waverley," &c. ... London: Printed for Hurst, Robinson, and Company, 90, Cheapside, and 8 Pall-Mall. 1824. J. Moyes, London. Published 19 April 1824 in London (*MC*) as the eighth in the Hurst, Robinson series. Notes: Following printed title cover, engraved vignette title-page and two plates, both painted by H. Corbould and engraved by Chas. Heath. The printed title lists five states of this issue: (1) 12° prints, 4s.; (2) Medium 8° prints, 6s.; (3) 4° proofs, 12s.; (4) Imperial 4° proofs on India paper, 15s.; (5) Columbier 4° proofs on India paper, before letters. Copy: (5) T/B.

A separate MS indicates that the captions are, for the vignette, "Stand not to look on a dying man, but haste to save the Queen.", for the plates: (1) 'Roland introduced to Sir Halbert Glendenning.'; (2) 'Roland Graeme offering his services to the Queen.'

146De] LONDON: Lowndes 1820
The Abbot; or, Mary, Queen of Scots, A Serious Melo-Dramatic Historical Burletta, in Three Acts, . . . London: Printed for J. Lowndes, Bow Street, Covent Garden, By Barnard and Farley, Skinner Street. 1820. Pages: *i-ii, 1* 2-62. Notes: Drama by Henry Roxby Beverly ('music selected from the most popular productions of Scottish Composers' not included) as performed at the Theatre of Variety, Tottenham Street, 18 September 1820, sixteen days after publication of the novel. The title-page also notes: 'Written and adapted to stage representation, from the popular production, entitled "The Abbot," and combining all the prominent incidents of that admired novel.' Price: One Shilling. Copies: BCL L; CtY(2) InU. References: Bolton 3636; Ford A1.

146Df] LONDON: Mason 1820
The Abbot of Kennaquair, A Romance; . . . From the pen of the Author of Waverly[!]. . . London: Printed and Published by W. Mason, 21, Clerkenwell Green. [1820]. Pages: *1-3* 4-36. Notes: Chapbook with coloured frontispiece. Pages 31-36 print the text of 'Anningait and Ajut'. Price: Sixpence. Copy: NNU-W.

UNITED STATES

146Dg] NEW YORK: Megarey 1821
Mary of Scotland, or The Heir of Avenel. A Drama, in Three Acts. Founded on the Popular Novel of "The Abbot,". . . . New-York: Published by Henry I. Megarey, 96, Broadway. W. Grattan, Printer. 1821. Pages: *i-iii* iv-viii *ix-xii, 1* 2-114. Notes: Drama by an unidentified author performed, according to Bolton, 17 May 1821 at the Anthony Street Theater, New York. According to the preface, this play proved that 'if so few American plays are exhibited on the stage, the cause is not so much to be sought for in the dearth of patronage, as in the absence or indolence of that genius which is necessary to call it into action.' Copies: CtY(2) MH MWA NN RPB. Reference: Bolton 3638.

ADDRESS TO THE KING!

147A] First Edition: 1820

[*caption title*] ADDRESS TO THE KING! | [*short French rule*].

Published in December 1820. Paper: Demy 8° in fours (203 x 125mm cut). Watermarks: *none*. Collation: *A*^{4} B-C^4. Pagination: *1*-2 text, 3-24 printed list of 1028 names and addresses. Printers' imprint at foot of page *1*: R. MENZIES, Printer.

Notes: Text begins: 'We, your Majesty's Dutiful and Loyal Subjects, Inhabitants of the City of Edinburgh, . . .' Five paragraphs in support of the present administration and against demagoguery. In the appended list of names, all male and apparently ordered according to time of signing, Scott's name is the 64th.

Copy: GU(Ea4-f.9[no.6]).

References: *Letters*, vi.317; Corson (2) page 184 (referring to his own [incomplete] copy, now unlocated).

BALLANTYNE'S NOVELIST'S LIBRARY

148A] First Printings: 1821-1824

Ballantyne's Novelist's Library. Vol. [I]-II [III-X]. . . . Edinburgh. 1821 [-1825].

Volume 1 published 1 January 1821 in London (*MC*); issued 25 January in Edinburgh (*EEC*). £1.8.0. A note in the *Letters* (vi.288-289), wrongly indicating publication in February, notes that John Ballantyne had sent the first volume to London on 17 November 1820. After his death 16 June 1821 the volumes continued to appear until 1825: total price for the complete issue, £14.

General Notes: The serial title, as cited above, and the volume numbers appear only on the half-titles. The first hint of such a 'Library', erroneously recalled by Scott as once entered in the *Quarterly Review*, actually appeared thirteen years before in the 'Literary Intelligence' section of the *Monthly Magazine*: 'Messrs. Murray, of London, and Ballantyne, of Edinburgh, have announced a splendid collection of the most esteemed Novels and Romances, printed from, and collated with, the best editions; including Translations, selected from Foreign Languages; with Critical and Biographical Prefaces, in twenty volumes, Royal 8vo' (1 April 1809, page 281). All such ideas were soon abandoned, however, upon the publication in 1810 of Mrs Barbauld's *British Novelists* in 50 volumes, an extensive issue which proceeded into a 'new edition' on 9 September 1820 (*MC*), four months before this more restricted series.

Upon the death of the proprietor in 1821, Constable then predicted an eventual failure for this edition: 'A collection of Novels must not be printed in a small type like a Newspaper . . . and in the present times of good and rather expensive taste, there will be no very great number of readers found for works requiring a magnifying glass or at all events spectacles' (*Letters*, vii.14,n.1). Nonetheless an Advertisement probably by Scott in the first, 1821 volume of this 1821-1824 edition announces an intention to reprint, not only 'The Works of the best of the English Novelists', but also 'selections from the German, French, and Italian. . . .' (A supposed 'second edition' of 1824, listed in *NUC*, is unrecorded in the library there cited.)

Copies: BCL E L(2); CtY(vols.2-9) NN(Berg: Joseph Marryat, Charles Dickens).

Reference: Thomson, page 15. For references to individual memoirs see below.

1] Ballantyne's Novelist's Library . . . . Vol. I. . . . 1821.

'PREFATORY MEMOIR TO FIELDING.', pages *i* ii-xxiv, dated from Abbotsford, 25 October 1820, *in*:

The Novels of Henry Fielding, Esq. . . . To Which Is Prefixed, A Memoir of the Life of the Author. London: Published by Hurst, Robinson, and Co. 90, Cheapside. Printed by James Ballantyne and Company, At the Border Press: For John Ballantyne, Edinburgh. 1821.

Published 1 January 1821 as noted above. References: Thomson, page 28. (Magnum Opus Edition 1834: *The Miscellaneous Prose Works*, iii.77-116 as 'Henry Fielding'.)

2] Ballantyne's Novelist's Library . . . . Vol. II. . . . 1821.

'PREFATORY MEMOIR TO SMOLLETT.', pages *i* ii-xlii, dated from Abbotsford, 1 June 1821, *in*:

The Novels of Tobias Smollett, M.D. Viz. Roderick Random, Peregrine Pickle, and Humphry Clinker. To Which [&c. as in volume 1]. . . Edinburgh. 1821.

Published 18 July 1821 in London (*MC*). £2.16.0 (for volumes 2-3).

Notes: Volume 3 continues with the text of *Ferdinand Count Fathom, Sir Launcelot Greaves,* and Smollett's translation of Cervantes's *Don Quixote,* but no contribution by Scott.

References: Thomson, page 63. (Magnum Opus Edition 1834: *The Miscellaneous Prose Works*, iii.117-190 as 'Tobias Smollett'.)

4] Ballantyne's Novelist's Library . . . . Vol. IV. . . . 1822.

[a] 'PREFATORY MEMOIR TO LE SAGE.', pages *i* ii-xxvii;
[b] 'PREFATORY MEMOIR TO CHRYSAL.', pages *xxviii* xxix-xxxvii, dated from Abbotsford, 20 September 1822, *in*:

The Novels of Le Sage, and Charles Johnstone. . . . To Which Are Prefixed, Memoirs of The Lives of the Authors. London, Published by Hurst, Robinson and Co. 90, Cheapside. Printed by James Ballantyne and Company, At the Border Press, Edinburgh. 1822.

Published 26 October 1822 in London (*MC*). £1.8.0.

Notes: 'Chrysal' was the popular reference for the work by Charles Johnstone identified on title as 'The Adventures of a Guinea'.

References: Thomson, [a] page 41; [b] page 37. (Magnum Opus Edition 1834: *The Miscellaneous Prose Works*, [a] iii.390-426 as 'Alain Rene Le Sage', [b] iii.427-440 as 'Charles Johnstone'.)

5] Ballantyne's Novelist's Library . . . . Vol. V. . . . 1823.

[a] 'PREFATORY MEMOIR TO STERNE.', pages *i* ii-xxii;
[b] 'PREFATORY MEMOIR TO GOLDSMITH.', pages *xxiii* xxiv-xxxix;
[c] 'PREFATORY MEMOIR TO JOHNSON.', pages *xl* xli-xlvi;
[d] 'PREFATORY MEMOIR TO MACKENZIE.', pages *xlvii* xlviii-lix;
[e] 'PREFATORY MEMOIR TO WALPOLE.', pages *lx* lxi-lxxviii;
[f] 'PREFATORY MEMOIR TO CLARA REEVE.', pages *lxxix* lxxx-lxxxvii, dated from Abbotsford, 1 March 1823, *in*:

The Novels of Sterne, Goldsmith, Dr Johnson, Mackenzie, Horace Walpole, and Clara Reeve. . . . To Which Are Prefixed, Memoirs of the Lives of the Authors. London: Published by Hurst, Robinson, and Co. 90, Cheapside, and 8, Pall Mall. Printed by James Ballantyne and Company, At the Border Press, Edinburgh. 1823.

Issued March 1823 in Edinburgh (*EM*). £1.8.0.

References: Thomson, [a] page 69, [b] page 32, [c] page 37, [d] page 43, [e] page 75, [f] pages 56-57. (Magnum Opus Edition 1834: *The Miscellaneous Prose Works*, [a] iii.273-298 as 'Laurence Sterne', [b] iii.231-259 as 'Oliver Goldsmith', [c] iii.260-272 as 'Samuel Johnson', [d] iv.*1* 2-19 as 'Henry Mackenzie', [e] iii.299-324 as 'Horace Walpole', [f] iii.325-336 as 'Clara Reeve'.)

6] Ballantyne's Novelist's Library . . . . Vol. VI. . . . 1824.

'PREFATORY MEMOIR TO RICHARDSON.', pages *i* ii-xlviii, dated from Abbotsford, 1 January 1824, *in*:

The Novels of Samuel Richardson, Esq. . . . In Three Volumes. To Which Is Prefixed, A Memoir of the Life of the Author. London: [&c. as in Volume 5 except:] . . . Edinburgh. 1824.

Published 31 January 1824 in London (*MC*). £4.4.0 (for volumes 6-8).

Notes: Volume 7 continues with *Clarissa Harlowe* after letter 93; volume 8 includes *Sir Charles Grandison*.

References: Thomson, page 57. (Magnum Opus Edition 1834: *The Miscellaneous Prose Works*, iii.*3* 4-76 as 'Samuel Richardson'.)

9] Ballantyne's Novelist's Library . . . . Vol. IX. . . . 1824.

[a] 'PREFATORY MEMOIR TO JONATHAN SWIFT.', pages *i* ii-xv;
[b] 'PREFATORY MEMOIR TO ROBERT BAGE.', pages xvi-xxxiv;
[c] 'PREFATORY MEMOIR TO RICHARD CUMBERLAND.', pages xxxv-lx, dated from Abbotsford, December 1824, *in*:

The Novels of Swift, Bage, and Cumberland; . . . With Prefatory Notices, &c. London: [&c. as in Volume 5 except:] . . . Edinburgh. 1824.

Published 10 January 1825 in London (*MLA*). £1.8.0. Typography: Page number xlix is misnumbered lxix; page number lx is misnumbered lxx.

References: Thomson, [b] page 13, [c] page 24. (Magnum Opus Edition 1834: *The Miscellaneous Prose Works*, [a] Not reprinted because of earlier one-volume version which begins Scott's edition of Swift's *Works*, [b] iii.441-464 as 'Robert Bage', [c] iii.191-230 as 'Richard Cumberland'.)

10] Ballantyne's Novelist's Library . . . . Vol. X. . . . 1825.

'PREFATORY MEMOIR TO MRS ANN RADCLIFFE.', pages *i* ii-xxxix, dated from Abbotsford, 1 September 1824, *in*:

The Novels of Mrs Ann Radcliffe . . . To Which Is Prefixed, A Memoir of the Life of the Author. London [&c. as in Volume 5 except:] . . . Edinburgh. 1824.

Published 10 January 1825 in London (*MLA*). £1.8.0.

References: Thomson, page 56. (Magnum Opus Edition 1834: *The Miscellaneous Prose Works*, iii.337-389 as 'Mrs Ann Radcliffe'.)

REPRINTS

FRANCE

PARIS: Baudry, Barrois [and others]
[~] The History of Tom Jones, . . with a Life of the Author, By Sir Walter Scott. 1831. (Collection of Ancient and Modern British Novels and Romances: *see* 288R.4-5.)

[~] The Life and Opinions of Tristram Shandy, Gentleman. . . . with a Life of the Author, by Sir Walter Scott. 1832. (Collection of Ancient and Modern British Novels and Romances: *see* 288R.38.)

PARIS: Didot and Galignani
[~] Biographical Memoirs. By Sir Walter Scott. 1830. (Collection of Modern English Authors: *see* 292R.27-28.)

[~] Lives of the Novelists. By Sir Walter Scott. 1825. (Collection of Modern English Authors: *see* 292R.6-7.)

GERMANY

148Ra] BERLIN: Schlesinger 1825
[Lives of the novelists. . . . Berlin, Printed for Adolph Martin Schlesinger. 1825. Two volumes.] Notes: It would appear that this edition was reprinted from the Didot and Galignani issue of the same title and date (*see* 292R.6-7). Copy reported in Staatsbibliothek zu Berlin (Haus 2). Reference: GDS 132, page 343.

148Rb] DRESDEN: Arnold 1825
'Prefatory Memoir by Sir Walter Scott.', pages *iii* iv-xxxviii, *in* The Vicar of Wakefield. A Tale by Oliver Goldsmith. A New Edition. . . . Dresden, Published by Arnold 1825. Copy: MH.

148Rc] FRANKFORT am MAIN: Broenner 1827
'Prefatory Memoir by Sir Walter Scott.', pages *III* IV-XXVI, *in* The Vicar of Wakefield. A Tale by Oliver Goldsmith. Francfort o. M. Printed by and for H. L. Broenner. 1827. Copy: MH.

148Rd] MARBURG: Krieger 1828
'Prefatory Memoir', pages *IX* X-XXVIII, *in* The Vicar of Wakefield. A Tale by Oliver Goldsmith. Marburg, bei Joh. Christ. Krieger und Comp. 1828. Pages: *I-III* IV-XXVIII, *1-3* 4-300. Notes: Scott's 'Prefatory Memoir' and the full text of *The Vicar of Wakefield* are in English, but all notes by the editor Karl Franz Christian Wagner and his 'Vorrede' are in German. Copy: MH.

ZWICKAU: Schumann
[~] Lives of the Novelists. 1826. (Pocket Library of English Classics: *see* 302R.125-127.) A collection deriving either from 148Ra or, as noted there, from 292R.6-7.

GREAT BRITAIN

148Re] LONDON: Goodhugh 1827
The English Gentleman's Library Manual; . . . By William Goodhugh, . . . London: Printed for William Goodhugh, 155, Oxford Street, and Goodhugh and Co. 4, Berkeley Square. 1827. Notes: Extracts from Scott's commentaries, some of them extensive, appear on pages 137, 143, 144, 148-149, 150-151. Copy: T/B.

UNITED STATES

148Rf] BOSTON: Cummings, Hilliard 1826
Lives of the Novelists. By Sir Walter Scott. . . . Boston: Cummings, Hilliard and Company. 1826. Two volumes. Pages 1: *i-vi*, *1* 2-240; 2: *i-iv*, *1* 2-227. Notes: Reset from the 1825 Philadelphia, Carey edition (*see* 148Rg), with the preliminary notice lineally reprinted (this

deriving ultimately from the Paris: Didot and Galignani edition, *see* 292R.6-7) and, as in that issue, omitting the Swift memoir. Copies: CtY MWA OCl PHi RPB ViU(2).

BOSTON: Wells and Lilly
[~] Biographical and Critical Notices of Eminent Novelists. 1829. (*see* 308R.3).

148Rg] PHILADELPHIA: Carey & Lea (and others) 1825
Lives of the Novelists. By Sir Walter Scott. . . . Philadelphia: H. C. Carey & I. Lea, R. H. Small, E. Parker, J. Grigg, Towar & Hogan, and Marot & Walter, and Collins & Hannay, New York. William Brown, Printer. 1825. Two volumes. Pages 1: *i-vi*, *1* 2-241; 2: *i-iv*, *1* 2-239. Notes: It is evident from the wording of the preliminary notice that this is a reprint of the Paris: Didot and Galignani edition, issued in the same year (*see* 292R.6-7) and, as in that edition, it omits the Swift memoir. This Philadelphia edition in turn was reprinted in Boston the following year (*see* 148Rf). Copies: MWA NjP PPL ViU. References: Kaser 703 (no cost entry.)

KENILWORTH

A certain degree of success, real or supposed, in the delineation of Queen Mary [in *The Abbot*], naturally induced the author to attempt something similar respecting "her sister and her foe," the celebrated Elizabeth. He will not, however, pretend to have approached the task with the same feelings; for the candid Robertson himself confesses having felt the prejudices with which a Scottishman is tempted to regard the subject; and what so liberal a historian avows, a poor romance-writer dares not disown. ('Introduction', 1 March 1831, *WN*, xxii.*iii*.)

149Aa] First Edition: 1821

KENILWORTH; | A ROMANCE.| BY THE AUTHOR OF WAVERLEY," "IVANHOE," &c. | [*short rule*] | [*one-line quotation from* The Critic] | [*short rule*] | IN THREE VOLUMES. | VOL. I [II-III]. | [*short Oxford rule*] | EDIN BURGH: | PRINTED FOR ARCHIBALD CONSTABLE AND CO.; | AND JOHN BALLANTYNE, EDINBURGH; | AND HURST, ROBINSON, AND CO., | LONDON. | [*dash*] | 1821.

Published 8 January 1821 in Edinburgh (*EEC*); issued 20 January in London (*MC*). £1.11.6. 10,000 copies (*EEWN11*.396). Binding: drab or blue boards with printed labels. Paper: Post 8° (195 x 122mm uncut). Watermarks: 1818 | 2; 1819 | 1; M | 1819 | 5; D & A Cowan | 1819 | *none* [7]; 1820 | 1 [4]; N 1820 | *none* [1, 3, 4, 6]; D & A Cowan | 1820 | 5 [9].

Typography: Printer's imprints read: (1) [*short rule*] | *Printed by James Ballantyne and Co. Edinburgh.*; (2) [*short rule*] | Edinburgh: | Printed by James Ballantyne and Co. ['& Co.' vols. 2-3]. In all volumes the preliminary fold (half-title and title) was set in duplicate, with title short Oxford rule (a) regular or (b) reversed, and verso (c) first without, (d) then with printer's imprint(1). Thus sets may exhibit any one of four combinations of these 'points' or, for the three volumes, twelve combinations altogether.

General Notes: Scott finished this book on 27 December 1820, printing was completed by 5 January 1821, and the main lot of copies destined for London, in unbound sheets, was dIspatched from Leith on 9 January. Meanwhile in Philadelphia the publisher Mathew Carey, on receiving advance sheets, now for the first time allowed the local *National Gazette* to print two extensive extracts immediately after he had composed his own first volume. Altogether some 10,200 words are cited: the first extract 3 March 1821 representing (in the Edinburgh edition) all of chapter I, the second 9 March quoting from volume 2, chapter V, pages 121.21 to 142.16 (volume 1, chapter XVII, in the Carey edition: *see* 149Rh).

Copies: (Volume 2, state 1): BCL(3) ES L O(2); MH NN(3) T/B TxU. (2): AN BCL E(2) L(2) O(4); CtY IdU InU(3) MH NN(3) NNU-W(2) TxU(2). Mixed or sophisticated copies: One or more sets (not located, but illustrated in Worthington, page *119*) have volume 3 of the second edition with a counterfeit first edition title, imprint in three lines.

References: J. H. Alexander (ed.), *EEWN11*; Church 540; Sterling 732; Thomson, pages 38-39; Van Antwerp(1) 12; Worthington 11 (with illustration). (Magnum Opus Edition 1831: *Waverley Novels*, xxii-xxiii.)

1] **KENILWORTH;** . . . VOL. I. . . . 1821.

Collation: π^2 A-U^8. Pagination: *i* half-title, *ii blank*, *iii* title-page, *iv* printer's imprint(1), *1* fly-title, *2 blank*, *3* 4-320 text, 320 printer's imprint(2).

Figures: A*3*-8/- 12-7, B24-5 31-6, C34-9 44-10, D63-1 64-2, E74-4 80-3, F90-6 96-5, G111-7 112-8, H125-10 126-9, I 137-12 143-11, K153-13 158-1, L163-7 169-6, M190-2 192-3, N204-4/1 206-5, O 221-9 222-8, P229-10 235-11, Q246-12 256-13, R267-2 272-1, S275-3 288-5, T292-7 299-6, U310-8 317-9.

2] **KENILWORTH;** . . . VOL. II. . . . 1821.

Collation: π^2 A-X^8 Y^2. Pagination: *i* half-title, *ii blank*, *iii* title-page, *iv* printer's imprint(1), *1* fly-title, *2 blank*, *3* 4-339 text, 339 printer's imprint(2), *340 blank*.

Figures: A13-11 14-10, B18-13 25-10/12, C41-3 47-4, D50-1 61-2, E79-6 80-5, F82-9 96-11, G106-8 108-7, H127-1 128-13, I 142-2 144-3, K146-4 157-5, L166-7 173-6, M178-8 188-9, N203-1 208-13, O 213-10 215-11, P227-3 237-2, Q252-4 255-5, R265-6 270-7, S283-11 285-10, T302-9 304-8, U318-12 320-13, X324-1 334-2, Y338-6/-.

Notes: Page 119 line 4 first word (1)'"Here', (2) '" ere'. The composior of the second edition, assuming rightly that a letter or two had dropped out of the (2) word, mistakenly altered it to read '"There'. Gathering Y2 is in a duplicate setting, page 338 either with line 16, last word 'having' and press-figure 6 or 'ha-' and no press-figure.

3] **KENILWORTH;** . . . VOL. III. . . . 1821.

Collation: π² A-Y⁸. Pagination: *i* half-title, *ii blank*, *iii* title-page, *iv* printer's imprint(1), *1* fly-title, *2 blank*, *3* 4-348 text, 348 printer's imprint(2), *1* 2-3 *4* Archibald Constable catalogue.

Figures: A4-3 15-4, B18-7 25-5, C47-9 48-8, D58-11 61-10, E68-12 78-13, F82-2 88-1, G98-3 112-4, H127-6 128-5, I 134-7 144-8, K158-9 160-10, L162-13 176-2, M191-12 192-11, N194-3 196-1, O 210-4(or 222-12) 216-5, P230-7 240-8, Q245-13 254-12, R261-6 262-11, S276-3 279-1, T297-9 299-10, U309-14 310-6, X326-5 329-4, Y339-7 345-8.

149Ab] Second Edition: 1821

KENILWORTH; | A ROMANCE. | BY THE AUTHOR OF "WAVERLEY," "IVANHOE," &c. | [*short rule*] | [*one-line quotation from* The Critic] | [*short rule*] | IN THREE VOLUMES. | VOL. I [II-III]. | SECOND EDITION. | [*short Oxford rule*] | EDINBURGH: | PRINTED FOR ARCHIBALD CONSTABLE AND CO.; | AND JOHN BALLANTYNE, EDINBURGH; AND HURST, ROBINSON, AND CO., | LONDON. | [*dash*] | 1821.

Published 3 March 1821 in Edinburgh (*EEC*, described as 'New Edition'); issued 6 June in London (*MC*). £1.11.6. 2000 copies (*EEWN11*.396). Binding: drab boards and printed labels. Paper: Post 8° (200 x 122mm uncut). Watermarks: *none*. Typography: Printer's imprints read invariably: (1) [*short rule*] | *Printed by James Ballantyne and Co. Edinburgh.*; (2) [*short rule*] | EDINBURGH: | Printed by James Ballantyne & Co.

General Notes: Excepting only U and X of the third volume, each of these reset sheets was machined by a single pressman, indicating leisurely work on this edition. Dr J. H. Alexander has determined that this new setting contains ninety substantive variants, several representing 'intelligent corrections' (*EEWN11*.409).

Copies: BCL E L; CtY.

1] **KENILWORTH;** . . . VOL. I. | SECOND EDITION. . . . 1821.

Collation: π² A-U⁸. Pagination: *i* half-title, *ii blank*, *iii* title-page, *iv* printer's imprint(1), *1* fly-title, *2 blank*, *3* 4-320 text, 320 printer's imprint(2).

Figures: A12-5, B23-6, C37-9, D52-8, E76-4, F96-13, G109-7, H118-3, I 137-10, K154-5, L167-12, M191-4, N195-13, O 214-8, P226-6, Q254-9, R269-7, S285-12, T304-10, U313-4.

2] **KENILWORTH;** . . . VOL. II. | SECOND EDITION. . . . 1821.

Collation: π^2 A-X^8 Y^2. Pagination: *i* half-title, *ii blank*, *iii* title-page, *iv* printer's imprint(1), *1* fly-title, *2 blank*, *3* 4-339 text, 339 printer's imprint(2), *340 blank.*

Figures: A5-11, B29-2, C48-13, D64-8, E79-13, F91-6, G110-2, H125-8, I 140-4, K148-3, L162-14, M188-10, N196-8, O 212-9, P238-7, Q250-3, R272-12, S274-9, T303-7, U318-4, X334-11, Y—.

3] **KENILWORTH;** . . . VOL. III. | SECOND EDITION. . . . 1821.

Collation: π^2 A-Y^8. Pagination: *i* half-title, *ii blank*, *iii* title-page, *iv* printer's imprint(1), *1* fly-title, *2 blank*, *3* 4-348 text, 348 printer's imprint(2), *1* 2-3 *4* Archibald Constable catalogue.

Figures: A13-8, B28-13, C41-2, D51-14, E72-5, F88-12, G104-9, H125-4/-, I 134-7, K150-3, L172-5, M180-12, N205-9, O 218-6, P238-7, Q244-3, R272-13, S288-8, T299-4, U307-7 320-1, X334-12 336-9, Y346-14.

REPRINTS

FRANCE

149Ra] PARIS: Amyot and Baudry 1821
Kenilworth; A Romance. By the Author of "Waverley," Ivanhoe,[!] etc. . . . Paris. Amyot, Bookseller, no 6, Rue de la Paix. Baudry, Bookseller in Foreign Languages; no 9, Rue du Coq-S.-Honoré; 1821. Two volumes. Pages 1: *i-iv*, *1* 2-383 *384*; 2: *i-iv*, *1* 2-389 *390.* The last page in each volume prints a Table of the chapters in the volume. Copy: E.

149Rb] PARIS: Baudry, Amyot, and Pinard 1821
Kenilworth; A Romance. By the Author of "Waverley," "Ivanhoe,[!] etc. . . . Paris. Baudry, Bookseller in Foreign Languages; no 9, Rue du Coq-S.-Honoré; Amyot, Bookseller, no 6, Rue de la Paix; Pinard, no 5, Quai Voltaire. 1821. A variant issue of 149Ra. Copies: BCL O. Reference: Kohler(1) 133 (with illustration).

PARIS: Baudry, Barrois [and others]
[~] Kenilworth. 1832. (Collection of Ancient and Modern British Novels and Romances: *see* 288R.21.)

PARIS: Didot and Galignani
[~] Kenilworth; A Romance. M DCCC XXI. (Collection of Modern English Authors: *see* 291R.34-36.)

PARIS: Glashin, Robertson [and others]
[~] Kenilworth. 1828. (The Complete Works of Sir Walter Scott, Bart.: *see* 295R.10-12.)

GERMANY

ZWICKAU: Schumann
[~] Kenilworth. 1824. (Pocket Library of English Classics: *see* 302R.74-77.)

UNITED STATES

149Rc] BOSTON: Parker 1821-1832
Kenilworth; A Romance. By the Author of "Waverley," "Ivanhoe," &c. . . . Boston: Samuel H. Parker, No. 12, Cornhill. 1821. Pages: *1-3* 4-402. Notes: Title-page reads 'Complete in one Volume.' With woodcut plan of Kenilworth Castle as frontispiece. Copies: MH MWA. (Also reissued 1822 in Novels Tales and Romances: *see* 305R.11).

[~] Kenilworth. 1828, 1829. (Waverley Novels: *see* 306R.21-22).

[~] Kenilworth. 1831, 1832. (Waverley Novels [Parker's Edition Revised] *see* 307R.21-22).

149Rd] HARTFORD: Goodrich, and Huntington and Hopkins 1821
Kenilworth; By the Author of Waverley, Ivanhoe, etc. Hartford: Samuel G. Goodrich, and Huntington and Hopkins. 1821. Pages: *1-3* 4-300. Copies: NN PU.

149Re] NEW YORK: Duyckinck 1821
[Kenilworth. New York, Evert Duyckinck, 1821. Two volumes.] Copy reported at MBU, but not located. Reference: S/S 6747.

149Rf] NEW YORK: Harper 1821
[Kenilworth.; By the Author of Waverley, Ivanhoe, &c. &c. . . . New York: Printed by James & John Harper, No. 189 Pearl-Street. 1821.] Two volumes. Copy reported at Hagley Museum and Library, Wilmington, Delaware (vol.2 only).

149Rg] NEW YORK: Seymour 1821
[Kenilworth; . . . New York, J. Seymour, 1821. Notes: Volume 2 has imprint: New York, Printed by J. & J. Harper, 1821.] Copy: not seen.

149Rh] PHILADELPHIA: Carey 1821
Kenilworth; By the Author of Waverley, Ivanhoe, &c. &c. . . . Philadelphia: M. Carey & Son —Chesnut Street. 1821. Two volumes. Pages 1: *i-iv*, *3* 4-290; 2: *i-iv*, *1* 2-321. Notes: After encountering some difficulty in receiving advance copy on the two previous occasions (144Rh, 146Re), Carey was now provided with an early set, announced his edition 16 February as 'In the Press' (*NG*), extracted portions of it as noted above in the *National Gazette* 3, 9 March (149Aa), and published his volumes on 10 March. On the 10th six other booksellers, though not appearing in any imprint, also separately advertised this novel. Copies: E E(vol.1) O; CtY InU MH NNU-W NNU-W(vol.1) PPL(2) RPB ViU. Reissued with one or both titles reading 'Second American Edition.': E(vol.2) O. Reference: Clarkin 1225.

149Ri] PHILADELPHIA: Crissy 1827
Kenilworth; A Romance. By The Author of "Waverley," "Ivanhoe," &c. &c. . . . Philadelphia: James Crissy, No. 14, South Seventh Street. 1827. Two volumes. Pages 1: *1-3* 4-257; 2: *1-3* 4-260. Copies: IdU NN T/B(vol.1).

149Rj] PHILADELPHIA: M'Carty & Davis 1824
Kenilworth: A Romance. By the Author of "Waverley," "Ivanhoe," &c. &c. . . . Fourth American Edition. Philadelphia, Published by M'Carty & Davis, No. 171, Market-Street. 1824. Two volumes. Pages 1: *1-3* 4-252; 2: *1-3* 4-288. Copy: PPL.

149Rk] PHILADELPHIA: Scott 1821
Kenilworth; A Romance. By the Author of "Waverley," "Ivanhoe," &c. &c. . . . Third American Edition. Philadelphia: Published by Edwin T. Scott, 61, North Eighth Street. 1821. Two volumes. Pages 1: *i-ii*, *1-3* 4-290; 2: *i-iv*, *1* 2-321. Notes: In large part a lineal reprint of Carey's 1821 edition (149Rh). Copies: NN PPL T/B(vol.2).

149Rl] PHILADELPHIA: Silver 1824
[Kenilworth; . . . 4th Amer. ed. Philadelphia, T. Silver, 1824.] Copy: not seen. Reference: S/S 17918.

DERIVATIVES

GREAT BRITAIN

149Da] BIRMINGHAM: Beilby & Knotts [and others] 1822
Kenilworth; or, The Earl of Leicester and Amy Robsart; A Tale. London: Printed for Beilby & Knotts, Birmingham; J. & C. Evans, London; Henry Mozley, Derby; and Oliver & Boyd. Edinburgh. 1822. Pages: *1-5* 6-36. Notes: Chapbook with hand-coloured woodcut frontispiece and title-page vignette included in pagination. 'Kenilworth' ends on page 34, but publication continues with a two-page essay entitled: 'Character of Queen Elizabeth.' Copies: E; TxU.

CHISWICK: Whittingham
[~] Kenilworth Illustrated. M DCCC XXI. (*see* next entry)

149Db] COVENTRY: Merridew and Son 1821
Kenilworth Illustrated; or, The History of the Castle, Priory, and Church of Kenilworth. . . . Chiswick: Printed by C. Whittingham, College House; For Merridew and Son, Coventry; John Merridew, Warwick; and W. and T. Radclyffe, Birmingham. Sold also by Longman, Hurst, and Co. Rodwell and Martin, and Hurst, Robinson, and Co. London; and Constable and Co. Edinburgh. M DCCC XXI. Pages *i-viii*, *1* 2-63 *64*, *1* 2-108 + 19 plates. Though not strictly a 'derivative' issue this 'beautiful antiquarian publication', as Scott later called it (378A,xxiii.203.note), was issued concurrently in parts with plates datng from 1 February 1820 to 1 December 1821. Scott received the earlier number(s) just as he was starting on his fictional account and was a subscriber to the final volume issue, one also sold by his own Edinburgh and London publishers. Copy: T/B(large paper with proof plates). References: Abbotsford, page 242; *EEWN11*.428, 473.

149Dc] EDINBURGH: Huie 1823

Kenilworth: A Historical Drama, Founded on the Celebrated Romance of the Same Name, by the Author of "Waverley," &c. &c. . . . [no imprint. 1822]. Pages: *1-5* 6-62. Notes: Play by Thomas J. Dibdin, written for Drury Lane, 14 February 1821, and on 8 March transferred to Covent Garden for five nights. Subsequently issued in revised form. Engraved frontispiece portrait 'Mrs. H. Siddons of the Theatre Royal Edinburgh, as Amy Countess of Leicester. Drawn and Engraved for the National Dramas by E. Mitchell and Published by James L. Huie 14 Infirmary Street Edinburgh 1822.' Dramatis personae for 1822 only. Page 62 begins: '(The Earl of Leicester, . . .'. Signatures: N-S. Copies: E; InU. (A variant issued in: Dramas from the Novels, Tales, and Romances: volume 1, number 3. *see* 323D). References: Bolton 3808; White, pp.125-126.

149Dd] FALMOUTH: Philp 1830

Kenilworth: A Tragedy in Five Acts. . . . Falmouth: Printed and Published by James Philp, and sold in London, by Simpkin and Marshall, Stationers' Court. 1830. Pages: *i-ii*, *1-5* 6-62. Notes: Anonymous drama. Statement on the title-page reads: 'This play is founded on Sir Walter Scott's celebrated Romance of Kenilworth, and adapted to theatrical representation.' Price One Shilling. The play is dedicated to Scott (see 519T). Copy: E. References: Bolton 3865; Ford L15.

149De] LONDON: Burn 1821

Laneham's Letter Describing the Magnificent Pageants Presented before Queen Elizabeth at Kenilworth Castle in 1575; . . . London: Printed for J. H. Burn, Maiden-Lane, Covent-Garden. 1821. Pages: *i-iii* iv-xvi *xvii-xviii*, *1* 2-114 *115*. Notes: With frontispiece of Queen Elizabeth. These letters, by Robert Laneham, are 'repeatedly referred to in the Romance of Kenilworth'. Copy: L.

149Df] LONDON: Chappell 1825

"The Bonny Owl," The Song of Master Goldthred, the Mercer of Abingdon, from Kenilworth, . . . London, Printed & Sold by Chappell & Co. Music Sellers to his Majesty, 50, New Bond Street. [watermarked 1819. 1821]. Pages: 1-5. Notes: Engraved sheet music with caption title and plate number: '1773'. Words from chapter 2 (first words: 'Of all the birds on bush or tree.'). Music composed by George Dance arranged for voice and pianoforte. Copy: L. Reference: G/T 10094.

149Dg] LONDON: Cole 1823

Kenilworth; or, The Golden Days of Queen Bess. . . . London: Printed by and for W. Cole, 10, Newgate-street. Price Sixpence. [1823]. Two parts. Pages 1: *1-3* 4-24; 2: *1-3* 4-28. Notes: Each part of this abbreviated prose version has a fold-out coloured woodcut frontispiece by George Cruikshank: the first is titled 'Tresillian taking Vengeance on Richard Varney' with imprint at foot reading: London. Pubd. Jany. 28, 1823, by Hodgson & Co. 10. Newgate Street. The second illustration is titled 'The Countess of Leicester decoyed into the Trap at Tony Fosters, loses her life." with imprint at foot reading: Pubd. April 1st 1823, by Hodgson & Co. 10, Newgate Street. The imprint of the 'Second Part' reads: London: Printed by and for Hodgson & Co. No. 10, Newgate Street. [Price Sixpence]. Copies: L; NjP. References: Douglas 476, 477; Cohn 460.

149Dh] LONDON: The Company of Booksellers 1822
Kenilworth Castle; or, Strange Things in the Reign of Elizabeth. A Romance of the Sixteenth Century: By the Celebrated Author of Waverley, Ivanhoe, Pirate, etc. . . . Epitomised by a Favorite Author. London: Printed for The Company of Booksellers. . . . [1822]. Pages: *1-2*, *7* 8-34. Notes: Chapbook with coloured woodcut frontispiece with two scenes. Price: Sixpence. Copy: E.

LONDON: Cumberland
[~] Kenilworth. A Drama. [1832]. (Cumberland's British Theatre: number 311. *see* 329D).

149Di] LONDON: Dean and Munday 1821
Kenilworth; or, A Tale of the Inn: A Romance of the Sixteenth Century; By the Celebrated Author of Waverley, and Ivanhoe. . . . London: Printed and Sold by Dean & Munday, Threadneedle-Street. [ca. 1821]. Pages: *1-5* 6-26. Notes: Chapbook epitome by Sarah S. Wilkinson, with coloured woodcut frontispiece and two scenes. Price: Sixpence. Copies: A BCL. Reference: Abbotsford, page 320.

149Dj] LONDON: Hurst, Robinson 1821
[*printed wrapper*] Illustrations of Kenilworth; A Romance. By the Author of "Waverley," "Ivanhoe," &c. . . . London: Printed for Hurst, Robinson, and Co. (Late Boydell), 90, Cheapside. 1821. Moyes, London. Published 8 January 1821 in London (*MC*) as the fifth in the Hurst, Robinson series. Notes: Following printed title cover, engraved vignette title-page and six plates, all drawn by C. R. Leslie, engraved by the artists cited below, and bearing a Hurst, Robinson imprint dated 1821. The printed title lists four states of this issue: (1) Medium 8° prints, 16s.; (2) Imperial 4° proofs, £1.4.0; (3) Imperial 4° proofs on India paper, £1.10.0; (4) Columbier 4° proofs on India paper, before letters, £1.16.0. Copies: (2) T/B; (4) T/B.

The engraved title begins 'Kenilworth A Romance' and bears a vignette inscription "Upstarted of a sudden Tony Foster himself, with a cudgel in his hand." engraved by J. Romney, Vol. 1, page 39, elsewhere captioned as 'Tony Foster refusing Tressilian admittance to Cumnor Place.' Plate captions and engraver:
(1) 'The Countess in the Drawing Room attended by Janet.' Chas. Heath;
(2) 'Wayland Smith relating the History of His Life.' Charles Rolls;
(3) 'The Gallantry of Sir Walter Raleigh.' John Scott;
(4) 'Mike Lambourne, drunk in the garden of Cumnor Place, abusing Tony Foster and the Astrologer.' J. Romney;
(5) 'The entry of Queen Elizabeth into Kenilworth Castle.' F. Engleheart;
(6) 'The meeting of Leicester & the Countess at Kenilworth.' Charles Rolls.

LONDON: Jarvis and Witton
[~] An Account of Kenilworth Castle *see* London: Wetton and Jarvis. An Historical Account of Kenilworth Castle (149Dl).

149Dk] LONDON: Lowndes 1821
Kenilworth: A Melo=Drama, in Two Acts. (Founded on the Novel of that Name.) . . . London: Printed for John Lowndes, 36, Bow-Street. [watermarked 1820. 1821]. Pages: *1-4*, *i-ii*, *5* 6-34. Notes: Drama by an unknown dramatist as performed at the Theatre Royal, Covent-

Garden, 8 March 1821. In the Advertisement, dated 12 March 1821, the Compiler' who 'by way of apology to the distinguished author of the novel' stresses the value of a two act drama as opposed to those of his competitors, notably Thomas Dibdin, for this play is not to be confused with Dibdin's which opened at the Surrey Theatre 14 February 1821. (Another version, by Planché, opened on 8 February.) The compiler also gives credit to Charles Farley's 'assiduity and abilities, in arranging the performance'. Price: Two Shillings. Copies: BCL; DLC NN. Reference: Bolton 3801.

LONDON: The Proprietors
[~] Kenilworth. A Melo-Drama. 1824. (The New English Drama: volume 3. *see* 340D).

LONDON: Richardson
[~] Amy Robsart. 1826. (*in* Old English Tales of Love and Chivalry. *see* 407E).

LONDON: Simpkin and Marshall
[~] Kenilworth. A Melo-Drama. 1824. (Oxberry's Edition: number 3. *see* 340D).

149Dl] LONDON: Wetton and Jarvis 1821
An Historical Account of Kenilworth Castle, in the County of Warwick. . . . Being an historical introduction to the Readers of the new novel, entitled, Kenilworth, by the author of Waverley, Ivanhoe, etc.; as well as to the visitors of that ancient and picturesque castle. London: Published by Wetton and Jarvis, 65, Paternoster-row; and Joseph Capes (Public Library), 111, Fleet-street; and sold by Francis Smith, Southam, Warwickshire. 1821. Pages: *i-iii* iv-vi, *7* 8-55. Notes: The account by J. Nightingale was issued simultaneously with the London issue of *Kenilworth* (*MC* 20 January 1821) with the comment: 'It is conceived that the perusal of this pamphlet will be a most interesting introduction to the visitors of that ancient and picturesque Castle, and to the readers of a Novel from so celebrated a pen.' Unfortunately, the *Morning Chronicle* gave the publishers as 'Jarvis and Witten' and the title as 'An Account of Kenilworth Castle'. The frontispiece is a plan of Kenilworth Castle, drawn by W. Merrington. Price on wrapper: One Shilling and Sixpence. Copy: L.

UNITED STATES

149Dm] PHILADELPHIA: Hickman and Hazzard 1822
Laneham's Letter describing the Magnificent pageants presented before Queen Elizabeth, at Kenilworth Castle: in 1575; Repeatedly referred to in the romance of Kenilworth; . . . Philadelphia: Printed and published by Hickman and Hazzard, No. 121, Chesnut-Street. 1822. Pages: *i-iii* iv-xvi *xvii-xviii*, *1* 2-114. A reprint of 149De. Copy: RPB.

EDITORIAL ON THE WHIGS AND THE TORIES

150A] First Printing: 1821

[Editorial on the Whigs and the Tories], page 17, *in*:

The Edinburgh Weekly Journal. Vol. XXIV. No. 1205.] Wednesday, January 17, 1821. [Price 7d Edinburgh—Printed by James Ballantyne, For himself and the other Proprietors.

Published 17 January 1821.

Notes: This editorial relates to the annual meeting 12 January of the Pitt and Fox clubs, whose celebrations are reported at length on pages 20-21.

Copy: E. References: Garside, pages 511-513. (Magnum Opus Edition: Not reprinted.)

ESSAY ON JOHN BULL

151A] First Printing: 1821

'LITERARY INFORMATION. Discovery of the remainder of the History of John Bull, from the MSS. of his learned and celebrated Biographer Sir Humphrey Polesworth.', page 30, *in*:

The Edinburgh Weekly Journal. Vol. XXIV. No. 1206.] Wednesday, January 24, 1821. [Price 7d Edinburgh—Printed by James Ballantyne, For himself and the other Proprietors.

Published 24 January 1821.

Notes: With some amendment, this contribution may well derive from Adam Ferguson, whose manuscript on the subject Scott in 1824 acknowledged as then in his possession (*see* 79Ac, volume 6).

Copy: E. References: Garside, pages 514-515. (Magnum Opus Edition: Not reprinted).

NORTHERN MEMOIRS

152A] First Scott Edition: 1821

NORTHERN MEMOIRS, | CALCULATED FOR | THE MERIDIAN OF SCOTLAND; | TO WHICH IS ADDED, | THE CONTEMPLATIVE AND PRACTICAL | ANGLER. | [*short rule*] | WRIT IN THE YEAR 1658, | BY |

RICHARD FRANCK, PHILANTHROPUS. | [*short rule*] | [*one-line quotation in Latin*] | [*short rule*] | NEW EDITION, | WITH | PREFACE AND NOTES. | [*short reversed Oxford rule*] | EDINBURGH: | PRINTED FOR ARCHIBALD CONSTABLE AND CO. EDINBURGH; | AND HURST, ROBINSON, AND CO. LONDON. | [*dash*] | 1821.

Published January 1821 in Edinburgh (*EM*, December 1820); issued 6 March in London (*MC*). 15s. 250 copies. Binding: Drab boards. Paper: Demy 8° (225 x 140mm uncut). Watermarks: D & A COWAN | 1819. Collation: π^2 a^4 b^2 a-c^8 A-Y^8 Z^4(±Z4)χ^8 $2A^2$. Pagination: *i* title-page, *ii blank*, *iii* Contents, *iv blank*, *1* 2-10 Preface dated from Edinburgh 3 January 1821, *11* poem, *12 blank*, *v* vi-xii letter from Philanthropus to Mr J. W. merchant in London, *xiii* xiv-l dedications, *li* facsimile of 1694 title-page, *lii blank*, *1* 2-359 text, *360 blank*, *361* fly-title, *362 blank*, *363* 364-379 Notes, 379 printer's imprint, *380* advertisement. Printer's imprint: [*short rule*] | EDINBURGH: | Printed by James Ballantyne and Co. Typography: After the preliminary fold, the first signature is unsigned, the second, '*b*', printed in italic. Page-number 57 is transposed as 75.

Figures: *a*8-3, *b*—, a xix-12, b xxiii-11, c xl-13, A14-3, B20-3, C41-4, D51-10, E68-7, F85-6, G99(or 103)-8, H125-1, I 142-2, K153-12, L166-10, M178-9, N202-9, O 221-7, P236-3, Q256-9, R265-12, S283-2, T304-8, U313-12, X329-12, Y345-9, Z356-9, χ 371-5, 2A—.

Notes: The purpose of this reissue is immediately set forth in the initial paragraph of Scott's Preface: 'The following reprint of a scarce book will afford, it is hoped, amusement as well to the topographical antiquary as to the lover of the angle, since it contains some curious particulars respecting the state of Scotland during the sixteenth century.' Actually the work relates particularly to the seventeenth century, and the original edition of 1694 (Wing F2064) appears to be about as common as this 1821 redaction.

Among his forty-two notes, Scott on page 373 has occasion to refer to his 1809 edition of the Somers' Tracts, i.588-589 (*see* 38A). A supposed 'second edition', again in 250 copies, was advertised in the *Morning Chronicle* 24 August, but this appears to be in error.

Copies: BCL E GU O P; CtY IdU InU NN.

LETTER ON THE TORIES

153A] First Printing: 1821

'TO THE EDITOR OF THE EDINBURGH WEEKLY JOURNAL.', pages 45-46, *in*:

The Edinburgh Weekly Journal. Vol. XXIV. No. 1208.] Wednesday, February 7, 1821. [Price 7d Edinburgh—Printed by James Ballantyne, For himself and the other Proprietors.

Published 7 February 1821.

Notes: An ironical report on a suspected Tory 'scheme to overthrow our liberties', signed 'A Moderate Whig.'

Copy: E. References: Garside, pages 515-517. (Magnum Opus Edition: Not reprinted).

PRIVATE LETTERS OF THE SEVENTEENTH CENTURY

154A] Projected Scott Edition: 1821

[Private Letters of the Seventeenth Century, 1821].

Paper: Demy 4° (278 x 223mm uncut). Watermarks: *none*. Collation: A-I^4. Pagination: *1*-2 Advertisement dated from London 20 March 1821, *3* 4-11 Dedication to The Noble Lord who will Understand it, signed T. H., *12 blank*, *13* 14-72 text of eleven letters. Figures: *none.*

Notes: This projected fictional edition, in collaboration with Lady Louisa Stuart, of correspondence supposedly discovered in the archives of a noble family was abandoned after Scott was persuaded that the letters represented a story better suited for another novel: advice adopted in *The Fortunes of Nigel*. It would appear, however, from a manuscript addition to the 1821 Advertisement, that Scott later thought this piece worth salvaging in its original incomplete form: 'The Letters being a selection from a large library are of different character but are chiefly judge[d] to contain some curiosity[.] Being honoured with no satisfaction from the noble Lord in expectation of which it was [illegible] years suppressed[,] it is now without ceremony given to the publisher. London 1st January 1832.' The MH copy with this MS addition, and other revisions on pages 23, 46, 63, 72, also contains a letter from Walter Maxwell-Scott, dated 14 September 1936, which states that this is the surviving copy referred to by Lockhart [vi.407-414].

Copies: E; MH. Reference: Douglas Grant (ed), *Private Letters of the Seventeenth Century*, Oxford: Clarendon Press, 1947.

ON THE CORONATION OF KING GEORGE IV

155A] First Printing: 1821

'TO THE EDITOR OF THE EDINBURGH WEEKLY JOURNAL.', page 237, *in*:

The Edinburgh Weekly Journal. Vol. XXIV. No. 1232. Wednesday, July 25, 1821. Price 7d Edinburgh—Printed by James Ballantyne, For himself and the other Proprietors.

Published 25 July 1821. Notes: Scott's letter is dated from London 20 July 1821, the day after the coronation.

Copy: E. References: (Magnum Opus Edition: Not reprinted, but quoted in Lockhart vi.345-357).

THE PIRATE

This brief preface may begin like the tale of the Ancient Mariner, since it was on shipboard [in 1814] that the author acquired the very moderate degree of local knowledge and information, both of people and scenery, which he has endeavoured to embody in the romance of the Pirate. ('Introduction', 1 May 1831, *WN*, xxiv.*iii*.)

156Aa] First, Edinburgh Edition, First Issue: 1822[1821]

THE | **PIRATE.** | BY THE AUTHOR OF "WAVERLEY, | KENILWORTH," &c. | [*short rule*] | [*two-line quotation from* The Tempest] | [*short rule*] | IN THREE VOLUMES. | VOL. I [II-III]. | [*short reversed Oxford rule*] | EDINBURGH: | PRINTED FOR ARCHIBALD CONSTABLE AND CO. | AND HURST, ROBINSON, AND CO., | LONDON. | [*dash*] | 1822.

Published 22 December 1821 in Edinburgh (*EEC*, but announced 6 and 13 December as to be published 24 December); issued 25 December in London (*MC*, prior notice 6 December 'On the 24th instant'). (In view of these dates, as well as the issues described below, simultaneous publication was probably intended.) £1.11.6. 10,000 copies.

Binding: drab, blue, green, or grey boards with printed labels. Paper: Post 8° (200 x 123mm uncut). Watermarks: Generally *none*, but in volumes 2-3 only, certain gatherings beginning with sheet P: London | 1818; D & A Cowan | 1819. Typography: In volume 1 and some copies of volumes 2-3 the first 'CO.' in publisher's imprint is followed by a semicolon. Printer's imprints read invariably: (1) [*short rule*] | *Printed by James Ballantyne and Co. Edinburgh*.; (2) [*short rule*] | Edinburgh: | Printed by James Ballantyne & Co.

General Notes: For the second time the Philadelphia firm of Mathew Carey, on receiving advance sheets, allowed the local *National Gazette* to quote several times from its own first volume (volume II of this Edinburgh edition): on 12 January 1822 the song from pages 44-45 as well as 'A Scene from the new novel' pages 119-131.19 and, on 15 January another song from pages 26-27—altogether about 2440 words. (As early as 9 May and 16 June 1821 this Philadelphia journal had announced that *The Buccaneer*, as then titled, was 'in the British press.') Concerning a missing chapter in the advance sheets for the Carey edition, *see* 156Ri.

Presentation copy: E('given me by the author Sir Walter Scott while as yet secret 1822' [Lady Louisa Stuart]). Other copies: BCL(3) E(4) ES ES(vols.1-2) L LU(2) LVA (Dyce) O(9) O*; CtY IdU InU(2) MH(3) NN(4) NNU-W(2) NNU-W(vols.1-2) T/B TxU ViU. Mixed copy: TxU(Wrenn: vol.2 of the next issue: *see* 156Ab). *With 4-page Longman catalogue December 1821.

References: Church 543; B. J. McMullin, *The Bibliotheck,* xvi (1989)[1992], 1-29 (with illustrations); Randall, pages 45-46; Sterling 718, 733; Thomson, page 53; Van Antwerp(1) 13; Worthington 12. (Magnum Opus Edition 1831: *Waverley Novels*, xxiv-xxv.)

1] THE | **PIRATE.** . . .VOL. I. . . . 1822.

Collation: π^2 a^4 A-C^8 D^8(±D8) E-U^8 X1. Pagination: *1* half-title, *2 blank, 3* title-page, *4* printer's imprint(1), *i* ii-vii Advertisement, dated 1 November 1821, *viii blank, 1* flytitle, *2 blank, 3* 4-322 text, 322 printer's imprint(2). Typography: Preliminary gathering 'a' exists in a triplicate setting, with page iv fifth line first word: (a) 'it', (b) 'then', (c) 'thumbs'. Signature C (page 33) is in lower case. Though D8 is normally integral (with figure 11 on page 64) in several copies there is a belated cancel without figure and in a duplicate setting, with or without a comma after 'day', line 8. Leaf X1 is also of a triplicate setting, with period in heading page 321 above the (a) first or (b) second vertical bar of 'h' in 'the' and, in the latter layout, line 20 a light or (c) heavy dash.

Figures: a ii-3 (or iv-2), A9-2 10-1/-, B27-14 32-3, C34-1/4 44-13, D50-12 64-11/-, E79-5 80-6, F95-8 96-10, G98-9 112-7, H127-3 128-13, I 137-1 142-2, K158-15 160-14, L174-8 176-6, M190-10 192-11, N206-9 208-5, O 218-8 224-12, P227-9 240-1, Q254-15 256-14, R266-12 272-13, S286-3 288-2, T298-5 304-4, U319-10 320-14, X—.

2] THE | **PIRATE.** . . . VOL. II. . . . 1822.

Collation: π^2 A^8 B^8(±B1) C-U^8 X^4 Y^2. Pagination: *1* half-title, *ii blank, iii* title-page, *iv* printer's imprint(1), *1* fly-title, *2 blank, 3* 4-332 text, 332 printer's imprint(2). Typography: Title-page verso is in a duplicate setting, with printer's imprint measuring either 57mm or 62mm. In some copies page 197 is misnumbered 19.

Figures: A15-5 16-7, B31-1 32-2, C47-9 48-8, D62-15 64-14, E79-3 80-8, F82-12 96-13, G109-8 110-5, H127-11 128-10, I 143-14 144-7, K159-9 160-1, L166-8 176-15, M189-2 190-3, N207-13 208-11, O 223-12 224-8, P237-2 238-3/4, Q255-6 256-7, R271-2 272-9, S287-1 288-15, T303-4 304-13, U318-14 320-5, X322-3, Y330-10/-.

Notes: The Philadelphia, Carey edition, set from uncorrected proofs, indicates that pages 16-17 originally read: 'He darted a glance at Mordaunt, as if for the purpose of imploring secrecy. The Udaller, . . .' Evidently, in Edinburgh, this text was corrected at press, just before the run on sheet A (through page 16) and during the run on B (page 17 on), and then read (state 1) [page 16, lines 22-24]: 'He darted a deprecatory glance at Mordaunt, as if for the purpose of imploring secrecy respect- [page 17, line 1] ing his tumble; and the Udaller, . . .' Also page 17, line 20, last word, then read incorrectly: 'their'. Thereafter a duplicate cancel (state 2) was prepared to replace the early uncorrected B1 leaves, this with the revised text, as cited above, and last word line 20 reading either 'their' or, correctly, 'there'.

3] THE | **PIRATE.** . . . VOL. III. . . . 1822.

Collation: π^2 A-X^8 Y^4 Z1. Pagination: *i* half-title, *ii blank, iii* title-page, *iv* printer's imprint(1), *1* fly-title, *2 blank, 3* 4-346 text, 346 printer's imprint(2). Typography: The final leaf Z1 is in a duplicate setting, with or without a period in the heading page 345.

Figures: A7-10 16-8, B31-15 32-12, C47-3 48-7/3, D63-14 64-8, E79-9 80-10, F95-12 96-1, G111-14 112-5, H127-7 128-13, I 143-1 144-6, K146-10 160-5, L175-9 176-8, M186-2 192-1, N194-6 200-14, O 210-3 224-7 (or 210— 224-10), P234-12 240-5, Q255-13 256-6, R267-9 272-10, S285-1 287-2, T299-12 304-9, U319— 320-3 (or 319-15 320-8), X335-5 336-14, Y344-13, Z—.

156Ab] First, London Edition, First Issue: 1822

THE | **PIRATE.** . . . VOL I [II-III]. . . . 1822.

Watermarks: Volumes 1-2 *none*; volume 3, as for previous issue. An augmented issue of 2000 copies prepared in London. Collation and pagination as for the first, Edinburgh edition, but without cancels (the text for these now integral and in final state), volume 2 printer's imprint(2) concluding 'and Co.' The preliminaries for all three volumes were provided by Constable, and so remain of the same setting as in his own Edinburgh issue.

General Notes: Though Ballantyne, according to Constable's directions, continues to be listed as the printer, Dr McMullin has conclusively demonstrated that, because of an unexpectedly large number of pre-publication orders, volumes 1-2 of this supplemental issue were hurriedly printed in London, the first by James Moyes, the second by William Lewis, neither of whom used press figures and thus require no further comment.

To complete this job Constable himself then sent to London, along with the requisite preliminaries, the whole of volume 3, this consisting essentially of a 2000-copy overrun of sheets O-Z, all just then being printed for his own Edinburgh edition, and a new setting of the previous sheets, where the type had already been distributed. Accordingly in this London issue sheets A-N of the third volume exhibit the new array of figures cited below.

3] Figures: A16-3, B31-12 32-9, C47-6 48-15, D63-9 64-8, E73-6 79-13, F95-9 96-14, G111-1/- 112-11, H127-6 128-13, I 142-14 144-2, K159-9 160-2, L175-3 176-15, M191-15 192-3, N200-11 207-5, O 210-3 (&c. as in Ednburgh issue).

Notes: Apart from (1) this regular new setting (2) some copies of this third volume have stray sheets from the previous setting, and so vary in their figures: thus, for example, F95-12 96-1, L175-9 176-8.

Copies: (1) E; CtY; (2) O.

156Ac] First Composite Edinburgh/London Issue: 1822

THE | **PIRATE.** . . . VOL I [II-III]. . . . 1822.

Watermarks: As for the First Edinburgh Issue.

General Notes: When Constable prepared the third volume for the London market (previous London issue) he apparently retained some copies to supplement his own earlier printing of the first two volumes (previous Edinburgh issue), thus producing, in effect, a mongrel set. The one copy observed is in an early binding and apparently unsophisticated.

Copy: CtY.

156Ad] First Composite London/Edinburgh Issue: 1822

THE | **PIRATE.** . . . VOL I [II-III]. . . . 1822.

Watermarks: Volumes 1-2 none; volume 3, as for previous issue.

General Notes: This is the reverse combination of the mongrel set described in the previous entry, now with the first two volumes of the London issue (unfigured) and the third of the original Edinburgh setting (figures A7-10 16-8, &c.). Evidently, in view of the next variant, Constable at this later time sent on to London most of the volume 3 remainders still reposing in his warehouse, including for this issue the extra preliminaries he had prepared for the complete set.

Copy: O(Dunston)+
+Extra-illustrated with 1825 engraved plates by Wright and Corbould (*see* 156Dk).

156Ae] Second Edition (London/Edinburgh Edition, Reissue): 1822
THE | **PIRATE.** . . . VOL. I [II-III] | SECOND EDITION. . . . 1822.

Published ca. 26 December 1821 in London and Edinburgh (McMullin note). Binding: blue or drab boards with printed labels. Paper: Post 8° (198 x 121mm uncut).

General Notes: A further issue of the mongrel set just described, now with a new title label, first two volumes of the London issue (unfigured) third volume with original Edinburgh figures (A7-10 16-8, &c.). The new preliminaries for all three volumes here were prepared by Moyes in London, this probably in a mistaken belief that a SECOND EDITION was then called for. Only a title-leaf was printed for the third volume, however, there to serve as a cancellans for the 'first edition' titles accompanying copies still remaining of this Edinburgh printing.

Copies: BCL E(3) L O(vols. 2-3); RPB+ T/B.
+With Longman, Hurst 4-page catalogue, December 1821, listing 58 'Popular Novels', including only three by Scott: *The Abbot, The Monastery,* and *Rob Roy*, 3d edition. This copy is in Southey's chintz 'Cottonian' binding.

156Af] Third Edition (First, Edinburgh Edition, Reissue): 1822

THE | **PIRATE.** . . . VOL. I [II-III] | THIRD EDITION. . . . 1822.

Published 27 February 1822 in Edinburgh (*EWJ*); issued 4 March in London (*MC*). £1.11.6. Binding: blue boards (O Dunston copy, rebacked) Paper: Post 8° (198 x 120mm uncut).

General Notes: This reissue is now entirely of Edinburgh manufacture, all volumes constituting remainders of the original issue and still retaining the cancel in volume 2. In one set (O), however, only volumes 1-2 are of this remainder and read 'Third Edition', volume 3 without edition notice representing sheets A-N of the second setting sent to London (of which, as noted above, some copies were retained in Edinburgh), sheet O onward of the earlier Edinburgh impression (figures A16-3, B31-12 . . . N207-5, O 210-3 &c. *see* 156Ab, Aa). Thus ends the most scrambled production among all of Scott's novels, one causing still further confusion when printed nine years later in the 'Magnum Opus' edition (*see* 348A.25).

Copies: BCL L. Mixed copy: O(Dunston).

REPRINTS

FRANCE

PARIS: Baudry, Barrois [and others]
[~] The Pirate. 1832. (Collection of Ancient and Modern British Novels and Romances: *see* 288R.22.)

PARIS: Didot and Galignani
[~] The Pirate. M DCCC XXII, 1826. (Collection of Modern English Authors: *see* 291R.37-39.)

GERMANY

156Ra] BERLIN: Schlesinger 1822
[The Pirate. . . . Berlin, Printed for Adolph Martin Schlesinger. 1822. Three volumes]. Copy: not seen. Reference: GDS 132, page 344.

ZWICKAU: Schumann
[~] The Pirate. 1824. (Pocket Library of English Classics: *see* 302R.78-81.)

UNITED STATES

156Rb] ALBANY: Hosford 1822
The Pirate; A Romance. By the Author of Waverley, Ivanhoe, &c. . . . Albany: Printed by E. and E. Hosford, No. 100 State-street. 1822. Two volumes. Pages 1: *i-iii* iv, *5* 6-224; 2: *1-3* 4-230. Copies: CtY PPL.

BOSTON: Munroe and Francis.
[~] The Pirate. 1822. (*see* 156Rd.)

156Rc] BOSTON: Parker 1822
The Pirate. By the Author of "Waverley, Kenilworth," &c. . . . Boston: Samuel H. Parker, No. 12, Cornhill. 1822. Pages: *i-iii* iv, *5* 6-407. Copy: DLC. Notes: (Also reissued 1822 in Novels Tales and Romances: *see* 305R.12).

[~] The Pirate. 1828, 1829. (Waverley Novels: *see* 306R.23-24).

[~] The Pirate. 1831, 1832. (Waverley Novels [Parker's Edition Revised] *see* 307R.23-24).

156Rd] BOSTON: Wells and Lilly & Munroe and Francis 1822
The Pirate. By the Author of "Waverley, Kenilworth," &c. . . . Boston: Published by Wells and Lilly, Court-Street; and by Munroe and Francis, Cornhill. 1822. Two volumes. Pages 1: *1-3* 4-315; 2: *1-3* 4-320. Notes: The names are reversed in Volume 2 imprint: Published by Munroe

and Francis, Cornhill; and by Wells and Lilly, Court-Street. With its blue boards and printed labels, this is a direct imitation of the original Edinburgh edition. Copies: O; MH (vol.2) NN.

156Re] HARTFORD: Goodrich, and Huntington & Hopkins 1822
The Pirate. By the Author of "Waverley, Kenilworth," &c. . . . Hartford: Samuel G. Goodrich, and Huntington & Hopkins. 1822. Pages: *i-iii* iv, *5* 6-305. Copies: CtY NjP.

156Rf] NEW YORK: The Booksellers 1822
The Pirate. By the Author of "Waverley," "Kenilworth," &c. . . . New-York: Printed for the Booksellers, by J. Seymour, 49 John-St. 1822. Two volumes. Pages 1: *i-iii* iv-v *vi*, *7* 8-231; 2: *1-3* 4-239. Notes: Some copies lack colon in title imprint. Volume 2 has imprint: New York: Printed for the booksellers by C. S. Van Winkle. Copies: NN NNU-W.

156Rg] NEW YORK: Borradaile 1822
The Pirate: A Romance. By the Author of Waverly[!], Kenilworth, &c. . . . New-York: Published by William Borradaile, Samuel Marks, Printer. 1822. Two volumes. Pages 1: *i-iii* iv-v *vi*, *3* 4-248; 2: *1-3* 4-245. Copies: E; DLC MWA PPL T/B.

156Rh] NEW YORK: Duyckinck and Collins & Hannay 1822
The Pirate; A Romance. By the Author of "Waverley," "Ivanhoe," "Kenilworth," &c. &c. . . . New-York: Published by E. Duyckinck, and Collins & Hannay. J. & J. Harper, Printers. 1822. Two volumes. Pages 1: *i-iii* iv-vi, *7* 8-231; 2: *1-3* 4-239. Notes: A variant issue of the 'Booksellers' edition (*see* 156Rf). Copies: MWA PPL.

156Ri] PHILADELPHIA: Carey 1822
The Pirate: A Romance. By the Author of Waverley, Ivanhoe, &c. . . . Philadelphia: M. Carey & Sons, Chesnut Street. 1822. Two volumes. Pages 1: *1-3* 4-293 *294-298*; 2: *1-2, 5* 6-343. Notes: Volume 2 title reads 'Pirate;' and 'Philadelphia: H. C. Carey & I. Lea—Chesnut Street. 1822.' Notes: Bound in drab printed boards. This first American edition, set from Edinburgh proofs, was extracted in the *National Gazette* 12, 15 January 1822 as noted above (156Aa), and then published 8 February (*NG*), at which time nine booksellers also advertized the book. On 31 July, in a letter to the *National Gazette*, the publisher reported that his advance copy originally omitted a chapter (in the Edinburgh edition volume 1, the last chapter XIII) which he then later printed and 'had it inserted in all the copies yet unsold, and given to those who had previously purchased it. . . .' This separate printing has not been discovered. Copies: E; InU NjP PPL RPB(vol.2 title of the issue next entered). References: Clarkin 1325; Randall, pages 45-46.

156Rj] PHILADELPHIA: Carey and Lea 1822
The Pirate: A Romance. By the Author of Waverley, Ivanhoe, &c. &c. . . . Philadelphia, H. C. Carey and I. Lea—Chesnut Street. 1822. Two volumes. Pages 1: *1-3* 4-293; 2: *1-2, 5* 6-339. Notes: On 1 January 1822 the *National Gazette* announced the publishing partnership of Henry C. Carey and Isaac Lea (Mathew Carey's son and son-in-law). Copy: ViU.

156Rk] PHILADELPHIA: Crissy 1826
The Pirate: A Romance. By the Author of "Waverley, Ivanhoe," &c. . . . Philadelphia: James

Crissy, No. 14, South Seventh Street. 1826. Two volumes. Pages 1: *1-3* 4-285; 2: *1-3* 4-295. Copies: IdU NN(2) PPL T/B.

DERIVATIVES

GREAT BRITAIN

156Da] EDINBURGH: Anderson 1824
[The Pirate. Edinburgh: Published by John Anderson, Junr. 55, North Bridge Street. 1824.] Copy: not seen. (Also issued in: Edinburgh Select British Theatre, 1824: number 4 [*see* 319D] and in: The Waverley Dramas, 1824: volume 1, play 4 [*see* 321D].)

156Db] EDINBURGH: Paterson, Roy 1830
[Love wakes & weeps. Edinburgh: Paterson, Roy & Co. (1830). Music composed by John Thomson arranged for voice and pianoforte by T. Bucher.] Copy: not seen. Reference: G/T 10676.

156Dc] LONDON: Bailey 1823
The Pirate; or, The Witch of the Winds. With the Adventures of Captain Cleveland and Minna Troil.... London: Printed by Joseph & H. W. Bailey, Chancery Lane. [ca.1823]. Pages: *1-3* 4-27 *28*. Notes: Chapbook with coloured folding frontispiece by Cruikshanks (George and Robert). Price: sixpence. Copy: A. Reference: Abbotsford, page 320; Cohn 652.

156Dd] LONDON: Birchall 1822
[1] Farewell to Northmaven, Claud Halcro's Song, In the Novel of The Pirate, (written by the Author of Waverley &c.). . . . London, Printed & Sold by Birchall & Co. 133, New Bond Street. [watermarked 1817 or 1822]. Pages: 1-5. Notes: Engraved sheet-music with caption title and plate number: '1251'. Words from chapter 12, there entitled 'Mary' (first words: 'Farewell to Northmaven, Grey Hillswicke, farewell!'). Music composed by John Clarke for voice and pianoforte. Price: 1/6. Copies: E L(2); MH. Reference: G/T 10617.

[2] Love Wakes & Weeps, Serenade, In the Novel of The Pirate (written by the Author of Waverley &c.) .... London, Printed & Sold by Birchall & Co. 133, New Bond Street. [1822]. Pages: 1-5. Notes: Engraved sheet-music with plate number '1250'. Words from chapter 23 (first words: 'Love wakes and weeps / While Beauty sleeps!'). Music composed by John Clarke for voice and pianoforte. Price: 1/6. Copies: L(2) O. Reference: G/T 10618.

156De] LONDON: Chappell 1822
[1] "Farewell to Northmaven," from the Novel of The Pirate.... London, Printed & Sold by Chappell & Co. Music Sellers to His Majesty, 50, New Bond Street. [1822]. Pages: 1-5. Notes: Engraved sheet music with a caption title and plate number '2009'. Words from chapter 12 (first words: 'Farewell to Northmaven Grey Hillswicke farewell'). Music composed by Samuel Webbe, Jr. arranged for voice and pianoforte. Price: 2s/-. Copy: L. Reference: G/T 10678.

[2] "Love Wakes and Weeps," The Pirate's Serenade, ... The Words by Sir Walter Scott Bart. ... London Printed & Sold by Chappell & Co. Music Sellers to His Majesty, 50 New Bond

Street [1822]. Pages: 1-5. Notes: Engraved sheet-music. Words from chapter 23 (first words: 'Love wakes and weeps while Beauty sleeps!'). Music composed by Marmaduke Charles Wilson arranged for voice and pianoforte or harp. Copy: O. Reference: G/T 10683.

[3] The Serenade, from the Novel of the Pirate,... London, Printed & Sold by Chappell & Co. Music Sellers to His Majesty, 50, New Bond Street. [watermarked 1822]. Pages: 1-4. Notes: Engraved sheet-music with caption title and plate number '2010'. Words from chapter 23 (first line: 'Love wakes and weeps'). Music composed by Samuel Webbe, Jr. arranged for voice and pianoforte. Copy: L. Reference: G/T 10679.

156Df] LONDON: Clementi 1824
"Love wakes and weeps," Serenade from the Pirate. London; Published by Clementi & Co. 26, Cheapside. [1824]. Pages: 1-3. Notes: Engraved sheet-music with caption title and plate mark 'Serenade by Mc. Murdie.' Words from chapter 23 (first words: 'Love wakes and weeps, While beauty sleeps,'). Song composed by Joseph MacMurdie arranged for voice and pianoforte. Price: 1/6. Copy: L. Reference: G/T 10649.

156Dg] LONDON: Company of Booksellers 1822
The Pirates, A Tale, Founded on Facts: ... And Epitomised from a Celebrated Novel of That Name. By a Favorite Author. London: Printed for the Company of Booksellers. [ca.1822]. Pages: *5-7* 8-66. Notes: Chapbook with coloured woodcut frontispiece. Price One Shilling. Copy: BCL.

156Dh] LONDON: Dean and Munday 1822
The Pirate, or, The Sisters of Burgh Westra: A Tale of the Islands of Shetland and Orkney. Epitomized from the Celebrated Novel of the Same Title, Written by the Author of Waverley, ... London: Printed and Sold by Dean and Munday, Threadneedle-Street. [plate dated 1822]. Pages: *1-2*, *5* 6-26. Notes: Chapbook abridged by Sarah Scudgell Wilkinson with a coloured fold-out woodcut frontispiece with four scenes. Price Sixpence. Copy: E.

156Di] LONDON: Goulding, D'Almaine, Potter 1822-1823
[1] [The Song of Harold. London: Goulding, D'Almaine, Potter & Co. (1822). Notes: Music composed by John Parry.] Copy: not seen. Reference: G/T 10659.

[2] Love wakes and weeps. A Serenade, From the highly Popular New Novel of The Pirate. . . . London Published by Goulding D'Almaine Potter & Co. 20, Soho Sq. & to be had at 7, Westmorland Street Dublin. [watermarked 1823]. Pages: 1-5. Notes: Engraved sheet-music with caption title. Words from chapter 23 (first words: 'Love wakes and weeps while beauty sleeps!). Music composed by John Parry arranged for voice and pianoforte. Price: 2/-. Copies: L; InU. Reference: G/T 10660.

156Dj] LONDON: Hawes 1832
The Pirate's Serenade... The Poetry by Sir Walter Scott... London, Published by W. Hawes, 355, Strand. [ca.1832]. Pages: *i-ii*, 1-5. Notes: Engraved sheet-music with plate number '692' and composer's signature below imprint. Words from chapter 23 (first words: 'Love wakes and weeps while Beauty sleeps!'). Music composed by George Hargreaves arranged for voice and pianoforte. Price: 2s. Copies: MH-M NN-L.

156Dk] LONDON: Hurst, Robinson 1825

[Illustrations of The Pirate]. Original printed wrapper not seen.. Lowndes (page 2229) appears to be in error since there are not seven plates in the only located copy, but as for *The Abbot* (146Dd) the three listed below, each serving as a frontispiece. The first, captioned 'The Shipwreck of Cleveland', was drawn by J. M. Wright, engraved by R. Baker, 'Published by Hurst, Robinson & Co. London, 1825.' The other two, painted by H. Corbould and engraved by [Charles] Heath, are respectively designated 'Pirate. Vol.2. p.129.' and 'Pirate. Vol.3. p.149 [corrected in pencil to 297]'. Copy: (bound in O copy 156Ad, shelfmark Dunston B[Scott] 166).

LONDON: Leigh

[~] Song, "Farewell to Northmaven." 1831. (The Harmonicon: number 7. *see* 337D[5].) Notes: Series initially printed for The Proprietors, published by Leigh. This title published by Longman, Rees, Orme, Brown, and Green.

[~] Serenade, 1832. (The Harmonicon: number 11. *see* 337D[9].) Notes: Series initially printed for The Proprietors, published by Leigh. This title published by Longman, Rees, Orme, Brown, Green, and Longman.

156Dl] LONDON: Lowndes 1822

The Pirate: A Musical Drama. In Three Acts. . . Founded on the Popular Novel of that Name: . . . London: Printed for John Lowndes, 36, Bow Street, Covent Garden. [watermarked 1821. 1822]. Pages: *1-5* 6-70. Notes: Drama by J. R. Planché, as performed at the Olympic Theatre on 14 January 1822, three weeks after publication of the novel. Engraved frontispiece. (Music by L. Reeve not included.) Copies: E; NN(2). References: Bolton 4042; Ford Q2.

156Dm] LONDON: Power 1830

The Pirate's Farewell, A Ballad. by Sir Walter Scott Bart. . . . London: Power [1830]. Pages: *1-2* 3-6. Notes: Engraved sheet music with plate number '1171'. Words from chapter 23 (first words: 'Farewell, Farewell, the voice you hear / Has left its last soft tone with you;'). Music composed by Mrs. Robert Arkwright arranged for voice and pianoforte. Price: 2s. Copy: L. Reference: G/T 10609.

156Dn] LONDON: Williams 1822

Farewell Merry Maids, The Celebrated Fisherman's Glee & Chorus, Sung in The Pirate. . . . London, Published by T Williams, 2, Strand & to be had of Mrs. Attwood Nassau St. Dublin. [unwatermarked. ca.1822]. Notes: Engraved sheet music with plate mark 'Farewell Merry Maids'. Words from chapter 22 (first words: 'Farewell merry maids, to dance to song and laugh'). Music composed by William Rooke arranged for voice and pianoforte. Price: 2/6. Copy: L.

156Do] SOUTHWARK: Barnes 1822

The Pirate. A melo dramatic romance, in three acts. Taken from the novel of that name, . . . 1822. Printed and published by W. Barnes, near St. George's Church, Southwark. And to be had of all Booksellers. Pages: *1-5* 6-64. Notes: This drama, presented as performed at the Surrey Theatre, 9 January 1822, was written by Thomas Dibdin who states in an 'Advertisement': 'Mr. Dibdin has most sincerely to thank the unexampled exertion of every Performer and

Artist, whose zeal and perseverance enabled him to produce the following Piece in fourteen days from the publication of the original Novel.' (music by John Sanderson not included). Price: 1s. 6d. Copies: L; CtY(2) InU. References: Bolton 4041; Ford Q1.

UNITED STATES

156Dp] BALTIMORE: Blake 1822-1823

[1] Love wakes and weeps, Serenade from the Pirate . . . Philadelphia, Published by G. E. Blake No. 13 south 5th. Street. [ca.1822]. Pages: 1-3. Notes: Engraved sheet-music. Words from chapter 23 (first words: 'Love wakes and weeps, While beauty sleeps;'). Music composed by J. MacMurdie for voice and pianoforte. Copy: MB.

[2] "Love wakes and weeps," Serenade, . . . The Words from The Pirate, by the Author of Waverly[!]. . . . Baltimore, Printed and published (by G. E. Blake, Philada.) for the Author, No. 19 second St., where may be had all his Published Compositions. [ca.1823]. Pages: *1-2* 3-10. Notes: Cover title. Engraved sheet-music. Words from chapter 23 (first words: 'Love wakes and weeps, While beauty sleeps;'). Music composed by Arthur Clifton for four-part chorus with pianoforte accompaniment. A later issue from the same plates was published in Philadelphia (*see* 156Dv). Copy: MB. Reference: Wolfe 1933.

156Dq] BALTIMORE: Carr 1822

Love Wakes and Weeps while beauty sleeps! A Serenade from The Pirate. . . Baltimore, Published & Sold by the Author at his Music Store, No. 78 1/2 Market Street. [1822]. Pages: *1-2*. Notes: Engraved sheet music with caption title. Words from chapter 23 (first words: 'Love wakes and weeps while beauty sleeps! O for Music's softest numbers,'). Music composed by Thomas Carr arranged for voice and pianoforte. At head of title: 'Armonica, No. 8. Copy Right.' Copy: DLC. References: G/T 10615; Wolfe 1682.

156Dr] BALTIMORE: Cole 1825

Love Wakes and Weeps. Written by Sir Walter Scott . . . . Baltimore, Published by John Cole No. 123 Market Street. [1825]. Pages: *1*-2. Notes: Engraved sheet-music with caption title and plate number '110' on page 2. Verso of page *1* is blank and pages are facing. Words from chapter 23 (first words: 'Love wakes and weeps, While beauty sleeps;'). At foot of page 2 just above plate number: 'Entered according to act of Congress March 5th.1825 by John Cole of Maryland.' Music adapted by John Cole as a duet with pianoforte accompaniment from a serenade by F. Blangini. Probably the title advertised in *NYEP* 20 April 1825. Copies: RPB(2). References: G/T 10621; Wolfe 876.

156Ds] BALTIMORE: Robinson 1822

The Pirate, A Melo Dramatic Romance. In Three Acts. Taken from the Novel by that Name, . . . Baltimore: Printed and Published by J. Robinson, Circulating Library and Dramatic Repository, 94, Market-street. 1822. Pages: *1-3* 4-57. Notes: Drama by Thomas Dibdin as performed at the Surrey Theatre. Copies: MWA NN.

156Dt] BOSTON: Carr 1822

[Love wakes and weeps while beauty sleeps! Boston: Carr (1822). Notes: Music composed by Thomas Carr.] Copy: not seen, but cf. 156Dq. Reference: G/T 10615.

156Du] BOSTON: Jackson 1822

["Love Wakes and Weeps". Serenade from The Pirate... Boston, Published & sold by E. W. Jackson, No. 44 Market St. (ca.1822). Notes: Music composed by Joseph MacMurdie.] Copy: not seen. Reference: Wolfe 5489.

156Dv] PHILADELPHIA: Blake 1823

[1] [Love Wakes and Weeps. Serenade from The Pirate. . . . Philadelphia, Published by G. E. Blake, No. 13 South 5th Street. (1823). Notes: Music composed by Joseph MacMurdie.] Copy: not seen, but cf. 156Dp. Reference: Wolfe 5487.

[2] [Love Wakes and Weeps. Philadelphia: Blake (1823). Notes: Music composed by Arthur Clifton.] Copy: not seen, but cf. 156Dp. Reference: G/T 10620.

156Dw] PHILADELPHIA: Willig 1822

[1] "Love Wakes and Weeps." Serenade, . . . The words from The Pirate, by the Author of Waverly[!], . . . Philadelphia. Published and Sold by Geo: Willig, 171 Chesnut St., where may be had all his published compositions. [ca.1822]. Pages: *1-2* 3-10. Notes: Engraved sheet music with title on page *1* and page *2* blank. Words from chapter 23 (first words: 'Love wakes and weeps While Beauty sleeps,'). Music composed by Arthur Clifton arranged for voice and pianoforte. An earlier issue from the same plates was published in Baltimore (*see* 156Dp[2]). Price: $1. Copies: InU MWA RPB(3). Reference: Wolfe 1933A.

[2] [Love Wakes and Weeps. Serenade from The Pirate. . . . Philad., Pub. by George Willig. (ca.1822). Notes: Music composed by J. MacMurdie. Probably the title advertised in *NYEP* 2 January 1822.] Copy: not seen. Reference: Wolfe 5488.

EXTRACTS IN ANTHOLOGIES

156E] From *The Pirate* there are eight extracts in six anthologies: 361[1]E.1,6 389.32,35 404.3 405(2)[3].1 405(3)[1].4 472.3.

THE FORTUNES OF NIGEL

Having, in the tale of the Heart of Mid-Lothian, succeeded in some degree in awakening an interest in behalf of one devoid of those accomplishments which belong to a heroine almost by right, I was next tempted to choose a hero [in George Heriot] upon the same unpromising plan . . . . I made free with the name of a person who has left the most magnificent proofs of his benevolence and charity that the capital of Scotland has to display. ('Introduction', 1 July 1831, *WN*, xxvi.*iii*-iv)

157Aa] First Edition, First Issue: 1822

THE | **FORTUNES OF NIGEL.** | BY THE AUTHOR OF "WAVERLEY, | KENILWORTH," &c. | [*short rule*] | [*one-line quotation from* Poetry of the Anti-Jacobin] | [*short rule*] | IN THREE VOLUMES. | VOL. I [II-III]. | [*short* *reversed Oxford rule*] | EDINBURGH: | PRINTED FOR ARCHIBALD CONSTABLE AND CO. EDINBURGH; | AND HURST, ROBINSON, AND CO., | LONDON. | [*dash*] | 1822.

Published concurrently in Edinburgh and London 29 May 1822 (*EWJ, MC*). £1.11.6. Binding: drab, blue, brown, or grey boards with printed labels. Paper: Post 8° (197 x 123mm uncut). Watermarks: London | 1818; D & A Cowan | 1819; [*Prince of Wales feathers*] | 1822. Typography: Printer's imprints read: (1) [*short rule*] | *Printed by James Ballantyne and Co. Edinburgh.*; (2) [*short rule*] | Edinburgh: | Printed by James Ballantyne & Co.

General Notes: According to precedent, beginning with *Kenilworth* (*see* 149Aa), on 4 and 22 May 1822, shortly before the publication of this novel, some 20,440 words (volume 1, chapter 1, and volume 2, chapter 6 in this Edinburgh edition) were extracted in the Philadelphia *National Gazette*, these deriving from proofs early shipped for the Carey & Lea edition (157Rf).

Two days after publication, on 31 May, Constable reported to Scott that 'The Smack Ocean, by which the new work was shipped [to London], arrived at the wharf on Sunday [26 May]; the bales were got out by *one* on Monday morning, and before halfpast ten o'clock 7000 copies had been dispersed from 90 Cheapside.' (This quotation, from Lockhart, vii.21, differs somewhat from that in *Letters*, vii.178n.) The novel was extracted in only one anthology, 372[1]E.8.

Copies: BCL E(3) ES L(2) O(13); CtY IdU InU(3) MH(2) MH* MH+ NN(3) NNU-W T/B TxU ViU.
*With additional unrevised proofs complete in 35 pages.
+With three undated catalogues issued by C. Chapple, Royal Library, Pall Mall in each volume.

References: Church 541; Sterling 734; Thomson, page 29; Van Antwerp(1) 14; Worthington 13. (Magnum Opus Edition 1831: *Waverley Novels*, xxvi-xxvii.)

1] THE | **FORTUNES OF NIGEL.** . . . VOL. I. . . . 1822.

Collation: π^2 a-b^8 A-T^8 U^4 *X*1. Pagination: *1* half-title, *2 blank, 3* title-page, *4* printer's imprint(1), *i* ii-xlviii Introductory Epistle signed Cuthbert Clutterbuck, Kennaquhair, 1 April 1822, *1* fly-title, *2 blank, 3* 4-313 text, 313 printer's imprint(2), *314 blank*. Typography: Final leaf *X*1 is in a duplicate setting, with rule above imprint page 313 measuring 21 or 24mm.

Figures: a xi-19 xvi-2, b xxx-3 xxxii-1, c xxxix-2 xliv-18, A10-4 12-6, B31-8 32-15, C47-12 48-9, D63-14 64-10, E79-11 80-13, F82-7/- 96-5, G99-4 112-6, H126-3 128-2, I 142-7 144-13, K155-9 160-8, L167-10 176-11, M186-12 189-1, N198-14 208-15, O 220-4 222-2, P239-1 240-7, Q255-5 256-15, R266-3 272-8, S274-1, T300-6 302-10, U312-9, *X*—.

2] THE | **FORTUNES OF NIGEL.** . . . VOL. II. . . . 1822.

Collation: π² A-X⁸. Pagination: *i* half-title, *ii blank, iii* title-page, *iv* printer's imprint(1), *1* fly-title, *2 blank, 3* 4-334 text, *335* printer's imprint(2), *336 blank.*

Figures: A10-13 16-12, B22-3 32-15, C42-16 45-17, D57-11 58-14, E66-5 77-8, F86-11 93-2, G111-8 112-4, H128-1, I 144-3, K155-9 156-18, L163-3 176-1 (or 163— 176-3), M186-14 192-15, N207-13 208-12, O 222-17 224-16, P237-10 239-2, Q247-1 256-3, R267-7 272-4, S284-8 287-9/-, T294-5 304-6, U319-11 320-12, X327-3/- 329-1/3. The later impression of sheet L recurs in the 'Second Edition'.

3] THE | **FORTUNES OF NIGEL.** . . . VOL. III. . . . 1822.

Collation: π² A-Y8 *Z*². Pagination: *i* half-title, *ii blank, iii* title-page, *iv* printer's imprint(1), *1* fly-title, *2 blank, 3* 4-349 text, 349 printer's imprint(2), *350 blank, 1* 2-6 Works published by Archibald Constable and Co. Printer's imprint(2) 'and Co.'

Figures: A15-7 16-5, B31-9 32-16, C47-18 48-6, D58-13 64-11, E79-19 80-2, F95-3 96-1, G111-9 112-14, H126-4 128-18, I 142-20 144-17, K159-11 160-12, L162-9 176-5, M186-14 192-13, N201-17/19 202-19, O 222-1 224-3/6, P238-12 240-8, Q254-14 256-16, R268-15/10 270-7/8, S274-5 288-8, T290-19 304-13, U319-15 320-17, X331-1 336-12, Y346-6 2-2, *Z*—. The later impression of sheets N, O, and R recur in the 'Second Edition'.

Notes: The last entry in Constable's list, page 6, cites as 'In the Press' a foolscap 8° edition of *The Poetry, . . . Contained in the Novels, Tales, & Romances* (265A). Some copies, including several in original boards, end with Y8, representing only the first two pages of this list.

157Ab] Second Edition (First Edition, Second Issue): 1822

THE | **FORTUNES OF NIGEL.** . . . IN THREE VOLUMES. | VOL. I [II-III]. | SECOND EDITION. . . . 1822.

Published 12 October 1822 in Edinburgh (*EEC*). £1.11.6. General Notes: Except as noted below this is a further issue of the first edition with new 'Second Edition' preliminaries.
Copies: BCL E O; CtY.

1] THE | **FORTUNES OF NIGEL.** . . . VOL. I. | SECOND EDITION. . . 1822.

Figures: As for first edition except: c xxxix— xliv-18/16.

2] THE | **FORTUNES OF NIGEL.** . . . VOL. II. | SECOND EDITION. . . 1822.

Figures: As for first edition except: L163-3 176-1 (or 163— 176-3).

3] THE | **FORTUNES OF NIGEL.** . . . VOL. III. | SECOND EDITION. . . 1822.

Figures: As for first edition except: N201-19, O 224-6, R268-10 270-8. No concluding advertisements.

157Ac] Third Edition (First Edition, Third Issue): 1822

THE | **FORTUNES OF NIGEL.** . . . IN THREE VOLUMES. | VOL. I [II-III]. | THIRD EDITION. . . . 1822.

General Notes: Except as noted below this is a further issue of the first edition with new 'Third Edition' preliminaries.

Copies: L; T/B.

1] THE | **FORTUNES OF NIGEL.** . . . VOL. I. | THIRD EDITION. . . 1822.

Figures: As for first edition except: xxxix— F82-1/-.

2] THE | **FORTUNES OF NIGEL.** . . . VOL. II. | THIRD EDITION. . . 1822.

Figures: As for first edition except: L163— 176-3, X327-3/- 329-3.

3] THE | **FORTUNES OF NIGEL.** . . . VOL. III. | THIRD EDITION. . . 1822.

Figures: As for first edition except: N201-19, O 224-6, R270-8.

REPRINTS

FRANCE

PARIS: Baudry, Barrois [and others]
[~] The Fortunes of Nigel. 1832. (Collection of Ancient and Modern British Novels and Romances: *see* 288R.23.)

PARIS: Didot and Galignani
[~] The Fortunes of Nigel. M DCCC XXII. (Collection of Modern English Authors: *see* 291R.40-42.)

GERMANY

157Ra] BERLIN: Schlesinger 1822
The Fortunes of Nigel. By the Author of "Waverley, Kenilworth," &c. . . . Berlin, Printed for Adolph Martin Schlesinger. 1822. Three volumes. Pages 1: *1-2*, *I* II-XXVIII, *1* 2-194; 2: *1-3* 4-211 *212*; 3: *1-3* 4-216. Copy: E. Reference: GDS 132, page 338.

157Rb] LEIPZIG: Herbig 1822
The Fortunes of Nigel. By the Author of "Waverley, Kenilworth," &c. . . . Leipzig: Printed for F. L. Herbig. MDCCCXXII. Three volumes. Pages 1: *1-2*, *I* II-XXIV, *1-3* 4-240; 2: *1-3* 4-256; 3: *1-3* 4-262 *263-264*. Notes: The last unnumbered leaf contains errata for all three volumes. Copy: NNU-W.

ZWICKAU: Schumann
[~] The Fortunes of Nigel. 1824. (Pocket Library of English Classics: *see* 302R.82-85.)

UNITED STATES

157Rc] BOSTON: Parker 1822-1832
The Fortunes of Nigel. By the Author of "Waverley, Kenilworth," &c. . . . Boston: Samuel H. Parker, No. 12, Cornhill. 1822. Pages: *1-3* 4-415 *416*. Copy: NNU-W. Notes: (Also reissued 1822 in Novels Tales and Romances: *see* 305R.13).

[~] The Fortunes of Nigel. 1828, 1829. (Waverley Novels: *see* 306R.25-26).

[~] The Fortunes of Nigel. 1831, 1832. (Waverley Novels [Parker's Edition Revised] *see* 307R.25-26).

157Rd] NEW YORK: The Booksellers 1822
The Fortunes of Nigel. By the Author of Waverley, Kenilworth, &c. . . . New-York: Printed for the Booksellers. 1822. Two volumes. Pages 1: *i-iii* iv-xxiv, *25* 26-276; 2: *1-3* 4-260. Copies: InU MWA.

157Re] NEW YORK: Longworth 1822
The Fortunes of Nigel. By the Author of Waverley, Kenilworth, &c. . . . New York: Published by Thomas Longworth. 1822. Two volumes. Pages 1: *i-iii* iv-xxvii *xxviii*, *29* 30-363; 2: not seen. Copy: NNU-W(vol.1).

157Rf] PHILADELPHIA: Carey, Lea, and Carey 1822
The Fortunes of Nigel, A Romance, By the Author of Waverley, Ivanhoe, &c. . . . Philadelphia: H. C. Carey and I. Lea, Chesnut Street, and H. C. Carey & Co. Broadway, New York. 1822. Two volumes. Pages 1: *i-ii*, *1* 2-310; 2: *i-iii* iv-xxii, *3* 4-316. Notes: The first American edition, set from Edinburgh proofs, from which pre-publication extracts appeared 4 and 22 May 1822 in the *National Gazette* (*see* 157Aa). The 'Introductory Epistle', provided in volume 2, in some copies has been transferred to volume 1 according to instructions from the publisher. In an extensive commentary published in the *Gazette* 31 July the Carey firm adverts to the late

receipt of this 'Epistle', remarking that it was then printed 'in the beginning of the second vol. in order to repair the deficiency as far as possible. . . .' It is further noted for this novel, and may be customary for others, that as soon as the first volume was printed it was 'bound up, and forwarded to Boston and elsewhere, subject to our orders, to guard against the edition, which, we presumed, would be published in New York, immediately upon receipt of the London copy.' (Probably the new Carey branch office in New York, as cited in the imprint, was established to forestall any such competition.) Still further it is remarked that, because the firm has an agent in England, who forwards them 'the new publications, in sheets, as they come from the press', they ordinarily would issue a work 'at least three weeks before any other copy could have arrived in this country.' Copies: E; MH MWA NN NNU-W PPL(2) RPB. References: Clarkin 1323; Randall, pages 48-49.

157Rg] PHILADELPHIA: Crissy 1825
The Fortunes of Nigel, A Romance, By the Author of "Waverley," &c. . . . Philadelphia: James Crissy, 14, South Seventh Street. 1825. Two volumes. Pages 1: *i-iii* iv-xxi *xxii*, *23* 24-268; 2: *1-3* 4-262. Copies: O; IdU NN T/B.

157Rh] PHILADELPHIA: Scott 1822
The Fortunes of Nigel, A Romance, By the Author of Waverley, Ivanhoe, &c. . . . Philadelphia: Published by Edwin T. Scott, No. 61 N. Eighth Street. 1822. Two volumes. Pages 1: *i-iii* iv-xx, *21* 22-285; 2: *1-3* 4-276. Notes: The first volume has a reversed Oxford dash above date in imprint; the second volume has a hyphen in 'Eighth-street' and eight points in place of the dash. Copies: CtY InU NjP NN PPL T/B(vol.2).

DERIVATIVES

GREAT BRITAIN

157Da] EDINBURGH: Anderson 1823
[George Heriot. Edinburgh: Published by John Anderson, Junr. 55, North Bridge Street. 1823.] Copy: not seen. (Also issued in: Edinburgh Select British Theater, 1823: volume 1 [*see* 319D] and in: The Waverley Dramas, 1823: volume 1, play 1. [*see* 321D].)

157Db] EDINBURGH: Constable and Hurst, Robinson 1822
Memoirs of George Heriot Jeweller to King James VI with an Historical Account of the Hospital founded by Him at Edinburgh. Edinburgh; Printed for Archibald Constable and Co. Edinburgh; and Hurst, Robinson and Co. London. 1822. Pages: *1-2*, *i* ii-viii, *1* 2-228. Notes: Engraved vignette title-page only, with frontispiece portrait of Heriot statue and three other engraved plates. The Advertisement commences: 'The following brief notice of the Life of George Heriot originated in a perusal of the Fortunes of Nigel, by the Author of Waverley, where he appears a prominent and interesting character.' Though the Memoirs are sometimes attributed to Constable, the publisher, the preliminary 'Sketch of the Life' (pages *1* 2-48) may owe something to Scott. Copies: E(2); CtY.

157Dc] EDINBURGH: Huie 1823
The Fortunes of Nigel; or, George Heriot. A Historical Drama, Founded on the Celebrated

Novel of the Former Title, By the Author of "Waverley," &c. &c. . . . [no imprint. Edinburgh: Printed for James L. Huie, 14 Infirmary Street. 1823.] Pages: *1-3* 4-70. Notes: Drama by William Henry Murray (from the text of Edward Fitzball's drama) as performed at the Theatre-Royal, Edinburgh, 6 February 1823. Engraved frontispiece portrait 'Mr. Murray of The Theatre Royal Edinburgh as George Heriot. Drawn and Engraved for the National Dramas by W. H. Lizars, and Published by James L. Huie 14 Infirmary Street, Edinburgh. 1823.' Copies: E; InU MH(prompt copy) NjP. (A variant issued in: Dramas from the Novels, Tales, and Romances, 1823: volume 1, number 5. *see* 323D). References: Bolton 4059; Ford G4; White, page 168.

LONDON: Cumberland
[~] The Fortunes of Nigel: A Melo-Dramatic Romance. [1831]. (Cumberland's Minor Theatre: number 32. *see* 330D).

157Dd] LONDON: Dean and Munday 1822
The Fortunes of Nigel: A Tale, By the Author of Waverley. . . . London: Printed and Sold by Dean and Munday, Threadneedle-Street. [ca.1822]. Pages: *1-5* 6-34. Notes: Epitomised from the original by Sarah Scudgell Wilkinson. Chapbook with folding coloured frontispiece included in pagination. Price: Six-pence. Copies: A O(J.Johnson). Reference: Abbotsford, page 320.

157De] LONDON: Hodgson 1825
The Fortunes of Nigel, Lord Glenvarloch; and Margaret Ramsay. An Interesting Narrative. London: Printed by and for Hodgson & Co. No. 10, Newgate-Street. [1825]. Pages: *1-3* 4-24. Notes: Chapbook with coloured fold-out woodcut frontispiece. Wrapper imprints may identify the publisher as either Hodgson or, later, William Cole, Hodgson's successor at the Newgate address. Price: Sixpence. Copies: E L; NNC(2).

157Df] LONDON: Longman, Hurst, Rees, Orme, and Brown 1823
Nigel; or, The Crown Jewels, A Play, in Five Acts, . . . Second Edition. London: Printed for Longman, Hurst, Rees, Orme, and Brown, Paternoster Row. 1823. Pages: *i-iii* iv-v *vi*, *1* 2-97 *98*. Notes: A variant issue of London, Wilks (157Di), with publisher and price now indicated on title-page. Price: Three Shillings. Copies: BCL E. Reference: Ford G2.

157Dg] LONDON: Lowndes 1822
The Fortunes of Nigel; or, King James I. and His Times. A Melo-Dramatic Romance, in Three Acts, Founded on the Popular Novel of the Same Name. By Sir Walter Scott. . . . London: Printed for John Lowndes, 36, Bow-Street, Covent-Garden. 1822. Pages: *1-3* 4-44. Notes: Drama by Edward Ball [Edward Fitzball], as first performed at the Surrey Theatre, on 25 June 1822, one month after publication of the novel. Price: 2s. 6d. Copies: DT E; CtY(2) InU MH NN PU(inscribed by the dramatist). References: Bolton 4055; Ford G1.

157Dh] LONDON: Marks 1822
The Fortunes of Nigel. A Melo-Drama, in Three Acts. . . . London: Printed and Published by J. L. Marks, 23, Russell Court, Covent Garden; and may be had of all booksellers. [ca.1822]. Pages: *1-3* 4-31 *32*. Notes: With coloured frontispiece. 'Sir Walter Scott' is cited on title-page, but there is no reference to the dramatist and no list of the actors. Price: Sixpence. Copy: TxU.

157Di] LONDON: Wilks 1823

Nigel; or, The Crown Jewels, A Play, in Five Acts, . . . London: [*Imprint entered from printer's imprint:* R. Wilks, Printer, 89, Chancery Lane, London.'] 1823. Pages: *i-iii* iv-v *vi, 1* 2-97 *98*. Notes: The play is as first performed at the Theatre Royal Covent Garden, 28 January 1823 and may well have been used for sale at the theatre, without the imprint (*see also* 157Df). The 'Induction' features a lady and 'an Author, in a cloak and black silk mask'. The author is quoted 'In me / You see—or, but for this disguise, would see— / An unknown champion in the muse's field, / But more consider'd still, as more conceal'd, / A guest in courts, in camps, in halls, in hovels— / In short—the Author—of the Scottish Novels.' Copies: O; CtY MH NN. References: Bolton 4058; Ford G2.

HALIDON HILL

158Aa] First Edition, First Impression: 1822

HALIDON HILL; | A | DRAMATIC SKETCH, | FROM | **SCOTTISH HISTORY.** | [*short rule*] | BY | SIR WALTER SCOTT, BART. | [*short Oxford rule*] | [*one-line quotation from Pope's* Essay on Criticism] | [*short reversed Oxford rule*] | EDINBURGH: | PRINTED FOR ARCHIBALD CONSTABLE AND CO., EDINBURGH; | AND HURST, ROBINSON, AND CO. LONDON. | [*short rule*] | 1822.

Published 25 June 1822 in Edinburgh (*EEC* 8 June, *EWJ* 26 June); issued 4 July in London (*MC*, also, this same date, mistakenly advertising a second edition). 6s. Binding: drab paper wrappers with title printed on front cover. Paper: Demy 8° (226 x 143mm uncut). Watermarks: B | 1821 | 1. Collation: A^8 B-G^8. Pagination: *1* half-title, *2 blank*, *3* title-page, *4 blank*, *5* dedication to Joanna Baillie, *6 blank*, *7* 8-14 Advertisement, *15* fly-title, *16 blank*, *17* Dramatis Personae, *18 blank*, *19* 20-109 text, *110 blank*, *111* Notes, *112 blank*. No printer's imprint.

Figures: *A*9-19 11-5, B29-10 30-2, C42-16 48-9, D58-17 64-8, E67-2 80-5, F91-9 96-16, G100-15 102-7.

Notes: As Scott explained to Byron the day after issue, this sketch was intended for Joanna Baillie's forthcoming *Collection of Poems* (166A) but, as it soon 'ran out of bounds', was now published separately. The author wished he could have dedicated it to Byron, 'your Lordship being in lineal descent half a Gordon as I am a fourth part a Swinton.'

Presentation copy: BCL('Richard Heber Esq from the author'). Other copies: BCL BCL(Henry Liddell, Lord Ravensworth) E(2)*c ES HS*a; CtY CtY*b CtY*c InU(3) InU*a MH*a NN(2) T/B TxU ViU.
*With (a) undated 8-page Constable catalogue, (b) 8-page Hurst, Robinson catalogue June 1822, (c) both catalogues.

References: *Letters*, vii.197; Ruff 171; Thomson, page 33; Tinker 1875; Van Antwerp(1) 20; Van Antwerp(2) 24(presentation copy, to Lord Montague [Montagu]). (Magnum Opus Edition 1834: *The Poetical Works*, xii.*3-5* 6-86.)

158Ab] First Edition, Second Impression, First Issue: 1822

HALIDON HILL: . . . [*short reversed Oxford rule*] . . . 1822.

Binding: drab paper wrappers with title printed on front cover. Paper: Demy 8° (224 x 142mm uncut). Watermarks: *none*. Collation: *A*†^{8} B†-D†^{8} †E-†G^8. Pagination: As for first impression. Typography: Page 14 has † below text as a sign that gathering *A*, although unsigned, now also has been reimpressed, along with the other daggered sheets. Figures: As for first impression.

Copies: BCL E E*a(inscribed by James Ballantyne to Mrs. [Charlotte Ellen] Gibson); IdU InU*a InU*b MH NNU-W*b PPL.
* With (a) undated 8-page Constable catalogue, (b) 8-page Hurst, Robinson catalogue June 1822.

Reference: Ruff 172.

158Ac] Second Edition (First Edition, Second Impression, Second Issue): 1822

HALIDON HILL: . . . [*short reversed Oxford rule*] | SECOND EDITION. . . . 1822.

Published 6 July 1822 (*The Scotsman*); issued 6 August in London (*MC*). 6s. Binding: drab printed paper wrappers. Paper: Demy 8° (228 x 140mm uncut). Watermarks: *none*. Notes: Except for title, in all respects identical to the previous issue.

Presentation copy: InU('From the Author' [recipient unknown]). Other copies: E; CtY* MH* TxU.
*With 8-page undated Constable catalogue.

Reference: Ruff 173.

REPRINTS

FRANCE

PARIS: Didot and Galignani
[~] Halidon Hill. M DCCC XXII. (Collection of Modern English Authors: *see* 290R[1B).

UNITED STATES

158Ra] NEW YORK: Campbell 1822
Halidon Hill; A Dramatic Sketch, from Scottish History. By Sir Walter Scott.... New-York: Published by Samuel Campbell and Son. E. B. Clayton, Printer. 1822. Pages: *1-5* 6-70 *71*. Notes: In some copies the colon in the imprint is missing. Copies: BCL; CtY MH MWA NN PU.

158Rb] PHILADELPHIA: Carey & Lea 1822
Halidon Hill; A Dramatic Sketch, from Scottish History. By Sir Walter Scott, Bart. . . . Philadelphia: Published by H. C. Carey & I. Lea. J. Maxwell, Printer. 1822. Pages: *1-7* 8-107 *108*. Copies: E O; MH MWA NN PU RPB T/B. References: Clarkin 1324; Kohler(1) 196 (with illustration).

CHRONOLOGICAL NOTES OF SCOTTISH AFFAIRS

159A] First Edition: 1822

CHRONOLOGICAL NOTES | OF | **SCOTTISH AFFAIRS,** | FROM 1680 TILL 1701; | BEING | CHIEFLY TAKEN FROM THE DIARY | OF | **LORD FOUNTAINHALL.** | [*short reversed Oxford rule*] | EDINBURGH: | PRINTED FOR ARCHIBALD CONSTABLE AND CO. EDINBURGH; | AND HURST, ROBINSON, AND CO. LONDON. | [*short French rule*] | 1822.

Published 17 July 1822 in Edinburgh (*EEC* 'Only 120 Copies printed.'). £1.16.0. Paper: Royal 4° (236 x 187mm cut). Watermarks: VALLEY FIELD | 1817 (double watermark, some copies of sheet 2I); D & A COWAN | 1819 (π, a, χ, *2P*-2Q); LONDON | 1819 (double watermarks, text sheets). Collation: π^2 a^2 A^4 B-$2N^4$ $2O^2$ χ^2 $2P^4$ $2Q^2$. Pagination: *i* half-title, *ii blank*, *iii* title-page, *iv blank*, *v* vi-viii Introduction, unsigned, but dated from Abbotsford 7 March 1822, *1* fly-title, *2 blank*, *3* 4-293 text, 293 printer's imprint(1), *294 blank*, *i* Errata, *ii blank*, *295* 296-306 Index, 306 printer's imprint(2). Printer's imprints: (1) [*short rule*] | EDINBURGH: | Printed by James Ballantyne & Co.; (2) [*short rule*] | EDINBURGH: | Printed by James Ballantyne and Co.

Figures: *A*4-9, B10-9, C22-9, D31-5, E40-5, F44-5, G56-5, H58-2, I 71-2, K79-6, L84-6, M95-8, N98-8, O 110-8, P120-9, Q122-9, R130-2, S140-2, T147-2, U154-2, X167-7, Y174-7/-, Z180-7, 2A 186-7, 2B 200-1/-, 2C 208-1, 2D 216-1, 2E 220-1, 2F 226-7/-, 2G 237-7/-, 2H 247-7, 2 I 250-7/-, 2K 261-7, 2L 268-7, 2M 280-7/-, 2N 284-9, 2 O 292-9, χ—, *2P*—, 2Q—.

Notes: In his Introduction Scott laments the ineradicable interpolations of one [Robert] Mylne in Sir John Lauder's manuscript diary, then in the Advocates' Library, but declines to specify his own responsibilities. The several irregularities at the end (in pagination, collation, double imprint, and absence of press figures) would indicate that the Errata, as well as the Index, were not originally intended.

An informative account of Scott's uneasy dealings over the decade 1815-1825 with the heir of Fountainhall, Sir Thomas Dick Lauder, is given in the Johnson monograph cited below.

Copies: BCL E L(2) O; NNU-W(Lauder copy, annotated, with inserts) PPL T/B TxU.

Reference: Edgar Johnson, *Sir Walter Scott in the Fales Library,* (Bibliographical Series No.4), New York: New York University Libraries, 1968, pages 37-43..

MILITARY MEMOIRS OF THE GREAT CIVIL WAR

160A] First Edition: 1822

MILITARY MEMOIRS | OF THE | **GREAT CIVIL WAR.** | BEING | **THE MILITARY MEMOIRS OF JOHN GWYNNE;** | AND | AN ACCOUNT | OF THE | **EARL OF GLENCAIRN'S EXPEDITION,** | AS GENERAL OF HIS MAJESTY'S FORCES, IN | THE HIGHLANDS OF SCOTLAND, | IN THE YEARS 1653 & 1654. | BY | A PERSON WHO WAS EYE AND EAR WITNESS TO EVERY | TRANSACTION. | WITH | **AN APPENDIX.** | [*short rule*] | EDINBURGH: | PRINTED FOR HURST, ROBINSON, AND CO. LONDON; | AND ARCHIBALD CONSTABLE AND CO. EDINBURGH. | [*short rule*] | 1822.

Published ca. July 1822 (advertised in Hurst, Robinson catalogue June 1822 [*see* 158Aa, Ab] as 'in the press' and of an 'impression limited to 350 copies'). Binding: drab or blue-green boards and printed label. Paper: Demy 4° (292 x 230mm uncut). Watermarks: *none*. Collation: π^2 a^4 b1 A^4 B-$2K^4$. Pagination: *i* half-title, *ii blank*, *iii* title-page, *iv* printer's imprint(1), *v* vi-xiv Introduction, dated from Abbotsford 21 December 1821, *1* fly-title for 'Military Memoirs', *2 blank*, *3* 4-153 text, *154 blank*, *155* fly-title for 'Earl of Glencairn's Expedition', *156 blank*, *157* 158-186 text, *187-189* 190-263 Appendix, 263 printer's imprint(2), *264 blank*. Printer's imprint: (1) [*short rule*] | EDINBURGH: | PRINTED BY JAMES BALLANTYNE AND CO.; (2) [*short rule*] | JAMES BALLANTYNE & Co. Printers, Edinburgh. Figures: none, an unusual feature since Ballantyne regularly uses these indices elsewhere.

Notes: As Scott's Introduction immediately declares (page *v*): 'The two following Narratives are put into a printed state, not because they give any new or particular information upon the subjects of the Great Civil War, but because it is desirable, for many reasons, to place beyond the reach of accident every personal narrative connected with that eventful period.' The first manuscript was presented to the editor by the Reverend John Grahame of Lifford, near Strabane, Ireland, and the second account (by John Graham, of Duchrie) was in the possession of Sir Alexander Don of Newton, representative of the Earl of Glencairn. The name of the first memorialist is correctly spelled Gwynne in title and Introduction, Gwyn in text and headlines.

Apart from the unfigured type-work, this edition is also unusual for its heavy leading (14 lines in 100mm), short type lines (100mm), and large paper (outer margins averaging 65mm). Obviously these measures were taken to enlarge the physical appearance of this edition.

Copies: BCL E(2) GU O(2); CtY MH(Thomas Carlyle bequest) NjP T/B TxU. Reference: (Magnum Opus Edition: Not reprinted).

CARLE, NOW THE KING'S COME!

161A] First Edition: 1822

[*caption title*] CARLE, NOW THE KING'S COME! | BEING NEW WORDS TO AN AULD SPRING. (first words: 'The news has flown frae mouth to mouth,'.)

Published before 14 August 1822 in Edinburgh. Unbound. Paper: Post 8° in twos (214 x 127mm uncut). Watermarks: *none*. Collation: *A-B*². Pagination: *1* 2-4 Part First; *1* 2-4 Part Second. Figures: *none*.

Notes: On 14 August, the day before King George IV arrived for his first royal visit to Edinburgh, the poem was reprinted in the *Edinburgh Weekly Journal.* The E proof has, in pencil following the 'First Part', a handwritten copy of the last stanza with the cryptic note following: 'Hogg's The Relics, II. 40.' After the proof there is, in a fair hand, a Latin translation, in manuscript, headed 'Carminis festivi Translatio'. The MH copy, possibly another proof, bears a note signed with initials 'AS' (Anne Scott, the author's daughter) supplying another stanza 'as it stood in the original MS'. The O specimen is described on the first page by John G. Wood as being the 'Original copy of Sir W Scotts Song on the Kings arrival'. On 15 August the London *Morning Chronicle* quotes the entire 'Part Second', a version here extending only to twenty-one of the twenty-three stanzas in the original printing.

Copies: E(proof, with Scott's MS corrections) O; MH.

References: Ruff 174 (with illustrations of proof pages 1 and 3). (Magnum Opus Edition 1834: *The Poetical Works*, x.369-380.)

REPRINT

GREAT BRITAIN

161R] STIRLING: Macnie 1822
Carle Now the King's Come; Composed on the Occasion of his Majesty, King George IV.'s

Visit to Scotland, in August 1822. In two parts. Stirling: Printed and Sold by W. Macnie, Bookseller. [1822]. Pages: *1-2* 3-8. Notes: Anonymous chapbook. (Poem begins on page *2*. First words: 'The news has flown frae mouth to mouth,'). Copies: L(2).

DERIVATIVE

GREAT BRITAIN

161D] LONDON: Birchall 1822

Carle Now the King's Come, Written on the occasion of His Majesty's Visit to Scotland by Sir Walter Scott Bart. . . . London, Printed & Sold by Birchall & Co. 133, New Bond Street. [1822]. Pages: 1-3. Notes: Engraved sheet-music with plate number: (1323). Words in full (first words: 'The news has flown frae mouth to mouth,'). Music composed by Marmaduke Charles Wilson arranged for voice and pianoforte. Price: 1s. Copy: O. Reference: G/T 9775.

EXTRACTS IN ANTHOLOGIES

161E] The poem 'Carle' was extracted in three anthologies: 361[1]E.9 381.1 413.4.

HINTS ADDRESSED TO THE INHABITANTS OF EDINBURGH

162A] First Edition: 1822

HINTS | ADDRESSED TO THE | **INHABITANTS OF EDINBURGH,** | AND OTHERS, | IN PROSPECT OF | His Majesty's Visit. | BY AN OLD CITIZEN. | [*short Oxford rule*] | EDINBURGH: | PRINTED FOR BELL AND BRADFUTE, | MANNERS AND MILLER, ARCHIBALD CONSTABLE AND CO. | WILLIAM BLACKWOOD, WAUGH AND INNES, | AND JOHN ROBERTSON. | [*dash*] | 1822.

Published August 1822 in Edinburgh. Paper: Demy 8° (220 x 145mm uncut). Watermarks: 1822. Collation: A^8 B^8. Pagination: *1* title-page, *2* printer's imprint(1), *3* 4-28 text of Hints, 29-32 'Carle, Now the King's Come!', 32 printer's imprint(2). Printer's imprints (1) and (2): [*short rule*] | Printed by George Ramsay & Co. Figures: *none.*

Notes: In this anonymous pamphlet published before the King's arrival, Scott, in charge of arrangements for the visit, gives a brief historical sketch and in some detail all the formalities, the itinerary, and the ceremonies attending the great event, 14-29 August 1822, as well as important practical advice. The poem 'Carle, Now the King's Come!', described on page 29 as already 'circulated on the occasion', represents the corrected version of the separately printed text (*see* 161A).

Copies: BCL E; InU NNU-W. References: Duval 968(with illustration). (Magnum Opus Edition: Not reprinted.)

SKETCH OF THE LIFE AND CHARACTER OF THE LATE LORD KINEDDER

163A] First Edition: 1822

[*wrapper title, within a black border*] SKETCH | OF THE | LIFE AND CHARACTER | OF THE LATE | **LORD KINEDDER.** | [*short reversed Oxford rule*] | EDINBURGH: | PRINTED BY JAMES BALLANTYNE AND CO. | [*dash*] | 1822.

Privately printed October 1822 in Edinburgh. Binding: Drab printed wrappers. Paper: 4° (240 x 186mm cut). Watermarks: *none*. Collation: A-B[4] C1. Pagination: *1* 2-18 text.

Notes: As remarked in a postscript on the last page, this account of William Erskine, who died 14 August 1822, 'was chiefly drawn up by the late Mr. Hay Donaldson, Writer to the Signet, the intimate friend of Lord Kinnedder, who followed him to the grave within a few weeks', or on 30 September. It is further observed in the 1871 Exhibit that 'There can be little doubt that the 'Sketch' was prepared for the press by Sir Walter Scott. Only a few copies were printed for private circulation. Erskine was one of his most confidential friends, and was intrusted to act on behalf of "the Author of Waverley" in the publication of *The Tales of My Landlord, etc.*' This memoir was reprinted in full in the *Edinburgh Annual Register, for 1822*, 1824, pages 363-368.

Copies: E(2). References: 1871 Exhibit, item 377. (Magnum Opus Edition: Not reprinted.)

THE DEATH OF DON PEDRO

164A] First Printing: 1822[1823]

'The Death Of Don Pedro', volume 1, pages 312-314, *in*:

The History of the Ingenious Gentleman, Don Quixote of La Mancha; Translated from the Spanish, By Motteux. A New Edition, with Copious Notes; and an Essay on the Life and Writings of Cervantes. In Five Volumes. Vol. I [II-V]. Edinburgh: Printed for Hurst, Robinson, and Co. London; and Archibald Constable and Co., Edinburgh. 1822.

Published 15 January 1823 in London (*MC*). £2.2.0.

Notes: The verse is in nine quatrains beginning 'Henry and King Pedro clasping, / Holding in straining arms each other;'. Apart from the poem, immersed in a note, and belatedly acknowledged by Lockhart as of Scott's own invention, this author quite possibly was concerned with many other aspects of this extensive edition. As he remarked to Constable, 'I meant to do it myself and made some progress but Lockhart being a much better Spaniard and having more time I gave him my materials.'

Copies: BCL E L P. References: *Letters*, vii.16; Ruff 191. (Magnum Opus Edition: Not reprinted.)

PEVERIL OF THE PEAK

Sooth to say I tired of it most d[am]nably and Ballantyne mutinied on me to make me put more strength and spirit into a fourth volume which . . . I wrote in 14 days as much too fast as the others were too slow. I hope to do much better things in my next [*Quentin Durward*] having an admirable little corner of history fresh in my head where the vulgar dogs of imitators have no sense to follow me. (Scott to J.B.S. Morritt, [11 January 1823], *Letters*, vii.308.)

165Aa] First Edition, First Issue: 1822[1823]

PEVERIL OF THE PEAK. | BY THE AUTHOR OF "WAVERLEY, | KENILWORTH," &c. | [*short rule*] | [*two-line quotation from the* British Essayist] | [*short rule*] | IN FOUR VOLUMES. | VOL. I [II-IV]. | [*short reversed Oxford rule*] | EDINBURGH: | PRINTED FOR ARCHIBALD CONSTABLE AND CO. EDINBURGH; | AND HURST, ROBINSON, AND CO. | LONDON. | [*dash*] | 1822.

Published ca. 7 January 1823 in Edinburgh; issued 21 January in London (*MC*). £2.2.0. (On 9 January Scott advised Terry that, while in transit to London, the book had been 'stopped ten days, having been driven back to Leith Roads by stress of weather.' *Letters*, vii.303.)

Binding: drab, blue, green, or grey boards with printed labels. Paper: Post 8° (196 x 126mm uncut). Watermarks: London | 1818 [Vol. 1, sheet M, in some copies]. Typography: All four title-pages, apparently imposed together (with their half-titles) on the same forme, (a) originally were printed 'CO.,' at end of third line in imprint; but in the course of press-work (b) the inappropriate comma was removed. Though usually mingled, in a few sets all volumes represent the first state (e.g. E Gilson 81, in blue boards) or the second state (E RB.s.244, in drab boards). Throughout the signatures and press figures are of a smaller type size than usual. Printer's imprints read invariably: (1) [*short rule*] | *Printed by James Ballantyne and Co. Edinburgh.*; (2) [*short rule*] | Edinburgh | Printed by James Ballantyne and Co.

General Notes: According to precedent, beginning with *Kenilworth* (*see* 149Aa), on 22 February 1823, shortly after the publication of this novel, some 9350 words (volume 2, chapter 9 in this Edinburgh edition) were extracted in the Philadelphia *National Gazette* as 'Chapter IV', these deriving from proofs early shipped for the Carey & Lea edition (165Rf).

Copies: BCL(4) E(2) ES O(17); CtY InU(2) MH(2) NN(5) NNU-W(2) T/B TxU ViU(2). Sophisticated copy: InU(copy 3: type-facsimile titles with LONDON on-line, second title watermarked 1823).

References: Church 542; Randall, pages 46-48; Sterling 735; Thomson, pages 52-53; Van Antwerp(1) 15(publisher's inscription, apparently to Harriot Coutts); Worthington 14. (Magnum Opus Edition 1831: *Waverley Novels*, xxviii, xxix-xxx.)

1] **PEVERIL OF THE PEAK.** . . . VOL. I. . . . 1822.

Collation: π^2 a-b^8 A-T^8. Pagination: *1* half-title, *2* advertisement, *3* title-page, *4* printer's imprint(1), *i* ii-xxxii Prefatory Letter signed 'Jonas Driasdust, Michaelmas-day, 1822, York.', *1* fly-title, *2 blank*, *3* 4-302 text, 302 printer's imprint(2), *303-304 blank*.

Figures: a xii-8 xiv-11, b xxiv-13 xxx-10, A11-1 12-3, B19-12 32-14, C46-3 48-1, D61-20 63-2, E74-19 77-13, F95-2 96-12, G111-15 112-8, H115-20 121-14, I 136-3 142-1, K147-13 160-17, L168-20 174-14, M187-15 192-12, N207-3 208-1, O 219-15 221-11, P230-13 240-2, Q242-12 256-8, R267-19 269-17, S274-3 288-1, T298-11 300-20.

Notes: The advertisement notes the publication 'This day', in foolscap 8°, at 7s.6d., the *Memoirs of George Heriot* (*see* 157Db).

2] **PEVERIL OF THE PEAK.** . . . VOL. II. . . . 1822.

Collation: π^2 A-T^8 U^8(±U1). Pagination: *i* half-title, *ii* advertisement, *iii* title-page, *iv* printer's imprint(1), *1* fly-title, *2 blank*, *3* 4-319 text, 319 printer's imprint(2), *320 blank*.

Figures: A10-14 16-8, B18-2 32-15, C47-5/12 48-19, D53-10 63-17, E75-13 80-'41'[14]/21/6, F86-8 96-7, G102-8 112-7, H114-10 125-5(or 128-12), I 131-15 144-16, K154-9/- 160-14/11, L167-15 176-13, M190-8 192-16, N201-12 202-10, O 219-6/8 224-15, P227-17 240-14, Q248-15 251-16, R269-14 271-16, S282-12 288-15, T301-13/- 302-17(or 302-17 304-11/13), U313-18 315-10. Among the variable figure assignments in sheets C, E, H, K, O, and T it will be noted that, in each instance, the variant cited last also recurs in the 'Second Edition.'

Notes: The advertisement notes as 'Just published', in foolscap 8°, at 9s., *The Poetry Contained in the Novels . . . of the Author of Waverley* (*see* 265A). The Philadelphia, Carey edition, apparently set from uncorrected proofs, indicates that leaf U1, page 306, line 7, in cancel state reading 'yesterday', originally read 'today'.

3] **PEVERIL OF THE PEAK.** . . . VOL. III. . . . 1822.

Collation: π^2 A^8(±A8) B-T^8 U^4 X^2. Pagination: *i* half-title, *ii blank*, *iii* title-page, *iv* printer's imprint(1), *1* fly-title, *2 blank*, *3* 4-315 text, 315 printer's imprint(2), *316 blank*. Typography: Cancel leaf A8 (pages 15-16) bears the direction line 'VOL. III.'

Since all sheets in this work bear two press figures, it may be presumed that the one now lacking in the A gathering (on the inner forme) originally appeared on cancellandum page 15.

Figures: A9-12, B31-11 32-9, C43-13 48-16, D52-14 59-17, E74-10 80-11, F83-7 89-15, G100-14 106-17, H122-16 128-11, I 139-12 140-10, K155-18 160-9, L163-15 169-14, M187-13 192-11, N205-16 207-7, O 219-9 224-7, P228-16 238-8, Q252-14 254-17, R271-13 272-15, S274-16 277-7, T298-19 304-9, U309-21 311-20, X—.

Notes: An 'Erratum' slip, usually found after title-page, or after text, is of a duplicate setting, reading: ERRATUM. VOL. III. | Page 227, line 13, *for* Fleet-prison, *read* Newgate.' The alternate setting reads '-Prison'. The Philadelphia, Carey edition, apparently set from uncorrected proofs, indicates that leaf A8, page 16, lines 1-2, in cancel state reading 'seated themselves', originally read 'kneeled down'. The Carey text does not copy the other, manuscript variants (as cited by Van Antwerp), all of which it seems had already been revised.

4] **PEVERIL OF THE PEAK.** . . . VOL. IV. . . . 1822.

Collation: π^2 A-P^8 Q^8(±Q7) R-U^8. Pagination: *i* half-title, *ii blank*, *iii* title-page, *iv* printer's imprint(1), *1* fly-title, *2 blank*, *3* 4-320 text, 320 printer's imprint(2).

Figures: A11-14 16-8, B30-11 32-18, C40-1 46-6, D62-10 64-13, E77-20 78-17, F90-19 93-21, G110-15 112-4, H127-18 128-3, I 140-9 143-12, K157-16 158-8, L169-5 171-7, M188-17/15 191-10, N207-1 208-6, O 219-19 224-21/19, P228-17 239-20, Q249-11 255-9, R271-14 272-13, S283-16 284-18, T297-7 303-3, U317-15 318-5. Among the variable figure assignments in sheets M and O it will be noted that, in both instances, the variant cited last recurs in the 'Second Edition'.

Notes: The Philadelphia, Carey edition, apparently set from uncorrected proofs, indicates that leaf Q7, page 253, lines 4-5, now reading 'betwixt his Grace and Chiffinch', originally read 'betwixt them'. (The original phrase, as reported by Van Antwerp, also occurs in the Butterwick copy, which uniquely represents the cancellandum.) Since the alteration was made at press, the integral revised state of leaf Q7 may be identified by the first word, page 253, line 6, reading 'Place', the cancel by the reading 'and'.

165Ab] Second Edition (First Edition, Second Issue): 1823

PEVERIL OF THE PEAK. . . . VOL. I [II-IV]. | SECOND EDITION. . . 1823.

Issued 26 February 1823 in London (*MC*, cited as 'New Edition'). Notes: A further issue, in all respects identical with the first edition except as noted below.

Copies: BCL L.

1] **PEVERIL OF THE PEAK.** . . . VOL. I. | SECOND EDITION. . . . 1823.
Notes: No variation observed.

2] **PEVERIL OF THE PEAK.** . . . VOL. II. | SECOND EDITION. . . . 1823.
Figures: E80-6, K160-11, T302-17 304-13.

3] **PEVERIL OF THE PEAK.** . . . VOL. III. | SECOND EDITION. . . . 1823.
Notes: No variation observed. Cancel A8 (pages 15-16) is still present and page 227 remains uncorrected.

4] **PEVERIL OF THE PEAK.** . . . VOL. IV. | SECOND EDITION. . . . 1823.
Figures: M188-17, O 224-19. Page 253 is in the revised state.

REPRINTS

FRANCE

PARIS: Baudry, Barrois [and others]
[~] Peveril of the Peak. 1832. (Collection of Ancient and Modern British Novels and Romances: *see* 288R.26.)

PARIS: Didot and Galignani
[~] Peveril of the Peak. M DCCC XXIII. (Collection of Modern English Authors: *see* 291R. 46-49.)

PARIS: Galignani
[~] Peveril of the Peak [with three other titles]. 1827. One volume. (*see* 294R[3].4.)

GERMANY

165Ra] BERLIN: Schlesinger 1823
Peveril of the Peak. By the Author of "Waverley, Kenilwoth," &c. . . . Berlin, Printed for Adolph Martin Schlesinger. 1823. Four volumes. Pages 1: *I-III* IV-XXIII *XXIV*, *1* 2-185; 2: *1-3* 4-192; 3: *1-3* 4-192; 4: *1-3* 4-200. Copy: E. Reference: GDS 132, page 344.

165Rb] LEIPZIG: Fleischer 1823
Peveril of the Peak. By the Author of "Waverley, Kenilworth," &c. . . . Leipzick: Printed for Ernst Fleischer. MDCCCXXIII. Four volumes. Pages 1: *I-III* IV-XXIV, *1-3* 4-230; 2: *I-II*, *1-3* 4-239; 3: *I-II*, *1-3* 4-240; 4: *I-II*, *1-3* 4-248. Copy: E. Reference: GDS 132, page 344(place given as Berlin).

ZWICKAU: Schumann
[~] Peveril of the Peak. 1824. (Pocket Library of English Classics: *see* 302R.86-90.)

UNITED STATES

165Rc] BOSTON: Parker 1823
Peveril of the Peak. By the Author of "Waverley, Kenilworth," &c. . . . Boston: Samuel H. Parker, No. 12, Cornhill. 1823. Pages: *i-iii* iv-xii, *13* 14-512. Copy: MWA. Notes: (Also reissued 1823 in Novels Tales and Romances: *see* 305R.14).

[~] Peveril of the Peak. 1828, 1829. (Waverley Novels: *see* 306R.27-28).

[~] Peveril of the Peak. 1832. (Waverley Novels [Parker's Edition Revised] *see* 307R.27-28).

165Rd] NEW YORK: Campbell and Son [and others] 1823
Peveril of the Peak; A Romance. By the Author of Waverley, Ivanhoe, Kenilworth, &c. &c. . . New-York: Printed by James & John Harper, For Messrs. S. Campbell and Son, Evert Duyckinck, E. Bliss and E. White, Collins and Hannay, W. B. Gilley, C. Wiley, Collins and Co. J. V. Seaman, G. Long, F. and R. Lockwood, R. and W. and G. Bartow; and T. Longworth, Savannah. 1823. Two volumes. Pages 1: *i-iii* iv-xiii *xiv*, *15* 16-360; 2: *1-3* 4-283. Copies: DLC PPL(vol.2) NNU-W NNU-W(vol.2) T/B.

165Re] NEW YORK: Duyckinck, Collins and Hannay [and others] 1823
Peveril of the Peak; A Romance. By the Author of Waverley, Ivanhoe, Kenilworth, &c. &c. . . New-York: Published by E. Duyckinck, Collins and Hannay, Collins and Co., and E. Bliss and E. White. J. & J. Harper, Printers. 1823. Two volumes. Pages 1: *i-iii* iv-xiii *xiv*, *15* 16-282; 2: *1-3* 4-283. Copy: MWA.

165Rf] PHILADELPHIA: Carey & Lea 1823
Peveril of the Peak. By the Author of "Waverley, Kenilworth," &c. . . . Philadelphia: H. C. Carey & I. Lea—Chesnut Street, and H. C. Carey & Co. No. 157, Broadway, New York. 1823. Three volumes. Pages 1: *1-2*, *i* ii-xxi *xxii-xxiv*, *1-2* 5-267; 2: *1-3* 4-298; 3: *1-2, 5* 6-199. Notes: The first American edition, set from Edinburgh proofs, extracted in the *National Gazette* 22 February 1823 (165Aa), and issued 1 March (*NG*). On the date of issue it was announced that, 'To gratify the great public anxiety' the firm was releasing only the first two volumes, as they had 'just received the remaining sheets, and hoped to deliver the 3d vol. on Saturday next' (7 March). The title imprints for volumes 2 and 3 give the Broadway address as 'No. 159'. Original board imprints, however, change to '159' only in volume 3. To complete the gathering, a blank leaf follows the 'Prefatory Letter' (pages *xxiii-xxiv*) in volume 1. Copies: E; CtY InU MH(2) MWA PPL(2). References: Clarkin 1394; Randall, pages 46-48.

165Rg] PHILADELPHIA: Crissy 1826
Peveril of the Peak. By the Author of "Waverley, Ivanhoe," &c. . . . Philadelphia: James Crissy, No. 14, South Seventh Street. 1826. Three volumes. Pages 1: *i-iii* iv-xxii, *23* 24-259; 2: *1-3* 4-264; 3: *1-3* 4-259. Copies: IdU NN T/B.

165Rh] PHILADELPHIA: The Trade 1823
Peveril of the Peak. By the Author of "Waverley, Kenilworth," &c. . . . Philadelphia: Published for the Trade. 1823. Two volumes. Pages 1: *1-2*, *i* ii-xii, *1* 2-309; 2: *1-3* 4-324. Copies: NjP NN PPL ViU.

DERIVATIVES

GREAT BRITAIN

165Da] COCKERMOUTH: Banks 1825
Peveril of the Peak; or, The Singular History of Julian Peveril and Alice Bridgenorth. A Tale, Founded on the last new Novel of the same Name, Written by The Author of Waverley. Cockermouth: Printed and Sold by Edward Banks. [1825]. Pages: *3-5* 6-42. Notes: A chapbook. Price Sixpence. Copy: O.

165Db] EDINBURGH: Anderson 1823
[Peveril of the Peak. Edinburgh: Published by John Anderson Junr. 55. North Bridge Street. 1823. Pages: *i-iv*, *1* 2-66 *67*.] Copy: not seen. (Also issued in: Edinburgh Select British Theatre, 1823: volume 7 [*see* 319D].)

[~] Peveril of the Peak. 1823. Pages: *i-vi*, *1* 2-66 *67-68*. (The Waverley Dramas, 1823: volume 1, play 5 [*see* 321D].)

165Dc] EDINBURGH: Huie 1823
Peveril of the Peak; a Melo-Dramatic Play, Founded on the Celebrated Romance of the Same Name, By the Author of "Waverley," &c., &c. . . . Edinburgh: Printed for James L. Huie, and sold by Oliver & Boyd, and Stirling & Slade, Edinburgh; G. & W. B. Whittaker, and Black, Young, and Young, London. 1823. Pages: *1-7* 8-55. Notes: Play by Edward Ball [Fitzball] (music by Dewar and Ware not included) as performed at the Theatre-Royal, Edinburgh. Engraved frontispiece portrait 'Miss S. Booth as Fenella. Drawn and Engraved for the National Dramas by W. H. Lizars and Published by James I. Huie 14 Infirmary Street Edinburgh. 1823.' Copies: E; InU NN. Reference: Bolton 4103. (A variant issued in: Dramas from the Novels, Tales, and Romances, 1823: volume 2, number 6. *see* 323D.)

165Dd] LONDON: Bensley 1823
Historical Notices of Edward and William Christian; Two Characters in Peveril of the Peak. [B. Bensley, Bolt Court, Fleet Street. 1823.] Pages: *1-3* 4-42. Notes: Fly-title only; imprint entered from printer's imprint. Copy: L.

LONDON: Cumberland
[~] Peveril of the Peak; or, The Days of King Charles II. [1831]. (Cumberland's Minor Theatre: number 42. *see* 330D.)

165De] LONDON: Dean & Munday 1823
Peveril of the Peak; or, The Singular History of Julian Peveril & Alice Bridgenorth, A Tale,

Founded on and taken from the last new Novel of the same Name, Written by The Author of Waverley. London: Printed and Sold by Dean & Munday, Thread-needle-Street. [1823]. Pages: *3-5* 6-36. Notes: Chapbook with folding coloured frontispiece with two scenes. Imprint may read '&' or 'and'. Price: Sixpence. Copies: BCL O(J.Johnson).

165Df] LONDON: Hodgson 1823

Peveril of the Peak; or, The Loves of Julian and Alice. Founded on the Novel of that Name, By the "Great Unknown!" London: Printed by and for Hodgson & Co. No. 10, Newgate Street. [1823]. Pages: *1-3* 4-24. Notes: Chapbook with a coloured fold-out woodcut frontispiece. Price: Sixpence. Copies: E NN.

165Dg] LONDON: Lowndes 1823

Peveril of the Peak, or, The Days of King Charles II. A Melo-Dramatic Romance, in Three Acts. Founded on the Popular Novel of the Same Name, by Sir Walter Scott. . . . London: Printed for John Lowndes, 36, Bow Street, Covent-Garden. [1823]. Pages: *1-5* 6-48. Notes: Drama by Edward Ball [Fitzball], as first performed at the Surrey Theatre on 6 February 1823, two weeks after publication of the novel. Price: 2s. 6d. Copies: BCL E; CtY(2) MH NN PU(inscribed by the dramatist 2 April 1823). References: Bolton 4103; Ford P1.

165Dh] LONDON: Welsh and Hawes 1826

Peveril of the Peak A Comic Opera, . . . London, Published at the Royal Harmonic Institution Argyll Rooms, 246, Regent Street, By Welsh & Hawes, Music Sellers (by special Appointment) to His Majesty, Their Royal Highnesses the Dukes of York, Clarence, Sussex & the Duchess of Kent . . . . [1826]. Pages: *i-iv*, 1-129. Notes: Engraved sheet music. Operatic libretto by I. Pocock; music composed by Charles E. Horn with the Overture arranged for pianoforte, the songs for voice and pianoforte as performed at the Theatre Royal Covent Garden, 17 October 1826. Each of the seventeen songs, except the last, is paged individually to allow for separate issue. Price: for the whole—unmarked; 1/6=(3); 2/-=(4-5)(8-9)(11)(15-16); 2/6=overture and (6)(10)(13-14); 3/-=(7)(12); 3/6=(2). Copy: L. References: Bolton 4108; G/T 10578.

MAC DUFF'S CROSS

166A] First Printing: 1823

'MAC DUFF'S CROSS, *A DRAMA.*' (first words: 'Nay, smile not, Lady, when I speak of witchcraft,'). pages *1-3* 4-20, *in*:

A Collection of Poems, Chiefly Manuscript, and from Living Authors. Edited for the Benefit of a Friend, By Joanna Baillie. London: Printed for Longman, Hurst, Rees, Orme, and Brown, Paternoster-Row. 1823.

Published April 1823 in London (advertisement following text).

Notes: The authorship of Scott's poetic drama, the first in the collection, is declared only in the table of 'Contents'. The list of 'Subscribers' Names' shows that he desired ten copies, while the King subscribed only for five. Judging by the one indirect presentation noted below, some or all of these ten may have been dispatched, at Scott's request, directly from the London publisher. That one copy, though in a later binding, oddly bears Scott's portcullis device (*Letters*, ii.168-169), an emblem seen on no other book outside the author's own library and now occasionally reproduced in this bibliography..

Apart from Scott, the persistent Miss Baillie secured some original verse from Wordsworth, Southey, Rogers, Campbell, and Crabbe.

Presentation copy: T/B('From Sir Walter Scott Bart. M[arianne] D. Maclean Clephane' [with Scott device]). Other copies: BCL L O(2); InU(2) NjP.

References: Kohler(3) 49; Ruff 178; Thomson, page 42; Van Antwerp(1) 22. (Magnum Opus Edition 1834: *The Poetical Works*, xii.*87-94* 95-111 (with the name Mac Duff spelled throughout as one word with a capital 'D'.)

REPRINT

GERMANY

166R] LEIPZIG: Rein 1824
[Macduff's Cross. A Drama. Macduff's Kreuz. Ein Drama von Walter Scott; . . . Leipzig, 1824. Notes: Issued in English and German, with the German translation by W. A. Lindau.] Copy: not seen.

QUENTIN DURWARD

In fact, the sensation which this novel, on its first appearance, created in Paris, was extremely similar to that which attended the original Waverley in Edinburgh, and Ivanhoe afterwards in London. For the first time Scott had ventured on foreign ground, and the French public, long wearied of the pompous tragedians and feeble romancers, . . . were seized with a fever of delight when Louis XI. and Charles the Bold started into life again at the beck of the Northern Magician. (Lockhart, vii.163.)

167Aa] First Edition, First Issue: 1823

QUENTIN DURWARD. | BY THE AUTHOR OF "WAVERLEY, | PEVERIL OF THE PEAK," &c. | [*short rule*] | [*four-line quotation in French*] | [*short rule*] | IN THREE VOLUMES. | VOL. I [II-III]. | [*short reversed Oxford rule*] | EDINBURGH: | PRINTED FOR ARCHIBALD CONSTABLE AND CO. EDINBURGH; | AND HURST, ROBINSON, AND CO. | LONDON. | [*dash*] | 1823.

Published concurrently 20 May 1823 in Edinburgh (*EEC* 3 May, *EWJ* 21 May), 20 May in London (*MC*), a month before the date given by Lockhart. £1.11.6. Binding: drab, green, or grey-green boards with printed labels. Paper: Post 8° (198 x 130mm uncut). Watermarks: seldom in volume 1; irregular thereafter. Typography: Printer's imprints read invariably: (1) [*short rule*] | *Printed by James Ballantyne and Co. Edinburgh.*; (2) [*short rule*] | EDINBURGH: | Printed by James Ballantyne and Co.

General Notes: On 3 May 1823, more than two weeks before issue, *The Museum* (London) offered 'very copious extracts', much to Constable's outrage (*Letters*, vii. 389,n.1); on the 10th (as noted in the *Morning Chronicle* on the 9th) the London *Literary Register* also printed a number of 'interesting Extracts'; and again on the 17th the *Literary Gazette* (pages 305-311), after admonishing the other journals for 'bragging of their priority of intelligence', excerpted several passages. Meanwhile, according to established practice, beginning with *Kenilworth* (*see* 149Aa), on 15 and 27 May, just before and after publication, some 6350 words (volume 1, xxvi-xxix, and 19-43 in this Edinburgh edition) were reproduced in the Philadelphia *National Gazette*, these deriving from proofs early shipped for the Carey & Lea edition. For Carey's difficulties with the CONCLUSION see the note to his edition (167Rd).

In an attempt to forestall all these early printings, by Carey or others, *Quentin Durward*, instead of disclosing its title in headlines, there cites only chapter numbers and headings. Though eventually quite successful, the book at first, coming only four months after *Peveril*, was regarded by Constable as '*too quick* for the pocket' and thus the subject of some anxious correspondence (*Letters*, viii.29,n.2).

Presentation copy: MH('From the Author' [not in Scott's hand]). Other copies: AN BCL BCL* E(3) L(2) O(14) O(3)+; CtY InU(2) MH NN(4) NNU-W(2) T/B TxU ViU.
*With 4-page Longman catalogue March 1823.
+Dunston copies with three 4-page catalogues, Longman March 1823, Longman May 1823, and Hurst, Robinson May 1823.

References: Church 544; Sterling 736; Thomson, pages 55-56; Van Antwerp(1) 16(publisher's inscription to Harriot Coutts 17 May 1823); Worthington 15. (Magnum Opus Edition 1831: *Waverley Novels*, xxxi-xxxii.)

1] **QUENTIN DURWARD.** . . . VOL. I. . . . 1823.

Collation: π^2 a-d^8 A-R^8 *S*^{2}. Pagination: *1* half-title, *2 blank*, *3* title-page, *4* printer's imprint(1), *i* ii-lxiii Introduction, *lxiv blank*, *1* fly-title, *2 blank*, *3* 4-273 text, 273 printer's imprint(2), *274-276 blank*.

Figures: a xv-16 xvi-15/18, b xxvii-15 xxix-13, c xlii-12 xlviii-9, d lvii-19 lix-15, A14-9 16-16, B25-18/14 27-5, C47-6 48-16, D58-11 64-10, E73-20/12 78-13, F95-10 96-21, G106-17 112-18, H126-16 128-14, I 137-12 139-9, K158-15 160-22, L173-19 175-23, M190-14 192-9, N207-20 208-10, O 219-13 220-17, P234-21 240-16, Q254-15 256-22, R269-18 270-11, *S*—. The alternate figure 14 in B recurs in the 'Second Editions'.

2] **QUENTIN DURWARD.** . . . VOL. II. . . . 1823.

Collation: π[2] A-U[8] X[4] Y[2]. Pagination: *i* half-title, *ii blank, iii* title-page, *iv* printer's imprint(1), *1* fly-title, *2 blank, 3* 4-331 text, 331 printer's imprint(2), *332 blank.*

Figures: A4-16/24 7-24/23, B30-12 32-19, C42-13 45-16, D58-21 60-11, E79-19/9 80-18, F95-21 96-12, G98-20 108-19, H125-15 127-17, I 142-14/22 144-14, K152-16 154-18, L174-13 176-11, M185-21 190-16, N205-9 206-20, O 222-10 224-12, P239-18 240-13, Q253-19 254-17, R267-15 272-23/15, S286-21 288-14, T301-15 303-17, U317-11 318-20, X326-18 328-12, Y—. Again the alternate figures, now in A, E, and R, also usually recur in the 'Second Editions'.

3] **QUENTIN DURWARD.** . . . VOL. III. . . . 1823.

Collation: π[2] A-Y[8] Z[4]. Pagination: *i* half-title, *ii blank, iii* title-page, *iv* printer's imprint(1), *1* fly-title, *2 blank, 3* 4-360 text, 360 printer's imprint(2).

Figures: A11-20 16-21, B25-14/10 31-19, C47-11 48-18, D63-23 64-20, E74-13 80-24, F95-17 96-9, G111-15 112-21, H125-14 127-25, I 137-23 139-18, K154-11 160-13, L174-19 176-9, M187-20 192-21, N206-23 208-18, O 219-11 224-13, P239-17 240-15, Q254-25 256-12, R271-24 272-14, S283-12 288-21, T302-19 304-20, U313-17 318-10, X334-15 336-9, Y350-17 352-9, Z357-11. The alternate figure 10 in B recurs in the 'Second Editions'.

167Ab] Second Edition (First Edition, Second Issue): 1823

QUENTIN DURWARD. . . . VOL. I [II-III]. | SECOND EDITION. . . . 1823.

Issued 25 August 1823 in London. (*MC*). Binding: drab boards with printed labels. Paper: Post 8° (197 x 124mm uncut).

General Notes: A further issue with titles still bold-face in first line and short reversed Oxford rule above imprint. Ordinarily the figures in this set are of the later variants noted above, but the second volume has mixed figures in two sheets: A4-16/24, E79-19/9.

Copies: BCL L L(vol.2). Mixed copy: O(2:'Second Edition' for volume 2 only).

167Ac] Second Edition (First Edition, Third Issue): 1823

QUENTIN DURWARD. . . . VOL. I [II-III]. | SECOND EDITION. . . . ROBINSON, AND CO. LONDON. | [*dash*] | 1823.

Binding: drab boards with printed labels. Paper: Post 8° (197 x 124mm uncut). Notes: A further issue with titles now of a uniform type-fount, first line in Roman type, without rule above imprint, and figures all in the later state of the impression.

Copies: E L(vols.1,3).

REPRINTS

FRANCE

PARIS: Baudry, Barrois [and others]
[~] Quentin Durward. 1832. (Collection of Ancient and Modern British Novels and Romances: *see* 288R.24.)

PARIS: Didot and Galignani
[~] Quentin Durward. M DCCC XXIII, 1827. (Collection of Modern English Authors: *see* 291R.43-45.)

PARIS: Glashin, Robertson [and others]
[~] Quentin Durward. 1827. (The Complete Works of Sir Walter Scott, Bart.: *see* 295R.1-3.)

PARIS: Lequien
[~] Quentin Durward. 1832. (Collection of the Best British Authors: *see* 297.5-8.)

GERMANY

167Ra] BERLIN: Schlesinger 1823
Quentin Durward. By the Author of "Waverley, Peveril of the Peak," &c. . . . Berlin, Printed for Adolph Martin Schlesinger. 1823. Three volumes. Pages 1: *i-ii*, *I* II-XLII, *1* 2-158 *159*; 2: *1-3* 4-195 *196*; 3: *1-3* 4-209 *210*. Copies: E; MH. Reference: GDS 132, page 337.

ZWICKAU: Schumann
[~] Quentin Durward. 1824. (Pocket Library of English Classics: *see* 302R.91-94.)

UNITED STATES

167Rb] BOSTON: Parker 1823-1832
Quentin Durward; A Romance. By the Author of "Waverley," "Ivanhoe," &c. &c. . . . Boston: Samuel H. Parker, No. 12, Cornhill. 1823. Pages: *i-iii* iv-xxii, *23* 24-407. Notes: Without engraved title-page. Copies: E; DLC(poor paper issue) MWA. Reference: Kohler(1) 7 (with illustration). (Also reissued 1823 in Novels Tales and Romances: *see* 305R.15).

[~] Quentin Durward. 1828, 1829. (Waverley Novels: *see* 306R.29-30).

[~] Quentin Durward. 1832. (Waverley Novels: [Parker's Edition Revised] *see* 307R.29-30).

167Rc] NEW YORK: Duyckinck and Campbell and Son [and others] 1823
Quentin Durward; A Romance. By the Author of Waverley, Ivanhoe, &c. &c. . . . New-York: Published by E. Duyckinck, S. Campbell and Son, William B. Gilley, E. Bliss and E. White,

Collins and Co., Collins and Hannay, and F. and R. Lockwood. J. & J. Harper, Printers. 1823. Two volumes. Pages 1: *1-3* 4-246; 2: *1-3* 4-264. Copies: CtY IdU NjP PPL T/B.

167Rd] PHILADELPHIA: Carey and Lea 1823
Quentin Durward; A Romance. By the Author of Waverley, Ivanhoe, &c. &c. . . . Philadelphia: H. C. Carey and I. Lea—Chesnut Street. 1823. Two volumes. Pages 1: *1-2, i* ii-xxxvi, *1* 2-271; 2: *1-3* 4-321. Notes: The first American edition, set from Edinburgh proofs, extracted in the *National Gazette* 15, 27 May (167Aa), and issued during the week following 14 June 1823 (*NG*). Later in a note 28 June to the *Gazette* the publisher printed the conclusion to this work: a section not received with the original copy but now made available *gratis* to the public. In some annoyance the Carey firm further remarks: 'Having paid Messrs. Constable & Co. a large sum to have the volumes forwarded several days previous to their appearance in London, those gentlemen were pledged to furnish them complete.' Copies: CtY MWA NNU-W PPL RPB. Reference: Clarkin 1395.

167Re] PHILADELPHIA: Crissy 1826-1827
Quentin Durward. A Romance. By the Author of "Waverley, Ivanhoe," &c. &c. . . . Philadelphia: James Crissy, No. 14, South Seventh Street. 1826 [1827]. Two volumes. Pages [1826] 1: *i-iii* iv-xxvi, *27* 28-279; [1827] 2: *1-3* 4-293. Copies: NN T/B(vol.1). Later issue with vol. 2 imprinted 'S. Seventh . . . 1827' (IdU).

167Rf] PHILADELPHIA: Wright 1823
Quentin Durward: A Romance. By the Author of Waverly[!], Ivanhoe, &c. &c. . . . Philadelphia: Printed by Robert Wright. 1823. Two volumes. Pages 1: *i-iii* iv-xxxii, *33* 34-272; 2: *1-3* 4-275. Copies: CtY NjP.

DERIVATIVES

GREAT BRITAIN

167Da] EDINBURGH: Huie [and others] 1823
Quentin Durward: A Drama, Founded on the Celebrated Novel of the Same Name, by the Author of "Waverley;" . . . Edinburgh: Printed for James L. Huie, 14 Infirmary Street, and Black, Young, and Young, Tavistock Street, Covent Garden, London. 1823. Pages: *1-5* 6-78 *79-80*. Notes: Drama by J. L. Huie, first performed at The Caledonian Theatre, Edinburgh, 23 June 1823. This edition is dedicated to Archibald Constable, publisher of the novel. Copies: L; CtY NN TxU. References: Bolton 4124; Ford R2.

167Db] LONDON: Chappell 1823
County Guy, A Song, from the Novel of Quentin Durward, . . . London, Printed & Sold by Chappell & Co. Music Sellers to His Majesty, 50, New Bond Street. [ca.1823]. Pages: 1-5. Notes: Engraved sheet music with caption title and plate number '2208'. Words from chapter 4 (first words: 'Ah! County Guy, the hour is nigh, The Sun has left the lea,'). Music composed by George Farquhar Graham arranged for voice and pianoforte. G/T says that 'the song was composed at Scott's request.' Price: 2/-. Copies: E L. Reference: G/T 10700.

167Dc] LONDON: Clementi 1825
Ah! County Guy, the celebrated Serenade in Quentin Durward, . . . London, Published by Clementi & Co. 26, Cheapside. [1825]. Pages: 1-5. Notes: Engraved sheet music with caption title and plate mark: 'Ah County Guy.'. Words from chapter 4 (first words: 'Ah! County Guy, the hour is nigh, / The sun is on the lea;'). Music composed by Burford George Henry Gibsone arranged for voice and pianoforte. Price: 1/6. Copy: L. Reference: G/T 10699.

167Dd] LONDON: Cole 1823
Quentin Durward: or, The fortunate Scotsman: being an account of his adventures at the court of France, and displaying the intrigues of Louis XI. and the violent, but open-hearted, conduct of Charles of Burgundy: with the barbarous murder of the Bishop of Liege, by William de la Marck, the wild-boar of the Ardennes. London: Printed by and for William Cole, 10, Newgate Street [ca.1823]. Pages: *1-3* 4-24. Notes: Chapbook with coloured folding woodcut frontispiece. Price: Sixpence. Copy: CtY.

167De] LONDON: Dean and Munday 1823
The History and Adventures of Quentin Durward and the Beautiful Isabelle, . . . from the Popular Novel of "Quentin Durward," by the Author of "Waverley." London: Printed and Sold by Dean and Munday, Threadneedle-Street. [ca.1823]. Pages: *1-3* 4-36. Notes: Chapbook with coloured woodcut frontispiece. Price: Six-pence. Copy: BCL.

167Df] LONDON: Goulding, D'Almaine, Potter 1823
. . . County Guy, The Poetry from "Quentin Durward"; . . . London, Published by Goulding, D'Almaine, Potter & Co. 20, Soho Square, and to be had at 7, Westmorland St, Dublin. [watermarked 1820 or 1821. 1823]. Pages: *1* 2-4. Notes: Engraved sheet music with composer's monogram stamped just below imprint and with plate mark: 'County Guy.'. Just above title is a four-line quotation from '"Quentin Durward" by the Author of "Waverly"[!] &c. Chap 4. Vol:1.' and just above music on page 2: 'The Poetry by the Author of "Waverly[!]".' Words from chapter 4 (first words: 'Ah! County Guy, the hour is nigh'). Music composed by Henry R. Bishop arranged for voice and pianoforte. Price: 1/6. Copies: L O; NNP. References: G/T 10687; Van Antwerp(2) 42o.

167Dg] LONDON: Hebert 1823
Quentin Durward: A Drama, in Three Acts. Founded upon the Novel of that Name. London: Printed for G. Hebert, 88, Cheap-side; Sold by Simpkin & Marshall, Stationers' Court. 1823. Pages: *1-3* 4-40. Notes: Written and arranged for representation by R Haworth. Price: One Shilling. Copy: CtY. Reference: Bolton 4126.

167Dh] LONDON: Hodgson 1825
[Quentin Durward; or, The Wild Boar of Ardennes. London: Hodgson [ca. 1825]. Notes: Drama by John Thomas Haines (music by T. Hughes not included) first performed at the Coburg Theatre, London, 9 June 1823, three weeks after publication of the novel.] Copy: not seen. Reference: Bolton 4123.

167Di] LONDON: Hodsoll 1823
[County Guy. London: Hodsoll (1823). Notes: Music composed by Augustus Voigt.] Copy: not seen. Reference: G/T 10718.

167Dj] LONDON: Knight 1823
Historical Illustrations of Quentin Durward, Selected from the Memoirs of Philip de Comines, and Other Authors. London: Printed for Charles Knight, 7, Pall-Mall East. MDCCCXXIII. Pages: *i-iii* iv-viii, *1* 2-166 *167-168*. Notes: Three portrait plates, engraved by Aglio; published by C. Knight, 7 Pall Mall East; frontispiece with caption 'Lovis XI. King of France.' with facsimile signature; plates 2 and 3 have captions 'Charles the Bold. Duke of Burgundy' and 'Phillip de Commines'[!] respectively. Copies: O; IdU InU NN(2).

167Dk] LONDON: Nathan 1823
[Ah! County Guy. London: Nathan (1823). Notes: Music composed by Isaac Nathan.] Copy: not seen. Reference: G/T 10709.

167Dl] LONDON: Platts 1830
County Guy. A Romance from Quentin Durward, . . . London, Printed & Sold by J. Platts, Music Seller, 9 John Street, near Regent Circus, Oxford St. [unwatermarked. ca.1830]. Pages: *1-6*. Notes: Engraved sheet music. Words from chapter 4 (first words : 'Ah County Guy, the hour is nigh,'). Music composed by Ernest Augustus Kellner arranged for voice and pianoforte. Price: 1/6. Copy: L. Reference: G/T 10704.

167Dm] LONDON: Rovedino 1823
County Guy, A Ballad, The Words from "Quentin Durward" by the Author of Waverly[!], . . . Published for Mr. T. Rovedino, 163, Sloane Street, by Birchall & Co. 133, New Bond Street. London. [1823]. Pages: *i-ii*, 1-5. Notes: Engraved sheet music with composer's signature in ink to right of imprint. Words from chapter 4 (first words: 'Ah! County Guy the hour is nigh,'). Music composed by Tommaso E. G. Rovedino arranged for voice, flute and harp. Copies: L; MH. Reference: G/T 10713. Variant copy with imprint reading: by Birchall & Co. 140, New Bond Street, London. Copy: MH.

167Dn] LONDON: Wybrow 1825
County Guy, from Sir Walter Scotts popular Romance of Quintin [!] Durward, . . . London, Printed by W. & S. Wybrow, 24 Rathbone Place. [1823]. Pages: *1* 2-3. Notes: Engraved sheet music with caption title and note below composer's name reading: 'This Arrangement is acknowledged by the Noble Author as being the best adapted to the Poetry.' Words from chapter 4 (first words: 'Ah! County Guy the hour is nigh,' Music composed by Sidney Waller for voice and pianoforte. Copy: MH.

167Do] YORK: Knapton, White and Knapton 1825
County Guy, A Ballad, . . The Words from Quentin Durward. York: Printed & Sold by Knapton, White & Knapton, Coney Street, and to be had in London at W. Bainbridge's Patent Flageolet Manufactory. 35 Holborn Hill. [unwatermarked. ca.1825]. Pages: 1-3. Notes: Engraved sheet music. Words from chapter 4 (first words: 'Ah County Guy the hour is nigh, The Sun has left the lea'). Music composed by Philip Knapton arranged for voice and pianoforte. Copies: E L; MH. Reference: G/T 10705.

UNITED STATES

167Dp] PHILADELPHIA: Klemm 1825
Ah County Guy. The celebrated Serenade in Quentin Durward Written by Sir Walter Scott. . . . Philadelphia, Published by J. G. Klemm. [ca.1825]. Pages: *1* 2-3. Notes: Engraved sheet music with caption title and plate number: '232'. Words from chapter 4 (first words: 'Ah! County Guy, the hour is nigh, The sun is on the lea'). Music composed by Burford G. H. Gibsone arranged for voice and pianoforte. Copies: PHi RPB. Reference: Wolfe 2999.

EXTRACTS IN ANTHOLOGIES

167E] The poem 'Ah! County Guy' was extracted in four anthologies: 389E.8 411 414[2].3 469.11.

LETTER ON PETERKIN'S CONDUCT

168A] First Printing: 1823

'LETTER from Sir WALTER SCOTT, Bart. to Mr Peterkin', pages 47-48, *in*:

Letter to the Landholders, Clergy, and other Gentlemen, of Orkney and Zetland, with relative Documents: and Correspondence betwixt J. A. Maconochie, Esq. Sheriff-Depute, and Alex. Peterkin. Edinburgh: Printed by John Moir. 1823.

Published ca. July 1823 in Edinburgh. Notes: This letter, dated 24 June, is one of several commending Alexander Peterkin's conduct, in reference to his dispute as Sheriff-Substitute with James Allan Maconochie.

Copy: E. References: *The Scott Newsletter*, 20 (Summer 1992), 12-13. (Magnum Opus Edition: Not reprinted.)

A BANNATYNE GARLAND

169A] First Edition: 1823

A | Bannatyne Garland, | Quhairin | The President Speaketh. (first words: 'Assist me, ye friends of old books and old wine,').

Printed 22 November 1823 in Edinburgh. 40 copies. Binding: coated green or marbled wrappers. Paper: Crown (or Large Post) 8° in half-sheets (202 x 129mm uncut). Watermarks: A COWAN | 1822. Collation: A^6. Pagination: *i-ii blank*, *1* caption title-page, *2 blank*, *3* 4-6 text, *7-10 blank*. Typography: The entire edition is printed in gothic type. Figures: *none*.

Notes: Scott as founder and president composed this song for the first dinner of the Club, 9 March 1823, when it was then sung by James Ballantyne. The verse of ten stanzas is signed on page 6: Finis, quoth the Knight of Abbotsford.

Copies: E GU* O(corrected proof copy); IdU MH NN NNP(Van Antwerp: signed W. A. [Drummond] Hay).
*With erroneous MS note 'Sung by Jas. Ballantyne at the anniversary dinner. 25. November 1823 Sir Walter Scott in the Chair.'

References: Duval 971 (with illustration); Ruff 177; Thomson, pages 14, 64; Van Antwerp(1) 21. (Magnum Opus Edition 1834: *The Poetical Works*, xi.377-382.)

THE BUKE OF THE HOWLAT

170A] First Edition: 1823

[Notes added by Scott to the Preface, pages xix-xxiii, and to the Appendix, page 5, relating to stanzas XIII-XIX] *in*:

The Buke of the Howlat. By Holland. [*woodblock vignette*]. Printed at Edinburgh. MDCCCXXIII.

Notes: This Bannatyne Club volume, later designated as number 3, bears David Laing's dedication dated 23 October 1823.

Copy: A NN. References: Abbotsford, page 276; *Letters*, viii.97. (Magnum Opus Edition: Not reprinted.)

ST RONAN'S WELL

The novel which follows is upon a plan different from any other that the author has ever written, . . . It is intended, in a word—*celebrare domestica facta*—to give an imitation of the shifting manners of our own time, and paint scenes, the originals of which are passing round us, so that a minute's observation may compare the copies with the originals. ('Introduction', '1 February 1832', *WN*, xxxiii.*iii*.)

171Aa] First Edition, First Issue: 1824[1823]

ST RONAN'S WELL. | BY THE AUTHOR OF "WAVERLEY, | QUENTIN DURWARD," &c. | [*short rule*] | [*two-line quotation from Wordsworth*] | [*short rule*] | IN THREE VOLUMES. | VOL. I [II-III]. | [*short reversed Oxford rule*] | EDINBURGH: | PRINTED FOR ARCHIBALD CONSTABLE AND CO. EDINBURGH; | AND HURST, ROBINSON, AND CO. | LONDON. | [*dash*] | 1824.

Published concurrently 27 December 1823 in Edinburgh (*EEC*); 29 December in London (*MC*). £1.11.6. 9800 copies, of which 7000 were shipped to Hurst, Robinson on 16 December 1823 (*EEWN16*.379). Binding: drab, cream, blue, rose, or blue-green boards with printed labels. Paper: Post 8° (195 x 123mm uncut). Watermarks:

1823 infrequently. Typography: Printer's imprints read invariably: (1) [*short rule*] | EDINBURGH: | PRINTED BY JAMES BALLANTYNE AND CO.; (2) [*short rule*] | EDINBURGH: | Printed by James Ballantyne & Co.

General Notes: According to established practice, beginning with *Kenilworth* (*see* 149Aa), on 25 November 1823, a month before the publication of this novel, some 6375 words (volume 1, chapter 1 in this Edinburgh edition) were extracted in the Philadelphia *National Gazette*, these deriving from proofs early shipped for the Carey & Lea edition (171Re).

A climactic scene in this novel, as now represented (vol.3, pages 301.16-303.18), was considerably altered at the insistence of Scott's squeamish printer and publisher. The original text is restored in the latest, definitive edition, *EEWN16.* 363.28-364.36 and the change, described as 'unique among the Waverley Novels', further discussed there on page 390.

Presentation copies: E('given me by the author (as yet secret) Sir Walter Scott [Lady] L[ouisa] Stuart'). Other copies: AN(2) BCL(2) E(4) ES L(2) O(16); CtY IdU InU(3) MH NN(5) NNU-W(2) RPB(2) T/B TxU ViU.

References: Church 546; Sterling 737; Thomson, page 59; Van Antwerp(1) 17(publisher's inscription to Harriot Coutts, with her date 1 January 1824); Mark A. Weinstein (ed.), *EEWN16*; Worthington 16. (Magnum Opus Edition 1832: *Waverley Novels*, xxxiii-xxxiv.)

1] **ST RONAN'S WELL.** . . VOL. I. . . . 1824.

Collation: π^2 A-T^8 U^4. Pagination: *i* half-title, *ii blank, iii* title-page, *iv* printer's imprint(1), *1* fly-title, *2 blank, 3* 4-310 text, 310 printer's imprint(2), *311-312 blank.*

Figures: A12-20 14-18, B22-17 32-16, C35-12 48-13 (or 35-12 48-12, or 35-13 48-12), D57-10 63-18, E73-21 78-22, F95-11 96-20, G111-15 112-18, H118-17 128-9, I 139-21 144-16, K151-13 156-12, L172-14 174-20, M186-12 192-11, N195-11 208-18, O 218-16 220-9, P239-18 240-16, Q255-11 256-14, R271-13 272-10, S287-18 288-16, T303-2 304-14, U308-11. The two alternate C figure records, occurring in a few copies, reappear in the 'Second Edition'.

2] **ST RONAN'S WELL.** . . . VOL. II. . . . 1824.

Collation: π^2 A-U^8 X^4. Pagination: *i* half-title, *ii blank, iii* title-page, *iv* printer's imprint(1), *1* fly-title, *2 blank, 3* 4-325 text, 325 printer's imprint(2), *326-328 blank.*

Figures: A15-19 16-18, B31-17 32-16, C45-10 46-14, D63-18 64-12, E77-9 79-15, F95-13 96-19, G111-20 112-12, H127-18 128-21, I 143-13 144-12, K159-16 160-14, L175-18 176-20, M191-19 192-21, N207-21 208-18, O 223-19 224-20, P237-21 238-16, Q255-14 256-20, R271-19 272-18, S287-17 288-15, T301-9 302-21, U317-20 318-16, X324-12.

3] **ST RONAN'S WELL.** . . . VOL. III. . . . 1824.

Collation: π^2 A-U^8 X^4. Pagination: *i* half-title, *ii blank, iii* title-page, *iv* printer's imprint(1), *1* fly-title, *2 blank, 3* 4-323 text, *324* printer's imprint(2), *325* advertisement, *326-328* Archibald Constable catalogue.

Figures: A13-12 14-17, B31-11 32-10, C47-21 48-13, D63-16 64-14, E79-20 80-17, F95-10 96-21, G110-13 112-12, H127-21 128-12, I 143-17 144-14, K159-21 160-20, L175-12 176-16, M186-20 192-21, N207-19 208-12, O 223-16/17 224-16/17, P239-21 240-20, Q255-17 256-11, R267-13 272-12, S285-15 286-14, T303-16 304-19, U319-20 320-21, X*327*-18/-.

171Ab] Second Edition (First Edition, Second Issue): 1824

ST RONAN'S WELL. . . . VOL. I [II-III]. | SECOND EDITION. . . . 1824.

General Notes: A further issue of the first edition sheets, with the alternate figures in volume 1 in later state.

Copies: L(2) O.

REPRINTS

FRANCE

PARIS: Baudry, Barrois [and others]
[~] St. Ronan's Well. 1832. (Collection of Ancient and Modern British Novels and Romances: *see* 288R.27.)

PARIS: Didot and Galignani
[~] St Ronan's Well. M DCCC XXIV. (Collection of Modern English Authors: *see* 291R. 50-52.)

GERMANY

171Ra] BERLIN: Schlesinger 1824
[St. Ronan's Well. . . . Berlin, Printed for Adolph Martin Schlesinger. 1824]. Copy: not seen. Reference: GDS 132, page 346.

ZWICKAU: Schumann
[~] St Ronan's Well. 1824. (Pocket Library of English Classics: *see* 302R.95-98.)

UNITED STATES

171Rb] BOSTON: Parker 1824
St. Ronan's Well. By the Author of "Waverley," "Quentin Durward," &c. Boston: Samuel H. Parker, No. 12, Cornhill. 1824. Pages: *1-3* 4-380. Copy: NN. Notes: (Also reissued 1824 in Novels Tales and Romances: *see* 305R.16).

[~] St. Ronan's Well. 1828, 1829. (Waverley Novels: *see* 306R.31-32.)

[~] St. Ronan's Well. 1832. (Waverley Novels [Parker's Edition Revised] *see* 307R.31-32.)

171Rc] NEW YORK: Duyckinck, Collins and Hannay, [and others] 1824
St. Ronan's Well. By the Author of "Waverley," "Quentin Durward," &c. . . . New-York: Printed by James & John Harper, for Messrs. Evert Duyckinck, Collins and Hannay, Collins and Co., and E. Bliss and E. White, 1824. Two volumes. Pages 1: *1-3* 4-231; 2: *1-3* 4-250. Copies: E; CtY NN. Reference: Kohler(1) 67 (with illustration).

171Rd] NEW YORK: Gilley, Long, [and others] 1824
St. Ronan's Well. By the Author of "Waverley," "Quentin Durward," &c. . . . New York: Printed by James & John Harper, for Wm. B. Gilley, George Long, F. & R. Lockwood, and James V. Seaman. 1824. Two volumes. Pages 1: *1-3* 4-'254'[245]; 2: *1-3* 4-250. Notes: In vol. 2 imprint Gilley's initials are given as 'W. B.' Copy: RPB.

171Re] PHILADELPHIA: Carey and Lea 1824
St. Ronan's Well; By the Author of Waverley, Ivanhoe, &c. . . . Philadelphia: H. C. Carey & I. Lea—Chesnut Street. 1824. Two volumes. Pages 1: *1-2, 11* 12-296; 2: *1-3* 4-288. Notes: The first American edition, set from Edinburgh proofs, extracted in the *National Gazette* 25 November 1823 (171Aa), and issued 19 February 1824 (*NG*). Copies: E; CtY MWA NN NNU-W PPL. Reference: Clarkin 1517.

171Rf] PHILADELPHIA: Crissy 1827
St. Ronan's Well; By the Author of Waverley, Ivanhoe, &c. . . . Philadelphia: James Crissy, No. 14, South Seventh Street. 1827. Two volumes. Pages 1: *1-3* 4-236; 2: *1-3* 4-263. Notes: A paginal reprint of the 1824 Wright edition (next entry). Copies: IdU NN T/B.

171Rg] PHILADELPHIA: Wright 1824
St. Ronan's Well, By the Author of Waverley, Ivanhoe, &c. . . . Philadelphia: Published at No. 4, South Front-street. R. Wright, Printer. 1824. Two volumes. Pages 1: *1-3* 4-236; 2: *1-3* 4-263. Notes: The title in volume 2 is followed by a semi-colon and the imprint substitutes 'D. Dickinson, printer.' for Wright. Copies: CtY DLC NjP.

DERIVATIVES

GREAT BRITAIN

171Da] EDINBURGH: Anderson 1824
[St. Ronan's Well. Edinburgh: Published by John Anderson, Junr. 55, North Bridge Street. 1824. (Also listed for issue in: Edinburgh Select British Theatre, 1824: number 15. *see* 319D.14 note. No copy of this variant has been seen.) Notes: No copy reported by Bolton, but attributed to James Robinson Planché and first performance recorded at the Adelphi, London 19 January 1824 (three weeks after publication of the novel), with a later performance at the Theatre Royal, Edinburgh.] Copy: not seen. References: Bolton 4260, 4262.

171Db] EDINBURGH: Bell and Bradfute [and others] 1826
The Cook and Housewife's Manual; containing the most Approved Modern Receipts . . . Edinburgh; Printed for the Author, and Sold by Bell & Bradfute, and Oliver & Boyd, Edinburgh; Longman, Rees, Orme, Brown, and Green, London; Robertson & Atkinson, Glasgow; and John Cumming, Dublin. 1826. Pages: [*1-2*] *3-7* 8-366. Notes: Compiler identified as 'Mrs Margaret Dods, of the Cleikum Inn, St Ronan's' (Mrs Christian Isobel Johnstone), but the 'Preface' and more especially the 'Introduction' (later designated 'Institution of the Cleikum Club') were later ascribed to Scott: *see* next entry. Copies: E O.

171Dc] EDINBURGH: Oliver and Boyd, Bell and Bradfute 1827-1828
[1] The Cook and Housewife's Manual; containing the most Approved Modern Receipts . . . The Second Edition; in which are given, A Compendium of French Cookery, . . Edinburgh; Printed for Oliver and Boyd, and Bell and Bradfute; Geo. B. Whittaker, London; Robertson and Atkinson, Glasgow; and William Curry, Jun. and Co. Dublin. 1827. Pages: *i-iv*, *1* 2-525 *526*, *1*-2. Notes: Compilation by 'Mrs Margaret Dods, of the Cleikum Inn, St Ronan's (Mrs Christian Isobel Johnstone), but the 'Preface' and more especially the 'Introduction', referred to in the Contents as 'Institution of the Cleikum Club', are ascribed to Scott in the *Monthly Review*, quoted in the last leaf of 'Reviews of the First Edition': 'We have no hesitation in saying, that if the humorous introduction is not written by Sir Walter Scott, the author of it possesses a singular talent of mimicking his best comic manner, and has presented us with an imitation of the great novelist, as remarkable for its fidelity, facility, and cleverness, as any-thing in the Rejected Addresses.' This second edition introduces as a further imitation of Scott's manner a 'Final Sederunt of the Cleikum Club' in theatrical form, pages *513* 514-525. Copy: O.

[2] The Cook and Housewife's Manual . . . The Third Edition; . . . 1828. Notes: This paginal reprint provides only a slight rearrangement of the material appearing in the second edition. Scott himself comments on this manual and, perhaps deliberately, provides a mangled rendition of the title in the last note to his final edition of the novel, *WN*, xxxiv.358-359. Copy: O.

171Dd] EDINBURGH: Oliver and Boyd, Simpkin and Marshall 1829
The Cook and Housewife's Manual . . . The Fourth Edition, Revised and Enlarged: . . . Published by Oliver & Boyd, Edinburgh; and Simpkin & Marshall, London. MDCCCXXIX.
Pages *1-4*, *i* ii-xii, *13* 14-552. Notes: Because of the extensive additions the 'Final Sederunt of the Cleikum Club' is omitted in this issue. Copy: T/B.

171De] LONDON: Dean and Munday 1824
Clara Mowbray; or, St. Ronan's Well: An Affecting Narrative. By the Author of Waverley, Kenilworth, Pirate, &c. London: Printed and Sold by Dean and Munday, Threadneedle-Street. [1824]. Pages: *1-5* 6-38. Notes: A chapbook. Coloured frontispiece counted in the pagination. Some copies have a comma after "Mowbray;'. Price: Six-pence. Copies: O(J. Johnson); NNU-W.

171Df] OTLEY: Walker 1825
St. Ronan's Well; or, The Fatal Effects of a Clandestine Marriage: A Scottish Tale. . . . Otley: Printed by William Walker. [1825]. Pages: *1-3* 4-24. Notes: A chapbook. Copy: E.

TO MONS. ALEXANDRE

172A] First Printing: 1824

'TO MONS. ALEXANDRE.', [first words: 'Of yore, in old England, it was not thought good'], page 133, *in:*

The Edinburgh Weekly Journal. Vol. XXVII. No. 1376.] Wednesday, April 28, 1824. [Price Sevenpence. Edinburgh—Printed by James Ballantyne, For himself and other Proprietors.

Published 28 April 1824 in Edinburgh.

Notes: The preliminary notice reports that, after performing at the Caledonian Theatre, this ventriloquist visited Scott and, on mentioning that he kept a sort of album, 'Sir Walter stept aside, while the carriage was getting ready for his guest's departure, and immediately presented to him the following good-humoured and characteristic lines.' The 16-line poem is dated from Abbotsford 23 April.

Copy: L. Reference: (Magnum Opus Edition 1834: *The Poetical Works*, x.363-364 as 'Lines, addressed to Monsieur Alexander, the celebrated ventriloquist'.)

REPRINTS

GREAT BRITAIN

172Ra] EDINBURGH: Ballantyne 1825
'TO MONS. ALEXANDRE.', *in*: The Edinburgh Annual Register, for 1824. Edinburgh: Printed by James Ballantyne and Co. Edinburgh; and Hurst, Robinson, and Co., London. 1825. Pages: Part II, pages 265-266. Notes: Lockhart erroneously gives this printing as the first (*PW*, x.364n). Copies: E L; PPL.

172Rb] LONDON: Robins 1827
'Lines to Monsieur Alexandre', page 140, *in*: The Gentleman's Pocket Magazine; and Album of Literature and Fine Arts. . . . 1828. Joseph Robins, Bride-Court, Bridge-Street, London. [1827]. Copy: NNP.

ROMANCE

173A] First Printing: 1824

['ROMANCE.' Volume VI, Part 2, pages 435-456, *in*:

Supplement to the Fourth, Fifth, and Sixth Editions of the Encyclopaedia Britannica. With Preliminary Dissertations on the History of the Sciences. Illustrated by Engravings. Volume Sixth. Part II. Edinburgh: Printed for Archibald Constable and Company, Edinburgh; and Hurst, Robinson, and Company, London. 1824.]

Published 1 May 1824 in Edinburgh (*EEC*), but dated April on page *865*. £1.5.0.

Notes: This and the two earlier essays Scott wrote for the *Encyclopaedia* (*see* 115A, 129A) are initialled at the end '(N.N.)'. Apparently this text, except for the last six lines ('The modern romance . . . impossibilities'), is reprinted without alteration in the 7th edition, volume XIX, pages 318-334, originally issued after 1836 and there initialled '(D.D.D.)'.

Copies: (Original part issue) not seen; (reissue with 1824 volume title) E GM. References: Thomson, page 58. (Magnum Opus Edition 1834: *The Miscellaneous Prose Works*, vi.*127-129* 130-216 as 'Essay on Romance'.)

REPRINT

FRANCE

PARIS: Didot and Galigmani
[~] Essays by Sir Walter Scott. 1828. (*see* 292R.8-9.) Also included are the two other *Encyclopaedia* essays titled 'Chivalry' and 'The Drama'.

LETTER ON THE CHIMNEYS AT ABBOTSFORD

174A] First Printing: 1824

[Letter on the Chimneys at Abbotsford] pages x-xi, *in*:

The Chimney-Sweeper's Friend, and Climbing-Boy's Album. . . . Arranged by James Montgomery. With Illustrative Designs by Cruikshank. London: Printed for Longman, Hurst, Rees, Orme, Brown, and Green, Paternoster-Row. 1824.

Published 17 May 1824 in London (*MC*). 9s.

Notes: This contribution is introduced in a separate paragraph: 'Sir Walter Scott, however, has contributed something towards this work, which will tell better in the end than even a poem from his own inimitable pen might have done. In a very obliging letter to the Editor, he says, "I assure you I am a sincere friend to the cause which you have so effectually patronised; and in building my house at this place (Abbotsford) *I have taken particular care*, by the construction of the vents, *that no such cruelty shall be practised within its precincts*. . . ." The entire paragraph on Scott's chimneys, together with a preliminary comment dated 4 January 1824, is given in the *Letters* (viii.147), which also prints a further commentary on 12 February (viii.177-178). Montgomery's dedication, to the King, is dated 24 April 1824. Cruikshank's designs are limited to a frontispiece and a print facing page 363.
Copies: E; CtY(2) InU NjP. Reference: (Magnum Opus Edition: Not reprinted.)

MEMORIAL NOTICES OF LORD BYRON AND ALEXANDER CAMPBELL

175A] First Printings: 1824

[1] '[Lord Byron]', pages 156-157, *and*

[2] 'MR. ALEXANDER CAMPBELL', page 158, *in*:

The Edinburgh Weekly Journal. Vol. XXVII. No. 1379.] Wednesday, May 19, 1824. [Price Sevenpence. Edinburgh—Printed by James Ballantyne, For himself and other Proprietors.

Published: 19 May 1824 in Edinburgh.

Notes: Scott's first obituary follows several preliminary notices on Byron's death and the beginning of an editorial column dated 18 May. The second on Campbell concerns an Edinburgh musician and editor of *Albyn's Anthology* (92A, 96A).

Copy: L. References: Thomson, page 19. (Magnum Opus Edition 1834: *The Miscellaneous Prose Works*, [1] iv.343-350, [2] not reprinted.)

REPRINTS

GREAT BRITAIN

175Ra] LONDON: Sherwood 1824
Character of Lord Byron. By Sir Walter Scott, Bart. Pages *169-170* 171-173, *in*: The Pamphleteer; Dedicated to Both Houses of Parliament. Vol. XXIV. . . . London: Printed by A. J. Valpy, Red Lion Court, Fleet Street. Sold by Sherwood and Co.; Black, Kingsbury, Parbury, and Allen; Longman and Co.; Simpkin and Marshall; W. Carpenter; London—Parker, Oxford—Barret, Cambridge—Macredie and Co. Edinburgh—Cumming, Dublin—and all other booksellers. 1824. Copies: BCL E; InU.

175Rb] LONDON: Murray 1824
Character of Lord Byron. [London, ca.1824]. Pages: *1-3* 4-8. Notes: A separate large-type setting with an engraved frontispiece portrait of Byron and 34 engraved plates illustrating Byron's works. The latter have John Murray imprints dated 1814 or 1819. Artists and engravers vary, but most are either by Thomas Stothard and W. Finden or by Richard Westall and Charles Heath. Copy: IdU.

EXTRACTS IN ANTHOLOGIES

175E] The Byron memorial was extracted in four anthologies: 356[1]E 356[2].1 361[2].1 395.1.

PHAROS LOQUITOR

176A] First Printing: 1824

'Pharos loquitor' (first words: 'Far in the bosom of the deep') [reproduction of Scott's manuscript on plate facing page 64], *in*:

An Account of the Bell Rock Light-House, . . . Drawn up by Desire of the Commissioners of the Northern Light-Houses, by Robert Stevenson, . . . Edinburgh: Printed for Archibald Constable & Co. Edinburgh; Hurst, Robinson & Co. 90. Cheapside; and Josiah Taylor, 59. High Holborn, London. 1824.

Published 29 May 1824 in Edinburgh (*EEC* 'Only 250 copies printed' of this elaborate edition). £5.5.0.

Notes: Six lines of verse written (as indicated on page 419) 30 July 1814 in a visitors' album at the lighthouse. On 22 February 1824 Scott returned to Stevenson proofs of a single sheet representing some prose text with the suggestion that 'situate' be altered to 'situated'. (E MS 785 f.3. Dr. Millgate, in reporting this note, advises us that it is accompanied by a corrected proof.) Copies in volume form (1) have the plate referred to in the text as the second title-page. Some have the plate with letters on India paper. In other copies (2) this plate and others concerning Bell Rock were sold in a portfolio of illustrations largely before letters.

Copies: (1) E L(2); InU. (2) E. References: Ruff 179. (Magnum Opus Edition 1834: *The Poetical Works*, x.355.)

REPRINT

GREAT BRITAIN

176R] LONDON: Robins 1827
'Pharos Loquitor' (first words: 'Far on the bosom of the deep'), page 357, *in*: The Gentleman's Pocket Magazine; and Album of Literature and Fine Arts. . . . 1828. Joseph Robins, Bride-Court, Bridge-Street, London. [1827]. Notes: At head of poem, not bracketted: All strangers visiting the Bell Rock light-house are presented with an album, in which they enter their names, with any remarks they may choose to make. Among the numerous insertions is the following: . . . Copy: NNP.

EPILOGUE for ST RONAN'S WELL

177A] First Printing: 1824

[Epilogue for St Ronan's Well], (first words: 'That's right, friend—drive the gaitlings back,'), page 181, *in*:

The Edinburgh Weekly Journal. Vol. XXVII. No. 1382.] Wednesday, June 9, 1824. [Price Sevenpence. Edinburgh—Printed by James Ballantyne, For himself and other Proprietors.

Published 9 June 1824 in Edinburgh.

Notes: The play, adapted from *St. Ronan's Well* by James Robinson Planché, was first produced in London 19 January 1824, then revived in Edinburgh at the Theatre Royal for one night 5 June and reviewed in the *Edinburgh Weekly Journal* 9 June. In the review Scott's epilogue was quoted and there 'ascribed to an eminent literary character.' Line 32, here reading 'Boyle's', was later corrected to 'Bayle's'.

Copies: E L. References: Bolton 4261; Ford U1; Thomson, page 65. (Magnum Opus Edition 1834: *The Poetical Works*, xi.369-373.)

REDGAUNTLET

The Jacobite enthusiasm of the eighteenth century, particularly during the rebellion of 1745, afforded a theme, perhaps the finest that could be selected, for fictitious composition, founded upon real or probable incident. ('Introduction', '1 April 1832', *WN*, xxxv.*iii*.)

178Aa] First Edition, First Issue: 1824

REDGAUNTLET. | A TALE OF THE EIGHTEENTH CENTURY. | BY THE AUTHOR OF "WAVERLEY." | [*short rule*] | [*two-line quotation from* As You Like It] | [*short rule*] | IN THREE VOLUMES. | VOL. I [II-III]. | [*short reversed Oxford rule*] | EDINBURGH: | PRINTED FOR ARCHIBALD CONSTABLE AND CO. EDINBURGH; | AND HURST, ROBINSON, AND CO. | LONDON. | [*dash*] | 1824.

Published 14 June 1824 in Edinburgh (E MS 21014,f.25v); issued 29 June in London (*MC*). £1.11.6. 10,000 copies. Binding: drab, blue or green boards with printed labels. Paper: Post 8° (198 x 124mm uncut). Watermarks: 1823; KEYS | 1823. Typography: In some copies the title of volumes 1 and 2 have a comma ending the first line, but in most this is corrected to a period. Printer's imprints read invariably: (1) [*short rule*] | EDINBURGH: | PRINTED BY JAMES BALLANTYNE AND CO.; (2) [*short rule*] | Edinburgh: | Printed by James Ballantyne and Co.

General Notes: According to established practice beginning with *Kenilworth* (*see* 149Aa) on 13 July 1824, a month after the publication of this novel, some 8450 words (volume 1, Letter IV, pages 52-85 in this Edinburgh edition) were extracted in the Philadelphia *National Gazette*, these deriving from proofs early shipped for the Carey & Lea edition (178Rf).

Presentation copy: E('given me by the author (as yet secret) Sir Walter Scott 1824' [Lady Louisa Stuart]). Other copies: AN BCL(3) E(5) L(3) O(13) O*a O*b; CtY(2) IdU InU MH*c(2) NN(2) NNU-W(2) T/B TxU ViU.
*With Longman 4-page catalogue (a) March 1824, (b) June 1824, (c) Constable undated 4-page catalogue.

References: Church 545; Randall, pages 49-50; Sterling 738; Thomson, page 56; Van Antwerp(1) 18(with publisher's inscription to Harriot Coutts, with her date 10 June 1824); Van Antwerp(1) 19(with illustration of cancel); G. A. M. Wood and David Hewitt (eds.), *EEWN17*; Worthington 17. (Magnum Opus Edition 1832: *Waverley Novels*, xxxv-xxxvi.)

1] **REDGAUNTLET.** . . . VOL. I. . . . 1824.

Collation: π^2 A-F^8 G^8(-G1-4,+G^4) H-O^8 P^8(±P4,P8) Q-U^8. Pagination: *i* half-title, *ii blank, iii* title-page, *iv* printer's imprint(1), *1* fly-title, *2 blank, 3* 4-319 text, 319 printer's imprint(2), *320 blank.*

Figures: A15-11 16-8, B31-6 32-8, C47-3 48-7, D63-12 64-14, E79-5 80-9, F95-16 96-17, G103-15 110-14 112-7, H125-9 127-16, I 143-2 144-3, K159-12 160-7, L175-16 176-15, M186-3 192-1, N207-14 208-5, O 223-16 224-9, P238-11, Q255-8 256-17, R267-9 272-4, S282-5 288-6, T303-3 304-4, U315-11 316-2.

Notes: Since the earlier portion of the Philadelphia, Carey edition apparently is now derived from corrected proofs, the original uncorrected text of the cancels, especially G1-4 (pages 97-104), cannot be determined from this source (although it appears that the four substitute leaves were imposed as a half sheet, distinctively figured 103-15), but proofs in an earlier state, at NNP, disclose that the substitute half-sheet, standardises the spelling of 'Birrenswork' (*EEWN17*.392). However, the cancellanda for P4 and P8 (as illustrated in part by Van Antwerp after page 134) exhibit various readings, for example: page 231, line 13 (1) cancelland: 'Laird and', (2) cancellans: 'Laird, Dougal MacAllum, and'. Page 239, line 24 (1) cancelland: 'Sir Robert', (2) cancellans: 'Sir John'. The two cancels P4 and P8, it should be further noted, are in duplicate settings which may be distinguished, the first at page 232, line 16, reading either 'would' or 'wad', the second at page 240, line 2 first word, reading either 'lowed' or 'followed'.

2] **REDGAUNTLET.** . . . VOL. II. . . . 1824.

Collation: π^2 A-U^8 X^4. Pagination: *i* half-title, *ii blank, iii* title-page, *iv* printer's imprint(1), *1* fly-title, *2 blank, 3* 4-328 text, 328 printer's imprint(2).

Figures: A15-8 (or 14-8) 16-9, B27-7 32-6, C47-4 48-12, D58-2 64-1, E77-9 78-12, F95-6 96-8, G111-8 112-17, H127-17 128-7, I 139-8 144-1, K159-9 160-12, L175-10 176-12, M187-4 192-7, N201-4 207-9/11, O 223-10 224-17, P239-15 240-12, Q251-11 256-16, R267-9 272-17, S287-11 288-8, T303-2 304-1, U319-9 320-17, X327-12.

Notes: The alternate A figure recurs in the 'Second Edition'.

3] **REDGAUNTLET.** . . . VOL. III. . . . 1824.

Collation: π^2 A-D^8 E^8(±E4) F-X^8. Pagination: *i* half-title, *ii blank, iii* title-page, *iv* printer's imprint(1), *1* fly-title, *2 blank, 3* 4-331 text, 331 printer's imprint(2), *332 blank, 333-336* Archibald Constable catalogue.

Figures: A15-7 16-17, B30-2 32-1, C43-3 48-17, D63-12 64-11, E79-15 80-9, F89-11 94-1, G111-17 112-12, H127-15 128-16, I 143-12 144-17, K159-10 160-8, L175— 176-11 (or 175-5 176-11/1), M191-9 192-13, N207-8 208-10, O 219—/17 224-15, P227-11 240-12, Q255-15 256-2, R269-17 271-9, S283-7 288-3, T303-11 304-10, U319-8 320-6, X328-12 330-5.

Notes: In the third portion of this text Carey appears to be setting from uncorrected proofs, a circumstance which indicates that cancel E4, now correctly reading '*Bellerophontis*' (page 71, line 16), was originally misspelled '*Bellephontes*'. In some copies leaf S5 (pages 281-282) also is a cancel, for reasons undetermined. The alternate figures for L and O usually recur in the 'Second Edition'. The catalogue lists, as already published, the 'new edition' of Swift's *Works* (*see* 79Ac), price £8.11.0.

178Ab] Second Edition (First Edition, Second Issue): 1824

REDGAUNTLET. . . . VOL. I [II-III]. | SECOND EDITION. . . . 1824.

General Notes: Except for the title-pages, a further issue with the several alternate press figures in second state and (a) all cancels still present, (b) except for volume 1, G^4, all cancel text now integral, apparently, and in revised state.

Copies: (state a) CtY. (b) O.

REPRINTS

FRANCE

PARIS: Baudry, Barrois [and others]
[~] Redgauntlet. 1832. (Collection of Ancient and Modern British Novels and Romances: *see* 288R.28.)

PARIS: Didot and Galignani
[~] Redgauntlet. M DCCC XXIV. (Collection of Modern English Authors: *see* 291R.53-55.)

GERMANY

178Ra] BERLIN: Schlesinger 1824
[Redgauntlet. . . . Berlin, Printed for Adolph Martin Schlesinger. 1824.] Copy: not seen. Reference: GDS 132, page 344. Reissued 1825 (copy reported at Stadtbibliothek Hannover).

ZWICKAU: Schumann
[~] Redgauntlet. 1825. (Pocket Library of English Classics: *see* 302R.113-116.)

UNITED STATES

178Rb] BOSTON: Parker 1824
Redgauntlet. A Tale of the Eighteenth Century. By the Author of "Waverley." . . . Boston: Samuel H. Parker, No. 12, Cornhill. 1824. Pages: *1-3* 4-390. Notes: Page number 193 has the

last two digits missing. Copies: O; MWA. (Also reissued 1824 in Novels Tales and Romances: *see* 305R.17).

[~] Redgauntlet. 1828, 1829. (Waverley Novels: *see* 306R.33-34).

[~] Redgauntlet. 1832. (Waverley Novels [Parker's Edition Revised]: *see* 307R.33-34).

178Rc] EXETER: Williams 1824
Redgauntlet. A Tale of the Eighteenth Century. By the Author of "Waverley.". . . Exeter, Published by J. & B. Williams, 1824. Two volumes. Pages 1: *1-3* 4-202; 2: *1-3* 207. Copy: MWA.

178Rd] NEW YORK: Borradaile and King 1824
Redgauntlet. A Tale of the Eighteenth Century. By the Author of "Waverly"[!]. . . . New-York: Published by William Borradaile, 130 Fulton-Street, and Solomon[!] King, 136 William-Street. 1824. Two volumes. Pages 1: *1-3* 4-266; 2: *1-3* 4-252. Notes: Volume 2 has the title pointed "By the Author of Waverly[!]" and imprint reversed to read 'New-York: Published by Solomon[!] King, 136 William Street, and William Borradaile, 130 Fulton-Street. 1824.' Copies: MWA RPB. Reference: Kohler(1) 68 (with illustration).

178Re] NEW YORK: Duyckinck, Collins [and others] 1824
Redgauntlet. A Tale of the Eighteenth Century. By the Author of "Waverley." . . . New=York: Printed by James and John Harper, for Evert Duyckinck, Collins & Co., Collins & Hannay, E. Bliss & E. White, A. T. Goodrich, Wm. B. Gilley, George Long, and H. I. Megary. 1824. Two volumes. Pages 1: *1-3* 4-264; 2: *1-3* 4-248. Copies: E; CtY.

NEW YORK: King and Borradaile *see* 178Rd.

178Rf] PHILADELPHIA: Carey and Lea 1824
Redgauntlet. A Tale of the Eighteenth Century. By the Author of "Waverley." . . . Philadelphia: H. C. Carey and I. Lea—Chesnut Street. 1824. Two volumes. Pages 1: *i-ii*, *1-3* 4-288; 2: *i-iv*, *1* 2-321. Notes: The first American edition, set from Edinburgh proofs, extracted in the *National Gazette* 13 July 1824 (178Aa), and issued 31 July (*NG*). Copies: CtY DLC MH NjP NNU-W PPL T/B. References: Clarkin 1516; Randall, pages 49-50.

178Rg] PHILADELPHIA: Crissy 1827
Redgauntlet. A Tale of the Eighteenth Century. By the Author of "Waverley." . . . Philadelphia: James Crissy, No. 14, South Seventh Street. 1827. Two volumes. Pages 1: *1-3* 4-245; 2: *1-3* 4-252. Copies: IdU NN.

178Rh] PHILADELPHIA: Sherman 1824
Redgauntlet. A Tale of the Eighteenth Century. By the Author of "Waverley." . . . Philadelphia: A. Sherman, Agt. 32, South Fourth Street. 1824. Two volumes. Pages 1: *i-ii*, *1* 2-248; 2: *i-ii*, *1* 2-250. Copies: E; NNU-W.

DERIVATIVES

GREAT BRITAIN

178Da] EDINBURGH: Anderson 1824
[Redgauntlet. Edinburgh: Published by John Anderson Junr. 55. North Bridge Street. 1824.] Notes: Bolton reports a play by an anonymous dramatist performed in July 1824 at the Surrey Theatre, London, and again at the Caledonian, Edinburgh 17 July, one month after publication of the novel.] Copy: not seen. References: Bolton 4287-4288. (Also issued in: Edinburgh Select British Theatre, 1824, volume 13 [*see* 319D] and in: The Waverley Dramas, 1824, volume 2, play 8[*see* 321D].)

178Db] YORK: Knapton, White and Knapton 1825
["For all our men were very, very merry". York: Knapton, White and Knapton (1825). Notes: Music composed by Philip Knapton.] Copy: not seen. Reference: G/T 10723.

REVIEW OF THE CORRESPONDENCE OF LADY SUFFOLK

179A] First Printing: 1824

'ART. XII.—*Letters to and from Henrietta, Countess of Suffolk',* pages 542-559, *in*:

The Quarterly Review. January, 1824. [No.60. volume 30 imprint:] London: John Murray, Albemarle Street. 1824.

Published 28 August 1824 in London (*MC*).

Copies: BCL L O; PPL.

References: Shine 718; Thomson, page 23, entered under John Wilson Croker, the editor. (Magnum Opus Edition 1835: *The Miscellaneous Prose Works*, xix.185-212 as 'Lady Suffolk's Correspondence'.)

LAYS OF THE LINDSAYS

180A] First (Suppressed) Edition: 1824

Lays of the Lindsays; | BEING | **POEMS** | BY | **THE LADIES** | OF | **THE HOUSE OF BALCARRAS.** | [*short reversed Oxford rule*] | EDINBURGH: | Printed by James Ballantyne and Company. | [*dash*] | 1824.

Printed, but then 'recalld & cancelld' 3 October 1824 (Scott to David Laing, *Letters*, viii.386). Binding: Drab boards. Paper: Demy 4° (270 x 210mm uncut). Watermarks:

A COWAN | 1822 (entered twice in a sheet). Collation: π^2 A^4 B-P^4 Q^2. Pagination: *1* title-page, *2 blank, i*-ii Contents, *1* fly-title for Poems by Lady Anne Barnard, *2 blank, 3* 4-6 Introduction (by Scott), *7* 8-72 text, *73* fly-title for Poems by Lady Elizabeth Scott Lindsay, *74 blank*, 75-83 text, *84 blank, 85* fly-title for Poems and Translations by the Lady Margaret Lindsay Fordyce, *86 blank*, 87-123 text, 123 printer's imprint, *124 blank*. Printer's imprint: [*short rule*] | EDINBURGH: | PRINTED BY JAMES BALLANTYNE AND CO. Figures: *none*.

Notes: In his introduction Scott remarks that he had been aware of the authorship of the 'long-contested ballad of "Auld Robin Gray"' from a very early period of his life, and that Lady Anne had eventually confided the circumstances in a letter of [8] July 1823. This he quotes at length (75 lines) and notes that he is printing not only the original ballad (pages 7-8), but Lady Anne's two continuations (pages 9-14). Not mentioned here is the occasion for this letter, written after Anne discovered that Scott had quoted from one of the continuations in *The Pirate* 1822 (156A), and that Scott himself, it seems—in an issue of Thomson's *Select Melodies* 1822 (405(3)[1]E, vol.3, page 33)—had ventured to provide another conclusion to the main ballad:

ADDED BY THE AUTHOR OF WAVERLEY

Nae langer she wept, her tears were a' spent,
Despair it was come, and she thought it content;
She thought it content, but her cheek it grew pale
And she droop'd like a lily broke down by the hail.

Despite Lord Crawford's contention that Lady Anne, 'nervous at the idea' of this intended issue for the Bannatyne Club, directed that the book be destroyed, it is clear that, as Scott reported to Laing, the suppression was at the instance of her younger sister, Lady Elizabeth, Countess Hardwicke. For the later authorized Bannatyne issue of Anne's poem alone *see* 182A.

Copies: A*E(Lord Crawford's copy, pages 75-78 reproduced from Abbotsford exemplar; CtY(Isabella Hayes from Lady Anne Barnard, November 1824) InU.
*Unsewn folded sheets.

Reference: Abbotsford, page 271.

TALES OF THE CRUSADERS
THE BETROTHED and THE TALISMAN

The "Betrothed" did not greatly please one or two friends, who thought that it did not correspond to the general title of "The Crusaders." They urged, therefore, that, without direct allusion to the manners of the Eastern tribes, and to the romantic conflicts of the period, the title . . . would resemble a playbill, which is said to have announced the tragedy of Hamlet, the character of the Prince of Denmark being left out. ('Introduction to The Talisman', '1 July 1832', *WN*, xxxviii.*iii*.)

181A] First Edition: 1825

TALES | OF THE CRUSADERS. | BY THE AUTHOR OF "WAVERLEY, | QUENTIN DURWARD," &c. | IN FOUR VOLUMES. | [*short rule*] | VOL. I [II-IV]. | The Betrothed. [*or, vols. III-IV:* The Talisman.] | [*short Oxford rule*] | EDINBURGH: | PRINTED FOR ARCHIBALD CONSTABLE AND CO. EDINBURGH; | AND HURST, ROBINSON, AND CO. LONDON. | [*dash*] | 1825.

Published 22 June 1825 in Edinburgh (*EWJ*); issued 11 July in London (*MC*, earlier announced on 20 June as to be published 'On Wednesday' [22 June]). £2.2.0. Binding: drab or blue boards with printed labels. Paper: Post 8° (199 x 123mm uncut). Watermarks: [infrequently] 1823; KEYS | 1825. Typography: Printer's imprints read: (1) EDINBURGH: | PRINTED BY JAMES BALLANTYNE AND CO.; (2) [*short rule*] | EDINBURGH: | Printed by James Ballantyne and Co. ['& Co.' vols. 2-4].

General Notes: Coincident with its issue ths novel was widely reviewed (22 June in *The Scotsman*, 25 June in *The Literary Chronicle* and *The Literary Gazette*, 27 June in *The Examiner*) and adapted in a dramatic production of 'The Talisman' 22 June at the Edinburgh Theatre Royal which continued for at least 19 performances (Bolton 4330). Moreover, according to established practice beginning with *Kenilworth* (*see* 149Ac), on 28 July, a month after publication, some 7225 words (volume 3, chapter 1 and part of chapter 2, through page 34.2 of this Edinburgh edition) were extracted in the Philadelphia *National Gazette*, these deriving from proofs early shipped for the Carey & Lea edition (181Re). The running-titles for volumes 1-2 ('The Betrothed') now represent a compromise between the two earlier practices, with serial title as the left headline and tale number and title as the right headline. In volumes 3-4 ('The Talisman') the procedure oddly reverts to the earlier practice with serial title only throughout.

Copies: AN BCL(3) E(2) E*a L(2) LU O(10); CtY IdU InU(3) MH MH*b NN NNU-W NNU-W*c T/B TxU TxU(vols.1-2).
*With 4-page Longman catalogue (a) April 1825, (b) September 1826, (c) Geo. B. Whittaker catalogue June 1825.

References: Church 547; Randall, page 50; Sterling 739; Thomson, pages 14-15, 71; Van Antwerp(1) 20 (publisher's inscription to Harriot Coutts with her date 22 June 1825); Worthington 18. (Magnum Opus Edition 1832: *Waverley Novels*, [1] xxxvii, [2] xxxviii.)

1] **TALES | OF THE CRUSADERS.** . . . VOL. I. | The Betrothed. . . . 1825.
Collation: π^2 a^8 b^4 c^2 A-U^8 X^4. Pagination: *i* half-title, *ii blank*, *iii* title-page, *iv* printer's imprint(1), *i* ii-xxviii Introduction, *1* fly-title, *2 blank*, *3* 4-327 text, 327 printer's imprint(2), *328 blank*.

Figures: a xv-15 xvi-12, b xxiv-10/14, c xxvi-1, A10-13 16-15, B18-10 32-17, C46-11 48-15, D63-12 64-9, E79-11 80-17, F94-10 96-2, G111-15 112-13, H126-15 128-9, I 142-13 144-12, K153-17 159-15, L162-11 176-13, M191-9 192-12, N194-10 208-11, O 211-1/- 224-17, P234-17 240-14, Q254-13 256-15, R267-10 272-11, S287-9 288-12, T303-14 304-17, U319-12 320-11, X322-11.

2] **TALES | OF THE CRUSADERS.** . . . VOL. II. | The Betrothed. . . 1825.

Collation: π^2 A-Y^8 Z^2. Pagination: *i* half-title, *ii blank*, *iii* title-page, *iv* printer's imprint(1), *1* fly-title, *2 blank*, *3* 4-355 text, 355 printer's imprint(2), *356 blank*. Typography: In some copies page 91 is misnumbered 95. Printer's imprint(2) reads: [*short rule*] | Edinburgh: | Printed by James Ballantyne & Co.

Figures: A15-17 16-10/-, B31-13/- 32-14, C47-14 48-9, D63-17 64-10, E79-15 80-13, F87-13 96-17, G111-10 112-9, H123-13 128-11, I 143-5 144-6, K159-7 160-1, L174-13 176-9, M191-2 192-6, N207-5 208-1, O 223-4 224-3, P234-9 240-13, Q255-12 256-9, R271-13 272-9, S287-10 288-9, T303-12 304-13, U319-8 320-9, X335-7 336-13, Y351-13 352-10, Z—.

3] **TALES | OF THE CRUSADERS.** . . . VOL. III. | The Talisman. . . . 1825.

Collation: π^2 A-G^8 H^8(±H7) I-U^8 X^4. Pagination: *i* half-title, *ii blank*, *iii* title-page, *iv* printer's imprint(1), *1* fly-title, *2 blank*, *3* 4-325 text, 325 printer's imprint(2), *326-328 blank*. Typography: On the title-page, in some copies, the second line of the imprint omits the final semicolon.

Figures: A15-15 16-11, B18-12 32-9, C47-10 48-11, D63-1 64-8, E75-12 80-9, F91-9 96-11, G107-4 112-3, H125-14 127-10 128-11, I 139-12 144-13, K158-5 160-1, L172-12 175-10, M191-9 192-13, N207-11 208-13, O 223-9 224-11, P239-14 240-10, Q243-12 256-11, R269-13 270-6, S287-15 288-8, T299-4 304-9, U319-12 320-6, X—.

Notes: Since the Philadelphia, Carey edition apparently now, in this portion, derives from corrected proofs, the original uncorrected text of cancel H7 (pages 125-126, 125 press-figure 14) cannot be determined. The present whereabouts of other evidence—either of the manuscript, last sold in 1920, or of the proof-sheets, auctioned in 1924—is also unknown.

4] **TALES | OF THE CRUSADERS.** . . . VOL. IV. | The Talisman. . . . 1825.

Collation: π^2 A-Z^8. Pagination: *i* half-title, *ii blank*, *iii* title-page, *iv* printer's imprint(1), *1* fly-title, *2 blank*, *3* 4-364 text, 364 printer's imprint(2), *1* 2-4 Archibald Constable catalogue. Typography: In some copies, page 12 footnote has 'sort' misspelled 'srot'.

Figures: A15-9 16-15, B31-11 32-13, C46-10 48-8, D63-15/- 64-11, E79-14 80-13,

F95-7 96-12, G109-10 111-6, H127-13 128-9, I 143-8 144-14, K157-15 158-6, L175-10 176-3, M191-9/- 192-13, N207-15 208-7, O 223-8 224-12, P239-14 240-13, Q254-15 256-10, R267-12 272-9, S287-13 288-11, T303-14 304-10, U318-11 320-15, X335-14 336-13, Y350-5 352-10, Z360-4 362-15.

REPRINTS

FRANCE

PARIS: Baudry, Barrois [and others]
[~] Tales of the Crusaders. 1832. (Collection of Ancient and Modern British Novels and Romances: *see* 288R.30-31.)

PARIS: Didot and Galignani
[~] Tales of the Crusaders. MDCCCXXV. (Collection of Modern English Authors: *see* 291R.56-59.)

GERMANY

181Ra] BERLIN: Schlesinger 1825
Tales of the Crusaders. By the Author of "Waverley," "Quentin Durward," etc. . . . Berlin, Printed for Adolph Martin Schlesinger. MDCCCXXV. Four volumes. Pages 1: *i-iii* iv-xix *xx*, *1* 2-191 *192*; 2: *1-3* 4-209 *210*; 3: *1-3* 4-191 *192*; 4: *1-3* 4-216. Copy: E. Reference: GDS 132, page 346 (reads 1815).

ZWICKAU: Schumann
[~] Tales of the Crusaders. 1826. (Pocket Library of English Classics: *see* 302R.120-135.)

UNITED STATES

181Rb] BOSTON: Parker 1825-1832
[Tales of the Crusaders. By the Author of "Waverley, Quentin Durward," &c. The Betrothed, and the Talisman. . . . Boston: Samuel H. Parker, No. 164, Washington-Street. 1825. Pages: *i-iii* iv-x, *11* 12-544.] Copy: not seen. Notes: (Also reissued 1825 in Novels Tales and Romances: *see* 305R.18).

[~] Tales of the Crusaders. 1825, 1829. (Waverley Novels: *see* 306R.35-36).

[~] Tales of the Crusaders. 1832. (Waverley Novels [Parker's Edition Revised]: *see* 307R.35-36).

181Rc] NEW YORK: Duyckinck, Collins, [and others] 1825
Tales of the Crusaders. By the Author of "Waverley, Quentin Durward," &c. . . . New-York: Published by E. Duyckinck, Collins & Hannay, Collins & Co., E. Bliss and E. White, and W. B. Gilley. J. & J. Harper, Printers. 1825. Four volumes. Pages 1: *1-5* 6-155; 2: *1-3* 4-156; 3:

1-3 4-144; 4: *1-3* 4-164. Notes: The first volume has an integral blank leaf before the title-page. Copies in publisher's bindings were issued as four volumes in two with printed paper boards and with spine reading below general title: 'Harper's Edition'. Copies: E; NjP NN (vols.1-2) NNU-W PPL(vols.3-4) RPB(inscribed 'August 1825') ViU.

181Rd] NEW YORK: Van Norden 1825
Tales of the Crusaders, By the Author of "Waverly,[!] Quentin Derward[!]," &c. . . . New-York: Printed by William Van Norden, 1825. Four volumes. Pages 1: *1-3* 4-150; 2: *1-3* 4-156; 3: *1-3* 4-146; 4: *1-3* 4-160. Copies: E(vols.1-2); MH NjP.

181Re] PHILADELPHIA: Carey & Lea 1825
Tales of the Crusaders. By the Author of "Waverley, Quentin Durward," &c. . . . Philadelphia: H. C. Carey & I. Lea—Chesnut Street. 1825. Four volumes. Pages 1: *1-2*, *i* ii-xi*xii*, *1* 2-163; 2: *i-ii*, *1* 2-177; 3: *i-ii*, *1* 2-168; 4: *i-ii*, *1* 2-180. Notes: The first American edition, set from Edinburgh proofs, extracted in the *National Gazette* 28 July (181A), and issued 30 July (*NG*) in 875 copies. Copies: CtY MH(vols.1-2) NNU-W PPL T/B. References: Kaser 12; Randall, page 50.

181Rf] PHILADELPHIA: Crissy 1825
Tales of the Crusaders. By the Author of "Waverley, Quentin Durward," &c. . . . Philadelphia: James Crissy, No. 14, South Seventh Street. 1825. Three volumes. Pages 1: *i-iii* iv-xiii*xiv*, *15* 16-243; 2: *1-3* 4-244; 3: *1-3* 4-236. Copies: E; IdU MWA NN(2) T/B. Reference: Kohler(1) 197(with illustration).

DERIVATIVES

GREAT BRITAIN

181Da] EDINBURGH: Anderson 1828
[The Talisman. Edinburgh: Published by John Anderson Junr. 55. North Bridge Street. 1828.] Copy: not seen. (Also issued in: The Waverley Dramas, 1828: volume 2, play 10. *see* 321D.)

181Db] LONDON: Cumberland 1826-1831
[1] The Knights of the Cross, or The Hermit's Prophecy: A New Musical Romance, in Three Acts. . . . London, 1826: Printed for John Cumberland, 19, Ludgate Hill. Pages: *1-5* 6-64. Notes: Drama by Samuel Beazley, founded in part on 'The Talisman' and on Boieldieu's 'Charles de France' (the music composed and selected by Henry R. Bishop not included), as first performed at the Theatre Royal, Drury Lane, 29 May 1826. Price: 2s. 6d. Copies: BCL; InU. Variant issue with text ending p.62 (CtY MH). References: Bolton 4335; Ford V3.

[2] The Knights of the Cross; or, The Hermit's Prophecy: A Romantic Drama, in Three Acts, . . . London: John Cumberland, 2, Cumberland Terrace, Camden New Town. [1831]. Pages: *1-5* 6-43. Notes: Drama by Samuel Beazley. This version is cited as 'printed from the acting copy . . . As performed at the Theatres Royal, London.' Copies: MH NN-L(prompt copy). (Also issued in: Cumberland's British Theatre, 1831: number 261, *see* 329D).

181Dc] LONDON: Goulding & D'Almaine 1826
I Ask'd of My Harp! Ballad. The Words Selected from the Tales of the Crusaders. . . . London, Printed by Goulding & D'Almaine. [watermarked 1825]. Pages: *i-ii*, *1* 2-5. Notes: Engraved sheet music. Words from *The Betrothed*, chapter 31 (first words: 'I ask'd of my harp, "Who hath injur'd thy chords?"). The music by George B. Herbert arranged for voice and pianoforte and dedicated to Sir Walter Scott (*see* 530T[1]). Copy: NNP. Reference: Van Antwerp(2) 42r.

EXTRACTS IN ANTHOLOGIES

181E] Only 'The Betrothed' is extracted, four times in two anthologies: 389E.20,22 426.1,2.

AULD ROBIN GRAY

182A] First Edition: 1825

AULD ROBIN GRAY; | A BALLAD. | BY THE | RIGHT HONOUR ABLE LADY ANNE BARNARD, | BORN LADY ANNE LINDSAY OF BALCARRAS. | [*short Oxford rule*] | EDINBURGH: | Printed by James Ballantyne and Co. | 1825.

Printed ca. June 1825 in Edinburgh. Paper: Post 4° (264 x 208mm uncut). Watermarks: A COWAN & SON | 1825; [Bannatyne Arms]. (Sheets *A* B are on laid paper). Collation: π^4 A^4 B^4. Pagination: *i blank*, *ii* engraving, *iii* title-page, *iv blank*, *1*-2 roster of Bannatyne Club members 1824, *3* dedication by Scott to the Bannatyne Club, *4 blank*, *1* 2-7 Introduction, *8 blank*, *9* 10-16 the Ballad, with Continuation and Second Continuation. Illustrations: The engraving, of a disconsolate woman, was drawn by C. Kirkpatrick Sharpe, engraved by W. H. Lizars. Figures: *none*.

Notes: There are at least three issues (1) list in two pages of thirty-one members, with the recipient's name in red; (2) no list, apparently for general distribution; (3) roster in four pages, after dedication, listing one hundred members, with no names in red. This title, later classed as the Club's ninth printing, offers only a portion of the poems originally intended (*see* 180A) and probably was prepared shortly after the death of Lady Anne on 6 May 1825.

Presentation copies: (issue 2) NNP('For Mrs. [Clementina Stirling?] Graham from her most respectful & affectionate friend Walter Scott'). (3) NNU-W([Inscribed, not by Scott] 'For Mrs. Fullarton with Sir Walter Scotts respectful & kind Complemens[!]'). Another copy: (issue 1) E(Earl of Minto).

PARLIAMENT-HOUSE WORTHIES

183A] First Printing: 1825

'PARLIAMENT-HOUSE WORTHIES.', pages 93-105 *in*:

Traditions of Edinburgh. By Robert Chambers. Vol. II. Edinburgh: Printed for W. & C. Tait, Princes Street. MDCCCXXV.

Published after 20 September 1825 (date of Chambers' concluding note).

Notes: Scott's contribution is attested in the copy at the Edinburgh Central Library, which contains, besides a portion of his manuscript draft, the corrected proof of his section. In this Scott deletes a footnote reference supplied by the grateful compiler, page 25: 'The greater part of the following article, and considerable portions of others which follow, are printed verbatim from notes contributed by a distinguished individual, whose affectionate remembrances of his "OWN ROMANTIC TOWN" have fortunately disposed him to assist in this commemoration of its curiosities.' Among the 'others' where Scott would be especially well informed are the seven sections appended to James Boswell's 'Court of Session Garland', these of eminent advocates (pages 168-179). It should also be noted that the volume itself is dedicated to Scott (*see* 516T).

The copy described above also originally contained an explanatory note to Chambers (*Letters*, ix.180-181), which has now been removed.

Copies: E(2) EP. Reference: (Magnum Opus Edition: Not reprinted.)

EPILOGUE in MARY STUART

184A] First Printing: 1825

'EPILOGUE. Written for a Tragedy, entitled "Mary Stuart," and intended to have been spoken by Mrs. H. Siddons. By Sir Walter Scott, Bart.' (first words: 'The sages—for authority pray look,'), pages 373-374, *in*:

The Literary Souvenir; or, Cabinet of Poetry and Romance. Edited by Alaric A. Watts. London: Printed for Hurst, Robinson and Co. 90, Cheapside, and 8, Pall-Mall. And A. Constable and Co. Edinburgh. 1825.

Published 23 November 1825 in London (*MC*). 12s.

Notes: A 38-line poem written presumably for the play (based on *The Abbot*) first performed at the Theatre Royal, Edinburgh, 4 July 1825, when Mrs Henry Siddons played the part of Mary Stuart (Bolton 3642). Subsequent to this publication Scott inserted two lines after the thirty-second line 'There is a talisman in that word Mary,'. These read: 'That unto Scottish bosoms all and some / Is found the genuine *open sesamum!*'

Copies: L O; MH NN. Reference: (Magnum Opus Edition 1834: *The Poetical Works*, xi.374-375, with the 40-line version).

FIVE
1826-1832

In early June 1825,[1] seven months before they were brought to sudden ruin, Walter Scott and his printer James Ballantyne were advised by their publisher of a new scheme which, if effected, would bring them far greater prosperity than any venture hitherto envisaged. What Constable enthusiastically proposed was that books should now be greatly reduced in price and issued continually, down to 'a three shilling or half-crown volume every month' and 'so good that millions must wish to have them, and so cheap that every butcher's callant may have them, if he pleases to let me tax him sixpence a-week!' (Lockhart, vii.382, 383). Previously Scott's own books had been directed to the higher, moneyed classes, with his triple-decker novels gradually priced upward from £1.1.0 to £1.11.6: now a prevailing charge at least three times the price for the piratical printings issued immediately in France and America[2] (and, indeed, more than thrice the equivalent cost of novels today).[3] The novels produced thus far were, of course, now also being sold in attractively designed collected sets, all carefully ordered in successive 8°, 12°, and 18° formats to catch less affluent readers (*see* preliminary note to 269Aa), but even the least costly of these were above what Constable had in mind and, in any event, were not available on a per-novel basis.

On receiving Scott's approbation at the June meeting, the publisher then hurried away to arrange for his new 'Constable's Miscellany', as the series was to be called, reluctantly acceded to Hurst, Robinson's demand that this exclude all work by the 'Author of Waverley'—in London still an 'immense property' yet unsold either in separate or collected editions—and eventually prevailed upon Scott to compose for the King (with his royal permission) a dedication in the first volume for the entire series.[4] That book, Basil Hall's *Voyage to Loo-Choo* (195A), though early announced for issue 4 February 1826, was soon overtaken by a sequence of disastrous events and did not appear until 6 January 1827. The interval marks the successive bankruptcies in January 1826 of Hurst, Robinson and Constable, followed immediately by the insolvency of Ballantyne and Scott, both of whom were then obliged to surrender all their assets into trusteeships safeguarding the interests of their creditors. A highly valued author accustomed to transactions in thousands of pounds was now so reduced in circumstance as to accept, somewhat ruefully, review payments as low as £10 (192A). Rather more generous was the £50 he could expect for advance copy of any new novels shipped to Philadelphia (206Aa), a fee earlier assessed by Constable as a publisher's perquisite.

Most gratifying of all, in these piratical times, was the £295 advance by Carey, the Philadelphia publisher, for early proofs of *The Life of Napoleon Buonaparte* (200Aa), all of which were later determined to be of an uncorrected state (200Rf). Before issue in Edinburgh it also appears that, for the first time, Scott was able to secure some financial arrangements for other foreign editions—£105 for a French translation by François Licquet, £105 again several weeks later for a Galignani edition in English, and possibly some fee for Zwickau editions both in German and English—all advantageous preliminary negotiations for a scholarly work of international interest, conducted internationally, and leading on 20 February 1827 to an announcement that the *Napoleon* would be 'published in English, French, and German, at Edinburgh, London, Paris, Leipsic, Berlin, and Vienna, on the same day.'[5]

Shortly after publication on 28 June, Scott remarked that this extensive biography was 'the most severe and labourious undertaking which choice or accident ever placed on my shoulders' (*Letters*, x.235-236), and its bibliographical intricacies certainly enforce this judgment. As with his earliest books so now with this last grand enterprise, the author continued to enlarge his work, here from four volumes as envisaged in 1825 to the nine issued in 1827. Additonally, beyond any previous endeavour, he also undertook far-ranging research not only on cartloads of books and journals sent to Abbotsford and Edinburgh but also in all available archives at London and Paris. Last-minute discoveries after presswork was underway required scores of errata listed on slips attached to the volumes, a few cancel leaves printed *ad hoc*, several others set in duplicate, and 122 more printed together for insertion throughout the work. Even as the first setting was being impressed a decision to hasten the issue by underprinting successive sheets necessitated in the second 'second edition' (200Ac) a resetting of 28 of the cancels earlier prepared, allowed the author one last opportunity for further revisions, and enlisted the simultaneous work of seven printers, two of them still unidentified. Altogether then in concept, extent, and complexity, Scott's *Napoleon* was a magnificent achievement.

Within a month after publication of his biography, on 21 July 1827, Scott's former publisher Archibald Constable died and, on that very day, he was advised that the ownership both of this work and of *Woodstock*, in dispute because of the Constable bankruptcy, had been adjudicated as entirely his—the first intimation that with the assistance of his new publisher Robert Cadell, earlier a partner in the Constable firm, he might eventually recover all rights to his literary property for the final collected edition he now contemplated.[6] As this objective was gradually realized, Scott by the end of the year was already considering a changed format for his miscellaneous prose works so that 'they might be made to range with the new set of novels' (*Letters*, x.345) and on later occasions negotiated with Longman and Murray, his London publishers, over the copyrights they held for some of his poems. While still engaged in annotating his novels, in April 1830, Scott also provided new introductions for his major verse. Thus it would appear that, while he lived to see only a portion of his complete work through the press, Scott's reference to his 'magnum opus' may appropriately encompass, as in this bibliography, all phases of the final production, the novels, poetry, and prose (348A-350A), ranging continuously from 1829 to 1836 through ninety volumes: truly a surpassing event quite 'unprecedented in English literature,' as Lockhart finally observed.

1. The meeting at Abbotsford, usually mentioned as occurring in May 1825 (a date presumed from the headline in Lockhart, vii.379, 381), would appear to range from Saturday through Monday, 4-6 June. At that time Scott, apparently accompanied by Lockhart, had hurriedly gone to his country home for a purpose undisclosed in the correspondence and remained there until 8 June before returning to London (*Letters*, ix.133).

2. *Kenilworth*, the first novel to be published at £1.11.6, cost for the Paris issue the equivalent of 8 shillings 11 pence (13 francs @ 9 pence: see list on L copy wrappers of *Redgauntlet* [291R.53-55], where all of Scott is advertised as 'at one third of the London prices') and for the Philadelphia printings the equivalent of only 7 shillings ($1.75 @ 25 cents a shilling: see *National Gazette* 31 March, 7 April 1821).

3. Based upon McCusker's 'Composite Commodity Price Index' record for 1821 (90.6, the date for *Kenilworth*) and 1991 (3627.3, the last entry cited), the appreciation factor is (x40), or £1.11.6 then = £63 or $100.80 now. John J. McCusker, *How Much Is That in Real Money?*, Worcester: American Antiquarian Society, 1992, pages 344, 350.

4. On 15 October 1825 the *Literary Gazette* (page 672) reported *Constable's Miscellany* as

then 'preparing for the press' and subtended a lengthy prospectus listing 53 items, the series to appear in weekly numbers, cost one shilling a number, three numbers to a volume. Though this scheme was not fully realized, the *Miscellany* eventually ran to 76 volumes. It would further appear that both of the earliest volumes directly involving Scott, the first and the fifth (195A, 198A), though prepared before the end of 1825, were long delayed in issue because of the Constable bankruptcy.

5. For these several arrangements see in order the *Journal*, pages 216, 233; *Allgemeine Zeitung* as cited in entry 302R.150-167; and the Philadelphia *National Gazette* for 20 February 1827. A random check of these editions indicates that, unlike the Carey, Philadelphia issue, all are based generally on texts in a later, corrected state, yet still earlier than the final state represented by the official Edinburgh publication.

6. The first public notice of this intention occurs six months before the formal Prospectus (225A) in a report from the 9 August 1828 *Literary Gazette* (page 510): 'A new edition of the Waverley Novels, the copyrights of which were purchased [19 December 1827] at the sale of Mr. Constable's property for above 8000*l*., is about to be produced, with illustrations, engraved from pictures by Wilkie, Leslie, Newton, and other distinguished artists. Sir Walter says they may now be considered as rather antiquated beauties, and therefore need a little more of ornament to set them off.' Actually the price was £8,500, and Scott's comments here on the value of some pictorial embellishment were reiterated two months later in more vigorous language (*Letters*, xi.7: cited below in introductory note for 348Aa).

CONTENTS OF CHAPTER FIVE

TRADITIONS AND RECOLLECTIONS DOMESTIC, CLERICAL, and LITERARY

185A] First Printing: 1826

[Five letters dated 10 October, 30 December 1810; 1 December 1811; September 1814; 4 November 1815] Volume 2, pages 636-637; 637-639; 644-645; 667-668; 684-685, *in*:

Traditions and Recollections, Domestic, Clerical, and Literary; In which are included Letters of Charles II. Cromwell, [and 17 others] . . . Sir Walter Scott, and Other Distinguished Characters. . . By the Rev. R. Polwhele. . . . Vol. II. London: Printed by and for John Nichols and Son, 25, Parliament Street. 1826.

Published 27 January 1826 in London (*MC*).

Notes: At the request of his clerical acquaintance Scott on 6 September 1824 reluctantly agreed to the printing of these letters, provided that he was afforded the opportunity of reviewing them before publication. Polwhele again printed these with others just after Scott's death in 1832 (*see* 257Aa).

Copies: E O; NN.

References: *Letters*, x.361. (Magnum Opus Edition: Not reprinted.)

FIRST LETTER ON THE PROPOSED CHANGE OF CURRENCY

These diatribes produced in Scotland a sensation not, perhaps, inferior to that of the Drapier's letters in Ireland; a greater one, certainly, than any political tract had excited in the British public at large since the appearance of Burke's Reflections on the French Revolution. (Lockhart, viii.242.)

186Aa] First Letter, First Journal Printing: 1826

'THE CURRENCY. TO THE EDITOR OF THE EDINBURGH WEEKLY JOURNAL.', pages 60-62 *in*:

The Edinburgh Weekly Journal. Vol. XXIX. No. 1471.] Wednesday, February 22, 1826. [Price sevenpence. Edinburgh—Printed by James Ballantyne, For himself and other Proprietors.

Published 22 February 1826 in Edinburgh.

Copy: E. References: Grant & Shaw Ltd, Catalogue 35 (1997), no.36; Thomson, page 43. (Magnum Opus Edition 1836: *The Miscellaneous Prose Works*, xxi.*269* 270-311 as 'Letters of Malachi Malagrowther. Letter I'.)

186Ab] First Letter, First Book Edition (First Impression): 1826

THOUGHTS | ON THE | **PROPOSED CHANGE OF CURRENCY,** | AND | OTHER LATE ALTERATIONS, | AS THEY AFFECT, OR ARE INTENDED TO AFFECT, | THE | **KINGDOM OF SCOTLAND.** | [*short rule*] | [*one-line quotation*] | [*short rule*] | EDINBURGH: | **Printed by James Ballantyne and Company.** | FOR WILLIAM BLACKWOOD, EDINBURGH. | [*dash*] | 1826.

Published 1 March 1826 in Edinburgh (*EWJ*). 2s. Binding: sewed. Paper: Demy 8° (226 x 147mm uncut). Watermarks: *none*. Collation: *A*^{8} B-C^8 D^4 F^2. Pagination: *1* title-page, *2 blank*, *3* 4-60 text, 60 printer's imprint: [*short rule*] | EDINBURGH: | PRINTED BY JAMES BALLANTYNE AND CO. Typography: Signature E (page 57) is missigned F. Figures: *A*—, B31-15 32-13, C48-7, D56-11, 'F'[E]—.

Notes: In this series of 'Letters' defending the issuance of Scottish banknotes Scott benefits from his work on Swift (*see* 79Aa) by patterning the Malachi Malagrowther letters on Swift's *Drapier's Letters*. In this first edition 'Malachi Malagrowther' is not mentioned on the title-page, but does appear as a signature on page 58 at end of text, and before the newly added postscript, pages 58-60.

Copies: E HS(Gladstone's copy, annotated) LU(Lord Holland) O; CtY MH NN NNU-W TxU.

Reference: Van Antwerp(2) 28a.

186Ac] First Letter, Second Edition (Second Impression, First Issue): 1826

A LETTER | TO THE | **Editor of the Edinburgh Weekly Journal,** | FROM | MALACHI MALAGROWTHER, Esq. | ON THE | **PROPOSED CHANGE OF CURRENCY,** | AND | OTHER LATE ALTERATIONS, | AS THEY AFFECT, OR ARE INTENDED TO AFFECT, | THE | **KINGDOM OF SCOTLAND.** | [*short rule*] | [*one-line quotation*] | [*short rule*] | SECOND EDITION. | EDINBURGH: | **Printed by James Ballantyne and Company,** | FOR WILLIAM BLACKWOOD, EDINBURGH. | [*dash*] | 1826.

Published 8 March 1826 in Edinburgh (*EWJ*); issued 13 March in London (*MC*). 2s. Binding: sewed. Paper: Demy 8° (226 x 147mm uncut). Watermarks: *none*. Collation: *A*^{8} B-C^8 D^4 F^2. Pagination: *1* title-page, *2 blank*, *3* 4-60 text, 60 printer's imprint: [*short rule*] | EDINBURGH: | PRINTED BY JAMES BALLANTYNE AND CO. Typography: Signature E (page 57) is again missigned F. Figures: *A*—, B31-13 32-6, C47-1 48-2, D56-14, 'F'[E]—.

Notes: Essentially a reimpression with revisions. Most of these were entered by Scott upon first edition proofs (E MS.4867), but not incorporated until this hurriedly produced second edition. The most extensive revision consists of two sentences added to the first paragraph on page 27: 'The Bank of Falkirk . . . the creditors.'; 'None of these bankruptcies . . . considerable loss.' (This substantial addition, of 39 words, was accomodated by extending the line-count on several pages before and after.) Further revisions also occurred which are not in the proofs; for example, 'Union' was inserted in the first quotation above, so that it begins 'The Union Bank of Falkirk . . .'

Copies: LU; CtY('Maria Edgeworth from Mrs. Younge').

186Ad] First Letter, Second Edition (Second Impression, Second Issue): 1826

A LETTER . . . FOR WILLIAM BLACKWOOD, EDINBURGH: AND | T. CADELL, STRAND, LONDON. | [*dash*] | 1826.

Notes: The addition of a London publisher to the imprint would signify a quickening interest in England concerning this Scottish problem.

Copies: BCL E O; CtY InU NN.

186Ae] First Letter, Third Edition (Third Impression): 1826

A LETTER . . .THIRD EDITION. . . . 1826.

Published 30 March 1826 in Edinburgh (*EEC*). 2s. Binding: sewed. Paper: Demy 8° (226 x 147mm uncut). Watermarks: *none*. Collation: A^8 B-C^8 D^4 E^2. Pagination: *1* title-page, *2 blank*, *3* 4-60 text, 60 printer's imprint: [*short rule*] | EDINBURGH: | PRINTED BY JAMES BALLANTYNE AND CO. Typography: Signature E (page 57) is now correctly signed. Figures: A15-12, B31-7 32-18, C47-11 48-14, D56-9, E—.

Notes: Except for the corrected signature, this is apparently an unaltered reimpression.

Copies: E('Walter Scott [Scott's eldest son] Major Kings Hussars') LU(2); NN RPB.

186Af] First Letter, Fourth Edition (Fourth Impression): 1826

A LETTER . . . FOURTH EDITION. . . . 1826.

Binding: sewed. Paper: Demy 8° (225 x 146mm uncut). Watermarks: *none*. Figures: A15-9, B32-3, C47-11/- 48-5, D—, E—.

Notes: Again this edition seems to be an unaltered reimpression: the hyphen at the end of page 29, line 17, missing in the early first edition proofs, is still omitted here. However, 'friend', correctly spelled page 45 line 22 in the proofs and first edition, is misprinted 'frined' from the second edition onward—an odd circumstance for a word embedded in the middle of the type-page.

Copies: E; TxU ViU.

SECOND LETTER ON THE PROPOSED CHANGE OF CURRENCY

187Aa] Second Letter, First Journal Printing: 1826

'THE CURRENCY. [*four-line quotation*] TO THE EDITOR OF THE EDINBURGH WEEKLY JOURNAL.', pages 60-62 *in*:

The Edinburgh Weekly Journal. Vol. XXIX. No. 1472.] Wednesday, March 1, 1826. [Price sevenpence. Edinburgh—Printed by James Ballantyne, For himself and other Proprietors.

Published 1 March 1826 in Edinburgh.

Copy: E. References: Thomson, page 43. (Magnum Opus Edition 1836: *The Miscellaneous Prose Works*, xxi.312-375 as 'Letter II'.)

187Ab] Second Letter, First Book Edition (First Impression): 1826

A | **SECOND LETTER** | TO THE | Editor of the Edinburgh Weekly Journal, | FROM | MALACHI MALAGROWTHER, Esq. | ON THE | **PROPOSED CHANGE OF CURRENCY,** | AND | OTHER LATE ALTERATIONS, | AS THEY AFFECT, OR ARE INTENDED TO AFFECT, | THE | **KINGDOM OF SCOTLAND.** | [*short rule*] | [*four-line quotation*] | [*short rule*] | EDINBURGH: | Printed by James Ballantyne and Company, | FOR WILLIAM BLACKWOOD, EDINBURGH. | [*dash*] | 1826.

Published 4 March 1826 in Edinburgh (*EEC*). 2s. Binding: sewed. Paper: Demy 8° (226 x 147mm uncut). Watermarks: *none*. Collation: A^8 B-E^8 F^2. Pagination: *1* title-page, *2 blank*, *3* 4-84 text, 84 printer's imprint: [*short rule*] | Edinburgh: | Printed by James Ballantyne and Co. Figures: A16-8, B32-2, C47-16, D—, E—, F—.

Notes: The title quotation, withdrawn in the 'Second Edition', here reads: 'When the pipes begin to play / Tuttie taittie to the drum, / Out claymore, and down wi' gun, / And to the rogues again!'

Copies: E(2) LU O(2); CtY(2) MH NN(2) RPB.

Reference: Van Antwerp(2) 28b.

187Ac] Second Letter, Second Edition (Second Impression): 1826
A | **SECOND LETTER** . . . SECOND EDITION . . . FOR WILLIAM BLACKWOOD, EDINBURGH: AND | T. CADELL, STRAND, LON DON. | [*dash*] | 1826.

Published 13 March 1826 in Edinburgh (*EEC*). 2s. Binding: sewed. Paper: Demy 8° (226 x 147mm uncut). Watermarks: *none*. Collation: *A*^{8} B-E^8 F^4. Pagination: *1* title-page, *2 blank*, *3* 4-86 text, 86 printer's imprint, *87-88 blank*. Printer's imprint: [*short rule*] | EDINBURGH: | Printed by James Ballantyne and Co. Figures: C48-1, E80-11.

Notes: Again as with the first letter there are numerous revisions in this reimpression, all extending the text to two extra pages. New footnotes appear on pages 29, 79, and 80, the first of these citing 'the old song' which appeared on the first edition title-page. Of this ditty Scott now remarks: 'I have laid it aside in this edition, some cautious friends thinking it liable to misinterpretation.'

Copies: BCL E HS(Gladstone's copy, annotated) LU(2); NN.

187Ad] Second Letter, Third Edition (Third Impression): 1826
A | **SECOND LETTER** . . . THIRD EDITION. . . . 1826.

Binding: sewed. Paper: Demy 8° (223 x 142mm uncut). Watermarks: *none*. Collation and pagination as for the 'second edition'. Figures: *A*12-14, B32-9/-, C48-17, D51-12, E80-11, F84-14.

Notes: Apparently this 'edition' is an uncorrected reimpression.

Copies: E(2) LU; TxU ViU.

THIRD LETTER ON THE PROPOSED CHANGE OF CURRENCY

188Aa] Third Letter, First Journal Printing: 1826

'THE CURRENCY. [*two-line quotation*] TO THE EDITOR OF THE EDINBURGH WEEKLY JOURNAL.', pages 60-62 *in*:

The Edinburgh Weekly Journal. Vol. XXIX. No. 1473.] Wednesday, March 8, 1826. [Price sevenpence. Edinburgh—Printed by James Ballantyne, For himself and other Proprietors.

Published 8 March 1826 in Edinburgh.

Copy: E. References: Thomson, page 43. (Magnum Opus Edition 1836: *The Miscellaneous Prose Works*, xxi.376-402 as 'Letter III'.)

188Ab] Third Letter, First Book Edition (First Impression): 1826

A | **THIRD LETTER** | TO THE | **Editor of the Edinburgh Weekly Journal,** | FROM | MALACHI MALAGROWTHER, ESQ. | ON THE | **PROPOSED CHANGE OF CURRENCY,** | AND | OTHER LATE ALTERATIONS, | AS THEY AFFECT, OR ARE INTENDED TO AFFECT, | THE | **KINGDOM OF SCOTLAND.** | [*short rule*] | [*two-line quotation*] | [*short rule*] | EDINBURGH: | **Printed by James Ballantyne and Company,** | FOR WILLIAM BLACKWOOD, EDINBURGH: AND | T. CADELL, STRAND, LONDON. | [*dash*] | 1826.

Published 13 March 1826 in Edinburgh (*EEC*); issued 20 March in London (*MC*). 1s. Binding: sewed. Paper: Demy 8° (226 x 147mm uncut). Watermarks: *none*. Collation: A^8 B^8 C^4. Pagination: *1* title-page, *2 blank*, *3* 4-39 text, 39 printer's imprint, *40 blank*. Printer's imprint: [*short rule*] | EDINBURGH: | Printed by James Ballantyne & Co. Figures: none.

Notes: This third letter remains unaltered in its several impressions.

Copies: BCL E(3) LU O(2); CtY InU MH NN(3).

Reference: Van Antwerp(2) 28c.

188Ac] Third Letter, Second Edition (Second Impression): 1826

A | **THIRD LETTER** . . . SECOND EDITION. . . . 1826.

Published 30 March 1826 in Edinburgh (*EEC*). 1s. Binding: sewed. Paper: Demy 8° (227 x 143mm uncut). Watermarks: *none*. Collation and pagination as for the previous impression. Figure: A16-8.

Notes: A reimpression, now with a single press figure.

Copies: E HS(Gladstone's copy, annotated) LU; CtY RPB ViU.

188Ad] Third Letter, Third Edition (Third Impression): 1826

A | **THIRD LETTER** . . . THIRD EDITION. . . . 1826.

Published 5 April 1826 in Edinburgh (*EWJ*). 1s. Binding: sewed. Paper: Demy 8° (227 x 143mm uncut). Watermarks: *none*. Collation and pagination as for the first edition. Figures: A16-3/6, B32-5, C—.

Notes: A reimpression, now with two press figures.

Copies: E(2) LU; TxU.

REVIEW OF PEPYS

189A] First Printing: 1826

'ART.I.—*Memoirs of Samuel Pepys*. . . . Edited by Richard, Lord Braybrooke.', pages *281* 282-314, *in*:

The Quarterly Review. [March, 1826. No.66, volume 33 imprint:]. London: John Murray, Albemarle Street. 1826.

Published 6 April 1826 in London (*MC*); issued 22 April in Edinburgh (*EEC*).

Notes: Scott began writing this review 27 December 1825 so that it might appear as the first article in the journal now under Lockhart's editorship. As so often, however, the issue was delayed.

Copies: BCL L O; PPL.

References: *Journal*, page 49; Thomson, page 52. (Magnum Opus Edition 1835: *The Miscellaneous Prose Works*, xx.94-152 as 'Pepys' Memoirs'. *MPW* incorrectly indicates the review appeared in a January 1826 number.)

WOODSTOCK

The busy period of the great Civil War was one in which the character and genius of different parties were most brilliantly displayed, and, accordingly, the incidents which took place on either side were of a striking and extraordinary character, and afforded ample foundation for fictitious composition. ('Introduction', '1 August 1832', *WN*, xxxix.*iii*.)

190A] First Edition: 1826

WOODSTOCK; | OR, | **THE CAVALIER.** | A TALE | OF THE | *YEAR SIXTEEN HUNDRED AND FIFTY-ONE.* | BY THE AUTHOR OF "WAVERLEY, | TALES OF THE CRUSADERS," &c. | [*short rule*] | [*one-line quotation from Chaucer*] | [*short rule*] | IN THREE VOLUMES. | VOL.

I [II-III]. | [*short reversed Oxford rule*] | EDINBURGH: | PRINTED FOR ARCHIBALD CONSTABLE AND CO. EDINBURGH; | AND LONGMAN, REES, ORME, BROWN, AND GREEN, | LONDON. | [*short rule*] | 1826.

Published concurrently 28 April 1826 in Edinburgh (*EEC* 15 April, to be published 'on Friday 28 April'); 28 April in London (*MC* 21 April, 'On Friday next, the 28th of April'). £1.11.6. Binding: drab boards or (a later issue?) slate cloth with printed labels. Paper: Post 8° (197 x 125mm uncut). Watermarks: none. Typography: Printer's imprints read: (1) [*short rule*] | EDINBURGH: | PRINTED BY JAMES BALLANTYNE AND CO.; (2) [*short rule*] | EDINBURGH: | Printed by James Ballantyne & Co.

General Notes: This novel was advertised in 1825 as 'in the press' just before Constable's bankruptcy, the *Literary Gazette* on 26 November indicating that it would be published 'On the 25th of January next'. According to established practice, beginning with *Kenilworth* (*see* 149Aa), on 20 May 1826, shortly after actual publication, some 9600 words (volume 1, chapter 8 of this Edinburgh edition) were extracted in the Philadelphia *National Gazette*, these deriving from proofs early shipped for the Carey & Lea edition (190Re). Several weeks before the extract, on 9 May, the Carey firm announced the novel as already 'In press' and gave the subtitle as 'a Tale of the Long Parliament': an indication that, contrary to Randall's conclusion (page 52), some of the advance copy was in an unrevised state. Two selections from this novel were extracted in the anthologies:389E.39, 404E.1.

In its various single leaves or partial gatherings, this book exhibits an unusual number of multiple settings, perhaps because at the time of printing more space than usual was available in the formes then engaged for presswork, either on this novel or other works.

Presentation copy: CtY('From the Author' [Henry Mackenzie signature on each of the three title-pages]). Other copies: BCL(8) E(2) E*b L+ L(2) O(22); IdU InU MH MH*a NN(3) NNU-W T/B TxU(Wolff) TxU(2) ViU.
+ page proofs, extensively corrected, with letters to James Ballantyne.
*With Longman catalogue of (a) 4 pages dated December 1825; (b) 12 pages dated August 1826.

References: Church 548; Randall, pages 51-52; Sterling 740; Thomson, page 77; Van Antwerp(1) 21 (Maria Edgeworth copy, illustrated); Worthington 19. (Magnum Opus Edition 1832: *Waverley Novels*, xxxix-xl.)

1] **WOODSTOCK;** | OR, | **THE CAVALIER.** . . . VOL. I. . . . 1826.

Collation: $\pi^8(\pm\pi2)$ A-T[8] U[4] X2. Pagination: *i* half-title, *ii* printer's imprint(1), *iii* title-page, *iv blank, v* vi-xvi Preface, *1* fly-title, *2 blank, 3* 4-315 text, 315 printer's imprint(1), *316 blank*. Typography: Except as noted below, printer's imprint (1) is used both on verso of half-title and on the last page.

Figures: π xv-6 xvi-7/-, A14-7/- 16-4, B30-14 32-12, C47-17 48-18, D57-13 59-9, E79-14 80-16, F86-13 96-17, G109-9/- 111-11, H121-14 123-11, I 141-14 142-12, K158-11 160-10, L171-15 176-14, M186-9 192-16, N194-3 208-8, O 223-12 224-4, P239-19 240-7, Q255-10 256-14, R270-9 272-6, S287-19 288-17, T303-15 304-18, U312-16, X—.

Notes: The integral half-title is in two states, with printer's imprint(1) on verso reading BALLANTINE or BALLANTYNE. However, the incorrect misprint cannot be regarded as an early issue, for at least one copy (E), in original boards, carries a late catalogue dated August 1826. The separate cancel title-leaf exists in a triplicate setting, with dash above date 13mm, 14mm, or 15mm in length. As Scott's own comments in the manuscript would indicate, the present title reference 'A Tale of the Year Sixteen Hundred and Fifty-one' is preferable to the earlier (cancelled) reading 'A Tale of Long Parliament Times' because that parliament 'has scarce been mentioned in the work.'

2] **WOODSTOCK;** | OR, | **THE CAVALIER.** . . . VOL. II. . . . 1826.

Collation: π^2 A-U^8 X^4 Y^2. Pagination: *i* half-title, *ii* printer's imprint(1), *iii* title-page, *iv blank, 1* fly-title, *2 blank, 3* 4-332 text, 332 printer's imprint(1). Typography: Printer's imprint (1) is used both on verso of half-title and on the last page.

Figures: A15-11 16-8, B31-14 32-2, C42-4 44-12, D63-7 64-9, E74-5 80-18, F94-13/- 96-1/-, G111-15 112-4, H127-3 128-5, I 137-12 139-7, K159-17 160-9, L175-18 176-6, M189-14 190-11, N206-18 208-2, O 223-5 224-7, P239-8 240-16, Q250-1 256-9, R271-14 272-12, S283-17 288-11, T303-18 304-13, U319-4 320-6, X328-3, Y330-9/-.

Notes: The preliminary fold exists in a duplicate setting, with the reversed Oxford rule on title either 13mm in length or 17mm. Final quarter-sheet Y (pages 329-332), though representing a considerable amount of text, also appears in a duplicate setting, with page 330 last line first word either 'tisement' (with or without press figure 9), or 'ment' and no press figure.

3] **WOODSTOCK;** | OR, | **THE CAVALIER.** . . . VOL. III. . . . 1826.

Collation: π^2 A-K^8 L^8(±L4) M-Z^8 2A1. Pagination: *i* half-title, *ii* printer's imprint(1), *iii* title-page, *iv blank, 1* fly-title, *2 blank, 3* 4-370 text, 370 printer's imprint(2). Typography: The printer's imprints are now in regular order.

Figures: A13-16 14-6, B31-2 32-9, C42-12 48-17/14, D63-18 64-11, E79-13 80-4, F95-14 96-7, G111-9 112-11, H122-9 128-11, I 143-14 144-12, K146-17 160-8, L167-17/- 175-7 176-2, M188-16 191-18, N194-4 204-6, O 218-2 224-8, P234-5 240-7, Q255-9 256-11, R269-16 271-17, S287-18 288-12/3, T303-7 304-3, U318-9 320-11, X335-1 336-8, Y344-2 350-14, Z362-10 368-13/16, 2A—.

Notes: Cancel leaf L4 occurs in a duplicate setting, page 167 with redundant figure 17 (in some copies) and 168 line 16 reading 'orders!—I', or 167 without figure and 168 reading 'orders—I'. Altogether, as exhibited in the manuscript, some ten additions or substitutions were made in the revised L4 text, the first, on page 167, line 7, adding 'rolled his eyes,'. Another duplicate setting appears in final leaf 2A1 (pages 369-370), with signature 'A' either centered below the 'c' and 'o', or under the first 'o' of 'colour'.

REPRINTS

FRANCE

PARIS: Baudry, Barrois [and others]
[~] Woodstock. 1832. (Collection of Ancient and Modern British Novels and Romances: *see* 288R34.)

PARIS: Didot and Galignani
[~] Woodstock. 1826, 1832. (Collection of Modern English Authors: *see* 291R60-62.)

PARIS: Galignani
[~] Woodstock [with six other titles]. 1827. One volume. (*see* 294R[3].5.)

GERMANY

190Ra] BERLIN: Schlesinger 1826
[Woodstock. . . . Berlin, Printed for Adolph Martin Schlesinger. 1826. Three volumes.] Copy reported by James Burmester. Reference: GDS 132, page 351.

ZWICKAU: Schumann
[~] Woodstock. 1826. (Pocket Library of English Classics: *see* 302R.138-141.)

UNITED STATES

190Rb] BOSTON: Parker 1826
[Woodstock; or The Cavalier. A Tale of the Year Sixteen Hundred and Fifty-one. . . . Boston: Samuel H. Parker, No. 164, Washington-Street. 1826. Pages: *1-3* 4-396.] Copy: not seen.
Notes: (Also reissued 1826 in Novels Tales and Romances: *see* 305R.19.)
[~] Woodstock. 1826, 1829. (Waverley Novels: *see* 306R.37-38.)

190Rc] NEW YORK: Borrodaile and Burgess 1826
Woodstock; or The Cavalier. A Tale of the Year Sixteen Hundred and Fifty-One. . . . By the Author of Waverley, Tales of the Crusaders, &c., &c. . . . New-York: W. Borrodaile, 114 Fulton-Street. and W. Burgess, Jun. 93 Fulton-Street. 1826. Two volumes. Pages 1: *1-3* 4-212; 2: not seen. Copy: MWA(vol.1). Reference: Kohler(1) 69 (with illustration).

190Rd] NEW YORK: Harper 1826
Woodstock; or The Cavalier. A Tale of the Year Sixteen Hundred and Fifty-One. . . . By the Author of Waverley, Tales of the Crusaders, &c. &c. . . . New York: Printed by J. & J. Harper, 327, Pearl St. 1826. Two volumes. Pages 1: *3-5* 6-283; 2: *3-5* 6-300. Notes: Variant issue of the Philadelpia, Carey & Lea edition, next entry. First leaf in both volumes is blank, but counted in the pagination. Copies: E O; NjP NN.

190Re] PHILADELPHIA: Carey & Lea 1826
Woodstock; or The Cavalier. A Tale of the Year Sixteen Hundred and Fifty-One. . . . By the Author of Waverley, Tales of the Crusaders, &c. &c. . . . Philadelphia: H. C. Carey & I. Lea, Chesnut Street. 1826. Two volumes. Pages 1: *1-2, 5* 6-283; 2: *1-2, 5* 6-300. Notes: The first American edition, set from Edinburgh proofs, announced 9 May 1826 as 'In press', extracted in the *National Gazette* 20 May (190A), and issued 27 May (*NG*) in 3000 copies. In a further communication to the *Gazette* 26 January 1827 Carey & Lea advised their readers that the preface, not provided originally with the text, was being issued gratis. Copies: IdU MH MWA NjP NNU-W(2) PPL(2) RPB T/B(2). References: Kaser 31; Kohler(1) 198 (with illustration); Randall, pages 51-52.

190Rf] PHILADELPHIA: Crissy 1826
Woodstock; or The Cavalier. A Tale of the Year Sixteen Hundred and Fifty-One. . . . By the Author of Waverley, Tales of the Crusaders, &c. &c. . . . Philadelphia: James Crissy, No. 14 South Seventh Street. 1826. Two volumes. Pages 1: *i-iii* iv-viii *ix-x*, *5* 6-283; 2: *1-2, 5* 6-300. Notes: A later variant issue of the Philadelphia, Carey & Lea edition (*see* preceding entry), now with preface correctly included. Copies: CtY IdU T/B(vol.1).

DERIVATIVES

GREAT BRITAIN

190Da] LONDON: Miller 1826
[1] Woodstock. A Play in Five Acts. Founded on the Popular Novel of That Name; . . . London: John Miller, New Bridge Street, Blackfriars. 1826. Pages: *i-vii* viii, *1* 2-86 *87-88*. Notes: Play by Isaac Pocock, as first performed at the Theatre Royal, Covent Garden, 20 May 1826, five days after another, unpublished version (by C. I. M. Dibdin) had opened across the Thames at the Surrey Theatre. The Prologue for the Pocock adaptation concludes with a quatrain:

> If then *this* Woodstock tale, in three hour's space,
> Culled from three volumes, briefly he can trace,
> Let your indulgence to his toil be shewn,—
> Give all your plaudits to the GREAT UNKNOWN.

Price: Three Shillings. Copy: E. References: Bolton 4406; Ford Y2.

[2] Woodstock. A Play in Five Acts. Founded on the Popular Novel of That Name; . . . London: John Miller, New Bridge Street, Blackfriars. 1826. Pages: *i-vii* viii, *1* 2-83. Notes: Presumably the second setting with text compressed (*see* previous entry). Copy: CtY.

190Db] LONDON: Power 1828
One Hour with thee! A Ballad by Sir Walter Scott Bart. . . . London, Published by J. Power, 34, Strand, Where may be had the following Songs. . . . [watermarked 1828.] Pages: *1* 2-7. Notes: Engraved sheet-music with plate mark: '1156'. Words from chapter 26 (first words: 'One hour with thee! When earliest day / Dapples with gold the eastern grey.') Music composed by Mrs Robert Arkwright arranged by Thomas Simpson Cooke for voice and pianoforte. Copy: L. Reference: G/T 10941.

FAIRY LEGENDS AND TRADITIONS

191A] First Printing: 1826

'TO THE AUTHOR OF IRISH FAIRY LEGENDS.', pages vii-xi, *in*:

Fairy Legends and Traditions of the South of Ireland. Second Edition. London. John Murray. MDCCCXXVI.

Second edition published in London by 29 April 1826 (*LG*, page 272).

Notes: A letter of appreciation, dated 27 April 1825, to Thomas Crofton Croker, the editor, for receipt of copy of the first edition. The letter expands at length on a comparison of Scottish and Irish fairy tales: this a further reiteration of Scott's lifelong interest in fairies and 'little personages'.

Copies: BCL O(Opie).

Reference: (Magnum Opus Edition: Not reprinted, but quoted in *Letters*, ix.94-97.)

REVIEWS OF KEMBLE and KELLY

192A] First Printing: 1826

'ART.IX. 1.—*Memoirs of the Life of John Philip Kemble, Esquire,* . . . By James Boaden. 2. *Reminiscences of Michael Kelly of the King's Theatre* . . . 2d Edition', pages 196-248, *in*:

The Quarterly Review. [June, 1826. No.67. volume 34 imprint:] London: John Murray, Albemarle Street. 1826.

Published 13 June 1826 in London (*MC*); issued 26 June in Edinburgh (*EEC*).

Copies: BCL L O; PPL.

References: Thomson, page 38. (Magnum Opus Edition 1835: *The Miscellaneous Prose Works*, xx.152-244 as 'Life of Kemble—Kelly's Reminiscences'. *MPW* incorrectly indicates the review appeared in an April 1826 number.)

REVIEW OF GALT

193A] First Printing: 1826

'THE OMEN.', pages 52-59, *in*:

Blackwood's Edinburgh Magazine. July, 1826. No. CXIV. Vol. XX. [volume imprint:] William Blackwood, Edinburgh; and T. Cadell, Strand, London. 1826.

Issued 30 June 1826 in London (*MC*).

Notes: On 23 June Scott received £10 only for this brief review, then plaintively remarked: 'Time was I would not have taken these small Tithes of mint and cummin but scornful dogs will eat dirty puddings and I with many depending on me must do the best I can with my time, God help me.' The author of the book, at first unknown to the reviewer, was later revealed to be John Galt.

Copies: L O; NjP PPL.

References: *Journal*, page 161, Thomson, page 30. (Magnum Opus Edition 1835: *The Miscellaneous Prose Works*, xviii.333-353.)

THE WORKS OF SHAKSPEARE

194A] Projected Scott Edition: 1826

[The Works of Shakspeare. London: A. Constable, 1826.]

Unpublished. Binding: drab boards. Paper: Demy 8° (225 x 145mm uncut). Watermarks: *none*. Typography: Printer's imprint reads invariably: [*short rule*] | EDINBURGH: | PRINTED BY JAMES BALLANTYNE AND CO.

General Notes: A projected edition of ten or more volumes, of which four odd volumes are known to survive: these without title pages or preliminaries. The first volume, unprinted, was to consist, as Scott remarked, of 'the prolegomena and Life & Times', his primary responsibility, but in general the editing was carried on by Lockhart. Archibald Constable, who first suggested the work in February 1822, wanted the edition to be 'readable' and with 'amusing notes': a suggestion well observed in the present performance. The work done up to 1826 also seems to have advanced beyond proof stage as surviving volumes are on fine quality ribbed wove paper and bear press figures. Upon Constable's bankruptcy at that later date, however, the three finished volumes remained in his warehouse and the project was finally abandoned. Constable's son later reported the sheets were sold as waste paper, and he doubted whether a single copy of this extensive project was then in existence.

Each play is prefaced by an introduction which relies heavily upon previous editors, Johnson, Malone, Reed, Rowe, and Steevens, and their conclusions. The same editors are quoted throughout in the footnotes. Many of the these notes are signed (S.), referring either to Steevens or, possibly, in some instances, to Scott himself.

Copies: E*a(vol.2); MB*b(vols.2-4).
*Acquired from (a) Abbotsford in 1934, (b) Thomas Rodd at a sale in Edinburgh.

References: *Letters*, ix.385, x.59, 66n, 76n.

2] [The Works of Shakspeare. . . . Vol. 2. . . . 1826].

Collation: A-2D^8 2E^4(-2E4). Pagination: *1* fly-title for *Two Gentlemen of Verona, 2 blank, 3* 4-102 text, *103* fly-title for *Comedy of Errors, 104 blank, 105* 106-185 text, *186 blank, 187* fly-title for *Love's Labour's Lost, 188 blank, 189-193* 194-320 text, *321* fly-leaf for *Merchant of Venice, 322 blank, 323* 324-438 text, 438 printer's imprint.

Figures: A—, B32-1, C48-4, D64-1, E80-1, F84-1, G112-1, H128-5, I 144-5, K160-2, L176-2, M*189*-6, N208-6, O 220-4, P240-4, Q256-4, R272-5, S288-1, T304-5, U320-5, X336-7, Y352-7, Z368-2, 2A 384-2, 2B 400-5, 2C—, 2D 432-2, 2E—.

3] [The Works of Shakspeare. . . . Vol. 3. . . . 1826].

Collation: A-2F^8 2G^4 2H1. Pagination: *1* fly-title for *Midsummer-Night's Dream, 2 blank, 3* 4-106 text, *107* fly-title for *Taming of the Shrew, 108 blank, 109* 110-225 text, *226 blank, 227* fly-title for *As You Like it, 228 blank, 229* 230-354 text, *355* fly-title for *Much Ado about Nothing, 356 blank, 357-361* 362-474 text, 474 printer's imprint. Typography: The single leaf, pages 43-44, is incorrectly imposed and appears between pages 38-39.

Figures: A16-2, B32-1, C48-2, D64-1, E80-1, F96-5, G*109*-5, H128-5, I 144-5, K160-4, L176-4, M192-3, N208-4, O 224-7, P240-7, Q253-2, R272-1, S288-1, T304-5, U320-8, X336-7, Y352-8, Z368-1, 2A 384-3, 2B 400-7, 2C 416-8, 2D 234-2, 2E 448-6, 2F 464-1, 2G 472-1, 2H—.

4] [The Works of Shakspeare. . . . Vol. 4. . . . 1826].

Collation: A-2I^8 2K^4 2L^2. Pagination: *1* fly-title for *Merry Wives of Windsor, 2 blank, 3* 4-129 text, *130 blank, 131* fly-title for *Measure for Measure, 132 blank, 133* 134-264 text, *265* fly-title for *All's Well that Ends Well, 266 blank, 267-271* 272-402 text, *403* fly-title for *Twelfth-Night: or, What You Will, 404 blank, 404-405* 406-524 text, 524 printer's imprint. Typography: Another example of misimposition: page 134 is imposed after 129, with final page of introduction for the next play, *Measure for Measure*, entered after concluding note to *Merry Wives of Windsor.*

Figures: A16-6, B31-1, C48-8, D64-1, E80-8, F96-3, G112-5, H128-5, I 144-7, K160-7, L—, M192-2, N208-6, O 224-6, P240-2, Q256-3, R272-7, S288-5, T304-3, U320-7, X336-8, Y352-8, Z—, 2A 384-5, 2B 394-7 400-2, 2C 416-5, 2D 432-7, 2E—, 2F 464-6, 2G 480-7, 2H 496-7, 2 I 512-5, 2K 520-5, 2L—.

Notes: There exists a proof sheet (E MS.8997.ff.40-41) of *All's Well That Ends Well*, pages 359-362, with manuscript corrections and a footnote in Lockhart's handwriting.

VOYAGE TO LOO-CHOO

195A] First Printing: 1826[1827]

[*steel engraving*] 'TO | His Majesty | KING GEORGE IV. | The Most generous Patron | even of the most humble attempts | towards the advantage of his Subjects: | This Miscellany, | designed to extend useful Knowledge | and elegant Literature; | By placing Works of Standard Merit, | within the attainment of every Class of | Readers; | Is most humbly Inscribed | BY HIS MAJESTY'S | Dutiful and Devoted Subject, | Archibald Constable.', *in:*

Voyage to Loo-Choo, and Other places in the Eastern Seas, in the year 1816. . . . and Notes of an Interview with Buonaparte at St Helena, in August 1817. By Captain Basil Hall, R.N. F.R.S. Edinburgh: Printed for Archibald Constable & Co. And Hurst, Robinson, & Co. London, 1826.

Published 6 January 1827 in Edinburgh (*EEC* 1 January); issued 16 January in London (*MC*). This book was first announced 28 December 1825 in *EWJ* for 'Saturday 4th Feb' [1826], but as several papers later remarked was then long delayed because of 'unfortunate circumstances', that is, Constable's bankruptcy. Illustrations: Scott's dedication leaf was engraved by W. H. Lizars, the engraved general title, preceding this, by W. Archibald. This title reads: 'Constable's Miscellany of Original and Selected Publications in the Various Departments of Literature, The Sciences & The Arts. Vol. I. Hall's Voyages [*vignette of Java*] Edinburgh: Printed for Archibald Constable & Co. And Hurst, Robinson & Co. London. 1826.' Scott had requested permission for the dedication in October 1825 and received the necessary licence on 20 December, just before Constable defaulted.

Notes: The Constable miscellany, the first to address the mass market for cheap literature, was the immediate prototype for other series selling generally at five shillings a volume. Apart from Scott's own later contribution to the Constable collecton (198A), see also Lardner's *Cabinet Cyclopaedia* (232Aa), Murray's *Family Library* (200D, 231A, 241Aa), and his own 'Magnum Opus' in 1829-1836 (348A-350A).

Copies: E GU O.

References: *Journal*, pages 28, 44. (Magnum Opus Edition: Not reprinted.)

MEMOIR OF THE DUKE OF YORK

196A] First Printing: 1827

[Memoir of The Duke of York], pages 13-14 *in*:

The Edinburgh Weekly Journal. VOL. XXX. No. 1517.] WEDNESDAY, JANUARY 10, 1827. [Price Sevenpence]. Printed by James Ballantyne, for himself and the other Proprietors.

Published 10 January 1827 in Edinburgh.

Notes: A two-paragraph note introduces Scott's commentary: 'The public will immediately trace in the observations which follow, the Master Hand to whom they are indebted for them.'

Copies: EP L.

References: Thomson, page 77. (Magnum Opus Edition 1834: *The Miscellaneous Prose Works*, iv.400-416.)

REPRINTS

GREAT BRITAIN

196Ra] LONDON: Marsh 1827
Memoir of the Duke of York. By Sir Walter Scott, Bart. London: Printed for William Marsh, Public Subscription Reading Rooms, 137, Oxford Street. 1827. Pages: *i-iv*, *1* 2-16, *1* 2-6. Notes: Scott's contribution concludes: '. . . we here offer an imperfect tribute.' To Scott's Memoir is subjoined, pages 15-16, a paragraph by Robert Southey. Copies: DN E.

196Rb] NEWCASTLE: Sykes 1827
An Account of the Death & Funeral Procession of His Royal Highness Frederick Duke of York; . . . To Which is subjoined, Sir Walter Scott's Character of His Royal Highness. Newcastle: Printed for John Sykes, Bookseller, Johnson's Head, 10, Pilgrim-Street. MDCCCXXVII. Pages: *1-5* 6-32. Includes the Scott memoir, pages 25-32. Each page has a black border. Copies: E; InU.

THE THEATRICAL FUND DINNER

197Aa] First Journal Printing: 1827

'THEATRICAL FUND DINNER' [Remarks as President of the Fund and Chairman of the Dinner, 23 February], pages 68-69, *in*:

The Edinburgh Weekly Journal. Vol. XXX. No. 1524. Wednesday, February 28, 1827. [Price Sevenpence. Edinburgh—Printed by James Ballantyne, for himself and the other Proprietors.

Published 28 February 1827 in Edinburgh.

Notes: Scott's public avowal of his authorship of the Waverley Novels first appears in this journal report, which was sent to him for 'correction' prior to publication. His account is preceded by a letter dated 'Monday' [26 February] stating that he does not have 'leisure to correct the copy' forwarded by the Editor (this printed in *Letters*, x.166).

Copies: EP L.

References: Thomson, page 72. (Magnum Opus Edition 1832: *Waverley Novels*, xli.*xxxv* xxxvi-lxxiii.)

197Ab] First Book Printing: 1827

[Remarks as President of the Fund and Chairman of the Dinner, 23 February], pages 4-22, *in*:

An Account of the First Edinburgh Theatrical Fund Dinner, Held at Edinburgh, On Friday 23d February 1827; . . . Edinburgh: John Anderson, Jun. 55. North Bridge Street; And Sold by Simpkin & Marshall, and Charles Tait, London; Robertson & Atkinson, Glasgow; and A. Brown & Co. Aberdeen. M.DCC.XXVII.

Published ca. 7 March 1827 in Edinburgh.

Notes: Scott was now at 'leisure' to revise this account, deriving from the *Edinburgh Weekly Journal*, and accordingly refines his explanations for remaining anonymous. For example, in referring to his 'long silence': 'Perhaps caprice might have a considerable share . . .' [first journal printing]; 'A variety of reasons had led to the concealment; perhaps caprice had the greatest share . . .' [first book printing, page 11, lines 12-13].

Copies: BCL E(2). Reference: Van Antwerp(1) 25.

MEMOIRS OF THE MARCHIONESS DE LA ROCHEJAQUELEIN

198A] First Scott Edition: 1827

MEMOIRS | OF THE | **MARCHIONESS** | **DE LA ROCHEJA QUELEIN.** | TRANSLATED FROM THE FRENCH. | [*short Oxford rule*] | EDINBURGH: | PRINTED FOR CONSTABLE AND CO. | [*short rule*] | 1827.

Published 31 March 1827 in Edinburgh (*EEC*); issued 5 April in London (*MC*). 3s.6d. Binding: blue-green silk over boards with printed label. Paper: 12° in sixes. (152 x 93mm uncut). Watermarks: *none*. Collation: π^2 A-2H^6 2I 1. Pagination: [*engraved title*], *i* title-page, *ii* printer's imprint(1), *iii*-iv Contents, *1* fly-title, *2 blank*, *3* 4-17 Preface, dated from Abbotsford 1 February 1826, *18 blank*, *19* 20-374 text, 374 printer's imprint(2). Printer's imprints: (1) EDINBURGH: | PRINTED BY JAMES BALLANTYNE AND CO.; (2) [*short rule*] | EDINBURGH: | PRINTED BY JAMES BALLANTYNE AND CO. Illustration: Engraved title reads in full: CONSTABLE'S MISCELLANY | OF | ORIGINAL AND SELECTED PUBLICATIONS | IN THE VARIOUS DEPARTMENTS | OF | LITERATURE, SCIENCE, & THE ARTS | MEMOIRS OF | THE MARCHIONESS OF LAROCHEJAQUELIN. | VOL.V. | [vignette engraved on steel by W. Miller, with caption 'Castle of Clisson'] | EDINBURGH: | PRINTED FOR CONSTABLE & Co. | 1827. Figures: *none*.

Notes: The memoir, dated by the author 1 August 1811, is chiefly concerned with the insurrection of La Vendée, begun in March 1793 and terminated with the defeat at Quibaron 20 July 1795. Scott's unsigned preface eventually led him 'to draw comparisons between the civil wars of England during the middle of the seventeenth century, and the revolution of France in the end of the eighteenth . . . ' (pages 13-16): comparisons he had first drawn to Southey in 1824. Beyond this account, as he frankly remarked in his *Journal*, he entered only a few additional notes (that is, those appearing on pages 60, 152-153, and 187). The text itself, with numerous other notes, is reprinted from the 1817 English 'second edition' of the *Memoirs*, published by Constable and Longman.

Copies: BCL EP; CtY IdU T/B TxU ViU.

References: *Letters*, viii.376; *Journal*, page 49. (Magnum Opus Edition: Not reprinted.)

REVIEW OF MACKENZIE

199A] First Printing: 1827

'ART.VIII.—*The Works of John Home, Esq. . . . to which is prefixed an Account of his Life and Writings*. By Henry Mackenzie', pages 167-216, *in*:

The Quarterly Review. [June 1827. No.71, volume 36 imprint:] London: John Murray, Albemarle Street. 1827.

Published 13 June 1827 in London (*MC*); issued 21 June in Edinburgh (*EEC*).

Copies: BCL L O; PPL. Reference: (Magnum Opus Edition 1835: *The Miscellaneous Prose Works*, xix.283-367 as 'Life and Works of John Home'.)

THE LIFE OF NAPOLEON BUONAPARTE

The work, devoured at first with breathless delight, had a shade thrown over it by [some] angry Lilliputians; but it has now emerged, slowly and surely, from the mist of suspicion—and few, whose opinions deserve much attention, hesitate to avow their conviction that, whatever may be the Polybius of the modern Hannibal, posterity will recognise his Livy in Scott. (Lockhart, ix.120.)

200Aa] First Edition, First Issue: 1827

THE | **LIFE** | OF | **NAPOLEON BUONAPARTE,** | EMPEROR OF THE FRENCH. | WITH A | PRELIMINARY VIEW OF THE FRENCH | REVOLUTION. | BY THE AUTHOR OF "WAVERLEY," &c. | [*short rule*] | IN NINE VOLUMES. | [*short rule*] | VOL. I [II-IX]. | [*short reversed Oxford rule*] | EDINBURGH: | Printed by Ballantyne and Co. | FOR LONGMAN, REES, ORME, BROWN, & GREEN, LONDON; | AND | CADELL & CO., EDINBURGH. | [*dash*] | 1827.

<SEE ACCOMPANYING ILLUSTRATION>

First announced as to be published 'in the course of March' 1827 (*LG* 3 March. page 144); published 28 June in Edinburgh (*EEC*); issued 'positively . . . Saturday June 30th' in London (*MC* 11 and 16 June). £4.14.6. 8000 copies (but reduced to 6000 in the course of printing: *see* 200Ac). Binding: drab, maroon, or green marbled boards and printed labels. Paper: Post 8° (196 x 123mm uncut). Watermarks: *none*.

Typography: As usual in multi-volume sets, the preliminary half-title/title fold was prepared in several settings to facilitate the printing in a single forme. These three settings may be differentiated on half-title verso, where the 'L' of 'LUCANI' is entered below:

'L' of 'LUCANI' entered below	Title *dash*	Volumes
second 's' of 'fecisse'	9mm	1,5
the 'r' of 'ruina'	10mm	2,3,6,7,9
second 'e' of 'fecisse'	11mm	4,8,9

It will be noted that, within this group, the preliminary fold for the 9th volume is in a duplicate setting, probably to bring the total count to an even number for efficient presswork. Printer's imprints read: (volumes 1-5) [*short rule*] | EDINBURGH: | Printed by James Ballantyne & Co.; (volumes 6-8) [*short rule*] | EDINBURGH: | PRINTED BY JAMES BALLANTYNE AND CO. (volume 9 omits JAMES).

General Notes: By November 1826 Scott was in such straitened circumstances that he readily agreed, upon the payment of £295, for the 'early transmission of proof sheets' to, and advance issue by the Philadelphia firm of Carey, Lea, Carey (*Letters*, x.123). Accordingly this firm, following its usual practice, on 1 March 1827 (*NG* 13 February) began to print 22 extensive extracts now in the new *American Quarterly Review*, its own journal: the first number (pages 189-222) quoting some 990 words, the second number (pages 578-603) about 9460 words. Shortly thereafter the firm apparently distributed its first two volumes, but was delayed in publishing the whole work until 21 August (200Rf). In the interim the Philadelphia journal numbers reached London, where from this secondary source two extensive extracts were again printed, 19 and 26 May 1827, in the *Literary Gazette* (pages 317-319, 331-332): a circuitous trans-Atlantic route to be repeated in 1831 on a larger and more devious scale (*see* 253A).

Meanwhile, on 20 February (*NG*) it was announced that *The Life of Napoleon* would be 'published in English, French, and German, at Edinburgh, London, Paris, Leipsic, Berlin, and Vienna, on the same day.' Whether this multinational simultaneous issue actually occurred at every locale, on the date appointed, cannot be determined.

In several copies of the first Edinburgh edition, first issue, after the errata list in volume 1, there is a further slip conveying this useful information:

DIRECTIONS TO THE BINDER

The Errata to go to the end of the respective volumes. Particular attention is requested to the cancels. When those of one volume make a sheet, only the first page is marked with the volume; when cancels of more than one volume are in a sheet, each leaf is marked with the volume it belongs to.

N.B.—A cancel of the first leaf of sheet O of Vol. VII. is inserted in *some* of the copies. It must be destroyed, and another, which will be found on the 12th sheet of cancels, substituted for it. In some of the copies, the *first* page of the 14th sheet of cancels is marked Vol.VII.—It should be Vol.VIII. All the cancels in that sheet belong to Vol.VIII.

THE

LIFE

OF

NAPOLEON BUONAPARTE,

EMPEROR OF THE FRENCH.

WITH A

PRELIMINARY VIEW OF THE FRENCH REVOLUTION.

BY THE AUTHOR OF "WAVERLEY," &c.

IN NINE VOLUMES.

VOL. I.

EDINBURGH:
Printed by Ballantyne and Co.
FOR LONGMAN, REES, ORME, BROWN, & GREEN, LONDON;
AND
CADELL & CO., EDINBURGH.

1827.

ENTRY 200Aa. THE TODD / BOWDEN COPY

The 122 cancels so printed, on two unnumbered and fourteen numbered sheets, in this extraordinary circumstance are, for each volume, all cited together within a single parenthesis. In any sequence cancels for adjacent leaves (e.g. II F5.F6) were regularly imposed together and are still found conjoined in one or more copies. Press figures on a cancel are enclosed in parentheses; those on cancellanda, and therefore no longer part of the book, are listed separately. Cancel leaves with one or two figures may result in a 3 or 4-figured gathering (as in vol. 1, sheet T); cancellanda with figures, when withdrawn, may leave a completely unfigured gathering (as in sheet A). Not in the original cancel sheets are certain other 'aberrant' leaves, printed before (or after?) these sequences, all of which are also noted separately.

Presentation copy: (Volume 1, state 1a) E('From the Author'). Other copies: (Volume 1, state 1a) E(2) ES. (1b) NNU-W. (2) BCL L(2) LU O; CtY IdU InU* NjP T/B TxU(2).
*With 12-page Longman catalogue June 1827.

Separate files of cancellanda: L(shelf-mark:610.g.14); PPL(UV3 50510D).

References: Duval 984; B. J. McMullin, 'Notes on Cancellation in Scott's *Life of Napoleon*,' *Studies in Bibliography*, 45 (1992), 222-231; William Ruff, 'Cancels in Sir Walter Scott's "Life of Napoleon",' *Edinburgh Bibliographical Society Transactions*, 3 (1949-1951), 139-151 [cites original readings from the L file]; Thomson, page 49; Van Antwerp(1) 26. (Magnum Opus Edition 1835: *The Miscellaneous Prose Works*, viii-xvi.)

1] THE | **LIFE** | OF | **NAPOLEON BUONAPARTE,** . . . VOL. I. . . . 1827.

Collation: π^2 $2\pi^4(-2\pi4)$ a^2 A-X^8 Y^6 (with 8 cancels, ± A8 L2 P8 Q3 Q7 T2 T6 Y5) + 16-line errata slip. Pagination: *1* half-title, *2* quotation, *3* title-page, *4 blank*, *i* ii-v Advertisement, dated from Edinburgh 7 June 1827, *vi blank*, *i* ii-iv Contents, *1* fly-title, *2 blank*, *3* 4-348 text, 348 printer's imprint.

Figures: A—, B31-12 32-11, C46-9 48-13, D62-10 64-7, E75-3 80-6, F94-9 96-10, G111-12 112-15, H122-5 128-11, I 143-9 144-16, K157-13 159-15, L175-10 176-16, M191-1 192-15, N205-11 206-3, O 223-15 224-10, P234-13/- 237-17, Q255-17 256-15, R271-17 272-15, S287-9/- 288-18, T298-10 (300-15) 304-13, U319-11 320-19, X330-19 336-11, Y(345-18). Figures on cancellanda: A15-15/5 16-7, Y345-12 346-14. The first cancellanda figure 15 appears in a defective O copy (27.302) where the cancellandum leaf A8 (pages 15-16) is still retained.

Notes: Apart from the eight identified cancels, all presumably filling the first, unnumbered cancel sheet, the first leaf of Scott's Advertisement occurs in two consecutive settings. In its earlier setting (1a) page *i* line 1 ends with 'have,' and is unsigned, ii line 1 reads 'was', a reading (1b) corrected at press to 'were'; in its later, cancel state (2) page *i* line 1 ends with 'Work,' and is signed with an asterisk '*' (the usual sign of a reprinting), ii line 1 is corrected to 'were'. The suggestion that (2) may have been done for Longman in London gains some credence in the fact that all the Edinburgh copies examined are of the earlier variant (1a or 1b) and the London copies are of variant (2). Copies seen elsewhere, and containing a Longman catalogue, also are of state (2).

2] THE | **LIFE** | OF | **NAPOLEON BUONAPARTE,** . . . VOL. II. . . . 1827.

Collation: π^2 a^2 b1 A-$2B^8$ (with 15 cancels, ± E1 F5.F6 H1 H4 H6 K3 K7 O5 Q8 R3 S4 Z2 2A5 2B6) + five-line errata slip. Pagination: *1* half-title, *2* quotation, *3* title-page, *4 blank*, *i* ii-v Contents, *vi blank*, *1* fly-title, *2 blank*, *3* 4-399 text, 399 printer's imprint, *400 blank*. Typography: Direction lines for cancels E1 and K7 (pages 65 and 157) also bear cancel sheet numbers 2 and 3. In some copies cancel leaf Z2 (pages 355-356) is misnumbered 255-256. The correct numbers recur in the second issue.

Figures: a ii-14, b—, A15-10/- 16-15, B31-11 32-19, C47-13 48-16, D63-3/7/19 64-6, E79-20 80-19, F(91-20) 96-15, G109-16 110-13, H127-6 128-12, I 143-11 144-7, K159-17 160-10, L166-6 176-13, M191-11 192-18, N203-6 208-9, O 218-(10) 223-10 224-13, P239-11 240-1, Q—, R270-3 272-14, S(280-6) 282-11 288-12, T297-9 299-14, U319-2 320-7, X330-8 333-13, Y350-5 352-10, Z(356-1/-) 366-11 368-6, 2A 382-9 384-12, 2B 397-1 398-14. Figures in cancellanda: F91-12, Q255-5 256-8.

Notes: Apart from the 15 'sheet' cancels two others, Q7 and Z1 (pages 253-254 and 353-354), both apparently printed earlier, may appear as replacements for erroneous leaves corrected at press.

3] THE | **LIFE** | OF | **NAPOLEON BUONAPARTE,** . . . VOL. III. . . . 1827.

Collation: π^2 a^2 *b*1 A-Y^8 (with 14 cancels, ± A4 B2 B6 D2 D8 G4 L2 M6.M7 R5 S4 X8 Y3.Y4) + six-line errata slip. Pagination: *1* half-title, *2* quotation, *3* title-page, *4 blank*, *i* ii-v Contents, *vi blank*, *1* fly-title, *2 blank*, *3* 4-350 text, 350 printer's imprint, *351-252 blank*. Typography: The direction line for A4 (page 7) also, in some copies, bears cancel sheet number 4. Another, unnumbered sheet was used, apparently, to print off the eight cancels starting with L2.

Figures: A15-11 16-9, B31-10 32-13, C43-12 48-14, D—, E72-1 78-5, F94-7 96-4, G(104-2) 111-12 112-11, H123-5 128-2, I 135-13 144-3, K158-10 160-13, L(164-9) 175-1 176-3, M178-5 192-6, N206-7 208-10, O 223-1 224-8, P235-4/- 240-11, Q255-12 256-13, R271-11 272-3, S283-7 288-5, T298-2 304-10, U319-11 320-7, X331-1, Y346-1 349-10. Figures on cancellanda: D63-8 64-2, X336-10.

Notes: Apart from the 14 'sheet' cancels three others, π2, K5, T2 (pages 3-4, 153-154, 291-292), all apparently printed earlier, may appear as replacements for erroneous leaves corrected at press.

4] THE | **LIFE** | OF | **NAPOLEON BUONAPARTE,** . . . VOL. IV. . . . 1827.

Collation: π^2 a^4 A-2A^8 (with 16 cancels, ± B8 D6 E2 E4 E6.E7 F7 L6 P3 R1 R8 S6 U3 Z2.Z3 Z5) + three-line errata slip. Pagination: *1* half-title, *2* quotation, *3* title-page, *4 blank*, *i* ii-viii Contents, *1* fly-title, *2 blank*, *3* 4-381 text, 381 printer's imprint, *382-384 blank*. Typography: Direction lines for E2 and R8 (pages 67 and 271) also bear cancel sheet numbers 6 and 5 respectively. In some copies page 245 is misnumbered 254.

Figures: a iii-10, A11-11 12-13, B26-8 29-13, C47-11 48-12, D54-5 64-1, E70-12 73-13, F95-7 96-10, G111-2 112-8, H122-4 128-10, I 138-3 141-6, K159-11 160-13, L174-12 176-11, M189-2 191-13, N207-9 208-7, O 215-5 224-1, P(230-9) 239-7 240-8, Q253-6 255-9, R(258-3) (272-16), S(284-2) 288-12, T303-10 304-11, U319-7 320-5, X334-9 336-6, Y351-9 352-10, Z367-12 368-13, 2A 379-10 380-11. Figures on cancellanda: R271-10 272-11.

5] THE | **LIFE** | OF | **NAPOLEON BUONAPARTE,** . . . VOL. V. . . . 1827.

Collation: π^2 a^4 A-2C^8 (with 25 cancels, ± A2 A4 F3 F6 G8 I4.I5 L2 L5 N7 P1 P4 P8.Q1 R2 S3 T8.U1 U8 X7 Y3 Y8 Z4 Z7 2C7) + five-line errata slip. Pagination: *1* half-title, *2* quotation, *3* title-page, *4 blank*, *i* ii-vii Contents, *viii blank*, *1* fly-title, *2 blank*, *3* 4-415 text, 415 printer's imprint, *416 blank*. Typography: Cancel U1, conjoined to T8, is unsigned. Direction lines for A2, I 5, T8 (pages *3*, 137, 303) also bear cancel sheet numbers 7, 8, 9.

Figures: a v-10, A15-13 16-11, B30-9 32-10, C47-13 48-11, D63-10 64-9, E79-10 80-12, F(86-8) 90-13 96-9, G107-9, H127-12 128-11, I 142-13 144-10, K159-13 160-11, L171-10 176-11, M191-11 192-10, N(206-14) 208-12, O 218-13 224-10, P238-9, Q(242-2) 255-9 256-10, R271-12 272-11, S(278-10/-) 287-10 288-9, T302-12, U—, X335-11 336-12, Y—, Z367-10 368-13, 2A 379-6 384-3, 2B 399-2 400-11, 2C 402-6/10 (414-4). Figures on cancellanda: G112- 10, N206-9, T304-11, U319-9 320-10, Y351-10 352-13, 2C 413-13.

6] THE | **LIFE** | OF | **NAPOLEON BUONAPARTE,** . . . VOL. VI. . . . 1827.

Collation: π^2 a^2 *b*1 A-2A^8 (with 16 cancels, ± A2.A3 C7 H6 I3 M6 N5 O 3 P4 P8 Q7 R8.S1 U4 X1 2A6) + eight-line errata slip. Pagination: *1* half-title, *2* quotation, *3* title-page, *4 blank*, *i* ii-vi Contents, *1* fly-title, *2 blank*, *3* 4-381 text, 381 printer's imprint, *382-384 blank*. Typography: Direction lines for A2 and C7 (pages *3* and 45) also bear cancel sheet numbers 11 and 10 respectively. Page 297 is misnumbered 299.

Figures: a ii-17, *b*—, A11-8 16-12, B31-10 32-13, C47-13 48-9, D63-10 64-12, E75-14 80-11, F95-10 96-13, G111-11 112-9, H127-2 128-4, I 142-14 144-10,

K158-9/- 160-11, L175-10 176-15, M(188-5) 191-5 192-13, N203-9 208-14, O 223-9 224-10, P227-15, Q(253-6/9) 255-10 256-11, R259-14/-, S285-15/'51'[15] 287-13, T290-5 304-9, U(311-13/14) 319-15 320-16, X335-10 336-12, Y351-12 352-14, Z366-10 368-16, 2A 377-7. Figures on cancellanda: P240-14, R272-9, 2A6-15.

7] THE | **LIFE** | OF | **NAPOLEON BUONAPARTE,** . . . VOL. VII. . . . 1827.

Collation: π^2 a^6 A-$2Q^8$ (with 18 cancels, ± A2 B8 C1 H3.H4 M7 O1 T5 Y4 2A5.2A6 2A7 2E4 2G3 2H3 2I 2 2M2 2M5) + in some copies, three-line erratum slip. Pagination: *1* half-title, *2* quotation, *3* title-page, *4 blank*, *i* ii-xi Contents, *xii blank*, *1* fly-title, *2 blank*, *3* 4-623 text, 623 printer's imprint, *624 blank*. Typography: Direction lines for A2, C1, H3 (pages *3*, 33, 117) also bear cancel sheet numbers 15, 13, 12, respectively.

Figures: a iii-18, A13-9 15-11, B—, C46-13 48-16, D63-7 64-12, E74-15 80-10, F94-16 96-10, G110-14 112-12, H126-10 128-16, I 142-7 144-12, K159-7 160-16, L174-8 176-4, M192-14, N207-15 208-11, O 222-9 224-16, P234-14 240-13, Q255-11 256-16, R271-15 272-13, S287-14 288-17, T302-9 304-16, U314-13 316-15, X330-10 336-16, Y351-12 352-9, Z366-13 368-15, 2A(381-14 382-12) 383-12 384-14, 2B 399-9 400-17, 2C 414-16 416-11, 2D 431-17 432-16, 2E 442-14 448-12, 2F 463-10 464-15, 2G(470-7) 473-12 479-13, 2H 495-10 496-16, 2I 510-6 512-7, 2K 526-14 528-11, 2L 543-10 544-16, 2M 559-12 560-15, 2N 573-13 575-11, 2 O 591-14 592-15, 2P 606-16 608-12, 2Q 621-12 622-17. Figures on cancellanda: B31-12 32-10, M190-13.

Notes: As noted in the binders' DIRECTIONS cancel leaf O1 superseded a cancel previously supplied, and is itself, it now appears, of a duplicate setting, page 210, lines 5 and 25, with or without a comma after 'army'. Apart from the 18 sheet cancels three others, A4, C3, E3 (pages 7-8, 37-38, 69-70), may appear as replacements for erroneous leaves corrected at press.

8] THE | **LIFE** | OF | **NAPOLEON BUONAPARTE,** . . . VOL. VIII. . . . 1827.

Collation: π^2 a^4 A-$2I^8$ $2K^4$ (with 9 cancels, ± A4 C3 C6 L1 L4 M7 R6 2F8 2G3) + seven-line errata slip. Pagination: *1* half-title, *2* quotation, *3* title-page, *4 blank*, *i* ii-viii Contents, *1* fly-title, *2 blank*, *3* 4-518 text, 518 printer's imprint, *519-520 blank*. Typography: Direction line for A4 (page 7) bears cancel sheet number 14 and in some copies (as noted in binders' DIRECTIONS) erroneously reads 'VOL. VII.' The recto of cancel 2G3 (page 469) is misnumbered 69.

Figures: a viii-3/-, A15-14/17 16-9, B31-12 32-16, C47-17 48-10, D63-9 64-12, E79-11 80-17, F95-14 96-16, G108-16 111-14, H127-16 128-10, I 142-9 144-17, K159-11 160-15, L174-12 176-10, M191-15, N203-16 208-14, O 218-12 224-10, P234-9 240-11, Q253-7 254-4, R(267-10/-) 271-10 272-12, S287-17 288-13,

T303-14 304-15, U315-16 320-18, X335-12 336-10, Y351-17 352-13, Z367-14 368-11, 2A 383-10 384-12, 2B 394-18 400-13, 2C 415-12 416-16, 2D 431-14/18 432-15, 2E 442-18 448-16/17, 2F 462-10, 2G 477-17 479-14, 2H 486-16 493-17, 2 I 511-11 512-9, 2K 517-15. Figure on cancellandum: 2F 464-18.

Notes: Cancel R6 is in a duplicate setting, with figure 10 present or absent on page 267.

9] THE | **LIFE** | OF | **NAPOLEON BUONAPARTE,** . . . VOL. IX. . . . 1827.

Collation: π^2 a^2 *b*1 A-X^8 Y1 a-l^8 m^6 (with one cancel, ± Y1). Pagination: *1* half-title, *2* quotation, *3* title-page, *4 blank*, *i* ii-vi Contents, *1* fly-title, *2 blank*, *3* 4-338 text, *i* fly-title, *ii blank*, *iii* iv-clxxxvii Appendix, clxxxvii printer's imprint, *clxxxviii blank*. Typography: Preliminary signatures *a* and *b* are in italic.

Figures: *a* iii-16, *b* vi-11, A15-12 16-14, B30-10 32-17, C46-13 48-11, D63-9 64-16, E68-15 78-12, F94-17 96-11, G111-9 112-17, H123-18 128-9, I 130-17 141-10, K159-12 160-17, L175-13 176-15, M186-9 192-9/18, N207-20 208-19, O 222-16 224-17, P230-14 237-10, Q255-11 256-1, R269-20 271-19, S285-17 287-7, T303-5 304-11, U315-7 320-13, X335-5 336-15/-, Y—, a xii-14 xiv-10, b xxx-7 xxxii-4, c xlii-13 xlviii-16, d liii-12 lxiii-13, e lxxviii-16 lxxx-15, f xciii-6 xcv-11, g cxi-6 cxii-7, h cxxvii-8 cxxviii-12, i cxliii-15 cxliv-13, k clvi-18 clviii-10, l clxxvi-12, m clxxxiii-4.

Notes: Cancel Y1 is in a duplicate setting, page 338 line 13 last word 'have' or 'steps'.

200Ab] Second Edition (First Edition, Second Issue): 1827

THE | **LIFE** | OF | **NAPOLEON BUONAPARTE,** | EMPEROR OF THE FRENCH. | WITH A | PRELIMINARY VIEW OF THE FRENCH | REVOLUTION. | BY THE AUTHOR OF "WAVERLEY," &c. | [*short rule*] | IN NINE VOLUMES. | [*short rule*] | VOL. I [II-IX]. | SECOND EDITION. | [*short reversed Oxford rule*] | EDINBURGH: | Printed by Ballantyne and Co. | FOR LONGMAN, REES, ORME, BROWN, & GREEN, LONDON; | AND | CADELL & CO., EDINBURGH. | [*dash*] | 1827.

Published 18 August 1827 in Edinburgh (*EEC*, but on 2 July indicating issue within a 'very few days'). £4.14.6. Paper: Post 8° (196 x 123mm uncut).

General Notes: A reissue of first edition remainders, now without half-titles and bearing newly-labeled cancel title-pages. Except as noted below all points earlier noted therefore remain the same.

Copy: E.

1] THE | **LIFE** | OF | **NAPOLEON BUONAPARTE,** . . . | VOL. I. | SECOND EDITION. . . . 1827.

Notes: The separate preliminary leaf remains as a [London] cancel, signed *, with page ii line 1 first word reading '1814' and with correction 'were'.

2] THE | **LIFE** | OF | **NAPOLEON BUONAPARTE,** . . . | VOL. II. | SECOND EDITION. . . . 1827.

Typography: Leaf Z2, though still a cancel, is now correctly numbered 355-356. Figures: In gathering D the figure is the last of those previously cited: D63-19.

3] THE | **LIFE** | OF | **NAPOLEON BUONAPARTE,** . . . | VOL. III. | SECOND EDITION. . . . 1827.

Figures: U319 is unfigured.

4] THE | **LIFE** | OF | **NAPOLEON BUONAPARTE,** . . . | VOL. IV. | SECOND EDITION. . . . 1827.

Notes: No variations observed.

5] THE | **LIFE** | OF | **NAPOLEON BUONAPARTE,** . . . | VOL. V. | SECOND EDITION. . . . 1827.

Figures: S278-10, 2C 402-11

6] THE | **LIFE** | OF | **NAPOLEON BUONAPARTE,** . . . | VOL. VI. | SECOND EDITION. . . . 1827.

Figures: Q253-6, U311-13.

7] THE | **LIFE** | OF | **NAPOLEON BUONAPARTE,** . . . | VOL. VII. | SECOND EDITION. . . . 1827.

Notes: No variations observed.

8] THE | **LIFE** | OF | **NAPOLEON BUONAPARTE,** . . . | VOL. VIII. | SECOND EDITION. . . . 1827.

Figures: A15-7, 2D 431-18, 2E 448-17.

9] THE | **LIFE** | OF | **NAPOLEON BUONAPARTE,** . . . | VOL. IX. | SECOND EDITION. . . . 1827.

Figures: b vi-17, M192-9, X336—, m clxxxiii—.

200Ac] Second Edition: 1827

THE | **LIFE** | OF | **NAPOLEON BUONAPARTE,** | EMPEROR OF THE FRENCH. | WITH A | PRELIMINARY VIEW OF THE FRENCH | REVOLUTION. | BY THE AUTHOR OF "WAVERLEY," &c. | [*short rule*] | IN NINE VOLUMES. | [*short rule*] | VOL. I [II-IX]. | SECOND EDITION. | [*short reversed Oxford rule*] | EDINBURGH: | Printed by Ballantyne and Co. | FOR LONGMAN, REES, ORME, BROWN, & GREEN, LONDON; | AND CADELL & CO., EDINBURGH. | [*dash*] | 1827.

Published: after 18 August 1827 in Edinburgh. £4.14.6. 2000 copies. Binding: blue-green boards with printed labels. Paper: Post 8° (194 x 122mm uncut).

General Notes: Through volume 3 sheet E this edition is essentially of the same setting as the first. Except for the three leaves noted below, however, all the original cancels in this early portion have now been reset and, without exception, carry volume direction lines on their rectos. This circumstance results from the fact that, when the decision was made in April 1826 (as the printer reached sheet E) to expedite the original issue by reducing the first edition from 8000 to 6000 copies, the original cancel-sheets thereafter prepared (at 6000 each) did not allow for the extra 2000 copies earlier produced, and the 28 earlier cancels therefore had to be redone. Moreover, it would appear that the gatherings in this first portion were now already sewn, a condition that necessitated (for copies still in original boards) the insertion of the cancels on rather large stubs.

After sheet E of the third volume, the volumes are reset but remain essentially as a paginal reprint with the previous cancel text now integral in this 2000-copy supplementary section. A few revisions occur here, as noted below. This final issue exceeded the expected demand, for the unsold stock three years later was sold to J. Dowding of Newgate Street, London, who then continually advertised sets at £2, less than half the original price (*Ath* 30 October 1830; *MLA* June 1831; *MC* 26 November 1831) and finally reduced even this price to £1.16.0 (*Ath* 18 August 1832).

Copies: E L O; IdU RPB T/B.

1] THE | **LIFE** | OF | **NAPOLEON BUONAPARTE,** . . . VOL. I. | SECOND EDITION. . . . 1827.

Collation and pagination: as for first edition. Figures: Generally as for first edition, but omitting the figures (T300, Y345) appearing only on original cancels.

Notes: The preliminary Advertisement may exist in the original settings of the first edition or represent, in a new setting, a combination of these readings (*i* line 1 ending 'have,' ii line 1 corrected to 'were'). Apart from the eight reset cancels (A8 L2 P8 Q3 Q7 T2 T6 Y5) two new cancels are entered in some copies, T3 and X4

L2 P8 Q3 Q7 T2 T6 Y5) two new cancels are entered in some copies, T3 and X4 (pages 293-294, 327-328), both also with direction lines and (in original bindings) on prominent stubs.

2] THE | **LIFE** | OF | **NAPOLEON BUONAPARTE,** . . . VOL. II. | SECOND EDITION. . . . 1827.

Collation and pagination: as for first edition. Figures: Again the preliminaries may be of the original setting (figure ii-14) or reset (iv-11). Figures on the old cancels (F91, O 218, S280, Z356) again are omitted on the new, but one of the new cancels (F6) bears its own figure: 91-18.

Notes: Among the reset cancels (E1 F5 F6 H1 H4 H6 K3 K7 O5 Q8 R3 S4 Z2 2A5 2B6) apparently only three, in this volume only (E1, K7, R3), are of the same setting as before, with the first two of these still exhibiting, on pages 65 and 157, their original sheet numbers 2 and 3.

3] THE | **LIFE** | OF | **NAPOLEON BUONAPARTE,** . . . VOL. III. | EDITION. . . . 1827.

Collation and pagination: as for first edition. Figures: As in first edition through sheet E, then: F89-17, G98-7 109-1, H126-13 128-9, I 143-11 144-15, K159-17 160-16, L171-12, M179-20 189-14, N202-10 208-15, O 223-15 224-14, P240- 14, Q245-2 250-18, R269-12 270-16, S279-2 288-11, T301-14 302-4, U319-9 320-12/17, X330-18 336-9, Y346-18 349-9.

Notes: Among the six reset cancels appearing through sheet E (π2 A4 B2 B6 D2 D8) there is one slight revision, leaf B2 page 20 line 5, previously reading 'prepare your future', now reads 'secure your future'. Beginning with the newly reset text portion, from sheet F (page 81) onward, the paper is of a poorer quality and, in some copies, somewhat discoloured.

Except for printing the 2000 copies sheets F-Y required to complete this third volume, Ballantyne did no further work on this job until the last, ninth volume.

4] THE | **LIFE** | OF | **NAPOLEON BUONAPARTE,** . . . VOL. IV. | SECOND EDITION. . . . 1827.

Collation and pagination: as for first edition, except no final blank leaf. Page 381 printer's imprint: [*short rule*] | EDINBURGH: | Printed by James Ballantyne & Co. Figures: A—, B32-8, C48-h, D64-*s*, E77-*s*, F96-*s*, G112-*s*/-, H128-*s*, I 144-*s*, K160-*s*, L176-*s*, M—, N208-*s*, O 221-*s*/- 224-*s*, P240-*s*, Q—, R272-*s*, S—, T304-*s*, U320-*s*, X336-*s*, Y352-*s*, Z368-13, 2A—. All *s* figures are in small fount italic.

Notes: Although the printer is still identified as Ballantyne, the peculiar press figures, not observed elsewhere in any Scott printing, must signify some other, unidentified printer.

5] THE | **LIFE** | OF | **NAPOLEON BUONAPARTE,** . . . VOL. V. | SECOND EDITION. . . . 1827.

Collation and pagination: as for first edition, except that the Contents now extend to page viii. Page 415 printer's imprint: [*short rule*] | EDINBURGH: | Printed by James Walker. Typography: In this setting, $2 is signed throughout, except for I 2 (page 131) which is missigned 2 I, and signatures B2, X2, Y2, Z2 (pages 19, 323, 339, 355) all of which are omitted. Figures: A16-2, B—, C48-1, D64-2.

Notes: The brief run of figures and odd $2 signing are due to the varying practice of printer Walker.

6] THE | **LIFE** | OF | **NAPOLEON BUONAPARTE,** . . . VOL. VI. | SECOND EDITION. . . . 1827.

Collation: As for first edition except a^4 and hence no *b*1. Pagination: As for first edition except *vii-viii blank*. Page 381 printer's imprint: [*short rule*] | Reprinted by the Heirs | of D. Willison. Typography: $2 signed except for Z2 (page 355) which is missigned 2Z. Figures: A—, B25-1 31-9.

Notes: Again another printing firm, the Willison heirs, displays a varying practice.

7] THE | **LIFE** | OF | **NAPOLEON BUONAPARTE,** . . . VOL. VII. | SECOND EDITION. . . . 1827.

Collation and pagination: as for first edition except for a^4 and b^2. Page 623 printer's imprint: [*short double rule*] | EDINBURGH: | PRINTED BY JOHN STARK. Typography: In some copies page-number 121 is misnumbered 221.
Figures: a viii-9/-, b—, A14-1 16-6, B26-3, C38-1, D58-4, E77-3 78-3, F90-1 92-6, G112-3, H120-6, I 138-1, K148-6 150-1, L170-4, M178-6 180-3, N—, O 218-3 224-6, P238-4, Q242-4, R258-5 268-2, S278-1, T290-3 300-6, U—, X334-6 336-1, Y344-4 346-3, Z362-6 368-1, 2A—, 2B 398-2 400-3, 2C 412-4, 2D—, 2E 443-1, 2F 450-6 464-3, 2G 476-5, 2H 488-1, 2 I 509-3, 2K—, 2L 530-2, 2M 546-1, 2N 566-4, 2 O 592-6, 2P 606-3, 2Q 616-4.

8] THE | **LIFE** | OF | **NAPOLEON BUONAPARTE,** . . . VOL. VIII. | SECOND EDITION. . . . 1827.

Collation and pagination: as for first edition. Page 518 printer's imprint: EDINBURGH: | PRINTED BY JAMES CLARKE & CO.

Figures: A16-3, B—, C47-2, D61-2, E78-2 80-3, F95-3 96-2/3, G100-1 111-2, 125-2 127-1, I—, K159-2, L175-3 176-1, M181-1 190-2, N207-3, O 223-2 224-3, P238-1, Q251-2, R267-2 272-2, S—, T300-3, U320-3, X—, Y338-3, Z363-1, 2A 381-2 382-1/-, 2B—, 2C 414-2, 2D—, 2E-446-1/-.

Notes: The later, unfigured portion 2F-2K (pages 449-518) may be the only part worked off by the designated printer, James Clarke, the earlier section being assigned to an small unidentified firm using figures 1, 2, 3.

9] THE | **LIFE** | OF | **NAPOLEON BUONAPARTE,** . . . VOL. IX. | SECOND EDITION. . . . 1827.

Collation and pagination: as for first edition except for new cancels H2 and X6. Page clxxxvii printer's imprint: [*short rule*] | EDINBURGH: | PRINTED BY BALLANTYNE AND CO.

Figures: *a* iv-18, *b* vi-19, A12-20, B27-14, C48-17, D59-13 64-12, E71-17 80-9, F94-17 96-14, G111-10 112-19, H126-11 128-15, I 144-17, K160-10, L175-18 176-12, M186-13 192-1, N207-10 208-19, O 223-10 224-17, P227-16 232-17, Q254-10 256-19, R271-15 272-20, S286-17/- 288-11, T301-15 303-10, U319-12 320-16, X335-19 336-15, Y—, a xv-11 xvi-15, b xix-1 xxxii-18, c xlvii-14 xlviii-17, d lxiii-10 lxiv-5, e lxxiii-8 lxxiv-3, f xcvi-4, g cxi-10 cxii-19, h cxxvii-10 cxxviii-17, i cxxxix-13 cxl-17, k clviii-18, l clxxv-12 clxxvi-14, m clxxxiii-4 clxxxv-16.

Notes: The two cancels exhibit several revisions of the first edition: H2 page 115, line 7: 1820] 1821; line 12: thirty] forty-two; page 116, line 4: nine or ten] twenty. X6 page 331, line 14: His habits . . . system.] *omit.*; line 17: life;] life;* [**additional 9-line footnote.*] In copy RPB the first leaf remains uncancelled and thus still exhibits the earlier readings.

The work here undoubtedly is by Ballantyne's large firm, again employing, as usual, figures ranging up to 18, 19, 20.

REPRINTS

FRANCE

PARIS: Didot and Galignani

[~] The Life of Napoleon Buonaparte. 1827. Nine volumes. (Collection of Modern English Authors: *see* 292R.10-18.)

[~] The Life of Napoleon Buonaparte. 1828. One volume. (Collection of Modern English Authors: *see* 294R.1.)

PARIS: Galignani

[~] The Life of Napoleon Bonaparte. 1827. One volume. (*see* 294R[3].6.)

200Ra] PARIS: Treuttel and Würtz 1827

The Life of Napoleon Buonaparte, Emperor of the French, With a Preliminary View of the French Revolution, By Sir Walter Scott. . . . Paris Treuttel and Würtz, Rue de Bourbon, No 17. Strasburg, Rue des Serruriers. 1827. Nine volumes. Pages 1: *1- 4*, *i* ii-iv, *1* 2-383; 2: *i-iv*, *1* 2-'339'[439]; 3: *i-iv*, *1* 2-416; 4: *i-iv*, *1* 2-446; 5: *i-iv*, *1* 2-496; 6: *i-iv*, *1* 2-407; 7: *i-iv*, *1*

2-708; 8: *i-iv*, *1* 2-635; 9: *i-iv*, *1* 2-436. Notes: In volume 1 frontispiece portrait of Napoleon, engraved by J. W. Cook. Titles for vols 2-9 read 'French;'. Copies: P P(vols 1-3).

GERMANY

200Rb] STUTTGART: Brodhagen 1827-1829
[The Life of Napoleon Buonaparte. . . . Stuttgart: Brodhagen, 1827-1829. 35 volumes.] Copy: Not seen. References: GDS 25 and 132.

STUTTGART: Franckh
[~] The Life of Napoleon Buonaparte. 1827. (Collection of the Master-Pieces of the Most Celebrated Ancient and Modern English Authors: *see* 301R.1-6.)

ZWICKAU: Schumann
[~] The Life of Napoleon Buonaparte, Emperor of the French. 1827-1828. (Pocket Library of English Classics: *see* 302R.150-167.)

UNITED STATES

200Rc] EXETER: Williams 1827-1834
The Life of Napoleon Buonaparte, Emperor of the French. With a Preliminary View of the French Revolution. By the Author of "Waverley," &c. . . . Exeter: J. & B. Williams. 1827. Two volumes. Pages 1: *i-iii* 'vi'[iv] *v* vi-xvi, *19* 20-494; 2: *i-iii* iv-xii, *13* 14-414, *i* ii-lxiv. Notes: In two-column format except for appendices in volume 2. Volume 1 frontispiece portrait of Napoleon, engraved by Thos. Kelly and imprinted Exeter, J. & B. Williams, 1827. Copies: P; IdU MH MWA(2). Reissued, with all retaining the '1827 portrait', 1828 (E P; CtY MH PU ViU[vol. 1]); 1832 (MWA); 1834 (MWA).

200Rd] NEW YORK: Harper 1827-1828
The Life of Napoleon Buonaparte, . . . By the Author of "Waverley," &c. . . . New-York: Printed and Published by J. & J. Harper. No. 82 Cliff-Street. 1827. Three volumes. Pages 1: *i-iii* iv *ix* x-xv *xvi*, *17* 18-516; 2: *i-iii* iv-viii, *9* 10-399; 3: *i-iii* iv-viii, *9* 10-368, *i* ii-lxix. Notes: With volume 1 portrait frontispiece. With the author's Advertisement reset (page iv first word 'On'), but otherwise printed from the 1827 Philadelphia, Carey, Lea & Carey plates (*see* 200Rf). Copies: MH PU ViU(vol.1). Reissued 1828 (1) with spine label reading in part 'Harper's Corrected Edition', apparently with the Carey plates corrected (E; MWA[vol.1]); (2) in printed boards reading: 'Alison's History of Europe 1815' with Harper imprint (MH).

200Re] PHILADELPHIA: Ayres 1827
The Life of Napoleon Buonaparte, . . . By the Author of "Waverley," &c. . . . Philadelphia: J. P. Ayres,—No. 63, S. Fifth Street. 1827. Three volumes. A variant issue of the 1827, Philadelphia, Carey, Lea & Carey edition (next entry), with both Advertisements, page iv of the setting first word reading 'has'. Copy: ViU(vol.1).

200Rf] PHILADELPHIA: Carey, Lea & Carey 1827
The Life of Napoleon Buonaparte, . . . By the Author of "Waverley," &c. . . . Philadelphia: Carey, Lea & Carey.—Chesnut-Street. Stereotyped by J. Howe. 1827. Three volumes. Pages 1: *i-iii* iv, *ix* x-xv *xvi*, *17* 18-516; 2: *i-iii* iv-viii, *9* 10-399; 3: *i-iii* iv-viii, *9* 10-368, *i* ii-lxix *lxx*, *i*-ii. Notes: Title-page of the first volume is preceded by an engraved frontispiece portrait of Napoleon and, in some copies, by a publisher's 'Advertisement' noting an irregularity in the receipt of copy. The author's own 'Advertisement', on a single leaf, is in a multiple setting, with first word page iv reading 'has', 'been', or 'On'. As on some previous occasions this publisher was setting his edition from uncorrected proofs, but the admitted irregularity here resulted in late arriving sections not filling the space allowed (volume 1 after page 134 two page numbers omitted), in three instances extending much beyond the allowed space (volume 1.260, *261-271 *272*; volume 2.136, *137-147 *148*; volume 2.*256-262: all with starred signatures and/or page numbers duplicating the numbers in sections which follow) and in one producing further disorder (volume 1.383-391 *392*: an extra chapter XXVII, similarly marked).

As noted above (200Aa) the earlier text was extracted in Carey's own Philadelphia journal, beginning 1 March 1827, but 'the whole of the Life' was not announced as received until 7 August and final issue thus delayed until 21 August (*NG*). Volume 3 concludes with an extensive list of errata followed by a note: 'The publishers of this edition think it proper to state, that all of the above errata were in the English edition, from which this was printed, but they have been subsequently corrected, either by lists of errata, or by cancelling the pages in which they occur.' Evidently, then, the original lists and cancels arrived only after the Philadelphia issue, in some 4083 copies, had been printed.

Copies: BCL E; CtY(2) MWA NNU-W NNU-W(vol.2) PHi PPL(2) RPB T/B TxU ViU. Reference: Kaser 80.

DERIVATIVES

GREAT BRITAIN

200Da] LONDON: Murray 1829
The History of Napoleon Buonaparte. . . . London: John Murray, Albemarle Street. MDCCCXXIX. Two volumes. Pages 1: *i-iii* iv-vii *viii*, *1* 2-303 *304*; 2: *i-iii* iv-ix *x*, *1* 2-379 *380*. Notes: Volumes I-II of 'The Family Library'. When J. G. Lockhart expressed some misgivings about starting Murray's new 'Family' series with this work, Scott in his letter of 30 October 1828 urged him to produce 'an epitome of the Life of Boney' based upon his own 'nine thick volumes'. Copy: T/B. Reference: *Letters*, xi.28.

UNITED STATES

200Db] NEW YORK: Collins & Hannay 1827
The Life of Napoleon Buonaparte, . . . By the Author of "Waverley," &c. Abridged by an American Gentleman. . . . Three Volumes in One. New-York: Published by Collins & Hannay. 1827. Pages: *i-iii*, *1* 2-381. Notes: With frontispiece portrait of Napoleon. Evidently abstracted from the Philadelphia, Carey, Lea & Carey edition (200Rf). The 'Editor's Advertisement' is dated from Philadelphia, September 1827. Copies: E L; MWA T/B.

ESSAY ON THE SUPERNATURAL IN FICTION: HOFFMANN

201A] First Printing: 1827

'ART. II.—*On the Supernatural in Fictitious Composition; and particularly on the Works of* Ernest Theodore William Hoffmann.', pages 60-98, *in*:

The Foreign Quarterly Review. [July, 1827. No. 1, volume 1 imprint:] London: Treuttel and Würtz, Treuttel, Jun. and Richter, Soho Square. 1827.

Published 27 July 1827 in London (*MC*); issued 2 August in Edinburgh (*EEC*). 7s.6d.

Notes: A later 'Notice to Correspondents' in Volume 2 of the *Review* (February 1828, pages *352* 353-354: *see* 211A), doubtless written by Scott himself, contraverts much of the legend cited in this review concerning one 'Captain M[acpherson]'.

Copies: BCL L O; NjP PU(2).

References: *Journal*, page 451; Thomson, page 35. (Magnum Opus Edition 1835: *The Miscellaneous Prose Works*, xviii.270- 332 as 'Novels of Ernest Theodore Hoffmann.')

LETTER ON DAVID WILKIE

202A] First Edition: 1827

[*caption title*] | LETTER | FROM | SIR WALTER SCOTT TO SIR ADAM FERGUSON, | DESCRIPTIVE OF A PICTURE PAINTED BY DAVID WILKIE, ESQ. R.A. | EXHIBITED AT THE ROYAL ACADEMY, 1818. | [*short Oxford rule*].

Printed ca. August 1827. Binding: issued unbound. Watermarks: J WHATMAN | 1827.

Collation: Post 4° in 2s (260 x 205mm cut). Pagination: *1* caption title, *1* 2-3 text of letter, *4 blank*. Figures: none.

Notes: The salutation is to 'My Dear Adam,' and the close reads 'Yours affectionately, Walter Scott. Abbotsford, 2nd August, 1827.' This letter, though uncollected, is highly evocative—particularly as it relates to the epitaph for the dog Maida—and, as noted below, is somewhat complicated textually. Other comments follow on from an earlier discussion of 7 March 1827 printed in *Letters*, x.166-170.

The Cambridge copy is designated #17 in a bound portfolio of ephemeral pieces gathered by Robert Balmanno, Secretary of the Incorporated Artists' Fund: the 'Gentleman' referred to in the first line of the letter, who in the 'List of Contents' states that this description of the Wilkie picture was provided at Balmanno's request.

The engraving, once enclosed in the volume, is now lacking. This letter was reprinted in full in the *London Weekly Review*, 13 October, and in the *Morning Chronicle,* 15 October 1827. The Yale exemplar has the original Scott letter to Balmanno, postmarked from Melrose 3 August 1827, sending heavily annotated proofs (in a different fount) for the published version and galley proofs (with a single manuscript revision) for the *Morning Chronicle* reprint.

Copies: C; CtY MH. Reference: (Magnum Opus Edition: Not reprinted.)

REPRINT

GREAT BRITAIN

202R] LONDON: Pickering 1828
'Letter from Sir Walter Scott', pages *33* 34-38 *in*: The Bijou; or Annual of Literature and the Arts. London William Pickering, Chancery Lane. 1828. Notes: Facing page *33* is a steel engraving of the family portrait in question, painted by David Wilkie, engraved by W. H. Worthington. The editor W.F., pages *v*-vi, expresses his appreciation to Scott for the letter and family portrait which are 'so pleasing a memorial of a writer to whose merits England, Europe, nay, the whole civilized world, has offered its homage and its praise.' References to Balmanno in the original edition are here represented by * * *. *The Bijou* is dedicated to Mrs John Gibson Lockhart (Scott's daughter Sophia), who is included in the portrait made before her marriage. This volume was issued (1) with the above imprint or (2) for American readers with an imprint reading: 'London William Pickering. Chancery Lane. & Thomas Wardle, Philadelphia. 1828.' Copies: (1) BCL O; InU(2) NN(Berg); (2) MWA.

LETTER ON PARK'S EMPLOYMENT

203A] First Printing: 1827

'ORIGINAL LETTER OF SIR WALTER SCOTT.', pages 220-221 *in*:

London Weekly Review and Journal of Literature and the Fine Arts. No. 14. Saturday, September 8, 1827. Price 8d. London: Printed for the Proprietor, and Published early every Saturday, by F. C. Westley, Bookseller, 159, (near Somerset House,) Strand. . . .

Published 8 September 1827 in London.

Notes: This uncollected letter to Archibald Park, dated from Edinburgh 17 February 1816, advises him on the possibility of a position either at Dunbar or on the Isle of Mull. The editor now publishes it 'because it does credit to Sir Walter Scott's humanity and condescension.'

Copy: LU.

LETTER TO GENERAL GOURGAUD

204A] First Printing: 1827

'LIFE OF NAPOLEON. TO THE EDITOR OF THE WEEKLY JOURNAL.', page 301 *in*:

The Edinburgh Weekly Journal. VOL. XXX. No. 1553.] WEDNESDAY, SEPTEMBER 19, 1827. [Price Sevenpence.] Printed by Ballantyne and Company, for the Proprietors.

Published 19 September 1827 in Edinburgh.

Notes: Scott's letter (dated from Abbotsford 14 September 1827) begins: 'Sir, I observed in the London papers which I received yesterday, a letter from General Gourgaud, which I beg you will have the goodness to reprint, with this communication and the papers accompanying it.' Accordingly the Gourgaud letter, dated 28 August, is reprinted on page 299, and Scott's supporting documents entered immediately following his own rejoinder.

Copies: EP L.

Reference: (Magnum Opus Edition: Not reprinted, but quoted in Lockhart ix.147-152.)

REVIEW OF ROBERT MONTEATH

205A] First Printing: 1827

'ART. VIII.—*The Forester's Guide and Profitable Planter.* By Robert Monteath.', pages 558-600, *in*:

The Quarterly Review. [October, 1827. No.72, volume 36 imprint:] London: John Murray, Albemarle Street. 1827.

Published 18 October 1827 in London (*MC*); issued 27 October in Edinburgh (*EEC*).

Copies: BCL O; PPL.

References: Thomson, page 48. (Magnum Opus Edition 1836: *The Miscellaneous Prose Works*, xxi.*1* 2-76 as 'On Planting Wastelands'.)

CHRONICLES OF THE CANONGATE
[First Series]
THE HIGHLAND WIDOW, THE TWO DROVERS, and THE SURGEON'S DAUGHTER

206Aa] First Edition: 1827

CHRONICLES | OF | **THE CANONGATE;** | BY | THE AUTHOR OF "WAVERLEY," &c. | [*short rule*] | [*one-line motto of the Canongate Arms*] | [*short rule*] | IN TWO VOLUMES. | VOL. I [II]. | [*short reversed Oxford rule*] | EDINBURGH: | PRINTED FOR CADELL AND CO., EDINBURGH; | AND SIMPKIN AND MARSHALL, LONDON. | [*dash*] | 1827.

Published concurrently 5 November 1827 in London (*MC*, but announced 2 October for 'Thursday, 1st November'); 8 November in Edinburgh (*EEC*, but publication previously announced 6 October 'on Friday 2nd Nov'). £1.1.0. Scott's Introduction was extracted in *EEC* 1 November. Binding: drab, blue, or grey boards with printed labels; one copy (Van Antwerp[1] 23) noted in wrappers with labels. Paper: Post 8° (198 x 127mm uncut). Watermarks: *none*. Typography: Printer's imprints read: (1) EDINBURGH: | PRINTED BY BALLANTYNE AND CO.; (2) [*short rule*] | EDINBURGH: | PRINTED BY BALLANTYNE AND CO. ['& CO.' vol. 2].

General Notes: According to established practice, beginning with *Kenilworth* (*see* 149Aa), on 29 November 1827, shortly after the publication of this novel, some 5100 words (volume 1, part of chapter 3 (pages 44-48) and the whole of volume 2, chapter 7 of this Edinburgh edition), were extracted in the Philadelphia *National Gazette*, these deriving from proofs early shipped for the Carey & Lea edition (206Re). The second extract, toward the end of the novel, would indicate that, on this particular occasion, the Philadelphia firm already possessed the entire set of text proofs. Since Scott's previous Edinburgh publisher, Archibald Constable, a bankrupt, had died earlier in the year, Carey paid the author £50 directly for this advance copy.

Two weeks before issue the *London Weekly Review* also began to print, now from the final text, two passages, the first 20 October (pages *305* 306-310) representing the whole of 'The Two Drovers', the second 3 November (pages 340-343) providing a brief extract from 'The Surgeon's Daughter.' Though both of these purportedly came 'by the circuitous route of Paris', the page references given (i.293-351 and ii.217-226 respectively) pertain only to the Edinburgh edition. Only 'The Two Drovers' was extracted in an anthology, 372[1]E.5.

A letter of transmittal dated by Scott 23 June 1827, printed in Van Antwerp(1) 22, and originally inserted by the Duchess of St Albans (formerly Harriot Coutts) in her copy of this novel, is four or five months earlier than Scott's dated Introduction or the established date of publication, and thus must be misplaced. Probably it refers to Scott's *Life of Napoleon,* the work which had taken 'a great deal of my time', ordered to be sent to her on the following day, and officially issued five days later on 28 June.

Presentation copy: NNP('Her Grace the Duchess of St. Albans, from the Author'). Other copies: BCL E(4) LVA(Dyce) O(2); IdU InU(2) T/B TxU.

References: *Letters*, x.230-232; Church 549; Madison, page 11; Randall, pages 52-54; Sterling 741; Thomson, pages 21, 34, 69, 74; Van Antwerp(1) 22, 23; Worthington 20. (Magnum Opus Edition 1832: *Waverley Novels*, ['The Highland Widow'] xli.*i-iii* iv-xxxiv, *1-3* 4-237, ['The Two Drovers'] xli.238-288, ['The Surgeon's Daughter'] xlviii.*147-149* 150-430.)

1] **CHRONICLES** | OF | **THE CANONGATE;** . . . VOL. I. . . . 1827.

Collation: π^2 a^8 b^4 c^2 A-M^8 N^8(±N6) O-Y^8. Pagination: *i* half-title, *ii blank*, *iii* title-page, *iv* printer's imprint(1), *i* ii-xxviii Introduction, signed Walter Scott, Abbotsford, 1 October 1827, *1* 2-351 text, 351 printer's imprint(2), *352 blank*.
Figures: a xiv-1 xvi-4, b xxiv-1, c—, A2-12 16-11, B32-6, C48-2, D64-3, E80-5, F89-6, G112-7, H128-5, I 144-2, K160-7, L176-6, M185-8, N204-13/- 208-5, O224-2, P238-19 240-9/15, Q243-7 256-5, R271-6 272-10, S286-19 288-13, T298-9 304-11, U319-12 320-14, X334-10 336-15, Y346-19 349-13.

Notes: In this issue page 31 lines 14/15 read, nonsensically, 'linea-/ments to'. The heading page 111, said to be corrected at press to 'CHAPTER VI.' in all issues seen remains uncorrected as 'CHAPTER VII.' The original N6 text, as exemplified in the Philadelphia Carey & Lea edition, page 204, line 15 reads 'mother—but I can remember, they'; the revised text 'mother—well I remember her words!—They'. Leaf N6 revised may be integral, or a cancel in a duplicate setting (with or without figure 13 on page 204).

In his Introduction, page xxvii, Scott observes that this work 'was meditated, and in part printed, long before the avowal of the novels took place', a remark which may account for the later resetting of sheets B-O in the second issue. Apart from various commentary, this volume consists of two chronicles, 'The Highland Widow' (pages 146-287) and 'The Two Drovers' (pages 293-351).

2] **CHRONICLES** | OF | **THE CANONGATE;** . . . VOL. II. . . . 1827.

Collation: π^2 A-D^8 E^8(±E1) F-$2A^8$. Pagination: *i* half-title, *ii blank*, *iii* title-page, *iv* printer's imprint(1), *1* 2-374 text, 374 printer's imprint(2), *1-2* 3-8 Cadell and Co. catalogue, *9-10 blank*.

Figures: A15-10 16-13, B31-9 32-10, C47-5 48-12, D62-4 64-6, E78-2 80-1, F93-12 94-10, G111-9 112-7, H123-11 128-10, I 143-1 144-2, K158-8 160-6, L163-11 176-10, M191-7 192-9, N202-5 208-4, O 223-3 224-12, P228-12 235-7, Q253-11

255-7, R265-11 267-4, S287-7 288-3, T297-2 303-6, U319-10 320-6, X334-5 336-8, Y346-12 352-11, Z361-6 366-3/-, 2A 370-10 '6'[380]-5.
Notes: Both in this and in the later issues, where the volume is of a common setting, there may be some cancellation involving one or two leaves:

D8(pages 63-64)	63.15	figure	E1(pages 65-66)
1) cancellandum	*wretch*	64-6	integral or cancellans
2) cancellans	*retch*	63-15	integral or conjugate cancellans with leaf D8

The original E1 text, as exemplified in the Philadelphia, Carey & Lea edition, page 65, lines 7-9 read 'Zilia de Monçada heard the question; and'; the revised text reads 'Zilia de Monçada heard the question, (which, being addressed to the father, Grey had inconsiderately uttered in French,) and'. The E1 revised text, when integral, is of a single setting (page 66 line 16 5th word 'care'), but as a cancel is of a duplicate setting ('care' or 'charge'), either of which may appear separately with D8 state (1) or conjugate with D8 state (2).

Again after some early and late commentary the story proceeds, pages 29-368, with the third chronicle, 'The Surgeon's Daughter'.

206Ab] Second Edition, First Issue: 1827

CHRONICLES | OF | **THE CANONGATE;** . . . IN TWO VOLUMES. | VOL. I [II]. . . . 1827.

Collation and pagination as for the first edition. Notes: Though not originally designated as a 'second edition', the major part of the first volume has been reset, as the figures cited below for sheets B-O would indicate. In the reset portion the first observed revision occurs at page 31, lines 14/15, now reading 'lineage / to'. Nonetheless, this issue must have been prepared immediately after the first, for leaf N6 is still subject to cancellation, as earlier described.

Variant figures: B30-1 32-5, C47-3 48-6, D62-9 64-5, E77-10 78-12, F95-2 96-8, G109-1/- 111-9, H127-10 128-7, I 141-12 142-9, K159-11 160-4, L175-9 176-7, M185-10 191-8, N202-10 208-1, O 219-4 224-5, P238-19 &c. as in previous issue.

Copies: BCL BCL* L(2) LU O(21); CtY DLC InU(2) MH(2) MH+(vol.2) NN(2) NNU-W RPB T/B TxU(2).
*With 4-page Longman catalogue September 1827.
+Vol. 2 interleaved with Scott's corrections and revisions for the Magnum Opus. Evidently this volume was originally joined with the one described in the next entry.

206Ac] Second Edition, Second Issue: 1828

CHRONICLES | OF | **THE CANONGATE;** . . . VOL. I [II]. | SECOND EDITION. . . . 1828.

Issued 15 April 1828 in London (*Ath*). £1.1.0. Binding: blue-green cloth with printed labels.

Notes: A further issue with later 'edition' reference and date. In volume 1 the P figure is of the later variant (240-15); volume 2 D8 is still a cancellandum, E1 a separate cancellans.

Copies: BCL; NN+(Berg: vol.1).
+Vol.1 interleaved with Scott's corrections and revisions for the Magnum Opus. For volume 2 see preceding entry.

REPRINTS

FRANCE

PARIS: Baudry, Barrois [and others]
[~] Chronicles of the Canongate. The Highland Widow. . . . 1832. (Collection of Ancient and Modern British Novels and Romances: *see* 288R.36.)

PARIS: Didot and Galignani
[~] Chronicles of the Canongate. 1827. (Collection of Modern English Authors: *see* 291R.63-64.)

PARIS: Galignani
[~] Chronicles of the Canongate [with two other titles]. 1830. One volume. (*see* 294R[3].7.)

PARIS: Glashin, Robertson [and others]
[~] Chronicles of the Canongate. 1827. (The Complete Works of Sir Walter Scott, Bart.: *see* 295R.8-9.)

GERMANY

206Ra] BERLIN: Schlesinger 1828
[Chronicles of the Canongate. . . . Berlin, Printed for Adolph Martin Schlesinger. 1828.]
Copy reported at Herzog-August-Bibliothek, Wolfenbuettel. Reference: GDS 132, page 337.

ZWICKAU: Schumann
[~] Chronicles of the Canongate . . . 1828. (Pocket Library of English Classics: *see* 302R.168-170.)

UNITED STATES

206Rb] BOSTON: Parker 1828-1829
Chronicles of the Canongate; By the Author of "Waverley, Ivanhoe," &c.&c. . . . Boston: Samuel H. Parker, No. 164, Washington-Street. 1828. Pages: *1-3* 4-346. Copy: MWA. Notes: (Also reissued 1828 in Novels Tales and Romances: *see* 305R20).

[~] Chronicles of the Canongate. 1828, 1829. (Waverley Novels: *see* 306R.39-40).

206Rc] NEW YORK: Collins and Hannay, &c. 1827
Chronicles of the Canongate; By the Author of "Waverley," &c. . . . New-York: Printed by J. & J. Harper, for Collins and Hannay, Collins and Co., and G. and C. Carvill,—Philadelphia, Carey, Lea and Carey, R. H. Small, and Towar and Hogan,—Boston, Richardson and Lord, and Hilliard, Gray, and Co. 1827. Two volumes. Pages 1: *1-2*, *i* ii-xii, *13* 14-259; 2: [*1-2*] *3-5* 6-242. A variant issue of the Carey edition (*see* 206Re). Copies: E; T/B.

206Rd] NEW YORK: Duyckinck, Collins and Hannay [and others] 1827
Chronicles of the Canongate; By the Author of "Waverley," &c. . . . New-York: Printed by J. & J. Harper, for E. Duyckinck, Collins and Hannay, Collins and Co., G. and C. Carvill, E. Bliss, O. A. Roorbach, and W. Burgiss;—and John Grigg, Philadelphia. 1827. Two volumes. Pages 1: *1-4*, *i* ii-xii, *13* 14-259; 2: *1-5* 6-242. Notes: In some copies the third line on title-page ends with a colon. A variant issue of the Carey edition (*see* next entry). Copies: O; CtY InU MH MWA PPL.

206Re] PHILADELPHIA: Carey, Lea & Carey 1827
Chronicles of the Canongate; By the Author of "Waverley," &c. . . . Philadelphia Carey, Lea & Carey—Chesnut Street. 1827. Two volumes. Pages 1: *1-4*, *i* ii-xii, *13* 14-259; 2:*1-5* 6-242. Notes: The first American edition, set from Edinburgh proofs, a portion of the text extracted in the *National Gazette* 29 November 1827 (*see* 206Aa), the 'Introduction' later received then extracted 13 December, and the book issued 15 December (*NG*) in 4125 copies. Title-pages were altered for three variant issues recorded as 206Rc, Rd, Rg, and the edition itself closely reprinted in another 1827 edition (Rf). Copies: E L; CtY(vol.2) MH MWA NN NNU-W PPL RPB T/B ViU. References: Kaser 105; Randall, pages 52-54.

206Rf] PHILADELPHIA: Clarke 1827
Chronicles of the Canongate; By the Author of "Waverley," &c. . . . Philadelphia: Published by L. B. Clarke, No.'s 32 & 33 Arcade, and at No. 4 South Front Street. 1827. Two volumes. Pages 1: *1-4*, *i* ii-xii, *13* 14-259; 2: *1-5* 6-242. Notes: This is of a different setting from the Philadelphia, Carey, Lea & Carey issue: *see* preceding entry. Paper spine labels read: 'Arcade Edition'. Title-page in volume 2 has 'Waverly'(!) spelled thus and the imprint reads: 'Philadelphia. L. B. Clarke, Arcade. 1827'. Copies: T/B ViU.

206Rg] PHILADELPHIA: Crissy 1827
Chronicles of the Canongate; By the Author of "Waverley," &c. . . . Philadelphia: J. Crissy, No. 14, S. Seventh Street. 1827. Two volumes. Pages 1: *1-4*, *i* ii-xii, *13* 14-259; 2: *1-5* 6-242. A variant issue of the Carey edition (*see* 206Re). Copies: IdU NN T/B (vol.1).

DERIVATIVES

GREAT BRITAIN

206D] GLASGOW: Booksellers 1828
Stories of The Two Drovers, and Countess of Exeter. Glasgow: Printed for the Booksellers. [1828?] Pages: *1-3* 4-24, Notes: Chapbook. 'The Two Drovers' fills pages *3*-23. At the foot of the title-page frame is '38', possibly alluding to a later date of issue. Copy: O(J.Johnson).

LONDON: Duncombe
[~] The Two Drovers. A Domestic Legendary Melo-Drama. [1828]. (Duncombe's Edition of the British Theatre: *see* 331D.75.)

THE BONNETS OF BONNIE DUNDEE

207A] First Printing: 1828[1827]

'THE BONNETS OF BONNIE DUNDEE' (first words: 'To the Lords of Convention 'twas Clavers who spoke,'; second line 'crown go down'), pages 29-33, *in*:

The Christmas Box. An Annual Present for Children. Edited by T. Crofton Croker, Esq. F.S.A. . . . London: William Harrison Ainsworth, Old Bond Street. M DCCC XXVIII.

Published 19 November 1827 in London (*Ath*). Notes: This poem is preceded by several pages of introduction and, for the juvenile reader, has twenty helpful footnotes also by the Editor. Scott later much revised the wording and included the poem, without title, in *Doom of Devorgoil*: the second line there reading 'crown shall fall'.

On half-title verso this anthology has the following note: 'The Publisher begs to inform the Composers of Music and Music-sellers, that Mr. James Power, of the Strand, Music-seller, is the only person authorized by him to publish *The Bonnets of Bonnie Dundee*, by Sir Walter Scott.' No such version is recorded. This note is the only indication given that Scott is the author of the poem.

Copies: E O; DLC.

References: Ruff 192. (Magnum Opus Edition 1834: *The Poetical Works*, xii.194-197 titled 'Song' to the air 'The Bonnets of Bonny Dundee.' and immediately documented by Lockhart with an 800-word footnote.)

EXTRACTS IN ANTHOLOGIES

207E] Under its original title of 'The Bonnets of Bonnie Dundee' the poem was extracted in two anthologies, 369[3]E.15 and 369[4]E.15; under other titles supplied by Thomson, in two more, 405(2)[3]E.6 and 405(3)[3]E.1

TALES OF A GRANDFATHER
[First Series]

I am persuaded both children and the lower class of readers hate books which are written *down* to their capacity and love those that are more composed for their elders and betters. I will make if possible a book that a child will understand yet a man will feel some temptation to peruse should he chance to take it up. It will require however a simplicity of style not quite my own. (24 May 1827, *Journal*, pages 308-309.)

208Aa] First Edition: 1828[1827]

TALES | OF | **A GRANDFATHER;** | BEING | **STORIES** | TAKEN FROM | **SCOTTISH HISTORY.** | HUMBLY INSCRIBED | TO | HUGH LITTLEJOHN, Esq. | IN THREE VOLS. | VOL. I [II-III]. | [*short reversed Oxford rule*] | PRINTED FOR CADELL AND CO. EDINBURGH; | SIMPKIN AND MARSHALL, LONDON; AND | JOHN CUMMING, DUBLIN. | [*dash*] | 1828.

Published 15 December 1827 in Edinburgh (*EEC*); 29 December in London (*MC*). 10s.6d. Binding: Half blue, green or maroon roan and marbled boards. Paper: Royal 18° in sixes (141 x 90 cut; machine-wove?). Watermarks: *none*. Illustrations: Described below are the engraved frontispieces and titles, both preceding the printed titles. Typography: Printer's imprints read: (1) EDINBURGH: | PRINTED BY BALLANTYNE AND CO.; (2) [*short rule*] | EDINBURGH: | PRINTED BY BALLANTYNE & CO. ['AND CO.' vol. 2]

General Typography: To indicate full-sheet order in this part-sheet 18° imposition, the first part of every three-section sheet, beginning with part-sheet D, is with few exceptions numbered successively to the right of the signature, thus: (page 37) D 2; (page 73) G 3; and so on every 18 leaves (36 pages). Hence, within each three-gathering sequence (marked here and below with a semicolon), no more than two press-figures appear, one for each forme. Though these figures remain constant throughout, in a few copies (including the set Scott presented to a godson four days after publication) the first signature in each full sheet (A,D,G,K,N,Q,T) also bears a dagger †, probably signifying an immediate reimpression before issue. At the time this godson of Scott's was one of five, as identified by Corson, and perhaps all entitled to copies. On 21 December Scott facetiously proposed that he 'might raise a corps of light infantry out of my spiritual clanship.'

General Notes: On 1 December, two weeks before issue, the Philadelphia *National Gazette* announced that the firm of Carey, Lea & Carey had 'just received a considerable part' of this work, but for this and the later Grandfather *Tales* offered no extracts, doubtless misconceiving these to be too juvenile for its more mature readers. In the anthologies this first tale was extracted only once, *see* 372[1]E.9.

Presentation copy: MH('Walter Scott Hughes with his godffectionate[!] godfathers Blessing' [vols 2-3 dated 19 December 1827]). Other copies: BCL E(2) HS (vols.1,3) O(4); CtY(vol.1) IdU NNU-W T/B(signed January 1828) TxU(vol.3).

References: *Letters*, x.142-143 as further noted by Corson(2), page 273; Thomson, page 70; Van Antwerp(1) 27. (Magnum Opus Edition 1836: *The Miscellaneous Prose Works*, xxii-xxiii.*1* 2-209.)

1] **TALES** | OF | **A GRANDFATHER;** . . . VOL. I. . . . 1828.

Collation: $\pi1$ $2\pi^2$ A-U^6. Pagination: [*frontispiece, engraved title*], *1* title-page, *2* printer's imprint(1), *i*-ii Preface, dated from Abbotsford 10 October 1827, *iii*-iv Contents (for ten chapters), *1* fly-title, *2 blank*, *3* 4-6 Dedication. To Hugh Littlejohn, Esq., *7* 8-239 text, 239 printer's imprint(2), *240 blank*. Illustrations: Engraved frontispiece drawn by W. Allan, engraved on steel by J. Horsburgh, with caption 'Hugh Littlejohn at His Grandfather's Gate'; title vignette by same illustrators. Typography: The printed title is in a triplicate setting, one with a semi-colon at the end of the third line and (1) a period after VOL.', (2) no period after 'VOL', the third (3) with a comma at the end of the third line and no period after 'VOL'. No sheet-numbers appear for signatures D and Q (pages 37, 181).

Figures: A12-5, B20-7; E56-3/- 60-8; G80-1 84-6; L128-4 132-7; N152-8, O 168-2; R203-7 204-3; T—, U—.

2] **TALES** | OF | **A GRANDFATHER;** . . . VOL. II. . . . 1828.

Collation: $\pi1$ $2\pi^2$ A-U^6 *X*1. Pagination: [*frontispiece, engraved title*], *1* title-page, *2* printer's imprint(1), *i* ii-iii Contents (for 11 chapters), *iv blank*, *1* fly-title, *2 blank*, *3* 4-241 text, 241 printer's imprint(2), *242 blank*. Illustrations: Engraved frontispiece drawn by H. Corbould, engraved on steel by W. H. Lizars, with caption 'A Scottish Chief shewing John de Vinne the English Army defiling through a Narrow Pass'; title vignette drawn and engraved on steel by W. H. Lizars. Typography: This title is in a duplicate setting, with the short Oxford rule either reversed or in normal order. Page 163 line 11 date 1482 is misprinted 1582. Signature T2 (page 221) is missigned 2T.

Figures: C35-3 36-5; F62-2 72-4; I 107-6 108-7; L122-8, M144-7; P179-7 180-4; Q191-2 192-8; T218-5 228-6; U240-3.

3] **TALES** | OF | **A GRANDFATHER;** . . . VOL. III. . . . 1828.

Collation: π1 2π² A-2C⁶ 2D⁴. Pagination: [*frontispiece, engraved title*], *1* title-page, *2* printer's imprint(1), *i* ii-iii Contents (for 9 chapters), *iv blank*, *1* fly-title, *2 blank*, *3* 4-320 text, 320 printer's imprint(2). Illustrations: Engraved frontispiece drawn and engraved on steel by W. H. Lizars, with caption 'Meeting of the Bishops of Dunkeld and Glasgow' and quotation beginning '"Ha! my Lord! . . ."'; title vignette by the same illustrator. Typography: This title also is in a duplicate setting, with the short Oxford rule either reversed or in normal order.

Figures: C35-8 36-7; D44-4, E60-5; G79-6, I 107-1; L131-4/5/- 132-2/-; P179-7 180-1; R203-4, S216-5; X251-7 252-2; Y270-6 272-8; 2B 300-1, 2D 314-3.

208Ab] Second Edition, First Issue: 1828

TALES | OF | **A GRANDFATHER;** | BEING | **STORIES** | TAKEN FROM | **SCOTTISH HISTORY.** | HUMBLY INSCRIBED | TO | HUGH LITTLEJOHN, ESQ. | IN THREE VOLS. | VOL. I [II-III]. | SECOND EDITION. | [*short rule*] | PRINTED FOR CADELL AND CO. EDINBURGH; | SIMPKIN AND MARSHALL, LONDON; AND | JOHN CUMMING, DUBLIN. | [*dash*] | 1828.

Issued 9 April 1828 in London (*MC*). 10s.6d. Binding: Half green or maroon roan and marbled boards. Paper: Royal 18° in sixes (140 x 90 cut; machine-wove?). Watermarks: *none*. Illustrations: Except as noted below for volume 2, engraved frontispieces and titles are as in first edition. Typography: Printer's imprints read invariably: (1) EDINBURGH: | PRINTED BY BALLANTYNE AND CO.; (2) [*short rule*] | EDINBURGH: | PRINTED BY BALLANTYNE & CO.

General Notes: The new Preface, dated more than four months after the first, indicates that the author has now 'carefully revised the present edition, corrected several errors and inaccuracies, and made numerous and large additions. . . .' The text, previously extending to 30 chapters, now ranges through 33. Concerning the 18° format see General Notes for the first edition.

Copies: BCL E(with Scott's MS revisions) O; NN.

1] **TALES** | OF | **A GRANDFATHER;** . . . VOL. I. | SECOND EDITION. | [*short rule*] . . . . 1828.

Collation: π1 2π² 3π² A-Z⁶ 2A⁴. Pagination: [*frontispiece, engraved title*], *1* title-page, *2* printer's imprint(1), *i* ii-iii Preface, dated from Abbotsford 22 February 1828, *iv blank*, *iii* iv-v Contents (for 12 chapters), *vi blank*, *1* fly-title, *2 blank*, *3* 4-6 Dedication. To Hugh Little-john, Esq., *7* 8-283 text, 283 printer's imprint(2), *284 blank*.

Figures: C35-2 36-7; F71-6 72-4; I 103-3 104-7; L131-8, M144-3; P179-4 180-1; S215-5 216-3; X248-7 252-3; Y260-6, Z276-8.

2] **TALES** | OF | **A GRANDFATHER;**. . . VOL. II. | SECOND EDITION. | [*short rule*] . . . . 1828.

Collation: π1 2π^2 A-F^6 G^6(±G2) H-Z^6 2A^6(-2A6). Pagination: [*frontispiece, engraved title*], *1* title-page, *2* printer's imprint(1), *i* ii-iv Contents (for 13 chapters), *1* fly-title, *2 blank*, *3* 4-286 text, 286 printer's imprint(2). Illustrations: In the engraved frontispiece the Scottish chief, bare-armed and wearing a headband with two feathers in the first edition, here is in full armor with a helmet bearing three plumes..

Figures: C35-8 36-6; F71-2 72-7; I 107-6 108-8; M143-5 144-2; P179-8 180-3; Q192-5, S215-7; X251-8 252-6; 2A 278-7 283-4.

Notes: Cancel leaf G2, with direction line 'VOL. II.' on recto, reads on page 76, lines 19-22, 'such Scottish noble as . . . royal house.', this revising a statement in the first edition (there page 75, lines 18-20) reading 'the Scottish noble who . . . royal family.'

3] **TALES** | OF | **A GRANDFATHER;**. . . VOL. III. | SECOND EDITION. | [*short rule*] . . . . 1828.

Collation: π1 2π^2 A-2C^6. Pagination: [*frontispiece, engraved title*], *1* title-page, *2* printer's imprint(1), *i* ii-iii Contents (for 8 chapters), *iv blank*, *1* fly-title, *2 blank*, *3* 4-306 text, 306 printer's imprint(2), *1* 2-6 Advertisements.

Figures: C35-6 36-8; E50-4, F72-8; I 107-3 108-1; M143-8 144-6; P179-8 180-6; R198-4, S215-6; X251-8 252-7; 2A 287-4 288-8; 2B 295-7 296-8/-.

208Ac] Third Edition (Second Edition, Second Issue): 1828

TALES | OF | **A GRANDFATHER;**. . . VOL. I [II-III]. | THIRD EDITION. . . . 1828.

Issued 30 May 1828 in London (*MC*, cited as 'New Edition'). Notes: A further issue with altered title-pages. Volume 2 leaf G2 (pages 75-76) remains a cancel. Copies: O O(vol.3); CtY(vol.3).

208Ad] Fourth Edition (Second Edition, Third Issue): 1828

TALES | OF | **A GRANDFATHER;**. . . VOL. I [II-III]. | FOURTH EDITION. . . . 1828.

Published in Edinburgh by 2 October 1828 (inscription in AN copy), issued 9 October in London (*MC*, cited as 'New Edition'). Notes: A further issue with altered title-pages. In volume 2 the figure page 72 is dropped, in some copies, and leaf G2 (pages 75-76) remains a cancel.

Copies: AN O; CtY(vol.2).

208Ae] Fifth Edition: 1828

TALES | OF | **A GRANDFATHER;** | BEING | **STORIES** | TAKEN FROM | **SCOTTISH HISTORY.** | HUMBLY INSCRIBED | TO | HUGH LITTLEJOHN, ESQ. | IN THREE VOLS. | VOL. I [II-III]. | FIFTH EDITION. | [*short rule*] | PRINTED FOR CADELL AND CO. EDINBURGH; | SIMPKIN AND MARSHALL, LONDON; AND | JOHN CUMMING, DUBLIN. | [*dash*] | 1828.

Binding: Half green or maroon roan, drab or marbled boards. Paper: Royal 18° in sixes (140 x 90 cut; machine-wove?). Watermarks: *none*. Illustrations: Engraved frontispieces and titles as in Second Edition. Typography: Printer's imprints read invariably: (1) EDINBURGH: | PRINTED BY BALLANTYNE AND COM PANY, | PAUL'S WORK, CANONGATE.; (2) [*short rule*] | EDINBURGH: | PRINTED BY BALLANTYNE AND CO. | PAUL'S WORK, CANONGATE.
General Notes: The extensive revisions which Scott entered in his copy of the second edition (first issue: 208Ab) now appear in this 'fifth edition', the first four being: 8.18 from] from all; 12.7 of the name of] named; 14.21 from] from the North of; 18.9 but] yet.

Copies: E(vols.1-2) E(vols.2-3) HS(vol.2) O; T/B(vols.2-3).

1] **TALES** | OF | **A GRANDFATHER;** . . . VOL. I. | FIFTH EDITION. | [*short rule*] . . . . 1828.

Collation: π1 2π^2 3π^2 A-Z^6 2A^4. Pagination: [*frontispiece, engraved title*], *1* title-page, *2* printer's imprint(1), *i* ii-iii Preface, *iv blank*, *iii* iv-v Contents (for 12 chapters), *vi blank*, *1* fly-title, *2 blank*, *3* 4-6 Dedication, *7* 8-283 text, 283 printer's imprint(2), *284 blank*. Printer's imprint(2) omits third line.

Figures: C35-8 36-2; F71-7; I 107-7 108-2; M134-8 144-5; P179-1 180-6; S215-7 216-5; X251-6 252-2; Z276-7, 2A 278-4.

2] **TALES** | OF | **A GRANDFATHER;** . . . VOL. II. | FIFTH EDITION. | [*short rule*] . . . . 1828.

Collation: π1 2π^2 A-2A^6. Pagination: [*frontispiece, engraved title*], *1* title-page, *2* printer's imprint(1), *i* ii-iv Contents (for 13 chapters), *1* fly-title, *2 blank*, *3* 4-286 text, 286 printer's imprint(2), *287-288 blank*. Typography: Sheet-number (3) is missing for G1r (page 73). In some copies the title-page imprint lacks a semicolon after EDINBURGH.

Figures: C35-6 36-1; E50-6, F72-3; H92-2, I 108-8; K120-1, M134-3; P179-5 180-2; R199-8, S215-7/-; T224-1, X252-5; Z276-4, 2A 278-3.

3] **TALES** | OF | **A GRANDFATHER;** . . . VOL. III. | FIFTH EDITION. | [*short rule*] . . . . 1828.

Collation: π1 2π² A-2C⁶. Pagination: [*frontispiece, engraved title*], *1* title-page, *2* printer's imprint(1), *i* ii-iii Contents (for 8 chapters), *iv blank*, *1* fly-title, *2 blank*, *3* 4-306 text, 306 printer's imprint(2), *1* 2-6 Cadell list.

Figures: C26-6 36-1; D44-8, E54-7; G80-4/-, I 108-6; M143-8 144-7; P179-5 180-2; Q182-8, S216-6; X251-4 252-6; 2A 287-7 288-1.

208Af] Sixth Edition: 1829

TALES | OF | **A GRANDFATHER;** | BEING | **STORIES** | TAKEN FROM | **SCOTTISH HISTORY.** | HUMBLY INSCRIBED | TO | HUGH LITTLEJOHN, ESQ. | IN THREE VOLS. | VOL. I [II-III]. | SIXTH EDITION. | [*short rule*] | PRINTED FOR CADELL AND CO. EDINBURGH; | SIMPKIN AND MARSHALL, LONDON; AND | JOHN CUMMING, DUBLIN. | [*dash*] | 1829.

Binding: Half black or maroon roan and drab boards. Paper: Royal 18° in sixes (140 x 88mm cut; machine-wove?). Watermarks: *none*. Illustrations: Engraved frontispieces and titles as in Second Edition and still dated 1828. Typography: Printer's imprints read: (1) EDINBURGH: | PRINTED BY BALLANTYNE AND COMPANY, | PAUL'S WORK, CANONGATE.; (2) [*short rule*] | EDINBURGH: | PRINTED BY BALLANTYNE AND COMPANY, | PAUL'S WORK, CANONGATE.

General Notes: Compared to the preceding editions, this printing frequently has no sheet-numbers and, as noted below, often omits the press-figures in certain sequences. Remainder copies were advertised under the title 'Sir Walter Scott's Stories from Scottish History', but still at the original price of 10s.6d (*MLA* March 1831, item 7).

Copies: E L; T/B TxU(vols.2-3).

1] **TALES** | OF | **A GRANDFATHER;** . . . VOL. I. | SIXTH EDITION. | [*short rule*] . . . . 1829.

Collation: π1 2π² *a*² A-Z⁶ 2A⁴. Pagination: [*frontispiece, engraved title*], *1* title-page, *2* printer's imprint(1), *i* ii-iii Preface, *iv blank*, *iii* iv-v Contents (for 12 chapters), *vi blank*, *1* fly-title, *2 blank*, *3* 4-6 Dedication, *7* 8-283 text, 283 printer's imprint(2), *284 blank*. Typography: Signature *a* is in italic. In some copies page 55 is misnumbered 5. Figures: 2π ii-11; G84-13, H86-9; Z 271-13.

2] **TALES** | OF | **A GRANDFATHER;** . . . VOL. II. | SIXTH EDITION. | [*short rule*] . . . . 1829.

Collation: π1 2π² A-Z⁶ 2A⁶(-2A6). Pagination: [*frontispiece, engraved title*], *1* title-page, *2* printer's imprint(1), *i* ii-iv Contents (for 13 chapters), *1* fly-title, *2 blank*, *3* 4-286 text, 286 printer's imprint(2). Printer's imprint(2) '& COMPANY.' Figures: M144-13; P180-18; Q182-9, S206-18; Y263-14 264-19.

3] **TALES** | OF | **A GRANDFATHER;** . . . VOL. III. | SIXTH EDITION. | [*short rule*] . . . . 1829.

Collation: π1 2π² A-2B⁶ 2C² *2D*1. Pagination: [*frontispiece, engraved title*], *1* title-page, *2* printer's imprint(1), *i* ii-iii Contents (for 8 chapters), *iv blank*, *1* fly-title, *2 blank*, *3* 4-306 text, 306 printer's imprint(2). Printer's imprint(1) '& COMPANY.' Figures: S212-19; T218-9, X242-15; 2B 296-18.

REPRINTS

FRANCE

PARIS: Didot and Galignani
[~] Tales of a Grandfather. 1828. Two volumes. (Collection of Modern English Authors: *see* 292R.19-20.)

PARIS: Galignani
[~] Tales of a Grandfather. 1828. Three volumes. (*see* 293R.1-3.)

GERMANY

208Ra] BERLIN: Schlesinger 1827
[Tales of a Grandfather. Berlin, Printed for Adolph Martin Schlesinger. 1827]. Copy reported at Landes-u. Hochschulbibliothek Darmstadt.

ZWICKAU: Schumann
[~] Tales of a Grandfather. First Series. (Pocket Library of English Classics: *see* 302R. 171-173.)

UNITED STATES

208Rb] BOSTON: Parker 1828
Tales of a Grandfather; Being Stories Taken from Scottish History. . . . Boston: Samuel H. Parker, No. 164, Washington Street. [1828]. Pages: *i-v* vi, *vii*-viii, *13* 14-386. Copy: RPB. Notes: Also reissued 1828 in Novels Tales and Romances: *see* 305R.21.

[~] Tales of a Grandfather. 1828. (Waverley Novels: *see* 306R.41.)

208Rc] BOSTON: Tupper 1828
Tales of a Grandfather, Being Stories Taken from Scottish History. . . . Boston. Hiram Tupper, Printer, Bromfield Lane. 1828. Two volumes. Pages 1: *i-v* vi, *7* 8-200; 2: *1-3* 4-261. Copies: BCL; CtY PPL.

208Rd] NEW YORK: Burgess 1828-1829
Tales of a Grandfather; Being Stories taken from Scottish History. . . . By Sir Walter Scott, Author of "Waverley," &c. &c. . . . New=York: Published by William Burgess, Jun. Juvenile Emporium, No. 97 Fulton-street. 1828. Two volumes. Pages 1: *i-iii* iv-viii, *9* 10-276; 2: *i-iii* iv-vi, 7-249. Notes: Printed title-pages preceded by engraved frontispieces and title-pages with vignettes, all copied from the Edinburgh edition. Copies of the engraved titles are dated either 1828 or 1829. Original printed boards distinguish several issues, (1) 'Second American Edition.'; (2) 'Fifth American Edition.' Copies: (1) MWA(vol.2); (2) MWA TxU; rebound CtY NN NN(vol.1) PPL(vol.2).

208Re] PHILADELPHIA: Carey, Lea and Carey 1828
Tales of a Grandfather, Being Stories taken from Scottish History. . . . Philadelphia: Carey, Lea & Carey, Chesnut Street. 1828. Two volumes. Pages 1: *1-7* 8-247; 2: *i-ii*, *1-3* 4-312. Notes: First American edition. Though the firm announced as early as 1 December 1827 that it had 'just received a considerable part' of this work, it was not published until 23 February 1828 (*NG*). 2500 copies were printed. Copies: E; DLC (vol.1) MWA MWA(vol.1) NjP NNU-W PHi. Reference: Kaser 110.

THE BANNATYNE MISCELLANY

209A] First Edition: 1827

THE | **BANNATYNE MISCELLANY;** | CONTAINING | ORIGINAL PAPERS AND TRACTS, | CHIEFLY RELATING TO THE | HISTORY AND LITERATURE | OF SCOTLAND. | [*short rule*] | VOLUME I. | [*short rule*] | [*arms of the Bannatyne Club*] | PRINTED AT EDINBURGH: | M.DCCC.XXVII.

Published ca. December 1827 in Edinburgh. Binding: in two parts, separately bound in orange boards with printed labels. Paper: Laid Post 4° (265 x 208mm uncut). Watermarks: [Bannatyne arms, countermark initials ACL]

Collation: ('PART FIRST.') π^6 a^2 A-H^4 I^4(-I4) K-N^4 χ1 O-Y^4; ('PART II.') Z^4 $2A^4$(2A2+2) 2B-$2K^4$ $2L^4$(2L3+1). Pagination: *1* title-page, *2 blank, 3* resolution to print this work 4 July 1823, signed David Laing, Secretary, *4 blank, i-iv* list of members, *v* vi-viii Contents [for both parts], Part First: *i* ii-iii Contents [for Part First], *iv blank, 1* fly-title, *2 blank,* 3-96 99-176 text, *177-178 blank*. Part II: *177* fly-title, *178 blank, 179* 180-356 text, 357-362 Index, 362 printer's imprint: [*short rule*] | EDINBURGH: | PRINTED BY BALLANTYNE AND CO. Typography: Direction lines read 'PART FIRST.', 'PART II.' Signatures 2A, 2B &c. are (unusually for Ballantyne) printed AA, BB &c. Signature M (page 89) is unsigned. Leaves S1, 2E1, 2F1, all fly-titles, are excluded in the pagination. A dagger is placed against page numbers 185-187, 269-270, representing the two-leaf and one-leaf inserts in the 'PART II' collation. Illustrations: Coloured folding plan of Edinburgh [about May 1544] facing page 184; view of The Royal Palace of Holy Rood House [about 1650] facing page 188.

General Notes: A Committee of Management of the Bannatyne Club, meeting at Scott's Edinburgh house in July 1823, resolved that printing begin, in successive parts or numbers, of a work to be entitled *The Bannatyne Miscellany,* containing a *Collection of Tracts and Original Papers, Relative to the History, Literature, and Antiquities of Scotland.* It was also resolved that this publication be 'under the joint superintendance of the PRESIDENT and SECRETARY.' Scott, as President, apart from assisting David Laing, as Secretary, in the general editing of this work, also contributed, in the first volume, the introduction, pages 3-6, the section titled 'Elegy on Sir Robert Kerr, of Cessford, First Earl of Roxburghe', pages *191* 192-196, and certain of the notes. Volumes 2-3 are generally credited to Laing alone. The book in complete form was later designated as number 21 in the Club series.

Some copies include additional inserts, such as, 'Rules of the Bannatyne Club, and Lists of the Members' for various dates. Bound after each part in the E copy are 'Rules of the Bannatyne Club', the first (of four leaves) inserted after PART FIRST presenting the initial regulations of 1823, with membership then limited to 31 (Article 1), the second (of five leaves) inserted after PART II, effective December 1827, with membership extended to 100. Following this second insert the E copy contains 11 leaves of text apparently intended as further cancels. (The increase in membership was voted at a meeting of the Club on 3 December 1827.)

Apart from the irregularities noted above, there appears to be a shift in the collation, with N page numbers 97-98 omitted but text continues, M gathering regularly in fours; or with numbers 97-98 present, but after M3 an inserted leaf numbered †101, 102†.

Copies: BCL E; NN(lists of 31 members, 1824, and of 87 members, February 1828).

References: *Letters*, viii.385. (Magnum Opus Edition: Not reprinted.)

REVIEW OF MOLIÈRE

210A] First Printing: 1828

'ART. X.--1. *Oeuvres de Molière, avec . . . une Vie de Molière.* Par M. Auger. . . 2. *Histoire de la Vie et des Ouvrages de Molière.* Par J. Taschereau.', pages 306-351, *in*:

The Foreign Quarterly Review. [February 1828. No.3, volume 2 imprint:] London: Treuttel and Würtz, Treuttel, Jun. and Richter, 30, Soho Square. 1828.

Published 23 February 1828 in London (*MC*); issued 27 March in Edinburgh (*EEC*).

Copies: BCL L O; NjP PU(2).

References: Thomson, page 48. (Magnum Opus Edition 1835: *The Miscellaneous Prose Works*, xvii.137-215 as 'Molière'.)

NOTICE TO CORRESPONDENTS

211A] First Printing: 1828

'NOTICE TO CORRESPONDENTS.', pages 352-354, *in*:

The Foreign Quarterly Review. [February 1828. No.3, volume 2 imprint:] London: Treuttel and Würtz, Treuttel, Jun. and Richter, 30, Soho Square. 1828.

Published 23 February 1828 in London (*MC*); issued 27 March in Edinburgh (*EEC*).

Notes: This notice immediately follows Scott's review of Molière. It is now attributed to Scott, who here acknowledges that much of the legend concerning one Captain Macpherson (cited in his review in Volume I entitled, 'On the Supernatural . . . .' *see* 201A) 'had done great injustice to the character of the unfortunate gentleman' and then provides a more favourable report. Even this did not suffice, however, for Scott on 1 April 1828 received a 'distressing letter' from Macpherson's daughter, who remained 'very angry'.

Copies: BCL L O; NjP PU(2).

References: *Journal*, page 451. (Magnum Opus Edition: Not reprinted.)

VERSES TO CUTHBERT SHARP

212A] First Printing: 1828

'Forget thee? No.' (first words: 'Forget thee? No; my worthy fere;—').

[*caption above the poem*] ' Written by one of the Guests at the Wellington Dinner, | to the Vice, who reminded him of a Promise to revisit | Sunderland, which he appeared to have forgotten.'

Printed 15 March 1828 in Edinburgh. 56 copies ordered by Sir Cuthbert Sharp. Slip broadside, printed on one side only. Paper unwatermarked (220 x 139mm cut).

Notes: On the 4th of October 1827 Scott was present at a dinner for the Duke of Wellington held in Sunderland for 204 seated guests (and probably given by Sir Cuthbert Sharp). Scott's close friend Robert Surtees refused to attend, saying that he could not endure 'bungalow' dinners!

Copies: O O(2 proof copies, with Scott MS and other memorabilia).

References: Ruff 183 (with illustration). (Magnum Opus Edition: Not reprinted.)

REVIEW OF STEUART

213A] First Printing: 1828

'ART. I.—*The Planter's Guide;* . . . By Sir Henry Steuart, Bart. LL.D., F.R.S.E. &c.', pages *303* 304-344, *in*:

The Quarterly Review. [March 1828. No.74, volume 37 imprint:] London: John Murray, Albemarle Street. 1828.

Published 25 March 1828 in London (*MC*); issued 10 April in Edinburgh (*EEC*).

Notes: The extract at Harvard, recorded as bearing the title 'On Ornamental Plantations and Landscape Gardening', actually is a separately bound copy of this review, the NUC record deriving from the headlines.

Copies: BCL L O; MH PPL.

References: Thomson, page 69. (Magnum Opus Edition 1836: *The Miscellaneous Prose Works*, xxi.77-151 as 'On Landscape Gardening'.)

RELIGIOUS DISCOURSES

214Aa] First Edition, First Issue: 1828

RELIGIOUS DISCOURSES. | BY A LAYMAN. | [*short rule*] | LONDON: | HENRY COLBURN, NEW BURLINGTON STREET. | MDCCCXXVIII.

Published 30 April 1828 in London (*MC* 28 April). 4s.6d. Paper: Demy 8° (220 138mm uncut). Binding: Drab wrappers with printed label. Watermarks: *none*. Collation: B^8 C-F^8. Pagination: *i* half-title, *ii blank*, *iii* title-page, *iv* printer's imprint(1), *v* vi-viii Preface, *9* fly-title for 'The Christian and the Jewish Dispensations Compared', *10 blank*, *11* 12-48 text, *49* fly-title for 'The Blessedness of the Righteous', *50 blank*, 51-79 text, *80* printer's imprint(2). Printer's imprints (1) and (2): LONDON: | IBOTSON AND PALMER, PRINTERS, SAVOY STREET, STRAND. Figures: *none*.

Notes: George Huntly Gordon, once an amanuensis for Scott, was a probationer for the ministry, but fearful of preparing two trial sermons, which Scott then graciously devised and, on 29 February 1828, corrected for the press. In his Preface (pages vi-viii) the unidentified recipient cites an extract from a 2 January letter signed 'W. S.' allowing the publication of these essays. Nonetheless the *Athenaeum* reviewer (7 May, pages 435-437) expressed surprise at the issuance of these 'sermons': 'It is not very creditable, under any circumstances, for a minister of religion to offer the results of another's inquiry after truth for his own.'

Presentation copy: PPL(from Scott to Melrose Library, received 6 December 1828). Other copies: BCL(Henry Liddell, Lord Ravensworth) E ES GU(2); CtY IdU MH* NNP* T/B TxU.
*With 8-page 'Works . . . by Henry Colburn,' dated 25 April 1828.

References: *Journal*, page 435; *Letters*, x.352; Thomson, page 57. (Magnum Opus Edition: Not reprinted.)

214Ab] Second Edition (First Edition, Second Issue): 1828

RELIGIOUS DISCOURSES. . . . [*short rule*] | SECOND EDITION. | [*short rule*] | LONDON: . . . MDCCCXXVIII.

Published 4 September 1828 in London (*MC*). 4s.6d. Notes: Except for the edition statement on title, this printing is identical to the original issue.

Copy: E.

REPRINTS

CANADA

214Ra] KINGSTON: Macfarlane 1828
[Religious Discourses. . . Kingston, U.C., Printed and published by James Macfarlane. 1828. Pages: 1-16.] Copy: not seen, reported in *NUC*.

FRANCE

PARIS: Didot and Galignani
[~] Religious Discourses. 1828. (Collection of Modern English Authors: *see* 292R.25.)

UNITED STATES

214Rb] BETHANY: Campbell 1831
[A Discourse on the Holy Spirit. By Walter Scott. . . . Second Edition, Enlarged and Improved. Bethany, Va. Printed by Alexander Campbell. MDCCCXXXI. Pages: 1-24.] Copy located at Virginia Baptist Historical Society, Richmond.

214Rc] NEW YORK: Collins & Hannay [and others] 1828
Religious Discourses. By a Layman. New-York: Printed by J. & J. Harper, Sold by Collins & Hannay, Collins and Co., W. B. Gilley, A. T. Goodrich, and O. A. Roorbach. 1828. Pages: *i-iii* iv-v *vi, 7-9* 10-48. In some copies the comma after Harper is changed to a period. Copies: E ES; CtY DLC NN(2) RPB. Reference: Kohler(1) 70 (with illustration).

214Rd] PHILADELPHIA: Carey, Lea and Carey 1828
Religious Discourses. By a Layman. Philadelphia: Carey, Lea and Carey—Chesnut Street. Sold in New York by G. and C. Carvill—in Boston by Monroe and Francis. 1828. Pages: *i-v* vi-viii, *9-11* 12-79. Notes: 1250 copies were printed. Copies: BCL; DLC IdU MWA NNU-W PPL.

LETTER ON PORTRAITS OF ILLUSTRIOUS PERSONAGES

215A] First Printing: 1828

Notes: This extensive commmendatory letter to the publisher Joseph Harding, dated from Abbotsford 25 March 1828, was first printed in an unlocated catalogue of the original illustrations exhibited in Pall Mall for the ongoing folio part-issue of Edmund Lodge's *Portraits of Illustrious Personages of Great Britain* and then immediately reprinted at length in the 3 May 1828 number of the *Literary Gazette* (pages 284-285). Thereafter it was printed in the prospectus for issues in smaller formats, in the volume issue, then in several other journals (*ELJ*, 22 November

1828; *EEC*, 25 May 1829), and finally collected 1832 in *Letters to Polwhele*, pages 95-99 (257Aa).

References: (Magnum Opus Edition: Not reprinted, but abbreviated version quoted in *Letters*, x.405-407.)

CHRONICLES OF THE CANONGATE
[Second Series]
ST VALENTINE'S DAY

216Aa] First Edition, First Issue: 1828

CHRONICLES | OF | **THE CANONGATE.** | Second Series. | BY | THE AUTHOR OF "WAVERLEY," &c. | [*short rule*] | [*one-line motto of the Canongate Arms*] | [*short rule*] | IN THREE VOLUMES. | VOL. I [II-III]. | [*short reversed Oxford rule*] | EDINBURGH: | PRINTED FOR CADELL AND CO., EDINBURGH; | AND SIMPKIN AND MAR SHALL, LONDON. | [*dash*] | 1828.

Published concurrently 15 May 1828 in Edinburgh (*EEC*); 15 May in London (*MC* 1 May, 'Thursday, May 15'). £1.11.6. Binding: drab, blue, or green boards with printed labels. Paper: Post 8° (198 x 121mm uncut). Watermarks: *none*. Typography: Printer's imprints read invariably: (1) EDINBURGH: | PRINTED BY BALLANTYNE AND CO.; (2) [*short rule*] | EDINBURGH: | PRINTED BY BALLANTYNE AND CO.

General Notes: According to established practice, beginning with *Kenilworth* (*see* 149Aa), on 27 May 1828, shortly after the publication of this novel, some 5950 words (volume 1, chapter 10 of this Edinburgh edition) were extracted in the Philadelphia *National Gazette*, these deriving from proofs early shipped for the Carey, Lea & Carey edition (216Rd). As the Philadelphia publisher had not yet been supplied with the general title, reference is there made only to the sub-title, 'St Valentine's Day'. This Chronicle was extracted only once in an anthology, 404E.2.

Presentation copy: NNP('From the Author' to the Duchess of St. Albans). Other copies: AN BCL(2) E(4) L(2) LU O(12); DLC IdU InU NN NNU-W T/B TxU.

References: Church 550; Randall, page 54; Sterling 742; Thomson, page 27; Van Antwerp(1) 24; Worthington 21. (Magnum Opus Edition 1832: *Waverley Novels*, as 'Saint Valentine's Day; or, The Fair Maid of Perth', xlii-xliii.)

1] **CHRONICLES** | OF | **THE CANONGATE.** | **Second Series.** | . . . VOL. I. . . . 1828.

Collation: π^2 A-X^8. Pagination: *i* half-title, *ii blank*, *iii* title-page, *iv* printer's imprint(1), *1* fly-title, *2 blank*, *3* 4-336 text, 336 printer's imprint(2).
Figures: A15-6 16-3, B31-8 32-13, C46-3 48-12, D62-10 64-9, E74-11 80-9, F82-5 96-15, G109-10 111-15, H127-11 128-13, I 131-15 144-1, K159-9 160-5, L175-12 176-7, M191-15 192-13, N207-7 208-4, O 223-13 224-16, P234-5 237-11, Q254-10 256-3, R269-14/'41' 271-13, S285-4/11 287-9, T302-13 304-12, U319-14 320-15, X335-10 336(or 333)-15. The 336 figure, entered inappropriately just below imprint on last text/imprint page, and so observed in a few copies, was soon transferred to a better position on page 333.

Notes: Chapter V (page 113) is misnumbered 'IV.', an error which disorders all later chapter numbers in this volume.

2] **CHRONICLES** | OF | **THE CANONGATE.** | **Second Series.** | . . . VOL. II. . . . 1828.

Collation: π^2 A-X^8. Pagination: *i* half-title, *ii blank*, *iii* title-page, *iv* printer's imprint(1), *1* fly-title, *2 blank*, *3* 4-336 text, 336 printer's imprint(2).

Figures: A15-14 16-16, B31-9 32-13, C46-15 48-14, D63-4 64-3, E75-11 80-7, F92-10 95-14, G98-5 109-12, H127-16 128-11, I 139-6 144-7, K155-15 157-9, L173-13 175-14, M191-8 192-10, N206-11 208-4, O 223-16 224-12, P239-10 240-15, Q255-6 256-9, R271-15 272-9, S277-13 283-11, T303-2 304-12, U319-16 320-4, X324-5 335-7/-.

3] **CHRONICLES** | OF | **THE CANONGATE.** | **Second Series.** | . . . VOL. III. . . . 1828.

Collation: π^2 A-Y^8 Z1. Pagination: *i* half-title, *ii blank*, *iii* title-page, *iv* printer's imprint(1), *1* fly-title, *2 blank*, *3* 4-348 text, 348 printer's imprint(2), *1* 2-6 Cadell and Company catalogue.

Figures: A15-8 16-15, B31-16 32-10, C47-6 48-7, D52-9 58-11, E79-2 80-13, F93-16 95-15, G111-12 112-10, H123-11 128-13, I 143-16 144-9, K159-11 160-15, L175-13 176-12, M185-10 190-9, N207-16 208-10, O 223-14 224-10, P237-4 238-13, Q255-12 256-16, R267-3 272-1, S287-15 288-11, T303-8 304-9, U319-11 320-13, X335-16 336-10, Y3-1 4-12, Z6-4.

216Ab] Second Edition (First Edition, Second Issue): 1828

ST VALENTINE'S DAY; | OR, | **THE FAIR MAID OF PERTH.** | BY | THE AUTHOR OF "WAVERLEY," &c. | FORMING THE | **Second Series** |

OF CHRONICLES OF THE CANONGATE. | [*short rule*] | [*one-line motto of the Canongate Arms*] | [*short rule*] | SECOND EDITION. | IN THREE VOLUMES. | VOL. I [II-III]. | [*short reversed Oxford rule*] | EDINBURGH: | PRINTED FOR CADELL AND CO., EDINBURGH; | AND SIMPKIN AND MARSHALL, LONDON. | [*dash*] | 1828.

Published 7 June 1828 in Edinburgh (*EEC*); issued 30 June in London (*MC*). £1.11.6. Binding: Blue-green cloth with printed labels. Paper: Post 8° (190 x 115mm cut). Watermarks: *none*.

General Notes: A continued issue of the first edition sheets with altered title-page and imprint on verso changed to a new style: EDINBURGH: | PRINTED BY BALLANTYNE AND COMPANY, | PAUL'S WORK, CANONGATE. In some copies the comma is omitted after second line of title-page. The original cloth binding for this 'second edition' is identical with that for the 'second edition' of *Chronicles*, first series (206Aa) and, in the BCL copies, bears the same bookseller's ticket (Prior & Co., 42 Ludgate Hill).

Copies: BCL E; CtY TxU(with Scott's extensive manuscript revisions for the Magnum Opus).

REPRINTS

FRANCE

PARIS: Baudry, Barrois [and others]
[~] Chronicles of the Canongate. Saint Valentine's Day. 1832. (Collection of Ancient and Modern British Novels and Romances: *see* 288R.37.)

PARIS: Galignani
[~] Chronicles of the Canongate. Second Series. 1828. (Collection of Modern English Authors: *see* 291R.65-67.)

GERMANY

216Ra] BERLIN: Schlesinger 1828
Saint Valentine's Day; or The Fair Maid of Perth. Chronicles of the Canongate. Second Series.... Berlin. Published by Adolph Martin Schlesinger. 1828. Three volumes. Pages 1: *1-3* 4-192; 2: *1-3* 4-192; 3: *1-3* 4-200. Copy: C. Reference: GDS 132, page 346.

ZWICKAU: Schumann
[~] Chronicles of the Canongate. Second Series. 1828. (Pocket Library of English Classics: *see* 302R.entry following 171-173.)

UNITED STATES

216Rb] BOSTON: Parker 1828
Chronicles of the Canongate. By the Author of "Waverley, Ivanhoe," &c. &c. Second Series. Boston: Samuel H. Parker, No. 164 Washington Street. 1829. Pages: *1-3* 4-264, *3* 4-260. Notes: The title-page notes 'Complete in One Volume' though, as indicated, there is double pagination and gatherings in the second section have direction line 'VOL. II.'] Copy: not seen. (Also reissued 1829 in Novels Tales and Romances: *see* 305R.22.)

[~] Chronicles of the Canongate. Second Series. 1828, 1829. (Waverley Novels: *see* 306R.42-43.)

216Rc] NEW YORK: Harper 1828
Chronicles of the Canongate. Second Series. By the Author of "Waverley," &c. . . . New York: Printed by J. & J. Harper, 82 Cliff Street. 1828. Two volumes. Pages 1: *1-2, 13* 14-264; 2: *1-2, 13* 14-257. Notes: A variant issue of Carey edition, next entry. Copies: E; CtY NN(2) PPL.

216Rd] PHILADELPHIA: Carey, Lea, and Carey 1828
Chronicles of the Canongate. Second Series. By the Author of "Waverley," &c. . . . Philadelphia: Carey, Lea, and Carey—Chesnut Street. 1828. Two volumes. Pages 1: *1-2, 13* 14-264; 2: *1-2, 13* 14-257. Notes: The first American edition, set from Edinburgh proofs, extracted in the Philadelphis *National Gazette* 27 May 1828 (216Aa), and issued 12 June (*NG*). Copies: CtY MB MH MWA NNU-W PPL ViU.

216Re] PHILADELPHIA: Crissy 1828
Chronicles of the Canongate. Second Series. By the Author of "Waverley," &c. . . . Philadelphia: J. Crissy, No. 14 S. Seventh Street. 1828. Two volumes. Pages 1: *1-2 13* 14-264; 2: *1-2 13* 14-257. Notes: A variant issue of the Carey edition, preceding entry. Copies: E; IdU T/B (vol.2).

DERIVATIVES

GREAT BRITAIN

216Da] LONDON: Goulding & D'Almaine 1828
[1] The Fair Maid of Perth. The Celebrated Scottish Ballad. . . London Pubd. by Goulding & D'Almaine, 20, Soho Square. & to be had at the Author's Music Warehouse. Belle Vue, Clapham. [unwatermarked. ca.1828.] Pages: *i-ii, 1* 2-5. Notes: Engraved sheet music with plate mark: 'The Fair Maid of Perth.' Words adapted by Richard Ryan, and dedicated by Permission to Sir Walter Scott Bart (*see* 530T[2]). Music by E. Solis arranged with symphonies and accompaniments for voice and pianoforte. Price: 2/. Copy: L.

[2] Yes Thou May'st Sigh, the Poetry from The Chronicles of the Canongate. Second Series . . . London Published by Goulding & D'Almaine, 20, Soho Square, Manufact-urers of Cabinet, Harmonic & Square Piano Fortes, where an elegant assortment for Sale or Hire may be seen. [ca.1828]. Pages: *i-ii* 1-5. Notes: Engraved sheet music with plate mark as for

title. Words from chapter 30 (first words as for title). Music by William Horsley arranged for voice and pianoforte. Price: 2/. Copy: MH.

LONDON: Leigh
[~] Song, "Yes, thou may'st sigh." 1832. (The Harmonicon: *see* 337D.6.) Notes: Series initially printed for the Proprietors, published by Leigh. This title was published by Longman, Rees, Orme, Brown, Green, and Longman.

216Db] LONDON: Power 1828
Poor Louise, A Ballad by Sir Walter Scott, Bart. . . . London Published by J. Power, 34, Strand. Where may be had the following Songs . . . . [unwatermarked. ca.1828]. Pages: *1-2* 3-7. Notes: Engraved sheet-music with plate number '1157'. Words from 'Saint Valentine's Day', chapter 10, 'The Lay of Poor Louise' (first words: 'Oh, poor Louise, the live long day / She roams from Cot to Castle gay'.) Music composed by Mrs Robert Arkwright arranged for voice and pianoforte. Text somewhat altered. Price: 2s. Copy: L. Reference: G/T 10853.

UNITED STATES

216Dc] NEW YORK: Mesier 1828
[The Lay of Poor Louise. New York: Mesier (1828). Notes: Song composed by William Ball.] Copy: not seen. Reference: G/T 10854.

THE DEATH OF KEELDAR

217Aa] First Printing: 1829[1828]

'THE DEATH OF KEELDAR. BY SIR WALTER SCOTT BART.', (first words: 'Up rose the sun o'er moor and mead;') pages *13* 14-17, *in*:
The Gem, A Literary Annual, Edited by Thomas Hood, Esq. . . . London: W. Marshall, 1, Holborn Bars. 1829.

Published 8 October 1828 in London (*Ath* 8 October, reviewed 15 October, pages 800-802). 12s.

Notes: An eight-line headnote begins: 'Percy or Percival Rede, of Trochend, . . .' Facing the text is an engraving of a huntsman mourning his dead hound, with caption 'The Death of Keeldar', painted by A. Cooper, engraved by A. W. Warren, with a Marshall 1829 imprint. In his preface (pages 4-5) Hood expresses his gratitude to the first contributor: 'To Sir Walter Scott—not merely a literary feather in my cap, but a whole plume of them—I owe, and with the hand of my heart acknowledge, a deep obligation. A Poem from his pen is likely to confer on the Book that contains it, if not perpetuity, at least a very Old Mortality.' Besides this tribute the publisher sent a 'handsome Silver Cup' acknowledged by Scott on 4 January 1829.

Scott was moved to compose this poem on receiving, 7 February 1828, what he then described as a 'beautiful sketch of a hunter who had by accident shot his own dog and was mourning over him, the horse standing by in mute sympathy.' On sending these lines to Cooper, 4 July, he indirectly suggested that the artist might consider sending further sketches, presumably for the Magnum Opus then in preparation.

Copies: EU L; InU(inscribed 27 December 1828) NjP(2) NN.

References: *Journal*, page 424; *Letters*, x.457, xi.87-88; Ruff 184. (Magnum Opus Edition: Not reprinted.)

217Ab] Second Printing: 1829[1828]

[*caption title*] THE DEATH OF KEELDAR. BY SIR WALTER SCOTT, BART.

Collation: A^4. Pagination: *i-ii blank*, *1* 2-5 text, *6 blank*. Notes: An offprint of the preceding issue, with the engraving, before letters, inserted before page *1*. This may be representative of the 'valuable proofs' Scott acknowledged along with the silver cup on 4 January 1829. The only known copy, in crimson moiré silk with gilt lettering, was presented to Lady Georgiana, Duchess of Bedford.
Copy: O.

REVIEW OF DAVY

218A] First Printing: 1828

'ART. IX.—*Salmonia, or Days of Fly-Fishing.* By an Angler.', pages 503-535, *in*:

The Quarterly Review. [October, 1828. No.76, volume 38 imprint:] London: John Murray, Albemarle Street. 1828.

Published 28 October 1828 in London (*MC*). Notes: The author of *Salmonia* was later identified as Sir Humphry Davy.

Copies: BCL L O; PPL.

References: Thomson, page 60. (Magnum Opus Edition 1835: *The Miscellaneous Prose Works*, xx.245-300 as 'Davy's Salmonia'.)

THE KEEPSAKE FOR MDCCCXXIX

219A] First Printings: 1828

1] 'MY AUNT MARGARET'S MIRROR.', pages *1* 2-44,

2] 'THE TAPESTRIED CHAMBER, OR THE LADY IN THE SACQUE.', pages 123-142,

3] 'DEATH OF THE LAIRD'S JOCK. TO THE EDITOR OF THE KEEPSAKE.', pages 186-192,

4] 'DESCRIPTION OF THE ENGRAVING ENTITLED A SCENE AT ABBOTSFORD.', pages 258-261, *in*:

The Keepsake for MDCCCXXIX. Edited by Frederic Mansel Reynolds. London: Published for the Proprietor, by Hurst, Chance, and Co., 65, St. Paul's Churchyard, and R. Jennings, 2, Poultry. [1828].

Published 1 November 1828 in London (review in *Literary Gazette*). £1.1.0.

Notes: The first two contributions were originally intended for the second series of the *Chronicles of the Canongate*, but then withdrawn at the insistence of Ballantyne and Cadell; a sketch of the third was sent on to Reynolds 11 March 1828; and Chief Commissioner Adam on 1 February advised Scott that he was willing to release the Landseer painting for the fourth. All the pieces are attributed to 'The Author of Waverley' and each provided with an engraved illustration imprinted Hurst, Chance, and Jennings and facing [1] page 33: 'The Magic Mirror' drawn by J. M. Wright, engraved by E. Portbury, printed by McQueen; [2] page 136: 'The Tapestried Chamber' drawn by F. P. Stephanoff, engraved by J. Goodyear, printed by E. Brain; [3] page 191: 'The Lairds Jock' drawn by H. Corbould, engraved by Charles Heath, printed by E. Brain; [4] page 258: 'Scene at Abbotsford' painted by Edwin Landseer, A.R.A., engraved by C. Westwood, printed by McQueen. This last piece, not later collected, chiefly concerns Scott's highland greyhound 'Maida'.

In reference to the previous volume of this annual Scott on 30 January 1828 observed only that 'the plates are beyond comparaison[!] beautiful. But the letterpress indifferent enough.' A month later, 24 February, Southey reported to Caroline Bowles: 'Will you believe that of this *Keepsake*, which is bought merely for presents, or for the sake of the engravings, he [Reynolds] has sold fifteen thousand copies! And for binding the next volume he has bespoken four thousand yards of red silk!'

Copies: BCL; CtY NN T/B.

References: *Journal*, pages 421, 422, 442; Thomson, pages 25, 49, 72. (Magnum Opus Edition 1832: *Waverley Novels*, [1] xli.*289-291* 292-346, [2] xli.*347-351* 352-373, [3] xli.*375-377* 378-385, [4] not reprinted.)

REPRINT

FRANCE

PARIS: Didot and Galignani
[~] Tales and Essays. 1829. (Collection of Modern English Authors: *see* 292R.26.)

TALES OF A GRANDFATHER [Second Series]

220Aa] First Edition: 1829[1828]

TALES | OF | **A GRANDFATHER;** | BEING | **STORIES** | TAKEN FROM | **SCOTTISH HISTORY.** | HUMBLY INSCRIBED | TO | HUGH LITTLEJOHN, ESQ. | IN THREE VOLS. | VOL. I [II-III]. | Second Series. | [*short rule*] | PRINTED FOR CADELL AND CO. EDINBURGH; | SIMPKIN AND MARSHALL, LONDON; AND | JOHN CUMMING, DUBLIN. | [*dash*] | 1829.

Published 27 November 1828 in Edinburgh (*EEC*); issued 4 December in London (*MC*, but advertised 3 and 13 November to be issued 'on the 27th'). 10s.6d. Binding: half maroon, green, or dark blue roan and drab boards. Paper: Royal 18° in sixes (140 x 91mm uncut). Watermarks: *none*. Illustrations: Unlike those in the First Series, the engraved frontispieces and titles are now inserted after a preliminary leaf, as indicated below. Typography: Printer's imprints read invariably: (1) EDINBURGH: | PRINTED BY BALLANTYNE AND COMPANY, | PAUL'S WORK, CANONGATE.; (2) [*short rule*] | EDINBURGH: | PRINTED BY BALLANTYNE AND COMPANY, | PAUL'S WORK, CANONGATE.

General Notes: Three weeks before issue, on 6 November 1828, the Philadelphia firm of Carey, Lea & Carey announced its edition as 'In the Press' (*NG*), an indication that this establishment was still receiving advance copy or proofs. This tale was extracted only once in an anthology, 372[2]E.1.

Copies: BCL(2) E HS O(2); MH* NN NNU-W T/B.
*With 8-page undated Cadell & Co. catalogue.

References: Thomson, pages 70-71; Van Antwerp(1) 28. (Magnum Opus Edition 1836: *The Miscellaneous Prose Works*, xxiii.*211-215* 216-402, xxiv, xxv.*1* 2-105.)

1] **TALES** | OF | **A GRANDFATHER;** . . . VOL. I. | Second Series. . . . 1829.

Collation: π^2 $2\pi1$ $3\pi^2$ A-C^6 D^6(±D2) E-2C^6 2D^4. Pagination: *1-2* advertisement, [*frontispiece, engraved title*], *3* title-page, *4* printer's imprint(1), *i*-ii Dedication to Hugh Littlejohn, dated from Abbotsford 15 October 1828, *i* ii-iv Contents, *1* fly-title, *2 blank*, *3* 4-320 text, 320 printer's imprint(2). Illustrations: Frontispiece portrait painted by Vandyke, engraved by W. H. Lizars, with caption 'James Graham, Marquis of Montrose.'; title vignette drawn and engraved by W. H. Lizars.

Figures: B24-6, C26-1; D47-1 48-2/8; H86-5 96-11; L143-7 144-4; O 158-16 168-9; S212-10/- 216-1; X251-6 252-5; Y264-10, Z275-9; 2C 311-16 312-11.

Notes: The text on cancel leaf D2 (pages 39-40) apparently was troublesome, for the corresponding passage in the succeeding edition is further revised.

2] **TALES** | OF | **A GRANDFATHER;** . . . VOL. II. | **Second Series.** . . 1829.

Collation: π^2 a^2 A^6(±A2) B-2A^6 2B^8. Pagination: *1-2 blank*, [*frontispiece, engraved title*], *3* title-page, *4* printer's imprint(1), *i* ii-iii Contents, *iv blank*, *1* fly-title, *2 blank*, *3* 4-304 text, 304 printer's imprint(2). Illustrations: Frontispiece portrait painted by Sir P. Lely, engraved by W. H. Lizars, with caption 'John Graham of Claverhouse, Viscount Dundee.'; title vignette drawn and engraved by W. H. Lizars. Typography: Section signature Y2 (page 257) is misprinted 2Y.

Figures: A8-7, B24-1; F71-4 72-9; G84-16, H86-9; K120-17, M144-10; N150-7, O 158-9; R203-7, S215-11; T227-16 228-5; Y259-11, 2A 288-9; 2B 291-11 301-9/-.

Notes: Again the text, now on cancel leaf A2 (pages *3*-4), was troublesome, being further revised in the succeeding edition.

3] **TALES** | OF | **A GRANDFATHER;** . . . VOL. III. | **Second Series.** . . 1829.

Collation: π^2 a^2 A-2E^6 *2F*^{2}. Pagination: *1-2 blank*, [*frontispiece, engraved title*], *3* title-page, *4* printer's imprint(1), *i* ii-iii Contents, *iv blank*, *1* fly-title, *2 blank*, *3* 4-332 text, 332 printer's imprint(2), *1* 2-8 Cadell catalogue. Illustrations: Frontispiece portrait engraved by W. H. Lizars with caption 'Andrew Fletcher of Saltoun.'; title vignette drawn and engraved by W. H. Lizars.

Figures: B23-13 24-6; F71-9 72-2; G79-4, H92-10; L131-7 132-5; P179-1 180-2; S215-7 216-16; U234-11, X247-9; Z276-11, 2A 288-16; 2B 300-13, 2C 302-7.

220Ab] Second Edition: 1829

TALES | OF | **A GRANDFATHER;** | BEING | **STORIES** | TAKEN FROM | **SCOTTISH HISTORY.** | HUMBLY INSCRIBED | TO | HUGH LITTLEJOHN, Esq. | IN THREE VOLS. | VOL. I [II-III]. | **Second Series.** | A NEW EDITION. | [*short rule*] | PRINTED FOR CADELL AND CO.

EDINBURGH; | SIMPKIN AND MARSHALL, LONDON; AND | JOHN CUMMING, DUBLIN. | [*dash*] | 1829.

Issued 6 June 1821 in London (*MC*). Binding: Half green or maroon roan with drab boards. Paper: Royal 18° in sixes (143 x 89mm cut). Watermarks: *none.* Illustrations: Engraved frontispieces and titles as in first edition. Typography: Printer's imprints read invariably: (1) EDINBURGH: | PRINTED BY BALLANTYNE AND COMPANY, | PAUL'S WORK, CANONGATE.; (2) [*short rule*] | EDINBURGH: | PRINTED BY BALLANTYNE AND COMPANY, | PAUL'S WORK, CANONGATE.

General Notes: As disclosed in the collation and pagination, the content of each of these volumes has been extended and, as noted in the previous edition, further revised. Remainder copies of this edition were advertised under the title 'Sir Walter Scott's Stories from Scottish History', but still at the original price of 10s.6d (*MLA*, March 1831, item 7).

Copies: E(2) LU; InU(vol.3) T/B TxU.

1] **TALES** | OF | **A GRANDFATHER;** . . . VOL. I. | **Second Series.** | A NEW EDITION. . . . 1829.

Collation: π^2 $2\pi1$ $3\pi^2$ A-K^6 L^6(±L2) M-2D^6 2E^4. Pagination: *1-2 blank*, [*frontispiece, engraved title*], *3* title-page, *4* printer's imprint(1), *i*-ii dedication, *i* ii-iv Contents, *1* fly-title, *2 blank*, *3* 4-331 text, 331 printer's imprint(2), *332 blank.*

Figures: C35-9 36-12; H91-11, I 108-16; K119-6, L128-11 M140-1; S212-5 216-16; 2A 283-11 287-2; 2D 323-9 324-10. Sheets 2 (D-F) and 5 (N-P) are unfigured, and sheet 4 (K-M) oddly figured thrice.

Notes: Pages 123-124 (L2) are in a revised state, with a cancel appearing in some copies. When compared with the corresponding pages 119-121 in the first edition, these exhibit the following variants and additional note:

123.20 now an] now as much as
123.22 son-in-law] step-son
124.8 him] his step-son
124.10 MacKinnon of Ulva,] MacQuarrie of Ulva,*

*By an error unpardonable in one who has read Boswell's tour to the Hebrides, and seen the late venerable Laird of MacQuarrie, the name of MacKinnon was inserted in the former editions. [Later references to MacKinnon are all corrected in the text.]

2] **TALES** | OF | **A GRANDFATHER;** . . . VOL. II. | **Second Series.** | A NEW EDITION. . . . 1829.

Collation: π^2 a^2 A-2C^6. Pagination: *1-2 blank*, [*frontispiece, engraved title*], *3* title-page, *4* printer's imprint(1), *i* ii-iii Contents, *iv blank*, *1* fly-title, *2 blank*, *3* 4-312 text, 312 printer's imprint(2). Typography: Page 244 is either misnumbered 118 or when corrected the 244 is inserted up side down.

Figures: A8-7, C32-5; D48-10, F66-4; H96-9, I 108-13; L127-1 128-5; S215-8 216-9; T228-12, X252-10; Y264-11 2A 288-3. Sheets 5 (N-P) and 9 (2B-2C) are unfigured.

3] **TALES** | OF | **A GRANDFATHER;** . . . VOL. III. | Second Series. | A NEW EDITION. . . . 1829.

Collation: π^2 a^2 A-2E^6 2F^6 2G^4(-2G4). Pagination: *1-2 blank*, [*frontispiece, engraved title*], *3* title-page, *4* printer's imprint(1), *i* ii-iii Contents, *iv blank*, *1* fly-title, *2 blank*, *3* 4-346 text, 346 printer's imprint(2), *1* 2-7 *8* advertisement headed 'Lately Published by Cadell and Co.'. Typography: In some copies page 145 is unnumbered.

Figures: A12-10, B23-11; H96-5, I 108-10; N156-3, P180-6; S212-11 216-16; 2E 336-12. Sheets 2 (D-F), 4 (K-M), and 7-9 (T-2D) are unfigured.

Notes: The last notice in the catalogue appended to some copies is of the pending issue on 1 June of the revised *Waverley Novels,* 18° hot pressed at 5s a volume.

REPRINTS

FRANCE

PARIS: Didot and Galignani
[~] Tales of a Grandfather. . . Second Series. 1829. Two volumes. (Collection of Modern English Authors: *see* 292R.21-22.)

PARIS: Galignani
[~] Tales of a Grandfather. . . . Second Series. 1828. Three volumes. (*see* 293R.4-6.) Copy: not seen.

GERMANY

220Ra] BERLIN: Schlesinger 1828
[Tales of a Grandfather. Second Series. Berlin, Printed for Adolph Martin Schlesinger. 1828]. Copy reported at Stadt-u. Universitätsbibliothek, Frankfurt am Main.

ZWICKAU: Schumann
[~] Tales of a Grandfather. Second Series. 1829. (Pocket Library of English Classics: *see* 302R. entry following 198.)

UNITED STATES

220Rb] BOSTON: Parker 1829
Tales of a Grandfather; . . . Second Series. . . . Boston: Samuel H. Parker, No. 164 Washington Street. 1829. Two volumes. Pages 1: *1-5* 6-233; 2: *1-3* 4-223. Copies: MWA RPB. Notes: Scott not identified on the title-page. (Also reissued 1829 in Novels Tales and Romances: *see* 305R.23.)

[~] Tales of a Grandfather. Second Series. 1829. (Waverley Novels: *see* 306R.44-45.)

220Rc] NEW YORK: Burgess 1829-1831
Tales of a Grandfather; Being Stories Taken from Scottish History. Humbly inscribed to Hugh Littlejohn, Esq. By Sir Walter Scott, Author of "Waverly(!)," &c. &c. . . . Second Series. New-York: Published by William Burgess, Juvenile Emporium, No. 97 Fulton-street. 1829. Two volumes. Pages 1: *i-v* vi-viii, *9* 10-332; 2: *i-iii* iv-v *vi*, *7* 8-320. Notes: Each printed title-page is preceded by a conjugate engraved frontispiece and vignette title-page dated 1829, all copied from the Edinburgh edition. Bound in printed boards which read 'Second American Edition'. Copies: E; MWA NjP NN(vol.2) NNU-W(vol.2). Reference: Kohler(1) 72 (with illustration). Reissued 1831 (NN[vol.2].)

220Rd] PHILADELPHIA: Carey, Lea & Carey 1829[1828]
Tales of a Grandfather; Being Stories taken from Scottish History . . . Second Series. Philadelphia: Carey, Lea & Carey, Chesnut Street. 1829. Two volumes. Pages 1: *1-4*, *9* 10-296; 2: *1-2* *5* 6-286. Notes: Three weeks before issue of the Edinburgh edition, on 6 November 1828, this first American edition was announced as 'In the Press' and then, before its own imprint date, published 23 December (*NG*). Copies: O; PPL T/B.

THE COURSER'S MANUAL

221A] First Printings: 1828

1] 'My Greyhounds' (first words: 'Remember'st thou my Greyhounds true?'), page vii,

2] 'Twas when fleet Snowball's head was waxen grey' (first words, with no title,) page lxxi,

3] 'The last dying Words of Bonny Heck, A Famous Greyhound in the Shire of Fife', (first words: 'Alas, alas, quo' bonny Heck,'), pages lxxii-lxxvi, included in a letter of transmittal dated 16 October 1828, *in*:

The Courser's Manual or Stud-Book. . . . By Thomas Goodlake, Esq. Liverpool: Printed by Harris and Co. for Geo. B. Whittaker, Ave Maria Lane, and Jos. Booker, Bond-Street, London. MDCCCXXVIII.

Published 28 November 1828 in London (*MC*).

Notes: The first Scott contribution is a four-line epigraph; the second, ten lines of untitled verse. The third, Scott's principal contribution, is the provision of an elegy which, as he reports, first appeared in James Watson's *A Choice Collection of Comic and Serious Scots Poems*, Edinburgh 1706. This version is preceded by an extensive 'notice' in Scott's letter of transmittal, acknowledging as his own a 'few glossarial notes'—actually twelve for this poem of fourteen six-line stanzas. Otherwise the elegy is modernized in its accidentals and, on comparison with the 1706 printing, exhibits two minor variants (line 43 Wily, Witty] witty, wily; 58 Amry] amby), both of which might be attributed to the printer.

Copies: E O; CtY.

References: (Magnum Opus Edition: Not reprinted, but the 'notice' quoted in *Letters*, xi.14-17.)

ESSAYS ON PLANTING AND GARDENING

222A] Projected Scott Edition: 1828

Notes: Scott first proposed this subject to Lockhart in December 1827 as one suitable for Murray's *Family Library*, this just after he had reviewed Robert Monteath's book on planting (*see* 205A). After an inexact reference to the project in the 'Literary Intelligence' section of *The Athenaeum*, 19 February 1828, where the title is given in reverse, no further publicity appears until the 15 November number of the *Edinburgh Literary Journal*, which notes that 'The indefatigable Author of Waverley is about to publish "Essays on Planting and Gardening," in one pocket volume.' Meanwhile, in another letter to Lockhart, 3 September, Scott acknowledged that his 'pop-gun might be accounted an act of rivalry' with other pending commentaries and, in effect, withdrew his proposal. References: *Letters*, x.321, 497.

PROCEEDINGS HELD UPON JOHN, MASTER OF SINCLAIR

223A] First Edition: 1828

PROCEEDINGS | IN | **THE COURT-MARTIAL,** | HELD UPON | **JOHN, MASTER OF SINCLAIR,** | CAPTAIN-LIEUTENANT IN PRESTON'S REGIMENT, | FOR | THE MURDER OF ENSIGN SCHAW | OF THE SAME REGIMENT, | AND | CAPTAIN SCHAW, OF THE ROYALS, | 17TH OCTOBER 1708. | WITH | **CORRESPONDENCE** | RESPECTING THAT TRANSACTION. | [*short rule*] | EDINBURGH: | PRINTED BY BALLANTYNE AND COMPANY. | MDCCCXXVIII.

Printed ca. December 1828 in Edinburgh. 52 copies (Dibdin). Binding: Roxburghe Club pink silk or maroon boards with black leather spine. Paper: Demy 4° (261 x

212mm uncut). Watermarks: J WHATMAN | 1808. Collation: $\pi^2(\pi 2+1)$ A-B^4 A-E^4 *F*1. Pagination: *1* title-page, *2 blank*, *3* undated dedication by Scott 'To the President and Members of the Roxburghe Club', *4 blank*, *1* roster, *2 blank*, *i* ii-xv Introduction, *xvi blank*, *1* 2-41 text, *42 blank*. No printer's imprint. Typography: The roster lists the recipient's name in red; some copies (for more general distribution?) substitute a two-page list (*1*-2) of the 31 members. Figures: *none.*

Notes: A cancelled dedication 'To the Members . . .' notes that the account is 'from an original and authentic manuscript in the Editor's possession', and is dated from Abbotsford 1 December 1828. It occurs alone in the E and DLC copies and is inserted after the final state described above in the NN and TxU(Bolland) copies. The manuscript materials, concerning both the Sinclairs and Schaws, Scott reports (page xv) were found 'among the papers of his deceased mother, who was related (according to the Scottish ideas of consanguinity)' to both families.

Scott was elected to the Roxburghe Club in 1823, but dined with the members only once, on 15 May 1828. Those then attending, he observed, were rather poor company: 'Lord Clive, besides whom I sate, was deaf though intelligent and goodhumourd, the Duke of Devonshire was still deafer.' [The enfeebled Duke, it may be remarked, was nineteen years younger than Scott.]

Copies: A(The Earl Gower) E(Abbot) GU(Edward Littledale) L[without roster] L(George Watson Taylor, M.P.) O(George Hibbert); DLC(The Duke of Devonshire, K.G.) InU(George Henry Freeling) MH(Thomas Ponton) NN(Viscount Clive) TxU(William Bolland) TxU(John Delafield Phelps).

References: Abbotsford, page 276; *Journal*, page 475; Dibdin, *Reminiscences*, i.468. (Magnum Opus Edition: Not reprinted.)

REVIEWS OF MORIER and FRASER

224A] First Printing: 1829

'ART. III.—[1.] *The Adventures of Hajji Baba of Ispahan in England.* 2. *The Kuzzilbash: a Tale of Khorasan.*', pages 73-99, *in*:

The Quarterly Review. [January, 1829. No.77, volume 39 imprint:] London: John Murray, Albemarle Street. 1829.

Published 28 January 1829 in London (*MC*, 26 January, 'On Wednesday' [28th]).

Notes: The two books were by James Justinian Morier and James Baillie Fraser.

Copies: BCL L O; PPL.

References: Thomson, page 48. (Magnum Opus Edition 1835: *The Miscellaneous Prose Works*, xviii.354-398 as 'Hajji Baba in England'.)

PROSPECTUS OF A NEW EDITION OF THE WAVERLEY NOVELS

225A] First Printings: 1829

'AUTHOR'S ADVERTISEMENT.', pages 5-8, *in*:

[*half-title:*] Prospectus of a New Edition of the Waverley Novels, with the Author's Notes, and New Introductions. [*title:*] Edinburgh, February 1829. WAVERLEY NOVELS. . . . Edinburgh: Published for the Proprietors, By Cadell & Company, Edinburgh; Simpkin and Marshall, London; And to be had of all Booksellers throughout the kingdom.

Published 16 February 1829 (*Letters,* xi.141). Scott's 'Advertisement' and other particulars are quoted at length in various papers, including *ELJ*, *EEC*, *EWJ* (7, 12, 25 March respectively and often thereafter). In his *Journal* for 4 March Scott observes: 'The prospectus of the magnum already issued only a week has produced such a demand among the trade that he [Cadell] thinks he must add a large number of copies that the present edition of 7000 may be increased to the demand—he talks of raising it to ten or 12,000.' [By the end of the year, according to Cadell's ledgers, the issue of the first two volumes had reached 30,750 copies.]

Notes: The first public intimation of a pending 'Magnum Opus' appeared six months before this formal prospectus, on 9 August 1828 (see above, page 614, note 6), where several artists were then identified as already engaged for the edition. Of this later, formal announcement there are at least three early issues: (1) first setting, no insert after page 10, page 12 reads: *The following are nearly ready for publication.*; (2) first setting, two-leaf insert containing as a specimen *Waverley* volume 2 pages 75-78; (3) second setting, two-leaf insert of *Guy Mannering* volume 4 pages 317-320, page 12 reads: *The following will shortly be published.* The order of issue is further confirmed by the punctuation in Scott's 'Advertisement', which, like that in the edition, is dated from Abbotsford January 1829:

(1)-(2)	(3)	text in vol. 1
5.12 the events,	the events,	*i*.12 the events
7.9 epithets,—	epithets—	iii.12 epithets—
alterations,	alterations,	alterations

In a later separate issue (T/B), dated 1 August 1829, Scott's text was removed to accomodate extensive excerpts from 26 reviews of the first two volumes, these issued together on 1 June (348Aa). It was then announced that, at the request of the booksellers, beginning on 1 August only one volume would be issued at a time. In the last issue observed (*see* 244A insert), a 16-page prospectus for a new monthly issue of the novels, dated December 1830, Scott's text was reset and reinserted, here with different lining and paged 5-9. The punctuation for this setting corresponds to that for (3) as cited above, but the article 'the', common to all of the earlier printings, has now been deleted.

A week after initial issue of the Prospectus, on 23 February 1829, Charles Heath, one of the engravers there listed, was so brash as to inform Scott that, as the pending edition consisted only of old works, 'the *Plates* will be a great attraction, particularly now when the Arts are so appreciated—much of the extensiveness of the sale will depend on their *excellence* both as to design and Engraving.' Two days later, however, the *Athenaeum* reviewer took immediate exception to these projected illustrations—'an invention of the devil' (pages *113*-114)—providing, as he later remarked, 'the gross substitution of a reality for our finest imaginings' (18 September 1830, page 589).

Copies: (Issue 1)EP. (2) O(J. Johnson). (3) O(J. Johnson).

References: *Journal*, pages 525,n.2, 527; Lockhart, ix.326; Millgate(4), pages 21, 125, n.51. (Magnum Opus Edition 1829: *Waverley Novels*, i.i-iv.)

REVIEW OF PITSLIGO

226A] First Printing: 1829

'LORD PITSLIGO.', pages 593-600, *in*:

Blackwood's Edinburgh Magazine. May, 1829. No. CLII. Vol. XXV. [imprint:] William Blackwood, No. 17, Prince's Street, Edinburgh; and T. Cadell, Strand, London.

Published ca. 30 April 1829 in Edinburgh. Notes: This account, in the form of a letter, actually is a review of Alexander Lord Pitsligo's *Thoughts concerning Man's Condition and Duties in This Life*.

Copies: L O; NjP PPL.

References: *Letters*, xi.227n. (Magnum Opus Edition: Not reprinted.)

ANNE OF GEIERSTEIN

227A] First Edition: 1829

ANNE OF GEIERSTEIN; | OR, | **THE MAIDEN OF THE MIST.** | BY | THE AUTHOR OF "WAVERLEY," &c. | [*short rule*] | [*two-line quotation from Shakespeare*] | [*short rule*] | IN THREE VOLUMES. | VOL. I [II-III]. | [*short reversed Oxford rule*] | EDINBURGH: | PRINTED FOR CADELL AND CO., EDINBURGH; | AND SIMPKIN AND MARSHALL, LONDON. | [*dash*] | 1829.

Published 20 May 1829 in Edinburgh (*EWJ*); issued 25 May in London (*MC*). £1.11.6. Binding: drab, grey-blue, grey-green, or tan boards with printed labels. Paper: Post 8° and 12° (208 x 125mm uncut). Watermarks: none. Typography: Printer's imprints (1) and (2) read invariably: [*short rule*] | EDINBURGH: | PRINTED BY BALLANTYNE AND COMPANY, | PAUL'S WORK, CANONGATE.

General Notes: According to established practice, beginning with *Kenilworth* (*see* 149Aa), on 12 May 1829, a week before the publication of this novel, some 6800 words (volume 1, chapter 2 in this Edinburgh edition) were extracted in the Philadelphia *National Gazette*, these deriving from proofs early shipped for the Carey, Lea & Carey edition (227Rc).

Copies: BCL(4) E(3) L(2) LU(2) O(16); CtY IdU InU(2) InU* MH+ NN NNU-W(2) T/B TxU(2) ViU(3).
*With 4-page Longman catalogue December 1828.
+Volumes 1, 3 are interleaved and with Scott's revisions and corrections throughout for the Magnum Opus Edition.

References: Church 551; Sterling 719, 743; Thomson, page 11; Van Antwerp(1) 25; Worthington 22. (Magnum Opus Edition 1833: *Waverley Novels*, xliv-xlv.)

1] **ANNE OF GEIERSTEIN;** . . . VOL. I. . . . 1829.

Collation: π^2 A-M^8 N-O^{12} Q-T^{12}. Pagination: *i* half-title, *ii blank, iii* title-page, *iv* printer's imprint(1), *1* fly-title, *2 blank, 3* 4-336 text, 336 printer's imprint(2). Figures: A15-3 16-14/4, B31-11 32-13, C47-5 48-1/-, D63-12 64-10, E79-16 80-11, F95-3 96-13, G110-10 112-9, H127-7 128-11, I 139-12 144-8, K154-11 160-17, L175-5 176-11, M191-16 192-9, N215-3 216-7, O 230-11 240-5, Q263-7/- 264-10, R286-8 288-5, S302-4/- 312-10, T—. As indicated, in some copies page 16 the figure 14 lacks the first digit, presumably dropped in the course of printing.

Notes: The shift from 8° to 12° at signature N and the absence of signature P indicate several uncertainties in the presswork.

2] **ANNE OF GEIERSTEIN;** . . . VOL. II. . . . 1829.

Collation: π^2 A-K^{12} L^{12}(±L12) M-O^{12} P^6(-P6). Pagination: *i* half-title, *ii blank, iii* title-page, *iv* printer's imprint(1), *1* fly-title, *2 blank, 3* 4-346 text, 346 printer's imprint(2). Typography: Section signature K2 (page 225) is missigned X2.

Figures: A14-4/- 24-1, B39-2 48-8, C71-16 72-12/-, D86-11 93-10, E—, F—, G—, H191-7 192-5, I—, K239-16 240-9, L251-11, M—, N—, O—, P343-11.

Notes: The manuscript text exhibits seven readings revised in cancel leaf L12, the first, page 263, line 5, earlier reading 'had', now altered to 'had been'.

3] **ANNE OF GEIERSTEIN;** . . . VOL. III. . . . 1829.

Collation: π^2 A-Q^{12}. Pagination: *i* half-title, *ii blank, iii* title-page, *iv* printer's imprint(1), *1* fly-title, *2 blank, 3* 4-381 text, 381 printer's imprint(2), *382 blank, 383-384* advertisement for Cadell and Company.

Figures: A23-12 24-10, B—, C—, D—, E106-13 112-14, F143-6 144-8, G154-14 168-12, H—, I 195-8 216-6, K238-3 240-6, L—, M274-2/16 280-8, N310-13 312-5, O—, P—, Q—.

Notes: The first entry in Cadell's 'Works Published' advertisement, perhaps a week or so ahead of time, is for volumes 1-2 in the 'New Edition of the Waverley Novels [Magnum Opus, *see* 348Aa] royal 18mo, price 10s., done up in cloth.—*(To be continued Monthly, and delivered with the Magazines and Reviews.)*'—that is, on 31 May 1829. It was later decided to issue only one volume a month.

REPRINTS

FRANCE

PARIS: Didot and Galignani
[~] Anne of Geierstein. 1829. (Collection of Modern Engllish Authors: *see* 291R.68-70.)

GERMANY

227Ra] BERLIN: Schlesinger 1829-1830
Anne of Geierstein; or, The Maiden of the Mist. By Sir Walter Scott. . . Berlin, Published by Adolph Martin Schlesinger, 1829-1830. Three volumes. Pages [1829] 1: *i-ii, 1* 2-192; [1830] 2: *i-ii, 1* 2-195 *196*; 3: *i-ii, 1* 2-214. Copy: O. Reference: GDS 132, page 338.

ZWICKAU: Schumann
[~] Anne of Geierstein. 1829. (Pocket Library of English Classics: *see* 302R.218-222.)

UNITED STATES

227Rb] NEW YORK: Harper 1829
Anne of Geierstein; or, The Maiden of the Mist. By the Author of "Waverley." . . . New=York: Printed for J. & J. Harper. 1829. Two volumes. Pages 1: *1-2, 13* 14-264; 2: *1-2, 5* 6-278. Notes: Variant issue of the Philadelphia, Carey edition, cited in the next entry, The pagination reflects the anticipation of receiving a Scott introduction, which did not arrive before the publication date. Copies: E; CtY(vol.1) DLC MWA NN(2) NNU-W TxU. Reference: Kohler(1) 71(with illustration).

227Rc] PHILADELPHIA: Carey, Lea and Carey 1829
Anne of Geierstein; or, The Maiden of the Mist. By the Author of "Waverley." . . . Philadelphia: Carey, Lea & Carey—Chesnut Street. 1829. Two volumes. Pages 1: *1-2, 13* 14-264; 2: *1-2, 5* 6-278. Notes: The first American edition, set from Edinburgh proofs, extracted in the *National Gazette* 12 May 1829 (227A), and issued 30 June (*NG*). Copies: E O; MH(vol.1) NNU-W PPL RPB ViU. Reference: Kohler(1) 199(with illustration).

REVIEW OF RITSON

228A] First Printing: 1829

'ART. V.—*Annals of the Caledonians, Picts, and Scots;* . . . By Joseph Ritson, Esq.', pages 120-162, *in*:

The Quarterly Review. [July, 1829. No.81, volume 41 imprint:] London: John Murray, Albemarle Street. 1829.

Published 20 July 1829 in London (*MC*); issued 25 July in Edinburgh (*EEC*).

Copies: BCL L O; PPL.

References: Thomson, page 57. (Magnum Opus Edition 1835: *The Miscellaneous Prose Works*, xx.301-376 as 'Ancient History of Scotland'.)

CHARACTER SKETCH OF CATHERINE COCKBURN

229Aa] First 8° Printing: 1829

[Character Sketch of Catherine Cockburn], volume 1, pages liv-lvii *in*:

The Scottish Songs; Collected and Illustrated by Robert Chambers, . . . Edinburgh: Printed by Ballantyne and Company, for William Tait, 78 Princes Street. MDCCCXXIX.

Octavo edition issued 5 August 1829 in London (*Ath*). 18s.

Notes: After a brief preface dated from Hanover Street, 27 April 1829, Chambers presents a lengthy 'Historical Essay on Scottish Song', where Scott's memoir is introduced page liv as follows: 'That the reader may have a just idea of the sort of good society which thus gave encouragement to Scottish song about the middle of the last century, I beg to introduce a brief characteristic notice of Mrs Cockburn, with which I have been politely favoured by Sir Walter Scott, her surviving friend.' The memoir, occupying nine paragraphs, notes that she was the author of 'The Flowers of the Forest' (pages 118-119), as a Rutherford of Fairnalee distantly related to Scott's mother, and composed some verse for his father. Fifteen of Scott's own poems also are represented in this anthology (*see* 369E[3]).
Copies: InU NN. Reference: (Magnum Opus Edition: Not reprinted.)

229Ab] First 12° Printing: 1829

[Character Sketch of Catherine Cockburn], volume 1, pages lx-lxiii *in*:

The Scottish Songs; Collected and Illustrated by Robert Chambers, . . . Edinburgh: Printed by Ballantyne and Company, for William Tait, 78 Princes Street. MDCCCXXIX.

Duodecimo edition issued concurrently with the octavo 5 August 1829 in London (*Ath*). 12s.

Notes: Though advertised as an 18°, this is actually a 12° in sixes, of a different setting from the 8° issue, thus with Scott's memoir differently paged. Priority of setting has not been determined, and the variant pagination requires a separate entry among the anthologies (*see* 369E[4]).

Copies: E E(vol.1); T/B.

REVIEWS OF COMTE DE MODENE and LE DUC DE GUISE

230A] First Printing: 1829

'ART. I.--1. *Mémoires du* Comte de Modene *sur la Revolution de Naples de* 1647. 2. *Le Duc de Guise à Naples . . . en* 1647 *et* 1648.', pages *355* 356-403, *in*:

The Foreign Quarterly Review. [August, 1829. No.8, volume 4 imprint:] London: Treuttel and Würtz, Treuttel, Jun. and Richter. 30, Soho Square. 1829.

Published 15 August 1829 in London (*MC*).

Notes: This, the first article in issue number 8, was at once recognized as Scott's, 'and it is every way worthy of his fame and genius' (*Ath*, 19 August, page 516).

Copies: BCL L O; NjP PU(2).

References: *Letters*, xi.132n.1,3. (Magnum Opus Edition: Not reprinted.)

THE LIFE OF GENERAL THE EARL OF PETERBOROUGH

231A] Projected Scott Edition: 1829

Scheduled for issue in London 1 September 1829.

Notes: Following upon a preliminary announcement 7 March 1829 in the *Edinburgh Literary Journal* that this *Life* would appear 'during the present year', Scott on 16

April noted in his Journal that it remained a deal still 'on hand', and the book accordingly appears in John Murray's May list of volumes forthcoming in his *Family Library* series (list inserted in the second volume T/B copy of Lockhart's *History of Napoleon Buonaparte*, issued 1 May, *see* 200Da). According to this monthly schedule Scott's work, as the 5th book, was due on 1 September, but nothing further is reported. Scott's interest in the General is noted as early as 1808 in the *Memoirs of Capt. George Carleton* (*see* 31Aa) and again 1811 in *The Vision of Don Roderick* (*see* 59Aa).

Reference: *Journal*, page 548.

THE HISTORY OF SCOTLAND

232Aa] First Edition, First (Primary) Issue: 1830[1829]

[*First title*] THE | **CABINET CYCLOPAEDIA.** | CONDUCTED BY THE | REV. DIONYSIUS LARDNER, LL.D. F.R.S. L.& E. | M.R.I.A. F.L.S. F.Z.S. Hon.F.C.P.S. M.Ast.S. &c. &c. | ASSISTED BY | EMINENT LITERARY AND SCIENTIFIC MEN. | [*dash*] | History. | [*dash*] | SCOTLAND. | BY | SIR WALTER SCOTT, BART. | VOL. I [II]. | [*short rule*] | LONDON: | PRINTED FOR | LONGMAN, REES, ORME, BROWN, AND GREEN, | PATERNOSTER-ROW; | AND JOHN TAYLOR, | UPPER GOWER STREET. | 1830.

[*Second, alternate title*] THE | **CABINET OF HISTORY.** | CONDUCTED BY THE | REV. DIONYSIUS LARDNER, LL.D. F.R.S. L.& E. | M.R.I.A. F.L.S. F.Z.S. Hon.F.C.P.S. M.Ast.S. &c. &c. | ASSISTED BY | EMINENT LITERARY MEN. | [*short rule*] | THE | **HISTORY OF SCOTLAND.** | BY | SIR WALTER SCOTT, BART. | VOL. I [II]. | [*short rule*] | LONDON: | PRINTED FOR | LONGMAN, REES, ORME, BROWN, AND GREEN, | PATERNOSTER-ROW; | AND JOHN TAYLOR, | UPPER GOWER STREET. | 1830.

[*Third, alternate title*] THE | **CABINET HISTORY** | OF | **ENGLAND, SCOTLAND, AND** | **IRELAND.** | BY | THE RIGHT HON. SIR JAMES MACKINTOSH, M.P. | SIR WALTER SCOTT, BART. AND | THOMAS MOORE, ESQ. | [*short rule*] | SCOTLAND. | VOL. I [II]. | [*short rule*] | LONDON: | PRINTED FOR | LONGMAN, REES, ORME, BROWN, AND GREEN, | PATERNOSTER-ROW; | AND JOHN TAYLOR, | UPPER GOWER STREET. | 1830.

Published 1 November 1829 (vol.1) and 1 March 1830 (vol.2) in London (*MC* 31

October; 30 November and 25 February for 'Monday March 1'). 6s. Binding: maroon cloth with printed labels. Paper: Royal 16° in eights (170 x 105mm uncut; machine-wove?). Watermarks: *none*.

General Notes: In his own Advertisement within the book, Scott differentiates this more scholarly account from his earlier, simplified *Tales of a Grandfather*. Unstated is the fact that, whereas the *Tales* carry the history forward to the close of the rebellion of 1745, this account concludes in 1603 with the accession of James VI to the throne of England. A separate eight-page 'Prospectus' in some copies sets forth the several objectives of the 'Cabinet Cyclopaedia' and cites Scott's *History of Scotland* as the first and fourth volumes in the collection: a designation not represented in the books.

Copies in original state have a half-title with an imprint on verso, an inserted engraved title, and the first printed title without imprint on verso. The second and third alternate titles, each with imprint on verso, in original issue are bound as a conjugate pair at the back of each volume and may be found folded with either title first. In all volumes the engraved title, which may follow either the half-title or the first title, the vignettes are by H. Corbould, engraved by E. Finden. Because of the vagaries of nineteenth century binders, the position and inclusion of printed and engraved title-pages in all privately bound volumes is highly variable. Whereever placed, the printer's imprints read, uniformly: (1) and (2) London: | Printed by A. & R. Spottiswoode, | New-Street-Square. There are no press figures.

Copies: Volume 1 engraved title (state 1) BCL L; InU MWA(engraved titles only) NN. (2) BCL E; CtY NN NNU-W T/B(engraved titles with second printed titles only) TxU.

References: Morse Peckham, 'Dr. Lardner's *Cabinet Cyclopaedia*,' *PBSA* 45 (1951), 37-58; Thomson, page 60; Van Antwerp(1) 31(engraved titles only, illustration of corrected page proofs after page 62). (Magnum Opus Edition: Not reprinted.

1] THE | **CABINET CYCLOPAEDIA.** . . . VOL. I. . . . 1830.

Collation: A-Z⁸. Pagination: *i* half-title, *ii* printer's imprint(1), [*engraved vignette title*], *iii* first title-page, *iv blank*, *v*-vi Advertisement, dated from Abbotsford 1 November 1829, *vii* viii-xii Contents, *1* 2-352 text, 352 printer's imprint(2). Typography: In some copies an errata slip is inserted. Page *v* is signed A3.

Notes: In all issues the first engraved title, beginning 'The | HISTORY of SCOTLAND' is in two states, dated (1) 1829 or (2) 1830. It will be noted that, as in certain volumes of his 'Magnum' *WN* series, Scott's Advertisement date is assigned to correspond with actual date of issue.

2] THE | **CABINET CYCLOPAEDIA.** . . . VOL. II. . . . 1830.

Collation: A⁶ B-2E⁸ 2F⁴. Pagination: *i* half-title, *ii* printer's imprint(1), [*engraved

vignette title], *iii* first title-page, *iv blank, v* vi-xii Contents, *1* 2-427 text, *428* Kings of Scotland, *429* 430-438 Index, 438 printer's imprint(2), *439* Errata, *440 blank.*
Typography: Page *v* is signed A3. Double signatures are represented as AA, BB, etc.

Notes: The engraved title is invariably dated 1830.

232Ab] First Edition, Second Issue: 1832

THE | **CABINET OF HISTORY.** | CONDUCTED BY THE | REV. DIONYSIUS LARDNER, LL.D. F.R.S. L.& E. | M.R.I.A. F.L.S. F.Z.S. Hon.F.C.P.S. M.Ast.S. &c. &c. | ASSISTED BY | EMINENT LITERARY MEN. | [*short rule*] | THE | **HISTORY OF SCOTLAND.** | BY | SIR WALTER SCOTT, BART. | VOL. I [II]. | [*short rule*] | LONDON: | PRINTED FOR | LONGMAN, REES, ORME, BROWN, GREEN, & LONGMAN, | PATERNOSTER-ROW; | AND JOHN TAYLOR, | UPPER GOWER STREET. | 1832.

General Notes: This issue is styled like the 1830 second, alternate title, without half-titles and with printer's imprint on the verso of the title-page. Engraved volume 1 title again may be dated (1) 1829, or (2) 1830. (Though other title variants dated 1832 have not been noted, in the 1835 issue all three variants appear in CtY, LU and NN copies respectively. Furthermore, in the CtY set, volume 2 is dated 1836.)

Copies: (state 1) BCL ES LU(vol.2). (2) IdU(engraved titles only).

REPRINTS

FRANCE

PARIS: Didot and Galignani
[~] History of Scotland. 1830. (Collection of Modern English Authors: *see* 292R.31-32)

GERMANY

232Ra] LEIPZIG: Leske 1830-1831
[The History of Scotland. . . . Leipzick und Darmstadt: C.W. Leske, 1830-1831. Two volumes.]
Copy reported at Landesbibliothek Wiesbaden. Reference: GDS 132, page 339.

ZWICKAU: Schumann
[~] The History of Scotland. 1830-1831. (Pocket Library of English Classics: *see* 302R.223-225, 230-232.)

UNITED STATES

232Rb] CAMBRIDGE: Hilliard and Brown 1830
The History of Scotland. By Sir Walter Scott, Bart. . . . Cambridge: Published by Hilliard & Brown. Boston: Hilliard, Gray, Little & Wilkins, and Carter & Hendee. New-York: G. & C. & H. Carvill. 1830. Two volumes. Pages 1: *i-iii* iv-x, *1* 2-338; 2: *i-iii* iv-x, *1* 2-417. Copies: MWA NNU-W(vol.1) T/B.

232Rc] NEW YORK: Harper 1830
The History of Scotland by Sir Walter Scott, Bart. . . . New-York: Harper & Brothers, 82 Cliff-St. [1830]. Notes: Variant issue, with undated imprint, of the 1830 Philadelphia, Carey & Lea edition, but without the general titles: *see* next entry. Copy: NN.

232Rd] PHILADELPHIA: Carey and Lea 1830
The History of Scotland. By Sir Walter Scott, Bart. . . . Philadelphia. Carey & Lea.—Chestnut Street. 1830. Two volumes. Pages 1: *iii-v* vi *vii* viii-xi *xii*, *13* 14-332; 2: *i-v* vi-xii, *13* 14-407. Notes: First American edition, announced 29 December 1829 as 'sent to press'; the first volume published 13 February 1830, the second volume on 8 May (*NG*). 1500 copies were printed. The specific title-pages cited above may be preceded by one or two general titles: (1) The Cabinet Cyclopaedia. Conducted by the Rev. Dionysius Lardner, . . . [and/or] The Cabinet of History. In a later state these general titles are amended to read: (2) The Cabinet Cyclopaedia, (Dionysius Lardner): volumes 100-101 [and/or] The Cabinet History of England, Scotland, and Ireland. (James Mackintosh, Scott, Thomas Moore). Copies: (1) CtY MWA RPB ViU(vol.1). (2) E; NjP(vol.1) NN(vol.2) PPL ViU(vol.1). References: Kaser 196; Kohler(1) 201(with illustration). Later issues are dated 1835 and, under the imprint of Carey, Lea & Blanchard, 1836 (ViU).

THE HOUSE OF ASPEN

233A] First Printing: 1829

'THE HOUSE OF ASPEN, A TRAGEDY. BY SIR WALTER SCOTT.', pages *1* 2-66, *in*:

The Keepsake for MDCCCXXX. Edited by Frederic Mansel Reynolds. London: Published for the Proprietor, by Hurst, Chance, and Co., 65, St. Paul's Churchyard, and R. Jennings, 62, Cheapside. [1829].

Published 14 November 1829 in London (*Ath* 11 November). Advance review in Edinburgh 24 October (*ELJ*, pages *285* 286-287).

In this play there are first printings of poetry: [1] 'Song' (first words: 'Joy to the victors! The sons of old Aspen!') pages 25-26; [2] 'Song' (first words: 'Sweet shone the sun on the fair lake of Toro') pages 28-29; [3] 'Rhein-Wein Leid[!]' (first words: 'What makes the troopers' frozen courage muster?') page 48. Song [2] is a variant of an 1806 poem 'The Maid of Toro' (21Aa); song [1] was extracted 1830 in a U.S. anthology (477E.1).

Notes: In the preliminary 'Advertisement', dated from Abbotsford, 1 April 1829, Scott admits that this play was written thirty years earlier and that he 'borrowed the substance of the story and a part of the diction from a dramatic romance called "Der Heilige Vehm" (The Secret Tribunal), which fills the sixth volume of the "Sagen den Vorzeit" (*Tales of Antiquity*), by Beit Weber.' A correspondent to the *Edinburgh Literary Journal* (2 January 1830, page 15) identified the 'Weber' pseudonym as that of Ludwig Leonhardt Waechter (or, rather, Georg Phillipp Ludwig Leonhard Wächter).

The play is illustrated with two engraved plates, both printed by McQueen and published by Hurst & Co., R. Jennings, and by Giraldon Bovinet, Galerie Vivienne, Paris. Facing page 33: 'George of Aspen and Isabella.' painted by F. P. Stephanoff, engraved by J. Mitchell; page 46, 'Isabella and Gertrude.' drawn by A. E. Chalon, R.A., engraved by F. Bacon.

Copies: BCL; CtY(2) NN T/B.

References: Ruff 186. (Magnum Opus Edition 1834: *The Poetical Works*, xii.*363-364* 365-441.)

REPRINTS

FRANCE

PARIS: Didot and Galignani
[~] The House of Aspen. 1830. (Collection of Modern English Authors: *see* 292R.29.)

UNITED STATES

233R] PHILADELPHIA: Alexander 1830
The House of Aspen, A Tragedy. By Sir Walter Scott. London--1829. Re-Published in Philadelphia. C. Alexander, Pr. 1830. Pages: *1-5* 6-69. Copies: MWA NN.

DERIVATIVE

UNITED STATES

233D] NEW YORK: Riley 1830
The Maid of Toro from the Musical Bijou for 1830. Written by Sr. Walter Scott. . . . New-York, Published by [Edward] Riley, 29, Chatham Street. [ca.1830]. Pages: *1* 2-3. Notes: Engraved sheet music. Words from act 3, scene 1 (first words: 'O! low shone the sun on the fair lake of Toro, And weak were the whispers'). Music composed by John Parry arranged for voice and pianoforte. Copy: MWA.

TALES OF A GRANDFATHER
[Third Series]

234A] First Edition: 1830[1829]

TALES | OF | **A GRANDFATHER;** | BEING | **STORIES** | TAKEN FROM | **SCOTTISH HISTORY.** | HUMBLY INSCRIBED | TO | HUGH LITTLEJOHN, Esq. | IN THREE VOLS. | VOL. I [II-III]. | 𝔗𝔥𝔦𝔯𝔡 𝔖𝔢𝔯𝔦𝔢𝔰. | [*short rule*] | PRINTED FOR CADELL AND CO. EDINBURGH; | SIMPKIN AND MARSHALL, LONDON; AND | JOHN CUMMING, DUBLIN. | [*dash*] | 1830.

Published concurrently 21 December 1829 in Edinburgh (*EEC* 10 and 21 December); 23 December in London (*MC*). Advance review in Edinburgh on 19 December (*ELJ*). 10s.6d. Binding: half green or maroon roan without labels or cloth and drab boards with printed labels. Paper: Royal 18° in 6s (150 x 92 uncut). Watermarks: *none*. Typography: Printer's imprints read: [*short rule*] | EDINBURGH: | PRINTED BY BALLANTYNE AND COMPANY, | PAUL'S WORK, CANONGATE. Illustrations: In this series the engraved frontispieces and titles now precede the printed title.

General Notes: A month before issue, on 24 November, the Philadelphia firm of Carey & Lea announced this work as 'In the Press' (*NG*), another indication that it was still receiving advance copy. Remainder copies of the original issue were later advertised under the title 'Sir Walter Scott's Stories from Scottish History', but still at the original price of 10s.6d (*MLA* March 1831, item 7).

Copies: BCL(2) E(2) HS+ LU O(5); CtY IdU InU(vols.2-3) NNU-W T/B TxU.
+With 2-page Cadell advertisement dated December 1829.

References: Thomson, page 70; Van Antwerp(1) 29. (Magnum Opus Edition 1836: The Miscellaneous Prose Works, xxv.*107-109* 110-433—xxvi.)

1] **TALES** | OF | **A GRANDFATHER;** ... VOL. I. | 𝔗𝔥𝔦𝔯𝔡 𝔖𝔢𝔯𝔦𝔢𝔰. ... 1830.

Collation: π^6 $2\pi^4$(-2π4) A-2C^6 2D^2. Pagination: [*frontispiece, engraved title*], *i* title-page, *ii* printer's imprint(1), *iii* iv-xii Prefatory Letter, dated from Abbotsford 1 December 1829, *iii* iv-vii Contents, *viii blank*, *1* fly-title, *2 blank*, *3* 4-316 text, 316 printer's imprint(2). Illustrations: The frontispiece engraved by W. H. Lizars is captioned 'The Chevalier de St. George.'; title vignette is drawn by S. Watson, engraved by W. H. Lizars.

Figures: As usual in this format the gatherings are numbered throughout, but now figured only in sheet 2: D42-18, E59-13.

2] **TALES** | OF | **A GRANDFATHER;** . . . VOL. II. | Third Series. . . . 1830.

Collation: π1 2π² A-2D⁶ 2E⁴. Pagination: [*frontispiece, engraved title*], *i* title-page, *ii* printer's imprint(1), *iii* iv-vi Contents, *1* fly-title, *2 blank*, *3* 4-331 text, 331 printer's imprint(2), *332 blank*. Illustrations: The frontispiece engraved by W. H. Lizars is captioned 'John Campbell, Duke of Argyle.'; title vignette is engraved by Stewart Watson, engraved by W. H. Lizars.

Figures: These now appear only in the sixth and seventh sheets: R198-7; U236-3 240-2.

Notes: Final gathering 2E, though representing a considerable amount of text (pages 325-331), is in a duplicate setting most easily differentiated by printer's imprint(2) page 331 reading either '&' or 'AND'.

3] **TALES** | OF | **A GRANDFATHER;** . . . VOL. III. | Third Series. . . . 1830.

Collation: π⁴ A-2H⁶ 2I⁸. Pagination: [*frontispiece, engraved title*], *1* title-page, *2* printer's imprint(1), *i* ii-v Contents, *vi blank*, *1* fly-title, *2 blank*, *3* 4-382 text, 382 printer's imprint(2), *1* 2-6 advertisements. Printer's imprint(1) first line ends in a period. Illustrations: The frontispiece engraved by W. H. Lizars is captioned 'Cameron of Lochliel.'; title vignette engraved by W. H. Lizars is captioned 'Flora.'. Typography: In some copies page 249 is unnumbered. Signatures 2F2 and 2H2 (pages 341, 365) are missigned 2H2 and 2H respectively. Figures: *none*.

REPRINTS

FRANCE

PARIS: Didot and Galignani
[~] Tales of a Grandfather. Third Series. 1830. (Collection of Modern English Authors: *see* 292R.23-24.)

GERMANY

ZWICKAU: Schumann
[~] Tales of a Grandfather. Third Series. 1830. (Pocket Library of English Classics: *see* 302R. entry following 223-225.)

UNITED STATES

234Ra] NEW YORK: Forbes 1830
Tales of a Grandfather; . . Third Series. New-York, S & D. A. Forbes, Printers, No. 29 Gold-Street. 1830. Two volumes. Pages 1: *1-3* 4-310; 2: *1-3* 4-333. Notes: Imprint for vol. 2 varies: New-York, Published by William Burgess, Jun. Juvenile Emporium. No. 79 Fulton-Street. On NN printed boards: vol. 1, 10th American edition; vol. 2. 2nd American ed. On PPL printed boards: vol. 1, Second American edition; vol. 2. Fourth American edition. Added engraved frontispieces and engraved titles reading 'Printed for Wm. Burgess, New York: 1830.' Copies: NN PPL.

234Rb] PHILADELPHIA: Carey and Lea 1830
Tales of a Grandfather; Being Stories taken from Scottish History. . . . Third Series. Philadelphia: Carey and Lea. 1830. Two volumes. Pages 1: *1-5* 6-304; 2: *1-5* 6-327. Notes: First American edition, announced 24 November as 'In the Press' (*NG*) but no further notice appears. 1500 copies were printed. Volume 2 title-page is pointed 'Grandfather:' and 'Philadelphia.' Copies: E; MWA NjP NNU-W(vol.1) PPL. References: Kaser 195; Kohler(1) 200(with illustration).

OBSERVATIONS ON THE HISTORY OF THE REGALIA

235A] First Printing: 1829

'OBSERVATIONS, &c. [OBSERVATIONS ON THE HISTORY OF THE REGALIA OF SCOTLAND]', pages *17* 18-51, *in*:

Papers relative to the Regalia of Scotland. Printed at Edinburgh; M. DCCC.XXIX.

Published in 1829.

Notes: Brief title is on page *17*, full title in headlines which follow. William Bell, in offering the volume, immediately declares page *vii* his indebtedness for the principal section: 'This Collection of Documents, connected with the Preservation of these Ancient Monuments of Scottish Royalty, in perilous Times, is presented to THE BANNATYNE CLUB, to whom the "Observations" will be acceptable, as being the joint Production of two of its most distinguished Members, who mainly originated, and who have conferred such important Services on the Club.' Scott doubtless is one of the compilers; the other may be either Thomas Thomson (Vice President) or David Laing (Secretary), both of whom were actively engaged since the founding of the Society. The book was later numbered 30 in the series.

Copy: E. Reference: (Magnum Opus Edition: Not reprinted.)

MEMOIR OF GEORGE BANNATYNE

236A] First Printing: 1829

'MEMOIR OF GEORGE BANNATYNE.', pages *3* 4-24 *in*:

Memorials of George Bannatyne. M.D.XLV.—M.DC.VIII. Printed at Edinburgh: M.DCCC.XXIX.

Published in 1829.

Notes: The Memorials were 'printed for the use of the Members [of the Bannatyne Club], under the superintendence of the PRESIDENT', Sir Walter Scott. This issue was later numbered 35 in the series.

Copies: BCL E(2) O; CtY NN.

Reference: (Magnum Opus Edition: Not reprinted.)

COMMENTARY ON LORD BYRON

237A] First Edition: 1830

[Commentary on Lord Byron], volume I, pages 614 note, 615-619, *in*:

Moore, Thomas. Letters and Journals of Lord Byron: With Notices of His Life, . . . London: John Murray, Albemarle-Street. MDCCCXXX.

Published in London: volume 1, 15 January 1830 (*Ath* 23 January), volume 2, 25 December (*Ath* review, pages *801* 802-804).

Notes: It is indeed remarkable that an Irish editor should dedicate to a Scottish novelist this work by an English poet (*see* 538T[5]). Scott's contribution is a lengthy comment on the Scott-Byron relationship, particularly as it flourished during Scott's visit to London in 1815. Apart from the dedication the work includes the first printing of three letters from Byron to Scott dated 6 July 1812, 12 January 1822, 4 May 1822 (vol.I, pages 359-360; vol.II, pages 569-571, 592-594). Also printed from Byron's journal, 24 November 1813 (I.page 450), is his estimate of Scott ('He is undoubtedly the Monarch of Parnassus, and the most *English* of bards') and (on page 451) his famous pyramid of the poets, with Scott transcending all: see his diagram reproduced above, page 166.

Copies: GU; NN T/B(Signet Library) TxU. Reference: *Journal*, pages 437, 575.

REPRINT

UNITED STATES

237R] NEW YORK: Harper 1830
Moore, Thomas. Letters and Journals of Lord Byron: With Notices of His Life. . . . New=York: Printed and Published by J. & J. Harper. Sold by Collins & Hannay, Collins & Co., G. & C. & H. Carvill, O. A. Roorbach, W. B. Gilley, E. Bliss, White, Gallaher & White, A. T. Goodrich, C. S. Francis, N. B. Holmes, M. Bancroft, M'Elrath & Bangs, W. Burgess, J. Leavitt, G. W. Bleecker, and J. P. Haven. 1830. Notes: At head of title: Harper's Stereotype Edition. Copy: NN.

REVIEW OF TYTLER

238A] First Printing: 1829[1830]

'ART. III.—*History of Scotland.* By Patrick Fraser Tytler, Esq., F.R.S.E. and F.A.S. Volumes 1 and 2.', pages 328-359, *in*:

The Quarterly Review. [November 1829. No. 82, volume 41 imprint:] London: John Murray, Albemarle Street. 1829.

Published 21 January 1830 in London (*MC*); issued 20 February in Edinburgh (*EEC*).

Notes: When Tytler visited Abbotsford in 1823, Scott suggested that he write a history of Scotland, but in this review regrets that the historian is unconcerned with any account prior to the advent of Alexander III in 1249. Tytler's history eventually extended in 1843 to nine volumes.

Copies: BCL L; PPL.

References: Thomson, page 74. (Magnum Opus Edition 1836: *The Miscellaneous Prose Works*, xxi.152-198 as 'Tytler's History of Scotland'.)

THE DOOM OF DEVORGOIL

These dramatic pieces, or at least the first of them, were long since written, for the purpose of obliging the late Mr Terry . . . for whom the Author had a particular regard. The manner in which the mimic goblins of Devorgoil are intermixed with the supernational machinery, was found to be objectionable, and the production had other faults, which rendered it unfit for representation [in 1818].' ('Preface', page *i*.)

239A] First Edition, Second Issue: 1830

THE | **DOOM OF DEVORGOIL,** | A MELO-DRAMA. | [*short rule*] |

AUCHINDRANE; | OR, THE | **AYRSHIRE TRAGEDY.** | [*short rule*] | BY SIR WALTER SCOTT, BART. | [*short reversed Oxford rule*] | PRINTED FOR | CADELL AND COMPANY, EDINBURGH; | AND SIMPKIN AND MARSHALL, LONDON. | [*dash*] | 1830.

Published concurrently 20 April 1830 in Edinburgh (*EWJ* 7 and 21 April), 21 April in London (*MC*). Pre-publication extracts appeared in *The Literary Gazette*, 17 April, pages 251-253. 9s. Binding: drab wrappers, drab boards, or (a later issue?) green cloth with printed label. Paper: Demy 8° (223 x 141mm uncut). Watermarks: *none*. Collation: *A*^{4} B*-I*^{8} *K^{8} L^{8} M*-N*^{8} O-P^{8} Q*^{8} *R-*S^{8} T*^{8} U^{8} *X^{8} Y*^{8}. Pagination: *1* half-title, *2* printer's imprint(1), *3* title-page, *4 blank*, *i* ii-iii Preface, *iv blank*, *7* Dramatis Personae for 'The Doom of Devorgoil', *8 blank*, *9* 10-176 text, *177* fly-title for 'Auchindrane', *178 blank*, *179* 180-208 Preface, 209-210 Dramatis Personae, *211* 212-337 text, *338* printer's imprint(2), *1* 2-4 Cadell advertisements dated 20 April 1830. Printer's imprints (1) and (2): [*short rule*] | EDINBURGH; | PRINTED BY BALLANTYNE AND COMPANY, | PAUL'S WORK, CANONGATE. Typography: Pages 202 and 275 are misnumbered 206 and 276. The signature for gathering L (page 151) always remains unstarred. Two other gatherings unstarred either to the right or to the left (O, P) have the asterisk on the verso of the signature leaf (pages 200, 216). Gathering U, however, may have the asterisk, (a) to the right of the signature, page 295, (b) to the left, or (c), as with the aberrant O and P, on the verso, page 296.

Figures: *A*—, B*22-13, C*38-2, D*54-6, E*70-13, F*83-18/-, G*102-6/-, H*—, I*134-14, *K—, L166-7, . . . *X326-18, Y*4-7. Sheets M-U have no figures.

Notes: The earlier printings of this play, without asterisks, formed part of the 1830 collected *Poetical Works* (267Ab.11 and 268A.2, these essentially of the same impression, but with different signatures and pagination). The idea for 'Auchindrane', not specifically mentioned in either Preface, came to Scott upon a reading of proofs for Pitcairn's *Trials*, the subject of Scott's last, 1831 article for the *Quarterly Review* (*see* 245A), a reading noted here on page 207.

Copies: (state a) InU. (b) O. (c) E(2) ES HS(with Gladstone's annotations) L; CtY IdU(2) InU(2) MH(Holland House) NNU-W(2) T/B(2) TxU(3).

References: Ruff 185; Thomson, page 26; Van Antwerp(1) 30. (Magnum Opus Edition 1834: *The Poetical Works*, 'The Doom of Devorgoil' xii.*113-114* 115-240, 'Auchindrane' xii.*241-242* 243-362.)

REPRINTS

FRANCE

PARIS: Didot and Galignani
[~] The Doom of Devorgoil. 1830. (Collection of Modern English Authors: *see* 292R.30.)

UNITED STATES

239R] NEW YORK: Collins and Hannay [and others] 1830
The Doom of Devorgoil, A Melo-Drama. Auchindrane; or, The Ayrshire Tragedy. By Sir Walter Scott, Bart. New-York: Printed by J. & J. Harper, 82 Cliff-St. Sold by Collins and Hannay, Collins and Co., G. and C. and H. Carvill, O. A. Roorbach, White, Gallaher, and White, A. T. Goodrich, W. B. Gilley, E. Bliss;—Philadelphia, Carey and Lea, J. Grigg, U. Hunt, Towar and Hogan, M'Carty and Davis, E. L. Carey and A. Hart, and J. Crissy;—Pittsburg, Hogan and Co.;—Baltimore, Cushing and Sons, W. and J. Neal, Joseph Jewett, and F. Lucas, Jr.;—Boston, Richardson, Lord, and Holbrook, Hilliard, Gray, and Co., Crocker and Brewster, Carter and Hendee, R. P. and C. Williams, and Wells and Lilly;—Albany, O. Steele, and Little and Cummings. 1830. Pages: *i-iii* iv, *5-7* 8-190 *191-192*. Copies: E O; CtY MH MWA NNU-W(2) ViU. Reference: Kohler(1) 73(with illustration).

DERIVATIVES

GREAT BRITAIN

LONDON: Leigh
[~] Song, "Constancy!" 1832. (The Harmonicon: *see* 337D.8.) Notes: Series initially printed for the Proprietors, published by Leigh. This title was published by Longman, Rees, Orme, Brown, Green, and Longman.

[~] Song, "When Friends are Met." 1830. (The Harmonicon: *see* 337D.2.)

EXTRACTS IN ANTHOLOGIES

233E] In *The Doom of Devorgoil* one song ('The Sun upon the Lake') was extracted in an anthology, 405(2)[3]E.7; another sometimes titled elsewhere as 'The Bonnets of Bonnie Dundee' is recorded among the reprints listed in entry 207E.

LETTER ON LARDNER'S CABINET CYCLOPAEDIA

240A] First Printing: 1830

'DR. LARDNER'S CYCLOPAEDIA' , page *3*, column 1 *in*:

The Times. No. 14,281 London. Saturday, July 17, 1830 Price 7d. [Page *4* imprint:] Printed and published by John Joseph Lawson, Printer, of Printing-house-square, near Apothecaries'-hall, Blackfriars, at the office in Printing-house-square.

Notes: On reading some intimation that the authors in the *Cabinet Cyclopaedia* merely lent their names to work done by others, Lardner on 9 July wrote *The Times* (10 July) requesting the name of the correspondent, and then, having received no satisfaction, on the 10th sent copies to the five persons in question—Scott, Macintosh, Southey, Moore, Campbell—each of whom briefly responded (in the order named) in letters published under the above heading on the 17th. Scott's report to Lardner, dated from Abbotsford on the 12th, reads: 'Dear Sir,—I am favoured with your letter of 10th July, and the copy of *The Time* newspapers, expressing, so far as I am concerned, the false and calumnious allegation that I am not the author of the work going under the name of the *History of Scotland*, published as mine in your *Cyclopaedia*. Nothing can be more false than such an assertion, as I either wrote with my own hand or dictated every line in that history. I am with regard, dear Sir, your most obedient, servant. WALTER SCOTT'

The five letters, together with Lardner's preliminary comment, were regarded as of such consequence as to be reprinted in the *Edinburgh Literary Journal*, 24 July 1830, pages 58-59.

Copy: E. (Microfilm copies: E L; NN TxU.)

LETTERS ON DEMONOLOGY AND WITCHCRAFT

You have asked of me, my dear friend, that I should assist the Family Library, with the history of a dark chapter in human nature, which the increasing civilisation of all well-instructed countries has now almost blotted out, though the subject attracted no ordinary degree of consideration in the older times of their history. ('Letter I' to Lockhart, page 2.)

241Aa] First Edition: 1830

LETTERS | ON | DEMONOLOGY AND WITCHCRAFT, | ADDRESSED TO | J. G. LOCKHART, ESQ. | BY | SIR WALTER SCOTT, BART. | [*short reversed Oxford rule*] | LONDON: | JOHN MURRAY, ALBEMARLE STREET. | [*dash*] | MDCCCXXX.

Published 14 September 1830 in Edinburgh (*EWJ* 20 September, 'on Tuesday was published'); issued 21 September in London (*MC* 20 September). 5s. Binding: printed tan cloth, front 'THE FAMILY LIBRARY No.XVI.' &c., back listing 15 volumes and number 1 of the Dramatic Series. Paper: Pot 16° in eights (156 x 98mm uncut). Watermarks: *none.*

Collation: π² a⁶(-a1) A-E⁸ F⁸(±F5) G-2B⁸ *2C*1. Pagination: *1* half-title, *2* printer's imprint(1), *3* title-page, *4 blank*, *i* ii-ix Contents, *x blank*, *1* 2-402 text, 402 printer's imprint(2). Printer's imprints: (1) and (2) [*short rule*] | EDINBURGH: | PRINTED BY BALLANTYNE AND COMPANY, | PAUL'S WORK, CANONGATE. Illustration: Frontispiece drawn by J. Skene, engraved by W. H. Lizars, with caption 'The Bow, Edinburgh, House of Major Weir.' and published by John Murray, London, 1830. (The account of Weir and his sister is given on pages 329-332.)

Figures: Q254-8 256-1, S287-6 288-3/16, U306-6 320-5, Y351-15 352-11, 2A 384-7, 2B 400-18, *2C*—.

Notes: Occasionally in the original issue of this work, bound before the preliminaries, is a 16-page issue of 'The Family Library Advertiser' for September 1830, listing books by various publishers. The original readings for cancellandum F5 (pages 89-90) are unknown.

The format is verified by the figures which, when they occur, are only in alternate gatherings (2A, 2B excepted). The earlier unfigured section apparently was printed in another shop, with type-lines for this measuring 68mm as against 67.5mm for the latter portion. Final leaf *2C*1 is in a duplicate setting, page 402 lines 4 and 6 with or without commas after 'proverb' and 'clear'. As Lockhart was aware, the supernatural was an abiding interest of Scott's and, in this extended treatise, allows him to refer rather indirectly to some of his earlier accounts (here further identified in parentheses by the bibliographical number):
[1] 'The Wild Huntsman', 1796: page 43. (no.1A above, then titled 'The Chase')
[2] 'On the Fairies of Popular Superstition', 1802: page 120. (8A.2)
[3] 'Thomas the Rhymer', 1802: pages 132-143. (8A.2)
[4] Reresby, *Memoirs*, 1813 [projected edition]: pages 269-270. (66A)
[5] 'The Eyrbiggia Saga', 1814: pages 100, 108-109. (76A)
[6] Kirk, *An Essay ... of Invisible People*, 1815: pages 90n, 163-166 . (83A)
Later on Scott also refers, even more indirectly, to articles now at press or still unwritten:
[7] Review of Pitcairn, *Trials*, 1831: pages 2, 145-160, 315-316. (245A)
[8] *Trial of Duncan Terig*, 1831: pages 370-373. (246A)
[9] [The Commissioners arrival at Woodstock, 13 October 1649]: pages 374-375. (This account discovered 3 July 1830 [*Journal*, page 605] and reported in the 'Introduction' to the 'Magnum' *Woodstock* [348A.39, pages vii-xv])
There are two binding issues, with back cover listing (1) as noted above, 15 volumes; (2) 16 volumes.

Copies: (issue 1) AN BCL E(2) E(3)* O(2) O(Douce)*; CtY(2) CtY(2)* IdU InU InU* MH NNU-W+ PPL. (2) O; TxU. (rebound) AN GU HS; MH MH* T/B.
*Extra-illustrated, after November 1830, with 12 plates by George Cruikshank (*see* 241D).
+Dated 'Septr 23 1830' and inscribed 'A[nne] Scott from Sophia Lockhart Demonology'.

References: Sterling 720; Thomson, page 25; Tinker 1877. (Magnum Opus Edition: Not reprinted.)

241Ab] Second Edition: 1831

LETTERS | ON | DEMONOLOGY AND WITCHCRAFT, | ADDRESSED TO | J. G. LOCKHART, ESQ. | BY | SIR WALTER SCOTT, BART. | SECOND EDITION. | LONDON: | JOHN MURRAY, ALBEMARLE STREET. | MDCCCXXXI.

Published 24 January 1831 in Edinburgh (*EEC*). 5s. Binding: printed tan cloth, front 'THE FAMILY LIBRARY No.XVI.' &c., back board listing 17 volumes. Paper: 16° in eights (155 x 97mm uncut). Watermarks: *none*. Collation: π^8(-π8) A-2A^8 2B^4(-2B4) 2C^4. Pagination: *1* half-title, *2* printer's imprint, *3* title-page, *4 blank*, *i* ii-ix Contents, *x blank*, *1* 2-390 text, *391* 392-396 'Note on a Passage in Sir Walter Scott's Demonology', *397-398* advertisements dated 1 January 1831. Printer's imprint: EDINBURGH: | PRINTED BY BALLANTYNE AND CO. PAUL'S WORK, CANONGATE.

Illustration: frontispiece drawn by J. Skene, engraved by W. H. Lizars, with caption 'The Bow, Edinburgh, House of Major Weir.' Typography: Second leaf in 2B gathering (page 387) is also signed 2B. This and the next part gathering 2C, comprising altogether fourteen pages, are set in duplicate with the following points of differentiation: page 387 head has the G of DEMONOLOGY above the 's' or 'o' of 'so'; page 390 is correctly numbered in the left margin or incorrectly numbered 490 in the right margin; the last period *397* is below either the 'a' or the 'n' of 'and'. Figures: *none*.

Notes: There are at least four binding issues: (1) tan printed cloth, as noted above, listing 17 volumes; (2) list extended to 65 volumes; front cover imprinted 'London: John Murray, Albemarle Street, and Thomas Tegg,, 73, Cheapside. MDCCC-XXXVIII. Price Five Shillings. Bradbury and Evans, Printers, Whitefriars.' (3) gilt title on spine: 'Demonology and Witchcraft' either in blind-stamped red cloth or, later, ca.1850, (4) diced brown cloth with a frontispiece now imprinted 'London, William Tegg & Co. Cheapside.' Volumes extra-illustrated by Cruikshank are cited below as a London derivative (241D).

Copies: (issue 1) PU. (2) T/B. (3) E; CtY. (4) E; NNU-W. (rebound) O; TxU.

REPRINTS

FRANCE

PARIS: Didot and Galignani
[~] Letters on Demonology and Witchcraft. 1831. (Collection of Modern English Authors: *see* 292R.33.)

UNITED STATES

241R] NEW YORK: Collins and Hannay [and others] 1830
Letters on Demonology and Witchcraft. . . . By Sir Walter Scott, Bart. New=York: Printed by J. & J. Harper, 82 Cliff-St. Sold by Collins & Hannay, Collins & Co., G. & C. & H. Carvill, and White, Gallaher, & White;—Philadelphia, Carey & Lea, John Grigg, Towar & J. & D. M. Hogan, U. Hunt, E. L. Carey & A. Hart, T. Desilver, jr., and M'Carty & Davis;—Baltimore, Cushing & Sons, J. Jewett, W. & J. Neal, and G. M'Dowell & Son;—Boston, Richardson, Lord, & Holbrook, Hilliard, Gray, & Co., and Carter & Hendee. 1830. Pages: *i-vii* viii-xi *xii*, *13* 14-338 *339-356*. Notes: Frontispiece as in first edition, but reengraved by J. Smillie for Harper's Family Library, 1830. At head of title 'Harper's Stereotype Edition.' Printed boards read on front: 'Harper's Family Library. No. XI.' and the first issue has on the back the eleven numbered volumes already published. This entry is under Collins and Hannay because the Harpers are only credited with printing the 1830-1831 issues. The copies distributed in Philadelphia by Carey and Hart were 'Just received' on 27 November 1830 (*NG*). Copies: E; IdU NjP NN PPL. Reissued 1831 (E; DLC NN PU TxU ViU), 1832 (NIC), 1833 (PPL), 1835 (E), 1836 (MWA), 1845 (NNU-W).

DERIVATIVE

GREAT BRITAIN

241D] LONDON: Robins 1830
Twelve Sketches Illustrative of Sir Walter Scott's Demonology and Witchcraft, by George Cruikshank. London: Published for the Artist, By J. Robins and Co. Ivy Lane, Paternoster Row. 1830. Notes: After the title-page there are twelve leaves, each headed 'PLATE I [II-XII].' and quoting from Scott's text, each then preceding the woodcut etching, these in final state d. Available separately are four states, all bearing, above the plate (proof states a-c) plate number only, or (final state d) plate number, page reference, and below in script: 'Designed Etched & Published [or Pubd] by George Cruikshank Novbr 1830.' Below this legend, in state d, are the captions, also in script:

(1) The "Corps de Ballet";
(2) The Spectre Skeleton;
(3) The Goddess Freya;
(4) Elfin Tricks;
(5) The Persecuted Butler;
(6) Elfin arrow Manufactory;
(7) Fairy Revenge;
(8) Puck in Mischief;
(9) "Black John" Chastising the Witches;
(10) Witches Frolic;
(11) "Tak aff the Ghaist!";
(12) The Ghost of Mrs Leckie.

A much later issue [2] of bound-in plates has the page reference at the top of each plate excised, but retains the script legend beneath. This exists with so-called mounted India 'proofs', and with other plates both coloured and uncoloured.

Copies: [issue 1] (a) India proofs: E*. Separate plates: E(2). Full text, with plates in one or more states, bound in: BCL E(2); CtY RPB. [2] InU MH.
* With additional engraved frontispiece portrait of Scott and with imprint: London. John Lofts. 368 Strand. Also with additional plate states b(proofs uncoloured); c(proofs coloured); d(full text plates).

References: Church 552; Cohn 188.

REVIEW OF SOUTHEY

242A] First Printing: 1830

'ART. V.—*The Pilgrim's Progress, with a Life of John Bunyan*. By Robert Southey, Esq., LL.D.', pages 469-494, *in*:

The Quarterly Review. [October 1830. No. 86, volume 43 imprint:] London: John Murray, Albemarle Street. 1830.

Published 13 October 1830 in London (*MC* 12 October).

Copies: BCL L; PPL.

References: Thomson, page 67. (Magnum Opus Edition 1835: *The Miscellaneous Prose Works*, xviii.74-117 as 'Southey's Life of John Bunyan'.)

THE EX-KING OF FRANCE

243A] First Printing: 1830

'THE EX-KING OF FRANCE', page 332, *in*:

The Edinburgh Weekly Journal. VOL. XXXIII. No. 1714.] Wednesday, October 20, 1830. [Price Sevenpence] Printed by Ballantyne and Company, for the Proprietors.

Published 20 October 1830 in Edinburgh.

Notes: Scott's unsigned and undated announcement of the imminent return of Charles X, as an exile, to Holyrood House, is described by the editor as 'an affective and impressive article.'

Copy: L. References: Johnson, page 1150. (Magnum Opus Edition: not reprnted, but quoted in Lockhart, ix.365-368.)

TALES OF A GRANDFATHER
[Fourth Series]
THE HISTORY OF FRANCE

244A] First Edition: 1831[1830]

TALES | OF | **A GRANDFATHER;** | BEING | **STORIES** | TAKEN FROM THE | **HISTORY OF FRANCE.** | INSCRIBED TO | MASTER JOHN HUGH LOCKHART. | IN THREE VOLS. | VOL. I [II-III]. | [*short rule*] | PRINTED FOR ROBERT CADELL, EDINBURGH; | WHITTAKER AND CO., LONDON; AND | JOHN CUMMING, DUBLIN. | [*dash*] | 1831.

Published concurrently 21 December 1830 in Edinburgh (*EEC* 11 and 23 December); 20 December in London (*MC*). 10s.6d. Binding: half green roan and drab boards or half maroon roan and marbled boards. Paper: Royal 16° in eights (146 x 92mm cut). Watermarks: *none*. Illustrations: Engraved frontispieces and titles, as described below, precede printed titles. Typography: Printer's imprints read: [*short rule*] | EDINBURGH: | PRINTED BY BALLANTYNE AND COMPANY, | PAUL'S WORK, CANONGATE.

General Notes: Unlike the earlier series, in which each full sheet is numbered and consists of three segments (A-C, D-F, &c.), the sheets in this last series were imposed with two segments each (A-B, C-D, E-F), and remain unnumbered. Remainder copies of this edition were soon advertised under the title 'Sir Walter Scott's Stories from the History of France', but still at the original price of 10s.6d (*MLA* March 1831, item 6).

Copies: BCL E E* HS* O(3)* O*(Opie); NNU-W* T/B*.
*With 16-page Cadell prospectus and catalogue, December 1830: *see* 225A.

References: Thomson, page 70; Van Antwerp(1) 32. (Magnum Opus Edition 1836: *The Miscellaneous Prose Works*, xxvii-xxviii.*1* 2-281.)

1] **TALES** | OF | **A GRANDFATHER;** . . . TAKEN FROM THE | **HISTORY OF FRANCE.** . . . VOL. I. . . . 1831.

Collation: π^4 A-T^8 U^6. Pagination: [*frontispiece, engraved title*], *1* title-page, *2* printer's imprint(1), *i* ii-vi Contents, *1* fly-title, *2 blank*, *3* 4-8 preface, dated from Abbotsford 29 July 1830, *9* 10-315 text, *316* printer's imprint(2). Illustrations: Frontispiece drawn and engraved by W. H. Lizars with caption 'Encounter between William the Conqueror and His Son Robert.'; title vignette by the same illustrator. Typography: In some copies the colon is omitted in printer's imprint(2).

Figures: A16-1, B32-6; C48-7, D52-18; F95-11 96-15; G112-7, H128-18; I 144-8, K157-6; L176-16, M189-10; N208-12, O 224-6; P240-10, Q256-15; R272-17,

S288-18; T304-18, U312-17. Excepting the third sheet (E-F) a figure appears in each part section of this volume.

2] **TALES** | OF | **A GRANDFATHER;** . . . TAKEN FROM THE | **HISTORY OF FRANCE.** . . . VOL. II. . . . 1831.

Collation: π^4 A-U^8 X^4 *Y*1. Pagination: [*frontispiece, engraved title*], *1* title-page, *2* printer's imprint(1), *i* ii-vi Contents, *1* fly-title, *2 blank*, *3* 4-329 text, 329 printer's imprint(2), *330 blank*. Illustrations: Frontispiece drawn and engraved by W. H. Lizars with caption 'Reception of the Pontiff Alexander the III by Henry & Louis.'; title vignette by the same illustrator.

Figures: A16-12, B32-8; C48-6, D64-3; E80-16, F84-2; G109-4, H128-12; I 141-5, K157-7; L176-1, M192-2; O 223-8 224-11; P—, Q—; R—, S—; T304-5, U320-1; X328-3, *Y*—. Excepting the seventh, eighth and ninth sheets (N-O, P-Q, R-S) a figure again appears in each part section of this volume. Typography: In some copies the figure 3, page 64, is inverted.

Notes: Leaf *Y*1 is in a duplicate setting, final period of printer's imprint(2) page 329 appearing below either the 'M' or the 'P' of 'COMPANY'.

3] **TALES** | OF | **A GRANDFATHER;** . . . TAKEN FROM THE | **HISTORY OF FRANCE.** . . . VOL. III. . . . 1831.

Collation: π^6 A-U^8 X^4 Y-Z^8. Pagination: [*frontispiece, engraved title*], *1* title-page, *2* printer's imprint(1), *i* ii-ix Contents, *x blank*, *1* fly-title, *2 blank*, *3* 4-360 text, 360 printer's imprint(2). Illustrations: Frontispiece drawn and engraved by W. H. Lizars with caption 'Intercession of Queen Philippa in behalf of the Burgesses of Calais.'; title vignette by the same illustrator. Figures: These now occur only in the sixth sheet: L176-2, M192-9.

REPRINTS

FRANCE

PARIS: Didot and Galignani
[~] Tales of a Grandfather; . . . from The History of France. First Series. 1831. (Collection of Modern English Authors: *see* 292R.34.)

UNITED STATES

244Ra] NEW YORK: Burgess 1831
Tales of a Grandfather, Fourth Series; Being Stories taken from the History of France. . . By

Sir Walter Scott, . . . New-York: Published by William Burgess, Juvenile Emporium, 97 Fulton-st. 1831. Two volumes. Pages 1: *1-3* 4-5, *vi* vii-x, *11* 12-297; 2: *i-iii* iv-viii, *7* 8-310. With engraved frontispiece and vignette title-pages, imprinted Wm. Burgess, New-York. 1831. Copies: MWA MWA(vol.1) NN(vol.2).

244Rb] PHILADELPHIA: Carey & Lea 1831

Tales of a Grandfather; Being Stories taken from the History of France. Inscribed to Master John Hugh Lockhart. . . . Philadelphia: Carey & Lea. 1831. Two volumes. Pages 1: *1-3* 4-6, *vii* viii-xii, *13* 14-232; 2: *i-iii* vi-xii, *13* 14-236. Notes: This edition was published on 17 February 1831 and, two days later, also advertised by three other Philadelphia booksellers: Thomas T. Ash, J. Grigg, and E. Littell (*NG*). 2375 copies were printed. In some copies page 13 is numbered. Copies: E; CtY IdU MWA(vol.2) NNU-W PPL. References: Kaser 244; Kohler(1) 202(with illustration).

REVIEW OF PITCAIRN

245A] First Printing: 1831

'ART. V.—*Trials, and other Proceedings, in matters Criminal, before the High Court of Justiciary in Scotland*; . . . By Robert Pitcairn, . . . Parts I-VI. Published by the Bannatyne Club.', pages 438-475, *in*:

The Quarterly Review. [February, 1831. No. 88, volume 44 imprint:] London: John Murray, Albemarle Street. 1831.

Published 19 February 1831 in London (*MC*).

Notes: This, Scott's last review, begins with a long account of the difficulty of publishing 'curiosities'—'ancient poems, ancient chronicles, ancient legends'—and thus the necessary function of private clubs like Bannatyne (of which he was still President), as well as of bibliophiles generally. Scott had access to Pitcairn's proofs and earlier twice referred to the first several parts (239A, 241Aa). The work was completed 1833 in three volumes under the general title *Criminal Trials in Scotland*.

Copies: BCL L O; PPL.

References: Thomson, page 53. (Magnum Opus Edition 1836: *The Miscellaneous Prose Works*, xxi.199-265 as 'Pitcairn's Criminal Trials'.)

TRIAL OF DUNCAN TERIG ALIAS CLERK

246A] First Edition: 1831

TRIAL | OF | DUNCAN TERIG ALIAS CLERK, | AND ALEXANDER BANE MACDONALD, | FOR | THE MURDER | OF | ARTHUR DAVIS, |

SERGEANT IN GENERAL GUISE'S REGIMENT OF FOOT. | JUNE, | A.D. M.DCC.LIV. | [*short rule*] | EDINBURGH: | PRINTED BY BALLANTYNE AND COMPANY. | [*short rule*] | 1831.

Issued ca. 5 March 1831 in Edinburgh. Binding: (presentation) half olive morocco and crimson boards. Paper: Demy 4° laid paper (270 x 207mm uncut). Watermarks on each leaf: Arms of the Bannatyne Club, with countermark AC&L.

Collation: π1 2π1 3π[2] *a*[4] *b*[4](-*b*4) *A*[4] B-F[4] G[4]. Pagination: *1* title-page, *2 blank*, *3* presentation to the Club by Walter Scott, dated February 1831, *4 blank*, *5-8* List of [then 100] Members, Scott listed first as President, *iii* dedication by Scott to Sir Samuel Shepherd, dated 15 February 1831, *iv blank*, *v* vi-xv Introduction, dated from Abbotsford, 18 March 1830, *xvi blank*, *1* fly-title for trial, *2 blank*, *3* 4-54 text, *55-56 blank*. No printer's imprint. Typography: Page x is misnumbered ix. Signature *b* is in italic. Figures: *none*.

Notes: In his Introduction Scott observes (page xi) that his connection with this curious trial 'is of an old standing, since, shortly after he was called to the bar in 1792, it was pointed out to him by Robert M'Intosh, Esq., one of the counsel in the case. . . .' The Bannatyne Club, originally limited to thirty-one members, on 3 December 1827 voted to increase the membership to one hundred. This 1831 book was later numbered 40 in the Bannatyne Club series.

Presentation copies: BLC('Miss Jane Erskine for her impressment in the services of Civil Law and Demonology from her affectionate friend the Editor, W.S. Abbotsford') BCL('To the Right Honourable Sir Samuel Shepherd, Bart. From the Editor'); CtY('Etra[Extra] Copy Major Scott from his affectionate father The Editor'). Other copies: E O; MH PU T/B.

THE LIFE OF SAMUEL JOHNSON

247A] First Printing: 1831

[Notes for Boswell's *Life*], volumes 1-3, *in*:

The Life of Samuel Johnson, LL.D. . . . By James Boswell, Esq. A New Edition. With Numerous Additions and Notes, by John Wilson Croker, . . . London: John Murray, Albemarle-Street. MDCCCXXXI.

Published concurrently 22 June 1831 in London (*Ath* 18 June); 23 June in Edinburgh (*EEC*). £3.

Notes: As detailed in the Bowden/Todd account, Scott contributed for the first three volumes of the Croker edition 84 notes, amounting altogether to some 7000 words. Seventy-seven of these informative commentaries relate, appropriately, to the *Journal of a Tour to the Hebrides*, incorporated by Croker in the *Life* itself.

Copies: E L; CtY T/B TxU.

Reference: Ann Bowden and William B. Todd, 'Scott's Commentary on *The Journal of a Tour to the Hebrides with Samuel Johnson*,' *Studies in Bibliography* 48 (1995), 229-248.

MEMORIAL INSCRIPTION FOR LORD HOPETOUN

248A] First Printing: 1831

ERECTED TO THE MEMORY OF | **JOHN, FOURTH EARL OF HOPETOUN,** | BY | HIS GRATEFUL COUNTRYMEN, . . . M.DCC. XXXI.
<SEE ACCOMPANYING ILLUSTRATION>

Printed ca. June 1831 in Edinburgh (*Ath* 9 July, page 446: 'we have seen a specimen . . .'). Paper: broadside, laid paper (383 x 235mm uncut). Watermarks: C WILMOTT | 1820; [posthorn within a shield] | W.

Notes: Eight years after the death of the Fourth Earl, in 1823, the family requested an epitaph from Scott. This he finally prepared, in 33 lines, and insisted that 'Ballantyne must set it up being indispensible at all those niceties of spaces, blocks, divisions & the style-lapidary.'

Copies: E(Abbot[3]).

References: *Letters*, xii.14. (Magnum Opus Edition: Not reprinted.)

LETTER ON CHATEAUBRIAND

249A] First Printing: 1831

'SIR WALTER SCOTT AND M. CHATEAUBRIAND.', page 252, *in*:

The Edinburgh Evening Post, and Scottish Literary Gazette. Vol. V.—No. 222. Edinburgh, Saturday Evening, August 6, 1831. . . . Price 7d. Edinburgh:—Printed for the Proprietors, by J. Glass, 19 Shakespeare Square.

Published 6 August 1831 in Edinburgh.

Notes: Scott's letter, dated from Abbotsford 29 July 1831, denies any knowledge of Chateaubriand's politics, as asserted in a previous number (23 June) of the *Post*. Elsewhere on page 252 the editor expresses his great pleasure in receiving this '*holograph* letter', but adds a footnote confessing some difficulty in decyphering it.

Copy: EP. References: *Letters*, xii.25,n.2; Scott Newsletter 6 (Spring 1985) 14-15. (Magnum Opus Edition: Not reprinted.)

ERECTED TO THE MEMORY OF

JOHN, FOURTH EARL OF HOPETOUN,

BY

HIS GRATEFUL COUNTRYMEN,

WHO,

RESISTING THE VARIOUS BLANDISHMENTS
HELD FORTH TO HIS ACCEPTANCE BY EXALTED RANK,
A LIBERAL FORTUNE, AND A WELL-CULTIVATED MIND, NAY,
EVEN THOSE AFFORDED BY THE PUREST DOMESTIC AFFECTION,
IN HIS EARLY YOUTH
DEDICATED HIMSELF TO THE MILITARY SERVICE OF HIS NATIVE COUNTRY,
DURING A LONG, BLOODY, AND EVENTFUL WAR OF TWENTY YEARS,
NEVER SHEATHED HIS SWORD TILL A COMPLETE TRIUMPH
WAS ACHIEVED FOR HIS COUNTRY,
AND THE WAR WAS ENDED BY THE PEACE OF PARIS IN 1815,
WHICH SEEMED TO ASSURE LASTING REPOSE TO EUROPE.
THEN AT LENGTH, WHEN HIS COUNTRY SEEMED
NOT LIKELY FOR A LONG TIME TO NEED HIS SERVICES,
HE RENDERED UP THE LIFE WHICH HE HAD PRESERVED THROUGH
MANY PERILS BOTH OF WOUNDS AND CLIMATE,
DYING IN PROFOUND PEACE IN THE

YEAR M.DCCC.XXIII.

IN THE COUNTRY WHERE HE HAD OFTEN LED THE BRITISH FORCES,
OFTEN AS A CONQUEROR, ALWAYS AS A HERO,
LEAVING THE NAME OF NO ONE MORE HONOURED
AMONG THE FOLLOWERS OF WELLINGTON.
HIS PEACEFUL AND SOCIAL TALENTS WERE SO ADMIRABLY
MINGLED WITH THOSE OF HIS PROFESSION, AS TO AUTHORIZE
THE WORDS OF THE LATIN POET,—

—— CUI PUDOR ET JUSTITIA RARA,
INCORRUPTA FIDES NUDAQUE VERITAS,
QUANDO ULLAM PACEM?

M.DCCC.XXXI.

ENTRY 248A. THE NATIONAL LIBRARY OF SCOTLAND (Abbot 111[37])
(illustration reduced)

A VISION OF THE CORONATION

250A] First Printing: 1831

'A VISION OF THE CORONATION.', (first words: 'The steady foxhound, staunch and true,'), page 620, *in*:

The Court Journal: Gazette of the Fashionable World. No. 124. Saturday, September 10, 1831. Price 1s. London: Printed for Henry Colburn; and published by W. Thomas, at the Office, 19, Catherine-street, Strand. Sold also by all Booksellers, Newsvenders, and Clerks of the Roads. Harjette & Savill, 107, St. Martin's-lane, Charing-cross.

Published 10 September 1831 in London.

Notes: This previously unrecorded 157-line poem, celebrating the investiture of William IV, and initialed 'W.S.', is introduced by the editor: 'The following verses have been sent us under cover. The initials at the end were not required to mark their illustrious author.' After printing this admirable paean the editor also provides a footnote to line 143: 'The illustrious author of the foregoing must also have had, in his dreams, a vision of the *Times*, which is the only paper, so far as we have seen, which has stated that the Princess Victoria was present at the Ceremony.'

On reprinting the poem, with its preamble and note, the Philadelphia *National Gazette*, 3 November 1831, immediately identified the piece as 'By Sir Walter Scott'.

Copy: CtY. Reference: (Magnum Opus Edition: Not reprinted.)

KING GATHOL'S CHAIR

251A] First Printing: 1831

'KING GATHOL'S CHAIR.', (first words: 'Dead were this spirit, by my fay'). pages 376-377, *in*:

Fraser's Magazine for Town and Country. October, 1831. No.XXI. Vol.IV. London: James Fraser, 215, Regent Street, John Anderson, Jun., Edinburgh; and Grant & Co. Dublin. M.DCCC.XXXI.

Published 1 October 1831 in London (*Ath*).

Notes: Scott's 86-line poem is one of eleven contributed to a section headed 'Coronation Coronal; Or, Verses on the Coronation of Their Majesties, King William IV. and Queen Adelaide. By the Most Eminent Poets of the Day.' Scott's contribution is the second, after a poem by Wordsworth, and follows the pattern of prefixing a letter—his from Abbotsford 18 September 1831 written in the 'bustle of departure for Naples'. Evidently Scott's poem, hitherto unrecorded, and some of the others were in response to a solicitation from the editor on the 13th, five days after the coronation.

Copies: E O; CtY.

Reference: (Magnum Opus Edition: Not reprinted.)

A HIGHLAND ANECDOTE

252A] First Printing: 1831

'A HIGHLAND ANECDOTE. BY SIR WALTER SCOTT, BART. TO THE EDITOR OF THE KEEPSAKE.', pages 283-286, *in*:

The Keepsake for MDCCCXXXII. Edited by Frederic Mansel Reynolds. London: Published by Longman, Rees, Orme, Brown, and Green. [1831].

Published 12 November 1831 in London (*Ath* review, pages 736-737). £1.1.0.

Notes: Since at the time of issue Scott had already departed on his last voyage, his very short contribution was no longer given the first position, nor even an illustration: distinctions which he had been accorded in his earlier appearances in *The Keepsake* (*see* 218A, 233A).

Copies: BCL; CtY MWA NN.

Reference: (Magnum Opus Edition: Not reprinted.)

TALES OF MY LANDLORD
[Fourth Series]
COUNT ROBERT and CASTLE DANGEROUS

The gentle reader is acquainted, that these are, in all probability, the last tales which it will be the lot of the Author to submit to the public. . . . The public have claims on his gratitude, for which the Author of Waverley has no adequate means of expression; but he may be permitted to hope, that the powers of his mind, such as they are, may not have a different date from those of his body; and that he may again meet his patronizing friends, if not exactly in his old fashion of literature, at least in some branch, which may not call forth the remark, that—Superfluous lags the veteran on the stage. (iv.329-330.)

253A] First Edition: 1832[1831]

TALES OF MY LANDLORD, | Fourth and Last Series, | COLLECTED AND ARRANGED | BY | JEDEDIAH CLEISHBOTHAM, |

SCHOOLMASTER AND PARISH-CLERK OF GANDERCLEUCH. | [*short rule*] | [*six-line quotation from* Don Juan] | [*short rule*] | IN FOUR VOLUMES. | VOL. I [II-IV]. | [*short Oxford rule*] | PRINTED FOR ROBERT CADELL, EDINBURGH; | AND WHITTAKER AND CO., LONDON. | [*dash*] | 1832.

Published concurrently 1 December 1831 in Edinburgh (*EEC*); 1 December in London (*MC*). £2.2.0. Binding: drab, blue, or blue-grey boards, or (a later issue?) in green cloth with printed labels. Paper: Royal 12° (205 x 122mm uncut). Watermarks: *none*. Typography: Printer's imprints read: [*short rule*] | EDIN BURGH: | PRINTED BY BALLANTYNE AND COMPANY, | PAUL'S WORK, CANONGATE.

General Notes: According to established practice, beginning with *Kenilworth* (*see* 149Aa), on 7 July 1831, five months before the publication of this novel, some 5100 words (volume 1, continuous extract from the end of chapter 3 to the middle of chapter 4, pages 86.22-114.16, in this Edinburgh edition) were extracted in the Philadelphia *National Gazette*, these deriving from proofs early shipped for the Carey & Lea edition (253Rb). This extract in turn was reprinted in the 20 August issue of *The Athenaeum* (pages *529* 530-532), where it was conjectured that, in order to secure American copyright, 'proof-sheets are regularly transmitted across the Atlantic . . . .' The conjecture is reprinted in the October *Lady's Magazine,* which thereupon reproduces *The Atheneum* text (pages 211-218): the fourth printing of this considerable extract before publication of the novel!

Scott twice alluded to this extraordinary business, on 25 and 29 August (E MS 1752,ff.360, 362), without realizing that it all began with Carey, but then advised Cadell on 11 September (f.376) that he would continue work on 'Count Robert to the necessary length. Of course you will take care nobody sees the cancelled sheets'. As Scott left Abbotsford on the 23rd, it is doubtful that he accomplished much more in the time remaining, and Lockhart is now held largely responsible for this first tale.

Still later, in the 'Introduction' to the published *Tales* (dated 15 October), this vexing matter is again discussed, first in the report 'that our hopeful scheme is entirely blown up. The Tales, on publishing which we reckoned with so much confidence, have already been printed; they are abroad all over America, and the British papers are clamorous' (page xxxviii). It is then queried 'whether this American production embraces the alterations [regarded as] necessary, before the work could be fitted to meet the public eye?' (xxxix). As no unequivocal response occurs in the further colloquy, we may now conjecture that, when the first portion was shipped to Carey ca. May 1831, the earliest 'cancelled sheets', if any, probably were included but, as the several collations cited below will indicate, many revisions still remained.

Copies: BCL(2) E L(2) O(8); CtY IdU InU(2) MH NN(2) T/B TxU(2) ViU(2).

References: Church 553; Randall, pages 54-55; Sterling 744; Thomson, pages 19, 22; Van Antwerp(1) 26; Worthington 23. (Magnum Opus Edition 1833: *Waverley Novels*, 'Count Robert of Paris', xlvi-xlvii.*1-3* 4-241, 'Castle Dangerous', xlvii.*243-245* 246-466—xlviii.*3-5* 6-146.)

1] **TALES OF MY LANDLORD,** | Fourth and Last Series, . . . VOL. I. . . . 1832.

Collation: *a*^{12}(-*a*1) *b*^{12} A-C^{12} D^{12}(±D10) E^{12}(±E1) F-N^{12} O^{6} P^{2} *Q*1(*Q*1+1). Pagination: *i* half-title, *ii blank, iii* title-page, *iv* printer's imprint(1), *v* vi-xliii Introduction, signed 'J.C.', Gandercleuch, 15 October 1831, *xliv blank, xlv* series title, *xlvi blank, 1* fly-title for 'Count Robert of Paris', *2 blank, 3* 4-329 text, chapters 1-11, 329 printer's imprint(2), *330 blank, 331* Errata, *332 blank.* Typography: Preliminary signatures *a* and *b* are in italics. Page 16 is misnumbered 6.

Figures: *a*—, *b*—, A22-4 24-8, B45-3 46-6, C69-7 71-5, D93-4 94-8/-, E111-3 120-8, F143-5 144-7, G165-7 166-6, H190-5 192-3, I 214-7 216-8, K218-3 240-7, L250-4 261-2, M267-2 288-7, N299-1 312-3, O 323-3, P—, *Q*—.

Notes: Cancel D10, page 92, lines 11, 24, reading 'the stoic . . . Elephantos' in the original text according to the Philadelphia *Gazette* extract and Carey edition, now reads 'that sect . . . . Elephans'. Cancel E1, page 97, line 14, originally reading 'always', now reads 'occasionally'. According to the errata leaf page 200, 4th line of motto, 'Gallaplune' should read 'Gallaphron' and page 243, line 18, 'position' should read 'precision'. As evident in the MH(Lowell) copy, this errata leaf was printed with the errata leaf for volume 2.

2] **TALES OF MY LANDLORD,** | Fourth and Last Series, . . . VOL. II. . . . 1832.

Collation: π^{2} A^{12}(-A1+A^{2}, ±A12) B-E^{12} F^{12}(±F12) G-N^{12} O^{8}(O8+1) *P*1. Pagination: *i* half-title, *ii blank, iii* title-page, *iv* printer's imprint(1), *v* series title, *vi blank, 1* fly-title for 'Count Robert of Paris', *2 blank, 3* 4-330 text, continued, 330 printer's imprint(2), *331* Errata, *332 blank.* Typography: The printer's imprint(2) lacks the short rule. In some copies page 4 lacks a page number and page 245 is misnumbered 248. Signature G2 (page 153) is missigned 2G.

Figures: A—, B47-3 48-8, C51-4 72-5, D95-6 96-8, E119-2 120-7, F—, G166-4 168-3, H191-4 192-1, I 213-3 214-4, K— [&c *none*]. It would appear that, beginning with sheet K in this volume, the Ballantyne printing office no longer used press-figures.

Notes: The A^{2} substitution allows for the extra 'Count Robert' fly-title, a leaf apparently overlooked in the original imposition. The original text for cancel A12 (pages 23-24) is unknown. Cancel F12, now reading, page 144, line 20, 'Household,' in the original text according to the Philadelphia, Carey edition read 'Haram,'. Again according to the errata, page 30, line 4, 'cost' should read 'zest', page 129, line 12, '*pruchie*' should read '*psyche*' and page 227, last line (wrongly cited as 'ninth line from foot') 'Hampton' should read 'Hampshire'.

3] **TALES OF MY LANDLORD,** | Fourth and Last Series, . . . VOL. III. . . . 1832.

Collation: π^2 A-O^{12} P^2(P2+1). Pagination: *i* half-title, *ii blank, iii* title-page, *iv* printer's imprint(1), *1* series title, *2 blank, 3* fly-title for 'Count Robert of Paris', *4 blank, 5* 6-211 text, concluded, *212 blank, 213* fly-title for 'Castle Dangerous', *214 blank, 215* 216-342 text, chapters 1-6, 342 printer's imprint(2). Typography: In some copies section signature L2 (page 249) is missigned 2L. Figures: *none.*

4] **TALES OF MY LANDLORD,** | Fourth and Last Series, . . . [*eight-line quotation from Robert Burns*] . . . . VOL. IV. . . . 1832.

Collation: π^2 A-N^{12} O^8 P1. Pagination: *i* half-title, *ii blank, iii* title-page, *iv* printer's imprint(1), *1* series title, *2 blank, 3* fly-title for 'Castle Dangerous', *4 blank, 5* 6-328 text, concluded, 328-330 postscript, dated from Abbotsford, September 1831, 330 printer's imprint(2). Typography: The printer's imprint(2) has a period after COMPANY. Section signature F2 (page 129) is missigned 2F. Figures: *none.*

REPRINTS

FRANCE

PARIS: Baudry, Barrois [and others]
[~] Tales of My Landlord. Fourth and Last Series. 1831. (Collection of Ancient and Modern British Novels and Romances: *see* 288R.18.)

PARIS: Didot and Galignani
[~] Tales of My Landlord. Fourth and Last Series. 1832. (Collection of Modern English Authors: *see* 291R.71-73.)

PARIS: Galignani
[~] Count Robert of Paris and Castle Dangerous. 1832. One volume. (*see* 294[3].8.)

GERMANY

LEIPZIG: Wigand
[~] Count Robert of Paris. 1832. (A Complete Edition of the Waverley Novels: *see* 300R.25-27.)
[~] Castle Dangerous. 1832. (A Complete Edition of the Waverley Novels: *see* 300R.28-29.)

UNITED STATES

253Ra] NEW YORK: Harper 1832

Tales of My Landlord, Fourth and Last Series, Collected and Arranged by Jedediah Cleishbotham, . . . New York: J. & J. Harper—No. 82 Cliff Street. 1832. Three volumes. Pages 1: *i-iii* iv-xvi, *17* 18-200; 2: *1-3* 14-226; 3: *1-3* 4-146. Notes: This issue evidently is based upon the Carey edition, next entry. Volume 2-3 have a changed imprint, more boldly presented: New=York: J. & J. Harper--82 Cliff Street. 1832. Contents: volume 1 'Castle Dangerous'; volumes 2-3 'Count Robert of Paris'. Copies: E O; NN NNU-W (vol.3).

253Rb] PHILADELPHIA: Carey and Lea 1832
Tales of My Landlord, Fourth and Last Series, Collected and Arranged by Jedediah Cleishbotham, . . . Fourth and Last Series, . . . Philadelphia: Carey and Lea—Chestnut Street. 1832. Three volumes. Pages 1: *i-iii* iv-xvi, *17* 18-200; 2: *1* 2-12 [+ title-leaf] *13* 14-226; 3: *1-3* 4-146. Notes: Some copies occasionally lacking preliminaries were issued with titles imprinted simply: Philadelphia: Carey & Lea. 1832. The first American edition, set from Edinburgh proofs, with the early 'Count Robert' text extracted in the *National Gazette* 7 July 1831 (*see* 253A), the complete 'Tales' edition announced for issue 'Very shortly' on 24 January 1832 and published 7 February (*NG*). Volume 1 prints 'Castle Dangerous', volumes 2-3 'Count Robert of Paris': an order reversing the Edinburgh sequence.

The disorder occurs because Carey, on receiving ca. June 1831 the first part of the text, assumed this to be yet another discrete novel and, in an undated catalogue (oddly included in the pagination as *1* 2-12: this replacing text later canceled?), accordingly listed it as 'Count Robert of Paris, a Romance of the Lower Empire. By the Author of Waverley. In 2 vols. 12mo. *Nearly ready*.' [Note the sub-title, later omitted in the Edinburgh edition.] Conformably the direction lines for his setting read 'Vol. I.' and 'Vol. II.' It would seem, however, that his early extract in the *Gazette*—five months before the Edinburgh issue—prompted Cadell (or Lockhart) to deny him any further copy: a circumstance that forced Carey to prepare the 'Castle' text as the first of the *Tales* and, when the other copy was finally received, to define the other tale on the disjunct general titles as 'VOL. II.' and 'VOL. III.' Nonetheless, the 'Introduction' and postscript are entered here first and last as in the Edinburgh edition.

Copies: CtY(2) MH MWA(vol.2) NjP NN(2) NNU-W(vols.2-3) PPL RPB T/B ViU. References: Kaser 299(no cost entry); Randall, pages 54-55.

LETTER ON THE WORD 'PYNE'

254A] First Printing: 1832

'Original Correspondence Sir Walter Scott', page 361, *in*:

The Literary Gazette; and Journal of Belles Lettres, Arts, Sciences, &c. No. 803. Saturday, June 9, 1832. Price 1s. [Printer's imprint:] London: Published every Saturday by W. A. Scripps, at the Literary Gazette Office, 7, Wellington Street, Waterloo Bridge, Strand, and 13, South Moulton Street, Oxford Street; . . .

Published 9 June 1832 in London.

Notes: As may be inferred from a headnote, the letter, undated from Abbotsford, apparently was written after 16 July 1831 to Baron de Fahnenberg, and alludes to Scott's use of the word 'pyne'.

Copy: L. References: *Letters*, xi.54, 343; Corson(2), page 307. (Magnum Opus Edition: Not reprinted.)

LETTER ON A BRONZE MEDAL OF SCOTT

255A] First Printing: 1832

Fac-Simile of an Autograph Letter of Sir Walter Scott Bart. Printed exclusively to accompany a Bronze Medal of Sir Walter Scott. Published Sepr 27, 1832 by Messrs Jennings and Chaplin, Cheapside & sold by S. Parker, Argyll Place and all Booksellers.

Published 27 September 1832 in London. Two-leaf fold (230 x 189mm cut). Paper unwatermarked.

Notes: This lithograph by C. J. Hullmandel is of a letter 29 May [1827] to Samuel Parker, Bronze Works, 12 Argyle Place, London, congratulating him on the bronze proof of two medals, one of George IV, the other of himself. The reproduction occupies the first two pages, the 'fac-simile' account given above appearing in print at the foot of the second page. In one of the E copies a pencilled note by Sir Walter Maxwell-Scott indicates that both medals are at Abbotsford, the King's medal remaining unfinished, Scott's bearing the date MDCCCXXVII. The facsimile letter, promptly issued upon the death of Scott, was reprinted several months later in *Letters to Polwhele* (pages 101-102, *see* 257Aa); the original, not in the collected *Letters*, is at Oxford (Bodl MS Autog c.24.f.162-3).

Copies: E(3). Reference: (Magnum Opus Edition: Not reprinted.)

LETTER ON LANDSCAPE ILLUSTRATIONS

256A] First Printing: 1832

Notes: This brief letter to the publisher Charles Tilt, postmarked from Melrose 14 May 1830, graciously acknowledges receipt of the first number of the *Landscape Illustrations of the Waverley Novels*, a work sent to Scott the week before. Tilt apparently was emboldened by the precedent just established in September 1832 (previous entry) and prepared an exact lithographic facsimile of this note, with address, red sealing wax, and black postmarks on the outer leaf, thus producing an insidious replica often passing (at a high price) as the original—but betrayed as a fake by watermarks dated at first (1) 1831, with outer address panel 'dust darkened' and, (2) in later printings, 1832, with all panel folds undusted. As with the preceding facsimile, this replica was shortly reprinted in *Letters to Polwhele* (page 100, *see* 257Aa). Tilt again reproduced the letter only (inner leaf) in his 1833 edition of *Portraits of the Principal Female Characters* (vol.3:*see* concluding note to 342D).

Copies: (Issue 1) NNP T/B. (2) NNP.

References: J. Herbert Cahoon, 'A Scott Facsimile', *The Book Collector* 6 (1957) 74; J. A. Stargardt (Marburg) Auction Catalogue 1-2 June 1976, item 260 (600DM estimate [=£250]); Maggs Catalogue 1091 [1989], item 324 (£350). (Magnum Opus Edition: Not reprinted, but quoted in *Letters*, xii.471, which cites location of the supposed original letter [another facsimile copy?].)

LETTERS ADDRESSED TO THE REV. R. POLWHELE

257Aa] First Edition, First Issue: 1832

LETTERS | OF | **SIR WALTER SCOTT;** | ADDRESSED TO | THE REV. R. POLWHELE; D. GILBERT, ESQ.; | FRANCIS DOUCE, ESQ. &c. &c. | ACCOMPANIED BY AN AUTOBIOGRAPHICAL MEMOIR OF | LIEUT.-GENERAL SIR HUSSEY VIVIAN, | BART. K.C.B. K.G.H. | [*short rule*] | LONDON: | J. B. NICHOLS AND SON, 25, PARLIAMENT STREET. | [*dash*] | 1832.

Published 1 December 1832 in London (*Ath*). Binding: green moiré silk or blue-grey boards with printed label on front board. Paper: Royal 12° (203 x 128mm uncut). Watermarks: *none*. Collation: π^2 A^4(A4+1) B-E^{12} F^6. Pagination: *1* title, *2 blank, i* Advertisement, *ii blank, iii* dedication to John Gibson Lockhart, *iv blank, v* vi-xii Introductory Lines, *1* 2-103 text, *104 blank, 1* 2-4 Nichols catalogue, 4 printer's imprint: [*short rule*] | J. B. Nichols and Son, 25, Parliament Street, London. Figures: *none*.

Notes: In a letter to The Rev. Polwhele, dated 6 October 1825 (page 84), Scott agreed to the publication of certain of his correspondence, saying: 'I have consented to your wish merely because it was your wish, and without any idea on my own part, that what was written for your own eye deserved a more extensive circulation.' The agreement apparently pertained only to the five letters earlier printed in Polwhele's 1826 *Traditions and Recollections* (see 185A), and not to the twenty-three others now issued posthumously. Letters numbered XXV-XXVII (pages 95-100), all addressed to other persons, were previously printed, the one to Joseph Harding, 25 March 1828, in a catalogue of Lodge's portraits (215A); the one to Samuel Parker, 29 May [1827] in a facsimile issue (255A); and the one to Charles Tilt, May 1830, also in facsimile (256A).

Copies: E HS O(Douce); CtY NNU-W PPL T/B.

Reference: (Magnum Opus Edition: Not reprinted.)

257Ab] First Edition, Second Issue: 1832

LETTERS | OF | **SIR WALTER SCOTT;** | . . . 1832.

Notes: To the original issue a 'Postscript' is added: a conjugate doubleton signed F5, paged *105* 106-108, inserted in that position, and initialed R.P. from Polwhele, 30 November [1832].

Copy: MH(with Polwhele's MS corrections and inscription to his wife).

257Ac] Second Edition (First Edition, Third Issue): 1832

LETTERS | OF | **SIR WALTER SCOTT;** | ADDRESSED TO | THE REV. R. POLWHELE; D. GILBERT, ESQ.; | FRANCIS DOUCE, ESQ. &c. &c. | [*short rule*] | SECOND EDITION. | [*short rule*] | LONDON: | J. B. NICHOLS AND SON, 25, PARLIAMENT STREET. | [*dash*] | 1832.

Binding: Purple moiré silk and printed label. Paper: Royal 12° (203 x 128mm uncut). Watermarks: none. Collation: $\pi^2(\pm\pi 1)$ $A^4(A4+1)$ B-C^{12} D^{12}(-D11,12) E^{12} (-E1,2,3,4+χ1) F^8. Pagination: *1* title-page, *2 blank*, *i* Advertisement, *ii blank*, *iii* dedication, *iv blank*, *v* vi-xii Introductory Lines, *1* 2-69 80-103 text, *104 blank*, *105* 106-108 Postscript, *1* 2-4 Nichols catalogue, 4 printer's imprint: [*short rule*] | J. B. Nichols and Son, 25, Parliament Street.

Notes: A further issue with some readjustment of the contents. The cancel defined as χ1 actually bears a direction line 'D11-E4' (in substitution for the six leaves on Sir Hussey Vivian, which are now withdrawn), but this signal cannot easily be entered in the collation. The substitute leaf covering the gap, paged on recto 69, and on verso 80, represents the first portion of Scott's letter XIX dated '1816', previously paged 79-80 in the first issue.

Presentation copy: HS('The Right Honble. W. E. Gladstone with Mr. Polwhele's very respectful Compts. Avonbury Vicarage May 1875'). Other copies: E O.

WILL OF SIR WALTER SCOTT

258A] First Printing: 1832

'Will of Sir Walter Scott.', page 396, *in*:

The Edinburgh Weekly Journal. VOL. XXXV. No. 1826.] Wednesday, December 12, 1832. [Price Sevenpence.] Printed by Ballantyne and Company, for the Proprietors.

Published 12 December 1832 in Edinburgh.

Notes: This summary account, with some provisions cited directly, concludes with a reference to the *Caledonian Mercury*; but no report has been located in that newspaper. The will, executed 4 February 1831, had then been deposited with Robert Cadell.

Copy: L.

THE BATTLE OF KILLIECRANKIE

259A] First Printing: 1833[1832]

'THE BATTLE OF KILLIECRANKIE.', (first words: 'The glorious Graham, of deathless fame,') pages 380-381, *in*:

Chambers' Edinburgh Journal. No. 48. Saturday, December 29, 1832. Price Three Halfpence. [Volume imprint:] Edinburgh: Published by William and Robert Chambers, 19, Waterloo Place; Orr and Smith, London; John Macleod, Glasgow; and sold by all booksellers. 1833.

Published 29 December 1832 in Edinburgh.

Notes: The poem, on the battle fought 26 July 1689, consists of nine 8-line stanzas, all representing a 'spirited Effusion' of a Latin poem published in 1769. According to an 1811 note from Alexander Hunter, quoted in this report (and now with Scott's MS poem at NNP), the verse was given to him 'about six years ago' *i.e.* in 1805. This first 1832 printing was unknown to Strout.

Scott's translation should not be confused with another poem by Bishop Skinner of Aberdeen, which has seven 8-line stanzas, an identical title, and first words reading: 'Clavers and his Highlandmen / Came down upon the raw, man;'.

Copy: E. References: Alan L. Strout, 'An Unpublished Ballad-Translation by Scott, *The Battle of Killiecrankie*,' *Modern Language Notes*, 30 (1939), 13-18. (Magnum Opus Edition: Not reprinted.)

CLAUSUS • TUTUS • ERO

SIX

COLLECTED EDITIONS

1. AUTHORIZED EDITIONS OF THE POETRY, NOVELS, AND PROSE (260A-287A)

As observed in the earlier part of this section, Scott's *Minstrelsy* and the separate major poems were deceptively conjoined in 1806-1817 under various *Works* titles (260Aa-Ad) and then, beginning in 1819, his lesser verse cobbled together in a supplemental volume eventually entitled *Miscellaneous Poems* (261Aa-Ae). Some thirteen issues appear under these several titles, all rather high-priced and offering, in the single volume, only one new poem: a brief epitaph on Mrs Euphemia Erskine. To extend the market to less affluent readers, the publisher thereupon proposed a complete *Poetical Works* in a cheaper twelve-volume 12° format (262A), this to include in the first volume, as a frontispiece, Raeburn's portrait of the author, in the tenth the Erskine epitaph, and in the twelfth, four new poems of greater length.

Early in 1819 Constable also purchased from Scott copyrights to the novels thus far published and, recognizing the continuing demand for his fiction, decided upon yet another and more elaborate scheme of continual appeal to every purse. This involved both novels and verse, all to be issued at first in a larger size, on better paper, adorned with vignette titles, and then correlated to proceed at appropriate intervals from 8° to less costly 12° and finally to the cheapest 'miniature' 18° issue. Over the first several years the chronological correlation is readily perceived in this Table.

Size	NOVELS	Vols	Price	Published	POEMS	Vols	Price	Published
8°	269Aa	12	£7.4.0	9 Dec 1819	263A	10	£6.0.0	4 Dec 1820
12°	270Aa	16	6.0.0	31 Mar 1821	*264A	8	3.12.0	24 Nov 1821
18°	271A	12	4.4.0	20 Sep 1823	*266Aa	10	3.3.0	31 May 1823

[* Of the six collections listed 264A is the only one issued without engraved titles; but 266Aa was also sold with extra engraved frontispieces for £3.13.0.]

Evidently this gradation in the novels was particularly appealing to Constable's associate firm in London, Hurst Robinson, which originally accepted only 650 of the 1500 copies prepared for the expensive 8° novels, but especially ordered 5000 sets of the newly designed 18° (David Hewitt [ed.], *EEWN3*.374-377).

As the double lettering in the Table might suggest, novels in the first two formats eventually in 1821-1825 went into further issues or editions, and the poems also in the last format, but here not until 1830 when further material was added. This last 18° poetical issue (266Ab) apparently represents the first printing of Scott's new introductions, preceding their occurrence in a final 8° publication of the same date (267Ab), where two further essays are introduced.

Among the carefully orchestrated collected editions it will be noted that, since by this time Scott had, essentially, discontinued the writing of verse, only the novel sequences continue in the original pattern, and then, for the most part, maintain the intervals between issues and the price structure first established, whatever the number of volumes: 8° at 12s a volume, 12° at 7s.6d, and 18° at 7s. (Again, however, as for the earlier separate editions, these volumes were available only as a set.) It is also noteworthy that in general, to maintain interest in these series, each 8-12-18° sequence was assigned a newly-devised collective title and begins with a 'banner' issue, that is, with one of the more prominent novels, or one representing a new departure. Thus [1] the first 1819 sequence, as represented in the Table above, is labelled 'Novels and Tales' and starts with *Waverley* (269Aa); [2] 1822 'Historical Romances', *Ivanhoe* (272A); [3] 1823 'Novels and Romances', *The Pirate* (275A); [4] 1827 'Tales and Romances', *St. Ronan's Well* (278A); and, posthumously under the same 4th collective title, [5] 1833 *Chronicles of the Canongate* (281A). In all, these five collective novel series, occasionally revised by Scott in one issue or another, range through 170 volumes, truly a notable achievement by the author's ingenious publishers.

It should also be observed that, as these series progressed, Scott from 1828 to 1831 used interleaved copies of the octavo editions to prepare for his 'Magnum Opus' (a set then handsomely bound by Cadell and now reposing in the National Library of Scotland); but on the first three occasions these octavos had, at the time of his revision, proceeded into later issues: thus for [1] 269Ac(2), [2] 272A(2), [3] 275A(2), but still first issue for [4] 278A. Since series [5] was not available in his lifetime, the texts represented here were revised on interleaved copies of the separate editions previously identified and cited again in entry 281A.

On 17 May 1827 the *Edinburgh Evening Courant* advertised the original issue both of [4] 'Tales and Romances' and of *The Miscellaneous Prose Works* (287A), a collection already at press before the 1826 bankruptcy and intended to bring together, revised in six volumes, all the readily available pieces not included in the poetry or novel volumes. Altogether, then, with the recovery of his last remainng copyrights in a December 1827 auction, Scott was ready in the following year to begin work on his comprehensive 'Magnum', using the texts just described. This was an enterprise eventually exceedng all that had gone before and thus properly serves as the subject of Chapter Seven.

2. COLLECTED REPRINT EDITIONS (288R-318R)

It has already been remarked that Scott's separate editions since 1805 were rapidly printed after, and in a few instances issued before, the British issue. When a sufficient number of his works had appeared, the more adventure-some booksellers then began to publish the author in collected form, first at Baltimore in 1812-1813 with *The Poetical Works* (303R), a curious amal-gam incorporating in its final volume a variant issue from Philadelphia. Thereafter his collected verse was frequently published, with the last in Scott's lifetime a single-volume 1829 Philadelphia issue (316R), continually reprinted in later years, but deriving originally from an 1827 Paris, Galignani edition.

The first comprehensive edition of all of Scott's works, ranging from 1819 through 1831 in 156 miniature 32° volumes, appears in Zwickau (302R), this presenting first some of his poetry, then the novels intermixed with other verse and prose, and at least four volumes evidently deriving also from earlier Galignani issues. A year later, in 1820, Galignani began his own series, a complex of five sequences in 145 volumes varying from 32° to Royal 8° (290R-294R). Here in the unnumbered 12° series comprising the 'Novels and Tales' (291R) it will be observed that the issue, now ordered as Galignani finally decreed in the original British sequence, according to the imprint states began—appropriately for French readers—with *The Abbot* (volumes here numbered 31-33), a popular novel followed by *Guy Mannering* (4-6), *Waverley* (1-3), *Ivanhoe* (25-27), *The Pirate* (37-39), and *Quentin Durward* (43-45). These six novels, as the record indicates, were in such demand as to require two or three editions, all the others being issued or reissued only from a single setting.

A much simpler operation, limited to 'The Novels Tales and Romances', was started 1821 by Parker in Boston (305R-307R) and, in Scott's lifetime, proceeded in British order through three sequences, the first in 23 volumes, the second in 45, and the third in 54, with this last dependent upon the 1829-1833 'Magnum Opus' and all occasionally reprinted. Similarly dependent is the Paris, Baudry 'Collection of Ancient and Modern British Novels and Romances' 1831-1833, with the Scott entries running to thirty volumes: a sequence which chronologically comes last in this discussion, but in our alphabetic geographical array is necessarily listed first. Since with few exceptions all of these foreign collections were issued (like the 'Magnum') in serial order, and thus could be purchased a volume or two at a time, the separate titles therein are cross-referenced among the separate reprint ('R') entries earlier described and not again listed in the Index.

Amid all this international activity the only 'collected' British reprint was an abortive series of abridgements (335D), advertised 6 October 1827 as to continue for about 48 numbers, and with the first number then issued containing all of *Waverley* and part of *Guy Mannering*. Very probably this brave project, starting just two months before Scott and Cadell recovered the last of the copyrights needed for their 'Magnum Opus', was regarded as an immediate threat to this larger enterprise, and therefore stopped by some high authority; but further information on this odd circumstance is unavailable.

3. COLLECTED DERIVATIVE EDITIONS (319D-346D)

Like the reprints just considered, the collected derivatives ('D') sometimes were issued serially and here represent several kinds of activity inspired by Scott, that is:
Illustrations: 322 324 325 328 334 341 342 346 [total entries: 224]
Plays: 319 321 323 329 330 331 333 340 347 [45]
Music: 336 337 339 344 [29]
Miscellaneous: 320 326 335 338 345 [5]
Quite apart from numerous separate 'D' derivatives described in earlier chapters, and relevant parodies or satires considered later (479S-503S), the 303 items recorded here in collected series would suggest that, if numbers have any signifance, the audience in Scott's time more often than not was aware of his various literary achievements only in these altered or debased versions.

CONTENTS OF CHAPTER SIX

1A. COLLECTED EDITIONS: POETRY

1B. COLLECTED EDITIONS: NOVELS

1C. COLLECTED EDITIONS: INTRODUCTIONS

1D. COLLECTED EDITIONS: PROSE

1A. COLLECTED EDITIONS: POETRY

Note: After repeatedly listing other, earlier poems in the notices for his latest separate work (13Ab, 24Aa, 28Af, 31Aa, &c), Scott's publishers eventually issued all of his poems collectively under various *Works* titles, the first apparently in 1806 as a five-volume octavo set, the last in the period 1813-1817 when the poems then ranged to nine or ten volumes. Generally these nonce collections consisted, at first of large-paper, later of ordinary copies, and thus, as the following account indicates, may differ from set to set.

260Aa] First, Five Volume Issue: 1806

THE | **WORKS** | OF | WALTER SCOTT, ESQ. | [*short Oxford rule*] | VOL. I [II-V]. | CONTAINING | [*specific title*]. | [*short reversed Oxford rule*] | EDINBURGH: | Printed by James Ballantyne and Co. | FOR LONGMAN, HURST, REES AND ORME, LONDON; AND | A. CONSTABLE AND CO. EDINBURGH. | 1806.

Published ca. November 1806 in Edinburgh; issued 7 March 1807 in London (*MH*). £5.5.0. Binding: Pink or blue-green boards with printed labels. Paper: Royal 8° (246 x 152mm uncut). Watermarks: J Whatman | 1804 [1805]. New preliminary gathering occasionally watermarked: J Whatman | 1806.

Notes: This original collective issue consists of a uniform impression especially prepared with an identical large-paper watermark, but with a new *Works* preliminary gathering replacing (in volumes 1-4) the original separate preliminaries. Press figures and other typographical evidence, however, reveal the original separate edition numbers to be as cited below.

Copies: EU(Corson); CtY+(Anne, Countess of Ormonde) DLC MH.
+With 16-page Longman catalogue 1 October 1806 (not listing the *Works*).

Reference: Ruff 58.

1-3] Minstrelsy of the Scottish Border. 3rd edition, 1806.
4] Sir Tristrem. 2nd edition, 1806. The substitute final preliminary leaf, listing 'Contents of the Fifth Volume', has not been transferred in the CtY and DLC copies examined.

5] The Lay of the Last Minstrel. 4th edition, 1806. Possibly because the 'Contents' leaf was not entered (in some copies) as a cancellans for the original fourth edition title, this leaf is sometimes here retained; but the prefixed *Works* title indicates that the collective issue is now augmented with 'Ballads and Lyrical Pieces' (signatures Y3-Y8, Z[8] 2A[6] 2B[2](2B2+1; 2B missigned M), pages *333* fly-title, *334 blank, 335* 336-382 text, 382 printer's imprint). As compared with the separate fourth edition, this large-paper reimpression also varies throughout in its press figures: *A*14-3, B31-3, C35-3, D63-3(or 64-7), E80-7/-, F82-3, G110-4 112-7, H128-7, I 131-4, K155-2, L172-2 174-3, M192-3, N194-4, O 224-3, P231-2 240-1, Q244-3 246-1, R265-4, S286-7, T303-4, U326-7, Y344-3, Z355-3, 2A 363-4, 'M'[2B] 381-2.

260Ab] Six Volume Issue: '1806'[1808]

THE | **WORKS** | OF | WALTER SCOTT, ESQ. | [*short Oxford rule*] | VOL. I [II-V], . . . 1806.

Notes: This issue, in ideal state still retaining the collective 1806 title for five volumes, now adds with its separate title only, as a sixth volume, the second edition, large-paper impression of *Marmion* (28Ad), of which 'A few Copies' were published in April 1808. The inserted catalogue in the regular paper issue of that edition (28Ac), and in the Carleton *Memoirs*, issued the same month (31Aa), price the one volume at £1.1.0, the six volumes at £6.6.0.

Copy: not seen. Reference: Ruff 58.

260Ac] Eight-Nine Volume Issue: 1812-1813

THE | **WORKS** | OF | WALTER SCOTT, ESQ. | [*short Oxford rule*] | VOLUME FIRST [SECOND-EIGHTH] | CONTAINING | [*specific title*]. | [*short reversed Oxford rule*] | EDINBURGH: | [*short Oxford rule*] | PRINTED FOR | LONGMAN AND CO. WILLIAM MILLER, AND JOHN MURRAY, | LONDON; AND FOR CONSTABLE AND CO. | AND JOHN BALLANTYNE AND CO. | EDINBURGH. | [*dash*] 1812.

Notes: This is an ordinary paper issue, containing only a single 'Works' title-leaf for each volume, without printer's imprint, followed (in volumes 4-8) with the original single volume edition title. The edition of volumes 1-3 has been determined by reference to the press-figures. The only copy located is of a later issue with a ninth volume added, bearing its own separate 1813 title-leaf, but no 'Works' title.

Copy: EU(Corson)

1-3] Minstrelsy of the Scottish Border. 5th edition, 1812. (Volume 2 is of the first issue [B20-4, F87-9] and volume 3 of the second issue [Y344-1]).
4] The Lay of the Last Minstrel. 13th edition, 1812.
5] Marmion; A Tale of Flodden Field. 8th edition, 1811.
6] Sir Tristrem; A Metrical Tale of the 15th Century. 3rd edition, 1811.
7] The Lady of the Lake. 9th edition, 1811.
8] The Vision of Don Roderick, 2nd edition, 1811; Ballads and Lyrical Pieces 4th edition, 1812.
9] Rokeby. 5th edition. 1813.

260Ad] Nine-Ten Volume Issues: 1813-1817

THE | **WORKS** | OF | WALTER SCOTT, ESQ. | [*short Oxford rule*] | VOLUME FIRST [SECOND-NINTH], | CONTAINING | [*specific title*]. | [*short reversed Oxford rule*] | EDINBURGH: | [*short Oxford rule*] | PRINTED FOR | LONGMAN AND CO. WILLIAM MILLER, AND JOHN MURRAY, | LONDON; AND FOR CONSTABLE AND CO. | AND JOHN BALLANTYNE AND CO. | EDINBURGH. | [*dash*] | 1813.

Watermarks: J WHATMAN | 1812 [evident in all issues noted below].

Notes: There are at least five issues under this collective 1813 bifolium, representing: *1* half-title, *2* printer's imprint, *3* title, *4 blank*. Printer's imprint: [*short Oxford rule*] | EDINBURGH: | Printed by James Ballantyne & Co.

1] First Issue:

THE | **WORKS** | OF | WALTER SCOTT, ESQ. . . . 1813.

Notes: In its original nine-volume issue, Scott's poems would range through *Rokeby*, none of any edition date later than 1813. A nine-volume Royal 8° set, however, is advertised for £11 in the *Morning Chronicle* as late as 29 March 1815. Copy: not seen.

2] Second Issue:

THE | **WORKS** | OF | WALTER SCOTT, ESQ. . . . 1813 [1815].

Notes: This issue, in ideal state still retaining the collective 1813 title originally prepared for nine volumes, now adds with its separate title only, as a tenth volume, *The Lord of the Isles*, published 2 January 1815. Evidently this is the ten-volume set advertised in *The Field of Waterloo*, issued 2 November 1815, as then available at £12.9.0. A partial large-paper set at CtY (with coronetted 'BV' initials on spine), separately described but not entered here since it has no collective titles, is of this time, with the tenth volume now of a 'second edition'. A collective-title issue, however, still remains unlocated.

3] Third Issue:

THE | **WORKS** | OF | WALTER SCOTT, ESQ. . . . 1813 [1816].

Notes: This large-paper issue again retains the original collective 1813 'Works' bifolium for the first nine volumes, but now also, in the only copy observed, the separate titles for all ten volumes, with the 4th and 7th each dated 1816. These separate titles immediately identify the editions as cited below.

Copy: BCL

1-3] Minstrelsy of the Scottish Border. 5th edition. 1812.
4] The Lay of the Last Minstrel. 15th edition. 1816.
5] Marmion; A Tale of Flodden Field. 9th edition. 1815.
6] Sir Tristrem; A Metrical Tale of the 15th Century. 3d edition. 1811.
7] The Lady of the Lake. 11th edition. 1816.
8] The Vision of Don Roderick. 3rd edition. 1815 and Ballads and Lyrical Pieces. 3rd edition. 1815.
9] Rokeby. 6th edition. 1815.
10] The Lord of the Isles. 2nd edition. 1815.

4] Fourth Issue

THE | **WORKS** | OF | WALTER SCOTT, ESQ. . . . 1813 [1817].

Notes: The first nine volumes, with collective titles, are of the same editions as the previous issue, though here without the inconvenient separate titles; the separate tenth volume is now of the fifth edition, 1815; and all volumes are of the regular paper impression. As Scott observed of this very set, in a letter 29 March 1817 to his friend Daniel Terry, it had by then become impossible 'to make up a large paper set . . . and after all, it is the *ex dono* which can alone give value to the volumes.'

Presentation copy: NNP+('For Mr [William] Atkinson, a slight testimony of grateful esteem from his obliged friend The Author').
+With inserted frontispiece of the 1805 James Saxon portrait.

5] Fifth Issue:

THE | **WORKS** | OF | WALTER SCOTT, ESQ. . . . 1813 [1817].

Notes: Again the set is of a regular paper impression, of the same editions as in the previous issue, but the earlier portion of the 6th volume is now made up of remainder sheets: gatherings a-d from 3d edition, 1st impression, 1811 (13Ac); e-f and text from 2d edition, 1806 (13Ab); g-h lacking.

Presentation copy: NNU-W('Edward Blore Esq from his obliged friend The Author Edinbrugh[!] 8th July 1817' [lacking vol. 10]).

Postscript: Apart from the octavo nonce collections described above, there is some indication that Scott or his publishers may once or twice have contrived to issue, without collective titles, quarto collections of any copies in that format still available. One notice of these appears in the London *Morning Chronicle* 18 January 1809, which advertised as uniform with the 4° *Marmion* 'SCOTT'S POETICAL WORKS, in 4to'. Though early collections of this kind have not been identified, an assemblage of five large-paper volumes issued 1808-1815 and now at NNU-W, all bearing the book label AUCHINCRUIVE, in a contemporary half-calf publishers' binding labeled 'SCOTT'S POETICAL WORKS', and described among the separate issues, would appear to be of this order: *see* 14An, 28Ab, 47Ab, 64Ab, 81Ab. Scott represented the trustees of this now defunct manorial estate before the Court of Session on 1 December 1798 (352A.11).

MISCELLANEOUS POEMS

261Aa] Trial Printing (Unpublished): 1819

BALLADS, &c. | THE | **BRIDAL OF TRIERMAIN,** | AND | **HAROLD THE DAUNTLESS.** | POEMS. | [*short Oxford rule*] | BY | WALTER SCOTT, Esq. | [*short reversed Oxford rule*] | EDINBURGH: | PRINTED FOR ARCHBALD CONSTABLE AND CO. EDINBURGH; | LONGMAN, HURST, REES, ORME, AND BROWN, PATERNOSTER-ROW; | AND HURST, ROBINSON, AND CO. 90, CHEAPSIDE, LONDON. | [*dash*] | 1819.

Paper: Demy 8° (227 x 144mm uncut). Watermarks: *none*. Collation: π^4 N-2H^8 U^8 2K^4 2L^2. Pagination: *i* half-title, *2 blank*, *3* title-page, *4 blank*, *5* Contents [for all three sections], *6 blank*, *7* Advertisement [for the Ballads], *8 blank*, *181* fly-title, *182 blank*, *183* 184-370 text, *365* fly-title for *Harold the Dauntless*, *366 blank*, *367* 368-510 *511* text, *511* printer's imprint, *512 blank*. Printer's imprint: [*short rule*] | Edinburgh: | Printed by James Ballantyne & Co. Typography: Sheets 2E-2G are misnumbered *321* 322-368. Figures: 189-10.

Notes: As the suppressed title and pagination would indicate, Constable originally intended this issue to contain two earlier sections.

Copy: E. Mixed copies (retaining suppressed π^4 with suppressed title, but with full first-issue text): O(J. Johnson); CtY. References: Ruff, pages 202-203(with illustration).

261Ab] First Edition, First Issue: 1820

MISCELLANEOUS | **POEMS.** | BY | WALTER SCOTT, ESQ. | [*short reversed Oxford rule*] | EDINBURGH: | PRINTED FOR ARCHIBALD CONSTABLE AND CO. EDINBURGH; | AND HURST, ROBINSON, AND CO. CHEAPSIDE, LONDON. | [*dash*] | 1820.

Published 13 March 1820 in Edinburgh (*EEC*); issued 29 March in London (*MC*). 14s. 500 copies. Binding: drab or blue boards with printed label. Paper: Demy 8° (228 x 146mm uncut). Watermarks: *none*. Collation: π^4 A-D^8 F^8 H^8 K^8 M-2H^8 U^8 2K^4 2L^2. Pagination: *i* half-title, *ii* printer's imprint(1), *iii* title-page, *iv blank*, *v* Advertisement, *vi blank*, *vii*-viii Contents, *1* fly-title for 'Miscellaneous Poems', *2 blank*, *3* 4-'180'[128] text, *181* fly-title for *The Bridal of Triermain*, *182 blank*, *183* 184-350 text and notes, *351* fly-title for 'Fragments', *352 blank*, *353* 354-363 text, *364 blank*, *365* fly-title for *Harold the Dauntless*, *366 blank*, *367* 368-510 *511* text, *511* printer's imprint(2), *512 blank*. Printer's imprints (1) and (2): [*short rule*] | EDINBURGH: | Printed by James Ballantyne & Co. Typography: To join with the following section (already printed in the preceding, abortive state) the first section is 'spread out' typographically, the fifth leaf of four successive gatherings (D, F, H, K) signed respectively E, G, I, L, and the pagination repeatedly moved upward: pages 38-51 numbered 48-61; pages 56-59 numbered 86-89; page 60 numbered 84; pages 61-92 numbered 91-122; pages 96-128 numbered 148-180. In the second section (beginning with fly-title page *181*) pages 422-468 are misnumbered 322-368 and pages 482, 483 are misnumbered 483, 482. In some copies 2K (page 501) is missigned X.

Figures: [misnumbered pages are cited without reference to the correct page number] A16-2, B24-15, C58-2, D91-15, F108-4, H115-2, K150-15, M175-9, N189-10, O 204-6, P—, Q233-7, R250-5, S267-5, T285-10, U308-5, X324-10, Y336-10, Z*353*-5, 2A 360-8, 2B 385-9, 2C 404-10, 2D 411-12, 2E 327-5, 2F 346-5, 2G 358-13, 2H 472-5, U494-12, 2K—, 2L—.

Notes: The advertisements state that this issue was 'printed uniformly with the octavo editions, in order to accomodate purchasers of sets of Mr Scott's Poetry in that size, which this volume will complete'—that is, the various 'nonce' cumulations described above (*see* 260Aa-Ad). The volume includes the first printing of the 'Epitaph on Mrs Erskine' (first words: 'Plain, as her native dignity of mind,' pages *147*-148), the wife of William Erskine (Lord Kinedder), who died 20 September 1819.

Copies: BCL E(2); CtY(2) IdU InU T/B TxU. References: Ruff 161, Van Antwerp(1) 19. (Magnum Opus Edition 1834: *Poetical Works*, xi.)

261Ac] First Edition, Second Issue: 1820

MISCELLANEOUS | **POEMS.** . . . 1820.

Collation: π[4] A-D[8] F[8] H[8] K[8] M[8] *A8* B-U[8] X[4] Y[2]. Pagination: *i* half-title, *ii* printer's imprint(1), *iii* title-page, *iv blank*, *v* Advertisement, *vi blank*, *vii*-viii Contents, *1* fly-title for 'Miscellaneous Poems', *2 blank*, *3* 4-'180'[128] text, *i* fly-title for *The Bridal of Triermain*, *ii blank*, *iii* iv-xii Preface, *1* 2-171 text, *172 blank*, *173* fly-title for *Harold the Dauntless*, *174 blank*, *175* 176-318 *319* text, *319* printer's imprint(2), *320 blank*.

Notes: This issue may be recognized as a hybrid, essentially, combining the first section of the preceding entry with the first section of the entry following, and thus representing all the typographical peculiarities of both. The one copy located is rebound, thus possibly a sophistication.

Copy: O(Dunston).

261Ad] First Edition, Third Issue: 1820

MISCELLANEOUS | **POEMS.** . . . 1820.

Binding: (1) Drab, blue, or green boards and (a later issue?) red or green cloth with printed label. Paper: Demy 8° (228 x 146mm uncut). Watermarks: *none*. Collation: π[4] A[8] B-U[8] X[4] Y[2](±Y2) Z-2G[8]. Pagination: *i* half-title, *ii* printer's imprint(1), *iii* title-page, *iv blank*, *v* Advertisement, *vi blank*, *vii*-viii Contents, *i* fly-title for *The Bridal of Triermain*, *ii blank*, *iii* iv-xii Preface, *1* 2-171 text, *172 blank*, *173* fly-title for *Harold the Dauntless*, *174 blank*, *175* 176-319 text, *320 blank*, *321* fly-title for 'Miscellaneous Poems', *322 blank*, *323* 324-448 text, 448 printer's imprint(2). Printer's imprints (1) and (2): [*short rule*] | EDINBURGH: | Printed by James Ballantyne & Co. Typography: Signature 2C (page 369) is repeated on page 371, and 2D (page 385) is missigned 3D.

Figures: A ix-10, B12-6, C—, D41-7, E58-5, F75-5, G93-10, H116-5, I 132-10, K144-10, L*161*-5, M168-8, N193-9, O 212-10, P219-12, Q235-5, R254-5/-, S266-13, T280-5, U302-12, X314-6, Y—, Z336-2, 2A 344-15, 2B 368-2, 2C 381-15, 2D 398-4, 2E 405-2, 2F 418-15, 2G 443-9.

Notes: Before it was decided to move the 'Miscellaneous Poems' section to the end of this volume, in state (1) leaf Y2 (page *319*) ended with a printer's imprint(2). After the decision was made, however, (2) a cancel leaf was supplied with Y2 signed and numbered 319, and the imprint withdrawn for later insertion on page 448.

So far as possible all of the previous setting is retained, but the sections are now reordered with new pagination and signatures: thus the fly-title for 'Miscellaneous Poems', signed A (page *1*) in the first issue, is now moved and accordingly signed

Z (page *321*). Within the text the press figures, however, remain unchanged, whatever the new page numbers: thus the page with figure 10, originally numbered 189, is now numbered ix, figure 6 originally on 204 is now on 12, &c.

Copies: (state 1) InU(leaf Y2 in both states) ViU; IdU InU. (2) E(2) O(3); CtY NNU-W. Reference: Ruff 162 ('Second Issue').

261Ae] First Edition, Fourth Issue: 1820[1829]

MISCELLANEOUS | **POEMS.** . . . 1820.

Published after 1 January 1829. Binding: Blue paper boards with vertical printed label 'Miscellaneous Poems' or drab boards with vertical printed label 'Bridal of Triermain, | and | Harold the Dauntless'.

Notes: A remainder issue, the Ruff copy with a Thomas Tegg catalogue reading on page 4: 'On Thursday, the first of January, 1829, was published. . . .'

Copy: not seen. Reference: Ruff 163.

THE POETICAL WORKS

262A] First Collected Edition: 1820

THE | **POETICAL WORKS** | OF | WALTER SCOTT, Esq. | [*short rule*] | IN TWELVE VOLUMES. | VOL. I [II-XII]. | [*short Oxford rule*] | EDINBURGH: | PRINTED FOR ARCH. CONSTABLE AND CO. EDINBURGH: | LONGMAN, HURST, REES, ORME, AND BROWN; | AND JOHN MURRAY, LONDON. | [*short rule*] | 1820.

Issued 21 January 1820 in London (*The Times*). 2000 copies. £3.12.0. Binding: boards. Paper: Crown 12° (162 x 97mm cut). Watermarks: *none*.

General Notes: This first integral collection exhibits some changes in spelling and punctuation, a few corrections throughout, and some additional verse in the last volume. Typography: Printer's imprints read: (1) [*short rule*] | *Printed by James Ballantyne and Company*.; (2) [*short rule*] | Edinburgh: | Printed by James Ballantyne and Co. [EDINBURGH: vols. 1, 3].

Copies: E; CtY InU T/B(Joseph John Gurney) TxGR. Reference: Ruff 160.

1] THE | **POETICAL WORKS** . . . IN TWELVE VOLUMES. | VOL. I. . . . 1820.

Collation: $\pi^2(\pi2+1)$ A-K[12] *L*1. Pagination: *1* half-title, *2* printer's imprint(1), *3* title-page, *4 blank, i* Contents, *ii blank, 1* fly-title for *The Lay of the Last Minstrel*,

2 blank, 3 dedication, *4 blank, 5* preface, *6 blank, 7* fly-title, *8 blank, 9* 10-135 text, Cantos 1-4, *136 blank, 137* fly-title, *138 blank, 139* 140-241 Notes, 241 printer's imprint(2), *242 blank.* Illustration: Frontispiece portrait drawn by Raeburn, engraved by C. Heath, with Constable imprint dated 1 January 1820. Typography: Section signature C2 (page 57) is omitted. In some copies the last number is dropped from page-number 132.

Figures: A12-1, B48-6, C50-2, D76-2, E108-4, F142-2, G164-1, H190-2, I 208-1, K238-1, *L*—.

2] THE | **POETICAL WORKS** . . . IN TWELVE VOLUMES. | VOL. II. . . . 1820.

Collation: $\pi^2(\pi2+1)$ A-K^{12} L^6. Pagination: *1* half-title, *2* printer's imprint(1), *3* title-page, *4 blank, i*-ii Contents, *1* fly-title for *The Lay of the Last Minstrel*, *2 blank, 3* 4-70 text, Cantos 5-6, *71* fly-title, *72 blank, 73* 74-105 Notes, *106 blank, 107* fly-title for *Ballads and Lyrical Pieces*, *108 blank, 109* 110-230 text and notes, *231* fly-title for 'Songs', *232 blank*, 233-250 text and notes, *251* printer's imprint(2), *252 blank.* Typography: Section signatures D2 and H2 (pages *81*, 177) are transposed as 2D and 2H respectively. Section signatures E2 and G2 (pages 105, 153) are omitted.

Figures: +1 *i*-9, A23-2, B*37*-9, C70-9, D84-2, E119-2, F133-2, G153-1/-, H185-6, I 203-2, K219-9, L246-12.

3] THE | **POETICAL WORKS** . . . IN TWELVE VOLUMES. | VOL. III. . . . 1820.

Collation: $\pi^2(\pi2+1)$ A-I^{12} K^{12}(-K12). Pagination: *1* half-title, *2* printer's imprint (1), *3* title-page, *4 blank, i* Contents, *ii blank, 1* fly-title for *Marmion*, *2 blank, 3* Advertisement, *4 blank, 5* dedication, *6 blank, 7* fly-title, *8 blank, 9* 10-173 text, Cantos 1-3, *174 blank, 175* fly-title, *176 blank, 177* 178-238 Notes, 238 printer's imprint(2). Typography: Section signatures A2, D2, H2 (pages *9, 81, 177*) are omitted.

Figures: A22-9, B39-1/-, C68-2, D75-6, E104-4, F*123*-6, G150-9, H187-6, I 207-4, K237-4.

4] THE | **POETICAL WORKS** . . . IN TWELVE VOLUMES. | VOL. IV. . . . 1820.

Collation: $\pi^2(\pi2+1)$ A-L^{12} M^6 *N*1. Pagination: *1* half-title, *2* printer's imprint(1), *3* title-page, *4 blank, i* Contents, *ii blank, 1* fly-title for *Marmion, 2 blank, 3* 4-209 text, Cantos 4-6, *210 blank, 211* fly-title, *212 blank, 213* 214-277 Notes, 277 printer's imprint(2), *278 blank.*

Figures: A22-2/9, B36-9, C60-4, D88-2/-, E117-6, F140-9, G164-4, H180-2, I 206-9, K224-6, L261-4/-, M272-1, *N*—.

5] THE | **POETICAL WORKS** . . . IN TWELVE VOLUMES. | VOL. V. . . . 1820.

Collation: $\pi^2(\pi2+1)$ A-L[12]. Pagination: *1* half-title, *2* printer's imprint(1), *3* title-page, *4 blank, i* Contents, *ii blank, 1* fly-title for *The Lady of the Lake, 2 blank, 3* dedication, *4 blank, 5* Argument, *6 blank, 7* fly-title, *8 blank, 9* 10-194 text, Cantos 1-4, *195* fly-title, *196 blank, 197* 198-263 Notes, 263 printer's imprint(2), *264 blank.* Typography: Section signature K2 (page 225) is omitted.

Figures: A24-12, B47-2, C67-9, D93-4, E110-2, F144-12, G159-12, H178-1, I 207-2, K240-8, L261-2.

Notes: Although text is provided in this volume for Cantos 1-4 of *The Lady of the Lake*, in order to regularize the size of all volumes, the extensive notes for Canto 4 were moved to volume 6, pages *105* 106-147.

6] THE | **POETICAL WORKS** . . . IN TWELVE VOLUMES. | VOL. VI. . . . 1820.

Collation: $\pi^2(\pi2+1)$ A-K[12] L[12](-L12). Pagination: *1* half-title, *2* printer's imprint (1), *3* title-page, *4 blank, i* Contents, *ii blank, 1* fly-title for *The Lady of the Lake, 2 blank, 3* 4-102 text, Cantos 5-6, *103* fly-title, *104 blank, 105* 106-183 Notes, *184 blank, 185* fly-title for 'Thomas the Rhymer', *186 blank, 187* 188-262 text and notes, 262 printer's imprint(2). Typography: Section signature I 2 (page 201) is omitted.

Figures: A13-2, B48-12, C62-9, D76-6, E120-12, F132-8, G156-12, H172-2, I 198-9, K237-6, L250-9.

7] THE | **POETICAL WORKS** . . . IN TWELVE VOLUMES. | VOL. VII. . . . 1820.

Collation: $\pi^2(\pi2+1)$ A-L[12]. Pagination: *1* half-title, *2* printer's imprint(1), *3* title-page, *4 blank, i* Contents, *ii blank, 1* fly-title for *Rokeby, 2 blank, 3* dedication, *4 blank, 5* Advertisement, *6 blank, 7* fly-title, *8 blank, 9* 10-187 text, Cantos 1-4, *188 blank, 189* fly-title, *190 blank, 191* 192-264 Notes, 264 printer's imprint(2). Typography: In some copies, page 117 is misnumbered 11. Section signature L2 (page 249) is omitted.

Figures: A15-9, B48-4, C58-6, D93-9, E110-1, F135-9, G159-9, H192-8, I 216-12, K*229*-13, L257-1/-.

8] THE | **POETICAL WORKS** . . . IN TWELVE VOLUMES. | VOL. VIII. . . . 1820.

Collation: $\pi^2(\pi 2+1)$ A-N^{12}. Pagination: *1* half-title, *2* printer's imprint(1), *3* title-page, *4 blank, i* Contents, *ii blank, 1* fly-title for *Rokeby, 2 blank, 3* 4-116 text, Cantos 5-6, *117* fly-title, *118 blank, 119* 120-161 Notes, *162 blank, 163* fly-title for *Harold the Dauntless, 164 blank, 165* 166-308 *309* text, *310* printer's imprint(2), *311-312 blank.* Typography: In some copies page 136 is misnumbered 16.

Figures: A15-6, B34-1, C72-12, D95-9, E108-12, F144-8, G149-2, H174-2, I 214-4, K*219*-9, L244-4, M288-8, N304-1.

9] THE | **POETICAL WORKS** . . . IN TWELVE VOLUMES. | VOL. IX. . . . 1820.

Collation: $\pi^2(\pi 2+1)$ A-L^{12} M^8 *N*1. Pagination: *1* half-title, *2* printer's imprint(1), *3* title-page, *4 blank, i* Contents, *ii blank, 1* fly-title for *The Lord of the Isles, 2 blank, 3* Advertisement, *4 blank, 5* fly-title, *6 blank, 7* 8-174 text, Cantos 1-4, *175* fly-title, *176 blank, 177* 178-281 Notes, 281 printer's imprint(2), *282 blank.* Typography: Section signature L2 (page 249) is transposed as 2L.

Figures: A24-8, B41-1, C72-8, D96-8, E110-13, F144-8, G166-13, H183-4, I 208-9, K218-9, L253-6, M267-1, *N*—.

10] THE | **POETICAL WORKS** . . . IN TWELVE VOLUMES. | VOL. X. . . . 1820.

Collation: $\pi^2(\pi 2+1)$ A-K^{12} *L*1. Pagination: *1* half-title, *2* printer's imprint(1) *3* title-page, *4 blank, i*-ii Contents, *1* fly-title for *The Lord of the Isles, 2 blank, 3* 4-105 text, Cantos 5-6, *106 blank, 107* fly-title for 'Songs and Miscellanies', *108 blank, 109* 110-168 Notes, *169* fly-title, *170 blank*, 171-241 text, 241 printer's imprint(1), *242 blank.* Typography: The page-number on page 172 is transposed to read 127. Section signature H2 (page 177) is omitted.

Figures: A*3*-2, B31-9, C72-12, D84-1/-, E120-12, F144-12, G157-2, H178-5, I 214-9, K240-12, *L*—.

11] THE | **POETICAL WORKS** . . . IN TWELVE VOLUMES. | VOL. XI. . . . 1820.

Collation: $\pi^2(\pi 2+1)$ A-K^{12} L^4. Pagination: *i* half-title, *ii* printer's imprint(1), *iii* title-page, *iv blank, v*-vi Contents, *1* fly-title for *The Bridal of Triermain, 2 blank, 3* 4-11 Preface, *12 blank, 13* 14-158 text, *159* fly-title, *160 blank, 161* 162-170 Notes, *171* fly-title for 'Fragments', *172 blank, 173* 174-183 text, *184 blank, 185* fly-title for 'Ballads from the German', *186 blank,* 187-248 text. No final printer's imprint.

Typography: Section signature F2 (page 129) is omitted and G2 (page 153) transposed as 2G. Page 228 is misnumbered 208.

Figures: A*23*-6, B37-2, C72-9, D86-4, E115-9, F131-9, G156-5 166-8, H192-8, I 96-5, K231-6, L245-10.

Notes: Throughout the entire edition sheet G of this volume alone bears two press figures, but there is no evidence of cancellation.

12] THE | **POETICAL WORKS** . . . IN TWELVE VOLUMES. | VOL. XII. . . . 1820.

Collation: π[4] A-I[12] K[8]. Pagination: *1* half-title, *2* printer's imprint(1), *3* title-page, *4 blank, i* ii-iii Contents, *iv blank, i* fly-title for *The Vision of Don Roderick [&c.], ii blank, iii* dedication, *iv blank, v* vi-viii Preface, *9* fly-title, *10 blank, 11* 12-71 text, *72 blank, 73* fly-title, *74 blank, 75* 76-105 Notes, *106 blank, 107* fly-title for 'Miscellaneous Poems', *108 blank, 109* 110-159 text, *160 blank, 161* fly-title for *The Field of Waterloo, 162 blank, 163* dedication, *164 blank, 165* 166-198 text, *199* fly-title, *200 blank, 201* 202-205 Notes, *206 blank, 207* fly-title for 'Miscellaneous', *208 blank, 209* 210-232 text, 232 printer's imprint(2). Typography: Section signature G2 (page 153) is signed G and I 2 (page *201*) is omitted. Last printer's imprint concludes: & Co.

Figures: π ii-1, A22-2, B42-4, C60-9, D95-12, E98-5, F128-1, G157-6/-, H191-12, I 203-5, K—.

Notes: The 'Miscellaneous Poems' section contains in succession apparently the first printings of [1] 'Farewell to Mackenzie' (first words: 'Farewell to Mackenneth, great Earl of the North,'), pages 148-150; [2] 'Imitation of the Preceding Song' (first words: 'So sung the old Bard, in the grief of his heart,'), pages 151-153, [3] 'War-Song of Lachlan' (first words: 'A weary month has wander'd o'er'), pages 154-156, [4] 'Saint Cloud' (first words: 'Soft spread the southern Summer night'), pages 157-159. Two of these poems were extracted in the anthologies, [1] in 362E.2 and 378E.13, [3] in 378E.11. (Reprinted in Magnum Opus Edition 1834: *Poetical Works*, [1-3] viii.390-396; [4] xi.295-296.)

263A] Second Collected Edition: 1821[1820]

[*engraved title*] THE | POETICAL WORKS | OF | SIR WALTER SCOTT, BARONET. | IN TEN VOLUMES. | VOL.I [II-X]. | [*volume title*] | [*vignette*] | EDINBURGH; | PRINTED FOR ARCHIBALD CONSTABLE AND CO. EDINBURGH; | LONGMAN, HURST, REES, ORME, AND BROWN; J. MURRAY; | AND HURST, ROBINSON, AND CO. LONDON. | [*French dash*] | 1821.

Published concurrently 4 December 1820 in Edinburgh (*EEC*); 2 December in London (*MC*). £6. Paper: Demy 8° (217 x 135mm cut). Watermarks: *none*.

General Notes: As indicated below, engraved titles are counted in the pagination, but not the collation. As the first collected 8° issue, and thus of a size corresponding to the separate works, certain of these volumes were also issued separately with printed titles, I-III as a 'fifth edition' of *Minstrelsy of the Scottish Border* (8Ai), VI as a 'tenth edition' of *Marmion* (28An).

By 1830 it is very doubtful that any of this 1821 issue remained with the publishers, as it had been superseded in 1825 by another 8° edition (267Aa). Accordingly the few sets still retaining 1821 engraved titles, but with (1) 1830 introductions and/or (2) an additional 1830 eleventh volume—all classified by Ruff (165) as a publishers' 'Second Issue'—are here regarded as copies made up by early owners and thus described below in entry 267Ab. In 1821 the new title vignettes are drawn by A. Nasmyth and engraved by W. H. Lizars. Concluding printer's imprints read: [*short rule*] | EDINBURGH: | Printed by James Ballantyne & Co. ['and Co.' vols. 4, 6-10]

Copies: BCL E ES GU*(vols. 1-4, 6-10); IdU InU NN(vols. 1-3, 8-10) T/B.
*This defective set has the title-page wording 'IN TEN VOLUMES.' carefully scraped away, except in volume 7, undoubtedly because the volume 10 title-page has been changed to appear to be volume 5.

Reference: Ruff 164.

1] [*engraved title*] THE | POETICAL WORKS . . . IN TEN VOLUMES. | VOL. I. | MINSTRELSY | [*vignette of the Castle of Newark*] . . . . 1821.

Collation: π^2 A-D^8 e-m^8 A-U^8. Pagination: [*i engraved title-page, ii blank*], *iii* list of vignettes, *iv blank, v*-'v'[vi] Contents, *i* fly-title, *ii blank, iii* dedication, *iv blank, v* vi-clxxxix Introduction and Appendices, *cxc blank, 1* section-title, *2 blank, 3* 4-321 text and notes of *The Minstrelsy of the Scottish Border*, Part First, 321 printer's imprint, *322 blank*. Illustration: Engraved frontispiece portrait with caption 'Sir Walter Scott, Baronet.', painted by Raeburn, engraved by W. T. Fry; published 1 January 1821[!] by Archibald Constable & Co. Edinburgh, and Longman, Hurst, Rees, Orme, & Brown, London. Typography: In some copies the first digit drops in one page number (lviii) and the last digit in two others (vi, cxviii).

Figures: A xiv-2, B xxix-6, C xlv-3, D lii-12, e lxxiii-3, f lxxxix-6, g c-2, h cxxiii-10, i cxxxv-8, k cxlix-1, l clxiii-7, m clxxxiv-9, A13-11, B20-8, C45-4, D63-10, E75-9, F90-2, G107-6, H118-4, I 138-1, K150-3, L178-10, M189-9, N210-8, O 217-6, P242-2, Q244-5, R265-11, S276-2, T306-1, U319-6.

Notes: The frontispiece date is some four weeks later than the date of issue.

2] [*engraved title*] THE | POETICAL WORKS . . . IN TEN VOLUMES. |

VOL. II. | MINSTRELSY | [*vignette of Branxholme*] . . . . 1821.

Collation: π1 A-2E^8 2F^4. Pagination: [*i engraved title-page, ii blank*], *v*-vi Contents, *1* fly-title, *2 blank, 3* 4-99 conclusion of *The Minstrelsy of the Scottish Border*, Part First, *100 blank, 101* fly-title, *102 blank, 103* 104-456 text of *The Minstrelsy*, Part Second, 456 printer's imprint. Typography: Page 291 is misnumbered 29.

Figures: A15-6, B24-10, C48-10, D58-10, E72-7, F82-3, G104-9, H120-9, I 139-2, K160-1, L175-2, M182-2, N196-6, O 224-9, P227-10, Q250-7, R270-2, S286-6, T302-6, U306-6/-, X327-5, Y348-4, Z364-7, 2A 379-9, 2B 400-6, 2C 413-10, 2D 431-4, 2E 446-10, 2F 453-7.

3] [*engraved title*] THE | POETICAL WORKS . . . IN TEN VOLUMES. | VOL. III. | MINSTRELSY | [*vignette of Smailholm Tower*] . . . . 1821.

Collation: π1 A-2G^8 2H^4. Pagination: [*i engraved title-page, ii blank*], *v*-vi Contents, *1* fly-title, *2 blank, 3* 4-145 conclusion of *The Minstrelsy*, Part Second, *146 blank, 147* fly-title for *The Minstrelsy*, Part Third, *148 blank, 149* 150-488 text, 488 printer's imprint. Typography: In the title-page imprint, the comma is omitted after 'Robinson'.

Figures: π vi-9/-, A*3*-6, B32-10, C48-10, D50-9, E75-11, F87-2, G104-5, H124-9, I 143-7, K151(or 158)-8, L168-9, M192-5, N204-9, O 223-5, P227-2, Q249-11, R265-7, S286-3, T303-5, U310-11, X336-9, Y346-3, Z361-3, 2A 382-7, 2B 389-2, 2C 405-1/-, 2D 422-6, 2E 438-7, 2F 458-5, 2G 478-11, 2H 483-6.

4] [*engraved title*] THE | POETICAL WORKS . . . IN TEN VOLUMES. | VOL. IV. | SIR TRISTREM | [*vignette of Bridge in the Rhymer's Glen*] . . . 1821.

Collation: π1 a-h^8 A-M^8 N^8(-N8=*2C*1) O-2B^8 *2C*1. Pagination: [*i engraved title-page, ii blank*], *iii* Contents, *iv blank, i* fly-title, *ii blank, iii* section-title, *iv blank, v* vi-xcvi Introduction, *xcvii* fly-title, *xcviii blank, xcix* c-cxxviii appendices, *1* section-title, *2 blank, 3* 4-204 text of *Sir Tristrem, 205* fly-title, *206 blank, 209* 210-262 description and abstract, *263* fly-title, *264 blank*, 265-374 Notes, *375* fly-title, *376 blank, 377* 378-401 glossary, 401 printer's imprint, *402 blank*. Typography: Signature a (page *i*) is missigned A and signature d (page xlix) is missigned c.

Figures: π *iii*-3, 'A'[a] xv-2, b xxviii-9, c xxxiv-11, 'c'[d] lxiii-6, e lxxix-10, f xciv-2, g c-7, h cxxii-2, A7-4, B31-6, C48-4, D58-10, E67-7, F94-2, G102-6, H115-3, I 142-11, K157-10, L176-10, M190-1, N197-9, O 224-5, P234-7, Q247-9, R260-8, S288-10, T293-4, U306-9, X336-4, Y346-10, Z354-9, 2A 373-2, 2B 386-5, *2C*—.

5] [*engraved title*] THE | POETICAL WORKS . . . IN TEN VOLUMES. | VOL. V. | LAY OF THE LAST MINSTREL | [*vignette of Melrose Abbey*] . . . 1821.

Collation: π1 A-2F^8 *2G*1. Pagination: [*i engraved title-page, ii blank*], *v*-vi Contents, *1* fly-title, *2 blank, 3* dedication, *4 blank, 5* preface, *6 blank, 7* section-title, *8 blank,* 9-206 text, *207* fly-title, *208 blank, 209* 210-347 Notes, *348 blank, 349* fly-title for 'Ballads', *350 blank,* 351-384 text, *385* fly-title for 'Songs', *386 blank,* 387-397 text, *398 blank, 399* fly-title for 'Fragments', *400 blank,* 401-411 text, *412 blank, 413* fly-title for 'Ballads from the German', *414 blank,* 415-465 text, 465 printer's imprint, *466 blank.* Typography: Page 224 is misnumbered 226. Direction line on page *289* reads VOL.IV.

Figures: A12-6, B28-11, C42-1, D58-6, E74-4, F86-1, G110-4, H119-13, I 132-13, K158-7, L175-10, M191-10, N202-2, O 220-7, P234-2, Q250-9, R265-2, S274-7, T296-10, U317-9, X324-3, Y338-5, Z366-2, 2A 379-3, 2B 390-3, 2C 410-6, 2D 423-4, 2E 441-3, 2F 463-9, *2G*—.

6] [*engraved title*] THE | POETICAL WORKS . . . IN TEN VOLUMES. | VOL. VI. | MARMION | [*vignette of the Linlithgow Palace*] . . . . 1821.

Collation: π1 A-2I^8. Pagination: [*i engraved title-page, ii blank*], *iii* Contents, *iv blank, 1* fly-title, *2 blank, 3* dedication, *4 blank, 5* Advertisement, *6 blank, 7* fly-title, *8 blank, 9* 10-383 text, *384 blank, 385* fly-title, *386 blank,* 387-512 Notes, 512 printer's imprint. Typography: Direction line on page 49 reads VOL. IX. Pages 391-392 are misnumbered 385-386.

Figures: A14-7, B23-9, C37-2, D58-5, E70-7, F85-7, G112-10, H118-6, I 132-6, K155-2, L168-7, M192-10, N205-2, O 216-5, P238-9, Q254-6, R267-5, S281-2, T301-9, U312(or 315)-6, X332-2, Y339-5, Z365-1, 2A 370-9, 2B 390-10, 2C 414-1, 2D 425-8, 2E 444-7, 2F 458(or 461)-7, 2G 467-10, 2H 487-10, 2I 510-10 511-13/ 3/-.

7] [*engraved title*] THE | POETICAL WORKS . . . IN TEN VOLUMES. | VOL. VII. | LADY OF THE LAKE | [*vignette of Stirling Castle*] . . . . 1821.

Collation: π1 A-2G^8 2H^8(-H8). Pagination: [*i engraved title-page, ii blank*], *v*-vi Contents, *1* fly-title, *2 blank, 3* dedication, *4 blank, 5* Argument, *6 blank, 7* section-title, *8 blank, 9* 10-296 text, *297* fly-title, *298 blank,* 299-439 Notes, *440 blank, 441* fly-title for 'Miscellaneous Poems', *442 blank, 443* 444-493 text, 493 printer's imprint, *494 blank.*

Figures: A12-2, B32-5, C47-3, D62-4, E80-6, F90-2, G108-7, H128-4, I 139-9, K154-12, L171-4, M190-9, N204-1, O 224-3, P232-4, Q244-12, R271-7, S286-1, T302-10, U308-10, X331-6, Y339-5, Z363-12, 2A 372-1, 2B 395-7, 2C 409-8, 2D 421-3, 2E 443-5, 2F 452-7, 2G 477-5, 2H 491-2.

8] [*engraved title*] THE | POETICAL WORKS . . . IN TEN VOLUMES. | VOL. VIII. | ROKEBY | [*vignette of Mortham Castle*] . . . . 1821.

Collation: π1 A-2G8 2H2. Pagination: [*i engraved title-page*, *ii blank*], *iii* Contents, *iv blank, 1* fly-title for *Rokeby, 2 blank, 3* dedication, *4 blank, 5* Adver-tisement, *6 blank, 7* section-title, *8 blank, 9* 10-304 text, *305* fly-title, *306 blank*, 307-419 Notes, *420 blank, 421* fly-title for *The Vision of Don Roderick, 422 blank, 423* dedication, *424 blank*, 425-427 Preface, *428 blank, 429* fly-title, *430 blank*, 431-483 text, Stanzas I-LXIII, 483 printer's imprint, *484 blank.* Typography: Direction line page 353 erroneously reads VOL. VII.

Figures: A11-4, B32-9, C37-1, D61-6, E71-9, F83-12, G112-9, H124-9, I 139-1, K154-11, L168-5, M179-4, N208-10, O 214-3, P235-4, Q245-1, R268-10, S286-6, T293-9, U310-7, X325-3, Y345-2, Z366-6, 2A 371-10, 2B 394-9, 2C 416-7, 2D 432-4, 2E 444-9, 2F 461-6, 2G 470-6, 2H—.

9] [*engraved title*] THE | POETICAL WORKS . . . IN TEN VOLUMES. | VOL. IX. | LORD OF THE ISLES | [*vignette of the Castle of Artornish*] . . . 1821.

Collation: π1 A-2H8 2 I2. Pagination: [*i engraved title-page, ii blank,*] *iii* Contents, *iv blank, 1* fly-title the *The Vision of Don Roderick, 2 blank, 3* 4-15 text concluded, *16 blank, 17* fly-title, *18 blank, 19* 20-51 Notes, *52 blank, 53* fly-title for *The Lord of the Isles, 54 blank, 55* Advertisement, *56 blank, 57* section-title, *58 blank, 59* 60-331 text, *332 blank, 333* fly-title, *334 blank*, 335-499 Notes, 499 printer's imprint, *500 blank.*

Figures: A12-5, B31-2, C36-4, D63-1, E72-4, F82-2, G100-9, H121-4, I 140-1, K158-9, L164-6, M192-4, N202-3, O 211-10, P230-9, Q244-7, R270-6, S282-10, T290-9, U317-6, X324-8, Y352-5, Z367-4, 2A 382-8, 2B 400-4, 2C 402-4, 2D 425-7, 2E 443-10, 2F 458-3, 2G 480-8, 2H 485-5, 2 I 498-8.

10] [*engraved title*] THE | POETICAL WORKS . . . IN TEN VOLUMES. | VOL. X. | MISCELLANIES | [*vignette of Abbotsford*] . . . . 1821.

Collation: π2 A-2G8 2H1. Pagination: [*i engraved title-page, ii blank*], *v* vi-vii Contents, *viii blank, 1* fly-title for *The Field of Waterloo, 2 blank, 3* dedication, *4 blank, 5* 6-49 text and notes, *50 blank, 51* fly-title for 'Songs and Miscellanies', *52 blank*, 53-150 text, *151* fly-title for *The Bridal of Triermain, 152 blank, 153* 154-162 Preface, 163-320 text and notes, *321* fly-title for 'Fragments', *322 blank*, 323-333 text, *334 blank, 335* fly-title for *Harold the Dauntless, 336 blank*, 337-481 text, *482* printer's imprint.

Figures: A12-6, B20-10, C47-4, D58-2, E74-3, F85-9, G98-4, H127-4, I 131-13, K154-12, L173-9, M190-12, N205-7, O 216-8, P240-10, Q256-7, R261-10, S284-5, T300-3, U317-7, X330-5, Y339-13, Z365-8, 2A 383-3, 2B 393-2, 2C 408-10, 2D 429-12, 2E 448-8, 2F 462-8/-, 2G 479-10, 2H—.

264A] Third Collected Edition: 1822[1821]

THE | **POETICAL WORKS** | OF | SIR WALTER SCOTT, BART. | [*short rule*] | IN EIGHT VOLUMES. | VOL. I [II-VIII]. | [*short reversed Oxford rule*] | EDINBURGH: | PRINTED FOR ARCH. CONSTABLE AND CO. EDINBURGH: | LONGMAN, HURST, REES, ORME, AND BROWN; | JOHN MURRAY; AND HURST, ROBINSON, AND CO., | LONDON. | [*dash*] | 1822.

Published 24 November 1821 in Edinburgh (*EEC*); issued 19 January 1822 in London. £3.12.0. 2000 copies (E MS.794,f.297b). Paper: Foolscap 12° (169 x 99mm cut). Watermarks: *none*. Typography: Printer's imprints read (1) [*short rule*] | Printed by James Ballantyne and Company.; (2) [*short rule*] | EDINBURGH: | Printed by James Ballantyne & Co. ['and Co.' vols 3, 6].

General Notes: Of this smaller and cheaper format, with printed titles, Longmans had only 52 sets remaining unsold in 1830, and thus was disregarded in the Cadell issues of that later date.

Copies: Volume 1, issue (1): E O; CtY MH. (2) E. References: Millgate(2); Ruff 167.

1] THE | **POETICAL WORKS** . . . IN EIGHT VOLUMES | VOL. I. . . 1822.

Collation: π^2 $2\pi1$ A-P^{12} Q^6 R^4. Pagination: *i* half-title, *ii* printer's imprint(1), *iii* title-page, *iv blank*, *v*-vi Contents, *1* fly-title for *Lay of the Last Minstrel*, *2 blank*, *3* dedication, *4 blank*, *5* preface, *6 blank*, *7* fly-title, *8 blank*, *9* 10-206 text, *207* fly-title, *208 blank*, *209* 210-345 Notes, *346 blank*, *347* fly-title for 'Miscellaneous Poems', *348 blank*, *349* 350-379 text, 379 printer's imprint(2), *380 blank*. Illustration: Frontispiece portrait by Raeburn, engraved by W. T. Fry, with caption 'Sir Walter Scott, Baronet' and Constable/Longman imprint dated January 1822[!]. Typography: Section signature O2 (page *321*) is omitted and P2 (page 345) is missigned P.

Figures: A21-5, B48-6, C72-7, D96-5, E120-2, F144-2, G147-2 168-4, H192-7, I 216-2, K229-12, L250-9, M288-1, N300-8, O 336-12, P360-7, Q366-8, R—.

Notes: Again the frontispiece is dated considerably after date of issue. Varying figures for sheet D signify two consecutive settings. (1) the first 96-5, cited above; (2) the second 76-2. The second (2) was prepared, it seems, when a short count was later discovered in the original issue. At the start, pages 73-78, the second compositor follows copy (1), regularly eliding past participles according to Scott's practice therein, but in the remaining pages 79-96 on some thirty-six occasions as regularly departs from copy by spelling the word in full. The first such lapse appears on page 79 line 4 where the word 'pass'd' becomes 'passed'.

2] THE | **POETICAL WORKS** . . . IN EIGHT VOLUMES | VOL. II. . . 1822.

Collation: π^2 $2\pi^2$(-$2\pi2$=$2\pi1$ of volume 1) A-Q^{12} R^8 S1. Pagination: *i* half-title, *ii* printer's imprint(1), *iii* title-page, *iv blank, v* Contents, *vi blank, 1* fly-title for *Marmion, 2 blank, 3* Advertisement, *4 blank, 5* dedication, *6 blank, 7* fly-title, *8 blank, 9* 10-302 text, Cantos 1-5, *303* fly-title, *304 blank, 305* 306-401 Notes, 401 printer's imprint(2), *402 blank.* Typography: Section signatures D2 and Q2 (pages *81*, 369) are omitted. Leaf S is in a duplicate setting, with or without the signature.

Figures: A24-9, B48-7, C72-5, D96-6, E117-5, F144-6, G165-10, H192-2, I 216-12, K240-9, L264-6, M288-5, N312-2, O 336-9, P360-6, Q384-7, R400-4, S—.

3] THE | **POETICAL WORKS** . . . IN EIGHT VOLUMES | VOL. III. . . . 1822.

Collation: π^2 $2\pi1$ A-P^{12} Q^8 R^2. Pagination: *i* half-title, *ii* printer's imprint(1), *iii* title-page, *iv blank, v*-vi Contents, *1* fly-title for *Marmion, 2 blank, 3* 4-81 text, Canto 6, *82 blank, 83* fly-title, *84 blank, 85* 86-113 Notes, *114 blank, 115* fly-title for *Ballads and Lyrical Pieces, 116 blank,* 117-296 text, *297* fly-title for 'Songs', *298 blank,* 299-316 text, *317* fly-title for 'Ballads from the German', *318 blank,* 319-380 text, 380 printer's imprint(2). Typography: Section signatures H2 and I 2 (pages 177, 201) are omitted.

Figures: A21-8, B48-5, C72-5, D96-2, E120-1, F144-8, G168-6, H192-7, I 216-6, K240-6, L264-4, M288-2, N312-4, O 333-10, P360-7, Q364-5, R—.

4] THE | **POETICAL WORKS** . . . IN EIGHT VOLUMES | VOL. IV. . . . 1822.

Collation: π^2 $2\pi1$ A-P^{12} Q^8 R^2. Pagination: *i* half-title, *ii* printer's imprint(1), *iii* title-page, *iv blank, v* Contents, *vi blank, 1* fly-title for *The Lady of the Lake, 2 blank, 3* dedication, *4 blank, 5* Argument, *6 blank, 7* fly-title, *8 blank, 9* 10-'264'[246] text, Cantos 1-5, *247* fly-title, *248 blank, 249* 250-380 Notes, 380 printer's imprint(2). Typography: Section signatures I 2 and M2 (pages 201, 273) are omitted. Page 246 is misnumbered 264.

Figures: A24-4, B40-10, C72-5, D96-7, E120-5, F144-7, G168-10, H180-10, I 216-10, K240-10, L264-5, M280-10, N312-9, O 335-9, P357-12, Q—, R379-10.

5] THE | **POETICAL WORKS** . . . IN EIGHT VOLUMES | VOL. V. . . 1822.

Collation: π^2 $2\pi1$ A-Q^{12} R1. Pagination: *i* half-title, *ii* printer's imprint(1), *iii* title-page, *iv blank, v*-vi Contents, *1* fly-title for *The Lady of the Lake, 2 blank, 3* 4-50 text, Canto 6, *51* fly-title, *52 blank, 53* 54-67 Notes, *68 blank, 69* fly-title for *The*

Bridal of Triermain, 70 blank, 71 72-226 text, *227* fly-title, *228 blank, 229* 230-238 Notes, *239* fly-title for *Harold the Dauntless, 240 blank, 241* 242-384 *385* text, *385* printer's imprint(2), *386 blank.* Typography: Leaf R is in a duplicate setting, with or without the signature.

Figures: A24-7, B45-10, C72-6, D96-7, E120-6, F144-9, G168-7/-, H192-1, I216-4, K220-2, L264-5, M288-5, N312-12, O 328-5, P357-8, Q384-9, R—.

6] THE | **POETICAL WORKS** . . . IN EIGHT VOLUMES | VOL. VI. . . . 1822.

Collation: π^2 $2\pi 1$ A-R^{12} S^6 T^2. Pagination: *i* half-title, *ii* printer's imprint(1), *iii* title-page, *iv blank, v* Contents, *vi blank, 1* fly-title for *Rokeby, 2 blank, 3* Advertisement, *4 blank, 5* dedication, *6 blank, 7* fly-title, *8 blank, 9* 10-304 text, *305* fly-title, *306 blank, 307* 308-423 Notes, 423 printer's imprint(2), *424 blank.* Typography: Page 231 is misnumbered 237. Section signature L2 (page *249*) is omitted.

Figures: A24-12, B48-6, C72-2, D93-5, E120-9, F144-6, G168-12, H192-5, I216-9, K240-6, L264-10, M288-5, N312-2, O 336-10, P352-6, Q384-9, R408-5, S416-4, T—.

7] THE | **POETICAL WORKS** . . . IN EIGHT VOLUMES | VOL. VII. . . . 1822.

Collation: π^2 $2\pi 1$ A-Q^{12} R^2. Pagination: *i* half-title, *ii* printer's imprint(1), *iii* title-page, *iv blank, v*-vi Contents, *1* fly-title for 'Miscellaneous Poems', *2 blank,* 3-37 text, *38 blank, 39* fly-title for *The Lord of the Isles, 40 blank, 41* Advertisement, *42 blank, 43* fly-title, *44 blank, 45* 46-260 text, Cantos 1-5, *261* fly-title, *262 blank, 263* 264-387 Notes, 387 printer's imprint(2), *388 blank.*

Figures: A21-12, B48-6, C52-2, D96-2, E120-6, F144-10, G148-12, H192-7, I216-1, K240-9, L264-10, M288-5, N300-6, O 336-7, P357-10/-, Q384-9, R386-9.

8] THE | **POETICAL WORKS** . . . IN EIGHT VOLUMES | VOL. VIII. . . . 1822.

Collation: π^2 $2\pi^2$ A-P^{12} Q^6. Pagination: *i* half-title, *ii* printer's imprint(1), *iii* title-page, *iv blank, v* vi-vii Contents, *viii blank, 1* fly-title for *The Lord of the Isles, 2 blank, 3* 4-57 text, Canto 6, *58 blank, 59* fly-title, *60 blank, 61* 62-100 Notes, *101* fly-title for 'Fragments', *102 blank, 103* 104-113 text, *114 blank, 115* fly-title for *The Vision of Don Roderick, 116 blank, 117* dedication, *118 blank, 119* 120-185 text, *186 blank, 187* fly-title, *188 blank, 189* 190-219 Notes, *220 blank, 221* fly-title for *The Field of Waterloo, 222 blank, 223* dedication, *224 blank, 225* 226-258 text, *259* fly-title, *260 blank, 261* 262-265 Notes, *266 blank, 267* fly-title for 'Songs and Miscellanies', *268 blank, 269* 270-366 text, 366 printer's imprint(2), *1* 2-6 list of Constable publications.

Figures: A24-12, B48-9, C72-8, D76-1, E120-2, F144-7, G168-7, H180-5, I 216-9, K240-4, L264-6/-, M288-12, N312-7, O 325-5, P360-10, Q365-5.

THE POETRY CONTAINED IN THE NOVELS, TALES, AND ROMANCES

265Aa] First Edition, First Issue: 1822

[*engraved title*] THE| **POETRY** | CONTAINED IN | THE NOVELS, TALES, | AND | ROMANCES, | OF | THE AUTHOR OF "WAVERLEY." | [*vignette*] | EDINBURGH: | PRINTED FOR ARCHIBALD,[!] CONSTABLE, & CO. | AND HURST, ROBINSON, & CO. | LONDON. | [*dash*] | 1822.

Issued 11 June 1822 in London (*MC* 10 June). 9s. 3000 copies. Binding: drab or pink boards or (a later issue?) green cloth with printed label. Paper: Foolscap 8° (171 x 106mm uncut). Watermarks: *none*. Collation: A^8 B-Z^8. Pagination: *i* half-title, *ii blank, [engraved title], iii* Advertisement, dated May 1822, *iv blank, v* vi-xvi Contents, *1* fly-title, *2 blank, 3* 4-345 text, 345 printer's imprint, *346 blank, 1* 2-6 advertisement listing illustrations by Nasmyth and Allan. Printer's imprint: London: | PRINTED BY JAMES MOYES, GREVILLE STREET. Illustration: The vignette, a distant view of Edinburgh from Craigleith, is drawn by the Rev. J. Thomson, engraved by J. Stewart. The engraved title (1) in the original issue is on heavy plate paper, (2) in a later issue on lighter paper watermarked 1824. (A duplicate plate of the first issue, seen in one copy only [AN], has no quotation marks around WAVERLEY and no comma after ARCHIBALD.) Figures: Not used by printer Moyes.

Notes: The Advertisement reports that, while the verse may be either original or borrowed, in some instances 'the author has not hesitated to alter considerably, either to supply defects of his own memory, or to adapt the quotation more explicitly and aptly to the matter in hand.' The concluding advertisement cites 16 engravings for the Waverley novels by Lizars from designs by Nasmyth in imperial 4° (£1.11.6), 8° (16s.), 12° (10s.) and 12 prints after designs by William Allan in Colombian India proofs (£ 3.3.0), imperial 4° on India (£2.12.6), 8° (£1.11.6), 12° (£1.4.0). The Lizars suite was first used as vignette title-pages in the 1821 12° *Novels and Tales* (270Aa); the Allan suite, issued 11 December 1820, was not incorporatd in any edition, though originally intended for the 8° series (269Aa), and thus is listed separately as entry 322D.

Copies: (issue 1) AN E(2) ES(2); IdU InU NNU-W. (2) InU TxU. Reference: Ruff 169.

265Ab] First Edition, Second (Remainder) Issue: post 1822

THE | **POETRY,** | CONTAINED IN | THE NOVELS, TALES, | AND | ROMANCES, | OF | THE AUTHOR OF "WAVERLY[!]." | [*short Oxford rule*] | EDINBURGH: | PRINTED FOR ARCHIBALD,[!] CONSTABLE, & CO. | AND HURST, ROBINSON, & CO. | LONDON. | [*dash*] | 1822.

Notes: This type-set tipped-in title-page, cited by Ruff and Tinker as of the first issue, is carelessly composed and on paper thicker than that used for the text (calibrating .13mm as against .10mm). It thus appears not to have been printed in Edinburgh but prepared after the engraved titles, in either issue, were no longer available.

Copies: E(2); CtY MH. References: Ruff 168; Tinker 1874.

265Ac] First Edition, Third (Remainder) Issue: 1827

MISCELLANEOUS POETRY, | CONTAINED IN | THE NOVELS, TALES, | AND | ROMANCES | OF | SIR WALTER SCOTT, BART. | Edinburgh: | PRINTED FOR ARCHIBALD CONSTABLE AND CO.; | AND HURST, ROBINSON, AND CO. | LONDON. [1827].

Notes: A further reissue with variant printed title, no date, and prepared after Scott had acknowledged his authorship of the novels.

Copy: CtY. Reference: Ruff 170.

THE POETICAL WORKS

266Aa] Fourth Collected Edition, First 18° Issue: 1823

[*engraved title*] THE | POETICAL WORKS | OF | SIR WALTER SCOTT, BARONET. | IN TEN VOLUMES. | VOL.I [II-X]. | [*volume title*] | [*vignette*] | EDINBURGH | Printed for Archibald Constable & Co. Edinburgh; Longman, Hurst, Rees, Orme & Brown; | J. Murray; and Hurst, Robinson and Co. London, | 1823.

Issued 31 May 1823 in London (*MC*). £3.3.0. Binding: drab boards with printed labels. Paper: Demy 18° (154 x 94mm uncut). Watermarks: *none*.

General Illustrations: At time of issue this 'miniature edition' was also available with ten plates by R. Smirke, price £3.13.6, all appearing as frontispieces except in the first volume. When present, these are engraved by the artists listed below, although without exception all title-page vignettes are 'Engraved on Steel by Chas.

Heath.' Volume 1 engraved portrait frontispiece imprint cites all four publishers and is undated; succeeding volume plates cite only Hurst, Robinson and are dated 1823. Punctuation for the lettering on the engraved title-pages varies slightly.

Typography: Ellipses marks in the following collations indicate a regular alternating sequence of six- and twelve-leaf gatherings in this 18° format, with the two segments imposed together to form a complete sheet, identified here by semicolons. Accordingly the press figures may both occur on one of the segments only (as in A-B through I-K, first volume), or one in each of the segments (L-M). Concluding printer's imprint reads: [*short rule*] | EDINBURGH: | Printed by James Ballantyne & Co. ['and Co.' vols 3-4]. Except for volumes 3, 4, and 6, other title-pages exhibit no spacing in the volume reference.

Copies: E; CtY(2) IdU MH*(vols.2-10) T/B*. Mixed copy, with second issue inserts of 1830 frontispiece and introductions: InU.
*Extra-illustrated with the 10 frontispiece Smirke plates described below.

Refrence: Ruff 175.

1] [*engraved title*] THE | POETICAL WORKS . . . IN TEN VOLUMES | VOL.I. | LAY OF THE LAST MINSTREL. | [*vignette of Melrose Abbey*] . . . 1823.

Collation: π^2 A^{12} B^6...R^{12} S^6 T^8(T4+1). Pagination: *i* half-title, *ii blank*, [*frontispiece, engraved title*], *iii* Contents, *iv blank, 1* fly-title, *2 blank, 3* dedication, *4 blank, 5* preface, *6 blank, 7* fly-title, *8 blank, 9* 10-206 text, Cantos 1-6, *207* fly-title, *208 blank, 209* 210-341 Notes, 341 printer's imprint, *342 blank.* Illustrations: Frontispiece portrait, painted by Sir H. Raeburn, engraved by R. Cooper, with caption 'Sir Walter Scott, Bart.'; plate (facing page *1* in some copies) with caption 'Lay of the Last Minstrel' and two-line quotation from the Introduction, engraved by J. Mitchell. Typography: Page 75 is misnumbered 57. Sheet 5 number (page 145) is lacking. Section signature M2 (page *209*) is omitted.

Figures: A10-10/- 13-16; D*71*-7 72-6; E74-6 85-10; G118-16 132-7; I 147-10 168-17; L193-7, M212-6; N231-7, O—; P256-5 263-6; R312-5, S323-7; T334-4.

Notes: In some copies page *ii* has an advertisement.

2] [*engraved title*] THE | POETICAL WORKS . . . IN TEN VOLUMES | VOL.II. | MARMION. | [*vignette of Linlithgow Palace*] . . . 1823.

Collation: π^2 A^{12} B^6...P^{12} Q^6 R^8(R4+1) S1. Pagination: *i* half-title, *ii blank*, [*frontispiece, engraved title*], *iii* Contents, *iv blank, 1* fly-title, *2 blank, 3* Advertisement, *4 blank, 5* dedication, *6 blank, 7* section-title, *8 blank, 9* 10-229 text, Cantos 1-4, *230 blank, 231* fly-title, *232 blank, 233* 234-308 Notes, 308 printer's imprint. Illustration: Frontispiece engraved by E. Portbury, with caption 'Marmion.' and two-line quotation from canto 2, stanza 31.

Figures: A22-10 24-4; C57-6, D68-17; F102-7 107-4; G129-6, H134-10; I 166-4 168-18; L201-18, M206-10; N219-10, O 247-4; P276-7, Q287-6; R306-5, S—.

3] [*engraved title*] THE | POETICAL WORKS . . . IN TEN VOLUMES | VOL. III. | MARMION & BALLADS. | [*vignette of Crichton Castle*] . . . 1823.

Collation: π^2 A^{12} B^6...P^{12} Q^6 R^4. Pagination: *i* half-title, *ii blank*, [*frontispiece, engraved title*], *iii* Contents, *iv blank, 1* fly-title for *Marmion, 2 blank, 3* 4-153 text, Cantos 5-6, *154 blank, 155* fly-title, *156 blank, 157* 158-206 Notes, *207* fly-title for *Ballads and Lyrical Pieces, 208 blank,* 209-296 text and notes, 296 printer's imprint. Illustration: Frontispiece engraved by J. H. Watt, with caption 'Marmion.' and three-line quotation from canto 6, stanza 32. Typography: Section signature D2 (page 65) is missigned B2.

Figures: A24-18, B—; C60-18, D62-4; E96-6, F98-7; G119-18 132-7; I 146-3 168-5; L202-6, M210-10; N224-18 238-10; P274-4, Q282-6; R291-11.

4] [*engraved title*] THE | POETICAL WORKS . . . IN TEN VOLUMES | VOL. IV. | LADY OF THE LAKE. | [*vignette of Stirling Castle*] . . . | 1823.

Collation: π^2 A^{12} B^6...P^{12} Q^6 R^8. Pagination: *i* half-title, *ii blank*, [*frontispiece, engraved title*], *iii* Contents, *iv blank, 1* fly-title, *2 blank, 3* dedication, *4 blank, 5* Argument, *6 blank, 7* section-title, *8 blank, 9* 10-194 text, Cantos 1-4, *195* fly-title, *196 blank, 197* 198-303 Notes, 303 printer's imprint, *304 blank.* Illustration: Frontispiece engraved by J. Mitchell, with caption 'Lady of the Lake.' and three-line quotation from canto 4, stanza 5. Typography: Section signature M2 (page 209) is omitted.

Figures: A24-4, B26-6; C39-4 40-6; E95-7 96-6; G119-7, H144-5; I 168-2, K179-4; L201-1 202-12; N220-4, O 251-2; P275-5, Q288-4; R—.

Notes: In some copies page *ii* has an advertisement for a separate issue of the Smirke illustrations occasionally appearing as frontispieces in this edition (*see* 334D[2]).

5] [*engraved title*] THE | POETICAL WORKS . . . IN TEN VOLUMES | VOL.V. | LADY OF THE LAKE. | & | BALLADS. | [*vignette of Bridge in the Rhymer's Glen*] . . . 1823.

Collation: π^2 A^{12} B^6...P^{12} Q^6 R^4. Pagination: *i* half-title, *ii blank*, [*frontispiece, engraved title*], *iii*-'vi'[iv] Contents, *1* fly-title for *Lady of the Lake, 2 blank, 3* 4-102 text, cantos 5-6, *103* fly-title, *104 blank, 105* 106-139 Notes, *140 blank, 141* fly-title, *142 blank*, 143-214 text and notes of 'Thomas the Rhymer', 215-224 'The Fire-King', *225* fly-title, *226 blank*, 227-294 'Ballads from the German', *295* printer's imprint, *296 blank.* Illustrations: Frontispiece engraved by Chas. Heath with caption 'Lady of the Lake.' and two-line quotation from canto 6, stanza 23. Typography: Page 189 is correctly signed L2, but page 191 is also redundantly signed L2.

Figures: B32-1 36-2; D67-4 71-8; E83-4 84-2; G119-5 121-2(or H138-2); I—, K174-4; L182-7 184-6; N219-2/-, O 246-4; P267-2 276-12; R293-4.

6] [*engraved title*] THE | POETICAL WORKS . . . IN TEN VOLUMES | VOL. VI. | ROKEBY. | [*vignette of Mortham Castle*] . . . 1823.

Collation: π^2 A^{12} B^6...R^{12} S^6 T^4. Pagination: *i* half-title, *ii blank*, [*frontispiece, engraved title*], *iii*-iv Contents, *1* fly-title for 'Miscellaneous Poems', *2 blank, 3* 4-68 text, *69* fly-title for *Rokeby, 70 blank, 71* Advertisement, *72 blank, 73* dedication, *74 blank, 75* fly-title, *76 blank, 77* 78-255 text, Cantos 1-4, *256 blank, 257* fly-title, *258 blank, 259* 260-332 Notes, 332 printer's imprint. Illustration: Frontispiece engraved by J. Mitchell, with caption 'Rokeby.' and two-line quotation from canto 5, stanza 35.

Figures: A16-6 23-5; C40-11, D62-1; E94-3 96-2; G110-4 132-5; I 148-11 154-6; L184-2 195-3; N226-6, O 247-1; P254-7, Q288-12; R299-1 309-12; T—.

7] [*engraved title*] THE | POETICAL WORKS . . . IN TEN VOLUMES | VOL.VII. | ROKEBY | & | BRIDAL OF TRIERMAIN. | [*vignette of Johnnie Armstrong's Tower*] . . . 1823.

Collation: π^2 A^{12} B^6...R^{12} S^6 T^2(T2+1). Pagination: *i* half-title, *ii blank*, [*frontispiece, engraved title*], *iii* Contents, *iv blank, 1* fly-title for *Rokeby, 2 blank, 3* 4-116 text, Cantos 5-6, *117* fly-title, *118 blank, 119* 120-159 Notes, *160 blank, 161* fly-title for *The Bridal of Triermain, 162 blank, 163* 164-171 Preface, *172 blank, 173* 174-318 text, 319 fly-title, *320 blank, 321* 322-330 Notes, 330 printer's imprint. Illustration: Frontispiece engraved by Chas Heath, with caption 'Bridal of Triermain.' and two-line quotation from canto 5, stanza 35. Typography: The last, separate leaf (pages 329-330) is signed T2.

Figures: A5-5, B32-3; C50-7, D66-2; E87-4 93-3; G122-6, H138-1; I 147-11, K180-5; L201-2 203-5; N231-7, O 244-6; P274-1 276-4; R298-3, S324-2; T327-11.

8] [*engraved title*] THE | POETICAL WORKS . . . IN TEN VOLUMES | VOL.VIII. | HAROLD the DAUNTLESS | RODERICK & MISCELLANIES. | [*vignette of Abbotsford*] . . . 1823.

Collation: π^2 A^{12} B^6...P^{12} Q^6 R^6. Pagination: *i* half-title, *ii blank*, [*frontispiece, engraved title*], *iii*-'vi'[iv] Contents, *1* fly-title for *Harold the Dauntless, 2 blank, 3* 4-147 text, *148 blank, 149* fly-title for *The Vision of Don Roderick, 150 blank, 151* dedication, *152 blank, 153* 154-155 Preface, *156 blank, 157* fly-title, *158 blank,*

159 160-219 text, *220 blank, 221* fly-title, *222 blank, 223* 224-253 Notes, *254 blank, 255* fly-title for *The Field of Waterloo, 256 blank, 257* dedication, *258 blank, 259* 260-292 text, *293* fly-title, *294 blank, 295* 296-299 Notes, 299 printer's imprint, *300 blank* Illustration: Frontispiece engraved by Chas. Heath, with caption 'Harold the Dauntless.' and two-line quotation from canto II, stanza VII. Typography: Section signature D2 (page 65) is omitted.

Figures: A13-7 15-4; C40-3, D68-1; E86-18 96-6; G111-5 129-6; I 167-4, K180-6; L195-1 201-3; N—, O 248-2; P273-6, Q278-4; R290-17. All full sheets are figured twice, excepting sheet 7 (N-O).

9] [*engraved title*] THE | POETICAL WORKS . . . IN TEN VOLUMES | VOL.IX. | LORD OF THE ISLES | [*vignette of Castle of Artornish*] . . . 1823.

Collation: π^2 A^{12} B^6...O^6 P^{12} Q1. Pagination: *i* half-title, *ii blank*, [*frontispiece, engraved title*], *iii* Contents, *iv blank, 1* fly-title for *Lord of the Isles*, *2 blank, 3* Advertisement, *4 blank, 5* section-title, *6 blank, 7* 8-174 text, Cantos 1-4, *175* fly-title, *176 blank, 177* 178-278 Notes, 278 printer's imprint. Illustration: Frontispiece engraved by Chas. Heath, with caption 'Lord of the Isles.' and two-line quotation from canto 1, stanza 8. Typography: Section signature P2 (page 261) is omitted. In some copies page 98 is misnumbered 78.

Figures: A13-4, B32-1/-; C48-2 50-5; E76-6, F98-3/-; G121-6 122-1; I 148-7, K170-5; L184-4, M206-3; N219-3 237-2; P262-1 268-3/-.

10] [*engraved title*] THE | POETICAL WORKS . . . IN TEN VOLUMES | VOL.X. | LORD OF THE ISLES | & | MISCELLANIES. | [*vignette of Castle of Newark*] . . . 1823.

Collation: π1 2π^2 A^{12} B^6...P^{12} Q^6 R^4 *S*1. Pagination: *i* half-title, *ii blank*, [*frontispiece, engraved title*], *iii* iv-v Contents, *vi blank, 1* fly-title for *Lord of the Isles, 2 blank, 3* 4-105 text, Cantos 5-6, *106 blank, 107* fly-title, *108 blank, 109* 110-166 Notes, *167* fly-title for 'Fragments', *168 blank*, 169-179 text, *180 blank, 181* fly-title for 'Songs and Miscellanies', *182 blank, 183* 184-280 text, *281* fly-title for 'Songs', *282 blank*, 283-297 text, 297 printer's imprint, *298 blank*. Illustrations: Frontispiece engraved by Chas. Heath, with caption 'Lord of the Isles.' and three-line quotation from canto 6, stanza 36.

Figures: B32-8 36-2; C39-5, D72-2; E82-8 93-6; G118-6 129-4; K170-3 175-1; L190-18 204-12; N228-6, O 251-2; P273-5, Q278-4. The entry of two figures in the 'outer forme' of B would indicate that this six-leaf segment (and others?) was not imposed in the normal way.

266Ab] Fourth Collected Edition, Second 18° Issue: 1830

[*engraved title*] THE | POETICAL WORKS | OF | SIR WALTER SCOTT, BARONET. | IN ELEVEN VOLUMES | VOL.I [II-XI]. | [*volume title*] | [*vignette*] | EDINBURGH | Printed for Cadell & Co. Edinburgh, and | Simpkin and Marshall, London. | 1830.

Published 21 April 1830 in London (*MC*); issued 2 June in Edinburgh (*EWJ*). £3.3.0. Illustrations: For this reissue of the 1823 edition volume 1 contains a new frontispiece portrait by David Wilkie, engraved by E. Smith, with caption 'Sir Walter Scott Bart' and Cadell imprint dated 1830. Succeeding volumes represent a reprint of the earlier Smirke frontispiece plates, now with an undated Cadell imprint. Title-page vignettes remain as before but, as described above, imprints reflect the new publishing arrangement. Punctuation for engraved title-page lettering varies slightly. Typography: Printer's imprint reads as in the earlier 1823 issue: [*short rule*] | EDINBURGH: | Printed by James Ballantyne & Co.' To verify the reissue the final signatures, pages, and press figures are again cited. Typography: Except for volumes 3, 4, 6, and 8, other title-pages exhibit no spacing in the volume reference.

General Notes: Since this augmented issue, like the one in 8° format (267Ab), was announced in London six weeks before the Edinburgh date, it would appear that Cadell had early sent on to his London associate the materials to be inserted there (chiefly the 2769 copies transferred from Longmans, a previous publisher) and then from a further printing completed his own stock. A separate 11th volume 'to complete former editions' was also provided first in London on 10 May (*see* 268A).

To five of the previous ten volumes have been added new introductions by Scott or other material, as cited below in angular brackets, and an eleventh volume containing additional works originally published after 1823. Because of the smaller format these are of a setting different from that occurring in the 8° issues described below. The dedication and introductions are all dated from Abbotsford, volumes 1, 2, 4, 6, 9, April 1830, volume 11 January 1830. This 18° issue was the first to receive an advance review in Edinburgh (*ELJ* 8 and 15 May, pages *265* 266-269, 280-282) and thus probably represents the first printing of the new material.

Copies: BCL E(2). References: Millgate(2); McMullin(2); Ruff 176.

1] [*engraved title*] THE | POETICAL WORKS . . . . IN ELEVEN VOLUMES | VOL.I. | LAY OF THE LAST MINSTREL | [*vignette of Melrose Abbey*] . . . . 1830.

Collation: π^2(π1+<a1>) <a-b^6 c^2 *d*1>...T^8(T4+1). Pagination: *i* half-title, *ii blank*, [*frontispiece, engraved title*], <*i*-ii dedication to Walter Francis Douglas, Duke of Buccleuch and Queensberry>, *iii* Contents, *iv blank*, <*i* ii-xxx Introduction>, . . . 341 printer's imprint, *342 blank*. Figures: <a—>, <a—, b xxiv-1, xxviii-3, *d*—>, . . . T334-4.

2] [*engraved title*] THE | POETICAL WORKS . . . . IN ELEVEN VOLUMES | VOL.II. | MARMION. | [*vignette of Linlithgow Palace*] . . . . 1830.

Collation: π^2 <a^6>...R^8(R4+1) S1. Pagination: *i* half-title, *ii blank*, [*frontispiece, engraved title*], *iii* Contents, *iv blank*, <*i* ii-xi Introduction, *xii blank*>, . . . 308 printer's imprint. Figures: <a vii-8/->, . . . R306-5, S—.

3] [*engraved title*] THE | POETICAL WORKS . . . . IN ELEVEN VOLUMES | VOL. III. | MARMION & BALLADS | [*vignette of Crichton Castle*] . . . . 1830.

Notes: Except for the substitution of a new frontispiece and engraved title-page, identical with 1823 issue.

4] [*engraved title*] THE | POETICAL WORKS . . . . IN ELEVEN VOLUMES | VOL. IV. | LADY OF THE LAKE | [*vignette of Stirling Castle*] . . . . 1830.

Collation: π^2 <a^6 b1>...Q^6 R^8. Pagination: *i* half-title, *ii blank*, [*frontispiece, engraved title*], *iii* Contents, *iv blank*, <*i* ii-xiii Introduction, *xiv blank*>, . . . 303 printer's imprint, *304 blank*. Figures: <a xi-7, b—>, . . . Q288-4; R—.

5] [*engraved title*] THE | POETICAL WORKS . . . . IN ELEVEN VOLUMES | VOL.V. | LADY OF THE LAKE | & | BALLADS | [*vignette of Bridge in the Rhymer's Glen*] . . . . 1830.

Notes: Except for the substitution of a new frontispiece and engraved title-page, identical with 1823 issue.

6] [*engraved title*] THE | POETICAL WORKS . . . . IN ELEVEN VOLUMES | VOL. VI. | ROKEBY | [*vignette of Mortham Castle*] . . . . 1830.

Collation: π^2 <a^6 b^2>...R12 S6 T4. Pagination: *i* half-title, *ii blank*, [*frontispiece, engraved title*], *iii*-iv Contents, <*i* ii-xv Introduction, *xvi blank*>, . . . 332 printer's imprint. Figures: <a—, b—>, . . . R309-12, S—; T—.

7] [*engraved title*] THE | POETICAL WORKS . . . . IN ELEVEN VOLUMES | VOL.VII. | ROKEBY | & | BRIDAL OF TRIERMAIN | [*vignette of Johnnie Armstrong's Tower*] . . . . 1830.

Notes: Except for the substitution of a new frontispiece and engraved title-page, identical with 1823 issue.

8] [*engraved title*] THE | POETICAL WORKS . . . . IN ELEVEN VOLUMES | VOL. VIII. | HAROLD THE DAUNTLESS | RODERICK &

MISCELLANIES | [*vignette of Abbotsford*] . . . . 1830.

Notes: Except for the substitution of a new frontispiece and engraved title-page, identical with 1823 issue.

9] [*engraved title*] THE | POETICAL WORKS . . . . IN ELEVEN VOLUMES | VOL.IX. | LORD OF THE ISLES | [*vignette of Castle of Artornish*] . . . . 1830.

Collation: π^2 <a^2 *b*1> A12...P^{12} Q1. Pagination: *i* half-title, *ii blank*, [*frontispiece, engraved title*], *iii* Contents, *iv blank*, <*i* ii-vi Introduction>, . 278 printer's imprint. Figures: <a—, *b*—>, . . . P268-3/-, Q—.

10] [*engraved title*] THE | POETICAL WORKS . . . . IN ELEVEN VOLUMES | VOL.X. | LORD OF THE ISLES | & | MISCELLANIES | [*vignette of Castle of Newark*] . . . . 1830.

Collation: π1(±π1) $2\pi^2$(±2π2)...Q^6 R^4 S1(-S1) <S-$2C^6$>. Pagination: *i* half-title, *ii* advertisement, [*frontispiece, engraved title*], *iii* iv-v Contents, *vi blank*, . . . 298 blank, <*299* fly-title for *Halidon Hill*, *300 blank, 301* 302-308 Advertisement, *309* Dramatis Personae, *310 blank, 311* 312-402 text, 403 Notes, *404* printer's imprint: EDINBURGH: | PRINTED BY BALLANTYNE AND COMPANY, PAUL'S WORK, CANONGATE.> Figures: . . . Q278-4; R—, S—, <T—, U331- 12, Z358-3, 2A—, 2B—, 2C—>.

Notes: The three cancels were used so that page *ii* now advertises Smirke's illustrations, page v enters in Contents *Halidon Hill*, and page 297 deletes the 1823 references 'THE END' and printer's imprint. The added 'dramatic sketch', first published in 1822, for some reason was omitted in the original 1823 issue of these *Works*.

11] [*engraved title*] THE | POETICAL WORKS . . . . IN ELEVEN VOLUMES | VOL.XI. | MACDUFFS CROSS &c. | [*vignette of Smailholm Tower*] . . . . 1830.

Collation: a^4 A-$2G^6$ $2H^4$. Pagination: *i* fly-title, *ii blank*, [*frontispiece, engraved title*], *iii* Contents, *iv blank, v* vi-vii Preface, *viii blank, 1* fly-title for 'MacDuff's Cross', *2 blank, 3* dedication, *4 blank, 5*-6 Introduction, *7* Dramatis Personae, *8 blank, 9* 10-33 text, *34 blank, 35* fly-title for 'The Doom of Devorgoil', *36 blank, 37* Dramatis Personae, *38 blank, 39* 40-206 text, *207* fly-title for 'Auchindrane', *208 blank, 209* 210-238 Preface, *239*-240 Dramatis Personae, *241* 242-367 text, 367 printer's imprint, *368 blank*. Printer's imprint: EDINBURGH | PRINTED BY ANDREW SHORTREDE, | THISTLE LANE. Illustrations: For this additional volume the frontispiece was again painted by R. Smirke, engraved by A. Duncan, with caption 'Halidon Hill' and three-line quotation from Act 2, Scene 2, the Cadell imprint dated 1 June 1830[!]; title-page vignette engraved by W. H. Lizars.

Figures: a—, A—, B18-3 20-1; E54-1 56-3; G80-1, I 107-3; L128-3 132-2; O 158-2, P179-3; S212-1 216-3; U235-2; Z276-3, 2A 288-1; 2B 300-2, 2D 324-1; 2F 343-5, 2G 360-2; 2H 362-3.

Notes: In this new setting, differing from the other volumes in its format, sheet-numbers are again used, beginning with a '2' for the second sheet (page 37). As a supplementary volume to the earlier 1823 ten-volume set, this was announced 10 May 1830 in London (*MC*) as then available separately for 9s.

267Aa] Fifth Collected Edition, First 8° Issue: 1825

[*engraved title*] THE | POETICAL WORKS | OF | SIR WALTER SCOTT, BARONET. | IN TEN VOLUMES. | VOL.I [II-X]. | [*volume title*] | [*vignette*] | EDINBURGH; | PRINTED FOR ARCHIBALD CONSTABLE AND CO. EDINBURGH; | LONGMAN, HURST, REES, ORME, AND BROWN; J. MURRAY; | AND HURST, ROBINSON, AND CO. LONDON. | [*French dash*] | 1825.

Published ca. August 1825 in Edinburgh. Binding: Drab boards with printed labels. Paper: Demy 8° (223 x 143mm uncut). Watermarks: *none.* General Illustrations: Title vignettes correspond to those previously used in the 8° 1821 edition (263A), all drawn by A. Nasmyth and engraved by W. H. Lizars. Typography: Except for volumes 3, 4, 7, and 8, other title-pages exhibit no spacing in the volume reference. Since Ballantyne's printer's imprint is highly variable, it is given in full for each volume.

Copies: E; DLC*. Reference: Ruff 180.
*Extra-illustrated in vols. 5-10 with six of the Smirke plates described for the 18° 1823 edition (266Aa).

1] [*engraved title*] THE | POETICAL WORKS . . . . IN TEN VOLUMES. | VOL.I. | MINSTRELSY. | [*vignette of Castle of Newark*] . . . 1825.

Collation: π1 a-m⁸ A-U⁸. Pagination: [*frontispiece, engraved title*], *v*-vi Contents, *i* fly-title, *ii blank, iii* dedication, *iv blank, v* vi-cxxxviii Introduction, *cxxxix* cxl-clxxxix appendices, *cxc blank, 1* section-title for Part First, *2 blank*, 3-321 text and notes, 321 printer's imprint, *322 blank*. Printer's imprint: [*short rule*] | EDINBURGH: | Printed by James Ballantyne and Co. Illustration: Frontispiece portrait of Scott, painted by Raeburn, engraved by W. T. Fry, dated August 1825. Typography: In some copies page xxxiii is misnumbered xxxii.

Figures: a—, b xxxii-11, c xlviii-9, d lxiv-5, e lxxx-8, f xcvi-13, g cxii-2, h cxxviii-6, i cxliv-14, k—, l clxxvi-13, m clxxxviii-12, A18-12, B34-10, C50-5, D66-9, E82-11, F95-8, G114-13, H—, I 146-7, K162-13, L178-8, M194-7, N210-7, O 226-9, P242-6, Q258-7, R270-3, S290-2, T306-7, U319-3.

2] [*engraved title*] THE | POETICAL WORKS . . . . IN TEN VOLUMES. | VOL.II. | MINSTRELSY | [*vignette of Branxholme*] . . . . 1825.

Collation: π1 A-2E^8 2F^4. Pagination: [*engraved title*], *v*-vi Contents, *1* fly-title, *2 blank, 3* 4-99 text, Part First, concluded, *100 blank, 101* fly-title for Part Second, *102 blank, 103* 104-456 text, 456 printer's imprint: [*short rule*] | EDINBURGH: | Printed by James Ballantyne & Co.

Figures: A16-10, B29-11, C48-4, D64-8, E80-3, F96-12, G112-8, H128-11, I 144-3, K160-7, L176-7, M192-5, N208-6, O 224-3, P—, Q253-7, R272-6, S288-10, T304-6, U320-7, X336-8, Y345-6, Z368-6, 2A 384-8, 2B 391-1, 2C 412-8, 2D 424-7, 2E 441-10, 2F 453-12.

3] [*engraved title*] THE | POETICAL WORKS . . . . IN TEN VOLUMES. | VOL. III. | MINSTRELSY. | [*vignette of Smailholm Tower*] . . . . 1825.

Collation: π1 A-2G^8 2H^4. Pagination: [*engraved title*], *v*-vi Contents, *1* fly-title, *2 blank,* 3-145 text for Part Second, concluded, *146 blank, 147* fly-title for Part Third, *148 blank, 149* 150-488 text, 488 printer's imprint: [*short rule*] | EDINBURGH: | Printed by JAMES BALLANTYNE & Co. Typography: Pages 206 and 219 are misnumbered 226 and 291 respectively.

Figures: A16-7, B32-6, C48-10, D61-8, E73-7, F93-13, G112-7, H120-7, I 144-13, K157-13, L176-10, M189-10, N208-9, O 224-7, P240-4, Q256-9, R261-12, S288-10, T304-10, U320-7, X—, Y352-11, Z364-6, 2A 384-8, 2B 400-10, 2C 416-4, 2D 432-12, 2E 448-8, 2F 460-7, 2G 480-10, 2H 487-10.

4] [*engraved title*] THE | POETICAL WORKS . . . . IN TEN VOLUMES. | VOL. IV. | SIR TRISTREM | [*vignette of Bridge in the Rhymer's Glen*] . . . . 1825.

Collation: π1 a-h^8 A-M^8 N^8(-N8=*2C*1) O-2B^8 *2C*1. Pagination: [*engraved title*], *1* Contents, *2 blank, i* section title, *ii blank, iii* fly-title, *iv blank, v* vi-xcvi Introduction, *xcvii* fly-title, *xcviii blank, xcix* c-cxxviii appendices, *1* section-title, *2 blank, 3* 4-204 text, *205* fly-title, *206 blank, 209* 210-262 description and abstracts, *263* fly-title, *264 blank*, 265-374 Notes, *375* fly-title, *376 blank*, 377-401 Glossary, 401 printer's imprint, *402 blank.* Printer's imprint: [*short rule*] | EDINBURGH: | Printed by James Ballantyne & Co. Typography: Signature a is missigned A. The break in pagination after page *206* is caused by the removal of the final Glossary leaf entered last as *2C*1. This is still retained as N8 in some copies.

Figures: 'A'[a] xvi-7, b xxxii-10, c xlviii-10, d lxiv-7, e lxxx-5, f xcii-10 g cxii-3, h cxxiv-3, A16-12, B32-6, C48-2, D61-3, E80-11, F92-9, G112-6, H121-13, I 138-6, K160-5, L176-2, M189-3, N—, O—, P240-3, Q256-9, R272-4, S288-1, T304-6, U320-7, X336-3, Y352-10, Z368-2, 2A 380-1, 2B 400-8, *2C*—.

5] [*engraved title*] THE | POETICAL WORKS . . . . IN TEN VOLUMES. | VOL.V | LAY OF THE LAST MINSTREL. | [*vignette of Melrose Abbey*] . . . . 1825.

Collation: π1 A-2F⁸ *2G*1. Pagination: [*engraved title*], *v*-vi Contents, *1* fly-title, *2 blank, 3* dedication, *4 blank, 5* preface, *6 blank, 7* section-title, *8 blank*, 9-206 text, *207* fly-title, *208 blank, 209* 210-347 Notes, *348 blank, 349* fly-title for 'Ballads', *350 blank*, 351-384 text, *385* fly-title for 'Songs', *386 blank*, 387-397 text, *398 blank, 399* fly-title for 'Fragments', *400 blank*, 401-411 text, *412 blank, 413* fly-title for 'Ballads from the German', *414 blank*, 415-465 text, 465 printer's imprint, *466 blank*. Printer's imprint: [*short rule*] | EDINBURGH: | Printed by JAMES BALLANTYNE and Co.

Figures: A16-1, B25-6, C48-5, D64-11, E80-7, F84-2, G112-13, H128-6, I 144-2, K160-10, L176-8, M192-1, N204-13, O 224-9, P240-7, Q256-7, R—, S285-11, T300-5, U320-10, X336-4, Y352-9, Z368-7, 2A—, 2B 388-9, 2C 405-6, 2D 432-9, 2E 445-11, 2F 464-7, *2G*—.

6] [*engraved title*] THE | POETICAL WORKS . . . . IN TEN VOLUMES. | VOL.VI. | MARMION. | [*vignette of Linlithgow Palace*] . . . . 1825.

Collation: π1 A-2I⁸. Pagination: [*engraved title*], *iii* Contents, *iv blank, 1* fly-title, *2 blank, 3* dedication, *4 blank, 5* Advertisement, *6 blank, 7* fly-title, *8 blank, 9* 10-383 text, *384 blank, 385* fly-title, *386 blank*, 387-512 Notes, 512 printer's imprint: [*short rule*] | EDINBURGH: | Printed by James Ballantyne and Co.

Figures: A16-12/13, B32-10, C48-5, D60-9, E77-4, F96-7, G112-14, H128-8, I 144-11, K160-13, L171-10, M192-9, N208-6, O 224-8, P240-13, Q256-12, R272-8, S288-6, T292-10, U308-11, X336-12, Y352-7, Z368-11, 2A 380-6, 2B 393-13/-, 2C 413-1, 2D 432-8, 2E 445-3, 2F 464-5, 2G 480-7, 2H 496-11, 2I 500-2.

7] [*engraved title*] THE | POETICAL WORKS . . . . IN TEN VOLUMES. | VOL. VII. | LADY OF THE LAKE. | [*vignette of Stirling Castle*] . . . . 1825.

Collation: π1 A-2G⁸ 2H⁸. Pagination: [*engraved title*], *v*-vi Contents, *1* fly-title, *2 blank, 3* dedication, *4 blank, 5* Argument, *6 blank, 7* fly-title, *8 blank, 9* 10-296 text, *297* fly-title, *298 blank*, 299-439 Notes, *440 blank, 441* fly-title for 'Miscellaneous Poems', *442 blank, 443* 444-493 text, 493 printer's imprint, *494-496 blank*. Printer's imprint: [*short rule*] | EDINBURGH: | Printed by James Ballantyne & Co.

Figures: A16-4, B32-9, C41-7, D64-6/-, E80-7, F96-12, G112-13, H128-7, I 144-4, K160-6, L176-8, M192-7, N208-5, O 224-4, P240-10, Q256-10, R272-7, S288-7, T304-6, U320-4, X336-10, Y352-8, Z368-5, 2A 384-13, 2B 400-7, 2C 416-8, 2D 432-9, 2E 444-4, 2F 464-3, 2G 477-13/-, 2H—.

8] [*engraved title*] THE | POETICAL WORKS . . . . IN TEN VOLUMES. | VOL. VIII. | ROKEBY | [*vignette of Mortham Castle*] . . . . 1825.

Collation: π1 A-2G⁸ 2H². Pagination: [*engraved title*], *iii* Contents, *iv blank, 1* fly-title for *Rokeby, 2 blank, 3* dedication, *4 blank, 5* Advertisement, *6 blank, 7* section-title, *8 blank, 9* 10-304 text, *305* fly-title, *306 blank*, 307-419 Notes, *420 blank, 421* fly-title for *The Vision of Don Roderick, 422 blank, 423* dedication, *424 blank*, 425-427 Preface, *428 blank, 429* fly-title, *430 blank*, 431-483 text, through Stanza 63, 483 printer's imprint, *484 blank*. Printer's imprint: [*short rule*] | Edinburgh: | Printed by James Ballantyne & Co.

Figures: A16-7, B32-12, C48-7, D—, E80-2, F92-7, G112-2, H128-7, I 144-13, K160-2, L176-12, M192-7, N208-5, O 224-14, P240-4, Q256-5, R272-7, S288-7, T301-4, U320-10, X326-1, Y352-3, Z368-5, 2A 384-5, 2B 400-8, 2C 416-13, 2D 432-12, 2E 448-4, 2F 457-10, 2G 480-2, 2H—.

9] [*engraved title*] THE | POETICAL WORKS . . . . IN TEN VOLUMES. | VOL.IX. | LORD OF THE ISLES | [*vignette of Castle of Artornish*] . . . 1825.

Collation: π1 A-2H⁸ 2 I². Pagination: [*engraved title*], *iii* Contents, *iv blank, 1* fly-title for *The Vision of Don Roderick, 2 blank,* 3-15 text concluded, *16 blank, 17* fly-title, *18 blank*, 19-51 Notes, *52 blank, 53* fly-title for *The Lord of the Isles, 54 blank, 55* Advertisement, *56 blank, 57* section-title, *58 blank, 59* 60-331 text, *332 blank, 333* fly-title, *334 blank*, 335-499 Notes, 499 printer's imprint, *500 blank*. Printer's imprint: [*short rule*] | Edinburgh: | Printed by James Ballantyne & Co.

Figures: A12-9, B32-12, C48-7, D64-3, E80-7, F88-4, G112-7, H128-5, I 144-2, K160-15, L176-8, M192-5, N208-3, O 224-4, P240-7, Q256-8, R272-1, S288-3, T304-4, U320-5, X336-2, Y352-5, Z368-1, 2A 384-3, 2B 400-1, 2C 416-3, 2D 432-8, 2E 448-11, 2F 464-4, 2G 480-13, 2H 496-11, 2 I—.

10] [*engraved title*] THE | POETICAL WORKS . . . . IN TEN VOLUMES. | VOL.X. | MISCELLANIES | [*vignette of Abbotsford*] . . . 1825.

Collation: π² A-2N⁸. Pagination: [*engraved title*], *v* vi-vii Contents, *viii blank, 1* fly-title for *The Field of Waterloo, 2 blank, 3* dedication, *4 blank, 5* 6-43 text and notes, *44 blank, 45* fly-title for 'Songs and Miscellanies', *46 blank*, 47-141 text,

142 blank, 143 fly-title for *The Bridal of Triermain, 144 blank, 145* 146-154 Preface, 155-312 text and notes, *313* fly-title for *Harold the Dauntless, 314 blank*, 315-458 *459* text, *460 blank, 461* fly-title for *Halidon Hill, 462 blank, 463* dedication, *464 blank, 465* 466-567 *568-569* text and notes, *569* printer's imprint, *570 blank, 1* 2-6 Works Published by Constable. Printer's imprint: [*short rule*] | EDINBURGH: | Printed by JAMES BALLANTYNE & Co. Typography: In the page-number for 387 the last digit is defective.

Figures: A16-2, B28-4, C48-15, D64-7, E77-10, F92-8, G108-9, H128-8, I 140-12, K160-9, L176-2, M192-15, N208-10, O 224-13, P240-7, Q256-9, R272-10, S288-5, T304-2, U318-15, X336-8, Y352-1, Z361-10, 2A 381-9, 2B 400-11, 2C 416-3, 2D 432-15, 2E 448-9, 2F 451-15, 2G 480-15, 2H 496-10, 2 I 512-9, 2K 528-9, 2L 542-13, 2M 560-2, 2N—.

267Ab] Fifth Collected Edition, Second 8° Issue: 1830

[*engraved title*] THE | POETICAL WORKS | OF | SIR WALTER SCOTT, BARONET. | IN ELEVEN VOLUMES | VOL.I [II-XI]. | [*volume title*] | [*vignette*] | EDINBURGH | Printed for Cadell & Co. Edinburgh. and | Simpkin and Marshall. London. | 1830.

Published 21 April 1830 in London (*MC*); issued 2 June in Edinburgh (*EWJ*). £6. Binding: tan boards with green cloth spine and printed labels. Paper: Demy 8° (223 x 143mm uncut). Watermarks: *none*. Illustrations: The newly engraved 1830 titles now have vignettes 'Engraved on Steel by Chas. Heath.' Typography: Except for volumes 3, 4, and 7, other title-pages exhibit no spacing in the volume reference.

General Notes: Since this augmented issue, like the one in 18° format (266Ab), was announced in London six weeks before the Edinburgh date, it would appear that Cadell had early sent on to his London associate the new materials to be inserted there (chiefly in the 709 copies transferred from Longmans, a previous publisher) and then from a further printing later completed his own stock in Edinburgh. Two further introductory essays for *Minstrelsy of the Scottish Border,* not reprinted in the 18° format, are first printed here in volumes 1 and 3 and dated from Abbotsford 1 March and April 1830 respectively. A separate 11th volume 'to complete former editions' was also provided first in London on 10 May (*see* 268A).

As for the 18° issue the new dedication in this 8°, the Introductions to volumes 5-9, and the Preface to volume 11, are all dated from Abbotsford, April 1830. Again as before collation and pagination of the new material is represented within angular brackets and, to differentiate this from the 1821 reissue, final signatures, pages, and press figures are repeated. The Smirke plates, now bearing an undated Cadell & Co. imprint, may appear as frontispieces, as noted below, or be inserted in the text.

Copies: T/B(prize set from Trinity College Cambridge) TxU. Mixed copy: CtY (Preface to vol. 11 inserted in vol. 1; lacks Introductions for vols. 1, 3). References: Millgate(2); McMullin(2); Ruff 181.

1] [*engraved title*] THE | POETICAL WORKS . . . . IN ELEVEN VOLUMES | VOL.I. | MINSTRELSY. | [*vignette of Abbotsford*] . . . . 1830.

Collation: π1 <*a*1 a*-e*^{8} f*^{2}> . . . U^{8}. Pagination: [*frontispiece, engraved title*], *v*-vi Contents, <*i*-ii dedication to Walter Francis, Duke of Buccleuch, dated from Abbotsford, April 1830, *i* ii-lxxxiii 'Introductory Remarks on Popular Poetry', dated from Abbotsford, 1 March 1830, *lxxxiv blank*> . . . *322*. Illustrations: Frontispiece titled 'Sir Walter Scott Bart.', painted by David Wilkie, engraved by E. Smith, published by Cadell & Co., 1830. Typography: First signature *a* is in italic; signature b* (page xvii) is incorrectly signed *b; page xxxiii in some copies is misnumbered xxxii. Figures: <d* lxiv-2> . . . U319-3.

2] [*engraved title*] THE | POETICAL WORKS . . . . IN ELEVEN VOLUMES | VOL.II. | MINSTRELSY | [*vignette of Smailholm Tower*] . . . . 1830.

Collation, pagination, and figures as for 1825 issue.

3] [*engraved title*] THE | POETICAL WORKS . . . . IN ELEVEN VOLUMES | VOL. III. | MINSTRELSY. | [*vignette of Castle of Newark*] . . . . 1830.

Collation: π1 <a†-e†^{8} f†^{2} g†^{8} h†^{4}> . . . 2H^{4}. Pagination: [*frontispiece, engraved title*], *v*-vi Contents, <*i* fly-title, *ii blank, iii* iv-lxxxiii 'Essay on Imitations of the Ancient Ballad', dated from Abbotsford, April 1830, *lxxxiv blank, lxxxv* fly-title, *lxxxvi blank, lxxxvii* lxxxviii-cviii appendices> . . . 488. Typography: Signature g† (page *lxxxv*) is missigned g*.

Figures: <a† vi-15, b†—, c† xlviii-5, d† lxii-14, e† lxxx-18, f†—, 'g*'[=g†] xcvii-17, h† cvii-14> , . . 2H 487-10.

4] [*engraved title*] THE | POETICAL WORKS . . . . IN ELEVEN VOLUMES | VOL. IV. | SIR TRISTREM | [*vignette of Bridge in the Rhymer's Glen*] . . . . 1830.

Collation, pagination, and figures as for 1825 issue.

5] [*engraved title*] THE | POETICAL WORKS . . . . IN ELEVEN VOLUMES | VOL.V | LAY OF THE LAST MINSTREL. | [*vignette of Melrose Abbey*] . . . 1830.

Collation: π1 <*a*^{8}(-*a*1) b^{8}> . . . *2G*1. Pagination: [*frontispiece, engraved title*], *v*-vi

Contents, <*i* ii-xv 'xviii'[xvi]-'xxxi'[xxix] Introduction, dated from Abbotsford, April 1830> . . . *466*. Figures: <*a* xii-18, b—> . . . 2F 264-7, *2G*—.

6] [*engraved title*] THE | POETICAL WORKS . . . . IN ELEVEN VOLUMES | VOL.VI. | MARMION. | [*vignette of Linlithgow Palace*] . . . 1830.

Collation: π1 <a[4] *b*1> . . . 2I[8.] Pagination: [*frontispiece, engraved title*], *1* Contents, *2 blank*, <*i* ii-x Introduction, dated from Abbotsford, April 1830> . . . 512. Figures: <*none*> . . . 2I 500-2.

7] [*engraved title*] THE | POETICAL WORKS . . . . IN ELEVEN VOLUMES | VOL. VII. | LADY OF THE LAKE. | [*vignette of Stirling Castle*] . . . . 1830.

Collation: π1 <a[4] b[2]> . . . 2H[8](2H8). Pagination: [*frontispiece, engraved title*], *v*-vi Contents, <*i* ii-xii Introduction, dated from Abbotsford, April 1830> . . . *494*. Figures: <*none*> . . . 2G 477-13/-, 2H—.

8] [*engraved title*] THE | POETICAL WORKS . . . . IN ELEVEN VOLUMES | VOL.VIII | ROKEBY | [*vignette of Johnnie Armstrong's Tower*] . . . . 1830.

Collation: π1 <*a*[8]> . . . 2H[2.] Pagination: [*frontispiece, engraved title*], *1* Contents, *2 blank*, <*i* ii-xiv Introduction, dated from Abbotsford, April 1830, *xv-xvi blank*> . . . *484*. Typography: Signature a is in italic. Figures: <*a* xi-16> . . . 2G 480-2, 2H—.

9] [*engraved title*] THE | POETICAL WORKS . . . . IN ELEVEN VOLUMES | VOL.IX. | LORD OF THE ISLES | [*vignette of Castle of Artornish*] . . . . 1830.

Collation: π1 <*a*[4](-*a*1)> . . . 2I[2.] Pagination: [*frontispiece, engraved title*], *1* Contents, *2 blank*, <*i* ii-vi Introduction, dated from Abbotsford, April 1830> . . . *500*. Figures: <*none*> . . . 2H 496-11, 2I—.

10] [*engraved title*] THE | POETICAL WORKS . . . . IN ELEVEN VOLUMES | VOL.X | [*vignette of Crichton Castle*] . . . . 1830.

Collation: . . . 2F[6.] Pagination: . . . *460*. Figures: 2F 451-15. Typography: In its earliest state the plate for the engraved title-page, originally reading 'VOL.XI.', has the last two sorts scraped away, leaving 'VOL.X'. A re-engraved state has the period after X.

Notes: There is no insert for this volume, but it is curtailed by the removal in this issue of the last section, *Halidon Hill*, a work transferred to the next volume.

11] [*engraved title*] THE | POETICAL WORKS . . . . IN ELEVEN VOLUMES | VOL.XI. | [*vignette of Mortham Castle*] . . . . 1830.

Collation: π1 2π[2] A-2F[8] 2G[6]. Pagination: [*frontispiece, engraved title*], *1* dedication to Joanna Baillie, *2 blank*, *i* ii-iii Preface, dated from Abbotsford, April 1830, *iv blank*, *1* fly-title for *Halidon Hill*, *2 blank*, *3* 4-11 Advertisement, *12 blank*, *13-15* 16-105 *106-107* text, *108 blank*, *109* fly-title for 'MacDuff's Cross', *110 blank*, *111* dedication, *112 blank*, *113*-114 Introduction, dated from Abbotsford, January 1830, *115-117* 118-141 text, *142 blank*, *143* fly-title for 'The Doom of Devorgoil', *144 blank*, *145-147* 148-314 text, *315* fly-title for 'Auchindrane', *316 blank*, *317* 318-346 Preface, undated, *347* 348-475 text, *476* printer's imprint: [*short rule*] | EDINBURGH: | PRINTED BY BALLANTYNE AND COMPANY, | PAUL'S WORK, CANONGATE. Illustrations: Frontispiece titled 'Halidon Hill' with a three-line quotation from act 2, scene 3, engraved by A. Duncan. One copy (CtY) substitutes as a frontispiece a plate properly attached to the previous volume: titled 'Harold the Dauntless' with a two-line quotation from canto 2, stanza 7, engraved by Chas Heath.

Figures: B31-19, C42-9, D59-9, E80-9, O 224-6, 2F 464-18.

Notes: As a supplementary volume to the earlier 1825 ten-volume set, this was, it seems, one of two alternatives announced 10 May in London (*MC*) as available separately for 18s. With *Halidon Hill* now removed from the preceding volume for inclusion here, this volume could properly supplement the 1821 edition, which lacked this text, but not the 1825 issue, which still contained it in the 10th volume. For that other alternative, see the description immediately following. (An 11th volume noted by McMullin, with an 1822 first edition of *Halidon Hill* inserted, apparently was made up to meet the requirement for 1821.)

268A] Collected Edition, Supplementary Volumes: 1830

[*printed title*] THE | **POETICAL WORKS** | OF | SIR WALTER SCOTT, BART. | IN ELEVEN VOLUMES. | [*short rule*] | VOL. XI. PART I [II]. | ESSAYS ON BALLAD POETRY, | AND | INTRODUCTIONS. | [*short Oxford rule*] | PRINTED FOR | CADELL AND COMPANY, EDIN BURGH; | AND SIMPKIN AND MARSHALL, LONDON. | [*dash*] | 1830.

Published 'to complete former editions' as 'Parts I and II' 10 May 1830 in London (*MC*); issued 2 June in Edinburgh (*EWJ*). 18s (9s each part). Binding: drab boards with printed label and title. Demy 8° (223 x 142mm uncut). Watermarks: *none*. Illustration: frontispiece portrait by Wilkie, as in preceding 11-volume issue.

General Notes: So far the record discounts, as irrelevant to official issue, the several occasions wherein private owners, on acquiring in 1830 new materials from the publisher, have 'updated' their own sets of *The Poetical Works* (*see* copy note for 266Aa)—a practice sometimes revealed by their retention of the title-pages originally supplied—and summarily treated what appears to be the first supplementary issue in circulation: the 1830 18° issue of a single setting. Of greater complexity are the variable 1830 8° issues originating in 1821 and 1825, of which the one just described had priority of publication on 21 April. In this it should now be noted, the new introductory matter is appropriately accorded, for each volume, introductory signatures (a,b, &c) and page numbers in roman letter. Once these sections had been prepared, with new 1830 title-pages, Cadell immediately had all type reimposed for the supplementary printing described below.

In this supplement two states occur, (1) with printer's imprint on half-title verso when the work consisted only of the first part, (2) with imprint removed and transferred to the last page when the work was extended to two parts. In either state, printer's imprint is: [*short rule*] | EDINBURGH: | PRINTED BY BALLANTYNE AND COMPANY, | PAUL'S WORK, CANONGATE.

A combined reissue of both parts in 1836, with a misleading title *The Miscellaneous Works* (L copy), has the sections in the first part, as defined below, ordered 2,3,1, but press figures and final imprint remain the same.

Copies: (state 1) E. (2) ES.

1] THE | **POETICAL WORKS** . . . VOL. XI. PART I. . . . 1830.

Collation: π^2 *a*1 ^{1}A†^{8} b^8 C-E^8 F1; ^{2}A-E^8 F1; ^{3}A†-E†^{8} F†^{2} G†^{8} H†^{4}. Pagination: *1* half-title, *2* printer's imprint, *3* title-page, *4 blank, i*-ii dedication to Walter Francis Douglas, Duke of Buccleuch and Queensberry, *1* fly-title, Introduction to the *Lay of the Last Minstrel, 2 blank, 3* 4-31 text, *32 blank; 1* fly-title, Introduction to *Marmion, 2 blank, 3* 4-12 text, *1* fly-title, Introduction to *The Lady of the Lake, 2 blank, 3* 4-14 text, *1* fly-title, Introduction to *Rokeby, 2 blank, 3* 4-16 text, *1* fly-title, Introduction to *The Lord of the Isles, 2 blank, 3* 4-8 text; *1* 2-83 Introductory Remarks on Popular Poetry, *84 blank, 1* fly-title, Essay on Imitations of the Ancient Ballad, *2 blank, 3* 4-83 text, *84 blank, 85* fly-title, Appendix, *86 blank, 87* 88-108 text. Typography: In the third sequence signatures C†, F†, and G† (pages 33, 81, *85*) are in lower case.

Figures: ^{1}A† 14-18, b25-7/-, C9-16, D6-18, E6-12; ^{2}D 64-2; ^{3}A† 6-15, C† 48-5, D† 62-14, E† 80-18, G† 97-17, H† 107-14.

Notes: It will be observed that in this alternate imposition the figures remain subtended to the same text-type page as that inserted in the preceding 11-volume issue; thus vol. 1 there, d* lxiv-2 = ^{2}D 64-2 here, vol.3 a† vi-15 = ^{3}A† 6-15 [&c], vol. 5 a xii-18 = ^{1}A† 14-18, and so on. From the three collational sequences it is also evident that this impression, though also intended 'to complete former editions', is designed for reference only: the gatherings are split apart whenever (as in Ruff's 165 'issue') previous owners mistakenly insert the text sections into their own copies.

2] [THE | **POETICAL WORKS** . . . VOL. XI. PART II. . . . 1830.]

Collation: A^2 $†^2$ B-Z^8 $2A^6$. Pagination: *1* fly-title, *2 blank, 3* dedication to Joanna Baillie, *4 blank, i* ii-iii Preface, *iv blank, 5*-6 Introduction [to the plays], *7-9* 10-33 text of 'MacDuff's Cross', *34 blank, 35* fly-title for 'The Doom of Devorgoil', *36 blank, 37-39* 40-206 text, *207* fly-title for 'Auchindrane', *208 blank, 209* 210-367 text, *368* printer's imprint: [*short rule*] | EDINBURGH: | PRINTED BY BALLANTYNE AND COMPANY, | PAUL'S WORK, CANONGATE. Typography: Instead of a printed title corresponding to that of 'PART I.' the only copy seen of this section (ES) has an engraved volume XI title with another 'I' added in ink, with the section bound in calf to match the previous part. Figures: H116-6, Z356-18.

Notes: As an alternative to the 11th volume published four weeks earlier, on 21 April (267Ab.11), this separate Part excludes *Halidon Hill*, thus rendering it an appropriate continuation of the 8° 1825 edition, which included this piece in the 10th volume (267Aa.10). Otherwise this is a reimposition of the 11th volume, with figures O 224-6, 2F 464-18 there = H116-6, Z356-18 here.

1B. COLLECTED EDITIONS: NOVELS
NOVELS AND TALES [WAVERLEY—MONTROSE]

269Aa] First Series, First 8° Edition, First Issue: 1819

[*engraved title*] NOVELS AND TALES | OF | THE AUTHOR OF WAVERLEY. | VOL. I [II-XII]. | [*volume title*] | [*vignette*] | EDINBURGH; | PRINTED FOR ARCHIBALD CONSTABLE AND Co. EDINBURGH; | LONGMAN, HURST, REES, ORME AND BROWN; | AND HURST, ROBINSON AND Co. | LONDON. | [*French dash*] | 1819.

Published 9 December 1819 in Edinburgh (*EEC*); issued 28 December in London (*MC*). £7.4.0. 1500 copies, of which 650 were shipped to Hurst, Robinson on 3 December (*EEWN3*.374). Binding: grey boards with printed labels. Paper: Royal 8° (227 x 145mm uncut). Watermarks: *none*. Illustrations: In each of the twelve volumes the title-page vignette is of Stirling Castle, drawn and engraved by W. & D. Lizars. Typography: Printer's imprints read: [*short rule*] | EDINBURGH: | Printed by James Ballantyne & Co. ['and Co.' vol. 4].

General Notes: For the more affluent readers of his novels Scott, in this first collected edition, is presented in the grandest manner, with large paper and type, as well as an array of illustrations intended here, eventually introduced 1822 in a later edition (269Ac), and fully displayed in the subsequent octavo sequences (269Ac[2], 272A, 275A, 278A, 281A). Eight months before publication of this first series Constable reported that he had commissioned a pictorial suite from William Allan, yet through some misadventure this was still being engraved in August 1820 (*Letters*, vi.254), issued 11 December (*see* entry 322D), but never incorporated in any edition. Nonetheless, one set of the novels in this original issue has been reported with the Allan plates later inserted (David Hewitt [ed.], *EEWN3*.373).

For other readers less expensive series in 12° and 18° soon followed in orderly progressions, as detailed below, and for publishers abroad the series now provided an impetus to start collections of their own: 1819 by the Brothers Schumann in Zwickau (302R), 1820 by Galignani in Paris (290R), and 1821 by Parker in Boston (305R).

Copies: BCL E ES(vols.1-10) L; CtY(2) T/B.

1] [*engraved title*] NOVELS AND TALES | OF | THE AUTHOR OF WAVERLEY. | VOL. I. | WAVERLEY. | [*vignette*] . . . . 1819.

Collation: A-2I^8 2K^4. Pagination: [*engraved title*], *i* fly-title, *ii blank, iii* iv-vi Preface to the Third Edition, *7* 8-208 211-521 text, chapters 1-47, 521 printer's imprint, *522 blank*. Typography: In some copies page 516 is misnumbered 51.

Figures: A *iii*-6, B26-7, C42-12, D50-1/-, E75-2, F96-1, G110-9, H116-6, I 144-8, K159-12, L162-12, M178-1, N202-6, O 218-9, P242-7, Q245-4, R263-11, S290-12, T303-7, U319-11, X333-4, Y354-12, Z366-13, 2A 374-8, 2B 393-8, 2C 413-6, 2D 422-9, 2E 444-3, 2F 453-9, 2G 482-2, 2H 491-9, 2 I 500-13, 2K 520-1.

Notes: The break in text pagination 208 | 211, occurring between the end of chapter 18 (sheet N) and the beginning of chapter 19 (sheet O), would seem to indicate a division of copy at this juncture and a numerical miscalculation when composition started on the latter part.

2] [*engraved title*] NOVELS AND TALES | OF | THE AUTHOR OF WAVERLEY. | VOL. II. | WAVERLEY. | GUY MANNERING. | [*vignette*] . . . . 1819.

Collation: A-2H^8 2I^4 *2K*1. Pagination: [*engraved title*], *1* fly-title for *Waverley*, *2 blank, 3* 4-263 text concluded, *264 blank, 265* fly-title for *Guy Mannering*, *266 blank, 267* 268-505 text, chapters 1-21, 505 printer's imprint, *506 blank*. Typography: Page 13 is misnumbered 31.

Figures: A16-8, B26-11/-, C48-3, D53-1/- 55-11, E80-7, F93-10/-, G111-8, H116-12, I 141-3, K154-12, L175-2, M190-10, N208-8, O 210-9, P240-7, Q248-2, R272-8/-, S281-6, T302-9, U316-5, X333-7/-, Y352-7, Z368-12, 2A 373-3, 2B 396-11, 2C 405-5, 2D 430-10, 2E 448-12, 2F 462-8 464-11, 2G 479-3 480-7, 2H 491-7, 2 I 504-11, *2K*—.

3] [*engraved title*] NOVELS AND TALES | OF | THE AUTHOR OF WAVERLEY. | VOL. III. | GUY MANNERING. | [*vignette*] . . . . 1819.

Collation: A-2H⁸. Pagination: [*engraved title*], *1* fly-title, *2 blank, 3* 4-495 text concluded, 495 printer's imprint, *496 blank.*

Figures: A7-6/- 16-8, B29-3, C42-7 48-11, D57-5 59-13, E80-8, F96-11, G105-6, H127-7, I 137-13 143-13, K156-12, L176-8, M182-3, N197-3, O 223-13, P236-4, Q253-10, R263-11, S284-13, T304-8, U316-10, X329-13, Y352-7, Z367-11, 2A 381-5, 2B 393-10, 2C 409-13, 2D 422-6, 2E 448-12, 2F 461-5, 2G 474-9, 2H 494-11.

4] [*engraved title*] NOVELS AND TALES | OF | THE AUTHOR OF WAVERLEY. | VOL. IV. | ANTIQUARY. | [*vignette*] . . . . 1819.

Collation: A-2G⁸. Pagination: [*engraved title*], *i* fly-title, *ii blank, iii* iv-v Advertisement, *vi blank, 7* 8-479 text, chapters 1-29, 479 printer's imprint, *480 blank.*

Figures: A8-3, B32-11, C41-10, D64-5, E80-4, F96-9, G99-11, H128-7, I 144-13, K160-5, L176-7, M192-8, N201-4, O 222-3, P234-13, Q248-5, R263-11, S286-9, T298-11, U320-14, X325-5, Y346-5, Z358-3, 2A 371-11, 2B 400-14, 2C 405-5, 2D 429-14, 2E 443-10, 2F 461-11, 2G 477-8.

5] [*engraved title*] NOVELS AND TALES | OF | THE AUTHOR OF WAVERLEY. | VOL. V. | ANTIQUARY. | ROB ROY. | [*vignette*] . . . . 1819.

Collation: A-2H⁸. Pagination: [*engraved title*], *1* fly-title for *The Antiquary*, *2 blank, 3* 4-253 text concluded, *254 blank, 255* fly-title for *Rob Roy*, *256 blank, 257* 258-259 Advertisement, *260 blank, 261* 262-493 text, chapters 1-13, 493 printer's imprint, *494-496 blank.*

Figures: A13-3, B28-10, C45-7, D61-10, E75-5, F96-5, G99-3, H121-4, I 141-12, K155-3, L176-10, M180-11, N205-10, O 221-3, P240-10, Q249-7, R272-6, S281-2, T292-11, U312-7, X334-3, Y352-14, Z364-10, 2A 382-11, 2B 397-7, 2C 410-11, 2D 432-8, 2E 446-14, 2F 457-3, 2G 475-11, 2H 484-8.

6] [*engraved title*] NOVELS AND TALES | OF | THE AUTHOR OF WAVERLEY. | VOL.VI. | ROB ROY. | [*vignette*] . . . . 1819.

Collation: A-2G⁸. Pagination: [*engraved title*], *1* fly-title, *2 blank, 3* 4-477 text concluded, 477 printer's imprint, *478-480 blank.* Typography: The title exhibits no spacing in the volume reference.

Figures: A16-12, B21-7, C46-11, D58-11, E80-7, F84-14, G109-5, H115-7, I 134-9, K150-3, L174-11, M191-12, N208-5, O 224-3, P229-7, Q256-5, R264-4, S288-14, T302-1, U308-10, X336-11, Y349-11, Z368-8, 2A 381-1, 2B 387-6, 2C 415-9, 2D 427-10, 2E 447-14, 2F 464-7, 2G 472-13.

7] [*engraved title*] NOVELS AND TALES | OF | THE AUTHOR OF WAVERLEY. | VOL. VII. | TALES OF MY LANDLORD. | [*vignette*] ... 1819.

Collation: A-2H[8] 2I[4](-2I 4). Pagination: [*engraved title*], *1* fly-title for the *Tales* [first series], *2 blank, 3* 4-16 Introduction, *17* fly-title for 'The Black Dwarf', *18 blank, 19* 20-260 text, *261* fly-title for 'Old Mortality', *262 blank, 263* 264-501 text, chapters 1-13, 501 printer's imprint, *502 blank.*

Figures: A7-9, B32-12, C48-12, D64-8, E77-5, F96-6, G112-3, H128-8, I 144-11, K153-14, L171-7, M192-11, N208-8, O 218-12, P239-14, Q256-7, R268-13, S286-12, T304-11, U320-13, X332-11, Y341-5, Z367-11, 2A 371-3, 2B 397-14/-398-5, 2C 405-11, 2D 427-5, 2E 442-10, 2F 453-3, 2G 466-6, 2H 493-11, 2I 498-13.

8] [*engraved title*] NOVELS AND TALES | OF | THE AUTHOR OF WAVERLEY. | VOL. VIII. | TALES OF MY LANDLORD. | [*vignette*] ... 1819.

Collation: A-2G[8] 2H[4] 2I[2]. Pagination: [*engraved title*], *1* fly-title for 'Old Mortality', *2 blank, 3* 4-491 text concluded, 491 printer's imprint, *492 blank.*

Figures: A13-10, B32-8, C39-9, D57-10, E73-7, F84-7, G109-10, H124-9, I 137-5, K160-8, L173-14 174-13, M182-7 192-11, N204-13, O 224-5, P232-14/-, Q256-8, R260-6, S283-11, T303-13, U312-14, X336-4, Y340-5, Z365-13, 2A 383-4, 2B 388-14, 2C 414-11, 2D 418-14, 2E 442-14, 2F 459-4 464-2, 2G 473-9, 2H 482-14, 2I *490*-8.

9] [*engraved title*] NOVELS AND TALES | OF | THE AUTHOR OF WAVERLEY. | VOL. IX. | TALES OF MY LANDLORD. | [*vignette*] ... 1819.

Collation: A-2G[8] 2H[4] 2I 1. Pagination: [*engraved title*], i fly-title for the *Tales*, Second Series, *ii blank, iii* iv-x introduction, *11* fly-title for 'The Heart of Mid-Lothian', *12 blank, 13* 14-490 text, chapters 1-26, 490 printer's imprint. Typography: Signatures 2A-2I are recorded as Aa-Ii.

Figures: A iv-1 vi-4, B28-10 30-11, C34-10 44-11, D54-12 64-6, E68-6 74-12, F82-4 92-11, G106-10 112-4, H116-11 126-1, I 130-6 136-10, K152-12 158-11, L164-1 170-6, M178-4 192-11, N194-4, O 222-1 224-10, P230-12 232-4, Q252-6 254-10, R268-1, S286-6 288-10, T294-1 304-10, U318-6 320-10, X322-6, Y338-4 352-10, Z362-10, 2A 370-4, 2B 398-1 400-6, 2C 402-6 412-10, 2D 426-4, 2E 436-6, 2F 462-10, 2G 478-4, 2H 486-11/-, 2I—.

Notes: The use of double-letter signatures Aa, Bb, &c. would indicate that this and the tenth volume were not printed by Ballantyne, as alleged in the imprint, but by some other printer who followed this scheme, probably George Ramsay. It should also be remarked that, while the other volumes regularly exhibit only one press figure in a sheet, volumes 9-10 usually display two.

10] [*engraved title*] NOVELS AND TALES | OF | THE AUTHOR OF WAVERLEY. | VOL. X. | TALES OF MY LANDLORD. | [*vignette*] . . . . 1819.

Collation: A-2G[8] *2H*1. Pagination: [*engraved title*], 1 fly-title for the *Tales* [second series], *2 blank, 3* 4-481 text of 'The Heart of Mid-Lothian' concluded, 481 printer's imprint, *482 blank*. Typography: Signatures 2A-2G again are recorded as Aa-Gg: see note to preceding volume.

Figures: A6-6, B30-4 32-1, C44-4 47-11, D50-12 56-4, E70-6 72-1, F88-1 90-7, G108-6 110-12, H118-4 124-11, I 134-7 140-1, K150-4 160-6, L172-12, M178-7 180-6, N202-1 205-6, O 218-12 220-4, P230-1 240-10, Q250-4 252-1, R260-4 266-10, S286-10, T294-4, U306-10 320-1, X324-1 326-10, Y344-4, Z364-10, 2A 382-1, 2B 392-4, 2C 414-10, 2D 430-1, 2E 446-1, 2F 450-4, 2G 478-10, *2H*—.

11] [*engraved title*] NOVELS AND TALES | OF | THE AUTHOR OF WAVERLEY. | VOL. XI. | TALES OF MY LANDLORD. | [*vignette*] . . . . 1819.

Collation: A-2G[8] 2H[4] 2I[2]. Pagination: [*engraved title*], *1* fly-title for the *Tales*, Third Series, *2 blank, 3* 4-492 text of 'The Bride of Lammermoor', chapters 1-26, 492 printer's imprint. Typography: Pages 225-240 (sheet P) are misnumbered 255-270; page 272 is misnumbered 372.

Figures: A9-5, B20-10, C48-7, D61-13, E80-5, F92-11, G104-7, H128-7, I 141-3, K160-6, L175-9, M186-11, N208-3, O 224-8, P'261'[231]-6, Q255-3/-, R'372'[272]-8, S288-13, T299-12, U308-4, X336-8, Y352-5, Z368-6, 2A 380-13, 2B 400-11, 2C 414-10, 2D 429-11, 2E 448-11, 2F 458-5, 2G 470-2, 2H 488-11, 2I—.

12] [*engraved title*] NOVELS AND TALES | OF | THE AUTHOR OF WAVERLEY. | VOL. XII. | TALES OF MY LANDLORD. | [*vignette*] . . . 1819.

Collation: A-2K[8]. Pagination: [*engraved title*], *1* fly-title for 'The Bride of Lammermoor', *2 blank, 3* 4-102 text concluded, *103* fly-title for 'A Legend of Montrose', *104 blank, 105* 106-114 Introduction, *115* 116-505 text, *506 blank, 507* fly-title for Glossary, *508 blank, 509* 510-527 text, 527 printer's imprint, *528 blank*.

Figures: A16-7, B32-8, C44-11, D60-7, E80-3, F91-2, G99-10, H115-3, I 131-4, K160-14, L168-1, M192-11, N208-7, O 224-3, P240-3, Q256-11, R261-11, S276-3, T299-11, U307-3, X327-7, Y341-3, Z355-7, 2A 384-14/-, 2B 395-11, 2C 403-12, 2D 427-14, 2E 441-6, 2F 451-14, 2G 475-1/-, 2H 485-1, 2 I 511-14, 2K 525-4.

269Ab] First Series, First 8° Edition, Second Issue: 1822

[*engraved title*] NOVELS AND TALES | OF | THE AUTHOR OF WAVERLEY | VOL. I [II-XII]. | [*volume title*] | [*vignette*] | EDINBURGH; | PRINTED FOR ARCHIBALD CONSTABLE AND Co. EDINBURGH; | AND HURST, ROBINSON AND Co. | LONDON. | [*dash*] | 1822.

Published 2 February 1822 in Edinburgh (*EEC*); issued 18 February in London (*MC*, 'New Edition'). £7.4.0. Paper: Royal 8° (227 x 145mm uncut). Watermarks: *none.*

General Notes: A remaindered reissue of the 1819 edition with the engraved title now bearing a variant imprint and later date. The vignette in all volumes, still of Stirling Castle, is here represented as drawn by Lizars and engraved by Archibald (surnames only). Possibly some copies may exhibit (as in the next issue) an early state of the first two volumes, with titles dated 1821.

Other than titles, five sheets are reset in this later issue, as signified by variant figures in the four volumes recorded below. The several resettings, with their variant figures, recur in the legitimate second edition next described (269Ac).

Copy: ES(vols.1-5, 7-12).

1] [*engraved title*] NOVELS AND TALES . . . VOL. I. . . . 1822.

Collation: . . . 519 text, chapters 1-47, 519 printer's imprint, *520 blank.* Notes: Final sheet 2K is reset, figured 518-7, and perhaps deliberately mispaged 497-519 to 'recover' the two page numbers originally lost in the first issue. As compared with 499 first word 'accents' in the earlier issue, this '497' first word is 'known', repeating part of the final word 'well-known' on the preceding page.

5] [*engraved title*] NOVELS AND TALES . . . VOL. V. . . . 1822.

Notes: Sheet U is reset, figured 320-14, with page 316 line 10, previously reading 'Wat', now reading 'Watt'.

7] [*engraved title*] NOVELS AND TALES . . . VOL. VII. . . . 1822.

Notes: Sheets O and 2H are reset, figured 217-5, 496-9, with page 220, line 22, previously beginning 'thed', now reading 'ed', and page 484 line 3, earlier starting 'tical', now reading 'cal'.

12] [*engraved title*] NOVELS AND TALES . . . VOL. XII. . . 1822.

Notes: Sheet A is reset, figured 16-6, with page 12 first word, previously 'to', now reading 'which'.

269Ac] First Series, Second 8° Edition: 1821[1822]

[*engraved title*] NOVELS AND TALES | OF | THE AUTHOR OF WAVERLEY | VOL. I [II-XII]. | [*volume title*]. | [*vignette*] | EDINBURGH; | PRINTED FOR ARCHIBALD CONSTABLE AND Co. EDINBURGH; | AND HURST, ROBINSON AND Co. LONDON. | [*French dash*] | 1821 [*or* 1822].

Published probably 2 February 1822 (*EEC*), concurrent with the preceding issue (269Ab). £7.4.0. Binding: drab boards with printed labels. Paper: Royal 8° (224 x 144mm uncut). Watermarks: none.

General Notes: The text-copy for this paginal resetting is of the preceding 8° 1822 issue, incorporating its several variant readings. In its earliest issue (1), not further described below, the title-vignettes, all of Stirling Castle, are again reused, imprint dates reading 1821 for volumes 1-2, corrected to 1822 thereafter. In the imprint of this issue, volume 3 and subsequent volumes have the 'LONDON.' standing alone on a fourth line. Later, as described below, (2) all volumes are dated 1822 and imprint 'LONDON.' stands alone. For this second issue the plates were newly engraved with specific titles for the 'Tales' volumes and relevant vignette scenes previously illustrating the 12° 1821 edition (*see* 270Aa), all painted by A. Nasmyth and engraved by W. H. Lizars, now enlarged for this 8° format. However, since the 12° extended to sixteen volumes, four of the vignettes there appearing (in volumes 4, 6, 9, 13) are here excluded.

General Typography: As before, the concluding printer's imprint reads: [*short rule*] | EDINBURGH: | Printed by James Ballantyne & Co. ['and Co.' vols. 6-9, 11]. Nonetheless, as the press figures for volumes 10-11 would indicate, the work for this latter section appears to have been done by Walker and Greig.

Copies: (issue 1) HS(Gladstone's set, annotated) O; CtY T/B. (2) E(Scott's interleaved set, revised ca. 1828).

1] [*engraved title*] NOVELS AND TALES | OF | THE AUTHOR OF WAVERLEY | VOL. I. | WAVERLEY. | [*vignette of Craigcrook Castle*] . . . 1822.

Collation: A-2I^8 2K^4. Pagination: [*engraved title*], *i* fly-title, *ii blank, iii* iv-vi Preface to the Third Edition, *7* 8-519 text, chapters 1-47, 519 printer's imprint, *520 blank.*

Figures: A12-7, B20-9, C38-4, D50-9, E80-5, F95-3, G107-6, H122-1, I 132-9, K150-6, L162-6, M186-3, N204-6, O 220-10, P226-8, Q250-9, R270-7, S286-2, T300-9/7, U314-1, X336-4, Y349-5, Z358-2, 2A 376-6, 2B 400-5, 2C 416-8, 2D 419-10, 2E 436-9, 2F 452-6, 2G 473-7, 2H 490-3, 2 I 502-9, 2K 518-7.

Notes: In this resetting the pagination is now entirely regular and continuous, correcting both the 208 | 211 break in the 1819 original issue and the subsequent 'correction' of 499 to 497 in the 1822 reissue. As regularly ordered the last word page 496 is properly 'well-' and the first word next page is 'known', the reading in the reissue.

2] [*engraved title*] NOVELS AND TALES | OF | THE AUTHOR OF WAVERLEY | VOL. II. | WAVERLEY. | [*vignette of Holyrood Palace*] . . . . 1822.

Collation: A-2H[8] 2I[4] *2K*1. Pagination: [*engraved title*], *1* fly-title for *Waverley, 2 blank, 3* 4-263 text concluded, *264 blank, 265* fly-title for *Guy Mannering, 266 blank, 267* 268-505 text, chapters 1-21, 505 printer's imprint, *506 blank.*

Figures: A16-5, B32-12, C48-6, D64-2, E80-9, F96-13, G112-2, H128-6, I 144-9, K160-6, L176-5, M192-10, N208-3, O 224-11, P240-10, Q256-8, R272-11, S288-7, T304-13, U320-11, X326-8 336-4, Y352-3, Z368-5, 2A 384-8, 2B 400-11, 2C 416-5, 2D 432-13, 2E 448-7, 2F 464-9, 2G 480-4, 2H 496-8, 2 I 504-12, *2K*—.

Notes: In the title of the earlier '1821' issue (with vignette of Stirling Castle) both novels are listed.

3] [*engraved title*] NOVELS AND TALES | OF | THE AUTHOR OF WAVERLEY | VOL. III | GUY MANNERING | [*vignette of Caerlavroc Castle*] . . . 1822.

Collation: A-2H[8]. Pagination: [*engraved title*], *1* fly-title, *2 blank, 3* 4-495 text concluded, 495 printer's imprint, *496 blank.* Typography: First issue title has periods after the 4th and 5th lines.

Figures: A16-11, B32-11, C48-3, D64-12, E80-11, F96-5, G112-11, H128-12, I 144-14, K160-5, L176-11, M192-3, N208-15, O 224-7, P240-13, Q256-9, R272-12, S288-6, T304-13/14, U320-3, X336-10, Y352-14, Z368-8, 2A 384-2, 2B 400-13, 2C 416-14, 2D 432-11, 2E 448-3, 2F 464-14, 2G 480-15, 2H 493-7.

4] [*engraved title*] NOVELS AND TALES | OF | THE AUTHOR OF WAVERLEY | VOL. IV. | THE ANTIQUARY. | [*vignette of Dundee*] . . . 1822.

Collation: A-2G[8]. Pagination: [*engraved title*], *i* fly-title, *ii blank, iii* iv-v Advertisement, *vi blank, 7* 8-479 text, chapters 1-29, 479 printer's imprint, *480 blank.* Typography: First issue title reads only 'ANTIQUARY.' in the 5th line.

Figures: A16-11, B32-3, C48-10, D64-15, E80-11, F96-1, G112-3, H128-10, I 144-15, K160-12, L176-11, M192-7, N208-6, O 220-8, P240-7, Q256-8, R272-12, S288-2, T304-6, U320-3, X336-13, Y352-3, Z365-2, 2A 384-1, 2B 400-14, 2C 416-2, 2D 432-15, 2E 448-1, 2F 464-13, 2G 477-15.

5] [*engraved title*] NOVELS AND TALES | OF | THE AUTHOR OF WAVERLEY | VOL. V. | ROB ROY. | [*vignette of the High Church, Glasgow*] . . . . 1822.

Collation: A-2H[8]. Pagination: [*engraved title*], *1* fly-title for *The Antiquary*, *2 blank, 3* 4-253 text concluded, *254 blank, 255* fly-title for *Rob Roy*, *256 blank, 257* 258-259 Advertisement, *260 blank, 261* 262-493 text, chapters 1-13, 493 printer's imprint, *494-496 blank.*

Figures: A13-15, B32-13, C44-13, D64-3, E80-15, F96-5, G112-13, H128-6, I 132-2, K160-12, L176-13, M179-13, N208-15, O 224-13, P240-12, Q245-8, R272-2, S288-14, T304-7, U320-14, X336-15, Y352-8, Z368-1, 2A 384-2, 2B 400-1, 2C 415-11 416-12, 2D 432-15, 2E 448-7, 2F 464-15, 2G 480-8, 2H 489-15.

Notes: In the title of the earlier issue (with vignette of Stirling Castle) both novels are listed.

6] [*engraved title*] NOVELS AND TALES | OF | THE AUTHOR OF WAVERLEY | VOL. VI. | ROB ROY. | [*vignette of Inversnaid Fort*] . . . . 1822.

Collation: A-2G[8]. Pagination: [*engraved title*], *1* fly-title, *2 blank, 3* 4-477 text concluded, 477 printer's imprint, *478-480 blank.* Typography: Page number 407 is tilted.

Figures: A16-6, B32-8, C48-9, D64-3, E79-10 80-11, F96-4, G112-3, H128-12, I 144-1, K160-6, L176-8, M192-12, N208-10, O 224-3, P240-12, Q256-10, R272-9, S288-8, T304-2, U320-9, X336-3, Y352-12, Z368-13, 2A 384-4, 2B 400-15, 2C 416-6, 2D 432-15, 2E 448-14, 2F 464-1, 2G 468-15.

7] [*engraved title*] NOVELS AND TALES | OF | THE AUTHOR OF WAVERLEY | VOL. VII. | OLD MORTALITY. | [*vignette of Craignethan*] . . . . 1822.

Collation: A-2H[8] 2I[4](-2I 4). Pagination: [*engraved title*], *1* fly-title for *Tales of My Landlord,* First Series, *2 blank, 3* 4-16 Introduction, *17* fly-title for 'The Black Dwarf', *18 blank, 19* 20-260 text, *261* fly-title for 'Old Mortality', *262 blank, 263* 264-501 text, chapters 1-13, 501 printer's imprint, *502 blank.* Typography: First issue title, fifth line, reads 'TALES OF MY LANDLORD.'

Figures: A13-7, B32-11, C48-9, D64-9, E80-12, F96-1, G110-2 112-11, H128-15, I 144-2, K160-5, L176-15, M192-13, N208-5, O 217-5, P240-8, Q256-14, R272-3, S288-3, T304-15, U317-15, X336-12, Y352-13, Z368-3, 2A 384-7, 2B 400-6, 2C 416-12, 2D 432-9, 2E 448-8, 2F 464-14, 2G 480-12, 2H 496-9, 2I 499-9.

8] [*engraved title*] NOVELS AND TALES | OF | THE AUTHOR OF WAVERLEY | VOL. VIII. | OLD MORTALITY. | [*vignette of Bothwell Bridge*] . . . . 1822.

Collation: A-2G^8 2H^4 2I^2. Pagination: [*engraved title*], *1* fly-title for *Tales of My Landlord*, First Series, *2 blank, 3* 4-491 text of 'Old Mortality' concluded, 491 printer's imprint, *492 blank*. Typography: First issue title, fifth line, reads 'TALES OF MY LANDLORD.' In some copies page 459 is misnumbered 45.

Figures: A16-14, B32-8, C48-3, D64-13, E80-1, F89-11, G112-15, H128-14, I 144-13, K160-6, L175-13 176-9, M192-5, N208-15, O 224-8, P240-6, Q256-11, R272-6, S288-2, T304-11, U320-8, X336-12, Y352-14, Z368-15, 2A 384-13, 2B 400-9, 2C 416-15, 2D 432-9, 2E 444-12/-, 2F 464-13, 2G 480-2, 2H 486-14, 2I—.

9] [*engraved title*] NOVELS AND TALES | OF | THE AUTHOR OF WAVERLEY | VOL. IX. | HEART OF MID LOTHIAN. | [*vignette of Heart of Mid-Lothian*] . . . . 1822.

Collation: A-2G^8 2H^4 2I 1. Pagination: [*engraved title*], i fly-title for *Tales of My Landlord*, Second Series, *ii blank, iii* iv-x introduction, *11* fly-title for 'The Heart of Mid-Lothian', *12 blank, 13* 14-490 text, chapters 1-26, 490 printer's imprint. Typography: First issue title, fifth line, reads 'TALES OF MY LANDLORD.'
Figures: A16-7, B32-3, C48-5, D64-5, E80-9, F89-2, G112-13, H128-1, I 144-5, K160-2, L175-5 176-1, M192-2, N208-11, O 224-6, P228-8, Q256-7, R272-8, S288-14, T304-7, U320-6, X336-7/-, Y352-6, Z368-6, 2A 384-7, 2B 400-10, 2C 416-1, 2D 432-2, 2E 448-2, 2F 464-8, 2G 480-13, 2H 488-5, 2I—.

10] [*engraved title*] NOVELS AND TALES | OF | THE AUTHOR OF WAVERLEY | VOL. X. | HEART OF MID LOTHIAN. | [*vignette of St Anthony's Chapel*] . . . . 1822.

Collation: A-2G^8 *2H*1. Pagination: [*engraved title*], 1 fly-title for the *Tales*, Second Series, *2 blank, 3* 4-481 text of 'The Heart of Mid-Lothian' concluded, 481 printer's imprint, *482 blank*. Typography: First issue title, fifth line, reads 'TALES OF MY LANDLORD.' Signatures 2A-2G are recorded as Aa-Gg.

Figures: A16-23, B32-58, C47-16, D63-58, E79-23, F95-16, G112-58, H128-23, I 143-16, K159-23, L175-58, M191-16, N207-58, O 223-16, P239-58, Q255-16, R271-23, S287-58, T303-58, U319-58, X335-16, Y351-16, Z367-23, 2A 383-58, 2B 399-23, 2C 415-16, 2D 430-58, 2E 447-23, 2F 463-90, 2G 480-5, *2H*—.

Notes: Both the double signature mode and the peculiar figures (here entered usually on the inner forme) indicate that this volume, though bearing James Ballantyne's imprint on the final leaf, was in fact printed by Walker and Greig.

11] [*engraved title*] NOVELS AND TALES | OF | THE AUTHOR OF WAVERLEY | VOL. XI. | THE BRIDE OF LAMMERMOOR. | [*vignette of Crichton Castle*] . . . . 1822.

Collation: A-2G^8 2H^4 2I^2. Pagination: [*engraved title*], *1* fly-title for the *Tales*, Third Series, *2 blank, 3* 4-492 text of 'The Bride of Lammermoor', chapters 1-26, 492 printer's imprint. Typography: First issue title, fifth line, reads 'TALES OF MY LANDLORD.'

Figures: A15-16, B31-23, C47-16, D64-23, E79-16, F95-23, G112-23, H127-16, I 143-23, K159-16, L175-16, M190-23, N207-16, O 223-23, P239-16, Q255-23, R271-16, S287-23, T303-16, U319-23, X335-16/23, Y351-16, Z368-58, 2A 382-16, 2B 399-58, 2C 415-58, 2D 431-58, 2E 447-58, 2F 463-16, 2G 478-16, 2H 488-10, 2I 491-15.

Notes: Again as in the previous entry the figures show that Walker and Greig, despite the Ballantyne imprint, are responsible for this volume, though the firm is now following the 1819-1822 copy-text in signing 2A-2I in the Ballantyne manner.

12] [*engraved title*] NOVELS AND TALES | OF | THE AUTHOR OF WAVERLEY | VOL. XII. | LEGEND OF MONTROSE. | [*vignette of Old Inverary*] . . . . 1822.

Collation: A-2K^8. Pagination: [*engraved title*], *1* fly-title for the *Tales*, Third Series, *2 blank, 3* 4-102 text of 'The Bride of Lammermoor' concluded, *103* fly-title for 'A Legend of Montrose', *104 blank, 105* 106-114 Introduction, *115* 116-505 text, *506 blank, 507* fly-title for Glossary, *508 blank, 509* 510-527 text, 527 printer's imprint, *528 blank*. Typography: First issue title, fifth line, reads 'TALES OF MY LANDLORD.' Page 106 is misnumbered 06.

Figures: A16-6, B32-5, C48-15, D64-13, E80-6/8, F96-14, G112-6, H128-8, I 144-14, K160-15, L176-1, M192-6, N208-15, O 224-12, P240-8, Q256-10, R266-7 272-1, S288-15, T304-13, U320-3, X336-2, Y352-9, Z368-14, 2A 384-7, 2B 397-11, 2C 416-10, 2D 432-15, 2E 437-6, 2F 464-9, 2G 480-13, 2H 496-14, 2I 512-5, 2K 525-8.

Notes: The figures, now entered regularly in the outer forme, are recognized as those employed by the Ballantyne office.

270Aa] First Series, First 12° Edition: 1821

[*engraved title*] NOVELS AND TALES | OF | THE AUTHOR OF WAVERLEY. | VOL. I [II-XVI]. | [*reversed Oxford dash*] | [*volume title*] | [*reversed Oxford dash*] | [*vignette*] | EDINBURGH; | PRINTED FOR

ARCHIBALD CONSTABLE AND Co. EDINBURGH; | AND HURST, ROBINSON AND Co. LONDON. | [*French dash*] | 1821.

Published 31 March 1821 in Edinburgh (*EEC*). 1500 copies. Not listed apparently in London before 31 August when the *Morning Chronicle* described this issue as foolscap octavo. £6. Paper: Demy 12° (165 x 98mm cut). Watermarks: *none.*

General Notes: The title-page vignettes now are of various scenes, each painted by Nasmyth and engraved by W. H. Lizars, all advertised in 265A as also available separately in 4° (not seen) and 8° (*see* 269Ac). Concluding printer's imprints read: [*short rule*] | EDINBURGH: | Printed by James Ballantyne & Co. ['and Co.' volumes 4-8, 10-11, 13-14].

Copies: (volume 1, state 1) E L O. (2) IdU.

1] [*engraved title*] NOVELS AND TALES | OF | THE AUTHOR OF WAVERLEY. | VOL. I. | [*reversed Oxford dash*] | WAVERLEY. | [*reversed Oxford dash*] | [*vignette of Craigcrook Castle*] . . . . 1821.

Collation: A^4 $A\text{-}P^{12}$ Q^6. Pagination: [*engraved title*], *i* fly-title, *ii blank, iii* iv-vii Preface to the Third Edition, *viii blank, 1* fly-title, *2 blank, 3* 4-372 text, chapters 1-33, 372 printer's imprint. Typography: Section signatures H2 and O 2 (pages 177, 321) are missigned 2H and 2O.

Figures: A23-9, B40-2, C59-15, D86-6, E118-1, F130-9, G167-8, H189-12, I216-3, K240-2, L262-6, M280-7, N290-10, O 326-3, P346-7, Q368-9.

Notes: Sheet A, (1) originally with figure 23-9, (2) apparently because of a short count was reset and then figured 24-11, a number not employed before the third volume..

2] [*engraved title*] NOVELS AND TALES | OF | THE AUTHOR OF WAVERLEY. | VOL. II. | [*reversed Oxford dash*] | WAVERLEY. | [*reversed Oxford dash*] | [*vignette of Holyrood Palace*] . . . . 1821.

Collation: $A\text{-}Q^{12}$ R^2. Pagination: [*engraved title*], *1* fly-title, *2 blank, 3* 4-388 text concluded, 388 printer's imprint. Typography: Below the vignette the artist's name is misspelled 'Naysmith'. Section signatures A2, I 2, and N2 (pages 9, 201, 297) are respectively missigned 2A, 2I, 2N.

Figures: A15-8, B43-6, C70-5, D87-9, E98-10, F131-5, G157-4, H189-3, I 205-1, K228-7, L253-9, M279-3, N301-4, O 315-3, P349-1, Q375-6, R—.

3] [*engraved title*] NOVELS AND TALES | OF | THE AUTHOR OF WAVERLEY. | VOL. III. | [*reversed Oxford dash*] | GUY MANNERING. | [*reversed Oxford dash*] | [*vignette of Caerlavroc Castle*] . . . . 1821.

Collation: A-P^{12} Q^{4}(-Q4). Pagination: [*engraved title*], *1* fly-title, *2 blank, 3* 4-365 text, chapters 1-32, 365 printer's imprint, *366 blank*. Typography: Section signature E2 (page 105) is missigned 2E.

Figures: A23-8, B37-11, C62-10, D88-1, E108-6, F144-5, G167-10, H170-8, I 213-4, K229-9, L242-9, M280-11, N312-5, O 314-8, P358-10, Q—.

4] [*engraved title*] NOVELS AND TALES | OF | THE AUTHOR OF WAVERLEY. | VOL. IV. | [*reversed Oxford dash*] | GUY MANNERING. | [*vignette of Dunure Castle*] . . . . 1821.

Collation: A-P^{12}. Pagination: [*engraved title*], *1* fly-title, *2 blank, 3* 4-360 text concluded, 360 printer's imprint. Typography: The vignette, extending further upward then usual, eliminates the dash above it.

Figures: A24-5/11, B39-7, C62-4, D93-3, E119-7, F134-3, G163-5, H178-4, I 203-7, K229-9, L261-2, M286-7, N299-4, O 322-5, P340-2.

5] [*engraved title*] NOVELS AND TALES | OF | THE AUTHOR OF WAVERLEY. | VOL. V. | [*reversed Oxford dash*] | THE ANTIQUARY. | [*reversed Oxford dash*] | [*vignette of Dundee*] . . . . 1821.

Collation: A^{12} B^{12}(±B9) C-P^{12} Q^{2}. Pagination: [*engraved title*], *1* fly-title, *2 blank, 3* 4-5 Advertisement, *6 blank, 7* 8-363 text, chapters 1-21, 363 printer's imprint, *364 blank.*

Figures: A13-7, B36-4, C69-6, D95-5, E108-7, F123-3, G166-10, H182-7, I 202-1, K234-10, L251-2, M285-9, N299-9, O 336-6, P350-1, Q362-1.

Notes: Cancel leaf B9 has a direction line 'VOL. V.' (page 41) to guide the binder. As compared against the 8° text this cancel leaf, page 41 line 10, alters 'patrae' to 'paterae' and 42 line 6 'demon' to 'daemon'.

6] [*engraved title*] NOVELS AND TALES | OF | THE AUTHOR OF WAVERLEY. | VOL. VI. | [*reversed Oxford dash*] | THE ANTIQUARY. | [*vignette of Abbey of Aberbrothwick*] . . . . 1821.

Collation: A-P^{12} Q^{6}(-Q6). Pagination: [*engraved title*], *1* fly-title, *2 blank, 3* 4-370 text concluded, 370 printer's imprint. Typography: Again, as in volume 4, the vignette extends further upward than usual, eliminating the dash above it. Section signature D2 (page 81) is missigned 2D.

Figures: A10-10, B46-6, C72-2, D88-9, E117-4, F124(or 144)-8, G157-7, H183-9, I 209-4, K229-6, L250-7, M286-7, N290-6, O 336-5, P358-11, Q367-5.

7] [*engraved title*] NOVELS AND TALES | OF | THE AUTHOR OF WAVERLEY. | VOL. VII. | [*reversed Oxford dash*] | ROB ROY. | [*reversed Oxford dash*] | [*vignette of High Church, Glasgow*] . . . 1821.

Collation: A-O^{12} P^{12}(-P12). Pagination: [*engraved title*], *1* fly-title, *2 blank, 3* 4-5 Advertisement, *6 blank, 7* 8-357 text, chapters 1-21, 357 printer's imprint, *358 blank.*

Figures: A24-8, B46-3, C72-7, D84-1, E120-5, F123-7, G167-13, H184-9, I 195-11, K226-1/-, L253-11, M274-4, N312-6, O 334-1, P339-6/13.

8] [*engraved title*] NOVELS AND TALES | OF | THE AUTHOR OF WAVERLEY. | VOL. VIII. | [*reversed Oxford dash*] | ROB ROY. | [*reversed Oxford dash*] | [*vignette of Inversnaid Fort*] . . . . 1821.

Collation: A^{12} B^{12}(±B2) C-I^{12} K^{12}(±K11) L-O^{12} P^{12}(-P12). Pagination: [*engraved title*], *1* fly-title, *2 blank, 3* 4-357 text concluded, 357 printer's imprint, *358 blank.*

Figures: A14-2, B35-9, C59-7, D96-11, E117-8, F141-10, G168-9, H189-2, I 206-7, K238-2 240-5, L255-10, M278-9, N301-5, O 328-9, P350-6.

Notes: As compared with the 8° edition text, cancel B2 exhibits on page 27 only two trifling variants: line 16 popery] Popery; line 21 nowte] nowt. Cancel K11, revealed by an extra press-figure on page 238, discloses on page 237, line 16, a somewhat more substantive variant: than might have been expected] than I expected.

9] [*engraved title*] NOVELS AND TALES | OF | THE AUTHOR OF WAVERLEY. | VOL. IX. | [*reversed Oxford dash*] | BLACK DWARF. | [*reversed Oxford dash*] | [*vignette of Canny Elshie's Cottage*] . . . . 1821.

Collation: π1 A-P^{12} Q^{6}(-Q6). Pagination: [*engraved title*], *i* dedication, *ii blank, 1* fly-title for *Tales of My Landlord*, First Series, *2* quotation, *3* 4-16 Introduction, *17* fly-title for 'The Black Dwarf', *18 blank, 19* 20-253 text, *254 blank, 255* fly-title for 'Old Mortality', *256 blank, 257* 258-369 text, chapters 1-7, 369 printer's imprint, *370 blank.*

Figures: A22-7, B48-11, C69-10, D87-9, E100-6, F133-8, G168-10, H176-7, I 216-10, K232-6, L263-10, M279-6, N312-5, O 325-3, P339-4, Q366-7.

10] [*engraved title*] NOVELS AND TALES | OF | THE AUTHOR OF WAVERLEY. | VOL. X. | [*reversed Oxford dash*] | OLD MORTALITY. | [*reversed Oxford dash*] | [*vignette of Craignethan*] . . . . 1821.

Collation: A-P^{12} Q^{6} *R*1. Pagination: [*engraved title*], *1* fly-title for *Tales of My Landlord.* First Series, *2* quotation, *3* section title for 'Old Mortality', *4 blank, 5*

6-373 text continued, *374* printer's imprint. Typography: In some copies page 362 is misnumbered 62.

Figures: A15-5, B35-5, C64-9, D87-6, E120-8, F—, G156-5, H190-6, I 213-5, K—, L264-9, M279-10, N296-7, O 324-8, P349-5, Q366-10, *R*—.

11] [*engraved title*] NOVELS AND TALES | OF | THE AUTHOR OF WAVERLEY. | VOL. XI. | [*reversed Oxford dash*] | OLD MORTALITY. | [*reversed Oxford dash*] | [*vignette of Bothwell Bridge*] . . . . 1821.

Collation: A-P[12] Q[8] R1. Pagination: [*engraved title*], *1* fly-title for *Tales of My Landlord*, First Series, *2* quotation, *3* section title for 'Old Mortality', *4 blank, 5* 6-244 text concluded, *245*-246 Peroration, *247* fly-title for *Tales of My Landlord*, Second Series. The Heart of Midlothian, *248 blank, 249* 250-378 text, chapters 1-7, 378 printer's imprint. Typography: Section signatures G2, L2, and N2 (pages 153, *249*, 297) are missigned 2G, 2L, 2N.

Figures: A11-13, B36-4, C64-5, D94-8, E113-7, F142-5, G166-13, H181-3, I 213-10, K240-2, L261-7, M287-9, N291-4, O 315-10, P350-5, Q372-8, R377-7.

12] [*engraved title*] NOVELS AND TALES | OF | THE AUTHOR OF WAVERLEY. | VOL. XII. | [*reversed Oxford dash*] | HEART OF MID-LOTHIAN. | [*reversed Oxford dash*] | [*vignette of the Heart of Mid-Lothian*] . . . . 1821.

Collation: A-P[12] Q[2]. Pagination: [*engraved title*], *1* fly-title for *Tales of My Landlord*, Second Series, *2* quotation, *3* section title for 'The Heart of Mid-Lothian', *4 blank, 5* 6-363 text continued, 363 printer's imprint, *364 blank.*

Figures: A23-10, B40-7, C63-1, D96-13, E111-3, F133-3, G157-5 167-3, H192-3, I 203-7, K231-9, L256-9, M287-9, N301-5, O 336-10, P359-9, Q362-4.

13] [*engraved title*] NOVELS AND TALES | OF | THE AUTHOR OF WAVERLEY. | VOL. XIII. | [*reversed Oxford dash*] | HEART OF MID-LOTHIAN. | [*reversed Oxford dash*] | [*vignette of Grass Market, Edinburgh*] . . . . 1821.

Collation: A-P[12] Q[6] R1. Pagination: [*engraved title*], *1* fly-title for *Tales of My Landlord.* Second Series, *2* quotation, *3* section title for 'The Heart of MidLothian', *4 blank, 5* 6-374 text continued, 374 printer's imprint. Typography: Section signature O 2 (page 321) is missigned 2 O.

Figures: A24-4, B35-7, C58-7, D86-10, E111-3, F133-10, G159-7, H176-9, I 216-2, K228-3, L251-10, M—, N312-2, O 335-10, P346-8, Q367-1, R—.

14] [*engraved title*] NOVELS AND TALES | OF | THE AUTHOR OF WAVERLEY. | VOL. XIV. | [*reversed Oxford dash*] | HEART OF MID-

LOTHIAN. | [*reversed Oxford dash*] | [*vignette of St Anthony's Chapel*] .... 1821.

Collation: A-P[12] Q[6] *R*1. Pagination: [*engraved title*], *1* fly-title for *Tales of My Landlord.* Second Series, *2* quotation, *3* section title for 'The Heart of Mid-Lothian', *4 blank, 5* 6-112 text concluded, *113* fly-title for *Tales of My Landlord.* Third Series. 'The Bride of Lammermoor', *114 blank, 115* 116-373 text, chapters 1-15, 373 printer's imprint, *374 blank.*

Figures: A10-1, B28-7, C71-2, D84-10, E99-10, F133-4, G160-2, H190-9, I 195-6, K219-2, L256-8, M288-9, N292-5, O 333-9, P360-2, Q366-6, *R*—.

15] [*engraved title*] NOVELS AND TALES | OF | THE AUTHOR OF WAVERLEY. | VOL. XV. | [*reversed Oxford dash*] | BRIDE OF LAM MERMUIR. | [*reversed Oxford dash*] | [*vignette of Crichton Castle*] .... 1821.

Collation: A-P[12] Q[6]. Pagination: [*engraved title*], *1* fly-title for *Tales of My Landlord.* Third Series, *2* quotation, *3* section title for 'The Bride of Lammermoor', *4 blank, 5* 6-301 text concluded, *302 blank, 303* fly-title for 'A Legend of Montrose', *304 blank, 305* 306-371 text, chapters 1-4, 371 printer's imprint, *372 blank.* Typography: The headline on page 307 is loose, reading: AL EGEND [*or* AL E GEND] OF MONTROSE.

Figures: A14-9, B37-8, C69-8, D82-6, E99-9, F142-6, G160-5, H189-7 190-12, I 195-4, K240-9, L253-12, M266-4, N311-7, O 333-5, P350-14, Q367-12.

Notes: Though Scott preferred an Anglicized spelling for his title, the title engraver reverts to the Scottish orthography: 'Lammermuir'.

16] [*engraved title*] NOVELS AND TALES | OF | THE AUTHOR OF WAVERLEY. | VOL.XVI. | [*reversed Oxford dash*] | MONTROSE. | [*reversed Oxford dash*] | [*vignette of Old Inverary*] .... 1821.

Collation: A-O[12] P1. Pagination: [*engraved title*], *1* fly-title for *Tales of My Landlord.* Third Series, *2* quotation, *3* section title for 'A Legend of Montrose', *4 blank, 5* 6-315 text concluded, *316 blank, 317* fly-title for Glossary, *318 blank, 319* 320-338 text, 338 printer's imprint. Typography: Section signature G2 (page 153) is omitted.

Figures: A23-3, B37-12, C58-1, D94-2, E109-5, F132-5, G160-11, H182-6, I 214-10, K239-6, L244-1, M274-11, N312-1, O 335-10, P—.

270Ab] First Series, Second 12° Edition: 1825

[*engraved title*] NOVELS AND TALES | OF | THE AUTHOR OF

WAVERLEY. | VOL. I [II-XVI]. | [*reversed Oxford dash*] | [*volume title*] | [*reversed Oxford dash*] | [*vignette*] | EDINBURGH; | PRINTED FOR ARCHIBALD CONSTABLE AND Co. EDINBURGH; | AND HURST, ROBINSON AND Co. LONDON. | [*French dash*] | 1825.

Paper: Demy 12° (165 x 99mm cut). Watermarks: *none.*

General Notes: Title-pages, including vignettes, are reprints of the 1821 12° edition, with the dates changed to 1825. Collation and pagination are also identical with the preceding edition but, as noted below, certain other points appear and, for a resetting, the press-figures differ throughout. Concluding printer's imprints read: [*short rule*] | EDINBURGH: | Printed by James Ballantyne & Co. ['and Co.' vols. 4, 6-8, 10-11].

Copies: E(vols. 2-16); NNU-W(vols.3-4) T/B*.
*Extra-illustrated with Tilt's 'Landscape Illustrations' (1830-1831) and 'Female Characters' (1832-1833): *see* 342D.

1] [*engraved title*] NOVELS AND TALES | OF | THE AUTHOR OF WAVERLEY. | VOL. I. | [*reversed Oxford dash*] | WAVERLEY. | [*reversed Oxford dash*] | [*vignette of Craigcrook Castle*] . . . . 1825.

Collation: a^4 A-P^{12} Q^6. Pagination: [*engraved title*], *i* fly-title, *ii blank, iii* iv-vii Preface to the Third Edition, *viii blank, 1* fly-title, *2 blank, 3* 4-372 text, chapters 1-33, 372 printer's imprint. Typography: Page 175 is misnumbered 157.

Figures: a—, A24-11, B48-11, C72-11, D96-9, E120-9, F144-15, G168-15, H192-11, I 216-12, K240-2, L264-17, M—, N—, O 336-6, P360-11, Q371-15.

2] [*engraved title*] NOVELS AND TALES | OF | THE AUTHOR OF WAVERLEY. | VOL. II. | [*reversed Oxford dash*] | WAVERLEY. | [*reversed Oxford dash*] | [*vignette of Holyrood Palace*] . . . . 1825.

Collation: A-Q^{12} R^2. Pagination: [*engraved title*], *1* fly-title, *2 blank, 3* 4-388 text concluded, 388 printer's imprint.

Typography: Page 225 omits section signature K2 but oddly bears a direction line 'VOL. II.' indicating a cancel. This appears not to be the case, and the text is identical with that for the 8° edition.

Figures: A24-4, B48-12, C72-16, D96-15, E120-16, F144-6, G168-2, H192-12, I 216-10, K240-10, L264-17/-, M288-12, N312-8, O 322-10, P360-8, Q384-15, R—.

3] [*engraved title*] NOVELS AND TALES | OF | THE AUTHOR OF WAVERLEY. | VOL. III. | [*reversed Oxford dash*] | GUY MANNERING. | [*reversed Oxford dash*] | [*vignette of Caerlavroc Castle*] . . . . 1825.

Collation: A-P[12] Q[4](-Q4). Pagination: [*engraved title*], *1* fly-title, *2 blank, 3* 4-365 text, chapters 1-32, 365 printer's imprint, *366 blank*. Typography: In some copies page 335 is unnumbered.

Figures: A24-17, B48-17, C72-14/4, D96-3, E120-15, F144-11, G168-15, H192-9, I 216-15, K240-16, L264-2, M288-15, N312-12, O 336-3, P360-7, Q363-17/-.

4] [*engraved title*] NOVELS AND TALES | OF | THE AUTHOR OF WAVERLEY. | VOL. IV. | [*reversed Oxford dash*] | GUY MANNERING. | [*reversed Oxford dash*] | [*vignette of Dunure Castle*] . . . . 1825.

Collation: A-P[12]. Pagination: [*engraved title*], *1* fly-title, *2 blank, 3* 4-360 text concluded, 360 printer's imprint.

Figures: A24-11, B48-15, C72-17, D96-2, E120-9, F144-9, G168-15, H192-3, I 216-15, K240-10, L264-15, M288-9, N312-6, O 336-5, P357-15.

5] [*engraved title*] NOVELS AND TALES | OF | THE AUTHOR OF WAVERLEY. | VOL. V. | [*reversed Oxford dash*] | THE ANTIQUARY. | [*reversed Oxford dash*] | [*vignette of Dundee*] . . . . 1825.

Collation: A-P[12] Q[2]. Pagination: [*engraved title*], *1* fly-title, *2 blank, 3* 4-5 Advertisement, *6 blank, 7* 8-363 text, chapters 1-21, 363 printer's imprint, *364 blank*.

Figures: A24-15, B48-8, C72-9, D96-12, E120-2, F144-12, G168-15, H192-13, I 216-17, K240-8, L264-4, M288-13, N312-9, O 336-6, P360-8, Q—.

6] [*engraved title*] NOVELS AND TALES | OF | THE AUTHOR OF WAVERLEY. | VOL. VI. | [*reversed Oxford dash*] | THE ANTIQUARY. | [*reversed Oxford dash*] | [*vignette of Abbey of Aberbrothwick*] . . . . 1825.

Collation: A-P[12] Q[6](-Q6). Pagination: [*engraved title*], *1* fly-title, *2 blank, 3* 4-370 text concluded, 370 printer's imprint.

Figures: A24-9, B48-17, C72-11, D96-13, E120-10, F136-1/-, G165-12, H192-10, I 216-8, K240-4, L264-15, M288-8, N312-13, O 336-9, P360-6, Q368-11.

7] [*engraved title*] NOVELS AND TALES | OF | THE AUTHOR OF WAVERLEY. | VOL. VII. | [*reversed Oxford dash*] | ROB ROY. | [*reversed Oxford dash*] | [*vignette of the High Church, Glasgow*] . . . . 1825.

Collation: A-O[12] P[12](-P12). Pagination: [*engraved title*], *1* fly-title, *2 blank, 3* 4-5 Advertisement, *6 blank, 7* 8-357 text, chapters 1-21, 357 printer's imprint, *358 blank*. Typography: Page 240 is misnumbered 204.

Figures: A24-11, B48-12, C72-9, D96-9, E120-17, F144-9, G168-10, H192-11, I

216-15, K '204'[240]-1, L264-3, M288-8, N312-5, O 336-7, P352-9.

8] [*engraved title*] NOVELS AND TALES | OF | THE AUTHOR OF WAVERLEY. | VOL. VIII. | [*reversed Oxford dash*] | ROB ROY. | [*reversed Oxford dash*] | [*vignette of Inversnaid Fort*] . . . . 1825.

Collation: A-O^{12} P^{12}(-P12). Pagination: [*engraved title*], *1* fly-title, *2 blank, 3* 4-357 text concluded, 357 printer's imprint, *358 blank.*

Figures: A24-1, B—, C72-12, D96-9, E120-4, F144-9, G168-17, H192-10, I216-15, K240-9, L264-13, M288-10, N312-2, O 336-9, P340-9.

9] [*engraved title*] NOVELS AND TALES | OF | THE AUTHOR OF WAVERLEY. | VOL. IX. | [*reversed Oxford dash*] | BLACK DWARF. | [*reversed Oxford dash*] | [*vignette of Canny Elshie's Cottage*] . . . . 1825.

Collation: π1 A-P^{12} Q^{6}(-Q6). Pagination: [*engraved title*], *i* dedication, *ii blank, 1* fly-title for *Tales of My Landlord*, First Series, *2* quotation, *3* 4-16 Introduction, *17* fly-title for 'The Black Dwarf', *18 blank, 19* 20-253 text, *254 blank, 255* fly-title for 'Old Mortality', *256 blank, 257* 258-369 text, chapters 1-7, 369 printer's imprint, *370 blank.*

Figures: A24-13, B48-17, C72-10, D96-9, E120-11, F144-10, G168-12, H192-8, I 216-12, K240-11, L264-7, M275-13, N309-17, O 336-11, P360-15, Q366-12.

10] [*engraved title*] NOVELS AND TALES | OF | THE AUTHOR OF WAVERLEY. | VOL. X. | [*reversed Oxford dash*] | OLD MORTALITY. | [*reversed Oxford dash*] | [*vignette of Craignethan*] . . . . 1825.

Collation: A-P^{12} Q^{6} *R*1. Pagination: [*engraved title*], *1* fly-title for *Tales of My Landlord*, First Series, *2* quotation, *3* section title for 'Old Mortality', *4 blank, 5* 6-373 text continued, 374 printer's imprint.

Figures: A24-13, B48-8, C72-13, D96-9, E120-12, F144-11, G168-12, H192-17, I 216-2, K240-10, L264-15, M288-12, N312-17, O 336-3, P360-13, Q372-6, *R*—.

11] [*engraved title*] NOVELS AND TALES | OF | THE AUTHOR OF WAVERLEY. | VOL. XI. | [*reversed Oxford dash*] | OLD MORTALITY. | [*reversed Oxford dash*] | [*vignette of Bothwell Bridge*] . . . . 1825.

Collation: A-P^{12} Q^{8} R1. Pagination: [*engraved title*], *1* fly-title for *Tales of My Landlord*, First Series, *2* quotation, *3* section title for 'Old Mortality', *4 blank, 5* 6-244 text concluded, *245*-246 Peroration, *247* fly-title for *Tales of My Landlord*, Second Series, *248 blank, 249* 250-378 text of 'The Heart of Mid-Lothian', chapters 1-7, 378 printer's imprint. Typography: In some copies the final digit in page number

264 is battered.

Figures: A24-10, B48-15, C72-8, D94-15, E120-6, F144-1, G168-17, H192-11, I 216-10, K240-12, L264-15, M288-11, N312-6, O 336-5, P357-4, Q376-12, R—.

12] [*engraved title*] NOVELS AND TALES | OF | THE AUTHOR OF WAVERLEY. | VOL. XII. | [*reversed Oxford dash*] | HEART OF MID-LOTHIAN. | [*reversed Oxford dash*] | [*vignette of the Heart of Mid-Lothian*] . . . 1825.

Collation: A-P[12] Q[2]. Pagination: [*engraved title*], *1* fly-title for *Tales of My Landlord*, Second Series, *2* quotation, *3* section title for 'The Heart of Mid-Lothian', *4 blank*, *5* 6-363 text continued, 363 printer's imprint, *364 blank*.

Figures: A24-11, B45-12, C63-10, D96-2, E120-7, F144-4, G168-8, H192-2, I 203-7 (or 216-2), K240-8, L264-8, M286-15, N312-3, O 336-1, P360-12, Q362-6.

13] [*engraved title*] NOVELS AND TALES | OF | THE AUTHOR OF WAVERLEY. | VOL. XIII. | [*reversed Oxford dash*] | HEART OF MID-LOTHIAN. | [*reversed Oxford dash*] | [*vignette of Grass Market, Edinburgh*] . . . . 1825.

Collation: A-P[12] Q[6] R1. Pagination: [*engraved title*], *1* fly-title for *Tales of My Landlord*. Second Series, *2* quotation, *3* section title for 'The Heart of Mid-Lothian', *4 blank*, *5* 6-374 text continued, 374 printer's imprint.

Figures: A24-15/5, B48-5, C72-8, D96-15, E120-9, F144-13, G168-12, H192-2, I 213-5, K240-15, L264-13, M288-9/-, N312-10, O 336-6, P360-7, Q372-6, R—.

14] [*engraved title*] NOVELS AND TALES | OF | THE AUTHOR OF WAVERLEY. | VOL. XIV. | [*reversed Oxford dash*] | HEART OF MID-LOTHIAN. | [*reversed Oxford dash*] | [*vignette of St Anthony's Chapel*] . . . . 1825.

Collation: A-P[12] Q[6] *R*1. Pagination: [*engraved title*], *1* fly-title for *Tales of My Landlord*. Second Series, *2* quotation, *3* section title for 'The Heart of Mid-Lothian', *4 blank*, *5* 6-112 text concluded, *113* fly-title for *Tales of My Landlord*. Third Series, *114 blank*, *115* 116-373 text of 'The Bride of Lammermoor', chapters 1-15, 373 printer's imprint, *374 blank*.

Figures: A24-5, B48-12, C72-8, D96-11, E120-3, F144-15, G168-7, H192-8, I 216-2, K240-10, L264-9, M288-10, N312-11, O—, P360-5, Q372-7, *R*—.

15] [*engraved title*] NOVELS AND TALES | OF | THE AUTHOR OF

WAVERLEY. | VOL. XV. | [*reversed Oxford dash*] | BRIDE OF LAMMERMUIR. | [*reversed Oxford dash*] | [*vignette of Crichton Castle*] . . . . 1825.

Collation: A-P^{12} Q^{6}. Pagination: [*engraved title*], *1* fly-title for *Tales of My Landlord.* Third Series, *2* quotation, *3* section title for 'The Bride of Lammermoor', *4 blank, 5* 6-301 text concluded, *302 blank, 303* fly-title for 'A Legend of Montrose', *304 blank, 305* 306-371 text, chapters 1-4, 371 printer's imprint, *372 blank.* Typography: As before, the engraver for the title uses the Scottish spelling 'Lammermuir'. In some copies page 25 is misnumbered 52.

Figures: A24-7, B40-14, C72-17, D96-13, E120-10, F144-7, G168-7, H192-4, I 216-11, K240-12, L264-6, M288-12, N309-5, O 336-13, P360-13, Q362-13.

16] [*engraved title*] NOVELS AND TALES | OF | THE AUTHOR OF WAVERLEY. | VOL. XVI. | [*reversed Oxford dash*] | MONTROSE. | [*reversed Oxford dash*] | [*vignette of Old Inverary*] . . . . 1825.

Collation: A-O^{12} P1. Pagination: [*engraved title*], *1* fly-title for *Tales of My Landlord.* Third Series, *2* quotation, *3* section title for 'A Legend of Montrose', *4 blank, 5* 6-315 text concluded, *316 blank, 317* fly-title for Glossary, *318 blank, 319* 320-338 text, 338 printer's imprint.

Figures: A24-13, B48-6, C64-13, D96-10, E—, F144-9, G168-1, H192-6, I 213-9, K240-10, L264-2, M288-9, N312-13, O 336-11, P—.

271A] First Series, 18° Edition: 1823

[*engraved title*] NOVELS AND TALES | OF | THE AUTHOR OF WAVERLEY. | IN TWELVE VOLUMES. | VOL. I [II-XII]. | [*volume title.*] | [*vignette*] | EDINBURGH; | PRINTED FOR ARCHIBALD CONSTABLE & Co. EDINBURGH; | AND HURST, ROBINSON, & Co. LONDON. | 1823.

Published 11 September 1823 in London (*MC*); issued 20 September in Edinburgh (*EEC*: described as a 'Miniature Edition'). £4.4.0. 5000 copies ordered by Hurst, Robinson were dispatched to London in several consignments, the last on 5 September (*EEWN3*.377) . Paper: Demy 18° (156 x 93mm uncut). Watermarks: *none*.

General Notes: The earlier London publcation date would indicate that Hurst, Robinson received all of the earlier printing, with Constable nine days later then announcing the availability of some minimal number later produced. On several occasions in 1822 Scott indicated that he was revising the proofs of this attractive 'miniature edition' and would continue to do so (*Letters* vii.170, 245), but the several editors of *EEWN* thus far have found relatively few revisions and the copy-text later used by Scott for his Magnum Opus was the 1821-1822 8° (269Ac[2]).

The 18° engraved title vignettes essentially are identical with those used for the preceding 1821 12° series, but the present versions—previously identified as painted by Nasmyth and engraved by W. H. Lizars—are now listed only as 'Engraved by Chas. Heath'. Since this 1823 series, in a smaller 'compressed' format, extends only to twelve volumes, four of the vignettes earlier employed in the sixteen-volume sequence (4, 7, 9, 13) are excluded here. (The 1822 8° edition earlier described 269Ac omits 4, 6, 9, 13.) The twelve frontispieces, first appearing in this 18° format, are all drawn by C. R. Leslie, engraved by the artists identified below, and carry the Hurst, Robinson imprint dated 1823.

For this 18° imposition, in alternating 12 and 6 leaf gatherings, numbers are entered on the first page of the full sheet, that is, 2 for C-D, 3 for E-F, &c., and no more than two press-figures thus are entered for any full sheet. In the following collations this regular alternation is indicated by ellipses marks. Concluding printer's imprint reads: [*short rule*] | EDINBURGH: | Printed by James Ballantyne & Co. ['and Co.' vol.2]

Copies: E L L* O; CtY MH(vols.1-8,11-12) T/B(vols.1-8,10-12) TxU(vols. 4,5, 8,11,12).
* MS notes by S. T. Coleridge: see further note to vol 5.

1] [*engraved title*] NOVELS AND TALES | OF | THE AUTHOR OF WAVERLEY. . . . VOL. I. | WAVERLEY. | [*vignette of Craigcrook Castle*]. . . . 1823.

Collation: A^{12} B^{6} . . . T^{12} U^{6} X^{10}. Pagination: [*engraved title*], *i* fly-title, *ii blank, iii* iv-vi Preface to the Third Edition, *7* 8-379 text, chapters 1-47, *380* printer's imprint. Illustrations: Frontispiece engraved by Chas. Heath, with caption 'Waverley.' and inscription 'Flora in the Glen of Glennaquoich.' Typography: Sheet number 1 (page *i*) is entered, unusually, but sheet numbers 4, 5, and 11 (pages 109, 145, 361) are omitted.

Figures: B35-10 36-7; C52-10, D68-6; E75-6 96-7; G122-6 132-18; H168-6, K179-10; L204-18, M215-4; N240-18, O 242-7; P273-6, Q278-10/-; R301-7 302-6; T348-10, U359-6; X362-4. In some copies the figure on page 204 is starred, perhaps indicating a further impression of this L-M forme.

2] [*engraved title*] NOVELS AND TALES | OF | THE AUTHOR OF WAVERLEY. VOL. II. | WAVERLEY, AND | GUY MANNERING. | [*vignette of Holyrood Palace*] . . . . 1823.

Collation: A^{12} B^{6} . . . T^{12} U^{6} X^{6}. Pagination: [*engraved title*], *i* fly-title for *Waverley*,

2 blank, 3 4-194 text concluded, *195* fly-title for *Guy Mannering*, *196 blank, 197* 198-372 text, chapters 1-21, 372 printer's imprint. Illustrations: Frontispiece engraved by Jas. Mitchell, with caption 'Waverley.' and inscription 'Mac-Ivor warned of his fate by The Grey Spirit.' Typography: Sheet-number 9 (page 289) is omitted.

Figures: A23-4 24-1/-; C40-1 59-3; E94-6 96-10; G118-7, H144-9; I 151-11 168-3; L204-6, M215-11; O 242-4 246-5; P254-1 288-2; R298-11, S324-2; T327-6 337-1; X366-5.

3] [*engraved title*] NOVELS AND TALES | OF | THE AUTHOR OF WAVERLEY. . . . VOL. III. | GUY MANNERING. | [*vignette of Caerlavroc Castle*] . . . 1823.

Collation: A^{12} B^{6} . . . T^{12} U^{6} X^{2}. Pagination: [*engraved title*], *1* fly-title, *2 blank, 3* 4-364 text concluded, 364 printer's imprint. Illustrations: Frontispiece engraved by J. Romney, with caption 'Guy Mannering.' and inscription 'Meg Merrilies compelling Dominie Sampson to eat.'

Figures: A23-6, B36-11; C49-2, D71-7; E75-3 76-4; H134-5 138-12; I 148-6, K176-7; L183-7, M216-4; O 248-2 252-5; Q283-6 284-1; R300-4, S320-5; T327-5, U354-6, X—.

Notes: Final gathering X^{2} is in a duplicate setting, either with or without sheet-number 11 on page 361.

4] [*engraved title*] NOVELS AND TALES | OF | THE AUTHOR OF WAVERLEY, . . . VOL. IV. | THE ANTIQUARY. | [*vignette of Dundee*] . . . 1823.

Collation: A^{12} B^{6} . . . T^{12} U^{6}(-U6). Pagination: [*engraved title*], *i* fly-title, *ii blank, iii*-iv Advertisement, *5* 6-358 text, chapters 1-29, 358 printer's imprint. Illustrations: Frontispiece engraved by E. Portbury, with caption 'The Antiquary.' and inscription 'The Antiquary incensed at the intrusion on his Sanctum Sanctorum.' Typography: Signature D (page 61) is missigned C. Section signature N2 (page 225) retains only the 2 in some copies and is omitted in others, apparently the result of a loose forme.

Figures: B30-5 35-1; C40-5 50-3; E86-4, F108-5; G111-6 120-2; K175-5 176-18; M206-4 211-3; O 248-4 252-5; P274-11, Q282-6; R291-3 312-5; T326-3, U354-1.

5] [*engraved title*] NOVELS AND TALES | OF | THE AUTHOR OF WAVERLEY. . . . VOL. V. | THE ANTIQUARY, AND | ROB ROY. | [*vignette of Abbey of Aberbrothwick*] . . . . 1823.

Collation: A^{12} B^{6} . . . T^{12} U^{6} X^{4}. Pagination: [*engraved title*], *1* fly-title for *The*

Antiquary, *2 blank, 3* 4-189 text concluded, *190 blank, 191* fly-title for *Rob Roy, 192 blank, 193* 194-195 Advertisement, *196 blank, 197* 198-368 text, chapters 1-13, 368 printer's imprint. Illustrations: Frontispiece engraved by C. Rolls, with caption 'The Antiquary.' and inscription 'Dousterswivel digging for treasure in Misticot's grave.' Typography: Section signature L2 (page 189) is missigned 2L. Sheet-number 11 (page 361) is omitted.

Figures: A13(or 36)-2 22-11; C38-11, D72-17; E107-17 108-12; G123-11/- 132-6; I 154-1 168-3; L182-17, M210-4; N240-3 O 251-2; Q278-3 282-6; S314-5 324-4; T339-5, U354-1; X—.

Notes: Coleridge, on receiving his volumes of this set, was chagrined to see that his friend Leslie had caricatured him in the drawing of Dousterswivel.

6] [*engraved title*] NOVELS AND TALES | OF | THE AUTHOR OF WAVERLEY. . . . VOL. VI. | ROB ROY. | [*vignette of Inversnaid Fort*] . . . . 1823.

Collation: A^{12} B^{6} . . . T^{12} U^{6}. Pagination: [*engraved title*], *1* fly-title, *2 blank, 3* 4-358 text concluded, 358 printer's imprint, *359-360 blank*. Illustrations: Frontispiece engraved by Chas. Heath, with caption 'Rob Roy.' and inscription 'Francis Osbaldistone & Diana Vernon in the library.' Typography: Sheet 7 (page 217) is misnumbered 4.

Figures: A24-6/-, B26-4; C39-3 40-2; E85-1, F104-4; H140-2 144-6; I 168-1, K170-3; L195-5 196-4; O 247-1 248-4; P267-5, Q282-6; S314-5/- 324-2; T340-1, U356-2.

7] [*engraved title*] NOVELS AND TALES | OF | THE AUTHOR OF WAVERLEY. . . . VOL. VII. | BLACK DWARF, & | OLD MORTALITY. | [*vignette of Craignethan*] . . . . 1823.

Collation: A^{12} B^{6} . . . T^{12} U^{6} X^{8}(-X8). Pagination: [*engraved title*], *1* fly-title for *Tales of My Landlord*. First Series, *2* quotation, *3* 4-13 Introduction, *14 blank, 15* fly-title for 'The Black Dwarf', *16 blank, 17* 18-193 text, *194 blank, 195* fly-title for 'Old Mortality', *196 blank, 197* 198-373 text, chapters 1-13, *374* printer's imprint. Illustrations: Frontispiece engraved by C. Rolls with caption 'The Black Dwarf.' and inscription 'The Black Dwarf in a frenzy of grief upon beholding the tomb of his affianced bride.' Typography: In some copies sheet-number 11 (page 361) is omitted and page 314 is misnumbered 431.

Figures: B26-5 36-6; C59-2 60-3; E74-5 96-6; G131-5 132-6; I 146-2 157-7; L182-5 204-1; N237-7, O 248-2; P256-6, Q284-2; R312-3, S323-1; U356-6 360-7; X372-5.

Notes: 'To His Loving Countrymen', the separately printed dedication leaf, usually omitted in this volume, when present may be inserted before or after the first fly-title.

8] [*engraved title*] NOVELS AND TALES | OF | THE AUTHOR OF WAVERLEY. . . . VOL. VIII. | OLD MORTALITY. | [*vignette of Bothwell Bridge*] . . . . 1823.

Collation: A^{12} B^{6} . . . T^{12} U^{6} X^{2}. Pagination: [*engraved title*], *1* fly-title for *Tales of My Landlord*. First Series, *2* quotation, *3* 4-364 text for 'Old Mortality' concluded, 364 printer's imprint. Illustrations: Frontispiece engraved by J. Romney, with caption 'Old Mortality.' and inscription 'King Charles the Second saluting Lady Bellenden.' Typography: In some copies sheet number 11 (page 361) is misnumbered 8.

Figures: B30-7 32-4; C60-6, D62-5; E94-3, F108-4; G123-2 129-5; I 166-7, K180-6; L183-2, M210-3; O 251-1 252-6; P276-7, Q278-2; S320-4 324-5; U359-7 360-6, X—.

9] [*engraved title*] NOVELS AND TALES | OF | THE AUTHOR OF WAVERLEY. . . . VOL. IX. | THE HEART OF MID-LOTHIAN. | [*vignette of the Heart of Mid-Lothian*] . . . . 1823.

Collation: A^{12} B^{6} . . . T^{12} U^{6} X^{4}. Pagination: [*engraved title*], *i* fly-title for *Tales of My Landlord*. Second Series, *ii* quotation, *iii* iv-viii introduction, *9* fly-title for 'The Heart of Mid-Lothian', *10 blank, 11* 12-367 text, chapters 1-26, 367 printer's imprint, *368 blank*. Illustrations: Frontispiece engraved by C. Rolls, with caption 'The Heart of Mid-Lothian.' and inscription 'The affecting scene between Effie Deans and her Sister in the Tolbooth.' Typography: Section signature B2 (page 29) is omitted and G2 (page 117) is signed H2. Sheet number 11 (page 361) is omitted.

Figures: B29-3 36-5; C59-7, D72-8; F98-5 108-2/-; H134-5 144-6; I 147-1, K180-3; L204-8, M212-4; N218-2 220-3; P255-7 273-5; R298-4 312-2; T345-1, U356-5; X365-8, 366-1.

10] [*engraved title*] NOVELS AND TALES | OF | THE AUTHOR OF WAVERLEY. . . . VOL. X. | THE HEART OF MID-LOTHIAN. | [*vignette of St Anthony's Chapel*] . . . . 1823.

Collation: A^{12} B^{6} . . . T^{12} U^{6}. Pagination: [*engraved title*], *1* fly-title for *Tales of My Landlord*. Second Series, *2* quotation, *3* 4-358 text of 'The Heart of Mid-Lothian' concluded, 358 printer's imprint, *359-360 blank*. Illustrations: Frontispiece engraved by Chas. Heath, with caption 'The Heart of Mid-Lothian.' and inscription 'The interview of Jeanie Deans with the Queen.' Typography: Sheet number 9 (page 289) is omitted.

Figures: A4-7, B32-6; C60-1, D71-2; E88-7, F98-4; G132-3, H143-2; I 167-6 168-8; L204-3, M212-1; N239-5, O 246-6; P267-7 276-4; R292-5, S314-3; T327-6 328-2, U—.

11] [*engraved title*] NOVELS AND TALES | OF | THE AUTHOR OF WAVERLEY. . . . VOL. XI. | THE BRIDE OF LAMMERMOOR. | [*vignette of Crichton Castle*] . . . . 1823.

Collation: A[12] B[6] . . . T[12] *U*1. Pagination: [*engraved title*], *1* fly-title for *Tales of My Landlord.* Third Series, *2* quotation, *3* 4-349 text for 'The Bride of Lammermoor', chapters 1-27, 349 printer's imprint, *350 blank.* Illustrations: Frontispiece engraved by Chas. Heath, with caption 'The Bride of Lammermoor.' and inscription 'The ominous incident at the Mermaiden's Fountain.' Typography: Signature S (page 313) is omitted.

Figures: A22-5 24-3; C39-4 60-2; E96-8, F107-1; H140-4 144-2; I 159-5 165-3; L196-2 202-1; N230-6 240-7; P267-5 276-8; R311-2 312-3; T337-7 338-6, *U*—.

12] [*engraved title*] NOVELS AND TALES | OF | THE AUTHOR OF WAVERLEY. . . . VOL. XII. | THE BRIDE OF LAMMERMOOR; | AND | A LEGEND OF MONTROSE. | [*vignette of Old Inverary*] . . . . 1823.

Collation: A[12] B[6] . . . T[12] U[6] X[8]. Pagination: [*engraved title*], *1* fly-title for *Tales of My Landlord.* Third Series, *2* quotation, *3* 4-71 text for 'The Bride of Lammermoor' concluded, *72 blank, 73* fly-title for 'A Legend of Montrose', *74 blank, 75* 76-81 Introduction, *82 blank, 83* 84-356 text, *357* fly-title for Glossary, *358 blank, 359* 360-376 text, 376 printer's imprint. Illustrations: Frontispiece engraved by Chas. Heath with caption 'A Legend of Montrose.' and inscription 'Dalgetty & Ranald of the Mist escaping through the Chapel.' Typography: Sheet number 11 (page 361) is omitted.

Figures: A22-5 24-7; C50-4 60-2; E94-1 96-3; G111-5 132-8; I 165-5, K176-3; L182-7 196-1; N239-4, O 246-6; P265N-7 274-2; R311-7, S324-5; T345-4 347-6, U—; X—.

HISTORICAL ROMANCES [IVANHOE—KENILWORTH]

272A] Second Series, 8° Edition: 1822

[*engraved title*] HISTORICAL ROMANCES | OF | THE AUTHOR OF WAVERLEY | VOL.I [II-VI]. | [*volume title*] | [*vignette*] | EDINBURGH; | PRINTED FOR ARCHIBALD CONSTABLE AND Co. EDINBURGH; | AND HURST, ROBINSON AND Co. | LONDON. | [*French dash*] | 1822.

Published 5 June 1822 in Edinburgh (*EWJ*); issued 15 July in London (*MC*). £3.12.0. 5000 copies, of which 2700 were dispatched to Hurst, Robinson (*EEWN11*.409) . Binding: drab boards with printed labels. Paper: Royal 8° (225 x 144mm uncut). Watermarks: *none.*

General Notes: Constable's increasing confidence in the sale of these collected series may be observed in the 5000 print run for this second sequence, some 3500 copies over the number originally ordered several years before for the first 8° series (269Aa). The title vignettes for these six volumes are painted by A. Nasmyth and engraved by W. Archibald. The first four have uniform concluding printer's imprints reading: [*short rule*] | EDINBURGH: | Printed by James Ballantyne & Co. Volume 5 as noted below was printed by Walker and Greig, and 6 by George Ramsay.

Copies: (Volume 1, issue 1): E ES; CtY(2) T/B(2). (2): E(Scott's interleaved set, revised 1829-1830) HS(Gladstone's set, annotated) L O.

1] [*engraved title*] HISTORICAL ROMANCES | OF | THE AUTHOR OF WAVERLEY | VOL.I. | IVANHOE. | [*vignette of Castle of Torquilstone*] . . . . 1822.

Collation: A-2I^8 2K^4 2L^2. Pagination: [*engraved title*], *i* fly-title, *ii blank, iii* iv-xxix Dedicatory Epistle, *xxx blank, 1* 2-494 text, chapters 1-29, 494 printer's imprint.

Figures: A xvi-12, B2-9, C18-13/14, D34-5, E46-14, F66-11, G82-10, H98-2, I 114-5, K130-15, L146-6/-, M162-4, N178-6, O 191-11, P210-8, Q226-12, R242-14, S258-15, T274-2, U290-3, X306-6, Y322-13, Z338-9, 2A 354-2, 2B 366-7, 2C 386-5, 2D 402-3, 2E 418-6, 2F 434-11, 2G 450-9, 2H 466-15, 2I 482-10, 2K 490-2, 2L 492--/11.

Notes: The final part-gathering 2L^2 (pages 491-494) is in two consecutive settings, page 492 first word: (1) 'her' and no press-figure; (2) 'ings' and figure 11. The latter setting, appearing in the set prepared for Scott's revisions, tends to regularize the composition (chiefly by eliminating many of the hyphens at line-end), but introduces two misprints (page 492 line 18, 'Maccabeus' for 'Maccabaeus'; page 494 line 7, 'it way' for 'it away'). As in other instances this second setting was probably necessitated by a late discovery of a shortage in this one gathering.

2] [*engraved title*] HISTORICAL ROMANCES | OF | THE AUTHOR OF WAVERLEY | VOL. II. | IVANHOE. | [*vignette of Glendearg*] . . . . 1822.

Collation: A-2K^8 *2L*1. Pagination: [*engraved title*], *1* fly-title for *Ivanhoe*, *2 blank, 3* 4-312 text concluded, *313* fly-title for *The Monastery*, *314 blank, 315* 316-356 Introductory Epistle, *357* 358-370 Answer, *371* fly-title, *372 blank, 373* 374-529 text, chapters 1-9, 529 printer's imprint, *530 blank.*

Figures: A16-12, B32-9, C48-14, D64-5, E80-7, F84(or 96)-8, G112-13, H128-15, I 144-12, K160-14, L176-2/-, M192-2, N208-6, O 224-13, P240-10, Q256-14, R272-7, S288-11, T304-2, U320-15, X336-12, Y352-13, Z368-12, 2A 384-14, 2B 400-15, 2C 416-16, 2D 432-15, 2E 448-13, 2F 464-6, 2G 480-12, 2H 496-13, 2I 512-5, 2K 528-10, *2L*—. A variant figure position in sheet F here signifies only an interrupted printing.

3] [*engraved title*] HISTORICAL ROMANCES | OF | THE AUTHOR OF WAVERLEY | VOL.III. | THE MONASTERY. | [*vignette of Abbey of St Mary, Kirkaldy*] . . . . 1822.

Collation: A-2I^8 *2K*1. Pagination: [*engraved title*], *1* fly-title, *2 blank, 3* 4-513 text concluded, 513 printer's imprint, *514 blank*. Typography: In some copies page 217 is unnumbered.

Figures: A16-9, B32-14, C48-7, D64-17, E80-2, F96-8, G112-10, H122-4 128-9, I 144-5, K160-10/-, L176-15, M192-12, N208-18, O 224-9/-, P240-16, Q256-8, R272-2, S288-10, T304-5, U320-13, X336-8, Y352-15, Z368-4, 2A 384-16, 2B 398-19 400-8, 2C 416-16, 2D 430-2 432-15, 2E 448-13, 2F 464-6, 2G 480-9, 2H 496-11, 2I 511-13 512-15, *2K*—.

4] [*engraved title*] HISTORICAL ROMANCES | OF | THE AUTHOR OF WAVERLEY | VOL.IV. | THE ABBOT. | [*vignette of Lochleven Castle*] . . . . 1822.

Collation: A-2I^8 2K^4 2L^2. Pagination: [*engraved title*], *i* fly-title, *ii blank, iii* iv-vi Introductory Epistle, *7* 8-523 text, chapters 1-26, *524* printer's imprint.

Figures: A16-16, B32-6/-, C48-5, D64-18, E80-6, F96-17, G112-16, H128-8, I 144-7, K160-18, L176-6, M189-14, N208-11, O 224-8, P240-9, Q256-14, R272-6, S288-17, T304-12, U306-14, X336-17/20, Y340-5, Z368-2, 2A 384-14, 2B 400-10, 2C 416-12, 2D 432-10, 2E 448-4, 2F 464-16, 2G 480-15, 2H 496-8, 2 I 512-12, 2K 519-5, 2L 522-15/-. Again the figure variants represent only interruptions in the presswork.

5] [*engraved title*] HISTORICAL ROMANCES | OF | THE AUTHOR OF WAVERLEY | VOL.V. | KENILWORTH. | [*vignette of Warwick Castle*] . . . . 1822.

Collation: A-2M^8 2N^4. Pagination: [*engraved title*], *1* fly-title for *The Abbot*, *2 blank, 3* 4-262 text concluded, *263* fly-title for *Kenilworth*, *264 blank, 265* 266-565 text, chapters 1-14, 565 printer's imprint, *566-568 blank*. Printer's imprint: [*short rule*] | Printed by Walker & Greig, | Edinburgh. Typography: Gatherings 2A-2N are signed Aa-Nn, according to Walker and Greig's practice.

Figures: A15-7 16-8, B26-1, C47-7 48-8, D63-4 64-1, E79-7, F95-4 96-1, G112-1, H127-7, I 143-4 144-1, K159-4 160-1, L175-7, M191-4 192-1, N206-4 208-1, O 223-7, P239-4 240-1, Q255-4 256-1, R271-7 272-8, S287-4 288-5, T303-1 304-4, U319-1 320-4, X335-7, Y351-1 352-4, Z367-1, 2A 384-1, 2B 399-1, 2C 415-1, 2D 431-7, 2E 447-1, 2F 463-1 464-4, 2G 479-7, 2H 495-1 496-4, 2I 511-8, 2K 527-4 528-1/-, 2L 543-7, 2M 559-1, 2N 564-7.

Notes: The peculiar combinations of press-figures elsewhere employed by Walker and Greig do not occur in this volume.

6] [*engraved title*] HISTORICAL ROMANCES | OF | THE AUTHOR OF WAVERLEY | VOL.VI. | KENILWORTH. | [*vignette of Remains of the Gateway*] . . . . 1822.

Collation: A-2I^8 2K^4 2L^2. Pagination: [*engraved title*], *1* fly-title, *2 blank, 3* 4-524 text concluded, 524 printer's imprint: [*short rule*] | Printed by George Ramsay and Company. Typography: Gatherings 2A-2L are signed Aa-Ll, according to Ramsay's practice.

Figures: A8-1 10-4, B28-4 30-1, C41-12, D60-4, E75-10 80-12, F82-12 96-10, G112-4, H128-1, I 134-4 144-11/-, K155-10 160-1, L174-12, M178-1 192-10, N202-4, O 214-10 220-1, P236-12 238-4, Q244-1, R258-12 268-11, S278-4 288-10, T290-12, U318-4 320-10, X330-12, Y350-11 352-1, Z364-11, 2A 370-10 384-4, 2B 400-4, 2C 406-1, 2D 426-11, 2E 445-12 446-10, 2F 458-4 464-11, 2G 466-10 468-1, 2H 486-11 496-12, 2I 512-4, 2K 520-1, 2L 522-11.

273A] Second Series, 12° Edition: 1822

[*engraved title*] HISTORICAL ROMANCES | OF | THE AUTHOR OF WAVERLEY | VOL.I [II-VIII]. | [*reversed Oxford dash*] | [*volume title*] | [*reversed Oxford dash*] | [*vignette*] | EDINBURGH; | PRINTED FOR ARCHIBALD CONSTABLE AND Co. EDINBURGH; | AND HURST, ROBINSON AND Co. LONDON. | [*French dash*] | 1822.

Published 12 October 1822 in Edinburgh (*EEC*, omnibus advertisement); issued 26 October in London (*MC*, described as foolscap 8°). £3.0.0. 1500 copies were originally proposed by Constable, the same number as that previously ordered for the first 12° series (270Aa), but somewhat later, apparently, Hurst, Robinson agreed to take 1620 (*EEWN8*.429-430). Paper: Demy 12° (169 x 99mm cut). Watermarks: *none*.

General Notes: The 12° engraved titles are comparable to those used for the preceding 8° series, with vignettes reappearing as follows (12° in parenthesis): 1-3=(1-3), 4=(5), 5=(8), 6=(7). For the extra volumes required for this sequence A. Nasmyth and W. Archibald prepared two further vignettes, (4) a ruined abbey and (6) a battlefield. Concluding printer's imprints read: [*short rule*] | EDINBURGH: | Printed by James Ballantyne and Co. ('& Co.' vol. 6-8).

Copies: BCL E L O; IdU NNU-W(vols.3-6) T/B*
*Extra-illustrated with Tilt's 'Landscape Illustrations' (1830-1832) and 'Female Characters' (1832-1833): see 342D.

1] [*engraved title*] HISTORICAL ROMANCES | OF | THE AUTHOR OF WAVERLEY | VOL.I. | [*reversed Oxford dash*] | IVANHOE. | [*reversed Oxford dash*] | [*vignette of Castle of Torquilstone*] . . . . 1822.

Collation: A-R^{12} S^{4}. Pagination: [*engraved title*], *i* fly-title, *ii blank, iii* iv-xxvii Dedicatory Epistle, *xxviii blank, 1* 2-385 text, chapters 1-24, 385 printer's imprint, *386-388 blank.* Typography: Pages 191 and 309 are misnumbered 190 and 310.

Figures: A xxiv-7, B20-10, C44-10, D68-8, E89-9, F116-7, G137-5, H164-7, I 188-6, K190-7, L236-5, M260-7, N281-6, O 308-4, P332-2, Q356-9, R380-12, S382-9.

2] [*engraved title*] HISTORICAL ROMANCES | OF | THE AUTHOR OF WAVERLEY | VOL.II. | [*reversed Oxford dash*] | IVANHOE. | [*reversed Oxford dash*] | [*vignette of Glendearg*] . . . . 1822.

Collation: A-R^{12} S1. Pagination: [*engraved title*], *1* fly-title, *2 blank, 3* 4-410 text concluded, 410 printer's imprint.

Figures: A24-5, B48-7, C72-12, D96-9, E120-5, F144-9, G168-1, H192-7, I 216-7, K240-5, L256-6/-, M288-12, N290-9, O 336-10, P360-10, Q384-12, R408-8, S—.

3] [*engraved title*] HISTORICAL ROMANCES | OF | THE AUTHOR OF WAVERLEY | VOL.III. | [*reversed Oxford dash*] | THE MONASTERY. | [*reversed Oxford dash*] | [*vignette of Abbey of St Mary, Kirkaldy*] . . . . 1822.

Collation: A-P^{12} Q1. Pagination: [*engraved title*], *1* fly-title, *2 blank, 3* 4-45 Introductory Epistle, *46 blank, 47* 48-60 Answer, *61* fly-title, *62 blank, 63* 64-362 text, chapters 1-17, 362 printer's imprint.

Figures: A24-5, B48-7, C72-10, D76-6, E120-12, F144-6, G168-10, H192-9, I 216-5, K240-4, L264-1, M288-7, N312-8, O 336-5, P352-8, Q--.

4] [*engraved title*] HISTORICAL ROMANCES | OF | THE AUTHOR OF WAVERLEY | VOL.IV. | [*reversed Oxford dash*] | THE MONASTERY. | [*reversed Oxford dash*] | [*vignette of a ruined Abbey*] . . . . 1822.

Collation: A-P^{12} Q^{6}(-Q6). Pagination: [*engraved title*], *1* fly-title, *2 blank, 3* 4-369 text concluded, *370* printer's imprint.

Figures: A24-1, B45-16, C72-9, D96-12, E120-6, F144-10, G168-10, H192-10, I 216-5, K240-7, L264-10, M288-5, N312-10, O 336-9, P360-2, Q364-7/-.

5] [*engraved title*] HISTORICAL ROMANCES | OF | THE AUTHOR OF WAVERLEY | VOL. V. | [*reversed Oxford dash*] | THE ABBOT. | [*reversed Oxford dash*] | [*vignette of Lochleven Castle*] . . . . 1822.

Collation: A-P^{12} Q^{6} S^{4}. Pagination: [*engraved title*], *1* fly-title, *2 blank, 3* 4-6 Introductory Epistle, *7* 8-378 text, chapters 1-21, *379* printer's imprint, *380 blank*. Typography: Section signature O 2 (page 321) is missigned 2 O. There is no gathering signed R.

Figures: A24-5, B48-5, C72-16, D93-12, E117-18, F144-17, G160-18, H192-6, I 216-16, K240-5, L261-17, M288-6, N311-19 312-4, O 336-2, P357-9, Q372-10, S—.

6] [*engraved title*] HISTORICAL ROMANCES | OF | THE AUTHOR OF WAVERLEY | VOL. VI. | [*reversed Oxford dash*] | THE ABBOT. | [*reversed Oxford dash*] | [*vignette of a battlefield*] . . . . 1822.

Collation: A-Q^{12} R1. Pagination: [*engraved title*], *1* fly-title, *2 blank, 3* 4-386 text concluded, 386 printer's imprint.

Figures: A24-9, B38-12, C72-5, D94-19 96-2, E120-17, F143-2 144-19, G168-8, H192-9, I 216-18, K238-2 240-5, L264-19, M288-10, N312-17, O 334-19 336-8/-, P360-17, Q384-9, R—.

7] [*engraved title*] HISTORICAL ROMANCES | OF | THE AUTHOR OF WAVERLEY | VOL.VII. | [*reversed Oxford dash*] | KENILWORTH. | [*reversed Oxford dash*] | [*vignette of Remains of the Gateway*] . . . . 1822.

Collation: A-Q^{12} R^{8}. Pagination: [*engraved title*], *1* fly-title, *2 blank, 3* 4-400 text, chapters 1-18, 400 printer's imprint.

Figures: A24-16, B48-5, C72-10, D96-5, E120-16, F133-6, G168-17, H192-16, I 216-19, K240-16, L264-19, M288-5, N312-9, O 336-9, P360-10, Q384-5, R397-9.

8] [*engraved title*] HISTORICAL ROMANCES | OF | THE AUTHOR OF WAVERLEY | VOL.VIII. | [*reversed Oxford dash*] | KENILWORTH. | [*reversed Oxford dash*] | [*vignette of Warwick Castle*] . . . . 1822.

Collation: A-Q^{12} R^{12}(-R12). Pagination: [*engraved title*], *1* fly-title, *2 blank, 3* 4-405 text concluded, 405 printer's imprint, *406 blank*.

Figures: A24-2, B48-19, C72-16, D96-17, E120-5, F144-9, G168-5, H189-18, I 216-6, K240-17, L264-9, M288-2/-, N312-7, O 334-2 336-8, P359-9 360-19, Q383-6 384-7, R386-1 400-3.

274A] Second Series, 18° Edition: 1824

[*engraved title*] HISTORICAL ROMANCES | OF | THE AUTHOR OF WAVERLEY | IN SIX VOLUMES | VOL. I [II-VI]. | [*volume title*] | [*vignette*]

| EDINBURGH; | PRINTED FOR ARCHIBALD CONSTABLE & Co. EDINBURGH; | AND HURST, ROBINSON & Co. LONDON. | 1824.

Published ca. February 1824. (*EEC* 22 January 1824, 'Nearly ready'). £2.2.0. About 5000 copies dispatched to Hurst, Robinson (*EEWN11*.409). Paper: Demy 18° (155 x 93mm uncut). Watermarks: *none*.

General Notes: As in the earlier series (271A) most of this 'miniature edition' would appear to have gone to London. The 18° engraved titles essentially are identical with those used for the earlier 8° series, each with the same vignette but Nasmyth now not identified, and Edwd. Finden inscribed as engraver. The frontispieces, new to this sequence, are described below: all bear the Hurst, Robinson imprint dated 1824. Ellipses marks in the following collations indicate a regularly alternating sequence 6° and 12° in this 18° format. Concluding printer's imprints read: (volumes 1-3) [*short rule*] | EDINBURGH: | Printed by James Ballantyne & Co.; (volumes 4-6) LONDON: | PRINTED BY J. MOYES, GREVILLE STREET.

Copies: E L L* O; CtY(vols.1-3,6) MH T/B(vols.3-6).
*MS notes by S. T. Coleridge.

1] [*engraved title*] HISTORICAL ROMANCES | OF | THE AUTHOR OF WAVERLEY . . . VOL. I. | IVANHOE. | [*vignette of Castle of Torquilstone*] . . . . 1824.

Collation: A^{12} B^{6} . . . X^{12} Y^{4}. Pagination: [*engraved title*], *i* fly-title, *ii blank, iii* iv-xxiii Dedicatory Epistle, *xxiv blank, 25* fly-title, *26 blank, 27* 28-392 text, chapters 1-29, 392 printer's imprint. Illustrations: Frontispiece painted by T. Stothard, engraved by J. Romney, with caption 'Ivanhoe.' and inscription 'The Black Knight & the Clerk of Copmanhurst carousing.' Typography: Section signature I 2 (page 153) is missigned 2 I.

Figures: A *iii*-8 xxi-6; D71-7 72-5; F107-2 108-6; H143-8 144-5; K179-4 180-6; M215-7 216-5; O 251-1 252-8; Q287-1 288-5; R311-2 312-7; U359-6 360-8; X384-5.

2] [*engraved title*] HISTORICAL ROMANCES | OF | THE AUTHOR OF WAVERLEY . . . VOL. II. | IVANHOE | AND THE | MONASTERY. | [*vignette of Glendearg*] . . . . 1824.

Collation: A^{12} B^{6} . . . X^{12} Y^{6} Z^{6} $2A^{6}$(-2A6). Pagination: [*engraved title*], *1* fly-title for *Ivanhoe*, *2 blank, 3* 4-233 text concluded, *234 blank, 235* fly-title for *The Monastery, 236 blank, 237* 238-417 text, chapters 1-9, 417 printer's imprint, *418 blank.* Illustrations: Frontispiece painted by T. Stothard, engraved by A. W. Warren, with caption 'Ivanhoe.' and inscription 'The trial of Rebecca.' Typography: Section signature A2 (page 9) is missigned 2A. Signature 2A (page 409) is missigned Y, and the section reference (page 415) is given as '2A'.

Figures: B32-1/- 36-2; C60-5, D71-4; E96-2, F98-3; G131-1, H144-5; I 147-4, K180-8; L204-6, M212-1; N240-2, O 251-7; P255-4 276-3; R312-6, S320-2; T347-7 348-5; X371-3 384-8; Z408-4.

3] [*engraved title*] HISTORICAL ROMANCES | OF | THE AUTHOR OF WAVERLEY . . . VOL.III. | MONASTERY. | [*vignette of Abbey of St Mary, Kirkaldy*] . . . . 1824.

Collation: A^{12} B^{6} . . . X^{12} Y^{2}. Pagination: [*engraved title*], *1* fly-title, *2 blank, 3* 4-387 text concluded, 387 printer's imprint, *388 blank.* Illustrations: Frontispiece painted by W. Brockedon, engraved by C. Rolls, with caption 'Monastery.' and inscription 'Edward Glendinning demanding an account of his brother of Sir Piercie Shafton.'

Figures: A24-6, B26-1; C38-2 60-8; E96-6, F107-1; G131-3 132-4; I 147-1 168-8; L183-7 204-6; N240-8, O 251-2; P276-5, Q287-1; R310-5 312-2; T347-3 348-2; X374-5 384-6; Y—.

4] [*engraved title*] HISTORICAL ROMANCES | OF | THE AUTHOR OF WAVERLEY . . . VOL.IV. | THE ABBOT. | [*vignette of Lochleven Castle*] . . . . 1824.

Collation: A^{12} B^{6} . . . X^{12} Y^{6} Z^{6}. Pagination: [*engraved title*], *1* fly-title, *2 blank, i* ii-iv Introductory Epistle, *7* fly-title, *8 blank, 9* 10-408 text, chapters 1-26, 408 printer's imprint. Illustrations: Frontispiece painted by H. Howard, engraved by Chas. Rolls, with caption 'Abbot.' and inscription 'Roland Graeme rescued from the water.' Typography: On the precedent of volume 1 the printer should have counted the first leaf as *i-ii* and the following epistle as *iii* iv-vi, a sequence which would then leave no gap in the numbering. Section signature P2 (page 261) is omitted. Figures: none used by printer Moyes.

Notes: Sheet numbers, regularly used by Ballantyne for volumes 1-3, are not employed for the Moyes printing of 4-6.

5] [*engraved title*] HISTORICAL ROMANCES | OF | THE AUTHOR OF WAVERLEY . . . VOL. V. | THE ABBOT | AND | KENILWORTH. | [*vignette of Warwick Castle*] . . . . 1824.

Collation: A^{12} B^{6} . . . X^{12} Y^{6} Z^{6}. Pagination: [*engraved title*], *1* fly-title for *The Abbot*, *2 blank, 3* 4-187 text concluded, *188 blank, 189* fly-title for *Kenilworth*, *190 blank, 191* 192-407 text, chapters 1-14, *408* printer's imprint. Illustrations: Frontispiece painted by A. Cooper, engraved by J. Romney, with caption 'The Abbot.' and inscription 'Roland Graeme rescuing Henry Seyton.' Figures: none used by printer Moyes.

6] [*engraved title*] HISTORICAL ROMANCES | OF | THE AUTHOR OF WAVERLEY . . . VOL.VI. | KENILWORTH. | [*vignette of Remains of the Gateway*] . . . . 1824.

Collation: A^{12} B^6 . . . X^{12} Y^6 Z^6 $2A^2$. Pagination: [*engraved title*], *1* fly-title, *2 blank*, *3* 4-412 text concluded, 412 printer's imprint. Illustrations: Frontispiece painted by H. Howard, engraved by Chas. Heath, with caption 'Kenilworth.' and inscription 'The Countess admiring the decorations of the Earl.' Facing page *3*, in a few copies, is a folding 'Ground Plan of Kenilworth Castle.' Typography: Section signatures N2 and P2 (pages 225, 261) are signed N5 and P5, numbers actually identifying the leaves. Signature 2A (page 409) is signed AA. Figures: none used by printer Moyes.

NOVELS AND ROMANCES [THE PIRATE—QUENTIN DURWARD]

275A] Third Series, 8° Edition: 1824[1823]

[*engraved title*] NOVELS AND ROMANCES | OF | THE AUTHOR OF WAVERLEY | VOL. I [II-VII]. | [*volume title*] | [*vignette*] | EDINBURGH; | PRINTED FOR ARCHIBALD CONSTABLE AND Co. EDINBURGH; | AND HURST, ROBINSON AND Co. | LONDON. | [*French dash*] | 1824.

Published 10 December 1823 in Edinburgh (*EWJ*); issued 12 January 1824 in London (*MC*). £4.4.0. Binding: Drab or blue boards or (later issues?) green paper wrappers or rose boards with printed labels. Paper: Royal 8° (224 x 142mm uncut). Watermarks: *none*. Illustrations: Title vignettes are drawn by A. Nasmyth and engraved (volume 1) by W. Miller or (volumes 2-7) by W. Archibald. The concluding printer's imprints read: [*short rule*] | EDINBURGH: | Printed by James Ballantyne and Co. [& Co. vol. 6].

Copies: (Volumes 3, 5, issue 1) E ES(2) HS(Gladstone's set, annotated) L O; CtY CtY(vols.3-7) NNU-W T/B. (2) E(Scott's interleaved set, revised ca. 1830).

1] [*engraved title*] NOVELS AND ROMANCES | OF | THE AUTHOR OF WAVERLEY | VOL. I. | THE PIRATE. | [*vignette of the Roost of Sumburgh*] . . . . 1824.

Collation: A-$2I^8$ $2K^4$ $2L^2$. Pagination: [*engraved title*], *i* fly-title, *ii blank*, *iii* iv-'vii' [viii] Advertisement, *9* 10-523 text, chapters 1-26, 523 printer's imprint, *524 blank*. Typography: Page viii is misnumbered vii.

Figures: A16-7, B32-5, C48-4, D64-3, E77-17, F96-13, G108-2/-, H128-6, I 144-1, K146-11, L176-4, M186-6, N208-10, O 224-8, P240-6, Q256-9, R272-11, S288-8,

T304-13, U320-3, X336-10, Y352-11, Z368-13, 2A 381-6, 2B 392-5, 2C 413-9, 2D 432-8, 2E 448-10, 2F 464-7, 2G 480-5, 2H 496-13, 2I 508-4, 2K 520-16, 2L 522-7.

2] [*engraved title*] NOVELS AND ROMANCES | OF | THE AUTHOR OF WAVERLEY | VOL. II. | THE PIRATE. | [*vignette of Burgh-Westra*] . . . . 1824.

Collation: A-2L⁸. Pagination: [*engraved title*], *1* fly-title for *The Pirate, 2 blank, 3* 4-291 text concluded, *292 blank, 293* fly-title for *The Fortunes of Nigel, 294 blank, 295* 296-332 Introductory Epistle, *333* fly-title. *334 blank, 335* 336-541 text, chapters 1-9, *542* printer's imprint, *543-544 blank.*

Figures: A16-8, B28-12, C41-10, D64-17, E80-12, F96-2, G112-10, H128-16, I 144-3, K160-1, L176-18, M192-8, N208-2, O 224-12, P238-12, Q256-17, R272-8, S288-1, T304-8, U320-15, X336-16, Y350-6, Z368-11, 2A 384-18, 2B 400-1, 2C 416-10, 2D 432-12, 2E 448-9, 2F 464-11, 2G 480-9, 2H 496-16, 2I 511-3, 2K 515-1 528-2, 2L 540-17.

3] [*engraved title*] NOVELS AND ROMANCES | OF | THE AUTHOR OF WAVERLEY | VOL. III. | THE FORTUNES OF NIGEL. | [*vignette of Whitehall*] . . . . 1824.

Collation: A-2H⁸. Pagination: [*engraved title*], *1* fly-title, *2 blank, 3* 4-493 text continued, *494* printer's imprint, *495-496 blank.* Typography: On page 375 the first digit of the press figure is upside down.

Figures: A4-16, B31-10 32-18, C46-10, D64-5, E66-1 80-18, F86-7 96-4, G98-11 112-17, H119-3 128-6, I 132-8 142-11, K153-12 159-9, L175-17 176-8, M190-10 192-9, N206-12 208-7, O 223-18 224-16, P234-16 240-8, Q256-5, R272-2, S287-8 288-7, T302-17 304-18, U310-2/- 317-3, X322-4 332-6, Y347-7 352-11, Z364-5 366-9, 2A 375-18 384-10, 2B 387-3 393-12, 2C 410-4, 2D 431-11 432-18, 2E 445-7 447-3, 2F 456-18 459-6, 2G 471-1 480-8, 2H 483-11 489-16.

Notes: In the original issue (1) sheet 2E (pages 433-448) has press figures as noted above, according to normal practice. However, when a copy was later interleaved for Scott, this sheet had been (2) reset without figures, apparently because of a shortage then discovered in the earlier printing. Originally page 438 line 7 first word read 'else,' in the later issue 'he'.

4] [*engraved title*] NOVELS AND ROMANCES | OF | THE AUTHOR OF WAVERLEY | VOL. IV. | THE FORTUNES OF NIGEL. | [*vignette of Camlet Moat*] . . . . 1824.

Collation: A-2I⁸. Pagination: [*engraved title*], *1* fly-title for *The Fortunes of Nigel, 2 blank, 3* 4-105 text concluded, *106 blank, 107* fly-title for *Peveril of the Peak,*

108 blank, 109 110-133 Prefatory Letter, *134 blank, 135* fly-title, *136 blank, 137* 138-'521'[512] text, chapters 1-18, '521'[512] printer's imprint. Typography: Page 512 is misnumbered 521.

Figures: A15-2, B30-7 32-13, C46-6 48-18, D54-4 64-9, E74-3 80-10, F91-8 96-1, G102-7 112-18, H127-9 128-5, I 143-8 144-4, K157-14 159-3, L166-1 169-13, M191-5 192-2, N205-3 206-10, O 222-9 224-7, P234-11 240-5, Q256-17, R270-4 272-2, S286-3 288-18, T303-17 304-2, U319-8 320-9, X335-10 336-12, Y347-3 352-6, Z367-2 368-17, 2A 378-1 384-9, 2B 399-13 400-17, 2C 410-6 416-10, 2D 430-9 432-12, 2E 448-1, 2F 462-6 464-5, 2G 480-8, 2H 496-1, 2I 505-2.

5] [*engraved title*] NOVELS AND ROMANCES | OF | THE AUTHOR OF WAVERLEY | VOL. V. | PEVERIL OF THE PEAK. | [*vignette of Castle of Holm-Peel*] . . . . 1824.

Collation: A-2H^8. Pagination: [*engraved title*], *1* fly-title, *2 blank, 3* 4-493 text continued, 493 printer's imprint, *494-496 blank.*

Figures: A14-9, B32-15/14, C48-5, D63-15 64-10, E76-2, F96-17, G112-11, H128-11, I 144-17, K160-10, L176-9, M192-15, N208-17, O 224-19, P240-11, Q256-9, R272-17, S288-7, T304-5, U320-15, X336-12, Y352-13, Z368-6, 2A 384-17, 2B 400-15, 2C 416-8, 2D 432-11, 2E 448-4, 2F 464-15, 2G 480-13, 2H 483-6.

Notes: In sheet B the press figure variation simply indicates a transfer in the course of the impression. As in volume 3, however, sheet 2D (pages 417-432) is in two issues: (1) with a figure, as noted above; (2) in the issue annotated by Scott, unfigured and reset. Originally page 420 line 4 first word read 'ed,' in the later issue 'sulted,'.

6] [*engraved title*] NOVELS AND ROMANCES | OF | THE AUTHOR OF WAVERLEY | VOL. VI. | PEVERIL OF THE PEAK. | [*vignette of Castle of Peronne*] . . . . 1824.

Collation: A-2G^8 2H^4 *2I*1. Pagination: [*engraved title*], *1* fly-title for *Peveril of the Peak, 2 blank, 3* 4-139 text concluded, *140 blank, 141* fly-title for *Quentin Durward, 142 blank, 143* 144-192 Introduction, *193* section title, *194 blank, 195* 196-489 text, chapters 1-14, *490* printer's imprint.

Figures: A10-11 16-7, B28-8 31-4, C42-6 48-7, D59-9 64-14, E79-16 80-5, F94-11 96-1, G106-7 112-5, H126-12 128-10, I 137-2, K158-7, L176-4, M188-7, N208-9, O 224-12, P237-4, Q255-6, R272-3, S288-4, T303-11 304-15, U320-1, X336-7, Y352-8, Z368-3, 2A 384-15, 2B 400-6, 2C 416-10, 2D 432-11, 2E 448-14, 2F 464-10, 2G 480-9, 2H 488-1, *2I*—.

7] [*engraved title*] NOVELS AND ROMANCES | OF | THE AUTHOR OF WAVERLEY | VOL. VII. | QUENTIN DURWARD. | [*vignette of Castle of Plessis-le-Tours*] . . . . 1824.

Collation: A-2G⁸. Pagination: [*engraved title*], *1* fly-title, *2 blank, 3* 4-479 text concluded, *480* printer's imprint. Typography: Page 457 is misnumbered 547.

Figures: A16-14, B32-15, C48-5, D64-12, E80-9, F96-15, G112-10, H128-7, I 144-13, K160-5, L176-8, M192-11, N208-13, O 224-14, P240-10, Q256-8, R272-11, S288-15, T304-4, U320-8, X336-7, Y352-15, Z368-14, 2A 384-6, 2B 400-16, 2C 416-6, 2D 432-15, 2E 448-9, 2F 464-11, 2G 477-2.

276A] Third Series, 12° Edition: 1824

[*engraved title*] NOVELS AND ROMANCES | OF | THE AUTHOR OF WAVERLEY | VOL. I [II-IX]. | [*reversed Oxford dash*] | [*volume title*] | [*reversed Oxford dash*] | [*vignette*] | EDINBURGH; | PRINTED FOR ARCHIBALD CONSTABLE AND Co. EDINBURGH; | AND HURST, ROBINSON AND Co. LONDON. | [*French dash*] | 1824.

Published 3 January 1824 in Edinburgh (*EEC*); issued 31 January in London (*MC*). £3.7.6. Paper: Demy 12° (166 x 98mm cut). Watermarks: *none*.

General Notes: The 12° engraved titles are comparable to those used for the preceding 8° series, with vignettes reappearing as follows (12° in parentheses): 1-4=(1-4), 5=(7), 6=(9), 7=(8). For the extra volumes required for this sequence A. Nasmyth and W. Archibald prepared two further vignettes, (5) lady and gentleman conversing and (6) a wayside inn. Concluding printer's imprints read: [*short rule*] | EDINBURGH: | Printed by James Ballantyne and Co. [& Co. vols. 2-9].

Copies: BCL E L; IdU T/B*.
*Extra-illustrated with Tilt's 'Landscape Illustrations' (1830-1832) and 'Female Characters' (1832-1833): see 342D.

1] [*engraved title*] NOVELS AND ROMANCES | OF | THE AUTHOR OF WAVERLEY | VOL. I. | [*reversed Oxford dash*] | THE PIRATE. | [*reversed Oxford dash*] | [*vignette of the Roost of Sumburgh*] . . . . 1824.

Collation: A-Q¹² R⁶. Pagination: [*engraved title*], *i* fly-title, *ii blank, iii* iv-viii Advertisement, *9* 10-394 text, chapters 1-20, 394 printer's imprint, *395-396 blank.* Typography: Page 317 is misnumbered 713.

Figures: A22-2, B46-4 48-17, C72-7, D95-7, E119-2, F141-11, G148-1, H183-3, I 208-7, K240-4, L263-13, M286-16, N312-2, O 316-17, P360-13, Q383-9, R390-12.

2] [*engraved title*] NOVELS AND ROMANCES | OF | THE AUTHOR OF WAVERLEY | VOL.II. | [*reversed Oxford dash*] | THE PIRATE. | [*reversed Oxford dash*] | [*vignette of Burgh-Westra*] . . . . 1824.

Collation: A-Q^{12} R^{6} S^{2}. Pagination: [*engraved title*], *1* fly-title, *2 blank, 3* 4-400 text concluded, 400 printer's imprint.

Figures: A24-10, B45-16, C72-10, D96-8, E117-12, F144-13, G168-17, H192- 10, I 216-16, K240-7, L264-9, M288-2, N312-6, O 336-8, P360-13, Q375-9, R396-6, S—.

3] [*engraved title*] NOVELS AND ROMANCES | OF | THE AUTHOR OF WAVERLEY | VOL.III. | [*reversed Oxford dash*] | THE FORTUNES OF NIGEL. | [*reversed Oxford dash*] | [*vignette of Whitehall*] . . . . 1824.

Collation: A-Q^{12} R1. Pagination: [*engraved title*], *1* fly-title, *2 blank, 3* 4-386 text, chapters 1-16, 386 printer's imprint. Typography: The direction line page 25 reads 'VOL.II.'

Figures: A24-5, B48-10, C62-6, D96-9, E120-15, F144-6, G168-15, H170-5, I 216-2, K239-10 240-9, L264-9, M288-12, N309-7, O 336-16, P351-5, Q376-12, R—.

4] [*engraved title*] NOVELS AND ROMANCES | OF | THE AUTHOR OF WAVERLEY | VOL. IV. | [*reversed Oxford dash*] | THE FORTUNES OF NIGEL. | [*reversed Oxford dash*] | [*vignette of Camlet Moat*] . . . 1824.

Collation: A-Q^{12} R^{4}. Pagination: [*engraved title*], *1* fly-title, *2 blank, 3* 4-392 text continued, 392 printer's imprint. Typography: Direction lines read irregularly: page 49, 'VOL.III.'; page 51, 'IV.'; page 73, 'VOL.III'.

Figures: A14-10/19, B48-4, C72-4, D96-5, E120-4, F144-17, G168-9, H191-2, I 216-5, K238-3, L256-6, M288-1, N312-16, O 336-10, P360-17, Q384-16, R386-11.

5] [*engraved title*] NOVELS AND ROMANCES | OF | THE AUTHOR OF WAVERLEY | VOL.V. | [*reversed Oxford dash*] | PEVERIL OF THE PEAK. | [*reversed Oxford dash*] | [*vignette of lady and gentleman conversing*] . . . . 1824.

Collation: A-P^{12} Q^{6}. Pagination: [*engraved title*], *1* fly-title for *The Fortunes of Nigel, 2 blank, 3* 4-57 text concluded, *58 blank, 59* fly-title for *Peveril of the Peak, 60 blank, 61* 62-370 text, chapters 1-14, 370 printer's imprint, *371-372 blank.*

Figures: A24-12, B48-12, C—, D96-2, E112-4, F144-16, G—, H189-9, I 216-17, K240-12, L264-5, M288-12, N309-17, O 336-10, P358-12, Q368-18.

6] [*engraved title*] NOVELS AND ROMANCES | OF | THE AUTHOR OF WAVERLEY | VOL.VI. | [*reversed Oxford dash*] | PEVERIL OF THE PEAK. | [*reversed Oxford dash*] | [*vignette of a wayside inn*] . . . . 1824.

Collation: A-O^{12} P^{6} Q^{2}. Pagination: [*engraved title*], *1* fly-title, *2 blank, 3* 4-351 text continued, 351 printer's imprint, *352 blank.*

Figures: A24-12, B48-5, C72-3, D96-8, E120-16, F144-8, G160-9, H192-10, I216-6, K240-10, L264-2, M288-10, N312-9, O 336-6, P348-13, Q—.

7] [*engraved title*] NOVELS AND ROMANCES | OF | THE AUTHOR OF WAVERLEY | VOL. VII. | [*reversed Oxford dash*] | PEVERIL OF THE PEAK. | [*reversed Oxford dash*] | [*vignette of Castle of Holm-Peel*] . . . . 1824.

Collation: A-F^{12} G^{12}(±G1) H-P^{12}. Pagination: [*engraved title*], *1* fly-title, *2 blank, 3* 4-357 text concluded, 357 printer's imprint, *358-360 blank.*

Figures: A24-16, B45-18, C72-10, D96-4, E120-8, F144-5, G168-17, H189-7, I 205-13, K240-3, L264-10, M288-7, N298-2, O 333-8, P349-3.

Notes: The original G1 cancellandum, preserved in the E copy, indicates that the cancellans page 146 line 2 revises 'answered' to 'replied' and line 10 corrects 'mih' to 'him'.

8] [*engraved title*] NOVELS AND ROMANCES | OF | THE AUTHOR OF WAVERLEY | VOL.VIII. | [*reversed Oxford dash*] | QUENTIN DURWARD. | [*reversed Oxford dash*] | [*vignette of Castle of Plessis-le-Tours*] . . . . 1824.

Collation: A-Q^{12} R1. Pagination: [*engraved title*], *i* fly-title, *ii blank, iii* iv-liv Introduction, *55* fly-title, *56 blank, 57* 58-386 text, chapters 1-16, 386 printer's imprint. Typography: Direction lines read irregularly: fly-title, 'VOL.III.'; page 169, 'VOL. VII.'; page 217, 'VOL. VII.'

Figures: A xxiv-16, B xlviii-10, C72-4, D96-2, E120-16, F144-3, G168-14, H192-3, I 205-6, K240-6, L264-1, M288-13, N312-8, O 336-5, P—, Q384-11, R—.

9] [*engraved title*] NOVELS AND ROMANCES | OF | THE AUTHOR OF WAVERLEY | VOL. IX. | [*reversed Oxford dash*] | QUENTIN DURWARD. | [*reversed Oxford dash*] | [*vignette of Castle of Peronne*] . . . . 1824.

Collation: A-S^{12} *T*1. Pagination: [*engraved title*], *1* fly-title, *2 blank, 3* 4-433 text concluded, *434* printer's imprint. Typography: Direction line page 73, 'VOL. VIII.' In some copies page 80 is misnumbered 82.

Figures: A24-15, B48-10, C72-15, D96-5, E120-9, F144-10, G168-11, H192-17, I

213-14, K240-7, L264-11, M288-2, N312-4, O 336-15, P360-2, Q384-15, R408-7, S429-17, *T*—.

277A] Third Series, 18° Edition: 1825

[*engraved title*] NOVELS AND ROMANCES | OF | THE AUTHOR OF WAVERLEY. | IN SEVEN VOLUMES. | VOL. I [II-VII]. | [*volume title*] | [*vignette*] | EDINBURGH; | PRINTED FOR ARCHIBALD CON STABLE, & Co. EDINBURGH, | AND HURST, ROBINSON, & Co. LONDON. | 1825.

Issued 8 January 1825 in London (*LG*). £2.9.0. Probably 5000 copies dispatched to London. Apparently not listed in Edinburgh before 2 May (*EEC*). Binding: drab boards with green cloth backs and printed labels (describing the issue as a 'Miniature Edition'). Paper: Demy 18° (154 x 94mm uncut). Watermarks: none.

General Notes: As in the earlier series (271A, 274A), most of this edition would appear to have been ordered by Hurst, Robinson, the Edinburgh issue being announced somewhat later. The title vignettes essentially are identical with those appearing the year before in the 8° seven-volume set, all drawn by A. Nasmyth (here throughout misspelled 'Naysmyth'), and now re-engraved by E. Finden. The frontispieces, first appearing in this 18° format, are described below. In all volumes the frontispieces bear the imprint: Published by Hurst, Robinson & Co. London, 1825. Ellipses marks in the following collations indicate a regularly alternating sequence 6° and 12° in this 18° format. Typography: Concluding printer's imprints reading: [*short rule*] | EDINBURGH: | Printed by James Ballantyne and Co. ['& Co.' vols. 1-2].

Copies: L L* O; CtY MH(vols.1-6) T/B.
* MS notes by S. T. Coleridge.

1] [*engraved title*] NOVELS AND ROMANCES | OF | THE AUTHOR OF WAVERLEY. . . . VOL. I. | THE PIRATE. | [*vignette of the Roost of Sumburgh*] . . . . 1825.

Collation: A^{12} B^{6} . . . X^{12} Y^{6}. Pagination: [*engraved title*], *i* fly-title, *ii blank*, *iii* iv-vii Advertisement, *viii blank*, *9* 10-395 text, chapters 1-26, 395 printer's imprint, *396 blank*. Illustration: frontispiece drawn by J. M. Wright, engraved by R. Baker, with caption 'The Pirate.' and inscription 'The shipwreck of Cleveland.'

Figures: A11-4 24-8; C46-2 52-7; E86-2, F108-7; G132-4, H134-2; I 167-2 168-1; L195-6, M210-1; N239-3 240-1; P276-6, Q278-3; R312-7, S314-2; T334-3 348-6; X384-4, Y386-6.

2] [*engraved title*] NOVELS AND ROMANCES | OF | THE AUTHOR OF

WAVERLEY. . . . VOL.II. | THE PIRATE, AND | THE FORTUNES OF NIGEL. | [*vignette of Burgh-Westra*] . . . . 1825.

Collation: A^{12} B^6 . . . X^{12} Y^6 Z^6 $2A^4$(-2A4). Pagination: [*engraved title*], *1* fly-title for *The Pirate*, *2 blank*, *3* 4-219 text concluded, *220 blank*, *221* fly-title for *The Fortunes of Nigel*, *222 blank*, *223* 224-255 Introductory Epistle, *256 blank*, *257* fly-title, *258 blank*, *259* 260-414 text, chapters 1-9, 414 printer's imprint. Illustration: frontispiece drawn by J. M. Wright, engraved by J. Mitchell, with caption 'The Fortunes of Nigel.' and inscription 'The Scene with Nigel, Trapbois, and Colepepper.' Typography: Section signature R2 (page 297) is missigned S2.

Figures: A24-8, B32-6; C51-6 60-1; E86-2, F108-4/-; G132-4, H134-3; I 167-2, K174-6; L191-2 204-4; N226-2 240-6; P276-4, Q284-7; R290-6 312-4; T347-7 348-2; X384-1; Z408-7.

3] [*engraved title*] NOVELS AND ROMANCES | OF | THE AUTHOR OF WAVERLEY. . . . VOL. III. | THE FORTUNES OF NIGEL. | [*vignette of Whitehall*] . . . . 1825.

Collation: A^{12} B^6 . . . T^{12} U^6 X^6 Y^1. Pagination: [*engraved title*], *1* fly-title, *2 blank*, *3* 4-373 text continued, 373 printer's imprint, *374 blank*. Illustration: frontispiece drawn by T. M. Wright, engraved by J. Romney, with caption 'The Fortunes of Nigel.' and inscription 'Nigel encountering the Murderers of Trapbois.'

Figures: A15-6 24-3; C59-7 60-5; E83-6 96-2; G132-1, H143-7; I 167-2 168-5; L203-7 204-4; N231-6, O 252-2; P256-4 262-3; R299-7 312-6; T335-1 348-5; X372-4.

4] [*engraved title*] NOVELS AND ROMANCES | OF | THE AUTHOR OF WAVERLEY. . . . VOL. IV. | THE FORTUNES OF NIGEL. | AND | PEVERIL OF THE PEAK. | [*vignette of Camlet Moat*] . . . . 1825.

Collation: A^{12} B^6 . . . X^{12} Y^4. Pagination: [*engraved title*], *1* fly-title for *The Fortunes of Nigel*, *2 blank*, *3* 4-81 text concluded, *82 blank*, *83* fly-title for *Peveril of the Peak*, *84 blank*, 85-106 Prefatory Letter, *107* fly-title, *108 blank*, *109* 110-392 text, chapters 1-18, 392 printer's imprint. Illustration: frontispiece drawn by T. M. Wright, engraved by J. Mitchell, with caption 'Peveril of the Peak.' and inscription 'The meeting of Peveril & Alice interrupted by Bridgenorth.' Typography: Section signatures E2 and H2 (pages 81, 137) are missigned C2 and G2.

Figures: A23-7 24-2; C58-6 60-5; E76-2 86-7; G111-1 132-3; I 166-6 168-5; L204-4, M206-7; N239-5 240-8; P275-7 276-2; R291-3 312-4; T347-5 348-8; X383-7 384-6.

5] [*engraved title*] NOVELS AND ROMANCES | OF | THE AUTHOR OF WAVERLEY. . . . VOL. V. | PEVERIL OF THE PEAK. | [*vignette of Castle of Holm-Peel*] . . . . 1825.

Collation: A^{12} B^{6} . . . T^{12} U^{6} X^{6}. Pagination: [*engraved title*], *1* fly-title, *2 blank, 3* 4-371 text continued, 371 printer's imprint, *372 blank*. Illustration: frontispiece painted by A. Cooper, engraved by C. Rolls, with caption 'Peveril of the Peak.' and inscription 'Sir Geoffrey Peveril opposing Bridgenorth in his pursuit of the Countess of Derby.'

Figures: A23-1 24-5; C59-2 60-4; E95-2 96-7; G111-1 132-8; I 167-2 168-7; L202-8 204-6; N240-5, O 251-1; P266-8 276-6; R311-2 312-7; T327-5 348-6.

6] [*engraved title*] NOVELS AND ROMANCES | OF | THE AUTHOR OF WAVERLEY. . . . VOL. VI. | PEVERIL OF THE PEAK, AND | QUENTIN DURWARD. | [*vignette of Castle of Peronne*] . . . . 1825.

Collation: A^{12} B^{6} . . . X^{12}. Pagination: [*engraved title*], *1* fly-title for *Peveril of the Peak, 2 blank, 3* 4-108 text concluded, *109* fly-title for *Quentin Durward, 110 blank, 111* 112-154 Introduction, *155* fly-title, *156 blank, 157* 158-382 text, chapters 1-14, *383* printer's imprint, *384 blank*. Illustration: frontispiece drawn by J. M. Wright, engraved by R. Baker, with caption 'Quentin Durward.' and inscription 'Quentin rescuing Isabelle at the sack of Schonwaldt.' Typography: Section signature S2 (page 317) is missigned L2.

Figures: A23-8 24-4; C59-3 60-5/6; E94-1 96-8; G131-2 132-7; I 158-5 168-4; L201-1, M206-2; N240-7, O 242-8; P267-2 276-4; R310-3 312-5; T347-12/1 348-7; X378-5 381-2.

7] [*engraved title*] NOVELS AND ROMANCES | OF | THE AUTHOR OF WAVERLEY. . . . VOL. VII. | QUENTIN DURWARD. | [*vignette of Castle of Plessis-le-Tours*] . . . . 1825.

Collation: A^{12} B^{6}. . . T^{12} U^{6} *X*1. Pagination: [*engraved title*], *1* fly-title, *2 blank, 3* 4-361 text of *Quentin Durward*, concluded, *362* printer's imprint. Illustration: frontispiece painted by W. Brockedon, engraved by C. Rolls, with caption 'Quentin Durward.' and inscription 'Quentin presenting to the Countess of Croye the letter of her Aunt'. Typography: In some copies signature O (page 241) is missigned P. Section signature P2 (page 261) is missigned I 2.

Figures: A23-8 24-7; C38-4, D67-2; E95-3 96-6; G131-5 132-1; I 154-3 168-7; L204-2; N230-2 240-7; P255-1, Q288-8; R298-3 312-7; T347-1 348-6.

TALES AND ROMANCES
[ST RONAN'S WELL—WOODSTOCK]

278A] Fourth Series, First 8° Edition: 1827

[*engraved title*] TALES AND ROMANCES | OF | THE AUTHOR OF WAVERLEY | VOL. I [II-VII]. | [*volume title*] | [*vignette*] | EDINBURGH; | PRINTED FOR CADELL AND Co. EDINBURGH, | AND LONGMAN, REES, ORME, BROWN AND GREEN | LONDON. | [*French dash*] | 1827.

Published 17 May 1827 in Edinburgh (*EEC*); issued 1 June in London (*MC*). £4.4.0. 1500 copies each of all three formats, 8°, 12°, and 18°, on 25 May 1826 were ordered to be printed by the Trustees administering Scott's affairs (*EEWN16*.394). Binding: drab boards with printed labels. Paper: Royal 8° (227 x 142mm uncut). Watermarks: *none*.

General Notes: Title vignettes are painted by J. Ewbank and engraved by W. H. Lizars, with volume 6 both painted and engraved by Lizars. The concluding printer's imprints read: [*short rule*] | EDINBURGH: | PRINTED BY JAMES BALLANTYNE AND CO.

Copies: BCL E E(Scott's interleaved copy, revised ca. 1830) ES(vols.5-7) L; CtY CtY* T/B.
*With undated 4-page Cadell catalogue.

1] [*engraved title*] TALES AND ROMANCES | OF | THE AUTHOR OF WAVERLEY | VOL. I. | St. RONAN'S WELL. | [*vignette of two men approaching a mansion*] . . . . 1827.

Collation: A-2H[8] 2I[4]. Pagination: [*engraved title*], *1* fly-title, *2 blank, 3* 4-503 text, chapters 1-26, *504* printer's imprint.

Figures: A16-4, B25-2, C48-6, D64-5, E80-1/-, F96-8, G112-5, H128-3, I 144-5, K160-6, L176-4, M192-1, N208-4, O 224-2, P240-8, Q256-5, R272-7, S288-3, T304-8, U320-4, X336-1, Y352-8, Z365-4, 2A 384-3, 2B 400-7, 2C 416-6, 2D 432-1, 2E 448-5, 2F 464-7, 2G 480-4, 2H 496-8, 2 I—.

2] [*engraved title*] TALES AND ROMANCES | OF | THE AUTHOR OF WAVERLEY | VOL. II. | St. RONAN'S WELL. | [*vignette of a church and a graveyard*] . . . . 1827.

Collation: A-2I[8] *2K*1. Pagination: [*engraved title*], *1* fly-title for *St Ronan's Well*, *2 blank, 3* 4-256 text concluded, *257* fly-title for *Redgauntlet*, *258 blank, 259* 260-513 text, letters 1-13, 513 printer's imprint, *514 blank.*

Figures: A16-3, B32-8, C48-1, D64-5, E80-7, F96-2, G112-7, H128-6, I 144-7,

K160-6, L176-1, M192-2, N208-4, O 224-3, P240-8, Q254-1, R—, S288-3, T304-7, U320-4, X336-1, Y352-6, Z368-7, 2A 384-7, 2B 400-3, 2C 416-4, 2D 432-7, 2E 448-5, 2F 464-1, 2G 480-8, 2H 496-1/-, 2 I 512-8, *2K*—.

3] [*engraved title*] TALES AND ROMANCES | OF | THE AUTHOR OF WAVERLEY | VOL. III. | REDGAUNTLET. | [*vignette of a lakeside cottage*] . . . . 1827.

Collation: A-2I^8 2K^4(-2K4). Pagination: [*engraved title*], *1* fly-title, *2 blank, 3* 4-518 text concluded, 518 printer's imprint.

Figures: A16-4, B29-1, C48-3, D64-4, E80-7, F96-6, G112-5, H128-2, I 144-7, K160-8, L176-2, M192-1, N206-3, O 224-6, P—, Q256-5, R272-3, S288-1, T304-5, U320-7, X336-5, Y352-5, Z368-8, 2A 384-2, 2B 400-6, 2C 416-8, 2D 432-6, 2E 448-3, 2F 464-1, 2G 480-7, 2H 496-5, 2 I 512-6, 2K 517-4.

4] [*engraved title*] TALES AND ROMANCES | OF | THE AUTHOR OF WAVERLEY | VOL. IV. | CRUSADERS. | [*vignette of a castle*] . . . . 1827.

Collation: A-2G^8 2H^4. Pagination: [*engraved title*], *1* fly-title for 'The Betrothed', *2 blank, 3* 4-25 Introduction, *26 blank, 27* 28-488 text, chapters 1-28, 488 printer's imprint.

Figures: A16-7, B32-12, C48-8, D64-11, E80-12, F96-10, G112-6, H128-2, I 144-8, K160-12, L176-6, M192-10, N208-4, O 224-12, P240-8, Q256-12, R272-10, S288-9, T304-2, U320-8, X336-3, Y352-6, Z368-7, 2A 384-11, 2B 400-13, 2C 416-7, 2D 432-6, 2E 448-12, 2F 464-7, 2G 480-7, 2H 486-6.

5] [*engraved title*] TALES AND ROMANCES | OF | THE AUTHOR OF WAVERLEY | VOL. V. | CRUSADERS. | [*vignette of a castle*] . . . . 1827.

Collation: A-2G^8 2H^4 2 I^2. Pagination: [*engraved title*], *1* fly-title for 'The Betrothed', *2 blank, 3* 4-90 text concluded, *91* fly-title for 'The Talisman', *92 blank, 93* 94-491 text, chapters 1-21, 491 printer's imprint, *492 blank*. Typography: In some copies page 257 is misnumbered 275.

Figures: A16-10, B28-6, C48-1, D64-13, E80-11, F96-8, G112-12, H128-12/-, I 144-12, K160-1, L176-8, M192-10, N—, O 224-1, P240-11, Q255-11, R272-5, S288-6, T304-4, U320-6, X336-2, Y352-6, Z363-3, 2A 384-7, 2B 400-13, 2C 416-11, 2D 429-9, 2E 448-9, 2F 462-14, 2G 480-6, 2H 488-2, 2 I—. Figure 12, page 128, is half-effaced in some copies, completely gone in others.

6] [*engraved title*] TALES AND ROMANCES | OF | THE AUTHOR OF WAVERLEY | VOL. VI. | CRUSADERS. | [*vignette of an enclosed well*] . . . . 1827.

Collation: A-K^8 L^8(L1+'L2'^{6}) M-2G^8 2H^2. Pagination: [*engraved title*], *1* fly-title for 'The Talisman', *2 blank, 3* 4-159 text concluded, *160 blank, 161* fly-title for *Woodstock*, *162 blank, 163* 164*-174* Preface, *163* 164-483 text, chapters 1-15, *484* printer's imprint.

Figures: A16-1, B32-6, C48-1, D64-7, E80-5, F96-8, G112-3, H128-7, I 144-3, K149-2, L*173-9 175-7, M192-8, N208-6, O 224-7, P240-5, Q256-8, R272-4, S288-3, T304-14, U320-3, X336-8, Y350-9, Z368-10, 2A 384-11, 2B 400-5, 2C 413-4, 2D 432-8, 2E 448-2, 2F 464-2, 2G 480-4, 2H—.

Notes: The inserted six-leaf 'L2' gathering, with starred page-numbers, represents the Preface, returned belatedly to (or temporarily mislaid by) the printer. Misplaced before this, as a paper apart in the E interleaved copy, are the heavily corrected proofs for the new Introduction to *Chronicles of the Canongate* (vol. 41 in the 'Magnum Opus'), these probably representing the last proofs attended by Scott, and dated by him 15 August 1831.

7] [*engraved title*] TALES AND ROMANCES | OF | THE AUTHOR OF WAVERLEY | VOL. VII. | WOODSTOCK. | [*vignette of a castle in the distance*] . . . . 1827.

Collation: A-2H^8 2I^4 2K^2. Pagination: [*engraved title*], *1* fly-title, *2 blank, 3* 4-507 text concluded, 507 printer's imprint, *508 blank.* Typography: Signatures 2A and 2B (pages 369, 385) are missigned A2 and B2.

Figures: A16-7, B32-16/6, C48-10, D64-5, E80-7, F96-6, G112-1, H128-2, I 144-4, K160-12, L176-9, M192-12, N208-12, O 224-3, P240-6, Q256-9, R272-7, S288-2, T304-4, U320-7, X336-2, Y352-7, Z368-2, 2A 384-7, 2B 400-2, 2C 416-8, 2D 432-8, 2E 448-7, 2F 464-6, 2G 480-2, 2H 496-5, 2 I 501-8, 2K—.

279A] Fourth Series, 12° Edition: 1827

[*engraved title*] TALES AND ROMANCES, | OF | THE AUTHOR OF WAVERLEY. | VOL. I [II-IX]. | [*double dash*] | [*volume title*] | [*double dash*] | [*vignette*] | EDINBURGH; | PRINTED FOR CADELL AND Co. EDINBURGH: | AND LONGMAN, REES, ORME, BROWN AND GREEN. | LONDON. | [*French dash*] | 1827.

Published 28 July 1827 in Edinburgh (*EEC*). £3.7.6. 1500 copies each of all three formats, 8°, 12°, and 18°, on 25 May 1826 were ordered to be printed by the Trustees administering Scott's affairs (*EEWN16*.394). Binding: Drab boards with printed labels. Paper: Demy 12° (178 x 102mm uncut). Watermarks: *none*. Illustrations: Since this smaller 12° format extends to nine volumes, two new title vignettes (for volumes 6 and 9) are now supplied. Two other vignettes (in volumes 3 and 4) reappear in reverse order. Throughout W. H. Lizars is recorded below title vignette as the engraver, but the artist is identified in only three volumes: J. Ewbank for volumes 2 and 5, J. B. Kidd for volume 6. Also in these three volumes only, LONDON is moved up on-line after GREEN. Concluding printer's imprints read: [*short rule*] | EDINBURGH: | PRINTED BY JAMES BALLANTYNE AND CO. ['& Co.' vols. 1, 6.].

Copies: BCL E E(vols.1-2, 5-9) L; IdU NNU-W(vols.5-6) T/B*.
*With July 1827 Longman catalogue.

1] [*engraved title*] TALES AND ROMANCES, | OF | THE AUTHOR OF WAVERLEY. | VOL.I. | [*double dash*] | ST. RONAN'S WELL. | [*double dash*] | [*vignette of two men approaching a mansion*] . . . 1827.

Collation: A-Q^{12}. Pagination: [*engraved title*], *1* fly-title, *2 blank, 3* 4-383 text, chapters 1-19, 383 printer's imprint, *384 blank.*

Figures: A24-3, B48-1, C72-6, D96-5, E120-4, F144-6, G168-5, H190-5, I 216-7, K240-2, L264-7, M288-4, N312-8, O 336-1, P360-1, Q364-2.

2] [*engraved title*] TALES AND ROMANCES, | OF | THE AUTHOR OF WAVERLEY. | VOL.II. | [*double dash*] | ST. RONAN'S WELL. | [*double dash*] | [*vignette of a church and a graveyard*] . . . . 1827.

Collation: A-R^{12}. Pagination: [*engraved title*], *1* fly-title, *2 blank, 3* 4-408 text concluded, 408 printer's imprint. Typography: Page 376 is misnumbered 76.

Figures: A16-6, B48-8, C72-3, D96-3, E120-2, F136-8, G168-4, H192-6, I 216-4, K240-2, L264-7, M288-4, N312-8, O 336-10, P360-1, Q384-3, R388-11.

Notes: In gathering C the four-leaf section inserted between pages 56 and 65 is usually folded wrongly, with pagination thus proceeding 59-60, 57-58, 63-64, 61-62.

3] [*engraved title*] TALES AND ROMANCES, | OF | THE AUTHOR OF WAVERLEY. | VOL.III. | [*double dash*] | REDGAUNTLET. | [*double dash*] | [*vignette of a castle*] . . . . 1827.

Collation: A-R^{12} S^{6} T^{4}(-T4). Pagination: [*engraved title*], *1* fly-title, *2 blank, 3* 4-426 text, chapters 1-22, 426 printer's imprint.

Figures: A24-12, B48-4, C72-10, D96-1, E120-6, F144-7, G168-5, H192-1, I216-10, K240-4, L264-2, M288-4, N312-12, O 336-10, P360-6, Q384-8, R408-10, S416-3, T424-2.

4] [*engraved title*] TALES AND ROMANCES, | OF | THE AUTHOR OF WAVERLEY. | VOL.IV. | [*double dash*] | REDGAUNTLET. | [*double dash*] | [*vignette of a lakeside cottage*] . . . . 1827.

Collation: A-Q^{12}. Pagination: [*engraved title*], *1* fly-title, *2 blank, 3* 4-383 text concluded, 383 printer's imprint, *384 blank.*

Figures: A24-5, B48-12, C72-10, D96-5, E120-6, F144-10, G168-7, H192-7, I 216-5, K240-7, L264-12, M288-13, N312-10, O 336-1, P360-6, Q381-5.

5] [*engraved title*] TALES AND ROMANCES, | OF | THE AUTHOR OF WAVERLEY. | VOL.V. | [*double dash*] | CRUSADERS. | [*double dash*] | [*vignette of a castle*] . . . . 1827.

Collation: A-Q^{12} R^{6} S1. Pagination: [*engraved title*], *1* fly-title for *Tales of the Crusaders*. Tale I. 'The Betrothed', *2 blank, 3* 4-26 Introduction, 27 28-398 text, chapters 1-21, 398 printer's imprint.

Figures: A24-10, B48-13, C72-5, D96-2, E120-7, F144-1, G168-1, H192-2, I 216-8, K240-3, L264-8, M288-7, N312-7, O 336-8, P360-8, Q384-2, R392-1/-, S—.

6] [*engraved title*] TALES AND ROMANCES, | OF | THE AUTHOR OF WAVERLEY. | VOL. VI. | [*double dash*] | CRUSADERS. | [*double dash*] | [*vignette of a distant lake*] . . . . 1827.

Collation: A-Q^{12} R^{6}. Pagination: [*engraved title*], 1 fly-title for *Tales of the Crusaders*. Tale I. 'The Betrothed', *2 blank, 3* 4-199 text concluded, *200 blank, 201* fly-title for *Tales of the Crusaders*. Tale II. 'The Talisman', *202 blank, 203* 204-394 text, chapters 1-9, 394 printer's imprint, *395-396 blank.*

Figures: A24-8, B39-2/-, C72-8, D96-2, E120-8, F144-1, G168-6, H192-3, I 216-7, K240-8, L264-6, M288-3, N312-11, O 336-4, P360-6, Q384-3, R386-4.

7] [*engraved title*] TALES AND ROMANCES, | OF | THE AUTHOR OF WAVERLEY. | VOL.VII. | [*double dash*] | CRUSADERS. | [*double dash*] | [*vignette of an enclosed well*] . . . . 1827.

Collation: A-Q^{12}. Pagination: [*engraved title*], *1* fly-title for *Tales of the Crusaders.* Tale II. 'The Talisman', *2 blank, 3* 4-383 text concluded, 383 printer's imprint, *384 blank.*

Figures: A24-13, B48-8, C59-1, D93-8, E120-7, F144-6, G168-7, H192-8, I 216-8/-, K240-5, L264-6, M288-2, N304-2, O 336-1, P360-5, Q381-5.

8] [*engraved title*] TALES AND ROMANCES, | OF | THE AUTHOR OF WAVERLEY. | VOL.VIII. | [*double dash*] | WOODSTOCK. | [*double dash*] | [*vignette of a castle in the distance*] . . . . 1827.

Collation: A-S^{12} T^{4}. Pagination: [*engraved title*], *1* fly-title, *2 blank, 3* 4-14 Preface, *15* 16-440 text, chapters 1-19, 440 printer's imprint. Typography: The printer's imprint omits 'JAMES'.

Figures: A23-2, B40-1, C72-4, D96-7, E—, F144-7, G168-7, H192-7, I 216-1, K232-1, L264-7, M288-7, N312-8, O 336-7, P360-7, Q384-1, R408-7, S432-5, T—.

9] [*engraved title*] TALES AND ROMANCES, | OF | THE AUTHOR OF WAVERLEY. | VOL.IX. | [*double dash*] | WOODSTOCK. | [*double dash*] | [*vignette of a castle in the distance*] . . . . 1827.

Collation: A-R^{12} S^{6} T^{4}. Pagination: [*engraved title*], *1* fly-title, *2 blank, 3* 4-426 text concluded, 426 printer's imprint, *427-428 blank.* Typography: Page 296 is misnumbered 96. The printer's imprint omits 'JAMES'.

Figures: A24-4, B48-2, C64-6, D96-7, E120-2/-, F144-5, G157-6, H192-1, I 216-2, K240-6, L264-7, M276-1, N312-8, O 336-3, P360-2, Q381-7, R408-2, S420-7, T—

280Aa] Fourth Series, First 18° Edition: 1828[1827]

[*engraved title*] TALES AND ROMANCES | OF | THE AUTHOR OF WAVERLEY | IN SEVEN VOLUMES. | VOL.I [II-VII]. | [*volume title*] | [*vignette*] | EDINBURGH; | PRINTED FOR CADELL AND Co. EDINBURGH; | AND LONGMAN, REES, ORME, BROWN AND GREEN. LONDON. | 1828[1827].

Published 27 October 1827 in Edinburgh (*EEC*). £2.9.0. 1500 copies each of all three formats, 8°, 12°, and 18°, on 25 May 1826 were ordered to be printed by the Trustees administering Scott's affairs (*EEWN16*.394). Paper: Demy 18° in sixes (149 x 96mm uncut). Watermarks: none. Illustrations: Unlike the three 18° sequences earlier issued, or the one following in 1833, this edition represents a new series of title vignettes as well as frontispieces. The vignette for volume 2 is both drawn and engraved by W. H. Lizars, for the other volumes drawn by J. B. Kidd and engraved by W. H. Lizars, with imprint uniformly dated 1828 in volumes 1-3, but as noted below 1827 or 1828 in each of the succeeding volumes 4-7. The frontispieces, all dated 1828 (except for 1827 volume 5), are drawn by William Heath and again engraved by Lizars (except for volume 7 engraved by J. Horsburgh), with Cadell and Longman imprint throughout. The printing was done by at least four firms, as indicated in volume descriptions, and unlike previous 18° formats is now imposed regularly in thirds (three signatures therefore to a sheet).

Copies: CtY(vols 4-7 dated 1827, 1828, 1827, 1828) T/B(vols 4-7 dated 1828, 1827, 1827, 1827).

1] [*engraved title*] TALES AND ROMANCES | OF | THE AUTHOR OF WAVERLEY . . . VOL.I. | ST. RONAN'S WELL. | [*vignette of distant castle on hill*] . . . . 1828.

Collation: A-2H^6. Pagination: [*engraved title*], *1* fly-title, *2 blank, 3* 4-371 text, chapters 1-26, 371 printer's imprint, *372 blank.* Printer's imprint: [*short rule*] | EDINBURGH: | PRINTED BY BALLANTYNE AND CO. Illustration: frontispiece with caption 'St. Ronan's Well.' and inscription 'Mowbray's interview with His Sister.'

Figures: C35-7; F72-6; I 108-8; M144-8; P180-1; S212-1 216-2; X251-7 252-6; Z266-7, 2A 288-6; 2D 323-7 324-1; 2E 335-3 336-6.

2] [*engraved title*] TALES AND ROMANCES | OF | THE AUTHOR OF WAVERLEY . . . VOL.II. | REDGAUNTLET. | [*vignette of footbridge*] . . . . 1828.

Collation: A-2H^6 2 I^4. Pagination: [*engraved title*], *1* fly-title, *2 blank, 3* 4-190 text of *St Ronan's Well* concluded, *191* fly-title for *Redgauntlet*, *192 blank, 193* 194-379 text through Letter XII, 379 printer's imprint, *380 blank.* Printer's imprint: [*short rule*] | EDINBURGH: | PRINTED BY BALLANTYNE AND CO. Illustration: frontispiece with caption 'Redgauntlet.' and inscription 'Wandering Willie, His Wife & Benjie discovered by Darsie Latimer.' Typography: Section signature B2 (page 17) is missigned 2B and signature E (page 49) is missigned F. The second digit in page number 141 is upside down.

Figures: C35-7 36-3; D38-7, F72-5; G80-2 84-7; K116-2, M144-6; P179-2 180-6; S215-3 216-4; X251-4 252-5; 2A 287-2 288-7; 2C 311-4, 2D 324-5; 2G 359-7; 2H 372-6, 2 I 374-1.

3] [*engraved title*] TALES AND ROMANCES | OF | THE AUTHOR OF WAVERLEY . . . VOL.III. | REDGAUNTLET. | [*vignette of two horsemen on a cliff*] . . . . 1828.

Collation: A-2I^6 2K1. Pagination: [*engraved title*], *1* fly-title, *2 blank, 3* 4-398 text concluded, 398 printer's imprint: [*short rule*] | Auchie, Printer, Edinburgh. Illustration: frontispiece with caption 'Redgauntlet.' and inscription 'Meeting of Father Buonaventure with Allan Fairford, Miss Arthuret, & Miss Seraphina.' Typography: Unlike Ballantyne, this and the other printers identified below do not use sheet numbers. Figures: *none.*

4] [*engraved title*] TALES AND ROMANCES | OF | THE AUTHOR OF WAVERLEY . . . VOL.IV. | THE BETROTHED | [*vignette of a castle on a hill*] . . . 1828.

Collation: A-2H^6 2*I*1. Pagination: [*engraved title*], *1* fly-title for *Tales of the Crusaders.* Tale I. 'The Betrothed', *2 blank, 3* 4-21 Introduction, *22 blank, 23* 24-373 text, chapters 1-29, 373 printer's imprint, *374 blank.* Printer's imprint: [*short rule*] | Auchie, Printer, Edinburgh. Illustration: frontispiece with caption 'The Betrothed.' and inscription 'Approach of Eveline to Her Aunt the Ancient Lady of Baldringham.' Typography: Section signatures A2, B2, C2, E2, and 2H2 (pages 5, 17, 29, 53, 365) are omitted. Page numbers 358, 359 are entered at inner margin and the headlines reversed. Figures: *none.*

5] [*engraved title*] TALES AND ROMANCES | OF | THE AUTHOR OF WAVERLEY. . . VOL.V. | THE BETROTHED. | [*vignette of a maiden by a spring*] . . . 1827.

Collation: A-2G^6 2H1. Pagination: [*engraved title*], *1* fly-title for *Tales of the Crusaders.* Tale I. 'The Betrothed', *2 blank, 3* 4-68 text concluded, *69* fly-title for Tale II. 'The Talisman', *70 blank, 71* 72-362 text, chapters 1-21. Illustration: frontispiece with caption 'The Talisman.' and inscription ' Sir Kenneth & the Emir at the Diamond of the Desert.' Typography: This unidentified printer uses volume direction lines for each six-leaf section of the sheet. Section signature Y2 (page 257) is missigned X2.

Figures: C36-1; I 108-1; S216-2; 2D 324-2.

6] [*engraved title*] TALES AND ROMANCES | OF | THE AUTHOR OF WAVERLEY . . . VOL.VI. | THE TALISMAN. | [*vignette of palm trees*] . . . . 1827.

Collation: A-2G^6 2H^6(-2H6). Pagination: [*engraved title*], *1* fly-title for *Tales of the Crusaders.* Tale II. 'The Talisman', *2 blank, 3* 4-119 text concluded, *120 blank, 121* fly-title for *Woodstock*, *122 blank, 123* 124-370 text, chapters 1-15, 370 printer's imprint: EDINBURGH: | PRINTED BY JAMES CLARKE AND CO. Illustration: frontispiece with caption 'Woodstock.' and inscription 'Scene with the Pastor and Master Tomkins in the Church at Woodstock.' Typography: Though the latter, *Woodstock* portion is entirely regular, the preceding sheets exhibit all manner of irregularities, viz: section signature A2 wrongly entered on page *3*; signature B (page 13) unsigned; section signatures D2-H2 (pages 41-89) signed D3-H3; signatures H, I (pages 85, 97) unsigned in some copies but with volume direction line; section signatures K2, L2, M2 (pages 113, 125, 137) unsigned. All of these variables would suggest composition of the earlier sheets in several different shops. In the later part signatures 2A-2H are signed Aa-Hh, a practice which probably may be attributed to printer Clarke: see next volume.

Figures: 2D 323-1; 2F 347-1.

7] [*engraved title*] TALES AND ROMANCES | OF | THE AUTHOR OF WAVERLEY . . . VOL.VII. | WOODSTOCK. | [*vignette of a woman by a spring*] . . . . 1827.

Collation: A-2H[6]. Pagination: [*engraved title*], *1* fly-title, *2 blank, 3* 4-372 text concluded, 372 printer's imprint: EDINBURGH: | PRINTED BY JAMES CLARKE AND CO. Illustration: frontispiece with caption 'Woodstock.' and inscription 'Wildrake's interview with Cromwell.' Typography: The last 2H signature (page 361) is signed Hh and thus, as in volume 6, may be attributed to printer Clarke.

Figures: 2A 288-2; 2D 324-1.

280Ab] Fourth Series, Second 18° Edition: 1828

[*engraved title*] TALES AND ROMANCES | OF | THE AUTHOR OF WAVERLEY | IN SEVEN VOLUMES. | VOL.I [II-VII]. | [*volume title*] | [*vignette*] | CADELL AND Co. EDINBURGH, | WHITTAKER AND Co. LONDON. | 1828.

Issued 5 May 1828 in London (*MC*, 'Second Edition'). £2.9.0. Paper: Demy 18° in sixes (cut). Watermarks: *none.*

General Notes: This 18° edition now exhibits in the imprint a different London publisher. As before, the title vignettes are drawn by J. B. Kidd and engraved by W. H. Lizars. The frontispieces are drawn by William Heath and again engraved by Lizars, with Lizars doing both the drawing and engraving for volume 3 and J. Horsburgh cited as the engraver for volume 7; all plates with Cadell and Whittaker imprint dated 1828.

Possibly this scarce issue, the only one in 18° format to go into a second edition, and then only six months after the first, represents the further order of 1000 copies requested by Cadell (*see* supplementary note in *EEWN17*.304, which, however, suggests 1829 as the date of issue). The printing was done by four firms, as indicated below.

Copy: L.

1] [*engraved title*] TALES AND ROMANCES | OF | THE AUTHOR OF

WAVERLEY . . . VOL.I. | ST. RONAN'S WELL. | [*vignette of distant castle on a hill*] . . . . 1828.

Collation: A-2H^6 2I^4(-2I4). Pagination: [*engraved title*], 1 fly-title, *2 blank, 3* 4-377 text, chapters 1-25, 377 printer's imprint, *378 blank.* Printer's imprint: [*short rule*] | EDINBURGH: PRINTED BY BALLANTYNE AND CO. Illustration: frontispiece with caption 'St. Ronan's Well.' and inscription 'Mowbray's interview with His Sister.' Typography: Section signatures L2 and M2 (pages 125, 137) are missigned 2L and 2M. Figures: *none.*

2] [*engraved title*] TALES AND ROMANCES | OF | THE AUTHOR OF WAVERLEY . . . VOL.II. | REDGAUNTLET. | [*vignette of a footbridge*] . . . . 1828.

Collation: A-2H^6 *2 I*^{4}(-*2 I*4.) Pagination: [*engraved title*], *1* fly-title, *2 blank, 3* 4-190 text of *St Ronan's Well* concluded, *191* fly-title for *Redgauntlet*, *192 blank, 193* 194-378 text through Letter XIII, 378 printer's imprint: EDINBURGH: | PRINTED BY THOMAS CONSTABLE. Illustration: frontispiece with caption 'Redgauntlet.' and inscription 'Meeting of Father Buonaventure with Allan Fairford, Miss Arthuret, & Miss Seraphina.' Typography: Section signature 2H2 (page 365) is unsigned. Figures: *none.*

Notes: It may be observed that the frontispieces for volumes 2-3 in the first 18° edition are here transposed.

3] [*engraved title*] TALES AND ROMANCES | OF | THE AUTHOR OF WAVERLEY . . . VOL.III. | REDGAUNTLET. | [*vignette of two horsemen on a cliff*] . . . . 1828.

Collation: A-2K^6. Pagination: [*engraved title*], *1* fly-title, *2 blank, 3* 4-396 text concluded, 396 printer's imprint: EDINBURGH: | Printed by ANDREW SHORTREDE, Thistle Lane. Illustration: frontispiece with caption 'Redgauntlet.' and inscription 'Wandering Willie, His Wife & Benjie discovered by Darsie Latimer.' Typography: This printer continues to use sheet-numbers for every three gatherings, 1 on A1, 2 on D1, &c. Figures: *none*

4] [*engraved title*] TALES AND ROMANCES | OF | THE AUTHOR OF WAVERLEY . . . VOL.IV. | THE BETROTHED | [*vignette of a castle on a hill*] . . . . 1828.

Collation: A-2G^6 2H^6(-2H6). Pagination: [*engraved title*], *1* fly-title for *Tales of the Crusaders.* Tale I. 'The Betrothed', *2 blank, 3* 4-21 Introduction, *22 blank, 23* 24-369 text, chapters 1-28, 369 printer's imprint, *370 blank.* Printer's imprint: [*short rule*] | EDINBURGH: | PRINTED BY JOHN STARK, OLD ASSEMBLY

CLOSE. Illustration: frontispiece with caption 'The Betrothed.' and inscription 'Approach of Eveline to Her Aunt the Ancient Lady of Baldringham.' Typography: Though not employing sheet numbers this printer still enters no more than two figures for every three 6-leaf gatherings: a circumstance confirming the imposition of three sections to a forme.

Figures: A10-3, C36-4; F62-3 72-4; G74-3, H90-4; K120-4, L128-3; N150-4, O 164-3; Q182-4; T228-4, X242-1; 2C 312-6; 2G 360-1.

5] [*engraved title*] TALES AND ROMANCES | OF | THE AUTHOR OF WAVERLEY . . . VOL.V. | THE BETROTHED. | [*vignette of a maiden by a spring*] . . . . 1828.

Collation: A-2H^6 2I^6(-2I 6). Pagination: [*engraved title*], *1* fly-title for *Tales of the Crusaders.* Tale I. 'The Betrothed', *2 blank, 3* 4-72 text concluded, *73* fly-title for Tale II. 'The Talisman', *74 blank, 75* 76-382 text, chapters 1-21, 382 printer's imprint: EDINBURGH: | Printed by ANDREW SHORTREDE, Thistle Lane. Illustration: frontispiece with caption 'The Talisman.' and inscription 'Sir Kenneth & the Emir at the Diamond of the Desert.' Typography: Section signature A2 (page 5) is omitted and 2A2 (page 281) is missigned 2. As in his earlier printing of volume 3, Shortrede employs sheet numbers but no press figures.

6] [*engraved title*] TALES AND ROMANCES | OF | THE AUTHOR OF WAVERLEY . . . VOL.VI. | THE TALISMAN. | [*vignette of palm trees*] . . . . 1828.

Collation: A-2H^6 2 I^4. Pagination: [*engraved title*], *1* fly-title for *Tales of the Crusaders.* Tale II. 'The Talisman', *2 blank, 3* 4-121 text concluded, *122 blank, 123* fly-title for *Woodstock, 124 blank, 125* 126-379 text, chapters 1-15, 379 printer's imprint, *380 blank.* Printer's imprint: [*short rule*] | EDINBURGH: | PRINTED BY JOHN STARK, OLD ASSEMBLY CLOSE. Illustration: Frontispiece with caption 'Woodstock.' and inscription 'Scene with the Pastor and Master Tomkins in the Church at Woodstock.' Typography: Page 233 is misnumbered 333 and direction line page 337 reads 'VOL. IV.' As in his earlier printing of volume 4, Stark does not use sheet numbers, but does enter press figures.

Figures: A8-1; D48-1; G74-3; M140-3 144-4; O 164-3, P180-4; S212- 4; T218-4 228-3; 2A 284-3 288-4; 2B 290-4, 2D 324-3; 2E 332-4, 2G 354-3; 2I 378-3.

7] [*engraved title*] TALES AND ROMANCES | OF | THE AUTHOR OF WAVERLEY . . . VOL.VII. | WOODSTOCK. | [*vignette of a woman by a spring*] . . . . 1828.

Collation: A-2H^6. Pagination: [*engraved title*], *1* fly-title, *2 blank, 3* 4-372 text concluded, 372 printer's imprint: EDINBURGH: PRINTED BY THOMAS CONSTABLE. Illustration: Frontispiece with caption 'Woodstock.' and inscription 'Wildrake's interview with Cromwell.' Figures: *none.*

Notes: This is the only volume in which the collation and pagination are, coincidentally, identical with the first 18° edition.

TALES AND ROMANCES [CHRONICLES OF THE CANONGATE—CASTLE DANGEROUS]

281A] Fifth Series, 8° Edition: 1833

[*engraved title*] TALES AND ROMANCES | OF | THE AUTHOR OF WAVERLEY | VOL. VIII [IX-XIV] | [*volume title*] | [*vignette*] | EDINBURGH; | PRINTED FOR ROBERT CADELL, EDINBURGH; | AND WHITTAKER & Co. LONDON. | [*French dash*] | 1833.

Issued 4 May 1833 in London (*Ath*). £5.8.0 (including the two-volume supplementary XV-XVI *Introductions*). Paper: Royal 8° (222 x 138mm uncut). Watermarks: *none*. Illustrations: Title vignettes are painted either by J. Ewbank (vol-umes 8, 11-14) or by D. O. Hill (volumes 9-10) and engraved by James Johnstone. Typography: The volume numbering for this series carries on from the previous issues. In volumes 8-11 printer's imprints read: (1) EDINBURGH: PRINTED BY BALLANTYNE AND COMPANY, PAUL'S WORK, CANONGATE.; (2) [*short rule*] | EDINBURGH: | PRINTED BY BALLANTYNE AND COMANY, | PAUL'S WORK, CANONGATE.; (3) [*short rule*] | PRINTED BY BALLANTYNE AND COMPANY, EDINBURGH. The entries in volumes 12-14, by three other printers, are cited below. Probably these others were engaged to speed up the issue before it was overtaken by the Magnum.

General Notes: This final sequence in all three formats, together with the two- or three-volume supplements for each (284A-286A), apparently were all issued simultaneously. Several days earlier, on 1 May 1833, was published the last, 48th volume of the Magnum *Waverley Novels* and, that same day, the first volume of the subsequent *Poetical Works*—certainly a marvelous concurrence.

Hitherto, as noted above, Scott in revising the text for his Magnum edition used an interleaved copy of these collected octavo series. For the novels reprinted in this latest (posthumous) sequence, however, he necessarily resorted to the earlier separate editions already identified (206Ab.2; 206Ac.1; 215Ab; 227A.1,3 [vol.2 not discovered]). *See* Claire Lamont, pages 39-40, in Iain Gordon Brown (ed.), *Scott's Interleaved Waverley Novels*.

Copies: E(2) ES L: CtY T/B.

8] [*engraved title*] TALES AND ROMANCES | OF | THE AUTHOR OF WAVERLEY | VOL. VIII | HIGHLAND WIDOW | [*vignette of waterfall and stream*] . . . . 1833.

Collation: *a-b*^{8} A-2G^8 2H^4. Pagination: [*engraved title*], *i* fly-title for *Chronicles of the Canongate*, *ii* Printer's imprint(1), *iii* iv-xxxi Introduction, dated from Abbotsford 1 October 1827, *xxxii blank*, *1* 2-120 Introductory, *121* fly-title for 'Highland Widow', *122 blank*, *123* 124-237 text, 238-242 Introductory for 'The Two Drovers', *243* 244-290 text, *291* fly-title for 'My Aunt Margaret's Mirror', *292 blank*, *293* 294-296 Introduction dated August 1831, *297* 298-354 text, 355 fly-title for 'The Tapestried Chamber', *356 blank*, *357* Introduction dated August 1831, *358 blank*, *359* 360-384 text, *385* fly-title for 'Death of The Laird's Jock', *386 blank*, *387* introduction [four lines] dated August 1831, *387* 388-396 text, *397* fly-title for *Saint Valentine's Day; or, The Fair Maid of Perth*, *398 blank*, *399* 400-414 Introductory, *415* 416-488 text, chapters 1-4, 488 printer's imprint(2). Typography: Preliminary signatures *a-b* are in italics.

Figures: *a* x-6, *b* xxiii-2, A16-1, B32-6, C44-3, D57-5, E80-2, F96-1, G112-5, H*123*-3, I 141-6, K157-5, L176-1, M192-5/-, N208-2, O 212-2, P240-1, Q254-5, R266-5, S288-1, T304-6, U315-2, X333-2, Y347-5, Z368-1, 2A 383-6, 2B 400-2, 2C *415*-5, 2D 432-6, 2E 448-1, 2F 462-2, 2G 480-5, 2H 486-6.

9] [*engraved title*] TALES AND ROMANCES | OF | THE AUTHOR OF WAVERLEY | VOL. IX | FAIR MAID OF PERTH | [*vignette showing distant view of a city*] . . . . 1833.

Collation: A-2H^8 2 I^2. Pagination: [*engraved title*], *1* fly-title, *2 blank*, *3* 4-500 text continued, 500 printer's imprint(2).

Figures: A16-2, B32-5, C48-3, D64-3, E80-5, F90-2, G109-5, H128-2, I 143-3, K157-2, L176-6, M189-5, N208-5, O 224-5, P240-1, Q—, R272-5, S288-2, T304-3, U320-3, X336-3, Y349-6, Z354-2, 2A 384-3, 2B 400-6, 2C 413-6, 2D 432-3, 2E 448-2, 2F 464-2, 2G 478-3/-, 2H 496-6, 2 I—.

10] [*engraved title*] TALES AND ROMANCES | OF | THE AUTHOR OF WAVERLEY | VOL. X | FAIR MAID OF PERTH | [*vignette of two boats*] . . . . 1833.

Collation: A-2H^8 2 I^8(-2I 8). Pagination: [*engraved title*], *1* fly-title for *The Fair Maid of Perth*, *2 blank*, *3* 4-236 text concluded, *237* fly-title for *Anne of Geierstein*, *238 blank*, *239* 240-509 text, chapters 1-12, 509 printer's imprint(2), *510 blank*.

Figures: A9-2, B—, C43-2, D64-2, E80-1, F95-7, G109-8, H128-1, I 144-7, K160-3, L169-6, M192-7, N207-2, O 224-6, P240-6, Q256-1, R272-2, S288-6, T291-2, U320-7, X336-1, Y352-6, Z368-2, 2A 384-7/-, 2B 389-6, 2C 416-2, 2D 432-1, 2E 442-8, 2F 464-8, 2G 479-8, 2H—, 2 I 501-8.

11] [*engraved title*] TALES AND ROMANCES | OF | THE AUTHOR OF WAVERLEY | VOL. XI | ANNE OF GEIERSTEIN | [*vignette of a castle in the distance*] . . . . 1833.

Collation: A-2H^8. Pagination: [*engraved title*], *1* fly-title, *2 blank, 3* 4-496 text continued, 496 printer's imprint(3).

Figures: A—, B32-8, C47-2/-, D64-4, E78-3, F96-4, G112-3, H128-4, I 144-4, K147-5, L176-2, M192-7, N195-2, O 224-7, P—, Q255-5, R272-4, S287-7, T292-6/-, U320-2, X336-4, Y352-4, Z368-6, 2A 378-3, 2B 400-3, 2C 415-5/1, 2D 426-7, 2E 448-4, 2F 462-5, 2G 478-4, 2H 493-2.

12] [*engraved title*] TALES AND ROMANCES | OF | THE AUTHOR OF WAVERLEY | VOL. XII | COUNT ROBERT OF PARIS | [*vignette of lakeshore*] . . . . 1833.

Collation: A-2I^8 2K^4 *2L*1. Pagination: [*engraved title*], *1* fly-title for *Anne of Geierstein, 2* printer's imprint(1), *3* 4-84 text concluded, *85* fly-title for *Tales of My Landlord*. Fourth Series, *86 blank, 87* 88-119 Introductory Address, *120 blank, 121* fly-title for 'Count Robert of Paris', *122 blank, 123* 124-521 text, chapters 1-17, 521 printer's imprint(2), *522 blank*. Printer's imprints: (1) EDINBURGH: PRINTED BY JAMES CLARKE & CO. OLD STAMP OFFICE.; (2) [*short rule*] | EDINBURGH: | PRINTED BY JAMES CLARKE AND CO. Typography: Signatures 2A-2K are signed Aa-Kk, according to Clarke's practice.

Figures: A16-2, B32-3, C46-1 48-2, D62-2/- 64-1, E79-2 80-1, F—, G110-2 112-1, H—, I 135-2 144-1, K158-1 160-2, L176-1, M178-2 192-1, N207-1 208-2, O 222-1, P235-1 240-3, Q254-3 256-1, R271-1 272-3, S286-3 288-1, T302-1 304-3, U309-2 315-1, X334-1 336-2, Y341-3 350-1, Z354-3 368-1, 2A 379-2, 2B 398-2/3 400-2, 2C 410-2 413-3, 2D 426-2 432-1, 2E 439-1 444-3, 2F 462-2 464-3, 2G 478-1 480-3, 2H 494-1 496-2, 2 I 510-3 512-1, 2K—, *2L*—.

13] [*engraved title*] TALES AND ROMANCES | OF | THE AUTHOR OF WAVERLEY | VOL. XIII | COUNT ROBERT OF PARIS | [*vignette of a city in the distance*] . . . . 1833.

Collation: A-2 I^8 2K^4. Pagination: [*engraved title*], *1* fly-title for 'Count Robert of Paris', *2 blank, 3* 4-313 text concluded, *314 blank, 315* fly-title for 'Castle Dangerous', *316 blank, 317* 318-520 text, chapters 1-12, 520 printer's imprint: [*short rule*] | EDINBURGH: | PRINTED BY NEILL & COMPANY, | OLD FISHMARKET. Typography: Gatherings 2A-2K are signed Aa-Kk, according to the practice of Neill & Company.

Figures: A8-3 11-2, B29-4 31-5, C48-4, D60-3, E71-5, F91-1, G100-4, H124-2, I 144-3, K149-5, L169-2, M—, N201-2, O 213-5, P238-1, Q253-4, R268-5, S281-2,

T301-4, U*317*-2, X325-3, Y352-2, Z357-1, 2A 381-4, 2B 395-2, 2C 413-5, 2D 425-4, 2E 440-5, 2F 460-3/-, 2G—, 2H 496-4, 2 I 508-5, 2K 519-1.

14] [*engraved title*] TALES AND ROMANCES | OF | THE AUTHOR OF WAVERLEY | VOL. XIV | CASTLE DANGEROUS | [*vignette of cottage and stream*] . . . . 1833.

Collation: A-2I^8 2K^4(-2K4). Pagination: [*engraved title*], *1* fly-title for *Tales of My Landlord.* Fourth Series, *2* printer's imprint(1), *3* fly-title for 'Castle Dangerous', *4 blank, 5* 6-165 text concluded, 165-166 postscript, dated from Abbotsford September 1831, *167* fly-title for 'The Surgeon's Daughter', *168 blank, 169* 170-474 text, *475* fly-title for Glossary, *476 blank, 477* 478-517 text, 518 printer's imprint(2). Printer's imprints (1) and (2): EDINBURGH: | Printed by ANDREW SHORTREDE, Thistle Lane.

Figures: A16-4/-, B—, C48-3, D56-3 61-3/-, E80-4, F88-2, G109-4, H125-3, I 137-3 142-6, K158-3, L164-4 174-4, M189-3, N201-4, O 219-3, P238-5, Q254-4, R264-4, S288-5, T304-4, U320-5, X336-4, Y351-4 352-5, Z368-1, 2A 379-1 384-5, 2B 400-3, 2C 416-4, 2D 430-3 432-1, 2E 445-4, 2F 464-4, 2G *477*-4 478-3, 2H—, 2 I 509-2, 2K—.

282A] Fifth Series, 16° Edition: 1833

[*engraved title*] TALES AND ROMANCES, | OF | THE AUTHOR OF WAVERLEY. | VOL. X [XI-XVII]. | [*reversed Oxford dash*] | [*volume title*] | [*reversed Oxford dash*] | [*vignette*] | EDINBURGH; | PRINTED FOR ROBERT CADELL, EDINBURGH; | AND WHITTAKER & Co. LONDON. | [*French dash*] | 1833.

Published 4 May 1833 in London (*Ath*). £4.2.6 (including the three-volume supplementary XVIII-XX *Introductions*). Binding: drab boards with printed labels. Paper: Demy 16° in eights (171 x 106mm uncut). Watermarks: *none.* Illustrations: Title-page vignettes correspond to those in the 8° edition, volumes 10, 13-17 drawn by J. Ewbank, 11-12 by D. O. Hill, all engraved by James Johnstone. The 17th volume, new in this 16° format, has an original design. Typography: Printer's imprints for volumes 10-13: [*short rule*] | Edinburgh:—Printed by J. HUTCHISON.; for volumes 14-16: EDINBURGH: PRINTED BY JAMES WALKER.; for volume 17, none declared. Press figures, appearing partially only in the 17th volume, confirm the format 16° in eights, for two gatherings here constitute a sheet with no more than two figures in each instance.

As in the 8° edition, other printers apparently were engaged to speed up this issue before it was overtaken, in the same year, by the last monthly volumes in the *WN* Magnum edition. To achieve a more uniform length the contents are somewhat re-ordered in volumes 10 and 17.

Copies: L; NNU-W(vols.10-16)*
*With 12-page Longman catalogue March 1833.

10] [*engraved title*] TALES AND ROMANCES, | OF | THE AUTHOR OF WAVERLEY. | VOL. X. | [*reversed Oxford dash*] | HIGHLAND WIDOW | [*reversed Oxford dash*] | [*vignette of waterfall and stream*] . . . 1833.

Collation: A-2D[8] 2E[6](-2E6). Pagination: [*engraved title*], *1* fly-title for *Chronicles of the Canongate*, *2 blank*, *3* 4-27 Introduction, dated from Abbotsford 1 October 1827, *28 blank*, *29* 30-144 Introductory, *145* fly-title for 'Highland Widow', *146 blank*, *147* 148-260 text, 261-265 Introductory for 'The Two Drovers', *266* 267-312 text, *313* fly-title for *Saint Valentine's Day; or, The Fair Maid of Perth*, *314 blank*, *315* 316-330 Introductory, 331-441 text, chapters 1-6, 441 printer's imprint, *442 blank*.

11] [*engraved title*] TALES AND ROMANCES, | OF | THE AUTHOR OF WAVERLEY. | VOL. XI. | [*reversed Oxford dash*] | FAIR MAID OF PERTH | [*reversed Oxford dash*] | [*vignette showing distant view of a city*] . . . 1833.

Collation: A-2C[8] 2D[6](-2D6). Pagination: [*engraved title*], *1* fly-title, *2 blank*, *3* 4-425 text continued, 425 printer's imprint, *426 blank*.

12] [*engraved title*] TALES AND ROMANCES, | OF | THE AUTHOR OF WAVERLEY. | VOL. XII. | [*reversed Oxford dash*] | FAIR MAID OF PERTH | [*reversed Oxford dash*] | [*vignette of two boats*] . . . 1833.

Collation: A-2C[8] 2D[4] 2E[2]. Pagination: [*engraved title*], *1* fly-title, *2 blank*, *3* 4-265 text of *The Fair Maid of Perth*, concluded, *266 blank*, *267* fly-title for *Anne of Geierstein*, *268 blank*, *269* 270-428 text, chapters 1-8, 428 printer's imprint. Typography: Page 241 is misnumbered 24.

13] [*engraved title*] TALES AND ROMANCES, | OF | THE AUTHOR OF WAVERLEY. | VOL. XIII. | [*reversed Oxford dash*] | ANNE OF GEIERSTEIN | [*reversed Oxford dash*] | [*vignette of castle in the distance*] . . . 1833.

Collation: A-2D[8] 2E[4](-2E4). Pagination: [*engraved title*], *1* fly-title, *2 blank*, *3* 4-437 text continued, 437 printer's imprint, *438 blank*. Typography: Page 377 is misnumbered 375.

14] [*engraved title*] TALES AND ROMANCES, | OF | THE AUTHOR OF WAVERLEY. | VOL. XIV. | [*reversed Oxford dash*] | COUNT ROBERT OF PARIS | [*reversed Oxford dash*] | [*vignette of a lakeshore*] . . . 1833.

Collation: A-2C[8] 2D[2]. Pagination: [*engraved title*], *1* fly-title, *2 blank*, *3* 4-252 text of *Anne of Geierstein*, concluded, *253* fly-title for *Tales of My Landlord.* Fourth Series, *254 blank, 255* 256-284 Introductory Address, dated 15 October 1831, *285* fly-title for 'Count Robert of Paris', *286 blank, 287* 288-'420'[440] text, chapters 1-6, '420'[440] printer's imprint. Typography: Pages 293-440 are misnumbered 273-420.

15] [*engraved title*] TALES AND ROMANCES, | OF | THE AUTHOR OF WAVERLEY. | VOL. XV. | [*reversed Oxford dash*] | COUNT ROBERT OF PARIS | [*reversed Oxford dash*] | [*vignette of a city in the distance*] . . . 1833.

Collation: A-2C[8]. Pagination: [*engraved title*], *1* fly-title, *2 blank, 3* 4-430 text continued, 430 printer's imprint, *431-432 blank.*

16] [*engraved title*] TALES AND ROMANCES, | OF | THE AUTHOR OF WAVERLEY. | VOL. XVI. | [*reversed Oxford dash*] | CASTLE DANGEROUS | [*reversed Oxford dash*] | [*vignette of a cottage and a stream*] . . . 1833.

Collation: A-2C[8]. Pagination: [*engraved title*], *1* fly-title for 'Count Robert of Paris', *2 blank, 3* 4-74 text concluded, *75* fly-title for 'Castle Dangerous', *76 blank, 77* 78-414 text, 414-416 postscript, dated from Abbotsford, September 1831, 416 printer's imprint.

17] [*engraved title*] TALES AND ROMANCES, | OF | THE AUTHOR OF WAVERLEY. | VOL. XVII. | [*reversed Oxford dash*] | SURGEONS DAUGHTER | [*reversed Oxford dash*] | [*vignette of a village lane*] . . . 1833.

Collation: A-2B[8]. Pagination: [*engraved title*], *1* fly-title for 'The Surgeon's Daughter', *2 blank, 3* 4-25 Prefatory, *26* 27-295 text, *296 blank, 297* fly-title for 'My Aunt Margaret's Mirror', *298 blank, 299* 300-302 Introduction dated August 1831, *303* 304-358 text, *359* fly-title for 'The Tapestried Chamber', *360 blank, 361* Introduction dated August 1831, *362 blank, 363* 364-387 text, *388 blank, 389* fly-title for 'Death of The Laird's Jock', *390 blank, 391* Introduction [four lines] dated August 1831, *391* 392-400 text. No printer's imprint.

Figures: A16-6; C36-5, D64-6; E80-6, F84-5; H126-5 128-6; K160-6 . . . R272-5, S288-6; T291-5 301-6; Y340-5; Z356-5, 2A 384-6; 2B 386-9.

Notes: As the only volume with press figures, this evidently was prepared by some printer other than the two previously involved.

283A] Fifth Series, 18° Edition: 1833

[*engraved title*] TALES AND ROMANCES | OF | THE AUTHOR OF

WAVERLEY | VOL. VIII [IX-XIII] | [*volume title*] | [*vignette*] | EDINBURGH; | PRINTED FOR ROBERT CADELL EDINBURGH. | AND WHITTAKER & Co. LONDON. | 1833.

Issued 4 May 1833 in London (*Ath*). £3.3.0 (including the three-volume supplementary XIV-XVI *Introductions*). Paper: Demy 18° in sixes (145 x 88mm cut). Watermarks: *none*. Illustrations: The title vignettes for volumes IX, X, XII and XIII were previously used for the prior issue volumes XI, XIII, XVI, and XVII; those newly prepared, for volumes VIII and XI, are described below. All frontispieces, new to this issue, and also described, bear a Cadell and Whittaker imprint dated 1833. Throughout the illustrations are engraved by James Johnstone. Printer's imprints, for volumes VIII-X: EDINBURGH: | Printed by ANDREW SHORTREDE, Thistle Lane.; for volumes XI-XIII: EDINBURGH: | PRINTED BY JOHN STARK, | OLD ASSEMBLY CLOSE. Again these other printers are employed to speed up the issue before the appearance, in this same year, of the *WN* Magnum edition.

Copies: L; CtY.

8] [*engraved title*] TALES AND ROMANCES | OF | THE AUTHOR OF WAVERLEY | VOL. VIII | HIGHLAND WIDOW | [*vignette of a woman attending a man at his bedside*] . . . . 1833.

Collation: A-2P^6 2Q^6(-2Q6). Pagination: [*engraved title*], *1* fly-title for *Chronicles of the Canongate*, *2 blank*, *3* 4-24 Introduction, dated from Abbotsford 1 October 1827, *25* 26-113 Introductory, *114 blank*, *115* fly-title for 'The Highland Widow', *116 blank*, *117* 118-202 text, *203* fly-title for 'My Aunt Margaret's Mirror', *204 blank*, *205* 206-247 text, *248 blank*, *249* fly-title for 'The Tapestried Chamber', *250 blank*, *251* Introduction dated August 1831, *252 blank*, *253* 254-272 text, *273* fly-title for 'Death of The Laird's Jock', *274 blank*, *275* introduction [four lines] dated August 1831, *275* 276-282 text, *283* fly-title for *Chronicles of the Canongate*. Second Series, *284 blank*, *285* 286-297 Introductory, *298* 299-465 text of *The Fair Maid of Perth*, chapters 1-11, *466* printer's imprint. Illustrations: The title vignette, newly prepared for this edition, was drawn by A. Fraser; frontispiece, by the same artist, is captioned 'Highland Widow'. Typography: In his work on this and the next two volumes, printer Shortrede uses sheet numbers, one for every three signatures in this 18° format.

Figures: C36-1; D48-1; G84-1; K120-3, M144-4; N156-2, P180-3; Q192-2, S216-1; T228-2, U236-3; 2A 288-3; 2D 323-3 324-1; 2F 348-3, 2G 360-1; 2H 372-1, 2K 396-3; 2L 408-2, 2N 432-1; 2 O 444-3, 2P 455-4.

9] [*engraved title*] TALES AND ROMANCES | OF | THE AUTHOR OF WAVERLEY | VOL. IX. | FAIR MAID OF PERTH. | [*vignette of a city in the distance*] . . . . 1833.

Collation: A-2N^6 2 O 1. Pagination: [*engraved title*], *1* fly-title for *Chronicles of the Canongate*. Second Series, *2 blank, 3* 4-434 text of *The Fair Maid of Perth*, concluded, 434 printer's imprint. Illustration: Frontispiece drawn by W. Allan with caption 'Fair Maid of Perth.'

Figures: A12-2/6, C36-3; D48-4, F72-6; G84-4, H86-3; M144-6; N156-3, P180-6; Q188-6 192-2; T228-4, X252-6; Y264-3, Z272-6; 2B 300-5, 2D 324-3; 2G 356-4 360-6; 2H 372-3, 2K 396-5; 2M 419-6.

10] [*engraved title*] TALES AND ROMANCES | OF | THE AUTHOR OF WAVERLEY | VOL. X. | ANNE OF GEIERSTEIN. | [*vignette of a castle in the distance*] . . . . 1833.

Collation: A-2M^6 2N^6(-2N6). Pagination: [*engraved title*], *1* fly-title, *2 blank, 3* 4-430 text continued, 430 printer's imprint. Illustration: frontispiece drawn by W. Mulready with caption 'Anne of Geierstein.'

Figures: A12-4, C36-6; D44-4 48-6; G84-6, I 108-5; K120-6, M144-5; N156-6, P180-5; Q192-5, S216-6; U240-5, X252-6; Y263-5 264-6; 2B 299-6 300-5; 2E 336-5, 2F 347-6; 2K 395-5 396-6; 2L 398-3.

11] [*engraved title*] TALES AND ROMANCES | OF | THE AUTHOR OF WAVERLEY | VOL. XI. | COUNT ROBERT OF PARIS. | [*vignette of a standing and a recumbent figure*] . . . . 1833.

Collation: A-2N^6 2 O^2. Pagination: [*engraved title*], *1* 2-199 text of *Anne of Geierstein*, concluded, *200 blank, 201* fly-title for *Tales of My Landlord*. Fourth Series, *202 blank, 203* 204-231 Introductory Address, dated 15 October 1831, *232 blank, 233* fly-title for 'Count Robert of Paris', *234 blank, 235* 236-436 text, chapters 1-12, 436 printer's imprint. Illustrations: The title vignette, newly prepared for this edition, was drawn by J. West, frontispiece was drawn by W. Boxall with caption 'Count Robert of Paris.' Typography: In his work on this and the next two volumes, printer Stark does not use sheet numbers, signs double-letter signatures as Aa, Bb, &c., but like the earlier printer continues to employ press figures, here at the beginning and the end of the book only.

Figures: B14-4 24-3; D48-6, E50-1 [then none until:] K120-1, M134-6; O 162-1, P170-4; Q188-3 192-4; T222-6, U230-1; Y254-6, Z276-1; 2B 296-4, 2D 318-3; 2E 336-6, 2G 350-1; 2H 362-4, 2 I 378-1; 2L 408-6.

12] [*engraved title*] TALES AND ROMANCES | OF | THE AUTHOR OF WAVERLEY | VOL. XII | CASTLE DANGEROUS. | [*vignette of a cottage and a stream*] . . . . 1833.

Collation: A-2M[6] 2N[4]. Pagination: [*engraved title*], *1* fly-title for 'Count Robert of Paris', *2 blank, 3* 4-310 text concluded, *311* fly-title for 'Castle Dangerous', *312 blank, 313* 314-427 text, chapters 1-8, 427 printer's imprint, *428 blank.* Illustration: Frontispiece drawn by C. Stanfield with caption 'Castle Dangerous.' Typography: Section signature T2 (page 221) is missigned 2T.

Figures: B18-1; E60-4, F68-6; G80-6, H90-1; L128-3 132-1; O 168-6, P170-4; Q192-3, S206-1; T222-4, U230-6; Y254-4, 2A 288-1; 2D 314-6 318-3; 2E 336-4, 2G 350-1; 2K 386-4 390-1; 2L 408-6, 2M 410-3.

13] [*engraved title*] TALES AND ROMANCES | OF | THE AUTHOR OF WAVERLEY | VOL. XIII. | THE SURGEON'S DAUGHTER. | [*vignette of a village lane*] . . . . 1833.

Collation: A-2S[6] 2T1. Pagination: [*engraved title*], *1* fly-title for 'Castle Dangerous', *2 blank, 3* 4-154 text concluded, 154-155 Scott's postscript, dated from Abbotsford, September 1831, *156 blank, 157* fly-title for 'The Surgeon's Daughter', *158 blank, 159*-160 Introduction, dated from Abbotsford, September 1831, *161* 162-178 Prefatory, *179* 180-379 text, *380 blank, 381* fly-title for 'The Two Drovers', *382 blank, 383* 384-386 Introductory, *387* 388-421 text, *422 blank, 423* fly-title for the Glossary, *424 blank, 425* 426-493 text, *494* printer's imprint. Illustration: frontispiece drawn by Frank Stone with caption 'The Surgeon's Daughter.' Typography: Page 74 is misnumbered 47 and the signature on page 413 is wrongly spaced as M m2. Gatherings 2 O-2Q so signed (pages 433-468), each without a signature on the third leaf, would appear to have been worked by someone other than Stark, the designated printer.

Figures: A8-1 12-4; E50-6, F72-4; G78-3, I98-1; L126-1, M134-3; P180-6; Q192-3 200-4; T228-1, X242-6; Y264-3, 2A 278-4; 2B 290-6, 2C 306-1; 2E 330-3, 2F 338-4; 2 I 374-6 384-1; 2L 408-1, 2M 410-6; 2Q 468-1; 2S 486-2 491-7.

1C. COLLECTED EDITIONS
INTRODUCTIONS, AND NOTES AND ILLUSTRATIONS

284A] First 8° Edition: 1833

INTRODUCTIONS, | AND | NOTES AND ILLUSTRATIONS, | TO THE | NOVELS, TALES, AND ROMANCES | OF THE | AUTHOR OF WAVERLEY. | [*short rule*] | VOL. I [II]. | [*titles*] | [*short rule*] | EDINBURGH: | PRINTED FOR ROBERT CADELL, EDINBURGH; | AND WHITTAKER & CO. LONDON. | 1833.

Issued 4 May 1833 in London concurrently with the 8° edition of volumes 8-13

(*Ath*). Also available separately. Paper: Royal 8° (222 x 138mm uncut). Watermarks: *none*. Typography: To indicate their supplementary status, the volume direction lines read XV and XVI.

General Notes: In all three formats, these supplementary volumes, containing new material in the Magnum Opus edition, were provided for owners of the five collected series already issued.

Copies: E(2) ES L; CtY T/B.

1] INTRODUCTIONS, . . . VOL. I. | WAVERLEY—THE ABBOT. . . . 1833.

Collation: π^2 A-2 O^8 2P^4 *2Q*1. Pagination: *i* half-title, *ii blank, iii* title-page, *iv blank, 1* section title, *2 blank, 3* 4-601 text, 601 printer's imprint, *602 blank.* Printer's imprint: [*short rule*] | EDINBURGH: | PRINTED BY BALLANTYNE AND COMPANY, | PAUL'S WORK, CANONGATE.

Figures: A16-3, B32-2, C48-2, D52-6, E79-3, F—, G107-2, H128-1, I 137-6, K160-1, L172-5/6, M190-2, N204-1/-, O 222-5/-, P240-2, Q256-6, R272-6, S282-2, T*303*-2, U320-6, X336-1, Y352-5, Z368-6, 2A 384-2, 2B 400-2, 2C 416-6, 2D 432-6, 2E 435-3, 2F 450-1, 2G 473-5, 2H—, 2 I 512-6, 2K 528-7, 2L 541-3, 2M 558-3, 2N *565*-5, 2 O 589-2, 2P 600-4, *2Q*—.

2] INTRODUCTIONS, . . . VOL. II. | KENILWORTH—CASTLE DANGEROUS. . . . 1833.

Collation: π^2 A-2P^8 2Q^4(-2Q4). Pagination: *i* half-title, *ii blank, iii* title-page, *iv blank, 1* section title, *2 blank, 3* 4-613 text, 613 Errata and printer's imprint, *614 blank.* Printer's imprint: [*short rule*] | PRINTED BY BALLANTYNE AND COMPANY, EDINBURGH. Illustration: Folding plate of 'Ground Plan of Kenilworth Castle' inserted before section title or text.

Figures: A—, B—, C48-1, D64-4, E77-7, F87-7/-, G98-7, H121-4, I 144-4, K—, L172-4, M—, N—, O *219*-4, P240-7, Q256-6, R*272*-4, S*285*-4, T295-5, U—, X*323*-5, Y341-4, Z—, 2A 374-4, 2B 400-1, 2C 414-3, 2D—, 2E 448-1, 2F 458-5, 2G 472-5, 2H 492-1, 2 I—, 2K—, 2L—, 2M—, 2N—, 2 O—, 2P 600-3 *607*-6, 2Q 610-5.

Notes: The 'Introductions' for certain of the works in this volume are dated long after Scott left Abbotsford—1 December 1831 (page 234), 1 February 1832 (page 271), 1 April (page 302), 1 July (page 357), 1 August (page 388)—but now appropriately (except for the first) bear no reference to his home. Such an arrangement derives from the 'Magnum Opus' volumes and corresponds to the actual issue date of the titles in question (vols. 31, 33, 35, 38, 39).

285A] First 16° Edition: 1833

INTRODUCTIONS, | AND | NOTES AND ILLUSTRATIONS, | TO THE | NOVELS, TALES, AND ROMANCES, | OF THE | AUTHOR OF WAVERLEY. | VOL. I [II-III]. | [*titles*] | EDINBURGH: | PRINTED FOR ROBERT CADELL, EDINBURGH; | AND WHITTAKER & CO. LONDON. | MDCCCXXXIII.

Issued 4 May 1833 in London concurrently with the 16° edition of volumes 10-17 (*Ath*). Also available separately. Binding: drab boards with printed labels. Paper: Royal 16° in eights (171 x 108mm uncut). Watermarks: *none*. Typography: Direction lines may be printed I, II, III or (as in NNU-W) XVIII, XIX, XX.

Copies: BCL L O; NjP NNU-W PPL.

1] INTRODUCTIONS, . . . VOL. I. | WAVERLEY—HEART OF MIDLOTHIAN. . . . MDCCCXXXIII.

Collation: π1 A-2F[8] 2G[4] *2H*1. Pagination: *i* title-page, *ii blank, 1* fly-title, *2 blank, 3* 4-474 text, 474 printer's imprint: [*short rule*] | Edinburgh:—Printed by J. HUTCHISON. Typography: In some copies the printer's imprint has a period rather than a colon after Edinburgh. Figures: *none.*

2] INTRODUCTIONS, . . . VOL. II. | BRIDE OF LAMMERMOOR—PEVERIL OF THE PEAK. . . . MDCCCXXXIII.

Collation: π1 A-2E[8] 2F1. Pagination: *i* title-page, *ii blank, 1* section title, *2 blank, 3* 4-450 text, 450 printer's imprint: [*short rule*] | Edinburgh:—Printed by J. HUTCHISON. Illustration: Folding plate of 'Ground Plan of Kenilworth Castle.' inserted before title or page 225. Typography: In some copies signature G (page 97) is represented by a black quad or remains unsigned. Page 243 is misnumbered 432. Figures: *none.*

3] INTRODUCTIONS, . . . VOL. III. | QUENTIN DURWARD—CASTLE DANGEROUS. . . . MDCCCXXXIII.

Collation: π1 A-2E[8] 2F1. Pagination: *i* title-page, *ii blank, 1* fly-title, *2 blank, 3* section title, *4 blank, 5* 6-449 text, 449 printer's imprint, *450 blank*. Printer's imprint: [*short rule*] | Edinburgh:—Printed by J. THOMSON. Typography: Page 161 is misnumbered 167. Figures: *none.*

Notes: The postdating of the introductions, remarked in the preceding 8° entry, also occurs here.

286A] First 18° Edition: 1833

INTRODUCTIONS, | AND | NOTES AND ILLUSTRATIONS | TO THE | NOVELS, TALES, AND ROMANCES | OF THE | AUTHOR OF WAVERLEY. | [*short rule*] | VOL. I [II-III]. | [*titles*] | [*short rule*] | EDINBURGH: | PRINTED FOR ROBERT CADELL, EDINBURGH; | AND WHITTAKER AND CO. LONDON. | [*short rule*] | 1833.

Issued 4 May 1833 in London concurrently with the 18° edition of volumes 8-13 (*Ath*). Also available separately. Paper: 18° in sixes (150 x 96mm uncut). Watermarks: *none*.

General Notes: Direction lines on half-titles are numbered I, II, III, but those on signature pages are listed as XIV, XV, XVI. Printer's imprints for volumes 1-2: EDINBURGH: | Printed by ANDREW SHORTREDE, Thistle Lane.; volume 3: EDIN BURGH: | PRINTED BY JOHN STARK, | OLD ASSEMBLY CLOSE.

Copies: L; CtY.

1] INTRODUCTIONS, . . . VOL. I. | WAVERLEY—HEART OF MID-LOTHIAN. . . . 1833.

Collation: π^2 A-2T^6 2U^2. Pagination: *i* half-title, *ii blank, iii* title-page, *iv blank, 1* fly-title, *2 blank, 3* 4-507 text, *508* printer's imprint. Typography: In some copies page 139 is misnumbered 13. Printer Shortrede, though ordinarily using sheet numbers, omits them for sheets 6, 8 (pages 181, 253) and in some copies 13 (page 433).

Figures: A12-2, C36-3; D48-1, E59-2; G83-4, I 107-2; K119-4 120-2; N156-2, P180-3; R194-5 199-4; T228-6, X252-3; Z271-6, 2A 288-2; 2B 300-3, 2C 311-2; 2E 336-4, 2F *347*-6; 2K 395-2; 2L 398-4 *408*-6; 2Q 467-6 468-4; 2R 475-2, 2S 488-4.

2] INTRODUCTIONS, . . . VOL. II. | BRIDE OF LAMMERMOOR—PEVERIL OF THE PEAK. . . . 1833.

Collation: π^2 A-2R^6 2S^4(-2S4). Pagination: *i* half-title, *ii blank, iii* title-page, *iv blank, 1* fly-title, *2 blank, 3* section title, *4 blank, 5* 6-486 text, 486 printer's imprint. Typography: Page 229 is misnumbered 22. Section signature 2H2 (page 365) is missigned 2.

Figures: A11-4 12-6; E*59*-5 60-4; H90-6, I 108-2; K120-2; N156-4, P180-3; Q192-3, R194-4; U239-6; Y264-5, 2A 288-2; 2D 324-5; 2E 336-4, 2F 347-2; 2 I 383-4, 2K 395-1; 2L 408-1, 2M 419-2; 2 O 444-2, 2Q 468-1; 2R 480-4.

3] INTRODUCTIONS, . . . VOL. III. | QUENTIN DURWARD—CASTLE DANGEROUS. . . . 1833.

Collation: π^2 A-2Q^6 2R^2. Pagination: *i* half-title, *ii blank, iii* title-page, *iv blank, 1* fly-title, *2 blank, 3* section title, *4 blank, 5* 6-471 text, *472* Addenda, *472* printer's imprint. Typography: Section signature O 2 (page 161) is unsigned. Printer Stark does not use sheet numbers and signs double signatures as Aa, Bb, &c.

Figures: A8-4 12-6; D48-6, F68-4; G74-4, I 108-1; K116-1, L132-6; N146-6 156-1; Q186-4, S212-3; T224-1, X246-6; Y264-1, 2A 278-4; 2B 294-4, 2D 314-1; 2E 326-6, 2F 348-4; 2 I 380-1, 2K 396-6; 2L 398-1 402-6; 2P 452-4 456-1.

Notes: The postdating of the introductions, remarked in the preceding 8° entry, also occurs here. The Addenda, supplied only for this edition, pertains to the spurious *Walladmor*.

1D. COLLECTED EDITIONS: PROSE

287A] First Edition: 1827

THE | MISCELLANEOUS | **PROSE WORKS** | OF | **SIR WALTER SCOTT, BART.** | IN SIX VOLUMES. | [*short rule*] | VOL. I [II-VI]. | [*title*] | [*short rule*] | EDINBURGH: | PRINTED FOR CADELL AND CO., EDINBURGH; AND | LONGMAN, REES, ORME, BROWN, AND GREEN, | LONDON. | [*dash*] | 1827.

Published 17 May 1827 in Edinburgh (*EEC*). £3.12.0. Binding: drab boards or (a later issue?) green cloth, with printed labels. Paper: Demy 8° (224 x 140mm uncut). Watermarks: *none*. Typography: Except as noted, printer's imprints (1) and (2) read: [*short rule*] | EDINBURGH: | PRINTED BY BALLANTYNE AND CO.

General Notes: Apart from slight revisions throughout and additional footnotes there are more significant additions, as noted below. An interesting hint concerning Scott's primary interests at the time appears in the concluding comment to the new advertisement in volume 3, page 4, where he confesses that 'the Critical Opinions are such as have occurred without much or profound study to one, too much of whose time has been spent in that "delightful lande of faerie," the seducing mazes of fictitious narrative.' In volume 4, page 49 (second state), Scott again refers to 'this most pleasant land of faery'. From Scott's letter to John Gibson, 1 July 1826, it appears that the first four volumes were completed before the crash six months earlier, and none of those remaining had as yet been sent to press.

Copies: (Volume 4, state 1) ES O; IdU T/B(vols. 4-5). (2) E L; CtY(2) InU. References: *Letters,* x.71; Thomson, page 63 (on Charlotte Smith, cf. volume 4).

1] THE | MISCELLANEOUS | **PROSE WORKS** . . . . VOL. I. | LIFE OF DRYDEN. . . . 1827.

Collation: π^2 a^8 A-2K^8 2L^4. Pagination: *1* half-title, *2 blank, 3* title-page, *4* printer's imprint(1), *i* ii-xi Advertisement, *xii blank, xiii* xiv-xv Contents, *xvi blank, 1* fly-title, *2 blank*, *3* 4-533 text, 533 printer's imprint(2), *534-536 blank*. Printer's imprint(2): [*short rule*] | EDINBURGH: | Printed by James Ballantyne & Co.

Figures: a iv-9, A16-7, B32-2, C48-10, D63-2, E80-7, F96-2, G112-2, H128-1, I 144-10, K160-9, L176-6, M192-8, N208-9, O 224-8, P240-10, Q256-8, R272-6, S288-9, T304-9, U320-7, X336-9, Y352-7, Z368-2, 2A 384-15, 2B 400-1, 2C 416-7, 2D 432-9, 2E 448-3, 2F 464-6, 2G 480-8, 2H 496-10, 2 I 512-15, 2K 528-7, 2L 532-1/-.

2] THE | MISCELLANEOUS | **PROSE WORKS** . . . . VOL. II. | LIFE OF SWIFT. . . . 1827.

Collation: π^2 $2\pi^2$ A-2K^8 2L^2. Pagination: *1* half-title, *2 blank*, *3* title-page, *4* printer's imprint(1), *i* ii-iii Contents, *iv blank*, *1* fly-title, *2 blank*, *3* 4-495 text, *496 blank*, *497* fly-title, *498 blank*, *499-500* 501-532 Appendix, 532 printer's imprint(2). Printer's imprint(2): [*short rule*] | EDINBURGH: | Printed by James Ballantyne and Co. Typography: In some copies signature A (page *1*) is unsigned.

Figures: A16-9, B32-12, C48-11, D64-17, E80-17, F96-12, G112-10, H128-5, I 144-9, K160-12, L176-10, M192-11, N208-17, O 224-3, P240-2, Q256-2, R272-9, S288-5, T304-3, U320-7, X336-6, Y352-4, Z368-11, 2A 384-9, 2B 400-6/-, 2C 416-7, 2D 432-8, 2E 448-4, 2F 464-6, 2G 480-5, 2H 492-15, 2 I 512-12, 2K 528-8, 2L—.

3] THE | MISCELLANEOUS | **PROSE WORKS** . . . . VOL. III. | BIOGRAPHICAL MEMOIRS. . . . 1827.

Collation: $\pi^2(\pi2+1)$ A-P^8 Q^8(±Q4,6) R-2L^8 2M^8(-2M8). Pagination: *i* half-title, *ii blank*, *iii* title-page, *iv* printer's imprint(1), *v* Contents, *vi blank*, *1* fly-title, *2 blank*, *3*-4 Advertisement, unsigned but dated from Abbotsford 1 September 1825, *5* 6-557 text, 557 printer's imprint(2), *558-560 blank*. Printer's imprint(2): [*short rule*] | EDINBURGH: | PRINTED BY JAMES BALLANTYNE AND CO. Some copies have no colon after 'EDINBURGH'.

Figures: A16-15, B32-2, C48-2, D64-6, E80-2, F96-6, G112-1, H128-9, I 144-3, K160-1, L176-8, M192-4, N208-2, O 224-5, P240-4, Q249-2, R272-14, S288-9, T304-9, U320-3, X336-12, Y352-2, Z368-2, 2A 384-2/7, 2B 400-10, 2C 416-7, 2D 432-10, 2E 448-10, 2F 464-10, 2G 480-14, 2H 496-10/13(or '31'), 2 I 512-7, 2K 528-5, 2L 544-5, 2M 547-2.

Notes: This edition reorders the fifteen 'Memoirs' first issued in 1820-1824, moving Samuel Richardson from eleventh to first position and arranging others according to this sequence:

1820-1824:	1	2	3	4	5	6	7	8	9	10	11	12	13	14	15
1827:	2	3	12	13	7	5	6	8	9	10	1	—	14	4	11

In this rearrangement it was prudent to delete the 1 January 1824 date originally subtended to the Richardson Memoir, as this is now followed by 2-Fielding and 3-Smollett, still dated 25 October 1820 and 1 June 1821. Two other deleted dates, perhaps from mere oversight, are those for Radcliffe and Johnstone, now ordered 11 and 13. Original 12-Swift is entirely canceled because of the full-scale *Life* in the preceding volume of this present series. (Lockhart's *MPW* retains the new order but moves 8-MacKenzie to the next volume). Original readings for cancels Q4 and Q6 (pages 247-248, 251-252) are unknown.

4] THE | MISCELLANEOUS | **PROSE WORKS** . . . . VOL. IV. | BIOGRAPHICAL MEMOIRS. . . . 1827.

Collation: $\pi^2(\pi 2+1)$ A-2G^8 *2H*1. Pagination: *i* half-title, *ii blank*, *iii* title-page, *iv* printer's imprint(1), *v* Contents, *vi blank*, *1* fly-title, *2 blank*, *3* 4-481 text, 481 printer's imprint(2), *482 blank*. Typography: Page *65* direction line is mislabeled 'VOL. V.'.

Figures: A16-5, B32-7, C48-4, D61-11, E80-2, F89-5, G112-2, H128-1, I 131-2, K160-6, L165-2, M192-6, N196-3, O 224-5, P240-7, Q256-6, R272-3, S288-5, T296-1/-, U309-7, X336-7, Y350-7, Z354-1 368-3, 2A 384-4, 2B 393-8, 2C 416-7, 2D 432-5, 2E 448-5, 2F 464-8, 2G 480-2, *2H*-. Throughout the six volumes sheet Z in this is the only one with two press figures.

Notes: Unlike the memoirs in the previous volume, all essentially reprinted from their first issue in 1820-1824, the ten essays in volume 4 represent considerable revision including the additional passages noted below.

Scott immediately attributes the first essay, on Charlotte Smith, to Mrs Dorset, 'sister of the subject of the Memoir,' but the postscript is certainly of his own composition. This addition, occupying the whole of sheet D, exists in two states: (1) with the sheet mispaged 33-47 and so run through the press with figure page '45'-3; (2) with the sheet later correctly paged 49-63 and now bearing the figure 61-11.

The third, Leyden memoir, entirely by Scott, now includes a new paragraph (pages 156-157) on the 'notice and patronage of Dr Robert Anderson of Edinburgh', together with an apologetic footnote not reprinted in Lockhart's *MPW* (see iv.149-150).

Though Scott early disclaimed the fifth, Defoe 'biographical sketch', attributing it to his 'late regretted friend' John Ballantyne, he revised the sketch itself for this volume (pages 258-279) and added the extensive sequel (pages 280-321).

Two sequels should also be noted in the ninth memoir on Byron, first a brief comment pages 400-401 ('Since this sketch first appeared . . . '), then an extensive commentary pages 401-461 ('When the preceding remarks on Lord Byron's death appeared in the newspapers . . .').

The tenth and last memoir, on the Duke of York, also has an additional paragraph, page 481 ('Since laying this hasty sketch . . .').

5] THE | MISCELLANEOUS | **PROSE WORKS** . . . . VOL. V. | PAUL'S LETTERS TO HIS KINSFOLK, &c. . . . 1827.

Collation: π^2 $2\pi^4$ A-2D^8 2E^4(-2E4) 2F-2I^8 2K^4 2L1. Pagination: *1* half-title, *2 blank*, *3* title-page, *4* printer's imprint(1), *i* ii-viii Contents, *1* 2-406 text of *Paul's Letters*, *407* fly-title, *408 blank*, *409* 410-439 appendices, *440 blank*, *441* fly-title for 'Abstract of the Eyrbiggia-Saga', *442 blank*, *443* 444-512 text, 512 printer's imprint(2). Typography: Page 91 is misnumbered 92.

Figures: A16-4, B32-15, C48-13, D61-9, E80-9, F96-13, G112-13, H128-13, I 144-4, K160-9, L176-8, M192-9, N208-15, O 224-15, P240-2, Q256-13, R272-2, S288-15, T304-2, U320-7, X336-8, Y352-1, Z368-3, 2A 384-8, 2B 400-2, 2C 416-13, 2D 432-7, 2E 437-13/-, 2F 454-6, 2G 470-1, 2H 486-8, 2 I 500-1, 2K 510-7, 2L—.

Notes: The short gathering 2E (pages 433-438) apparently reflects an early decision to conclude the volume with *Paul's Letters*, a text now ending with five lines on 2F1 (page 439).

6] THE | MISCELLANEOUS | **PROSE WORKS** . . . . VOL. VI. | CHIVALRY, ROMANCE, THE DRAMA. . . . 1827.

Collation: $\pi^2(\pi 2+1)$ A-I^8 K^8(±K5) L-2F^8 2G^4(-2G4). Pagination: *i* half-title, *ii blank*, *iii* title-page, *iv* printer's imprint(1), *v* Contents, *vi blank*, *1* fly-title for 'An Essay on Chivalry', *2 blank*, *3* 4-151 text, *152 blank*, *153* fly-title for 'An Essay on Romance', *154 blank*, *155* 156-256 text, *257* fly-title for 'An Essay on the Drama', *258 blank*, *259* 260-470 text, 470 printer's imprint(2). Printer's imprint(2) usually: [*short rule*] | EDINBURGH: | PRINTED BY JAMES BALLANTYNE AND CO. Some copies have no colon after 'EDINBURGH'. Typography: In some copies page 14 is misnumbered 41.

Figures: A16-3, B32-4, C48-1, D64-10, E80-11, F96-2, G112-7, H128-3, I 144-11, K160-2, L176-6, M192-13, N208-13, O 224-3, P240-4, Q256-2, R272-13, S288-7, T304-7, U320-3, X336-8, Y352-2, Z368-8, 2A 384-2, 2B 400-1, 2C 416-1, 2D 419-5, 2E 448-12, 2F 464-8, 2G 469-4.

Notes: The occasion for cancel K5, a fly-title (page *153*), is unknown.

2. COLLECTED REPRINT EDITIONS (288R-318R)

Preliminary Note: Since most of the poems and novels among the collected reprints were originally issued serially, or otherwise made available separately, these entries have also been identified by cross-reference from the previous accounts of separate editions and are not further cited in the index.

FRANCE

288R] PARIS: Baudry, Barrois [and others] 1831-1833
Collection of Ancient and Modern British Novels and Romances. Paris: 1831-1832.
General Notes: The 30 Scott entries in this Collection are reprinted from the Magnum Opus edition, 1829-1833. Series numbers are indicated only on half-titles and wrappers, both of which are sometimes removed to facilitate sale as separate editions. In the course of printing the title imprint goes through the four states listed below. Evidently, before starting this series, Baudry was distributing Didot and Galignani volumes as early as April 1822 (*see* 291R.37A) as well as separately printing a few works (47Ra, 149Ra-Rb). The imprints below exhibit minor changes in punctuation throughout, but substantive changes between each are shown.

IMPRINT 1: Paris, Baudry's Foreign Library, Rue du Coq-Saint-Honoré. Sold also by Theophile Barrois, Jun., Rue Richelieu; Truchy, Boulevard des Italiens; Amyot, Rue de la Paix; and Librairie des Etrangers, Rue Neuve-Saint-Augustin. 1831.
2: [As for imprint 1, except:] Rue de la Paix; Librairie des Etrangers, Rue Neuve-Saint-Augustin; and French and English Library, Rue Vivienne. 1831-1832.
3. [As for imprint 2, except:] Rue du Coq, Near the Louvre. 1832.
4: [As for 3 except:] Paris, Baudry's European Library, . . . Librairie des Etrangers, 55, Rue Neuve-Saint Augustin;. 1832.

1] Waverley, or 'Tis Sixty Years Since. [imprint 1] 1831. Pages: *i-iv*, *1* 2-632. Copy: E. Reference: Kohler(1) 92(with illustration).
2] Guy Mannering, or The Astrologer. [imprint 1] 1831. Pages: *i-ii*, *1* 2-532. Copy: E. Reference: Kohler(1) 97(with illustration).
3] The Antiquary. [imprint 1] 1831. Pages: *i-iv*, *1* 2-512. Copy: E. Reference: Kohler(1) 101(with illustration).
4-5] The History of Tom Jones, . . . By Henry Fielding, Esq. With a Life of the Author, By Sir Walter Scott. [imprint 1] 1831. Scott's 'Life', Vol. 4, pages: *i* ii-xxviii. Notes: The remainder of this and the fifth volume is a reprint of the novel as issued 1821 in *Ballantyne's Novelist's Library* (148A). Copies: P(vol.4); CtY.
6] Ivanhoe, A Romance. [imprint 1] 1831. Pages: *i-v* vi-xxxii, *1* 2-548. Copies: E L P.
10] Rob Roy. [imprint 1] 1831. Pages: *1-4*, *i* ii-lxviii *lxix-lxx*, *1* 2-478. Copies: E L O. Reference: Kohler(1) 107(with illustration).
12] Tales of My Landlord. . . . First Series. Black Dwarf.—Old Mortality. [imprint 1] 1831. Pages: *1-4*, *i-iii* iv-xvi, *1* 2-606. Notes: The glossary mentioned on the title-page is included in volume 14. Copies: E L. Reference: Kohler(1) 103(with illustration).
13] Tales of My Landlord. . . . Second Series. The Heart of Mid-Lothian. [imprint 1] 1831. Pages: *1-4*, *i-v* vi-xviii, *1* 2-589. Notes: The glossary mentioned on the title-page is included in volume 14. In some copies page 589 is unnumbered. Copies: E L P; NjP. Reference: Kohler(1) 111.
14] Tales of my Landlord. . . . Third Series. The Bride of Lammermoor.—A Legend of Montrose. [imprint 1] 1831. Pages: *1-4*, *i* ii-x *xi-xii*, *1* 2-578, *1* 2-8. Notes: Issued with a glossary advertised on the title-pages for volumes 12-14. Copies: E(2) L P. Reference: Kohler(1) 114(with illustration).
18] Tales of My Landlord, . . . Fourth and Last Series. Count Robert of Paris.—Castle Dangerous. [imprint 1 or 2] 1831. Pages: *i-v* vi-xix *xx*, *1* 2-630. Copies: (imprint 1) E L P.

(2) E L; NN. Reference: Kohler(1) 188(with illustration).

19] The Monastery. [imprint 2] 1832. Pages: *1-4*, *i* ii-lviii *lix-lx*, *1* 2-492. Copies: E(2) L P. Reference: Kohler(1) 126(with illustration).

20] The Abbot, Being the Sequel to The Monastery. [imprint 2] 1832. Pages: *1-4*, *i* ii-xi *xii*, *1* 2-568. Copies: E L P. Reference: Kohler(1) 130(with illustration).

21] Kenilworth. [imprint 2] 1832. Pages: *1-4*, *i* ii-viii, *9* 10-504. Notes: Issued with a ground plan of Kenilworth Castle. Copies: E L P; NNU-W. Reference: Kohler(1) 134 (with illustration).

22] The Pirate. [imprint 2] 1832. Pages: *i-v* vi-xv *xvi*, *1* 2-498. Copies: E(2) L P; NjP NN. Reference: Kohler(1) 140(with illustration).

23] The Fortunes of Nigel. [imprint 2] 1832. Pages: *i-v* vi-xxxi *xxxii*, *1* 2-500. Copies: E(2) L P; NN.

24] Quentin Durward. [imprint 2] 1832. Pages: *1-4*, *i* ii-xxxii, *1* 2-486. Copies: E L. Reference: Kohler(1) 151(with illustration).

26] Peveril of the Peak. [imprint 2] 1832. Pages: *1-4*, *i* ii-xlii *xliii-xliv*, *1* 2-587. Copies: E(2) L P; NN. Reference: Kohler(1) 146(with illustration).

27] St. Ronan's Well. [imprint 2] 1832. Pages: *i-v* vi-viii, *1* 2-463. Copies: E(2) L P; NN. Reference: Kohler(1) 157(with illustration).

28] Redgauntlet, A Tale of the Eighteenth Century. [imprint 2] 1832. Pages: *i-v* vi-xiv *xv-xvi*, *1* 2-477. Notes: Some copies have xiv misnumbered 'x'. Copies: E(2) L; NN. Reference: Kohler(1) 163(with illustration).

30] Tales of the Crusaders. . . . Tale I. The Betrothed. [imprint 3] 1832. Pages: *1-4*, *i* ii-xxi *xxii*, *1* 2-399. Notes: Copies: E(2) L(2) P; CtY(with Baudry catalogue [1836]) NN. Reference: Kohler(1) 168/169(with illustrations).

31] Tales of the Crusaders. . . . Tale II. The Talisman. [imprint 3] 1832. Pages: *1-4*, *i* ii-xiv, *1* 2-401. Copies: E(2) L P; NN. Reference: Kohler(1) 168/169(with illustrations).

34] Woodstock; or, The Cavalier. A Tale of the Year Sixteen Hundred and Fifty-One. [imprint 4] 1832. Pages: *1-4*, *i* ii-xxxix *xl*, *1* 2-504. Copies: E(2) L P; NN. Reference: Kohler(1) 172(with illustration).

36] Chronicles of the Canongate. The Highland Widow.—The Two Drovers. My Aunt Margaret's Mirror.—The Tapestried Chamber. The Surgeon's Daughter. [imprint 4] 1832. Pages: *1-4*, *i* ii-xxxvii *xxxviii*, *1* 2-'328'[428]. Copies: E(2) L P; NjP NN. Reference: Kohler(1) 177(with illustration).

37] Chronicles of the Canongate. Saint Valentine's Day; or, The Fair Maid of Perth. [imprint 4] 1832. Pages: *1-4*, *i* ii-v *vi*, *1* 2-509. Copies: E(2) L P; NN. Reference: Kohler(1) 180(with illustration).

38] The Life and Opinions of Tristram Shandy, Gentleman. By Lawrence Sterne, A.M. With a Life of the Author, By Sir Walter Scott. [imprint 4] 1832. Scott's 'Life', pages: *i* ii-xix. Copies: O P.

Subsequent volumes, as listed below, were issued after 1832 and thus are not represented in this bibliography. In addition, most of the titles listed above were reissued after 1832.

40] Anne of Geierstein. 1833.

43] Tales of a Grandfather. First Series. 1833.

44] Tales of a Grandfather. Second Series. 1833.

45] Tales of a Grandfather. Third Series. 1833.

46] Notices and Anecdotes. 1833.

289R] PARIS: Didot 1826

Select British Novels, Tales, and Historical Romances; edited by J. W. Lake, Esq. Paris. Firmin Didot and Sons, Rue Jacob, No 24; L. Laurent, at Toulon. 1826. Notes: An abortive unnumbered series.

[1-2] A Legend of Montrose, By Sir Walter Scott, Bart. 1826. Two volumes. Pages 1: *i-viii*, *1* II-XLVII *XLVIII*, *1* 2-201; 2: *i-viii*, *1* 2-224. Notes: In each volume a blank leaf is integral and precedes the half-title. The preliminary 'Literary Sketch' by J. W. Lake, in the final note, page XXXI, promises further commentary in 'the remaining productions of Walter Scott', but no further works appear to have been issued under this collective title. Copy: P.

290R-294R] PARIS: Didot and Galignani [imprints 1-2 and 5] and Galignani only [imprints 6-7] and Galignani and Didot [imprints 3-4] (12° series) 1820-1832

Collection of Modern English Authors. Paris: 1820-1832.

General Notes: This unnumbered 12° series title, when given, is on wrappers only and the imprint thereon often reverses the order in title imprint. In the course of printing the title imprint goes through the seven states listed below, often with variations in punctuation. As an unnumbered collection this and other sequences have been labelled, ordered, and numbers assigned according to the 1832 Galignani 'List' in the L copy of 291R.71—a record arranging the titles in three groups here indicated as 290R, 291R, 292R. Further series in small and large formats in this complex publishing programme are assigned indicators 293R, 294R. Reference to paper variants, or issues not in the 'List', derives from an 1828 'New Publications' catalogue in the ViU copy of 294R.1. Successive editions of a title are cited under a single number: i.e. [1A] and [1B]. All editions are promoted in advertisements and on wrappers as costing less than the London prices: ranging from one-third less to even 'one eighth of the London prices.'

IMPRINT 1: Paris: Published by P. Didot, Sen. Rue du Pont-de-Lodi, and Galignani, 18, Rue Vivienne. [*Roman numerals:*] 1820.

2: Paris: Published by P. Didot, Senior, Rue du Pont-de-Lodi, and A. and W. Galignani, 18, Rue Vivienne. [*Roman numerals:*] 1820-1821.

3: Paris: Published by A. and W. Galignani, 18, Rue Vivienne, and P. Didot, Sen. Rue du Pont-de-Lodi. [*Roman numerals:*] 1821-1822.

4: Paris: Published by A. and W. Galignani, 18, Rue Vivienne, and P. Didot, Senior, Rue du Pont-De-Lodi. [*Roman numerals:*] 1821-1823.

5: Paris: Printed by Jules Didot, Sen. for A. and W. Galignani, Rue Vivienne. [*Roman numerals:*] 1824.

6: Paris: Published by A. and W. Galignani, At the English, French, Italian, German, and Spanish Library, No 18, Rue Vivienne. [*Roman numerals:*] 1825-1826.

7: Paris: Published by A. and W. Galignani, At the English, French, Italian, German, and Spanish Library, No 18, Rue Vivienne. [*Arabic numerals:*] 1825-1832.

290R] 'Complete Poetical Works'

[1A-7A] The Poetical Works of Sir Walter Scott. [imprint 3] M DCCC XXI. Seven volumes. Notes: Engraved frontispiece portrait in volume 1 of Scott as a young man by Raeburn. The 'Poetical Works' title above is in bold at the head of the title-page, with the specific title in

a much smaller fount at mid-page. Copies: BCL(with 4-page Baudry catalogue dated 1823) E P; CtY. Reference: Kohler(1) 80(with illustration).
1] The Lay of the Last Minstrel. Pages: *i-vi, 1-5* 6-231.
2] Marmion. Pages: *i-vi, 1-5* 6-332.
3] The Lady of the Lake. Pages: *i-vi, 1-5* 6-299.
4] Rokeby. Pages: *i-vi, 1-5* 6-274.
5] Ballads and Miscellaneous Pieces. Pages: *i-v* vi-vii *viii, 1-3* 4-313.
6] The Lord of the Isles. Pages: *i-vi, 1-3* 4-291.
7] The Bridal of Triermain.—The Vision of Don Roderick.—The Field of Waterloo.—Ballads, etc. etc. etc. Pages: *i-v* vi-vii *viii, 1-3* 4-317.
[1B] Halidon Hill; A Dramatic Sketch, from Scottish History. By Sir Walter Scott, Bart. [imprint 3] M DCCC XXII. Pages: *i-vii* viii-xiii *xiv, 15-17* 18-85 *86-87*. Notes: Issued after the first collected edition of 1821 and still available in 1828, though included in volume 7 of *The Poetical Works* published in 1826 (cf. next entry). Copies: E P.
[1C-7C] The Poetical Works of Sir Walter Scott. [imprint 6] MDCCCXXVI. Seven volumes. Notes: There are two issues: (1) Engraved frontispiece portrait in volume 1 of a young Scott (as in 1A) and preliminaries paged *i-vi*; (2) portrait of a mature Scott by F. Sieurac and (as noted below) an additional memoir postdating 1826. The 'Poetical Works' title above is in bold at the head of the title-page, with the specific title in a smaller fount at mid-page. The imprint 'No' before '18' appears only in volumes 3-5 and 7. Issued on 'vellum paper' and also in 'large type'. Copies: (Issue 1) P. (2) BCL(vols. 1-2, 5-7) L(vols.1-2, 5-7); T/B.
1] The Lay of the Last Minstrel. Pages: *1-2, i-v* vi-lxx, *1-5* 6-214. Notes: The new preliminary section (in the second issue) represents a revision of J. W. Lake's 'Literary Sketch' 1826 (*see* 289R[1]), now called a 'Memoir' of Scott, concluding with a comment (page lxvii) on the meeting of his creditors 26 May 1826 and a final note (page lxx) on his reply 19 September 1827 to General Gourgaud (*see* 204A): this a year after the title date of the present edition.
2] Marmion. Pages: *i-vi, 1-5* 6-320.
3] The Lady of the Lake. Pages: *i-vi, 1-5* 6-279.
4] Rokeby. Pages: *i-vi, 1-5* 6-265.
5] The Lord of the Isles. Pages: *i-vi, 1-3* 4-285.
6] Miscellaneous. Pages: *i-v* vi, *1-3* 4-282.
7] The Vision of Don Roderick—Halidon Hill—Ballads, and Miscellaneous Pieces. Pages: *i-v* vi-vii *viii, i-v* vi, *7* 8-347.

291R] 'Novels and Tales'
Preliminary Note: It will be observed that, while Galignani finally, in the 1832 list, arranged the novels in original British order, the firm in 1820 started its series—appropriately for a French publisher—with *The Abbot* (31A-33A), representing imprint 1. The original wrappers, still reading 'Collecton of Modern English Authors', cites this series as appearing two volumes a month, each volume available separately, and sold at a reduced price for subscribers.
[1A-3A] Waverley; or, 'Tis Sixty Years Since. [imprint 3] M DCCC XXI. Three volumes. Pages 1: *i-v* vi-viii, *1* 2-239; 2: *i-iv*, *1* 2-247; 3: *i-iv*, *1* 2-248. Copies: BCL E; T/B. Reference: Kohler(1) 90(with illustration).
[1B-3B] Waverley; or, 'Tis Sixty Years Since. [imprint 6] MDCCCXXV. Three volumes. Pages 1: *i-v* vi-viii, *1* 2-258; 2: *i-iv*, *1* 2-265; 3: *i-iv*, *1* 2-266. Copies: E(2) L O(2); NNU-W. Reference: Kohler(1) 91(with illustration).

[1C-3C] Waverley; or, 'Tis Sixty Years Since. By Sir Walter Scott. . . . New Edition, . . . [imprint 7] 1830. Three volumes. Pages 1: *1-4*, *i* ii-lxxxi *lxxxii*, *1* 2-258; 2: *i-iv*, *1* 2-265; 3: *i-iv*, *1* 2-299. Notes: Includes the [1829] author's introduction and notes. Copy: BCL.

[4A-6A] Guy Mannering; or, The Astrologer. By the Author of "Waverley." [imprint 2] M DCCC XXI. Three volumes. Pages 1: *i-iv*, *1* 2-226; 2: *i-iv*, *1* 2-229; 3: *i-iv*, *1* 2-235. Copies: BCL E O; NNU-W T/B. Reference: Kohler(1) 95(with illustration).

[4B-6B] Guy Mannering; or, The Astrologer. By the Author of "Waverley." [imprint 7] 1826. Three volumes. Pages 1: *i-iv*, *1* 2-242; 2: *i-iv*, *1* 2-245; 3: *i-iv*, *1* 2-252. Copies: E(2) P. Reference: Kohler(1) 96(with illustration).

[4C-6C] Guy Mannering; or, The Astrologer. By Sir Walter Scott. New Edition, with the Author's Notes, etc. [imprint 7] 1830. Three volumes. Pages 1: *1-4*, *i* ii-xxiii *xxiv*, 1 2-242; 2: *i-iv*, *1* 2-245; 3: *i-iv*, *1* 2-270. Notes: Includes the [1829] author's introduction and notes. Copy: BCL.

[7-9] The Antiquary. By the Author of "Waverley" and "Guy Mannering." [imprint 4] M DCCC XXI. Three volumes. Pages 1: *i-v* vi-vii *viii*, *1* 2-221; 2: *i-iv*, *1* 2-228; 3: *i-iv*, *1* 2-235. Notes: Some copies have two or three plates drawn by C. R. Leslie, engraved by E. Portbury, bearing the imprint: Hurst, Robinson & Co., London, 1823 (*see* 334D[4]). Copies: BCL(with 4-page Baudry catalogue 1823) E(2) L O P; T/B. Reference: Kohler(1) 100(with illustration).

[10-13] Tales of My Landlord, First Series. [imprint 2] M DCCC XXI. Four volumes. Pages 1: *1-4*, *i-iii* iv-xv *xvi*, *1* 2-225; 2: *i-iv*, *1* 2-227; 3: *i-iv*, *1* 2-232; 4: *i-iv*, *1* 2-230. Copies: BCL E L P(vols.1-2); NNU-W T/B.

[14-17] Tales of My Landlord, Second Series, [imprint 4] M DCCC XXI. Four volumes. Pages 1: *1-4*, *i* ii-vii *viii*, *1* 2-216; 2: *i-iv*, *1* 2-216; 3: *i-iv*, *1* 2-222; 4: *i-iv*, *1* 2-251. Notes: In some copies of volume 1, page-numbers ii and iv are lacking. Copies: BCL E(2) L P; T/B. Reference: Kohler(1) 110(with illustration).

[18-20] Rob Roy. By the Author of "Waverley," "Guy Mannering," and "The Antiquary." [imprint 2] M DCCC XXI. Three volumes. Pages 1: *i-v* vi-vii *viii*, *1* 2-217; 2: *i-iv*, *1* 2-216; 3: *i-iv*, *1* 2-233. Copies: BCL E P(vols.2-3); NNU-W T/B. Reference: Kohler(1) 106(with illustration).

[21-24] Tales of My Landlord, Third Series, [imprint 4] M DCCC XXI. Four volumes. Pages 1: *i-iv*, *1* 2-222; 2: *i-iv*, *1* 2-216; 3: *i-iv*, *1* 2-229; 4: *i-iv*, *1* 2-220. Copies: BCL E L P; T/B.

[25A-27A] Ivanhoe; A Romance. By the "Author of Waverley," etc., etc. [imprint 3] M DCCC XXI. Three volumes. Pages 1: *1-4*, *i-iii* iv-xxiv, *1* 2-231; 2: *i-iv*, *1* 2-246; 3: *i-iv*, *1* 2-276. Copies: BCL(with 4-page Baudry catalogue 1823) E O. Reference: Kohler(1) 118(with illustration).

[25B-27B] Ivanhoe; A Romance. By the Author of "Waverley," etc. etc. etc. [imprint 6] MDCCCXXV. Three volumes. Pages 1: *1-4*, *i-iii* iv-xxiv, *1* 2-251; 2: *i-iv*, *1* 2-265; 3: *i-iv*, *1* 2-296. Copies: BCL E. Reference: Kohler(1) 119(with illustration).

[28-30] The Monastery. A Romance. By the Author of "Waverley," "Ivanhoe," etc. [imprint 3] M DCCC XXI. Three volumes. Pages 1: *1-4*, *i* ii-lxxi *lxxiii*, *1* 2-173; 2: *i-iv*, *1* 2-223; 3: *i-iv*, *1* 2-232. Copies: BCL E(2) P(vol.2); T/B. Reference: Kohler(1) 125 (with illustration).

[31A-33A] The Abbot. By the Author of "Waverley." [imprint 1 or 2] M DCCC XX. Three volumes. Pages 1: *1-4*, *i* ii-iv, *1* 2-238; 2: *i-iv*, *1* 2-243; 3: *i-iv*, *1* 2-252. Notes: It would appear that this is the first novel to be published by Galignani, as it is the only one to bear (in one copy) imprint 1. Copies: (Issue imprint 1) P. (2) E L(with additional engraved title by Chas. Heath and 4 plates, imprinted by Hurst, Robinson, 1824: *see* 146Dd). Reference: Kohler(1) 129(with illustration).

[31B-33B] The Abbot. By The Author of "Waverley." [imprint 2] M DCCC XXI. Three volumes. Pages 1: *i-v* vi-viii, *1* 2-238; 2: *i-iv*, *1* 2-242; 3: *i-iv*, *1* 2-249. Copies: BCL E(2) O.

[34-36] Kenilworth; A Romance. By the Author of "Waverley," "Ivanhoe," etc. [imprint 3] M DCCC XXI. Three volumes. Pages 1: *i-iv*, *1* 2-242; 2: *i-iv*, *1* 2-260; 3: *i-iv*, *1* 2-263. Copies: BCL E(2) L O. Reference: Kohler(1) 132(with illustration).

[37A-39A] The Pirate. By the Author of "Waverley," "Ivanhoe," etc. [imprint 3] M DCCC XXII. Three volumes. Pages 1: *1-4*, *i* ii-iv, *1* 2-241; 2: *i-iv*, *1* 2-249; 3: *i-iv*, *1* 2-260. Copies: BCL BCL(with 8-page Baudry catalogue April 1822) E(2) L; CtY. Reference: Kohler(1) 139(with illustration).

[37B-39B] The Pirate. By the Author of "Waverley," "Ivanhoe," etc. [imprint 7] 1826. Three volumes. Pages 1: *1-4*, *i* ii-iv, *1* 2-260; 2: *i-iv*, *1* 2-268; 3: *i-iv*, *1* 2-281. Copies: BCL E O P.

[40-42] The Fortunes of Nigel. By the Author of "Waverley," "Kenilworth," etc. [imprint 3] M DCCC XXII. Three volumes. Pages 1: *1-4*, *i* ii-xxxvii *xxxviii*, *1* 2-235; 2: *i-iv*, *1* 2-256; 3: *i-iv*, *1* 2-262. Notes: Some copies have a period rather than a colon after Paris. Copies: BCL E(2); NNU-W T/B. Reference: Kohler(1) 142(with illustration).

[43A-45A] Quentin Durward. By the Author of "Waverley," "Peveril of the Peak," etc. [imprint 4] M DCCC XXIII. Three volumes. Pages 1: *1-4*, *i* ii-xlviii, *1* 2-207; 2: *i-iv*, *1* 2-251; 3: *i-iv*, *1* 2-272. Copies: BCL E; NNU-W. Reference: Kohler(1) 149(with illustration).

[43B-45B] Quentin Durward. By the Author of "Waverley," etc. etc. [imprint 7] 1827. Three volumes. Pages 1: *1-4*, *i* ii-xl, *1* 2-221; 2: *i-iv*, *1* 2-269; 3: *i-iv*, *1* 2-290. Notes: Remarkably, in the year Jules Didot printed this edition, his relative at the same address, Julius Didot, printed the Glashin edition (295R.1-3). Copies: E(2) P; T/B. Reference: Kohler(1) 150(with illustration).

[46-49] Peveril of the Peak. By the Author of "Waverley," "Kenilworth," etc. [imprint 4] M DCCC XXIII. Four volumes. Pages 1: *1-4*, *i* ii-xxv *xxvi*, *1* 2-229; 2: *i-iv*, *1* 2-237; 3: *i-iv*, *1* 2-240; 4: *i-iv*, *1* 2-244. Copies: BCL E L P; T/B. Reference: Kohler(1) 145 (with illustration).

[50-52] St Ronan's Well. By the Author of "Waverley," "Quentin Durward," etc. [imprint 5] M DCCC XXIV. Three volumes. Pages 1: *i-iv*, *1* 2-234; 2: *i-iv*, *1* 2-245; 3: *i-iv*, *1* 2-241. Copies: BCL E(2) O P. Reference: Kohler(1) 156(with illustration).

[53-55] Redgauntlet. A Tale of the Eighteenth Century. By the Author of "Waverley," etc. [imprint 5] M DCCC XXIV. Three volumes. Pages 1: *i-iv*, *1* 2-242; 2: *i-iv*, *1* 2-247; 3: *i-iv*, *1* 2-246. Copies: BCL(2) E(2) L O; NNU-W T/B. Reference: Kohler(1) 162(with illustration).

[56-59] Tales of the Crusaders. By the Author of "Waverley," "Quentin Durward," etc. [imprint 6] MDCCCXXV. Four volumes. Pages 1: *1-4*, i-xxiii *xxiv*, *1* 2-275; 2: *i-iv*, *1* 2-291; 3: *i-iv*, *1* 2-270; 4: *i-iv*, *1* 2-299. Notes: Volumes 1-2 contain *The Betrothed* and 3-4 *The Talisman*. Copies: BCL E(2) L(vols.1-2) P; NNU-W. Reference: Kohler(1) 167 (with illustration).

[60-62] Woodstock; or, the Cavalier; A Tale of The Year Sixteen Hundred and Fifty-one. By the Author of "Waverley," "Tales of the Crusaders," etc. [imprint 7] 1826. Three volumes. Pages 1: *i-iv*, *1* 2-259; 2: *i-iv*, *1* 2-278; 3: *i-iv*, *1* 2-306. Copies: E; T/B. References: Kohler(1)

172(with illustration). Reissued ca.1832 with Scott's preliminary introduction, volume 1 pages *i* ii-xii, inserted before text (BCL E O; NNU-W).

[63-64] Chronicles of the Canongate. By Sir Walter Scott. [imprint 7] 1827. Two volumes. Pages 1: *1-4, i* ii-xx, *1* 2-283; 2: *i-iv, 1* 2-299. Copies: BCL E O P; T/B TxU. Reference: Kohler(1) 176(with illustration).

[65-67] Chronicles of the Canongate. Second Series. By Sir Walter Scott. [imprint 7] 1828. Three volumes. Pages 1: *i-iv, 1* 2-266; 2: *i-iv, 1* 2-266; 3: *i-iv, 1* 2-277. Copies: BCL E(2); T/B TxU. Reference: Kohler(1) 179(with illustration).

[68-70] Anne of Geierstein; or, The Maiden of the Mist. By Sir Walter Scott. [imprint 7] 1829. Three volumes. Pages 1: *i-iv, 1* 2-268; 2: *i-iv, 1* 2-275; 3: *i-iv, 1* 2-298. Copies: BCL E L P; IdU T/B. Reference: Kohler(1) 184(with illustration).

[71-73] Tales of My Landlord, Fourth and Last Series, Collected and Arranged by Jedediah Cleishbotham. [imprint 7] 1832. Three volumes. Pages 1: [*1-4, i* ii] iii-xxvi, *1* 2-361; 2: *i-iv, 1* 2-295; 3: *i-iv, 1* 2-341. Notes: Volumes 1 and 2 contain *Count Robert of Paris*, volume 3 *Castle Dangerous.* Copies: BCL L P.

292R] 'Miscellaneous Prose Works'

[1] Goetz of Berlichingen, with the Iron Hand. A Tragedy, from the German of Goethe. By Sir Walter Scott. [imprint 7] 1826. Pages: *1-4, i* ii-viii, *9* 10-187 *188*. Notes: In the preliminaries, page *3*, 'Notice of the Publisher' reads: 'It is presumed that the following translation first given to the public in the year 1799, will be perused with a high degree of curiosity and interest, as one of the earliest of those varied literary labours which have since, given such a brilliant and imperishable celebrity to the name of Sir Walter Scott.' Copies: BCL E(2) P; CtY OCl. Reference: Kohler(1) 85(with illustration). Reissued 1829 (not seen, *see* Kohler[2] 55).

[2-3] Memoirs of Jonathan Swift, D. D. Dean of St Patrick's, Dublin. By Sir Walter Scott. [imprint 6] MDCCCXXVI. Two volumes. Pages 1: *i-v, 1-2,* vi-x, *1* 2-311; 2: *i-v*vi, *1* 2-259. Notes: The 'Notice of the Publisher', inserted in the preliminaries, reads: 'The admirers of Sir Walter Scott will be gratified by the separate publications of these Memoirs, which will complete our Edition of his Works [*a premature statement*]. They are now for the first time published distinct from the Works of Swift, with which, at the price of upwards of eight guineas, they can only be purchased in London. Those who possess old Editions of Swift will find these Memoirs a valuable addition to that work. Paris, Dec. 15, 1825.' In some copies the 'Notice of the Publisher' is inserted in the second volume. Copies: BCL DN E(2) P; CtY NjP PPL ViU. Reference: Kohler(1) 175 (with illustration).

[4-5] Memoirs of John Dryden. By Sir Walter Scott. [imprint 6] MDCCCXXVI. Two volumes. Pages 1: *i-iv, 1-2, v* vi-vii *viii, v*-vi, *1* 2-277; 2: *i-vi, 1* 2-219. Notes: In the preliminaries, page *1*, 'Notice of the Publisher', dated 15 March 1826 reads: 'The admirers of Sir Walter Scott will be gratified by the separate publication of these Memoirs, which will complete our edition of his works [*statement still premature*]. They are now for the first time published distinct from the works of Dryden [*sic*], with which, at the price of upwards of eight guineas, they can only be purchased in London. Those who possess old editions of Dryden will find these Memoirs a valuable addition.' Copies: BCL E(3) P; MH PPL.

[6-7] Lives of the Novelists. By Sir Walter Scott. [imprint 7 without 'No' before '18'] 1825. Two volumes. Pages 1: *i-viii, 1* 2-268; 2: *i-vi, 1* 2-256. Notes: First separate edition of fourteen biographical notices and critical remarks. In some copies volume 1, page 268 is

misnumbered 68. The 'Notice of the Publisher' (volume 1, page *v*) concludes: 'We beg leave to suggest that these productions of Sir Walter Scott, thus attainable at a trifling expence, cannot be obtained in England but by purchasing the whole collection of the Novelist's Library.' This page exists in two settings, the first sentence of the 'Notice' ending either with the word '*Library.*' *or* 'Romances.' Contents: volume 1: Fielding, Le Sage, Smollett, Charles Johnstone, Sterne, Mrs Radcliffe; volume 2: Richardson, Johnson, Goldsmith, Walpole, MacKenzie, Clara Reeve, Robert Bage, Richard Cumberland. The 'Prefatory Memoir to Jonathan Swift' is omitted here because of the pending issue of a more extensive Scott account [2-3 above]. Copies: AN BCL E(3) L(2) O; CtY InU NNU-W OCl T/B.

[8-9] Essays by Sir Walter Scott. [imprint 7] 1828. Two volumes. Pages 1: *i-vi, 1* 2-237; 2: *i-iv, 1* 2-202. Notes: Volume 1, page *v* reads: 'Notice by the Publishers. The contents of these volumes are extracted from the Supplement to the *Encyclopaedia Britannica*, and cannot consequently be procured in England separately.' Contents: volume 1 'Chivalry' and 'Romance'; volume 2 'The Drama'. Copies: BCL E(2) P.

[10-18] The Life of Napoleon Buonaparte, Emperor of the French. With a Preliminary View of the French Revolution. By Sir Walter Scott. [imprint 7] 1827. Nine volumes. Pages 1: *1-4, i* ii-ix *x, 1* 2-361; 2: *i-v* vi-xi *xii, 1* 2-413; 3: *i-v* vi-x, *1* 2-381; 4: *i-v* vi-xiii *xiv-xvi, 1* 2-415; 5: *i-v* vi-xii, *1* 2-454; 6: *i-v* vi-xi *xii, 1* 2-384; 7: *i-v* vi-xvi, *1* 2-661; 8: *i-v* vi-xiv, *1* 2-583; 9: *i-v* vi-x, *1* 2-397. Notes: Volume 1 has frontispiece with two portraits and two signatures engraved by J. J. Wedgwood. Copies: BCL E P(vols.1-3); CtY T/B.

[19-20] Tales of a Grandfather; being Stories taken from Scottish History. [imprint 7] 1828. Two volumes. Pages 1: *1-4, i* ii-viii, 1 2-259; 2: *1-4, i* ii-iv, *1* 2-338. Copies: BCL E P.

[21-22] Tales of a Grandfather; being Stories taken from Scottish History. . . . Second Series. [imprint 7] 1829. Two volumes. Pages 1: *i-v* vi-xi *xii, 1* 2-360; 2: *i-v* vi-viii, 2-348. Copies: BCL E P; IdU(vol.2).

[23-24] Tales of a Grandfather; being Stories taken from Scottish History. . . . Third Series. [imprint 7] 1830. Two volumes. Pages 1: *i-v* vi-xvi, *1* 2-368; 2: *i-v* vi-ix *x, 1* 2-393. Copies: BCL P.

[25] Religious Discourses. By Sir Walter Scott. [imprint 7] 1828. Pages: *i-v* vi-viii, *9-11* 12-68. Copies: BCL E L P.

[26] Tales and Essays by Sir Walter Scott. [imprint 7] 1829. Pages: *1-6, i-iii* iv-xxxv *xxxvi, 1* 2-269. Notes: Of the selections, three are Scott reprints from *The Keepsake for 1829* ('The Tapestried Chamber', 'My Aunt Margaret's Mirror', and 'Death of the Laird's Jock'). In addition, there are four other Scott reprints ('The Letter of Sir Walter Scott to Sir Adam Ferguson', 1827; 'Phantasmagoria'; 'Abstract of the Eyrbiggia-Saga' 1814; 'Essay on the Life and Writings of Molière', 1828). Washington Irving's essay, 'Abbotsford', included in the Introduction, should not be confused with the essay in *The Keepsake*, 'Description of the Engraving entitled A Scene at Abbotsford.' NCBEL apparently is in error in citing an 1829 French edition of the two reprints first mentioned above. Copies: BCL E L P. Reference: Kohler(1) 84(with illustration.)

[27-28] Biographical Memoirs. By Sir Walter Scott. [imprint 7] 1830. Two volumes. Pages 1: *i-viii, 1* 2-243; 2: *i-vi, 1* 2-224. Notes: First book edition. As the contents show, this is a reprint, not from *Ballantyne's Novelist's Library* (previously issued as volumes 6-7 above), but from other, separate introductions or memorials written by Scott. The 'Notice of the Publishers' reads in part: 'The importance justly attached to every production of Sir Walter Scott, would doubtless secure a favourable reception to any republication of this nature—but it is submitted that even a peculiar value may be assigned to Biographical Notices, and

opinions on contemporary talent, by so eminent a judge and accurate a delineator of human nature, feeling, and character.' Contents: volume 1: Memoirs of Charlotte Smith, Sir Ralph Sadler, John Leyden and Anna Seward; volume 2: Memoirs of Daniel De Foe, The Late Duke of Buccleuch and Queensberry, Lord Somerville, King George III, Lord Byron, The Duke of York. Copies: BCL E O; CtY.

[29] The House of Aspen, A Tragedy. By Sir Walter Scott. [imprint 7] 1830. Pages: *1-4*, *i* ii-iv *v-vi*, *7* 8-102. Copies: E(2) O P.

[30] The Doom of Devorgoil, A Melo-Drama. Auchindrane; or, The Ayrshire Tragedy. By Sir Walter Scott. [imprint 7] 1830. Pages: *1-4*, *i*-ii, *3-7* 8-228. Copies: E O P.

[31-32] History of Scotland. By Sir Walter Scott. . . . [imprint 7 with a period after 'No.'] 1830. Two volumes. Pages 1: *i-v* vi, *1* 2-426; 2: *i-iv*, *1* 2-527. Copies: BCL; T/B.

[33] Letters on Demonology and Witchcraft, Addressed to J. G. Lockhart, Esq. By Sir Walter Scott, Bart. [imprint 7] 1831. Pages: *i-iv*, *1* 2-431. Copies: BCL E P; T/B.

[34] Tales of a Grandfather; being Stories taken from the History of France. First Series, [imprint 7] 1831. Two volumes. Pages 1: *i-v* vi-xiv, *1* 2-340; 2: *i-v* vi-xii, *1* 2-349. Notes: The publisher designated this work as 'First Series' in anticipation of further volumes on France. Copies: BCL P; T/B.

PARIS: Galignani (above 12° series with single imprint) *see* Didot and Galignani.

293R] PARIS: Galignani (18° and 32° collection) 1828-1829

[*Miscellaneous titles*]. Notes: This unnumbered miniature series, the first two sets in 18°, the remaining volumes in 32°, all apparently bear imprint 7: Paris: Published by A. and W. Galignani, At the English, French, Italian, German, and Spanish Library, No 18, Rue Vivienne. 1825-1832. The series is advertised among the 'New Publications' in volumes 19, 21 of the preceding 12° collection (copy P). Copies: volumes (1-3) P; (4-13) not seen.

[1-3] Tales of a Grandfather; Being Stories Taken from Scottish History. 1828. Three volumes. Pages 1: *i-v* vi-x, *1* 2-247; 2: *i-v* vi-vii *viii*, *1* 2-252; 3: *i-v* vi-viii, *1* 2-337.

[4-6] [Tales of a Grandfather. Second Series.]
[7] [The Lay of the Last Minstrel.]
[8] [Marmion.]
[9] [The Lady of the Lake.]
[10] [Rokeby.]
[11] [The Lord of the Isles.]
[12-13] [A Legend of Montrose.]

294R] PARIS: A. and W. Galignani (Royal 8° collections) 1827-1834

[1] The Life of Napoleon Bonaparte, Emperor of the French. With a Preliminary View of the French Revolution. By Sir Walter Scott. Paris: Published by A. and W. Galignani, No 18, Rue Vivienne. 1828. One volume in Royal 8°. Pages: *i-v* vi-xx, *1* 2-858. Notes: Frontispiece with two portraits of Napoleon and two of his signatures. Copies: DN E(2) L O; ViU.

[2] The Poetical Works of Sir Walter Scott. Complete in One Volume. Paris: Published by A. and W. Galignani, No 18, Rue Vivienne. 1827. One volume in Royal 8°. Pages: *i-vii* viii-xxxiii *xxxiv*, *1* 2-489. Notes: With an engraved frontispiece portrait and a memoir of Scott by J. W. Lake (this apparently a revised and much extended version of an essay published earlier in the year by Baudry: *see* 356E[2]). The 1828 list records issues in 'vellum paper' and 'large vellum paper'. Copies: BCL E P; CtY NNU-W T/B. Reference: Kohler(1) 81(with illustration). Reissued 1831 with preliminaries extended to pages xxxix *xl* and text to page 490.

[3] The Prose Works of Sir Walter Scott. Paris Published by A. and W. Galignani, No 18, Rue Vivienne. 1827-1834. Ten-volume collection in Royal 8°, printed in a two-column format. Two issues are found: (1) without notes, hence before publication of volume 10 in 1834; (2) with notes, added either by owner or publisher in or after 1834. The first five volumes of issue (2) were later titled *The Works of Sir Walter Scott.*

1] Waverley. Guy-Mannering. Antiquary. Rob Roy. Ivanhoe. 1827. Pages: *i-iv, 1* 2-771. Notes: With an engraved frontispiece portrait of Scott and title-page vignette of a harp. Copies: (1) L. (2) P.

2] Tales of my Landlord [The Black Dwarf. Old Mortality. The Heart of Midlothian. The Bride of Lammermoor. A Legend of Montrose]. The Monastery. 1827. Pages: *i-iv, 1* 2-750. Copies: (1) L. (2) P.

3] The Abbot. Kenilworth. The Pirate. The Fortunes of Nigel. Quentin Durward. 1827. Pages: *i-iv, 1* 2-840. Copies: (1) L. (2) P.

4] Peveril of the Peak. St-Ronan's Well. Redgauntlet. Tales of the Crusaders [The Betrothed. The Talisman.] 1827. Pages: *i-iv, 1* 2-769. Copies: (1) L. (2) P.

5] Woodstock. Memoirs of Swift. Life of Dryden. Lives of the Novelists. Paul's Letters to his Kinsfolk. Goetz of Berlichingen. Essays (Chivalry. The Drama. Romance). 1827. Pages: *i-iv, 1* 2-720. Copies: (1) L. (2) P.

6] The Life of Napoleon Bonaparte. 1827. Pages: *i-iv, 1* 2-858. Copies: (2) P; TxU.

7] Chronicles of the Canongate. Anne of Geierstein. Tales of a Grandfather. 1830. Pages: *i-iv, 1* 2-870. Copies: (1) L. (2) P.

8] Count Robert of Paris and Castle Dangerous, forming the fourth and last series of "Tales of My Landlord." 1832. Pages: *1-2, i-iii* iv-viii, *1* 2-215. Notes: A volume added to this Royal 8° series in order to complete the 'Waverley Novels'. Copy: (1) P. In 1834, after the period covered by this bibliography, two additional volumes were issued:

9] History of Scotland. Biographical Memoirs. Religious Discourses. House of Aspen. Doom of Devorgoil. Letters on Demonology and Witchcraft. History of France. Robert of Paris. Castle Dangerous. Tales and Essays [The Tapestried Chamber. My Aunt Margaret's Mirror. Phantasmagoria. Abstract of the Eyrbiggia-Saga. Moliere. Death of Laird's Jock]. Glossary.

10] Supplementary Volume: Containing Notes, Historical and Illustrative, By the Author, Glossary, etc. Notes: The Sections are separately paged for insertion by owners or issuance by the publishers at the end of each of the original eight volumes.

PARIS: Galignani and Didot (12° series) *see* Didot and Galignani.

295R] PARIS: Glashin, Robertson [and others] 1827-1828

The Complete Works of Sir Walter Scott, Bart. Paris: 1827 [1828.]

General Notes: Collective title and volume numbers appear only on the half-title, in Roman numerals. In the course of printing the title imprint goes through the four states listed below. It should be observed that the printer's first name, spelled 'Julius' here, is a relative at the same address as 'Jules' in the Galignani series.

IMPRINT 1: Paris: Printed by Julius Didot, Senior, for Glashin, 35, Rue de L'Odéon; Robertson, 8, Rue du Bouloy; Furlong, 178, Rue Montmartre; Bobée and Ingray[!], 14, Rue de Richelieu. 1827.

2: Paris: Printed by Julius Didot, Senior, for Glashin, 35, Rue de L'Odéon; Robertson, 8, Rue du Bouloy; Furlong, 179, Rue Montmartre; and to be had also of Bobée and Hingray, Booksellers, 14, Rue de Richelieu. 1827.

3: Paris: Printed by Julius Didot, Senior, for Glashin, 35, Rue de L'Odéon, and Robertson, 8, Rue du Bouloy. To be had also of Bobée and Hingray, Booksellers, 14, Rue de Richelieu. 1828.
4: Paris: Printed by Julius Didot, Senior, for Glashin, 10, Rue Vivienne, and Robertson, 8, Rue du Bouloy. To be had also of Bobée and Hingray, Booksellers, 14, Rue de Richelieu. 1828.

1-3] Quentin Durward. By Sir Walter Scott, Bart. with Notes Explanatory of the Scottish Dialect. [Volume 1 imprint 1 or 2] [Volumes 2-3 imprint 2] 1827. Three volumes. Pages 1: *i-v* vi-li *lii*, *1* 2-200; 2: *i-iv*, *1* 2-243; 3: *i-iv*, *1* 2-266. Notes: The printing office for this edition also in the same year printed the Galignani edition (291R. 43B-45B). Copies: [imprint 2] P; [imprint 1] T/B.
4-7] Tales of My Landlord, First Series. By Sir Walter Scott, Bart. With Notes Explanatory of the Scottish Dialect. [imprint 3] 1827. Four volumes. Pages 1: *i-v*, vii[!]-xviii, *xix-xx*, *1* 2-232; 2: *i-iv*, *1* 2-228; 3: *i-iv*, *1* 2-228; 4: *i-iv*, *1* 2-235. Notes: Volume 1 contains 'The Black Dwarf'; volumes 2-4 'Old Mortality'. Copy: P.
8-9] Chronicles of the Canongate. By Sir Walter Scott, Bart. With Notes Explanatory of the Scottish Dialect. [imprint 3] 1827. Two volumes. Pages 1: *1-2*, *i* ii-xxi *xxii*, *1* 2-270; 2: *i-iv*, *1* 2-277. Copy: P.
10-12] Kenilworth. By Sir Walter Scott, Bart. with Notes Explanatory of the Scottish Dialect. [imprint 4] 1828. Pages: 1: *i-iv*, *1* 2-239; 2: *i-iv*, *1* 2-258; 3: *i-iv*, *1* 2-257. Copies: P; T/B.

296R] PARIS: Ledoux 1830
The Works of Sir Walter Scott. Paris: Printed for E. Ledoux and Son, Booksellers, No 9, Rue Guénégaud. 1830.
General Notes: Title-pages read 'A New Edition, With the Author's Notes'. Some copies have an engraved frontispiece and one additional engraved plate in each volume. Volume numbers for this abortive series are entered only on half-titles.
1] Waverley; or, 'Tis Sixty Years Since. 1830. Pages: *i-iv*, *1* 2-632. Copies: E P.
2] Guy Mannering. 1830. Pages: *i-iv*, *1* 2-532. Copy: E.
3] The Antiquary. 1830. Pages: *i-iv*, *1* 2-512. Copies: E P.

297R] PARIS: Lequien 1832
Collection of the Best British Authors. Paris: Printed for Lequien, Bookseller, No 47, Quai des Augustins. 1832.
General Notes: In a preliminary statement in *Ivanhoe* the publisher gives his reasons for starting this abortive, unnumbered series with Scott: 'The study of the English language is daily diffusing itself more and more over France; but the high price at which English books are sold, has hitherto prevented the greater part of those who have studied it with great success, from appretiating[!] its litterature[!], otherwise than through the medium of translations. The best of them is but a feeble representation of the style and elegance of expression of an author. Thus to judge of a language, thus to attempt to set a value on its beauties, vould[!] be like forming one's opinion of an object, when seen through a false prism. . . . A volume of this Collection will appear in succession every week, dating from the 26th. january 1832.' Neither of the works listed below include Scott's final Magnum Opus introductions and notes, the first dated 1 September 1830, the second 1 December 1831 (347A.16, 31).
[1-4] Ivanhoe; A Romance. By the Author of "Waverley," etc. etc. 1832. Pages 1: *i-ix* x-xxxvi, *1* 2-179; 2: *1-5* 6-282; 3: *i-iv*, *1* 2-273; 4: *1-5* 6-261. Four volumes. Copies: E P.
[5-8] Quentin Durward. By the author of "Waverley," etc. etc. 1832. Four volumes. Pages

1: *1-5* 6-244; 2: *1-5* 6-269; 3: *1-5* 6-250; 4: *1-5* 6-286. Copies: E P(vols.1-2). Reference: Kohler(1) 152(with illustration).

GERMANY

298R] BRUNSWICK: Vieweg 1827

[1] The Poetical Works of Sir Walter Scott, Bart. . . . Brunswick, Printed for Frederick Vieweg by Fred. Vieweg and Son. 1827. Pages: *1-2*, *i-ii*, *1* 2-485. Copy: E(Anthony Trollope). Reference: GDS 132, page 351 (for this or following entry).

[2] The Poetical Works of Sir Walter Scott, Bart. . . . Brunswick, Printed for Frederick Vieweg by Fred. Vieweg and Son. 1827. Pages: *i-ii*, *1* 2-503, *I*-II. Notes: The addition of *Halidon Hill* accounts for the extra pages—a fact explained on page *486*. Copy: NNU-W. Reference: GDS 132, page 351 (for this or preceding entry).

299R] FRANKFORT AM MAIN: Broenner 1826-1834

The Poetical Works of Walter Scott. Francfort O. M. Printed by and for H. L. Broenner. 1826. Pages: *i-iv*, *1* 2-482 *483*. General Notes: Issued with engraved vignette title-page only and there described as 'Complete in One Volume'. On half-title verso it is indicated that this edition is available in ten different cities from a specified bookseller: Amsterdam, J. Müller & Comp; Brussels, J. Frank; Copenhagen, F. Brummer; Leyden, H. W. Hazenberg; Milan, J. Meiners; Moscow, Oelsner; Paris, Ponthieu; [St] Petersburg, Schwetschke; Philadelphia, J. G. Ritter; and Venice, J. B. Missiaglia. Unlike other one volume collections this includes poetry from the novels and (pages 481-482) Explanatory Notes. Copies BCL E P; T/B. References: GDS 132, page 351; Kohler(1) 20 (with illustration). Reissued as 'The Second Edition' 1834 (E).

300R] LEIPZIG: Wigand 1831-1833

A Complete Edition of the Waverley Novels. With Introductory Notes by the Author. Pest, Leipsic and London: Printed for Otto Wigand. 1831-1832. 29 volumes. General Notes: This series was reprinted from the Magnum Opus edition, 1829-1833, now with corrections of the press by Dr. Johann Gottfried Flügel (the corrector also of the early Tauchnitz editions). In the preliminaries of a complete copy a series title-page faces the title-specific title-page. Ordinarily three volumes are issued in one publisher's cloth binding. The editions are entered here under Leipzig since both Wigand and Flügel were residents of that city, and the title-pages are set up to show the most important publishing city, Leipzig, in the middle of the imprint with publishing outlets, Pest and London, on either side.

1-3] Waverley; or, 'Tis Sixty Years Since. 1831. Three volumes. Pages 1: *i-v* vi-lxxxviii, *1-3* 4-167; 2: *1-7* 8-249; 3: *1-7* 8-262. Notes: Volume 1 has a note for Chapter XVII on page 167. Copies: E O.

4-6] Guy Mannering. 1831. Three volumes. Pages 1: *i-vii* viii-xxxii, *1-3* 4-183; 2: *1-7* 8-223; 3: *1-7* 8-219. Copy: L.

7-9] The Antiquary. 1831. Three volumes. Pages 1: *i-v* vi-xx *xxi-xxii*, *1-3* 4-194; 2: *1-7* 8-204; 3: *1-7* 8-214. Copy: E.

10-12] Rob Roy. 1831. Three volumes. Pages 1: [*i-ii*] *iii-vii* viii-cxx, *1-3* 4-131; 2: [*1-7*] 8-240; 3: [*1-7*] 8-224. Copy: E.

13] [The Black Dwarf. 1831. One volume.] Copy reported at Gräflich Solms-Laubach'sche Bibliothek, Laubach.

14-16] Old Mortality. 1831. Three volumes. Pages 1: *i-ix* x-xxiv, *1* 2-191; 2: *1-9* 10-232; 3: *1-9* 10-215. Copy: E.
17-20] [The Heart of Midlothian. 1831. Four volumes.] Copy reported at Gräflich Solms-Laubach'sche Bibliothek, Laubach.
21-22] The Bride of Lammermoor. 1832. Two volumes. Pages 1: [*i-ii*] *iii-ix* x-xxiv, *1* 2-217; 2: [*1-2*] *3-9* 10-252. Copy: L.
23-24] [A Legend of Montrose. 1832 Two volumes.] Copy reported at Gräflich Solms-Laubach'sche Bibliothek, Laubach.
25-27] [Count Robert of Paris. 1833(?). Three volumes.] Copy reported at Landesbibliothek Wiesbaden.
28-29] [Castle Dangerous. 1833(?). Two volumes.] Copy reported at Landesbibliothek Wiesbaden.

301R] STUTTGART: Franckh 1827
Collection of the Master-Pieces of the Most Celebrated Ancient and Modern English Authors). 1827. Notes: An abortive series extending only to one work:
1-6] [The Life of Napoleon Buonaparte.... Stuttgart: Franckh, 1827. Six volumes. Notes: Edited by Charles Weil.] Copy reported at Herzog-August-Bibliothek, Wolfenbuettel. Reference: GDS 25, page 144.

302R] ZWICKAU: Schumann 1819-1831
Pocket Library of English Classics. The Works of Walter Scott, Esq.... Zwickau: Printed for the Brothers Schumann. 1819-1831. 156 Scott volumes of 232 in the entire series.
General Notes: This series represents the English authors most read in Germany and early in the program (cf. 1825 list, vol.117) identifies Scott as the most popular writer (85 volumes), then Byron (30), Thomas Moore (4) and Southey (2). There is some indication (cf. vols.125-127, 192-198) that certain of the Schumann texts derive not from the original editions, but from the Paris issues of Galignani.

Each volume was sold with or without an engraved copperplate frontispiece. The one copy located in original wrappers (vol.23) has front cover reading 'Pocket Edition', a variant of the text title cited above. Complete preliminaries may include, for each volume, three title-pages, successively: (1) general series with number for Pocket Library [PL]; (2) consecutive author series number for Walter Scott works [WS]; (3) title-specific for genre sequence, romances or poetical works [R or P]. 'Corrections' are generally on the last page of the last volume if needed for a given title. The list below is ordered by general PL number; WS and (where appropriate) R or P numbers, if given, are cited within brackets after each entry. (Early editions of the poetry, through WS volume 25, have no differential R or P title-pages.) For 7-8, 12-13 pagination is given for the copies seen, not the earlier editions reported. References: GDS 110, pages 13-14; Kohler(1) 218(with examples of 3 titles illustrated).

7-8] [The Lay of the Last Minstrel. 1819. Two volumes. Pages 1: *1-13* 14-173 *174-176*; 2: *1-9* 10-174 *175*]. Notes: [WS 1-2, second title numbers: the beginning of the Walter Scott sequence]. Copy reported at Stadtbibliothek Mainz. Reissued 'Second Edition' 1829 (T/B).
12-13] [The Lady of the Lake. 1819. Two volumes. Pages 1: *1-9* 10-224; 2: *1-7* 8-188]. Notes: [WS 3-4]. Copy reported at Stadtbibliothek Mainz. Reissued 'Second Edition' 1825 (T/B).

17-18] Rokeby. In Six Cantos. 1821. Two volumes. Pages: 1: *1-11* 12-222; 2: *1-7* 8-157. Notes: [WS 5-6]. Copy: T/B.

23] 1. The Vision of Don Roderick. — 2. The Field of Waterloo. — 3. Poems. 1821. Pages: *I-VI* VII-XV *XVI*, *1-2* 3-189 *190-191*. Notes: Page *191* lists a correction. [WS 7]. Copies: T/B T/B(original wrappers).

24-25] The Lord of the Isles. 1821-1822. Two volumes. Pages: 1: *I-IV*, *1-2* 3-212 *213*; 2: *1-6* 7-222. Notes: [WS 8-9]. Copy: T/B.

28-31] Waverley, or 'Tis Sixty Years Since. 1822. Four volumes. Pages 1: *I-VI* VII-XII, *1-2* 3-212; 2: *1-6* 7-221; 3: *1-6* 7-224; 4: *1-6* 7-224. Notes: In some copies volume 1, page VII is unnumbered and volume 2, page 7 is unnumbered. [WS 10-13; R 1-4]. Copies: BCL E; T/B(2). Notes: Among all editions of the novels, English or foreign, this would appear to be the first, in 1822, to name 'Walter Scott' as the author. Reissued 'Second Edition' 1822.

32-35] Guy Mannering; or, The Astrologer. By the Author of "Waverley." 1822. Four volumes. Pages 1: *1-7* 8-221; 2: *1-7* 8-221 *222-223*; 3: *1-7* 8-220; 4: *1-7* 8-205, *206-207*. Notes: Title-page imprints have 'Schumann' spelled 'Schuhmann'. Volume 2, page *223*, lists 'Corrections' for volume 2; volume 4, page *207*, lists 'Corrections' for volumes 3 and 4. [WS 14-17; R 5-8]. Copies: BCL E; T/B.

36-39] The Antiquary. By the Author of "Waverley" and "Guy Mannering." 1822. Four volumes. Pages 1: *1-7* 8-222; 2: *1-7* 8-191; 3: *1-7* 8-222; 4: *1-7* 8-221 *222-223*. Notes: Title-page imprints have 'Schumann' spelled 'Schuhmann' in volumes 1-2. Volume 4, page *223*, lists 'Corrections' for each of the volumes. [WS 18-21; R 9-12]. Copies: BCL E; T/B.

40-43] Rob Roy. By the Author of "Waverley." 1822. Four volumes. Pages 1: *I-VII* VIII-X, *11-13* 14-205; 2: *1-7* 8-188; 3: *1-7* 8-190; 4: *1-7* 8-204 *205*. Notes: Title-page imprints have 'Schumann spelled 'Schuhmann'. Volume 4, page *205*, lists 'Corrections' for each of the volumes. [WS 22-25; R 13-16]. Copies: BCL E; T/B.

46-47] [Tales of My Landlord. The Black Dwarf. 1822.] Two volumes. Notes: [WS 26-27; R 17-18]. Copy reported at Stadtbibliothek Mainz.

48-51] Tales of My Landlord, Collected and Arranged by Jedediah Cleishbotham. Old Mortality. 1822. Four volumes. Pages 1: *1-7* 8-212; 2: *1-7* 8-192; 3: *1-7* 8-220 *221*; 4: *1-7* 8-190 *191*. Notes: Volume 3, page *221*, lists 'Corrections' for volumes 1-3 and volume 4, page *191*, lists 'Corrections' for volume 4. [WS 28-31; R 19-22]. Copies: E; T/B.

52-56] The Heart of Mid-Lothian, A Romance, By the Author of "Waverley." 1822. Five volumes. Pages 1: *I-VII* VIII-XII, *1-3* 4-244; 2: *1-7* 8-252; 3: *1-7* 8-186; 4: *1-6* 7-188; 5: *1-7* 8-186 *187-188*. Notes: Volume 5, pages *187-188*, list 'Corrections'. [WS 32-36; R 23-27]. Copies: BCL E(vols.2-5); T/B(vols.3-5).

57-59] Tales of My Landlord, Collected and Arranged by Jedediah Cleishbotham, The Bride of Lammermoor. 1823. Three volumes. Pages 1: *1-7* 8-191; 2: *1-7* 8-206; 3: *1-7* 8-224. Notes: [WS 37-39; R 28-30]. Copy: T/B.

60-61] [The Legend of Montrose. 1823.] Two volumes. Notes: [WS 40-41; R 31-32]. Copy reported at Stadtbibliothek Mainz.

62-65] Ivanhoe; A Romance. By "The Author of Waverley," etc. 1823. Four volumes. Pages 1: *I-IX* X-XXXII, *1* 2-208; 2: *1-7* 8-221; 3: *1-7* 8-223; 4: *1-7* 8-237 *238-240*. Notes: Volume 4, pages *239-240*, lists 'Corrections'. [WS 42-45; R 33-36]. Copies: E; T/B. Reissued as 'Second Edition' 1834 with Scott's new introduction and notes (T/B).

66-69] The Monastery. A Romance. By The Author of "Waverley." 1824. Four volumes. Pages 1: *1-7* 8-222 223; 2: *1-7* 8-207; 3: *1-7* 8-189; 4: *1-7* 8-205 *206-207*. Notes: Volume 4, page *207*, lists 'Corrections'. [WS 46-49; R 37-40]. Copies: BCL E; T/B.

70-73] The Abbot. By the Author of "Waverley." 1824. Four volumes. Pages 1: *1-7* 8-192; 2: *1-7* 8-224; 3: *1-7* 8-224; 4: *1-7* 8-203 *204-205*. Notes: Volume 4, page *205*, lists 'Corrections'. [WS 50-53; R 41-44]. Copies: BCL E; T/B.
74-77] Kenilworth; A Romance. By the Author of "Waverley," "Ivanhoe," etc. 1824. Four volumes. Pages 1: *1-7* 8-221; 2: *1-7* 8-223; 3: *1-7* 8-224; 4: *1-7* 8-223 *224*. Notes: Volume 4, page 224, lists 'Corrections'. [WS 54-57; R 45-48]. Copies: BCL E L; T/B.
78-81] The Pirate. By the Author of "Waverley." 1824. Four volumes. Pages 1: *1-7* 8-221; 2: *1-7* 8-224; 3: *1-7* 8-238; 4: *1-7* 8-219 *220-221*. Notes: Volume 4, page *221*, lists 'Corrections' for each of the volumes. [WS 58-61; R 49-52]. Copies: BCL E O; T/B.
82-85] The Fortunes of Nigel. By the Author of "Waverley, Kenilworth," etc. 1824. Four volumes. Pages 1: *1-7* 8-224; 2: *1-7* 8-224; 3: *1-7* 8-224; 4: *1-7* 8-222 *223-224*. Notes: Volume 4, pages *223-224*, lists 'Corrections'. [WS 62-65; R 53-56]. Copies: E; T/B.
86-90] Peveril of the Peak. By the Author of "Waverley, Kenilworth," etc. 1824. Five volumes. Pages 1: *1-7* 8-224; 2: *1-7* 8-222; 3: *1-7* 8-222; 4: *1-7* 8-240; 5: *1-7* 8-222 *223*. Notes: Volume 5, page *223*, lists 'Corrections'. [WS 66-70; R 57-61]. Copies: BCL; T/B.
91-94] Quentin Durward. By the Author of Waverley. 1824. Four volumes. Pages 1: *1-7* 8-238; 2: *1-7* 8-208; 3: *1-7* 8-224; 4: *1-7* 8-219 *220-221*. Notes: Volume 4, page *221*, lists 'Corrections'. [WS 71-74; R 62-65]. Copies: BCL E; T/B(2).
95-98] St Ronan's Well. By the Author of "Waverley, Quentin Durward," etc. 1824. Four volumes. Pages 1: *1-9* 10-222; 2: *1-7* 8-221; 3: *1-7* 8-191; 4: *1-7* 8-206 *207-208*. Notes: Volume 4, pages *207-208*, lists 'Corrections' for each of the volumes. [WS 75-78; R 66-69]. Copies: BCL E; T/B.
113-116] Redgauntlet. A Tale of the Eighteenth Century. By the Author of "Waverley." 1825. Four volumes. Pages 1: *1-7* 8-224; 2: *1-7* 8-190; 3: *1-7* 8-223; 4: *1-7* 8-206 *207-208*. Notes: Volume 4, pages *207-208*, list 'Corrections'. [WS 79-82; R 70-73]. Copies: BCL E; T/B.
117] Ballads and Lyrical Pieces. By Walter Scott, Esq. 1825. Pages: *I-X*, *1* 2-209 *210-213*. Notes: Pages *211-213* give a useful list of the Pocket Library 'Already published.' There is no specific P title-page. [WS 83]. Copies: O; T/B.
118-119] Marmion. A Tale of Flodden Field. . . . By Walter Scott, Esq. 1825. Two volumes. 1: *I-XI* XII, *1-3* 4-291; *1-9* 10-160. Notes: The specific title-pages have no P numbers. Text of cantos in volume 1, notes in volume 2. [WS 84-85]. Copy: O; T/B. Reference: GDS 110, page 14.
125-127] Lives of the Novelists. By Sir Walter Scott. 1826. Three volumes. Pages 1: *I-XII*, *1* 2-179; 2: *I-VIII*, *1* 2-183; 3: *I-VIII*, *1* 2-182 *183*. Notes: The preliminary notice in volume 1, and thus presumably the entire text, derives from the Paris 1825 Galignani edition (292R.6-7). Volume 3, page *183*, lists 'Corrections'. [WS 86-88]. Copies: E; T/B.
128-129] Paul's Letters to His Kinsfolk. 1826. Two volumes. Pages 1: *1-7* 8-222; 2: *1-7* 8-239 *240*. Notes: Volume 2, page *240*, lists 'Corrections'. [WS 89-90; R 74-75]. Copies: BCL E; T/B.
130-135] Tales of the Crusaders. By the Author of "Waverley, Quentin Durward," etc. 1826. Six volumes. Pages 1: *I-VII* VIII-XXXII, *1-3* 4-189; 2: *1-7* 8-206; 3: *1-7* 8-207; 4: *1-7* 8-206; 5: *1-7* 8-221; 6: *1-7* 8-190. Notes: Volumes 1-3 'The Betrothed'; 4-6 'The Talisman'. [WS 91-96; R 76-81]. Copy: E.
136] The Bridal of Triermain, or The Vale of Saint John. In Three Cantos. 1827. Pages: *I-IX* X-XX, *1-3* 4-140. Notes: [WS 97]. Copies: BCL E.
137] Harold The Dauntless; A Poem, in Six Cantos. By the Author of "The Bridal of

Triermain." 1827. Pages: *1-7* 8-157. Notes: In some copies there is no quotation mark after 'Triermain.' [WS 98]. Copies: BCL E; T/B.
138-141] Woodstock; or, The Cavalier. A Tale of the Year Sixteen Hundred and Fifty-One. By the Author of "Waverley, Tales of the Crusaders," etc. 1826. Four volumes. Pages 1: *I-VII* VIII-XVI, *1-3* 4-207; 2: *1-7* 8-222 *223*; 3: *1-7* 8-256; 4: *1-7* 8-222. Notes: Volume 2, page *223* lists 'Corrections.' [WS 99-102; R 82-85]. Copies: BCL; T/B.
150-167] The Life of Napoleon Buonaparte, Emperor of the French. With a preliminary view of the French Revolution. By the Author of "Waverley," etc. 1827-1828. Eighteen volumes. Pages (1827) 1: *1-7* 8-303; 2: *1-9* 10-251; 3: *1-9* 10-256; 4: *1-9* 10- 255; 5: *1-9* 10-222; 6: *1-9* 10-252; (1828) 7: *1-9* 10-253; 8: *1-9* 10-256; 9: *1-9* 10-222; 10: *1-9* 10-222; 11: *1-9* 10-254; 12: *1-9* 10-254; 13: *1-9* 10-256; 14: *1-9* 10-222; 15: *1-9* 10-256; 16: *1-9* 10-256; 17: *1-9* 10-254; 18: *1-9* 10-303. Notes: [WS 103-120]. On the Schumann firm's activities the *Morning Chronicle* 30 March 1826 reported a news release from the *Allgemeine Zeitung* that the first volume of Scott's *Life* 'has lately been published in London; that it will consist of five large vols. 8vo. and be all published by the end of August; that a Dr Barrmann is making a translation, which they [the Schumanns] will publish, in seven pocket volumes (with copper-plates), the first two to be delivered to the subscribers in June, & the whole before the end of the year. They will also print an edition in English, and the price to be about fifteen pence a volume.' In all essentials the report is premature. Both the Barrmann translation and this English edition appeared in 1827-1828 and are based upon the corrected Edinburgh text, not issued until 28 June 1827. Copies: BCL; T/B.
168-170] Chronicles of the Canongate [first series]; By the Author of "Waverley," etc. 1828. Three volumes. Pages 1: *I-VII* VIII-XXXII, *1* 2-189; 2: *1-7* 8-223; 3: *1-7* 8-224. Notes: [WS 121-123; R 86-88]. Copies: BCL; T/B.
171-173] Tales of a Grandfather [first series]; Being Stories Taken from Scottish History. Humbly inscribed to Hugh Littlejohn, Esq. 1828. Three volumes. Pages 1: *I-VII* VIII-XII, *1-5* 6-212; 2: *I-VII* VIII-X *XI-XII*, *1* 2-212; 3: *I-VII* VIII-IX *X-XII*, *1* 2-210. Notes: [WS 124-126; R 89-91]. Copy: BCL.
???-???] [Chronicles of the Canongate (second series); By the Author of 'Waverley," etc. (1828-1829).] Four volumes. Notes: [WS 127-130; R 92-95]. Copy reported at Stadtbibliothek Mainz.
192-194] Memoirs of Jonathan Swift, D.D. . . . By Sir Walter Scott. 1829. Three volumes. Pages 1: *I-IX* X-XII, *1* 2-212; 2: *I-VI* VII-VIII, *1* 2-216; 3: *I-VI* VII-VIII, 1-181. Notes: The preliminary 'Notice of the Publisher' is a verbatim reprint of the one earlier appearing in the 1826 Galignani edition 292R.2-3. [WS 131-133]. Copy: T/B.
195-197] Memoirs of John Dryden. By Sir Walter Scott. 1829. Three volumes. Pages 1: *I-VIII* IX-XIV *XV-XVI*, 1-192; 2: *I-VII* VIII, *1* 2-213; 3: *I-VI* VII-VIII, 1-244. Notes: Volume 3 includes, pages *189* 190-213, 'Religious Discourses'. [WS 134-136]. The preliminary 'Notice of the Publisher' is a verbatim reprint of the one earlier appearing in the 1826 Galignani edition 292R.4-5. Copy: T/B.
198] Goetz of Berlichingen, with The Iron Hand. A Tragedy, from the German of Goethe. By Sir Walter Scott. 1829. Pages *I-IX* X-XVI, *1* 2-254. Notes: The preliminary 'Notice of the Publishers', and thus presumably the entire text, is reprinted from the 1826 Galignani edition 292R.1. Also included, pages *231-232* 233-254, 'Mac Duff's Cross'. [WS 137]. Copies: E; T/B.
???-???] [Tales of a Grandfather (second series) 1829. Four volumes.] Notes: [WS 138-

141]. Copy reported at Gesamthochschul-Bibliothek, Kassel.
218-222] Anne of Geierstein; . . . By the Author of "Waverley," etc. 1829. Five volumes. Pages 1: *1-7* 8-206; 2: *1-7* 8-189; 3: *1-7* 8-208; 4: *1-7* 8-188; 5: *1-7* 8-189. [WS 142-146]. Copy: T/B.
223-225] The History of Scotland. By Sir Walter Scott. 1830. Three volumes. Pages 1: *1-11* 12-208; 2: *1-7* 8-203 *204-206*; 3: *1-7* 8-189. Notes: Continued as volumes 230-232. [WS 147-149]. Copy: T/B.
???-???] [Tales of a Grandfather (third series) 1830. Four volumes.] Notes: [WS 150-153]. Copy reported at Stadtbibliothek Mainz.
230-232] The History of Scotland. By Sir Walter Scott. 1831. Three volumes. Pages 4: *1-7* 8-256; 5: *1-7* 8-252; 6: *1-7* 8-219 *220-221*. Notes: Concluded from volumes 223-225. [WS 154-156]. Copy: T/B.

GREAT BRITAIN

LONDON: Wigand
[~] A Complete Edition of the Waverley Novels. (GERMANY, LEIPZIG: Wigand: *see* 300R.)

HUNGARY

PEST: Wigand
[~] A Complete Edition of the Waverley Novels. (GERMANY, LEIPZIG: Wigand: *see* 300R.)

UNITED STATES

303R] BALTIMORE: Cushing 1813-1815
The Poetical Works of Walter Scott, Esq. Vol. I [II-V]. Baltimore Published by Joseph Cushing 1813. Notes: Engraved titles with vignette. Most volumes seen have a frontispiece: usually a pertinent Cushing plate, often with a portrait of Scott. The printed titles, some with variant dates as listed below, have for volumes 1-3, 5 no Cushing address and cite above date 'William Fry, Printer.' Volume 4, however, reads: . . . Cushing, No. 6, North Howard-Street. Fry and Kammerer, Printers. 1812.
1] The Vision of Don Roderick. Ballads and Lyrical Pieces. 1813. Pages: *i-ix* x-xi *xii, 13-15* 16-276. Copies: CtY InU MWA NN RPB ViU.
2] The Lay of the Last Minstrel. The Twelfth Edition. 1812. Pages: *1-9* 10-228. Copies: CtY MWA NN ViU. The original Baltimore edition was issued separately in 1811 (14Rb), but this 'Twelfth Edition' presumably refers to the Edinburgh Eleventh of 1810 (14Ar).
3] Marmion. 1812. Pages: *1-13* 14-324. Copies: DLC MWA NN PHi RPB ViU.
4] The Lady of the Lake. 1812. Pages: *1-13* 14-274. Copies: E; CtY MWA NNU-W RPB ViU.
5] Rokeby. 1813. Pages: *i-viii, 1* 2-267. Notes: A variant issue of the second (separate) 1813 Philadelphia, Bradford and Inskeep edition (*see* 64Re[2]). Copies: CtY DLC IdU MWA PPL ViU.

304R] BOSTON: Bedlington 1827-1828

The Poetical Works of Sir Walter Scott. . . . Boston: Published by Timothy Bedlington. 1828. Seven volumes. Notes: The printed titles with volume numbers, as described above, are preceded by engraved frontispieces and half-titles, the latter indicating the specific titles noted below. The half-titles are dated 1827 volumes 1-3, 1828 volumes 4-7. Copies: CtY NN.

1] The Lay of the Last Minstrel. Pages: *i-iii* iv, *5-11* 12-304.
2] Marmion. Pages: *1-11* 12-341.
3] The Lady of the Lake. Pages: *1-9* 10-292.
4] Rokeby. Pages: *1-11* 12-281.
5] Lord of the Isles. Pages: *1-9* 10-306.
6] Bridal of Triermain. Pages: *1-7* 8-268.
7] Harold the Dauntless. Pages: *1-7* 8-310. Notes: Last page unnumbered in some copies.

305R-307R] BOSTON: Parker 1821-1832

305R. FIRST PARKER SERIES] The Novels Tales and Romances of the Author of Waverley. . . . Boston, Samuel H. Parker, 12 Cornhill, 1821-1829. 23 volumes.
Notes: There are three numbered Parker series, here classified as 305, 306, 307. This first series consists of a reissue of the original printings, which often predate the series by several years. The new engraved series title-page with vignette precedes the printed title as originally issued in the separate book form. The information below is taken from this engraved title-page. Certain titles also have a comma after 'Novels' in the series title and some difference in the imprint pointing. The numbering of these volumes appears just before the individual titles on the engraved title-page. Following series date, the date of this original volume issue is cited in brackets. A poor paper issue was announced as being published without plates, hence no engraved title-page. In this first series the imprints are in three states:
IMPRINT 1: Boston. Samuel H. Parker. 12 Cornhill. 1820-1824.
2: Boston. Samuel H. Parker. 164 Washington St. 1824-1825.
3: Boston. Samuel H. Parker. 164 Washington-Street. 1826-1829.

1] Waverley. [imprint 1] 1822 [1820]. Pages: *i-iii* iv, *5* 6-384. Notes: Page 327 is misnumbered 237. Copies: DLC DLC(poor paper issue) MWA.
2] Guy Mannering. [imprint 1] 1822 [1821]. Pages: *1-3* 4-360. Copies: DLC DLC(poor paper issue) MWA.
3] The Antiquary. [imprint 1] '1820' [1821]. Pages: *1-3* 4-360. Copies: DLC DLC(poor paper issue) MWA.
4] Rob Roy. [imprint 1] 1822 [1821]. Pages: *i-iii* iv, *5* 6-352. Copies: DLC DLC(poor paper issue) MWA.
5] Tales of my Landlord, 1st series: Black Dwarf and Old Mortality. [imprint 1] 1821 [1821]. Pages: *i-iii* iv-vii *viii, 9* 10-483. Copies: DLC(2) TxU.
6] Tales of my Landlord 2nd. Series. . . . The Heart of Mid-Lothian. . . . [imprint 1] 1821 [1821]. Pages: *i-iii* iv-vi, *7* 8-480. Copies: DLC(2) MWA.
7] Tales of my Landlord 3d. Series The Bride of Lammermoor—Legend of Montrose. [imprint 1] 1822 [1821]. Pages: *1-3* 4-460, *1* 2-14. Notes: The last section is the 'Glossary of The Scottish Words and Phrases in the Novels, Tales, and Romances, of the Author of Waverley.' Copies: DLC DLC(poor paper issue) MWA.

8] Ivanhoe. [imprint 1] 1822 [1820]. Pages: *i-v* vi-xiv, *15* 16-412. Copies: DLC MWA.
9] The Monastery. [imprint 1] 1822 [1820]. Pages: *i-iii* iv-xxxix *xl*, *41* 42-384. Copies: DLC MWA.
10] The Abbot. [imprint 1] 1822 [1820]. Pages: *1-2*, *i*-ii, *3* 4-382. Copies: DLC DLC(poor paper issue) MWA.
11] Kenilworth. [imprint 1] 1822 [1821]. Pages: *1-3* 4-402. Notes: With woodcut plan of Kenilworth Castle as frontispiece. Copies: DLC MWA.
12] The Pirate. [imprint 1] 1822 [1822]. Pages: *i-iii* iv, *5* 6-407. Copies: DLC DLC (poor paper issue).
13] The Fortunes of Nigel. [imprint 1] 1822 [1822]. Pages: *1-3* 4-415 *416*. Copies: DLC DLC(poor paper issue) MWA.
14] Peveril of the Peak. [imprint 1] 1823 [1823]. Pages: *i-iii* iv-xii, *13* 14-512. Copies: DLC(2) MWA.
15] Quentin Durward. [imprint 1] 1823 [1823]. Pages: *i-iii* iv-xxii, *23* 24-407. Copy: MWA. Reference: Kohler(1) 7(with illustration).
16] St. Ronan's Well. [imprint 2] (1824) [1824]. Pages: *1-3*, 4-380. Copies: DLC DLC(poor paper issue).
17] Redgauntlet. [imprint 1] 1824 [1824]. Pages: *1-3* 4-390. Notes: Page number 193 has only the first digit. Copies: DLC(poor paper issue) MWA. Reissued: [imprint 2] (1824) [1824] (DLC).
18] Tales of the Crusaders. [imprint 3] 1825 [1825]. Pages: *i-iii* iv-x, *11* 12-544. Copies: DLC(2) MWA.
19] Woodstock. [imprint 3] 1826 [1826]. Pages: *1-3* 4-396. Copy: MWA. Reissue with pagination reading *i-iii* iv-vi, *3* 4-396. (O; DLC).
20] Chronicles of the Canongate. [imprint 3] 1828 [1828]. Pages: *1-3* 4-346. Copies: DLC DLC(poor paper issue) MWA.
21] Tales of a Grandfather. [imprint 2] (1828) [1828]. Pages: *i-v* vi-viii *13* 14-386. Notes: Although undated and unnumbered, this volume falls in The Novels, Tales and Romances sequence, even though there is no series designation on the engraved title-page: *see* second series below, vol. 23. Copies: DLC(2).
22] Chronicles of the Canongate. 2nd Series. St Valentine's Day. [imprint 2] (1829) [1829]. Pages: *1-3* 4-264, *3* 4-260. Notes: The single printed title-page notes 'Complete in One Volume' though, as indicated, there is double pagination and duplicate gatherings in the second section with direction lines reading 'VOL. II.' Copies: DLC(2) MWA PU.
23] Tales of a Grandfather, 2nd. Series. [imprint 2] (1829) [1829]. Pages: *1-5* 6-233 *234*, *3* 4-223. Notes: Although numbered in The Novels, Tales and Romances sequence, the engraved title gives the volume number but does not give the series title because this title does not fall into the category of novel, tale, or romance. The type-set title-page reads 'Complete in One Volume', even though the volume has double pagination and duplicate gatherings in the second section with direction lines reading 'VOL. II.' Copies: DLC(2) MWA.

306R. SECOND PARKER SERIES] Waverley Novels. . . . Boston. 1826-1829.
Notes: 45 volumes. With engraved frontispiece in each volume, two volumes occasionally bound together. Except for the first title, the authorship is generally defined as 'By the Author of "Waverley," &c., &c.' This second series title 'Waverley Novels' appears above

the imprint on the title-page. Only the spine label identifies this setting as 'Parker's Second Edition'. Volume 41 below is in the style of the 'Waverley Novels' series and is numbered 41 on the spine as if it were a part of that series, yet it is now identified as 'Parker's Stereotype Edition' on the spine and as 'Stereotype Edition' on the title-page with no volume number. The concluding advertisement further specifies that the Waverley series, in 40 volumes, is also available in 'A Second Quality, on Paper not quite so fine—without Plates'. In this series there is only imprint 4: Boston: Samuel H. Parker, No. 164 Washington-Street.

1-2] Waverley; or, 'tis Sixty Years Since. [imprint 4] 1826. Two volumes. Pages 1: *i-iii* iv, *5* 6-263; 2: *i-ii*, *3* 4-245. Copy: E. Reference: Kohler(1) 2(with illustration). Reissued 1829 (L; CtY).
3-4] Guy Mannering; or, The Astrologer. [imprint 4] 1826. Two volumes. Pages 1: *1-3* 4-251; 2: *1-3* 4-229. Copy: E. Reissued 1829 (L; CtY[vol.3].)
5-6] The Antiquary. A Romance. [imprint 4] 1827. Two volumes. Pages 1: *i-iii* iv, 5-238; 2: *1-3* 4-242. Copy: E. Reissued 1829 (L; CtY).
7-8] Rob Roy. A Romance. [imprint 4] 1827. Two volumes. Pages 1: *i-iii* iv, *5* 6-234; 2: *1-3* 4-233. Copy: E. Reissued 1828 (L), 1829(L).
9-10] Tales of My Landlord. First Series. [imprint 4] 1827. Two volumes. Pages 1: *i-v* vi-x, *11* 12-318; 2: *1-3* 4-319. Copy: E. Reissued 1829 (L; CtY).
11-12] Tales of My Landlord. Second Series. [imprint 4] 1827. Two volumes. Pages 1: *i-iii* iv-vi, *7* 8-304; 2: *1-3* 4-326. Copy: E. Reissued 1829 (L; CtY[vol.11].)
13-14] Tales of My Landlord. Second[Third] Series. [imprint 4] 1827. Two volumes. Pages 1: *1-3* 4-312; 2: *1-3* 4-294, *1* 2-14. Notes: In reissues the title is corrected to 'Third'. Pages *1* 2-14 in volume 2 provide a 'Glossary of The Scottish Words and Phrases . . .'. Copy: E. Reissued 1829 (L; CtY).
15-16] Ivanhoe, A Romance. [imprint 4] 1827. Two volumes. Pages 1: *1-3* 4-256; *1-3* 4-281. Copies: E O. Reissued 1829 (L).
17-18] The Monastery. A Romance. [imprint 4] 1827. Two volumes. Pages 1: *1-3* 4-241; *1-3* 4-245. Copy: E. Reissued 1829 (L; CtY).
19-20] The Abbot; Being the Sequel of The Monastery. [imprint 4] 1827. Two volumes. Pages 1: *i-iii* iv, *5* 6-252; 2: *1-3* 4-257. Copy: E. Reissued 1829 (L; CtY [vol.19]).
21-22] Kenilworth; A Romance. [imprint 4] 1828. Two volumes. Pages 1: *1-3* 4-275; 2: *1-3* 4-261. Copy: E. Reissued 1829 (L; CtY).
23-24] The Pirate. [imprint 4] 1828. Two volumes. Pages 1: *1-3* 4-262; 2: *1-3* 4-268. Copy: E. Reissued 1829 (L; CtY[vol.24].)
25-26] The Fortunes of Nigel. [imprint 4] 1828. Two volumes. Pages 1: *1-3* 4-267; 2: *1-3* 4-280. Copy: E. Reissued 1829 (L; CtY).
27-28] Peveril of the Peak. [imprint 4] 1828. Two volumes. Pages 1: *i-iii* iv-xv *xvi*, *17* 18-336; 2: *1-3* 4-335. Copy: E. Reissued 1829 (L; CtY MH[vol.1]).
29-30] Quentin Durward. [imprint 4] 1828. Two volumes. Pages 1: *i-iii* iv-xxviii, *29* 30-272; 2: *1-3* 4-264. Copy: E. Reissued 1829 (L; CtY).
31-32] St. Ronan's Well. [imprint 4] 1828. Two volumes. Pages 1: *1-3* 4-242; 2: *1-3* 4-257. Copy: E. Reissued 1829 (L; CtY).
33-34] Redgauntlet. A Tale of the Eighteenth Century. [imprint 4] 1828. Two volumes. Pages 1: *1-3* 4-249; 2: *1-3* 4-257. Copy: E. Reissued 1829 (L; CtY[vol.1] MH).
35-36] Tales of the Crusaders. [imprint 4] 1825 Two volumes. Pages 1: *i-iii* iv-xiii *xiv*, *15* 16-376; 2: *1-3* 4-369. Copies: E; ViU. Reissued 1829 (L).

37-38] Woodstock; or, The Cavalier. [imprint 4] 1826. Two volumes. Pages 1: *i-iii* iv-vii *viii*, *9* 10-264; 2: *1-3* 4-285. Copy: E. Reissued 1829 with volume 1 pagination *1-3* 4-264 (L; CtY).
39-40] Chronicles of the Canongate. [imprint 4] 1828. Two volumes. Pages 1: *1-3* 4-198; 2: *1-3* 4-194. Copy: E. Reissued 1829 (L; CtY).
41] Tales of A Grandfather. [imprint 4] 1828. Pages: *i-v* vi-viii, *13* 14-386, *1*-2. Notes: *See* headnote for this series for comment. Copies: E; CtY MB.
[42-43] Chronicles of the Canongate. Second Series. [imprint 4] 1828. Two volumes. Pages 1: *1-3* 4-264; 2: *1-3* 4-260. Notes: Because of the erroneous numbering of the previous, non-Waverley book, these volumes are numbered 42-43. Copy: E. Reissued 1829 (L; CtY).
[44-45] Tales of a Grandfather. Second Series. [imprint 4] 1829. Two volumes. Pages 1: *1-5* 6-233; 2: *1-3* 4-223. Notes: Again the spine label reads 'Parker's Second Edition', but now without any Waverley reference on the title-page. Copy: CtY.

307R. THIRD PARKER SERIES] Waverley Novels. . . . Parker's Edition, Revised and Corrected, with a general preface, an introduction to each novel, and notes, historical and illustrative, by The Author. Boston. Samuel H. Parker, 164 Washington-Street. 1829 [1830-1832].
Notes: 54 volumes. Series title and volume number at head of each title and on spine label, which also reads 'Parker's Revised Edition' and specific title. Each volume in this third series has an engraved frontispiece usually re-engraved from the drawings in the 'Magnum Opus', which now provides the text for this issue. All titles were issued in two volumes, except for volumes 45-47 (3) and 48 (1). Volume 41 has a preliminary notice: 'In consequence of not receiving one of the English Volumes, the publication of vols. 39 and 40 . . . is necessarily postponed.' (The note perhaps explains the lack of these volumes in certain sets.) A second notice reprints an Edinburgh January 1833 Prospectus for Scott's *Poetical Works* and lists the 54 prose volumes now at press in this Boston edition.

Beginning with volume 45 in 1834, and continuing with all 1834 reprints of earlier volumes, the imprint omits the street number, reading only: Boston: Samuel H. Parker, Washington Street. 1834. Volume 48 is the first volume of seven to bear, in its first issue, at head of title and on spine label, the series title 'Waverley Tales', but the numbering from 48-54 carries on from the 'Waverley Novels'. In a remainder issue with variant labels, however, the reading there still continues mistakenly as 'Waverley Novels.' Volumes reissued in 1836 have a combined imprint, generally reading: Published by Samuel H. Parker, Boston, for Desilver, Thomas, and Co. Philadelphia, 1836. Through 1832, the limit of this bibliography, the imprint reverts to number 3:
Boston: Samuel H. Parker, 164 Washington-Street.

1-2] Waverley. [imprint 3] 1829. Two volumes. Pages 1: *i-iii* iv, *5* 6-54 *55-56*, *1* 2-272; 2: *1-3* 4-255. Copy: E. Reissued 1830 (CtY[2] MH MWA); 1832 (PPL).
3-4] Guy Mannering. [imprint 3] 1830. Two volumes. Pages 1: *1-3* 4-20, *1-3* 4-258; 2: *1-3* 4-236. Copies: E; CtY(2) MH MWA NNU-W. Reissued 1831 (PPL).
5-6] The Antiquary. [imprint 3] 1830. Two volumes. Pages 1: *i-iii* iv, *5* 6-14, *3-5* 6-241; 2: *1-3* 4-246. Copies: E; CtY(2) MH MWA. Reissued 1832 (PPL, T/B).
7-8] Rob Roy. [imprint 3] 1830. Two volumes. Pages 1: *i-iii* iv, *5* 6-79 *80*, *5* 6-234 *235*; 2: *1-3* 4-239. Copies: E; CtY(2) MH MWA. Reissued 1832 (PPL).
9-10] Tales of My Landlord. First Series. [imprint 3] 1830. Two volumes. Pages 1: *i-v* vi-

x, *3* 4-324; 2: *1-3* 4-331. Copies: E; CtY MH MWA. Reissued 1832 (CtY PPL).
11-12] Tales of My Landlord. Second Series. [imprint 3] 1830. Two volumes. Pages 1: *i-iii* iv-ix *x, 3* 4-321; 2: *1-3* 4-330. Copies: E; CtY(2) MH MWA. Reissued 1832 (PPL).
13-14] Tales of My Landlord. Third Series. [imprint 3] 1830. Two volumes. Pages 1: *1-3* 4-14, *3* 4-315; 2: *1-3* 4-297. Copies: E; CtY(2) MH MWA. Reissued 1832 (PPL).
15-16] Ivanhoe; A Romance. [imprint 3] 1831. Two volumes. Pages 1: *i-iii* iv-xiv, *3* 4-263; 2: *1-3* 4-287. Copies: E; CtY MH MWA. Reissued 1832 (CtY[vol.15] PPL).
17-18] The Monastery; A Romance. [imprint 3] 1831. Two volumes. Pages 1: *i-iii* iv-xix *xx, 1-3* 4-246; 2: *1-3* 4-252. Copies: E; CtY(2) MH MWA. Reissued 1832 (PPL).
19-20] The Abbot. [imprint 3] 1831. Two volumes. Pages 1: *i-iii* iv-ix *x, 3* 4-260; 2: *1-3* 4-264. Copies: E; CtY(2) MH MWA. Reissued 1832 (PPL).
21-22] Kenilworth. [imprint 3] 1831. Two volumes. Pages 1: *i-iii* iv-x, *3* 4-280; 2: *1-3* 4-264 *265*. Page *265* is a woodcut print of Kenilworth Castle 'as it appeared in 1620': an illustration not deriving from the 'Magnum Opus' edition. Copies: E; CtY(2) MH MWA. Reissued 1832 (PPL).
23-24] The Pirate. [imprint 3] 1831. Two volumes. Pages 1: *i-iii* iv-vii *viii, 1-3* 4-271; 2: *1-3* 4-274. Copies: E; CtY(2) MH MWA. Reissued 1832 (PPL).
25-26] The Fortunes of Nigel. [imprint 3] 1831. Two volumes. Pages 1: *i-iii* iv-x, *3* 4-276; 2: *1-3* 4-285. Copies: E; CtY(2) MH MWA NNU-W. Reissued 1832 (PPL).
27-28] Peveril of the Peak. [imprint 3] 1832. Two volumes. Pages 1: *1-3* 4-38, *iii* iv-xv *xvi, 17* 18-357; 2: *1-3* 4-351. Copies: E; CtY(3) MH MWA(vol.2).
29-30] Quentin Durward; A Romance. [imprint 3] 1832. Two volumes. Pages 1: *1-3* 4-13 *14, iii* iv-xxviii, *29* 30-278; 2: *1-3* 4-272. Copies: E; CtY(2) MH MWA NNU-W PPL(vol.1).
31-32] St. Ronan's Well. [imprint 3] 1832. Two volumes. Pages 1: *1-3* 4-7 *8, 1-3* 4-245; 2: *1-3* 4-260. Copies: E; CtY(2) MH MWA NNU-W.
33-34] Redgauntlet. [imprint 3] 1832. Two volumes. Pages 1: *1-3* 4-14, *3* 4-256; 2: *1-3* 4-260. Copies: E; CtY(2) MH MWA.
35-36] Tales of the Crusaders. [imprint 3] 1832. Two volumes. Pages 1: *1-3* 4-12, *i-iii* iv-xiii *xiv, 15* 16-379; 2: *1-3* 4-372. Copies: E; CtY(2) MH PPL(vol.1).
Subsequent volumes in this series, as listed below, were first issued after 1832 and thus are not represented in this bibliography. As noted above many of the earlier titles were reissued between 1832 and 1836.
37-38] Woodstock. 1833.
39-40] Chronicles of the Canongate. First Series. 1833.
41-42] Chronicles of the Canongate. Second Series. 1833. Notes: *see* headnote for this series for comment on volume 41.
43-44] Anne of Geierstein. 1833.
45-47] Tales of My Landlord. Fourth Series. 1834.
48] Tales of a Grandfather; . . . First Series. 1834. Notes: *see* headnote for this series for comment on volume 48.
49-50] Tales of a Grandfather; Second Series. 1834.
51-52] Tales of a Grandfather; Third Series. 1834.
53-54] Tales of a Grandfather; Fourth Series. 1834.

308R] BOSTON: Wells and Lilly 1829
The Miscellaneous Prose Works of Sir Walter Scott, Bart. . . . Vol. I [II-VI]. . . .Boston: Wells and Lilly—Court-Street. 1829.

Notes: Six volumes. In each case the volume begins with a numbered general title-page, as described above, followed by a specific unnumbered title-page as identified below.
1] Life of John Dryden. Pages: *i-v* vi-xii, *13* 14-330. Copies: InU MWA NjP NNU-W PPL T/B.
2] Life of Jonathan Swift. Pages: *1-4, i* ii-iii *iv, 5* 6-364. Copies: InU MWA NjP PPL T/B.
3] Biographical and Critical Notices of Eminent Novelists. Pages: *i-ii, 1-7* 8-344. Copies: InU MWA(2) NjP NNU-W PPL T/B.
4] Biographical Memoirs. Pages: *i-ii, 1-5* 6-301. Copies: InU NjP NNU-W T/B.
5] Paul's Letters to his Kinsfolk. Pages: *1-4, i* ii-viii, *9* 10-323. Copies: InU NjP T/B.
6] An Essay on Chivalry, Romance, The Drama. Pages: *1-7* 8-293. Copies: InU PPL T/B.

309R] EXETER: Williams 1831
Waverley Novels. Exeter; Published by J. & B. Williams. John C. Gerrish, Printer. 1831. Notes: Waverley Novels [at head of title-page]. 'Revised and corrected, with introduction and notes by the author.' The title-page layout would indicate that this abortive series is reset from the two-volume Boston, Parker issue, but now as a cheaper edition in small type and thus 'Complete in One Volume.'
[1] Waverley; or, 'Tis Sixty Years Since. . . . 1831. Pages: *1-3* 4-455. Copies: E; CtY MWA.

310R] FREDERICKSBURG: Withers 1824
The Poetical Works of Sir Walter Scott. . . . Fredericksburg, Virginia: E. D. Withers. 1824. Seven volumes. Notes: All volumes have a frontispiece painted by R. Smirke and engraved by various American artists. Copy: ViU.
1] Lay of the Last Minstrel. Pages: *i-iii* 'ix'[iv] *v-x, 11* 12-288.
2] Marmion. Pages: *1-11* 12-324.
3] The Lady of the Lake. Pages: *1-9* 10-275.
4] Rokeby. Pages: *1-11* 12-270.
5] The Lord of the Isles. Pages: *1-9* 10-287.
6] Bridal of Triermain. Pages: *1-7* 8-'276'[266].
7] Harold the Dauntless. Pages: *1-7* 8-261.

311R] NEW YORK: Collins and Hannay [and others] 1829
Novels and Tales by Sir Walter Scott. Harper's Revised Stereotype Edition. [specific title] . . . New-York: Printed by J. and J. Harper, 82 Cliff-St. Sold by Collins and Hannay, Collins and Co., G. and C. and H. Carvill, W. B. Gilley, E. Bliss and O. A. Roorbach;—Philadelphia, Carey, Lea, and Carey, J. Grigg, Towar and Hogan, U. Hunt, H. Cowperthwaite, E. Littell and Brother, and M'Carty and Davis;—Albany, O. Steele. 1829. Notes: Though reproducing the engraved dedication to the King, in anticipation of reprinting the entire 'Magnum Opus', this abortive series, extending apparently only to the first novel, probably could not prevail against the ongoing Boston, Parker issue (*see* 307R).
[1-2] Waverley; or, 'Tis Sixty Years Since. . . . Corrected by the Author. . . . 1829. Two volumes. 1: *i-iii* iv-v *vi, 7* 8-254; 2: not seen. Copy: University of Georgia (vol.1).

312R] NEW YORK: Eastburn 1818
The Poetical Works of Walter Scott, Esq. Illustrated with Engravings from the designs of

Richard Westall, Esq. R.A. . . . New-York, Published by James Eastburn & Co. 1818. Six volumes. Notes: Each volume has an engraved frontispiece and vignette title-page, as well as a separate printed title-page reading: [title, as cited below] By Walter Scott, Esq. New-York: Published by J. Eastburn and Co. Literary-Rooms, Broadway. [date]. Apart from the frontispiece portrait in volume 1, drawn by H. Raeburn, all frontispiece illustrations and title vignettes are drawn by Richard Westall and engraved by P. Maverick & Durand.

1] The Lay of the Last Minstrel, A Poem. 1818. Pages: *1-7* 8-306. Notes: Pages *249-251* 252-306 represent 'The Dance of Death, and Other Poems'. Copies: E; CtY MWA (2) NN PU.

2] The Vision of Don Roderick. Ballads and Lyrical Pieces. 1818. Pages: *i-vii* viii-ix *x, 11-15* 16-286. Notes: Pages *83-89* 90-286 represent the Ballads. Copies: E; CtY MWA (2) NN PU.

3] Marmion; A Tale of Flodden Field. 1818. Pages: *i-viii, 9-11* 12-359. Copies: E; CtY MWA(2) NN.

4] The Lady of the Lake: A Poem. 1818 [or 1819]. Pages: *i-viii, 9-11* 12-348. Notes: Pages *315-321* 322-348 represent *The Field of Waterloo.* Copies: E; CtY MWA(2) NN.

5] Rokeby: A Poem. 1818. Pages: *i-viii, 9-11* 12-300. Copies: E; CtY MWA(2) NN PU.

6] The Lord of the Isles. A Poem. 1818. Pages: *i-vi, 7-9* 10-324. Copies: E; CtY MH MWA(2) NN PU.

313R] PHILADELPHIA: Carey 1820

The Search after Happiness; Or, The Quest of Sultaun Solimaun; with Other Poems. By Walter Scott, Esq. Philadelphia: M. Carey and Son. 1820. Pages: *1-5* 6-148. Notes: The title poem first appeared in *The Sale Room*, No. V., Saturday, 1 February 1817. In addition to the title poem, twenty-one other poems are presented here, including selections from *Albyn's Anthology*, George Thomson's musical publications, and *The Edinburgh Annual Register,* as well as ballads from the German. None of these were in the 1816 selection issued by Carey and Wells and Lilly in 1816 under the title: *The Dance of Death and Other Poems* (*see* 315R). Copies: O; CtY InU MH MWA NN PPL RPB.

314R] PHILADELPHIA: Carey and Lea 1831

Autobiography of Sir Walter Scott. Bart. Philadelphia: Carey & Lea—Chestnut Street. 1831. Pages: *i-iii* iv-viii, *9* 10-288. Notes: With an engraved frontispiece portrait and spine label reading: Cabinet Library No. III. This is a pastische excerpted from the introductions published thus far in the 'Magnum Opus' editions and *Collected Poems*, together with a reprint of 14 Appendixes and the addition, as XV, of Washington Irving's 'A Sketch of Abbotsford'. It is stated that the compiler, Henry D. Gilpin, has used 'scrupulous care' in piecing together this information.

In announcing the forthcoming issue of this compilation, the Philadelphia *National Gazette* on 16 August 1831 remarked: 'A sketch of his own life by an author like Sir Walter Scott must possess great interest. Having seen some portion of it, we are satisfied that the expectation which it may excite will not be disappointed.' Publication was announced 6 October. Copies: E(2) O; CtY(2) DLC IdU MWA NNU-W PPL PU TxU. Reference: Kohler(1) 203(with illustration).

315R] PHILADELPHIA: Carey and Wells and Lilly 1816

The Dance of Death, and Other Poems. By Walter Scott, Esq. Philadelphia: Published by M. Carey, No. 121, Chesnut Street, and by Wells and Lilly, Boston. William Fry, Printer.

1816. Pages: *i-v* vi *vii-viii*, *1* 2-62 *63-64*. Notes: The title poem first appeared in the *Edinburgh Annual Register for 1813*, published in 1815. The twenty-two poems in this selection do not include any in the selection issued by Carey in 1820 under the title: *The Search after Happiness; . . . . with Other Poems* (*see* 313R). Copies: DLC MWA PPL(2). Reference: Clarkin 934.

316R] PHILADELPHIA: Crissy and Grigg 1829-1835
The Poetical Works of Sir Walter Scott, With a Sketch of His Life, . . . Philadelphia. Published by J. Crissy and J. Grigg. Stereotyped by J. C. & J. Maxwell, Jr. 1829. Pages: [*i-ii*] *iii-vii* viii-xxviii, *1* 2-443. Notes: The J. W. Lake 'Memoir of Sir Walter Scott' preceding the text apparently is reprinted from the 1826 Paris, Galignani edition (290R.1C). With eight engraved plates, including the frontispiece portrait of Scott drawn by Raeburn. Copy: PPL. Reissued 1830(E); variant issue 1830 with the portrait assigned to Leslie (DLC) and without other plates; reissued without plates 1833 (E; MWA); 1834; 1835.

317R] PHILADELPHIA: Maxwell 1827-1828
The Poetical Works of Sir Walter Scott, Bart. . . . Philadelphia: J. Maxwell, Agent.—63, S Fifth St. 1827. Five volumes with a uniform title throughout. Pages 1: *i-iii* iv, *9-10* 11-172; 2: *1-7* 8-303; 3: *1-7* 8-287; 4: *1-5* 6-288; 5: *1-5* 6-277. Notes: Frontispiece portrait of Scott in volume 1. Copy: NNU-W(vols. 2-5). Reissued 1828 (NNU-W.[vol. 1]).

318R] PHILADELPHIA: Pomeroy 1824
The Poetical Works of Sir Walter Scott. . . . Philadelphia: R. W. Pomeroy—63, S. Fifth St. 1824. Seven volumes. Pages 1: *i-iii* 'ix'[iv] *v-x*, *11* 12-288; 2: *1-11* 12-324; 3: *1-9* 10-275; 4: *1-11* 12-270; 5: *1-9* 10-287; 6: *1-7* 8-266; 7: *1-7* 8-261. Notes: Publisher uses a uniform title for each volume with contents not given on title-pages. Each volume has frontispiece painted by R. Smirke, re-engraved by G. B. Ellis. Copies: MWA MH(vols.1-3,5-7) NNU-W.

COLLECTED DERIVATIVE EDITIONS

Preliminary Note: As with certain of the collected reprints listed in the preceding account (288R-318R), the plays recorded in this 'D' section were also available separately, and accordingly have also been identified by cross-reference from the earlier lists of separate derivatives.

GREAT BRITAIN

319D-321D] EDINBURGH: Anderson 1823-1825
319D] Edinburgh Select British Theatre. . . . Edinburgh: Published by John Anderson, Jun. 55, North Bridge Street, Edinburgh. 1823-1825. Notes: Also referred to as: Anderson's Edition. Edinburgh Select British Theatre. Engraved frontispiece and vignette title-page: there is no type-set title-page. Each title was also issued separately: refer to bracketted number following titles below.

1] George Heriot or The Fortunes of Nigel. 1823. Pages: *i-iv*, *1* 2-77. Notes: Drama by W. H. Murray, as performed at The Theatre Royal, Edinburgh. Engraved frontispiece 'George

Heriot, Edinburgh Published by John Anderson, Junr.' and title-page with vignette 'Heriot's Hospital' Engd. by W. H. Lizars.' Copies: E; NN. References: Bolton 4059; Ford G4. [Separate issue: 157Da].

2] Ivanhoe or the Jewess, A Drama Founded on the Celebrated Romance of Ivanhoe, By the Author of Waverley. 1823. Pages: *i-iv*, *1* 2-79. Notes: Drama by John William Calcraft [John William Cole]. Copies: C ES; NjP. References: Bolton 3362; Ford K7. [140Db].

3] The Battle of Bothwell Bridge; A Drama in Five Acts. [on wrappers: 1823]. Pages: *i-iv*, *1* 2-80. Notes: Drama by John William Calcraft [John William Cole], as performed at The Theatre Royal Edinburgh. Copy: E. References: Bolton 1320; Ford O 4. [98Db].

4] The Pirate; or, Minna & Brenda. A Drama. Founded on the Celebrated Novel of The Pirate. [1824]. Pages: *1* 2-53 *54-56*. Notes: This drama, probably written by J. W. Calcraft, was first performed in Edinburgh 29 March. Copies: C; NN. References: Bolton 4050; Ford Q5. [156Da].

7] Peveril of the Peak or The Days of Charles II. 1823. Pages: *i-iv*, *1* 2-66 *67*. Notes: Drama by Edward Fitzball [Edward Ball], as performed at the Theatre Royal, Edinburgh. Copies: C E. References: Bolton 4103; Ford P2. [165Db].

8] Montrose or The Children of the Mist. A Drama founded on the Legend of Montrose. Published by John Anderson Junr. 55. North Bridge Street, Edinburgh. 1823. Pages: *i-iv*, *1* 2-67. Notes: Drama by Isaac Pocock (music by Sir Henry Bishop not included) as performed at the Theatre Royal, Edinburgh, 13 March 1822. Copies: MH NN. Reissued 'Second Edition' 1823 (C E[2]). References: Bolton 3290; Ford M4. [135Db].

12] [Waverley. 1824.] Drama by John William Calcraft, as performed at the Theatre Royal, Edinburgh, 22 May 1824. Copy: not seen. References: Bolton 373; Ford X3. [77Db].

13] Redgauntlet A Drama; Founded on the Tale of the Same Name by the Author of Waverley &c. &c. 1824 [1825]. Pages: *i-ii*, *1* 2-61. Notes: Drama by William Henry Murray as performed at the Theatre Royal, Edinburgh, 27 May 1825. Copies: C E. References: Bolton 4289; Ford S2. [178Da].

14] Mary Queen of Scots or Loch-Leven Castle. A Drama Founded on The Abbot. 1825. Pages: *i-iv*, *1* 2-112 *113-116*. Notes: Drama tentatively attributed to Daniel Terry, as performed at the Theatre Royal, Edinburgh, 3 October(?) 1825. The back wrapper lists fourteen titles in the series with number 15 'St. Ronan's Well' at press (but apparently unpublished: cf. Bolton 4261; Ford U1). Copy: NN. References: Bolton 3644; Ford A3. [146Da].

320D] Illustrations of the Author of Waverley: Being Notices and Anecdotes of Real Characters, Scenes, and Incidents, Supposed to be Described in his Works. MDCCCXXV. John Anderson, Jun. Edinburgh, 55, North Bridge-Street, and Simpkin & Marshall, London. Pages: *i-v* vi, *1* 2-227. Notes: The Preface by the author, Robert Chambers, states this edition has 'greater correctness of language and more copious information.' With an engraved frontispiece showing a veiled portrait of the Author of Waverley. First 1823 edition not seen. This 'Second Edition' MDCCCXXV copies: ES; T/B.

321D] The Waverley Dramas. . . . John Anderson, Jun. Edinburgh, 55, North Bridge Street; and Simpkin & Marshall, London. MDCCCXXIII. Two volumes. Pages 1: *1-4*; 2: *1-2* [then separately paged plays as noted below]. Notes: In advertisements: 'The Dramas from the Works of the great Author of Waverley will be kept in Volumes by themselves, as a more suitable classification than diffusing them through miscellaneous Volumes.' Each title was also issued separately: refer to bracketted number following titles below. Most titles, as noted below, are variant issues of those collected in Anderson's *Edinburgh Select British Theatre* (ESBT), nos. 1-15 (*see* 319D). For the dedication to Scott *see* 504T[2].

VOLUME 1: 1] George Heriot or The Fortunes of Nigel. 1823. Notes: Variant issue of ESBT number 1. Copies: ES; NjP. [Separate issue: 157Da].

2] [Ivanhoe.] Notes: Presumably a variant issue of ESBT number 2. Copy: not seen. [140Db].

3] The Battle of Bothwell Bridge. A Drama in Five Acts. [1823]. Notes: Variant issue of ESBT number 3. Copies: ES; NjP. [98Db].

4] The Pirate or Minna & Brenda, A Drama. Founded on the Celebrated Novel of The Pirate, By the Author of Waverley &c. [no imprint, no date]. A different title and setting of ESBT number 4. Pages: *i-vi*, *1* 2-53 *54-56*. Copies: ES; NjP. [156Da].

5] Peveril of the Peak or The Days of Charles II. 1823. Pages: *i-vi*, *1* 2-66 *67-68*. Notes: Variant issue of ESBT number 7. Copies: ES; NjP. [165Db].

VOLUME 2: 6] Montrose or the Children of the Mist. 1823. Notes: Variant issue of ESBT number 8 'Second Edition'. Copy: ES. [135Db].

7] [Waverley]. Notes: Presumably variant issue of ESBT number 12. Copy: not seen. [77Db].

8] Redgauntlet A Drama. 1824. Notes: Variant issue of ESBT number 13. Copy: ES. [178Da].

9] Mary Queen of Scots or Loch-Leven Castle. 1825. Notes: Variant issue of ESBT number 14. Copy: ES. [146Da].

10] The Talisman A Drama, in Three Acts. 1828. Pages: *i-ii*, *1* 2-60. Notes: Drama by W. H. Murray as performed at The Theatre-Royal, Edinburgh, 22 June 1825. Copies: C ES. [181Da].

322D] EDINBURGH: Constable and Hurst, Robinson 1820

[wrapper title] Illustrations of the Novels and Tales entitled Waverley, Guy Mannering, The Antiquary, Rob Roy, The Black Dwarf, Old Mortality, The Heart of Mid-Lothian, The Bride of Lammermoor, and A Legend of Montrose, . . . Edinburgh: Published by Archibald Constable and Co. Edinburgh; and Hurst, Robinson, and Co. London. 1820. Moyes, London. Notes: Issued 11 December 1820 (*MC*) as the third in the Hurst. Robinson series. Notes: Following printed title-cover, engraved vignette title-page and twelve plates, all drawn by William Allan and engraved by the artists cited below. This suite was issued in four states: (1) 12° at 24s; (2) 8° at £1.11.6, (3) 4° India paper proofs, Imperial 4° £2.12.6, (4) proofs before letters, Colombier 4° £3.3.0.

Since the only copy discovered of the complete suite is without letters, a ready comparison is facilitated by assigning plate and then design numbers according to the nine works identified in the general title; captions are taken from a separate listing. Copy: (State 4) T/B.

Title vignette: title 3, W. H. Lizars; plates:

1] 'The Quarrel at Luckie Macleary's, between the Baron of Bradwardine and the Laird of Balmawhapple' title 1, C. Warren.

2] 'The conclusion of Flora's Song in the Glen of Glennaquoich' 1, F. Engleheart.

3] 'Meg Merrilies predicting the fall of the house of Elangowan' 2, H. Cook.

4] 'Meeting of Meg Merrilies, Brown, and Dinmont, at the ale-house in Cumberland' 2, Chas Warren.

5] 'The Antiquary buying fish from Mrs. Mucklebackit' 3, Henry Meyer.
6] 'The Laird of Monkbarns arming himself on the alarm of invasion' 3, Chas. Warren.
7] 'The fight in the public-house, at the Clachan at Aberfoil, between Baillie Jarvie and Major Galbraith's party' 4, J. Romney.
8] 'Isabella Vere's midnight visit to the Black Dwarf's hut' 5, F. Engleheart.
9] 'Burley's concealment in the hay-loft in Milnwood' 6, F. Engleheart.
10] 'Breakfast scene with Captain Knockdunder at Knocktarlitie' 7, J. Romney.
11] 'Lucy Ashton and the Master of Ravenswood pledging their love at the Mermaiden's Fountain' 8, J. Romney.
12] 'Captain Dalgetty consigning Gustavus to the care of the Children of the Mist' 9, Chas. Heath.

323D] EDINBURGH: Huie 1823
Dramas from the Novels, Tales, and Romances of The Author of "Waverley." . . . . Edinburgh: Printed for James L. Huie, 14 Infirmary Street. 1823. Notes: Two volumes. In its final issues volume 1 only has the collective printed title described here, an additional engraved frontispiece, vignette title, and preliminary leaves paged *i-viii* ix-xii (these including a dedication to 'the unknown' Scott), followed by individual plays as ordered below. The plays included usually are a random combination of separate printings (each play separately signed) or of a uniform printing (with signatures continuing throughout the volume: a uniform printing noted only in volume 1 of the InU set). Volumes 5-7 as noted below were also published 1823, in a different setting, by Anderson in Edinburgh.

Some later impressions read on wrappers: Edinburgh: Printed for James L Huie Reprinted for Stirling and Kenny. The plays, without an imprint on the title-page, were originally issued either as a program for use in the theatres or under the collective title. Although difficult to differentiate, for each title issued separately, refer to bracketted number following titles below. For titles thought to have been issued as a part of the series, see copies noted here.

VOLUME 1: 1] Rob Roy; A National Drama, . . . [1822]. Pages: *1-5* 6-60. Copies: InU NN. [Separate issue: *i-5* 6-68. *see* 112De]. Play by an anonymous dramatist, originally managed by William Henry Murray, as first performed at the Theatre Royal, Edinburgh, 15 February 1819. References: Bolton 1531; Ford T4.
2] The Heart of Mid-Lothian; A Romantic National Drama, . . . [1822]. Pages: *1-5* 6-63. Copy: InU. [Separate issue: *1-7* 8-66. *see* 122Dc]. Drama probably by William Henry Murray as performed at the Theatre Royal, Edinburgh, 23 February 1820. References: Bolton 2436; Ford I5.
3] Kenilworth; A Historical Drama, . . . [1822]. Pages: *1-5* 6-62. Notes: Dramatis Personae for 1822 and 1823; page 62 begins '*of the Trap;*'. Copies: E L; InU NN(2) NNP. [Separate issue: Dramatis Personae for 1822 only. *see* 149Dc]. Drama by Thomas Dibdin as performed at the Theatre Royal. Edinburgh, 2 July 1822. References: Bolton 3814; Ford L9.
4] The Antiquary; A National Drama, [1822]. Pages: *1-7* 8-66. Copies: InU NN. [Separate issue: *1-7* 8-64. *see* 94Da]. Drama probably by William Henry Murray as performed at the Theatre Royal, Edinburgh, 10 January 1822. References: Bolton 1291; Ford B3.
5] Fortunes of Nigel; or George Heriot. A Historical Drama, . . . [1823]. Copy: not seen. [Separate issue: *i-ii*, *1-3* 4-70. *see* 157Dc]. This drama by William Henry Murray is apparently the same version as that published 1823 by Anderson (*see* 319D[1]). References: Bolton 4059; Ford G4.

VOLUME 2: 6] Peveril of the Peak; A Melo-Dramatic Play, 1823. Copy: not seen. [Separate issue: *1-7* 8-55. *see* 165Dc]. This drama by Edward Fitzball [Ball] is apparently the same version as that published 1823 by Anderson (*see* 321D[5]). References: Bolton 4103; Ford P2.

7] Ivanhoe; A Historical Drama, 1823. Copy: not seen. [Separate issue: *1-7* 8-76. *see* 122Dc]. This drama, perhaps by John William Calcraft, is apparently the same version as that published 1823 by Anderson (*see* 319D[2]). References: Bolton 3362; Ford K7.

8] Guy Mannering; or, The Gypsey's Prophecy. A Musical Drama [1823] Pages: *[i-ii]*, *1-5* 6-60. Copies: InU NN. [Separate issue: *1-5* 6-68. *see* 82Da]. Drama by Daniel Terry as performed at the Theatre Royal, Edinburgh, 22 October 1822. References: Bolton 514; Ford H1.

EDINBURGH: Stirling and Kenney

[~] Huie's National Dramas see Edinburgh: Huie. Dramas from the Novels, Tales, &c. of The Author of "Waverley". *see* 323D.

324D] LONDON: Baldwin, Cradock, and Joy; W. Fearman 1819-1829

The Lady's Magazine, Or Entertaining Companion for the Fair Sex. Vol.50, No.8. for August, 1819 [No.9. for September, 1819—New Series, Vol.10, No.12. for December, 1829]. London: Printed by S. Hamilton, Whitefriars, For Baldwin, Cradock, and Joy, Paternoster-Row; and W. Fearman, Library, New Bond Street: Where Favors from Correspondents (post-paid) will be received.

Notes: Each of the monthly numbers listed below contains one or more plates, the first usually facing first page of text, which then introduces, often with some comment, an abstract from the novel illustrated. The following account records in order an assigned number, plate caption, names of artist and engraver as given on the plate, date of the magazine number, and facing page of text. Copies: L(1818-1821, others not examined); CtY (lacking nos. for 1820).

1]	The Bride of Lammermoor.	T. Stothard/ J. Heath.	August	1819.	*339*
2]	A Legend of Montrose.	" " " "	September	1819.	*387*
3]	The Black Dwarf.	" " " "	October	1819.	*435*
4]	The Heart of Mid-Lothian.	" " " "	November	1819.	497
5]	The Heart of Mid-Lothian.	" " " "	December	1819.	*529*
6]	Ivanhoe.	R. Westall/ " "	February	1820.	[101]
7]	Ivanhoe.	" " " "	March	1820	121
8]	Ivanhoe.	" " " "	April	1820	169
9]	Monastery.	T. Stothard/ " "	May	1820	*225*
10]	Monastery.	" " " "	June	1820	*281*
11]	Abbot.	H. Corbould/Heath.	November	1820	*569*
12]	Abbot.	" " " "	January	1821.	47
13]	Kenilworth.	Stothard/ Heath.	May	1821.	272
14]	Kenilworth.	" "	"	"	274
15]	Kenilworth.	" "	"	"	327
16]	Pirate.	Corbould/ Heath.	February	1822.	101
17]	Pirate.	H. Corbould/ Heath.	March	1822.	161
18]	Pirate.	Corbould/ Heath.	April	1822.	216

19] Tales of the Crusaders.	[Unidentified]	September	1825.	542
20] Tales of the Crusaders.	T.M. Wright/ A. Duncan.	October	1825.	623
21] Tales of the Crusaders.	“ “ “ “	November	1825.	688
22] Tales of the Crusaders.	“ “ / E.G. Pakins.	December	1825.	744
23] Tales of the Crusaders.	H.C. Slous/T. Woolnoth.	March	1826.	162
24] Tales of the Crusaders.	“ “ / Chas. Heath.	April	1826.	200
25] Woodstock.	H.C. Slous/ E. Stalker.	May	1826.	274
26] Woodstock.	“ “ “ “	June	1826.	330
27] Woodstock.	“ “ “ “	July	1826.	400
28] Woodstock.	“ “ “ “	August	1826.	449
29] Woodstock.	“ “ “ “	September	1826.	500
30] Woodstock.	“ “ “ “	October	1826.	567
31] Chronicles ... Canongate.	H.C. Slous/ Hamilton.	November	1827.	608
32] Chronicles ... Canongate.	“ “ “ “	December	1827.	655
33] Chronicles ... Canongate.	“ “ “ “	January	1828.	44
34] Chronicles ... Canongate.	“ “ “ “	February	1828.	103
35] Chronicles Second Series.	T. Meadows/ C.R.	June	1828.	321
36] Chronicles Second Series.	“ “ / G.A. Periam.	July	1828.	377
37] Chronicles Second Series.	“ “ “ “	September	1828.	496
38] Chronicles Second Series.	“ “ “ “	December	1828.	661
39] Anne of Geierstein.	J. Sargent/ R.G. Reeve.	October	1829.	548
40] Anne of Geierstein.	J.S./ “ “	November	1829.	601
41] Anne of Geierstein.	J. Sargent/ “ “	December	1829.	660

325D] LONDON: Baldwyn 1823-1824

[*wrapper title*] Illustrations of the Novels and Tales of the Author of Waverley: A series of portraits of eminent historical characters introduced in those works. Accompanied with biographical notices. parts 1-7. London, 1823. No more published. Proofs priced at 14s (Lowndes). Copy: L. This first issue was subsequently published under a collective, engraved title: Portraits Illustrative of the Novels, Tales, & Romances of the Author of "Waverley." London. Published by C. Baldwyn, Newgate street. [1824]. Each of the 32 portrait plates in this volume issue is followed by two unnumbered pages of letterpress text. The volume in 1832 was reissued by Evans (*see* 332D).

The following record cites in order: plate (here assigned a number); artist or source of the portrait, caption and, in brackets, further reference taken from the text. All plates are engraved by R. Cooper. Copies: NNU-W(2) T/B TxU.

1] Sir W. W. Wyron's picture; 'The Young Chevalier' [Charles Edward Stuart, 1720-1778]
2] Mr Whincop's picture; 'Colonel Gardiner' [1688-1745]
3] Sir Walter Scott's picture; 'Rob Roy' [Robert M'Gregor]
4] Sir I. Medina; 'Duke of Montrose' [James Graham]
5] Picture at Strawberry Hill; 'Countess of Suffolk' [d.1767]
6] Lord Leven's picture; 'Graham of Claverhouse' [d.1689]
7] W. Aikman; 'Duke of Argyle' [d.1661]
8] Sir Peter Lely; 'Marquis of Athol' [1635-1703]
9] Zucchero; 'Mary of Scotland' [1542-1587]
10] [unstated]; 'Earl of Morton' [d.1581]

11] Marc Garrard; 'Lord Hunsdon' [1524-1596]
12] Lely; 'Duke of Monmouth' [1649-1685]
13] Kneller; 'Queen Caroline' [1682-1737]
14] [unstated]; 'Earl of Leicester' [1532-1588]
15] Lely; 'Duke of Lauderdale' [1616-1682]
16] From a rare Print; 'General Dalzell' [d.1685]
17] I. Oliver; 'Queen Elizabeth' [1533-1603]
18] [unstated]; 'Lord Burleigh' [1520-1598]
19] Zucchero; 'Sir Francis Walsingham' [1536-1590]
20] [unstated]; 'Sir Walter Raleigh' [1552-1618]
21] Vertue; 'King John' [1166-1216]
22] Mr Radclyffe's picture; 'Earl of Sussex [1526-1583]
23] Vandyck; 'Marquis of Montrose' [1612-1650]
24] W. Aikman; 'Duke of Argyle' [1678-1743]
25] Duke of Portland's picture; 'Earl of Southampton' [1573-1624]
26] Sir P. Lely; 'Archbishop Sharp' [1618-1679]
27] Vertue; 'Richard, I' [1157-1199]
28] Scougal; 'George Heriot' [1563-1624]
29] C. Jansen; 'Duke of Buckingham' [1592-1628]
30] Scarce print by Pass; 'James 1' [1566-1625]
31] Rare print by Delaram; 'Charles, Prince of Wales' [1600-1649]
32] Picture at Holyrood; 'Earl of Murray' [James Stewart, d.1570]

326D] LONDON: Bumpus 1825
The Common-Place Book of Literary Curiosities, Remarkable Customs, Historical and Domestic Anecdotes, and Etymological Scraps. . . . London: John Bumpus, 85, Newgate-Street. MDCCCXXV. Pages: *i-ii*, *1* 2-423 *424-426*. Notes: Title identifies the author as 'The Rev. Dr. Dryasdust, of York, somewhile preface-writer to the Great Unknown.' The volume has three wood engravings including a coloured frontispiece signed W. Heathern and labelled [page] '124. Buck Skin Breeches.' Copy: T/B.

327D] LONDON: Chapman and Hall 1832-1833
Landscape Illustrations of the Prose and Poetical Works of Sir Walter Scott, Bart. With Portraits of the Principal Female Characters . . . London: Chapman and Hall, 186, Strand; Moon, Boys, and Graves, Pall Mall; James Fraser, 215, Regent Street. M. DCCC. XXXII [-M. DCCC. XXXIII].
Notes: Title from wrappers. 24 parts, with 5 plates and accompanying letterpress to a part, at 2s.6d. Part III cover adds the names of Oliver and Boyd, Edinburgh; J. Cumming, Dublin; and Rittner and Goupil, Paris. An 'Address', back cover of Part I, indicates that the 'present form' is a reissue at a reduction in price [of the Tilt series], and a similar notice in Part XV advertises 40 plates published 'this day' in *Landscape Illustrations*, volume 1 (apparently the only Chapman volume published [copy T/B]). The unnumbered plates are dated June 1832-September 1833. Illustrations for the Poetical Works, prepared for Chapman and Hall, though indicated on the part titles, were not included. An announcement for these, however, appears in the final part as another part series to begin 17 August [1833]. All these late Chapman and Hall plates are identified below under Tilt (*see* 342D[2]), the original publisher.

Copies: NN PPL. Reference: Maggs Catalogue 1120 (1990), item 248(with illustration page 82).

328D] LONDON: Colnaghi 1829

The Lithographic Album of Sir Walter Scott's Readers or 12 sketches by the following distinguished Artists R. P. Bonington, P. Delaroche et E. Lami London. Published by Colnaghi Son et Co., No 11, Pall-Mall East. 1829. Notes: 12 unnumbered india paper proofs. Title information from wrapper only. Printed by Villain and except for plate 1 dated 1 December 1828. Proofs for plates 1-4, 6-8 and 12 are sketched by Eug. Lami, 5 and 9 are by R. T. Bonington, 10 and 11 by P. Delaroche. Copy: LVA.

1] [no caption]
2] William Deloraine in Melrose-Abbey.
3] Fitz James sorrowing over his expiring Horse.
4] James the V at Stirling Castle.
5] A Duel between Frank and Rashleigh.
6] Loch-Ard Scene of Morris's Drowning.
7] Battle on Bothwell Bridge.
8] Jeanny[!] Deans embarking for Rosneath.
9] The escape from Argyle-Castle.
10] Queen Mary at Loch-Leven Castle.
11] A Fight in Higt[!] Street Edinburgh.
12] Hamish and his Mother.

329D-330D] LONDON: Cumberland 1829-1832

329D] Cumberland's British Theatre, with Remarks, Biographical and Critical, . . . 1829-1832. Notes: Edited by George Daniel, printed from the acting copies, with descriptions of the costumes, cast of the characters, entrances and exits, relative positions of the performers, and the whole of the stage business, as performed in the theatres in London. Each volume has a steel engraved portrait as a frontispiece. Each title has a wood-cut frontispiece illustration from a drawing taken in the Theatre by Robert Cruikshank and engraved by G. W. Bonner. The titles are arranged under the unique serial number of the item, usually found only on printed wrappers. Numbers in brackets before copies signify first the volume number, and then the number of the play within the volume.
IMPRINT 1: London: John Cumberland, 6, Brecknock Place, Camden New Town. [1829-1830].
2: London: John Cumberland, 2, Cumberland Terrace, Camden New Town [1830-1832].

177] The Maid of Judah; or, The Knights Templars: A Serious Opera, In Three Acts. (Dramatised from Sir Walter Scott's Ivanhoe,) . . . [imprint 1] [1829]. Pages: *1-5* 6-63. Notes: Libretto by Michael Rophino Lacy (music composed by Gioachino Rossini not included) as performed at Covent Garden 7 March 1829. Woodcut frontispiece titled 'The Maid of Judah.' [25; 5]. Copies: L O(2); InU TxU. References: Bolton 3384; Ford K10. Reissued: [imprint 1] [1830] (NN).
231] The Antiquary: A Musical Play, in Three Acts, from Sir Walter Scott, Bart. to Which is Prefixed A Memoir of his Life. [imprint 2] [1832]. Pages: *1-3* 4-77. Notes: The anonymous 'Memoir' was probably written by George Daniel, the author of the fifteen-stanza poem 'On the Death of Sir Walter Scott' (pages 17-20) and 'Remarks' on 'The Antiquary', which follow before the text of the play begins on page *27* (music by Henry Bishop not included). The play, by Daniel Terry, was first performed at Covent Garden 25 January 1820. With a woodcut frontispiece titled 'The Antiquary', drawn by R. Cruikshank. [31; 3]. Copies: E L; CtY InU RPB. References: Bolton 1275; Ford B2.
261] The Knights of the Cross; or, The Hermit's Prophecy: A Romantic Drama, in Three Acts, from Sir Walter Scott, Bart. [imprint 2] [1831?]. Pages: *1-5* 6-43. Notes: Drama by

Samuel Beazley based on 'The Talisman' (music by Sir Henry Bishop not included) performed at Drury Lane 29 May 1826. Woodcut frontispiece titled 'The Knights of the Cross.' with caption "Comrade. The hound! The hound!—Strike him, or he strangles me!". [34; 6]. Copies: MH TxU. References: Bolton 4335; Ford V3.

285] Rob Roy: A Romantic Drama, In Three Acts. [imprint 2] [1831]. Pages: *1-5* 6-45. Notes: Drama by George Soane, first performed at the Drury Lane 25 March 1818. Woodcut frontispiece titled 'Rob Roy' but not identified as by Cruikshank/Bonner, although in the same style. [36; 10]. Copy: L. Reference: Bolton 1451.

311] Kenilworth. A Drama, in Two Acts, (From Sir Walter Scott Bart.) [imprint 2]. [1832?] Pages: *1-5* 6-35. Notes: Drama by Thomas Dibdin(?) (so stated on title-page and in introduction) as performed at Covent Garden 8 March 1818. In the Advertisement, dated 12 March 1821, the 'Compiler' who 'by way of apology to the distinguished author of the novel' stresses the value of a two act drama as opposed to those of his competitors, notably Thomas Dibdin; for this play is not to be confused with Dibdin's which opened at the Surrey Theatre 14 February 1821. This may be an adaptation of Dibdin's title by A. Bunn. Woodcut frontispiece is titled 'Kenilworth' but there are signatures for neither Cruikshank nor Bonner. [39; 6]. Copies: L; CtY. References: Bolton 3801; Ford L6.

[?] Guy Mannering; or, The Gipsy's Prophecy. A Musical Play, in Three Acts. [imprint 2] [1831?]. Pages: *1-5* 6-60. Notes: Drama by Daniel Terry with help from Scott, first performed at Covent Garden 12 March 1816. Woodcut frontispiece titled 'Guy Man-nering'. [43; 6]. Copy: L. References: Bolton 409; Ford H1.

330D] Cumberland's Minor Theatre, with Remarks, Biographical and Critical. . . 1828-1832. Notes: Edited by George Daniel. Printed from the acting copies, as performed at the Metropolitan Minor Theatres. Except for the volume frontispiece (a steel engraving) all numbers have a woodcut frontispiece drawn by Robert Cruikshank and engraved by G. W. Bonner which is included in the pagination and in each case titled after the play. Although most plays were presented with musical scores, no music is present in this series. Individual plays when issued separately had wrappers. The titles are arranged under the unique serial number of the item, usually found on the printed wrappers. Numbers preceding the copy record [in brackets] represent the volume number and the number of the play in each volume.

Volumes 1-5 were issued before 1833: later volumes fall outside of the period of this bibliography. Although it is apparent that the miscellaneous titles included in this series were published at various times as separate issues, no individual titles have been seen, perhaps because of their ephemeral nature. The following imprints are marked by insignificant changes in title-page punctuation.

IMPRINT 1: London: John Cumberland, 19, Ludgate Hill. [1826-1829]
2: London: John Cumberland, 6, Brecknock Place, Camden New Town. [1829-1830].
3: London: John Cumberland, 2 Cumberland Terrace, Camden New Town. [1830-1832].

2] The Heart of Mid-Lothian: A Melo-Dramatic Romance, in Three Acts, [imprint 1. 1828]. Pages: *1-5* 6-54. Notes: Play by Thomas Dibdin, first performed at the Royal Circus (Surrey) Theatre, 13 January 1819. Casts given for performances in '1809'[1819] and in 1828. [1, 2]. Copies: E; InU(3) NN-L(prompt copy) T/B. In some copies the '1809' has been corrected. Reissued with Imprint 2, 1829 (InU) and Imprint 3, 1831 (E: CtY NNP). References: Bolton 2421; Ford I 1.

17] Ivanhoe; or, The Jew's Daughter: A Romantic Melo-Drama, In Three Acts. [imprint 2] [1829]. Pages: *1-5* 6-64. Notes: Drama by Thomas Dibdin. Cast of Characters as performed at the Surrey Theatre, 20 January 1820. [2, 8]. Copies: InU NjP RPB T/B. Reissued with [imprint 3] [1831] (DT; CtY(2) InU). References: Bolton 3333; Ford K1.

22] The Lady of the Lake: A Melo-Dramatic Romance, in Two Acts, (From Sir Walter Scott.) [imprint 2] [1829]. Pages: *1-5* 6-31. Notes: Drama by Thomas Dibdin. Cast of Characters, as performed at the Surry[!] Theatre [24 September] 1810. [3, 4]. Copies:CtY InU(2) NjP NN. Reissued: [imprint 3] [1830] (CtY[2] InU[3].) Reference: Bolton 49.

32] The Fortunes of Nigel: A Melo-Dramatic Romance, In Three Acts. [imprint 3]. [1831]. Pages: *1-5* 6-56. Notes: Drama by Edward Fitz-Ball (Ball). Cast of Characters for the Surrey Theatre [28 June] 1822 and for the Pavilion [27 September] 1830. [4, 5]. Copies: CtY InU(4) MH NN T/B. References: Bolton 4055, 4079; Ford G1.

42] Peveril of the Peak; or, The Days of King Charles II. A Dramatic Romance, In Three Acts, (From Sir Walter Scott, Bart.) [imprint 3] [1831]. Pages: *1-5* 6-53. Notes: Drama by Edward Fitz-Ball (Ball). Dramatis Personae for Surry[!] Theatre, 6 February 1823. [5, 6]. Copies: E; CtY NN T/B. References: Bolton 4103; Ford P1.

44] Waverley; or, Sixty Years Since: A Scottish Drama, in Three Acts, (From Sir Walter Scott,). [imprint 3] [1831]. Pages: *1-5* 6-48. Notes: Drama by Edward Fitz-Ball (Ball). Cast of Characters for the Coburg Theatre, 8 March 1824. [5, 8]. Copies: L; CtY InU NN T/B. References: Bolton 372; Ford X2.

331D] LONDON: Duncombe 1828

Duncombe's Edition of the British Theatre. London. 1828. Notes: The following entry appears to be the only play in the Duncombe Edition published before 1833—the cut-off date for this bibliography:

75] The Two Drovers. A Domestic, Legendary Melo-Drama. In Two Acts. London: Printed and published by J. Duncombe, 19, Little Queen Street, Holborn. [1828]. Pages: *1-5* 6-24. Notes: Melodrama by Henry Goff, as performed at the Surrey Theatre 4 February 1828, with engraved frontispiece counted in the pagination. At head of title: 'Duncombe's Edition'. (On wrapper: Duncombe's Acting Edition of the British Theatre: number 75). Copies: CtY NN(ms date 'June 1833'). Reissued with date '1831' [but printer's imprint ca.1837] (L). References: Bolton 4447; Ford W1.

332D] LONDON: Evans 1832

[*wrapper title*] Illustrations of the Novels and Tales of the Author of Waverley: A Series of Portraits of Eminent Historical Characters introduced in Those Works accompanied with Biographical Notices.... London: Edward Evans, 22, Fleet-Street; R. Griffin & Co., Glasgow; & Stillies, Brothers, Edinburgh. M.DCCC.XXXII. W. Lewis, Finch-Lane. Notes: Issued in seven parts, at 2s.6d. each, with four or five plates to a part, each plate followed by two unnumbered pages of letterpress. The plates and commentary represent a reissue of the London: Baldwyn [1823-1824] publication (*see* 325D). Copies: L; MB.

333D] LONDON: Hodgson 1822

Hodgson's Juvenile Drama. London: Printed by and for Hodgson and Co. No. 10, Newgate-street. Price: Sixpence. [1822]. Notes: Series title at head of each title-page, but unnumbered. Dramas stated to be by well-known playwrights 'adapted to Hodgson's theatrical characters and scenes'. As these were not performed in the repertory theatres they are listed only by page reference in Bolton and remain unrecorded in Ford.

1] Guy Mannering; or, The Gipsey's Prophecy: A Drama, in Three Acts. [1822]. Pages: *1-3* 4-24. Notes: The original playwright is unidentified. Copies: E L. Reference: Bolton, page 59.
2] The Heart of Mid Lothian; or, The Lily of St. Leonard's. A Drama, in Three Acts. [1822]. Pages: *1-3* 4-24. Notes: The original playwright is identified by Bolton as Thomas J. Dibdin. Copies: E L; InU. Reference: Bolton, page 261.
3] Montrose; or, The Children of the Mist: A Drama, in Three Acts. [1822]. Pages: *1-3* 4-26. Notes: The original playwright is unidentified. Copies: E L; CtY. Reference: Bolton, page 335.
4] Ivanhoe; or, The Jew of York: A Drama, in Three Acts. [1822]. Pages: *1-3* 4-24. Notes: Drama by Alfred Bunn, adapted for Hodgson from Thomas J. Dibdin's play 'Ivanhoe': or 'The Jew's Daughter'. Copies: E L; CtY InU. Reference: Bolton, page 345.
5] Rob Roy Macgregor; or, Auld Lang Syne: A Drama, in Three Acts. [1822]. Pages: *1-3* 4-28. Notes: The original playwright is unidentified. Copies: E L(2). Reference: Bolton, page 166.

334D] LONDON: Hurst, Robinson 1823-1825
1] [wrapper title] Illustrations of the Novels and Romances of "The Author of Waverley," entitled The Pirate, Fortunes of Nigel, Peveril of the Peak, and Quentin Durward. . . . London: Published by Hurst, Robinson, and Co. 90 Cheapside, and 8 Pall Mall; and Archibald Constable and Co., Edinurgh. 1825. J. Moyes, London. Notes: Issued first with the 18° edition, January 1825, and the seven frontispiece plates by various artists there described (277A). The wrapper title verso lists five states of this separate issue: (1) 12° prints, 8s.; (2) Medium 8° prints, 12s.; (3) 4° proofs, 18s.; (4) Imperial 4° proofs on India paper, £1.4.0; (5) Colombier 4° proofs on India paper, before the letters, £1.10.0. Copy: (5) T/B.

2] [Illustrations of the Poetical Works of Sir Walter Scott, Baronet. . . . Published by Hurst, Robinson & Co. 1823.] Notes: Printed wrapper title not seen. Issued separately 16 June 1823 (*MC*) as the first of a series illustrating collected works in 18° format. This suite of 10 plates after R. Smirke was later used in the 1823 edition of the *Poetical Works*, published 30 October, and the plates are there described (266Aa). An advertsement cites five states of the separate issue: (1) 12° 12s.; (2) 8° 18s.; (3) 4° proofs £1.10.0; (4) proofs on India paper, £1.18.0; (5) Colombier 4° proofs before the letters, £2.10.0. Separate copy: not seen.

3] [wrapper title] A New Series of Illustrations of the Historical Romances of "The Author of Waverley," entitled Ivanhoe, The Monastery, The Abbot, and Kenilworth. . . . London: Published by Hurst, Robinson, and Co. 90 Cheapside, and 8 Pall-Mall; and Archibald Constable and Co., Edinburgh. 1824. J. Moyes, London. Notes: Issued first with the 18° edition, published in February 1824, and the six frontispiece plates by various artists there described (274A). The wrapper title verso lists five states of the separate issue: (1) 12° 6s.; (2) Medium 8° 9s.; (3) 4° proofs 15s.; (4) Imperial 4° proofs on India paper, £1.0.0; (5) Colombier 4° proofs on India paper, before the letters, £1.5.0. Copy: (5) T/B.

4] [wrapper title] A New Series of Illustrations of the Novels and Tales entitled Waverley, Guy Mannering, The Antiquary, Rob Roy, The Black Dwarf, Old Mortality, The Heart of Mid-Lothian, The Bride of Lammermoor, and A Legend of Montrose, . . . London: Published by Hurst, Robinson, and Co. 90 Cheapside, and 8 Pall-Mall; and Archibald Constable and Co., Edinburgh. 1823. J. Moyes, London. Notes: Issued 18 September 1823 (*MC*) concurrently with the 18° edition and the 12 plates after C. R. Leslie there described (271A). The back wrapper of the 12° printing lists the seven Hurst, Robinson suites previously issued (in order of issue: 140Dk, 322D, 144De, 82Dg, 149Dj, 334D[2], 334D[4], and 146Dd['preparing']). After the present suite three others appeared in 1824 and 1825 (334D[3], 156Dk, 334D[1]).

The printed wrapper verso lists five states of this separate issue: (1) 12° 12s.; (2) Medium 8° 18s.; (3) 4° proofs £1.10.0; (4) Imperial 4° proofs on India paper, £1.18.0; (5) Colombier 4° proofs on India paper, before the letters, £2.10.0. Copies: (1) CtY; (5) T/B.

335D] LONDON: Knight and Lacey 1827

[*wrapper title*] 1. Price Sixpence. . . . Novels, Tales and Romances, By Sir Walter Scott, Bart. . . . Abridged and illustrated by Sholto Percy, . . . London: Printed for Knight and Lacey, 55, Paternoster-Row; And sold by all Booksellers and Dealers in Periodical Works. [1827]. Notes: This aborted series, intended to extend from *Waverley* to *Woodstock*, was advertised 6 October 1827 in the *Morning Chronicle* to begin 31 October and eventually to comprise 'about 48 numbers at 6d, 12 parts at 2s.' The editor (*recte* Joseph Clinton Robertson) was the principal editor of the 'Percy Anecdotes', one of which had been dedicated to Scott (*see* 524T), and the engraver engaged for this first number (including a frontispiece, title, and two text plates) was W. Read. In this number pages *1* 2-98 present the abridgement of *Waverley*, *99* 100-118 informative notes provided by the editor, *119-121* 122-168 the first part of an abridged *Guy Mannering,* this part ending in mid-sentence. Probably Scott's publishers intervened to stop this daring enterprise, realizing that an unauthorized series containing texts much *reduced* eventually might greatly impair the sale of of a considerably *augmented* series: one eventually realized in the *Magnum Opus* of 1829-1833. Copy: (Number 1) L.

336D] LONDON: Lee 1830

[An unnamed series of six numbers of engraved sheet music ca. 1830 based on the novels]. London, Leoni Lee Music Seller to his Majesty, 17, Old Bond Street. Notes: 'Each No. is embellished with Pictorial Illustrations from the Novels—& is complete in itself.' Each has 12 lithographed pictures as a frame on the title-page wrapper. Music is a divertimento for the pianoforte arranged, for each title, upon appropriate & characteristic Scottish & other melodies by Neville Butler Challoner. Copy: E(number 1: title page hand-coloured).

337D] LONDON: Leigh 1828-1832

The Harmonicon, A Journal of Music. . . London, Printed for the Proprietors, Published by Samuel Leigh, No. 18, Strand. Notes: Journal which includes both letter press [I] and engraved sheet music [II] in each monthly issue. Scott appears regularly in the engraved sheet music from February 1828 to October 1832. The music for Scott's words in each case is arranged for voice and pianoforte. Scott's songs are now assigned consecutive numbers. IMPRINT 1: London: Published for the Proprietors, by Samuel Leigh, 18, Strand. 1828-1830.

2: London: Printed for Longman, Rees, Orme, Brown, and Green, Paternoster-Row. 1831.

3: London: Printed for Longman, Rees, Orme, Brown, Green, and Longman, Paternoster-Row. 1832.

1] Scottish Air, "Jock O' Hazeldean." . . . The Poetry by Sir Walter Scott. [imprint 1]

February 1828. Notes: (first words: 'Why weep ye by the tide, ladie?), pages 12-13. The heading attributes this poem to Thomson's "A Select Collection of Scottish Songs", volume 5; however, the first printing was in Albyn's Anthology 1816. The symphonies and accompaniments were composed by Hummel. This music was issued separately as well. Copies: E L(2); CtY. Reference: G/T 10057.

2] Song, "When Friends are Met," from the "Doom of Devorgoil," by Sir Walter Scott. [imprint 1] December 1830. Notes: (first words: 'When friends are met o'er merry cheer, And laughing eyes are laughing near,' in act 2, scene 1), pages 501-503. Music composed by Finlay Dun. Copies: L(2).

3] Annot Lyle's Song, From Musical Illustrations of the Waverley Novels, [imprint 2] July 1831. Notes: (first words: 'Wert thou like me, in life's low vale,' from 'A Legend of Montrose', chapter 2), pages 136-137. Music composed by Miss Eliza Flower. Copies: E L(2); CtY.

4] War-Song, "To Horse! to Horse!—the Standard Flies." . . . The Words by Sir Walter Scott. [imprint 2] August 1831. Notes: (first words as title), pages 154-155. Music composed by Miss Smith. Copies: E L(2); CtY.

5] Song, "Farewell to Northmaven," . . . [imprint 2] September 1831. The Poetry by Sir Walter Scott, From The Pirate. Notes: (first words: 'Farewell to Northmaven, Grey Hillswicke, farewell!' from The Pirate, chapter 12), pages 168-169. Music composed by George Hogarth. Copies: E L(2); CtY. References: G/T 10638.

6] Song, "Yes, thou may'st sigh." Sung by Louise, in Sir Walter Scott's Novel, The Fair Maid of Perth. [imprint 3] February 1832. Notes: (first words as title from The Chronicles of the Canongate. Second Series, chapter 30), pages 34-35. Music composed and presented to The Harmonicon by John Thomson. Copies: E L(2); CtY.

7] "Ave Maria!" Words by Sir Walter Scott: . . . [imprint 3] March 1832. Notes: (first words: 'Ave Maria! Maiden mild! Listen to a maiden's prayer:' from The Lady of the Lake, canto 3, stanza 29), pages 54-55. Music composed by Fanny Mendelsohn-Bartholdy. Copies: E L(2); CtY.

8] Song, "Constancy!" The Poetry by Sir Walter Scott, Bart. [imprint 3] June 1832. Notes: (first words: 'When the tempest's at the loudest, On its gale the eagle rides;' from The Doom of Devorgoil, act I, scene 2), pages 94-96. Music composed and presented to The Harmonicon by George Hogarth. Copies: E L(2); CtY.

9] Serenade, . .—The Words by Sir Walter Scott, Bart., from his Novel, The Pirate. [imprint 3] October 1832. Notes: (first words: 'Love wakes and weeps, While beauty sleeps!', from The Pirate, chapter 23), pages 196-197. Music composed by Mrs. P. [Virtue] Millard. Copies: E L(2); CtY. References: G/T 10651.

338D] LONDON: Longman, Hurst, Rees, [and others] 1823-1824

Illustrations, Historical, Biographical, and Miscellaneous, of the Novels by the Author of Waverley; . . . London: Longman, Hurst Rees, Orme, and Browne, Pater-Noster-Row. 1823-[1824]. Notes: Three volumes. Pages 1 (1823): *1-3* 4-349 *350-352*; 2 (1824): *i-iv, 1* 2-461; 3 (1824) *i-ii, 1* 2-410 *411-412*. Notes: Prose text. The author, Richard Warner, intent upon presenting the *actual realities* of the works by this unknown author, early calculates (volume 1, page 8) that the public has paid £396,500 for the volumes published thus far, through *Peveril of the Peak*. Copy: L.

LONDON: Longman, Rees, Orme, Brown, and Green

[~] The Harmonicon 1831. *see* 337D.

339D] LONDON: Novello 1831
[Musical Illustrations of the Waverley Novels, London: Novello, 1831.] Notes: Engraved sheet-music for voice and chorus and pianoforte arranged by Eliza Flower for voice and pianoforte. An original set, as described below, has not been located.
1] 'Hail to thee, thou holy herb' (first words as title, from *Waverley*, chapter 24). Reference: G/T 10916.
2] 'Rose Bradwardine's Song—or St. Swithin's Chair' [St Swithin's Chair] (first words: 'On Hallow-Mass Eve,' from *Waverley*, chapter 13). Reference: G/T 10916.
3] 'Lucy Ashton's Song' (first words: 'Look not thou on beauty's charming', from *The Bride of Lammermoor,* chapter 3). Reference: G/T 9767.
4] 'Norman the Forester's Song' (first words: 'The monk must arise when the matins ring', from *The Bride of Lammermoor*, chapter 3). Reference: G/T 9767.
5] 'Meg Merrilies' Chant' (first words: 'Wasted, weary, wherefore stay', from *Guy Mannering*, chapter 27). Reference: G/T 9830.
6] 'Death to Madge Wildfire' (first words: 'Our work is over—over now', from *The Heart of Mid-Lothian*, chapter 38). Reference: G/T 9861.
7] 'Then in my gown of sober grey' (first words as title, from *The Monastery*, the motto heading chapter 32 by 'The Cruel Lady of the Mountains'). Reference: G/T 10538.
8] 'Farewell to Northmaven'['Mary.'] (first words as title, from *The Pirate,* chapter 12). Reference: G/T 10629.
9] 'Love wakes and weeps' (first words as title, from *The Pirate*, chapter 23). Reference: G/T 10629.
10] 'Louis Kerneguy's Song' (first words: 'An hour with thee!—When earliest day', from *Woodstock*, chapter 26). Reference: G/T 10944.
11] 'A health to King Charles' (first words: 'Bring the bowl which you boast' from *Woodstock*, chapter 20). Reference: G/T 10944.

340D] LONDON: The Proprietors
[~] The Harmonicon. Printed for The Proprietors, published by Thomas Leigh. 1818-1830. *see* 337D.

The New English Drama, with Prefatory Remarks, Biographical Sketches, and Notes, Critical and Explanatory. 1818-1825. Notes: Twenty volumes, with Scott derivatives appearing in the three volumes listed below. Notes: All volumes edited by William Oxberry as performed at the Theatres Royal. At the head of each title: 'Oxberry's Edition.' The numbers preceding title are assigned, with 'A' and 'B' entered to differentiate editions of the same play. Figures in brackets prior to the copy record represent the volume number and then the play number in each volume.
IMPRINT 1: Published 1820, by Simpkin & Marshall, Stationers Ct. & Chapple Pall Mall.
2: London. Published for the Proprietors, by W. Simpkin, and R. Marshall, Stationers' Court, Ludgate-Street; and C. Chapple, 66, Pall-Mall 1820.
3: London. Published for the Proprietors by W. Simpkin and R. Marshall, Stationers' Court, Ludgate-Street; C. Chapple, 66, Pall-Mall; and Sold by W. and J. Lowndes, 9, Brydges-Street, Covent-Garden.
4: London. Published for the Proprietors, by W. Simpkin, and R. Marshall, Stationers' Court, Ludgate Street; and C. Chapple, 59, Pall-Mall. 1820-1824
5: London, Published for the Proprietors, by W. Simpkin and R. Marshall, Stationers' Hall

Court, Ludgate Street; and C. Chapple, Royal Library, 59, Pall-Mall. 1826.

1A] Rob Roy Macgregor; or, Auld Lang Syne. An Opera. [imprint 1] 1820. Pages: *1-2*, *i* ii-iii *iv-vi*, *1* 2-69. Notes: Words by Isaac Pocock (music by John Davy not included). First performed at Covent Garden 12 March 1818. [10, 5]. Copies: PBL TxU. References: Bolton 1450; Ford T3. Reissued [imprint 4] 1820 TxU; [1821] (E, NN).
1B] Rob Roy Macgregor; or, Auld Lang Syne. An Opera; [imprint 4] 1822. Pages: *i-iii* iv-v *vi-ix* 10-77. [10, 5]. Copy: MH.
1C] Rob Roy Macgregor; or, Auld Lang Syne An Opera: . . . [imprint 5] 1826. Pages: *1-7* 8-72. Notes: Second page of 'Remarks' misnumbered page *ii*. Copy: CtY.

2A] Guy Mannering; or, The Gipsey's Prophecy! A Musical Play. . . [imprint 2] [1820]. Pages: *1-2*, *i*-ii *iii-iv*, *1* 2-63 *64*. Notes: Words by Daniel Terry (music composed by Henry R. Bishop not included) with engraved frontispiece portrait. 'Persons Represented' given for '1820' in Covent-Garden [17 September 1819] and in Drury-Lane [7 October 1819]. There is no reference to Scott on the title-page, but an oblique allusion occurs in the preliminary remarks, when referring to Mr. Terry: 'Guy Mannering is selected and arranged from the novel with the hand of a master.' [12]. Copies: E L O. Reissued 'Second Edition' 1820; 'Third Edition' 1820; 'Fourth Edition' 1820; 'Fifth Edition' 1820. References: Bolton 461-462; Ford H1.
2B] Guy Mannering; or, The Gipsey's Prophecy! A Musical Play. . . . [imprint 4] 1821. Pages: *1-2*, *i*-ii, *5-7* 8-69 *70-72*. Notes: Words by Daniel Terry (music composed by Henry R. Bishop not included) as it was performed at the Theatres Royal. Copies: DN TxU. Reissued 1824 (PBL PU).

3] Kenilworth. A Melo-Drama. [imprint 4] 1824. Pages: *i-iii* iv *v-vi*, *1* 2-61. Notes: Drama as performed at the Theatres Royal. The preliminary remarks by Oxberry state that the drama 'is a compilation from the novel,—from a play of the same name printed at Edinburgh [by Huie, *see* 323D.3]—and from another acted and published in London'. Frontispiece portrait of 'Mrs. Bunn as Queen Elizabeth: engraved by T. Kinnersley. . .' Performed at Drury Lane, 5 January 1824. [19, 5]. Copies: DN L; CtY DLC MB PBL TxU. References: Bolton 3832; Ford L12.

341D] LONDON: Sharpe 1812

[wrapper title] Illustrations to Glenfinlas,. And Other Ballads, &c. With the Vision of Don Roderick; . . . . From the Designs of R. Westall, Esq. R.A. London, Published by John Sharpe, Piccadilly. [1812]. Notes:With engraved vignette title beginning 'Glenfinlas' and six plates: four for *Ballads and Lyrical Pieces* dated 4 May 1812; two for *The Vision of Don Roderick* dated 4 June 1812 and 4 May 1812. The 'Glenfinlas' title, taken from the first poem in the *Ballads*, now covers usually late reprints of the two works identified (that is, in 24Aa, Ac, Ae-Ai, and 59Af-Ai and possibly in other issues). Separate issues of these *Illustrations* were advertised in the *Morning Chronicle* 25 June as [1] in 4° at £1.11.6 (not seen by Ruff) and [2] in 8° at 15s. Not advertised, but represented by one copy, with the wrapper title, is [3] a larger Colombier 4°, with plates on India paper, price £1.15.0. Separate copies: [1] O. [2] MH. [3] T/B. Reference: Ruff 118.

The plates deriving from the Westall designs were engraved by the following artists:
Title: W.B. Cooke, with two lines from 'Vision of Don Roderick', stanza 33
1] Richd Golding, with caption 'Glenfinlas.' and two lines from page 12.

2] Anker Smith, caption 'Cadyow Castle.' and two lines from page 50.
3] F. Engleheart, caption 'Thomas the Rhymer.' and two lines from page 130.
4] F. Engleheart, caption 'Helvellyn.' and two lines from page 180.
5] Saml. Noble, caption 'Vision of Don Roderick.' and one line from stanza 8, page 32.
6] A. Raimbach with caption as for 5 and two lines from stanza 21, page 42.

LONDON: Simpkin & Marshall
[~] The New English Drama. Oxberry's Edition. 1820-1824. *See* 340D.

342D] LONDON: Tilt 1830-1833
[1] [*wrapper title*] Landscape Illustrations of the Waverley Novels. From Drawings by [12 to 16 names]. Engraved by William and Edward Finden. London: Charles Tilt, Fleet Street; John Andrews, New Bond Street; Thomas Ireland, Jun., Edinburgh; Wardle, Philadelphia; Rittner & Co. Paris, MDCCCXXX [MDCCCXXXI]. Ibotson and Palmer, Printers,] [Savoy Street, Strand. Notes: The original issue of these plates, ordered generally as dated, from April 1830 to December 1831, four plates to a part in twenty parts. The part and order within is specified (in parentheses) in the list subtended to the 1832 volume description given below. Though the wrapper heading reads throughout 'Dedicated, By Permission, to The King', no dedication appears here or later. The 4-plate parts originally were priced at 4s, India proofs royal 4° 7s, Proofs before letters Imperial 4° (50 only) 10s. Copy: O(Dunston).

[2] Landscape Illustrations of the Waverley Novels, with Descriptions of the Views. London: Charles Tilt, Fleet Street. MCCCXXXII. Notes: Two volume issue of the parts described above. Pages 1: *i-vii* + 38 unnumbered plates; 2: *i-v* + 42 unnumbered plates. Two volumes, 1 'Waverley to Legend of Montrose', 2 'Ivanhoe to Woodstock'. Notes: The unsigned 'Advertisement' is dated from London 16 December 1831. Original issue of the plates with Tilt imprints, dated 1830-1832, those in volume 1 with facing letterpress descriptions paged 1-38, those in 2 with letterpress paged 39-80. The list of plates designates location in the 'New Edition' only through Vol 31 [1831], the last issued at the time the volumes were being prepared. Copies: E L; IdU NNU-W.

Illustrations: Altogether, for this extensive enterprise, 24 artists were engaged and four engravers (a number exceeded only by those concurrently engaged for Scott's 'Magnum Opus', 348Aa). The following record cites in order: plate number (assigned from facing descriptive text-page); artist/engraver; caption; book title; date of Tilt publisher imprint; (original part number and date in later Chapman and Hall issue [*see* 327D]):
VOLUME 1: 1] D. Roberts/E. Finden; 'Room at Abbotsford'; Waverley; December 1831. (original part number XX. plate 1; later Chapman and Hall issue, July 1832).
2] G. Barret/E. Finden; 'Mirkwood Mere'; Waverley; June 1830. (III.4).
3] J.D. Harding/E.F. Finden; 'Doune Castle'; Waverley; April 1830. (I.2).
4] G.F. Robson/E. Finden; 'Stirling Castle'; Waverley; April 1831. (XII.2; July 1832).
5] G.F. Robson/E. Finden; 'Linlithgow'; Waverley; February 1831. (X.2; July 1832)
6] G. Cattermole[1]/E. Finden; 'White Horse Inn'; Waverley; June 1831. (XIV.3; July 1832).
7] P. Dewint/E. Finden; 'Penrith'; Waverley; April 1830. (I.3).
8] D. Roberts/E. Finden; 'Caerlaverock Castle'; Guy Mannering; August 1830 [spelled 'Carlaverock' in text]. (IV.3).
9] W. Westall/E. Finden; 'Windermere'; Guy Mannering; April 1830. (I.4).
10] P. Dewint/E. Finden; 'Distant view of Skiddaw'; Guy Mannering; June 1830. (II.1)

11] Copley Fielding/Edward Finden; 'Waste of Cumberland'; Guy Mannering; 1 May 1830. (II.4).

12] C. Stanfield/E. Finden; 'Frith of Forth'; Guy Mannering; October 1831. (XVIII.4; July 1831).

13] Copley Fielding/Edwd Finden; 'Solway Firth from Allonby'; Guy Mannering; June 1830. (III.1).

14] C. Stanfield/E. Finden; 'North Queen's Ferry'; Antiquary, October 1830. (VI.1).

15] H. Purser/E. Finden; 'Home Castle'; Antiquary, May 1831 [spelled 'Hume' in text]. (XIII.2; August 1832).

16] G. Barret/E. Finden; 'London from Highgate; Rob Roy; July 1830. (IV.4).

17] W. Westall/E. Finden; 'Glasgow Cathedral'; Rob Roy; June 1830. (III.3).

18] G.F. Robson/E. Finden; 'Inch Cailleach'; Rob Roy; February 1831. (X.4; September 1832).

19] G.F. Robson/E.F. Finden; 'Loch Ard'; Rob Roy; May 1830. (II.3).

20] G.F. Robson/E.F. Finden; 'Ben Lomond'; Rob Roy; August 1831. (XVII.4; September 1832).

21] Copley Fielding[1]/E.F. Finden; 'Manor Glen'; Black Dwarf; April 1831. (XII.4; September 1832).

22] W. Daniell/E.F. Finden; 'Dunottar Castle'; Old Mortality; May 1830 [spelled 'Dunnottar' in text]. (II.2).

23] D. Roberts/W. Finden; 'Bothwell Bridge'; Old Mortality; March 1831. (XI.2).

24] R.R. Reinagle/E. Finden; 'Bothwell Castle'; Old Mortality; September 1830. V.3).

25] A. Nasmyth/E. Finden; 'Tolbooth'; Heart of Mid-Lothian; 1 August 1830. (IV.2).

26] G. Barret/E. Finden; 'St. Anthony's Chapel'; Heart of Mid-Lothian; November 1830. (VII.2).

27] G.F. Robson/E.F. Finden; 'Durham'; Heart of Mid-Lothian; August 1830. (IV.1).

28] P. De Wint/E. Finden; 'Newark Castle'; Heart of Mid-Lothian; June 1830. (III.2).

29] D. Roberts/E. Finden; 'Dunbarton Castle'; Heart of Mid-Lothian; December 1830. (VIII.1).

30] J.D. Harding[1]/E. Finden; 'Holy Loch'; Heart of Mid-Lothian; 1 September 1830. (V.2).

31] Wm. Daniell/Wm. Finden; 'Arran'; Heart of Mid-Lothian; April 1830. (I.1).

32] S. Prout[1]/E. Finden; 'Goldingham'; Bride of Lammermoor; September 1831 [spelled 'Coldingham' in text]. (XVIII.2; October 1832).

33] Copley Fielding/E. Finden; 'Fast Castle'; Bride of Lammermoor; March 1831. (XI.1; November 1832).

34] Copley Fielding[1]/E. Finden; 'Links of Eymouth'; Bride of Lammermoor; May 1831 [spelled 'Eyemouth' in text]. (XIII.1; November 1832).

35] G.F. Robson/E. Finden; 'Dunstafnage'; Legend of Montrose; January 1831. (IX.3; November 1832).

36] W. Daniell/E.F. Finden; 'Pier at Inverary'; Legend of Montrose; December 1830. (VIII.3).

37] J.B. Fraser/E. Finden; 'Loch Awe and Ben Cruachan'; Legend of Montrose; November 1830. (VII.3).

38] G.F. Robson/E.F. Finden; 'Inverlochy Castle'; Legend of Montrose; December 1830. (VIII.2).

342D] LONDON: Tilt. Landscape Illlustrations *continued*

VOLUME 2: 39] P. De Wint/E. Finden; 'Wharncliffe'; Ivanhoe; April 1831. (XII.3; November 1832).
40] G. Cattermole/E. Finden; 'Castle of Ashby'; Ivanhoe; June 1831. (XIV.1; November 1832).
41] P. De Wint/E. Finden; 'Jorvaulx Abbey'; Ivanhoe; January 1831. (IX.4).
42] P. De Wint/E. Finden; 'Conisborough Castle'; Ivanhoe; December 1831 [spelled 'Coningsburgh' in text]. (VIII.4).
43] F. Nash/E. Finden; 'York Minster'; Ivanhoe; March 1831. (XI.3; December 1832).
44] W. Westall[1]/E. Finden; 'Old Bridge of Tweed'; Monastery; June 1831. (XIV.2; December 1832).
45] D. Roberts/W. Finden; 'Cross of Melrose'; Monastery; August 1831. (XVI.1; December 1832).
46] S. Prout/E. Finden; 'St. Mary's'; Abbot; September 1830. (V.1).
47] C. Stanfield/W. Finden; 'Edinburgh Castle'; Abbot; November 1830. (VII.1).
48] T. Stothard/W. Redclyffe; 'High Street Edinburgh'; Abbot; August 1831. (XVI.2; December 1832).
49] H. Gastineau/E. Finden; 'Loch Leven'; Abbot; February 1831. (X.3; January 1833).
50] D. Roberts/E. Finden; 'Niddrie Castle'; Abbot; December 1831. (XX.4; January 1833).
51] D. Roberts/E. Finden; 'Castle of Crookstone'; Abbot; July 1831. (XV.3; January 1833).
52] Copley Fielding/Edwd. Finden; 'Frith of Cumberland and Galloway'; Abbot; July 1831. (XV.1; January 1833).
53] J. Constable/E. Finden; 'Warwick from the Kenilworth Road'; Kenilworth; May 1831. (XIII.4; July 1833).
54] George Barret/E. Finden; 'Warwick Castle'; Kenilworth; May 1831. (XIII.3; January 1833).
55] P. De Wint/E. Finden; 'Kenilworth Castle'; Kenilworth; January 1831. (IX.2).
56] C. Fielding[2]/Edw. Finden; 'The Hill of Hoy'; Pirate; October 1830. (VII.4).
57] W. Daniell/E. Finden; 'Kirkwall, Orkney'; Pirate; January 1831. (IX.1; February 1833).
58] C. Fielding[2]/Edw. Finden; 'Stromness'; Pirate; October 1830. (VI.3).
59] W. Purser[2]/E. Finden; 'St. Magnus'; Pirate; October 1830. (VI.2).
60] D. Roberts[1]/E. Finden; 'St. Cuthberts'; Fortunes of Nigel; November 1831. (XIX.4; February 1833).
61] D. Roberts[3]/E. Finden; 'Whitehall'; Fortunes of Nigel; February 1831. (XIV.4; March 1833).
62] D. Roberts/E. Finden; 'Heriots Hospital'; Fortunes of Nigel; December 1831. (XX.3; March 1833).
63] H. Gastineau/Edwd. Finden; 'Castle Rushin'; Peveril of the Peak; March 1831. (XI.4; March 1833).
64] H. Gastineau/E. Finden; 'Peel Castle'; Peveril of the Peak; September 1830. (V.4; March 1833).
65] S. Austin/E. Finden; 'Liverpool 1664'; Peveril of the Peak; October 1831. (XIX.1; March 1833).
66] D. Roberts/E. Finden; 'The Tower 1670'; Peveril of the Peak; February 1831. (X.1; March 1833).
67] S. Prout/E. Finden; 'Tours'; Quentin Durward; August 1831. (XVII.2; April 1833).
68] S. Prout/W. Finden; 'Namur'; Quentin Durward; October 1830. (VI.4).

69] S. Prout/E. Finden; 'Liege'; Quentin Durward; July 1831. (XV.4; April 1833).
70] W. Brockedon/E. Finden; 'Peronne'; Quentin Durward; December 1831. (XX.2).
71] W. Westall[1]/E. Finden; 'Nidpath Castle'; St. Ronan's Well; August 1831. (XVI.4; July 1833).
72] A. Chisholm/E. Finden; 'Dumfries from the south'; Redgauntlet; October 1831. (XIX.3; July 1833).
73] Copley Fielding/E. Finden; 'Solway Sands'; Redgauntlet; April 1831. (XII.1; May 1833).
74] G. Cattermole[1]/E. Finden; 'Craigevar Castle'; Redgauntlet; October 1831. (XVIII.1; May 1833).
75] D. Roberts[1]/E. Finden; 'Lagg Castle'; Redgauntlet; August 1831. (XVI.3; August 1833).
76] G. Barret/Finden; 'Solway Frith'; Redgauntlet; October 1831. (XVIII.3; August 1833).
77] C. Fielding[4]/E. Finden; 'Powis Castle'; Tales of the Crusaders; September 1831. (XVII.1; August 1833).
78] W. Westall/E. Finden; 'Woodstock from Blenheim'; Woodstock; November 1831. (XIX.2; August 1833).
79] W. Westall[5]/E. Finden; 'Woodstock'; Woodstock; August 1831. (XVII.3; September 1833).
80] W. Evans/E. Finden; 'Round Tower Windsor, 1660'; Woodstock; July 1831. (XV.2; September 1833).

1. 'From a Sketch by J. Skene'. 2. 'From a Sketch by the Marchioness of Stafford'. 3. 'From a Sketch by Hollar'. 4. 'From a Sketch by Lady Lucy Clive'. 5. 'From a Drawing in the collection of George III'.

In 1833, beyond the range of this bibliography, Tilt issued as 'Vol. III' a further series of plates under the general title 'Portraits of the Principal Female Characters . . . to which are added, Landscape Illustrations' (copy T/B), this including 36 portraits bearing 1832-1833 imprints of Chapman & Hall, four supplemental landscapes for works issued after *Woodstock* (the last novel portrayed in the previous volume) and, in the preliminaries, a facsimile of the Scott letter to Tilt postmarked 14 May 1830 (*see* 256A).

344D] LONDON: Willis 1828

Waverly[!] Melodies. No. 1, . . . Being the first of a Series which will comprise the greater part of the Songs of the Waverly[!] Novels, . . . London, Published by I. Willis & Co. Egyptian Hall, Piccadilly, and 7, Westmorland Street, Dublin. [1828]. Notes: Engraved sheet music with plate number '501' and pages: *i-ii*, *1* 2-9. Music composed anonymously by Eliza Flower arranged for voice and pianoforte. 'Inscribed by Permission to Sir Walter Scott Bart.' (*see* 549T). Price: 1/-. Copy: L. Includes:
1] 'False Love', (first words: 'False love! and hast thou play'd me this, In summer among the flow'rs?', from *Waverley*, chapter 20), pages 2-3.
2] 'The Knight's To the Mountain. (Duett)', (first words: 'The Knight's to the mountain his bugle to wind; [second line the same], /The Lady's to greenwood her garland to bind', from *ibid.* chapter 9), pages 4-6.
3] 'Wasted, weary, wherefore stay?', (first words: 'Wasted, weary, wherefore stay, wrestling thus with earth and clay?', from *Guy Mannering,* chapter 27), pages 7-9.

UNITED STATES

BALTIMORE: Le Pelletier
Journal of Music. [1810]. (*see* 47Dav)

345D] BOSTON: Goodrich 1828
Beauties of the Waverley Novels. Boston: Published by Samuel G. Goodrich No. 141 Washington-Street. 1828. Pages: *1-3* 4-456. Notes: Engraved frontispiece and undated vignette title-page precede printed title. Synopsis and paraphrase of each novel: *e.g. Ivanhoe*, pages 197-235. Copies: P; ViU.

346D] PHILADELPHIA: Hall 1826-1828
Illustrations from The Spy, The Pioneers, and The Waverley Novels, With Explanatory and Critical Remarks. Philadelphia: Published at the Port Folio Office, No. 64, South Fourth-Street, by Harrison Hall. R. Wright, Printer. 1826. Notes: Eleven unnumbered engraved plates with accompanying text-pages, the first seven for the J. F. Cooper books, the remaining four for Scott. Each of the Scott plates is imprinted H. Hall. Copy: MWA. Illustrations: the following record cites in order: plate number (here supplied); artist/engraver; caption; inscription; date (as in plate imprint):
8] R. Westall/C. G. Childs; Guy Mannering; 'Julia Mannering serenaded from the lake'; 1823.
9] R. Westall/F.K. & W.T.; Guy Mannering; 'The dead body of Kennedy discovered on the beach'; 1823.
10] Stothard/C. G. Childs; The Heart of Mid Lothian; 'Trial of Effie Deans.'; 1823.
11] C. R. Leslie/C. G. Childs; The Bride of Lammermoor; 'The ominous incident at the Mermaid's Fountain'; 1824.
Reissued 1828 with C. Alexander given as printer, plates 8-10 retaining 1823 dates, plate 11 omitted (DLC MWA).

347D] PHILADELPHIA: Poole 1826
Lopez and Wemyss' Edition. The Acting American Theatre. Containing the most Popular Plays, as they are performed at the Philadelphia Theatre; . . . [1826]. Notes: Issued in brown wrappers with an engraved frontispiece portrait and a general title preceding the title specific title-page for each number. At head of title for general title and specific title: 'Lopez and Wemyss' Edition. The Acting American Theatre.' The series number appears only on the wrapper. Only one Scott play is represented:
5] Marmion; or, The Battle of Flodden Field. A Drama in Five Acts. Philadelphia: Published by A. R. Poole, and Ash and Mason: P. Thompson, Washington: H. W. Bool, Baltimore: E. M. Murden, New York, for the Proprietors, and to be had of all the Principal Booksellers in the United States. [1826]. Pages: *1-7* 8-62. Notes: Drama by James N. Barker as performed in Philadelphia in 1826. Wrapper dated 1826. Price to non-subscribers: Fifty Cents. Copies: CtY DLC InU MWA NN. Reference: None in Bolton, but note his citations of earlier date in entries 14, 16.

SEVEN
MAGNUM OPUS

1. WAVERLEY NOVELS (348A)

The complex history of Scott's final literary endeavour has already been greatly elucidated: first in Jane Millgate's *Scott's Last Edition*, an admirable study tracing the evolution of the text from early contemplation to eventual presswork; then in *Scott's Interleaved Waverley Novels*, an elaborate, illustrated account by Iain Gordon Brown and others of the author's procedure in revising his copytexts for this extensive 48-volume series; and most recently, since 1993, in the 'Essays on the Text' and collations provided by the editors of the ongoing *EEWN* project. Accordingly the present record may be regarded as bibliographical addenda, with a few particulars already advanced for the Prospectus to this 1829-1833 edition (225A), and other accounts given below both for this novel sequence (348A) and for two subsequent series 1833-1836 (349A-350A) which may be encompassed in the term 'Magnum Opus'.

Still deserving of preliminary comment for the *Waverley Novels* is the author's concern over the pictorial enhancement of his work, a matter little regarded in his earlier years, but of increasing interest in later time. Apparently the first solicitation was of Abraham Cooper, R.A., who had earlier illustrated his 'Death of Keeldar' (216Aa), and now, on 4 July 1828, was asked to consider providing some further 'decorations' for Cadell's 'extensive literary undertaking' (*Letters*, x.457). In the next several months Scott's correspondence is replete with suggestions for Cadell, appeals to several other artists and, at last, an admission that, whatever its textual merit, the work must be made 'superior by illustrations & embellishments as a faded beauty dresses and lays on [a] prudent touch of rouge to compensate for want of her juvenile graces' (xi.7). Apart from any aesthetic consideration, the new graphic displays also had an appreciable pecuniary value, as the publisher later reported: 'Without plates 5000 less of the Waverley Novels would have sold at a difference on the whole work of £13,000 clear' (xi.493,n.2).

Thus, not unexpectedly, near the conclusion of the 'General Preface' to these novels (i.xxxix), Scott expressed his appreciation to Cooper and, at this early date, five other 'artists of distinction'. Eventually, when all was done, some 73 persons had been engaged for the ninety-six illustrations, including 35 artists and 38 engravers, with (again) 38 of these individuals appearing for the first time in our bibliographical record. As our index discloses, those most frequently employed, among the artists, were Cooper (7 entries), Alexander Fraser (8), Edwin Landseer (7) and, among the engravers, Charles Fox (6), Joseph Goodyear (7), Robert Graves (11), James Mitchell (6), Charles Rolls (6), and Samuel Sangster (6). Those least involved, with one entry each, include Scott's old associates William Allan (vol. 42), Charles Heath (vol. 20), and W. H. Lizars (vol. 1), along with some twenty-four individuals perhaps commisioned for a single work with which they were especially familiar, and maybe half-a-dozen youngsters apprenticed to relatives of the same surname (*see* index entries for Duncan, Engleheart, Fraser, Rolls, Stephanoff). Whether known or unknown in the present records of their profession, all of these artisans contributed in some variable measure to a production which, as Cadell then declared, was 'unprecedented in the Annals of Literature'.

Because of the unexpected demand, evident even before publication, and subsequent enlargements of issue to 30,000 or more copies, the *Literary Gazette* reported, first on 5 December 1829 that all of the steel-engraved plates were then being cut in duplicate so that there would be no loss in definition, and again on 16 October 1830 that a new edition was in preparation: this eventually published, the first volume, on 1 January 1831 (*see* 348Ac). Meanwhile, in these first several years, Cadell was issuing in various states two separate collections of illustrations, amounting to 159 plates altogether (348D), arranging the sale of his superfluous book stock, still partially under his own imprint, for an American issue (348Ab) and, shortly thereafter, disposing of his extra text plates only for a European issue in parts and volumes (348Ad-Ae)—truly unprecedented exploits also for an enterprising publisher.

Apart from the Cadell exploitation six other series were immediately precipitated by the original Magnum issue, two of them in Paris and Boston representing the complete range (288R, 307R), another in Leipzig selecting eleven of the novels and tales (300R), one in Paris proceeding only through the first three novels (296R), and two in the United States, at Exeter and New York (309R, 311R), producing only *Waverley.* The abortive New York venture is especially noteworthy, for some fourteen booksellers were here joined to carry on the great event—duly celebrated at the outset with a replica of the original engraved dedication—only to be overwhelmed, apparently, by a long-established Boston firm that for a decade had been continually publishing Scott's novels (305R-307R).

2. THE POETICAL WORKS (349A)

It is readily apparent that, once started on the final revisons for his Waverley Novels, Scott intended to incorporate in his 'Magnum Opus' all of his other writings, and to this end made certain arrangements, some carried out before his death in 1832, others later by J. G. Lockhart. For his poetry, as for his novels, an early task was to prepare a series of introductions, those for his own verse first appearing in an 18° edition already available (266Ab), two other essays for the *Minstrelsy* then added in another, 8° edition (267Ab), both collections, so augmented, then it seems being reissued concurrently on 21 April 1830.

Within a year thereafter the author also acceded to Cadell's decision to engage J. M. W. Turner as sole artist for the collected *Poetical Works*—this on the assurance that his name alone would increase the sale by 5000 copies—conducted Turner around to likely sites for illustration and, as before, advanced various notions as to subject and technique (*Letters*, xi.485-486, 493). Before leaving in September 1831 for his last voyage, to Malta, he also again, as on the previous occasion, entered on interleaved copies some final revisions. All these, it may be supposed, Lockhart thereafter incorporated in the collected edition, along with excerpts from the extant MSS and first edition, contemprary reviews, and his own annotations. To establish a seamless connection with the series that had gone before, both publisher and editor then deliberately timed the first volume of this collected poetry for 1 May 1833, the issue date of the last volume of the novels, and so continued with a monthly issue of the twelve volumes through 1 April 1834.

3. THE MISCELLANEOUS PROSE WORKS (350A)

On 1 May 1834, in strict adherence to their monthly schedule, publisher Cadell and editor Lockhart then issued the first of twenty-eight volumes in the third sequence of the 'Magnum Opus', and for these miscellaneous works, deriving essentially from the single revised collection of 1827 (287A), at once expressed their intent now to arrange the whole 'as nearly as possible, in chronological order, thus illustrating the course of the author's studies and exertions; and accompanied with notes, in which occasional mistakes are rectified, deficiencies filled up, and the observations of contemporray critics quoted or condensed' ('Notice', i. *iii*). It appears, then, that the editorial policy continued much as before, and continuity was further assured by the appointment of J. M. W. Turner for most of the illustrations.

When this third project was at last concluded, with a final issue on 1 August 1836, Lockhart could revel in an unparalleled accomplishment, this of 88 volumes representing, essentially, all the work of Sir Walter Scott. And yet, as noted below (350A.29-30), two supplementary volumes appeared shortly thereafter, and various reissues from the original stereotype plates ranged through 1846.

CONTENTS

348Aa] Final Revised Edition, First Impression, First Issue: 1829-1833

[*engraved title*] WAVERLEY NOVELS. | VOL. I [II-XLVIII]. | [*dash*] | [*novel title*]. | [*vignette*] | [*quotation*] | PRINTED FOR CADELL & COMPANY, EDINBURGH, | AND SIMPKIN AND MARSHALL, LONDON. | 1829 [1830-1833].

Published concurrently in Edinburgh and London at 5s a volume, the first two volumes, comprising *Waverley*, 1 June 1829, each volume thereafter at monthly intervals, beginning 1 August—the whole originally projected as 40 volumes, but finally extending to 48 volumes, the last issued on schedule 1 May 1833. On the proleptic dates applied to Scott's new Introductions, these ordinarily corresponding to the predetermind date of the monthly issue, see among other references the notes to volumes 16, 24, 31.

Binding: Red cloth with printed labels. Paper: Royal 18° in sixes, volumes 1-13; double foolscap 16° in eights, volumes 14-48 (172 x 110mm uncut). Watermarks: *none.* Illustrations: The engraved frontispiece and vignette title for each volume is described below, and the separate issue of all 96 engravings further cited in the 'Derivative' section (348D[1]). For an edition containing all engravings in 'proof impressions' 12s extra was charged.

Typography: Throughout the original issue may be distinguished from the second British impression by the engraved title imprint dates: 1829 (volumes 1-7), 1830 (8-19), 1831 (20-32), 1832 (33-43), 1833 (44-48). In this first impression the title engraver may enter either a comma or a period after EDINBURGH. Otherwise the title imprint ordinarily reads, volumes 1-14 as described above; volumes 15-19: PRINTED FOR R. [16-17 ROBERT] CADELL & COMPANY, EDINBURGH. | AND WHITTAKER & Co. LONDON.; volume 20: PRINTED FOR R. CADELL & COMPANY, EDINBURGH, | AND WHITTAKER, TREACHER & Co. LONDON.; volumes 21-48: PRINTED FOR ROBERT CADELL, EDINBURGH. |AND WHITTAKER & Co. LONDON.

In each volume the final printer's imprint reads: EDINBURGH: | PRINTED BY BALLANTYNE & COMPANY, | PAUL'S WORK, CANONGATE. [AND COMPANY, vols. 6-48]. Before the 37th volume in some copies, as noted below, and in all copies from 37 onward, there is also a printer's imprint (1) on verso of the half-title reading: PRINTED BY BALLANTYNE AND COMPANY, PAUL'S WORK, EDINBURGH. [with variant in vol.26]. With this same volume 37, issued 1 June 1832, the books regularly contain a press figure in every other gathering: this probably indicating a shift from the half-sheet imposition of a single gathering for 'work and turn' to double half-sheets—two successive signed gatherings—'worked together' (cf. Gaskell, figure 60). Before this shift, as Dr Jane Millgate has determined (pages 35, 38), two steam presses acquired by Ballantyne had begun work, tentatively in volume 12, through the first half of text in volume 16, and regularly thereafter.

In parentheses following the collation, notice is made of Cadell's inserted catalogues still appearing in some few copies, these generally with date corresponding to issue-date of the volume in question. In certain volumes the final gathering may be imposed to accomodate these lists.

Though all sets in the first copy record below are essentially of the original 1829-1833 impression, some volumes may exhibit, over this long issue period, slight variations in the stereotype plates (as described in the separate volume notes) and even in one case (volume 25) two distinct settings throughout. Generally, both for the illustrations and for the text, the later variant appears in the first collected impression, an indication that the duplicate, reserved plate was retained in uncorrected state and thus appears only in the second impression. In a few instances, however, the variants (as observed immediately in the first note) may result from a late adjustment, later even than the dates of the second impression '1830'[1831]-1834.

An appreciable number of mixed sets are listed both for the first and second British impressions, these mostly occurring, it may be supposed, when sheets of the second printing were stacked with those of the first and indiscriminately mixed upon later binding and issue.

Copies: AN BCL E(Octavius Suard, later Andrew Lang) E(vols. 1-2) E(vols. 1-9, 11-48) O(Douce); CtY(vols.3-48) InU MH NNU-W(2) TxU. Mixed copies [2d impression volume(s) noted in brackets]: O(Dunston: vols. 3-7, 10, 18-19, 41-43, 46-48, [8-9, 15, 20-21, 31-34, 37-40]); CtY(vols. 3-24, 27, 29-48, [25, 28]), IdU(vols. 1-41, [42]), T/B(vols. 1-25, 27-48, [26]).

References: I. Brown; Millgate (4); Thomson, pages 9-10.

1] [*engraved title*] WAVERLEY NOVELS. | VOL. I. | [*dash*] | WAVERLEY. | [*vignette*] | [*three-line quotation*] . . . . 1829.

Collation: π1(=vol.48,*2K*1) a^2 a-h^6 χ1 i^4, A-2C^6 2D^4. Pagination: [*frontispiece, engraved title, dedication*], *1-2* Contents of the Waverley Novels, *i* ii-iv Advertisement, dated from Abbotsford January 1829, *i* ii-xl General Preface, dated from Abbotsford 1 January 1829, *xli* xlii-xcvi Appendix, *1* fly-title, *2 blank, xcvii* xcviii-civ Introduction, *1* fly-title, *2 blank, 3* 4-8 Preface to the Third Edition, *9* 10-320 text, chapters 1-29, 320 printer's imprint (+4-page prospectus dated 1 June 1829). Illustrations: Frontispiece drawn by F. P. Stephanoff, engraved by R. Graves, with caption 'Waverley.' and three-line quotation beginning: '"Flora introduced a few irregular strains . . ."'; published 1 June 1829 by Cadell & Co. and Simpkin & Marshall. Title vignette drawn by E. Landseer, engraved by W. Raddon, is followed by a quotation beginning: '"He then invited his guest to a morning ride . . . ."' The third plate, 'Engd. on Steel' by W. H. Lizars, represents Scott's letter to the King, dated from Abbotsford 1 January 1829, and formally dedicating this entire 'Collection of Works of Fiction' to George IV.

Typography: Preliminary signatures are in italics. Advertisement page *i* direction line in a few copies is 'Vol. i.', but generally 'vol. i.', all letters in small caps as elsewhere. (The second, 1830 impression has no direction line.) In some copies section signature A2 (page 5) is omitted. Section signature T2 (page 221) is transposed as 2T.

Notes: As observed in the collation given above for 'ideal copy', a few copies have a Contents leaf for the 48 volumes (π1), here inserted as instructed in the 48th volume. Some also exhibit a portrait of Scott by John Watson Gordon transferred arbitrarily from volume 33.

2] [*engraved title*] WAVERLEY NOVELS. | VOL. II. | [*dash*] | WAVERLEY. | [*vignette*] | [*four-line quotation*] . . . . 1829.

Collation: A-2M^{6}. Pagination: [*frontispiece, engraved title*], *1* fly-title, *2 blank, 3* 4-420 text concluded, 420 printer's imprint (+2-page undated catalogue). Illustrations: Frontispiece drawn by G. S. Newton, engraved by Charles Rolls, with caption 'Waverley.' and four-line quotation beginning: '"They found the good old careful officer, . . ."'; published 1 June 1829 by Cadell & Co. and Simpkin & Marshall. Title vignette drawn by J. Stephanoff, engraved by R. Graves, is followed by a quotation beginning: '"It makes me young again to see you here, Mr. Waverley! . . ."' Typography: Printer's imprint is below a short rule.

3] [*engraved title*] WAVERLEY NOVELS. | VOL. III. | [*dash*] | GUY MANNERING. | [*vignette*] | [*three-line quotation*] . . . . 1829.

Collation: *a*1 a-b^{6} c^{4} A-2C^{6}. Pagination: [*frontispiece, engraved title*], *1* fly-title, *2 blank, i* ii-xxxi Introduction, dated from Abbotsford January 1829, *xxxii blank, 1* fly-title, *2 blank, 3* 4-311 text, chapters 1-29, *312* printer's imprint (+14-page catalogue dated 1 August 1829). Illustrations: Frontispiece drawn by C. R. Leslie, engraved by A. Duncan, with caption 'Guy Mannering.' and two-line quotation beginning '"He grinned like an ogre, . . ."'; published 1829 by Cadell & Co. and Simpkin & Marshall. Title vignette drawn by W. Kidd, engraved by C. G. Cooke, is followed by a quotation beginning '"Jock moved on westward, ..."' Typography: The first signature is in italic. In some copies the printer's imprint is omitted.

4] [*engraved title*] WAVERLEY NOVELS. | VOL. IV. | [*dash*] | GUY MANNERING. | [*vignette*] | [*two-line quotation*] . . . . 1829.

Collation: A-2H^{6} 2I^{4}(-2I3). Pagination: [*frontispiece, engraved title*], *1* fly-title, *2 blank, 3* 4-373 text concluded, 374-378 Additional Note, 378 printer's imprint. (Variant issue 2 I^{6} (2 I5+1), the additional leaves comprising an 8-page catalogue dated 1 September 1829.) Illustrations: Frontispiece drawn by William Kidd, engraved by James Mitchell, with caption 'Guy Mannering.' and two-line quotation beginning '"A forfeit! a forfeit! . . ."'; published 1829 by Cadell & Co. and Simpkin & Marshall. Title vignette drawn by Abram Cooper, engraved by J. C. Edwards, is followed by a quotation beginning: '"'Donner and blitzen!' said Hatteraick, . . ."'

5] [*engraved title*] WAVERLEY NOVELS. | VOL. V. | [*dash*] | THE ANTIQUARY. | [*vignette*] | [*five-line quotation*] . . . . 1829.

Collation: a[6] b[4] *a*1 A-2D[6] *2E*1. Pagination: [*frontispiece, engraved title*], *i* ii-xix Advertisement, *xx blank, xxi* fly-title, *xxii blank, 1* half-title, *2 blank, 3* 4-325 text, chapters 1-21, 325 printer's imprint, *326 blank* (+18-page catalogue dated 1 October 1829). Illustrations: Frontispiece drawn by C. Stanfield, engraved by J. Phelps, with caption 'The Antiquary.' and three-line quotation beginning '"Oldbuck took him kindly by the arm, . . ."'; published 1829 by Cadell & Co. and Simpkin & Marshall. Title vignette drawn by Abram Cooper, engraved by Ambrose Warren, is followed by a quotation beginning '"The Steed alarmed by the boy's cries . . . ."' Typography: Signature *a* on the single fly-leaf is in italic.

6] [*engraved title*] WAVERLEY NOVELS. | VOL. VI. | THE ANTIQUARY. | [*vignette*] | [*four-line quotation*] . . . . 1829. | [*short Oxford rule*].

Collation: A-2E[6] 2F[2]. Pagination: [*frontispiece, engraved title*], *1* fly-title, *2 blank, 3* 4-340 text concluded, 340 printer's imprint (+16-page catalogue dated 1 November 1829). Illustrations: Frontispiece drawn by F. P. Stephanoff, engraved by J. Romney, with caption 'The Antiquary.' and four-line quotation beginning '"You will find them but samples of womankind— . . . ."', published 1829 by Cadell & Co. and Simpkin & Marshall. Title vignette drawn by E. Landseer, engraved by J. Mitchell, is followed by a quotation beginning 'She came down accordingly, . . .' Typography: Engraved title has no dash below volume reference. Section signature N2 (page 149) is omitted.

Notes: The engraved title is in two states: (1) quotation in five lines, the last a single word, no rule below date; (2) quotation is adjusted to four full lines, below date a short Oxford rule. Despite the catalogue date, a Sunday, this volume doubtless, as usual, was issued officially on Monday, 2 November: cf. note to volume 24.

7] [*engraved title*] WAVERLEY NOVELS. | VOL. VII. | [*dash*] | ROB ROY. | [*vignette*] | [*four-line quotation*] . . . . 1829.

Collation: *a-l*[6] *m*[2] A-Y[6]. Pagination: [*frontispiece, engraved title*], *i* fly-title, *ii blank, iii* iv-v Advertisement to the First Edition, dated 1 December 1817, *vi blank, vii* viii-cxviii Introduction, undated, *cxix* cxx-cxxxv Appendix, *cxxxvi blank, 1* half-title, *2 blank, 3* 4-263 text, chapters 1-17, 263 printer's imprint, *264 blank* (+8-page catalogue). Illustrations: Frontispiece drawn by W. Kidd, engraved by S. Davenport, with caption 'Rob Roy.' and five-line quotation beginning '"Ah!—Eh!—Oh!" exclaimed the Bailie, . . ."'; published 1829 by Cadell & Co. and Simpkin & Marshall.

Title vignette drawn by A. E. Chalon, engraved by H. C. Shenton, is followed by a quotation beginning 'She poured herself forth to my infant ear . . . .' Typography: Title imprint reads: 'SIMPKIN &'. Preliminary signatures are in italics. Section signatures *a*2 and O2 (pages v and 161) are omitted. A short rule precedes the printer's imprint.

Notes: The new Introduction, by far the longest of any provided for this edition, most often refers to Burt's *Letters from a Gentleman in the North of Scotland* (pages l, lxix, cxxx), a frequent reference also as early as 1810 in *The Lady of the Lake* (47Ac). Now the reference is to the 1818 Jamieson edition of Burt (127Aa) and—though unspecified by name—to Scott's second contribution therein (ii.*338* 339-370). In several copies a † appears to the right of the signature on page 73, indicating a later printing of sheet G. Scott presented *Rob Roy* in this edition (volumes 7-8) to Mary Morritt, presumably a relative of J. B.S. Morritt (Tinker 1876).

8] [*engraved title*] WAVERLEY NOVELS. | VOL. VIII. | [*dash*] | ROB ROY. | [*vignette*] | [*six-line quotation*] . . . . 1830.

Collation: A-2H^6 2 I^4 *2K*^{2}. Pagination: [*frontispiece, engraved title*], *1* fly-title, *2 blank, 3* 4-380 text concluded, 380 printer's imprint, 381-384 Postscript. (Variant issue, *2K*^{4} [2K2+1], the additional pages constituting a leaf inserted and 4-page undated catalogue.) Illustrations: Frontispiece drawn by C. R. Leslie, engraved by A. W. Warren, with caption 'Rob Roy.' and four-line quotation beginning '"I started up in amazement— . . ."'; published 1830 by Cadell & Co. and Simpkin & Marshall. Title vignette drawn by A. Cooper, engraved by W. Raddon, is followed by a quotation beginning '"I wadna hae kenn'd the creature," . . .'

Notes: The Suard set, usually received upon issue, has this volume inscribed 1 January 1830, the official date of publication.

9] [*engraved title*] WAVERLEY NOVELS. | VOL. IX. | [*dash*] | OLD MORTALITY. | [*vignette*] | [*three-line quotation*] . . . . 1830.

Collation: π1 *a-b*^{6} *c*^{4}(-*c*4) A-2H^6 2 I^2. Pagination: [*frontispiece, engraved title*], *1* dedication, *2 blank, i* fly-title for *Tales of My Landlord*. First Series, *ii* quotation, *iii* iv-xiv Introduction, *xv* fly-title for 'The Black Dwarf', *xvi blank, xvii* xviii-xxix Introduction, undated, *xxx blank, 1* 2-217 text, *218 blank, 219* fly-title for 'Old Mortality', *220 blank, 221* 222-238 Introduction, undated, *239* 240-374 text, chapters 1-8, 374 printer's imprint, *375-376* advertisement, dated 1 January 1830. Illustrations: Frontispiece drawn by D. Wilkie, engraved by R. Graves, with caption 'Old Mortality. Page 353 Vol. IX.'; published 1830 by Cadell & Co. and Simpkin & Marshall. Title vignette drawn by J. Burnet, engraved by C. Fox, is followed by a quotation beginning 'The child set down its water pitcher, . .".' Typography: The preliminary signatures are in italic. Section signature C2 (page 29) is omitted.

Notes: All but a few copies lack the preliminary dedication leaf, for the reason given in the note to volume 11. The concluding advertisement is (1) wrongly dated 1 January 1830, as described above; (2) correctly dated 1 February 1830, extends to three leaves paged *1* 2-6, and occupies a gathering now imposed as 2 I^4.

10] [*engraved title*] WAVERLEY NOVELS. | VOL. X. | [*dash*] | OLD MORTALITY. | [*vignette*] | [*four-line quotation*] . . . . 1830.

Collation: A-2L^6 2M^4. Pagination: [*frontispiece, engraved title*], *1* fly-title, *2* quotation, *3* 4-416 text continued, 416 printer's imprint (+4-page catalogue dated 1 March 1830). Illustrations: Frontispiece drawn by A. Cooper, engraved by Charles Rolls, with caption 'Old Mortality. Page 129. Vol. X.'; published 1830 by Cadell & Co. and Simpkin & Marshall. Title vignette drawn by D. Wilkie, engraved by F. Engleheart, is followed by a quotation beginning '"Although I had never seen the old man before, . . ."' Typography: Section signature B2 (page 17) is omitted.

11] [*engraved title*] WAVERLEY NOVELS. | VOL. XI. | [*dash*] | HEART OF MID-LOTHIAN. | [*vignette*] | [*three-line quotation*] . . . 1830.

Collation: A-M^6 N^6(N3+1) O-2M^6. Pagination: [*frontispiece, engraved title*], *1* fly-title for 'Old Mortality', *2* quotation, *3* 4-136 text concluded, 137-138 Peroration, *139* fly-title for [*Tales of My Landlord.* Second Series]. 'The Heart of Mid-Lothian', *140 blank, 141* 142-149 Introduction, dated from Abbotsford 1 April 1830, *150 blank*, 151*-152* Postscript, *151* 152-161 prolegomenon, *162 blank, 163* 164-419 text, chapters 1-14, 419 printer's imprint, *420 blank* (+2-page undated advertisement). Illustrations: Frontispiece drawn by J. Burnet, engraved by W. H. Watt, with caption 'Heart of Mid-Lothian.' and three-line quotation beginning '"He found her gazing . . ."'; published 1830 by Cadell & Co. and Simpkin & Marshall. Title vignette drawn by Alexr Fraser, engraved by Wm. Finden, followed by a quotation beginning '"There's just twenty-five guineas . . . ."' Typography: Section signature R2 (page 197) is omitted. A short rule precedes the printer's imprint.

Notes: In a few copies there is pasted to leaf A1 a dedication page with direction line 'VOL. IX.' and, before this, a slip reading: 'NOTICE TO THE BINDER. The page beginning with, "To his Loving Countrymen," which is attached to this Volume, is requested to be placed at the beginning of Vol. IX.' Accordingly, in all other copies examined, this leaf is withdrawn, but then usually discarded.

12] [*engraved title*] WAVERLEY NOVELS. | VOL. XII. | [*dash*] | HEART OF MID-LOTHIAN. | [*vignette*] | [*five-line quotation*] . . . 1830.

Collation: A-2L^6. Pagination: [*frontispiece, engraved title], 1* fly-title for *Tales of My Landlord*, Second Series, *2* quotation, *3* 4-408 text of 'The Heart of Mid-Lothian' continued, 408 printer's imprint (+6-page undated catalogue). Illustrations:

Frontispiece drawn by W. Kidd, engraved by S. Sangster, with caption 'Heart of Mid-Lothian.' followed by three-line quotation beginning '"Hark ye," he exclaimed from the window, . . ."'; published 1830 by Cadell & Co. and Simpkin & Marshall. Title vignette drawn by Jas. Stephanoff, engraved by H. Rolls, is followed by a quotation beginning '"This filled up the measure of Madge's self-approbation . . ."' Typography: In some copies signature S (page 205) is omitted.

13] [*engraved title*] WAVERLEY NOVELS. | VOL. XIII. | [*dash*] | BRIDE OF LAMMERMOOR. | [*vignette*] | [*four-line quotation*] . . . 1830.

Collation: A-2I^6 2K^4. Pagination: [*frontispiece, engraved title*], *1* fly-title for *Tales of My Landlord*, Second Series, *2* quotation, *3* 4-234 text of 'The Heart of Mid-Lothian' concluded, *235* fly-title for *Tales of My Landlord*, Third Series. 'The Bride of Lammermoor', *236 blank, 237* 238-255 Introduction, undated, *256 blank, 257* 258-392 text, chapters 1-8, 392 printer's imprint (+4-page catalogue dated 1 June 1830). Illustrations: Frontispiece drawn by F. P. Stephanoff, engraved by J. Goodyear, with caption 'Bride of Lammermoor.' and four-line quotation beginning 'She was unabled to accomplish her purpose, . . .'; published 1830 by Cadell & Co. and Simpkin & Marshall. Title vignette drawn by R. Farrier, engraved by W. Ensom, is followed by a quotation beginning '"In a small and rude garden, . . ."' Typography: The frontispiece plate is in two states, with the third word in the quotation reading (1) 'unabled', (2) corrected to 'unable', the excised 'd' leaving a further space in the line. (In the 1831 second impression, from a different plate, the first text state reappears.)

14] [*engraved title*] WAVERLEY NOVELS. | VOL. XIV. | [*dash*] | BRIDE OF LAMMERMOOR. | [*vignette*] | [*four-line quotation*] . . . . 1830.

Collation: A-Z^8 2A^2. Pagination: [*frontispiece, engraved title*], *1* fly-title *Tales of My Landlord*, Third Series, *2* quotation, *3* 4-370 text of 'The Bride of Lammermoor' concluded, 370 printer's imprint, *1*-2 advertisement dated 1 July 1830. Illustrations: Frontispiece drawn by E. Landseer, engraved by W. Finden, with caption 'Bride of Lammermoor.' and five-line quotation beginning 'Lucy lay senseless on the ground. . . .'; published 1830 by Cadell & Co. and Simpkin and Marshall. Title vignette drawn by Thos. Duncan, engraved by S. Sangster, is followed by a quotation beginning '"Am I?" said the old man, ..."' Typography: In some copies signature 2A (page 369) is omitted.

15] [*engraved title*] WAVERLEY NOVELS. | VOL. XV. | [*dash*] | A LEGEND OF MONTROSE. | [*vignette*] | [*four-line quotation*] . . . . 1830.

Collation: *a-b*^{8} *c*^{6} A-X^8 *Y*^{2}. Pagination: [*frontispiece, engraved title*], *i* fly-title for *Tales of My Landlord*, Third Series, *ii* quotation, *iii* iv-xix Introduction to 'A Legend of Montrose', xx-xxiii Appendix, *xxiv blank*, xxv-xxxi Postscript, dated from

Abbotsford 1 August 1830, *xxxii blank, xxxiii* xxxiv-xliii Introduction, *xliv blank, 1* fly-title, *2 blank, 3* 4-337 text, 337 printer's imprint, *338 blank*, 1-2 undated advertisement. Illustrations: Frontispiece drawn by R. Lauder, engraved by H. Rolls, with caption 'A Legend of Montrose. Page 127 Vol.XV.'; published 1830 by R. Cadell & Co. and Whittaker & Co. Title vignette drawn by W. Boxall, engraved by F. Bacon, is followed by a quotation beginning '"One little maiden alone, . . ."' Typography: The preliminary signatures are in italic.

Notes: Despite the date assigned to Scott's postscript, a Sunday, this volume doubtless was issued officially on Monday, 2 August: cf. note to volume 24.

16] [*engraved title*] WAVERLEY NOVELS. | VOL. XVI. | [*dash*] | IVANHOE. | [*vignette*] | [*five-line quotation*] . . . . 1830.

Collation: *a-b*^{8} *c*^{6} A-Y^{8}. Pagination: [*frontispiece, engraved title*], *i* fly-title, *ii blank, iii* iv-xxii Introduction, dated from Abbotsford 1 September 1830, *xxiii* xxiv-xliv Dedicatory Epistle, *1* fly-title, *2 blank, 3* 4-348 text, chapters 1-24, 348 printer's imprint, *1* 2-4 advertisement dated 1 September 1830. Illustrations: Frontispiece drawn by John Martin, engraved by E. Portbury, with caption 'Ivanhoe.' and five-line quotation beginning '"Here," she said, "I take my stand. . . .'; published 1830 by R. Cadell & Whittaker & Co. Title vignette drawn by J. Cawse, engraved by W. J. Taylor, is followed by a quotation beginning '"Gurth", said the Jester, "I know thou thinkest me a fool, . . ." Typography: The preliminary signatures are in italic. Chapter VII (page 99) is misnumbered VIII, and all later chapters therefore misnumbered.

Notes: About this issue a reviewer in *The Athenaeum* immediately observed (4 September, page 546): 'The humour of dating the prefatory matter *1st of September*, we profess not to understand, having seen the volume nearly a month ago'.

17] [*engraved title*] WAVERLEY NOVELS. | VOL. XVII. | [*dash*] | IVANHOE. | [*vignette*] | [*three-line quotation*] . . . . 1830.

Collation: A-2B^{8}. Pagination: [*frontispiece, engraved title*], *1* fly-title, *2 blank, 3* 4-397 text concluded, 397 printer's imprint, *398 blank, 1*-2 undated advertisement (+4-page catalogue dated 1 October 1830). Illustrations: Frontispiece drawn by W. Boxall, engraved by R. Graves, with caption 'Ivanhoe.' and five-line quotation beginning '"No, lady," answered Rebecca, . . .'; published 1830 by R. Cadell & Whittaker & Co. Title vignette drawn by S. A. Hart, engraved by S. Davenport, is followed by a quotation beginning '"Back Dog!" said the Grand Master; . . .'.

18] [*engraved title*] WAVERLEY NOVELS. | VOL. XVIII. | [*dash*] | THE MONASTERY. | [*vignette*] | [*four-line quotation*] . . . . 1830.

Collation: *a-f*^{8} *g*^{2} A-Q^{8} R^{4} *S*^{2}. Pagination: [*frontispiece, engraved title*], *i* fly-title, *ii blank, iii* iv-xxxi Introduction, dated from Abbotsford 1 November 1830, *xxxii blank, xxxiii* fly-title, *xxxiv blank, xxxv* xxxvi-lxxxiv Introductory Epistle, *lxxxv* lxxxvi-c Answer to the Introductory Epistle, *1* 2-265 text, chapters 1-17, 265 printer's imprint, *266 blank*, 1-2 undated advertisement (+12-page catalogue dated 1 November 1830, first page announcing a 'new monthly issue' 1 January 1831 of this collected edition). Illustrations: Frontispiece drawn by G. S. Newton, engraved by E. Finden, with caption 'The Monastery.' and five-line quotation beginning '"Abbot Boniface was seated in his highbacked chair. . . ."'; published 1830 by Cadell & Co. and Whittaker & Co. Title vignette drawn by A. Chisholm, engraved by T. S. Engleheart, is followed by a quotation beginning 'The exiled family then set forward. . . .' Typography: The preliminary signatures are in italic.

Notes: The early Suard set (as well as AN and another copy cited in Millgate[4], page 125, n.63) retains on title two entries immediately effaced in other copies of the original issue: Just below the vignette name Engleheart, 'Printed by Renner, Sears & Co' and the imprint, second line, 'And Simpkin and Marshall, London' (now inapplicable, superseded by Whittaker & Co. in volume 15). In a later issue fly-title verso *ii* bears a one-line printer's imprint(1).

19] [*engraved title*] WAVERLEY NOVELS. | VOL. XIX. | [*dash*] | THE MONASTERY. | [*vignette*] | [*five-line quotation*] . . . . 1830.

Collation: A-Y^8 Z^4. Pagination: [*frontispiece, engraved title*], *1* fly-title, *2 blank, 3* 4-356 text concluded, 356 printer's imprint, 1-4 undated advertisement (+12-page catalogue arranged as in volume 18, but now dated December 1830). Illustrations: Frontispiece drawn by D. Wilkie, engraved by C. Fox, with caption 'The Monastery.' and five-line quotation beginning 'Henry Warden was led in, . . .'; published 1830 by R. Cadell & Co. and Whittaker & Co. Title vignette drawn by A. Fraser, engraved by F. Engleheart, is followed by a quotation beginning '"He was courteous, however, and offered Halbert a share . . . ."'

Notes: The early, Suard uncorrected state of this volume now does not have the Renner, Sears line below the vignette, but still retains the superseded Simpkin and Marshall title imprint. In copy AN and others the line now correctly reads 'and Whittaker & Co. London.' In a later issue fly-title verso *ii* bears a one-line printer's imprint(1).

20] [*engraved title*] WAVERLEY NOVELS. | VOL. XX. | [*dash*] | THE ABBOT. | [*vignette*] | [*four-line quotation*] . . . . 1831.

Collation: *a*^{8} *b*^{4} A-Y^8. Pagination: [*frontispiece, engraved title*], *i* fly-title, *ii blank, iii* iv-xv Introduction, dated from Abbotsford 1 January 1831, *xvi blank, xvii* fly-title, *xviii blank, xix* xx-xxii Introductory Epistle, *xxiii* fly-title, *xxiv blank, 1* 2-352 text, chapters 1-20, 352 printer's imprint (+12-page catalogue arranged as in volume 18, but now dated 1 January 1831; +2-page undated advertisement). Illustrations: Frontispiece drawn by A. E. Chalon, engraved by Charles Heath, with caption 'The

Abbot.' and five-line quotation beginning '"But it is over—and I am Mary Stuart once more. . . .'; published 1831 by Robert Cadell, and Whittaker & Co. Title vignette drawn by E. Landseer, engraved by W. H. Watt, is followed by a quotation beginning 'Wolf marked the object of her anxiety, . . .'. Typography: The preliminary signatures are in italics.

Note: This is the only volume to include the name Treacher in title imprint.

21] [*engraved title*] WAVERLEY NOVELS. | VOL. XXI. | [*dash*] | THE ABBOT. | [*vignette*] | [*four-line quotation*] . . . . 1831.

Collation: A-Y^{8} Z^{4}. Pagination: [*frontispiece, engraved title*], *1* fly-title, *2 blank, 3* 4-359 text concluded, 359 printer's imprint, *360 blank* (+8-page catalogue dated 1 February 1831, preceded in some copies by a two-page slip). Illustrations: Frontispiece drawn by J. Burnett, engraved by W. Finden, with caption 'The Abbot.'; published 1831 by Robert Cadell and Whittaker & Co. Title vignette drawn by D. O. Hill, engraved by W. Miller, is followed by a quotation beginning '"They landed, and while the abbot returned thanks aloud to Heaven, . . ."'

Notes: In some copies the separately inserted catalogue is incorporated into the last gathering, which then collates Z^{8}.

22] [*engraved title*] WAVERLEY NOVELS. | VOL. XXII. | [*dash*] | KENILWORTH. | [*vignette*] | [*three-line quotation*] . . . . 1831.

Collation: *a*^{8} A-X^{8} Y^{4}. Pagination: [*frontispiece, engraved title*], *i* fly-title, *ii blank, iii* iv-xv Introduction, dated from Abbotsford 1 March 1831, *xvi blank, 1* fly-title, *2 blank, 3* 4-344 text, chapters 1-17, 344 printer's imprint (+4-page catalogue dated 1 March 1831). Illustrations: Frontispiece drawn by C. R. Leslie, engraved by J. Goodyear, with caption 'Kenilworth.' and three-line quotation beginning '"But this other fair collar, so richly wrought, . . .'; published 1831 by Robert Cadell and Whittaker & Co. Title vignette drawn by C. R. Leslie, engraved by W. H. Watt, is followed by a quotation beginning '"Is it not of an absolute fancy Janet? . . ."' Typography: The preliminary signature is in italic.

Notes: In some copies the separately inserted catalogue is incorporated into the last gathering, which then collates Y^{6}.

23] [*engraved title*] WAVERLEY NOVELS. | VOL. XXIII. | [*dash*] | KENILWORTH. | [*vignette*] | [*five-line quotation*] . . . . 1831.

Collation: A-2A^{8} 2B^{8}(-2B8). Pagination: [*frontispiece, engraved title*], *1* fly-title, *2 blank, 3* 4-397 text concluded, 397 printer's imprint, *398 blank* (+4-page advertisement dated 1 April 1831). Illustrations: Frontispiece drawn by A. Cooper, engraved by A. W. Warren, with caption 'Kenilworth.' and four-line quotation beginning 'Janet re-entered the postern door, and locked it behind her,' published

1831 by Robert Cadell, and Whittaker & Co. Title vignette drawn by A. Fraser, engraved by T. Engleheart, is followed by a quotation beginning '"I swear it," said Alasco, "that the elixir thou hast there in the flask . . .'.

Notes: A fold-out 'Ground Plan of Kenilworth Castle' is inserted, usually between pages 396 and 397.

24] [*engraved title*] WAVERLEY NOVELS. | VOL. XXIV. | [*dash*] | THE PIRATE. | [*vignette*] | [*five-line quotation*] . . . . 1831.

Collation: a^8 b^2 A-Y^8 Z^8(-Z8). Pagination: [*frontispiece, engraved title*], *i* fly-title, *ii blank*, *iii* iv-xi Introduction, dated from Abbotsford 1 May 1831, *xii blank*, *xiii* fly-title, *xiv blank*, *xv* xvi-xix Advertisement, *xx blank*, *1* 2-366 text, chapters 1-20, 366 printer's imprint (+2-page catalogue dated 2 May 1831). Illustrations: Frontispiece drawn by J. Inskipp, engraved by C. Rolls, with caption 'The Pirate.' and four-line quotation beginning '"That error shall be presently mended" said Brenda; . . .'; published 1831 by Robert Cadell and Whittaker & Co. Title vignette drawn by W. Fraser, engraved by S. Sangster, is followed by a quotation beginning '"So saying, the pedlar seized one of the man's cold hands, . . .' Typography: The preliminary signatures are in italic. In some copies page xvii is misnumbered xvi.

Notes: After neglecting twice before (in volumes 6 and 15) to signal the precise issue whenever the first monthly date falls on a Sunday, the publisher now correctly dates his catalogue on the next day, Monday the second, the official time of publication. Unfortunately, however, the date early assigned to Scott's introduction remains uncorrected.

25] [*engraved title*] WAVERLEY NOVELS. | VOL. XXV. | [*dash*] | THE PIRATE. | [*vignette*] | [*five-line quotation*] . . . . 1831.

Collation: A-Z^8 $2A^4$(-2A4). Pagination: [*frontispiece, engraved title*], *1* fly-title, *2 blank*, *3* 4-373 text concluded, 373 printer's imprint, *374 blank*. Illustrations: Frontispiece drawn by C. Stanfield, engraved by J. Mitchell, with caption 'The Pirate.' published 1831 by Robert Cadell and Whittaker & Co. Title vignette drawn by A. Cooper, engraved by Freebairn, is followed by a quotation beginning 'She could not help looking back . . . .'

Notes: The 1831 issue exists in a duplicate setting throughout (first words 18.24 brave visage] bold visage; 33.24 to] ruin; 373.11 "a] ture), with a few copies (T/B) representing a mixture. As the word 'brave' occurs in all previous editions of *The Pirate*; 'bold' (and other variants?) may well constitute a final revision in proof. Nonetheless, the 'brave' setting, though probably composed earlier, like other variants of lesser consequence (in volumes 13, 37, 38), was retained in stereotype and later used for the second, 1833 British impression (348Ac). A CtY copy of that impression is of still later issue, without Ballantyne imprint on page 373 but imprint on *374*: [*short rule*] | PRINTED BY W. H. LIZARS, EDINBURGH. Lastly it may be observed that this is the only volume issued without a Cadell catalogue.

26] [*engraved title*] WAVERLEY NOVELS. | VOL. XXVI. | [*dash*] | THE FORTUNES OF NIGEL. | [*vignette*] | [*four-line quotation*] . . . 1831.

Collation: *a-c*^{8} *d*^{4}(-*d*4) A-X^{8} Y^{8}(-Y8). Pagination: [*frontispiece, engraved title*], *i* fly-title, *ii* printer's imprint(1), *iii* iv-xvii Introduction, dated from Abbotsford 1 July 1831, *xviii blank, xix* fly-title, *xx blank, xxi* xxii-liv Introductory Epistle, *1* 2-350 text, chapters 1-17, 350 printer's imprint(2) (+2-page advertisement dated 1 July 1831). Illustrations: Frontispiece drawn by A. Cooper, engraved by C. Rolls, with caption 'The Fortunes of Nigel', and six-line quotation beginning "I cram'd the sifflication into his hand, . . ."; published 1831 by Robert Cadell, and Whittaker & Co. Title vignette drawn by W. Boxall, engraved by Augs. Fox, is followed by a quotation beginning "Jin Vin, threw himself into the great leathern chair, . . ." Typography: The preliminary signatures are in italic.

Notes: In a later 1831 issue fly-title verso *ii* bears a one-line printer's imprint(1), with 'EDINBURGH:' the last word as usual, or 'EDINBURGH.' the first word. The T/B copy is of the 1833 second impression but, unlike the variant noted in the preceding volume, still retains Ballantyne imprint (2).

27] [*engraved title*] WAVERLEY NOVELS. | VOL. XXVII. | [*dash*] | THE FORTUNES OF NIGEL. | [*vignette*] | [*four-line quotation*] . . . 1831.

Collation: A-2A^{8} 2B^{2}. Pagination: [*frontispiece, engraved title*], *1* fly-title, *2 blank, 3* 4-388 text concluded, 388 printer's imprint (+4-page catalogue dated 1 August 1831). Illustrations: Frontispiece drawn by R. Smirk [!], engraved by S. Davenport, with caption: 'The Fortunes of Nigel', and five-line quotation beginning "Metaphors are no arguments, . . ."; published 1831 by Robert Cadell, & Whittaker & Co. Title vignette drawn by J. W. Wright, engraved by S. Sangster, is followed by a quotation beginning "The goldsmith, who had complied with great accuracy . . ."

28] [*engraved title*] WAVERLEY NOVELS. | VOL. XXVIII. | [*dash*] | PEVERIL OF THE PEAK. | [*vignette*] | [*four-line quotation*] . . . . 1831.

Collation: *a-e*^{8} *f*^{4} χ1 A-R^{8}. Pagination: [*frontispiece, engraved title*], *i* fly-title, *ii blank, iii* iv-xiv Introduction, dated from Abbotsford 1 July 1831, *xv* xvi-lxi appendices, *lxii blank, lxiii* fly-title, *lxiv blank, lxv* lxvi-lxxxvii Prefatory Letter, *lxxxviii blank, i* fly-title, *ii blank, 1* 2-271 text, chapters 1-14, 271 printer's imprint, *272 blank* (+4-page catalogue dated 1 September 1831). Illustrations: Frontispiece drawn by R. P. Bonnington, engraved by W. Ensom, with caption 'Peveril of the Peak.' and six-line quotation beginning "Then, by Heaven", answered Julian, . . .; published 1831 by Robert Cadell and Whittaker & Co. Title vignette drawn by J.

Webster, engraved by F. Bacon, is followed by a quotation beginning "Yet naturally bold and high-spirited, . . ." Typography: The preliminary signatures are in italics.

Notes: The date assigned to Scott's introduction, the same as that given for volume 26, is here two months before actual date of issue, as attested by the Cadell catalogue.

In a later issue fly-title verso *ii* bears a one-line printer's imprint(1). The CtY copy again, as in volume 25, is a later issue of the 1833 second impression, now with the Ballantyne imprint on page 271 replaced by one reading: EDINBURGH: | STEVENSON & CO. PRINTERS, | THISTLE STREET.

29] [*engraved title*] WAVERLEY NOVELS. | VOL. XXIX. | [*dash*] | PEVERIL OF THE PEAK. | [*vignette*] | [*five-line quotation*] . . . . 1831.

Collation: A-X^8 Y^8(-Y8). Pagination: [*frontispiece, engraved title*], *1* fly-title, *2 blank, 3* 4-349 text continued, 349 printer's imprint, *350 blank* (+4-page catalogue dated 1 October 1831). Illustrations: Frontispiece drawn by R. P. Bonnington, engraved by W. H. Watt, with caption 'Peveril of the Peak.' and six-line quotation beginning "A slender foot and ankle, was the only part . . . ."; published 1831 by Robert Cadell, & Whittaker & Co. Title vignette drawn by A. Fraser, engraved by R. Graves, is followed by a quotation beginning 'The landlady offered Peveril a glass . . . .' Typography: A short rule is entered above the printer's imprint.

30] [*engraved title*] WAVERLEY NOVELS. | VOL. XXX. | [*dash*] | PEVERIL OF THE PEAK. | [*dash*] | [*vignette*] | [*three-line quotation*] . . . 1831.

Collation: A-Y^8. Pagination: [*frontispiece, engraved title*], *1* fly-title, *2 blank, 3* 4-352 text concluded, 352 printer's imprint (+4-page catalogue dated 1 November 1831). Illustrations: Frontispiece drawn by C. R. Leslie, engraved by J. Goodyear, with caption 'Peveril of the Peak.' and five-line quotation beginning "Peveril unclasped his arms . . . ."; published 1831 by Robert Cadell, & Whittaker & Co. Title vignette drawn by D. Wilkie, engraved by Chas. Fox, is followed by a quotation beginning "The dwarf imparted to Peveril a volume . . . ."

31] [*engraved title*] WAVERLEY NOVELS. | VOL. XXXI. | [*dash*] | QUENTIN DURWARD. | [*vignette*] | [*four-line quotation*] . . . . 1831.

Collation: *a-d*^{8} *e*^{4}(-*e*1) A-U^8 X^6. Pagination: [*frontispiece, engraved title*], *i* fly-title, *ii blank, iii* iv-xxi Introduction, dated from Abbotsford 1 December 1831, *xxii blank, xxiii* fly-title, *xxiv blank, xxv* xxvi-lxx Introduction, *1* 2-331 text, chapters 1-17, 331 printer's imprint, *332 blank* (+2-page catalogue dated 1 December 1831 and 1-page slip advertisement). Illustrations: Frontispiece drawn by R. P. Bonnington, engraved by E. Goodall, with caption 'Quentin Durward.' and four-line quotation beginning: "His opponent, seeing himself . . ."; published 1831 by

Robert Cadell & Whittaker & Co. Title vignette drawn by J. W. Wright, engraved by J. Mitchell, is followed by a quotation beginning 'The mountain chivalry of Quentin Durward . . . .' Typography: Preliminary signatures are in italic. In a later issue fly-title verso *ii* bears a one-line printer's imprint(1).

Notes: Scott left Abbotsford 23 September 1831, ten weeks before the date assigned to his Introduction, and by this later time had journeyed to Malta.

32] [*engraved title*] WAVERLEY NOVELS. | VOL. XXXII. | [*dash*] | QUENTIN DURWARD. | [*vignette*] | [*four-line quotation*] . . . . 1831.

Collation: A-2B^8 2C1. Pagination: [*frontispiece, engraved title*], *1* fly-title, *2 blank, 3* 4-402 text concluded, 402 printer's imprint (+2-page advertisement dated 1 January 1832). Illustrations: Frontispiece drawn by R. Lauder, engraved by J. Horsburgh, with caption 'Quentin Durward.' and three-line quotation beginning "Quentin hastily raised her from the ground, . . ."; published 1831 by Robert Cadell & Whittaker & Co. Title vignette drawn by E. Landseer, engraved by R. Graves, is followed by a quotation beginning "At length the speed of the pseudo herald, . . ."

Notes: Though the advertisement is dated 1 January, a Sunday, this volume doubtless was issued officially on the following day.

33] [*engraved title*] WAVERLEY NOVELS. | VOL. XXXIII. | [*dash*] | ST. RONAN'S WELL. | [*vignette*] | [*four-line quotation*] . . . . 1832.

Collation: *a*^{6} A-X^8 Y^2. Pagination: [*frontispiece, engraved title*] *i* fly-title, *ii blank, iii* iv-x Introduction, dated from Abbotsford 1 February 1832, *1* fly-title, *2 blank, 3* 4-340 text, chapters 1-19, 340 printer's imprint (+2-page advertisement dated 1 February 1832). Illustrations: Frontispiece portrait painted by John Watson Gordon in 1830, engraved by John Horsburgh, with caption 'Sir Walter Scott, Bart.', published 1832 by Robert Cadell, and Whittaker & Co. Title vignette drawn by C. R. Leslie, engraved by J. Goodyear, is followed by a quotation beginning "Mr. Winterblossom was also distinguished for possessing a few curious engravings, . . ." Typography: The preliminary signature is in italic.

Notes: As noted above, the frontispiece portrait is sometimes transferred to the first volume. Scott's dated Introduction is in two states, page x (1) with an Abbotsford reference, as indicated above, (2) the reference excised as an evident anomaly, but the assigned date still retained (cf. volume 31).

34] [*engraved title*] WAVERLEY NOVELS. | VOL. XXXIV. | [*dash*] | ST. RONAN'S WELL. | [*vignette*] | [*three-line quotation*] . . . . 1832.

Collation: A-Y^8 Z^4. Pagination: [*frontispiece, engraved title*], *1* fly-title, *2 blank, 3* 4-359 text concluded, 359 printer's imprint, *360 blank* (+2-page undated advertisement). Illustrations: Frontispiece drawn by W. Mulready, engraved by R.

Graves, with caption 'St. Ronan's Well.' and five-line quotation beginning "The minister of St. Ronan's was so intently engaged in studying the book . . . ."; published 1832 by Robert Cadell & Whittaker & Co. Title vignette drawn by J. Wood, engraved by W. Chevalier, is followed by a quotation beginning '"Slowly and with a feeble hand, . . ."

35] [*engraved title*] WAVERLEY NOVELS. | VOL. XXXV. | [*dash*] | REDGAUNTLET. | [*vignette*] | [*four-line quotation*] . . . . 1832.

Collation: a^8 b^4 A-X^8. Pagination: [*frontispiece, engraved title*], *i* fly-title, *ii blank, iii* iv-xxiii Introduction, dated 1 April 1832, *xxiv blank, 1* fly-title, *2 blank, 3* 4-336 text, letters 1-13, chapters 1-7, 336 printer's imprint (+2-page undated advertisement; + 4-page prospectus for *Tait's Edinburgh Magazine*). Illustrations: Frontispiece drawn by A. Fraser, engraved by J. Mitchell, with caption 'Redgauntlet.'; published 1832 by Robert Cadell & Whittaker & Co. Title vignette drawn by J. Inskipp, engraved by R. Graves, is followed by a quotation beginning "I was induced at last to lend the rod . . . ." Typography: Preliminary signatures are in italic.

Notes: Again Scott's Introduction is dated conformably to date of issue, but unlike previous assignments (in volumes 31, 33) a reference to Abbotsford is now prudently omitted. Nonetheless, as 1 April was a Sunday, this volume doubtless was issued officially the following day.

36] [*engraved title*] WAVERLEY NOVELS. | VOL. XXXVI. | [*dash*] | REDGAUNTLET. | [*vignette*] | [*four-line quotation*] . . . . 1832.

Collation: A-Z^8 2A^6. Pagination: [*frontispiece, engraved title*], *1* fly-title, *2 blank, 3* 4-379 text concluded, 379 printer's imprint, *380 blank* (+4-page undated catalogue). Illustrations: Frontispiece drawn by D. O. Hill, engraved by Agus. Fox, with caption 'Redgauntlet.' and four-line quotation beginning "Are ye come light-handed, ye son of a toom whistle?"; published 1832 by Robert Cadell and Whittaker & Co. Title vignette drawn by W. Kidd, engraved by J. Horsburgh, is followed by a quotation beginning "The identical Peter . . .'

37] [*engraved title*] WAVERLEY NOVELS. | VOL. XXXVII. | [*dash*] | THE BETROTHED. | [*vignette*] | [*four-line quotation*] . . . . 1832.

Collation: *a-b*^{8} c^6 A-2G^8 2H^4(-2H4). Pagination: [*frontispiece, engraved title*], *i* fly-title for *Tales of the Crusaders*. 'The Betrothed', *ii* printer's imprint(1), *iii* iv-xx Introduction, dated from Abbotsford 1 June 1832, *xxi* fly-title, *xxii blank, xxiii* xxiv-xli Introduction, *xlii blank, xliii* fly-title, *xliv blank, 1* 2-485 text, 485 printer's imprint(2), *486 blank* (+4-page undated catalogue). Illustrations: Frontispiece drawn by E. Landseer, engraved by R. Graves, with caption 'The Betrothed.'; published 1832 by Robert Cadell & Whittaker & Co. Title vignette drawn by A.

Fraser, engraved by J. Goodyear, is followed by a quotation beginning "Once more, where is Peterkin Vorst, who should have kept this post? . . . ." Typography: Preliminary signatures are in italic. Beginning with this volume two printer's imprints regularly appear, as cited in General Notes above.

Figures: X336-2, Z368-1, 2B 400-1, 2D 429-2, 2F 461(or 464)-1.

Notes: Again the Introduction is in two states, page xx (1) with Abbotsford reference and date, (2) with both reference and date excised. (The later 1834 impression, however, was printed from an uncorrected plate and thus retains both notations.) The double printer's imprints and the press figures, now first appearing, indicate from here through volume 48, signify a shift in the printing procedure, now probably involving a new 'work and turn' imposition (Gaskell, figure 60). Only two figures are entered as Ballantyne at this time had only two machine presses.

38] [*engraved title*] WAVERLEY NOVELS. | VOL. XXXVIII. | [*dash*] | THE TALISMAN. | [*vignette*] | [*three-line quotation*] . . . . 1832.

Collation: *a*[8] *b*[4](-*b*4) A-2G[8] 2H[4] *2I*[4](-*2I*1). Pagination: [*frontispiece, engraved title*], *i* fly-title for *Tales of the Crusaders*. 'The Talisman', *ii* printer's imprint(1), *iii* iv-xii Introduction, dated 1 July 1832, *xiii* xiv-xxii Appendix, *1* fly-title, *2 blank, 3* 4-494 text, 494 printer's imprint(2) (+4-page catalogue dated 2 July 1832). Illustrations: Frontispiece drawn by Watson Gordon, engraved by Charles Rolls, with caption 'The Talisman.' and four-line quotation beginning '"The Nubian slipped the leash, and the hound rushing on, . . ."'; published 1832 by Robert Cadell & Whittaker & Co. Title vignette drawn by W. Gordon, engraved by S. Sangster, is followed by a quotation beginning '"Christian and Saracen, sat down together on the turf, . . ."' Typography: In a few copies the new printer's imprint(1), reading 'AND COMPANY' as usual, was mistakenly imposed on verso of the second fly-leaf, requiring the setting of another, reading 'AND CO', for the first leaf. The second entry was then withdrawn, leaving the variant imprint(1) on the first leaf. Page number xiv is occasionally omitted.

Figures: A16-1, C48-2, E80-1, G108-2, I 144-2, L176-1, N208-1, P240-2, Q—, R—, T304-1, X336-2, Z368-1/-, 2B 400-2, 2D 432-1, 2F 464-1, 2H 494-?/-. The last figure, if present, is battered beyond recognition.

Notes: As usual, presumed date of issue 1 July 1832 is assigned as the date for the new Introduction, here without reference to Abbotsford. (Again, however, the second British impression is from plates in an earlier state not appearing in this issue: with Abbotsford cited after the Introduction and the July date repeated after the Appendix. At this time, however, Scott was at his hotel in London, stricken with a stroke.) Since 1 July 1832 fell on a Sunday, however, actual date of issue is cited for the catalogue, 2 July.

39] [*engraved title*] WAVERLEY NOVELS. | VOL. XXXIX. | [*dash*] | WOODSTOCK. | [*vignette of a dog*] . . . . 1832.

Collation: *a-d*^{8} *e*^{6} A-Y^8 Z^8(-Z8). Pagination: [*frontispiece, engraved title*], *i* fly-title, *ii* printer's imprint(1), *iii* iv-xxi Introduction, dated 1 August 1832, *xxii blank, xxiii* xxiv-lxiv Appendix, *lxv* fly-title, *lxvi blank, lxvii* lxviii-lxxvi Preface, *1* fly-title, *2 blank, 3* 4-366 text, chapters 1-18, 366 printer's imprint(2) (+4-page catalogue dated 1 August 1832). Illustrations: Frontispiece drawn by W. Boxall, engraved by Charles Fox, with caption 'Woodstock.' and six-line quotation beginning '"Sir Henry Lee sat in a wicker arm-chair by the fire, . . ."'; published 1832 by Robert Cadell, and Whittaker & Co. Title vignette drawn by E. Landseer, engraved by W. Raddon, is followed by a caption reading '"Bevis."' but, in this volume, no quotation. Typography: Preliminary signatures are in italic.

Figures: *a* xvi-2, *c* xlviii-2, *e* lxxii-2, A16-2, C48-1, E80-1, G112-2, I 144-1, M192-1, N208-1, P240-2, R272-1, T304-2, X336-1.

Notes: In all copies of both impressions the assigned Introduction date is now given without reference to Abbotsford. A later issue of this first impression carries a catalogue dated 1 September 1832.

40] [*engraved title*] WAVERLEY NOVELS. | VOL. XL. | [*dash*] | WOODSTOCK. | [*vignette*] | [*three-line quotation*] . . . . 1832.

Collation: A-2A^8 2B^4 *2C*^{2}. Pagination: [*frontispiece, engraved title*], *1* fly-title, *2* printer's imprint(1), *3* 4-395 text concluded, 395 printer's imprint(2), *396 blank* (+4-page catalogue dated 1 September 1832 and 1-page slip advertisement). Illustrations: Frontispiece drawn by J. Inskipp, engraved by Augs. Fox, with caption 'Woodstock.' and four-line quotation beginning '"His daughter took some needle-work, . . .".'; published 1832 by Robert Cadell, and Whittaker & Co. Title vignette drawn by W. Collins, engraved by W. Humphreys, is followed by a quotation beginning '"As Phoebe Mayflower was reflecting, . . ."'

Figures: A13-1, C48-2/-, E80-1, G112-2, I 144-1, L176-2, N208-1, P240-2/-, R272-2, T304-2, X336-1, Z368-2, 2B 392-1.

41] [*engraved title*] WAVERLEY NOVELS. | VOL. XLI. | [*dash*] | THE HIGHLAND WIDOW. | [*vignette*] | [*four-line quotation*] . . . . 1832.

Collation: *a-d*^{8} *e*^{6}(-*e*1) A-2A^8 *2B*1. Pagination: [*frontispiece, engraved title*], *i* fly-title for *Chronicles of the Canongate*, *ii* printer's imprint(1), *iii* iv-xxxiv Intro-duction, dated from Abbotsford 15 August 1831, *xxxv* xxxvi-lxxiii Appendix, *lxxiv blank, 1* fly-title, *2 blank, 3* 4-120 text (introductory), *121* fly-title for 'The Highland Widow', *122 blank, 123* 124-237 text, 238-242 Introductory for 'The Two Drovers', *243* 244-288 text, *289* fly-title for 'My Aunt Margaret's Mirror', *290 blank, 291* 292-294

Introduction, dated August 1831, *295* 296-346 text, *347* fly-title for 'The Tapestried Chamber', *348 blank, 349* Introduction, dated August 1831, *350 blank, 351* 352-373 text, *374 blank, 375* fly-title for 'Death of the Laird's Jock', *376 blank, 377* introduction [one sentence], dated August 1831, *377* 378-385 text, 385 printer's imprint(2), *386 blank* (+4-page catalogue dated 1 October 1832, listing full order of publication through volume 48, May 1833). Illustrations: Frontispiece drawn by A. Fraser, engraved by J. Mitchell, with caption 'The Highland Widow.'; published 1832 by Robert Cadell and Whittaker & Co. Title vignette drawn by A. Fraser, engraved by W. H. Watt, is followed by a quotation beginning '"I must obey you mother, I feel I must, said Hamish . . . .' Typography: Preliminary signatures are in italic.

Figures: *a* xvi-2, *c* xlviii-1, A16-2, C48-1, E80-2, G112-2, I 144-1, L176-2, N208-1, P240-2, R272-1, T304-2, X336-1, Z368-1.

42] [*engraved title*] WAVERLEY NOVELS. | VOL. XLII. | [*dash*] | FAIR MAID OF PERTH. | [*vignette*] | [*three-line quotation*] . . . . 1832.

Collation: A-2A⁸. Pagination: [*frontispiece, engraved title*], *i* fly-title for *Chronicles of the Canongate*. Second Series. 'Saint Valentine's Day; or, The Fair Maid of Perth', *ii* printer's imprint(1), *iii* iv-xii Preface, dated from Abbotsford 15 August 1831, *1* fly-title, *2 blank, 3* 4-17 Introductory, 18-383 text, chapters 1-17, *384* printer's imprint(2) (+4-page catalogue dated 1 November 1832). Illustrations: Frontispiece drawn by W. Allan, engraved by Chas. Fox, with caption 'Fair Maid of Perth'; published 1832 by Robert Cadell, and Whittaker & Co. Title vignette drawn by D. O. Hill, engraved by W. Miller, is followed by a quotation beginning '"He beheld stretched beneath him, the valley of the Tay, . . ."'

Figures: A16-2, C62-2/-, E80-2, G112-1, I 144-1, L176-2/-, N208-1, P240-2, R272-2, T304-1, X336-2, Z368-1.

43] [*engraved title*] WAVERLEY NOVELS. | VOL. XLIII. | [*dash*] | FAIR MAID OF PERTH. | [*vignette*] | [*three-line quotation*] . . . . 1832.

Collation: A-2A⁸ 2B⁶(-2B1). Pagination: [*frontispiece, engraved title*], *1* fly-title, *2* printer's imprint(1), *3* 4-393 text concluded, 393 printer's imprint(2), *394 blank* (+6-page catalogue dated 1 December 1832). Illustrations: Frontispiece drawn by T. Duncan, engraved by J. Horsburgh, with caption 'Fair Maid of Perth.' and four-line quotation beginning '"At the foot of a rock which commanded the view in every direction, . .".'; published 1832 by Robert Cadell, and Whittaker & Co. Title vignette drawn by D. O. Hill, engraved by W. Miller, is followed by a quotation beginning '"A lute" said the Duke of Rothsay, listening; . . ."'

Figures: A16-1, C48-2, E80-1, G105-2, I 137/-, L176-2, N208-2, P—, Q254-1, R272-2, T292-1, X336-2, Z368-1, 2B—.

44] [*engraved title*] WAVERLEY NOVELS. | VOL. XLIV. | [*dash*] | ANNE OF GEIERSTEIN. | [*vignette*] | [*two-line quotation*] . . . . 1833.

Collation: *a*^{8} *b*^{6} A-2A^8 2B^2. Pagination: [*frontispiece, engraved title*], *i* fly-title, *ii* printer's imprint(1), *iii* iv-xxvii Introduction, dated from Abbotsford 17 September 1831, *xxviii blank, 1 fly-title, 2 blank, 3* 4-387 text, chapters 1-18, 387 printer's imprint(2), *388 blank* (+18-page catalogue dated January 1833, pages *1* 2-11 being a 'Prospectus of a New Edition of the Poetical Works', volume 1 to be issued 1 May). Illustrations: Frontispiece drawn by W. Mulready, engraved by R. Graves, with caption 'Anne of Geierstein.' and seven-line quotation beginning '"As Margaret spoke, she tore from her hair the sable feather and rose, . . ."'; published 1833 by Robert Cadell; and Whittaker & Co. Title vignette drawn by R. T. Bone, engraved by W. Humphrys, is followed by a quotation beginning '"Ha! Scharfgerichter," said the knight, . . ."'

Figures: b xxiii-2, A16-2, C48-1, E80-2/-, G112-1, I 144-2, L169-1, N208-2/-, P—, Q254-1, R272-2, T304-2, X336-1, Z368-2.

45] [*engraved title*] WAVERLEY NOVELS. | VOL. XLV. | [*dash*] | ANNE OF GEIERSTEIN. | [*vignette*] | [*four-line quotation*] . . . . 1833.

Collation: A-2A^8 2B^2. Pagination: [*frontispiece, engraved title*], *1* fly-title, *2* printer's imprint(1), *3* 4-388 text concluded, 388 printer's imprint(2) (+18-page catalogue as in volume 44). Illustrations: Frontispiece drawn by J. West, engraved by C. Rolls, with caption 'Anne of Geirstein.'[!] and six-line quotation beginning '"Young man," said "the Queen, the contemplation of a question so doubtful almost deprives me of reason". . . .'; published 1833 by Robert Cadell, and Whittaker & Co. Title vignette drawn by J. W. Wright, engraved by Josh. Rolls, is followed by a quotation beginning '"Annette sped up a narrow turnpike stair to a closet or dressing room, . . ."'

Figures: A16-1, C48-2, E80-1, G100-2, I 144-1, L176-2, N208-1, P240-2, R272-1, T304-1, Y351-1, Z368-2, 2B—.

Notes: In some copies the frontispiece spelling of 'Geirstein' has been corrected.

46] [*engraved title*] WAVERLEY NOVELS. | VOL. XLVI. | [*dash*] | COUNT ROBERT OF PARIS. | [*vignette*] | [*three-line quotation*] . . . . 1833.

Collation: *a-b*^{8} *c*^{8}(-*c*8) A-2A^8 2B^8(-2B8). Pagination: *frontispiece, engraved title*], *i* fly-title for *Tales of My Landlord.* Fourth and Last Series, *ii* printer's imprint(1), *iii* iv-xiv Advertisement, initialed 'J. G. L.' (Lockhart) and dated from London 1 March 1833, *xv* xvi-xlv Introductory Address, *xlvi blank, 1* fly-title for 'Count Robert of Paris', *2 blank, 3* 4-397 text, chapters 1-19, 397 printer's imprint(2), *398 blank* (+16-page catalogue again dated January 1833, but with the previous half-title leaf withdrawn and the remainder renumbered). Illustrations: Frontispiece drawn by

W. Boxall, engraved by W. Greatbatch, with caption 'Count Robert of Paris.' and five-line quotation beginning 'Without a moment's hesitation the Frank seated himself in the vacant throne of the Emperor, . . .'; published 1833 by Robert Cadell, and Whittaker & Co. Title vignette drawn by J. West, engraved by J. Goodyear, is followed by a quotation beginning 'The assassin hovered less than an instant over the sleeper, as if to mark the interval . . . .'

Figures: a xvi-1, A8-1, C48-2, E80-1/-, G112-2, K147-1, L176-2/-, N208-2, P240-2, R272-1, T304-2, X336-2, Z368-1, 2B—.

47] [*engraved title*] WAVERLEY NOVELS. | VOL. XLVII. | [*dash*] | CASTLE DANGEROUS. | [*vignette*] | [*two-line quotation*] . . . . 1833.

Collation: A-2F^8 *2G*1. Pagination: [*frontispiece, engraved title*], *i* fly-title for *Tales of My Landlord*. Fourth and Last Series, *ii blank, 1* fly-title for 'Count Robert of Paris', *2* printer's imprint(1), *3* 4-241 text concluded, *242 blank, 243* fly-title for 'Castle Dangerous', *244 blank, 245* 246-255 Introduction initialed 'W. S.' (forwarded from Naples in February 1832), *256* 257-274 Appendix, *275* fly-title, *276 blank, 277* 278-466 text, chapters 1-10, 466 printer's imprint(2) (+16-page catalogue as in volume 46). Illustrations: Frontispiece drawn by C. Stanfield, engraved by S. Sangster, with caption 'Castle Dangerous.'; published 1833 by Robert Cadell, & Whittaker & Co. Title vignette drawn by A. Fraser, engraved by Chas. Fox, is followed by a quotation beginning '"The trooper, wrapping part of a mantle round her head, . . ."'

Figures: A16-1, C48-1, E80-2, G112-1, I 144-2/-, L176-1, N196-2, P240-2, S286-1, U307-1, X336-1/2, Z368-1, 2B 388-1, 2D 432-2, 2F 464-6.

48] [*engraved title*] WAVERLEY NOVELS. | VOL. XLVIII. | [*dash*] | THE SURGEON'S DAUGHTER. | [*vignette*] | [*three-line quotation*] . . . . 1833.

Collation: A-2G^8 2H^4 2I^2 *2K*1(-*2K*1=vol.1,π1). Pagination: [*frontispiece, engraved title*], *1* fly-title for *Tales of My Landlord.* Fourth and Last Series, *2* printer's imprint(1), *3* fly-title for 'Castle Dangerous', *4 blank, 5* 6-145 text concluded, 145-146 postscript, dated from Abbotsford September 1831, *147* fly-title for 'The Surgeon's Daughter', *148 blank, 149*-150 Introduction, initialled W.S. and dated from Abbotsford September 1831, *151* 152-157 Appendix to Introduction, initialled J.T. (Joseph Train) and dated from Castle Douglas July 1832, *158 blank, 159* fly-title, *160 blank, 161* 162-430 text, *431* fly-title for Glossary to the Waverley Novels, *432 blank, 433* 434-492 text, *493-494* Contents of the Waverley Novels. No printer's imprint(2). (+8-page catalogue dated 1 May 1833, page *1* announcing the publication 'This day' of the *Poetical Works*, volume 1.) Illustrations: Frontispiece drawn by Frank Stone, engraved by J. Goodyear, with caption 'The Surgeon's Daughter.'; no publishers' imprint. Title vignette drawn by Frank Stone, engraved by Robt.Graves, is followed by a quotation beginning: '"It may be out of it, then, madam", answered Miss Grey. . . .'

Figures: A16-2, C36-1, E80-2, G112-1, I 137-1, L176-2, N205-1/-, P240-2, R269-1, T304-2, X336-2, Z368-1, 2B 400-2, 2D 429-1, 2F 452-9/-.

Notes: In a few copies, after the final leaf of Contents, there appears a slip reading: 'The Binder will cut off the leaf of Contents, and insert it after the Titlepage of Volume I.' Though the collations for 'ideal copy' in volumes 1 and 48 accordingly reflect this transfer, the printer's advice usually was ignored.

348Ab] Final Revised Edition, First Impression, First American Issue: 1829-1833 [1831-1834]

WAVERLEY NOVELS. | VOL. I [II-XLVIII]. | [*specific title*] | PRINTED FOR | CADELL AND COMPANY, EDINBURGH; | AND THOMAS WARDLE, PHILADELPHIA. | 1829 [1830-1833].

Issued in Philadelphia ca. 1831-1834. Binding: As for first British issue, in red cloth with printed labels (ViU volumes 24-25, 37, 43), or in contemporary half-red morocco of British manufacture, red marbled boards, coated cream endpapers (PPL). Except for the newly printed titles, inserted after the engraved titles originally prepared, and several other peculiarities listed below, all volumes of this issue apparently are identical with those of the first British issue and often carry the original Cadell catalogues.

General Notes: From a partial record (NNP MA 3556, page 94) it would appear that, about two years after starting the Magnum Opus, Cadell arranged with his longtime confederate Wardle for a serial issue of his old stock in America and, to bring his agent up to date, quickly dispatched in small numbers some ten or twelve volumes at a time, the last of these shipments (and the only one recorded) on 3 August 1831 consisting of 25 copies each, @ 2s.9d, for volumes 14-25. That same day, as this account further indicates, Cadell then began to ship 150 copies each of the succeeding novels as they became available: thus 3 August (volumes 26-27), 4 November (28-30), 23 December (31-32), 10 March 1832 (33-34), and 9 May, the last entry, (35-36). That the consignments continued in this orderly sequence is evident in another partial account (NNP MA 3555, pages 35, 39, 43, 47), where Cadell enigmatically records receipts 'from Philadelphia' of £250 on 16 August 1831 and £100 on 30 June 1832, then 'from Wardle' of £100 again on 15 December 1832 and 30 June 1833: two months after publication of the last, 48th volume in the original British issue.

Variant states: The imprints on the titles which Cadell affixed to these exported volumes are irregular and occasionally deviate from the wording on the preceding engraved plates. Volumes 14-16 (1) may continue to read CADELL . . . 1830 as in the engraved titles or (2) be of later state reading ROBERT CADELL . . . 1831, a full name not used until volume 17 in the original issue, with a date not occurring until the following year. Printed title date for volume 8 is 1829 (a year before first issue), volumes 18-19 is 1831, and 31-35 is either 1832 or 1833 (all a year or so after first issue). Some irregularity also appears in the use of engraved titles from the second British issue, as in ViU volume 31 dated 1833 and 42 dated 1834. Altogether, then, the Wardle issue does not consist entirely of unmixed remainder copies, but to some extent includes a reprinting, as further defined in the next section.

Reimpression symbols: Generally a †, the usual sign of a reimpression, appears after three signatures in volume 7 (G, N, T) and, with few exceptions, after every third signature in volumes 8-13 (in 'thirds' because three signatures in this section of the work constitute a full sheet). Press figures, however, remain as cited in the first British issue for volumes 37-48. As would be expected, where Cadell's advertisements are in several states (volumes 9, 21, 22) this issue generally represents the latter version.

Copies: (state 1): ViU. (2): PPL.

348Ac] Final Revised Edition, Second (British) Impression: 1830[1831]-1834

[*engraved title*] WAVERLEY NOVELS. | VOL. I [II-XLVIII]. | [*dash*] | [*novel title*] | [*vignette*] | [*quotation*] | PRINTED FOR ROBERT CADELL, EDINBURGH, | AND WHITTAKER & Co. LONDON. | 1830 [1831-1834].

Published concurrently in Edinburgh and London, the first volume 1 January 1831 (preliminary notice slip dated 1 November 1830 prefixed to volume 18 of first impression) and then continuing in monthly intervals until issue of the 48th volume 1 December 1834.

Notes: This second, continual reimpression, in unmixed state, may be readily distinguished by the later engraved title imprint dates: 1830 (volumes 1-2), 1831 (3-14), 1832 (15-24), 1833 (25-36), 1834 (37-48). Throughout the publishers are recorded as above (the final state of the earlier impression) and, except for volume 41, the terminal printer's imprint reads: EDINBURGH: | PRINTED BY BALLANTYNE AND COMPANY, | PAUL'S WORK, CANONGATE. The press figures, first appearing in volume 37 of the original impression, usually do not occur in this impression but, as noted above for volumes 13, 25, 37, and 38, the plates now used may occasionally derive from stereotype in an earlier state or setting.

Copy: L. Mixed copies [1st impression remainder volumes noted in brackets]: E(vols. 1-12, 15-22, 24-25, 27, 29-30, 35-41, 43-48 [13-14, 23, 26, 28, 31-34, 42]); CtY(vols. 1-24, 27-34, 38 [25-26, 35-37, 39-48]) TxU(Evelyn Waugh: 1-7, 9-14, 17, 19, 31, 42 [8, 15-16, 18, 20-30, 32-41, 43-48]).

348Ad] Final Revised Edition, Second (Continental) Impression, Part Issue 1835-1839

[*wrapper title:*] PART 1[2-240]. BY APPOINTMENT OF THE EXECUTORS. PRICE 1S. | [*ornamental frame*] TO BE PUBLISHED EVERY SATURDAY, . . . THE | WAVERLEY NOVELS; | PRINTED FROM | **Sir Walter Scott's own Edition,** | THE ONLY ONE CONTAINING HIS | LAST NOTES, INTRODUCTIONS, & CORRECTIONS. | ILLUSTRATED, | BY | J.M.W. TURNER, ESQ., R.A. [*and 15 others*] | FISHER, SON, & CO., LONDON & PARIS.

General Notes: Just as the 38th volume of the second British impression was issuing from the press, Cadell on 24 January 1834 approached the London firm of Jones & Co., proposing that 'a new Current' might be given to the novels and, when this offer was declined, then on 11 February wrote to Fisher Son & Co. with a similar proposition. Four days later this firm made a counter-offer that apparently was accepted: that they secure their own paper and plates and have 'exclusive sale in our line of business for at least seven years' (E MS 920,ff.19-20). Their 'line', it seems, was primarily with a European clientele and their immediate concern to enlist the services of the eminent artist identified first on their title-page. Turner had just then concluded his work for the Cadell issue of the *Poetical Works* (349A), the final volume of that collection appearing 1 April 1834.

Wrapper titles differ slightly throughout the course of the Fisher issue, with George Cruikshank's name added as another prominent illustrator beginning with number 8. Among all the undated weekly numbers the first 64 evidently were printed in 1834-1836, the chronological limit of the original *Magnum* issue, each part consisting of five or six gatherings in the newly arranged imposition described for the succeeding volume issues.

Copy: NN(Arents). Reference: Cohn 730.

Contents of the original weekly parts issued in 1834-1836:
1-10] Waverley. (Concluded in part 11, pages 417-420)
11-18] Guy Mannering. (Concluded in part 19, pages 321-378)
19-27] The Antiquary. (Concluded in part 28, pages 321-340)
28-36] Rob Roy. (Concluded in part 37, pages 353-384)
37-47] Tales of My Landlord. First Series.(Concluded in part 48, pages 129-138)
48-58] Tales . . . . Second Series. (Concluded in part 59, pages 225-234)
59-64] Tales . . . .Third Series. ('The Bride of Lammermoor' only, concluded in part 65, pages 353-370. The following tale bears a volume 15 title-page dated 1837: see notes to volume issue below.)

348Ae] Final Revised Edition, Second (Continental) Impression, Volume Issue:1836-1839

WAVERLEY NOVELS. | VOL. I[II-XIII]. | [*short rule*] | [*specific title and volume number*] | [*quotation*] | [*short rule*] | FISHER, SON, & CO., LONDON; | AND QUAI DES GRANDS AUGUSTINS, PARIS. 1836.

48 volumes with the first 13 issued during 1836. Binding: blue cloth with titles in gilt on spine.

General Notes: Except for printed title-leaves and illustrations these volumes were printed from the Ballantyne plates with the pages reimposed for 16° in eights and, in certain volumes, a † entered irregularly to indicate this imposition. The original 1836 reimpression, in part or volume issue, again bears the Ballantyne imprint; later impressions may carry the imprint of T. Constable or Stevenson & Co. Illustrations: Volumes 1-13 have a frontispiece and two text plates with imprint reading: 'Fisher, Son & Co. London & Paris. 1836.', captions in English and French. Printer's imprints: (1) on verso of title: EDINBURGH: PRINTED BY BALLANTYNE AND CO., PAUL'S WORK.; (2) on last page of text, as for (1) or: EDINBURGH: | PRINTED BY BALLANTYNE & [*or* AND] COMPANY, | PAUL'S WORK, CANONGATE.

1-2] Waverley. 1836. Two volumes. Pages 1: *1-2*, *i* ii-civ, *1-3* 4-320; 2: *1-3* 4-420. Copies: BCL(vol.1) E; NN. Reissued 1838 (BCL vol.2).
3-4] Guy Mannering. 1836. Two volumes. Pages 1: *1-2*, *i* ii-xxxi *xxxii*, *3* 4-311; 2: *1-3* 4-378. Copies: BCL(vol.2) E; NN T/B. Reissued 1838 (BCL vol.1).
5-6] The Antiquary. 1836. Two volumes. Pages 1: *1-2*, *i* ii-xix *xx*, *1-3* 4-325; 2: *1-3* 4-340. Copies: BCL E; NN.
7-8] Rob Roy. 1836. Two volumes. Pages 1: *i-iii* iv-cxxxv *cxxxvi*, *1-3* 4-263; 2: *1-3* 4-384. Copies: BCL(vol.2) E; NN T/B. Reissued 1838 (BCL vol.1).
9-11] Tales of my Landlord.—I[II-III]. First Series. 1836. Three volumes. Pages 1: *i-ii*, *1-2*, *iii* iv-xix *xxx*, *1* 2-374; 2: *1-3* 4-416; 3: *1-3* 4-419. Notes: Contents: Volume 1 'The Black Dwarf' and 'Old Mortality', chapters 1-8; volume 2 'Old Mortality' continued; volume 3 'Old Mortality' concluded and 'The Heart of Mid-Lothian', chapters 1-18. Copies: BCL E; NN.
12-13] Tales of my Landlord.—IV[-V]. Second Series. 1836. Two volumes. Pages 1: *1-3* 4-408; 2: *1-3* 4-392. Notes: Contents: Volume 1 'The Heart of Mid-Lothian' continued; volume 2 'The Heart of Mid-Lothian' concluded and 'The Bride of Lammermoor', chapters 1-8. Copies: E; NN. Reissued 1837 (BCL vol.2), 1838 (BCL vol.1).

Subsequent volumes, as listed below, were originally issued after 1836, final date of the Magnum Opus, and thus are not represented in detail in this bibliography.

14-15 Tales of My Landlord. Third Series. 1837

31-32 Quentin Durward. 1838
33-34 St. Ronan's Well. 1838

16-17 Ivanhoe. 1837
18-19 The Monastery. 1837
20-21 The Abbot. 1837
22-23 Kenilworth. 1837
24-25 The Pirate. 1837/1838
26-27 The Fortunes of Nigel. 1838
28-30 Peveril of the Peak. 1838
35-36 Redgauntlet. 1838
37-38 Tales of the Crusaders. 1838
39-40 Woodstock. 1838
41-43 Chronicles of the Canongate. 1838
44-45 Anne of Geierstein. 1838
46-48 Tales of MyLandlord. Fourth Series. 1838/1838/1839

DERIVATIVES

GREAT BRITAIN

348D] EDINBURGH: Cadell & Co. 1829-1833

[1] Illustrations of the Waverley Novels . . . Edinburgh: Published [*date*] by Cadell and Co. [*or* R. Cadell and Company] and Moon, Boys & Graves, 6, Pall Mall, London.
Notes: Title is taken from a Cadell prospectus issued 1 September 1829 (E copy), publishers' imprint from the 48 vignette titles in the E set. The accompanying 48 frontispiece plates have variant imprint: Edinburgh. Published [*date*] by Cadell & Co. [*or* Robert Cadell] & Moon, Boys & Graves, London. All 96 plates are identified in the preceding description of the first British volume issue (348Aa). In this separate issue, however, the quotation is placed above the vignette.

The prospectus announces the first 'Part I.', 16 plates, for issue 14 December, that is, several weeks before the appearance of the last two plates in *Rob Roy* volume 8, published 1 January 1830. At that time (and presumably throughout) the plates were advertised as available in five states: (1) 8° prints, 12s; (2) 4° French proofs, £1.0.0; (3) 4° India proofs, £1.4.0; (4) 4° Colombier proofs before letters [priced the following month at £1.15.0]; (5) Etchings, £1.1.0. Apart from these there exists (6) a suite of 96 enlarged steel engravings (plates average 200 x 150mm) in 25 copies only. Copies: (1) E(suite with 12 prints added from another series); (6) LVA.

[2] A Series of Sketches of the Existing Localities alluded to in the Waverley Novels. Etched from Original Drawings by James Skene, Esq. . . . Edinburgh: Printed for Cadell and Co., Edinburgh; Simpkin and Marshall, and Moon, Boys, and Graves, London. 1829. Pages: *1-5* 6-172. This work, originally issued in 21 numbers, extending over the period 1829-1831, was performed by a very close friend of Scott's and bears a lengthy dedication to him (*see* 508T[1]). 'The Preliminary Notice', dated from Edinburgh June 1829, further indicates that the task 'coincides with the wishes' of the author and attempts at 'strict fidelity; with this proviso, that such subjects as are now in ruins, are, where practicable, restored to the state they were in at the particular period assumed by the Author of Waverley.' Below the last page of text 172 appears 'End of Volume First', but no further text was published. Copies: (small-paper) E GU; InU. (large paper) ES; CtY NNU-W.

Illustrations: The following record lists in order a plate number (here assigned), caption, text heading page reference to Scott quotation, page numbers (in parentheses) of facing descriptive text, issue number given at foot of the first page whenever this is cited. It will be noted that, after *Guy Mannering*, the reference shifts from the earlier three-volume sets to the multi-volume series then just issuing of the Magnum Opus.

(1) Doune Castle; Waverley ii.78. (pages 9-10)
(2) Stirling Castle; Waverley ii.90. (pages 11-12)
(3) Palace Gate [Holyrood]; Waverley ii.94. (pages 13-14)
(4) White Horse Inn; Waverley ii.106. (page 15), No.2.
(5) Battle of Prestonpans; Waverley ii.168. (pages 16-17)
(6) Carlisle Castle; Waverley ii.390. (page 18)
(7) Caerlaverock Castle; Guy Mannering i.58. (pages 19-21), No.III.
(8) Court of Caerlaverock; Guy Mannering i.62. (pages 22-23)
(9) Rueberry Castle; Guy Mannering i.138. (pages 24-25, *26 blank*)
(10) Tod Willie; Guy Mannering ii.53. (pages 27-28), No.IV.
(11) Gleneaple; [Guy Mannering] iii.78. (pages 29-30)
(12) The Torrs Cave; [Guy Mannering] iii.285. (pages 31-33, *34 note indicating absence of localites in* The Antiquary)
(13) Glasgow 1764; Rob Roy viii.23. (pages 35-36), No.V.
(14) Glasgow Cathedral; Rob Roy viii.27. (pages 37-40)
(15) Barony Kirk [Glasgow]; Rob Roy viii.33. (pages 41-43, 'No.V.' on 43, *44 blank*)
(16) Aberfoyle; Rob Roy viii.161. (pages 45-46), No.VI.
(17) Lochard; Rob Roy viii.208. (pages 47-48)
(18) Ford of Alianan; Rob Roy, viii.259. (pages 49-50)
(19) Lediart; Rob Roy, viii.311. (pages 51-52), No.VII.
(20) Inversnaid; Rob Roy viii.318. (pages 53-54)
(21) Creek on the Shore of Loch Lomond; Rob Roy viii.318. (page 55, 'No.VII' on 55, *56 blank*)
(22) Manor Glen; Black Dwarf ix.3. (pages '51'-'53'), No.VIII.
(23) The Dwarf's Hut; Black Dwarf ix.44. (pages 54-57)
(24) The Dwarf's Grave; Black Dwarf ix.212. (pages 58-60)
(25) The Martyr's Tomb; Old Mortality ix.245. (pages 61-62), No.IX.
(26) Craignethan Castle; Old Mortality x.48. (pages 63-65)
(27) The Conventicle; Old Mortality x.95. (pages 66-68)
(28) Bothwell Bridge; Old Mortality x.355. (pages 69-71), No.X.
(29) The Black Linn; Old Mortality xi.95,99. (page 72)
(30) The Creehope Linn; Old Mortality xi.100. (pages 73-75, *76 blank*)
(31) The Heart of Mid-Lothian; Heart of Mid-Lothian xi.175. (pages 77-79), No.'IX'[XI].
(32) The Guard House; Heart of Mid-Lothian xi.247. (pages 80-83)
(33) The Grassmarket; Heart of Mid-Lothian xi.210. (pages 84-86)
(34) The Netherbow Port, Heart of Mid-Lothian xi.246. (pages 87-89), No.XII.
(35) Salisbury Crags; Heart of Mid-Lothian xi.285. (pages 90-92)
(36) The Parliament Close; Heart of Mid-Lothian xii.117. (pages 93-96)
(37) Wintoun House; Bride of Lammermoor xiv.135. (pages 97-99), No.XIII.
(38) Fast Castle; Bride of Lammermoor xiii.362. (pages 100-102)
(39) Eymouth; Bride of Lammermoor xiv.50. (pages 103-104)
(40) Earnsheugh; Bride of Lammermoor xiii.287. (pages 105-106), No.XIV.
(41) Coldingham Priory; Bride of Lammermoor xiii.289. (pages 107-109)
(42) Links of Eymouth; Bride of Lammermoor xiv.128,363. (pages 110-111, *112 blank*)
(43) Dunstafnage Castle; Legend of Montrose xv.134,143. (pages 113-115), No.XV.
(44) Inveraray Castle; Legend of Montrose xv.157. (pages 116-118)
(45) Inverlochy Castle; Legend of Montrose xv.269. (pages 119-121, *122 blank*)

(46) Vale of the Don; Ivanhoe xvi.123,xvii.330. (pages 123-126), No.XVI.
(47) Rotherwood; Ivanhoe xvi.35. (pages 127-129)
(48) Ashby; Ivanhoe xvi.212. (pages 130-131, *132 blank*)
(49) Jervaulx [Abbey]; Ivanhoe xvii.175. (page 133), No.XVII.
(50) Conningsburgh [Castle]; Ivanhoe xvii.331. (pages 134-138)
(51) Fontevraud [Vault]; Ivanhoe xvii.397. (pages 139-142)
(52) Melrose Abbey; Monastery xviii.2. (pages 143-145), No.XVIII.
(53) Bastel House [Darnick]; Monastery xviii.5. (pages 146-148)
(54) Coomsley [Tower]; Monastery xviii.10. (pages 149-150)
(55) Nameless Deen [Dean]; Monastery xviii.13. (pages 151-152), No.XIX.
(56) Old Bridge of Tweed; Monastery xviii.64. (pages 153-154)
(57) Melrose [Cross]; Monastery xix.333. (pages 155-157, *158 blank*)
(58) The Kirk of Field; The Abbot, xx.225. (pages 159-161), No.XX.
(59) Loch Leven Castle; The Abbot xx.347. (pages 162-163)
(60) Niddrie Castle; The Abbot xxi.299,301. (pages 164-165, *166 blank*)
(61) Crookstown [Crookstone] Castle; The Abbot xxi.327. (pages 167-168), No.XXI.
(62) Dundranen [Dundrennan] Abbey; The Abbot xxi.343. (pages 169-170)
(63) Port Mary; The Abbot xxi.349,350. (pages 171-172)

2. THE POETICAL WORKS

349A] Final Revised Edition: 1833-1834

[*engraved title*] THE | POETICAL WORKS | OF | SIR WALTER SCOTT, BARt. | VOL.1 [2-12]. | [*vignette*] | EDINBURGH,1833 [1834]. PRINTED FOR ROBERT CADELL,& WHITTAKER & Co. LONDON.

Published concurrently in Edinburgh and London, first volume 1 May 1833 at 5s (*EEC* 29 April), simultaneously with the 48th and last volume of *WN*. The final, 12th volume was issued on schedule 1 April 1834. Binding: purple cloth with printed labels. Paper: Royal 16° in eights (170 x 107mm uncut). Watermarks: *none*. Illustrations: All frontispieces and title vignettes are by J. M. W. Turner, as engraved by the persons identified below. Title volume numbers for 4-6, 9 are in Roman letters and punctuation may vary slightly from that given above.

Printer's imprints read: (1) EDINBURGH: PRINTED BY BALLANTYNE AND CO., PAUL'S WORK.; (2) PRINTED BY BALLANTYNE AND CO., PAUL'S WORK, EDINBURGH. Certain popular volumes (5-8) soon went out of print and were reimpressed, without press figures, by other printers:

Stevenson & Co. Copies: NNU-W(vol.8) RPB(6,8).
Macpherson & Syme Copies: NN(8) RPB(5).
Thomas Constable Copies: NN(7) RPB(7).

The person last named must have been engaged 1837 or later as he is designated 'Printer to Her Majesty'. Another Stevenson impression, observed in the 12th, T/B volume, was issued as late as 1851.

General Notes: Ordinarily, as specified in the following collations, the half-title is bound as a fly-title, following the engraved frontispiece and title-page. In his 'Advertisement' to the first volume Lockhart reports that this edition derives from Scott's final, interleaved copy with his last notes (all dated 1831), now with further annotation by the editor (entered here in brackets). The plates of airs in the first four volumes are transcribed, he indicates, from MSS in Scott's library. As with the previous *WN* sequence, Cadell inserts various catalogues, sometimes dated conformably with the volume issue date, and still retained in a few copies. These again are noted in parentheses following pagination.

A reissue of volumes 6-11 appears as a six-volume set with preliminary undated printed titles reading *The Select Poetry* (copies E L), this in several bindings as suitable for Christmas presents in 1835 (advts inserted in *MPW*, vols 19, 20).

Copies: E(3) O(Douce); IdU NNU-W ViU. Copies with later impressions, as noted above: NN NNU-W RPB T/B. Reference: Millgate(2), especially pp.345-351.

1] [*engraved title*] THE | POETICAL WORKS . . . VOL.1. | [*vignette of Smailholm Tower*] | EDINBURGH, 1833, . . . LONDON.

Collation: $\pi^4(\pi 1+1)$ A-2C^8 2D^6. Pagination: [*frontispiece, engraved title*], *1* fly-title for *Minstrelsy of the Scottish Border, 2 blank, i* Contents, *ii blank, iii* iv-viii Advertisement, signed J.G.L., dated from London 12 March 1833, *1*-2 dedication, *3* fly-title, *4 blank, 5* 6-91 Introductory Remarks on Popular Poetry, *92 blank, 93* fly-title for *Minstrelsy of the Scottish Border*, *94 blank, 95* dedication, *96 blank, 97* 98-239 Introduction, 240-291 appendices, *292 blank, 293* fly-title, *294 blank*, 295-428 text, 428 printer's imprint(2). No imprint(1). (+4+2 page catalogue dated 1 May 1833.) Illustrations: Frontispiece engraved by E. Goodall with caption 'Carlisle.'; title vignette engraved by E. Goodall (with caption misspelled 'Smallholm'); portrait of Scott engraved by W. Read, facing page *3* in some copies; one leaf of engraved music for 'The Battle of Otterburn' following page 368, three leaves for 'Johnie Armstrong' following page 416.

Figures: B30-2 32-1; D64-1; E80-1; G109-1; I 144-1; L176-1; N208-1; P240-1; R265-2; T297-2; X329-2; Z360-2; 2B 393-2. Excepting the first full sheet (A-B), all sheets in this half-sheet imposition are figured only once.

2] [*engraved title*] THE | POETICAL WORKS . . . VOL.2. | [*vignette of Johnnie Armstrong's Tower*] | EDINBURGH, 1833. . . . LONDON.

Collation: A^2 A-Y^8 Z^4. Pagination: [*frontispiece, engraved title*], *i* fly-title for the *Minstrelsy*, *ii blank, iii-iv* Contents, *1* fly-title, *2* printer's imprint(1), *3* 4-360 text continued, 360 printer's imprint(2) (+4-page catalogue dated 1 June 1833). Illustrations: Frontispiece engraved by R. Brandard with caption 'Jedburgh Abbey.'; title vignette engraved by E. Goodall; two leaves of engraved music for 'Dick o' the Cow' following page 62, one leaf for 'The Lord Maxwell's Good Night' following page 140, two leaves for 'The Battle of Bothwell Brigg' following page *246*.

Figures: A6-2; C48-1; F95-2; G105-2; I 137-2; L173-2; O 222-2; P237-1; R269-1; T297-2; X333-1/-. Again every full sheet is figured only once.

3] [*engraved title*] THE | POETICAL WORKS . . . VOL. 3. | [*vignette of Lochmaben Castle*] | EDINBURGH, 1833. . . . LONDON.

Collation: π^2 A-Y^8. Pagination: [*frontispiece, engraved title*], *1* fly-title for the *Minstrelsy*, *2* printer's imprint(1), *3*-4 Contents, *1* fly-title, *2 blank, 3* 4-348 text continued, 348 printer's imprint(1), *349-350 blank* (+4-page catalogue dated 1 July 1833). Illustrations: Frontispiece engraved by R. Wallis with caption 'Kelso.'; title vignette engraved by J. T. Willmore; two leaves of engraved music for 'The Douglas Tragedy' following second fly-title, two leaves for 'The Dowie Dens o' Yarrow' following page 150, one leaf for 'The Wife of Usher's Well' following page 262.

Figures: C41-2; E73-2/-; G112-1/-; I 142-2 144-3; M192-1; N196-2; R272-1; U317-1; X335-1/-. Excepting A-B and F-Q, both without figures, and H-I here figured twice, all full sheets as usual are figured only once.

4] [*engraved title*] THE | POETICAL WORKS . . . VOL.IV. | [*vignette of Hermitage Castle*] | EDINBURGH, PRINTED 1833, . . . LONDON.

Collation: π^2 A-$2A^8$ $2B^2$. Pagination: [*frontispiece, engraved title*], *i* fly-title for the *Minstrelsy, ii* printer's imprint(1), *iii*-iv Contents, *1* fly-title, *2 blank, 3* 4-78 Essay on Imitations of the Ancient Ballad, 79-87 Appendix, *88 blank, 89* fly-title, *90 blank*, 91-388 text concluded, 388 printer's imprint(1) (+4-page catalogue dated 1 August 1833). Illustrations: Frontispiece engraved by E. Goodall with caption 'Caerlaverock Castle.'; title vignette engraved by R. Wallis; one leaf of engraved music for 'True Thomas' following page 116, three leaves for 'Glenfinlas' following page 168.

Figures: A16-2; D64-1; F82-1; H125-1; L176-2; O 212-1; Q256-1; Y352-1; 2A 384-1. Excepting I-K, R-S, and T-U, all without figures, the full sheets are figured once.

5] [*engraved title*] THE | POETICAL WORKS . . . VOL. V. | [*vignette of Bemerside Tower*] | EDINBURGH, PRINTED 1833, . . . LONDON.

Collation: π^2 a^8 A-$2G^8$ $2H^6$ 2I 1. Pagination: [*frontispiece, engraved title*], *1* fly-title for *Sir Tristrem, 2* printer's imprint(1), *3* Contents, *4 blank, iii* iv-xvi Advertisement [by Lockhart] dated July 1833, *xvii* fly-title, *xviii blank, 1* 2-94 Introduction, 95-127 appendices, *128 blank*, *129* fly-title, *130 blank, 131* 132-353 text, *354 blank, 355* fly-title, *356 blank*, 357-367 Account of the German Romances [by Henry Weber], *368 blank, 369* fly-title, *370 blank*, 371-462 Notes, *463* fly-title, *464 blank*, 465-493 Glossary, 493 printer's imprint(1), *494 blank* (+ 6-page undated catalogue). Illustrations: Frontispiece engraved by W. Miller with caption 'Dryburgh

Abbey.'; title vignette engraved by J. Horsburgh; plate engraved by Jas. Johnstone titled 'Fac-Simile of the commencement of Sir Tristem' facing page 139. Typography: On page *iii* the direction '*vol. v.*' and signature *a* are in italics.

Figures: B32-1/-; E80-2, F96-2; K160-1; M184-2; U320-1; 2C 416-2. In this and succeeding volumes there are relatively few figures, or none.

6] [*engraved title*] THE | POETICAL WORKS . . . VOL. VI. | [*vignette of Newark Castle*] . . . EDINBURGH,1833, . . . LONDON.

Collation: π^2 A-2A^8(-2A8). Pagination: [*frontispiece, engraved title*], *i* fly-title for *The Lay of the Last Minstrel, ii* printer's imprint(1), *iii* Contents, *iv blank, 1* Advertisement [by Lockhart] undated, *2 blank, 3* fly-title, *4 blank, 5* 6-31 Introduction, *32 blank, 33* fly-title, *34 blank, 35* dedication, *36 blank*, 37-221 text, *222 blank, 223* fly-title, *224 blank*, 225-288 appendices, *289* fly-title for 'Ballads from the German', *290 blank*, 291-359 text, *360 blank, 361* fly-title for 'Songs', *362 blank*, 363-372 text, *373* fly-title for 'Fragments', *374 blank*, 375-382 text, 382 printer's imprint(1) (+4-page undated catalogue). Illustrations: Frontispiece engraved by W. Miller with caption 'Melrose.'; title vignette engraved by W. J. Cooke. Typography: Page 232 is misnumbered 238. Figure: T304-2.

Notes: In his 'Advertisement' Lockhart notes that Scott revised the text in the autumn of 1831 and this edition is printed from his interleaved copy. Unlike the later poems, the original MS for this, he reports, is no longer extant. Apart from reference also to first-edition readings Lockhart, beginning with this volume, and continuing through his edition of the *Miscellaneous Prose Works*, frequently provides excerpts from contemporary reviews. Concerning these it was remarked: 'Some will like and others dislike the notes from Jeffrey, and others of the critic's ungentle craft, which are hung to the text, like rough burrs at the fringe of a king's mantle. We like them: they show through what ordeals the sons of light must come.' (*Athenaeum*, 9 November 1833, review of volume 7, pages 750-751.)

7] [*engraved title*] THE | POETICAL WORKS . . . VOL.7. | [*vignette of Ashestiel*] | EDINBURGH, 1833, . . . LONDON.

Collation: π^2 A-2B^8 2C^2. Pagination: [*frontispiece, engraved title*], *i* fly-title for *Marmion, ii* printer's imprint(1), *iii* Contents, *iv blank, 1* Notice [by Lockhart] undated, *2 blank, 3* fly-title, *4 blank, 5* 6-14 Introduction, *15* fly-title, *16 blank, 17* dedication, *18 blank, 19-22* 23-363 text, *364 blank, 365* fly-title, *366 blank*, 367-404 Appendix, 404 printer's imprint(1) (+6-page catalogue dated 1 November 1833). Illustrations: Frontispiece engraved by W. Miller with caption 'Edinburgh.'; title vignette engraved by J. Horsburgh; folding plate engraved by Jas. Johnstone, facsimile of *Marmion* MS, facing page 219. Figures: R259-5, S286- 6, U317-4/-, Z368-1.

Notes: Lockhart now regularly cites variants from the original MS as well as the interleaved copy 'finally revised . . . in the summer of 1831', and at one point (page 284, canto 5, stanza 32, line 9) for the first time restores, as 'necessary to the *rhyme*,' the line 'In that inviolable dome,'.

8] [*engraved title*] THE | POETICAL WORKS . . . VOL. 8. | [*vignette of Loch Achray*] | EDINBURGH, 1834, . . . LONDON.

Collation: π^2 A-2A^8 2B^6. Pagination: [*frontispiece, engraved title*] *1* fly-title for *The Lady of the Lake, 2* printer's imprint(1), *i*-ii Contents, *1* fly-title, *2 blank, 3* 4-14 Introduction, *15* fly-title, *16 blank, 17* dedication, *18 blank, 19* 20-301 text, *302 blank, 303* fly-title, *304 blank*, 305-353 Appendix, *354 blank, 355* fly-title for 'Miscellaneous Poems', *356 blank, 357* 358-396 text, 396 printer's imprint(1) (+4-page catalogue dated 1 December 1833). Illustrations: Frontispiece engraved by W. Miller with caption 'Loch Katrine.'; title vignette engraved by W. Miller. Figures: U318-2, X336-3, Z368-1.

Notes: Again Lockhart cites variants from the original manuscript.

9] [*engraved title*] THE | POETICAL WORKS . . . VOL. IX. | [*vignette of Bowes' Tower*] | [EDINBURGH, 1834, . . . LONDON.]

Collation: π^2 A-2D^8 2E^4. Pagination: [*frontispiece, engraved title*], *i* fly-title for *Rokeby* and *The Vision of Don Roderick, ii* printer's imprint(1), *iii* Contents, *iv* Erratum, *1* 2-3 Notice [by Lockhart] undated, *4 blank, 5* fly-title, *6 blank, 7* 8-20 Introduction, *21* fly-title for *Rokeby*, *22 blank, 23* dedication, *24 blank, 25* 26-305 text, *306 blank, 307* fly-title, *308 blank*, 309-353 Appendix, *354 blank, 355* fly-title for *The Vision, 356* note, *357* 358-360 Preface, *361* fly-title, *362 blank, 363* dedication, *364 blank*, 365-426 text, *427* fly-title, *428 blank*, 429-440 Appendix, 440 printer's imprint(1) (+4-page catalogue dated 1 January 1834). Illustrations: Frontispiece engraved by John Pye with caption 'Junction of the Greta and the Tees.' The title vignette, engraved by Edwd Webb, extends so far down the page that the publishers' imprint, if any, does not appear. Typography: In printer's imprint page *ii*, 'CO.,' in some copies omits the comma. Figures: C48-2; E80-3; I 144-2.

Notes: On page 241 Lockhart indicates that for Note P (pages 345-349) 'the author in his interleaved copy has made considerable additions.' Again numerous variants are also cited from the original manuscripts of both poems.

10] [*engraved title*] THE | POETICAL WORKS . . . VOL. 10. | [*vignette of Staffa*] | EDINBURGH, 1834. . . . LONDON.

Collation: π^2 A-Z^8 2A^6. Pagination: [*frontispiece, engraved title], 1* fly-title for *The Lord of the Isles, 2* printer's imprint(1), *i*-ii Contents, *1*-2 Notice [by Lockhart] undated, *3* fly-title, *4 blank, 5* 6-10 Introduction, *11* fly-title, *12 blank, 13* 14-276 text, *277* fly-title, *278 blank*, 279-352 Appendix, *353* fly-title for 'Occasional Pieces', *354 blank, 355* 356-380 text, 380 printer's imprint(1) (+16-page catalogue dated January 1834, pages 1-7 representing a Prospectus for *MPW*). Illustrations: Frontispiece engraved by Henry LeKeux with caption 'Loch Coriskin.'; title vignette engraved by E. Goodall. Figures: B32-3, E80-2, G112-3, I 144-1, L173-3, N208-1, P240-2, X336-3.

Notes: Variants from the original manuscript are cited for the major work and, among the lesser pieces, for 'Carle, Now the King's Come!'

11] [*engraved title*] THE | POETICAL WORKS . . . VOL.11. | [*vignette of Mayburgh*] | EDINBURGH:1834, . . . LONDON.

Collation: π^2 A-2A^8. Pagination: [*frontispiece, engraved title*], *1* fly-title, *2* printer's imprint(1), *i*-ii Contents, *1* fly-title for the *Bridal of Triermain, 2 blank, 3* 4-15 Preface, *16 blank, 17* fly-title, *18 blank*, 19-138 text, 139-141 Appendix, *142 blank, 143* fly-title for *Harold the Dauntless, 144* note, 145-254 text, *255* fly-title for *The Field of Waterloo, 256* Advertisement, *257* dedication, *258 blank*, 259-291 text, *292 blank, 293* fly-title for 'Songs and Miscellanies', *294 blank*, 295-382 text, 382 printer's imprint(1), *383-384* advertisements (+8-page catalogue dated February 1834). Illustrations: frontispiece engraved by W. Miller with caption 'Skiddaw'; title vignette engraved by J. Horsburgh. Figures: *none*.

Notes: Of the three major works the manuscript of the second apparently was not available to Lockhart. Among the twenty-eight lesser, miscellaneous poems the last four, pages 369-382, it is noted in the Contents list, are now first collected; but of these only one appears to be a first printing: 'Inscription for the Monument of the Rev. George Scott' (first line: 'To youth, to age, alike, this tablet pale'), page 376.

12] [*engraved title*] THE | POETICAL WORKS . . . VOL.12. | [*vignette of Abbotsford*] | EDINBURGH, 1834, . . . LONDON.

Collation: π^2 A-2 O^8 *2P*^{2}. Pagination: [*frontispiece, engraved title*], *i* fly-title, *ii* printer's imprint(1), *iii* Contents, *iv blank, 1* Advertisement [by Lockhart] undated, *2 blank, 3* fly-title for *Halidon Hill, 4 blank, 5* 6-12 Preface, *13* fly-title, *14 blank, 15* Dramatis Personae, *16 blank*, 17-86 text, *87* fly-title for 'MacDuff's Cross', *88 blank, 89* dedication, *90 blank, 91*-92 Introduction, *93* Dramatis Personae, *94 blank*, 95-111 text, *112 blank, 113* fly-title for 'The Doom of Devorgoil', *114 blank*, 115-117 Preface, *118 blank, 119* Dramatis Personae, *120 blank*, 121-240 text, *241* fly-title for 'Auchindrane', *242 blank*, 243-269 Preface, *270 blank, 271*-272 Dramatis Personae, 273-362 text, *363* fly-title for 'The House of Aspen', *364 blank*, 365-368 Advertisement, *369*-370 Dramatis Personae, 371-441 text, *442 blank, 443* fly-title for *Goetz of Berlichingen, 444 blank*, 445-450 Preface, *451*-452 Dramatis Personae, 453-564 text, *565* fly-title, *566 blank, 567* 568-593 Index, *594* printer's imprint(1),

595-596 advertisements. (+8-+2-page catalogue April 1834). The pagination above represents (2) the final state of the text. An earlier state (1) has the Goetz text ending on page 561, then *562 blank, 563* fly-title, *564 blank, 565* 566-593 Index [&c]. Illustrations: Frontispiece engraved by W. Miller with caption 'Berwick-upon-Tweed'; title vignette engraved by Henry LeKeux. Typography: In a later impression (T/B) with engraved title dated 1851 and final imprint that of Stevenson & Co., beginning with signature 2D (page 417), the letter is repeated in lower-case italic, e.g.: 2D*d*.

Figures: C48-2, F95-2, P237-2, S287-3, Z365-3, 2E 446-3. A later printing (NN) represents only the last figure, and later impressions (1851) contain none.

Notes: Among these plays manuscript variants are recorded only for the first, third, and fourth.

3. THE MISCELLANEOUS PROSE WORKS

350A] Final Revised Edition: 1834-1836

[*half-title*] THE | MISCELLANEOUS PROSE WORKS | OF | SIR WALTER SCOTT, BART. | VOL. I [II-XXVIII]. | [*short rule*] | [*specific title*].
[*title-page*] [*specific title*] | BY | SIR WALTER SCOTT, BART. | [*short rule*] | ROBERT CADELL, EDINBURGH; | WHITTAKER AND CO., LONDON. | 1834 [1835-1836].

Published concurrently in Edinburgh and London at 5s a volume, first volume 1 May 1834, thereafter at monthly intervals, concluding with the 28th volume on schedule 1 August 1836. Binding: maroon cloth with green printed labels. Paper: Royal 16° in eights (170 x 107mm uncut). Watermarks: *none*.

Typography: The collective title and series volume number, as given above, appear only on the half-titles. Accordingly, to define each volume, both half-titles and full titles are recorded below. Throughout, in the first impression, the title imprint reads as above. Both on verso of half-title and at the end of text the printer's imprint reads invariably (1) and (2): EDINBURGH: PRINTED BY BALLANTYNE AND CO., PAUL'S WORK. As observed in the 'Napoleon' sequence 8-16 certain volumes were immediately reissued without title date or dated 1835-1840, most with variant printer's imprints, and thirteen of the subsequent volumes were also reimpressed in the period 1843-1846. Press figures, gradually phased out in the *Poetical Works* 1833-1834, do not appear in this continuing series of volumes. Illustrations: Inserted between the printed half-title and title-page are an engraved frontispiece and title, the latter with heading THE | PROSE WORKS and representing a vignette. With the few exceptions noted below the illustrations are again drawn by J. M. W. Turner. As indicated, however, different engravers are employed from volume to volume. Below the frontispiece and/or title vignette the plate imprint, if present, reads uniformly in the first impression: EDINBURGH: PUBLISHED 1834 [1835-1836] BY ROBERT CADELL; & WHITTAKER & Co. LONDON.

General Notes: An eight-page Prospectus dated February 1834 (and prefixed to an E copy volume 11 of the *Poetical Works*) announces publication on 1 May, observing further, with reference to the *Life of Napoleon*: 'The Editorship of this work is particularly dwelt upon in Sir Walter Scott's last will, and that document contains minute directions as to the manner in which the task should be fulfilled.' Lockhart further remarks, in the prefatory 'Notice' to the first volume (page iv), that the text for the *Life* is 'corrected and partly annotated by the Author; marginal dates are appended, in compliance with his instructions [and the work] is enriched with Maps of the Emperor's Campaigns.'

Another occasional slip in volume 20 of this series notes that these miscellaneous works could be purchased by subject-groups, from one to nine volumes: a circumstance evident in three of the partial sets cited below. These are sometimes in distinctive bindings and regularly occur without half-titles, which, if present, would immediately disclose the short set as part of a larger sequence.

Cadell's account for 1 July 1834 indicates an initial printing of 5000 copies (NNP MA 3555,f.251) and, under date of 30 June 1836 (f.255), shortly before publication of the final volume, notes a summary payment of £1505 from Thomas Wardle, this apparently for an unstated number of the total issue, '(in bds)', for distribution in America. Unlike an earlier arrangement for the novels, however (348Ab), no special Edinburgh-Philadelphia title-leaves seem to have been provided for this consignment and thus no way of detecting the exported issue.

Copies: E(4); CtY(vols.1-2, 10, 12, 15-17, 19-21, 26), CtY(vols.8-10, 14-15 [reissues 1835-1840, 11-13, 16] 'Life of Napoleon') IdU NN NNU-W(vols. 3-4 'Biographical Memoirs', inscribed by Maria Edgeworth to Mrs Grimshaw) NNU-W (vols.22-26 [incomplete part-set, lacking 27-28] 'Tales of a Grandfather') T/B(vols.1-3, 6, 8, 14-15, 18-21 [reissues 1835-1840, 9, 11-13, 16; reissues 1843-1846, 4-5, 7, 10, 17, 22-28]) ViU(vols 3-25, 27-28).

1] [*half-title*] THE | MISCELLANEOUS PROSE WORKS . . . VOL. I. . . . [*printed title*] THE LIFE | OF | JOHN DRYDEN. | BY | SIR WALTER SCOTT, BART. | [*short rule*] . . . . 1834.

Collation: $\pi 1(\pi 1+1)$ a^4 A-2E^8 2F^2(2F2+1). Pagination: *1* half-title, *2* printer's imprint(1), [*frontispiece, engraved title*], *i* title-page, *ii blank, iii*-iv Notice [by Lockhart] dated March 1834, *v* vi-vii Advertisement, *viii blank, ix*-x Contents, *1* 2-453 text, 453 printer's imprint(2), *454 blank* (+8-page catalogue 1 May 1834, a reprint of February 1834 Prospectus for this edition). Illustrations: Frontispiece portrait drawn by Sir G. Kneller, engraved by J. Horsburgh, with caption 'John

Dryden.' and 1834 imprint. Title vignette engraved by J. Horsburgh, with caption 'Dryden's Monument in Westminster Abbey.' Typography: Preliminary signature *a* is in italic.

2] [*half-title*] THE | MISCELLANEOUS PROSE WORKS . . . VOL. II. . . . [*printed title*] MEMOIRS | OF | JONATHAN SWIFT, D.D. | DEAN OF ST PATRICK'S, DUBLIN. | BY | SIR WALTER SCOTT, BART. | [*short rule*] . . . . 1834.

Collation: a^4(*a*1+1) A-2H^8 2I^4(2I4+1). Pagination: *1* half-title, *2* printer's imprint(1), [*frontispiece, engraved title*], *i* title-page, *ii blank, iii*-iv Advertisement, *v* vi-vii Contents, *viii blank, 1* 2-447 text, *448 blank, 449* fly-title, *450 blank, 451-452* 453-505 Appendix, 505 printer's imprint(2), *506 blank* (+4-page undated catalogue). Illustrations: Frontispiece portrait drawn by Bindon, engraved by Horsburgh, with caption 'Jonathan Swift, D.D.' Title vignette drawn by G. F. Sargent, engraved by J. Horsburgh, with caption 'Swift's Monument in St. Patrick's Cathedral.' and 1834 imprint. Typography: Preliminary signature *a* is in italic.

3] [*half-title*] THE | MISCELLANEOUS PROSE WORKS . . . VOL. III. . . . [*printed title*] BIOGRAPHICAL MEMOIRS | OF | EMINENT NOVELISTS, | AND OTHER DISTINGUISHED PERSONS. | BY | SIR WALTER SCOTT, BART. | VOL. I. | [*short rule*] . . . . 1834.

Collation: π2(π2+1) A-2F^8. Pagination: *i* half-title, *ii* printer's imprint(1), [*frontispiece, engraved title*], *iii* title-page, *iv blank, v* Contents, *vi blank, 1*-2 Advertisement, *3* 4-464 text, 464 printer's imprint(2). Illustrations: Frontispiece portrait 'Engraved by J. Horsburgh from a scarce Print' with caption 'Tobias Smollett, M.D.' and 1834 imprint. Title vignette drawn by J. M. W. Turner, engraved by W. Miller, with caption 'Dumbarton Castle and River Leven.' and 1834 imprint.

Notes: This volume includes thirteen of the authors included in the 1821 Ballantyne series, excluding only Mackenzie and Swift.

4] [*half-title*] THE | MISCELLANEOUS PROSE WORKS . . . VOL. IV. . . . [*printed title*] BIOGRAPHICAL MEMOIRS | OF | EMINENT NOVELISTS, | AND OTHER DISTINGUISHED PERSONS. | BY | SIR WALTER SCOTT, BART. | VOL. II. | [*short rule*] . . . . 1834.

Collation: π^2(π2+1) A-2C^8. Pagination: *i* half-title, *ii* printer's imprint(1), [*frontispiece, engraved title*], *iii* title-page, *iv blank, v* Contents, *vi blank, 1* 2-416 text, 416 printer's imprint(2). Illustrations: Frontispiece portrait drawn by Colvin Smith, engraved by J. Horsburgh, with caption 'Henry Mackenzie.' and 1834 imprint. Title vignette drawn by W. Allan, engraved by J. Horsburgh, followed by a quotation from Julia de Roubigne beginning 'I had fainted it seems. . . .' and 1834 imprint.

Notes: The first Memoir is of Henry Mackenzie (1745-1831), the only author then still alive among those celebrated in the 1821 series.

5] [*half-title*] THE | MISCELLANEOUS PROSE WORKS . . . VOL. V. . . . [*printed title*] PAUL'S LETTERS | TO | HIS KINSFOLK, | AND | ABSTRACT OF THE EYRBIGGIA-SAGA. | BY | SIR WALTER SCOTT, BART. | [*short rule*] . . . 1834.

Collation: π1 2π^4(2π4+1) A-2B^8 2C^8(-2C8). Pagination: *1* half-title, *2* printer's imprint(1), [*frontispiece, engraved title*], *3* title-page, *4 blank, 5* Advertisement [by Lockhart], *6 blank, i* ii-vi Contents, *1* 2-340 text of *Paul's Letters*, 341-354 appendices, *355* fly-title for the 'Abstract', *356 blank, 357* 358-413 text, 413 printer's imprint(2), *414 blank.* Illustrations: Frontispiece drawn by J. M. W. Turner, engraved by W. Miller, with caption 'Brussels.' Title vignette drawn by J. M. W. Turner, engraved by W. Miller, with caption 'Hougoumont.' and 1834 imprint.

6] [*half-title*] THE | MISCELLANEOUS PROSE WORKS . . . VOL. VI. . . . [*printed title*] ESSAYS | ON | CHIVALRY, ROMANCE, | AND | THE DRAMA. | BY | SIR WALTER SCOTT, BART. | [*short rule*] . . . . 1834.

Collation: π1(π1+2) A-2A^8 2B^4 2C^2. Pagination: *i* half-title, *ii* printer's im-print(1), [*frontispiece, engraved title*], *iii* title-page, *iv blank, v* Contents, *vi blank, 1* fly-title for 'An Essay on Chivalry' [1818], *2 blank, 3* 4-126 text, *127* fly-title for 'An Essay on Romance' [1824], *128 blank, 129* 130-216 text, *217* fly-title for 'An Essay on the Drama' [1819], *218 blank, 219* 220-395 text, 395 printer's imprint(2), *396 blank.* Illustrations: Frontispiece drawn by J. M. W. Turner, engraved by W. Miller, with caption 'Jerusalem'. Title vignette drawn by J. M. W. Turner, engraved by J. Horsburgh, with caption 'Shakespeare's Monument in Stratford Church.' and 1834 imprint. Typography: A later printing omits printer's imprint(1).

7] [*half-title*] THE | MISCELLANEOUS PROSE WORKS . . . VOL. VII. . . . [*printed title*] PROVINCIAL ANTIQUITIES | OF | SCOTLAND. | BY | SIR WALTER SCOTT, BART. | [*short rule*] . . . . 1834.

Collation: *a*^{4} A-2E^8 2F^4 *2G*1. Pagination: *1* half-title, *2 blank,* [*frontispiece, engraved title*], *3* title-page, *4 blank, i*-ii Contents, *iii* Advertisement [by Lockhart], *iv blank, 1* fly-title for 'An Essay on Border Antiquities', *2 blank, 3* 4-141 text, 142-153 appendices, *154 blank, 155* fly-title for 'Provincial Antiquities of Scotland', *156 blank, 157* 158-457 text, 457 printer's imprint, *458 blank.* No preliminary printer's imprint. Illustrations: Frontispiece drawn by J. M. W. Turner, engraved by W. Miller, with caption 'Norham Castle.' Title vignette drawn by J. M. W. Turner, engraved by W. Miller, with caption 'New Abbey near Dumfries.' and 1834 imprint. Typography: Preliminary signature *a*, in italic, is on page *iii*. Signature 2F (page

449) is missigned F.

8] [*half-title*] THE | MISCELLANEOUS PROSE WORKS . . . VOL. VIII. . . . [*printed title*] LIFE | OF | NAPOLEON BUONAPARTE, . . . BY | SIR WALTER SCOTT, BART. | VOL. I. | [*short rule*] . . . . 1834.

Collation: π[8] A-2B[8]. Pagination: 1-4 Cadell advertisement, *5* half-title, *6* quotation from Lucan with translation, printer's imprint(1), [*frontispiece, engraved title*], *i* title-page, *ii blank, iii*-iv Advertisement [by Lockhart], *v* vi-viii Advertisement, *ix* x-xii Contents, *1* 2-397 text of 'View of the French Revolution, chapters 1-11, 397 printer's imprint(2), *398-400 blank*. Illustrations: Frontispiece portrait drawn by J. Isabey, engraved by C. Rolls, with caption 'Napoleon Bonaparte. 1802.' and (in some copies) 1834 imprint. Title vignette drawn by J. M. W. Turner, engraved by W. Miller, with caption 'Hotel de Ville, Paris.' and 1834 imprint. Typography: In some copies an erratum slip dated 10 November 1834 is inserted before half-title, reading: 'Owing to a mistake in the *Lettering*, the name of William Miller is adhibited to the Vignette to this Volume, in place of J. Horsburgh.' The mistake was not corrected in later printings.

9] [*half-title*] THE | MISCELLANEOUS PROSE WORKS . . . VOL. IX. . . . [*printed title*] LIFE | OF | NAPOLEON BUONAPARTE, . . . BY | SIR WALTER SCOTT, BART. | VOL. II. | [*short rule*] . . . . 1835.

Collation: π[6] A-2C[8] 2D[2]. Pagination: 1-2 Cadell advertisement, *3* half-title, *4* printer's imprint(1), [*frontispiece, engraved title*], *5* title-page, *6 blank, i* ii-vi Contents, *1* 2-317 text of 'View of the French Revolution' concluded, 318-398 text of 'Life of Napoleon Buonaparte', chapters 1-2, *399* 400-420 appendices, 420 printer's imprint(2). Illustrations: Frontispiece drawn by J. M. W. Turner, engraved by W. Miller, with caption 'Brienne.' Title vignette drawn by J. M. W. Turner, engraved by J. Horsburgh, with caption 'Napoleon's Logement Quai Conti.' and 1835 imprint. Map facing page *1* of text, engraved by S. Hall, with caption 'North Italy' and 1835 imprint. Typography: In some copies a redundant printer's imprint appears on page *6*. Occasionally an undated erratum slip remains at end of text, reading: 'The name Las Cases, by an error of the printer, appears in this Volume as Las Casas.' The error was not corrected in later printings.

10] [*half-title*] THE | MISCELLANEOUS PROSE WORKS . . . VOL. X. . . . [*printed title*] LIFE | OF | NAPOLEON BUONAPARTE, . . . BY | SIR WALTER SCOTT, BART. | VOL. III. | [*short rule*] . . . . 1835.

Collation: π[4](π4+1) A-2C[8] 2D[8](-2D8). Pagination: *1* half-title, *2* printer's imprint(1), [*frontispiece, engraved title*], *3* title-page, *4 blank, i* ii-vi Contents, *1* 2-415 text, chapters 3-15, *416 blank, 417* 418-429 appendices, 429 printer's imprint(2), *430 blank*. Illustrations: Frontispiece drawn by J. M. W. Turner, engraved by W. Miller, with caption 'Placenza.' Title vignette drawn by J. M. W. Turner, engraved by W. Miller, with caption 'Venice.' and 1835 imprint. Map facing page *1* of text, engraved by S. Hall, with caption 'Egypt and Syria' and 1835 imprint.

11] [*half-title*] THE | MISCELLANEOUS PROSE WORKS . . . VOL. XI. . . . [*printed title*] LIFE | OF | NAPOLEON BUONAPARTE, . . . BY | SIR WALTER SCOTT, BART. | VOL. IV. | [*short rule*] . . . . 1835.

Collation: π1 2π^4 A-2A^8 2B^4 2C1. Pagination: *1* half-title, *2* printer's imprint(1), [*frontispiece, engraved title*], *3* title-page, *4 blank, i* ii-vi Contents, *1* 2-352 text, chapters 16-29, *353* 354-394 appendices, 394 printer's imprint(2). Illustrations: Frontispiece drawn by J. M. W. Turner, engraved by W. Miller, with caption 'Verona.' Title vignette drawn by J. M. W. Turner, engraved by W. Miller, with caption 'Vincennes.' and 1835 imprint. Map facing page *1* of text, engraved by S. Hall, with caption 'North Italy' and 1835 imprint. This map may have been prepared too late for the original issue, as it is lacking in most copies.

12] [*half-title*] THE | MISCELLANEOUS PROSE WORKS . . . VOL. XII. . . . [*printed title*] LIFE | OF | NAPOLEON BUONAPARTE, . . . BY | SIR WALTER SCOTT, BART. | VOL. V. | [*short rule*] . . . . 1835.

Collation: π^4(π4+1) A-Z^8 2A^6 *2B*1. Pagination: *1* half-title, *2* printer's imprint(1), [*frontispiece, engraved title*], *3* title-page, *4 blank, i* ii-v Contents, *vi blank, 1* 2-381 text, chapters 30-40, 381 printer's imprint(2), *382 blank.* Illustrations: Frontispiece drawn by J. M. W. Turner, engraved by W. Miller, with caption 'St. Cloud.' Title vignette drawn by J. M. W. Turner, engraved by W. Miller, with caption 'Mayence.' and 1835 imprint. Two maps facing page *1* of text, engraved by S. Hall, with captions 'North Germany and Prussia' and 'Central & South Germany', both with 1835 imprints. Again one of these maps, the first, may have been prepared too late for original issue, as it is lacking in most copies.

13] [*half-title*] THE | MISCELLANEOUS PROSE WORKS . . . VOL. XIII. . . . [*printed title*] LIFE | OF | NAPOLEON BUONAPARTE, . . . BY | SIR WALTER SCOTT, BART. | VOL. VI. | [*short rule*] . . . . 1835.

Collation: π^6 A-2C^8 *2D*1. Pagination: *1* half-title, *2* printer's imprint(1), [*frontispiece, engraved title*], *3* title-page, *4 blank, i* ii-vii Contents, *viii blank, 1* 2-405 text, chapters 41-55, *406 blank, 407* 408-417 Appendix, 417 printer's imprint(2), *418 blank.* Illustrations: Frontispiece drawn by J. M. W. Turner, engraved by J. Horsburgh, with caption 'Milan.' Title vignette drawn by J. M. W. Turner, engraved by W. Miller, with caption 'The Simplon.' and 1835 imprint.

14] [*half-title*] THE | MISCELLANEOUS PROSE WORKS . . . VOL. XIV. . . . [*printed title*] LIFE | OF | NAPOLEON BUONAPARTE, . . . BY | SIR WALTER SCOTT, BART. | VOL. VII. | [*short rule*] . . . . 1835.

Collation: π^6 A-2D^8 2E^2 *2F*1. Pagination: *1* half-title, *2* printer's imprint(1), [*frontispiece, engraved title*], *3* title-page, *4 blank, i* ii-vii Contents, *viii blank, 1* 2-432 text, chapters 56-71, *433* 434-438 Appendix, 438 printer's imprint(2). Illustrations: Frontispiece drawn by J. M. W. Turner, engraved by W. Miller, with caption 'Paris.' Title vignette drawn by J. M. W. Turner, engraved by W. Miller, with caption 'Malmaison.' and 1835 imprint. Map facing page *1* of text, engraved by S. Hall, with caption 'Russia' and 1835 imprint.

15] [*half-title*] THE | MISCELLANEOUS PROSE WORKS . . . VOL. XV. . . . [*printed title*] LIFE | OF | NAPOLEON BUONAPARTE, . . . BY | SIR WALTER SCOTT, BART. | VOL. VIII. | [*short rule*] . . . . 1835.

Collation: π^6(-π6) A-2D^8 2E^4(-2E4). Pagination: *1* half-title, *2* printer's im-print(1), [*frontispiece, engraved title*], *3* title-page, *4 blank, i* ii-vi Contents, *1* 2-438 text, chapters 72-88, 438 printer's imprint(2). Illustrations: Frontispiece portrait drawn by Ches. Steuben, engraved by R. Graves, with Napoleon's signature '1815' and 1835 imprint. Title vignette drawn by J. M. W. Turner, engraved by W. Miller, with caption 'Fontainbleau.' and 1835 imprint. Map facing page *1* of text, engraved by S. Hall, with caption 'France' and 1835 imprint.

16] [*half-title*] THE | MISCELLANEOUS PROSE WORKS . . . VOL. XVI. . . . [*printed title*] LIFE | OF | NAPOLEON BUONAPARTE, . . . BY | SIR WALTER SCOTT, BART. | VOL. IX. | [*short rule*] . . . . 1835.

Collation: π^4 A-2B^8 2C^6. Pagination: *1* half-title, *2* printer's imprint(1), [*frontispiece, engraved title*], *3* title-page, *4 blank, i* ii-iv Contents, *1* 2-310 text, chapters 89-97, 311-342 Conclusion, *343* 344-412 appendices, 412 printer's imprint(2). Illustrations: Frontispiece drawn by J. M. W. Turner, engraved by W. Miller, with caption 'Field of Waterloo.' Title vignette drawn by J. M. W. Turner, engraved by E. Goodall, with caption 'The Bellerophon. Plymouth Sound.' and 1835 imprint.

17] [*half-title*] THE | MISCELLANEOUS PROSE WORKS . . . VOL. XVII. . . . [*printed title*] | PERIODICAL CRITICISM. | BY | SIR WALTER SCOTT, BART. | VOL. I. | [*short rule*] | POETRY. | [*short rule*] . . . . 1835.

Collation: π^2(π2+1) A-Y^8 Z^8(-Z8). Pagination: *i* half-title, *ii* printer's imprint(1), [*frontispiece, engraved title*], *iii* title-page, *iv blank, v* Contents, *vi blank, 1* 2-366 text, 366 printer's imprint(2). Illustrations: Frontispiece portrait by Watson Gordon, engraved by W. H. Lizars, with caption 'Francis Jeffrey, Esqr. Now Lord Jeffrey.'

and 1835 imprint. Title vignette drawn by D. O. Hill, engraved by W. Miller, with caption 'Craig Crook Castle, near Edinburgh. . . .' and 1835 imprint. Typography: For this volume only, the final imprint(2) reads: [*short rule*] | PRINTED BY BALLANTYNE AND CO., PAUL'S WORK, CANONGATE.

18] [*half-title*] THE | MISCELLANEOUS PROSE WORKS . . . VOL. XVIII. . . . [*printed title*] | PERIODICAL CRITICISM. | BY | SIR WALTER SCOTT, BART. | VOL. II. | [*short rule*] | ROMANCE. | [*short rule*] . . . . 1835.

Collation: $\pi^2(\pi2+1)$ A-2A^8 2B^8(-2B8). Pagination: *i* half-title, *ii* printer's imprint(1), [*frontispiece, engraved title*], *iii* title-page, *iv blank, v* Contents, *vi blank, 1* 2-398 text, 398 printer's imprint(2). Illustrations: Frontispiece 'Engraved by G. B. Shaw from a Portrait by Wm. Hoppner, R.A. in possession of John Murray, Esqr.' with caption 'Wm. Gifford, Esqr.' and 1835 imprint. Title vignette drawn by J. M. W. Turner, engraved by W. Miller, with caption 'Chiefswood Cottage, near Abbotsford. For some Years the Summer retreat of J. G. Lockhart, Esqre.' and 1835 imprint.

19] [*half-title*] THE | MISCELLANEOUS PROSE WORKS . . . VOL. XIX. . . . [*printed title*] | PERIODICAL CRITICISM. | BY | SIR WALTER SCOTT, BART. | VOL. III. | [*short rule*] | MISCELLANEOUS. | [*short rule*] . . . . 1835.

Collation: $\pi^2(\pi2+1)$ A-Z^8. Pagination: *i* half-title, *ii* printer's imprint(1), [*frontispiece, engraved title*], *iii* title-page, *iv blank, v* Contents, *vi blank, 1* 2-367 text, 367 printer's imprint(2), *368 blank.* Illustrations: Frontispiece portrait by Sir Hy. Raeburn, engraved by Hy. Haig, with caption 'John Home.' and 1835 imprint. Title vignette engraved by W. H. Lizars, with caption 'Culloden House. . . .' and 1835 imprint.

20] [*half-title*] THE | MISCELLANEOUS PROSE WORKS . . . VOL. XX. . . . [*printed title*] | PERIODICAL CRITICISM. | BY | SIR WALTER SCOTT, BART. | VOL. IV. | [*short rule*] | MISCELLANEOUS. | [*short rule*] . . . . 1835.

Collation: $\pi^2(\pi2+1)$ A-Z^8 2A^4. Pagination: *i* half-title, *ii* printer's imprint(1), [*frontispiece, engraved title*], *iii* title-page, *iv blank, v* Contents, *vi blank, 1* 2-376 text, 376 printer's imprint(2). Illustrations: Frontispiece drawn by D. O. Hill, engraved by W. Richardson, with caption 'The Pavilion on the Tweed, near Abbotsford.' Title vignette drawn by D. O. Hill, engraved by J. Horsburgh, with caption 'The Peel Tower in the Village of Darnick. near Abbotsford' and 1835 imprint.

21] [*half-title*] THE | MISCELLANEOUS PROSE WORKS . . . VOL. XXI. . . . [*printed title*] | PERIODICAL CRITICISM. | BY | SIR WALTER SCOTT, BART. | VOL. V. | [*short rule*] | MISCELLANEOUS—(CONCLUDED). | [*dash*]

| LETTERS OF MALACHI MALAGROWTHER | ON THE CURRENCY. | [*short rule*] . . . . 1836.

Collation: $\pi^2(\pi2+1)$ A-2B[8] 2C1. Pagination: *i* half-title, *ii* printer's imprint(1), [*frontispiece, engraved title*], *iii* title-page, *iv blank, v* Contents, *vi blank, 1* 2-402 text, 402 printer's imprint(2). Illustrations: Frontispiece drawn by D. O. Hill, engraved by W. Forrest, with caption 'Allanton, Lanarkshire.' Title vignette drawn by J. M. W. Turner, engraved by W. Miller, with caption 'Rhymers Glen. Abbotsford' and 1836 imprint.

22] [*half-title*] THE | MISCELLANEOUS PROSE WORKS . . . VOL. XXII. . . . [*printed title*] TALES OF A GRANDFATHER. | BY | SIR WALTER SCOTT, BART. | VOL. I. | [*short rule*] | SCOTLAND. | [*short rule*] . . . . 1836.

Collation: π^2 $a^4(a2+1)$ A-2A[8] 2B[4](-2B4). Pagination: *1* half-title, *2* printer's imprint(1), [*frontispiece, engraved title*], *3* title-page, *4 blank, i* ii-iii Preface, *iv blank, v*-vi Contents, vii-ix Dedication,*x blank, 1* 2-389 text, 389 printer's imprint(2), *390 blank.* Reissued 1846 (T/B). Illustrations: Frontispiece drawn by J. M. W. Turner, engraved by W. Miller, with caption 'Edinburgh.' Title vignette drawn by J. M. W. Turner, engraved by J. Horsburgh, with caption 'Dunfermline.' and 1836 imprint. Typography: Preliminary signature *a* is in italic.

23] [*half-title*] THE | MISCELLANEOUS PROSE WORKS . . . VOL. XXIII. . . . [*printed title*] TALES OF A GRANDFATHER. | BY | SIR WALTER SCOTT, BART. | VOL. II. | [*short rule*] | SCOTLAND. | [*short rule*] . . . . 1836.

Collation: π^4 A-2B[8] 2C1. Pagination: *1* half-title, *2* printer's imprint(1), [*frontispiece, engraved title*], *3* title-page, *4 blank, i* ii-iii Contents, *iv blank, 1* 2-402 text, 402 printer's imprint(2). Illustrations: Frontispiece drawn by J. M. W. Turner, engraved by W. Miller, with caption 'Stirling.' Title vignette drawn by J. M. W. Turner, engraved by W. Miller, with caption 'Craigmillar Castle, near Edinburgh.' and 1836 imprint.

24] [*half-title*] THE | MISCELLANEOUS PROSE WORKS . . . VOL. XXIV. . . . [*printed title*] TALES OF A GRANDFATHER. | BY | SIR WALTER SCOTT, BART. | VOL. III. | [*short rule*] | SCOTLAND. | [*short rule*] . . . . 1836.

Collation: π^4 A-2B[8] 2C[4](-2C4). Pagination: *1* half-title, *2* printer's imprint(1), [*frontispiece, engraved title*], *3* title-page, *4 blank, i* ii-iii Contents, *iv blank, 1* 2-406 text, 406 printer's imprint(2). Reissued 1846 (T/B). Illustrations: Frontispiece drawn by J. M. W. Turner, engraved by W. Miller, with caption 'Dunnstaffnage.'

Title vignette drawn by J. M. W. Turner, engraved by W. Miller, with caption 'Linlithgow.' and 1836 imprint.

25] [*half-title*] THE | MISCELLANEOUS PROSE WORKS . . . VOL. XXV. . . . [*printed title*] TALES OF A GRANDFATHER. | BY | SIR WALTER SCOTT, Bart. | VOL. IV. | [*short rule*] | SCOTLAND. | [*short rule*] . . . . 1836.

Collation: π^4 A-2D^8 *2E*1. Pagination: *1* half-title, *2* printer's imprint(1), [*frontispiece, engraved title*], *3* title-page, *4 blank, i* ii-iv Contents, *1* 2-433 text, 433 printer's imprint(2), *434 blank.* Illustrations: Frontispiece drawn by J. M. W. Turner, engraved by W. Miller, with caption 'Glencoe.' Title vignette drawn by J. M. W. Turner, engraved by W. Miller, with caption 'Killiecrankie.' and 1836 imprint.

26] [*half-title*] THE | MISCELLANEOUS PROSE WORKS . . . VOL. XXVI. . . . [*printed title*] TALES OF A GRANDFATHER. | BY | SIR WALTER SCOTT, Bart. | VOL. V. | [*short rule*] | SCOTLAND. | [*short rule*] . . . 1836.

Collation: π^4 A-2D^8 2E^2. Pagination: *1* half-title, *2* printer's imprint(1), [*frontispiece, engraved title*], *3* title-page, *4 blank, i* ii-iii Contents, *iv blank, 1* 2-436 text, 436 printer's imprint(2). Illustrations: Frontispiece drawn by J. M. W. Turner, engraved by W. Miller, with caption 'Inverness.' Title vignette drawn by J. M. W. Turner, engraved by W. Miller, with caption 'Fort Augustus. Loch Ness.' and 1836 imprint.

27] [*half-title*] THE | MISCELLANEOUS PROSE WORKS . . . VOL. XXVII. . . . [*printed title*] TALES OF A GRANDFATHER. | BY | SIR WALTER SCOTT, Bart. | VOL. VI. | [*short rule*] | FRANCE. | [*short rule*] . . . . 1836.

Collation: π^4(π4+1) A-Z^8 2A8(-2A8). Pagination: *1* half-title, *2* printer's imprint(1), [*frontispiece, engraved title*], *3* title-page, *4 blank, i* ii-vi Contents, *1* 2-4 dedication, *5* 6-382 text, 382 printer's imprint(2). Illustrations: Frontispiece drawn by J. M. W. Turner, engraved by W. Richardson, with caption 'Rouen.' Title vignette drawn by J. M. W. Turner, engraved by J. Horsburgh, with caption 'Calais.' and 1836 imprint.

28] [*half-title*] THE | MISCELLANEOUS PROSE WORKS . . . VOL. XXVIII. . . [*printed title*] TALES OF A GRANDFATHER. | BY | SIR WALTER SCOTT, Bart. | VOL. VII. | [*short rule*] | FRANCE. | [*short rule*] . . . 1836.

Collation: π^4 2π^2 A-Y^8 Z^6. Pagination: *1* half-title, *2* printer's imprint(1), [*frontispiece, engraved title*], *3* title-page, *4 blank, i*-ii Notice [by Lockhart], dated 1 August 1836, *iii* iv-vii Contents, *viii blank, 1* 2-281 text, *282 blank, 283* 284-363 General Index, 363 printer's imprint(2), *364 blank.* Illustrations: Frontispiece drawn by J. M. W. Turner, engraved by W. Forrest, with caption 'Chateau d'Arc, near Dieppe.' Title vignette drawn by J. M. W. Turner, engraved by J. Horsburgh, with caption 'Abbeville.' and 1836 imprint.

Notes: As so often with the Scott introductions in *WN*, the date assigned to the Lockhart notice here is proleptic, indicating actual issue date for this final volume. In it Lockhart observes: 'This Volume concludes the Collected Works of Sir Walter Scott, which have reached, in Monthly issues, the term of seven years and four months, an extent for the writings of one individual unprecedented in English literature.' The total issue thus has extended from 1 June 1829 through eighty-eight months and comprised first the novels (48 volumes), then the poems (12), and finally these *Miscellaneous Prose Works* (28).

SUPPLEMENTARY VOLUMES

29-30] [*half-title*] THE | PROSE WORKS | OF | SIR WALTER SCOTT, BART. | VOL. XXIX [XXX]. | [*short rule*] | HISTORY OF SCOTLAND. | VOL I [II]. [1836]

General Notes: Though Lockhart, in the preceding 28th volume, notes that 'several volumes could have been added', the 1830 *History of Scotland* in Lardner's *Cyclopaedia* was necessarily excluded because it still belonged 'to the Proprietors of that work.' Cadell's account book, however, shows that by 31 December 1836 he had acquired the plates and impressed 3000 copies for his own issue (NNP MA 3555, f.256). These then were bound in the same cloth and green labels as the 1834-1836 *MPW* set, but with the original 1830 engraved titles (the first with additional line NEW EDITION above vignette), and newly printed half-titles as described above. The half-titles displace the original printed preliminaries, both volumes now (after engraved title and new half-title) starting with leaf A3 (page *v*). For the original issue *see* 232A.

Copies with supplementary volumes 29-30: CtY IdU.

CLAUSUS • TUTUS • ERO

APPENDICES

Legal Papers; Anthologies; Satires, Parodies, and Imitations; Tributes and Dedications

APPENDIX 1: LEGAL PAPERS

APPENDIX 1: LEGAL PAPERS (351A-353A)

Though Scott's varied legal career extended from 15 May 1786, when he was apprenticed to his father, to 7 December 1831, the date of his last judgement as Sheriff-Depute of Selkirkshire, the pertinent records printed in his lifetime, and now located, range only from 1792 to 1806 and relate solely to his activities as an Advocate in the Court of Session. Even in this brief period, however, the author is exhibited in a capacity little regarded in previous studies and thus requires separate notice in this present account.

351A] First Edition 1792

DISPUTATIO JURIDICA, | AD TIT. XXIV. LIB. XLVIII. PAND. | DE CADAVERIBUS DAMNATORUM. | QUAM, | FAVENTE NUMINE, | EX AUCTORITATE CLARISSIMI AC CONSULTISSIMI VIRI | D. HENRICI ERSKINE, | DE NEWHALL, | INCLYTÆE FACULTATIS JURIDICÆE DECANI: |NEC NON | Ex ejufdem FACULTATIS Confenfu et Decreto, | Pro ADVOCATI Munere confequendo, | Publicae Difquifitioni subjicit | GUALTERUS SCOTT, *Auct. et Refp.* | Ad diem 10. Julii, hor.loc.fol. | EDINBURGI: | Apud BALFOUR et SMELLIE, | Facultatis Juridicae Typographos. | [short rule] | M,DCC,XCII.

Printed: 10 July 1792, the date indicated on title (four days after the degree was awarded, 6 July, and one day before Scott 'assumed the gown with all its duties and honours' (Lockhart, i.83). Binding: wrappers. Paper: 4° in twos (232 x 176mm cut). Watermarks: laid, fleur-de-lys within a shield and initials GR (Heawood 1856). Collation: A^2 B-D^2. Pagination: *1* title-page, *2* Imprimatur, *3* dedication, *4* blank, *5* 6-13 text, *14 blank*, *15* Annexa, *16 blank*. Figures: none.

Notes: Scott's thesis for admission to the Faculty of Advocates, regarded by one recent commentator as 'a very creditable piece of legal Latin' (Buchan, page 40 note), by another as 'probably written for him by a hack, as the custom then was' (Daiches, page 59). Title translated: 'Concerning the Disposal of the Dead Bodies of Criminals.' Imprimatur reads: 'Edinburgi, 6. Julii 1792. Imprimatur. William Miller. David Williamson.' Miller (1755-1846) was raised to the Bench in 1795 as Lord Glenlee; Williamson (1761-1837) was elevated to the Bench in 1811 as Lord Balgray. The dedication reads: 'Viro Nobili Roberto Macqueen de Braxfield, Inter Quaesitores de Rebus Capitalibus Primario, Inter Judices de Rebus Civilibus, Senatori Dignissimo, Perito Haud Minus Quam Fideli Juris Interpreti; Adeoque, In Utroque Munere Fungendo, Scelera Sive Debita Severitate Puniendo, Sive Suum Cuique Tribuendo et Tuendo, Prudentia Pariter Atque Justitia, Insigni; Hasce Theses Juridicas, Summa cum Observantia, Sacras Esse Voluit Gualterus Scott.' The dedicatee, Macqueen of Braxfield (1722-1799), in 1788 was appointed Lord Justice-Clerk (or President of the Supreme Criminal Court) of Scotland. Though of limited issue, there are two printings, one (a) on thick paper, gilt edged, as described above, the other (b) on thinner paper with one or more half-sheets watermarked 'F S' [Freeman Spicer?]. In the variant issue (b) the last two leaves appear to be disjunct.

Presentation copy: (issue a) Dutch gilt decorated wrappers: E('William Keith Esqr. from his affectionate Cousin most respectfull humble Serv. The Author'). Other copies: (issue a) BCL(crimson morocco gilt [?]presentation binding); GU(Dutch gilt decorated wrappers, marked as once owned by Principal [John] Lee, then by David Laing). (Issue b in marbled wrappers): E. Reference: Johnson, pages 80n, 84.

SESSION PAPERS

352A] EDINBURGH: Court of Session 1793-1804

Preliminary note: This record of Scott's pleadings, though based upon a thorough search through the Session Papers collection in the Signet Library—all unfortunately unindexed by advocate—cannot be regarded as definitive, as it includes very few papers from Scott's first five years of practice (1792-1796) and none from the last two years (1805-1806) before he relinquished his post to become a Clerk of Session. Moreover, the record also excludes non-sessional papers deposited elsewhere, such as those pertaining to Scott's first recorded trial, that of M'Naught in May 1793 (extracted in Lockhart, i.281-286, from E MS 1627), and incidental papers in print or manuscript form produced after 1806 (e.g. the triplies lodged in 1810 on behalf of James Ballantyne re Thomas Kerr, his apprentice, Scottish Record Office, CS.236 [B/16/4]).

Despite its shortcomings the 66 printed papers preserved in the Signet Library collection amply illustrate Scott's various professional activities as an Advocate. In particular, they show the style he used to draft petitions (the first surviving example 352.2, it will be noted, located only at the National Library of Scotland) and five other formularies (each first appearing as 352.1, 3, 7, 13, and 29). Among several litigations continuing beyond a single process, the most protracted involves one John Scott, himself a Writer to the Signet and thus in the heading designated as 'Party' against Alexander Brodie. Of the papers filed by Walter Scott on John Scott's behalf the first is dated 25 June 1801, the fifth and last 8 March 1803.

Other persons having some familial or social connection with Scott, beyond any legal context, include three further Writers to the Signet, his father Walter (352.3, 5), his younger brother Thomas (352.52), and Alexander Keith (352.1, 50), a cousin and older brother of William, noted above as a recipient of his thesis (351) and cited again, perhaps, as the respondent to a petition on 29 May 1801 (352.33). Throughout this period, however, the Writer who most regularly instructed Scott was William Riddell of Camieston, whose assistance Scott early solicited in 1799 for a position as Sheriff-Depute of Selkirkshire. That same year, according to newly enacted law, the printer most frequently employed for Scott's legal papers identifies himself as David Willison (352.19), father-in-law of Scott's literary publisher Archibald Constable. Three other legal parties well known to Scott, and all involved in litigation in 1802, were his cousin Hugh Scott of Harden (18 June), the Marquis of Abercorn, later dedicatee of *The Lady of the Lake* (11 December), and Sir William Eliott of Stobs (12, 30 December). Altogether, then, the Scott record exemplifies a rather closely affiliated society.

The following account cites in order, first the date of the paper and name, as given, of the agent (a Writer of the Signet unless noted otherwise), next the opening and closing words, Scott's signature, then the page count, applicable notes, and volume entry location in the Signet Library. Two papers are deposited elsewhere (352.2, 29), the second here illustrated as the only known exemplar of a Scott process in the High Court of Judiciary.

Because of their special purpose, the normal issue of these legal papers probably did not exceed twenty-five copies: a sufficient number for the Lords of Session and interested parties. All names in these proceedings, as a class apart, are identified by a left bracket [in the General Index.

352A.1] 1793 12 November. Alex. Keith.
Answers for Charles Dempster and Son, Merchant in St Andrew's and Agents for the Bank of Scotland in that place; to the Petition and Complaint of Andrew Cathcart, Distiller in Paisley. . . . In respect whereof, &c. WALTER SCOTT.
Pages: *1* 2-7. Copy: ES[359(16)].

352A.2] 1796 21 January. C. Bremner.
Unto the Right Honourable the Lords of Council and Session, The Petition of John Baillie, residing in Glasgow. . . . According to Justice, &c. WALTER SCOTT.
Pages: *1* 2-17. Notes: MS annotation 22 June 1796 'Refused unanimously'. Copy: E[BCL.D2849(39)].

352A.3] 1797 20 April. Walter Scott.
Memorial for Messrs Eden, Ridley, and Company, Bankers in Newcastle, and Walter Scott, Writer to the Signet, their Attorney, Chargers, against Dr Stuart Threipland and Others, Suspenders. . . . In respect whereof, &c. WALTER SCOTT.
Pages: *1* 2-11. Copy: ES[377(54)].

352A..4] 1797 13 June. Wm Riddell.
Unto the Right Honourable the Lords of Council and Session, The Petition of Robert Pearson, Residenter in Leith. . . . According to justice, &c. WALTER SCOTT.
Pages: *1* 2-7. Copy: ES[385(57)].

352A.5] 1797 22 June. Walter Scott.
Unto the Right Honourable the Lords of Council and Session, The Petition of John James Marquis of Abercorn, Heritable Proprietor of the Seedhill Mills of Paisley, and William Langmuir, Tacksman of the said Mills. . . . According to justice, &c. WALTER SCOTT.
Pages: *1* 2-27. Copies: ES[372(9), 383(26)].

352A.6] 1797 24 November. John Scott.
Unto the Right Honourable the Lords of Council and Session, The Petition of William Redhead Tenant in Chatto. . . . According to justice, &c. WALTER SCOTT.
Pages: *1* 2-18. Notes: MS note 1 December 1797 'Refuse'. Copy: ES[367(1)].

352A.7] 1797 5 December. Joseph Gillon.
Consent by the Heritors of Melrose Parish, in Process of Augmentation. [no formal close] WALTER SCOTT.
Pages: *1* 2-3. Notes: Both here and in the paper of 2 February 1799 Gillon is identified only as a 'Writer', but another record of 22 May 1800 refers to him as an 'Attorney'. Copy: ES[398(10)].

352A.8] 1798 15 February. Wm Riddell.
Unto the Right Honourable the Lords of Council and Session, The Petition of William Vair, Son of the Deceased John Vair, late Merchant in Melrose, and Nelly Vair, Relict of the said James Vair. . . . According to justice, &c. WALTER SCOTT.
Pages: *1* 2-7. Copy: ES[392(41)].

352A.9] 1798 20 June. Jo. Scott.
Memorial and Abstract of the Prepared State in the Process for a Warrant to sell, at the instance of Thomas Watson and James Watson, only surviving Children of the deceased Dr James Watson Physician in Kelso, and Mrs Elizabeth Turnbull, widow of the said Dr James Watson, and others their Tutors-dative, against Alexander Watson, presently residing at Fisher-row, only brother of the said deceased Dr James Watson. . . . In respect whereof, &c. WAL. SCOTT.
Pages: *1* 2-12. Notes: Scott's oddly printed signature as advocate occurs only here and in the next paper. Copy: ES[402(19)].

352A.10] 1798 6 July. Jo. Scott.
Unto the Right Honourable the Lords of Council and Session, The Petition of James Ballantyne, Senior, Merchant in Boulogne, and Thomas Ballantyne tenant in Wheathope, youngest Son and universal disponee of the deceased George Ballantyne tenant in Craig of Douglas. . . . According to justice, &c. WAL. SCOTT.
Pages: *1* 2-8. Copy: ES[396(88)].

352A.11] 1798 1 December. H. Davidson.
Answers for Mr. William Keith, Trustee for Allan M'Dougall Writer to the Signet, and his Creditors, and for the Trustees of the late Richard Oswald, Esq. of Auchincruive, and others, Creditors of Captain Archibald M'Laine of Lochbuy; to the Petition of Allan M'Laine, eldest lawful Son of the deceased Gillean M'Laine, Tacksman of Seallaster, in the Island of Mull. . . In respect whereof, &c. WALTER SCOTT.
Pages: *1* 2-13 + 1-2 Appendix. Copy: ES[393(41)].

352A.12] 1799 4 January. Ja. Ferguson.
Memorial for William Henderson, Esq; Agent for the Bank of Scotland at Aberdeen, Charger; In the Suspension at the instance of Alexander Duthie, Stocking Manufacturer there. . . . In respect whereof, &c. WALTER SCOTT.
Pages: *1* 2-13. Copy: ES[401(2)].

352A.13] 1799 15 January. J. Scott.
Duplies for John Maxwell of Broomholm, William Keir in Minholm, and Thomas Baittie of Crieve, three of His Majesty's Justices of the Peace for the County of Dumfries; William Dalgleish Constable in Langholm, and Christopher Murray in Glebe Field or Limiecleugh, Defenders; to the Replies for John Bell in Nether-Hole House, Pursuer. . . . In respect whereof, &c. WALTER SCOTT.
Pages: *1* 2-11. Copy: ES[400(18)].

352A.14] 1799 2 February. Jos. Gillon.
Unto the Right Honourable the Lords of Council and Session, The Petition of Archibald Jamieson, Merchant in Greenock. . . . According to Justice, &c. WALTER SCOTT.
Pages: *1* 2-8. Copy: ES[399(51).

352A.15] 1799 28 June. Party.
Answers for William Riddell of Camiestown, Writer to the Signet, Trustee for Mrs Charlotte Wood alias Gillespie, and for Rollo Gillespie, Esq. her husband to the Petition for the creditors

of Alexander Ferguson, Esq. of Craigdarroch, and Common Agent in the Process of Ranking and Sale of his Estates. . . . In respect whereof, &c. WALTER SCOTT.
Pages: *1* 2-7. Copy: ES[405(27)].

352A.16] 1799 20 November. Wm Riddell.
Unto the Right Honourable the Lords of Council and Session, The Petition of Mary & Betty Nicols, Daughters of the late John Nicol, some time in Coaltown of Wemyss. . . . According to justice, &c. WALTER SCOTT.
Pages: *1* 2-7. Copy: ES[409(24)].

352A.17] 1799 30 November. John Scott.
Answers for John Maxwell of Broomholm, William Keir in Minholm, and Thomas Baittie of Crieve, three of His Majesty's Justices of the Peace for the County of Dumfries; William Dalgleish constable in Langholm, and Christopher Murray in Glebefield or Limiecleugh, to the Petition of John Bell in Netherholehouse. . . . In respect whereof, &c. WALTER SCOTT.
Pages: *1* 2-21 + *1* 2-23 Appendix. Copies: ES[408(15)]; NNP(Maidment).

352A.18] 1799 5 December. Ja. Ferguson.
Answers for Margaret Bowie, Wife of John Fraser, Merchant in Edinburgh, and for the said John Fraser for his Interest; to the Petition for Robert Bowie, residing in Edinburgh. . . . In respect whereof, &c. WALTER SCOTT.
Pages: *1* 2-10. Copy: ES[408(18)].

352A.19] 1799 17 December. Wm Riddell.
Answers for Mary and Betty Nicols, Daughters of the late John Nicol, some time in Coaltown of Wemyss; to the Petition of Thomas Page, Mason in Dunshalt. . . . In respect whereof, &c. WALTER SCOTT. Printed by D. Willison, Craig's Close, Edinburgh.
Pages: *1* 2-13. Notes: According to the 1799 Act a printer's imprint is now required, and is hereafter usually entered by David Willison, father-in-law of Scott's publisher Constable. Copy: ES[408(32)].

352A.20] 1800 28 January. Wm Riddell.
Unto the Right Honourable the Lords of Council and Session, The Petition of John Crombie, residing at Kirkland, near Methill. . . . According to justice, &c. WALTER SCOTT. Printed by D. Willison, Craig's Close, Edinburgh.
Pages: *1* 2-10 + *1* 2-12 Appendix. Copy: ES[410(42)].

352A.21] 1800 26 February. Wm. Riddell.
Answers for Andrew Hardie, Tenant in Bridgehaugh, James Dickson, Tenant in Morrick, and George Pringle, Tenant in Fans, Managers for the Children of the deceased Thomas Pringle, Tenant in Blainslie, to the Petition for Katharine Hardie, in Earlstown, and Kennedy Noble, her Husband, for his interest. . . . In respect whereof, &c. WALTER SCOTT. Printed by D. Willison, Craig's Close, Edinburgh.
Pages: *1* 2-15. Copy: ES[414(53)].

352A.22] 1800 22 May. Jos. Gillon.
Unto the Right Honourable the Lords of Council and Session, The Petition of Mrs Mary

Scott, alias Aitchison, Spouse of Robert Aitchison, Lieutenant in His Majesty's Navy, and the said Robert Aitchison for himself, and his right and interest, and Joseph Gillon, Writer in Edinburgh, his Attorney. . . . According to justice, &c. WALTER SCOTT. Printed by D. Willison, Craig's Close, Edinburgh.
Pages: *1* 2-11. Copy: ES[416(31)].

352A.23] 1800 28 May. H. Davidson.
Unto the Right Honourable the Lords of Council and Session, The Petition of Francis Scott, Esq. [and 15 others] being the whole heritable Creditors of the deceased Dugald Campbell, Esq; of Edderline, with consent of Mr Cornelius Elliot, Common Agent in the Ranking of his Creditors. . . . According to justice, &c. WALTER SCOTT.
Pages: *1* 2-7 + *1* 2-4 Appendix. Notes: No printer's imprint. Copy: ES[416(50)].

352A.24] 1800 26 June. W. Riddell.
Answers for Andrew Hardie, Tenant in Bridgehaugh, James Dickson, Tenant in Morrick, and George Pringle, Tenant in Fans, Managers for the Children of the deceased Thomas Pringle, Tenant in Blainslie; to the Petition for Katharine Hardie, in Earlstown, and Kennedy Noble, her Husband, for his Interest. . . . In respect whereof, &c. WALTER SCOTT. Printed by D. Willison, Craig's Close, Edinburgh.
Pages: *1* 2-10. Copy: ES[415(60)].

352A.25] 1800 26 June. Ja. Ferguson.
Duplies for Margaret Bowie, Wife of John Fraser, Merchant in Edinburgh, and the said John Fraser for his interest, to the Replies for Robert Bowie residing in Edinburgh. . . . In respect whereof, &c. WALTER SCOTT. Printed by Alex. Smellie, Anchor Close, Edinburgh.
Pages: *1* 2-9. Copy: ES[415(59)].

352A.26] 1800 5 July. Party.
Unto the Right Honourable the Lords of Council and Session, The Petition and Complaint of John Scott, Writer to the Signet. . . . According to justice, &c. JOHN SCOTT, WALTER SCOTT. Printed by D. Willison, Craig's Close, Edinburgh.
Pages: *1* 2-12 + *1* 2-7 Appendix. Notes: Earlier references to the letters Walter Scott wrote in this matter appear in the 2 January 1800 Duplies for John Tod, Writer to the Signet [ES(422[11])]. Copy: ES[417(10)].

352A.27] 1800 26 November. Wm. Riddell.
Unto the Right Honourable the Lords of Council and Session, The Petition of Mrs Mary Scott, alias Aitchison, Spouse of Robert Aitchison, Lieutenant in His Majesty's Navy, and the said Robert Aitchison for himself, and his right and interest, and Joseph Gillon, Writer in Edinburgh, his Attorney. . . . According to justice, &c. WALTER SCOTT. Printed by D. Willison, Craig's Close, Edinburgh.
Pages: *1* 2-13. Copy: ES[418(40)].

352A.28] 1800 16 December. Alex. Wood.
Memorial and Abstract of the Prepared State in the Process of Sale, at the instance of William Riddell of Camiestown, Writer to the Signet, and others, Trustees of the deceased Robert Riddell of Glenriddel, against the Heir and Creditors of the deceased John Carre of Cavers,

Esquire. . . . In respect whereof, &c. WALTER SCOTT. Printed by D. Willison, Craig's Close, Edinburgh.
Pages: *1* 2-11. Copy: ES[424(39)].

352A.29] 1801 7 January. Wm. Riddell, Jos. Gillon.
Information for George Elliot, late Horse-dealer in Hawick, present Prisoner in the Tolbooth of Edinburgh, against His Majesty's Advocate. . . . In respect whereof, &c. WALTER SCOTT. Printed by D. Willison, Craig's Close, Edinburgh.
Pages: *i-ii*, *1* 2-43. Notes: In brackets before caption title: '[HIGH COURT OF JUSTICIARY.]' An eloquent defence, on the grounds of irrelevancy, of a person charged with vending forged guinea notes in October 1799. Contrary to the usual supposition, Scott was involved, at least in this one case, while the High Court was sitting in Edinburgh. Copy: NNP(Maidment <SEE ILLUSTRATION>).

352A.30] 1801 14 May. Wm Riddell.
Unto the Right Honourable the Lords of Council and Session, The Petition of Alexander Carre Esq. of Caverse. . . . According to justice, &c. WALTER SCOTT. Printed by D. Willison, Craig's Close, Edinburgh.
Pages: *1* 2-9. Copy: ES[429(17)].

352A.31] 1801 15 May. Wm Riddell.
Unto the Right Honourable the Lords of Council and Session, The Petition of John Walker, Spirit-Dealer in Leith. . . . According to justice, &c. WALTER SCOTT. Printed by D. Willison, Craig's Close, Edinburgh.
Pages: *1* 2-8. Copy: ES[429(18)].

352A.32] 1801 20 May. Wm Riddell.
Unto the Right Honourable the Lords of Council and Session, The Petition of Miss Margaret Hunter, presently residing in Musselburgh, Daughter of the deceased William Hunter Writer in Melrose; and Mr John Mercer Writer in Melrose, her Curator at law, for his Interest. . . . According to justice, &c. WALTER SCOTT. Printed by D. Willison, Craig's Close, Edinburgh.
Pages: *1* 2-18, Copy: ES[429(29)].

352A.33] 1801 29 May. H. Davidson.
Answers for Mr William Keith, Trustee for Allan Macdougall, Writer to the Signet, and his Creditors; to the Petition of Samuel Crawford [and four others] and other Creditors of the Said Archibald Campbell. . . . In respect whereof, WALTER SCOTT.
Pages: *1* 2-11. Notes: No printer's imprint. Copy: ES[426(39)].

352A.34] 1801 25 June. Party.
Answers for John Scott, Writer to the Signet, to the Petition of Alexander Brodie, Tacksman of Ormiston, and of William Brodie, residing there. . . . In respect whereof, &c. WALTER SCOTT. Printed by D. Willison, Craig's Close, Edinburgh.
Pages: *1* 2-17. Notes: Legally this process began when John Scott on 14 May 1799 purchased a farm in Ormiston (over which Alexander Brodie had a lease) and there, it is claimed, did

7. JANUARY 1801.

INF.—GEO. ELLIOT,

AGAINST

HIS MAJESTY'S ADVOCATE.

WM. RIDDELL, W. S. } Agents.
JOS. GILLON,

[HIGH COURT OF JUSTICIARY.]

INFORMATION

FOR

GEORGE ELLIOT, late Horſe-dealer in *Hawick*, preſent Priſoner in the Tolbooth of *Edinburgh*,

AGAINST

HIS MAJESTY'S ADVOCATE.

THE pannel ſtands before your Lordſhips in circumſtances of peculiar diſtreſs and calamity—diſtreſs which he feels the more acutely, becauſe he cannot but be conſcious that it has, in a great meaſure, been the conſequence of his own miſconduct. In addition to the miſery occaſioned by an impriſonment of fourteen long months paſſed under the apprehenſion of a ſhameful and impending death, he has to lament that in which his wife and two infant children have been through him involved.

D. WILLISON, PRINTER.]

Both

ENTRY 352A.29. THE PIERPONT MORGAN LIBRARY (PML 127659.5)
(illustration reduced)

some damage to the crops and land. Allegations and counter charges continued until 8 March 1803. Copy: ES[426(62)].

352A.35] 1801 12 November. Party.
Unto the Right Honourable the Lords of Council and Session, The Petition of John Scott, Writer to the Signet. . . . According to justice, &c. WALTER SCOTT. Printed by D. Willison, Craig's Close, Edinburgh.
Pages: *1* 2-9. Copy: ES[432(47)].

352A.36] 1801 14 November. Wm Riddell.
Answers for George Pringle [and five others] to the Petition of John Grays [and six others]. . . . In respect whereof, &c. WALTER SCOTT. Printed by D. Willison, Craig's Close, Edinburgh.
Pages: *1* 2-11. Copy: ES[428(41)].

352A.37] 1801 17 November. John Scott.
Answers for John Maxwell Esq. of Broomholm, to the Petition of Robert Hyslop [and four others]. . . . In respect whereof, &c. WALTER SCOTT. Printed by D. Willison, Craig's Close, Edinburgh.
Pages: *1* 2-15. Copy: ES[428(42)].

352A.38] 1801 16 December. Wm Riddell.
Unto the Right Honourable the Lords of Council and Session, The Petition of John Nixon, Merchant in Hawick, Trustee upon the Sequestered Estate of Walter Lunn, Merchant or Travelling Packman, lately residing in Hawick. . . . According to justice, &c. WALTER SCOTT. Printed by D. Willison, Craig's Close, Edinburgh.
Pages: *1* 2-11. Notes: Both this and the following petition bear a headnote reading: '[Their Lordships are respectfully requested to read this Paper along with another Petition, presented of the same date, for the same Party.]' Copy: ES[433(37)].

352A.39] 1801 16 December. Wm Riddell.
Unto the Right Honourable the Lords of Council and Session, The Petition of John Nixon, Merchant in Hawick, Trustee upon the Sequestered Estate of Walter Lunn, Merchant or Travelling Packman, lately residing in Hawick. . . . According to justice, &c. WALTER SCOTT. Printed by D. Willison, Craig's Close, Edinburgh.
Pages: *1* 2-9. Notes: See preceding petition. Copy: ES[433(38)].

352A.40] 1802 25 February. Wm Riddell.
Unto the Right Honourable the Lords of Council and Session, The Petition of Mrs Isobel Douglas, in Jedburgh, Relict of John Douglas, Tenant in Kaims. . . . According to justice, &c. WALTER**352A.41]** 1802 9 March. Wm Riddell.
Unto the Right Honourable the Lords of Council and Session, Commissioners for Plantations of Kirks and Valuation of Teinds, The Petition of John Borthwick Esq. of Crookstown. . . . According to justice, &c. WALTER SCOTT. Printed by D. Willison, Craig's Close, Edinburgh.
Pages: *1* 2-3. Copy: ES[440(67)].

352A.41] 1802 9 March. Wm. Riddell.
Unto the Right Honourable the Lords of Council and Session, Commissioners for Plantations of Kirks and Valuation of Teinds, The Petition of John Borthwick Esq. of Crookstown....According to justice, &c. WALTER SCOTT. Printed by D. Willison, Craig's Close, Edinburgh
Pages: *1* 2-3. Copy: ES[434(67)].

352A.42] 1802 10 March. Wm. Riddell.
Unto the Right Honourable the Lords of Council and Session, The Petition of William Elliot, Tenant of Milnburnholm. . . . According to justice, &c. WALTER SCOTT. Printed by D. Willison, Craig's Close, Edinburgh.
Pages: *1* 2-10 + *1* 2-6 Appendix. Copy: ES[442(25)].

352A.43] 1802 1 April. Tho. Burns.
Answers for William Marshall, Tenant at Kettlestone, to the Petition of Agnes Gillespie, Spouse of William Irvine for his interest. . . . In respect whereof, &c. WALTER SCOTT.
Pages: *1* 2-8. Notes: No printer's imprint. Copy: ES[441(18)].

352A.44] 1802 25 May. Party.
Answers for John Scott, Writer to the Signet, to the Petition of Alexander Brodie, of Carey-Street, Lincoln-Inn-Fields, in the County of Middlesex, Gentleman. . . . In respect whereof, &c. WALTER SCOTT. Printed by D. Willison, Craig's Close, Edinburgh.
Pages: *1* 2-10. Copy: ES[441(53)].

352A.45] 1802 18 June. Dav. Thomson.
Answers for Hugh Scott, Esq. of Harden; to the Petition of William Purves Tenant in Broomhouse, and Andrew Purves Tenant in Burnfoot. . . . In respect whereof, &c. WALTER SCOTT. Printed by Mundell & Son, Royal Bank Close, Edinburgh.
Pages: *1* 2-18. Copy: ES[443(29)].

352A.46] 1802 2 July. W. Riddell.
Answers for John Nixon, Merchant in Hawick, Trustee upon the Sequestrated Estate of Walter Lunn, Merchant, or Travelling Packman, lately residing in Hawick, to the Condescendence for the said Walter Lunn. . . In respect whereof, &c. WALTER SCOTT. Printed by D. Willison, Craig's Close, Edinburgh.
Pages: *1* 2-5. Copy: ES[443(46)].

352A.47] 1802 14 October. Wm Riddell.
Information for Robert Stewart, Weaver and Portioner in Gattonside, George Stewart, his Son, and James Hay, Merchant in West Gordon, against Peter Watherstone, Merchant in Earlstoun. . . . In respect whereof, &c. WALTER SCOTT. Printed by D. Willison, Craig's Close, Edinburgh.
Pages: *1* 2-18 + *1* 2-13 Appendix. Copy: ES[439(51)].

352A.48] 1802 18 November. D. Wardlaw.
Unto the Right Honourable the Lords of Council and Session, The Petition of James Stuart, Tenant in Blyth. . . . According to justice, &c. WALTER SCOTT. [Printed by] J. Moir,

Royal Bank Close. [Edinburgh.]
Pages: *1* 2-12. Notes: Both here and in the paper of 9 December Wardlaw is identified simply as a 'Writer'. Copy: ES[446(16)].

352A.49] 1802 25 November. Party.
Unto the Right Honourable the Lords of Council and Session, The Petition of John Scott, Writer to the Signet. . . . According to justice, &c. WALTER SCOTT. Printed by D. Willison, Craig's Close, Edinburgh.
Pages: *1* 2-17. Notes: It is indicated that the lawsuit with Alexander Brodie has now been engaged for 'two years past'. Walter Scott is later cited as an alternate advocate in Brodie's Answers of 9 December 1802, Appendix Page 3, date 18 June [ES(444[43])]. Of this November petition there are two issues, (1) page 17 first of 14 lines, (2) then in the 'rectified' version of 35 lines. Copies: Issue (1): ES[446(32)]; (2): ES[446(29)].

352A.50] 1802 1 December. Ja. Ferguson.
Information for Alexander Keith, Esq; of Dunnottar. . . . In respect whereof, &c. WALTER SCOTT.
Pages: *1* 2-22. Notes: No printer's imprint. Copy: ES[458(35)].

352A.51] 1802 9 December. D. Wardlaw.
Unto the Right Honourable the Lords of Council and Session, The Petition of James Stuart, Tenant in Blyth. . . . According to justice, &c. WALTER SCOTT. [Printed by] J. Moir, Royal Bank Close. [Edinburgh.]
Pages: *1* 2-9. Copy: ES[446(69)].

352A.52] 1802 11 December. T. Scott.
Answers for the Most Noble John James Marquis of Abercorn to the Petition of the Magistrates of Musselburgh. . . . In respect whereof, &c. WALTER SCOTT.
Pages: *1* 2-19. Notes: No printer's imprint. Copy: ES[444(49)].

352A.53] 1802 12 December. Wm Riddell.
Unto the Right Honourable the Lords of Council and Session, The Petition of Sir William Eliott of Stobs, Baronet. . . . According to justice, &c. WALTER SCOTT. Printed by D. Willison, Craig's Close, Edinburgh.
Pages: *1* 2-17. Copy: ES[455(68)].

352A.54] 1802 14 December. Wm Riddell.
Unto the Right Honourable the Lords of Council and Session, The Petition of John Nixon, Merchant in Hawick, Trustee upon the Sequestrated Estate of Walter Lunn, Merchant or Travelling Packman, lately residing in Hawick; and of the Creditors of the Said Walter Lunn, Defenders. . . . According to justice, &c. WALTER SCOTT. Printed by D. Willison, Craig's Close, Edinburgh.
Pages: *1* 2-9. Copies: ES(2)[446(71), 455(52)].

352A.55] 1802 30 December. Wm Riddell.
Unto the Right Honourable the Lords of Council and Session, The Petition of Sir William Eliott of Stobs, Baronet. . . . According to justice, &c. WALTER SCOTT. Printed by D.

Willison, Craig's Close, Edinburgh.
Pages: *1* 2-18. Copy: ES[446(79)].

352A.56] 1803 13 January. Ja. Ferguson.
Unto the Right Honourable the Lords of Council and Session, The Petition of Robert Fair Seedsman in London, and his Mandatory. . . . According to justice, &c. WALTER SCOTT.
Pages: *1* 2-9 + *1* 2-7 Appendix. Notes: No printer's imprint. Copy: ES[448(6)].

352A.57] 1803 29 January. Wm Riddell.
Information for Corrybine Morris Venner Esq. and others, Heirs and Executors of the deceased James Lauder Esq. of Whitslade,—Defenders, against Mrs Elizabeth Helen Turner, alias Lauder, Relict of the said deceased James Lauder,—Pursuer. . . . In respect whereof, &c. WALTER SCOTT. Printed by D. Willison, Craig's Close, Edinburgh.
Pages: *1* 2-17. Copy: ES[449(14)].

352A.58] 1803 8 March. Party.
Unto the Right Honourable the Lords of Council and Session, The Petition of John Scott, Writer to the Signet. . . . According to justice, &c. WALTER SCOTT. Printed by D. Willison, Craig's Close, Edinburgh.
Pages: *1* 2-8. Notes: Apparently this is the final petition in a process against Alexander Brodie, which began on 25 June 1801. Copy: ES[453(13)].

352A.59] 1803 17 May. Wm Riddell.
Unto the Right Honourable the Lords of Council and Session, The Petition of Thomas Oliver, late Tenant of Burneyknow, now in Broadlee. . . . According to justice, WALTER SCOTT. Printed by D. Willison, Craig's Close, Edinburgh.
Pages: *1* 2-17. Copy: ES[453(39:defective copy)].

352A.60] 1803 26 May. A. & W. Douglas.
Unto the Right Honourable the Lords of Council and Session, The Petition of James Jardine, in Larieston. . . . According to Justice, &c. WALTER SCOTT. Printed by R. Allan, Edinburgh.
Pages: *1* 2-11 + *1* 2-7 Appendix. Copies: ES[456(11)]; NNP(Maidment).

352A.61] 1803 2 July. Wm Riddell.
Unto the Right Honourable the Lords of Council and Session, The Petition of Richard Blackett and Francis Walker, Tenants in Nisbet. . . . According to justice, &c. WALTER SCOTT. Printed by D. Willison, Craig's Close, Edinburgh.
Pages: *1* 2-7. Copy: ES[457(30)].

352A.62] 1803 6 July. Wm Riddell.
Answers for Alexander Carre Esq. of Caverse, Heir served and retoured to the deceased John Carre Esq. of Caverse, his Brother-german, to the Petition for the Right Honourable Francis Charteris, Earl of Wemyss. . . . In respect whereof, &c. WALTER SCOTT. Printed by D. Willison, Craig's Close, Edinburgh.
Pages: *1* 2-39 + *1* 2-21 Appendix. Copy: ES[454(7)].

352A.63] 1803 6 December. Riddell & Gillon.
Unto the Right Honourable the Lords of Council and Session, The Petition of Mrs Janet Rutherfurd alias Easton of Albany, North America; and for James Hall, Tenant in Hindhope; and John Rutherfurd, Saddler in Jedburgh, her Attornies, to the Petition of Walter Barrie, late Tenant in Longraw.... In respect whereof, &c. WALTER SCOTT. Printed by D. Willison, Craig's Close, Edinburgh.
Pages: *1* 2-13. Copy: ES[454(43a)].

352A.64] 1803 8 December. Wm Riddell.
Unto the Right Honourable the Lords of Council and Session, The Petition of Alexander Carre Esquire of Caverse, his Brother-german. According to justice, &c. WALTER SCOTT. Printed by D. Willison, Craig's Close, Edinburgh.
Pages: *1* 2-31. Copy: ES[455(35)].

352A.65] 1804 1 February. Wm Riddell.
Unto the Right Honourable the Lords of Council and Session, The Petition of Robert Stewart, Weaver and Portioner in Galtonside, George Stewart his Son, and James Hay, Merchant in West Gordon. . . . According to Justice, &c. WALTER SCOTT. Printed by D. Willison, Craig's Close, Edinburgh.
Pages: *1* 2-21. Copy: ES[460(11)].

352A.66] 1804 22 February. Party.
Answers for Harry Davidson, Writer to the Signet, Factor for Allan Macdougall, Writer to the Signet, and his Creditors; to the Petition of Hugh Stevenson, Merchant in Oban, for himself, and with John Stevenson, Merchant in Oban, for the Oban Brewing Company; and of Hugh Stevenson, Manager of the Oban Tanwork Company. . . . In respect whereof, &c. WALTER SCOTT.
Pages: *1* 2-8 + *1* 2-6 Appendix. Notes: No printer's imprint. Copy: ES[460(2)].

352A.67] 1804 23 February. Riddell & Gillon.
Unto the Right Honourable the Lords of Council and Session, The Petition of John Nixon, Merchant in Hawick, Trustee upon the Sequestrated Estate of Walter Lunn, Merchant or Travelling Packman, lately residing in Hawick. . . . According to justice, &c. WALTER SCOTT. Printed by D. Willison, Craig's Close, Edinburgh.
Pages: *1* 2-16. Copy: ES[460(34)].

352A.68] 1804 23 February. Riddell & Gillon.
Unto the Right Honourable the Lords of Council and Session, The Additional Petition of John Nixon, Merchant in Hawick, Trustee upon the Sequestrated Estate of Walter Lunn, Merchant or Travelling Packman, lately residing there.... According to justice, &c. WALTER SCOTT. Printed by D. Willison, Craig's Close, Edinburgh.
Pages: *1* 2-5. Notes: The 6 September 1804 Answers for Alexander Hay Borthwick and others to these Nixon petitions are inserted immediately thereafter in this volume 460. No further Scott pleadings have been located through 1806, the last year of his advocacy. Copy: ES[460(34)].

SUBSTANCE OF THE SPEECHES

353A] First Printing: 1807
[Speeches, motions, and votes], pages 32-48, 144-149, and 176, *in*:

Substance of the Speeches delivered by some Members of the Faculty of Advocates, at the Meeting on the 28th February, Adjourned to the 2d of March, and at the Meeting held on the 9th of March, 1807, for Considering the Bill entitled "An Act for better regulating the Courts of Justice in Scotland, and the Administration of Justice therein, and establishing Trial by Jury in certain Civil Cases." Edinburgh: Printed by James Ballantyne and Co. Sold by Bell and Bradfute, Manners and Miller, and A. Constable and Co. Edinburgh; and John Murray, London. 1807.

Notes: In the first session, 28 February, Scott objected to the 'very peculiar form, in which the business had been brought forward by the proposers of the motion' (page 32), then indicated that 'the disease, in this case, is but of a trifling nature, and the remedy affects the vitals of the constitution' (page 35), and further argued that the bill displayed 'a rage of imitating English forms and practices . . .' On 2 March, with reference to an amendment by the Solicitor General, 64 members voted for the motion, 62 including Scott and Walter Blair, Dean of Faculty, voted against. On 9 March Scott and 12 others 'delivered their sentiments' concerning other motions.

Copies: BCL E.

Postscript. Scott was appointed Sheriff-Depute of Selkirkshire on 16 December 1799. Of his later activities in this position some of the documentary evidence has been lost, but 114 manuscript processes have survived. These papers include the pleadings lodged on behalf of the litigants and Scott's interlocutors and judgments, the first (on busines accounts) dated 26 November 1800, the last (on the price of turnips) 7 December 1831. All of these proceedngs, generally processed by his Substitute in Selkirk, are summarized in Chisholm (pages 113-216) and 45 of them discussed at greater length (pages 12-110). Reference: John Chisholm, *Sir Walter Scott as a Judge*, Edinburgh: W. Green & Son, 1918.

APPENDIX 2: EXTRACTS IN ANTHOLOGIES

Since only six anthologies have been previously listed in Ruff (page 281), hardly enough to justify Hazlitt's assertion that Scott in 1824 was still 'the most popular of our living poets' (392E), it seems advisable to represent here in some detail the 164 books now discovered. Even a casual survey of this record, however, will immediately disclose a chaotic situation, with excerpts apparently copied parasitically one from another, and with progressive textual corruption evident throughout. The first entry cited below, quoting one of Scott's most famous expressions, is printed elsewhere either without a title, or with nine different labels variously supplied by the compilers; and all sixteen entries convey three variant readings in the initial line. Another piece titled 'The Knight Errant' only in American issues frequently provides as well the first-line misprint 'Dunvis', this originally in the earliest U.S. musical rendition (88Dk) and then, several years later, in the earliest U.S. anthologies (442E and 461E). Still another, 'The Foray', in its initial line, may alter 'steers' to 'deer' (389E.34). As variations of this order cannot be assessed adequately, either in the explanations that follow or in the General Index, a separate account of all extracts is given, by anthology 'E' suffix, in the entry for the first 'A' printing or, if of a considerable number, in a separate 'E' group following all entries for the 'A', 'R' and 'D' printings. Thus after these citations, 47E records 102 extracts from *The Lady of the Lake,* the largest number for any one poem. Altogether these anthologies represent some 662 extracts.

To avoid a multiplicity of particulars when (in brief accounts) none is required, other references to this E appendix will cite the extract numbers here assigned only when these number more than five. *The Universal Songster* (389E) provided 40 excerpts, the greatest number among all these issues; and *Elegant Extracts in Poetry* (408E[1]) required a conger of 56 publishers, the most extensive group in this bibliography. Hazlitt's own collection of Scott's poetry and that of other contemporary poets (392E) was the only one formally suppressed, it seems, for invasion of copyright; and Benjamin F. French's concoction (465E[1-2]), copyrighted in the United States, is so mangled as to defy analysis. Also left without further comment are other imponderables concerning false attributions, elisions in the verse, et cetera.

As examples of changing taste it is well to note, finally, that 'The Sun upon the Weirdlaw Hill', barely recognized in these anthologies (119E), is yet acclaimed by a recent critic as Scott's 'best short poem' (Pearson, page 134), and that 'Proud Maisie', then totally ignored, appears to be the poem most often reprinted in present-day compilations. Even the enthusiastic collector Van Antwerp ([1], pages 105-106) once interrupted his biblography to quote 'Proud Maisie' in full, remarking that this 'tenderly mournful song . . . has haunted my memory since boyhood.'

BELGIUM

354E] BRUSSELS: Berthot 1825-1826

Specimens of English Verse, Selected chiefly from Modern Poets. Brussels: Printed by C. J. De Mat and H. Remy; and sold by Berthot, Marché au Bois; Frank, German Bookseller, Rue de La Putterie; and Ewbank, English Bookseller, Rue Royale. 1825. Notes: Edited by R. F. Eusden. Includes brief extracts from Scott in English in the introductory section on 'Observations on English Versification' as well as more copious examples by verse type. Copy: T/B. Reissued 1826 (L).

Includes: (1) anonymously 'Our Native Land!' (first words: 'Breathes there the man, with soul so dead,' from *The Lay of the Last Minstrel*, canto 6, stanza 1), page 110; (2) 'The Aged Minstrel' (first words: 'And said I that my limbs were old;' from *ibid*, canto 3, stanza 1), page 111; (3) 'Song. To the Moon' (first words: 'Hail to thy cold and clouded beam,' from *Rokeby*, canto 2, stanza 33), pages 114-115; (4) 'Coronach' (first words: 'He is gone on the mountain,' from *The Lady of the Lake*, canto 3, stanza 16), pages 144-145.

FRANCE

355E] PARIS: Barrois 1818

The Beauties of English Poetry; or, Extracts from the most Eminent British Poets. A New Edition. London: And sold at Paris, by Theophilus Barrois, junior, Bookseller, No. 11, Quai Voltaire. 1818. Copy: L.

Includes: (1) 'The Last Minstrel' (first words: 'The way was long, the wind was cold,' from *The Lay of the Last Minstrel*, Introduction), pages 248-249; (2) 'The Dying Bard' (first words: 'Dinas Emlinn Lament, for the moment is nigh,' from *ibid,* pages 256-257); (3) 'The Cypress Wreath' (first words: 'O Lady! twine no wreath for me,' from *Rokeby*, canto 5, stanza 13), pages 336-337; (4) 'Roderick the Warrior' (first words: 'The summer dawn's reflected hue', from *The Lady of the Lake*, canto 3, stanzas 2-3), pages 346-348.

356E] PARIS: Baudry [and others] 1824-1827

[1] The Life and Genius of Lord Byron, . . with Additional Anecdotes and Critical Remarks from Other Publications; To which is prefixed A Sketch on Lord Byron's Death, by Sir Walter Scott, Bart. Paris, Printed for Baudry, English, Italian, Spanish, Portuguese and German Library, 9, Rue du Coq S.-Honoré. 1824. Notes: Edited in English by Cosmo Gordon. Copy: O.

Includes: 'A Character of Lord Byron by Sir Walter Scott,' pages 3 4-10.

[2] The Living Poets of England. Specimens of the Living British Poets, With Biographical and Critical Notices and An Essay on English Poetry. . . . Paris, Printed for L. Baudry, 9 Rue du Coq-Saint-Honoré; Robée et Hingray, Rue de Richelieu; A. et W. Galignani, Rue Vivienne. 1827. Two volumes. Notes: In addition to quotations, volume 2 also contains a lengthy essay 'On the Comparative Merits of Scott and Byron, As Writers of Poetry' by 'G.P.' (pages *136* 137-162) and a 'Memoir of Sir Walter Scott' by 'L.' (pages *214* 215-216). The 'Memoir', here of six paragraphs only, is recognized as the early draft of an essay by J. W. Lake which, later in 1827, was extended to some 24,000 words in a Galignani edition (*see* 294R[2]). Copy: InU.

VOLUME 2 includes: (1) 'A Character of Byron' (begins 'Amidst the general calmness'), pages 168-171; (2) 'Retrospect of Juvenile Years' (first words: 'Thus, while I ape the measure wild', from *Marmion*, Introduction), pages *217* 218-219; (3) 'The Last Minstrel' (first words: 'The way was long, the wind was cold,' from *The Lay of the Last Minstrel*, Introduction), pages 219-222; (4) 'Deloraine goes to the Grave of Michael Scott' (first words: 'If thou would'st view fair Melrose aright,' from *ibid*, canto 2, stanza 1), pages 222-230; (5) 'A Bridal' (first words: 'Breathes there the man, with soul so dead,' from *ibid*, canto 6, stanza 1), pages 231-234; (6) 'The Trial of Constance' (first words: 'In low dark rounds the arches hung,' from *Marmion*, canto 2, stanza 18), pages 234-243; (7) 'Court of James of Scotland' (first words: 'Old Holy-Rood rung merrily', from *ibid*, canto 5, stanza 7), pages 243-248; (8) 'Lochinvar. Lady Heron's Song' (first words: 'O, young Lochinvar is come out of the west,' from *ibid*, canto 5, stanza 12), pages 248-250; (9) 'The Battle' (first words: 'And why stands Scotland idly now,' from *ibid*, canto 6, stanza 20), pages 250-256; (10) 'The Death of Roderick Dhu' (first words: 'Thus, motionless, and moanless, drew', from *The Lady of the Lake*, canto 6, stanza 21), pages 256-264; (11) 'Wilfred's Song' (first words: 'The blood left Wilfred's ashen cheek;' from *Rokeby*, canto 5, stanza 12), pages 265-267; (12) 'Hunting Song' (first words: 'Waken, lords and ladies gay,' from *Queenhoo-Hall*), pages 267-268; (13) 'The Violet' (first words: 'The violet in her green-wood bower,' from *English Minstrelsy*), pages 268-269; (14) 'To a Lady. With Flowers from a Roman Wall' (first words: 'Take these flowers, which, purple waving,' from *ibid*), page 269; (15) 'The Bard's Incantation' (first words: 'The forest of Glenmore is drear,' from *ibid*), pages 269-271.

357E] PARIS: Renouard 1825
Popular Ballads and Songs, From Traditional Manuscripts, and Scarce Editions. Paris: Printed by Paul Renouard, N. 22, Rue de l'Hirondelle, for Antoine-Augustin Renouard. 1825. Notes: Edited by Baron François Adolphe Loève-Veimars. Notes: Loève-Veimars brought out a French prose translation of this anthology titled *Ballades, Légendes et Chants Populaires*, this also published by Renouard in 1825. In French 'Alice' of the second poem becomes 'Adélaide'. Copy: MH. Reference: Kohler(3) 865.
Includes: (1) 'Lochinvar' (first words: 'O, Young Lochinvar is come out of the west!' from *Marmion*, canto 5, stanza 12), page 6; (2) 'Frederick and Alice' (first words: 'Frederick leaves the Land of France') pages 20-21; (3) 'The Brignal's Banks' (first words: 'O Brignal banks are wild and fair,' from *Rokeby*, canto 3, stanza 16), page 26; (4) 'The Cypress Wreath' (first words: 'O Lady, twine no wreath for me,' from *ibid*, canto 5, stanza 13), page 29; (5) 'Jock of Hazeldean' (first words: 'Why weep ye by the tide, ladie?'), page 82; (6) 'Donald Caird' (first words: 'Donald Caird's come again,'), pages 85-86.

GREAT BRITAIN

358E] ABERDEEN: King [and others] 1831
The Beauties of Modern British Poetry, Systematically Arranged. . . . Aberdeen: George King, 36, St. Nicholas Street; Waugh & Innes, Edinburgh; W. Collins, Glasgow; and Whittaker, Treacher, & Co. London. 1831. Notes: Edited by David Grant. Copy: E.
Includes: (1) 'Fancied Happiness' (first words: 'Wo to the youth whom Fancy gains', from *Rokeby*, canto 1, stanza 31), pages 35-36; (2) 'Paternal Affection. I.' (first words: 'Some feelings are to mortals given', from *The Lady of the Lake*, canto 2, stanza 22), page 36; (3) 'The Bible. I.' (first words: Within this awful volume lies', from *The Monastery*, chapter

12), page 44; (4) 'Helvellyn'[!] (first words: 'I climbed the dark brow of the mighty Hellvellyn,'), pages 89-90; (5) 'Hebrew Hymn' ['Rebecca's Hymn'] (first words: 'When Israel, of the Lord beloved', from *Ivanhoe*, chapter 40), pages 93-94; (6) 'Time. IV.' ['The Gathering'] (first words: 'Time rolls his ceaseless course. The race of yore', from *The Lady of the Lake*, canto 3, stanza 1), page 97; (7) 'Time VI.' ['The Aged Carle'] (first words: 'Why sitt'st thou by that ruined hall', from *The Antiquary*, chapter 10), page 98; (8) 'The Last Day. I' ['Hymn for the Dead'] (first words: 'That day of wrath! that dreadful day!', from *The Lay of the Last Minstrel*, canto 6, stanza 30), page 105; (9) 'Love. I.' (first words: 'In peace, love tunes the shepherd's reed', from *ibid.*, canto 3, stanza 2), page 120; (10) 'Love. II.' (first words: 'True Love's the gift which God has given', from *ibid.*, canto 5, stanza 13), page 120; (11) 'Childhood's Tear' (first words: 'The tear, down childhood's cheek that flows', from *Rokeby*, canto 4, stanza 11), page 133; (12) 'Woman. I.' (first words: 'O Woman! in our hours of ease', from *Marmion*, can-to 6, stanza 30), page 135; (13) 'The Love of Country. IV.' (first words: 'Breathes there a man with soul so dead', from *The Lay of the Last Minstrel*, canto 6, stanza 30), pages 143-144; (14) 'Macrimmon's Lament' (first words: 'Macleod's wizard flag from the grey castle sallies', from *Albyn's Anthology*, 1818), page 151; (15) 'The Rose. II.' (first words: 'The Rose is fairest when 'tis budding new', from *The Lady of the Lake*, canto 4, stanza 1), page 246; (16) 'The End of Autumn' (first words: Autumn departs—but still his mantle's fold', from *The Lord of the Isles*, 'Introduction'), pages 261-262; (17) 'Silence after Thunder' (first words: 'Hast thou not marked, when, o'er thy startled head', *ibid.*, canto 3, stanza 1), page 286; (18) 'Loch Katrine' (first words: 'One burnished sheet of living gold', from *The Lady of the Lake*, canto 3, stanza 1), pages 308-309; (19) 'The Highlands' (first words: 'Stranger! if e're thine ardent step hath traced', from *The Lord of the Isles*, canto 4, stanza 1), page 363.

359E] BELFAST: Simms and M'Intyre 1820

Belfast Improved Edition of The Little Warbler, Being a Selection of the Most Popular and Esteemed Scotch, English, and Irish Songs. . . . Belfast: Printed by Simms and M'Intyre Donegall-Street. [1820]. Five volumes. Notes: A miniature set for children, with coloured folding woodcut frontispiece and extra vignette title. Copy: InU.

VOLUME 1 includes: (1) [anonymous] 'MacGregor's Gathering' (first words: 'The moon's on the lake, and the mist's on the brae', from *Albyn's Anthology*, 1816), pages 66-67; (2) [anonymous] 'The Heath this Night' (first words: 'The heath this night must be my bed,' from *The Lady of the Lake*, canto 3, stanza 23), pages 68-69.

VOLUME 5 includes: (3) 'Donald Caird's Come Again' (first words as title), pages 116-118.

360E] CORK: Bolster 1818

Harmonica; or, Elegant Extracts of English, Scotch, and Irish Melodies from the Most Approved, Popular, and Modern Authors. . . . Cork: Printed by John Bolster, Bookseller and Stationer, No. 7, Goold's-Buildings, Patrick-Street. 1818. Copy: L. Reissued with undated cancel title: The Harmonica, Being a Choice Collection of English, Irish, and Scottish Songs . . . . London: Printed for the Booksellers' (L).

Includes: (1) 'To horse! To horse! the standard flies' ['War-Song of the Royal Light Dragoons'] (first words as title), page 6; (2) 'Oh, say not, my love,' (first words: 'Oh, say not, my love, with that mortified air,' not first published in *The Bridal of Triermain* as said, but issued first in *The Edinburgh Annual Register for 1808*, Vol. 2—Part 2, 1811, as Scott's imitation of

Thomas Moore), page 7; (3) 'The heath this night must be my bed' (first words as title, from *The Lady of the Lake*, canto 3, stanza 23), page 8; (4) 'A Weary Lot is thine, fair maid' (first words as title, from *Rokeby*, canto 3, stanza 28), page 10; (5) 'Oh! rest thee, Babe' (first words: 'Oh! slumber, my darling, thy sire is a knight' / Thy mother a lady, so lovely and bright!', not from Scott's *Guy Mannering*, as said, but from Daniel Terry's play, *Guy Mannering, or The Gipsey's Prophecy*, 1816, the poem itself written by Scott), page '18'[13]; (6) 'The Cypress Wreath' (first words: 'O Lady, twine no wreath for me / Or twine it of the cypress tree;' from *Rokeby*, canto 5, stanza 13), page 15; (7) 'Song to the Moon' (first words: 'Hail to thy cold and cloudless beam, / Pale pilgrim of the troubled sky!' from *ibid*, canto 1, stanza 33), page 15; (8) 'It chanced that Cupid on a Season' (first words as title, from *Paul's Letters to His Kinsfolk*, letter 9), page 17; (9) [anonymous] 'Ill fares the bark with tackle riven' (first words as title from *Harold the Dauntless*, canto 3, 'Song' in stanza 9), page 19; (10) [anonymous] 'She may be fair' (first words as title from *ibid*, canto 3, 'Song' in stanza 10.), page 19; (11) 'The Troubadour' (first words: 'Glowing with love, on fire for fame, / A Troubadour that hated sorrow' from *Paul's Letters to His Kinsfolk*, letter 9), page 20; (12) 'The Harp' (first words: 'I was a wild and wayward boy, / My childhood scorned each childish toy;' from *Rokeby*, canto 5, stanza 18), page 30; (13) 'Where shall the lover rest' (first words as title from *Marmion*, canto 3, stanzas 10-11), page 33; (14) 'Hail to the Chief' ['Boat Song'] (first words: 'Hail to the chief, who in triumph advances! / Honour'd and bless'd be the ever-green Pine!' from *The Lady of the Lake*, canto 2, stanza 19), page 36; (15) 'It was Dunois, the young and brave' ['Romance of Dunois'] (first words: 'It was Dunois, the young and brave, bound for Palestine,' from *The Edinburgh Annual Register for 1813*, 1815 [1816]), page 47; (16) 'The last words of Marmion' (first words: 'A light on Marmion's visage spread, / And fired his glazing eye;' from *Marmion*, canto 6, stanza 32), page 53; (17) 'From the brown crest of Newark' ['On the Lifting of the Banner'] (first words: 'From the brown crest of Newark its summons extending, / Our signal is waving in smoke and in flame;' from *The Ettricke Garland*), pages 58-59; (18) 'O dread was the time' [Song for the Anniversary Meeting of the Pitt Club] (first words: 'O dread was the time, and more dreadful the omen, / When the brave on Marengo lay slaughter'd in vain,'), page 65; (19) 'Awake on your hills, on your islands awake' (first words as title from *Waverley*, chapter 22), page 68; (20) 'Lochinvar' (first words: 'O, young Lochinvar has come out of the west, / Through all the wide Border his steed was the best' from *Marmion*, canto 5, stanza 12), page 70; (21) 'My wayward fate I needs must plain' (first words as title, from 'The Resolve'), page 87; (22) 'The gathering of Clan-Connell' [Pibroch of Donnell-Dhu] (first words as true title), page 107; (23) 'Merrily bounds the bark' (first words: 'Merrily, merrily, bounds the bark, / She bounds before the gale;' from *The Lord of the Isles*, canto 4, stanza 7), page 126; (24) 'The Patriot' (first words: 'Breathes then[!] the man with soul so dead, / Who never to himself hath said' from *The Lay of the Last Minstrel*, canto 6, stanza 1), page 209; (25) 'Nora's Vow' (first words: 'Hear what highland Nora said, / "The Erlie's son I will not wed,' from *Albyn's Anthology*, I, 1816), page 210; (26) 'Pibroch of Donuil Dhu' [slightly variant text of item 22 above] (first words: 'Pibroch of Donuil Dhu,/ Pibroch of Donuil'), page 211; (27) 'O for the voice of that wild horn. To the memory of Edward the Black Prince' [identified correctly as from 'Rob Roy, by the author of "Waverly(!)]"', from chapter 2 (first words: 'O for the voice of that wild horn, / On Fontarabian echoes borne'), page 229; (28) [anonymous] 'Thy hue, dear pledge, is pure and bright,' [identified only as from 'Tales of My Landlord vol. 3rd'], specifically from *Old Mortality*, chapter 23 (first words as title), page 229.

361E] EDINBURGH: Anderson 1822-1825

[1] The Common-Place Book of British Song; . . . Edinburgh: John Anderson, Jun. 55. North Bridge-Street; Waugh & Innes; and W. Hunter, Edinburgh: Beilby & Knotts, Birmingham; and T. Tegg, London. 1823. Notes: The editor is identified only as 'J'. Copies: E L. References: Kohler(3) 316; Ruff, page 281.
Includes: (1) 'Love Wakes and Weeps' (first words as title, from *The Pirate*, chapter 23), page 26; (2) ['Lullaby of an Infant Chief'] (first words: 'Oh! Rest Thee, Babe' ['Oh! Hush thee, my babie, thy sire'] from the play *Guy Mannering, or The Gipsey's Prophecy*, 1816: the poem itself written by Scott), page 43; (3) 'O Brignal Banks!' (first words: 'O, Brignal banks are wild and fair,' from *Rokeby*, canto 3, stanza 16), pages 46-47; (4) 'There is Mist on the Mountain' (first words: 'There is mist on the mountain, and night on the vale,' from *Waverley*, chapter 22), pages 54-56; (5) 'Lochinvar' (first words: 'O, young Lochinvar is come out of the west!' from *Marmion*, canto 5, stanza 12), pages 65-67; (6) 'Farewell! Farewell! The Voice You Hear' (first words as title, from *The Pirate*, chapter 23), pages 141-143; (7) 'The Cypress Wreath' (first words: 'O Lady, twine no wreath for me,' from *Rokeby*, canto 3, stanza 13), page 195; (8) 'Jock of Hazeldean' (first words: 'Why weep ye by the tide, ladie?'), pages 244-245; (9) 'Carle, Now the King's Come' (first words: 'The news has flown frae mouth to mouth,') pages 250-255; (10) 'Donald Caird's Come Again' (chorus first, then first words: 'Donald Caird can lilt and sing,'), pages 315-317; (11) (first words: 'O! Rest Thee, Babe' ['A Lullaby of an Infant Chief']), page 43, a repetition of (2), again showing careless editing.

[2] The Common-Place Book of Prose; Second Series: . . . Edinburgh: John Anderson, Jun. 55. North Bridge-Street, Edinburgh: and Thomas Tegg, London. 1825. Notes: As in the preceding entry, the editor is 'J'. Copy: E.
Includes: (1) 'On the Death of Lord Byron' (begins: 'Amidst the general calmness of the political atmosphere'), pages 73-77; (2) 'Wandering Willie's Tale' (first words: 'All joy was bereft me the day that you left me,'), pages 294-317.

[3] The Poetical Common-Place Book, Consisting of an Original Selection of Standard and Fugitive Poetry; . . . Edinburgh: John Anderson, Jun. 55. North Bridge Street; Waugh & Innes; John Robertson; Macredie & Co.; and W. Hunter, Edinburgh: Beilby & Knotts, Birmingham; and T. Tegg, London. 1822. Notes: The editor, W.C., was William Clapperton. Both this and the 'second edition' of 1824 (with the same poems) have a frontispiece portrait of Scott engraved by J. Horsburgh. Copies: E L; CtY(2).
Includes: (1) 'Love of Country' (first words: 'Breathes there the man with soul so dead,' from *The Lay of the Last Minstrel*, canto 6, stanza 1), pages 34-35; (2) 'Elegy on the Death of Charles Gough' ['Hellvellyn'] (first words: 'I climb'd the dark brow of the mighty Helvellyn[!],'), pages 107-108; (3) 'Melrose Abbey' (first words: 'If thou wouldst view fair Melrose aright,' from *The Lay of the Last Minstrel*, canto 2, stanza 1), page 247.

362E] EDINBURGH: Colquhoun 1823

The Pocket Songster; or, Caledonian Warbler. A Collection of Popular Scotch Songs, and a Selection of new Ones. . . Edinburgh: Colquhoun, 221, High Street; and the Principal Booksellers. Also by Purvis & Aitken, Lyceum Court, Nelson Street, and the Principal Booksellers, Glasgow. 1823. Copy: E.
Includes: (1) 'The Massacre of Glencoe' (first words: '"O Tell me, Harper, wherefore flow'),

pages 352-354; (2) 'Farewell to M'Kenzie [Mackenzie]' (first words: 'Farewell to Mackeneth [Mackenneth], great Earl of the North,), pages 358-359; (3) 'Donald Caird's Come Again' (first words of chorus as title; first words of song: 'Donald Caird can lilt and sing:'), pages 366-367.

363E] EDINBURGH: Douglas 1828

The Poetical Melange. . . . Edinburgh: Published by George A. Douglas, 19. Castle Street; And sold by Charles Tilt, London; and W. Curry Jun. and Company, Dublin. MDCCCXXVIII. Three volumes. Notes: This 'first adventure in the commerce of literature', as noted in Douglas's 'Advertisement', is dedicated to Scott (see 510T). Copies: InU NN.
VOLUME 1 includes: (1) 'Decisive Charge at Waterloo' (first words: 'On came the whirl-wind—like the last', from *The Field of Waterloo*, stanza 11), pages 23-25; (2) 'The Last Minstrel' (first words: 'The way was long, the wind was cold,' from *The Lay of the Last Minstrel*, Introduction), pages 40-45; (3) 'Landing of the British Army in Portugal' (first words: '—The shout grew loud—', from *The Vision of Don Roderick*, stanza 55), pages 97-99; (4) 'Helvellyn[!]' (first words: 'I climbed the dark brow of the mighty Helvellyn[!],'), pages 185-187;
VOLUME 2 (5) 'On Melrose Abbey' (first words: 'If thou would'st view fair Melrose aright,' from *The Lay of the Last Minstrel*, canto 2, stanza 1), page 121;
VOLUME 3 (6) 'Warnings Foreboding the Fate of Rosabelle' (first words: 'O listen, listen, ladies gay!' from *ibid*, canto 6, stanza 23), pages 182-184; (7) 'From The Lady of the Lake' (first words: 'They bid me sleep—they bid me pray,' from canto 4, stanza 22), pages 218-219; (8) 'The Death of Marmion' first words: 'With fruitless labour Clara bound,' from *Marmion*, canto 6, stanza 32), pages 229-231.

364E] EDINBURGH: Fairbairn [and others] 1824

[The Poetical Scrap Book, consisting of an original selection of English poetry: . . . Edinburgh: Printed for John Fairbairn, Bell & Bradfute, Manners & Miller, William Whyte & Co., Oliver & Boyd, William Oliphant, Waugh & Innes, Stirling & Kenney, John Robertson, and Macredie & Co., Edinburgh; and T. Tegg, London. 1824. Notes: Edited by William Clapperton.] Apparently a variant issue of the Anderson edition, 361R[3]. Copy: not seen. Reference: Kohler(3) 1149.

EDINBURGH: Griffin

[~] Jacobite Melodies, 1823-1825. *see* GLASGOW: Griffin 375E.

EDINBURGH: Hurst, Robinson.

[~] Literary Gems, 1826. *see* LONDON: Hurst, Robinson 395E.

365E] EDINBURGH: Martin 1832

A Selection of Scots, English and Irish Songs . . . Edinburgh; Printed & Sold by R. Martin, Music Seller. [1832]. Two volumes. Notes: Engraved sheet music throughout except for preliminary matter. Words by various poets arranged for the pianoforte. Copy: E.
VOLUME 1 includes: '"Soldier Rest thy War Fare O'er" from *The Lady of the Lake*; Written by Walter Scott, Esqr.' (first words as title, from canto 1, stanza 31), pages 26-30. For an earlier issue *see* 368E

366E] EDINBURGH: Oliver and Boyd 1822-1827
[1] The Scrap Book; A Collection of Amusing and Striking Pieces In Prose and Verse, . . . Second edition, Improved and Enlarged. . . . Edinburgh; Oliver & Boyd, High-Street: Sold also by G. & W. B. Whittaker, London; Henry Mozley, Derby; Beilby & Knotts, Birmingham; John Cumming, and Hodges and MacArthur, Dublin; and William Turnbull, Glasgow. 1822. Notes: Edited by John M'Diarmid. With the exception of number 6, Scott is not mentioned and most of the excerpts are identified only by title. Copy: GU.
VOLUME 1 includes: (1) 'Interview between Waverley and Fergus MacIvor, at Carlisle, Previous to the Execution of the Latter' (first words: 'After a sleepless night, the first dawn of morning found Waverley on the esplanade.' from *Waverley*, chapter 69), pages 25-30; (2) 'Scene in Ivanhoe' (first words: 'It was upon the second morning after this happy bridal.' from *Ivanhoe*, final chapter), pages 30-34; (3) 'Rural Peace—Scenery of the Clyde' (first words: 'It was upon a delightful summer evening,' from *Old Mortality*, chapter 37), pages 34-35; (4) 'Description of the Laigh Kirk of Glasgow, near the era of the Rebellion in 1745' (first words: 'Conceive, Tresham, an extensive range of low-browed, dark, and twilight vaults,' from *Rob Roy*, chapter 20), pages 72-75; (5) 'A Morning in the Highlands—Punishment of a spy, whose Employers had betrayed Rob Roy MacGregor' (first words: 'I shall never forget the delightful sensation' from *ibid.* chapter 30), pages 107-110; (6) 'Anecdotes, Illustrative of the State of the Highlands after the Rebellion of Forty-Five' [footnote reads 'Written, we have little doubt, by Sir Walter Scott] (first words: 'The field of Culloden, and the scenes of cruelty which followed it,' not located), pages 173-177; (7) 'Landing of the English in Portugal' (first words: 'Don Roderick turn'd him as the shout grew loud—' from *The Vision of Don Roderick*, stanzas 55-60), pages 348-349; (8) 'The Combat of Fitz-James and Roderick Dhu' (first words: 'Then each at once his faulchion drew,' from *The Lady of the Lake*, canto 5, stanzas 14-16), pages 362-364; (9) 'Kemble's Final Exit from the Edinburgh Stage' (first words: 'As the worn war-horse, at the trumpet's sound,' (the 36-line version of 'The Farewell Address'), pages 396-397; (10) 'A Highland Coronach' [Coronach] (first words: 'He is gone on the mountain,' from *The Lady of the Lake*, canto 3, stanza 16), pages 427-428.

[2] The Scrap Book; A Collection of Amusing and Striking Pieces In Prose and Verse, . . . Volume II. Second edition, Revised and Improved. . . . Edinburgh; Published by Oliver & Boyd, Tweeddale-Court; and Geo. B. Whittaker, London. 1825. Notes: Edited by John M'Diarmid. Copy: E. Reissued the same date as 'Third Edition, Improved and Enlarged' (GU).
VOLUME 2: (11) 'Storming of Front-de-Boeuf's Castle' (first words: 'It was not, however, by clamour that the contest was to be decided,' from *Ivanhoe*, chapter '30'[29]), pages 178-181; (12) 'Bridal and Death of Lucy Ashton' (first words: 'Glancing wide over hill and dale,' from *The Bride of Lammermoor*, chapter 34), pages 185-191; (13) 'The Character and Poetry of Lord Byron' (first words: 'It has been reserved for our own time to produce one distinguished example' from Scott's review of 'Childe Harold's Pilgrimage, Canto III.' in the *Quarterly Review*, 1816), pages 303-308; (14) 'Clan Connell, A Pibroch.' (first words: Pibroch of Donell Dhu, from *Albyn's Anthology*, 1816), pages 397-398; (15) 'Lochinvar' (first words: 'O, young Lochinvar is come out of the west,' from *Marmion*, canto 5, stanza 12), pages 441-443; (15) 'Caledonia' (first words: 'Breathes there the man with soul so dead,' from *The Lay of the Last Minstrel*, canto 6, stanzas 1-2), pages 447-448.

[3] Specimens of Sacred and Serious Poetry, from Chaucer to the Present Day; . . . Edinburgh, Oliver & Boyd, Tweeddale-Court; and Geo. B. Whittaker, London. 1827. Notes: Edited by John Johnstone. Copy: E. Reference: Kohler(3) 754.
Includes: (1) 'The Last Judgment' (first words: 'That day of wrath, that dreadful day' from *The Lay of the Last Minstrel*, canto 6, stanza 31), pages 459-460; (2) 'Hymn of the Hebrew Maid' (first words: When Israel, of the Lord beloved,) from *Ivanhoe*, chapter 40), pages 460-461; (3) 'Time' (first words: '"Why sitt'st thou by that ruin'd hall,' from *The Antiquary*, chapter 10), pages 461-462.

367E] EDINBURGH: Purdie 1821-1824
[1] [*engraved title page*] The Scotish Minstrel A Selection from the Vocal Melodies of Scotland Ancient & Modern . . . Edinburgh Published & Sold by Robt. Purdie at his Music & Musical Instrument Warehouse No. 70 Princes Street. [1821,1824]. Six volumes. Notes: Edited by Robert Archibald Smith. Engraved sheet music throughout except for preliminary matter. Words by various poets arranged for voice and pianoforte. *DNB* states: 'The editor erred in allowing certain female coadjutors without acknowledgment, to tamper with the original words of some of the older songs.' Price: 8s. each. Copies: BCL E(2) E(vol.5); NN-L T/B(with booksellers ticket [Edinburgh: William Whyte] below title-page imprint on vols 3, 4, 6). Reference: Kohler(3) 1348.
VOLUME 1 includes: (1) 'The Foray' (first words: 'The last of our[!] steers on our board has been spread,' from Clarke's *Twelve Vocal Pieces*), pages 70-71;
VOLUME 2: (2) 'Hail to the Chief' ['Boat Song'] (first words: 'Hail! to the Chief who in triumph advances, Honour'd and bless'd', from *The Lady of the Lake*, canto 2, stanzas 19-20), pages 14-15;
VOLUME 3: (3) 'The Cypress Wreath' (first words: 'O, Lady, twine no wreath for me,', from *Rokeby*, canto 5, stanza 13), page 36, without music;
VOLUME 5: (4) 'Blue Bonnets' (first words: 'March, March, Ettrick and Teviotdale! Why, my lads, dinna ye march', from *The Monastery*, chapter 25), pages 10-11.

[2] The Scotish Minstrel A Selection from the Vocal Melodies of Scotland Ancient & Modern . . . Second Edition. Edinburgh Published & Sold by Robt. Purdie at his Music & Musical Instrument Warehouse No. 83 Princes Street. [1821-1824]. Six volumes. Notes: Edited by R. A. Smith. Engraved sheet music throughout except for preliminary matter, but in this edition the Index to each volume is engraved rather than letterpress. Essentially reset, the same as the first edition, but with additions and subtractions throughout: i.e. (1) Scott's name is now added to each Scott poem, instead of only being in the Index; (2) 'The Cypress Wreath' which filled in at the foot of a page has now been dropped. Copy: E.

[3] The Scotish Minstrel A Selection from the Vocal Melodies of Scotland Ancient & Modern . . . Third Edition. Edinburgh. Published & Sold by Robt. Purdie, at his Music & Musical Instrument Warehouse No. 83 Princes Street. [1821-1824]. Six volumes. Notes: Edited by R. A. Smith. Engraved sheet music throughout except for preliminary matter, but in this edition, as in the second, the Index to each volume is engraved rather than letterpress. As for second edition with (1) Scott's name at foot of each Scott poem; (2) 'The Cypress Wreath' dropped. Copy: E.

368E] EDINBURGH: Robertson 1820
A Selection of Scots, English and Irish Songs . . . Edinburgh; Printed & Sold by D. Robertson, Music Seller. No. 21 South College Street. [1820]. Two volumes. Notes: Engraved sheet music throughout except for preliminary matter. Words by various poets arranged for the pianoforte. Copy: E(vol.2). For a later issue see 365E.
VOLUME 1 includes: '"Soldier Rest thy War Fare O'er" from *The Lady of the Lake*; Written by Walter Scott, Esqr.' (first words as title), pages 26-30.

369E] EDINBURGH: Tait 1829
[1] The Scottish Ballads; . . . Edinburgh: Printed by Ballantyne and Company, for William Tait, 78 Princes Street. MDCCCXXIX. Notes: The 8° edition, collected and illustrated by Robert Chambers. An early rendering of 'Jock of Hazelgreen' is included on pages 284-287, giving the background for Scott's version. Copies: O(2).
Includes: *The Eve of St John* (first words: 'The Baron of Smaylho'me* rose with day,'), pages 345-351. [The starred footnote describing 'Smaylho'me, or Smailholm Tower' and its importance, with reference to Scott, appears to have been added by Chambers.]

[2] The Scottish Ballads; . . . Edinburgh: Printed by Ballantyne and Company, for William Tait, 78 Princes Street. MDCCCXXIX. Notes: A 12° in sixes edition of the preceding work, collected and illustrated by Robert Chambers. Again includes *The Eve of St John* (first words: 'The Baron of Smaylho'me rose with day,'), pages 388-395 and the early version of 'Jock of Hazeldean', pages 319-323. Copies: E(2); CtY T/B.

[3] The Scottish Songs; . . . Edinburgh: Printed by Ballantyne and Company, for William Tait, 78 Princes Street. MDCCCXXIX. Two volumes. Notes: The 8° edition, collected and Illustrated by Robert Chambers. Copies: InU NN.
VOLUME 1 includes: (1) 'A Weary Lot is Thine' (first words: 'A weary lot is thine, fair maid,' from *Rokeby*, canto 3, stanza 28), page 13; (2) 'Donald Caird' (first words: 'Donald Caird can lilt and sing,'), pages 56-57; (3) 'From the Brown Crest of Newark' [The Lifting of the Banner] (first words: 'From the brown crest of Newark its summons extending' from *Ettricke Garland*), pages 62-63; (4) 'Nora's Vow' (first words: 'Hear what Highland Nora said:'), page 92; (5) 'O Hush thee, My Baby' ['A Lullaby for an Infant Chief'] (first words: 'O hush thee, my baby! Thy sire was a knight,' from the play *Guy Mannering, or The Gipsey's Prophecy*, 1816, the poem itself written by Scott), page 187; (6) 'The Cypress Wreath' (first words: O lady, twine no wreath for me,' from *Rokeby*, canto 5, stanza 13), pages 200-201; (7) 'Young Lochinvar' ['Lochinvar'] (first words: 'O, young Lochinvar has come out of the west;' from *Marmion*, canto 5, stanza 12), pages 207-209; (8) 'Where Shall the Lover Rest' (first words as title, from *ibid*, canto 3, stanza 10), page 219;
VOLUME 2 (9) 'Blue Bonnets over the Border' (first words: 'March, march, Ettrick and Teviotdale,' from *The Monastery*, chapter 25), page 436; (10) 'Jock o' Hazeldean' (first words: '"Why weep ye by the tide, ladye—'), pages 440-441; (11) 'Pibroch of Donuil Dhu' (first words as title), pages 502-503; (12) 'Waken, Lords and Ladies Gay!' [Hunting Song] (first words as title), pages 552-553; (13) 'The Foray' (first words: 'The last of our[!] steers on the[!] board has been spread,' from *Twelve Vocal Pieces*), pages 558-559; (14) 'MacGregor's Gathering' (first words: The moon's on the lake, and the mist's on the brae,'

from *Albyn's Anthology*, 1816), page 563; (15) 'The Bonnets of Bonnie Dundee' (first words: 'To the Lords of Convention, 'twas Clavers who spoke,' from *The Christmas Box*), pages 612-614.

[4] The Scottish Songs; . . . Edinburgh: Printed by Ballantyne and Company, for William Tait, 78 Princes Street. MDCCCXXIX. Two volumes. Notes: A 12° edition of the preceding work, collected and illustrated by Robert Chambers. Copies: E E(vol.1); T/B.
VOLUME 1 includes: (1) 'A Weary Lot is Thine' (first words: 'A weary lot is thine, fair maid,' from *Rokeby*, canto 3, stanza 28), page 14; (2) 'Donald Caird' (first words: 'Donald Caird can lilt and sing,'), pages 63-64; (3) 'From the Brown Crest of Newark' [The Lifting of the Banner] (first words: 'From the brown crest of Newark its summons extending' from *Ettricke Garland*), pages 69-70; (4) 'Nora's Vow' (first words: 'Hear what Highland Nora said:'), pages 103-104; (5) 'O Hush Thee, My Baby' ['A Lullaby for an Infant Chief'] (first words: 'O hush thee, my baby! Thy sire was a knight,' from the play *Guy Mannering, or The Gipsey's Prophecy*, 1816, the poem itself written by Scott), pages 210-211; (6) 'The Cypress Wreath' (first words: 'O lady, twine no wreath for me,' from *Rokeby*, canto 5, stanza 13), pages 224-226; (7) 'Young Lochinvar' ['Lochinvar'] (first words: 'O, young Lochinvar has come out of the west;' from *Marmion*, canto 5, stanza 12), pages 233-234; (8) 'Where Shall the Lover Rest' (first words as title, from *ibid*, canto 3, stanza 10), pages 245-246;
VOLUME 2: (9) 'Blue Bonnets over the Border' (first words: 'March, march, Ettrick and Teviotdale,' from *The Monastery*, chapter 25), page 490; (10) 'Jock o' Hazeldean' (first words: '"Why weep ye by the tide, ladye—'), pages 495-496; (11) 'Pibroch of Donuil Dhu' (first words as title), pages 565-566; (12) 'Waken, Lords and Ladies Gay!' [Hunting Song] (first words as title), pages 621-622; (13) 'The Foray' (first words: 'The last of our[!] steers on the[!] board has been spread,'), page 628; (14) 'MacGregor's Gathering' (first words: The moon's on the lake, and the mist's on the brae,'), page 633; (15) 'The Bonnets of Bonnie Dundee' (first words: 'To the Lords of Convention, 'twas Clavers who spoke,' from *The Christmas Box*), pages 689-691. For Scott's original contribution concerning the character of Mrs. Catherine Cockburn see 229A [1829].

370E] EDINBURGH: Charles Thomson 1828
Forty Choice Poetical Extracts. . . Printed from Copper Plates. . . . Edinburgh. Published by Charles Thomson Engraver No. 19 Shakespeare Square—and to be had of all Booksellers 1828. Copy: E.
Includes: 'The Landing of the British in Spain' (first words: 'It was a dread yet spirit stirring sight', from *The Vision of Don Roderick*, stanzas 56-59), plate 36.

371E] EDINBURGH: George Thomson 1826
Twenty-Five Additional Scottish Airs, with Songs, and Symphonies and Accompaniments . . . Composed for this Work by Haydn, Hummel, Beethoven, &c. Forming a Second Part to Vol. V. . . . Edinburgh: Printed for G. Thomson, 140, Princes Street, By John Moir, 21, West Register Streeet. 1826. Notes: A supplemental volume to the 1826 London: Preston folio series (405E(2)[2]), with two Scott reprints in the main text and another in a separately paged Appendix. Copies: L(Hirsch, without Appendix) L(with Appendix).
Includes: (1) 'Why weep ye by the tide, Ladye' ['Jock of Hazeldean'] (first words as title, from *Albyn's Anthology*, 1816, music arranged by Hummel; (2) 'Pibroch of Donuil Dhu' (first words as title, from *ibid*, 1816), pages 234, music unidentified; (3) 'The Troubadour'

(first words: 'Glowing with love, on fire for fame,' from *Paul's Letters to His Kinsfolk*, letter 9), page '2nd.125', music arranged by Weber.

372E] GLASGOW: Blackie, Fullarton 1828-1829
[1] The Casquet of Literary Gems. . . . . Blackie, Fullarton, and Co., East Clyde Street, Glasgow; and A. Fullarton and Co., Edinburgh. MDCCCXXVIII. Two volumes. Notes: Edited by Alex. Whitelaw. Copies: L; InU.
VOLUME 1 includes: (1) 'Siege of Torquilstone' (begins: 'A moment of peril is often also a moment of open-hearted kindness and affection', from *Ivanhoe*, chapter 30), pages *3* 4-8; (2) 'Edinburgh' (first words: 'Still on the spot Lord Marmion stay'd,' from *Marmion*, canto 4, stanza 30), page 112; (3) 'The Imprisoned Huntsman' (first words: 'My hawk is tired of perch and hood,' from *The Lady of the Lake*, canto 6, stanza 24), page 43; (4) 'Interview between Effie and Jeanie Deans' (begins: 'Shame, fear, and grief had contended for mastery', from *The Heart of Mid-Lothian*, chapter 20), pages 184-186;
VOLUME 2 (5) *The Two Drovers* (begins: 'It was the day after the Doune fair when my story commences', from *Chronicles of the Canongate*, First Series), pages 4-13; (6) 'The Dance of Death' (first words: 'Night and Morning were at meeting'), pages 67-68; (7) 'Hymn of the Hebrew Maid' (first words: 'When Israel, of the Lord beloved,' from *Ivanhoe*, chapter 40), page 148; (8) 'Margaret Ramsay and the Lady Hermione' (after a six-line motto beginning 'By this good light, a wench of matchless mettle!', prose begins: 'When Mistress Margaret entered the Foljambe apartment,' from *The Fortunes of Nigel*, chapter 19), pages 217-220; (9) 'The Story of Sir William Wallace' (begins: 'I told you, my dear Hugh, that Edward the First of England had reduced Scotland', from *Tales of a Grandfather*, first series, chapter 7), pages 277-283.

[2] The Casquet of Literary Gems. . . . Second Series. . . . Glasgow: Blackie, Fullarton, & Co; A. Fullarton & Co., Edinburgh; J. M. Leckie, Dublin; James Duncan, and Simpkin & Marshall, London. MDCCCXXIX. Two volumes. Notes: Edited by Alex. Whitelaw. Copy: L.
VOLUME 1 includes: (1) 'The Darien Scheme' (begins: 'Human character, whether national or individual,' from *Tales of a Grandfather*. Second Series, chapter 26), pages 215-221; (2) 'Scene from "Old Mortality"' (begins: 'The Laird of Milnwood kept up all old fashions which were connected with economy.', from chapter 8), pages 327-334;
VOLUME 2 (3) 'The Fiery Cross' (first words: 'The summer dawn's reflected hue,' from *The Lady of the Lake*, canto 3, stanzas 2-24), pages 353-357.

373E] GLASGOW: Booksellers 1810-1829
[1] Hurrah for the Bonnets of Blue. . . . Glasgow: Printed for the Booksellers. 1829. Notes: Chapbook. Copies: E L O(2) O(2: J.Johnson); CtY. Includes anonymously: (1) 'The Cypress Wreath' (first words: 'O lady twine no wreath for me,' from *Rokeby*, canto 5, stanza 13), pages 4-5; (2) 'The Captive Maniac' (first words: 'They bid me sleep, they bid me pray' from *The Lady of the Lake*, canto 4, stanza 22), page 8.

[2] Seven Popular Songs. The Lily of France. Blue Bonnets over the Border... Glasgow: Printed for the Booksellers. 41. [1821]. Notes: Chapbook. Copy: O.
Includes: 'Blue Bonnets over the Border' (first words: 'March, march, Ettrick and Teviotdale,' from *The Monastery*, chapter 25), page 2.

[3] Tam Glen. Young Dunois. . . . Glasgow: . . . Printed for the booksellers. 1823. Notes: Chapbook. Copy: L.
Includes anonymously: 'Young Dunois' [Romance of Dunois] (first words: 'It was Dunois the young and brave, was bound for Palestine,' from *The Edinburgh Annual Register for 1813*, 1815 [1816]), pages 3-4.

[4] Tullochgorum. Ca' the Ewes to the Knowes. The heath this night must be my bed. She's fair and fause. Glasgow—Printed for the Booksellers. [1810]. Notes: Chapbook. Copy: L.
Includes anonymously: 'Soldier's Song' (first words: 'The heath this night must be my bed,' from *The Lady of the Lake*, canto 3, stanza 23), pages 6-7.

[5] Young Lochinvar; To which are added, The Rose of Dunmore, Scottish Whisky, . . . Glasgow: Printed for the Booksellers. 1828. Notes: Songster. Copies: E L(3) O(2) O(J.Johnson); MB.
Includes anonymously: 'Young Lochinvar' ['Lochinvar'] (first words: 'O! Young Lochinvar has come out of the west,' from *Marmion*, canto 5, stanza 12), pages 2-3.

374E] GLASGOW: Duncan 1808
Young Lochinvar. To which are added, Will ye gang to the North Highlands wi' me, and The Twa Drunken Snabs. Glasgow: Printed and Sold, Wholesale and Retail, by T. Duncan 159, Saltmarket. [1808?] Notes: Chapbook. Copies: L(2).
Includes anonymously: 'Young Lochinvar' ['Lochinvar'] (first words: 'O! Young Lochinvar has come out of the west,' from *Marmion*, canto 5, stanza 12), pages 2-3.

375E] GLASGOW: Griffin 1823-1825
[1] Jacobite Melodies: A Collection of the Most Popular Legends, Ballads, and Songs of the Adherents to the House of Stuart, from 1640, Till the Termination of the Rebellion in 1746. . . . Edinburgh: Printed by W. Aitchison: Published by R. Griffin &. Co. Glasgow, and T. & J. Allman, London. MDCCCXXIII. Notes: With an engraved frontispiece and engraved title-page, in addition to a typeset title-page. Copies: E L. References: Ruff, page 281, which reports 'five poems'. (Ruff may have counted the traditional poem 'Carle an the King Come' [Song XVI, pages 21-22] from which Scott derived his 'Carle, Now the King's Come'.) Reissued 1825 with imprint: Glasgow: Published by Richard Griffin & Co. 75, Hutcheson-Street, MDCCCXXV (E). In 1829 Griffin also published an anthology similarly titled *Jacobite Minstrelsy*, but which contained no selections from Scott.
Includes: (1) 'Song CXIII. The Gathering of the Clans' (first words: 'There is mist on the mountain, and night on the vale,' from *Waverley*, chapter 22), pages 168-170; (2) 'Song CXXII. Gathering of Clan Conuil' (first words: 'Pibroch of Donuil Dhu,'), pages 181-182; (3) 'Song CXXIII. Gathering of Macgregor' [Macgregor's Gathering] (first words: 'The moon's on the lake, and the mist's on the brae,'), page 183; (4) 'Song CLII. Blue Bonnets over the Border,' (first words: 'March, march, Ettrick and Teviotdale,' from *The Monastery*, chapter 25), pages 226-227. Authorship for each is identified in the text, but not in the 'Contents': the first three as by Sir Walter Scott, the last as 'By the Author of "Waverly[!]." Only text is given.

[2] Lyrical Gems: A Selection of Moral, Sentimental, and Descriptive Poetry, from the Works of the Most Popular Modern Writers. . . . Glasgow: Printed for Richard Griffin &

Co., and Daniel Weir, Greenock. MDCCCXXV. Notes: The entries are all noted only as by 'The Author of *Waverley*'. Copy: InU.
Includes: (1) 'To an Oak Tree' (first words: 'Emblem of England's ancient faith,' from *Waverley*, chapter 29), pages 218-219; (2) 'The Orphan Maid' (first words: 'November's hail-cloud drifts away,' from *A Legend of Montrose*, chapter 9), pages 219-220; (3) 'Ancient Gaelic Melody' (first words: 'Birds of omen dark and foul,' from *ibid*, chapter 6), page 221; (4) 'Flora Mac Ivor's Song' (first words: 'There is mist on the mountain, and night on the vale,' from *Waverley*, chapter 22), pages 317-319; (5) 'The Crusader's Return' (first words: 'High deeds achieved of knightly fame,' from *Ivanhoe*, chapter 18), pages 319-310; (6) 'The Barefooted Friar' (first words: 'I'll give thee, good fellow, a twelvemonth or twain,' from *ibid*), pages 321-322.

376E] GLASGOW: Khull 1819
The Harp of Caledonia . . . [Volume 3] Glasgow, Printed & published by E. Khull & Co. 1819. Notes: Engraved title-page. Volumes 1-2 were issued by Khull and other publishers, *see* 378E. Copy: InU.
Includes: (1) 'Pibroch of Donnel Dhu' (first words as title), pages 420-421; (2) 'Allan-a-Dale' [Allen-a-Dale] (first words: 'Allan-a-Dale has no faggot [fagot] for burning;' from *Rokeby*, canto 3, stanza 30), page 442; (3) 'The Harper' (first words: '"Summer eve is gone and past;' from *ibid*, canto 5, stanzas 7, 9), pages 443-444.

377E] GLASGOW: Smith [and others] 1816
The Pocket Encyclopedia of Scottish, English, and Irish Songs. . . . Glasgow: Printed by Andrew & James Duncan, and Sold by J. Smith & Son, A. & J. M. Duncan, W. Turnbull, and Brash & Reid; A. Constable & Co. J. Ballantyne, and P. Hill, Edinburgh; B. Crosby & Co. and Longman, Hurst, Rees, Orme, & Brown, London. 1816. Two volumes. Copy: O.
Includes: (1) 'The Heath' (first words: 'The heath this night must be my bed,' from *The Lady of the Lake*, canto 3, stanza 23), pages 97-98; (2) 'The last Words of Marmion' (first words: 'The war, that for a space did fail, from *Marmion*, canto 6, stanza 32), page 131. Scott, as well as other poets, is only identified in the Index.

378E] GLASGOW: Sommerville, Fullarton, Blackie 1819-1821
The Harp of Caledonia: A Collection of Songs, Ancient and Modern, (Chiefly Scottish.) . . . Glasgow: Printed by Edward Khull & Co. For Sommerville, Fullarton, Blackie, & Co. Sold by John Smith & Son, A. & J. Duncan, James Brash & Co. Reid and Henderson, M. Ogle, Wm. Turnbull, T. Ogilvie, and Murray & Bonnard, Glasgow; Wm. Blackwood, Edinburgh; and George Cowie & Co. London. 1819. Three volumes. Copies: E(vols.1-2) E(vol.2). Reference: Ruff, page 281. Reissued 1821 (L).
VOLUME 1 includes: (1) 'Song from Marmion' (first words: 'Where shall the lover rest,' from *Marmion*, canto 3, stanza 10), pages 49-50; (2) 'Young Lochinvar' ['Lochinvar'] (first words: 'O, Young Lochinvar has come out of the west,' from *ibid*, canto 5, stanza 12), pages 50-51; (3) 'Soldier's Song on the Eve of a Battle' (first words: 'The heath this night must be my bed,' from *The Lady of the Lake*, canto 3, stanza 23), page 248; (4) 'The Captive Maniac' (first words: 'They bid me sleep, they bid me pray,' *ibid.*, canto 4, stanza 22), page 250; (5) 'The Captive Huntsman' [Lay of the Imprisoned Huntsman] (first words: 'My hawk is tired of perch and hood,' *ibid*, canto 6, stanza 24), page 251; (6) 'Song' (first words: 'O Brignal banks are wild and fair,' from *Rokeby*, canto 3, stanza 16), pages 292-294; (7) 'Song. The

Cypress Wreath' (first words: 'O Lady, twine no wreath for me,' *ibid*, canto 5, stanza 13), pages 297-298; (8) 'Song. To the Moon' (first words: 'Hail to thy cold and clouded beam,' *ibid.*, canto 1, stanza 33), pages 301-302; (9) 'Song.' (first words: 'A weary lot is thine, fair maid,' *ibid*, canto 3, stanza 28), page 309;
VOLUME 2: (10) 'Song. Written for [sung at] the Anniversary of the Pitt Club of Scotland' (first words: 'O Dread was the time, and more dreadful the omen,'), pages 163-164; (11) 'War Song of Lachlan High Chief of Maclean' (first words: 'A weary month has wandered o'er'), page 167; (12) '[On] The Massacre of Glencoe' (first words: 'O Tell me, Harper, wherefore flow'), pages 168-170; (13) 'Farewell to M'Kenzie, High Chief of Kintail' (first words: 'Farewell to Mackenneth, great Earl of the North,') pages 173-174; (14) 'The Bard's Incantation' (first words: 'The forest of Glenmore is drear,'), pages 175-177;
VOLUME 3: Issued by Khull alone, with three further entries (*see* 367E).

379E] HAWICK: Armstrong 1811
The Banquet of Euphrosyne: A Selection of the most approved Songs, Scottish and English. . . . Hawick: Printed and Sold by R. Armstrong, Sold also by A. Rutherfurd, Kelso;—W. Renwick, Jedburgh;—P. Jollie & Sons, Carlisle;—J. Reid, Berwick;—and Peter Hill, Edinburgh. 1811. Copy: E.
Includes: (1) 'Lochinvar' (first words: 'O, young Lochinvar is come out of the west,' from *Marmion*, canto 5, stanza 12), pages 242-243; (2) 'Where shall the Lover, &c.' (first words: 'Where shall the lover rest,' from *ibid*, canto 3, stanza 10-11) pages 244-245; (3) 'The Heath, &c.' (first words: 'The heath this night must be my bed,' from *The Lady of the Lake*, canto 3, stanza 23), pages 245-246; (4) 'The Maniac's Song' (first words: 'They bid me sleep, they bid me pray,' from *ibid.*, canto 4, stanza 22), pages 246-247; (5) 'War Song of the Royal Edinburgh Light Dragoons' (first words: 'To horse! to horse! the standard flies,' from volume 3 of *Minstrelsy of the Scottish Border*), pages 249-251.

380E] KILMARNOCK: Crawford 1821
The Ayrshire Melodist: or, the Muses' Delight. . . Kilmarnock: Printed by H. Crawford, Bookseller. 1821. Notes: Songster. Copy: O(J.Johnson).
Includes anonymously: 'Annot Lyle' (first words: 'Wert thou like me in life's low vale,' from *A Legend of Montrose*, chapter 21), pages 15-16.

381E] LEITH: Burnet 1824
The Royal Scottish Minstrelsy: Being A Collection of Loyal Effusions Occasioned by the Visit of His Most Gracious Majesty George IV. to Scotland, August 15, 1822. Leith: Published by James Burnet, and Sold by all the Booksellers. 1824. Notes: In the Preface, dating from Leith 14 August 1824, the publisher claims all credit for this collection and makes no reference to Scott for any assistance in this compilation. Copies: E O; CtY InU. Reference: Ruff, page 281.
Includes: (1) 'Carle now the King's Come! By Sir Walter Scott, Bart.' (first words: 'The news has flown frae mouth to mouth,'), pages 1 2-12; (2) 'Lines added to the King's Anthem, Ascribed to Sir Walter Scott, Bart. and Sung at the Theatre while His Majesty was about to retire.' (7 lines, first words 'Bright beams are soon o'ercast,'), page 229. Another poem, sometimes attributed to Scott, also exists as a separate broadside (copy: CtY): (3) 'A Voice from the Highlands' (9 quatrains, first words: 'The peak of yon mountain is shining in light,'), pages 32-34.

382E] LONDON: Baker 1822
Selections from the British Poets, Commencing with Spenser, and including the Latest Writers. Southampton: Printed by Thomas Baker; and Published by Him, 18, Finsbury Place, London. 1822. Notes: Compiled by John Bullar. Copy: T/B.
Includes: (1) 'The Last Minstrel' (first words: 'The Way was long, the wind was cold,' from *The Lay of the Last Minstrel*, Introduction), pages 293-296; (2) 'War' (first words: 'The hunting tribes of air and earth' from *Rokeby*, canto 3, stanza 1), page 308; (3) 'Helvellyn[!]' (first words: 'I climbed the dark brow of the mighty Helvellyn[!]'), pages 322-323.

LONDON: Barrois *see* PARIS: Barrois (355E).

383E] LONDON: Batchelar 1824
Batchelar's Cossack Song Book: Being a Choice selection of new and popular Songs. . . London: Printed and sold by T. Batchelar, 115, Long Alley Moorfields. [1824?]. Copy: CtY.
Includes: '2. Dunois the brave' ['Romance of Dunois'] (first words: 'I[t] was Dunois the young and brave,' from *The Edinburgh Annual Register for 1813*, 1815), page 2.

LONDON: Birchall, Lonsdale, and Mills
[~] A Collection of Glees, Canons, and Catches. *see* 406E.

LONDON: Booksellers
[~] The Harmonica, Being a Choice Collection . . . London: Printed for the Booksellers. 1818. Notes: A reissue of the Cork: Bolster edition with cancel title-page, *see* 360R.

384E] LONDON: Boys 1826
Laconics or the Best Words of the Best Authors. London: Printed for T. Boys, Ludgate Hill. 1826. Three volumes. Copy: L. For later editions *see* 412E, 466E
VOLUME 1 includes: (1) 'MLXXX' (first words: 'Swift, in his "[A Serious and Useful] Scheme to make an Hospital for Incurables,"' from Scott's edition of *The Works of Jonathan Swift*, volume 9, page 537), page 222;
VOLUME 2 (2) 'DCLIII' (first words: 'Nay, dally not with time, the wise man's treasure,' from *The Monastery*, motto [Old Play], chapter 8), page 164; (3) 'DCLXXVII' (first words: 'I knew Anselmo. He was shrewd and prudent,' *The Antiquary*, title-page motto), page 171; (4) 'MLVIII' (first words: 'Nay, if she love me not, I care not for her:', from *ibid*, motto [Old Play], chapter 44), page 280; (5) 'MXCII' (first words: 'Heaven first, in its mercy, taught mortals their letters', from *Guy Mannering*, motto [Pope, imitated], chapter 17), page 288; (6) 'MCCCXIX' (first words: 'He strikes no coin, 'tis true, but coins new phrases,' from *The Monastery*, motto [Old Play], chapter 15), page 350;
VOLUME 3 (7) 'MXXIII' (first words: 'Fortune, you say, flies from us—She but circles,' from *The Antiquary*, motto [Old Play], chapter 43), page 330.

385E] LONDON: Bumpus [and others] 1824
The Beauties of the Poets, Lyric and Elegiac, Selected from the most Admired Authors. . . . London: Printed for John Bumpus, Holborn; T. Bult, 72, Baker Street, Portman Square; Hailes, Museum, Piccadilly; Clarke, Royal Exchange; Bossange and Co. Great Marlborough Street; also, R. Griffin & Co. Glasgow; and J. Cumming, Dublin. 1824. Notes: Edited by

James Ely Taylor. Copy: CtY.
Includes: (1) 'The Last Minstrel' (first words: 'The way was long, the wind was cold,' from *The Lay of the Last Minstrel*, Introduction), pages 114-118; (2) 'Landing of the British Army in Portugal' (first words: '——— The shout grew loud—/ A varied scene the changeful vision show'd,' from *The Vision of Don Roderick*, stanzas 55-60), pages 160-162; (3) 'Decisive Charge at Waterloo' (first words: 'On came the whirlwind—like the last' from *The Field of Waterloo*, stanzas 11-12), pages 171-172; (4) 'Helvellyn[!]' (first words: 'I climb'd the dark brow of the mighty Helvellyn[!]), pages 175-176.

386E] LONDON: Clark [and others] 1824
The First Volume of Poetry; Revised, Improved, and Considerably Enlarged, Containing the Most Favorite Pieces, as performed at The Noblemen and Gentlemen's Catch Club, The Glee Club, [and eight others] .... London: Printed for The Editor: and may be had of him, No. 25, Stangate Street, Bridge Road, Lambeth; at the Argyle Rooms, and of Messrs. Clementi's and Co. 25, Cheapside. 1824. Notes: In this collection reference is usually made to the composer and the publication representing the lyrics, rather than the author of the words. Copies: CtY InU. Reference: Kohler(3) 451.
Lacking titles, the first words include: (1) 'In peace, love tunes the shepherd's reed,' (from *The Lay of the Last Minstrel*, canto 3, stanza 2), pages 120-121; (2) 'Some feelings are to mortals given,' (from *The Lady of the Lake*, canto 2, stanza 22), pages 239-240; (3) 'Shepherds, I have lost my love,' [attributed erroneously to Scott]), page 241; (4) 'She paused, then blushing led the lay,' (from *The Lady of the Lake*, canto 1, stanza 32), pages 246-247; (5) 'The rose is fairest when 'tis budding new,' (from *ibid*, canto 4, stanza 1), page 277; (6) 'The harp's wild notes, though hush'd the song,' (from *The Lay of the Last Minstrel*, canto 5, conclusion), page 369; (7) 'Full well our Christian sires of old,' (from *Marmion*, canto 6, Introduction), page 397; (8) 'Wert thou like me, in life's low vale,' (from *A Legend of Montrose*, chapter 21), page 433.

LONDON: Cramer, Addison, and Beale
[~] Collection of Glees, Canons, and Catches. 1824. *see* 406E

387E] LONDON: Dean and Munday 1820-1827
[1] Beauties of Melody; A Collection of the most Popular Airs, Duets, Glees, &c. ... Also a Selection of the Best and Most Approved Irish Melodies; ... Interspersed with many of the Beautiful Scotch Melodies, ... London: Printed and Sold by Dean and Munday, Threadneedle-Street. [1827]. Notes: With engraved frontispiece portrait of John Braham, Esqr. dated 1 November 1827. Music included, arranged for voice and pianoforte. Copy: CtY.
Includes: (1) [anonymously] 'All the Blue Bonnets are over the Border' (first words: 'March, march, Ettrick and Teviotdale, Why, my lads' from *The Monastery*, chapter 25), pages 13 14-18; (2) 'Jock o' Hazeldean... The Words Written by Sir Walter Scott' (first words: 'Why weep ye by the Tide, lady? Why weep ye'), pages 255-257.

[2] The London Minstrel: Being a Collection of the most approved English, Irish, and Scotch Songs, Glees, Duets, &c. .. London: Printed for Dean and Munday, Threadneedle-Street 1820. Notes: Music printed with letter press throughout, arranged for voice, flute and violin. Also issued with engraved frontispiece and vignette title-page with imprint of Dean and

Munday and Newman. Copies: E; CtY. Reissued 1825 with imprint extended: 'and A. K. Newman and Co. Leadenhall-Street' (O[J.Johnson]). Includes anonymously: 'The Troubadour!' (first words: 'Glowing with love, on fire for fame', from *Paul's Letters to His Kinsfolk*, letter 9), pages 102-104.

388E] LONDON: Edwards 1824

Beauties of the British Poets; with Notices, Biographical and Critical. By F. Campbell, Esq. . . . London: Printed by Richard Edwards, 6, Crane Court, Fleet Street. 1824. Two volumes. Notes: Volume 1 has an engraved frontispiece portrait of Scott. Copy: T/B.

VOLUME 1 includes: (1) 'Love of Country' (first words: 'Breathes There a Man with Soul so Dead' from *The Lay of the Last Minstrel*, canto 6, stanzas 1-2), page 16; (2) 'Lady of the Lake' (first words: 'Never did Grecian chisel trace' from *The Lady of the Lake*, canto 1, stanzas 18-19), pages 115-116; (3) 'The Combat of Fitz-James and Roderick Dhu' (first words: 'Then each at once his faulchion drew,' *ibid*, canto 5, stanzas 14-16), pages 248-249; (4) 'Bertram Risingham' (first words: 'On his dark face a scorching clime,' from *Rokeby*, canto 1, stanzas 8-9, canto 3, stanza 3, and canto 6, stanza 21), pages 306-307; (5) 'Landing of the English in Portugal' (first words: 'Don Roderick turn'd him as the shout grew loud— ' from *The Vision of Don Roderick*, stanzas 55-60), pages 324-325; (6) 'Decisive Charge at Waterloo' (first words: 'On came the whirlwind—like the last' from *The Field of Waterloo*, stanzas 11-12), pages 341-342.

VOLUME 2 (7) 'Helvellyn' [!] (first words: 'I climbed the dark brow of the mighty Helvellyn [!]'), pages 4-5; (8) 'The Last Minstrel' (first words: 'The way was long, the wind was cold,' from *The Lay of the Last Minstrel*, Introduction), pages 130-133; (9) 'Young Lochinvar' ['Lochinvar'] (first words: 'O, young Lochinvar is come out of the west,' from *Marmion*, canto 5, stanza 12), pages 292-294.

389E] LONDON: Fairburn [and others] 1825-1832

The Universal Songster; or, Museum of Mirth: Forming the Most Complete, Extensive, and Valuable Collection of Ancient and Modern Songs in the English Language: . . . London: Printed for John Fairburn, Broadway, Ludgate-Hill; Simpkin and Marshall, Stationers' Court; and Sherwood, Gilbert, and Piper, Paternoster-Row. 1825. Three volumes, with volumes 2-3 dated 1826. Notes: The engraved Cruikshank title-pages are successively dated 11 June 1825, 21 January 1826, 22 May 1827. Copies: O; CtY InU. In a later issue the Cruikshank plates are undated, a preliminary frontispiece is dated 'Jany 1832', and the title imprints read 'Publishd by Jones and Co., Temple of the Muses, Finbury Square.' (T/B, vols.1-2). Reference: Cohn 820.

VOLUME 1 includes: (1) 'It was Dunois the Young and Brave' ['Romance of Dunois'] (first words: 'It was Dunois the young and brave, was bound for Palestine,' from *The Edinburgh Annual Register for 1813*, 1815 [1816]), pages 37-38; (2) 'A Weary Lot is Thine, Fair Maid' (first words as title, from *Rokeby*, canto 3, stanza 28), page 52; (3) 'The Heath this Night must be my Bed' (first words as title, from *The Lady of the Lake*, canto 3, stanza 23), page 109; (4) 'Our Vicar still Preaches, that Peter and Poule' [Soldier's Song] (first words as title, from *The Lady of the Lake*, canto 6, stanza 5), page 124; (5) 'The Last Words of Marmion' (first words: 'The war, that for a space did fail,' from *Marmion*, canto 6, stanza 32), page 140; (6) 'The Gathering of Clan Connell' (first words: 'Pibroch, of Donnell [Donuil] Dhu!'), page 152; (7) 'The Cavalier' (first words: 'While the dawn on the mountain was misty and gray,' from *Rokeby*, canto 5, stanza 20), page 157; (8) 'Ah! County Guy' (first words: 'Ah, County Guy! the hour is nigh,' from *Quentin Durward*, chapter 4), page 158;

(9) 'Twist ye! Twine ye! (first words: 'Twist ye! twine ye! ever so', from *Guy Mannering*, chapter 4), page 192; (10) 'How Swiftly wears the Summer Night' (first words: 'Hail to the cold and clouded beam,' from *Rokeby*, canto 1, stanza 33), page 297; (11) 'Hail to the Chief Who in Triumph Advances' (first words as title, from *The Lady of the Lake*, canto 2, stanzas 19-20), page 309; (12) 'Awake! On your Hills,—On your Islands, Awake! (first words as title, from *Waverley*, chapter 22), page 321; (13) 'Merrily, Merrily Bounds the Bark' (first words as title, from *The Lord of the Isles*, canto 4, stanzas 7, 9-11), page 345; (14) 'It Chanced that Cupid, on a Season' (first words as title, from *Paul's Letters to His Kinsfolk*, Letter 9), page 384; (15) 'Wake, Maid of Lorn' (first words: 'Wake, maid of Lorn, the moments fly', from *The Lord of the Isles*, canto 1, stanza 4), page 402; (16) 'Where shall the Lover Rest?' (first words as title, from *Marmion*, canto 3, stanzas 10-11), page 431; (17) 'Nora and the Erlie's Son' ['Nora's Vow'] (first words: 'Hear what Highland Nora said,'), page 444. Volume 1 also falsely attributes: 'Behold Me, sung Hassan, The Fearless and Free' to Walter Scott. The Vocal Library [London, Whittaker 1824] appears to be the earliest to imply that Walter Scott might have written this poem by listing it as by 'Scott'. Pirates unfortunately failed to realize that either Alexander Scott or John Scott of Amwell, both also included, might also be the author.
VOLUME 2 (18) 'I'd Rather Dwell Alone' ['The Resolve'] (first words: 'My wayward fate I needs must plain,') pages 67-68; (19) 'Yon Organ! Hark! How Soft, How Sweet' (first words as title, attributed to 'Sir Walter Scott' but written by John Scott of Amwell under the title 'Hearing Music'), page '67'[167]; (20) 'Soldier, Wake—The Day is Peeping' (first words as title, from *The Betrothed*, chapter 19), pages 234-235; (21) 'He is Gone on the Mountain'['Coronach'] (first words as title, from *The Lady of the Lake*, canto 3, stanza 16), pages 251-252; (22) 'The Truth of Woman' (first words: 'Woman's faith and woman's trust,' from *The Betrothed*, chapter 20), page 265; (23) 'Childhood, Happiest Stage of Life' (first words as title, attributed to 'Sir Walter Scott' but written by John Scott of Amwell with title 'To Childhood'), pages 279-280; (24) 'Breathes There a Man with Soul so Dead' (first words as title, from *The Lay of the Last Minstrel*, canto 6, stanza 1), page 310; (25) 'My Harp Alone' (first words: 'I was a wild and wayward boy,' from *Rokeby*, canto 5, stanza 18), page 354; (26) 'From the Brown Crest of Newark' ['Lifting of the Banner'] (first words: 'From the brown crest of Newark its summons extending'), pages 371-372; (27) 'Allen-a-Dale' (first words: 'Allen-a-Dale has no faggot for burning,' from *Rokeby*, canto 3, stanza 30), page 397; (28) 'The Death-Song of a Welsh Bard' ['The Dying Bard'] (first words: 'Dinas Emlinn, Lament! for the moment is nigh'), page 420.
VOLUME 3 (29) 'Hunters Watch so Narrowly, Narrowly' (first words: 'The toils are pitched, and the stakes are set,' from *The Lady of the Lake*, canto 4, stanza 25), page 23; (30) 'The Lonely Isle' (first words: 'Not faster yonder rowers might', *ibid*, canto 2, stanza 2), page 36; (31) 'Jock O' Hazel-Dean [Hazeldean]' (first words: 'Why weep ye by the tide, Lady?'), page 58; (32) 'Farewell to Northmaven' (first words as title, from *The Pirate*, chapter 12), page 67; (33) 'November's Hail-Cloud Drifts Away' ['The Orphan Maid'] (first words as title, from *A Legend of Montrose*, chapter 9), pages 95-96; (34) 'The Last of the Deer' ['The Foray'] (first words: 'The last of the deer [steers] on our board has been spread'), pages 104-105; (35) 'Farewell, Merry Maidens' (first words: 'Farewell, merry maidens, to song, and to laugh,' from *The Pirate*, chapter 22), page 128; (36) 'Oh! Listen, Listen, Ladies, Gay' (first words as title, from *The Lay of the Last Minstrel*, canto 6, stanza 23), pages 238-239; (37) 'The Blue Bonnets are Over the Border' (first words: 'March, march, Ettrick and Teviotdale!', anonymously from *The Monastery*, chapter 25), page 242; (38) 'Love is Heaven,

and Heaven is Love' (first words: 'In peace, Love tunes the shepherd's reed,' from *The Lay of the Last Minstrel*, canto 3, stanza 2), page 248; (39) 'Here's a Health to King Charles' ['Glee for King Charles'] (first words: 'Bring the bowl which you boast,' from *Woodstock*, chapter 20), page 326; (40) 'Soldier, Rest! Thy Warfare O'er' (first words as title, from *The Lady of the Lake*, canto 1, stanza 31), page 344.

390E] LONDON: Goulding and D'Almaine 1829
The Musical Bijou, An Album of Music, Poetry, and Prose, for MDCCCXXX. . . . London: Goulding and D'Almaine, 20, Soho Square. [1829]. Notes: This annual was edited by F. H. Burney. Copies: E L. Reference: G/T 10441.
Includes: 'The Maid of Toro. By Sir Walter Scott, Bart.', (first words: 'O, low shone the sun on the fair lake of Toro,') pages 16-20[engraved music], 21[letterpress]. Music composed by J. Parry arranged for voice and pianoforte.

391E] LONDON: Gray 1820
[engraved title] The New Musical and Vocal Cabinet. Comprising a Selection of the most Favorite English, Scotch, & Irish Melodies. . . . London: Publish'd by H. Gray No. 2 Barbican. [1820?] Notes: Some of the stereotype plates appear also in the same title published by Thomas Kelly in 1820 (*see* 398E). Copies: E L.
VOLUME 1 includes: (1) 'The Heath this Night, From "The Lady of the Lake"' (first words: 'The heath this night must be my bed,' from canto 3, stanza 23), pages 215-217;
VOLUME 2: (2) 'Our Vicar still preaches that Peter and Poule. ['Soldier's Song'] . . . Words by Walter Scott.' (first words as title from *ibid*, canto 6, stanza 5), pages 114-117; (3) 'The Lonely Isle' (first words: 'Not faster yonder rowers' might Flings' from *ibid*, canto 2, stanzas 2-3), pages 136-138; (4) 'Ave, Maria. . . .By Walter Scott.' (first words: 'Ave Maria maiden mild, Listen to a maiden's pray'r;' from *ibid*, canto 3, stanza 29), pages 287-289.

392E] LONDON: Hall 1824
Select British Poets, or New Elegant Extracts from Chaucer to the Present Time, With Critical Remarks. . . . London: Published by Wm. C. Hall, and Sold by All Booksellers. 1824. Notes: This anthology, edited by William Hazlitt, was withdrawn due to infringements of copyright in the section reprinting modern poetry. The paragraph on Scott in the 'Critical List of Authors' reads: 'Sir WALTER SCOTT is the most popular of our living poets. His excellence is romantic narrative and picturesque description. He has great bustle, great rapidity of action and flow of versification, with a sufficient distinctness of character, and command of the ornaments of style. He has neither lofty imagination, nor depth or intensity of feeling; vividness of mind is apparently his chief and pervading excellence.' Copies: O; CtY InU.
Includes: (1) 'The Last Minstrel' (first words: 'The way was long, the wind was cold,' from *The Lay of the Last Minstrel*, Introduction), page 668; (2) 'Margaret at her Father's Bier' (first words: 'Can piety the discord heal,' from *ibid.*, canto 1, stanzas 8-12), pages 668-669; (3) 'Deloraine goes to the Grave of Michael Scott' (first words: 'If thou would'st view fair Melrose aright,' from *ibid*, canto 2, stanzas 1-22), pages 669-671; (4) 'A Bridal' (first words: 'Breathes there a man, with soul so dead,' from *ibid.*, canto 6, stanzas 1-6), pages 671-672; (5) 'The Trial of Constance' (first words: 'In low dark rounds the arches hung,' from *Marmion*, canto 2, stanzas 18-33), pages 672-675; (6) 'Court of James of Scotland' (first words: 'Old Holy-Rood rung merrily' from *ibid*, canto 5, stanzas 7-11) pages 675-676; (7) 'Lochinvar. Lady Heron's Song' (first words: 'O, young Lochinvar is come out of the west,' from *ibid*,

canto 5, stanzas 12-13), page 676; (8) 'The Battle' (first words: 'And why stands Scotland idly now,' from *ibid*, canto 6, stanzas 20-26), pages 676-678; (9) 'The Death of Roderick Dhu' (first words: 'Thus, motionless, and moanless, drew' from *The Lady of the Lake*, canto 6, stanzas 21-29 and the Conclusion) pages 678-680; (10) 'Wilfrid's Song' (first words: 'The blood left Wilfrid's ashen cheek;' from *Rokeby*, canto 5, stanza 12-13 [which includes 'The Cypress Wreath']), pages 680-681; (11) 'Hunting Song' (first words: 'Waken, lords and ladies gay,' from *Queenhoo Hall*, chapter IV), page 681; (12) 'The Violet' (first words: 'The violet in her greenwood bower,'), pages 681-682; (13) 'To a Lady, with Flowers from a Roman Wall' (first words: 'Take these flowers, which, purple waving,'), page 682; (14) 'The Bard's Incantation, Written under the Threat of Invasion in the Autumn of 1804' (first words: 'The forest of Glenmore is drear,'), page 682.

393E] LONDON: Harris 1823
Poetical Gems; A Collection of Pieces, from the Most Admired Authors, . . Published Sept. 20th. 1823, by Harris & Son. Notes: Engraved title-page: the printed front board gives the imprint as 'London: J. Harris and Son, St. Paul's Church-yard.' Copy: O.
Includes: 'Teviot' (first words: 'Sweet Teviot! on thy silver tide' from *The Lay of the Last Minstrel*, canto 4, stanza 1), page 4.

394E] LONDON: Hurst, Chance 1828
The Poetical Album; And Register of Modern Fugitive Poetry. . . [First Series]. London: Hurst, Chance, and Co. St. Paul's Church-Yard. 1828. Notes: Edited by Alaric A. Watts. Copies: CtY InU. Reference: Kohler(3) 1141.
Includes: 'Mirkwood Mere' (first words: 'Late, when the Autumn evening fell,' from *Waverley*, chapter 5), page 150.

395E] LONDON: Hurst, Robinson 1825-1826
Literary Gems. . . Edinburgh: Printed for Hurst, Robinson, & Co. 5, Waterloo Place, Pall-Mall, London; and M'Lachlan & Stewart, Edinburgh. 1826. Notes: The engraved title-page, which precedes the letterpress title, reads: 'Printed for Hurst, Robinson & Co. London; and Maclachlan & Stewart, Edinburgh. 1826.' Copies: O; CtY.
Includes: (1) 'On the Death and Character of Lord Byron, by Sir Walter Scott, Bart' (first words: 'Amidst the general calmness of the political atmosphere, we have been stunned', from the *Edinburgh Weekly Journal*), pages *1* 2-7; (2) 'Phantasmagoria: Said to have been Written by the Author of *Waverley*, &c. [Letter] To the Veiled Conductor of Blackwood's Magazine.' (first words: 'There are few things so much affected by the change of manners and circumstances, as the quality and the effect of evidence.'), pages 293-306.

396E] LONDON: Jones 1826-1832
The Beauties of the Poets of Great Britain, . . . London: Printed for Jones & Co. Acton Place. 1826. Copy: L.
Includes: 'Helvellyn[!]. Walter Scott.'), volume 3, pages *325* 326-327.

[~] The Universal Songster [1832]. (*see* 389E)

397E] LONDON: Joy 1829
The Legendary Cabinet: A Collection of British National Ballads, Ancient and Modern;

From the Best Authorities.... London: W. Joy, 66, St. Paul's Church-yard. MDCCCXXIX. Notes: This anthology was edited by the Rev. J. D. Parry. Copies: E; CtY.
Includes: (1) 'The Gray Brother. A Fragment. By Sir Walter Scott' (first words: 'The Pope he was saying the high, high Mass,') pages *371* 372-375; (2) 'Hunting Song' (first words: 'Waken, lords and ladies gay!' from *Queenhoo Hall*, chapter IV), page 413. The last song is erroneously attributed to Joseph Strutt.

398E] LONDON: Kelly 1820
[engraved title] The New Musical and Vocal Cabinet Comprising a Selection of the most Favorite English Scotch & Irish Melodies. . . . London, Published by Thos. Kelly 17 Paternoster Row 1820. Two volumes. Notes: With music and words printed throughout by letterpress. The stereotype plates also appear in the same title published by Henry Gray in 1820[?] (*see* 391E). Music arranged for voice, violin and flute. Copies: E(vol.1); CtY(vol.1) RPB.
VOLUME 1 includes: (1) 'The Heath this Night from *The Lady of the Lake*' (first words: 'The heath this night must be my bed,' from canto 3, stanza 23), pages 215-217;
VOLUME 2: (2) 'Our Vicar still preaches that Peter and Poule. [Soldier's Song]. . . Words by Walter Scott.' (first words as title, from *ibid*, canto 6, stanza 5), pages 114-117; (3) 'The Lonely Isle. . . .By Walter Scott.' (first words: 'Not faster yonder rowers' might / Flings from their oars the spray' from *ibid*, canto 2, stanzas 2-3), pages 136-138; (4) 'Ave Maria. . . . By Walter Scott.' (first words: 'Ave, Maria, maiden mild, Listen to a maiden's pray'r;' from *ibid,* canto 3, stanza 29), pages 287-289.

399E] LONDON: Lacey 1829
The Juvenile Bijou: A Christmas and New Year's Gift, or Birth-Day Present. . . . London: Edward Lacey, 76, St. Paul's Church-yard. [ca.1829]. Copy: InU.
Includes: 'The Violet', (first words: 'The violet, in her greenwood bower'), page 33.

400E] LONDON: Longman, Hurst, Rees, Orme, and Brown 1813-1834
[1] The British Melodist; or, National Song-Book; . . . London: Sold by Longman, Hurst, Rees, Orme, and Brown; Baldwin, Cradock, and Joy; G. & W. B. Whittaker; Edwards and Knibb; W. Wright; Ogle Duncan, and Cochrane; Simpkin and Marshall; R. N. Rose: Henry Mozley, Derby; and John Stacy, Norwich. [1818]. Notes: At head of title: 'Second Edition, Corrected.' Copy: O(J.Johnson).
Includes: (1) [anonymously] 'Oh! Rest Thee Babe' (first words: 'Oh! slumber my darling, thy sire is a knight,'), page 84; with a (2) 'Parody on "Oh, Rest thee, Babe."' (first words: 'Oh, hush thee, my darling, the hour will soon come, / When thy Sire from the ale-house half drunk will reel home;' from the play, *Guy Mannering, or The Gipsey's Prophecy*, 1816: the poem itself written by Scott), page 185.

[2] Classical English Poetry for the Use of Schools, and Young Persons in General. The Eighth Edition. . . . London: Printed for Longman, Hurst, Rees, Orme, and Brown, Paternoster-Row; and to be had of all Booksellers in Town and Country. 1813. Notes: Collected by Dr. Mavor and Mr. Pratt. The 'Advertisement' page iv notes: 'To this Eighth Edition, some pieces have been introduced from the works of several modern poets of deserved eminence.' Apart from the three selections, all identified in the Contents as by 'Walter Scott', there are eight others by one 'Scott', determined to be John Scott of Amwell. Price: 6s. bound. Copy: L.

Reissued with slightly variant imprints as 'New Edition' in 1820 (T/B), 1823 (L O), 1828 (L), 1834 (InU).
Includes: (1) 'The Patriot' (first words: 'Breathes there the man with soul so dead,' from *The Lay of the Last Minstrel*, canto 6, stanza 1), pages 236-237; (2) 'The Last Minstrel' (first words: 'The way was long, the wind was cold,' *ibid*, Introduction), pages 336-337; (3) 'The Dying Bard' (first words: 'Dinas Emlinn lament, for the moment is nigh' from the pre-publication issue of *The Lay of the Last Minstrel*), page 350.

401E] LONDON: Longman, Rees, Orme, Brown, and Green 1827
Select Specimens of English Poetry, from the Reign of Elizabeth to the Present Time: . . . London: Printed for Longman, Rees, Orme, Brown, and Green, Paternoster-Row. 1827.
Notes: With an Introduction by George Walker. Copy: InU.
Includes: (1) *The Lay of the Last Minstrel* [seven excerpts, first words: (1) 'The way was long, the wind was cold,' from Introduction; (2) 'When kindness had his wants supplied,' from Introduction; (3) 'If thou would'st view fair Melrose aright,' from canto 2, stanza 1; (4) 'Again on the Knight look'd the Churchman old,' from canto 2, stanzas 7-12; (5) 'He paused: the listening dames again', from canto 4, conclusion; (6) 'Breathes there the man, with soul so dead,' from canto 6, stanza 1; (7) 'That day of wrath, that dreadful day,' from canto 6, stanza 31); pages *555* 556-562]; (2) *Marmion* [ten excerpts, first words: (8) 'Along the bridge Lord Mamion rode,' from canto 1, stanza 5); (9) '"Here is a holy Palmer come,' from canto 1, stanza 23; (10) 'The summoned Palmer came in place;', from canto 1, stanza 27; (11) 'Thus, while I ape the measure wild', from canto 3, Introduction; (12) 'No summons calls them to the tower,' from canto 3, stanza 2; (13) 'Nor less did Marmion's skilful view', from canto 5, stanza 2; (14) 'Next Marmion marked the Celtic race,' from canto 5, stanza 5; (15) 'Volumed and vast, and rolling far,' from canto 6, stanza 25; (16) 'They parted, and alone he lay;' from canto 6, stanza 29; (17) 'With fruitless labour, Clara bound,' from canto 6, stanza 32), pages 562-575]; (3) *The Lady of the Lake* [five excerpts, first words: (18) 'The western waves of ebbing day', from canto 1, stanza 11; (19) 'But scarce again the horn he wound,' from canto 1, stanza 17; (20) 'Far up the lengthened lake were spied', from canto 2, stanza 16; (21) '"Have, then, thy wish!"—he whistled shrill', from canto 5, stanza 9; (22) 'Harp of the North, farewell! The hills grow dark,' from Conclusion), pages 575-583].

402E] LONDON: Murray 1827-1832
[1] Hymns Written and Adapted to the Weekly Church Service of the Year. . . . London: John Murray, Albemarle-Street. MDCCCXXVII. Notes: This compendium of hymns arranged by the Right Rev. Reginald Heber, D.D. Copies: BCL O; InU NjP.
Includes: 'Sixth Sunday after Epiphany.—No.II. Walter Scott' ['Hymn for the Dead'] (first words: 'That day of wrath, that dreadful day,' from *The Lay of the Last Minstrel*, canto 6, stanza 31), page 43. In addition to minor punctuation changes, there are two textual changes of religious significance: line 4 here reads 'Whom shall he trust that dreadful day? rather than as in the first edition 'How shall he meet that dreadful day?'. Line 11 here reads 'Be Thou, oh Christ! the sinner's stay,' rather than 'Be THOU the trembling sinner's stay,'. From an analysis of the Preface by Amelia Heber, the bishop's widow, it is apparent that she first supposed that Scott had provided an original hymn, but in later editions she identifies the contribution as from *The Lay of the Last Minstrel*.

[2] [engraved title] Hymns Written or Selected . . . 1828. 4th. Edition. Notes: Scott's text is on page 31. Copy: O.

[3] Hymns Written and Adapted . . . A New Edition. . . . MDCCCXXVIII. Notes: Scott's text remains on page 31. Copy: O.

[4] Hymns Written and Adapted . . . A New Edition. . . . MDCCCXXXII. Notes: Scott's text still unchanged is on page 37, though slight alterations appear in the text of other authors. Copies: L O.

403E] LONDON: Pitts 1820
[1] The Cobourg Songster. . . . Pitts Printer Toy and Marble Warehouse 6, Great St Andrew Street 7 Dials [1820?]. Copy: CtY.
Includes: [anonymously] '17. Dunoise[!] the Brave' ['Romance of Dunois'] (first words: 'It was Dunois the young and brave,' from *The Edinburgh Annual Register for 1813*, 1815 [1816]), page 7.

[2] The New Covent Garden Annual Songster. . . . Printed and Sold by J. Pitts, Wholesale Toy 6, Great St. Andrew Street, Seven Di[als]. [1820]. Copy: CtY.
Includes anonymously: '5. Oh! Rest thee Babe (first words: 'Oh! Slumber, my darling' from a derivative play *Guy Mannering, or The Gipsey's Prophecy*, 1816: the poem itself written by Scott), page 3.

404E] LONDON: Power 1830
A Set of Six Songs, . . . The Words Selected by Permission from the Poems of Mrs. Hemans, Mrs. Opie, Sir Walter Scott, Bart. Mr. Willm. Spencer and Mr. Thos. Moore, . . . London, Published by J. Power, 34, Strand. [1830]. Four sets. Notes: Engraved sheet-music. Each set is a separate volume with title-page and six songs included, words and music. Volume 1 has no set number under imprint, price 10/6; volume 2 has no set number under imprint, price 12/; volume 3 has 'Third Set' under imprint, price 10/6; volume 4 has 'Fourth Set' under imprint, price 12/. Songs composed by Mrs. Robert Arkwright and previously published, but arranged by Thomas Simpson Cooke in this compilation. Copies: L(2) O. References: G/T 10941, G/T 10853 and G/T 10609.
VOLUME 1 includes: (1) 'One hour with thee!' (first words: 'One hour with thee!—When earliest day', from *Woodstock*, chapter 26), pages 19-21. Notes: plate number: '1145'; (2) 'Poor Louise.' (first words: 'Oh! poor Louise the livelong day' from *Chro-nicles of the Canongate*, 'Saint Valentine's Day', chapter 10), pages 22-27;
VOLUME 3: (3) 'The Pirates's Farewell.' (first words: 'Farewell, Farewell the voice you hear,' from *The Pirate*, chapter 23), pages 3-6. Notes: plate number: '1171'; (4) 'Alice Brand.', (first words: 'Merry merry it is in the good greenwood,' from *The Lady of the Lake*, canto 4, stanza 12), pages 7-11. Notes: Plate number '1171'.

405E] LONDON: Preston and George Thomson 1822-1831
[Note: To facilitate references among the variously arranged reprints issued by these publishers, the record below represents (1) the single Welsh Collection of 1809, (2) the folio Scottish Collections 1822-1831, and (3) the quarto Scottish Collections 1822-1839. Although these reprints are frequently advanced as original issues, parenthetical citations identify the

actual first printings. Since these collections are generally a mixture of engraved sheets and letter-press sheets with a repetition of page numbers, most references give one page number preceded by 'pages'. Preston and Thomson collections containing original printings of Scott material (dated 1814, 1817, 1818) are listed in the main section 72A, 107A, 119A. See also 371E

405E(1) Welsh 1809

A Select Collection of Original Welsh Airs Adapted for the Voice United to Characteristic English Poetry never before Published, With Introductory & Concluding Symphonies and Accompaniments for the Piano Forte or Harp, Violin & Violoncello Composed Chiefly by Joseph Haydn. . . . Vol 1. . . . London Printed & Sold by Preston, 97, Strand, And by G. Thomson the Editor & Proprietor Edinburgh. [1809]. Notes: Engraved sheet music interspersed with letter press leaves: published 10 July 1809 in Edinburgh (*EEC*). The undated engraved title-page exhibits two issues, priced (1) £1.1.0, then later (2) 15s. Copies: (issue 1) BCL E L(inscribed 'For Stationers Hall') O(inscribed 'For Stationers Hall'); CtY. (2) CtY. References: Ruff 78(vol.1).

Includes two Scott reprints: (1) 'The Last Words of Cadwallon (The Dying Bard). Written for this Work by Walter Scott, Esq.' (first words: 'Dinas Emlinn lament, for the moment is nigh,' with the pre-publication issue of *The Lay of the Last Minstrel*), pages 6, with musical arrangement by Joseph Haydn, according to the Index to the Airs; (2) 'The Norman Horse Shoe. Written for this Work By Walter Scott, Esq.' (first words: 'Red glows the forge in Striguil's bounds,' from *loc cit.*), pages 25, with musical arrangement by Kozeluch, according to the Index to the Airs.

405E(2) Scottish, Folio series 1822-1831

[1] [*engraved heading*] New Edition, with Additions by Beethoven & Frontispiece by Wilkie 1822. [title] A Select Collection of Original Scottish Airs for the Voice with Introductory & Concluding Symphonies & Accompaniments . . . by Pleyel Kozeluch & Haydn . . . London Printed & Sold by T. Preston 71 Dean St. Sold also by G. Thomson, the Editor & Proprietor, Edinburgh. [1822]. Copy: E. Reference: Ruff 82.

Includes two Scott reprints: (1) 'Lullaby of an Infant Chief. The Song written by Sir Walter Scott, Bart. and here published by express Permission.' (first words: 'O hush thee, my babie, thy sire was a knight,' from a derivative play, *Guy Mannering, or The Gipsey's Prophecy*, 1816: the poem itself written by Scott), pages 34, music arranged by Kozeluch; (2) 'Nora's Vow. Written by Sir Walter Scott, Bart. and here published by express Permission of the Proprietors—1822.' (first words: 'Hear what Highland Nora said:' from *Albyn's Anthology* I, 1816), pages 37, music arranged by Kozeluch.

[2] [*engraved heading*] New Edition. 1826. With many Additions & Improvements. [*title*] A Select Collection of Original Scottish Airs for the Voice with introductory & Concluding Symphonies & Accompaniments . . . by Pleyel Haydn Weber Beethoven &c. . . . London Printed & Sold by Preston 71. Dean St. Soho And by G. Thomson the Editor & Proprietor Edinburgh. [1826]. Notes: In this five-volume folio series, the first volume has two Scott reprints as in the preceding issue, the second has none, the third, fourth and fifth have reprints as listed below. The attributions for the Introductory and Concluding symphonies and for the Accompaniments are from the 'Index to the Airs' in each volume of the P copy. Copies: L(Hirsch) P.

VOLUME 3 includes: (1) 'The Troubadour. Written by Sir Walter Scott, Bart. And here Published by Permission of the Proprietors' (first words: 'Glowing with love, on fire for fame,' from *Paul's Letters to His Kinsfolk*, 1815, chapter 9), pages '2d 125' and '2nd 125', music arranged by Weber.
VOLUME 4: (2) 'The heath this night must be my bed. Written by Sir Walter Scott, Bart. And Here Published by Permission of the Proprietors' (first words as title, from *The Lady of the Lake*, canto 3, stanza 23), page 183, music unidentified.
VOLUME 5: (3) 'The Maid of Isla, (Imitated from the Gaelic.) Written for this Work by Walter Scott, Esq.' (first words: 'O Maid of Isla, from yon cliff,' from *A Select Collection of Original Scottish Airs*, 1818), pages 209, composed/arranged by Beethoven; (4) 'The Sun upon the Weirdlaw Hill. Written for this Work by Walter Scott, Esq.' (first words as title, from *ibid*, 1818), pages 215, composed/arranged by Beethoven; (5) 'Farewell to the Muse. Written for this Work by Walter Scott, Esq.' (first words: 'Enchantress, farewell, who so oft has decoy'd me,' from *ibid*, 1818), pages 217, the air composed by George Kinloch, with the Symphonies and Accompaniments by Beethoven; (6) 'Donald Caird. Written by Sir Walter Scott, Baronet, and here Published by Express Permission.' (first words: 'Donald Caird can lilt and sing,' from *Albyn's Anthology*, 1818), pages 224, the air arranged by George Thomson, the Editor; (7) 'On Ettrick Forest's Mountains Dun. Written for the Work by Sir Walter Scott, Bart.' (first words as title, from *A Select Collection of Original Scottish Airs*, 1818), page 228, composed/arranged by Haydn; page 228 is incorrectly cited as 226 in the 'Index to the Airs.' 'Donald Caird' is followed by 'Rob Roy. Written and Presented to the Editor by David Thomson, Galashiels, in 1822'. A footnote begins: 'Sir Walter Scott, who is strongly suspected of the resuscitation of Rob Roy, . . .' Apparently, for volume 5, certain composers were later engaged for an 1831 augmented issue: see next entry.

[3] [*engraved heading*] New Edition, 1831.—With many Improvements.— [*title*] The Melodies of Scotland, with Symphonies and Accompaniments for the Piano Forte, Violin &c by Pleyel, Haydn, Beethoven, Weber, Hummel, &c. . . . London: Printed and Sold by T. Preston, 71, Dean Street, Soho, and by G. Thomson Baxter's Place Edinburgh.. Five volumes. Notes: Dedication dated 30 March 1831. Title-pages initialed G.T. and volume numbers entered in ink. Copy: DLC.
VOLUME 1 includes: (1) 'Farewell to Northmaven' (first words as title, from *The Pirate*, chapter 12), pages 10, music arranged by Pleyel; (2) 'The Banner of Buccleuch' ['The Lifting of the Banner'] (first words: 'From the brown crest of Newark its summons extending', from *The Ettricke Garland*), pages 32, music arranged by Beethoven; (3) 'Lullaby of an Infant Chief' (first words: 'O hush thee my babie' from a derivative play, *Guy Mannering, or The Gipsey's Prophecy*, 1816: the poem itself was written by Scott), page 34, music arranged by Kozeluch; (4) 'Nora's Vow' (first words: 'Hear what Highland Nora said:', from *Albyn's Anthology*, 1816), page 37, music arranged by Kozeluch.
VOLUME 2: (5) 'There Came Three Merry Men' (first words: 'There came three merry men from south, west, and north,' from *Ivanhoe*, chapter 40), pages 87, music arranged by Haydn; (6) 'On the Hero of Killicrankie[!]' (first words: 'To the Lords of Convention, 'twas Clavers who spoke,' from *Christmas Box*, 1828), pages 100, composer/arranger unidentified.
VOLUME 3: (7) 'The Sun upon the Lake is Low' (first words as title, from *The Doom of Devorgoil*), pages 104, music arranged by Haydn; (8) 'The Troubadour' (first words: 'Glowing with love, on fire for fame,' from *Paul's Letters to His Kinsfolk*, chapter 9), pages 125 '2nd music arranged by Weber; (9) 'The Foray' (first words: 'The last of our steers on the board

has been spread,' from Clarke's *Twelve Vocal Pieces*), pages 129, music by Haydn. In the volume 3 index the first words of 'The Resolve' appears, but neither the poem nor the page number is entered.
VOLUME 4: (10) 'Wert thou like me in life's low vale' (first words as title, from *A Legend of Montrose*, chapter 21) pages 154, music by Haydn; (11) 'The heath this night must be my bed' (first words as title, from *The Lady of the Lake*, canto 3, stanza 23), pages 183, composer/ arranger unidentified.
VOLUME 5: (12) 'The Maid of Isla' (first words: 'O Maid of Isla, from yon cliff,' from *A Select Collection of Original Scottish Airs*, 1818), pages 209, composer/arranger unidentified; (13) 'The Sun upon the Weirdlaw Hill' (first words as title, from *ibid*), pages 215, music arranged by Hummel; (14) 'Enchantress Farewell' (first words as title, from *ibid*), pages 217, music arranged by Beethoven; (15) 'Donald Caird' (first Words: 'Donald Caird can lilt and sing,' from *Albyn's Anthology*, 1818), pages 224, music arranged by Thomson; (16) 'On Ettrick Forest's Mountains Dun' (first words as title, from *A Select Collection of Original Scottish Airs*, 1818), pages 228, music arranged by Haydn; (17) 'Why weep ye by the tide, Ladye' [Jock of Hazeldean] (first words as title, from *Albyn's Anthology*, 1816), pages 231, music arranged by Hummel; (18) 'Pibroch of Donuil Dhu' (first words as title, from *ibid*), pages 242, music arranged by Hummel; (19) 'The Orphan Maid' (first words: 'November's hail-cloud drifts away,' from *A Legend of Montrose*, chapter 9), pages 249, music arranged by Hummel. Volume 5 identifies composers not specified in the earlier 1826 folio issue (see previous entry.)

405E(3) Scottish, Quarto series 1822-1839
[1] [*engraved title*] The Select Melodies of Scotland, Interspersed with those of Ireland and Wales, . . . London, Printed & Sold by Preston, 71. Dean St. & G. Thomson, Edinburgh. [1822-1823]. Five volumes. Notes: Quarto series with engraved music and letterpress, both usually with the same page number. All volumes signed on title-page by George Thomson. Words by various poets arranged for pianoforte by the following composers: Pleyel, Kozeluch, Haydn and Beethoven. In volume 3 page 33 there is a quatrain by Scott appended to another poem (*see* 180A). Copies: E(vols.1,2,3,5) E(vols.2,3) L(2); PU(vol.5). References: (2) G/ T 9808-9809; (3) G/T 10342; (5) G/T 10397; Ruff 81.
VOLUME 1 includes: (1) 'Nora's Vow. Written by Sir Walter Scott, Bart. and here Published by express permission of the Proprietors—1822.' (first words: 'Hear what Highland Nora said:—' from *Albyn's Anthology*, 1816), pages 36, music composed by Kozeluch; (2) 'The Dying Bard to His Harp. The song written for this work by Sir Walter Scott, Bart.' (first words: 'Dinas Emlinn lament, for the moment is nigh,' with the pre-publication edition of *The Lay of the Last Minstrel*), pages 49, music composed by Haydn.
VOLUME 2: (3) 'From the Brown Crest of Newark, &c. Written by Sir Walter Scott, Bart. On The Lifting of the Banner of the House of Buccleuch, at a great foot-ball match on Carterhaugh. Here published by Express Permission.' (first words: 'From the brown crest of Newark its summons extending,' from *The Ettricke Garland*), pages 2, the air composed by Nathaniel Gow, arranged by Beethoven; (4) 'Serenade . . . . From a M.S. by Smith. 1822.' (first words : 'Love wakes and weeps, While Beauty sleeps!' from *The Pirate*, chapter 23), pages 13-14; (5) 'He's dear to me tho' far frae me. The song written by by[!] Sir Walter Scott, Bart. and here published by Express Permission.' (first words: 'O hush thee, my babie, thy sire was a knight,' from a derivative play, *Guy Mannering, or The Gipsey's Prophecy*, 1816: the poem itself was written by Scott), pages 32, arranged by Kozeluch.

VOLUME 3: (6) 'Pibroch of Donald [Donuil] Dhu, or, The Pipe Summons of Donald the Black. Written for Albyn's Anthology, by Sir Walter Scott, Bart. and here Published by Express Permission' (first words as title, from *Albyn's Anthology*, 1816), pages 4; (7) 'Jock of Hazeldean. A Border Melody. The first Stanza of this Ballad is ancient: The others were written for Albyn's Anthology, By Sir Walter Scott, Bart. and are here published by Express Permission.' (first words: 'Why weep ye by the tide, Ladye,' from *ibid.*), pages 7; (8) 'The Resolve. Written in Imitation of an old English Poem, by Sir Walter Scott, Baronet. Here first united with the music, by permission.' (first words: 'My wayward fate I needs must plain,' from the *English Minstrelsy*), pages 22, music arranged by Haydn; (9) 'Donald Caird. Written by Sir Walter Scott, Baronet, and here published by express Permission. (first words: 'Donald Caird can lilt and sing' from *Albyn's Anthology*, 1818), pages 29; (10) 'Young Terence Macdonough. ['The Return to Ulster'] The Song written for this work, by Sir Walter Scott, Baronet.' (first words: 'Once again, but how chang'd, since my wand'rings began—' from *A Select Collection of Original Irish Airs*, 1814), pages 42, music arranged by Beethoven from an air by Carolan; (11) 'The Sheriff's Fancy, A Hunting Song, Written by Sir Walter Scott, Bart. and here published by Express Permission.' (first words: 'Waken lords and ladies gay, Upon the mountain dawns the day;' from *Queenhoo Hall*), pages 47, music arranged by Beethoven.

VOLUME 4 (12) 'The Troubadour. By Sir Walter Scott, Baronet. The Air composed for the Song by G. Thomson, 1822.' (first words: 'Glowing with love, on fire for fame.' from *Paul's Letters to His Kinsfolk*, chapter 9), pages 9; (13) 'The Monks of Bangor's March. The Song written for this Work by Sir Walter Scott, Baronet.' (first words: 'When the heathen trumpet's clang' from *A Select Collection of Original Welsh Airs*, volume 3, 1817), pages 48, music arranged by Beethoven.

VOLUME 5 [1823] (14) 'The Maid of Isla, (Imitated from the Gaelic) Written for this Work by Sir Walter Scott, Bart.' (first words: 'O Maid of Isla, from yon cliff, That looks on troubled wave and sky,' from *A Select Collection of Original Scottish Airs*, 1818)), pages 8, music arranged by Beethoven; (15) 'Romance of Dunois. The words from the French by Sir Walter Scott Bart. The Music composed by G. F. Graham Esqr. in 1822.' (first words: 'It was Dunois, the young and brave, was bound for Palestine,' from *The Edinburgh Annual Register for 1813*, 1815 [1816]), pages 11; (16) 'On Ettrick Forest's Mountains Dun. Written for this Work by Sir Walter Scott, Bart.' (first words as title from *A Select Collection of Original Scottish Airs*, 1818), pages 18, music arranged by Haydn; (17) 'The Cypress Wreath. The Words by Sir Walter Scott, Bart.' (first words: 'O Lady, twine no wreath for me,' from *Rokeby*, canto 5, stanza 13), pages 29; (18) 'Kinloch. The following Farewell to the Muse was written for this work during illness, by Sir Walter Scott, Bart. The Air composed by George Kinloch, Esq. of Kinloch.' (first words: 'Enchantress, farewell, who so oft has decoy'd me,' from *A Select Collection of Original Scottish Airs*, 1818), pages 30, the air by Kinloch was arranged by Beethoven. One of the L copies of this issue is inscribed 'For Stationers hall' with volume 4 further dated 'Novr. 1822.' and the vignette identified as drawn by Stothard, engraved by Ranson.

[2] [*engraved title*] Thomson's Collection of the Songs of Burns, Sir Walter Scott Bart. and Other Eminent Lyric Poets Ancient & Modern United to the Select Melodies of Scotland, and of Ireland & Wales with Symphonies & Accompaniments for the Piano Forte by Pleyel, Haydn, Beethoven &c. The whole composed for & Collected by George Thomson F.A.S. Edinburgh In Six Volumes.... London. Printed & Sold by Preston 71. Dean Street. Hurst,

Robinson & Co. Cheapside. and G. Thomson, Edinburgh. Etd. at Sta. Hall. [colophon dated 1822 vols. 1-3, none vols. 4-5, 1824 vol.6. Preface dated March 1822 vol. 1, 2 May 1825 vol. 6]. Notes: An intermediate 4° collection with contents essentially as for the preceding issue (but excluding the entry there for volume 2 pages 13-14), and now adding a sixth volume. Copies: L(Hirsch); DLC.
VOLUME 6: (1) 'Parting. The Song by Sir Walter Scott Bart.' (first words: 'The heath this night must be my bed,' from *The Lady of the Lake*, canto 3, stanza 23), pages 38, music arranged by Beethoven; (2) 'The Bold Dragoon. The Plain of Badajos. ['British Light Dragoons'] Written for this work during the war in Spain, by Sir Walter Scott, Bart.' (first words: 'Twas a Marechal of France, and he fain would honour gain,' from *A Select Collection of Original Irish Airs*, 1814), pages 59, music arranged by Beethoven.

[3] [*engraved title*] Thomson's Collection of the Songs of Burns, Sir Walter Scott Bart. and Other Eminent Lyric Poets Ancient & Modern United to the Select Melodies of Scotland, and of Ireland & Wales with Symphonies & Accompaniments for the Piano Forte by Pleyel, Haydn, Beethoven &c. The whole composed for & Collected by George Thomson F.A.S. Edinburgh In Six Volumes. . . . London. Printed & Sold by Preston 71. Dean Street. Hurst, Robinson & Co. Cheapside. and G. Thomson, Edinburgh. Etd. at Sta. Hall. Price added below title-page imprint on volumes 1-3, 5-6: 8/ each. [colophon dated 1828 vol. 1; 1831 vol. 2; 1822 vol. 3; none vols 4-5; 1824 vol. 6. Preface dated May 1825 vols. 5-6]. Notes: Essentially a reissue of the preceding 1822-1825 4° collection, but with new entries for the second volume. Copies: E ES L; CtY(vol.3 a reissue 1839). References: G/T 10566; 9749.
VOLUME 2 includes: (1) 'Song On the Hero of Killiecrankie. Written by Sir Walter Scott, Bart. Here published by the Special Permission of the Proprietor, 1831.' (first words: 'To the Lords of Convention, 'twas Clavers who spoke,' from *The Christmas Box*, 1828), page 18; (2) 'Lullaby of an Infant Chief' (first words: 'O hush thee my babie, thy sire was a knight;' from a derivative play, *Guy Mannering, or The Gipsey's Prophecy*, 1816: the poem itself was written by Scott), page 31, music arranged by Kozeluch.

406E] LONDON: The Proprietor 1824
A Collection of Glees, Canons, and Catches. . . . London: Published for the Proprietor, by Cramer, Addison, and Beale, 201 Regent Street. [1824] Volume 3. Notes: Engraved sheet music. Words from various poets set to music composed by John Wall Callcott and edited by William Horsley. Copies: E(2).
VOLUME 3 includes: (1) 'Glee. Rosabelle.' (first words: 'O listen, listen ladies, listen ladies gay!' from *The Lay of the Last Minstrel*, canto 6, stanza 23), pages 102-107; (2) 'Glee. Melrose.' (first words: 'If thou would'st view fair Melrose aright, Go visit it by the pale moonlight,' from *ibid*, canto 2, stanza 1), pages 118-124.

407E] LONDON: Richardson 1826
Old English Tales of Love and Chivalry; Humour, Enterprise, and General Interest. . . . London: Published by T. Richardson, 98, High Holborn: Sold by Sherwood & Co. Paternoster Row; Simpkin & Co. Stationers' Court; W. Hunter, Edinburgh: and all Booksellers. 1826. Notes: Frontispiece portrait of Sir Walter Scott, engraved by R. Cooper, published by T. Richardson, 98 High Holborn. Contains 22 tales in twelve separately paged chapbook versions (each of twenty-four pages, with a woodcut vignette at head). Both of the original Scott

novels below are mentioned in the dedication to Scott (540T). Copy: T/B.
Includes: (1) the first chapbook titled 'Amy Robsart' (from *Kenilworth*); (2) the eighth 'The Young Jewess' (from *Ivanhoe*).

408E] LONDON: Rivington [and others] 1814-1816
[1] Elegant Extracts in Poetry, Selected for the Improvement of Young Persons. . . . London: Printed for F. C. and J. Rivington; G. Wilkie; J. Nunn; J. Cuthell; W. Clarke and Sons; Cadell and Davies; Scatcherd and Letterman; Longman, Hurst, Rees, Orme and Brown; Lackington, Allen and Co.; T. Boosey; J. and A. Arch; John Richardson; J. M. Richardson; E. Cox and Son; A. K. Newman, and Co.; E. Lloyd; J. Booker; S. Bagster; Darton, Harvey, and Darton; Black, Parry, and Co.; J. Black; W. Baynes; K. Williams; W. Stewart; J. Mawman; H. T. Hodgson; J. Booth; R. Dutton; J. Hatchard; Law and Whittaker; W. Ginger; Wingrave and Collingwood; J. Asperne; J. Harris; R. Scholey; T. Tegg; Baldwin, Craddock and Joy; D. Walker; Sherwood, Neely and Jones; Gale and Fenner; Taylor and Hessey; J. Faulder; J. Bohn; R. Saunders; C. Brown; W. Hone; R. Rees; Ogles, Duncan and Cochran; T. Hamilton; Walker and Edwards; B. Reynolds; John Robinson; Simpkin and Marshall; J. Harper; and for Wilson and Sons, York, and Doig and Stirling, Edinburgh. 1816. Copy: T/B.
Includes: (1) 'The Last Minstrel' (first words: 'The way was long, the wind was cold,' from *The Lay of the Last Minstrel*, 'Introduction.'), pages 571-572; (2) 'Melrose Abbey, and the Charm of the Wizard, Michael Scott' (first words: 'If thou wouldst view fair Melrose aright,' *ibid*, canto 2, stanza 1), pages 572-574; (3) 'Force of Love' (first words: 'And said I that my limbs were old;' *ibid*, canto 3, stanza 1), page 574; (4) 'Introduction to Canto Second of Marmion' (first words: 'When, musing on companions gone,' *ibid*), pages 576-577; (5) 'Trial of Constance' (first words: 'While round the fire such legends go,' *ibid*, canto 2, stanza 17), pages 577-579; (6) 'Song of Fitz-Eustace' (first words: 'Where shall the lover rest,' *ibid*, canto 3, stanza 10), pages 579-580; (7) 'Banquet at Holyrood House. Where James IV. of Scotland held his Court' (first words: 'Through this mixed crowd of glee and game,' *ibid*, canto 5, stanza 8), pages 580-581; (8) 'Lochinvar.—Lady Heron's Song' (first words: 'O, young Lochinvar is come out of the west,' *ibid*, canto 5, stanza 12), page 581; (9) 'Harp of the North' (first words: 'Harp of the North! that mouldering long hast hung', from *The Lady of the Lake*, canto 1, Introduction), page 581; (10) 'Portrait of Ellen' (first words: 'The boat had touch'd this silver strand,' *ibid*, canto 1, stanza 17), page 582; (11) 'The Harper' (first words: 'As died the sounds upon the tide,' *ibid*, canto 2, stanza 4), page 582; (12) 'The Sacrifice' (first words: '"Twas all prepared;—and from the rock," *ibid*, canto 3, stanza 8), pages 582-583; (13) 'The Wedding' (first words: 'A blithesome rout, that morning tide,' *ibid*, canto 3, stanza 20), pages 583-584; (14) 'Farewell Address to the Harp of the North' (first words: 'Harp of the North, farewell! The hills grow dark,' *ibid*, conclusion), page 584.

[2] The Poetical Register, and Repository of Fugitive Poetry, for 1810-1811. London: Printed for F. C. and J. Rivington, No 62, St. Paul's Church Yard. 1814. Copies: L(2); NN. References: Ruff 137 [incorrectly describing (1) as first printing: *see* 63A].
Includes under 'Fugitive Poetry': (1) Words Addressed to Ronald [Ranald] Macdonald, Esq. Laird of Staffa. Written in the Album, at Ulva, (first words: 'Staffa! sprung from high Macdonald,'), page 231; (2) 'Prologue to Miss Baillie's "Family Legend," a Tragedy.' (first words: 'Tis sweet to hear expiring summer's sigh',), pages 470-471.

410E] LONDON: Seeley and Burnside 1828

[1] The Beauties of the British Poets. . . . Published by R. B. Seeley and W. Burnside; and Sold by L. B. Seeley and Sons, Fleet Street, London. MDCCCXXVIII. Notes: With a few introductory observations, by the Rev. George Croly. Engraved title-page precedes typeset title-page. First issue with preliminaries not included in the text pagination. Copies: O; T/B. Includes: (1) 'The Last Minstrel' (first words: 'The way was long, the wind was cold,' from *The Lay of the Last Minstrel*, 'Introduction'), pages *243* 244-246; (2) 'The Tomb of Michael Scott' (first words: 'By a steel-clenched postern door,' *ibid*, canto 2, stanzas 9-22), pages 247-252; (3) 'The Trial of Constance' (first words: 'While round the fire such legends go,' from *Marmion*, canto 2, stanzas 17-33), pages 253-263; (4) 'Song' (first words: 'The heath this night must be my bed,' from *The Lady of the Lake*, canto 3, stanza 23), page 264.

[2] The Beauties of the British Poets. . . . Published by R. B. Seeley and W. Burnside; and Sold by L. B. Seeley and Sons, Fleet Street, London. MDCCCXXVIII. Notes: Second issue, as for the first except that preliminaries are included in text pagination: Scott's text therefore numbered as follows (1) pages *269* 270-272; (2) pages 273-278; (3) pages 279-289; (4) page 290. Copy: L. For a later reprint of this anthology see 463E.

411E] LONDON: Sherwood, Jones 1824

The Beauties of Modern Literature, in Verse and Prose; . . . London: Printed for Sherwood, Jones, and Co. Paternoster-Row. 1824. Notes: Edited by M. M'Dermot. Copies: L; CtY InU.

Includes anonymously: 'Song from "Quentin Durward"' (first words: '"Ah! County Guy, the hour is nigh, . . .', from *Quentin Durward*, chapter 4), page 50.

412E] LONDON: Sustenance and Stretch 1829-1831

[*engraved title*] Laconics or the Best Words of the Best Authors. Fourth Edition. London: Sustenance & Stretch, 14, Percy Street. 1829. Three volumes. Notes: A line-for-line reprint of the first edition published in London, T. Boys, 1826. (*see* 384E). Copy: L. Reissued 'Fourth Edition. London: S. W. Sustenance. 162, Piccadilly. 1831' (T/B).

413E] LONDON: Taylor 1825

The Songs of Scotland, Ancient and Modern; . . . London: Printed for John Taylor, Waterloo-Place, Pall-Mall. 1825. Notes: Edited by Allan Cunningham and fulsomely dedicated to Scott (*see* 545T).. Copies: E(3) O(2); TxU(3).

VOLUME 4 in the section entitled 'Songs of Living Lyric Poets' includes: (1) 'Pibroch of Donuil Dhu' (first words as title from *Albyn's Anthology*, 1816), pages 205-206; (2) 'Nora's Vow' (first words: 'Hear what Highland Nora said,—', from *ibid*), pages 215-216; (3) 'Jock of Hazeldean' (first words: 'Why weep ye by the tide, ladie!' from *ibid*), pages 224-225; (4) 'Carle, Now the King's Come!' (first words: 'The news has flown frae mouth to mouth,'), pages 243-245; (5) 'The Norman Horseshoe' (first words: 'Red glows the forge in Striguil's bounds,' with pre-publication edition of *The Lay of the Last Minstrel*), pages 250-251; (6) 'A Weary Lot is Thine' (first words: 'A weary lot is thine, fair maid,' from *Rokeby*, canto 3, stanza 28), page 256; (7) 'Waken, Lords and Ladies Gay' [Hunting Song] (first words as title from *Queenhoo Hall*, chapter 4), pages 257-258; (8) 'The Foray' (first words: 'The last of our steers on the board has been spread,' from Clarke's *Twelve Vocal Pieces*), page 272; (9) 'The Captive Huntsman' (first words: 'My hawk is tired of perch and hood,' from *The*

Lady of the Lake, canto 6, stanza 24), page 288; (10) 'Allan-a-Dale' (first words: 'Allen-a-Dale has no faggot for burning,' from *Rokeby*, canto 3, stanza 30), pages 294-295; (11) 'Marmion' (first words: 'Where shall the lover rest,' from *Marmion*, canto 3, stanza 10), pages 310-311; (12) 'Young Lochinvar' ['Lochinvar'] (first words: 'O, young Lochinvar is come out of the west,' *ibid.* canto 5, stanza 12), pages 313-315; (13) 'The Cypress Wreath' (first words: 'O Lady, twine no wreath for me,' from *Rokeby*, canto 5, stanza 13), pages 316-317; (14) 'Brignal Banks' (first words: 'O, Brignal banks are wild and fair,' *ibid*, canto 3, stanza 16), pages 345-347; (15) 'Donald Caird' ['Donald Caird's Come Again'] (chorus first, then first words: 'Donald Caird can lilt and sing,' from *Albyn's Anthology*, 1818), pages 349-350.

414E] LONDON: Tegg 1825-1830
[1] The Sky-Lark: A Choice Selection of the most admired popular Songs, . . . London: Published by Thomas Tegg, 73, Cheapside; R. Griffin and Co. Glasgow; and M. Baudry, Paris. [1825]. Notes: Additional title-page engraved on steel is dated 1825. Music included, arranged for voice, violin, and flute. Copies: E; CtY(2).
Includes anonymously: (1) 'Glowing with Love' (first words: 'Glowing with love, on fire for fame', from *Paul's Letters to His Kinsfolk*, letter 9), pages 80-81; (2) 'Dunois the Brave' ['Romance of Dunois'] (first words: 'It was Dunois the young and brave, was bound for Palestine,' from *The Edinburgh Annual Review for 1813*, 1815 [1816]), pages 126-127; (3) 'Allen-a-Dale' (first words: 'Allen-a-Dale has no faggot for burning,' from *Rokeby*, canto 3, stanza 30), pages 230-232; (4) 'The Cypress Wreath' (first words: 'Oh lady twine no wreaths[!] for me,' from *ibid*, canto 5, stanza 13), pages 238-240; (5) 'In Peace, Love Tunes' (first words: 'In peace love tunes the shepherd's reed,' from *The Lay of the Last Minstrel*, canto 3, stanza 2), pages 277-278; (6) 'Soldier Rest!' (first words: 'Soldier Rest, thy warfare o'er,' from *The Lady of the Lake*, canto 1, stanza 31), pages 282-283; (7) 'Huntsman, Rest!' (first words: 'Huntsman, rest! thy chase is done,' from *ibid*, canto 1, stanza 32), pages 284-285.

[2] The Thrush: A choice selection of the most admired popular songs, . . . London: Published by Thomas Tegg, 73, Cheapside; R. Griffin and Co. Glasgow; M. Baudry, Paris; J. Cumming, Dublin; and sold by all Booksellers. [1830]. Notes: With additional title-page engraved on steel dated 1 January 1830. Music arranged for voice, violin, and flute. Copies: CtY(2).
Includes anonymously: (1) 'Blue Bonnets over the Border' (first words: 'March, march, Ettrick and Teviotdale, / Why my lads dinna ye march' from *The Monastery*, chapter 25), pages 1-2; (2) 'Jock of Hazeldean' (first words: 'Why weep ye by the tide, lady,' from *Albyn's Anthology*, I), pages 270-271; (3) 'County Guy' (first words: 'Ah County Guy, the hour is nigh, / The Sun has left the Lea,' from *Quentin Durward*, chapter 4), pages 312-313; (4) 'The Last Words of Marmion' (first words: 'The war that for a space did fail,' from *Marmion*, canto 6, stanza 32), pages 316-317; (5) 'Lochinvar' (first words: 'Oh, young Lochinvar is come out of the west,' from *ibid*, canto 5, stanza 12), pages 322-324.

415E] LONDON: Whittaker 1824
The Vocal Library; being the Largest Collection of English, Scottish, and Irish Songs ever printed in a Single Volume. . . London: Printed for G. B. Whittaker, Ave-Maria Lane. Price 10s.6d. bound in red. 1824. Notes: Songster. All but (1), which is anonymous, are identified as by 'W. Scott', not to be confused with John Scott of Amwell, who in most anthologies of the period is identified only as 'Scott.' Copy: CtY. Reference: Ruff page 281.

Includes: (1) [anonymous] 'Waken, Lords and Ladies' [Hunting Song] (first words: 'Waken, lords and ladies gay,' from *Queenhoo Hall*, chapter IV), page 38; (2) 'Pibroch of Donnell [Donuil] Dhu' (first words: 'Pibroch of Donnell[!] Dhu,' from *Albyn's Anthology*, 1816), page 63; (3) 'Merrily Bounds the Bark' (first words: 'Merrily, merrily, bounds the bark,' a 27-line corruption from *The Lord of the Isles*, canto 4, stanzas 7, 9-11), page 419; (4) 'The Last Words of Marmion' (first words: 'The war that for a space did fail,' from *Marmion*, canto 6, stanza 32), page 559; (5) 'Where Shall the Lover Rest' (first words as title, from *ibid*, canto 3, stanzas 10-11), page 596; (6) 'Oh! Rest Thee, Babe.' ['Lullaby of an Infant Chief'] (first words: 'Oh! slumber, my darling, Thy sire is a knight') from a derivative play, *Guy Mannering, or The Gipsey's Prophecy*, 1816: the poem itself was written by Scott], page 626; (7) 'In Peace Love Tunes' (first words: 'In peace love tunes the shepherd's reed,' from *The Lay of the Last Minstrel*, canto 3, stanza 2), page 641; (8) 'Go Forth my Song' (first words: 'Go forth my song upon thy vent'rous way,' from *The Lord of the Isles*, conclusion), page 660; (9) 'Wake, Maid of Lorn' (first words: 'Wake, maid of Lorn, the moments fly,' from *ibid*, canto 1, stanza 4), page 662; (10) 'Boat Song' (first words: 'Hail to the chief who in triumph advances,' from *The Lady of the Lake*, canto 2, stanzas 19-20), page 663; (11) 'Lochinvar' (first words: 'Oh young Lochinvar is come out of the West,' from *Marmion*, canto 5, stanza 12), page 669.

416E] LONDON: Whittaker, Treacher 1829
The Anthology: An Annual Reward Book for Youth. Consisting of Amusing and Instructive Selections from the Best Authors. . . . London: Printed for Whittaker, Treacher, & Co. Ave Maria Lane. 1829. Notes: Edited by the Rev. J. D. Parry. Copies: InU MH.
Includes: 'Bruce's Voyage' (first words: 'Merrily, merrily, bounds the bark,' a pastiche from *The Lord of the Isles*, canto 4, stanza 7 through the last line of canto 5, stanza 34), pages 238-242.

417E] LONDON: Wightman and Cramp 1826
Beauties of the Modern Poets; . . . A New Edition; Corrected, Enlarged, and Rearranged. London: Wightman and Cramp, 24, Paternoster Row. MDCCCXXVI. Notes: Edited by David Carey. Earlier 'editions' of this anthology were published by Wright (*see* 419E below). States of this title are based on the variant spelling of the word 'Allsoul' in number (4). Copies (state a, page 158: Allsoul's) T/B; (state b: Allsouls') L.
Includes: (1) 'The Battle of Bannockburn' (first words: 'It was a night of lovely June,' from *The Lord of the Isles*, canto 6, stanza 19), pages 84-96; (2) 'Blanche of Devan' (first words: 'All in the Trosach's glen was still,' from *The Lady of the Lake*, canto 4, stanza 20), pages 112-118; (3) 'The Orphan Maid' (first words: 'November's hail-cloud drifts away,' from *A Legend of Montrose*, chapter 9), pages 138-139; (4) 'Geraldine' [Fitztraver] (first words: ''Twas Allsoul's Eve, and Surrey's heart beat high,' from *The Lay of the Last Minstrel*, canto 6, stanza 16), pages 158-159; (5) 'My Native Land' (first words: 'Breathes there the man with soul so dead,' *ibid*, canto 6, stanza 1), pages 169-173; (6) 'Combat of the Border Chiefs, Musgrave and Deloraine' (first words: 'Ill would it suit your gentle ear,' *ibid*, canto 5, stanza 21), pages 194-197; (7) 'Forest Scenery' (first words: ''Tis merry in greenwood, thus runs the old lay,' from *Harold the Dauntless*, canto 2, stanza 1), pages 213-216.

418E] LONDON: Williams 1820

The Harmonist in Miniature A Collection of Ancient & Modern Catches, Glees, Canons, Epigrams &c. . . . London Published by T. Williams, Music Seller; 29, Tavistock Street, Covent Garden. [ca.1820]. Price: 10/-. Copy: CtY.
Includes anonymously with music: 'Hie Away' (first words: 'Hie away hie away Over bank and over brae' from *Waverley*, chapter 12), pages 77-80.

419E] LONDON: Wright 1820-1821

Beauties of the Modern Poets; Being selections from the works of the most popular authors of the present day; . . . London: Printed for William Wright, 46 Fleet-Street. 1820. Notes: Edited by David Carey. Copies: L; InU. Reissued as 'New Edition' 1821 (L) and reset 1826 with different contents (417E). Reference: Kohler(3) 251.
Includes: (1) 'The Last Minstrel' (first words: 'The way was long, the wind was cold,' from *The Lay of the Last Minstrel*, 'Introduction'), pages 87-90; (2) 'Combat of the Border Chiefs, Musgrave and Deloraine' (first words: 'Ill would it suit your gentle ear,' from *ibid*, canto 5, stanza 21), pages 121-125; (3) 'My Native Land' (first words: 'Breathes there the man, with soul so dead,' *ibid*, canto 6, stanza 1), pages 132-136; (4) 'Jock of Hazeldean' (first words: 'Why weep ye by the tide, ladie,' from *Albyn's Anthology*, 1816), pages 145-146; (5) 'Forest Scenery' (first words: ''Tis merry in greenwood, thus runs the old lay,' from *Harold the Dauntless*, canto 2, stanza 1), pages 155-159; (6) 'Song' (first words: 'Oh, say not, my love, with that mortified air,' from *The Edinburgh Annual Register for 1809*, 1811), pages 202-203.

420E] MANCHESTER: Wardle and Bentham 1814-1815

The Magazine of the Muses: A Selection of Poems from the Most Esteemed Modern Authors. . . . Manchester: Printed by Wardle and Bentham, Market-Street. 1814. Notes: Edited by John Stagg. Copy: InU. Reissued 1815 (InU).
Includes (1) 'Monody to the Memory of Nelson, Pitt, and Fox' (first words: 'To mute and to material things' from *Marmion*, Introduction to canto first), pages 60-66; (2) 'Lay of the Imprisoned Huntsman' (first words: 'My hawk is tired of perch and hood,' from *The Lady of the Lake*, canto 6, stanza 24), pages 159-160; (3) 'The Death of Rosae' (first words: 'O listen, listen, ladies gay!' from *The Lay of the Last Minstrel*, canto 6, stanza 23), pages 330-332.

421E] NEWCASTLE: Fordyce 1820

Cork Leg Songster. . . Printed & Sold by W. & T. Fordyce, Dean-street, Newcastle Sold also by J. Whinham & Co. Scotch-street, Carlisle. [ca.1820]. Copy: O(J.Johnson).
Includes: 'Macgregor's Gathering' (first words: 'The moon's on the lake, and the mist's on the brae,' from *Albyn's Anthology*, 1816), page 7.

422E] NEWTON-STEWART: M'Nairn 1826

Seven Excellent Songs. The year that's awa. Blue Bonnets over the Border. The Laird o' Cockpen. Jock o' Hazeldean. . . Newton-Stewart Printed and Sold, Wholesale and Retail, by J. M'Nairn. [1826]. Notes: Chapbook. Copy: O.
Includes anonymously: (1) 'Blue Bonnets over the Border' (first words: 'March, march, Ettrick and Tivotdale[!]' from *The Monastery*, chapter 25), pages 4-5; (2) 'Jock O' Hazeldean' (first words: '"Why weep ye by the tide lady?"' from *Albyn's Anthology*, 1816), pages 5-6.

423E] NORWICH: Stacy 1820

British Melodies, Containing some of the Minor Pieces, and other Extracts, from the Works of the Modern Poets. . . . Printed for the Editor, (Not for Sale) By John Stacy, Norwich. [ca.1820]. Notes: Edited by J. H. R. Copies: BCL; CtY.

Includes: (1) 'The Cypress Wreath' (first words: 'O Lady twine no wreath for me,' from *Rokeby*, canto 5, stanza 13), pages 3-4; (2) 'Wandering Willie' (first words: 'All joy was bereft me the day that you left me,' from Whyte's *Collection of Scottish Airs*), pages 17-18; (3) 'Hunting Song' (first words: 'Waken lords and ladies gay,' from *Queenhoo Hall*, chapter IV), pages 70-71; (4) 'The Last Minstrel' (first words: 'The way was long, the wind was cold,' from *The Lay of the Last Minstrel*, Introduction), pages 117-120; (5) 'To a Lady, with Flowers from a Roman Wall' (first words: 'Take these flowers which, purple waving,'), page 141; (6) 'The Violet' (first words: 'The violet, in her greenwood bower,' from the *English Minstrelsy*), pages 141-142; (7) 'On The Lifting of the Banner of the House of Buccleuch, at a great Foot-ball Match on Carterhaugh' (first words: 'From the brown crest of Newark its summons extending,' from *The Ettricke Garland*), pages 159-160; (8) 'Harp of the North' (first words: 'Harp of the North, farewell! The hills grow dark,' from *The Lady of the Lake*, Conclusion), pages 171-172; (9) 'Farewell to the Muse' (first words: 'Enchantress, farewell, who so oft has decoy'd me,' from *A Select Collection of Original Scottish Airs*, volume 5, 1818), page 177; (10) 'Monody on Nelson, Pitt, and Fox' (first words: 'To mute and to material things' from *Marmion*, introduction to canto first), pages 214-219; (11) 'My Country' (first words: Breathes there the man, with soul so dead,' from *The Lay of the Last Minstrel*, canto 6, stanzas 1-2), pages 233-234; (12) 'The Field of Waterloo' (first words: 'Look forth, once more, with soften'd heart' from *The Field of Waterloo*, stanzas 20-23), pages 237-239; (13) 'Conclusion' (first words: 'Call it not vain:—they do not err,' from *The Lay of the Last Minstrel*, canto 5, stanzas 1-2), pages 243-244.

424E] PAISLEY: Caldwell 1826

Watty's Travels to Carlisle, in Search of a Place . . . . Paisley: Printed by G. Caldwell. 1826. Notes: Chapbook. In some copies page 5 is unnumbered. Copies: E(2) L(2) O O(J.Johnson); CtY.

Includes: 'Blue Bonnets over the Border' (first words: 'March, march, Ettrick and Teviotdale,' from *The Monastery*, chapter 25), pages 5-6.

425E] PAISLEY: Morrison 1818

The Vocal Casquet: . . Paisley: Published by R. Morrison. [1818]. Notes: Songster. Copy: O(J.Johnson).

Includes anonymously: 'The Macgregors' Gathering' (first words: 'The moon's on the lake, and the mist's on the brae,' from *Albyn's Anthology*, 1816) pages 15-16.

426E] SHEFFIELD: Todd 1826

The Selected Poetry which Appeared in The Sheffield Mercury for the Year 1825. Sheffield: Printed by and for Wm. Todd, Mercury Office. 1826. Notes: Also includes, by another writer, an anonymous tribute 'To the Great Unknown' (lines 26-28 'May be Sir Walter Scott—/Perhaps not!/Why dost thou so conceal and puzzle curious folks?'), pages 62-64. Copy: T/B.

Includes two 'Songs, from Tales of the Crusaders.' By the Author of *Waverley*.': (1) (first words: 'Soldier, wake—the day is peeping,' from *The Betrothed*, chapter 19), pages 85-86; (2) (first words: 'Woman's faith, and women's trust', *ibid*, chapter 20), page 86.

427E] STIRLING: The Booksellers 1808
Young Lochinvar, To which are added, The Rose of Dunmore, Scottish Whiskky,[!] . . . Stirling: Printed for the Booksellers. [1808?]. Notes: Chapbook. Copy: L.
Includes anonymously: 'Young Lochinvar' ['Lochinvar'] (first words: 'O! Young Lochinvar has come out of the west,' from *Marmion*, canto 5, stanza 12), pages 2-3.

428E] STIRLING: Johnstone 1820
Four Excellent Songs; . . . Stirling: Printed by E. Johnstone, Bookseller. [ca.1820]. Notes: Chapbook. Copies: E L O(2: J.Johnson); CtY(2).
Includes anonymously: 'Jock o' Hazledean[!]' (first words: 'Why weep ye by the tide, lady?' from *Albyn's Anthology*, 1816), pages 5-6.

429E] STIRLING: Macnie 1820-1825
[1] The Blue Bonnets o'er the Border; To which are added, My Peggy is a Young Thing, The Heaving of the Lead, . . . Stirling: Printed and Sold, Wholesale and Retail, by W. Macnie, Bookseller. [1820?]. Chapbook. Copy: L.
Includes anonymously: 'The Blue Bonnets o'er the Border' (first words: 'March, march, Ettrick and Tiviotdale![!]', from *The Monastery*, chapter 25), pages 2-3.

[2] The Woodman; To which are added, . . Jock of Hazeldean, . . Stirling: Printed and Sold, Wholesale and Retail, by W. Macnie, Bookseller [1825?]. Notes: Chapbook. Copies: O(2: J.Johnson); CtY.
Includes anonymously: 'Jock of Hazeldean' (first words: '"Why weep ye by the tide, lady?"' from *Albyn's Anthology*, 1816), pages 4-5.

UNITED STATES

430E] ALBANY: Loomis 1815-1822
[1] The Columbian Harmonist, or Songster's Repository; Being a Selection of the Most Approved Sentimental, Patriotic, and Other Songs. Albany: Printed and sold by G. J. Loomis & Co. Corner of State and Lodge-Streets. 1815. Copy: CtY.
Includes anonymously: 'Where shall the Lover Rest' (first words as title, from *Marmion*, canto 3, stanzas 10-11), pages 41-42.

[2] The Minstrel, or A New and Choice Selection of the Most Admired Songs. Albany: Printed by G. J. Loomis & Co. State-Street. 1822. Copy: MWA.
Includes: (1) 'Lochinvar' (first words: 'Oh, young Lochinvar is come out of the west,' from *Marmion*, canto 5, stanza 12), pages 52-53; (2) 'Far from Love and Thee, Mary' (first words: 'The heath this night must be my bed,' from *The Lady of the Lake*, canto 3, stanza 23), pages 149-150; (3) 'Hail to the Chief' ['Boat Song'] (first words: 'Hail! to the chief who in triumph advances,' *ibid*, canto 2, stanzas 19-20), pages 198-199.

[3] The Songster's Museum, or A New Selection of the Most Popular Songs, Moral, Sentimental, Humourous, and Patriotic. Albany: Printed by G. J. Loomis & Co. State-Street. 1822. Copy: MWA.
Includes: (1) 'Lochinvar' (first words: 'Oh, young Lochinvar is come out of the west,' from

Marmion, canto 5, stanza 12), pages 52-53; (2) 'Far from Love and thee, Mary' (first words: 'The heath this night must be my bed,' from *The Lady of the Lake*, canto 3, stanza 23), pages 149-150; (3) 'Hail to the Chief' ['Boat Song'] (first words: 'Hail! to the chief, who in triumph advances,' *ibid*, canto 2, stanzas 19-20), pages 198-199. Numbers (2) and (3) are attributed to Scott in the Index.

431E] BALTIMORE: Bool and Vicary 1828
The Warbler, Containing a Collection of Modern and Popular Songs, . . . Baltimore: Published by H. W. Bool, Jr. 60, Market Street, and Henry Vicary, 50, Pratt Street 1828. Notes: Falsely attributed to Scott is: 'Wha'll be King but Charlie.' (first words: 'The news, frae Moid art cam yestreen,'), pages 61-62. This poem appears to have been first attributed to Scott in a song copyrighted by Dubois & Stodart, 3 October 1826. After this date, many examples of sheet-music appeared with this title. Copy: MWA.
Includes: (1) 'All the Blue Bonnets over the Border' (first words: 'March, March, Etrick[!] and Tiviotdale[!]', anonymously from *The Monastery*, chapter 25), pages 2-3; (2) 'The Knight Errant' ['Romance of Dunois'] (first words: 'It was Dunois, the young and brave, was bound for Palestine,' from *The Edinburgh Annual Register for 1813*, 1815 [1816]), pages 51-52.

432E] BALTIMORE: Lucas 1817
The Diamond Songster; Containing the Most Approved, Sentimental and Lively, Scottish, Irish, and National Songs. Baltimore: Published by Fielding Lucas, Jun'r. 138 Market Street. Pomeroy & Toy, print. 1817. Notes: With an engraved title. Copy: MWA. Reference: Lowens 540.
Includes anonymously: 'Lochinvar' (first words: 'O, young Lochinvar is come out of the west,' from *Marmion*, canto 5, stanza 12), page 124.

433E] BALTIMORE: Nickerson 1829
The Universal and Theatrical Songster; or Museum of Mirth: Being a Collection of the Most Admired and Popular Songs and Recitations, . . . Baltimore: Engraved and published by C. V. Nickerson. B. Edes, Printer. 1829. Notes: This songster also has 'Sam Jones. A Parody on the Knight Errant', pages 13-14. . Copy: MWA.
Includes anonymously: 'The Knight Errant' ['Romance of Dunois'] (first words: 'It was Dunois, the young and brave was bound for Palestine,' from *The Edinburgh Annual Register for 1813*, 1815 [1816]), pages 12-13.

434E] BALTIMORE: Sands and Neilson 1831
The Warbler, Containing a Collection of Modern and Popular Songs, . . By an Amateur. Third Edition. Baltimore: Printed by Sands & Neilson. 1831. Notes: Songster which falsely attributes to Scott, 'Wha'll be King but Charlie' (first words: 'The news, frae Moid art cam yestreen,'), pages 80-81. Copy: CtY.
Includes: (1) 'All the Blue Bonnets over the Border' (first words: 'March, March, Etrick[!] and Tiviotdale[!]' from *The Monastery*, chapter 25), page 28; (2) 'The Knight Errant. ['Romance of Dunois'] Walter Scott' (first words: 'It was Dunois, the Young and brave, was bound for Palestine,' from *The Edinburgh Annual Register for 1813*, 1815 [1816]), pages 71-72.

435E] BALTIMORE: Wood 1831
The American Naval and Patriotic Songster. . . . Baltimore: Published by P. N. Wood, Market street. Wm. Wooddy, Printer. 1831. Copy: CtY.
Includes anonymously: (1) 'Soldier, Rest! Thy Warfare o'er.' (first words as title, from *The Lady of the Lake*, canto 1, stanza 31), pages 228-229; (2) 'The Last Words of Marmion' (first words: 'The war, that for a space did fail', from *Marmion*, canto 6, stanza 32), page 232.

436E] BOSTON: Belcher 1811
The Minstrel; A Collection of Ballads and Legendary Tales. . . . Boston, Printed by J. Belcher. 1811. Copies: MWA(2). Reference: Lowens, page 120.
Includes: (1) 'Alice Brand' (first words: 'Merry it is in the good green wood,' from *The Lady of the Lake*, canto 4, stanza 12), pages 23-27; (2) 'Lochinvar' (first words: 'Oh, young Lochinvar is come out of the west,' from *Marmion*, canto 5, stanza 12), pages 106-108.

437E] BOSTON: Deming 1829
Old Grimes And All the Blue Bonnets Over the Border. . . . Sold Wholesale and Retail by L. Deming, No. 1, South side of Faneuil Hall, Boston. [ca.1829-1830]. Notes: Broadside. Copy: RPB.
Includes anonymously: 'All the Blue Bonnets . . .' (first words: 'March, March, Etrick[!] and Tivotdale[!],' from *The Monastery*, chapter 25).

438E] BOSTON: Dutton and Wentworth 1826
The Merry Songster, Being an Excellent Collection of Patriotic, Facetious, Love, Merry, Rum, Comic, Laughable and Whimsical Songs. . . . Boston: Dutton and Wentworth . . . Printers, No. 4. Exchange Street. 1826. Copy: MWA.
Includes: 'The Knight Errant' ['Romance of Dunois'] (first words: 'It was Dunois the young and brave,' from *The Edinburgh Annual Register for 1813*. 1815 [1816]), page 11.

439E] BOSTON: Parker 1816
[*engraved title*] The Orphean Lyre, Containing A Collection of the most Harmonious Glees, Catches & Duets; Arranged with Accompaniments for the Pianoforte. Boston Published by S. H. Parker at the Union Circulating Library. No. 4. Cornhill. [1816]. Copy: CtY. References: (1) Wolfe 1833; (2) Wolfe 1841; (3) Wolfe 1870.
Includes: (1) 'It was a Night of Lovely June.' (from *The Lord of the Isles*, canto 6, stanza 19), pages 6-9; (2) 'Merrily, Merrily, Bounds the Bark.' (from *ibid*, canto 4, selected lines from stanzas 7. 9-12), pages 14-20; (3) 'Edith of Lorn.' [*music by*] Dr. J. Clarke' (from *ibid*, canto 1, selected lines from stanzas 1-3), pages 28-33.

440E] BOSTON: Swan 1821
The Songster's New Pocket Companion Embracing the Most Popular New Songs, sung at the Different Theatres in the United States. . . Second Edition. Boston. T. Swan. 1821. Copy: MWA. References: Lowens 555 note.
Includes 'The Last Words of Marmion' (first words: 'The war, that for a space did fail,' from *Marmion*, canto 6, stanza 32), pages 57-58.

441E] BOSTON: [*publisher unidentified*] 1830
Oh What a Row! Or the Adventures of a Steam Ship together with The Knight Errant. . . . A large assortment of songs can be found at No. 1 Market Square, corner of Merchant's Row, Boston [ca.1830]. Notes: Broadside. Copy: L.
Includes anonymously: 'Romance of Dunois' (first words: 'It was Dunois, the young and brave, was bound for Palestine', from *The Edinburgh Annual Register for1813*. 1815 [1816]).

442E] CHARLESTOWN: Baker 1822
The Musical Cabinet, Contaning a Selection of All the New and Fashionable Songs . . . Charlestown: Published by T. M. Baker, At His Circulating Library, Main Street. 1822. Notes: With music arranged for voice and pianoforte. Copies: CtY RPB. Reference: Wolfe 4351.
Includes anonymously: 'The Knight Errant' ['Romance of Dunois'] (first words: 'It was Dunvis[!] the young and brave, was bound for Palestine,' from *The Edinburgh Annual Register for 1813*. 1815 [1816]), pages 13-15.

443E] CINCINNATI: James 1832
The Eolian Songster, A Choice Collection of the Most Popular Sentimental, Patriotic, Naval, and Comic Songs. . . . Cincinnati: Published by U. P. James, No. 167 Walnut Street. [copyright 1832]. Copy: CtY.
Includes: (1) 'Hail to the Chief.['Boat Song']—By W. Scott' (first words: 'Hail to the Chief, who in triumph advances,' from *The Lady of the Lake*, canto 2, stanzas 19-20), pages 28-30; (2) 'The Knight Errant. ['Romance of Dunois']—By W. Scott' (first words: 'It was Dunois, the young and brave, was bound for Palestine,' from *The Edinburgh Annual Register for 1813*, 1815 [1816]), pages 68-69; (3) [anonymous and with music] 'The Blue Bonnets over the Border' (first words: 'March, March, Etrick[!] and Tiviot-dale[!],' from *The Monastery*, chapter 25), pages 82-83.

444E] CORNISH: Cole 1827
The Muse; Or Flowers of Poetry; . . . Cornish, Maine: Published and Sold by the Author. 1827. Notes: The editor of this collection, Samuel W. Cole, says in the introduction that he 'has endeavored, by "blending the useful with the sweet," to combine pleasure and improvement, to excite chaste, delicate, and pleasurable emotions'. Copies: DLC T/B.
Includes: (1) 'Hellvellyn' (first words: 'I climb'd the dark brow of the mighty Hellvellyn,'), pages 110-112; (2) 'Dirge. On Mungo Park, supposed to be drowned in the Nile' (first words: 'Hope no more! in peace he sleepeth,' [not identified elsewhere but ascribed here to 'W. Scott'], pages 128-129; (3) 'The Patriot' (first words: 'Breathes there a man with soul so dead,' from *The Lay of the Last Minstrel*, canto 6, stanza 10), pages 135-136; (4) 'The Last Words of Marmion' (first words: 'Recitative: The War, that for a space did fail,' 'Air. A light on Marmion's visage spread' from *Marmion*, canto 6, stanza 32), pages 179-180.

445E] HARTFORD: Andrus 1824-1830
[1] The Wreath; A Collection of Poems, from Celebrated English Authors. . . . Hartford: Published by Silas Andrus. Johnstone & Van Norden, Printers. 1824. Notes: This is a secondary issue, reimpression of *The Wreath* published 1824 in New York by Johnstone & Van Norden, which in turn is a literal reprint of *The Wreath* published 1821 in New York by Gilley and Megarey. (see 456E[2] and 455E). Copies: CtY MWA. Further reissued without

printer's imprint in 1824(CtY), 1826(CtY), 1827 (MWA), 1828, (MWA), 1830(InU[2], MWA).
Includes: 'Boat Song' (first words: 'Hail to the chief who in triumph advances!', from *The Lady of the Lake*, canto 2, stanzas 19-20), pages 195-196.

[2] The Songster's Museum. A New and Choice Collection of Popular Songs, Selected from the Best Authors. Hartford: Published by Silas Andrus. 1825. Notes: This is exactly the same as the 1824 New York issue by Johnstone and Van Norden. (see 456E[1]) and the 1825 Hartford issue by Benton (see 446E[1]) except that the latter two have in common a rough woodcut as title-page vignette. Copy: MWA.
Includes anonymously: (1) 'The Knight Errant' ['Romance of Dunois'] (first words: 'It was Dunois the young and brave,' from *The Edinburgh Annual Register for 1813.* 1815 [1816]), pages 44-45; (2) 'Hail to the Chief' ['Boat Song'] (first words: 'Hail to the Chief, who in triumph advances,' from *The Lady of the Lake*, canto 2, stanzas 19-20), pages 66-67.

446E] HARTFORD: Benton 1825-1835
[1] The Songster's Museum. A New and Choice Collection of Popular Songs, Selected from the Best Authors. Hartford: Published by Henry Benton. 1825. Notes: This is exactly the same as the 1824 New York issue by Johnstone and Van Norden (see 456E[1]) and the 1825 Hartford issue by Andrus (see 445E[2]) except for a variant woodcut as title-page vignette. Copy: MWA.
Includes anonymously: (1) 'The Knight Errant' ['Romance of Dunois'] (first words: 'It was Dunois the young and brave,' from *The Edinburgh Annual Register for 1813*, 1815 [1816]), pages 44-45; (2) 'Hail to the Chief' ['Boat Song'] (first words: 'Hail to the Chief, who in triumph advances,' from *The Lady of the Lake*, canto 2, stanzas 19-20), pages 66-67.

[2] The Songster's Museum. . . . Hartford Published by Henry Benton 1826. Notes: A reissue of the 1825 edition (see above) with (1) a rough title woodcut of a drinking scene or (2) a more polished woodcut vignette of a lady at a piano. Copies: (1) DLC; (2) CtY. Further reissued 1829 (DLC MWA), 1835 (CtY MWA).

447E] HARTFORD: Goodrich 1818
Elegant Extracts of Poetry from the Works of Modern Authors. Hartford: Published by S. G. Goodrich. 1818. Printed by Hamlen and Newton. Notes: This 'pocket volume' represents one selection each from eleven of the 'celebrated living bards in Great-Britain.' Copies: O; MWA.
Includes: 'The Combat' (first words: 'Fair as the earliest beam of eastern light,' from *The Lady of the Lake*, canto 5, stanzas 1-17), pages 49 50-59.

448E] NEW HAVEN: Babcock 1820-1825
[1] Songs for Gentlemen. Patriotic, Comic, and Descriptive. Sidney's Press: Published by J. Babcock and Son, New-Haven, and S. Babcock and Co. Charleston. 1825. Notes: Includes a 'Parody on "Hail to the Chief."' (first words: 'Hail to our Chief! now he's wet through with whiskey;'), pages 73-74. An earlier 1818 edition (CtY) is devoted almost entirely to songs relating to the War of 1812 with no Scott included. Copies: CtY MWA. Reference: Lowens 642 (1820 edition).
Includes anonymously: (1) 'Hail to the Chief' ['Boat Song'] (first words: 'Hail! to the chief, who in triumph advances,' from *The Lady of the Lake*, canto 2, stanzas 19-20), pages 88-89; (2) 'The Troubadour' (first words: 'Glowing with love, on fire for fame,' from *Paul's Letters*

to His Kinsfolk, letter 9), pages 133-134; (3) 'The Knight Errant.' ['Romance of Dunois'] (first words: 'It was Dunois, the young and brave, was bound for Palestine,' from *The Edinburgh Annual Register for 1813*, 1815 [1816]), pages 138-139.

[2] Songs for Ladies, Lively, Pathetic, and Sentimental. Sidney's Press. Published by John Babcock & Son, New-Haven, and S. & W. R. Babcock, Charleston. 1820. Copy: CtY. Reference: Lowens 643 note.
Includes anonymously: 'Lochinvar' (first words: 'Oh, young Lochinvar is come out of the west,' from *Marmion*, canto 5, stanza 12), pages 115-117.

[3] Songs for Ladies, Lively, Pathetic, and Sentimental. Sidney's Press: Published by J. Babcock and Son, New-Haven, and S. Babcock and Co. Charleston. 1825. Copy: MWA. Reference: Lowens 643 note.
Includes anonymously: (1) 'Lochinvar' (first words: 'Oh, young Lochinvar is come out of the west,' from *Marmion*, canto 5, stanza 12), pages 99-100; (2) 'Where shall the Lover Rest' (first words as title, from *ibid*, canto 3, stanzas 10-11), pages 137-138.

449E] NEW HAVEN: Maltby 1823
The Vocal Cabinet: A New Collection of the Most Approved Songs, Duets, Catches, &c. Some of which are with Music. . . New-Haven: Printed by A. H. Maltby and Co. 1823. Copies: CtY MWA.
Includes anonymously: (1) 'Boat Song' (first words: 'Hail to the chief, who in triumph advances,' from *The Lady of the Lake*, canto 2, stanzas 19-20), pages 36-37; (2) 'The Knight Errant'['Romance of Dunois'] (first words: 'It was Dunois, the young and brave, was bound for Palestine,' from *The Edinburgh Annual Register for 1813*, 1815 [1816]), pages 55-56; (3) 'Where Shall the Lover Rest' (first words as title, from *Marmion*, canto 3, stanzas 10-11), page 68; (4) 'The Troubadour' (first words: 'Glowing with love, on fire for fame', from *Paul's Letters to His Kinsfolk*, letter 9), page 79; (5) 'Young Lochinvar' ['Lochinvar'] (first words: 'O young Lochinvar is come out of the west,' from *Marmion*, canto 5, stanza 12), pages 114-115.

450E] NEW YORK: Anderson 1826
Beauties of the British Poets: or A Pocket Dictionary, Containing the Most Admirable Passages, . . . New-York: J. S. Anderson, 327 Pearl-Street. J. & J. Harper, Printer. 1826. Notes: This is a paginal reprint of a 1824 Philadelphia title (471E) which reads *Quotations from the British Poets; being A Pocket Dictionary of their Most Admired Passages.* Accordingly the 12 excerpts listed there are not again cited here, but these quotations are also entered in the General Index. Copies: CtY InU.

451E] NEW YORK: Birch 1832
The Souvenir of Harmony. Glees from the Works of the Most Celebrated Composers. . . Entered According to the Act of Congress in the year 1832 by Thos. Birch . . . New York. Notes: Engraved sheet music.
Includes: 'The Bark Before the Gale . . . Written by Sir Walter Scott' (first words: 'Merrily merrily, goes the bark, before the gale she bounds,' from *The Lord of the Isles*, canto 4, stanza 11). Copy: MWA(so recorded, but copy later, in 1997, unlocated).

452E] NEW YORK: Borrodaile 1823
The Blackbird, Being A Choice Collection of the Most Popular American, English, Irish, and Scotch Songs. New-York, Published by Wm. Borrodaile. 1823. Copy: MWA. (For an 1828 reimpression see 457E.)
Includes anonymously: (1) 'O Brignal Banks!' (first words: 'O Brignal banks are wild and fair,' from *Rokeby* canto 3, stanzas 16-18), pages 10-11; (2) 'Where shall the Lover Rest' (first words as title, from *Marmion* canto 3, stanzas 10-11), pages 21-22.

453E] NEW YORK: Clayton & Van Norden 1828
The Flowers of Melody: A Select Collection of Scottish, English, Irish, and American Songs. . . . New-York: Printed by Clayton & Van Norden, 64 Pine-street. 1828. Notes: Selected and arranged by John Graham. Without music. Also, falsely attributed to Scott, are two poems: 'Behold me, Sung Hassan' (first words: 'Behold me, sung Hassan, the fearless and free,'), page 88, and the first poem in the Appendix 'Wha'll be King but Charlie' (first words: 'The news frae Moidart cam' yestreen,') pages 379-380. Copy: MWA.
VOLUME 2 includes: (1) 'The Knight Errant' ['Romance of Dunois'] (first words: 'It was Dunois, the young and brave, was bound for Palestine,' from *The Edinburgh Annual Register for 1813*, 1815 [1816]), pages 10-11; (2) 'The Last Words of Marmion' (first words: 'The war that for a space did fail', from *Marmion*, canto 6, stanza 32), pages 126-127; (3) 'The Cypress Wreath.' (first words: 'O! Lady, twine no wreath for me,' from *Rokeby*, canto 5, stanza 13), pages 162-163.

454E] NEW YORK: Dearborn 1811
The Songsters Repository; Being a choice selection of the most Esteemed Songs many of which have not heretofore been published. . . . New York Published by Nathl. Dearborn No. 171 Willm. St. 1811. Notes: Engraved title-page and frontispiece. Copies: CtY DLC.
Includes: (1) '"The Heath this Night must be my bed."' (first words as title, incorrectly cited as from 'Marmion'[!] [*The Lady of the Lake*], canto 3, stanza 23), pages 27-28; (2) (first words: 'Where shall the lover rest,' from *Marmion*, canto 3. stanzas 10-11), pages 41-42; (3) 'The Hunting Scene' (first words: 'The toils are pitch'd, and the stakes are set,' from *The Lady of the Lake*, canto 4, stanza 25), page 105.

455E] NEW YORK: Gilley and Megarey 1821
The Wreath; A Collection of Poems, from Celebrated English Authors. New-York: Published by W. B. Gilley and H. I. Megarey. J. Seymour, printer. 1821. Copies: CtY MWA.
Includes: 'Boat Song' (first words: 'Hail to the Chief who in triumph advances!', from *The Lady of the Lake*, canto 2, stanzas 19-20), pages 199-200.

456E] NEW YORK: Johnstone and Van Norden 1824
[1] The Songster's Museum. A New and Choice Collection of Popular Songs, Selected from the Best Authors. New-York Johnstone and Van Norden, Printers. 1824. Notes: This issue appears to be the first of several similar printings: see also 445E[2], 446E[1]. The collection also includes a song imitating Scott [see 502S]: 'Hail to the Day. Tune—Hail to the Chief (first words: 'Hail to the day which arises in splendour,"), pages 5-6. Copy: MWA.
Includes anonymously: (1) 'The Knight Errant' ['Romance of Dunois'] (first words: 'It was Dunois the young and brave,' from *The Edinburgh Annual Register for 1813*, 1815 [1816]),

pages 44-45; (2) 'Hail to the Chief' ['Boat Song'] (first words: 'Hail to the Chief, who in triumph advances,' from *The Lady of the Lake*, canto 2, stanzas 19-20), pages 66-67.

[2] The Wreath; A Collection of Poems, from Celebrated English Authors. . . . Johnstone and Van Norden, Printers. New York: 1824. Notes: This is the primary literal reissue of *The Wreath* published 1821 in New York by Gilley and Megarey. For the secondary reissue see 445E[1]. Copies: CtY(2) MWA.
Includes: 'Boat Song' (first words: 'Hail to the Chief who in triumph advances!', from *The Lady of the Lake*, canto 2, stanzas 19-20), pages 195-196.

457E] NEW YORK: King 1828-1831
[1] The Blackbird, Being A Choice Collection of the Most Popular American, English, Irish, and Scotch Songs. New-York: Published by S. King, and Sold Wholesale and Retail, at His Store, No. 150, William-Street. 1828. A reprint of 452E. Copy: MWA.
Includes anonymously: (1) 'O Brignal Banks!' (first words: 'O Brignal banks are wild and fair,' from *Rokeby* canto 3, stanzas 16-18), pages 10-11; (2) 'Where shall the Lover Rest' (first words as title, from *Marmion* canto 3, stanzas 10-11), pages 21-22.

[2] The Universal Songster; A New Collection of the Most Fashionable, Popular, Sentimental Comic, Patriotic and Naval Songs. Together with Catches, Glees, &c. New-York: Published by Solomon King. 1831. Copy: MWA.
Includes anonymously: (1) 'Hail to the Chief' ['Boat Song'] (first words: 'Hail to the chief, who in triumph advances,' from *The Lady of the Lake*, canto 2, stanzas 19-20), pages 29-30; (2) 'The Troubadour' (first words: 'Glowing with love, on fire for fame,' from *Paul's Letters to His Kinsfolk*, letter 9), pages 129-130; (3) 'The Knight Errant' ['Romance of Dunois'] (first words: 'It was Dunois, the young and brave, was bound for Palestine,' from *The Edinburgh Annual Register for 1813*, 1815 [1816]), pages 148-149.

458E] NEW YORK: Nafis 1829
The American Songster, Containing a Choice Selection of About One Hundred and Fifty Modern and Popular Songs . . . Stereotype Edition. New-York: Published by N. C. Nafis, 278 Pearl Street. Philadelphia; John B. Perry, 88½ North 2d Street. [1829]. Copy: CtY.
Includes anonymously: 'The Moon's on the Lake, or, MacGregor's Gathering' (first words: 'The moon's on the lake, and the mist's on the brae,' from *Albyn's Anthology*, 1816), pages 125-126.

459E] NEW YORK: Riley 1829
The Musical Bijou for 1830. New-York, Published by Riley, 29, Chatham Street. [1829]. Notes: Engraved sheet music. Music composed by John Parry arranged for voice and pianoforte. Copy: E.
Includes: 'The Maid of Toro' (first words: 'O! low shone the sun on the fair lake of Toro, / And weak were the whispers that wav'd the dark wood;'), pages *1* 2-3.

460E] NEW YORK: Singleton 1820
The Melodist, comprising A Selection of the most Favourite English, Scotch, and Irish Songs, . . . New-York: Published by George Singleton At the Office of the Ladies' Literary Cabinet, 194 Greenwich-street. Printed by Broderick and Ritter, No. 2 Dey-street 1820. Notes: Edited by G. S. Thornton. Copy: CtY.

Includes anonymously: 'The Heath this Night." (first words: 'The heath this night must be my bed,' from *The Lady of the Lake*, canto 3, stanza 23), pages 218-219 with music.

461E] NEW YORK: Smith 1824
The Melodist, Comprising a Selection of the Most Favourite English, Scotch, and Irish Songs, arranged for the Voice, Flute, or Violin. New-York: Sold by W. & P. C. Smith, Printers and Booksellers, 59 Fulton-street. 1824. Notes: With music. Copies: MWA PPL RPB. References: Lowens 638 note; Wolfe 4355.
Includes: (1) 'The Knight-Errant.' ['Romance of Dunois'] (first words: It was 'Dunvis'[!] The young and brave,' from *The Edinburgh Annual Register for 1813*, 1815 [1816], the translation attributed here to the original author and composer, Hortencia, late Queen of Holland, [*recte* Duchesse de St Leu]), pages 29-30; (2) 'Ave, Maria' (first words: 'Ave, Maria, maiden mild,' from *The Lady of the Lake,* canto 3, stanza 29), pages 105-106.

462E] NEW YORK: Smith and Forman 1814
The Nightingale, or Musical Companion, being A Collection of Entertaining Songs. New-York; Printed and sold by Smith & Forman, At the Franklin Juvenile Bookstores, 195 and 213 Greenwich-Street. 1814. Copy: CtY.
Includes anonymously: 'Where shall the Lover Rest' (first words as title, from *Marmion,* canto 3, stanzas 10-11), pages 42-43.

463E] NEW YORK: Wells 1831
The Beauties of The British Poets. . . . New-York: C. Wells, 157 Broadway. 1831. Notes: 'With a few Introductory Observations, by the Rev. George Croly.' This issue is an exact reprint of London: Seeley and Sons, *see* 410E[2]. Copies: CtY NjP.
Includes: (1) 'The Last Minstrel' (first words: 'The way was long, the wind was cold,' from *The Lay of the Last Minstrel,* 'Introduction'), pages *269* 270-272; (2) 'The Tomb of Michael Scott' (first words: 'By a steel-clenched postern door,' *ibid,* canto 2, stanzas 9-22), pages 273-278; (3) 'The Trial of Constance' (first words: 'While round the fire such legends go,' from *Marmion*, canto 2, stanzas 17-33), pages 279-289; (4) 'Song' (first words: 'The heath this night must be my bed,' from *The Lady of the Lake*, canto 3, stanza 23), page 290.

464E] NEW YORK: White, Gallaher and White 1830
Poetry for Schools: Designed for Reading and Recitation. The whole selected from the best Poets in the English Language. . . . Second Edition Revised and Corrected. New-York: Published by White, Gallaher and White. Alex. Ming Jr. Printer. 1830. Notes: The section on Sir Walter Scott begins with a two-page essay on his work and characteristics and continues with informative notes interspersed throughout the verse. Copies: CtY InU.
Includes: (1) 'The Last Minstrel' (first words: '"The way was long, the wind was cold,' from *The Lay of the Last Minstrel*, Introduction), pages 147-149; (2) (first words: '"Hushed is the harp—the Minstrel gone."' from *ibid*, Conclusion), pages 149-150; (3) 'As passed the Dwarf the outer court,' from *ibid*, canto 3, stanzas 12-20), pages 153-155; (4) (first words: '"Earl Morton was lord of that valley fair,"' from *ibid*, canto 4, stanzas 10-12), pages 156-158; (5) (first words: '"Fast as the fatal symbol flies,' from *The Lady of the Lake*, canto 3 stanza 14 merged with part of stanza 24), pages 158-159; (6) (first words: '"I grant him liberal, to fling' from *ibid*, canto 2, stanza 14), page 159; (7) (first words: '"_________ the evening

fell, / 'Twas near the time of curfew;' from *The Lay of the Last Minstrel*, canto 3, stanzas 24-31), pages 160-163; (8) (first words: '"Sweet Teviot! on thy silver tide"', from *ibid*, canto 4, stanzas 1-2), page 164.

465E] PHILADELPHIA: Ash & Mason and DeSilver 1826-1828
[1] The Beauties of Sir Walter Scott, and Thomas Moore Esquire; selected from their works; with Historical and Explanatory Notes. By a Gentleman of Philadelphia. Philadelphia: Ash & Mason, and T. DeSilver. L. R. Bailey, Printer. 1826. Notes: With frontispiece drawn by R. Westall and engraved by G. Fairman with three-line caption beginning: 'Th' enchantress now begins her spell;'. On title-verso the publishers record their copyright as 18 September 1826. This is a pastiche of forty-one selections from Scott (pages *1* 2-168) and eleven from Moore (pages 169-236) with the 'notes' generally taken from the poets' own editions: the whole performance so garbled as to prevent any separate entries. Copies: CtY NNU-W.

[2] The Beauties of Sir Walter Scott, and Thomas Moore, Esquire; selected from their works; with Historical and Explanatory Notes. . . . Tenth Edition—Enlarged. Philadelphia: [1828]. Notes: With engraved frontispiece of *The Lady of the Lake*, painted by R. Smirke, engraved by J. W. Steele. No publisher or printer is cited and the date 1828 appears only on the front board. The editor, now identified on title verso as Benjamin F. French, received a copyright 1 December 1827 for this title, then described as a second edition. This supposedly 'enlarged 10th' edition has only forty selections from Scott (pages *1* 2-165) as well as the eleven from Moore (pages 169-236). Copies: RPB T/B.

466E] PHILADELPHIA: Carey, Lea and Carey 1829
Laconics or the Best Words of the Best Authors. With the Authorities. . . . First American Edition. Philadelphia: Carey, Lea & Carey—Chesnut Street. Sold, in New York, by G. & C. & H. Carvill,—In Boston, by Munroe & Francis. 1829. Three volumes. Notes: This edition retains the Roman designations used in the London edition, T. Boys, 1826 (see 384E) but is entirely reset. Copies: O; CtY.
VOLUME 1 includes: (1) 'MLXXX' (first words: 'Swift, in his "[A Serious and Useful] Scheme to make an Hospital for Incurables,"' from Scott's edition of *The Works of Jonathan Swift*, volume 9, page 537), pages 214-215;
VOLUME 2: (2) 'DCLIII' (first words: 'Nay, dally not with time, the wise man's treasure,' from *The Monastery*, motto [Old Play], chapter 8), page 160; (3) 'DCLXXVII' (first words: 'I knew Anselmo. He was shrewd and prudent,' from *The Antiquary*, title-page motto), page 166; (4) 'MLVIII' (first words: 'Nay, if she love me not, I care not for her:', from *ibid*, motto [Old Play], chapter 44), page 266; (5) 'MXCII' (first words: 'Heaven first, in its mercy, taught mortals their letters', from *Guy Mannering*, motto [Pope, imitated], chapter 17), page 272; (6) 'MCCCXIX' (first words: 'He strikes no coin, 'tis true, but coins new phrases,' from *The Monastery*, motto [Old Play], chapter 15), page 328;
VOLUME 3: (7) 'MXXIII' (first words: 'Fortune, you say, flies from us—She but circles,' from *The Antiquary*, motto [Old Play] chapter 43), page 298.

467E] PHILADELPHIA: Grigg 1827-1832
[1] Grigg's Southern and Western Songster: Being a Choice Collection of the Most Fashionable Songs, many of which are original. Second Edition, Greatly Enlarged. Philadelphia: Published by John Grigg, No. 9, N. Fourth-Street, And for sale by Booksellers

and Country Merchants generally in the Southern and Western States. Clark & Raser, Printers, 33 Carter's Alley. 1827. Copy: MWA.
Includes (1) 'Hail to the Chief' ['Boat Song'] (first words: 'Hail to the Chief, who in triumph advances,' from *The Lady of the Lake*, canto 2, stanzas 19-20), pages 45-46; (2) 'Lochinvar' (first words: 'O young Lochinvar is come out of the west,' from *Marmion*, canto 5, stanza 12), pages 46-47; (3) 'The Cypress Wreath' (first words: 'O Lady, twine no wreath for me,' anonymously from *Rokeby*, canto 5, stanza 13), page 119; (4) 'The Knight Errant' ['Romance of Dunois'] (first words: 'It was Dunois, the young and brave, was bound for Palestine,' from *The Edinburgh Annual Register for 1813*, 1815 [1816]), page 135.

[2] Grigg's Southern and Western Songster: Being a Choice Collection of the Most Fashionable Songs, many of which are original. New Edition, Greatly Enlarged. Philadelphia: Published by J. Grigg, No. 9, N. Fourth-St. 1829. Notes: Also, falsely attributes, to Scott, 'Wha'll be King but Charlie' (first words: 'There's news from Moidart cam' yestreem,'), page 273. Only selections (1)-(4) appeared in the earlier, 1827 edition. Copies: InU MWA. Reissued 1831 (MWA), 1832 (MWA).
Includes: (1) 'Hail to the Chief' ['Boat Song'] (first words: 'Hail to the Chief, who in triumph advances,' from *The Lady of the Lake*, canto 2, stanzas 19-20), pages 40-41; (2) 'Lochinvar' (first words: 'O young Lochinvar is come out of the west,' from *Marmion*, canto 5, stanza 12), pages 41-42; (3) 'The Cypress Wreath' (first words: 'O Lady, twine no wreath for me,' anonymously from *Rokeby*, canto 5, stanza 13), page 106; (4) 'The Knight Errant' ['Romance of Dunois'] (first words: 'It was Dunois, the young and brave, was bound for Palestine,' from *The Edinburgh Annual Register for 1813*, 1815 [1816]), page 118; (5) 'Allen-a-Dale' (first words: 'Allen-a-Dale has no fagot for burning,' from *Rokeby*, canto 3, stanza 30), page 262; (6) 'The Blue Bonnets are over the Border' (first words: 'March, march, Ettrick and Teviotdale!', anonymously from *The Monastery*, chapter 25), page 264; (7) 'The Harper's Song' (first words: 'Summer eve is gone and past,' from *Rokeby*, canto 5, stanzas 7, 9), pages 281-282; (8) 'Wake, Maid of Lorn' (first words: 'Wake, maid of Lorn, the moments fly', from *The Lord of the Isles*, canto 1, stanza 4), page 297; (9) 'Where shall the Lover Rest' (first words as title, from *Marmion*, canto 3, stanzas 10-11), pages 302-303.

468E] PHILADELPHIA: Hart 1829
The Aeolian Harp, or Songster's Cabinet; Being a Selection of the Most Popular Songs and Recitations; Patriotic, Sentimental, Humorous, &c. Published by S. Hart & Son, Philadelphia. 1829. Copy: MWA. Reference: Lowens 533 note.
Includes 'Where shall the Lover Rest' (first words as title, from *Marmion* canto 3, stanzas 10-11), pages 87-88.

469E] PHILADELPHIA: Key and Biddle 1832
The Singer's Own Book: A Well-Selected Collection of the Most Popular Sentimental, Amatory, Patriotic Naval and Comic Songs. Philadelphia: Key & Biddle—6 Minor Street. [1832]. Notes: Falsely attributed to Scott, is 'Hassan the Brave' (first words: 'Behold me, sung Hassan, the fearless and free,'), pages 9-10. Copy: MWA.
Includes, all anonymously unless noted otherwise: (1) 'Where shall the Lover rest!' (first words as title, from *Marmion*, canto 3, stanzas 10-11), pages 11-12; (2) 'The Harper's Song' (first words: 'Summer eve is gone and past,' from *Rokeby*, canto 5, stanzas 7, 9), page 58; (3) 'The Troubadour' (first words: 'Glowing with love, on fire for fame,' from *Paul's Letters to His*

Kinsfolk, letter 9), pages 80-81; (4) 'All the Blue Bonnets are over the Border' (first words: 'March, march, Ettrick and Teviotdale!', from *The Monastery*, chapter 25), pages 113-114; (5) 'Hail to the Chief' ['Boat Song'] (first words: 'Hail to the chief, who in triumph advances,' from *The Lady of the Lake*, canto 2, stanzas 19-20), pages 121-122; (6) 'Allen-a-Dale' (first words: 'Allen-a-Dale has no fagot for burning,' from *Rokeby*, canto 3, stanza 30), pages 196-197; (7) 'He is gone on the Mountain' (first words as title, from *The Lady of the Lake*, canto 3, stanza 16), page 207; (8) 'Merrily Bounds the Bark' (first words: 'Merrily, merrily, bounds the bark,' from *The Lord of the Isles*, canto 4, stanzas 7, 9-11), page 220; (9) '"Wert Thou like Me.—Annot Lyle's Song." Words by Sir W. Scott.' (first words: 'Wert thou like me, in life's low vale,' from *A Legend of Montrose*, chapter 21), page 252; (11) 'Ah! County Guy' (first words as title, from *Quentin Durward*, chapter 4), page 296; (12) 'Marmion' (first words: 'The war that for a space did fail,' from *Marmion*, canto 6, stanza 32), page 300.

470E] PHILADELPHIA: Key, Mielke & Biddle 1832
The Singer's Own Book: . . . Philadelphia: Key, Mielke & Biddle—181 Market Street. New Edition. [1832]. Notes: A variant state of the original Key and Biddle issue (*see* 469E), now with an additional name in the imprint and oddly reading 'New Edition'. Copies: MWA(2).

PHILADELPHIA: Perry. *see* New York: Nafis (458E).

471E] PHILADELPHIA: Pomeroy 1824
Quotations from the British Poets; being A Pocket Dictionary of their Most Admired Passages. . . . Philadelphia: R. W. Pomeroy, Fifth, below Walnut St. 1824. Notes: With an engraved title-page dated 1825. This text was used for a New York reprint [Anderson, 1826. *see* 450E] with a title reading *Beauties of the British Poets; or A Pocket Dictioary, Containing the Most Admirable Passages*. Copy: T/B.
Includes: (1) 'Abbey. Melrose Abbey' (first words: 'If thou would'st view fair Melrose aright,' from *Lay of the Last Minstrel*, canto 2, stanza 1), page 5; (2) '*Lady of the Lake*. Description of' (first words: 'Never did Grecian chizzel trace' from *The Lady of the Lake*, canto 1, stanzas 18-19), pages 110-111; (3) 'Loch Katrine' (first words: 'Gleaming with the setting sun,' from *ibid*, canto 1, stanza 14 and canto 3, stanzas 1-2), pages 118-119; (4) 'Minstrel. Described' (first words: 'Amid the strings his fingers strayed,' from *The Lay of the Last Minstrel*, Introduction), page 142; (5) 'Minstrel. His Retreat' (first words: 'Hushed is the harp—the minstrel gone.' from *ibid*. [Conclusion]), pages 142-143; (6) Scenes. Of our Native Land' (first words: 'Breathes there the man with soul so dead,' from *ibid*, canto 6, stanzas 1-3), pages 196-197; (7) 'Soldiers. English, Scottish, and Irish' (first words: 'A various host—from kindred realms they came,' from *The Vision of Don Roderick*, stanzas 58-60), pages 212-213; (8) 'Statesmen. Fox and Pitt' (first words: 'With more than mortal powers endowed,' from *Marmion*, Introduction to Canto First), page 223; (9) 'Teviot' (first words: 'Sweet Teviot! on thy silver tide' from *The Lay of the Last Minstrel*, canto 4, stanza 1-2), page 234; (10) 'Time. Ceaseless Sweep of.' (first words: 'Time rolls his ceaseless course' from *The Lady of the Lake*, canto 3, stanza 1), page 238; (11) 'War. Beacon Blaze of.' (first words: 'So pass'd the day—the evening fell,' from *The Lay of the Last Minstrel*, canto 4, stanzas 24-27), pages 253-254; (12) 'Warnings. Foreboding the Fate of Rosae.' (first words: 'O listen, listen, ladies gay!' from *ibid*, canto 6, stanza 23), pages 256-258.

472E] PHILADELPHIA: Poole 1827

Le Souvenir, or, Picturesque Pocket Diary for 1827. . . . Philadelphia: A. R. Poole, 66 Chesnut Street, And sold by P. Thompson, Washington: Bliss & White, W. E. Gilley, G. & C. Carvill, H. I. Megarey, and E. T. Goodrich, New York: Hilliard, Gray & Co. and Monroe & Francis, Boston: F. Lucas & E. I. Coale, Baltimore: C. Hall, Norfolk: I. Williams, Savannah: Babcock & Co. and J. Mill, Charleston: D. C. Hotchkiss, New Orleans: and all the principal Book-sellers in the United States. 1827. Copy: MWA.
Includes, all anonymously: (1) 'Rebecca's Hymn' (begins with prose: '"It was in the twilight of the day . . . . we have ventured thus to translate into English."', then first words of verse: 'When Israel, of the Lord beloved,' from *Ivanhoe*, chapter 40'), pages 9-10; (2) 'The Orphan Maid' (begins with ['Literal Translation', (which in the text is a footnote following verse)], first words of prose: 'The hail-blast had drifted away upon the wings', then first words of verse: 'November's hail-cloud drifts away,' from *A Legend of Montrose*, chapter 9), pages *16* 17-18; (3) 'Song' (first words: '"Love wakes and weeps", from *The Pirate*, chapter 23), page 18.

473E] PHILADELPHIA: [*no publisher identified*] 1818

Banks of Schuylkill. Lochinvar. The Toast. or Here's to the Maiden of Bashful fifteen. Bright Phoebus. to which is added, The Land of Potatoe's O. Printed in the Year, 1818. Notes: Chapbook. Copy: MWA.
Includes: 'Lochinvar. A favorite song, written by Walter Scott, Esq.' (first words: 'O, Young Lochinvar is come out of the west,' from *Marmion*, canto 5, stanza 12), pages 3-4.

474E] RICHMOND: Cottom 1814

The American Star: Being a Choice Collection of the most approved Patriotic and other Songs. . . . Richmond: Published by Peter Cottom, At his Law and Miscellaneous Bookstore, second Door above the Eagle Tavern. 1814. Copy: CtY.
Includes anonymously: (1) 'Lochinvar. Lady Heron's Song' (first words: 'O young Lochinvar is come out of the west,' from *Marmion*, canto 5, stanza 12), pages 31-32; (2) 'Coronach' (first words: 'He is gone on the mountain,' from *The Lady of the Lake*, canto 3, stanza 16), pages 32-33; (3) 'The Cypress Wreath' (first words: 'O Lady, twine no wreath for me,' from *Rokeby*, canto 5, stanza 13), pages 33-34.

475E] RICHMOND: Nash and White 1824

The Vocal Standard, or, Star Spangled Banner; Being the Latest and Best Selection ever offered to the Public, Particularly of American Patriotic Songs; . . . Richmond. Published by John H. Nash, Bookseller; and Thomas W. White, Printer; Richmond, Virginia. 1824. Notes: Headlines throughout read 'Star Spangled Banner'. Copy: MWA.
Includes anonymously: (1) 'Boat Song' (first words: 'Hail to the chief who in triumph advances,' from *The Lady of the Lake*, canto 2, stanzas 19-20), pages 125-126; (2) 'Young Lochinvar' ['Lochinvar'] (first words: 'O young Lochinvar is come out of the west,' from *Marmion*, canto 5, stanza 12), pages 148-149; (3) 'The Knight Errant' ['Romance of Dunois'] (first words: 'It was Dunois, the young and brave, was bound for Palestine,' attributed to 'the late Queen of Holland', but Scott translation from *The Edinburgh Annual Register for 1813*, 1815 [1816]), page 152; (4) "Where shall the Lover Rest' (first words as title, from *Marmion*, canto 3, stanzas 10-11), page 183.

476E] WASHINGTON: [*publisher given only as*] B. 1826
The Patriotic Songster; Being A Collection of the Most Approved Patriotic, and Other Songs. Washington: Published by John B., 9th Street. 1826. Copy: MWA. Reference: Lowens 523 note.
Includes anonymously (1) 'Wake, Maid of Lorn' (first words: 'Wake, Maid of Lorn! the moments fly,' from *The Lord of the Isles*, canto 1, stanza 4), pages 149-150; (2) 'Merrily, Merrily, Bounds the Bark' (first words as title, from *ibid*, canto 4, stanzas 7, 9-11), pages 151-152.

477E] WINDSOR: [*no publisher identified*] 1830
The New-England Pocket Songster; A Choice Collection of Popular Songs, New and Old. Windsor, 1830. Notes: Only place cited in imprint. Falsely attributed to Scott, 'Wha'll be King but Charlie' (first words: There's news from Moidart cam' yestreen,'), pages 22-23. Copy: MWA.
Includes: (1) 'Joy to the Victors!' (first words: 'Joy to the victors! the sons of old Aspen!', from 'The House of Aspen', act 2, scene 2), pages 19-20; (2) 'Wake, Maid of Lorn' (first words: 'Wake, maid of Lorn, the moments fly', from *The Lord of the Isles*, canto 1, stanza 4), page 31; (3) 'Hail to the Chief' ['Boat Song'] (first words: 'Hail to the Chief, who in triumph advances,' anonymously from *The Lady of the Lake*, canto 2, stanzas 19-20), page 50; (4) 'The Cypress Wreath' (first words: 'O Lady, twine no wreath for me,' anonymously from *Rokeby*, canto 5, stanza 13), pages 71-73.

478E] WOODSTOCK: Colton 1831
The Songster: A New and Choice Collection of Popular Songs Selected from the Best Authors. Woodstock, Vt. Published by R. Colton, 1831. Copy: MWA
Includes anonymously: 'Hail to the Chief' ['Boat Song'] (first words: 'Hail to the Chief, who in triumph advances,' from *The Lady of the Lake*, canto 2, stanzas 19-20), pages 66-67.

APPENDIX 3: SATIRES, PARODIES, and IMITATIONS

As it is occasionally difficult to determine precisely which of Scott's writings prompted the satires and parodies (S) listed below, all issues of this genre have been arrayed together, with further cross-reference given among the derivative (D) items of the particular work, when that is apparent. Obviously the early poetic epics, all exalting what might be regarded as mere commonplace, were most often subject to ridicule.

GREAT BRITAIN

479S] EDINBURGH: Ballantyne 1812
[1] 'The Magic Mirror. Addressed to Walter Scott, Esq. By John Wilson.', pages *cvii-cxiv* in: *The Edinburgh Annual Register for 1810.* Vol. Third—Part Second. Edinburgh: Printed by James Ballantyne and Co. For John Ballantyne and Co. Edinburgh; Longman, Hurst, Rees, Orme, and Brown; and John Murray, London. 1812. Notes: As the pagination would indicate, this is a late insert, entered just before the sections on 'New Publications' and 'Index'. The poem itself is described in its 'private' separate issue, perhaps issued simultaneously and recorded in the next entry. Copy: L.

[2] The Magic Mirror. Addressed to Walter Scott, Esq. By John Wilson, Author of "The Isle of Palms," &c. (Author's Copy.) Edinburgh: Printed by James Ballantyne and Co. 1812. Pages: *i-ii, 1-3* 4-21. Notes: As if in a dream, the poet imagines a Figure reproving him for coming into the 'romantic realm'. The title itself is modeled upon the pre-publication issue of *The Vision of Don Roderick* and reference is made to all of Scott's other major poems, as well as to some verse by Wordsworth and Coleridge. The first note reports that 'This poem appeared in the Edinburgh Annual Register for 1810', the preceding entry. Copy: L.

480S] EDINBURGH: Lawrie 1809
The Goblin Groom; A Tale of Dunse. . . . Edinburgh: Printed by Alex. Lawrie & Co. For Alex. Lawrie, Edinburgh; and J. Ridgway, London. 1809. Pages: *i-x, 1-3* 4-125. Notes: A particularly insulting parody of *The Lay of the Last Minstrel* by R. O. Fenwick, addressed 'To Walter Marrowfat, Gardener to His Grace the D__ of B____H.' J.B.S. Morritt notified Scott that it was a 'bloody satire . . . wh of course breaks your rest, & has destroyed yr appetite' (*Letters*, ii.306,n.1). This piece, dismissed by Corson as 'quite a harmless poem' ([2], page 58), sometimes has been wrongly described as ridiculing *Marmion.* Copies: CtY IdU(extensively annotated) InU.

481S] LONDON: Adams 1826
The Wasp. A Literary Satire . . . London: Published by W. Adams, 14, York Street, Covent Garden, . . . 1826. Notes: Number 5 (28 October) includes: (1) 'Sir Walter Scott's new Poem. Dear Murray' [(Letter) To John Murray, 24 October 1826] and verse titled (2) 'The Landladie' (first words of Introduction: 'The moon is smallest when we see it new'; first

words of text: 'The Landladie sat in her pride of place,'). Number 6 (4 November) includes: (3) 'Letter from Sir Walter Scott to Mr. Murray' [dated from Paris 30 October]. Letter (1) reports that Scott departs for Paris in the morning to work on his life of Napoleon, but wants to give the poem to Murray before he leaves for inclusion in The Wasp. Verse (2), of 55 lines, is described as 'a sketch from the commencement of a poem that I have in hand'. All these missives, chronologically wrong or weak imitations, occur in a periodical professedly representing a waspish view. Copy: L.

482S] LONDON: Cadell and Davies 1809
Wallace: or, The Fight of Falkirk; A Metrical Romance. London: Printed for T. Cadell and W. Davies, Strand, By J. M'Creery, Black-Horse-Court, Fleet-Street. 1809. Pages: *i-iii* iv-viii, *1* 2-248. Notes: A lengthy parody in the style and subject of *The Lay of the Last Minstrel* and *Marmion* published anonymously by Margaret (Holford) Hodson. (see also second edition: 491S[6]). Copies: E; TxU(Auchincruive label with signature of Richard Alexander Oswald). References: *Letters*, ii.301, 306.

483S] LONDON: Cawthorn 1814
The Lay of the Scottish Fiddle. A Poem. In Five Cantos. Supposed to be Written by W— S—, Esq. First American, from the Fourth Edinburgh Edition. London: Printed for James Cawthorn, Cockspur-Street. 1814. Pages: *i-iii* iv-xvi, *1* 2-222 *223-224*. Notes: In this parody of *The Lay of the Last Minstrel* by J. K. Paulding a new 'Preface of the English Editor' is prefixed to Paulding's 'Preface' to the 1813 New York edition (see 501S). A 'second' Cawthorn edition (not located, but advertized in London [*MC*] 21 October 1820) wrongly attributes this burlesque to Washington Irving. Scott regarded this as 'a piece of tolerable dull Trans-Atlantic Wit . . . which however I take to be the highest compliment I ever received, since it blends me with the Naval reputation of my country' (*Letters*, iii.466). Copies: BCL E; CtY T/B TxU. Reference: BAL 15688.

484S] LONDON: Colburn 1811
The Lay of the Last Minstrel, Travesty. . . . The Virgin Edition. London: Sold by H. Colburn, 50, Conduit-Street, Bond-Street; John Anderson, Edinburgh; and John Cumming, Dublin. 1811. Pages: *i-viii, 1-3* 4-237 *238-240.* Notes: Attributed to 'O. Neville', obviously an unsympathetic Englishman, who suggests, page *3*: 'It is particularly requested, that the following Poem may be read with the Original, line for line—without which, the parody will be entirely lost . . . .' Copies: BCL E; CtY('With the authors[!] compliments') CtY PU T/B. Reference: Kohler(3) 1071.

485S] LONDON: Crosby 1814
The Lay of the Poor Fiddler, A Parody on The Lay of the Last Minstrel, with notes and illustrations. By an Admirer of Walter Scott. . . . London: Published by B. and R. Crosby & Co. and sold by all booksellers. 1814. Pages: *1-5* 6-167 *168*. Notes: Probably written by John Roby, who also parodied *Rokeby* (*see* 497S[1-3]). Price: Five Shillings. Copies: E L; CtY.

486S] LONDON: Dwyer 1810
The Caledonian Comet. . . . London: Printed for W. Dwyer, 29, Holborn Hill. 1810. Pages: *i-v* vi, *7* 8-22. Notes: A satirical poem attributed to John Taylor, who has 'come forward to

check the progress of false taste', especially 'the Old Ballad style of poetry'. Scott as the 'Comet' first appears in line 31. Copies: L(inscrbed to Alexander Chalmers); CtY(inscribed to Mrs [Elizabeth] Inchbald).

487S] LONDON: Fearman 1820-1821

[1] Tales of My Landlord, New Series, Containing Pontefract Castle. . . . London: Printed for William Fearman, New Bond Street. 1820. Three volumes. Pages 1: *1-4, i* ii-xlvi *xlvii-xlviii, 1* 2-226; 2: *i-iv, 1* 2-290 *291-292*; 3: *i-iv 1* 2-319 *320*. Notes: The problems with this spurious work are laid out in great detail from the perspective of the plagiarist, William Fearman, in the 42-page preliminaries entitled 'The Publisher's Preface.' Volume 2, page 288 is misnumbered 88. Copies: BCL E(2) L; CtY(2) MH NNU-W. References: Lockhart, vi.39-40; Maggs Catalogue 1120, item 239; Thomson, page 54.

[2] Tales of My Landlord, New Series, Containing The Fair Witch of Glas Llyn. . . . London: Printed for William Fearman, New Bond-Street. 1821. Three volumes. Pages 1: *1-2, i* ii-xcvi, *1* 2-256; 2: *i-ii, 1* 2-360; 3: *i-ii, 1* 1 2-368. Notes: As in the earlier Fearman plagiarism (previous entry), this title begins with extensive rambling preliminaries: 'The Author to his book' (53 pages) and 'The Publisher's Preface' (42 pages). In the first the anonymous author concludes: 'Lastly, I as solemnly aver, that whatever may have been said or shall be said to the contrary, Pontefract and his younger brother are as much the sons of the reputed author of "Waverley," as "the Monastery" and "the Abbot."' Fearman devotes almost all of his 'Preface' to a vigorous defense of Pontefract Castle as a political warning of rebellions to come. Copies: O; InU.

LONDON: Hazard.

[~] Marmion Travestied. 1809. *see* 497S[4].

488S] LONDON: Hookham 1822-1825

[1] The Bridal of Caölchairn; and Other Poems. By John Hay Allan, Esq. London: Printed for T. Hookham, Old Bond Street; and W. and C. Tait, Prince's Street, Edinburgh. 1822. Notes: Apart from the title poem there are other imitations with titles such as: 'Lines to a Lady, with some Hair' and 'Lines in Return for a Set of Sporan Tassels.' The author's actual name was John Sobieski Stuart. See further 489S. Copy : L.

[2] New Landlord's Tales; or, Jedediah in the South. London: Printed for T. Hookham, Old Bond Street. 1825. Two volumes. Pages 1: *i-iv, 1* 2-347 *348*; 2: *i-iv, 1* 2-351 *352*. Notes: This parody consists of five stories ('But Just in Time', 'Friar Robert's Walk', 'The Red Man of Nagy Retsky', 'Constancy, in the Nineteenth Century', and 'Substance of Some Traditions respecting Grimmfer the Wizard') with an introduction by 'Jedediah Cleishbotham' explaining his reasons for moving southward from Gandercleugh, Scotland, to 'the pleasantly situated village of Dulwich, near London, within three doors of the Greyhound Inn.' Copies: L; CtY.

489S] LONDON: Hurst, Robinson 1822

The Bridal of Caölchairn; and Miscellaneous Poems. By Sir Walter Scott, Bart. Fifth Edition. London: Printed for Hurst, Robinson, and Co.: and Archibald,[!] Constable, and

Co. Edinboro'. 1822. Pages: *i-iv, 1-2* 3-344. Notes: A variant issue of the 1822 London, Hookham edition (*see* 488S[1]), with the authorship now attributed to Scott. Copies: E L O.

490S] LONDON: Iley 1818

Tales of My Landlady. . . . London: Printed for M. Iley, Somerset Street, Portman Square, and may be had of all booksellers. 1818. Three volumes. Pages 1: *i-ii, 1* 2-339; 2: *i-ii, 1* 2-261; 3: *i-ii, 1* 2-343 *344*. Notes: The title-page reads: 'Edited by Peregrine Puzzlebrain. Assistant to the Schoolmaster of Gandercleugh.' in direct imitation of Scott's first *Tales of my Landlord*, published about a year earlier. This parody was advertised in *MC* 26 February 1818. Price: £1.1.0. Copy: MH.

491S] LONDON: Longman, Hurst, Rees, Orme and Brown 1810-1817

[~] The British Melodist (including parody on 'Oh Rest thee, Babe'). *see* 400E[1]

[1] The Poetic Mirror, or The Living Bards of Britain. . . . London: Printed for Longman, Hurst, Rees, Orme, and Brown; and John Ballantyne, Edinburgh. 1816. Notes: A parodic anthology produced anonymously by James Hogg in retaliation for Scott's (and other poets: Byron, Wordswoth, Coleridge, Southey, and J. Wilson) refusal to contribute to a legitimate fund-raising anthology. Two enclosures are attributed to Scott: (1) 'Epistle to Mr R. S****[Southey].' dated 'Melrose, Teviotdale, August 3.' (first words: 'Dear S****, while the southern breeze / Floats, fresh'ning, from the upland leas,'), pages *27-29* 30-51; (2) 'Wat O' the Cleuch' in three cantos (first words: 'Wat 'o the Cleuch came down through the dale,'), pages *53-55* 56-129. The first 'contribution' is generally attributed to Thomas Pringle and the second to Hogg. Copies: L O; CtY.

[2] The Poetic Mirror, . . . Second Edition. . . . 1817. Notes: This reset text appears to be invariant except for the correction of an erratum noticed in the original issue pertaining to Scott's first 'contribution': page 49, line 1, previously 'not treacherous', is here corrected to 'and treacherous'. Copies: O; InU.

[3] Poetical Vagaries; containing . . . . The Lady of the Wreck, or Castle Blarneygig; . . . London: Printed for The Author; and sold by Longman, Hurst, Rees, Orme, and Brown, Paternoster-Row. 1812. Pages: *35-39* 40-111. Notes: A parody in two cantos by George Colman, The Younger, who has written 'a Short Epick Poem, stuff'd with Romantick Knick-knackeries; and interlarded with Songs, and Ballads, à la mode de Chevy Chace, Edom o Gordon, Sir Lancelot du Lake, &c. &c.' Dedicated 'To the Author of the Lady of the Lake;' see 534T[1]). Copy: L.

[4] Poetical Vagaries; containing . . . . The Lady of the Wreck, or Castle Blarneygig; . . . The Second Edition . . . London; Printed for Longman, Hurst, Rees, Orme, and Brown, Paternoster-Row, 1814. Pages: *37-41* 42-121. Notes: A revised and extended text, as observed in the pagination. For the dedication see 534T[1]. Copy: DLC.

[5] The Prince of the Lake, or O'Donoghue of Rosse, A Poem, In Two Cantos. . . . London: Printed for Longman, Hurst, Rees, Orme and Brown, Paternoster-Row; J. Cumming, Dublin; and J. Bolster, Cork. 1815. Pages: *i-viii, 1-3* 4-119 *120*. Notes: A Poem by M. J. Sullivan, of the Middle Temple. The verse concludes, pages 118-119, with three stanzas addressed to

Walter Scott, Esq. The *London Chronicle* for 1815 (page 604) notes: 'This Poem is put into the mouth of a minstrel, in imitation of Mr. Walter Scott, whose metre has also been adopted.' Copy: E.

[6] Wallace: or The Fight of Falkirk; A Metrical Romance. By Miss Holford. Second Edition. London: Printed for Longman, Hurst, Rees, Orme, and Brown, Paternoster-Row. 1810. Pages: *i-v* vi-vii *viii, 1* 2-252. Notes: As in the first edition (*see* 482S) except for identification of author and omission of Preface. Copies: E; TxU.

492S] LONDON: Longman, Hurst, Rees, Orme, Brown, Green 1824
Warreniana; With Notes, Critical and Explanatory, by the Editor of A Quarterly Review. . . . London: Printed for Longman, Hurst, Rees, Orme, Brown, and Green, Paternoster-Row. 1824. Notes: A collection of parodies by William Frederick Deacon, with a quote on title-page from Byron: 'I have even been accused of writing Puffs for Warren's Blacking.' Includes: 'The Battle of Brentford Green, A Poem in two Cantos. By Sir W—S—.' (first words: 'Day set on Regent Street, Pall Mall,'), pages *147* 148-162. An earlier prose essay 'By B.M.' on the Sable School of Poetry' presumes to attribute the Scottish novels to Sir William Curtis (page 79) and provides a series of notes to justify this ascription (pages 196-199). Copies: CtY InU T/B.

493S] LONDON: Miller 1812-1833
Rejected Addresses: Or The New Theatrum Poetarum. . . . London: Printed for John Miller, 25, Bow-Street, Covent Garden. 1812. Notes: A collection of parodies by James and Horace Smith, pertaining to the rebuilding of the Drury Lane Theatre. Includes: 'A Tale of Drury Lane. By W. S.' (first words: Survey this shield all bossy bright;'), pages *44* 45-53, this with headnote, 'To be spoken by Mr. Kemble in a suit of the Black Prince's armour borrowed from the Tower.' The book was continually reprinted but not 'carefully revised' until the 18th edition (published by John Murray, 1833), where there is a tribute to Scott's indulgence on its first publication (pages xviii-xix) and various notes, together with an illustration, then added to his 'contribution' (pages 64-77). Copy: L.

494S] LONDON: Phillips 1814
[1] The Knight of the Cross, The Favorite Harper's Song, Sung . . . in the Grand Melo Drame, called the Hag of the Lake, . . . London Published by W. Phillips Little Tower Hill. [1814]. Pages: *1-3*. Notes: Engraved sheet music with caption title. No author given for the three stanzas of parodic, satiric verse. Music composed and arranged by Montague P. Corri for voice and harp or pianoforte with German flute. Given as performed at the 'Royalty Theatre'. Price: 1s. Copy: L.

[2] Liberty, A Favorite Song sung . . . in the Grand Melo Drame, called the Hag of the Lake, . . . London Published by W. Phillips Little Tower Hill. [1814]. Pages: *1-3*. Notes: Engraved sheet music with caption title. No author given for the two stanzas of parodic verse. Music composed and arranged by Montague P. Corri for voice and pianoforte with German flute, as performed at the 'Royalty Theatre'. Price: 1s. Copy: L.

495S] LONDON: Richardson 1815
[1] The Ass on Parnassus; and From Scotland, Ge Ho!! comes Roderigh vich Neddy Dhu,

Ho! Ieroc!!! Cantos I. II. Of a Poem, entitled What are Scot's Collops? A Prophetic Tale; Written in Imitation of The Lady of the Lake. . . . London; Printed by A. J. Valpy, Took's Court, Chancery Lane; Sold by J. M. Richardson, No. 23, Cornhill, Opposite the Royal Exchange. [1815]. Pages: *i-iii* iv, *5* 6-36. Notes: A parody by 'Jeremiah Quiz'. On the last page of this part issue two additional cantos are cited as 'Preparing for the Press: 'Marmion-Feats' and 'Neddy'' Price: Three Shillings and Sixpence. Copies: L; CtY.

[2] The Ass on Parnassus. . . . London; Printed by A. J. Valpy, Took's Court, Chancery Lane; Sold by J. M. Richardson, No. 23, Cornhill, Opposite the Royal Exchange. [1815]. Notes: The collected issue now extends to page 134 and includes two further cantos [III] 'Marmion Feats' and [IV] 'Neddy, A Tale of Chalk-Farm'. Copy: DLC.

496S] LONDON: Taylor and Hessey 1825
Walladmor: "Freely translated into German from the English of Sir Walter Scott." And now freely translated from the German into English. . . . London: Printed for Taylor and Hessey, 93 Fleet Street, and 13 Waterloo Place, Pall Mall. 1825. Two volumes. Pages 1: *i-v* vi-xxx *xxxi-xxxii, 1* 2-247; 2: *i-vi, 1* 2-311 *312*. Notes: The original German imitation of Scott, by 'Willibad Alexis' [Georg Wilhelm Häring], was issued in Berlin 1824, then in the *London Magazine* 10 (October 1824, pages 353-82) fully analyzed by Thomas de Quincey, who thereupon ridiculed it further in this 'free' English translation. Erratum for volume 1 in volume 2, page *312*. For dedications to Scott by the translator and by the translator to the spurious German translator *see* 546T. Copies: E L O; CtY InU(remainder issue in one volume, publisher's red blind-stamped binding). Reference: Thomson, pages 74-75.

497S] LONDON: Tegg 1809-1813
[1] Jokeby, A Burlesque on Rokeby, A Poem, in Six Cantos, . . . London: Printed for Thomas Tegg, No. 111, Cheapside; W. Allason, 31, Bond Street; J. Dick, Edinburgh; and J. Cumming, Dublin. 1813. Pages: *i-iv, 1* 2-224. Notes: 'By an Amateur of Fashion' or, rather, John Roby. Copies: E O; IdU MH TxU.

[2] Jokeby, A Burlesque on Rokeby. A Poem, in Six Cantos, . . . The Fifth Edition, enlarged. London: Printed for Thomas Tegg, No. 111, Cheapside; W. Allason, 31, Bond-Street; J. Dick, Edinburgh; and J. Cumming, Dublin. 1813. Pages: *1-5* 6-216. Notes: With coloured frontispiece. This issue was published 23 July (*MC*), only five months after the original publication of *Rokeby*. There appear to be no intervening 'editions'. Copies: E L(2) O(2); CtY T/B.

[3] Jokeby, A Burlesque on Rokeby. A Poem, in Six Cantos, . . . The Sixth Edition, corrected and enlarged. London: Printed for Thomas Tegg, No. 111, Cheapside; Wm. Allason, No. 31 Bond-Street; C. Chapple, Pall-Mall; J. Blacklock, Royal Exchange; J. Dick, and J. Sutherland, Edinburgh; Brash and Reid, Glasgow; J. Cumming, and C. La Grange, Dublin, and all other Booksellers. 1813. Pages: *1-5* 6-216. Notes: With coloured frontispiece. In this and subsequent stereotyped reissues the 'corrections' remain undetected, but on page *4* a lengthy 'Encomium on Jokeby' is reprinted from Drakard's paper 4 July 1813. Here it is noted that Scott's disease is either 'cacoethes scribendi, or itch for writing' or simply 'an itching palm.' Copies: E L; CtY. Reissued as a 'Seventh Edition' (BCL L), 'Eighth Edition' (E L; NNU-W), 'Ninth Edition' (TxU).

[4] Marmion Travestied; A Tale of Modern Times. . . . London: Printed by G. Hazard, Beech-Street, for Thomas Tegg, III, Cheapside, London. 1809. Pages: *i-ix* x-xix *xx, 1-3* 4-277. Notes: Apparently the first extensive travesty of Scott, and dedicated to him by 'Peter Pry' (Thomas Hill). The Edinburgh newspapers were taken aback by this heresy, *EEC* 19 August 1809 announcing it as MARMION TRAVESTIED! and *EWJ* 6 September exclaiming MARMION TRAVESTIED!!! The latter reports a regular issue at 9s, large paper at 12s. Copies: CtY IdU NNU-W TxU.

498S] [LONDON]: [*publisher unknown*] 1808
Sir Albon: A Fragment. O Imitatores servum pecus! [no place, no date. watermarked 1807] Pages: *1-3* 4-15. Notes: One gathering beginning with a half-title headed as above. The first poem, in the style of Scott, is dated 27 February 1808, five days after the publication of *Marmion*. Copy: CtY.

499S] MONTROSE: Smith 1820
Bauldy Baird. . . . Printed for, and Sold by M. Smith & Co., Booksellers, &c. High-street, Montrose. [ca. 1820]. Notes: Slip-ballad parody with the following footnote to the title: '*This Song is a Parody on Sir Walter Scott's humorous one of "Donald Caird." It seems to possess no inconsiderable portion of spirit, and is sung with great effect.' (first words: 'Bauldy Baird's come again!') [Popular Songs—No. 10]. Copy: NN.

UNITED STATES

BALTIMORE: Nickerson
[~] The Universal and Theatrical Songster (includes the parody 'Sam Jones'). *see* 433E.

500S] BOSTON: Wells and Wait 1813
Jokeby, A Burlesque on Rokeby, A Poem....in Six Cantos. By an Amateur of Fashion. . . Published by W. Wells and T. B. Wait and Co. Boston, and Eastburn, Kirk and Co. N. York. 1813. Pages: *i-iv, 1* 2-218. Notes: Probably written by John Roby (*see* 497S), although often erroneously ascribed to the American writer James Kirke Paulding. Bound in drab printed boards with advertisements on back board for Scott's *Ballads and Lyrical Pieces, The Lay of the Last Minstrel, Marmion, The Lady of the Lake,* and *Rokeby*. Copies: E; CtY MH MWA NN(Berg).

NEW HAVEN: Babcock
[~] Songs for Gentlemen (includes a parody on 'Hail to the Chief'). *see* 448E.

501S] NEW YORK: Inskeep and Bradford 1813
The Lay of the Scottish Fiddle: A Tale of Havre de Grace. Supposed to be written By Walter Scott, Esq. . . . New-York: Published by Inskeep & Bradford, and Bradford & Inskeep, Philadelphia, 1813. Pages: *1-3* 4-262. Notes: A satirical parody of *The Lay of the Last Minstrel* by J. K. Paulding on the British at Havre de Grace during the War of 1812. Described on title as the 'First American, from the Fourth Edinburgh Edition.' Concerning Scott's reaction *see* 483S. Copies: E(2); DLC MWA PPL. Reference: BAL 15688.

502S] NEW YORK: Johnstone and Van Norden 1824
The Songster's Museum. A New and Choice Collection of Popular Songs, Selected from the Best Authors. New-York Johnstone and Van Norden, Printers. 1824. Notes: Includes a song imitating Scott: 'Hail to the Day. Tune—Hail to the Chief (first words: 'Hail to the day which arises in splendour,"), pages 5-6. *See also* 456E. Copy: MWA.

503S] PHILADELPHIA: Carey 1815-1817
[1] The Ass on Parnassus; . . . [Cantos I. II.] of a Poem, entitled What are Scot's Collops? A Prophetic Tale: Written in Imitation of The Lady of the Lake. . . . Philadelphia: Published by Mathew Carey, No. 121, Chesnut Street. 1815. Pages: *i-iii* iv, *5* 6-29. Notes: Imitation by Jeremiah Quiz. Canto 1 is titled 'The Ass on Parnassus'; 2: 'From Scotland, Ge Ho!!'. The printed boards are dated 15 May 1815. A sequel, with continuing pagination and cantos 3-7, was published in 1815 under the title Marmion Feats. (see next entry). Copy: CtY.

[2] Marmion Feats; . . . [Cantos III-VII] of a Poem entitled What are Scot's Collops? A Prophetic Tale; Written in Imitation of The Lady of the Lake. Being a sequel to The Ass on Parnassus, . . . Philadelphia: Published by Mathew Carey, No. 121, Chesnut Street. 1815. Pages: *31-35* 36-108. Notes: Following the title, the title-page lists each of the concluding cantos. Canto 3 is titled 'Marmion Feats; A Day before the Tournament'; 4: 'Neddy'; 5: 'Jeremiah and the Ass'; 6: 'Bartholomew Fair'; 7: 'From England Ge Ho!'. The first two cantos were published in 1815 under the title The Ass on Parnassus. (*see* preceding entry). Copy: CtY.

[3] The Poetic Mirror; or, The Living Bards of Britain. . . . Philadelphia: Published by M. Carey and Son, Chesnut-Street, Sold also by Wells and Lilly, Boston. 1817. Notes: A parodic anthology produced anonymously by James Hogg (*see* 491S[1]) which includes two poems falsely attributed to Scott: (1) 'Epistle to Mr. R. S*** [Southey].' dated 'Melrose, Teviotdale, August 3.' (first words: 'Dear S****, while the southern breeze'), pages *21-23* 24-37; (2) 'Wat o' the Cleuch' in three cantos (first words: 'Wat o' the Cleuch came down through the dale,'), pages *39-41* 42-90. As in the London edition, the table of Contents misspells 'Cleuch' as 'Cleugh'. Copies: CtY DLC MWA.

APPENDIX 4: TRIBUTES and DEDICATIONS (504T-560T)

After Samuel Johnson's 'declaration of independence' against Lord Chesterfield, in 1755, the production of dedications appears to have declined somewhat, Johnson himself in his lifetime receiving only eight and William Cowper merely four. Yet if these slight measures mark any tendency, Scott must be ranked as a notable exception in all later time, for seventy-two addresses to this author have now been discovered: a count still excluding numerous reprints and the pro forma listings cited in entry 506. In the early years these testimonials are primarily from his Scottish associates, but then increasingly from his admirers among the English and American literati, with the London publisher John Murray (538) hospitably issuing no fewer than five of the more remarkable dedications. As exhibited in the following table, eventually in 1820, upon the publication of *Ivanhoe* and the announcement of Scott's baronetcy, the yearly tributes on average increased several fold over the previous rate.

1807	509[1]	1820	518 521 531 538[3] 541 544 559
1808	509[2] 549	1821	528 538[1]
1809	547	1822	512 524
1810	505[1] 536 542	1823	504[2] 506 517 520 532
1811	505[3]	1825	515 516 535 545 546 548 552
1812	505[2] 529 534[1]	1826	526[1] 530[1] 540 543
1814	534[2]	1828	507 510 530[2] 537 538[2] 550
1815	504[1] 514 551	1829	508[1] 526[2] 533
1816	523	1830	519 522 538[5] 553 554
1817	525 538[4]	1831	508[2] 527[1] 539
1818	511	1832	527[2]

Altogether, over the long period represented in this account, only four years pass without some published tribute to an author universally admired and respected, an ever ready help to aspiring litterateurs, 'the Delight and Ornament of his Country' (520), and a 'Matchless Genius' (521).

GREAT BRITAIN

504T] EDINBURGH: Anderson 1815-1823

[1] Berguer, Lionel Thomas. Stanzas. Inscribed to Walter Scott, Esq. . . . Edinburgh: Printed by George Ramsay and Company, For John Anderson and Company, Edinburgh; and Longman, Hurst, Rees, Orme, and Brown, London. 1815. Copy: L.

Dedication (as 'Advertisement'): 'I can offer no apology for the publicaton of these desultory Stanxas, but my admiration for Mr. Scott. If my powers of poetry were but commensurate with this feeling, they would need no apology whatever. Edinburgh, 27th November 1815.'

[2] The Waverley Dramas. . . . John Anderson, Jun. Edinburgh, 55, North Bridge Street; and Simpkin & Marshall, London. MDCCCXXIII. Notes: For the collection itself *see* 321D. Copies: ES; NjP.

Dedication: 'To The Author of Waverley, these dramas, founded on his works, are respectfully dedicated. Edinburgh, 30th July, 1823.'

505T] EDINBURGH: Ballantyne 1810-1812

[1] Baillie, Joanna. The Family Legend. Edinburgh: Printed by James Ballantyne and Co. For John Ballantyne and Co. Hanover-Street; and Longman, Hurst, Rees, and Orme, Paternoster-Row, London. 1810. Notes: Scott provided the two-page prologue for this volume (*see* 46A). Dedication reprinted in second edition, 1810, and repeated in the New York City edition, November 1810. Copies: E; DLC.

Dedication: 'To Walter Scott, Esq. Whose friendly zeal encouraged me to offer it to the notice of my indulgent countrymen, I inscribe this play.'

[2] Hartstonge, Matthew Weld. Minstrelsy of Erin, or Poems Lyrical, Pastoral, and Descriptive. Edinburgh: Printed by James Ballantyne and Co. for John Ballantyne and Co. Edinburgh; Longman and Co. London; and J. Cumming, and M. N. Mahon, Dublin. 1812. Notes: For a discussion of Scott's involvement as editor of this work, *see* 69A. Hartstonge later inscribed a novel to the author of Waverley (*see* 548T). Copies: L O.

Dedication: 'To Walter Scott, Esq.' (followed by a sixteen-line poem beginning: 'To thee shall Erin's lay belong,').

[3] [Locker, Edward Hawke.] Catalonia, A Poem; With Notes Illustrative of the Present State of Affairs in the Peninsula. Edinburgh: Printed for John Ballantyne & Co. Hanover-Street; and for Longman, Hurst, Rees, Orme, and Brown, London. 1811. Notes: Nine lines from *The Vision of Don Roderick*, stanza 47, appear on the title-page. Copy: L. Reference: *Letters*, iii.67,n.1.

Dedication: 'To Walter Scott, Esq. My dear Sir, Great part of this little ballad was written in a leisure hour, soon after the fall of Figueras. It may seem strange, that the sight of your beautiful Poem of Don Roderick induced me to take it up again instead of destroying it, . . .' followed by another full page of dedication, signed 'The Author. His Majesty's Ship Caledonia, off Toulon, Sept. 16, 1811'.

506T] EDINBURGH: Bannatyne Club 1823-1830

Murray, David. Poems by Sir David Murray of Gorthy. Edinburgh: Reprinted by James Ballantyne and Co. MDCCCXXIII. Notes: This was the second title issued by the Club, according to the record given in the 1867 List of Members. Fourteen later titles are similarly dedicated pro forma to Scott, all identifying him as president: 3-8, 10, 14-15, 17, 20, 27, 34, 37. Copies: E EU O.

Dedication (by the editor): 'This the Second Impression of the Poems of Sir David Mvrray[!], is respectfully dedicated and presented to Sir Walter Scott of Abbotsford, and to the Other Members of The Bannatyne Club, by Thomas Kinnear.'

507T] EDINBURGH: Blackwood 1828

Smyth, Amelia Gillespie. Tales of the Moors: or, Rainy Days in Rossshire. . . William Blackwood, Edinburgh: and T. Cadell, Strand, London. M.DCCC.XXVIII. Notes: This work is occasionally ascribed to Caroline Bowles Southey. Copies: E O.

Dedication: 'To Sir Walter Scott, Baronet, these pages are respectfully and gratefully inscribed by the Author.'

508T] EDINBURGH: Cadell 1829-1831

[1] Skene, James. A Series of Sketches of the Existing Localities alluded to in the Waverley Novels. . . . Edinburgh: Printed for Cadell and Co., Edinburgh; Simpkin and Marshall, and Moon, Boys and Graves, London. 1829. *See* 348D[2]. Copies: E GU; InU.

Dedication: 'To Sir Walter Scott, Bart. My dear Sir Walter, Permit me to interpose the aegis of your powerful name for the protection of an attempt which your encouragement alone could excuse, and to inscribe to the Author of Waverley a performance which, without his aid and countenance, could lay little claim to notice. But there are subjects of such engrossing interest in themselves, that even trifles connected with them are permitted to catch up a gleam of reflected lustre, which serves to compensate for want of intrinsic merit; and where that borrowed gleam is so needful as in the present instance, I rely on the habitual indulgence of nearly forty years' uninterrupted intimacy and friendship, that the favour of your name will be kindly accorded for the introduction Of your affectionate friend, J. Skene. Edinburgh, July, 1829.'

[2] [Ferrier, Susan]. Destiny; or, The Chief's Daughter. . . . Edinburgh: Printed for Robert Cadell, Edinburgh; and Whittaker and Co., London. 1831. Notes: On Ferrier's ten-day visit to Abbotsford in October 1830 Scott promised her a better price for this last novel and did so: £1,700 from Cadell. (Johnson, page 1120). Copies: E; CtY InU.

Dedication: 'To Sir Walter Scott, Baronet, These volumes are respectfully dedicated by an obliged friend, though anonymous Author. Edinburgh, March 15, 1831.'

509T] EDINBURGH: Constable 1807-1817

[1] Hogg, James. The Mountain Bard; Consisting of Ballads and Songs, Founded on Facts and Legendary Tales. . . . Edinburgh: Printed by J. Ballantyne and Co. For Arch. Constable and Co. Edinburgh, and John Murray, London. 1807. Notes: The third [second?] edition of 1817 (as well as another 'third edition' of 1821, *see* 513T) alters the dedication to read 'Affectionate Friend' and subtends a dateline 'Mitchelslack, Sept. 27, 1807'. The prefatory letter to the 'Memoir' was provided by Scott, and copies were made available in large paper (222 x 138mm) as well as the regular issue (185 x 115mm uncut). Copies: L O; CtY InU NjP(Robert Southey's 'Cottonian Library') NjP TxU.

Dedication: 'To Walter Scott, Esq. Sheriff of Ettrick Forest, and Minstrel of the Scottish Border, The Following Tales are Respectfully Inscribed by His Friend and Humble Servant, The Author.'

[2] Weber, Henry (editor). The Battle of Flodden Field; A Poem of the Sixteenth Century. With the Various Readings of the Different Copies; Historical Notes, a Glossary, and an Appendix containing Ancient Poems and Historical Matter relating to the Same Event. . . . Edinburgh: Printed by James Ballantyne and Co. For Archibald Constable and Co. Edinburgh, and John Murray, London. 1808. Notes: The Preface reports (page ix) 'No less than three editions saw the light between the years 1770 and 1790, which have all become scarce', and later (page xv) mentions a 1664 issue 'in the possession of W. Scott, Esq. and I am not acquainted with the existence of any other copy.' Scott is especially thanked for 'advice as to the general plan of the publication' and the 'materials, without which the text could not have received any degree of authority' (page xxiv). It has also been suggested that Scott provided all of the elaborate appendices, pages 251-389. Copies: (regular issue: 226 x 136mm uncut) E; CtY TxU ViU; (large paper: 243 x 155mm uncut) InU.

Dedication: 'To Walter Scott, Esq. &c. &c. &c. This Republication of the Rude and Unadorned Metrical History of An Event, To which He has Lately Given that Celebrity, which None but the Poet Can Bestow, Is Inscribed by His Obliged Friend and Faithful Servant, Henry Weber.'

510T] EDINBURGH: Douglas 1828
Douglas, George A. The Poetical Melange... Edinburgh: Published by George A. Douglas, 19. Castle Street; and sold by Charles Tilt, London; and W. Curry Jun. and Company, Dublin. MDCCCXXVIII. Notes: For further information about this three-volume set as an anthology and Scott's inclusion in it, *see* 363E. Copies: InU NN.
Dedication: 'To Sir Walter Scott, Bart. These Volumes are, by Permission, Respectfully dedicated by His obedient and obliged servant, George A. Douglas.'

511T] EDINBURGH: Gow and Galbraith 1818
[*engraved title*] [Gow, Nathaniel, compiler] The Ancient Curious Collection of Scotland consisting of Genuine Scotch Tunes with their Original Variations . . . Edinburgh. Published by Gow & Galbraith, Music Sellers to His Majesty. 60 Princes Street & to be had of John Gow & Son. Music Sellers to his Majesty. 162 Regent Street London. [1818]. Copy: E. A variant issue has the imprint: Robertsons of 39, Princes Street (E).
Dedication: 'Dedicated to Sir Walter Scott Bart. To whose indefatigable researches Scotland is indebted for the recovery of her most Interesting Antiquities. by Nathaniel Gow.'

512T] EDINBURGH: [Laing] 1822
Laing, David (editor). Select Remains of the Ancient Popular Poetry of Scotland. Printed at Edinburgh. [published by David Laing] MDCCCXXII. Notes: The advertisement also reports that 'The entire impression does not exceed one hundred and eight copies.' Copies: E L O; InU. References: *Letters*, vii.292-293; *PW*, i.34.
Dedication (at conclusion of 'The Advertisement', pages 9-10): 'The present work must necessarily have a very limited circulation, yet, trusting that such a Collection is neither unworthy of publick attention, nor of the care that has been bestowed in forming it, the Editor, with all due feeling of grateful esteem, would inscribe it as a slight but sincere tribute of respect to THE DISTINGUISHED AUTHOR, to whom, of all others, the Literature of his Native Country is most deeply beholden:—Whose zeal in its cause has been shewn, no less in a friendly and generous encouragement of those engaged in its cultivation, than in his own successful exertions in behalf of the unregarded and traditionary productions of former ages;—and Who has, at the same time, so eminently sustained and extended the reputation of our national literary character, by those original compositions which have shed so much lustre over the MINSTRELSY AND ROMANCE OF SCOTLAND, and have happily displayed the extent and fertility of his own surpassing Genius.'

513T] EDINBURGH: Oliver and Boyd 1821
Hogg, James. The Mountain Bard; consisting of Legendary Ballads and Tales... The Third Edition, Greatly enlarged... Edinburgh; Oliver & Boyd, High-Street: Sold also by G. and W. B. Whittaker, Ave-Maria Lane, London; and William Turnbull, Glasgow. 1821. As indicated for the first edition (509T[1]), the dedication here is slightly altered. Copies: GU L InU.

EDINBURGH: Robertsons
[~] The Ancient Curious Collection of Scotland. *see* 511T.

514T] EDINBURGH: Schetky 1815
Normans Song and the Coronach from the Lady of the Lake Written by Walter Scott Esqr. . . Edinburgh: Published by G: Schetky Junr. 58 Hanover Street, and to be had at all the Music Shops. Notes: Engraved sheet music. In two parts, with dedication only on the title-page for part II. Copy: InU.
Dedication: 'To Walter Scott Esqr, Sir The kind applause You were pleas'd to bestow upon these Songs induces me to Dedicate them to You as a Mark of Respect from Sir, Your very Obedient Servant J. G. C. Schetky.'

515T] EDINBURGH: Stirling and Kenney [and others] 1825-1836
The Scottish Tourist, and Itinerary; or, A Guide to the Scenery and Antiquities of Scotland and the Western Islands. . . . Edinburgh: Printed for Stirling & Kenney; and John Fairbairn, Waterloo Place, Edinburgh; and James Duncan, London. 1825. Notes: The dedication is to be found in all editions from the first (above) to the sixth in 1836. Interestingly a description of Abbotsford is only a sentence without a plate in the first, but gradually increases until in the sixth there is substantial attention over nine pages. The plate, in all editions from the third to the sixth, is drawn by J. B. Kidd and engraved by W. H. Lizars with the caption 'Abbotsford. The Seat of Sir Walter Scott Baronet.' The punctuation in the dedication and the details of the imprint change over the years, but Stirling & Kenney continue to be involved in what must have been a most successful title. Copies: E[editions: 1 3-6] L[1-2 5] O[1-2 4 6]; NN[4 6].
Dedication: 'To Sir Walter Scott, Bart. of Abbotsford, this work is respectfully dedicated by the Publishers. Edinburgh, 29th August 1825.'

516T] EDINBURGH: Tait 1825
Chambers, Robert. Traditions of Edinburgh. . . . Vol. II. Edinburgh: Printed for W. & C. Tait, Princes Street. MDCCCXXV. Notes: For Scott's contribution to this volume*see* 183A. The first volume is inscribed to Charles Kirkpatrick Sharpe, another enthusiastic contributor. Copies: E(2) EP.
Dedication: 'To Sir Walter Scott, Bart. The Second Volume of the Traditions of Edinburgh is respectfully and gratefully inscribed.'

517T] EDINBURGH: Webster 1823
Sharpe, Charles Kirkpatrick. A Ballad Book. [Edinburgh, 1823]. Notes: Thirty copies. Although there is no title-page imprint, page 124 has a printer's imprint from Edinburgh: 'Webster, Printer, Horse Wynd.' Copies: E(2) O('Presented to Francis Douce Esq, by his obliged servant David Laing'). Reference: *PW*, i.25, 84.
Dedication: 'To Sir Walter Scott, Bart. This Trifle, which the Editor deems most unworthy of his Acceptance, is, by his kind Permission, Gratefully Dedicated.'

518T] EDINBURGH: [*no publisher*] 1820
Alfred; or The Magic of Nature. A Tragedy, in Five Acts. Edinburgh. 1820. Notes: The author is anonymous. Copy: A. References: Abbotsford, page 165; Corson(2), page 174.
Dedication: 'To Sir Walter Scott, of Abbotsford, Bart. This Tragedy, is humbly dedicated,

as a Mark of Admiration of His Genius, and of respect for his private worth, by his faithful, though unknown servant, The Author.'

519T] FALMOUTH: Philip 1830

Kenilworth: A Tragedy. Falmouth: Printed and Published by James Philip, and sold in London, by Simpkin and Marshall, Stationers' Court. Price one shilling. 1830. The playwright is anonymous. Copy: E. References: Bolton 3865; Ford L15.

Dedication: 'To Sir Walter Scott, Bart. Sir, In dedicating this play to you, I conceive there needs little more be said, than to ask pardon for the liberty I have taken in so doing, . . . Most of your works that I have seen dramatized, are dedicated to you, under the idea, perhaps, that consanguinity demanded it. . . .'

520T] GLASGOW: Griffin 1823

The Beauties of Scottish Poets, Ancient and Modern, . . . Glasgow: Richard Griffin and Co. Hutcheson-Street; and Thomas Tegg, Cheapside, London. 1823. Notes: Interestingly, there are no Scott poems in this anthology. Copies: E GU O; CtY.

Dedication: 'To Sir Walter Scott, Bart. This Volume of the Beauties of Scottish Poets, is respectfully inscribed, chiefly in admiration of those Talents, which indisputably constitute Him, at once the Delight and the Ornament of his Country.'

521T] GLASGOW: Johnstone [*and others*] 1820

Montrose; A National Melo-Drama. In Three Acts. Glasgow: Printed for C. Johnstone & Co. J. Brash & Co. Reid & Henderson, William Turnbull and Thomas Ogilvie; A. Constable & Co. William Blackwood and Fairburn & Anderson, Edinburgh; Longman & Co. and C. Chapple, 66, Pall Mall, London. 1820. The playwright is anonymous. Copies: BCL; CtY. References: Bolton 3288; Ford M3.

Dedication: 'To The Unknown, but Immortal Author of Waverley, The Writer of the Following Piece Presumes to Inscribe It, with Sentiments of Enthusiastic Admiration for his Matchless Genius.'

522T] GLASGOW: Smith 1830

The College Album for MDCCCXXX. A Selection of Original Pieces. Edited by Students in the University of Glasgow. Glasgow: Printed for John Smith and Son; Bell & Bradfute, Edinburgh; and H. Colburn and R. Bentley, London. MDCCCXXX. Notes: Scott is listed as subscribing for two copies. This tribute may be one consequence of a collegiate controversy when, on 15 November 1828, Scott was elected Lord Rector of the University of Glasgow, but 'declinsd the dubious honour'. Copy: GU. References: Corson(2), pages 305-306; *Edinburgh Literary Journal*, 22 November 1828, page 28.

Dedication: 'To Sir Walter Scott, Bart., This volume is, by permission, respectfully dedicated by his ever obliged humble servants, The Editors.'

523T] LONDON: Baldwin, Cradock, and Joy 1816

Campbell, Dorothea Primrose. Poems. . . . London: Printed for the Authoress; and Published by Baldwin, Cradock, and Joy, Paternoster-Row. 1816. Notes: Scott subscribed for four copies. The volume also includes (pages 156-157) a poem entitled 'On hearing some of Walter Scott's Poems recited by Mr. E*****, Advocate, Edinburgh. Lerwick, 1814.'—this almost certainly in reference to Scott's close friend William Erskine, then Sheriff of Orkney

and Zetland. It is of interest that Miss Campbell's earlier book, also titled *Poems* (privately published at Inverness, 1811, with a very different arrangement and inclusion), was dedicated to the controversial Jane, Duchess of Gordon. Copies: E L O.
Dedication: 'To Walter Scott, Esq. the following poems are, with his kind permission, most humbly and respectfully inscribed, by Dorothea Primrose Campbell.'

524T] LONDON: Boys 1822-1823
[*engraved title*] Percy, Sholto and Reuben. The Percy Anecdotes Original and Select ... London; Printed for T. Boys, Ludgate Hill. 1822. Illustration: Frontispiece portrait of Scott dated 1 November 1820 'Engraved with permission of John Murray Esqr. from a Painting by T. Phillips Esq. R.A. by W. T. Fry.' Notes: In original wrappers, not seen, this was probably subtitled 'Anecdotes of Imagination', number 12 in the monthly series issued by the pseudonymous authors, Joseph Clinton Robertson and Thomas Byerley. Scott's own work is not mentioned here, but he would be interested in the account of omens in the Scottish Highlands (pages 23-24), 'Second Sight' (page 113), and 'Spirit of Darkness' (pages 115-116). Copy: T/B. Reissued with another number as Volume XI in the first collected edition 1823 (O).
Dedication: 'To Sir Walter Scott, Bart. These Anecdotes of Imagination are Respectfully Dedicated, by His Devoted Admirers and Most Obedient Humble Servants, Sholto Percy Reuben Percy.'

525T] LONDON: Cawthorn 1817
O'Meara, D. A. Marmion; or, The Fight of Flodden. . . . London: Printed for J. Cawthorn, No. 5, Catherine Street, Strand, Bookseller to Her Royal Highness the Princess of Wales. 1817. Notes: For comments on this title as a derivative of *Marmion*, *see* 28Df. Copy: NN.
Dedication: 'The following melo-dramatic romance is respectfully dedicated to Walter Scott, Esq. author of the celebrated poem upon which it is founded.'

526T] LONDON: Colburn 1826-1830
[1] Carne, John. Letters from the East. . . London: Henry Colburn, New Burlington Street 1826. First edition, in a single volume. Copies: L O; CtY. In the second edition of 1826 (MH), reissued in 1828 (NN), as well as in the Colburn and Bentley third edition of 1830 (NjP), the dedication begins 'These volumes are . . . .'
Dedication: 'To Sir Walter Scott, Bart. This volume is, by his permission, inscribed, with every sentiment of the highest respect, by the author.'

[2] James, G. P. R. Richelieu, A Tale of France. . . London: Henry Colburn, New Burlington Street. 1829. Copies: E O. Notes: For a revision of this effusive dedication *see* 527T[1].
Dedication: 'To .... My Dear Sir, Your name is too great a one to be trifled with, and therefore, I do not put it at the head of this page. Should your anticipations in favour of this work be realized, and its success be equal to my utmost hopes, I dedicate it to you in testimony both of my gratitude for your kindness, and my admiration for your genius; but should the hand of criticism cut it short hereafter, or the frost of neglect wither it in the bud, I take a humbler tone, and beg you only to accept my thanks for your good wishes and kind encouragement. If it should succeed, you will, I am sure, receive the work with some pleasure on my account;—if it fail, you will still accept it as the only means I have of expressing my feeling of obligation towards you; and, at all events, you will understand my motive for not

prefixing your name to the Dedication of a book, the fate of which is yet doubtful. The Author.'

527T] LONDON: Colburn and Bentley 1830-1832
[~] Carne, John. Letters from the East . . . Third Edition. 1830. See 526T[1].

[1] James, G. P. R. Richelieu. A Tale of France. . . . Second Edition, Revised. . . . London: Henry Colburn and Richard Bentley, New Burlington Street. 1831. Notes: The remarkable dedication cited below is followed by a reprint of the first, anonymous dedication which is transcribed in 526T[2]. Copy: L.
Dedication: 'Dedication of the Second Edition. To Sir Walter Scott, Bart. My Dear Sir, When first this book was offered to the public, I was totally unknown to the world; and, though your kind encouragement gave me confidence to venture forth and try that world's uncertain smile, I could not prevail upon myself to risk your name, as the promoter of what might prove an unsuccessful attempt, however much I might long to express openly my sense of the great obligations you had conferred.

'For this reason—and this reason only—your name did not appear in the dedication of the first edition; but such motives no longer exist, and I now offer you a book that has been successful. I once almost feared that your goodness of heart might have biassed your opinion in my favour; but the public, who decide without such sympathies, have justified your judgment; and I am proud to be grateful towards him in whose kindness all my success took its rise.

'My admiration of your genius—my delight in every page that your hand has produced, I need hardly—and can hardly express. Yet I wish I could do so; for, without entering into all that I feel towards you, you cannot fully comprehend that value of your approbation to Your most truly, G.P.R. James. Edinburgh.'

[2] [Bulwer Lytton, Sir Edward]. Eugene Aram. A Tale. . . . London: Henry Colburn and Richard Bentley, New Burlington Street. 1832. Notes: This dedication is reprinted verbatim in the 1832 New-York, J. & J. Harper (CtY); 1834 London, Richard Bentley (CtY); and the 1836 Paris, Baudry editions. Copies: CtY NjP(Parrish).
Dedication: 'To Sir Walter Scott, Bart. &c. &c. Sir, It has long been the high and cherished hope of my ambition to add my humble tribute to the rich and numberless offerings that have been laid upon the shrine of your genius. At each succeeding Book that I have given to the world, I have paused to consider, if it were worth inscribing with your great name, and at each I have played the procrastinator, and hoped for that morrow of better desert which never came. . . . You have left us for a while; . . . Whatever the honours that await you abroad, you have left the gratitude, the homage, the very hearts of two mighty Nations to watch over your fame at home. You, I feel assured, will not deem it presumptuous in one, . . . to inscribe an idle work with your illustrious name:—a work which, however worthless in itself, assumes something of value in his eyes when thus rendered a tribute of respect to you. THE AUTHOR OF "EUGENE ARAM." London, December 22, 1831.'

528T] LONDON: Colnaghi 1821
Stuart, Sir James. [Etchings from Scott & Byron.] London: Published by Colnaghi, 1821. Notes: The three etchings inspired by Scott derive from *The Lady of the Lake* (2) and *Marmion*

and have brief quotations on facing pages. Copy: T/B. Reference: Corson(2), page 152.
Dedication: 'Inscribed to Sir Walter Scott, Bart.'

529T] LONDON: Falkner and Christmas 1812
Heather, William Edward. The Harp, Third Song, From Canto Five of Walter Scott's Popular Poem of Rokeby, . . . London, Printed by Falkner & Christmas (Late M. Kelly) 9, Pall Mall. . . . [paper watermarked 1812]. Notes: Engraved sheet-music. Music composed for voice 'with an accompanyment[!] expressly for Harp or Piano Forte,' . . . Copies: E; NN.
Dedication: 'Respectfully inscribed to Walter Scott Esqr. by William Edward Heather.'

530T] LONDON: Goulding and D'Almaine 1826-1828
[1] I Ask'd of My Harp! Ballad. The Words Selected from the Tales of the Crusaders. . . . London, Printed by Goulding & D'Almaine, 20, Soho Square, to be had at 7, Westmorland St. Dublin & of all Music Sellers, in the United Kingdom. [watermarked 1825. ca.1826]. Notes: Engraved sheet music with music composed by George B. Herbert. Copy: NNP.
Dedication: '. . . composed & respectfully dedicated to Sir Walter Scott Bart.'

[2] The Fair Maid of Perth. The Celebrated Scottish Ballad. London Pubd. by Goulding & D'Almaine, 20, Soho Square. & to be had at the Author's Music Warehouse, Belle Vue, Clapham. [unwatermarked. ca. 1828]. Notes: Engraved sheet music with music composed by E. Solis. Copy: L.
Dedication: '. . . and Dedicated by Permission to Sir Walter Scott Bart.'

531T] LONDON: Goulding, D'Almaine, Potter 1820
Stevenson, Sir John. Alice Brand, from the Lady of the Lake, A Glee . . . . London, Printed by Goulding, D'Almaine, Potter & Co. 20, Soho Square, & 7, Westmoreland Street, Dublin. [paper watermarked 1820]. Notes: Engraved sheet-music. Copy: E.
Dedication: 'Composed and Dedicated to Walter Scott Esqr. (Author of the Words) by Sir John Stevenson Mus Doc.'

532T] LONDON: Huie 1823
Dramas from the Novels, Tales, and Romances of the Author of "Waverley." Edinburgh: Printed for James L. Huie, 14 Infirmary Street. 1823. Copies: E; InU.
Dedication: 'To the unknown, but immortal, author of Waverley, these dramas founded on his highly celebrated productions, are, with the highest sentiments of respect and admiration, dedicated by his most obedient and very humble servant, The Publisher.'

533T] LONDON: Jones 1829
Britton, John. Modern Athens! Displayed in a Series of Views: or Edinburgh in the Nineteenth Century: . . . London: Published by Jones & Co. Temple of the Muses, Finsbury Square. 1829. Notes: With an additional engraved title dated 1 January 1829. Pages 66-68 represent an extensive description of Abbotsford, 'altogether sui generis' and 'a place destined to enduring fame'. Adorning this is a drawing 'most respectfully inscribed' to Scott by Thomas H. Shepherd, the artist for all of the engravings in the volume. Facsimile issues in 1969 and 1978 are dated 1831 on printed title. Copies: L; T/B.
Dedication: 'To To[!] Sir Walter Scott, Bart. &c. &c. &c. Dear Sir Walter, However

Scotland may be indebted to a Buchanan, a Robertson, a Sinclair, or a Chalmers, she owes much greater obligations to the inimitable Author of Waverley; who, by a series of literary Works of unprecedented merit and consequent popularity, has given a powerful interest and an intense value to Scottish History, as well as to the Antiquities, Scenery, and Customs of the country. Pre-eminent talent thus adorns and irradiates all that it touches. To no other person, therefore, however illustrious by birth, or exalted in station, can the present Publication be addressed so appositely and so consistently. It will zealously endeavour to deserve his favourable notice, by emulating that principle which pervades all his own Works—i. e. to impart information through the medium of amusement. . . . With respect and esteem, I remain, Dear Sir Walter, Yours, very sincerely, John Britton.'

534T] LONDON: Longman, Hurst, Rees, Orme, and Brown 1812-1814
[1] Colman, George. Poetical Vagaries; containing . . . . The Lady of the Wreck, or Castle Blarneygig; . . . London: Printed for the Author; and Sold by Longman, Hurst, Rees, Orme, and Brown, Paternoster-Row, 1812. Copy: L. Revised 1814 as a 'Second Edition' (491S[4]).
Dedication: [page 37, following section title] 'To the Author of The Lady of the Lake, whose gifted Muse needs no meretricious colourings upon her Beauty; whose Charms might disdain a veil of Obsoleteness, to obscure them; The following Poem, of The Lady of the Wreck, or Castle Blarneygig, is respectfully inscribed, by His Admirer.'

[2] Bond, Elizabeth. Letters of a Village Governess; Descriptive of Rural Scenery and Manners; With Anecdotes of Highland Children; . . . Vol. I [II]. London: Printed for the Author, By E. Blackader, Took's Court, Chancery Lane, And sold by Longman, Hurst, Rees, Orme, and Brown, Paternoster Row; Manners and Miller, Edinburgh; And may be had from the Authoress, at Mr. Macdoual's, 154, New Bond Street. 1814. Notes: In the 'List of Subscribers' Scott and Mrs Scott are down for one common copy each and their friends the Morritts for five each of the fine copies. Copy: L.
Dedication: 'To Walter Scott, Esq. Sheriff of Ettrick Forest, and Minstrel of the Scottish Border.'

535T] LONDON: Mayhew 1825
The Moon's on the Lake. The Celebrated Scotch Song of the MacGregor's Gathering. . . London Mayhew & Co. Music Sellers to the Royal Family, 17, Old Bond Street. [ca. 1825].
Notes: Engraved sheet-music. Copy: L.
Dedication [on title]: 'Dedicated to Sir Walter Scott, (the Author of the Poetry) . . . .'

536T] LONDON: Monzani 1810
Where shall the Lover rest. The Song of Fitz-Eustace, From Marmion, . . . Published by the Author [composer] & Sold by Monzani & Co., No. 3 Old Bond Street, London. [1810].
Notes: Engraved sheet-music. Music composed by Barham Livius. Copy: L. Reference: G/T 10492.
Dedication [on title]: 'Inscribed to Walter Scott Esqr.'

537T] LONDON: Mori & Lavenu 1828
The Rose and the Thistle, Arranged as a Duet . . . . London, Published by the Author, No. 33, Gervard[!] Street, Soho Square, & Sold by Messrs. Mori & Lavenu, 28, New Bond Street, Messrs. A. Lee & Co. Regent's Quadrant, & I Willis, Egyptian Hall, Piccadilly. [1828].

Notes: Engraved sheet music. Music arranged by Maria Hinckesman from the tune to which Prince Charles and Lady Eleanor Wemyss danced at the last ball given in Holyrood Palace in the year 1745. Copy: L.
Dedication: '. . . & most Respectfully Dedicated (by permission) to The Dowager Countess of Morton, Mrs. Ramsay (of Edinburgh) Mrs. Kerr (of Chatto & Sunlaws) Sir Peter Murray Threepland Bart. Sir Walter Scott Bart. & Sir Thomas Strange, by Maria Hinckesman.'

538T] LONDON: Murray 1817-1830
[1] Byron, Lord. Sardanapulus, A Tragedy. The Two Foscari, A Tragedy. Cain, A Mystery. . . . London: John Murray, Albemarle-Street. 1821. Notes: There are no dedications for the first two plays in this volume. Scott received an advanced copy on 13 December 1821, six days before publication. In an earlier 1814 dedication (to Thomas Moore, in *The Corsair*) Byron observed that 'Scott alone, of the present generation, has hitherto completely triumphed over the fatal facility of the octo-syllabic verse; and this is not the least victory of his fertile and mighty genius.' The *Cain* dedication is regularly reprinted in the early London editions, in the New York 1822 edition, but not in the 1830 (London: William Crofts) edition. Copy: TxU. Reference: Johnson page 775.
Dedication for *Cain*: 'To Sir Walter Scott, Bart. This mystery of Cain is inscribed, by his obliged friend, and faithful servant, The Author.'

[2] Croker, T. Crofton. Fairy Legends and Traditions of the South of Ireland. Part II. London. John Murray. MDCCCXXVIII. Notes: Both Part I, 1825, and Part III, 1828, are dedicated to other persons. Copy: NN. Reference: *Letters*, x.242, n5.
Dedication: 'To Sir Walter Scott, Bart. This volume is inscribed, in admiration of his genius, and in gratitude for his kindness, by T. Crofton Croker.'

[3] Irving, Washington. The Sketch Book of Geoffrey Crayon, Gent. . . . Third Edition. London: John Murray, Albemarle-Street. 1820. Notes: The dedication, omitted in the first edition (published earlier in 1820 by John Miller) and also in the second (issued by Murray), occurs in this third immediately after Scott was gazetted as a baronet and is repeated in Murray's 'new edition' of 1821 (L). The author's 'Advertisement', dated February 1820, indicates that these desultory papers, published in America, have now been revised for issue in England to forestall piracies in that country. Copy: L.
Dedication: 'To Sir Walter Scott, Bart. This work is dedicated, in testimony of the admiration and affection of the author.'

[4] Maturin, Charles R. Manuel; A Tragedy, in Five Acts; as performed at The Theatre Royal, Drury-Lane. By the Author of Bertram. London: John Murray, Albemarle-Street. 1817. Price 4s. 6d. Copy: NN. References: *Letters*, xii.356-357, 359.
Dedication: 'To Walter Scott, Esq. This Tragedy is Dedicated by The Author. Primâ dicte mihi, summâ dicende Camoenâ / —— quod spiro et placeo (si placeo) tuum est.'

[5] Moore, Thomas. Letters and Journals of Lord Byron: With Notices of His Life, . . . London: John Murray, Albemarle-Street. MDCCCXXX. Notes: It is a remarkable circumstance that an Irish editor should dedicate to a Scottish novelist this work by an English poet. The two volumes also include a contribution by Scott and several letters from Byron to him, as noted in 237A. Copies: GU; NN T/B TxU. References: *Journal*, pages 437, 575.

Dedication: 'To Sir Walter Scott, Baronet, These volumes are inscribed, by his affectionate friend, Thomas Moore. December, 1829.'

539T] LONDON: Pickering 1831

Greene, Robert. The Dramatic Works of Robert Greene, to which are added his Poems. With some account of the Author, and Notes, by the Rev. Alexander Dyce, B.A. Vol. I [II]. . . . London: William Pickering. 1831. Copy: L.

Dedication: 'To Sir Walter Scott, Bart., This work is inscribed, as a slight mark of admiration for his genius, and respect for his character, by his obedient servant, Alexander Dyce.'

540T] LONDON: Richardson 1826

Old English Tales of Love and Chivalry; Humour, Enterprise, and General Interest. . . London: Published by T. Richardson, 98, High Holborn: Sold by Sherwood & Co. Paternoster Row; Simpkin & Co. Stationers' Court; W. Hunter, Edinburgh: and all Booksellers. 1826. Notes: This volume contains two derivative stories in chapbook format: from *Kenilworth* and *Ivanhoe* respectively (*see* 407E). It is interesting that this explicit attribution of authorship, in London, occurs a year before Scott's own public admission. Copy: T/B.

Dedication: 'There is no man in existence to whom the lovers of the beautifully romantic portion of Old English History are more indebted than the powerful author of "Kenilworth" and "Ivanhoe." Impressed as the Proprietors of this Work, in common with the great mass of English readers, are with sentiments of profound admiration at the talent displayed in, and deep gratitude for the delight afforded by, the English Historical Tales we have mentioned; to that "great Northern Wizard," by whose wand many of the characters of old times, which are dearest to the hearts and memories of Englishmen, are brought forth in all the pride of truth and vitality; from whose works, like those of our mighty Bard, we always rise refreshed, and to which we return as to old and much-loved friends; to SIR WALTER SCOTT, BARONET, the author of "Ivanhoe" and "Kenilworth," with feelings of the utmost possible respect, we take leave to dedicate the present series of "Old English Tales of Love and Chivalry, Humour, Enterprise, and General Interest."'

541T] LONDON: Roach 1820

Dibdin, Thomas. Ivanhoe; or, The Jew's Daughter; A melo dramatic Romance. . . . London: Printed and published by Roach and Co: Public Library, Russell Court, Drury Lane. Price 2s. 6d. 1820. Copies: E; InU. References : Bolton 3333; Ford K1.

Dedication: 'With sentiments of profound veneration, and grateful recollection of services, emanating from their splendid talents, and greatly honouring the Surrey Theatre; this dramatic essay is respectfully inscribed to Jedediah Cleishbotham, School Master of Gandercleuch; and Lawrence Templeton, Esq. of Topping-Wold, near Egremont, in the County of Cumberland.'

542T] LONDON: Schetky 1810

Schetky, J. G. C. Norman's Song, and the Coronach. From the Lady of the Lake Written by Walter Scott Esqr. . . . London, Published by G. Schetky Junr. No. 6. Gt. Pulteney Street, Golden Square, And to be had at Mr. Birchall's & Mr. Chappel's Music Shops New Bond Street. [1810]. Copy: L

Dedication: 'To Walter Scott Esqr. Sir The kind applause You were pleas'd to bestow upon these Songs induces me to Dedicate them to You as a Mark of Respect from Your very Obedient Servant J. G. C. Schetky.'

543T] LONDON: Sherwood, Gilbert, and Piper 1825
The Spirit of the Public Journals, for the year M.DCCC.XXV: . . . London: Printed for Sherwood, Gilbert, and Piper, Paternoster-Row. 1826 [1825]. Copies: L(preliminaries in separate envelope); T/B.
Notes: In this third and last volume of a new series the elaborate frontispiece 'tribute', here to Scott, and illustrated on page 294 above, follows two inferior representations of the King and the recently deceased Byron. An extensive description identifies the portrait as taken from an [Andrew Geddes] miniature by Woolnoth and the emblematic border by Hawksworth, with the escutcheons containing eight scenes from Scott's poems, each illustrated in the account by a quotation. To the right, 'The Stag, the ancient Crest of the Scotts, surmounts a Trophy, composed of a Tilting and Battle Shield, a Buckler and *Pavisse*, a Lance and Gonfanon, with the Buccleuch motto, of Love and Loyalty, A M O. The Harp, the tilting Helmet, with the Buccleuch Crest, the Basnot, the Scotch Bonnet, &c. furnish out the Trophy; and in the left hand corner is the favourite Sporting Hound [Maida] of the Bard, who has lately closed his career of faithful attachment. . . .' Reference: 1871 Exhibit, item 151.

544T] LONDON: Simpkin and Marshall 1820
Beazley, Samuel. Ivanhoe; or, The Knight Templar. London: Printed by W. Smith, King Street, Long Acre; Sold by Simpkin and Marshall, Stationers' Court, Ludgate Street; Sherwood, Neely, and Jones, Paternoster Row; And C. Chappel, 66, Pall Mall. 1820. Copies: BCL C E L; DLC InU ViU. References: Bolton 3338; Ford K4.
Dedication: 'To the unknown Author of IVANHOE, and the rest of those Novels, which have for the last Seven Years entertained the reading part of the Population of England, and rescued our Country from the disgrace of those numerous Romances, which have brought discredit on the Works of Fiction in this Country.'

545T] LONDON: Taylor 1825
Cunningham, Allan. The Songs of Scotland, Ancient and Modern; with An Introduction and Notes. London: Printed for John Taylor, Waterloo-Place, Pall-Mall. 1825. Four volumes.
Notes: This anthology also includes, presumably with permission, fifteen extracts from Scott (413E). The first quotation below is from page *1*, the second appears on pages 254-255, before Cunningham's signature and the date February 1825. This is undoubtedly the longest (albeit interrupted) dedication Scott ever received. Copies: E(3) O(2); TxU(3).
Dedication: 'Scottish Songs. To Sir Walter Scott, Bart. To speak in your presence of Scottish song—to hope you will listen while I seek to trace its history, describe its varied character, and, with an honest heart and a liberal mind, examine the productions of the lyrists of our native land, seems something like the man who spoke to the sun concerning the source of light: for who can know so much about lyric lore, or bring so much knowledge and genius to illustrate it, as yourself? In supposing myself seated beside you with free license of speech, I imagine your patience equal at least to my presumption. . .

'I commenced this desultory Introduction by addressing myself to ONE who has done more for the instruction and delight of mankind than any author since the days of Shakspeare. I imagined him seated beside me, and listening, with his usual benevolence, to all I had to say on a subject with which he was far better acquainted than myself. If I have omitted all allusion to his presence as I wandered along, it was more from tenderness to him than from any idle vanity of my own. It could not be supposed that all I said would merit the sanction of his judgment or his taste; . . .'

546T] LONDON: Taylor and Hessey 1825
De Quincey, Thomas (*English editor*). Walladmor... London: Printed for Taylor and Hessey, 93 Fleet Street, and 13 Waterloo Place, Pall Mall. 1825. Notes: For a full understanding of the implications of this imitation *see* 496S. The Dedication below continues for eight full pages. In addition, there is a 'Dedication to W***s, the German 'Translator' of Walladmor' signed 'Translator' (that is, Thomas de Quincey). Copy: O.
Dedication: 'German "Translator's" Dedication to Sir Walter Scott, Bart. Sir,—Uncommon it may certainly be, but surely not a thing quite unheard of, that a translator should dedicate his translation to the author of the original work: and, the translation here offered to your notice—being, as the writer flatters himself, by no means a common one,—he is the more encouraged to take this very uncommon liberty.

'Ah Sir Walter!—did you but know to what straits the poor German translator of Walter-Scottish novels is reduced, you would pardon greater liberties than this. Ecoutez. First of all, comes the bookseller and cheapens a translator in the very cheapest market of translation-jobbers that can be supposed likely to do any justice to the work. Next,—the sheets, dripping wet as they arrive by every post from the Edinburgh press, . . .'

547T] LONDON: Tegg 1809
'Pry, Peter' [Hill, Thomas]. Marmion Travestied; A Tale of Modern Times. . . London: Printed by G. Hazard, Beech-Street, For Thomas Tegg, III, Cheapside, London. 1809. Notes: One of the earliest Scott burlesques: see 497S[4]. Copies: CtY IdU NNU-W TxU.
Dedication: 'To Walter Scott, Esq. Advocate, &c. &c. &c. This travesty is inscribed by the Author.'

548T] LONDON: Whittaker 1825
Hartstonge, Matthew Weld. The Eve of All-Hallows; or, Adelaide of Tyrconnel; A Romance. . . . London: For G. B. Whittaker, Ave Maria Lane. 1825. 3 vols.
Notes: This is the second work dedicated by Scott's Irish friend (cf. 505T[2]) and, as David Vander Meulen informs us, appears to be of Irish manufacture, with a Dublin bookseller's label on front cover and paper watermarked 'Killeen'. Very probably it was prepared in anticipation of Scott's visit to Ireland later in the year. Copy: ViU.
Dedication: 'To Sir Walter Scott, of Abbotsford, Bart., &c. &c. &c. (with whose kind permission,) the following Tale of Erin is respectfully inscribed, by his ever obliged friend and faithful servant, The Author. Molesworth-street, Dublin, February 1, 1825.

549T] LONDON: Wilkinson 1808
Lochinvar, Lady Heron's Song, in Marmion, A Tale of Flodden Field, . . . London, Printed for the Author by Wilkinson & Compy, late Broderip & Wilkinson, 13 Haymarket [watermarked 1807. ca.1808]. Notes: Engraved sheet music. Music composed by John Clarke. Copy: E. Reference: G/T 10464.
Dedication: 'Composed and respectfully dedicated to Walter Scott Esqr.'

550T] LONDON: Willis 1828
Waverly[!] Melodies. No. 1, . . . Being the first of a Series which will comprise the greater part of the Songs of the Waverly[!] Novels, . . . London, Published by I. Willis & Co. Egyptian Hall, Piccadilly, and 7, Westmorland Street, Dublin. [1828]. Notes: Engraved sheet music (*see* 344D) with plate number '501'. Music composed anonymously by Eliza

Flowers arranged for voice and pianoforte. Includes: 'False Love', 'The Knight's To the Mountain', and 'Wasted, weary, wherefore stay?'. Copy: L.
Dedication: 'Inscribed by Permission to Sir Walter Scott Bart.'

551T] NEWCASTLE: Hodgson 1815
Bedingfeld, Thomas and George Pickering. Poetry, Fugitive and Original; . . . Newcastle: Printed and sold by S. Hodgson, Union-Street; Sold also by Mr. Charnley, Messrs. Akenhead, and Mr. Finlay, Newcastle; and Messrs. Cradock and Joy, Paternoster-Row, London. 1815. Notes: Edited by James Ellis. Copy: MH. Reference: Corson(2), page 110.
Dedication: To Walter Scott, Esquire, this Collection of Poetry, which in a Great Measure owes its Existence to a Wish expressed by him, is Inscribed, with Sentiments of High Admiration, and Sincere Regard, by The Editor.

552T] PETERHEAD: Smith [*and others*] 1825-1827
Buchan, Peter. Gleanings of Scotch, English, and Irish, Scarce Old Ballads, Chiefly Tragical and Historical; . . . Peterhead: Printed by P. Buchan, and Sold by Lewis Smith, Aberdeen; A. Sangster, and G. Mudie, Peterhead; A. & J. Wilson, Banff; G. Maitland, Elgin; W. & D. Laing, and J. Dick & Co. Edinburgh; & W. Sutherland, London. 1825. Notes: An elaborate printed cover, over the same sheets, bears the date 1827 (illustration in Duval 107). Copies: E O; CtY.
Dedication: 'To Sir Walter Scott, Bart. the Following Gleanings of Ancient Song are Dedicated, with Every Veneration and Respect, by his most Obedient Servant, The Editor.'

553T] SUNDERLAND: Robson 1830
Robson, Thomas. [*engraved title*] The British Herald, or Cabinet of Armorial Bearings of the Nobility & Gentry of Great Britain & Ireland, . . . Sunderland, Printed for the Author by Turner & Marwood. 1830. Three volumes. Copy: NN.
Dedication: 'To Sir Walter Scott, Bart. This work is, by permission, most respectfully dedicated, as a tribute of respect to his brilliant genius, which, in its unexampled fertility, has created a new species of literature, and displayed, in living semblance, all the deeds, qualities, and characters, which constitute the pride and boast of heraldry.'

UNITED STATES

554T] BALTIMORE: Willig 1830
The Captive Knight. The Words by Mrs. Hemans. The Music by Her Sister. . . . Baltimore Published by Geo. Willig Jr. [1830]. Notes: Engraved sheet-music. Copy: MWA. With lithograph illustration and dedication on caption title (MWA).
Dedication: [*on title-page*] '. . . and both [*the words and the music*] Respectfully dedicated to Sir Walter Scott.'

555T] BOSTON: Bradlee 1830
The Captive Knight. The Words by Mrs. Hemans. The Music by Her Sister. Boston: Published by C. Bradlee, 164 Washington Street. [1830]. Notes: Engraved sheet-music with title in capital italics. Copy: MWA. Variant issue of 554T with title in capital roman type (MWA[2]).
Dedication: [*on title-page*]'. . . and both [*the words and the music*] Respectfully dedicated to Sir Walter Scott.'

Moore, Thomas. Letters and Journals of Lord Byron: With Notices of His Life. . . . New-York: Printed and Published by J. & J. Harper. Sold by Collins & Hannay, Collins & Co., G. & C. & H. Carvill, O. A. Roorbach, W. B. Gilley, E. Bliss, White, Gallaher & White, A. T. Goodrich, C. S. Francis, N. B. Holmes, M. Bancroft, M'Elrath & Bangs, W. Burgess, J. Leavitt, G. W. Bleecker, and J. P. Haven. 1830. Notes: At head of title: Harper's Stereotype Edition. Reprinted from the London edition (*see* 538T[5]). Copy: NN.
Dedication: 'To Sir Walter Scott, Baronet, These volumes are inscribed, by his affectonate friend, Thomas Moore. December, 1829.

557T] NEW YORK: Longworth 1810
Baillie, Joanna. The Family Legend. New-York: Published by D. Longworth, At the Dramatic Repository, Shakspeare-Gallery. Nov.—1810. Notes: Reprinted from the Edinburgh edition (*see* 505T[1]). Copies: E; MH MWA NjP NN-L(prompt copy) PPL PU.
Dedication: 'To Walter Scott, Esq. whose friendly zeal encouraged me to offer it to the notice of my indulgent countrymen, I inscribe this play.'

558T] NEW YORK: Mesier 1830
The Captive Knight. A Ballad, The Words by Mrs. Hemans, The Music by Her Sister, . . . N—York Publid. by E. S. Mesier, 28, Wall—st. [1830]. Notes: Engraved sheet-music. A variant issue of 554T. Copy: MWA.
Dedication: [*on title-page*]'. . . and both [*the words and the music*] Respectfully dedicated to Sir Walter Scott.'

559T] NEW YORK: Riley 1820
The White Maid of Avenel, A Serenade. The Words from the Romance of the Monastery. New York Published by E. Riley. 29 Chatham St. [1820?]. Notes: Engraved sheet-music. Song composed by Mrs. Colonel Stewart arranged for voice and piano-forte. Copies: MH MWA.
Dedication: 'Composed and Dedicated to Sir Walter Scott'.

560T] PHILADELPHIA: Carey and Lea 1831
[Ferrier, Susan]. Destiny; or, The Chief's Daughter. . . . Philadelphia: Published by Carey and Lea. 1831. Two volumes. Notes: Reprinted from the Edinburgh edition (*see* 508T[2]). Copy: MWA.
Dedication: 'To Sir Walter Scott, Baronet, these volumes are respectfully dedicated by an obliged Friend, though anonymous Author.'

INDEX 1: WORKS BY SIR WALTER SCOTT

For ease of reference this index lists all of the original Scott 'A' printings and editions, with page references if any indicated first within angular marks, primary entry numbers recorded thereafter ordinarily in roman type with **bold-face** numbers identifying the major works. All subsequent reprints, derivatives, and extracts retain the primary number but substitute the letter suffixes 'R', 'D', and 'E' respectively. Bracketed notes further define certain entries. Titles in brackets are supplied for untitled entries. Starred items bear the author's'name on title without his specific authorization. Certain of the titles listed are cited again in Index 2 if they are later used for other purposes.

INDEX 2: GENERAL INDEX

This index records generally, with minimal commentary, all aspects of Scott's bibliographical history, excluding only the original printings listed in the preceding account. Page references, if any, are indicated first within angular marks, followed by primary item numbers in roman type.

A bracket **[** in the left margin identifies, as a class apart, the persons named (sometimes exclusively) in the course of Scott's early legal activity (351A-353A) with 'WS' further denoting, in this class, a Writer to the Signet. Persons in other trades or professions relevant to the author's literary career are distinguished by bracketed letters, including (with total entries here in parentheses):
[a] artist (105) **[c]** composer (136) **[d]** dramatist (32) **[e]** engraver (114)
Also defined in the broadest sense, with a certain place of business, are the publishers, book and music sellers, most of whom are engaged in eight cities:
[pB] Boston (43) **[pD]** Dublin (27) **[pE]** Edinburgh (105) **[pG]** Glasgow (24)
[pL] London(330) **[pNY]** New York(109) **[pPA]**Paris(28) **[pP]**Philadelphia(80)
These computerized calculations include the changing house-styles of firms over a considerable period, but do not extend to entries with two sigla [a + e, &c], nor to other printer/publisher/bookseller shops in lesser numbers elsewhere. However identified, the record discloses an array of names undisclosed in present bibliographical records.

CLAUSUS • TUTUS • ERO